37ᵀᴴ Edition 1992

Library and Book Trade Almanac

Editor ☐ Catherine Barr
Contributing Editor ☐ Filomena Simora
Consultant ☐ Patricia Harris
Publisher ☐ Marion Sader

R. R. Bowker
A Reed Reference Publishing Company
New Providence, New Jersey

Published by R. R. Bowker,
a Reed Reference Publishing Company
Copyright © 1992 by Reed Publishing (USA) Inc.
All rights reserved
Printed and bound in the United States of America
Bowker is a registered trademark of Reed Publishing (USA) Inc.

International Standard Book Number 0-8352-3224-7
International Standard Serial Number 0068-0540
Library of Congress Catalog Card Number 55-12434

ISBN 0 - 8352 - 3224 - 7

9 780835 232241

Contents

Part 1
Reports From the Field

Federal Agency and Federal Library Reports

National Association Reports

Part 2
Legislation, Funding, and Grants

Legislation

Funding Programs and Grant-Making Agencies

Part 3
Library/Information Science
Education, Placement, and Salaries

Part 4
Research and Statistics

Library Research and Statistics

Book Trade Research and Statistics

Part 5
Reference Information

Part 6
Directory of Organizations

Preface

The state of the economy, the plight of the homeless, the effects of censorship, and the issue of copyright were major preoccupations of librarians and information specialists during 1991. The year's *Bowker® Annual* looks at these issues in special reports by Christinger Tomer, Ingrid Lesley, and John Harer, and in the trio of articles on legislation affecting libraries, publishers, and the information industry. Also included in this year's *Annual* are reports on the Second White House Conference, Library Networking and Cooperation in 1991, and the Reagan and Nixon Presidential Libraries.

In keeping with current interest in the ever-unfolding changes in Europe, the International Reports section features an assessment of the problems facing Eastern Europe's libraries, along with an update on library issues in Western Europe. Marjorie Bloss tells us about the Moscow coup in the IFLA report, *Publishers Weekly*'s Herbert Lottman and John Baker give us the lowdown on the Frankfurt Book Fair; and Gwynneth Evans reports on the Canadian Library Community.

Part 3 features professional information for librarians, present and aspiring. Margaret Myers's Guide to Employment Sources points jobseekers in the right directions, and there are lists of accredited library schools and scholarship sources, as well as a report by Fay Zipkowitz on salary levels.

The *Annual* contains the usual range of information on funding and grants and statistics from average book prices to library acquisition expenditures to the cost of expanding libraries themselves. This year, we also included "Expenditures for Resources in School Library Media Centers FY 1989–1990" by Marilyn L. Miller and Marilyn Shontz. Highlights from the National Center for Education Statistics' 1990 Public Library Survey summarize findings on staffing, expenditures, collection size, and circulation.

Reference information in Part 5 includes publishers' toll-free numbers, information on obtaining ISBNs and ISSNs, and lists of notable books and literary prizes of 1991.

To make the index more "user-friendly," this year we have added a separate Index of Organizations and a handy list of acronyms. Many other changes took place at the *Annual* this year, among them a new Bowker editor and a move toward electronic publishing. Thanks are owed to Karin Cigol, who did all the keyboarding, however complex, with skill and good grace, and to Roy Crego, production executive editor, who made the transition to electronic publishing very smooth.

We would also like to thank Consultant Patricia Harris, executive director of the National Information Standards Organization, who helped us select topics and authors for special reports and other features, and Contributing Editor Filomena Simora, who for more than fifteen years has brought continuity to the *Annual* with her meticulous and thoughtful editing.

Finally, we thank all who contributed information for the *Annual*, especially the organizations that replied to our questionnaires, helping to make the directory section an accurate and dependable reference tool.

We hope you will find this volume, like its predecessors, chock full of useful facts, figures, and reports from the library and publishing world—all to keep you fully informed on current issues and trends.

Catherine Barr
Editor

In Memoriam

Frank L. Schick, 1918–1992
Bowker Annual Consultant, 1968–1984

Part 1
Reports from the Field

News of the Year

LJ News Report:
1991 Library Budgets — Hard Times Continue

Judy Quinn
Senior News Editor, *Library Journal*

Michael Rogers
Assistant News Editor, *Library Journal*

In January 1991, when *Library Journal* first reported the results of its national study of library budgets, we noted that it was too soon to tell if then-occurring state budget shortfalls would spiral into long-term recession. Unfortunately we can tell now: The bleak financial picture continues. The following reports from state librarians and other librarians across the country confirm that significant budget cuts are occurring at state and local levels.

Library Staff Layoffs, Freezes

It is not only materials collections that are suffering from the budget blow; this crisis is also taking a human toll. According to a recent survey of library personnel managers conducted by the American Library Association's Office for Library Personnel Resources, 42 percent of respondents said they had to deal with reductions in staffing levels in 1991, and, of those, 43 percent had to terminate, furlough, or reduce the hours of some employees. Almost half — 45 percent — believe their libraries will experience budget cuts in 1992, while 29 percent expect budgets to stay at the 1991 level. The New York State Library Association adopts a rather ghoulish take on the problem: It now maintains an "Index of Misery" detailing the latest blows.

Library Use Greater than Ever

Libraries are struggling to meet service demands under these budget cuts, and the demands are rising. Librarians across the country — 371 respondents to a *Library Journal* questionnaire mailed to the 846 public library systems with book budgets in excess of $100,000 listed in R. R. Bowker's *American Library Directory* — told *Library Journal* that despite recent budget cuts, their libraries are being used more now than ever.

Note: Adapted from *Library Journal*, January 1992.

From 1988 to 1989, these libraries reported an average increase in circulation of 4.3 percent, and in 1990 the average increase jumped to 7.8 percent.

More than 70 percent of the respondents believe 1991 will be a record year for circulation, with many pointing to the economy as the reason for the growth. "We are experiencing a considerable number of customers whose jobs are either 'at risk' or 'gone,' " reports Herschel V. Anderson of Arizona's Mesa Public Library. "Many others seem to be preparing themselves for job shifts or starting their own firms." "Certainly the economy plays a role," confirms Ellen Bell, director of the Washington County Public Library, Marietta, Ohio. "People have told me that they used to buy from bookstores the items that they now get from us."

Libraries are also filling in the gaps of other education services squeezed by the recession. "The closing of school libraries, the development of 'colleges without walls' and often without libraries, as well as budget cuts at the local universities and neighboring public libraries are bringing more people in for books and help," Duluth (MN) Public Library's Jan Schroeder notes acerbically.

Indeed, the level of frustration was extremely high as *Library Journal* conducted interviews for this report. When we asked if rising circulation figures are an effective statistic to lobby for funding, we heard many guffaws. "Now all anyone wants to hear is zero budget increase," notes Fairfield (CT) Public Library's Bruce Kershner.

Local Victories

Still, there's some hope on individual battlefields, as local public libraries succeed in maintaining (but rarely significantly increase) their funding. Still others are scurrying to establish new sources of income, such as endowments or new taxes. The Pennsylvania Library Association effectively lobbied against a periodicals tax that passed the legislature and, when enacted later in 1992 (California is still struggling with a similar tax), would have cost libraries in the state millions of dollars a year. Dallas Public Library Director Pat O'Brien sent *Library Journal* a slew of clippings about a threatened $500,000 cut that was forestalled in 1991 by public outcry and a last-minute discovery of city funds to maintain current funding. More funding may soon come to all Texas libraries as previous property tax abatements, lifted recently to help the state recover from the recession that hit here earlier, add to state coffers.

Also hoping for more cash are Arkansas libraries, which began a new marketing campaign in January 1992 to launch an almost year-long lobbying campaign for a November 1992 ballot item to lift the present one-mill tax cap to five mills. West Virginia libraries will ask for levy funding to be approved by simple majority, instead of the current 60 percent approval needed. In Lincoln County, Oregon, and Salinas, Michigan, voters have established new library districts to create new tax bases for library funding. Says Jan Buvinger, director of the Charleston County Library in South Carolina: "It is my opinion that winning a public referendum is the most effective and possibly the only way to influence the outcome of the budgeting process positively."

What stance should libraries take in this budget crisis? "Should we consolidate to still provide basic services, or should we let the cuts dramatically show?" Illinois State Librarian Bridget Lamont mused to *Library Journal*, "It's hard to know." Perhaps through *Library Journal's* 1992 National Library Budgets Roundup, we'll have the answer.

State Reports

Alabama

"We do not have time to compile war stories," Alice Stephens, acting head of library operations at the Alabama Library Service, wearily notes. This agency's FY 1992 operating budget was cut by $389,000 from the previous year and thus received $2,489,064 for agency operations and $5,861,037 for grants and state aid, including state funds and projected federal Library Services and Construction Act (LSCA) monies. Alabama Library Service has lost 35 percent of its staff positions in the last two years, and Stephens says she is getting reports of similar layoffs in rural and mid-sized libraries in the state. The governor and other state legislators are planning to hold hearings on possible tax reform (to limit taxes) in 1992, so librarians in the state are forming a phone network to educate legislatures on the importance of library funding.

Alaska

"The dollar figure rose, but the situation deteriorated," notes Alaska State Library's George V. Smith. Although appropriations for state library and archive administration rose from $5,983,900 to $6,065,900 from FY 1991 to FY 1992, a cost of living adjustment of 5 percent was not figured in the budget. The state library recently laid off five workers and closed its media services section. The archives division reduced one position to half time and left a second vacant. There is some good news in the state, however. Smith says that although there have been some cutbacks in public libraries in the state, there are not many.

Arizona

"Worst year in a decade," is the grim news from Sharon G. Womack, director of Arizona's Department of Library Archives and Public Records. Cuts of 1 percent to 5 percent in FY 1991/1992 appropriations are in progress.

Arkansas

In October 1991, following a first quarter downturn in the Arkansas economy, the state imposed a 7.8 percent reduction in the FY 1992 state agency budget allocations, says John A. Murphey, Jr., state librarian. The cut eliminated the state library's book budget and forced cancellation of about 60 percent of its periodicals. In addition, unfilled state library personnel positions will remain frozen.

California

The California State Library budget was cut $7,990,789 from the 1991 operating budget of $59,842,000. The State Law Library was consolidated with the State Reference and Information Center to decrease operations expenditures by $500,000. Efforts to maintain the State Library budget, aid to public libraries, and adequate funding to preserve federal LSCA allocations are continuing.

Colorado

"Those who call attention to themselves get cut," says Colorado State Librarian Nancy Bolt. "We are laying low and building rapport behind the scenes." Obviously, this method has worked to some degree: The threatened 7.5 percent cut to the state library's FY 1992 budget was reduced to smaller cuts. Bolt received a 2 percent increase for distributions programs and a mid-year budget cut of only 1.5 percent for state library operations. She's predicting deeper cuts for FY 1993, however, and the state library has already had to eliminate 7.5 full-time equivalent employees and has cut its newsletter production from 12 issues a year to six. Bolt says a tax limitation measure will be on the ballot in 1992, so libraries in the state need to watch the issue carefully.

Connecticut

Since 1986, the Connecticut State Library has lost $600,000 in purchasing power for library materials due to the loss of inflationary increases. In FY 1992, purchasing power was further reduced by $49,000. Since FY 1988, state-funded full-time positions in the state library have fallen from 160 to 108. Since April 1991, all existing vacant positions have been eliminated. The FY 1992 budget for personnel services was reduced by an additional $40,298, but a plan to close the library for five days has eliminated the need for another tier of layoffs. The state library was asked to submit three budgets for FY 1993, with 10, 15, and 20 percent reductions. State aid grants to public libraries would be eliminated under all three.

Florida

The recession has finally cast a shadow on the Sunshine State; the governor and cabinet wanted to slash $579 million from a $29 billion budget in 1991, only to have the Florida Supreme Court wrest budget control from them and give it to the state legislature. The legislature finally approved the FY 1992 budget in mid-December, and the Florida State Library, originally in danger of losing three staff positions, retained much of its 1991 level funding, although the $90,000 book budget, monies usually drawn from the state's general tax revenue fund, was cut. Florida State Librarian Barratt Wilkins says, "I've never seen Florida quite this bad off" — he's experienced about five mandated budget cuts in the last two years. In FY 1991, the state library originally received $18.7 million to distribute state aid to libraries, but before these monies were distributed, the allocation was cut to $17.3 million. Although the cut was unfortunate, the amount is still an increase from the $16 million allotted the previous year. On the horizon: Florida's secretary of state has on his priority list a $5 million appropriations bill to help libraries in rural counties, most hit by the current ten-mill levy cap instituted in the state.

Georgia

The Georgia State Library budget for FY 1992 is $2,271,396, down from the 1991 allotment of $2,345,529. In previous years, the state library agency took all cuts that came along, and state aid to public libraries usually went up at the same time. In FY 1992, state aid was also cut. The technical amount of the cut is 5 percent. The effect is worse than that amount suggests, says State Librarian Joe Foresee, but Georgia is better off than many other states in library funding. Georgia public libraries will be trying for continuation or modest increases in certain categories of state aid.

Idaho

It was an "outstanding year" for the Idaho State Library, says State Librarian Charles Bolles. He received funds to add three permanent positions. He says his state suffered more in the early 1980s, and diversification away from just an agricultural economic base has helped make the recession "slacken off." Bolles also received a 5 percent increase in the 1992 budget, for a new total of $1.1 million—still inadequate funding even in this sparsely populated state. Something that could squeeze funds further is a "1 percent initiative" that would require a ballot issue whenever a library in the state raises its budget more than 1 percent. There was a similar initiative in 1978, but the true spirit of it was never enacted.

Illinois

State Librarian Bridget Lamont says she had a last-minute cut of $2.5 million from the $60–$70 million FY 1992 state library budget. The cut was primarily in funding of designated sites in the Illinois Library and Information Network (ILLINET). Lamont says problems in her state arise not so much from local cuts as from a growing tax reform movement. The "collar counties" surrounding the Chicago area, for example, just approved a property tax cap and Lamont's agency just finished a study that shows one out of five libraries in the area will be drastically affected.

Indiana

The Indiana State Library is at least managing to hold on to previous levels, with a FY 1992 operations budget of $2,456,735, a 3 percent increase from FY 1991. Although out-of-state travel budgets for state library staff have been cut in half, the state library managed to get previous hiring and equipment purchasing freezes lifted. Libraries in the state are surviving, but Indiana State Library Associate Director Martha Roblee reports of a new Committee to Restore Indiana Property Tax Controls that may try to change this in the next legislative session.

Iowa

State Librarian Shirley George, who was in the process of leaving her four-year post to become City Librarian in Beaverton, Oregon, in December 1991, says that her agency received cumulative cuts totaling 12.8 percent over the preceding 18 months and lost about six positions during that time. She is pleased that two years earlier, however, the state agency had received a 90 percent increase for funding of various new programs.

Kansas

State Librarian Duane Johnson reports a FY 1992 reduction of 3 percent. He says some areas of his budget cannot be decreased, but other areas are decreased as much as 20 percent. His materials budget, for example, received a 17 percent cut. FY 1993 will mean similar reductions, and Johnson reports that local library budgets are under similar pressure. "At best, local economies and local library budgets are operating in no-growth circumstances." Some change may be ahead as a newly released Kansas Library Association/State Library study outlines plans to encourage local library levy increases and develop a statewide networking system supported by state money. Johnson expects some discussion of these issues by the 1993 state legislative session.

Kentucky

Michelle Gardner, deputy commissioner of the Kentucky Department for Libraries and Archives, says the state library's budget for FY 1992 is $16,819,600, an increase over prior years only to accommodate annual personnel increments and inflation. Although the state library association continues to lobby for increased state aid, a local effort by the Louisville Free Public Library to establish a special taxing district failed for the second time in five years (but by a close 52 percent to 48 percent margin) in the November 1991 election.

Maine

The state library FY 1991 budget was reduced 15 percent. So far there has been a cut of 13 percent for FY 1992. Nine state library positions were lost in FY 1991. "There has been no expansion in anything," laments State Librarian J. Gary Nichols.

Maryland

State library network funding was reduced 25 percent in FY 1992, and public library aid was reduced $400,000. Most public libraries are experiencing budget deficits, with many systems instituting furloughs and additional closed hours. Not only is the Baltimore County Public Library cutting staff salaries and the state squashing prison library service, but the Enoch Pratt Free Library just reported a loss of $1.3 million in state funding for FY 1993 and will close eight of 28 branches, lay off 40 employees, and furlough staff. Staff at the Prince George's County and Southern Maryland Regional systems are also being furloughed.

Massachusetts

John Ramsey of the Massachusetts Board of Library Commissioners says that since FY 1980, libraries in the state have had level or below-level funding. More than 29 percent of Massachusetts public libraries report some branch closings and overall reduced hours.

Michigan

James Fry of the Library of Michigan says the state library agency received a 9.2 percent reduction in its FY 1990/1991 budget for state aid to 366 public libraries and 16 library cooperatives, to a final total of $9,710,878. In the 1991/1992 budget, the legislature showed strong support for libraries and increased state aid by $1.5 million, 15 percent above the previous year's level, which more than restores the 9.2 percent cut of 1990/1991. However, the Library of Michigan budget was reduced by $459,000 in the 1991/1992 fiscal year, and the agency's staff has been reduced by 20 positions through attrition and loss of all part-time positions. A few of the 20 vacancies will be filled in 1991/1992, but most will remain vacant. Evening hours were discontinued when the Library of Michigan's operating budget was reduced 9.2 percent in 1990/1991.

Two proposals to reduce local property taxes supporting public schools are being prepared for a statewide referendum in November 1992, which could threaten some school library service. A joint committee of the Library of Michigan Board of Trustees and the Michigan Library Association continues to work on alternative sources of public library funding, with recommendations due in 1992.

Minnesota

"This is by far the largest budget cut the Department of Education has had," says State Librarian Bill Asp. For FY 1992, the Minnesota Department of Education budget was cut 23 percent, and the state library agency (which is part of this department) was cut 15.8 percent — "so far," says Asp. Five state library staff members have been laid off. Some good news: Most libraries in the state seem to be holding their own, and the state legislature increased its appropriations for multitype library cooperatives and held appropriations for aid to public library service at the FY 1991 level. Even better, in FY 1993, public library service appropriations should increase significantly due to a new funding formula.

Missouri

State Librarian Monteria Hightower phoned in her FY 1992 budget: $1,492,263, a 16 percent cut from the previous year. As for local war stories, Hightower reports that "everyone is being cut," especially since Missouri is still paying some $71 million in settlements on desegregation suits in the 1970s.

Montana

Another better-is-actually-worse scenario at the Montana State Library: State Librarian Richard T. Miller's FY 1992 budget of $1,508,155 is an increase, but a mandated 8 percent reduction in state general revenue expenditures by the Governor's budget office and the underfunding of state salaries by the legislature are causing major budgetary difficulties. In January 1992, the legislature is calling a special session just to discuss revenue shortfalls, and the state library expects to have to lobby to retain some positions. Local public libraries are severely restricted under the state's Initiative 105 (I-105), a taxing and spending limitation passed years ago. Although an attempt was made to strike down the initiative in local jurisdictions in 1991, the bill did not pass the legislature. The library community will probably try again in the next legislative session to have public libraries exempted from I-105 or to repeal it altogether.

Nebraska

The Nebraska Library Commission's budget for FY 1992 is based on a freeze for aid to local governments (which includes regional library systems, public libraries, and ILL compensation) and an across-the-board 2 percent operations decrease. The aid freeze continues for 1992/1993, and the state library operating budget reduction is 3 percent. State Library Director Rod Wagner says the state's current method of property tax valuation has been declared unconstitutional by the state supreme court, and the last legislative session failed to resolve the issue.

New Hampshire

Kendall Wiggin, New Hampshire State Librarian, notes that his FY 1992 budget, $2,584,038, is down 7.5 percent from 1991. His book budget is down 40 percent from FY 1990. The state library has lost nine positions since 1990, including the state law librarian, and is currently under a hiring freeze. The law library is now closed two days a week. Several larger public libraries in the state have had budget reductions, but Wiggin can't offer a bailout. "The severe recession and budget crisis make it unlikely we will see much happen at the state level."

New Jersey

The New Jersey State Library budget was reduced by 1 percent from FY 1991. The operating budget is $3,616,000. State aid level is an increase from FY 1991 but a 16 percent reduction from FY 1990. State aid is $13,112,000.

Many regional systems are attempting to cut ILL networks, despite much public outcry. The New Jersey Library Association (NJLA) is also watching the effect of a new financial disclosure bill that requires volunteers, including library trustees, to divulge their incomes in an organization's accounting records. One trustee of the Dover Free Public Library wrote an angry letter to the *Newark Star Ledger* refusing to disclose income. NJLA President Pat Tumulty says this bill has not caused a major wave of library trustee resignations yet.

New Mexico

State Librarian Karen Watkins reports a FY 1992 budget of $2,898,100, 4 percent above the previous year. She has no budget battle war stories, either at the local or state level. "Things are peaceful for the time being," she says.

North Carolina

State Librarian Howard McGinn reports that North Carolina had a reduction from the previous year of $184,416 to end up with a FY 1992 budget of $14,371,233. After the start of FY 1991, a $190,450 reduction was ordered but has since been restored because of improvement in the economy. McGinn told *Library Journal* that lobbying efforts by librarians resulted in the restoration of $250,000 in state aid and the passing of a $700 million bond issue that includes $10 million for public library construction.

North Dakota

North Dakota State Library's Cynthia Larsen exclaimed excitedly that the state library budget for FY 1992 is "looking pretty good! Our legislature met in January 1991 and made an appropriation that was actually about 12 percent higher than the previous year." The increased budget was the result of heavy lobbying by librarians. Larsen told *Library Journal* that there were two major library issues in North Dakota in 1991. "The biggest thing under discussion was money we wanted for networking. They ended up giving us the money, but they didn't really see the value of it. The other thing that libraries were almost completely divided in half about was the setting up of a regional system. We received money to do a pilot study, but half the librarians want it and the other half don't."

Oklahoma

The FY 1992 state library budget is $6,768,884, an increase from the previous year to accommodate the creation of a CD-ROM bibliographic database of the holdings of approximately 300 library outlets.

Oregon

"This is the first serious downturn our budget has had after several years of gain," says State Librarian Jim Scheppke. He's lost three full-time equivalent staff, had his materials budget cut by one-third, and state aid cut 5 percent. Ballot Measure 5, a citizen initiative that limits property taxes to 1.5 percent of assessed property valuation when fully implemented, passed in November 1991. To counteract damage from this tax reform, Oregon Governor Barbara Roberts is working hard to overhaul the tax system. "It will be difficult for any of us to gain ground unless she succeeds," notes Scheppke.

Pennsylvania

State Librarian Sara Parker says overall appropriations for the operation of the state library are down, but there is a $1.5 million increase in state aid to public libraries and a new $350,000 program for distance learning. Pennsylvania did not settle its FY 1992 budget until the first week of August. In the final negotiations, libraries were caught in a $48 million line item veto that the governor made because of tax loopholes and special programs in the budget passed by the legislature. The $2 million Statewide Library Card program was among several reductions made to cultural agencies and programs that had strong legislative support.

Rhode Island

According to State Librarian Barbara Weaver, Rhode Island's State Library ended up on the budget casualty list. "Right now it's looking dismal. The forecast for the whole Northeast is that the recovery is going to take several years, and New England is the place that's supposed to take longer than anywhere else: about five to eight years. Our budget will definitely be less than last year." Weaver told *Library Journal* that each department in state government has been required to present a budget that looks at a 15 percent reduction over the current year and "in addition," she said, "the projection for the current fiscal year shows that there's going to be something like a $50 million shortfall, so we're all being asked to take cuts."

Lobbying efforts for increases eventually became the pleas of the drowning. "I think what's happening is that there is no more money, and so all that the libraries are doing is lobbying for at least a fair share so that no agency is cut below any other," Weaver told *Library Journal*. "One of the things we have done in this agency is renegotiate the lease on our building, and we're giving up about 15 percent of our space effective April 1. We also expect that there are some services that will have to be cut back or discontinued. Since the budget reduction hasn't yet been approved by the government, we can't say what those services might be." The Providence Public Library announced that it is going to be closing branches and cutting back on branch library hours because the city of Providence is cutting back.

South Carolina

South Carolina State Department of Education's Jim Johnson says the state library services operating budget and state aid for public libraries proposed at this time will be about the same as FY 1991, an approximate 6 percent reduction from FY 1990. However, the revenue forecast is gloomy; therefore additional cuts may be made before the FY 1992 budget is adopted. The state had a hiring and nonessential spending freeze for the first quarter of FY 1991. Public libraries in the state are in many cases experiencing no-growth budgets. "There have been several capital improvement initiatives; that's about it," says Johnson.

South Dakota

"We're talking about flat, flat, flat for many years now," says Jane Kolbe of the South Dakota State Library regarding the "modest increases" for FY 1992. "We just get squeezed in every possible way. Occasionally we have received part of the small increases that have gone for staff hours, and sometimes we've had to absorb parts of those. Probably the most desperate part of our financial situation is that we have not had any staff increases for the last ten years. Almost everything we do has increased and changed a lot, and we have only a very modest staff to manage that."

Tennessee

After suffering a 9 percent midyear reduction of state funds during FY 1990/1991, the budget for the Tennessee State Library and Archives and the Tennessee Regional Library System was cut by 14 percent for FY 1991/1992, resulting in the loss of 17 positions in the state library and archives and 12 in the regional library system. Despite intensive lobbying of the Tennessee General Assembly, no relief was forthcoming for FY 1991/1992, nor any funds lost during FY 1990/1991 restored. Now there is an additional reduction of 15 percent for FY 1991/1992. "We may also face additional reductions during the current fiscal year if sales tax collections, on which Tennessee depends so heavily, do not improve," says State Librarian Edwin Gleaves. "No one on staff remembers cuts of this magnitude in the last quarter-century. The recession (with a capital R), plus Tennessee's regressive tax structure, continue to take their toll."

Texas

State Librarian Bill Gooch sent the *Library Journal* survey questionnaire to library directors of the state's major systems to give *Library Journal* a barometer of the state's economic scene. Here are some highlights from these reports.

Steve Brown, director of the Brazonia County Library System, says his FY 1992 budget is $1,884,080, with city contributions estimated at approximately $180,000. Funding is approximately the same as FY 1991, which is to say that support is down due to rising usage and cost. However, some property tax exemptions have been lifted in the state, so new revenues may come in the next few years. Brown is anticipating launching bond issues next spring to build new branches. "Public support looks good, but success will depend on the course of the national economy," says Brown. "We have a persistent group of supporters and a philosophy of honesty in making budget requests; that is, we don't play the game of requesting more than we need in anticipation of cuts. This has worked well to build trust into our budget requests."

Flora Wilhite, city librarian, Sterling Municipal Library, Baytown, Texas, reports an FY 1992 budget of $1,082,031, an increase of $73,255 from the previous year. A local bond referendum for library building expansion passed in May 1991. Jeff Rippel, library director of the Lubbock public library system, says his new FY 1992 budget is only 1.5 percent higher than the previous year's. "Considering the state of the local economy, the increase is good," Rippel says. "I also got back two frozen positions. In addition, we got capital projects funding of $175,000 for final records conversion, the key to our automation project." The library also was given a public relations boost when First Lady Barbara Bush attended a literacy program fundraiser, an event that netted $120,000.

Utah

The Utah State Library's budget for FY 1992 contained two significant increases: An additional $106,000 for state grants to local public libraries (completing an initial goal set in 1987) and a new paraprofessional position in the library for the blind and physically handicapped. "Overall, a very successful year," says State Librarian Amy Owen. "We received a small increase in our base budget as well as monies to cover increased costs in ongoing programs." Although Utah's economy is stable and growing slowly, notes Owen, "no one expects the coming legislative session to be an easy sell."

Vermont

"Better than 1991 but not as good as 1990" is how Vermont State Library's Patricia Klinck is viewing the state library's FY 1992 budget of $2,228,000. As a result, staff is down about 20 percent from 1990. Klinck is rising to the challenge. "It's not good but we're having to look at services very differently. You can't do things the way you did in 1965 anymore," she says.

The cutbacks have forced the library to take more advantage of automated services and to eliminate subservices like 16mm film. "Our automated system is online all the time, and 95 percent of our interlibrary loan in the state now is done by electronic mail. It's saving us dramatic amounts of money. We can control our own destinies in a lot better ways. I frankly don't think all the cutbacks have hurt us that terribly much. We have to ask ourselves very differently what is information going to look like in the 1990s, and we have to look to our own needs and how this whole new world is impacting, and it's a dramatic departure."

Virginia

The Virginia State Library received a $3 million reduction in its FY 1992 budget allocation for a total state appropriation of $16,849,844, with the rest of its $21,416,926 budget coming from federal funds. State Librarian John Tyson says that libraries had been voted full funding, but because of a shortfall in the budget, the general assembly of the Virginia state legislature has asked for a postponement of its implementation.

Tyson predicts that the effect of the FY 1992 aid as it now stands will be "devastating" to smaller libraries. "Approximately 65 percent of our libraries will end up with less money than last year," he says.

West Virginia

State Librarian Fred Glazer says his agency received $7,679,025 for operations and $10,446,062 for state aid to public libraries for FY 1992, as compared with FY 1991 funds of $7,655,484 and $10,220,784.

Wisconsin

The Wisconsin State Library FY 1992 budget is $1,667,800, representing a decrease of $17,200 from FY 1991. In addition to this decrease, all state agencies are required to cut 10 percent in 1991/1992 and 5 percent in 1992/1993 in materials and supplies and capital outlay funds. As the state considers library materials capital outlay, the acquisitions budget will probably be decreased. The legislature increased aid to public library systems in 1991/1992 by 6 percent. The 1992/1993 appropriation was vetoed and was being considered in a mini-budget session in January 1992.

The Wisconsin state legislature also appropriated $539,000 to permit five public library systems to convert to multitype library systems. The governor vetoed this initiative and he also required that three of the systems that had received LSCA funds to demonstrate the concept be continued on LSCA funding. Bills are again being introduced to advance this initiative.

Local library budgets in the state are stable, and the state library is still projecting a 6 percent increase in local library expenditures. Milwaukee County just appropriated $2,775,000 to replace the Milwaukee County Federated Library System's automated circulation system; the Milwaukee Public Library reports a $150,000 increase in the acquisitions budget and is building a new branch library. Support in some urban counties is increasing but support in depressed rural areas tends to be flat.

Wyoming

The State Library, as with all state agencies, has just submitted a plan to reduce spending in the next biennium (July 1, 1992–June 30, 1994) by 12 percent. Jerry Krois, deputy state librarian, says the support level for public libraries in the state has changed little from FY 1991, as property valuation is the key to funding. Only a few of the 23 county libraries saw increased valuation, resulting in slightly higher budgets, and several counties saw continued cuts of up to 22 percent. Although per capita dollars for libraries in Wyoming are currently higher than the national average, funds for staffing, resources, and facilities are still inadequate to offer wages that compete with other local government jobs, to purchase current resources, or keep facilities open and decently maintained.

Krois is watching out for a possible "Unfair Competition" bill that may be introduced in the next state legislative session. Such a bill could define services and activities that libraries and governments offer as unfair to private business.

SLJ News Report: 1991 Unfinished Business

Lillian N. Gerhardt

Editor in Chief, *School Library Journal*

GraceAnne A. DeCandido

Executive Editor, *School Library Journal*

Alan P. Mahony

Assistant News Editor, *School Library Journal*

There is usually a library connection to the biggest national and international headlines in any given year — 1991 was no exception.

For instance, the biggest international headlines in 1991 attached to the Persian Gulf war and the Soviet Union's sudden crumble from enforced communism into various degrees of capitalism. At first glance, these events may not suggest strong connections to libraries and librarians in the United States, but the ties are there. The American Library Association was the first national organization to denounce the rush to war in the Persian Gulf, which was declared on January 16, during ALA's Midwinter Meeting in Chicago. This action put a chill on ALA's relations with members of the Bush administration, and it turned up the heat under the lingering question of whether ALA should take positions on issues not directly related to libraries.

As to the swift meltdown of the Iron Curtain, the most immediate business beneficiary is likely to be American children's book publishing as the separated Soviet republics reevaluate their publishing agreements with the United States; it's likely to bring us new writers and artists and allow ours a bigger audience — through libraries.

It's tempting to hunt the library connection in all the national news headlines, too. For instance, where is the library tie to the Anita Hill v. Clarence Thomas story? Easy to spot. As the hearings on Thomas's confirmation as Supreme Court justice became locked on Hill's charges of sexual harassment, the Senate's Judicial Committee failed to explore (among many other important topics) Thomas's views on intellectual freedom and a host of First Amendment issues. Therefore, Thomas was seated on the Supreme Court without his position on ALA's top priority having been examined.

School Library Journal's news and features editors decided to forgo the thrill of pursuing the library connection to every general-news headline in order to recap and follow up on some of the big library news stories reported in *SLJ* in 1991.

The White House Conference

The second White House Conference on Library and Information Services, held in July 1991, may prove key to the future of U.S. libraries. Five years of planning by the combined youth services groups of the American Library Association (the American Association of School Librarians, the Association for Library Service to Children, and the Young Adult Library Services Association) culminated in a strong showing for library services to the young at the conference. Participants in the Washington,

Note: Adapted from *School Library Journal*, December 1991.

D.C.-based conference endorsed the youth services resolution by a wide margin, over all of the other 90-odd resolutions.

After the hard work of the more than 700 delegates and alternates to the conference, the true test of WHCLIS lies in turning those resolutions into legislation supported with substantial funding. The WHCLIS summary report, *Information 2000: A Strategy for Library and Information Services for the 21st Century,* was given to President Bush in November. Of the 95 policy recommendations and 15 priority issues, the chief concerns are youth literacy, a national computer network, increased funding for libraries, marketing strategy for libraries, and a national preservation policy.

ALA President Patricia Glass Schuman hosted the two-hour teleconference "A Library and Information Services Action Agenda for the 90s" broadcast nationwide on December 10. Jointly sponsored by ALA and the College of DuPage in Glen Ellyn, Illinois, the teleconference summarized WHCLIS and its resolutions and mapped their implementation. Viewers were able to call in or fax their comments and suggestions during the broadcast. Contact the College of DuPage Teleconference Office for further information or to order a video of the event (708-858-6090).

The WHCLIS summary report is available for $6 from the Government Printing Office (202-783-3238). A 20-minute video that not only summarizes WHCLIS highlights but also includes excerpts from addresses by the President, the First Lady, Secretary of Education Lamar Alexander, Senator Paul Simon (D-Ill.), and Representative Major Owens (D-N.Y.) can be ordered from Encyclopaedia Britannica Educational Corporation (800-554-9862, ext. 6565), for $20 plus $4 shipping.

Librarians in Russia

Two groups of librarians went to the Soviet Union in 1991, and both made history. "We came, we saw, we conquered," was how Erik Mollenhauer characterized his visits to the Soviet Union in October with six school librarians and 72 other educators from New Jersey, including Betty Kramer, president of the New Jersey Education Association. The group traveled to Chelyabinsk, Nizhni Tagil, and Magnitogorsk, cities within the Russian republic that have been closed to the outside world for the past 50 years. Mollenhauer, who oversees "Hands Across the Water," an exchange program offered by the Educational Information and Resource Center, said the Russian children responded positively to the American visitors.

"American librarians and teachers carry themselves differently from their Russian counterparts," Mollenhauer told *SLJ.* "I think it is more than just their clothing or the language. The kids noticed our group's spontaneity immediately. One young girl told me that the main difference between her teachers and the guests is that American teachers smile a lot. 'They smile for no single reason at all,' she said."

In March 1992, the Russian teachers who hosted the group came for a three-week stay in the United States. Although "Hands Across the Water" is currently offered only in New Jersey, Mollenhauer said he has received requests from Texas, Missouri, Florida, and other states.

American librarians were also present at the International Federation of Library Associations and Institutions meeting that took place in Moscow during the short-lived Soviet coup. The IFLA conference went on, and librarians did what they do best — tried to get the word out.

CLASP in New York City

A year of planning among the New York Public Library's branch system and the city's public schools, funded by the DeWitt Wallace–Reader's Digest Fund, bore fruit in the November announcement of a $3.6 million, three-year grant called the DeWitt Wallace–Reader's Digest Connecting Libraries and Schools Project (CLASP). Its function is to forge new links among teachers, school and public librarians, and parents.

CLASP will fund a variety of outreach programs, after-school and special programs for children, bilingual workshops for children, and workshops for teachers. More than $1 million will be used to buy new books for the participating branch libraries in response to the increased demand expected from the program. Sources close to CLASP said the hope is that the project will become a national model. A total of 107 schools and 23 of NYPL's 83 branch libraries will become part of the program. Project director Stephen Del Vecchio called school and public libraries "the greatest places in their neighborhoods" for children to find "adventure and discovery." NYPL's associate director for programs and services, Kay Ann Cassell, stressed that this community-based collaboration was meant to "establish library use among students at the critical early stages of their intellectual development."

Business in Education

Miami

Anne Ryan is the sole library media specialist at South Pointe Elementary (Miami), the first public school in the United States to be run by a private company. *The New York Times* noted that this public school aims to turn a profit (November 6, p. B9). Although Education Alternatives, the company in charge of running South Pointe, employs no librarians in the private schools it operates in Minneapolis and Phoenix, Ryan is a member of the staff at the Miami school.

"When I arrive in the morning, the children are lined up outside the library waiting for me," Ryan told *SLJ*. "They're very happy students."

Classes are welcome in the library at any time of the day: Typically, teachers will lead their classes down to the media center to conduct research on a topic that was first discussed in class. Furthermore, students are granted free time on a daily basis to stop in and view a filmstrip, check out a book, or just browse through a magazine.

"We're very flexible," Ryan said. "If a teacher consults with me, I can prepare formal presentations for a class. Or I can assist the students with whatever they are working on. It's a jack-of-all-trades type of media center." Currently, Ryan is assisted in the library by parent volunteers. But she noted that she would welcome some permanent part-time help. "I need a clerk, and the principal is making every effort to find us one," Ryan told *SLJ*.

Chelsea, Massachusetts

While Boston University's School of Education finishes its second year of supervising the public schools in Chelsea, the city's financial situation grows ever more desperate. During the summer of 1991, Chelsea slid into virtual bankruptcy and was in receivership at year's end. B.U. administrators were forced to lay off nearly one third of the city's teachers and terminate some new programs.

Earl Adreani, special assistant to the dean of the School of Education and director of library media services at B.U., said one of the three librarians employed in the city's six schools was reassigned to a classroom as a fourth-grade teacher; another was laid off; and the third remained at the high school, serving a population of 800 students. The city's four elementary schools no longer have a librarian.

Boston University's original plan for overhauling Chelsea's school system required the city to maintain its level of funding. Unfortunately, the $11.6 million school budget fell short of the amount spent on the schools *before* the partnership started, $4.3 million less than university officials said they needed to implement their plans for the city's students. As a result, the university laid off 87 teachers and restructured the school district by eliminating the junior high and reconfiguring the high school program.

"Despite the loss of so many of their colleagues, the teachers have responded fantastically," Adreani said. "It is a difficult situation, but they have remained positive. This is a very dedicated group."

According to Adreani, the university's next goal is to cooperate fully with James Carlin, who was appointed receiver by Governor William F. Weld. Since B.U. took over as supervisor for the school system, Chelsea students' scores on both the Scholastic Aptitude Test (SAT) and state basic-skills tests have improved. Nearly twice as many students are taking the SAT. The number of students going on to college also has increased, from 46 percent when B.U. first stepped in, to 55 percent of the 1991 graduating class.

Dollars and Sense

Unquestionably, the biggest news of 1991 was the fact that the states and the cities and their suburbs are running out of money to support public services. Despite surveys of voters that show public education and literacy as their top priorities, the tax funds allocated to public schools and their libraries continue to diminish. Local surveys in both major cities and rural areas repeatedly show that public libraries are ranked first or second in importance and esteem among community services, but funding for public libraries receded in 1991, too.

Throughout the year, politicians regularly announced that the general economy was on its way out of recession and on the road to recovery. These statements were propped up by data from the politicians' pet economists. Translation: "On the way out of recession" means we're still in one, and "on the road to recovery" means we're still sick.

Although the stalled and ailing economy is the result of poor business conditions resulting from poor business decisions, the stewards of educational and cultural institutions increasingly look to big business for both largesse and leadership. A vote needs to be taken on whether this is the biggest irony of public service in 1991 or just a stretch of contagious naïveté.

In 1991, foundation grants helped to fuel ongoing public and school library services programs and meld them into the sort of cooperation toward "family literacy" that foundations as well as the general public favor. At the state and local levels, school library media staff and children's public librarians are submitting project proposals that win support. Even though the general climate seems right, funding for nationally influential library demonstration or research projects continues to elude the separate efforts of ALA's three youth services divisions; the divisions can only bask for a time in their combined achievement of top billing at WHCLIS II before members ask, "What will you do for me next?"

1992

"The Right to Know" is ALA President Pat Schuman's theme for her presidential year. *SLJ* editors predict that *SLJ* readers in school and public libraries everywhere can and will put an extra spin on that theme to successfully demonstrate the binding professional principle *"The Right to Know Insures the Right to Grow."*

PW News Report: Playing for High Stakes

John F. Baker
Editor in Chief, *Publishers Weekly*

Publishers today are perplexed, anxious, disturbed. They have survived a decade of upheaval, corporate takeovers and mergers, a rapidly changing retail environment, growing debt burden — only to run into a thoroughly unorthodox recession whose effects are unpredictable and whose possible duration is unguessable. They have responded in varying ways: by tightening lists (production of new titles went down a whopping 17.2 percent from 1989 to 1990, and 1991 promises a further double-digit cut); by shrinking staff; by printing more frequently and in smaller quantities, in an adaptation of the "just in time" Japanese industrial approach; and still, all too often, by paying ever-riskier sums in pursuit of major authors with proven track records as bestsellers, or of personalities, like "Magic" Johnson or Gen. H. Norman Schwarzkopf, who might catch the ever-fickle and often fleeting public imagination.
Listen to some of their concerns:

- "I worry that people will find books too high-priced, that the recession will affect their willingness to pay; that's a real concern. Such a perception could cause the business to contract," says Peter Jovanovich, president and chief executive officer of newly rescued Harcourt Brace Jovanovich.
- "I think there are one or two huge accounts out there that could be in difficulty in the year ahead, and that a big bad-debt writeoff could be looming," says Thomas McCormack, chairman and chief executive officer of St. Martin's Press.
- "I worry whether as an industry we're spending too much money on too many books," says Larry Kirshbaum, president of Warner Books.
- "I worry about the strength of some of our customers. A successful business has to have all its parts strong, and some of our customers are weaker than they should be," says Jack Hoeft, president and chief executive officer of the Bantam Doubleday Dell Publishing Group.

Note: Adapted from *Publishers Weekly,* January 1, 1992.

- "I'm anxious about Baker & Taylor's new ownership. It's very important to us, and we need to know whether it will be as responsive to our needs as the former one," says Eric Rohmann, sales director at Princeton University Press.
- "I worry that publishers are pulling back on their selling efforts at a time when they should be selling harder than ever. When a publisher cedes orders to wholesalers, he's giving up his influence over booksellers," says Leonard Shatzkin, publishing consultant.
- "I'm concerned about what we hear about price resistance out there. I don't always see it on individual titles, and I'd like some realistic data on it. And I don't see any indication among agents and authors that they understand what tough times we're in, and that's not healthy," says William Shinker, senior vice president and publisher of the HarperCollins trade group.
- "My biggest concern is that the industry as a whole will not understand that there's a ceiling on how many copies you can sell. More people may be reading books, but they're passing them along," says Susan Petersen, president of Ballantine Books.
- "We're concerned, as always, about returns, overprinting, how to get the right number of books into the right outlets at the right time," says Michael Jacobs, president of Viking Penguin.

Concern about Retailers

What nearly all these comments have in common is their concern about the retail marketplace: its significance to publishers, and their apparent inability to sufficiently influence what happens there.

One of the first things a successful publisher needs to do is to become thoroughly familiar with the world of the bookseller. When, a year or so ago, Bantam Doubleday Dell sent some of its top executives into the field to see how the retail half lives — and sells its books — it was regarded as newsworthy. Surely it should be routine. And every year, when we at *Publishers Weekly* enumerate some of the year's more expensive flops and offer booksellers' comments on why the much-bally-hooed books failed, the signs of lack of communication are plain to see. Surely it behooves publishers to pay closer attention to their most expert customers.

Obviously, publishers and booksellers are never going to agree about discount points and pricing. But perhaps these are not even the issue. Leonard Shatzkin believes — and we are inclined to agree — that stock turn is the most important measure of profitability for a bookseller. If a store can turn over stock more frequently, and not have money tied up in excessive inventory, it will quickly show a higher profit than if it over-buys and has to return. And publishers can play a key role in this, for it should be every publisher's imperative to help make bookstores more profitable. The moves among a number of publishers to shrink sales forces and depend more on telemarketing are counterproductive in this regard. More, not fewer, sales calls would help guide booksellers toward the kind of ordering that profits both sides. At a time when publishers are trying, as many now are, to reduce their initial printings and instead go back to press quickly as needed, frequent and smaller buys from bookstores, coupled with much lower returns, would fit in beautifully with this new strategy.

What all booksellers are looking for, and all publishers ought to consider, is free freight. Publishers that offer it usually find that their orders increase — and many booksellers tell us it is a major consideration in their buying decisions. With the growth in the number of chain superstores and large independents carrying deep stock, backlist clearly will become increasingly important in the years ahead. Michael Jacobs at Viking Penguin described backlist sales in the last six months of 1991, fueled by delayed billing and stock offers, as "phenomenal" and added: "I think this will be a Christmas season driven by backlist and classics. In hard times people look for books that have stood the test of time." Larry Kirshbaum suggests that even the outstanding success of *Scarlett* was due in part to the same yearning: "The irony is that it was consumer uncertainty that probably helped: Here was a familiar story." And he has launched a new advertising program concentrating on backlist stars. Jack Hoeft says Bantam Doubleday Dell is planning to spur backlist sales in 1992 by price reductions on some major authors in paperback: selling Robert Ludlum's titles for $3.99, for example.

The Returns Question

Returns remain one of the most intransigent problems facing the industry today. Nearly all the publishers queried for this article mentioned the high level of returns in Spring 1991 as one of the factors that made the year particularly difficult. And implicit in the comments of several was anxiety about Spring 1992, when stores check inventory after what seems almost certain to be a less-than-triumphant Christmas sales season. Is this a burden that must continue to be borne indefinitely? Surely, if publishers can print in smaller quantities and booksellers can order more rationally — and more frequently — this absurd relic of a time when publishers were trying any device to increase their bookstore presence could be reconsidered. Harcourt attempted to remove the returns cushion unilaterally a few years ago, but had to give up when nobody followed suit; this is a case where there has to be general industry agreement to at least try it, or nothing will ever happen. We think the time has come to consider it — and in the new year we will be convening a roundtable of publishers and booksellers to discuss the implications of such a major change. But for now, let us simply say that current trends, including the greater rationalization of ordering, the "just in time" printing and stocking mechanisms and the increasing interest in backlist (traditionally return-proof) make a new look at the old returns habit imperative.

Of course we know, all too well, the arguments against it: That it would lead booksellers to stock more cautiously, thus severely limiting the chances of first novels, risky nonfiction, midlist books in general. But surely it must have become clear by now that the American book-buying public is by no means as monolithic and predictable as the bestseller syndrome would have us believe. How else to account for the huge success of "destination" stores, like Tattered Cover, Oxford, Borders, and perhaps now Waterstone's, whose driving force is a depth of stock most stores could not dream of? If, as we believe, there is a book hunger in America that is not appeased by the basic frontlist-bestseller offerings, then may it not be for small numbers of a wide range of books, rather than very large numbers of a few? And where is the basic returns argument then?

Current Conditions

Most publishers we talked to showed varying degrees of anxiety about the current sales picture. Kirshbaum finds it (apart from *Scarlett*) "troublesome, an unforgiving marketplace." Hoeft sees it as "sluggish," with Christmas sales "crucial;" Rohmann and Petersen both have "fingers crossed," Jovanovich finds things "pretty flat," Mc-Cormack "pretty bleak so far," Shinker finds it "difficult to get a handle on the marketplace," and Jacobs wonders whether the very good crop of fall titles will sell through Christmas.

There was general agreement that budgetary moves had been called for, and taken. Kirshbaum called Warner "leaner, meaner, and cleaner" (meaning that inventory has been deliberately kept down). He thinks twice about any large buy, and is cautious on initial printings. Jovanovich sees "everybody getting more selective and sensible, buying only the things they really want to buy," which he contrasts with the auction fevers of the early to mid-eighties. "When we bid $3.6 million for John Jakes's *California Gold*—which eventually went for $4.5 million—someone asked me, 'Are you nuts?' I'm sure more people would ask that today." Jacobs: "We've become a lot more cognizant of operating expenses, keeping them down, cutting titles back. We're anxious about overpaying for projects." Shinker is "tightening systems, printing tighter," and plans to operate through 1992 with the same staffing levels as in 1990, though, he says business is up 20 percent. "If you can leverage sales with the same overhead, it obviously improves your bottom line."

Bright Spots in 1991

What bright spots did they see? Hoeft was gratified that Bantam Doubleday Dell, thanks partly to the success of John Grisham's long-running bestseller *The Firm,* was able to offer its usual Christmas bonus, and suggested that "we many be the only publisher who can say that." Kirshbaum, of course, had *Scarlett,* "which really carried us, though the sales velocity on our other titles is not what it should be." McCormack said St. Martin's was "feeling no pain," after two years that were "the best in our history," mostly owing to several bestsellers in the mass market division, including *Not Without My Daughter, Silence of the Lambs,* and *September.* Petersen took comfort in being "author-driven rather than category-driven," adding that "the readers who remain will be there because they have to be." And she determinedly instills into her sales representatives the notion of Now-ness: that stores should be able to react swiftly to a sudden spurt of public interest in a subject. Shinker has found frequent, smaller printings a good strategy, and comments that "initial advances are not necessarily a good indicator of final sales," when the house often sells, in the end, four or five times the initial printing.

But there is still all too little attention paid in publishing these days to *creating* books, as opposed to shopping for them from authors and agents—a point Michael Jacobs makes. "I think there's a challenge to become better *commissioners* of work. As publishers we should have the book ideas, but agents have become the brain trust of publishing—an unhealthy sign. We should be list builders too, creating a coherent publishing program."

The Electronic Revolution

And what of the electronic revolution that, with the advent of the Sony Data Discman and similar players, seems on the verge of turning many readers into viewers of CD-ROM and interactive products? Lee Simmons, former publisher at Arbor House and president of Franklin Spier, now connected with an investment firm, is unhappily convinced that "trade publishers are so myopic that they'll miss the electronic revolution altogether." He predicts, as do many industry observers, that conventional reference publishing as we know it — dictionaries, encyclopedias, thesauruses — will be marginalized within five years. He even sees cookbooks as likely to be all-electronic before long, transferred to the CD medium.

In fact many of the publishers we talked to had considered this new technology to some extent, and had decided it wasn't for them, as least for the present. Jacobs sees the revolution so far in terms of more and more electronic publishers seeking rights. Rohmann said Princeton had "so far let it go by, while trying to think of everything else." Bantam Doubleday Dell, says Hoeft, is "looking at the possibilities," which he finds "exciting," and he adds that parent company Bertelsmann has been heavily involved in the new materials. For McCormack, electronics is simply an additional medium, not a supplanting one, which he avers "will not impact books like the VCR impacted the movie industry." HarperCollins, says Shinker, is using desktop technology extensively in the pre-press process, and insists contractually on manuscripts on disc from its authors. And of course Simon & Schuster and Random House have both been investing heavily in the new technology.

Role of Agents and Packagers

How is publishing changing in other ways? For one thing, the continued pruning of personnel is leading to longer work weeks for in-house editorial staff and, of course, a greater dependence on packagers and their product. Steve Ettlinger, president of the American Book Producers Association, says the organization receives an average of 10 calls a day inquiring about membership, many from newly dismissed editorial people, and he and his members are now being approached by publishers who never previously used packagers. "They're after ideas especially," he says. "These days publishers often don't have the luxury of being able to generate ideas." Clearly, this is an important publishing function that is being abdicated, to agents as well as to packagers, as Jacobs has noted.

Georges Borchardt, president of the new agents' federation, the Association of Authors' Representatives, says: "We seem to spend more and more time listening to publishers complaining and moaning," but adds waspishly: "What irritates me more than anything is that their problems are often of their own making." As an example, he cites a number of cases where he has received royalty statements showing such low sales that he asked for the rights back. "Then they look around and find they have let the book go out of stock. And if you let a backlist book go out of stock, you've lost sales you'll never recover." This, he finds, is all to common.

The net impression is that many publishers, despite the sophisticated tools at their fingertips, do not think as carefully about how they operate in the marketplace as they might. They are making much-needed economies, but still are too often bound by unquestioned, traditional procedures. Tough times call for changes that draw on publishing's very real strengths. In the new year, we'd like to become involved in helping them to make such changes.

Special Reports

Library Services for Special User Groups

1991 Trends and Selected Innovative Services for Immigrants, the Homeless, Children after School, the Disabled, and the Unemployed

J. Ingrid Lesley

Chief, Arts and Letters Division
Chicago Public Library/Harold Washington Library Center

The library world today focuses much attention on special user groups—immigrants, the homeless, the unemployed, students after school, and the disabled. With the possible exception of the disabled, these are the "special classes of readers" listed in Cannons's *Bibliography of Library Economy, 1876–1920.*[1] Andrew Carnegie's concept of the public library as a social force to serve the worker, the unemployed, children, the foreign-born, and immigrants remains as valid today as it was a century ago, and its users have not changed that drastically.

Throughout its history, the public library has been the place to learn, study, and read, the community center for special groups. Good librarians have always asked the same questions: Who lives in the community? What are their needs? How do we best meet them? Should the library be reaching out to others in the community? The *Bibliography of Library Economy* indexes such articles as "How Shall the Library Help the Working Man?" "Traveling Libraries of Foreign Books," and "The Library and the Foreign Born." *Library Literature, 1921–1932,* the supplement to Cannons's *Bibliography,* includes articles on libraries and the unemployed during the years of the Great Depression.[2]

Effective solutions to these challenges may incorporate high tech delivery systems and immense funding, but they may also be low tech, low-cost reinterpretations of solutions from the past. Librarians have a choice between *Star Wars* and *Small Is Beautiful.* Each approach works in its place. The common denominator of the two approaches is the commitment of librarians to the information and reading needs of these groups. The opportunities and challenges for providing information on services, programs, and guidelines to meet the needs of children after school, immigrant groups such as the Spanish-speaking, and the disabled have become professional standards by which librarians may measure other services, collections, and programs.[3]

With this in mind, let us look at some innovative, and some time-honored, ways of meeting information needs of the homeless, unemployed, new immigrants, and students after school.

The Unemployed

Who Are They?

Some have said that most Americans are four paychecks away from being without a roof over their heads. As 1991 ended, unemployment lines drew new ranks of the "new or about to be homeless," many threatened by lack of a paycheck for the first time in their middle-class lives. Accountants, engineers, lawyers, financial types, and especially those with service sector jobs (except for health care) stood in these lines. The "concerted drive to squeeze costs and improve profits has resulted in extensive cost-cutting, job freezes, layoffs, consolidations and takeovers."[4] "Unemployment, now at 6.8 percent, is expected to hover above 6 percent for years."[5]

In the 1980s, almost four out of five workers were employed in 21 million new service sector jobs in what has been called "the engine that powered the great American job machine."[6] The engine is idling and almost stalled in today's economy. According to the Bureau of Labor Statistics, the unemployment rate in blue-collar occupations—a broad category covering more than 30 million Americans, from skilled craftspeople to manual laborers—stood at 9.1 percent in November 1991.[7] By contrast, white-collar unemployment was 4.1 percent.

The decline in service sector jobs parallels the decline in the early 1980s of "the racked smokestack industry." "Economists say the slump in service productivity is partly a result of the huge influx of inexperienced workers in the 1970s and the 1980s. They also say that service companies failed to use computers effectively. And finally, they say, the service sector has simply had just too much capacity."[8]

Coping with Unemployment

What can a library do to help users cope with unemployment? Activities range from what might be called traditional—establishment of a job and business center in the library—to far-reaching high tech programs incorporating computers and cable TV.

In times of high unemployment, the circulation of the public library increases. Today's public librarians must respond to the needs of both the unemployed and the business community. Any person out of work in 1991 needs a résumé, and many libraries offer personal computers with résumé software for patrons to use. In Arkansas, the Pine Bluff Jefferson County Library System used a $6,500 grant to furnish and stock the William H. Kennedy Business Center in the central library. The center, which opened in October 1991, has a public access computer with résumé software that is heavily used. The William H. Kennedy Business Center works closely with the Arkansas Small Business Development Center to provide information on how to start a business in such areas as child-care, janitorial, and food service.[9]

Memphis, TN: From a Converted Bluebird Bus to Cable TV

The Memphis/Shelby County Public Library, in a joint venture with the Tennessee Department of Employment Security (TDES), broadcasts daily job listings on cable TV. The library's Jobfile cable program is now two years old. During its first year, more than 650 people found jobs through Jobfile, and calls are still coming in at a rate of 150 to 275 a day.

Judith Drescher, director of libraries for Memphis/Shelby County Public Library, says that Jobfile is the direct outgrowth of earlier library efforts to take job data and résumé information to the people in a 35-foot Bluebird bus converted to a traveling library.[10] The bus is equipped with an online computer system connected to the library's collection, a fax machine, a video camcorder, a telephone, and personal computers with résumé-writing software. Funds to purchase the bus came from United Way, Tennessee Library Services and Construction Act, and the county government.

"When TDES heard we were putting our collection about jobs on the road, they came to us and said the system they were using wasn't working well — having people sit and wait to sign up for posted jobs," says Drescher, "and we agreed to download all the jobs that were listed with TDES every morning into the library system's online computer."

The Memphis/Shelby County Public Library manages a cable TV station, so the next step was to turn this information into a daily program — Jobfile. "Now, the only visit job seekers have to make to the TDES office is to register, list qualifications, and obtain a special number," says Drescher. "After that, they can watch the job listings at home on TV — we broadcast them twice daily, between 5 A.M. and 7 A.M. and from 1 P.M. to 3 P.M. — and then they can telephone TDES for more information about any particular job." TDES helped the program get started with a $75,000 challenge grant.

Because not everyone has cable TV, Jobfile is shown daily at all city branch libraries (the 1 P.M. broadcast), and the 5 A.M. listings are videotaped and available at each branch by 10 A.M. for replay on videocassette recorders. Each month, more than 1,000 people request the Jobfile tapes.

To support the unemployed further, the library system established job/career centers in five branches and the main library that include software for analyzing a person's skills and information on how to get and keep a job and how to start a small business.

Memphis has not been as affected by the recession as many other cities. The mobile unit, called JOBLINC, reaches the underemployed as well as the unemployed. The bus goes to companies in the process of downsizing. "We park in company parking lots, in grocery store lots, by churches, and in shopping malls," says Drescher, "making four or five stops a day." JOBLINC has been to high school job fairs and to conventions in Memphis.

The JOBLINC user has access to 5.5 million titles in the library's collection using the online database, in addition to the job information carried on the bus and at the career centers in the libraries. Jobfile program tapes are available, and popular, there too. "We're proud to share in this partnership with Employment Security," says Drescher. "Jobfile is meeting the library's goal of giving people information they need. In fact, I think that we are doing this so successfully that the word is: 'If you want a job, go to the library. They can help you there.' "

Helping the New Immigrant

Legislation enacted in 1990 is expected to increase diversity among immigrants to America. The Immigration and Naturalization Service forecasts that legal immigration will exceed 700,000 a year starting in 1992.[11] Many will have no family or relatives in the United States but will have highly prized work skills, as engineers and scientists, or will plan to make significant business investments, as multinational executives and managers. California, New York, Texas, Florida, Illinois, and New Jersey "are expected to get three of every four new immigrants, who will be joining already-large minority populations in those states."[12]

The preconference "Community Connections: Planning Library Services for a Culturally Diverse Population," of the Fourth National Public Library Association Conference, March 19–20, 1991, focused on serving the new immigrants of the 1990s. Gary Strong, state librarian of California, stated: "When I go into the public library and see no one inside, I know that no attempts to change the library to relate to a community's ethnic groups have taken place."[13] Empty libraries are those that do not respond to changes in the population.

Serving the New Asian American

Cities are still the ports of entry to the United States. More than 58 percent of California's immigrants come to Los Angeles and New York City's latest wave of immigration is the second-largest in its history.[14] Immigrants usually locate among relatives and friends in urban areas. In New York, for example, ownership of gas stations, dry cleaners, greengrocer's shops, pharmacies, machinery repair shops, child-care facilities, and unfranchised fast-food businesses is in the hands of entrepreneurial immigrants who have developed special niches, "virtually monopolizing certain businesses or professions and slowly changing the commercial, political, and cultural profile of the city."[15] More than 85 percent of the 1,600 greengroceries in the metropolitan area are Korean-owned and -run, according to sociologists.[16]

Kenji Ima, professor of sociology at San Diego State University, states that in 1960 the United States had less than 1 million Asians; in 1990, there were 7 million, 3 percent of the country's population and the fastest-growing community of color. In this population group, there is diversity in language, education, and income. The group includes Vietnamese, Chinese Vietnamese, Khmer, Lao, and Hmong. By 2000, 75 percent of all Asians in the United States will have immigrated since 1980 or will be a child of someone who has. Ninety percent of Hmong live in poverty, according to Ima.[17]

New immigrants value libraries in different ways. In the Los Angeles China Town branch, highest use is among language-proficient adults. When the Chicago Public Library Cultural Center closed for the move to the new Harold Washington Library Center, the Foreign Language Section staff observed extraordinarily high use of the library on the last day, July 13, 1991. This day marked a shutdown on news from home for the city's diverse polyglot readers until the new center opened its doors on October 7, 1991.

Susan Ma, senior librarian at Rosegarden Branch Library in San Jose, California, encourages librarians to visit language bookstores and to buy direct.[18] She cautions against relying on bookstore staff and recommends that librarians bring a language user to help select materials and identify subject areas for purchase.

Library advisory committees, task forces, and partnerships in which librarians and ethnic leaders plan programs, collections, and services together are valuable models. They have the added benefit of drawing users, as leaders carry the word of the library to their constituents.

Chicago, IL: Ancient Korean Poetry and a Kayagum Concert

Chicago's Korean Town, whose heart is at Lawrence and Kimball streets, is the port of entry for newcomers, with 40 percent of the population Korean. The neighborhood library, the Albany Park Branch, and the Chicago Public Libraries Foreign Language Section collaborated with the suburban libraries of Lincolnwood, Morton Grove, and Skokie on "Korean-Americans and the American Public Library," a Library Services and Construction Act (LSCA) Title I project that targeted this group and its community leadership to develop library services, cultural programs, and collections. The suburban libraries serve second- and third-generation Korean Americans.

A 13-member Korean-American Library Advisory Committee, spearheaded by Consul Jung-ho Park of the city's Korean Consulate, helped project librarians learn more about Korean Americans and to outline 13 cultural programs. These included a Kayagum concert, performances of the mask dance, the Farmers' Dancing Band and the Women's Chorus, Korean poetry, painting and song contests, ancient poetry and folktales, book reviews in the Korean-language newspaper, and a seminar on the Korean immigrant family. These programs drew an audience of 2,772. The highlight of the series was a reception in the State of Illinois Center, May 20, 1991, hosted by Lura Lynn Ryan, wife of Secretary of State George H. Ryan, for the artists in the Korean Children's Art Exhibition.

A Korean Business Computer Workstation was set up at the neighborhood library, and a series of computer and business skills programs was presented. A colorful poster and a bilingual brochure, designed by Aesop Rhim, were distributed to businesses, shops, restaurants, and schools. The brochure highlighted the libraries' story times, after-school homework sessions, interlibrary loan service, reading programs, and hours of service.

Through the committee, the librarians were able to benefit from the creativity and talents of program participants, and a coordinator fluent in Korean and English was hired. The committee worked with librarians to introduce the American public library to the targeted population in the city and three suburbs.

LSCA Title V Programs

In 1991, $976,000 was appropriated for Title V, Section 501 of the Library Services and Construction Act, Foreign Language Materials Acquisition Program. Some libraries have responded to the downturn in the economy and changes in the demographics of their service area with innovative services and collections. Thirty-one public libraries in 13 states received grants to improve community library services, especially for immigrants. The libraries will use the grants to purchase foreign-language materials. Before Title V, libraries sought LSCA Title I grants to develop foreign-language collections, to hire staff to direct programs, and to retrofit collections and train staff to meet the needs of targeted user groups. As Gary E. Strong, state librarian of California, pointed out: "You cannot support ongoing operations with donations. Materials alone won't do it. You need staff, libraries with sensitive signages, and outreach people with contacts in the community."[19]

Chandler Library, AZ: Self-Help for Hispanic Americans

Karen Drake, librarian of the Chandler Public Library, Arizona, will use the $32,000 LSCA Title V grant to purchase Spanish-language nonfiction for young adults and adults.[20] She will also buy books offering practical self-help and information on citizenship, general educational development, home improvement, childbirth, pregnancy, and how to succeed in job interviews. Says Drake: "The materials will primarily be on living and coping skills and general basic education, plus some materials on English as a second language for high school students."

Tucson–Pima, AZ: Basic Life Skills for Mexican Americans

Laura Thomas Sullivan, librarian of the Tucson–Pima Public Library, has targeted the 29.3 percent of the metropolitan population of 405,390 who are Spanish-speaking, a group of long-term Mexican-American residents and newcomers from Mexico and Central America.[21] "We will purchase materials that address basic life skills, the manuals to prepare oneself to get a G.E.D. (General Equivalency Diploma) certificate, parenting techniques, and repairing small engines," said Sullivan. These materials will further develop the Spanish-language collections in the library system. Sullivan plans on marketing the new materials on Spanish-language radio stations. Social service agencies will be surveyed to determine the needs of their clients.

Huntsville, AL: An Unusual Southern Town

According to Gabrielle Liddon of Huntsville Madison County (Alabama) Public Library, Huntsville is unusual for a southern town because it attracted engineers from all over the United States in the 1950s and its population grew from 15,000 to 100,000. The library will use its $35,000 LSCA, Title V grant to develop new collections in the Eastern European languages.[22] "We will be buying as many materials as possible until the money runs out," says Liddon. The languages include Latvian, Czech, Romanian, Bulgarian, Serbo-Croatian, and Russian. In addition, the library will augment contemporary fiction and nonfiction in African languages, Arabic, Persian, and Turkish. Liddon also plans to build the library's collection of Vietnamese, Cambodian, and Laotian materials.

Alhambra and Fresno, CA: Serving Hmong, Khmer, Lao,
and Vietnamese Immigrants

Deborah Kaye Clark, librarian of the Alhambra Public Library, California, serves a community whose population of 82,000 is 37 percent Asian. She plans to develop collections in Vietnamese and Mandarin Chinese.[23]

Lydia Kuhn, librarian at Fresno County Free Library, says her community has the highest number (18,500 in 1987) of Hmong residents in California, where 47,000 live. The 1990 census counted 54,410 Asians and Pacific Islanders in Fresno County's total population of 667,490. Kuhn believes that this group was undercounted, as "many of the Southeast Asian refugees were afraid of the government's paperwork."[24] The library will purchase books, tapes, and videos in Hmong, Lao, Khmer, Vietnamese, and Spanish. Kuhn says: "It will be difficult to locate the Hmong materials. Recently, Fresno had a Hmong New Year's Festival and a lot of vendors came. We will work with them on obtaining the Hmong materials." A French priest invented a writing system for the Hmong less than a generation ago.

Rolling Meadows, IL: Celebrating Cinco de Mayo

Roselinda V. Davis, librarian at the Rolling Meadows, Illinois, Public Library, will use an LSCA, Title V grant of $10,320 to develop a Spanish-language collection in a Rolling Meadows Police Neighborhood Resource Center.[25] "Our goal is to place children's books, fiction, videos, board books for babies, and reference materials in the center. The grant provides the money for the materials, and now we are trying to get donations for the wood to build the shelving," says Davis. A grand opening for the satellite library is planned for May 5, 1992, a festival day (Cinco de Mayo) for Spanish-speaking Americans.

Queens Borough Public Library, NY: The New Americans Project

The Queens Borough (NY) Public Library System with its 62 branches circulated 13.2 million books, magazines, and tapes in 1990. This library system is unique for its multilingual users and collections.[26] "But it is more than the sheer volume of books that makes Queens extraordinary. It has become a warren of diverse cultures, ethnic groups, languages, and religions, created by the immigrant tide that has shaped the borough in the last decade."[27]

When faced with staff layoffs, reduced hours, and library closings in the borough of 2 million people, Constance B. Cooke, the Queens Borough System director, stated: "The library is their lifeline."[28] The library's New Americans Project, initiated in 1977, offers such lifeline programs as "How to Get a Job," "Living in America," "How to Deal with a Landlord," "How to Get a Green Card," and "The Rights of Immigrants."

For the many immigrants in Queens, the branch library is "a comfortable link between the lands they left and the new one they are tentatively discovering, offering them classes in how to cope with American life while providing books and magazines in languages they know."[29] To learn English, an immigrant in Queens may go to just about any branch in the library system. The New Americans Project teaches 3,500 people a year.

The fourth-highest circulation in the Queens Borough Library System is at the Elmhurst Branch, where eight out of ten library users are Asian. Linna Yu, the branch manager, says the branch is "the first stop for many immigrants who have never seen a library before. They read and read and read."[30]

Adriana Tandler, head of the New Americans Project, says one of every three of the borough's 2 million residents was born in another country.[31] The newest immigrants are Chinese, Korean, and Asian Indians. The system's 62 branches offer 75 English as Second Language classes. "Students in these classes are from more than 70 countries. Registration begins at 10 A.M.; and there are people in line at 5 A.M. in February in below-freezing temperatures. For every 3,000 students registered, we have to turn away just as many."

The project's Coping Skills Program is targeted to Spanish, Chinese, and Korean speakers. Bilingual lawyers, teachers, and counselors offer programs on topics that help immigrants adjust to life in the United States — on starting a small business, parenting, and dealing with the stresses of being an immigrant. Tandler received $12,772 in LSCA, Title V funds to develop two new Korean-language collections. These materials will augment the system's Korean-language collections, for which there is high demand, as evidenced by circulation statistics and requests by library users for newer materials.

Serving Children after School

To many, Memphis/Shelby County's Jobfile program — established with the cooperation and funding of the state employment department and using high-end technology
such as computers and cable TV — may seem the epitome of expanded library services.
Although not all of us can afford activity on this level, sometimes working on a small
scale can produce worthwhile results. Take the case of McAllen, Texas.

McAllen, TX: Outreach in a Police Substation

McAllen is located seven miles north of the Mexican border. One day, while Gerard
Mittelstaedt, director of the McAllen Memorial Library, was sitting next to the police
chief at a meeting of city department heads, the police chief told him that a public
service officer was helping some youngsters with homework after school at a police
substation.[32] Police substations were built in neighborhoods where the police department needed better relations with the public, areas of moderate and potentially high
crime "where the people basically look upon the police with suspicion," says Mittelstaedt. "One of the public service officers . . . was really good at doing math," Mittelstaedt explains, "and this project came about when a kid came to the officer and
asked him if he could help him with a hard math problem."

The substation had an old dictionary and a couple of books. Mittelstaedt and his
staff augmented the McAllen Police Department's Program of Helping Youngsters
by putting together for seven police substations core reference collections of the
World Book Encyclopedia, Webster's Dictionary, a thesaurus, the *World Almanac,*
an atlas, and the *Statistical Abstract.* At Mittelstaedt's request, the staff of the South
Texas Library System gave a workshop on using these reference books.

Mittelstaedt notes that his library had wanted to do outreach in McAllen but was
limited by funds. After-school hours at the library are "very, very busy," he says. Indeed, the McAllen Memorial Library has more traffic (313,000 patrons a year) than
the local airport (250,000 travelers). But, says Mittelstaedt, "If you keep your eyes
open, sometimes a solution will come your way."

South Hollis, NY: Storytelling, Puppets, and Help for Latchkey Children

For many youngsters living in big cities, the public library may be the only safe haven
after school. No doubt that is the case for many of the 12- to 15-year-olds who attend
the daily "latchkey" program at the South Hollis Branch of the Queens Borough Library, in New York City.

The South Hollis after-school program, and similar programs at 11 other Queens
Borough Library branches, offer children an hour of homework help and an hour of
recreational activity, such as crafts, storytelling, puppets, and actors. The program is
funded through an LSCA, Title I grant, and in each branch it is operated by a part-time
employee hired specifically for that purpose. "We tried using volunteers at first," reports
Mimi Koren, director of public relations, "but they didn't come regularly. The program
depends upon the reliable presence of a regular paid staff person."[33]

Salisbury, NC: Stories to Go

Marian Lytle, children's librarian, Rowan Public Library, Salisbury, North Carolina,
and her staff saw an opportunity to reach children who might not be exposed to
books by taking a refurbished bookmobile and Stories to Go to three- to five-year-

olds in day-care, Head Start, and preschool settings.[34] As the Rowan Public Library established more branches, the bookmobile was serving fewer users. Phillip Barton, director of the Rowan Public Library, had the idea of combining the day-care outreach service staff with the bookmobile service.

Lytle's goal was to provide reading as an early intervention for illiteracy. "The earlier the exposure to literature and to share it in the child's own home with family, the greater the chance that the child will have the desire to read," she says. A grant of $8,500 from the Cannon, Proctor, and Margaret C. Woodson, Inc., foundations and the local Hoechst-Celanese plant augmented library funds to develop the bookmobile collection.

Children (as well as staff members) at 33 day-care centers are now regular borrowers of books, kits, and other materials from the bookmobile. Inmates of the North Carolina Piedmont Correctional Center overhauled the bookmobile's engine, worked on the body, and repainted the vehicle inside and out to make it appealing to the 800 or so children who use the library on wheels each month. The children are registered for library cards and given book bags. They may take books home or read them at the centers.

The Homeless: Give Them a Voice

The belt tightening in today's economic climate is mirrored in the retrenchment as the public confronts the homeless. In the last three years, however, some libraries have collaborated with service providers and community agencies to establish reading rooms and collections for homeless people.

In cooperation with the Baltimore County (Maryland) Coalition for the Homeless, the Baltimore County Public Library distributed a "Street Card" folded into a brochure listing food, health, shelter, winter-only, legal, and other services on one side and income/welfare and employment programs on the other. Street Card lists addresses, hours of service, and telephone numbers.

The San Francisco Public Library found a way to register homeless borrowers who had no address.[35]

The Chicago Public Library cosponsored the "Voices Louder Than Words" reading and panel discussion, November 21, 1991, with 38 other organizations, including Booksellers for Social Responsibility, Guild Books, the Chicago Coalition for the Homeless, READ Illinois, Clara's House Shelter, PEN, Travelers and Immigrants Aid, and the Marshall Field department store's bookshop. Participants included Dino, Jackie and Southern Comfort, homeless poets from the Los Angeles Writers Coalition, and Joseph Groller and Diana Schooler, former homeless writers from Nashville, Tennessee. Short-story writer Robert Bosell read "The Products of Love," and Antonya Nelson read "The Facts of Air" from the anthology *Voices Louder Than Words*. Poet Cindy Salach, winner of the city's Poem for Prague Contest for "You Have the Right NOT to Remain Silent" and the city's cultural ambassador, read poems written by women in the city's shelters. The program was taped by Edward Lifson for a Thanksgiving Day National Public Radio broadcast on the Bob Edwards Morning Edition.

From 1990 until its move to the new Harold Washington Library in July 1991, the Chicago Public Library Cultural Center distributed a Help the Loop Area Homeless card in cooperation with Travelers and Immigrants Aid. The library's Visual and

Performing Arts Department exhibited poems written by formerly homeless men and women, in November and December 1991, created as letterpress prints by students at the University of Western Kentucky under the direction of Professor Veronic Koss in conjunction with the Voices Louder Than Words program.

Mail a Book to the Homebound

Jo De Lapo, branch manager, Queens Village, Queens Borough Public Library, serves six nursing homes and 500 individual shut-ins, using the U.S. mail. De Lapo and her staff mailed 13,000 items in 1991. "They call all the time and write notes and letters requesting science fiction, mysteries, biographies, and bestsellers," she says, "and they write beautiful thank-you letters." The mail-a-book collection is purchased with funds from the Queens Village budget, augmented by special services funds.

The Library as Infrastructure

Librarian of Congress James Billington said libraries are infrastructure, not frills.[36] The continuance and growth of the community depend on its libraries. Yet one of the greatest challenges facing libraries today is not how to serve "special users" but how to serve at all. Library budget cuts have resulted in reductions in hours, staff, and materials. At the same time, some libraries have had increases in circulation and hours. On the CBS-TV program "Sunday Morning," Charles Kuralt told viewers that there is "something that feels wrong when the public library, the intellectual heart and soul of America, has to curtail hours or close its doors."[37]

In the Consumers in the Information Age survey conducted by Louis Harris and Associates and sponsored by Equifax, Inc., more than six out of ten Americans (66 percent of respondents) reported using the services of the public library in 1990.[38] This figure is 15 percent higher than reported by the 1978 Gallup poll. The survey also revealed that 91 percent of the respondents borrowed books, 77 percent used reference materials, 49 percent read newspapers and magazines, and 25 percent used library computer terminals.[39] (The "computer literate" may constitute a special user group. They tend to be young — 45 percent between 18 and 24 years of age — and well educated — 36 percent have college or postgraduate experience.)

In suburban Chicago, Mark West, Elk Grove Village Library administrator, reports that for some years his library has been exploring ways to increase the accessibility of the library.[40] "All of the bordering libraries to Elk Grove Village, the Schaumburg Township District Libraries, Arlington Heights Memorial Library, and the Mount Prospect and Bensenville Public Libraries, were open until 10 P.M. and the public's expectation for these later hours was confirmed in a response to a patrons' requests and a citizens' survey," says West. The Elk Grove Village Public Library is now open 77 hours a week, Friday evenings and Sundays in summer, and until 10 P.M. Monday through Friday during the academic year. From 8 to 9 P.M. is the hour of heaviest use, primarily by high school students, who have part-time jobs, responsibilities at home, and extracurricular activities after school. "It can be 7 P.M. before a youngster is ready to come to the library and study," adds West.

For the first time since World War II, the San Diego (California) Central Library will be open Sunday afternoons, 1–5 P.M., October to April.[41] The city of San Ramon, California, surveyed its citizens, and nearly 25 percent of the respondents answered the question "What one thing would most likely increase your use and satisfaction with the library?" with "more hours," particularly Sunday afternoons and after 8 P.M. on weeknights.[42]

Luren Dickinson, director of the Findlay–Hancock County (Ohio) Public Library, applied for a grant of $24,000 to cover personnel costs for the first year and 50 percent of the costs in the second year for the central library to be open on Sundays, Labor Day through Memorial Day, 1–5 P.M. through Spring 1993.[43] The library is the second in the 26-county northwest Ohio area to have Sunday hours for the full academic year. According to Dickinson, there has been a steady increase in use and circulation has gone up weekly. Who are the users? "We get plenty of students – and these are the most serious of students, librarians tell me – a limited number of homeless, and a lot of local and family history usage from the elderly," says Dickinson.

Circulation at the Brooklyn Public Library has increased in the face of cuts leaving 46 of the system's 58 branches open only two days a week, cuts that affect children, job seekers, and immigrants in adult literacy programs.[44]

Circulation at the Richland County (South Carolina) Public Library increased 12 percent over 1990, with individual branches registering increases of up to 50 percent.[45] The regional library is the third-busiest in the state. Director David Warren points to the economy, a new regional library, and an automated public access catalog as some reasons for the increases.

Support to keep the neighborhood libraries of the Chicago Public Library open came from the city's legislators who were absolutely opposed to cuts in hours. Funding for part-time staff to keep these libraries open will come from the tax on admission to offtrack betting, rental fees for use of meeting rooms and the restaurant in the new Harold Washington Library Center, and the Chicago Library Foundation.

The Last Word

History does repeat itself. The problems we face as this century closes seem much like those that marked its beginning: waves of immigration; economic recession; a growing gap between the haves and have-nots; homeless men, women, and families; children who come to the library after school because no one is home – these patterns of earlier times are being repeated today. But the latest word in technology is not necessarily the last word in library services. High tech is fine for those who can get it – for those who can afford it and have the means to apply it. But the small-scale solutions that meet local needs with purely local resources are equally important. Librarians might co-opt the slogan of the ecology movement: "Think globally, act locally."

The biggest problem, however, is not how librarians serve this or that user group – after all, we have always served a library usership composed of groups – but whether we serve at all. The library that is not open when potential users need it is not meeting their needs, no matter how good its intentions.

Notes

1. "C – Special Classes of Readers," in Cannons's *Bibliography of Library Economy, 1876–1920* (Chicago: American Library Association, 1927).

2. *Library Literature, 1921-1932,* a supplement to Cannons's *Bibliography of Library Economy* (Chicago: American Library Association, 1934), pp. 119-120.

3. For example, Frances Smardo Dowd, *Latchkey Children in the Library and Community: Issues, Strategies and Programs* (Phoenix, Ariz.: Oryx Press, 1991); Salvador Guerena, ed., *Latino Librarianship: A Handbook for Professionals* (Jefferson, N.C.: McFarland, 1990); Adela Artola Allen, ed., *Library Services for Hispanic Children: A Guide for Public and School Librarians* (Phoenix, Ariz.: Oryx Press, 1987); RASD, *Guideline for Library Services to Hispanics,* prepared by Library Services to the Spanish-Speaking Committee (Chicago: Reference and Adult Services Division, American Library Association, 1988); J. Ingrid Lesley, "The Homeless in the Public Library," *Libraries and Information Services Today: The Yearly Chronicle, 1991 Edition,* ed. June Lester (Chicago: American Library Association, 1991), pp. 12-22; and Amado M. Padillo, *Public Library Services for Immigrant Populations in California: A Report to the State Librarian of California* (Sacramento: California State Library Foundation, 1991).

4. Sylvia Nasar, "Employment in Service Industry, Engine for Boom of 80s, Falters," *New York Times,* January 2, 1992, pp. A1, C5.

5. Ibid.

6. Ibid.

7. Steve Lohr, "Accepting the Harsh Truth of a Blue-Collar Recession," *New York Times,* December 25, 1991, pp. 1, 24.

8. Nasar, pp. A1, C5.

9. Interview with Roger Saft, reference librarian and director of the William H. Kennedy Business Center, Pine Bluff Jefferson County Library System, Arkansas, January 1992.

10. Interview with Judith Drescher, director of libraries, Memphis/Shelby County Public Library and Information Center, January 1992.

11. Martha Farnsworth Riche, "We're All Minorities Now," *American Demographics* 13, 10 (October 1991), 26-34.

12. Ibid.

13. J. Ingrid Lesley, notes from Preconference: Community Connections: Planning Library Services for a Culturally Diverse Population, March 19-20, 1991, Fourth National Conference, Public Library Association.

14. Donatella Lorch, "Ethnic Niches Creating Jobs That Fuel Immigrant Growth," *New York Times,* January 12, 1991, pp. 1, 14.

15. Ibid.

16. Ibid.

17. Lesley, notes.

18. Ibid.

19. Ibid.

20. Interview with Karen Drake, librarian, Chandler Public Library, Arizona, January 1992.

21. Interview with Laura Thomas Sullivan, librarian, Tucson-Pima Public Library, Arizona, January 1992.

22. Interview with Gabrielle Liddon, project director, Huntsville Madison County Public Library, Alabama, January 1992.

23. Interview with Deborah Kaye Clark, librarian, Alhambra Public Library, California, January 1992.

24. Interview with Lydia Kuhn, librarian, Fresno County Free Library, California, January 1992.

25. Interview with Roselinda V. Davis, librarian, Rolling Meadows Public Library, Illinois, January 1992.

26. Donatella Lorch, "Queens Polyglot Libraries, Nation's Busiest, Await Deep Cuts," *New York Times,* June 13, 1991, p. B10.

27. Ibid.

28. Ibid.

29. Ibid.

30. Ibid.

31. Interview with Adriana Tandler, head, Queens Borough Public Library's New Americans Project, January 1992; QBPL press release no. 71, November 22, 1991.

32. Interview with Gerard Mittelstaedt, director, McAllen Memorial Library, Texas, January 1992.

33. Interview with Mimi Koren, director of public relations, Queens Borough Public Library, January 1992; and Lorch, "Queens Polyglot Libraries."

34. Interview with Marian Lytle, children's librarian, Rowan Public Library, Salisbury, North Carolina, January 1992.

35. Mary N. Landgraf, "Library Cards for the Homeless," *American Libraries* 22, no. 10 (November 1991), 945–950.

36. Frankie Pelzmen, "Upfront News Washington Observer," in "Room with a View," *Wilson Library Bulletin* (October 1991), 19.

37. "CBS News Features Crisis in America's Libraries," *Library Hotline,* July 15, 1991, p. 1.

38. Alan F. Westin and Anne L. Finger, *Using the Public Library in the Computer Age: Present Patterns, Future Possibilities* (Chicago: American Library Association, 1991).

39. Ibid.

40. Interview with Mark West, administrator, Elk Grove Village Public Library, Illinois, January 1992.

41. "For the first time since W.W. II, San Diego Public Library will be open on Sundays . . . ," *Library Hotline,* October 21, 1991, p. 6.

42. "City of San Ramon, California, Survey," *Library Hotline,* August 5, 1991, p. 3.

43. Interview with Luren Dickinson, director, Findlay-Hancock County Public Library, Ohio, January 1992.

44. "Borrowing Increases in the Face of Cuts: Brooklyn Public Library," *Library Hotline,* November 18, 1991, and July 15, 1991, p. 1.

45. Interview with Sarah Linder, chief, Main Library, and David Warren, director, Richland County Public Library, Columbia, South Carolina, January 1992.

A New Decade for Intellectual Freedom:
Of Heroes and the Bill of Rights

John B. Harer

Head, Circulation Division
Sterling C. Evans Library
Texas A&M University
College Station, TX

One of the world's greatest documents, the Bill of Rights, the first ten amendments to the U.S. Constitution, was ratified two hundred years ago, in 1791. Few professionals are as affected by intellectual freedom matters as are librarians. Both the ALA Library Bill of Rights, adopted in 1939, and its Freedom to Read Statement reflect librarians' commitment to the principles of the First Amendment. In communities small and large, librarians have stood with public officials, teachers, library trustees, library staff, and volunteers to defend the First Amendment when it was challenged by an individual or a group. Confronted with an array of issues from protecting the confidentiality of library patrons' reading choices to guarding against a challenge to a library resource, librarians need to know the constitutional heritage of the United States, use common sense, and constantly be vigilant against the forces of repression.

Intellectual Freedom Awards

What librarians have done is indistinguishable from the deeds performed by many courageous people in all walks of life. Society likes to reward its more memorable heroes, and the library/publishing profession is no exception. The following were recognized in 1991 for extraordinary and courageous accomplishments in defense of intellectual freedom.

- C. James Schmidt, former chairperson of the ALA Intellectual Freedom Committee and currently with the Research Libraries Group, received the coveted Robert B. Downs Intellectual Freedom Award. Cosponsored by the Greenwood Press and the Graduate School of Library Science at the University of Illinois at Urbana–Champaign, the award recognizes a professional librarian for his or her significant contributions in defense of the First Amendment.

- Christopher Merrett, deputy university librarian at the University of Natal in Pietermaritzburg, South Africa, won the John Phillip Imroth Memorial Award for Intellectual Freedom, an ALA award granted to a person or group who has demonstrated extraordinary courage in defense and support of intellectual freedom. Merrett received the award for years of courageous support of the principles of intellectual freedom for all peoples in South Africa.

- The Oregon Intellectual Freedom Clearinghouse received the Intellectual Freedom Round Table State Program Award for 1991. Sponsored by IFRT and funded by Social Issues Resources Series, Inc. (SIRS), the award recognizes the most creative and successful state library association intellectual freedom committee program or project. A cooperative effort of the Oregon state government, the Oregon Library Association and Educational Media Association, and the American Association of University Women, the Oregon Clearinghouse has sponsored several events and workshops and published numerous reports to keep various constituencies informed about intellectual freedom issues.

- David R. Bates, public information officer at the Houston Public Library, won the Texas Library Association/SIRS Intellectual Freedom Award. A longtime supporter of intellectual freedom and a frequent speaker and presenter of workshops, Bates is contributing editor on intellectual freedom to the *Texas Library Journal* and the *Library Administration and Management Journal*.[1]

- Representative Don Edwards (D–Calif.) received the 1991 James Madison Award honoring champions of the public's right to know for his leadership in defense of civil liberties and privacy. Sponsored by the Coalition on Government Information, the award was first established in 1989.[2]

Seven individuals received the Hugh M. Hefner First Amendment Award in October 1991:

- Allan Adler, the leading litigating attorney under the Freedom of Information Act, was given the award for publishing. His efforts have vastly increased public access to information from the federal government.

- Debbie Nathan received the Hefner award for print journalism. A free-lance journalist, Nathan has worked tirelessly to defend day-care workers falsely accused of sexual abuse.

- The award for arts and entertainment was given to Bell Lewitzky, founder of the Lewitzky Dance Company, for standing up against the National Endowment for the Arts anti-obscenity pledge.

- James Dana, president of the Great Lakes Booksellers Association, was awarded the Hefner prize for book publishing. Dana was instrumental in combating repressive Michigan censorship legislation.

- Traci Bauer, editor in chief of the *Southwest Standard,* the student paper at Southwest Missouri State University, won the law award. She successfully won the right to access campus crime reports.

- The Hefner award for government was given to Sydney Schanberg, associate editor of *New York Newsday*. Schanberg was in the forefront of efforts to end Pentagon censorship during the Persian Gulf war.

- Inez Austin was recognized for individual conscience as a whistle-blower at the Westinghouse Hanford Tank Farms.[3]

Notable Resources

In the bicentennial year of the Bill of Rights, a number of publications and resources were produced to aid librarians and others to understand the principles of the Bill of Rights and report on the state of intellectual freedom.[4]

Two resources are central to any effort to remain current on intellectual freedom. A bimonthly publication of the Office for Intellectual Freedom (OIF), the *Newsletter on Intellectual Freedom,* is an excellent source of information on issues and trends facing all types of institutions. The *Intellectual Freedom Manual,* also published by OIF, is recommended as a guide for libraries developing policy and for professionals facing challenges. The fourth edition will be available in Spring 1992. OIF has also developed a database of censorship incidents and other challenges to intellectual freedom.

The Modular Education Program on Confidentiality in Libraries was field-tested in 1991. Attendees of a postconference to the Public Library Association's annual conference in San Diego saw two modules of the program successfully tested: "Policy Writing" and "Technology and Confidentiality." The "Legislative" module was tested at the Arizona/Mountain Plains Library Association conference in October 1991. The program features manuals for trainers and workbooks for participants, all designed to instruct individuals and groups about intellectual freedom and confidentiality of library records.

The American Library Association, through the Office for Intellectual Freedom, and the American Bar Association's Commission on Public Understanding about the Law will publish the Bill of Rights Bicentennial Resource Kit to celebrate the occasion. The kit includes a resource book and four poster-size reproductions of public service announcements used in billboard displays that celebrated freedoms guaranteed by the Bill of Rights. The resource book is designed to assist in showcasing the Bill of Rights, including publicity aids and activity ideas.

The American Library Association also published *Information Freedom and Censorship: World Report, 1991,* by William Shawcross, chairperson of the London-based Article XIX International Centre on Censorship. The report gives an extensive country-by-country analysis of the results of the only human rights survey focusing on freedom of expression.

Three other resources that became available in 1991 are *The First Amendment Handbook* by the Reporters' Committee for Freedom of the Press, a booklet of postcards to help legislators lobby for intellectual freedom, and a booklet from the American Society of Newspaper Publishers. The *Handbook* is an excellent guide to such First Amendment issues as confidential sources, libel, invasion of privacy, the Freedom of Information Act, copyright, and access. The "Ban Censorship" postcards are available at B. Dalton and Crown bookstores and include a foreword by People for the American Way. *Celebrate the First Amendment: A Newspaper Editor's Guide to Celebrating the 200th Anniversary of the First Amendment* is a 52-page booklet of information and suggestions for ways to celebrate the Bill of Rights.

The Intellectual Freedom Climate

Despite the celebration of the Bill of Rights' dynamic two-hundred-year survival, support for its principles may be eroding in the face of what seem to be insurmountable obstacles. A survey conducted by Robert Wyatt, professor at Middle Tennessee State University, and David Neft of Gannett, Inc., revealed that Americans " 'believe they believe' in free expression but, on close inquiry, 'it is obvious that they don't.' "[5] A majority of the respondents would give the press far less protection than political speech, for example. Given specific situations and asked if they would protect the action all the time, sometimes, or not at all, a substantial plurality would not protect many such acts at all. Twenty-eight percent would not allow newspapers to editorialize on a current political campaign. Reporters criticizing the military would be banned by 23 percent, and the reporting of classified material would not be allowed by 48 percent of those surveyed.

A number of highly charged national debates have demonstrated that intellectual freedom as a national ethic has deteriorated among the public. Most visible are the machinations over "political correctness." According to Greg Sawyer, dean of students at the University of North Texas, there is no political correctness movement; the term has been devised by adversaries of multicultural diversity on college campuses and elsewhere.[6]

Two nationally televised Public Broadcasting System programs, a special edition of "Firing Line" and a national town meeting debate moderated by Fred Friendly, showcased the issue before the American public. The town meeting was illustrative of the division within the scholarly and civil liberties communities over the procedures for dealing with "hate speech" and what is seen as political correctness in some circles. Speakers such as Nat Hentoff argued against policies that developed a list of prohibited words, calling them censorship of the worst kind. Others on the panel, students and professors from Stanford, for example, called for sanctions by universities for words and comments of racial and sexual harassment. The "Firing Line" broadcast encapsulated the two sides of the issue.

As Michael Kinsley, the moderator of the program, wrote in a recent article for the *New Republic,* the argument against political correctness is a strategy exemplified either by William F. Buckley's seminal work *God and Man at Yale,* which argues not for objectivity in academia but for conservative orthodoxy, or by Dinesh D'Souza's *Illiberal Education,* which relies heavily on isolated anecdotes.[7] If conservative orthodoxy is the ultimate goal, as suggested by Kinsley, then the United States could be in for another round of speech censorship that would bleed into library services.

ALA Intellectual Freedom Committee

The ALA Intellectual Freedom Committee, assisted by the Office for Intellectual Freedom, addresses through policy making those phenomena that contribute to the climate of intellectual freedom, especially in libraries. Political correctness aroused some worry and debate within the committee in 1991, but several national events augured serious implications for libraries and the expressive rights of all citizens.[8]

First and foremost was the alarming U.S. Supreme Court ruling in *Rust* v. *Sullivan.* The decision to uphold regulations prohibiting abortion clinics funded by federal monies from providing patients with information about abortion services relied heavily on the logic that dictating policy on ideological grounds was justified if institutions received federal subsidies. Although Chief Justice William Rehnquist acknowledged in his majority opinion that a university is a traditional place for the open exchange of ideas that should not be tampered with, the decision does not include language to prevent the federal government from dictating that a library receiving federal dollars cannot hold abortion or pro-choice materials. Some legal scholars suggest that this will not occur, but the decision does not indicate where the court would stand on the issue for libraries.

Second, as the national economy fluctuates and threatens the stability of the country and of its citizens, the fallout is manifested in the growing ranks of the poor and the homeless. Faced with the problems of the poor in using library services and the desire to improve services to this group, libraries are caught in the inevitable struggle between providing access and protecting shrinking resources. Their dilemma was brought to bear on the committee in two ways. A suit on behalf of a homeless person in Morristown, New Jersey, *Kreimer* v. *Morristown,* divided the ranks of library professionals. Although the New Jersey Library Association, among others, supported the Morristown Public Library's attempts to regulate behavior in the library, the Intellectual Freedom Committee, through ALA, and the Freedom to Read Foundation joined the suit by the American Civil Liberties Union to protect the right of access to library services for all citizens, including the homeless and the poor.

The committee also was concerned about the growing trend toward fee-based access to new and, possibly, to traditional services to enhance dwindling financial support. Two hearings on fees for library services were held in 1991, one at the ALA Midwinter meeting in Chicago and the second at the annual ALA conference in Atlanta. At both, the right to receive information was recognized as corollary to the right of free expression and fees and restrictive regulations were viewed as barriers to information access.

Third, the U.S. government's control over the press and treatment of Arab-American citizens during the Persian Gulf war drew outcries. Ground rules set for the press corps by the Pentagon contained severe limitations similar to those instituted during the Grenada invasion of 1983. A small group of news organizations, selected with an apparent conservative bias, were given official credentials. The guidelines included a military review process and travel restrictions that some news media called an attempt to manage the reporting of the war. Furthermore, before the breakout of hostilities, President Bush issued an executive order imposing an embargo on Iraq and Iraqi-controlled Kuwait. The original order followed established precedent and exempted library and scholarly materials. But a second order reversed the precedent, banning books and the exchange of library information. ALA Council adopted a resolution calling for less restrictive censorship guidelines for the press and two resolutions on the embargo by the United States and the United Nations. Another resolution condemned the intimidation of Arab-American citizens by FBI agents under the guise of protecting them from harassment by other Americans.

Reinterpreting the Library Bill of Rights

Interpretations of the Library Bill of Rights intended to guide professionals are an integral part of the *Intellectual Freedom Manual.* From time to time the interpretations must be reexamined to address changes in the profession and the society as a whole resulting from state and federal legislation on information access, political and economic pressures, or specific problems that affect libraries. At the 1991 ALA Midwinter Conference, the committee revised the interpretation on exhibit spaces and meeting rooms because of a challenge to the Oxford (Mississippi) Public Library's policy on meeting room use. A lawsuit brought by Concerned Women for America objected to the exclusion of religious services as a valid room use. The Intellectual Freedom Committee rewrote this interpretation as two separate interpretations, one for exhibit spaces and bulletin boards and one for meeting rooms. The committee recommended that policies governing meeting room use be written in inclusive rather than exclusive language and that policies limiting room use to library-sponsored activities be permitted as long as they are applied to all organizations.

Interpretations of the Library Bill of Rights need to be revised to address perceived and potential infractions by libraries and professionals. The committee completed all its revisions in 1991, in preparation for the new edition of the *Intellectual Freedom Manual* and also to alert the profession to a number of possible dangers:

- The tendency in selecting materials and in providing access to services to obstruct use by minors. (The committee revised "Free Access to Libraries for Minors.")
- Use of administrative policies and procedures to create barriers to such groups as minors, the homeless, and the poor. ("Regulations, Policies, and Procedures Affecting Access to Library Resources and Services" replaced "Administrative Policies and Procedures. . . .")
- Creating collections with restricted access to protect materials from loss or theft or to segregate potentially controversial materials. The revised version of "Restricted Access to Library Materials" includes the reminder that the goal is to establish free and open access, though preservation issues may have overriding considerations in some cases.

Universal Declaration of Human Rights and Free Expression

Fallout from controversy over *The Starvation of Young Black Minds,* by Robert Wedgeworth and Lisa Drew, carried over into the debate over adoption of the United Nations Declaration of Human Rights, particularly Article 19 dealing with expressive rights. This was by no means the only international issue the committee had to face, and librarians were becoming increasingly aware that they could no longer view intellectual freedom in a parochial way. Iran's death threat against Salman Rushdie, Israeli press censorship, and the Iraq-Kuwait war were recent dilemmas with grave consequences for the profession.

As the South African controversy began to unfold in 1990, ALA realized that the Library Bill of Rights did not address international issues. This led the Intellectual Freedom Committee to develop "The Universal Right to Free Expression," an interpretation of the Library Bill of Rights originally begun as "The Free Flow of Information." Its language sets a philosophical base for the expressive rights of all people in the world, incorporating not only Article 19 but also Articles 18 and 20 of the UN Universal Declaration of Human Rights. ALA could not adopt the UN document as policy without setting a bad precedent, and such a step seemed impractical as well. After all, the association had never adopted the U.S. Constitution or Bill of Rights as policy. The ALA Library Bill of Rights codifies the principles of the profession, even as they apply to international concerns, without embroiling libraries in issues that only indirectly affect them. The "Universal Right to Free Expression" makes it clear that government oppression and censorship in any form cannot be tolerated.

Intellectual Freedom Update

The Intellectual Freedom Committee is faced with myriad topics each time it meets, and its work on many issues extends over several years. Two types of government intervention in expressive rights have preoccupied library professionals over the last two years. The FBI Library Awareness Program is particularly reprehensible because of its violation of privacy implications. The committee monitored the program, which sought information from librarians on the reading habits of foreign nationals, and obtained reports from librarians on their requests for personal files held by the FBI. A Midwinter report on these results indicated that the FBI does not view the program as a problem. The FBI returned most requests for personal files, denying their existence.

In 1990, ALA had brought suit against the federal government for enforcing the record-keeping and forfeiture provisions of the Child Protection and Obscenity Enforcement Act of 1988. Although the case, *ALA* v. *Thornburgh,* was argued on appeal, Congress passed the Child Restoration and Penalties Enhancement Act, which changed most of the objectionable language of the previous law. However, the committee, through ALA, and the Freedom to Read Foundation once again brought suit against the federal government, charging that the new law was an unconstitutional burden on the conduct of library services. The new challenge succeeded in laying aside enforcement until regulations are made. The committee will continue to monitor this latest legislative attempt to broaden the scope of obscenity enforcement.

In other matters, a resolution introduced and tabled at ALA's 1990 annual conference calling for publication of the paperback edition of *The Satanic Verses* was dropped from consideration. In a vain attempt to get the Iranian death sentence lifted, Salman Rushdie renounced its publication and embraced Islam. The National Endowment for the Arts was reauthorized, but language prohibiting obscene art is still included, though the anti-obscenity pledge was eliminated.

Recent Developments

Vigilance is as much the byword for the Intellectual Freedom Committee as for any library professional. As the committee struggles with unresolved controversies and routine matters, new difficulties always arise, sometimes in the most surprising ways. At the ALA annual conference, the committee was suddenly faced with an explosive issue within the profession. A Langston Hughes quotation was removed from publicity for the Gay and Lesbian History Month celebration at the Los Angeles Public Library on orders from the director. Several — primarily African-American — staff members objected to the assertion that Hughes was gay. Asked to prepare a resolve against such censorship, the committee did so by revising the interpretation "Regulations, Policies, and Procedures Affecting Access to Library Resources and Services."

Other issues raised during the annual conference have nationwide implications for at least the near future. First, the committee prepared a resolution against the Pornography Victims Compensation Act, a bill introduced into Congress during the spring term, noting that, if the bill is enacted, libraries could be held liable for financial compensation as distributors under the law's definitions of the same. At the very least, enforcement of the act would have a chilling effect on libraries.

Second, the committee heard a disturbing report of congressional action to reduce the Smithsonian's funding due to a comment entered in a visitor's book by Librarian of Congress James Billington on inaccuracies he noted in a western art exhibit. Billington's comment prompted some Representatives to press to limit Smithsonian funding on ideological grounds. The committee passed a resolution voicing its concern over the revision of text accompanying the art display and the trend in Congress to tie funding to a narrow point of view.

As the conference progressed, committee members were saddened by news of Supreme Court Justice Thurgood Marshall's resignation. The departure of this champion of civil rights and the First Amendment is seen as a severe blow to expressive and civil rights. As the makeup of the Court grows even more conservative, there is great trepidation about the direction it will take in the next several years. ALA Council passed a resolution honoring Justice Marshall that had been recommended by the committee.

Conclusion

All those who have defended intellectual freedom, even in a small way, have helped protect the expressive rights of all people. The ALA Library Bill of Rights and its interpretations inspire and reinforce librarians' dedication to the principles of intellectual freedom and vigilance against the forces of censorship. The document educates library professionals, staff, and other responsible individuals and guides them in their daily lives.

Beyond the Library Bill of Rights, the greatest resource within ALA lies within the Office for Intellectual Freedom. OIF is the anchor within the association that supports the Intellectual Freedom Committee and professionals in need. Its good counsel is the result of years of study and experience. Its publishing activities and other projects are aimed at broadening the understanding of all citizens, not just library professionals, of the First Amendment. The new decade holds serious challenges for the committee. Though its foundation for meeting these is strong, we must all be constantly vigilant to protect the ideals of intellectual freedom.

Notes

1. Information here and elsewhere in this report was obtained from the Office for Intellectual Freedom's *Memorandum,* a monthly newsletter; minutes of the IFC 1991 Midwinter meeting; and the author's notes as a committee member.
2. "Rep. Edwards Honored," *Newsletter on Intellectual Freedom* 40, no. 4 (July 1991): 122.
3. Playboy Foundation public announcement, Oct. 17, 1991.
4. Information on recent publications was obtained from several 1991 issues of the Office for Intellectual Freedom's *Memorandum*.
5. "Survey Finds Weak Support for Free Expression," *Newsletter on Intellectual Freedom* 40, no. 4 (July 1991): 122.
6. Speech given by W. Greg Sawyer at the Drive-in for Diversity conference, Texas A&M University, Nov. 22, 1991.
7. Michael Kinsley, "TRB from Washington: P.C.B.S.," *New Republic,* May 20, 1991: pp. 8, 50.
8. The information in the remainder of this report was obtained from the minutes of the Intellectual Freedom Committee's 1991 meetings and the 1991 Intellectual Freedom Committee Reports to Council by Chairperson Gordon Conable.

WHCLIS: The Second White House Conference on Library and Information Services

Rhea Farberman

Director, Public Affairs
White House Conference on Library and Information Services

On July 9–13, 1991, 700 delegates from all 50 states and six U.S. territories, the District of Columbia, and the Native American community convened in Washington, D.C., at the second national White House Conference on Library and Information Services to consider the future role of library and information services in a rapidly changing society. The culmination of many years of grass-roots activity and interest, the conference stemmed directly from a joint congressional resolution (PL 100-382) calling on the president to authorize and request a second White House Conference.

The seeds of the 1991 conference were planted more than a decade ago at the first national conference on library and information services when the Information Age and the personal computer were in their infancy. The 1979 conference produced 64 policy recommendations including one that "a White House or federal Conference on Library and Information Services be held every decade to establish the national information goals and priorities for the next decade, to assure effective transfer of knowledge to citizenry, and to accomplish this goal in light of accelerated changes in information and technology practices."

Designing the Conference

Planning for the second White House Conference began in 1985 with the creation of the White House Conference Preliminary Design Group. The 17-member committee appointed by the National Commission on Libraries and Information Science was charged with suggesting the scope and focus of the conference.

In its December 1985 report, the group identified three overarching themes for the conference: "increased productivity, literacy, and sound government decision making" as "critical to the health of our nation." Calling libraries "information agencies in an information society" and "indispensable to the economic well-being of our nation," the group proposed that the second White House Conference consider ways for libraries:

- To make information accessible to all people through networks that link the resources of public, university, school, and special libraries
- To provide business and industry improved access to needed information
- To ensure access to new information technology
- To support formal education for literacy more effectively
- To best extend literacy and other basic information services to people in rural areas and the disadvantaged
- To support lifelong learning for people of all ages, conditions, and abilities
- To serve as effective information centers for all citizens

- To make use of technology to store, analyze, and transmit information needed by government decision makers and the public

A secondary purpose of the conference would be to increase public support for libraries and appreciation for the importance of the nation's information resources.

Fine-tuning the Platform

Thousands of Americans had the opportunity to participate in the democratic process and express their support for libraries and access to information by taking part in preconference activities.

During the five grueling days of the national conference in Washington, delegates fine-tuned the recommendations that had "funneled up" from the grass-roots level into a coherent platform consisting of 95 policy recommendations. Following are the priority recommendations that are expected to focus legislative initiatives at both the state and federal levels.

- Adoption of an Omnibus Children and Youth Literacy Initiative
- Creation and funding of the National Research and Education Network (NREN)
- Sufficient funding for libraries to provide the information resources needed for increased U.S. productivity and competitiveness
- Creation of a model library marketing program
- Literacy initiatives including the development of a national training model for library literacy programs
- Adoption of a national information preservation policy
- Development of networks connecting rural, small, urban, and tribal libraries
- Creation of library programs and materials for multicultural, multilingual populations
- Amendments to copyright legislation respective to new and emerging information technologies
- Expansion of the Freedom of Information Act to ensure access to all nonexempt information whether received by the federal government or created at public expense regardless of physical form or characteristics
- Designation of libraries as educational institutions for lifelong learning and inclusion of libraries in all legislation, regulations, and policies designed to support and improve American education

In the words of conference Cochairperson Richard Akeroyd, "The WHCLIS platform recommends programs and policies which would strengthen the role of libraries as educational institutions, ensure access to information for more Americans and teach literacy skills. When they are implemented, these recommendations will allow our national information infrastructure to meet the challenges of a more diverse American society, more complex information technologies, and a more complex world." Specifically, the proposals suggest ways library and information services can advance literacy, productivity, and democracy and make library services for young people and underserved populations a priority.

Some members of the library community have expressed concern that the sheer number of recommendations (95) may hinder the implementation process. But a review of the recommendations clearly reveals the small number of overarching themes that are of utmost importance to the delegates. "If even half of the resolutions passed by the conference are acted upon, we will see significant change in this country in terms of access to information for all Americans," concludes John Tyson, state librarian of Virginia and a conference delegate.

Information 2000: Library and Information Services for the 21st Century, the summary report of the conference, was presented to President Bush in November 1991. The president transmitted the report with his response to Congress in February 1992. Governors and state library officials also received a copy, and the report is available for public review at federal depository libraries nationwide.

WHCLIS: "A Process, Not an Event"

Bill Asp, director of the Minnesota State Office of Library Development and Services and a member of the White House Conference Advisory Committee, calls WHCLIS "a process, not an event." Indeed, the 95 policy recommendations adopted by delegates to the national conference in July 1991 were the results of years of planning and the input of thousands of Americans.

"The timing of the second White House Conference created high hopes and high expectations for the process," states Akeroyd, state librarian of Connecticut as well as conference cochairperson and chairperson of the conference advisory committee. "During the 1990s, we will face new and exciting opportunities for libraries to play center stage in American education and economic development, but we are also facing declining resources for libraries. Many libraries are being asked to do more with less and are looking to the WHCLIS recommendations for help and direction."

"This conference really is the voice of the American people concerning library and information services," Charles Reid, conference cochairperson, said at the close of the conference, and it remains true today. "This process has identified the priority for national policy into the next decade for library and information services in relationship to access to information, education, and American productivity," Reid concluded. The mandate of Public Law 100-382 has been met; the full impact of the 1991 WHCLIS, however, is yet to be measured.

The Process Continues: The Virginia Library and Information Services Task Force*

The Virginians who participated in the Virginia Governor's Conference on Library and Information Services were determined to see their deliberations and work bear fruit. To ensure that the agenda established at the Governor's Conference would stay before the people of the commonwealth, they passed Resolution 18, calling for the establishment of a group to follow up on the resolutions and undertake grass-roots implementation of the recommendations.

*John C. Tyson, state librarian, and Frank Freimarck, VLIST cochairperson, supplied our information on developments in Virginia.

In response to that resolution, State Librarian John Tyson appointed the Virginia Library and Information Services Task Force (VLIST). The 22-member task force of citizens and librarians, Governor's Conference and White House Conference delegates, observers, and volunteers is chaired by Trist McConnell and Fran Freimarck, Virginia's delegates to the White House Conference. Ida Patton of the state library's Public Library Development Division is staff liaison.

VLIST identified action already taken on Governor's Conference resolutions and issued a report. To create a framework for implementation of the remaining resolutions, VLIST grouped the resolutions and recommendations under four main initiatives: Libraries and Productivity; Library Cooperation; Library Services for Children and Youth; and Creating an Understanding of Libraries.

Libraries and Productivity is aimed at ensuring that librarians assist each individual in the commonwealth in reaching his or her potential for acquiring and applying skills as a productive worker or responsible citizen. Among its priorities is recognition of libraries by the governor and the legislature as an integral part of all plans for state education and telecommunication.

Library Cooperation is aimed at building and maintaining the Virginia Library and Information Network (VLIN) to allow equitable access and participation for all citizens and libraries. The network will be an example of public/private partnership to build a solid and more effective information infrastructure for Virginia's future economic and social health. Of paramount importance is that through state, local, and private funding, all libraries in the commonwealth will be able to convert bibliographic records to machine-readable format. In addition, libraries in the state will have a microcomputer and modem to access the online database and transfer data. This initiative also seeks to promote cooperative collection development among Virginia libraries.

Library Services for Children and Youth is intended to ensure that the Commonwealth of Virginia meet the library-related needs of its children and youth. Among its priorities is the establishment of a statewide, resource sharing network that includes school libraries with media programs as equal partners with public libraries and ensures all youth access to the state's library and information resources. This initiative seeks to develop a partnership between school and public libraries to provide comprehensive library services to children and young adults. It provides grants to colleges and universities for the development and support of both undergraduate and graduate programs that prepare library and information service providers to serve children and young adults.

Creating an Understanding of Libraries will position libraries at the center of the information sector in the twenty-first century. To achieve this initiative, libraries need sound infrastructure and policy. Priorities include a comprehensive, statewide marketing plan and fostering an understanding of libraries and their services. The plan will emphasize the library as a resource to meet the educational, business, and personal needs of the community.

VLIST held its first public meeting January 16, 1992, the afternoon of the Virginia Library Association's Legislative Day. Participants received VLIST's report and proposed initiatives with enthusiasm and interest. The next steps are to identify responsible individuals who are willing to become involved, and specific strategies for implementing the priorities established for each initiative.

Conference Postscript: Evaluating the Process

Approximately three weeks after the conclusion of WHCLIS, a conference evaluation form was sent to delegates. Members of the delegations were asked 21 questions on how the conference was conducted, ranging from the recommendations development process and selection of speakers to lodging accommodations.

Four hundred and thirty-two delegates (62 percent of the total voting delegation) responded to the survey. An overwhelming majority, 77 percent, rated the conference as successful. Seventy-four percent called the meal function speakers excellent. The keynote speakers were also rated as excellent by 83 percent of the respondents.

Respondents strongly supported the role of state and preconference activities in their preparation for the national forum. Eighty-six percent categorized their state's preconference activity as "timely, meaningful, and good preparation for the White House Conference."

Regarding the functioning of the conference, most delegates rated the process by which issues produced at the state level were fine-tuned for consideration at the national forum as excellent (26 percent), good (39 percent), or acceptable (30 percent). However, those casting their vote in the good range were also expressing the belief that some changes could improve the process.

The most frequent concern of the respondents was the amount of time available at the conference to complete the recommendations debate process. In the final analysis, the greatest detraction of the conference process seems to have been an overloaded schedule.

The following is a sample of what delegates said about WHCLIS.

Phyllis Heroy (Baton Rouge, LA): "Overall, WHCLIS was handled well. I enjoyed the great variety of speakers and issues presented. The major concern I have is the extreme rush under which the recommendations had to be considered, discussed, and formulated."

Trist McConnell (Williamsburg, VA): "The conference was exhilarating and productive. The extent to which the president and Congress adopt and support our recommendations and resolutions is the ultimate measure of the conference's success."

Calvin Potter (Kohler, WI): "Those in the political arena need a clear and simple message. For the next conference, direct the states to submit a limited number of resolutions to be considered. Overall, it appears that we accomplished our objective; now we can move on to the implementation phase."

Anonymous: "Concerning the recommendations, I was pleased in the end. The process, however, was frustrating because of the lack of time and voting methods. There were so many issues, too many special interests, and not enough thought to the broad perspective."

Vicki Fischo (Frankfort, KY): "I consider WHCLIS one of the most enlightening opportunities it has been my experience to enjoy. It epitomized the democratic process and forged in me a renewed respect for our imperfect but unparalleled form of government. Where else but in the United States of America could such an exercise have taken place?"

Linda Harris (Las Cruces, NM): "Was the week worth the taxpayers' investment in us? I say yes. First, because people like me, and the mayor from Florida, and the library volunteer from Kansas, should have a stake in what happens to the nation's libraries. Plus, no plan for public education reform should be considered without its national partner—the public library. Our job was and is to give voice to that partnership."

Library Networking and Cooperation in 1991*

JoAn S. Segal

Associate Executive Director, Programs
American Library Association

The economic conditions afflicting the world in general, and the library world in particular, played a major part in library networking and cooperative activities in 1991. If cooperation was originally conceived as a frugal practice, librarians have learned over the years that it has its financial and political trade-offs. Yes, cooperative purchasing may bring prices down, but purchasing arrangements do not happen without someone expending time. Interlibrary borrowing can be substituted for some purchases, but growth in interlibrary loan (ILL) activity may demand more staff in that area and faculty members are happiest when they can have their own copies. Indeed, shared cataloging has reduced the professional time spent on minutiae, but participation in users' groups and lobbying for agreed system modifications take top-level catalogers days of meeting time.

Librarians have pressured local, state, and regional networks to reduce libraries' expenses in these areas. Local systems that do not feed into national databases appear increasingly attractive in the short-range, fiscally constrained environment. Based as they are on traditional concepts of hierarchical interlibrary loan protocols, local and statewide databases and resource-sharing systems represent the view that one should seek needed networking and cooperation resources close to home before going far afield. In an interesting article that appears at first to be the history of one consortium, Becky Lenzini and Ward Shaw assert:

> In the highly networked environment which has emerged in the last 10 years, geographic proximity is no longer a defining or limiting characteristic. . . . Partnerships are now forming around common goals or common notions, rather than geographic location.
>
> One of the challenges that this distance independence creates is to find ways to deliver physical or electronic documents directly to users wherever they happen to be and without concern for their specific relationship with the lending library. . . .
>
> These new methods of information delivery can be and will be competitive in price and convenience with the traditional collection model.[1]

In January 1991, nearly 100 invitees attended a seminar for Research Libraries Group (RLG) librarians and OCLC research library users, "Local Systems and Bibliographic Utilities: Data Exchange Options."[2] In his keynote address, Gerald R. Lowell declared that "the spread of local systems, coupled with the existence of more than one bibliographic utility, now inhibit successful data exchange and national-level resource sharing."[3] He cites several factors for the difficulty in exchanging data. Among them are differing methods of implementing local systems, variety in the design and use of bibliographic utilities, different ways of designing local workflow, technological challenges, and differences in institutional environments. He recommends three key attributes for a successful data exchange program: flexibility, cost-effectiveness, and workflow efficiency. Lowell advocates consolidating the Research

---

*This article reaches back to October 1990 for news not reported until early 1991 and closes with a few items published as late as November 1991.

Libraries Information Network (RLIN) and OCLC (the Online Computer Library Center) and having the Library of Congress use this consolidated database for cataloging data and the production of MARC records. According to Lowell, librarians need to see local systems and bibliographic utilities as equally important parts of a national information network.[4]

After encouraging signs of a possible link between the RLIN and OCLC databases, member libraries in late summer rejected an RLG-OCLC negotiated agreement.[5] Lamenting this development, Marshall Keys, NELINET executive director, remarked on the importance of a national bibliographic database and on the breakdown of this dream.[6]

Librarians, who have spearheaded the development of standardized cooperative forms of data interchange and who have begun to impress on others the necessity and importance of cooperatively developed standards in this area, are under the greatest pressure to abandon their lofty collaborative goals. Networkers must fend off these pressures and continue to provide leadership in the development of information standards and data-sharing activities despite the difficult economic conditions.

Major Developments

General

One of the end-of-year shocks in the library community was the sale of NOTIS to Ameritech, following on the heels of recent court decisions that allowed the "Baby Bells" to invest in the information business.[7] Brian Alley expresses the concern that the links between libraries via online public access catalogs (OPACs) and circulation systems may be altered if such services are provided by one or more companies with very different philosophies from the cooperative stance that has historically existed in library networking and cooperation.

Telecommunications

Larry Learn continues to publish his "Telecommunications News and Perspectives" column in *Library Hi Tech News*. Learn provides readers with rare opportunities to become familiar with telecommunications concepts and developments.

National Research and Education Network

History and Philosophy

The *ALA Washington Office Analysis* has kept the library world well informed about the status of National Research and Education Network (NREN) legislation. The June 6, 1991, issue describes three versions of the High-Performance Computing Act of 1991.[8]

Roberta Corbin traces the development of national networks and NREN from the formation of ARPANET in 1969 through NSFNET, BITNET, and Internet. She describes the governmental role, the organization of the Coalition for Networked Information, technological and political implications, and the role librarians can play in conjunction with others in the dreamed-of NREN.[9]

The May 1991 issue of *NELINET Liaison* gives a clear and practical description of Internet and BITNET. Author Mary McKenna includes some references.[10]

In his analysis of NREN and its philosophical underpinnings, Milo Nelson points out the difficulty in imagining a network with both educational and research goals. He expresses misgivings about the speed with which NREN is progressing, yet he is hopeful about making education less "rooted to space and sites," with a basic change in the way education and information are received.[11]

The research of Charles McClure and others on NREN received the Jesse H. Shera Award for the best research in library/information science for 1990.[12] With an extensive history of its development, the research report includes valuable resource materials from the National Science Foundation and the National Academy of Science, among other organizations.[13]

Continued expansion and upgrading of NSFNET is involving more researchers throughout the nation.[14] Kenneth King, president of EDUCOM, billed NSFNET the "interim NREN" at the Net 1991 meeting, held March 20–22. Attendees showed optimism about national networking.[15]

Developments

Library Perspectives on NREN, edited by Carol Parkhurst, was published by the Library Information and Technology Association (LITA).[16] The monograph contains materials from the NREN packet that LITA issued in 1990.

The Senate passed its version of NREN on September 11, which went to conference committee to merge with the House of Representatives' version that passed in July.[17] On December 9, 1991, President Bush signed the bill and it became PL 102-1194.[18]

Conferences

The second Networks for Networkers Conference was held in Washington, D.C., in December 1990. In March 1991, an attractive document containing a synthesis of the papers from the conference and a summary of its resolutions was prepared for delegates to the White House Conference on Library and Information Services (WHCLIS). All delegates received a copy. In addition to the results of the conference, the document contains excellent background summaries on library networks, computer networking, and telecommunications concepts. Among the key issues it elaborates for the delegates are NREN; new technology and information access; network support for scholarly research and for citizen access to information; and library and information research, innovation, and standards. The document urges library professionals to form information alliances and to move away from library-centered networks, embracing multitype information providers and becoming a component of a large network of providers.

It presents a comprehensive vision of information access: "Anyone who wants a piece of information or data can obtain it, if it exists, and use it productively, and communicate with anyone else as needed, at his/her desk, without undue effort, in a short time, at a reasonable cost, and be confident of the quality and integrity of the process."

As measures of the presentation's success, the NREN resolution was the second most highly supported item on the WHCLIS delegates' agenda, and several networking resolutions were included in the final list of WHCLIS outcomes.[19]

Key Publications

Bibliographic Utilities

Irene Hoadley discussed the future of library "utilities" in her address to the Mountain Plains and Utah Library Associations (MPLA/ULA) in May 1990. The paper found its way into the published literature in February 1991. Hoadley urges more cooperation among bibliographic utilities, believes utilities should serve libraries, not end users and not networks, and describes a complete "information cycle" for libraries and users, including bibliographic data for monographs and journals and full-text electronic document delivery.[20]

Sheila Intner, reacting to discussions between OCLC and RLG, focused on the history of library networks in her "Interfaces" column in May.[21] Her insightful analysis of the development of OCLC in comparison with other "utilities" includes a description of what she believes to be the three steps OCLC took to ensure its future survival: (1) funding of a research and development unit; (2) constant updating of its hardware, software, and telecommunications systems; and (3) development of new products and services based on the Online Union Catalog (OLUC). She also notes two "troublesome trends" that have had a negative impact on RLIN: (1) the constant need for major changes in hardware, software, and telecommunications because of progress in computing; and (2) the continuing financial distress among research libraries. Intner deplores the developments that seemed at the time to herald the convergence of national bibliographic utilities into one network, predicting that the emergence of one national database would result in a monopoly opposed to local control and the power of librarians.

Ron Miller published his views on utilities and networks in *Information Today* in May. He suggests that networks and utilities will have to face two major issues during a transitional period: services to libraries and their clients and management concerns. According to Miller, the provision of a major cataloging database will continue to be a core service, but the loading of new databases will become an important function. He warns that the communications networks of the utilities must be used carefully to safeguard copyright and ensure that their primary function is served. He believes niche specialties will develop, such as the UnCover products from the Colorado Alliance of Research Libraries (CARL). Management issues include revenue generation in an environment where charging patterns are fluid, competition among organizations that are also trying to find ways to work together toward a common cause, and a trend toward integration. Miller believes in integration and connectivity of services from many sources and by many parties, and he sees great pressure being brought to bear to make access to outside databases, many of them international, available (transparently) on the local OPAC (online public-access catalog).[22]

Interlibrary Loan

In February, Mary Jackson reported on the Interlibrary Loan Discussion Panel at OCLC in October 1990, which raised several issues of importance to public, academic, and state libraries. The growth in ILL traffic only emphasizes the discrepancy between the speed at the "front end" of the process—verifying, locating, requesting, and confirming—and the roadblocks yet to conquer in the fulfillment and delivery of documents. A major issue involves how libraries are compensated for ILL services. Concern increases when lending activity far exceeds borrowing. Suggestions for ways to absorb costs include a national coupon system. A second major issue is the disparity between bibliographic and physical access; here, suggestions for improvement include turnaround time standards and improved access to local collections. The panel suggested that several existing cost models be reviewed and one chosen for a cost study.

The panel also discussed "free" or "universal" access, recommending it be examined at a national ILL conference. Other topics were balance in borrowing and lending, turnaround time from request to receipt, and a national union catalog, now under challenge by state and regional union catalogs. A final issue was training for ILL practitioners and improved communication among them. A national interlibrary loan conference was suggested.[23]

In her June 1991 column, Jackson touches on several other aspects of resource sharing. She describes an ILL electronic discussion group and the significance of instantaneous debate of ILL issues. This specialized "list server" is typical of the way in which librarians have responded to the available technology to link themselves with others having similar interests. The column also includes a useful ILL reading list for resource sharers.[24]

Miscellaneous

Anne Woodsworth and Thomas B. Wall's *Library Cooperation and Networks* indicates the extent to which the field has matured. Designed for use in library schools, their monograph includes definitions, history, and practical examples, with such material as sample bylaws, participant agreements, and survey instruments appended.[25]

Bernard Sloan's *Linked Systems for Resource Sharing* presents an overview of automated resource sharing, detailed descriptions of the ILLINET Online and IRVING projects, and nitty-gritty details of the planning, funding, management, and evaluation of linked systems. Sloan urges librarians to move beyond the behind-the-scenes aspects of library automation and to use such systems more for resource sharing.[26]

Local, State, Regional, National, and International Library Networking

Local

In May, the directors of the member libraries of the Association of Big Eight Universities (ABEU) and other regional research libraries met at Kansas State University to discuss the growing inability of individual research libraries to purchase publications for researchers and students. They proposed that ABEU libraries serve as the nucleus for a regional library cooperative sharing research library resources. Among the activities to be implemented are a regional OCLC union list of serials, digital fax document delivery, and use of a commercial courier service. Keeping records on the libraries' ability to purchase needed information sources will be emphasized, and such data will be analyzed to keep university faculty and administrators informed about library acquisition problems.[27]

State

The New York State Library will join the New York State Education and Research Network (NYSERNet), thereby gaining access to Internet, starting a staged replacement for New York State Interlibrary Loan (NYSILL) network telecommunications, and building the capability for a statewide E-mail network.[28]

The Florida Library Information Network (FLIN) now has 109 online participants in its OCLC Group Access network, enabling libraries to share resources. The state also makes available the Florida Information Resource Network (FIRN), which provides access to the online catalogs of all state university system libraries and two community colleges.[29]

The first library to come up on the Ohio Library and Information Network (OhioLINK) was the University of Cincinnati, in December 1991. Following soon are Miami University, Bowling Green, Case Western Reserve, Central State, and Wright State. OhioLINK, a research network established for faculty, students, businesses, and the public, will provide access to the holdings of participant libraries via campus computer terminals and personal computers.[30] The network is expected to be the largest shared system in the United States, linking more than 2,500 concurrent users via direct and network access across the state to a database of more than 20 million items held by 18 state and private institutions in the consortium.[31]

Maine is moving toward the creation of a statewide network of major academic and public resources. The URSUS system currently includes the Maine State Library, the State Law and Legislative Reference libraries, the University of Maine, and Colby, Bowdoin, and Bates colleges.[32]

Regional: OCLC-Related

Table 1 includes the major bibliographic databases currently operating networks for the transmission of bibliographic data. Table 2 lists the regional networks of OCLC and the states served by them.

AMIGOS

AMIGOS Bibliographic Council, Inc., inaugurated or expanded several services in 1991. The Specialized Cataloging Services help a variety of libraries, from small col-

Table 1 / Bibliographic Databases

Database	Characteristics
OCLC, Online Computer Library Center	Serves 10,000 libraries of all types; largest database; has own national telecommunications network.
RLIN, the Research Libraries Information Network	Online library service of the Research Libraries Group. Targeted to research libraries, has own national telecommunications network.
UTLAS	Based in Canada, serving libraries throughout the world.
WLN, the Western Library Network	Regional database for Northwest U.S. & Canada known for quality and authority control. Formerly part of Washington State Library, now independent.

Table 2 / OCLC Regional Networks

Name	Chief Area Served
AMIGOS Bibliographic Council, Inc. (AMIGOS)	TX, AZ, NM, OK
Bibliographical Center for Research (BCR)	CO, UT, WY, KS, IA
CAPCON	Washington DC Metro area
Federal Library and Information Network (FEDLINK)	Federal libraries anywhere
ILLINET/OCLC Services	IL
Indiana Cooperative Library Services Authority (INCOLSA)	IN
Michigan Library Consortium (MLC)	MI
MINITEX	MN, SD, ND
Missouri Library Network Corporation (MLNC)	MO
Nebraska Library Commission (NEBASE)	NE
NELINET, Inc.	New England
OCLC Pacific Network (PACNET Headquarters)	WA, OR, CA
OHIONET	OH
PALINET	Eastern PA, NJ, DE, MD
Pittsburgh Regional Library Center (PRLC)	Western PA, WV
Southeastern Library Network (SOLINET)	AR, VA, NC, SC, FL, GA, AL, MS, LA, KY, TN
SUNY/OCLC Network	NY
Wisconsin InterLibrary Services (WILS)	WI

Note: These networks provide a variety of services, both cooperative (such as group buying plans) and automated (reference services, personal computers, CD-ROM application in addition to OCLC), and training. The particular mix of services varies.

lege to large university and public libraries, to alleviate cataloging backlogs and staff shortages.[33] The AMIGOS Collection Analysis System provides a computer analysis of bibliographic files, offering libraries data on overlap and unique titles in defined subject categories.[34] The network signed a retrospective agreement with Washington University in Saint Louis, Missouri, for the conversion of some 586,000 titles.[35]

With the appointment of the AMIGOS Preservation Service (APS) Advisory Council[36] and of Tom Clareson as preservation service manager, progress was made in implementing APS, a project funded by the National Endowment for the Humanities.[37] A funding packet for the support of preservation activities was issued and a preservation survey was initiated in the fall.[38]

AMIGOS moved to larger offices at reduced rent.[39] Its educational activities included the seminar "The Selector's Role in Preservation: Building Collections That Will Last," offered in conjunction with the AMIGOS Fall 1991 Conference,[40] and the workshop "Library Binding as a Preservation Tool," cosponsored by SOLINET and led by SOLINET Preservation Officer Lisa Fox in December 1991.[41] The Spring 1991 membership conference, held May 8–10, featured a general session on library funding that was addressed by W. David Penniman and Ray M. Fry.[42] The keynote speech by Edward G. Holley, OCLC board president, focused on OCLC and the future of its work with networks in providing maximum access to information at the lowest cost.[43]

The fall 1991 conference was expanded to five days, with two and a half days of training seminars preceding the general session on the OCLC/AMIGOS Collection Analysis CD and on collection development and its relationship to preservation and technical services. An exciting forum on visions of possibilities for library patrons dominated one morning session. The conference concluded with a seminar on hard-disk management for IBM PCs.[44]

Bibliographical Center for Research

Although OCLC services continue to be the major focus of the Bibliographical Center for Research (BCR), the network extended offers for new cooperative discounts on CD-ROM products and library supplies throughout the year. Much staff time has been spent on training, with more than 200 sessions scheduled throughout the region between August 1991 and April 1992,[45] especially as libraries were being trained on the new PRISM system. By December 10, all libraries in the region had been trained on PRISM and PASSPORT.[46]

In May, Amy Owen (Utah state librarian) was elected president and Brice Hobrock (director, Kansas State Libraries) was chosen vice president.[47] At the membership meeting, Louella Wetherbee presented the results of her study, carried out for the Network Advisory Committee, on the effects of shared local systems on the national bibliographic database. Her findings were published in fall 1991.[48]

BCR serves as a clearinghouse for information on preservation projects in the region. Articles in its newsletter highlight such projects.

CAPCON

CAPCON's annual membership meeting in June included reports on OCLC developments, NREN, and elections for the board of advisors.[49] Sharon Rogers was reelected to the OCLC Users' Council.[50] The network's continuing education activities included several new training sessions.[51] Between September and December, more than 50 sessions were offered on such topics as OCLC features, classification, various software packages, databases, strategic planning, user satisfaction, copyright law, and cataloging music recordings.[52]

Federal Library and Information Center Committee

The parent group of the FEDLINK network moved along in support of pre–White House Conference and NREN activities. Mary Berghaus Levering became executive director. [For additional information, see the report on FLICC activities later in Part 1 — Ed.]

ILLINET/OCLC

The Illinois state network's extensive OCLC training program is carried out completely by volunteer instructors, coordinated by the Illinois State Library and two ILLINET Users' Group committees.[53] In 1990, 67 workshops were held. By November, every ILLINET/OCLC library had switched to the Sprint network and was trained on PRISM.[54] Beth Sandore continued as chairperson of the Illinois OCLC Users' Group Executive Committee.[55] The group published *Books Format I: Illinois OCLC Users' Group Introductory Workbook — A Self-Help Manual.*[56]

Michigan Library Consortium

The Michigan Library Consortium (MLC) specialized in CD-ROM products and information in 1991.[57] MLC offered 12 automation seminars between September and December.[58]

MINITEX Library and Information Network

In its request for additional funding, MINITEX, which is based in Minneapolis, cited the following facts regarding services: (1) 130 Minnesota postsecondary and state agency libraries participate in MINITEX programs, supported by state appropriations to the Higher Education Coordinating Board at the University of Minnesota; (2) 95 additional libraries participate, including public libraries in Minnesota, through the Office of Library Development and Services; and (3) libraries in North and South Dakota participate through contracts that provide funding. Document delivery, the union list of serials, and online cataloging are core MINITEX services provided at no charge to participating libraries; periodical exchange and reference are secondary services provided on a reimbursement basis.[59] The Minnesota state legislature approved a budget for MINITEX that includes a 12 percent increase over the biennium.[60]

Training is also an important aspect of network services. Sessions include cataloging and classification, OCLC features, the Minnesota Union List of Serials (MULS), and CD-ROM products.[61] A task force reviewed MULS and recommended continuation of the service.[62]

MINITEX serves as a regional clearinghouse to track canceled titles. Libraries use this information as they evaluate journal collections.[63]

In the fall, MINITEX revived the *MINITEX Messenger* to replace the *Communications Memo,* thus returning to a more formal newsletter to disseminate information both in the region and throughout the country.[64] Statistics show that MINITEX received 4 percent more document delivery requests in FY 1991 than in 1990.[65]

Missouri Library Network Corporation

The Missouri Library Network Corporation (MLNC), in Saint Louis, continues to provide Missouri libraries with OCLC and other services. Group purchasing services for CD-ROM products, training on CD-ROM, OCLC, database searching, and provision of OCLC services are MLNC's major activities.[66]

NEBASE

The Nebraska state network, NEBASE, features information on CD-ROM technology along with the usual information about OCLC, interlibrary loan, and training opportunities.[67] Under the new Resource Sharing Participation Program announced by Rod Wagner, Nebraska state librarian, the NELCMS system was eliminated and libraries in Nebraska were asked to use OCLC exclusively for interlibrary loans. The Nebraska Library Commission (State Library) offered to subsidize part of the cost of in-state borrowing and lending. An interlibrary loan fee has been adopted for loans processed through system resource libraries.[68] The new Nebraska Coalition for Networked Information includes the Nebraska Library Commission, the Nebraska Department of Education, the University of Nebraska—Lincoln (Computing Resource Center), the Nebraska State College System, and the Department of Administrative Services, Division of Communications. Its mission is to promote the creation of and access to information resources in networked environments in support of research and education throughout Nebraska.[69]

NELINET

The annual financial issue of the *NELINET Liaison* is a gem of clarity written "in plain English." NELINET members can feel secure that the network's finances are in order and that they understand the financial picture.[70] A strong provider of OCLC services and training, NELINET continues to provide New England libraries with basic automation services.

OHIONET

The OHIONET board and staff set out to develop a strategic plan for the network using the services of the Carroll Group, a consulting firm. Each month, the newsletter *Ohionetwork* carried news of its development. A brief presentation at the annual membership meeting in May was followed by questions and suggestions. A questionnaire was distributed in the summer, and in August the staff analyzed the network's strengths, weaknesses, opportunities, and dangers. In September, the board and senior staff management examined the mission and operating principles and how the staff might support the mission. At the annual program meeting, Julie Virgo, the planning consultant, and Joel Kent, OHIONET executive director, reviewed the work completed to date on the plan. Members expressed strong support for staff development and training, particularly in technology; a clearinghouse of consultants, including OHIONET members with special expertise; an unbiased source of information about vendors and library technology products; education about networks, their development, and how to get on them; document delivery services; value-added services for access to electronic resources; information on cooperative collection development; and expertise on writing requests-for-proposals or bids. The consultant will continue to work with the network until planning operations are concluded. The financial situation improved as FY 1989/1990 was ending, with net revenue of more than $327,000. Every issue of *Ohionetwork* contained announcements of extensive training opportunities.[71] At year's end, Joel Kent resigned as executive director.[72]

PALINET

The PALINET Long-Range Strategic Plan was adopted December 4, 1990, and appeared in the February 1991 issue of *PALINET News*.[73] Every issue of the *News* includes listings of training opportunities. John Zenelis is the president of the PALINET Board of Trustees.[74]

SOLINET

Frank Grisham, SOLINET executive director, received the Rothrock Award from the Southeastern Library Association (SELA) at its annual conference.[75] In his state-of-the-network address, Grisham discussed the results of the SOLINET Member Needs Assessment Project.[76]

In his keynote address at the annual meeting and conference in Atlanta May 2–3, "Networked Information Resources and Services," Paul Peters examined the activities of the Coalition for Networked Information, NREN, and prospects for the future.[77] The board approved the long-range strategic plan and budget. Gail Kennedy was elected to succeed Susan Nutter as chairperson and Barbara Williams Jenkins was elected vice chairperson.[78]

The SOLINET Preservation Program published *Choosing and Working with a Conservator.*[79] In a test of SOLINET's own disaster procedures, its offices suffered flooding from a burst pipe and survived at least partly because of established disaster contingency procedures.[80]

SOLINET has made its 2.4-million-title Library Data Conversion System available on compact disc for use by libraries in in-house retrospective conversion systems. SOLINET staff later process the tapes of records produced at the library.[81]

SOLINET announced that it would move to new offices about half a mile from its current location because of economic conditions. The network will gain space and reduce costs. It will have a larger and better equipped training facility, more conference space, and better parking rates.[82]

SUNY/OCLC

The SUNY/OCLC Network's Resource Sharing Advisory Group drafted a networkwide ILL agreement to encourage more liberal use of interlibrary loan throughout New York State. The network will maintain and publish a list of the signing libraries.[83] SUNY/OCLC Online Information Retrieval Services (SOIRS) offers members group discount rates via CD-ROM and other tailored plans.[84]

In May, the SUNY/OCLC Network Advisory Committee (SONAC) endorsed a new category of participation, associate participant, for libraries within an institution with a centralized cataloging facility but decentralized resource sharing.[85]

Wisconsin Interlibrary Services

New Tech News, published by the Wisconsin Interlibrary Services (WILS), continues to be an outstanding resource for those interested in new technology. Its coverage is not limited to library applications and includes all kinds of technological news, such as VDT hazards, systems lacking standardized commands, NREN and various statewide network configurations, the life span of CD-ROM discs (three–five years!), book reviews, CD-ROM networking — wonderful news items not seen elsewhere.[86]

Regional: Non-OCLC Networks

Colorado Alliance of Research Libraries

An excellent history of the Colorado Alliance of Research Libraries (CARL) provides more than the story of a particular system and how it developed.[87] Always innovative and not risk-averse, CARL leaders relied from the beginning on state-of-the-art technology and pioneered such ideas as incorporating nonbibliographic databases into the system, including nonlibrary entities, and creating the article access service UnCover. Lenzini and Shaw suggest that we must be willing to move into the delivery of a fundamentally important service, but that in doing so we will have to deal with unfamiliar competitors from the private sector, and we will be attracting the attention of the administrators of our institutions, who will also want a part of the action.

CARL Systems introduced its new document delivery service, UnCover 2, in Fall 1991. UnCover 2 is designed for selection and ordering, as well as ILL requests, from the UnCover database. CARL is working with the Copyright Clearance Center and individual publishers to provide royalty fee information.[88]

Cooperative Library Agency for Systems and Services

The Cooperative Library Agency for Systems and Services (CLASS) continues to offer members a wide range of services, including discounts on online services, publications, library supplies, microcomputer software, and CD-ROM products. It also offers workshops and seminars on topics of current interest and consulting services.[89] In late 1990, CLASS merged with A.S.I.A. (Asian Shared Information and Access) to gain collection development, retrospective conversion, and technical processing of Asian language materials.[90]

Western Library Network

The Western Library Network (WLN) moved forward after its recent transition to private nonprofit corporation status with Ron Miller as executive director. New services include the Conspectus Service, the MARC Record Service, LaserPac CD-ROM Catalogs, and the BCL3 Collection Comparison Service.[91]

The Conspectus Service is designed to facilitate collection assessment. It is based on the standard subject descriptors and collection codes used for the North American Collections Inventory Project and the RLG Conspectus. The database software allows libraries to generate five types of reports.[92] The BCL3 Collection Comparison Service allows libraries to compare their collections against the latest edition of *Books for College Libraries*.[93]

New search and sort features have been added for WLN users. They may now sort large sets of bibliographic records by date, format, and title; select without keying in reference numbers; and browse through the bibliographic file.[94]

WLN announced that it would work with UMI Data Courier to convert records in several Data Courier databases to complete-USMARC format.[95] PolarPak, a CD-ROM database of citations to literature on the arctic and polar regions, was also released.[96]

National Networking

Medical Libraries

The National Network of Libraries of Medicine is the new name for the 25-year-old Regional Medical Library Network, but operations will continue much the same as before. The network comprises eight regional medical libraries, 136 resource libraries, and 3,300 local health science libraries, with support from the National Library of Medicine through contracts with the regional medical libraries. The new eighth region is New England, with headquarters in Farmington, Connecticut. New five-year contracts will help health professionals in inner cities and rural areas learn about network services. Major activities of the network include interlibrary loan, reference services, training and consultation, and online access to MEDLINE and other databases.[97]

Library of Congress

The Library of Congress (LC) introduced CDMARC Bibliographic, the LC-USMARC database on CD-ROM, in August. The database contains more than 4 million records on six discs, cumulated quarterly.[98] LC also released CDMARC Names, the complete LC name authority file containing 2.3 million personal, corporate, series, and title authority records on three CD-ROM discs.[99]

OCLC (Online Computer Library Center)

The attractive OCLC annual report, celebrating 20 years of online service, offered the center an unprecedented opportunity to extol its history and growth. President K. Wayne Smith notes that in 1990–1991 traditional services were greatly strengthened and new products and services were developed. The high-speed, packet-switched X.25 New Network was installed, with more than 3,000 modem sites and 8,250 workstations converted. The PRISM service was inaugurated, allowing libraries to use the new network and the OCLC system more effectively; training of librarians is proceeding apace. During the conversion, duplicate systems were in operation. FirstSearch, a low-cost reference service for library patrons, is now operational. Although the EPIC service did not grow at the expected rate, it has been well reviewed and use increased steadily during the year. Financially, OCLC is still strong, although it had less revenue in 1991 than in the previous year. The Local Systems Division was sold. The cost of duplicating services during conversion to the New Network and PRISM reduced the contribution to equity. OCLC acquired MAPS, the MicrogrAphic Preservation Service, Inc., which does preservation microfilming for libraries, archives, and museums. New strategic alliances with other major organizations resulted in new products and services, such as the Faxon/Document Delivery Service and serials table-of-contents database, the Silver Platter/CD Services, and the AAAS/electronic science journal.[100]

Also published was a summary of OCLC's Strategic Plan, which graphically describes the environment in which the center operates, including libraries, and assesses corporate strengths and weaknesses, opportunities and risks. OCLC's plan builds on its strong technology platform, enabling it to enhance existing products and services while developing new ones. OCLC intends to maintain its position as a world-class source of bibliographic information by enhancing cataloging and resource sharing and to move beyond bibliography to become a world-class provider of reference services, including full-text information. This means becoming fully integrated into the "digital, broadband, global community" so that OCLC can provide "information to people in the form required, when and where needed, and at an affordable price."

The center was featured in the October *Chronicle of Higher Education* in an attractive illustrated spread, clearly making the point that OCLC is moving from a library-oriented service to one that provides information to end users.[101]

As in past years, the amount of information in the library press concerning OCLC indicates its tremendous level of activity.

EPIC. The EPIC service, for searching the OCLC database by subject, keyword, or key phrase and for Boolean searches, finished its first year in operation. Terry Ballard suggests that free practice time might improve and encourage use.[102] Databases were added throughout the year.[103] The addition of EPIC to OCLC's Library School Program means no-cost searching of the major part of the database.[104] OCLC also announced that EPIC is connected to Internet[105] and is available on Sundays.[106]

Research. One of OCLC's strengths has always been research and development. Michael McGill and Martin Dillon describe these activities in an article in *Colorado Libraries.*[107] OCLC announced that the U.S. Department of Education had granted $48,675 to support three-quarters of the cost of an investigation and analysis of Internet resources.[108] In addition, Cornell University and OCLC agreed to proceed with the Chemical Online Retrieval Experiment (CORE), a project to develop and test an online information system in light of its impact on a community of scholars.[109]

Marketing. In July, OCLC announced that it was creating a Library Market Research Panel to help monitor developments and trends in member libraries, measure user satisfaction and opinion, and allow member libraries greater participation in surveys and opinion research.[110]

New York Public Library Link. The New York Public Library (NYPL) was the first institution to link its internal network (NYPLNET) with the OCLC telecommunications network. The link, based on the X.25 OSI standard, will connect NYPL research and branch libraries to the OCLC system for cataloging and resource sharing.[111]

RLG Cooperation. The Research Libraries Group (RLG) and OCLC signed a cooperative agreement that encourages increased participation in the RLG Preservation Program. OCLC is subsidizing program fees for eligible OCLC member institutions not already affiliated with the program that are not RLG members.[112] After months of negotiating, RLG member libraries voted in spring 1991 not to create an intersystem link between the OCLC and RLIN databases.[113]

New Services. After extensive field testing, FirstSearch, OCLC's online reference tool for end users, became available in late fall. Extensive online help is available to make the database friendly to nonlibrarians, in the hope that people will use it at home and in their offices. Some libraries will offer FirstSearch through their OPAC or LAN (local area network), linked to OCLC with an OCLC Communications Controller.[114]

Other. OCLC donated $10,000 to create an Information Center database in the headquarters library of the American Library Association.[115] In February, OCLC and UTLAS broke off discussions regarding OCLC's acquisition of UTLAS.[116] William Gray Potter, director of university libraries, University of Georgia, was elected vice president/president of the OCLC Users' Council.[117]

International. Some 162,446 bibliographic records from the National Library of Australia were processed through the OCLC TAPECON service, the largest group of records ever processed in OCLC's international operations.[118] OCLC use in France will be expanded under an agreement between OCLC and three French education and information organizations.[119]

Research Libraries Information Network

March headlines introduced a year of ups and downs for the Research Libraries Group (RLG) and its Research Libraries Information Network (RLIN). "What Is Happening to the Research Libraries Group?" was the headline for a report on the March 7–8 meeting of the RLG board of governors. RLG had just completed the most successful fiscal year in its history.[120] As a result of changes in the environment, RLG would reformulate its governance and management structures, reshape the RLIN database, and shift to new business directions. It would also investigate an intersystem link with OCLC.[121]

After the June board meeting, RLG announced new membership, governance, and dues structures that heralded the restructuring called RLG92. Targeting new, nonlibrary organizations for membership, RLG intends to broaden links between research libraries and other major cultural institutions such as museums, scholarly societies, archives, publishers, university presses, information agencies, and peer research institutions outside North America.

RLG announced that RLG92 must achieve economies in operational costs; a special commission was appointed to consider how RLIN could better meet member needs. The emphasis will not be on online cataloging, now widely available from a variety of other sources, but on the "collaborative creation of access to new and untapped resources."[122]

As the end of the year approached, RLG published *RLG in Perspective: Focusing Collaboration in the 1990s,* which describes the organization's plans for meeting the needs of research libraries and related organizations. Institutions will need to work collectively on projects they cannot do alone, using RLG to enhance their resources.[123]

RLIN introduced Arabic-script capability to its system, becoming the only online bibliographic network in the world to support such script and the only one to support the entire JACKPHY menu of languages that use non-Roman scripts (defined by the Library of Congress as Arabic, Chinese, Hebraic, Japanese, Korean, Persian, and Yiddish); RLIN also supports Cyrillic script.[124]

A new online resource was added to RLIN, the Ei Page One database of tables of contents of engineering journals and conference proceedings. Ei also offers delivery of full-text articles, with requests generated from the online system.[125]

In keeping with its new orientation toward other organizations, RLG published *Information Needs in the Sciences: An Assessment,* surveying current information sources in the sciences and identifying types of information needed by science researchers. Companion publications are *Information Needs in the Humanities* (1988) and *Information Needs in the Social Sciences* (1989).

RLG has developed a new workstation, called the Document Transmission Workstation (DTW), that "will allow any scholar to access not only its home institution's online catalog, but also RLIN, and possibly other databases through RLIN." DTW allows the user to scan, store, and transmit articles, papers, and similar documents from one workstation to another, where they can be printed on demand.[126]

RLG will survey micropublishers regarding the quality, storage conditions, and location of microform master negatives under a contract with the Commission on Preservation and Access. The survey will produce a directory of micropublishers, tabulated survey results, and a narrative analysis.[127] RLG and Chadwyck-Healey will publish on CD-ROM a related publication, the *RLIN Preservation Masterfile,* containing about a half-million citations for books and journal titles, with information about the microfilm master negative for works needing preservation reformatting.[128]

The RLG publication *Computer Files and the Research Library* explores research libraries' problems with machine-readable data files (MRDFs). Four coauthors report on issues related to collecting, describing, and providing access to computer files, offering some solutions.[129]

International Networking

Nancy Melin Nelson of Computers in Libraries International reported in May on her company's February conference, which emphasized networks. Topics included systems in schools, commercial and industrial organizations, cooperative systems, hypermedia, indexing languages, and expert systems.[130]

Two recent publications are helpful in identifying networking activities abroad, but both have significant limitations. *European Library Networks,* by Karl W. Neubauer and E. R. Dyer, is current only to the end of 1989, but it does focus on computerized networks at the regional and national levels in Europe and it has an extensive bibliography.[131] *The Unesco Network of Associated Libraries: An Introduction* is a brief booklet describing the formation of the Unesco Network of Associated Libraries (UNAL). Its purpose is to foster communication among libraries in different countries rather than facilitate the exchange of computerized data.[132]

Conclusion

In another active year of library networking and cooperation, libraries continued to integrate exciting new technologies. Key players at local, state, and national levels tested the waters for major cooperative projects but rejected them and embarked on independent tracks while duplicating each other's efforts. The year's activities are ample evidence that librarians are still willing to cooperate—up to a point. The full impact of the economic downturn has not yet been felt as this is being written; 1992 will be crucial for cooperation on many fronts. Major networking institutions' efforts to woo end users and nonlibrary organizations may have far-reaching consequences, as may the entry of the Baby Bells onto the library and information scene.

Notes

1. Rebecca T. Lenzini and Ward Shaw, "Creating a New Definition of Library Cooperation: Past, Present, and Future Models," *Library Administration and Management* 5, no. 1 (Winter 1991): 37–40.
2. "Special Section: Report from the OCLC/RLG Seminar," *Information Technology and Libraries* 10, no. 2 (June 1991): 99–120.
3. Gerald R. Lowell, "Local Systems and Bibliographic Utilities: Data Exchange Options: Keynote Address," *Information Technology and Libraries* 10, no. 2 (June 1991): 99.
4. Ibid., 99–104.
5. K. Wayne Smith, "OCLC Issues Statement on Cessation of RLG-OCLC Talks," *Action for Libraries* 17, no. 10 (October 1991): 1–2.
6. Marshall Keys, "National Bibliographies and Local Systems," *NELINET Liaison* 13, no. 7 (July 1991): 1, 5.
7. Brian Alley, "Belling the Cat," *Technicalities* 11, no. 10 (October 1991): 1.
8. "Committee-Reported NREN Bills: Analysis and Excerpts," *ALA Washington Office Analysis,* June 6, 1991.
9. Roberta A. Corbin, "The Development of the National Research and Education Network," *Information Technology and Libraries* 10, no. 3 (September 1991): 212–220.
10. "Internet and BITNET: Access and Services," *NELINET Liaison* 13, no. 5 (May 1991): 1–3.
11. Milo Nelson, "Editing Down Our Ideas about NREN: The Present Dog Won't Hunt," *Information Today* 8, no. 6 (June 1991): 37–39.
12. "All about NREN," *Technicalities* 11, no. 8 (August 1991): 2.
13. Charles R. McClure, Ann F. Bishop, Philip Doty, and Howard Rosenbaum, *The National Research and Education Network (NREN) Research and Policy Perspectives* (Norwood, N.J.: Ablex, 1991).

14. Ken Horning, "Remaining Eight Nodes Will Move to T3," *Link Letter* 3, no. 6 (January/February 1991): 1, 10.

15. Ellen Hoffman, "National Net '91 Convenes in Washington, D.C.," *Link Letter* 4, no. 1 (March/April 1991): 1, 8.

16. Carol A. Parkhurst, ed., *Library Perspectives on NREN: The National Research and Education Network* (Chicago: Library Information and Technology Association, 1991).

17. "Senate Version of NREN Passes," *Library Hotline* 20, no. 38 (September 23, 1991): 1.

18. ALANET broadcast message, December 10, 1991.

19. *Networks for Networkers II Conference,* prepared by Barbara Evans Markuson, INCOLSA, for the Library of Congress from the papers prepared for the conference (Washington, D.C.: Library of Congress, 1991).

20. Irene Hoadley, "The Future of Library Utilities," *MPLA Newsletter* 35, no. 4 (February 1991): 1–2, 4.

21. Sheila S. Intner, "Requiem for a Database," *Technicalities* 11, no. 5 (May 1991): 4–7.

22. Ron Miller, "The Utility Perspective," *Information Today* 8, no. 5 (May 1991): 42–43.

23. Mary E. Jackson, "Library to Library: ILL: Issues and Actions," *Wilson Library Bulletin* (February 1991): 102–105.

24. Mary E. Jackson, "Library to Library," *Wilson Library Bulletin* (June 1991): 97–100.

25. Anne Woodsworth and Thomas B. Wall, *Library Cooperation and Networks: A Basic Reader* (New York: Neal-Schuman, 1991).

26. Bernard Sloan, *Linked Systems for Resource Sharing* (Boston: G. K. Hall, 1990).

27. "University Library Directors Meet to Discuss Cooperative Efforts," *Library Hotline,* May 27, 1991, p. 3.

28. "State Library to Join Education and Research Network," *Library Hotline,* April 8, 1991, p. 3.

29. "Cooperative Networks Flourish in Florida," *Library Hotline,* April 22, 1991, p. 2.

30. "OhioLINK: A Single Resource of Over 16 Million Volumes," *Information Retrieval and Library Automation* 27, no. 4 (September 1991): 7.

31. "Innovative Interfaces to Install OhioLINK System," *Library Hi Tech News,* no. 84 (September/October 1991): 24.

32. "Maine Advances toward Statewide Network," *Wilson Library Bulletin* (June 1991): 11.

33. "AMIGOS' Specialized Cataloging Services Serve Diverse Group of Libraries," *Information Today* 8, no. 6 (June 1991): 47.

34. "AMIGOS Collection Analysis Systems," *Library Hotline,* July 8, 1991, pp. 4–5.

35. "AMIGOS Signs Retrospective Conversion Agreement with Washington University," *Information Today* 8, no. 10 (November 1991): 44.

36. News release, Dallas: AMIGOS Bibliographic Council, March 1, 1991.

37. "Tom Clareson Named AMIGOS Preservation Service Manager," *Que Pasa?* 12, no. 2 (April 1991): 2.

38. "Fund Raising Packet Available," *Que Pasa?* 12, no. 3 (July 1991): 5.

39. "Mission Accomplished," *Que Pasa?* 12, no. 3 (July 1991): 1.

40. News release, Dallas: AMIGOS Bibliographic Council, October 2, 1991.

41. News release, Dallas: AMIGOS Bibliographic Council, October 23, 1991.

42. "The Future of Funding for Libraries," *Que Pasa?* 12, no. 2 (April 1991): 1, 5.

43. "Membership Meeting Highlights," *Que Pasa?* 12, no. 3 (July 1991): 4.

44. "AMIGOS Expands Conference to Five Days," *Que Pasa?* 12, no. 4 (October 1991): 1, 5.

45. "BCR Workshop Schedule Sent in July," *Action for Libraries* 17, no. 8 (August 1991): 5.

46. Gretchen Redfield, "PRISM/PASSPORT Training Completed in BCR Region," *Action for Libraries* 17, no. 12 (December 1991): 1.

47. "BCR Board Elects Officers for FY 1991-92," *Action for Libraries* 17, no. 6 (June 1991): 1.

48. "Wetherbee Study of Effect of Shared Local Systems on National Bibliographic Database to Be Published," *Action for Libraries* 17, no. 6 (June 1991): 3.

49. "CAPCON Holds Annual Membership Meeting," *CAPCON Newsletter* (Summer 1991): 1-2.

50. "Sharon Rogers Re-elected to Users Council," *CAPCON Newsletter* (Summer 1991): 2.

51. "New CAPCON Training Courses to Be Offered," *CAPCON Newsletter* (Fall 1991): 1.

52. "CAPC0N Fall 1991 Workshop and Demonstration Calendar," *CAPCON Newsletter* (Fall 1991): 7-8.

53. "IOUG/ISL Training Program," *Information Bulletin,* February 6, 1991, pp. 1-2.

54. Jean Wilkins, "ILLINET/OCLC Manager's Report," *Illinois OCLC Users' Group, Inc. Newsletter,* no. 56 (April 1991): 1.

55. "Highlights of the IOUG Executive Committee Meeting January 11, 1991," *Illinois OCLC Users' Group, Inc. Newsletter,* no. 56 (April 1991): 4-5.

56. *Books Format I: Illinois OCLC Users' Group Introductory Workbook* (Springfield: Illinois OCLC Users' Group, 1991).

57. *Automation Highlights* (Lansing: Michigan Library Consortium, 1991).

58. MLC Automation Training Seminars 1991 Schedule (Lansing: Michigan Library Consortium, 1991).

59. MINITEX, *HECB 1992-92 Biennial Budget Request,* 1991.

60. "Status of MINITEX and Other Minnesota Library Appropriations," *MINITEX Communications Memo,* June 14, 1991, pp. 1-3.

61. *MINITEX Communications Memos,* March-September 6, 1991.

62. "MULS Task Force Report Complete," *MINITEX Communications Memo,* June 14, 1991, p. 4.

63. MINITEX Serials Cancellation Database Grows," *MINITEX Communications Memo,* September 6, 1991, p. 2.

64. "Why MINITEX Messenger?" *MINITEX Messenger,* October 23, 1991, p. 1.

65. "MINITEX Year-End Document Delivery Statistics—Up 4%," *MINITEX Messenger,* October 23, 1991, pp. 7-8.

66. *MLNC Watch,* no. 4 (1991).

67. *NEBASE from Here and There* 3, no. 5 (January 1991): 2-5.

68. "Resource Sharing Program Changes," *NEBASE News* 3, nos. 7-8 (March-April 1991): 1.

69. "Networked Information Coalition," *NEBASE News* 4, no. 1 (August 1991): 1.

70. *NELINET Liaison* 13, no. 2 (February 1991).

71. *Ohionetwork* 13, nos. 1-11 (November 1991).

72. "Joel Kent Resigns as Executive Director," *Ohionetwork* 13, no. 11 (November 1991): 1.

73. "PALINET Board of Trustees Adopts Long-Range Strategic Plan," *PALINET News,* no. 70 (February 1991): 1, 3.

74. "Meet the Board," *PALINET News,* no. 70 (February 1991): 3.

75. Elizabeth Curry, "Interstate Cooperation High at SELA/TLA," *SOLINEWS* 17, no. 3 (Winter 1991): 4.

76. "SOLINET: State of the Network Program," *SOLINEWS* 17, no. 3 (Winter 1991): 5.

77. Liz Hornsby and Joanne Gray, "SOLINET Annual Meeting/Conference Draws Members to Atlanta," *SOLINEWS* 17, no. 4 (Spring 1991): 1.

78. Joanne Gray, "Board Meeting Highlights," *SOLINEWS* 17, no. 4 (Spring 1991): 3.

79. Barbara Brown, "Preservation News," *C&RL News* 52, no. 5 (May 1991): 309.

80. Jane Pairo with Cynthia Wilkinson, "SOLINET Offices Survive Water Damage," *SOLINEWS* 17, no. 4 (Spring 1991): 4.

81. "SOLINET Now Offers ReCon Option on CD," *SOLINEWS* 17, no. 4 (Spring 1991): 7.

82. Joanne Gray, "SOLINET to Relocate Offices," *SOLINEWS* 18, no. 1 (Summer 1991): 3.

83. "SUNY/OCLC Network ILL Agreement," *SOL: Messages from SUNY/OCLC Network* 4, nos. 1/2 (January/February 1991): 1.

84. "SUNY/OCLC Online Information Retrieval Services (SOIRS)," *SOL: Messages from SUNY/OCLC Network* 4, nos. 3/4 (March/April 1991): 3.

85. "New Participation Category," *SOL: Messages from SUNY/OCLC Network* 4, nos. 5/6 (May/June 1991): 1.

86. *New Tech News,* January 7–November 1991.

87. Rebecca T. Lenzini and Ward Shaw, "Creating a New Definition of Library Cooperation: Past, Present, and Future Models," *Library Administration and Management* 5, no. 1 (Winter 1991): 37–40.

88. "CARL System Introduces Companion Service to UnCover," *Library Hi Tech News,* no. 86 (November 1991): 12–13.

89. CLASS membership promotional materials (San Jose, Calif., 1991).

90. "A.S.I.A. Becomes Part of CLASS," *Information Today* 7, no. 10 (November 1990): 50.

91. WLN promotional material (Lacey, Wash., 1991).

92. Susan Johnson, "The WLN Conspectus Service and Collection Assessment," *Information Retrieval and Library Automation* 26, no. 11 (April 1991): 1–4.

93. "WLN Announces New BCL3 Collection Comparison Service," *Library Hi Tech News,* no. 77 (December 1990): 7.

94. "WLN Adds Major New Online Search Features," *Library Hi Tech News,* no. 83 (July/August 1991): 20.

95. "WLN to Participate in Joint Project with UMI/Data Courier," *Information Today* 8, no. 9 (October 1991): 3.

96. "WLN," *Advanced Technology/Libraries* 20, no. 10 (October 1991): 10–11.

97. "National Network of Libraries of Medicine (NN/LM): A Rose by Any Other Name . . . ," *Information Retrieval and Library Automation* 27, no. 4 (September 1991): 8.

98. "LC Introduces MARC on CD-ROM," *Library Hotline,* August 26, 1991, pp. 3–4.

99. "LC Releases CDMARC Names," *Advanced Technology/Libraries* 19, no. 9 (September 1990): 6.

100. K. Wayne Smith, "To the Membership," *OCLC Annual Report* 1990/91, p. 1.

101. David L. Wilson, "Researchers Get Direct Access to Huge Data Base," *Chronicle of Higher Education,* October 9, 1991, pp. A24, A28.

102. Terry Ballard, "OCLC's EPIC: Reports from the Field," *Computers in Libraries* 11, no. 4 (April 1991): 47–49.

103. "New Additions on EPIC," *Information Today* 8, no. 7 (July/August 1991): 2.

104. "Dateline: Dublin, Ohio: EPIC Price Reduction for Library Schools," *Information Today* 8, no. 6 (June 1991): 1.

105. "OCLC's EPIC," *Information Retrieval and Library Automation* 26, no. 9 (February 1991): 6–7.

106. "EPIC Service Now Available on Sundays," *Information Today* 8, no. 4 (April 1991): 34.

107. Michael McGill and Martin Dillon, "Library Research Activities at OCLC Online Computer Library Center," *Colorado Libraries* (December 1990): 41–46.

108. "U.S. Department of Education Provides Grant for Internet Research," *Library Hotline,* August 12, 1991, p. 3.

109. "Cornell, OCLC to Proceed with CORE Project," *Advanced Technology/Libraries* 20, no. 9 (September 1991): 7–8.

110. "OCLC Creates Library Market Research Panel," *Library Hotline,* July 1, 1991, p. 3.

111. "NYPL Links Internal Network to OCLC System," *Advanced Technology/Libraries* 20, no. 10 (October 1991): 8–9.

112. "RLG, OCLC Sign Preservation Agreement," *Advanced Technology/Libraries* 20, no. 2 (February 1991): 5–6.

113. "RLG Terminates Discussions with OCLC: OCLC Issues Statement," *Advanced Technology/Libraries* 20, no. 8 (August 1991): 1–2.

114. "OCLC's FirstSearch for End-Users," *Information Retrieval and Library Automation* 27, no. 6 (November 1991): 6.

115. "OCLC Donates $10,000 for ALA Information Center Database," *Advanced Technology/Libraries* 20, no. 10 (October 1991): 2.

116. "OCLC and Thomson Canada Limited End UTLAS Acquisition Talks," *Library Hotline,* March 4, 1991, p. 1.

117. "OCLC Users Council Elects William Gray Potter Vice President/President Elect," *Library Hi Tech News,* no. 80 (April 1991): 16.

118. "OCLC Processes Largest International Tapecon Project," *Library Hotline,* January 21, 1991, p. 3.

119. "OCLC and French Libraries Extend Network Alliance," *Information Today* 8, no. 4 (April 1991): 9.

120. "RLG Reports Record Year," *Advanced Technology/Libraries* 20, no. 6 (June 1991): 7–8.

121. "What Is Happening to the Research Libraries Group?" *Library Hotline,* March 25, 1991, p. 1.

122. "RLG Begins Reorganization," *Information Retrieval and Library Automation* 27, no. 3 (August 1991): 8–9.

123. "Research Libraries Group Publication Outlines Support for Research Information Needs," *Library Hi Tech News,* no. 78 (November 1991): 9–10.

124. "RLIN Intros Arabic-Script Cataloging," *Information Today* (October 1991): 37.

125. "Research Libraries Group Adds Ei Engineering Citations and Document Delivery to RLIN," *Library Hi Tech News* (January/February 1991): 23.

126. "RLG's Document Transmission Workstation: LIR Is First Electronic Library," *Information Today* 8, no. 3 (March 1991): 55.

127. "RLG to Conduct Survey of Micropublishers," *Advanced Technology/Libraries* 20, no. 10 (October 1991): 3–4.

128. "RLIN Preservation Masterfile," *Information Hotline* 23, no. 6 (June 1991): 3.

129. "Research Libraries Group Publication on Computer Files and the Research Library Now Available," *Library Hi Tech News,* no. 79 (March 1991): 19.

130. Nancy Melin Nelson, "Networking in the U.K. and France," *Information Today* 8, no. 5 (May 1991): 15–17.

131. Karl W. Neubauer and E. R. Dyer, eds., *European Library Networks* (Norwood, N.J.: Ablex, 1990).

132. *The Unesco Network of Associated Libraries: An Introduction* (Paris: Unesco, 1990).

The Nixon and Reagan Presidential Libraries

Frank L. Schick

Consultant, Bethesda, MD

From George Washington to Richard Nixon, presidential papers were considered the private property of the president, to be disposed of as he saw fit. Although all presidents have been aware of the historical importance of their records, many have been lost, sold, stolen, given away, or destroyed. Until the 1930s, the Library of Congress, some state historical societies, and a few special libraries had collected and maintained the most complete sets of the papers of individual presidents. Franklin D. Roosevelt developed the concept of the presidential library constructed and equipped by private funds and maintained and administered in perpetuity by the National Archives. All later presidents, and Herbert Hoover retroactively, deposited their papers in presidential libraries.

Following the Watergate scandal and President Nixon's resignation in 1974, Congress enacted the Presidential Recordings and Materials Preservation Act (PL 93-526) to ensure the preservation and public availability of the Nixon papers and related materials, placing them in the custody of the General Services Administration and mandating that they be stored in the Washington, D.C., metropolitan area. Despite President Nixon's objections, the Supreme Court upheld these regulations. Nixon fought an unsuccessful series of legal battles seeking to gain control of his papers and tapes or to force the federal government to pay him for their use.[1] Nixon's presidential papers are maintained in the Nixon Presidential Materials Project of the National Archives in Alexandria, Virginia. The Richard Nixon Library in Yorba Linda, California, houses his pre- and postpresidential papers and, unlike the other presidential libraries, is privately maintained. In 1978, Congress passed the Presidential Records Act (PL 95-591), which established the public ownership of and access to future presidential papers. The first president legally bound to comply with this law was Ronald Reagan; presidents Ford and Carter voluntarily complied.[2]

The Nixon and Reagan libraries were dedicated in 1990 and 1991 in California. President Bush plans to locate his library at Texas A & M University in College Station, Texas.

Nixon Presidential Materials Project

In compliance with PL 93-526, the National Archives organized the Nixon Presidential Materials Project in an 80,000-square-foot former warehouse in Arlington, Virginia. In 1994, the project will be moved to a larger National Archives building under construction in College Park, Maryland.

In 1987, the National Archives began releasing the Nixon materials, with some exceptions, for public access; the process will continue as papers and tapes are declassified. The materials include all Nixon records from 1969 to 1974, consisting of approximately 40 million pages of text stored in standard classified folders; 950 reels of tape covering some 4,000 recorded hours; and 1,200 pictures and audiovisual materials. The book collection holds approximately 10,000 gift books and all federal documents published during Nixon's administration. Some 30,000 presidential gifts are kept in boxes; selections have been made available for exhibit in the Nixon Library in Yorba Linda and other libraries and museums. Declassified documents, tapes, and visual materials can be used in a small research and reading room.

Richard Nixon Library and Birthplace

Shortly after his inauguration, Richard Nixon established a White House liaison office with the National Archives. His vice-presidential and other prepresidential papers were stored in the Federal Archives and Records Center building in Laguna Niguel, California. Although his presidential papers had to remain in the Washington, D.C., area, the Nixon Archives Foundation was incorporated in 1983 to collect funds for and supervise erection of a library similar to the presidential libraries operated by the U.S. government and to donate the facility to the federal government if and when it will be permitted to accept it.

The original plan was to establish the library on a 13-acre tract near Nixon's home in San Clemente, California. By 1987, the foundation had collected pledges of $24 million to build the facility. During summer 1988, however, environmental and building clearance delays developed. At about the same time, the city of Yorba Linda, less than 30 miles from Los Angeles, offered the foundation, at no cost, a 9-acre site adjoining the Nixon birthplace. President Nixon and his family greatly preferred this location, and the decision was made to restore to its original condition the small, 900-square-foot farmhouse erected by Nixon's father in 1912. The restoration cost about $450,000. The house is furnished with some original Nixon family possessions, including the piano Nixon practiced on as a boy, his high chair, and the bed he was born in, as well as other items that reflect early twentieth century middle-class American life.

Facing the house, across an attractive garden and reflecting pool, stands the Richard Nixon Library, a simple 53,000-square-foot single-story building consisting of three red-tiled pavilions. The museum is on the ground floor; the library is in the basement. The building, which cost approximately $21 million to construct, was dedicated July 19, 1990. On July 20, the museum opened to the general public. Research facilities will become available in 1992 at the earliest. The facility now holds only Nixon's postpresidential papers; decisions will be made at a later date concerning copies of prepresidential and presidential papers to be included.

Visitors are introduced to the museum by a 25-minute film of Nixon's life. A display of 30 enlarged Nixon covers of *Time* magazine leads the visitor to the exhibit areas. A large center hall features dramatic life-size statues of nine men and one woman whom Nixon considered the greatest leaders among his contemporaries: Konrad Adenauer, Leonid Brezhnev, Chou En-lai, Winston Churchill, Charles de Gaulle, Nikita Khrushchev, Mao Tse-tung, Golda Meir, Anwar Sadat, and Shiguru Yoshida. The Watergate room features audiotape machines playing excerpts from several Watergate tapes. Other exhibits illustrate Nixon's road to the presidency, his campaigns, the TV debates with John F. Kennedy, video displays concentrating on foreign affairs, and a Pat Nixon area. Unlike most presidential libraries, which show the Oval Office, this one features a replica of the Lincoln Sitting Room in the White House.

Ronald Reagan Presidential Library

The Reagan Presidential Foundation was incorporated in 1985 to finance and plan the Reagan Presidential Library. The original plans called for the Presidential Library and a separate Public Affairs Institute to be located near the Hoover Institute on the campus of Stanford University, where Reagan's California governorship papers had already been deposited. When campus opposition developed over the Public Affairs Institute, the foundation announced the need for a larger site in Southern California that could accommodate the library and the institute. More than thirty proposals were submitted. A 100-acre site on a hilltop in Simi Valley in Ventura County, 40 miles northeast of Los Angeles, donated by the real estate development firm Blakley Swartz, was finally accepted. Hugh H. Stubbins's Spanish mission-style design for the Stanford University campus building was adapted to the new hilltop location. The library officially opened November 4, 1991.

The Reagan Presidential Library complex of 153,000 square feet, constructed at a cost of $60 million, is by far the largest and most expensive of the ten presidential facilities and has the most extensive collection of presidential papers and audiovisual records, tapes, photographs, and films. By November 1991, the foundation had raised $57.2 million to cover building costs; it plans to raise another $6.5 million and to collect an additional $11.3 million in pledges to pay for construction loans and endowments for the Reagan Center for Public Affairs. Because Congress restricted the size of presidential libraries to 70,000 square feet in order to limit the National Archives administrative costs, the foundation will have to bear the continuing cost of administering and maintaining the excess library space.

Visitors are first directed to the auditorium to view a film about the life of President Reagan, featuring his background and major achievements. The museum galleries are organized chronologically, from Reagan's boyhood to Hollywood, the California governorship, and the 1976 and 1980 presidential campaigns. Approximately half of the display area is dedicated to the Reagan presidency, covering foreign policy, the economy, and life in the White House. A metal wall is engraved with the names of famous Soviet dissidents; other walls bear the signatures of all previous presidents and the names of major donors to the library. The facility also has a replica of the Oval Office, extensive displays of Reagan memorabilia, and a large gift shop.

The archives has a large reading room and listening areas for researchers; materials are being made available as they are declassified. An area has been set aside for the planned Ronald Reagan Center for Public Affairs; there are elaborate facilities for meetings and receptions and a suite of offices for the Reagans' use. On clear days, visitors standing on the terrace can see a large section of the Berlin Wall amid the reddish-brown California hills. Ronald and Nancy Reagan plan to be buried on the hillside below the wall.

Notes

1. Tracy Thompson, "Federal Judge Rules against Nixon on Papers, Tapes. Former President Had Sought Unspecified Damages from the Government," *Washington Post,* December 14, 1991, p. A8.
2. Frank L. Schick, with Renee Schick and Mark Carroll, *Records of the Presidency: Presidential Papers and Libraries from Washington to Reagan* (Phoenix, Ariz.: Oryx Press, 1989), pp. 239–250.

The Effects of the Recession on Academic and Public Libraries

Christinger Tomer

Assistant Professor
School of Library and Information Science
University of Pittsburgh, Pittsburgh, PA 15260

For about 25 years following World War II, the United States enjoyed unparalleled prosperity. In the last two decades, however, spendthrift government, the arms race, and unrealistically low taxes have combined to drive the U.S. economy to the verge of bankruptcy. Virtually every component of the social infrastructure has suffered, as the means or the willingness to fund agencies and institutions has diminished.

Now, in early 1992, the recession that began in the second half of 1989, not long after George Bush assumed the presidency, shows evidence of deepening, exacerbating already serious problems for many nonprofit institutions, including academic and public libraries.[1] In the case of libraries, long-standing financial problems have grown worse during the recession, in large part because the cost of acquiring new books and journals has continued to rise at a rate well in excess of the rate of inflation, and far higher than the rate at which budgets have been growing, if they have been growing at all.

Traditionally, libraries have been viewed as a sound investment in the future. Specific circumstances might produce a different notion of how the investment ought to be made or maintained, but librarians and library supporters have usually been united in the conviction that adequate support for libraries is necessary for community development, whether the community is defined politically or academically.

In principle, this conviction is rarely challenged. In practice, however, cuts in library funding often come early and hit hard, because library patrons usually make up a minority in the community from which the library draws support, because the qualitative effects of reduced library funding are often neither immediate nor obvious, and because assessing libraries as long-term investments is too complex for the cost-benefit models in which many planners and decision-makers place confidence.

The conventional wisdom is that the future of the library, at least as we know it today, is unclear. Beneath such an expression, one senses among librarians and scholars the fear that agencies dedicated to collecting, organizing, and providing access to printed materials will soon be obsolete.

This article shows how the recession is affecting academic and public libraries, and how librarians are responding to what many regard as critical problems. It also considers how these problems and the ways libraries tackle them are likely to influence the future of libraries.

Academic Libraries

Colleges and universities in the United States are struggling with intense financial problems. Tuition at many schools is increasing faster than anticipated, appropriations for higher education are being slashed in many states, some institutions have furloughed staff and faculty or asked employees to forgo salary increases or fringe benefits, and in many places repairs or improvements have been deferred until the financial crisis abates.

Whither academic libraries? According to Herbert S. White, academic library funding has declined "steadily and consistently" since at least 1972.[2] More to the point, there are signs that the decline has been more acute in recent years. Costs, particularly of books and journals, have been rising at extrainflationary rates, while budgets have become so inelastic that many academic libraries have been forced to cut acquisitions budgets deeply. Indeed, merely labeling library budgets "inelastic" may grossly understate the problem. According to a 1991 survey by the Association of Research Libraries, 52.7 percent of the libraries polled suffered a budget reduction in 1991, and more than 60 percent expected one in 1992.[3] Of the libraries that received higher funding during 1991, almost all reported that the increase did not cover the increase in operating costs.[4]

The consequences? According to the experts, the men and women who direct research libraries, the financial crisis sweeping through higher education is forcing research libraries to redefine their mission. A generation or two ago, the idea of a comprehensive collection was tenable. Today, it smacks of the fantastic. A generation ago, the Association of Research Libraries considered preserving all of its collective holdings. Today, that seems ludicrous. No one knows if or how research libraries will maintain traditional commitments to scholarship past, present, or future.

At Stanford University, to meet a savings goal of $3.1 million, the administration is considering several proposals, including reducing library staff 10 percent, merging a number of departmental libraries, and closing the undergraduate library. (The proposal to close the library is especially painful because Stanford has long prided itself on the quality of its undergraduate library services.) At nearby San Jose State University, library support for 1992 has been cut 10 percent, public service hours have been reduced 16 hours a week, and book acquisitions are expected to decrease 25 percent, from 16,000 new titles in 1991 to 12,000 in 1992. At Florida Atlantic University, library funding has dropped from $3.1 million to $1.3 million in two years. In the process, librarians have reduced the number of serial subscriptions by 30 percent.[5]

For a subscription rate to increase 10 percent annually is not unusual—the average rate of increase for 1991 was 11.7 percent, with the average annual subscription costing $104.36; in fact, the average price of U.S. periodicals has increased almost 400 percent since 1977, and 72 percent since 1986. Nor is it unusual for subscription rates in such areas as the basic sciences, medicine, and engineering to increase at much higher rates. In 1991, the cost of a subscription for a medical serial rose 14.7 percent, to average $249.94; in 1977, the average cost was $51.31. In engineering, the cost of a serial subscription rose 15.3 percent in 1991, to average $160.13; in 1977, the average cost was $35.77.[6] In serial services, i.e., indexing and abstracting services, the average subscription rose 9.3 percent in 1991, with the biggest increases in business (11.7 percent) and science and technology (9.1 percent).[7] Taking a longer view, increases in the cost of serial services covering the humanities, law, science and technology, and general periodical literature have been well above average since 1977.[8] (Averaging has a tendency to mask related problems, such as cost overruns due to significant, unexpected increases in subscription rates. For example, cost overruns on serials at Harvard were as high as $500,000 annually in the late 1980s, and the major academic libraries at Yale, Stanford, Michigan, Ohio State, and the University of

California at Berkeley have experienced similar difficulties. In the late 1980s and early 1990s, many academic libraries, including those at Harvard, Yale, and Stanford, were requesting 15 to 25 percent increases in their serial budgets to keep pace with rising prices and prevent overruns.)

At many institutions, library staff vacancies have been left unfilled. At the University of Minnesota — Twin Cities, where the size of the library staff is seriously inadequate, 23 positions are vacant, and there is a freeze on hiring. At the University of Pittsburgh, 16 professional positions have been left open, more or less permanently.

At institutions as affluent as Yale University, budgetary problems have forced libraries to neglect the physical plant. At Yale's Sterling Memorial Library, because of leaks in the roof and around windows, librarians must cover segments of the collection with plastic sheeting on rainy days to prevent water damage.

Like many major research libraries, Sterling Memorial faces the added problems and expense of dealing with physical deterioration of collections and preserving fragile documents or their contents. According to Millicent Abell, Yale's university librarian, almost 40 percent of the collection, or about 3.5 million volumes, are no longer usable (presumably meaning that the items are too fragile to be used under normal conditions without sustaining physical damage. Most are likely books and journals published between 1850 and 1950.) Abell says: "Given the fact that we're considered one of the meccas of scholars, we have a special responsibility for preservation." Yet, the $300,000 that Yale allocated for preservation in 1992 represents only two thirds of the amount Abell believes is necessary to meet basic needs in this area.[9]

The problem is emblematic of those faced by contemporary libraries. Although preserving fragile books, journals, and manuscripts is without doubt an important function, the requisite investment does not increase the informativeness of a collection, nor is it likely to increase use significantly. Consequently, U.S. research libraries, which had difficulty reconciling their curatorial mission with obligations to readers in better times, may be able to preserve only a fraction of the materials at risk, as colleges and universities demand more immediate, more tangible return on library expenditures.[10] The good news, if there can be any in such a situation, is that in keeping with prevailing economies, preservationists, librarians, and scholars, too long preoccupied with issues like mass deacidification and technologies such as micrographic reproduction, will be forced to develop more rigorous selection criteria for preservation and to use electronic technology more extensively for processing, storage, display, and reproduction.

Another issue that typifies the bind of so many academic libraries is technology. The ability to keep pace with new information technologies has become a standard by which libraries, particularly research libraries, are judged. Some technologies offer clear economic advantages. Consortia for shared cataloging, such as OCLC and the Research Libraries Group, have already greatly improved cataloging quality and the efficiency of related technical processes. The number of full-text database services is growing and database vendors are offering licensing deals that place campuswide access within financial reach of many medium- and large-sized academic library systems. Network-based facsimile services will soon transform interlibrary loan services and perhaps create a more favorable environment for collaborative collection development and management. On the horizon are libraries of electronic books akin to the volumes that can be reviewed via SONY's DATA DISCMAN, and on-demand publishing services that will allow readers to reach across a network and copy — for a fee — an article, book, or relevant portions thereof.[11]

But information technology is still expensive, particularly when used as a basis for more generally distributed services. As many librarians have discovered in recent years, waxing lyrical about the virtues of the online public access catalog or the full-text database is one matter, but finding the money to finance the servers, terminals, printers, and licenses to support this mode of delivery is another.

Other problems worry librarians in the academic sector. In the rush to deal with spiraling serial costs, many libraries are not developing book collections. Librarians are most concerned about the adverse effects of such neglect on undergraduate programs, where books are often more important than journals. Yet, the decline in book buying is not likely to affect just undergraduate programs. Clearly, many disciplines within the humanities and the social sciences rely heavily on monographic literature, and imagining how graduate programs in these areas will be able to sustain quality without a steady, substantial influx of new books is difficult.

Public Libraries

The situation for public libraries is even worse than for academic libraries. In a survey of state library agencies by *American Libraries* in late 1991, only Ohio reported favorable conditions for public libraries. Missouri reported "livable" conditions. Except for libraries in states affected adversely by the decline in oil prices, such as Texas, Oklahoma, Colorado, and Wyoming, public libraries in the Mountain states and the Southwest are reasonably stable. So, too, are public libraries in the South, with the exception of Virginia, where a massive deficit has resulted in a 15 percent cutback in support for all state agencies. In Illinois and Minnesota, conditions were "unsettled." In Iowa and Indiana, conditions appear to be acceptable, at least for now, although in each the state library was about to sustain a significant reduction in state support. In most other states, conditions ranged from "grim" to "dire" to "critical."

Not surprisingly, libraries in New England, and in the heart of the Middle Atlantic region, New York, Pennsylvania, and New Jersey, may be in the worst situation. Many have long-term economic problems, such as dwindling tax revenues, structural unemployment, rapidly rising expenditures for basic social and welfare services, and a physical infrastructure that is deteriorating rapidly. The recent downturn in the economy has exacerbated an already bad situation.

In Massachusetts, the governor proposed a 10 percent decrease in funding for libraries for 1992, eliminating support for automated resource sharing networks. Because 30 percent of the state's libraries have already reduced public service hours and more than one third have further diminished the state's ability to generate revenues, one can expect public libraries in Massachusetts to suffer grievously in the next couple of years.

In New York, where the state's $6 billion deficit is necessitating drastic cuts in many areas, Governor Cuomo has proposed a 10 percent reduction in support for libraries. However, because Cuomo's proposed cuts for programs in other areas, such as the arts and public broadcasting, run as high as 50 percent, public library users in New York may ultimately consider themselves lucky.

In New York City, however, the Public Library's financial problems are so serious that it has announced plans to reduce the 1992 serial budget 30 percent, a projected savings of more than $800,000. An even worse example is Queens Borough (New York) Public Library, a system devastated by the recession. The Queens Library system—founded 95 years ago with the Long Island City Public Library—has long been a pioneer in community service, with foreign-language collections, adult learning centers, library services to persons with disabilities, and literacy programs for older adults and immigrants. During the last four years, however, more than 135 library jobs have been lost and library hours have been shortened as the result of a 26 percent budget reduction. A hiring freeze in effect since October 1990 has left the system with only 750 employees to serve 1.9 million people. Worse yet, city funding for FYs 1991–1992 was slashed $6.1 million, forcing the system to reduce weekend hours at branch libraries. Ironically, the Queens Borough Public Library has had among the highest annual circulation rates in the nation—13.5 million items in 1989–1990, 13.2 million in 1990–1991.[12]

In Pennsylvania, where the state government faces a revenue shortfall of $700 to $800 million and chronic economic problems, the situation for public libraries is slightly better. Governor Robert Casey's budget reduction measures include withdrawing $2 million in state aid for libraries and $250,000 in funding for the statewide library card reimbursement program. In New Jersey, the state legislature is considering a bill that would eliminate minimum funding requirements for public libraries. The fear is that this will license municipal officials to reduce support for local public libraries disproportionately.

Public libraries in Kansas, Michigan, and Nebraska are facing substantial loss of funding. In the last two fiscal years, funding for public libraries in Michigan has been reduced 2.5 percent and 9.2 percent, respectively, with devastating results. The Detroit Public Library has had to trim its operating budget by $900,000, cutting public service hours in half at six branches, slashing acquisition budgets for materials and equipment, and forcing management to freeze hiring and promotions. (Detroit voters approved a million dollar levy for library services, but income from this measure will not be available until July 1992.) In Kansas, all regional library systems are being obliged to curtail service as the result of already-imposed cuts, and the legislature is considering an additional 5 percent reduction in funding for public libraries. In Nebraska, changes in the source of most public library funding has resulted in millions of dollars in lost tax income.

Another example of the cruel ironies born of hard times is Sherwood Regional Library in Mount Vernon, Virginia.[13] In February 1991, the library closed its doors for extensive renovations. Carpeting was replaced, the parking lot was enlarged, the interior was repainted, and a huge wing was added, almost doubling the size of the facility. Some $3.1 million was spent to renovate and expand Sherwood into the second-largest library in the extensive Fairfax County system, yet its doors will remain locked after the work is completed in April 1992 unless Fairfax County officials find the necessary operating funds.

Tax revenue has dropped sharply, leaving the county with a $138 million shortfall in the budget year that starts July 1, 1992. In an effort to reduce spending, officials imposed a strict hiring freeze and are considering not opening buildings that require new employees. (This policy may also affect the new $4.3 million Centreville Regional Library scheduled to open later in 1992.) Because Sherwood's librarians were transferred when it was closed, the library system will need special permission to fill nine positions. How much would it cost to reopen the Sherwood Regional Library? Fairfax County officials estimate about $175,000.

In California and Washington, where economic instability has complicated and hampered public funding for almost two decades, public libraries have "critical" problems. Taxpayers in Los Angeles and San Francisco voted a few years ago to build new central libraries, but other cities in California are facing cuts that would eliminate branches with low circulation, replace rural libraries with bookmobile service, and consolidate libraries that are close together. For example, faced with a $500,000 budget shortfall, the San Diego County Library system, which has an operating budget of $9.5 million supporting 32 branches and two bookmobiles, has recommended closing 7 branches.

Libraries in three categories have been targeted for closure: (1) libraries in communities that have more than one county library; (2) libraries that circulate fewer than 10 items an hour; and (3) libraries open less than 20 hours a week that are no more than 15 miles from another branch. For immediate help in balancing the budget, San Diego County's Board of Supervisors approved an increase in book fines. The fine on overdue books was raised from 10 cents to 20 cents a day, the fine on children's books was doubled from 5 cents to a dime each day, and fines can be charged for up to 50 days. Supervisors also approved adding a $10 fee to the replacement cost of lost materials. The new policies are expected to generate approximately $70,000 in additional income.[14]

Librarians in Oregon reported that good economic conditions were "getting better," although libraries were experiencing a temporary budgetary problem in adjusting to a shortfall stemming from a new statutory limit on property tax.

During times of economic hardship the public library historically has become even more important to city residents. Today, public libraries provide resource manuals and trade magazines to help patrons search for employment. They offer books, videos, and films that provide inexpensive entertainment, and basic reading material for people no longer able to afford newspapers, magazines, and books. But social programs are out of political fashion, and pressure is mounting to demonstrate on a quantified basis that public libraries are relevant and useful and merit investment of public funds. As a result, an increasing number operate like for-profit bookstores, and fewer operate as agencies dedicated to the commonweal.[15]

Professional Responses

In higher education, the response to these problems has been largely predictable. Early on, academic librarians identified serial costs as the primary culprit, and devised tactics for dealing with the problem mainly in those terms. But a surprising number of librarians have been willing to consider fundamental changes in the role of the academic library and in its activities.

In the related areas of collection development and management, if academic librarians have responded predictably, they also have been forceful. Many libraries have terminated a large number of serial subscriptions and significantly decreased the number of new books added to collections. Additional economies have been sought through reduced expenditure on binding, a moratorium on the purchase of new serial titles, canceling and restricting approval plans, reducing or stopping expensive purchases, or negotiating deeper discounts from jobbers and vendors.

In terms of technology, information technology until recently offered little help where librarians needed it most, i.e., in controlling serial costs. With indexes and abstracting publications on CD-ROM many librarians were able to attract new users and increase use of certain collections. But CD-ROM technology was not without limitations, not the least of them being that access to CD-ROM sources could not be offered across networks at that time; in most instances, implementation of CD-ROM sources was in the "single machine, single user" mode, most machines being overpriced microcomputers based on outdated microprocessor technology.

Now, however, librarians' efforts to use information technology to solve financial problems are about to bear fruit. An important element in this evolving strategy is the inclusion of publishing in the collective mission of libraries. As Lloyd Davidson of Northwestern University pointed out at the October 1991 meeting of the American Society for Information Science, publishing has the potential to generate income for libraries, enhance the availability of certain types of material, and advance efforts to reduce the cost of acquiring information resources through cooperative publishing and distribution arrangements. With the availability of sophisticated yet inexpensive desktop publishing software, and with access to high-speed networks like BITNET and Internet, academic librarians are in a position to produce "research reports and primary data generated at their home institutions, software, electronic bulletin board or news service extracts, and bibliographic databases."[16]

At the 1991 meeting of the Society for Scholarly Publishing, publishers, librarians, and scholars gathered in Washington, D.C., to consider the possibilities of electronic publishing. One of the principal speakers, William Arms, vice president for academic services at Carnegie-Mellon University, presented a series of notions about electronic publishing and the role that networks may be expected to play in the near future. Arms urged publishers to be more imaginative in their vision of electronic publishing, suggesting that they focus more on the needs of end-users. In terms of networking and network use, Arms predicted that the increasing number of individuals regularly using the services of Internet will force progressively more formal modes of operation; specifically, Arms believes that there will be: (1) changes in pattern for network subsidies; (2) charges related to volume of use; (3) more explicit, more extensive rules and regulations governing use of Internet and allied resources; (4) more commercial use; and (5) more governmental oversight. Arms also believes that in no more than 10 years Internet will be a commercial enterprise. An examination of the High Performance Computing Act of 1991, the so-called NREN bill, and related documentation suggests that Arms's sense of Internet as a commercial enterprise will be vindicated, given the expectation that nine of every ten dollars used to capitalize the National Research and Education Network (NREN) will come from private sources.

In that vein, librarians and other interested parties will be watching the progress of the new electronic journal, the *Online Journal of Current Clinical Trials,* scheduled to appear in April 1992. *Clinical Trials* is a cooperative venture involving the American Association for the Advancement of Science (AAAS) and OCLC (Online Computer Library Center). According to its founding editor, *Clinical Trials* "will be the first journal to make immediately available findings that could save or extend the lives of critically ill patients."[17] The journal, which will be fully abstracted in *Biosis,* will provide hypertext links to abstracts of cited articles, enabling readers to scan a journal article's reference within a pop-up window on the screen without leaving the issue they are reading. Although a number of electronic journals are already available through computer networks, *Clinical Trials* is probably the first electronic journal to incorporate hypertext links from typeset text to charts and graphics.

AAAS, the world's largest general science organization, developed the editorial focus for *Clinical Trials*. OCLC, a nonprofit corporation that links 13,000 libraries in 46 countries by means of a computer network, developed the technology and programming for the new journal; AAAS developed the editorial content and focus. Subscribers will be able to access the journal with a 286 or higher-level IBM-compatible personal computer equipped with Windows 3.0 software, a VGA graphics monitor, a modem, and 2 megabytes of RAM. (OCLC plans to release a Macintosh-compatible version of the software in 1993.) The journal uses an interface called GUIDON, developed by OCLC's Thomas Hickey, to provide the typeset articles and illustrations. Subscribers with less powerful equipment will receive articles, some tables, and equations in text form through a command interface.

According to Paul Nicholson, AAAS executive officer and publisher of *Clinical Trials,* the aim of the journal is to "combine the rigorous standards of the most prestigious research journals in medicine with the immediacy of online technology."[18] Authors of research articles will be able to communicate with editors and AAAS either by electronic or surface mail. Similarly, computer networks will be used to link authors, editors, and peer reviewers. Authors will submit articles by network, modem, in hard copy, or on diskette. Manuscripts will be sent to peer reviewers and comments collected from them electronically. The intent is to eliminate "the weeks and even months of delay that occur in print journals between the time that peer review is completed and actual publication" of research articles and to make new articles available to subscribers within 24 hours of peer-reviewed acceptance. (By comparison, even the most timely print journals, such as the *New England Journal of Medicine,* take at least two months, and often longer, to review and accept a research article, and then another two to three months to publish it. The hope is that by managing the publication process electronically, journal publishers will be able to reduce the time between submission and publication by at least three months.)

The editors of *Clinical Trials* expect to provide subscribers with the latest findings several times a week. When subscribers log into the system, an automatic alert will accompany articles published since they last logged on. This feature is particularly important as research findings are continually being published. Automatic alerts notify subscribers of letters, rebuttals, or retractions related to articles they select. Subscribers will be able to register areas of special interest and will be notified by fax when new articles are published. They will also be able to search the *Clinical Trials* database by key word, subject, author or title, and view an article's abstract, full text, references, or graphics in any order.[19]

In the event that *Current Clinical Trials* succeeds, it will almost certainly be followed by a flurry of interest in electronic formats among publishers of professional and scholarly journals now offered as print-on-paper documents. The reasons? The development of sufficiently large markets for electronic journals in subject areas such as medicine, business, and the basic sciences will enable publishers to maintain high revenues while slashing operating costs as much as 75 to 80 percent by eliminating printing, binding, and postage.

There are no guarantees, but the benefits of libraries functioning as electronic publishers and using electronic delivery systems for serial publications may combine to alleviate the budgetary pressures that afflict almost every college and university library in the United States. However, Paul Zahray and Marvin Sirbu, public policy analysts at Carnegie Mellon University, offer a cautionary note. There are at least two reasons to be concerned. A dilemma of new technology may occur where groups of libraries benefit from the publication of electronic journals only if they collaborate. Also, "when a publisher is able to impose royalties on the new service, his profit maximizing strategy may be to charge a royalty that precludes the new service."[20]

The situation before public libraries is much more troubling. Public investment has been on the decline since the 1950s.[21] Astronomical sums of money have been squandered on unproductive, unnecessary aspects of the military-industrial complex, and in the process the tax burden has been shifted from the rich to the poor, widening the gap between them, and greatly weakening the infrastructure of communities. Shortfalls in funding make the problems of the public school or library obvious, and at the heart of the problem is a diminishing sense of community and a growing sense of differentiation.

For more than 100 years, from the end of the Civil War through the end of the Vietnam War, taxpayers in cities and towns all across the country provided a steady stream of tax money to finance library services. Arthur Curley, director of the Boston Public Library, believes that in many places they still do, notwithstanding the problems that have so greatly diminished the desire to support the public sector. In an article on public library funding, Curley suggests that there is a strong connection between local tax structures and public library support, that public libraries able to seek direct approval of bond issues and levies often succeed where libraries encumbered by more convoluted schemes for support do not, and that "strategies for public library funding in the 1990s must include legislative efforts to increase the ability of libraries to go directly to the public."[22] Beyond that, he believes that we need a national public library network, full federal funding for the depository library program, and legislation that recognizes and provides funding for urban public libraries to play special roles (offering research facilities to the general public and often coordinating countywide or regional library services). Curley concludes: "More than all else, these strategies must be based on a reassertion of the fundamental relationship of the public library to the cultural, educational, civic, and economic health of the nation."[23]

Notes

1. How bad is the recession? In January 1992, shortly after returning from an economic mission to Japan, President Bush admitted "that this economy is in free fall." Economic growth is expected to be minimal in 1992. The projected federal budget deficit for 1992 is between $250 and $350 billion, and that estimate presumes a low rate of inflation. Budget planners expect debt service to constitute about 25 percent of the federal government's expenditures in 1992, and substantial cuts in funds for a number of traditional social programs, such as Library Services and Construction. Even more important, 8.9 million men and women are "officially unemployed," as of this writing. Estimates of the number of unemployed who are no longer actively seeking work, and therefore not included in the official count, vary greatly, especially in an election year, but the level of unemployment is certainly far greater than indicated by federal government data.

2. White, Herbert S. "The Tragic Cost of Being Reasonable," *Library Journal* 116 (February 15, 1991): 166.

3. From *ARL Statistics, 1990–1991*. Washington, D.C.: Association of Research Libraries (forthcoming).

4. Regularly denied the increases necessary to keep pace with inflation, major research libraries like those at Tulane University, the University of Pennsylvania, and the University of North Carolina at Chapel Hill have experienced an annual decline in buying power of 15 to 20 percent. To cite an example, at Virginia Polytechnic Institute an already strained serial

budget was reduced $300,000 for 1992, owing to the disparity between the budget and funding.

5. Nicklin, Julie, "Threat to Scholarly Resources: Rising Costs and Dwindling Budgets Force Libraries to Make Damaging Cuts in Collections and Services," *The Chronicle of Higher Education* (February 18, 1992): A28.

6. Carpenter, Kathryn Hammell, and Adrian W. Alexander, "Price Index for U.S. Periodicals: The 31st Annual Survey of U.S. Periodical Prices," *Library Journal* 116 (April 15, 1991): 52–60.

7. According to the American National Standard for Library and Information Sciences and Related Publishing Practice — Library Materials — Criteria for Price Indexes, ANSI Z39.20-1983, a serial service is "a periodical publication that revises, cumulates, abstracts, or indexes information in a specific field on a regular basis by means of new or replacement issues, pages, or cards, intended to provide information otherwise not readily available."

8. Shroyer, Andrew, "Price Index for U.S. Serial Services: The 28th Annual Survey of U.S. Serial Services," *Library Journal* 116 (April 25, 1991): 60–61.

9. Nicklin, Julie, *The Chronicle of Higher Education*, op. cit.

10. One of the first serious proposals for systematic preservation of research library holdings in the United States was offered to Congress by the Association of Research Libraries in 1965, as it deliberated various aspects of Lyndon Johnson's "Great Society."

11. Gherman, Paul. "Setting Budgets for Libraries in the Electronic Era," *The Chronicle of Higher Education* (August 14, 1991): A36.

12. *Newsday,* December 15, 1991.

13. *Washington Post,* February 2, 1992. With 125,000 books, magazines, videotapes, and other items, the Sherwood Regional Library was one of six regional libraries in Fairfax offering extensive reference resources and computerized databases. In the year before it closed, Sherwood's patrons circulated 581,696 items — the equivalent of seven books for every man, woman, and child in the area it serves. In 1989, prior to the onset of the recession, voters approved a bond measure that included money for the library's renovation.

14. *Los Angeles Times,* November 14, 1991.

15. In the midst of such travail is the traditionally underpaid librarian, whose economic standing, though diminished, has diminished only slightly compared to the financial ravages endured by academic and public libraries. In 1990, the most recent year for which data are available, beginning salaries rose roughly 3 percent. The salaries of librarians, in general, rose 4.3 percent, with reference, children's, and young adult services librarians garnering the most substantial increases. In 1991, salaries went up an average 7.6 percent; unfortunately, the greatest increases were enjoyed mainly by directors, associate directors, and department heads, although collection development librarians and subject bibliographers did receive the highest proportional increases. During this two-year interval, the cost of living, as measured by the Consumer Price Index, rose about 5 percent each year. So, librarians may not have been moving ahead economically, but they have not been falling back as alarmingly as the libraries that they run. Yet the raises offered librarians have often been below the averages reported for white collar workers in general, local and state government employees in particular. (The year 1991 was an exception, when raises for librarians outpaced raises for white collar workers in general by 4 percent. Yet providing the backdrop for such increases in 1991 were the many reports of hiring freezes, staff reductions, and early retirements.) Moreover, salaries for professional librarians are embarrassingly, distressingly low: In 1990, the average starting salary for public librarians was a paltry $23,420, the average salary for academic librarians only slightly better at $24,641. In terms of the profession as a whole, reference librarians made an average $28,227 in 1989, $29,999 in 1990, and $31,523 in 1991. Children's librarians made an average $26,008 in 1989, $27,669 in 1990, and $29,872 in 1991. Worse yet, real income for most U.S. workers has steadily declined for

the last 20 years, which means that the purchasing power of a librarian's salary, even when adjusted for inflation, is 15 to 25 percent below what it was in 1972. In her survey of 1990 placements and salaries, Fay Zipkowitz reports another telling statistic: Only about 55 percent of the men and women who received graduate library degrees in 1990 "were known to be employed either in professional or nonprofessional positions in libraries or information-related work, as were 65 percent of the 1989 graduates and 64 percent of the 1988 graduates." [Zipkowitz's report appears in Section 3 of *The Bowker Annual—Ed.*] No less disturbing is Zipkowitz's finding that 48 percent of 1990 graduates hold full-time, professional positions, 8 percent less than in 1988 or 1989. In this context most programs responding to Zipkowitz's survey reported "no significant difficulty in placing 1990 graduates," which may mean that the job markets closest to library education's major programs are highly saturated, that graduates committed to living in those areas are often forced to accept part-time and/or clerical positions, and that placement officers tend to discount geographically immobile graduates in more subjective assessments of their own effectiveness. Sources of the data are: (1) Lynch, Mary Jo, "The 1990 Salary Survey: Smaller Increases than in 1989," *American Libraries* (November 1990): 951; Lynch, Mary Jo, "Good News? Librarians' Salaries Increase an Average of 7.6 Percent for 1991," *American Libraries* (November 1991): 976; and Zipkowitz, Fay, "Placements and Salaries 1990: Losing Ground in the Recession," *Library Journal* (November 1, 1991): 44–50. Lynch's salary surveys poll full-time professional librarians in academic and public libraries, and therefore are not indicative of salary patterns in school or special libraries.

16. Evans, Nancy H., "Conference Report: ASIS 54th Annual Meeting: Systems Understanding People," *Library Hi Tech News* (December 1991): 1–2.

17. Wilson, Martin. "AAAS Plans Electronic Journal Venture With OCLC," *Information Today* 10 (October 1991): 19.

18. Ibid.

19. The annual subscription price for *Clinical Trials* will be $110, which includes unlimited on-line access to research findings.

20. Zahray, Paul, and Marvin Sirbu, "The Provision of Scholarly Journals by Libraries via Electronic Technologies: An Economic Analysis," *Information Economics and Policy* 4 (1989/1990): 127–154.

21. For evidence, you need look no further than the highways and bridges in your hometown. During the Eisenhower presidency, more than 6 percent of the nonmilitary budget, or about 4 percent of the Gross National Product (GNP), was devoted to maintaining the nation's physical infrastructure. By the 1980s, the figure had fallen to 1.2 percent of the nonmilitary budget, or about 3 percent of GNP. In another telling comparison, in 1963, the United States spent 2.3 percent of GNP on new highways, bridges, and other aspects of the public systems of transportation and communication; in 1989, the figure had fallen to 1 percent of GNP. In public education, the figures are slightly better. Funding for public education continues to increase, although at rates significantly lower than those that characterized support from the 1950s through the early 1970s. Perhaps more relevant in the long term is that the United States ranks ninth in the world in per capita expenditure for public education, and that libraries must compete with schools, public works, and public safety for insufficient federal support. For more information, see Robert B. Reich, *The Work of Nations: Preparing Ourselves for 21st Century Capitalism* (New York: Knopf, 1991).

22. Curley, Arthur, "Funding for Public Libraries in the 1990s," *Library Journal* 115 (January 1990): 67.

23. Ibid.

International Reports

International Federation of Library Associations and Institutions

Marjorie E. Bloss
Director, Technical Services Division
Center for Research Libraries

The International Federation of Library Associations and Institutions (IFLA) began primarily as a European-based organization in 1927. Today, its scope is most certainly international. With more than 1,200 members (predominantly associations and institutions) from 129 countries, it can be considered the United Nations of the library world. Although the annual IFLA conference is similar — in organization, activities, and the topics discussed — to library conferences in the United States, the many different cultures and perspectives represented give it an extra dimension.

The IFLA Organization

IFLA consists of 32 sections (or standing committees) and 11 round tables that funnel information to eight divisions. Association and institutional members elect section and round table members. Every two years, section members elect section officers who in turn elect division officers. Divisional chairpersons form the Professional Board, which oversees the program activities of the organization. The Executive Board, which is responsible for general policy, management and finance, and external communications, is also elected every two years.

Like other library associations, IFLA has some sections that deal with the form or function of library activities (cataloging, serial publications, preservation and conservation, and electronic data processing); others concentrate on a type of library. Underlying the activities of the sections are IFLA's five core programs: Universal Availability of Publications; Universal Bibliographic Control International MARC; Universal Dataflow and Telecommunications; Preservation and Conservation; and Advancement of Librarianship in the Third World.

As a vehicle for informing divisions, sections, and round tables of one another's activities, IFLA prepares the Medium-Term Program (MTP) every six years. The resulting document has its roots in the sections and round tables, which evaluate their progress since the last MTP and identify the activities (topical meetings, conferences, seminars and workshops, studies and publications) that they intend to work on during the next six years. Each division is also responsible for its own Medium-Term Program, and for ensuring that the goals and objectives of the sections are in line with those of the division.

The Annual Conference

The fifty-seventh annual IFLA conference in Moscow August 17–24, 1991, was to be an important one. Not only were the usual meetings (programs) and workshops scheduled, but 1991 was an election year for officers, and the year to put the finishing touches on the MTP for 1992–1997. But unanticipated events in Moscow added to the already full agenda and shifted the perspective from libraries to international politics.

Preconference Concerns

Even before the conference, many who planned to attend were apprehensive, because it was to be held in Moscow. IFLA headquarters in the Hague received a number of inquiries concerning a possible change in venue or cancellation of the conference altogether in the preceding months. Neither alternative was an option, however, and preparations went on as planned.

During spring and early summer 1991, a primary concern – the push for independence by various Soviet republics – although far from resolved, appeared under control. In a letter to registrants, IFLA headquarters attempted to reassure them that the staff was working closely with the Organizing Committee in Moscow headed by Ludmila Koslova and that plans for the conference were progressing well.

First Council Meeting

At final count, 1,492 delegates attended the fifty-seventh annual IFLA conference in Moscow (527 from the Soviet Union and 965 from other countries), dispelling concern over whether there would be enough delegates to constitute a quorum for elections. During the first two days, delegates elected officers of standing committees and the following members of the Executive Board: Marcelle Beaudiquez (France); Warren Horton (Australia); Robert D. Stueart (United States); Eeva-Maija Tammekann (Finland); and Marta Terry (Cuba). Robert Wedgeworth (United States) was elected the new IFLA president.

Another important agenda item brought up for discussion at the first council meeting was a proposal to restructure IFLA for more effective coordination of professional activities and assimilation of IFLA's Core Programs by divisions and sections. Hope Clement (Canada), chairperson of the Professional Board, summarized its activities during 1989–1991. Besides coordinating IFLA's professional activities, the board had accomplished the goals set forth in the 1986–1991 Medium-Term Program. The draft of the fourth MTP (1992–1997) was almost complete and would be finalized later in 1991.

The Opening and Plenary Sessions

The opening session of the conference was scheduled for Monday afternoon August 19, 1991, at the Rossiya Hotel, not far from Red Square. Nothing could possibly have prepared conference attendees for the series of events that began Monday morning, the morning of the coup d'état.

Everyone who attended the conference has a tale of how they first learned of the coup. At the Sovincentre (the conference site, located close to the Russian "White House"), delegates were told that Gennadi Yanayev had taken over because Gorbachev, vacationing at his dacha in the Crimea, was too ill to govern. Despite delegates' concern and frustration over the lack of news, conference activities went on as planned with a morning of programs and papers.

In the afternoon, Intourist buses transported delegates from their hotels to the Rossiya, taking circuitous routes due to the growing number of detours. Nikolai Gubenko, the Soviet minister of culture, was to speak at the opening session and delegates were hopeful that he would be able to answer some of their questions. But Gubenko's knowledge of events differed little from theirs, and he recommended that the conference proceed as scheduled. This recommendation was echoed by IFLA President Hans-Peter Geh.

Geh welcomed the audience to the conference, whose theme was "Libraries and Culture: Their Relationship," pointing out that cultural development is dependent on individual freedom, which in turn relies on good management. Libraries, he said, play key roles in both areas. Geh then described IFLA's newly adopted Long-Term Policy. Its objectives include strengthening the role of libraries in their communities, improving the general public's access to literature, and developing and applying new technologies. The Long-Term Policy emphasizes the central role of libraries in society both as cultural and educational institutions and as agents for promoting literacy.

Gubenko then gave the plenary address, citing the importance of culture in uniting nations and reminding the delegates that peace depends on valuing one another's cultures. He underscored the need to share information to promote culture, but said that libraries are, at times, incapable of providing requested information due to underfunding. He concluded by emphasizing the importance of funding for cultural institutions because "culture is the main moral support of nations."

Should the Conference Continue?

On Tuesday, August 20, conference activities proceeded as scheduled as delegates stayed in touch with their embassies and shared information with one another, mostly from CNN reports and Intourist guides. The citizens of Moscow went about their daily routines, taking the political events in stride, but delegates were encouraged to take subways rather than taxis and buses because no one knew when or where street barricades would be erected. An 11:00 P.M. curfew was announced for that evening.

With the killing of three people at the Russian "White House," the mood turned somber on Wednesday. Several delegations had already been called home and others were making arrangements to leave Moscow before the scheduled conclusion of the conference. The question "Should the conference continue?" was paramount in everyone's mind. IFLA officers decided to cancel the workshops scheduled for Thursday and to hold an abbreviated closing session that day.

Although elections for the divisions and the Professional Board were scheduled for Thursday, outgoing President Hans-Peter Geh and Professional Board Chairperson Hope Clement decided to hold elections immediately because of the diminishing number of attendees. As many IFLA delegates were at the Sovincentre attempting to learn about the latest political developments, this entailed tracking down colleagues who served in the same division and presenting them with write-in ballots. Thus members and officers were elected for both the divisions and the Professional Board.

Those elected to the Professional Board were David W. G. Clements (United Kingdom), chairperson; Erland Nielsen (Denmark), representing the Division of General Research Libraries; Derek Law (United Kingdom), representing the Division of Special Libraries; John Day (United States), representing the Division of Libraries Serving the General Public; Nancy John (United States), representing the Division of Bibliographic Control; Ulrich Montag (Germany), representing the Division of Collections and Services; Sally McCallum (United States), representing the Division of Management and Technology; Ian Johnson (United Kingdom), representing the Division of Education and Research; and Gboyega Banjo (Nigeria), representing the Division of Regional Activities.

Reception at the Kremlin

A reception for IFLA delegates sponsored by the Soviet government was scheduled for Wednesday evening at the Kremlin, although delegates were highly skeptical that it would take place. At the beginning of committee meetings on Wednesday afternoon, delegates were informed that the reception would begin earlier than scheduled and as a result, late-afternoon meetings were canceled. At 3:45, committee meetings were interrupted with an announcement. The coup was over. Gorbachev was returning to Moscow, and the remaining "Gang of Eight" was airborne, but would be arrested as soon as their plane touched down.

The reception at the Kremlin that evening was an event that those who were present will never forget. There were many toasts, much smiling, even more dancing, and undoubtedly a few tears of joy. What could have been an extremely grim gathering turned into a euphoric celebration.

The Closing Session

The jubilation of the evening before spilled over into IFLA's closing session the next day. Nikolai Gubenko received a standing ovation when he announced that he had resigned from the position of minister of culture because he felt he could not support the coup's ruling committee.

The Executive Board had canceled all conference activities after Wednesday (except for this final abbreviated session), including the second council session at which a number of resolutions would have been brought forth. Consequently, those resolutions were read in condensed form during the closing session. Two centered on IFLA's policy on South Africa, a general resolution advocated use of permanent paper, and another called for a global forum to develop a network to inform librarians of the ratification and implementation of documents in their respective countries. Resolutions presented to the Professional Board focused on maps and the skills required for their handling, UNIMARC, and preservation and conservation.

Thus ended the fifty-seventh IFLA annual meeting. Those who stayed to the end will not forget IFLA in Moscow in 1991 for a long time. For those who left before the coup was over, the words of incoming President Robert Wedgeworth are most appropriate. "It has all been a very exciting time for those of us who stayed the course. But we must not think ill of our colleagues who left early. Put simply, they missed the best part of the conference."

Frankfurt Book Fair, 1991: Quarrelsome but Quiet

Herbert R. Lottman
International Correspondent, *Publishers Weekly*

With reporting by John F. Baker
Editor in Chief, *Publishers Weekly*

A pair of events seemed to set the scene at the 43rd Frankfurt Book Fair, held October 9–14, 1991. Chancellor Helmut Kohl entered through a front gate one morning for a whirlwind walk-through of the exhibits. At that very moment, East Germany's wizard spymaster Markus Wolf—the "Carla" of John le Carré's novels—slipped out a side door after promoting a tell-all memoir at the stand of his German publisher, Schneekluth. (Wolf had been indicted, extradited from Austria, and is free on bail awaiting trial.) These could be symbols of the fair as focal point of German and world news for one week each year, but also of the strain on security services and of the opening to the East and its temptations. The collapse of the Soviet empire, the civil war in Yugoslavia, events in the Middle East—all had echoes inside the fair pavilions, often in the books on offer.

A Serious Concern

But for many American visitors, for some of their British trading partners, and for the agents who usually serve as go-betweens, an overriding concern was geographic in a different sense. The hall set aside for U.S. exhibitors (with Canada, Japan, and Israel) seemed too far from the action. The context was a fair grown too big for the space available and the sheer impossibility of placing all the major players in a single hall. Somebody had to go. "It's a situation we've never had before—a reduction in space," noted a book fair spokesman. In most areas there was sufficient room to allow normal growth—but only if the Americans were kept out of international Hall 4. And there the problems began.

The shift to Hall 3 had been announced early in 1991, when protests from leading U.S. groups led fair director Peter Weidhaas to meet with American publishers in June during the ABA show in New York. At the time, several major players threatened significant reductions in stand size and personnel if the transfer to Hall 3 was maintained. By fair time only the Bantam Doubleday Dell (BDD) group and Simon & Schuster had actually reduced booth space, but a number of other houses joined them in sending fewer key people to the fair—often 25 percent fewer.

For Jack Hoeft and Alun Davies of BDD, the shift to a new location provided an opportunity to review "what BDD really needed at Frankfurt." The tentative answer was nearly 25 percent less space, 50 percent fewer people. S&S cut its exhibit area by 40 percent. One large U.S. group increased its space, and, with newcomers, the American section was slightly larger. But the absence of familiar faces (including S&S's Richard Snyder) was evident, and no matter that publishers were ready to admit that market conditions called for reduced Frankfurt budgets.

Note: Adapted from *Publishers Weekly,* November 1, 1991.

In his New York meeting with publishers, fair director Weidhaas had pleaded for a chance to show how the new floor plan—which kept British publishers in Hall 4, adjacent to Hall 3—would work. But as the days passed, the complaints continued. A *PW* reporter found that a brisk walk (the only way one walks at Frankfurt) took him from the lower level of American Hall 3 to the Literary Agents Center in only 50 seconds and to the door of the lower level of Hall 4 in 90. The worst trip was from the British section of Hall 4 to the lower level of Hall 3, and that took only two minutes—longer if you were at the far end of either hall. But the issue was serendipity, chance meetings, spur-of-the-moment dropping-in at the stand of a favorite partner. Everybody had a yardstick to measure the reduced traffic. Bruno Quinson of Henry Holt, who used to have to fight off catalog-grabbers, found himself with a third of the pile still on the counter the day before closing. Even the Japanese, who shared Hall 3 with the United States, were complaining about the isolation; the fair had "lost energy," one confided. "Of course the American section is quiet," one neutral observer quipped, "because all the Americans are over in the British section—the busiest place in the fair."

Agent John Brockman was one who didn't mind the absence of some American publishing folk: "Why should they be here when the market is driven by agents?" Hearst's Howard Kaminsky had his own solution: If truly trade publishers were separated from the rest (the rest including "scanners and sci-tech houses"), there would be room enough for the former in international Hall 4.

Keeping his promise, Peter Weidhaas met on Saturday morning (the fourth day of the fair) with all the Americans who wanted to talk about the issue—a total of 70. The meeting opened with a warning by Nicholas Veliotes, president of the Association of American Publishers, that the space issue was "a serious concern." (AAP circulated a questionnaire during the fair asking for comments on the relocation; early returns were heavily negative.) "Have you decided to keep us in Hall 3 next year?" asked Frans Gianotten of Addison-Wesley. "Yes," Weidhaas replied. "Then why are we here?" That was the tone of the exchange.

There were specific complaints. "The hall smells terrible," said one, referring to the pervasive sewage smell at both sides of the lower level. Ronald Algrant of Hearst reminded Weidhaas that he had promised to reconsider the relocation if it worked out badly: "It was as bad as we thought it would be." Penguin's Peter Mayer feared that the fair's management was thinking in "geopolitical terms"—Britain as part of Europe, when in fact American and British publishers do most of their business with each other. "You destroyed a pattern of trading," declared BDD's Davies, who said that some Americans had been so angry that they decided not to attend the meeting. Weidhaas, who explained why fairground logistics made the move necessary, went on: "We can't change our layout every year. It doesn't help you or any other publishers."

There was a suggestion (from Lee Selverne of Worldwide Media) to alternate with the British in Halls 3 and 4. Frankfurt authorities did seem to hesitate to remove exhibitors from the "weak" countries, the Third and even the Second World, from Hall 4 to make room for the Americans. But "this is a business fair, and the weight of business should govern how the fair is conducted," declared an American. Ulrich Wechsler, chairman of the fair's board, pointed out that if a change is made, "we have to put a strong group in Hall 3, and you are the foremost group in the rights business; everybody comes to you. That was our idea in making the change." "What we would like to know before we leave is, will there be a reconsideration?" AAP's Veliotes summed up. Wechsler promised that there would be. "We need the answer quickly," Veliotes responded.

Echoes of Political Change

And as if that weren't enough distraction, there was the matter of Iran, excluded two years back because of the official call for the murder of author Salman Rushdie and others (including publishers) responsible for publication of *The Satanic Verses*. Iranians had been readmitted to the 1991 fair in the interests of universality, until angry protests from German publishers forced the fair's management to rescind the invitations. Frankfurt management had denied that Iranian participation was canceled because of protests from Klaus Piper of R. Piper Verlag and other publishers, instead attributing the decision to security considerations.

Then there was Yugoslavia — a crisis that developed under the eyes of fair visitors, as the initial stand arrangement placing Serbs opposite Croats was changed so that the latter were regrouped in the adjacent aisle, in a "Croatia" exhibit (though Croatia was not yet recognized as a country in the fair catalog). All the while, fairgoers could watch the civil war on their hotel TV, including the bombing of the Croatian capital, Zagreb. The Croatian stand, the center of intense activity, featured war posters and postcards bearing an ironic "Greetings from Croatia," showing scenes of destruction by bombing.

The surprise was the turnout at the traditional Sunday morning breakfast of the Motovun Group of copublishers and packagers of East and West, a group originated as a joint project of Serb and Croat publishers (the hilltop village of Motovun is in Croatia). The war apparently hadn't discouraged 89 publishing people (including newcomers) from attending; two of the most applauded were from "the capital of Slovenia, former Yugoslavia."

The new Russia was present and active at the fair, symbolized by that old leviathan, Progress, now apparently privatized and open to real-world dealing. Typical of the change was the situation at Novosti — Novosti Publishers, of the parent Novosti Press Agency, a Brezhnev-era baby, disappeared after the failed August coup. *PW* talked with Novosti Publishers' director Alexander Eininov and Vladimir V. Grigoriev, deputy director for acquisitions and rights, who seemed ready for Frankfurt trading despite the unresolved issue of Novosti's corporate structure. Meanwhile, Grigoriev continued to peddle state secrets, including new biographies of Trotsky and Lenin by Stalin biographer Dmitry Volkogonov, whose *Triumph and Tragedy* was acquired by George Weidenfeld in an early *glasnost* negotiation. The Trotsky book, based on heretofore closed archives, "restores the historical truth," a Novosti prospectus promises. There is also Gorbachev's account of the coup and *Health and Power* by Yevgeny Chazov, doctor to Brezhnev and his Kremlin successors, which promises to tell how a leader's health influences decision-making.

And Poland's Grzegorz Boguta, who wears so many hats, seemed ubiquitous at this Frankfurt. Obviously the man who made a worldwide publishing sensation of the underground press Nowa seemed the right person to bring Poland's publishing bureaucracy, not excluding the Warsaw Book Fair, into the market economy. Escorted through the Czechoslovak exhibit — once a scene of dreary conformity — by editor Dennis Verecky of Československý Spisovatel, *PW* couldn't help focusing on all the new publishers, each with a handful of titles. "Small publishers didn't even exist before November 1989," Verecky observed.

The day before the fair, East Germany's best-known literary imprint was sold to a consortium of West German businessmen who promised to retain Aufbau's managing director, Elmar Faber, and to maintain the house's cultural mission. *PW* met Ingo-Eric Schmidt-Braul, new managing director of East Berlin's Volk & Welt, which had been the Communist regime's imprint for translations. Taken over by the Treuhandanstalt, the government body responsible for former East German properties, Volk & Welt is to be kept alive; Schmidt-Braul himself is a Westerner, with experience in several real-world publishing houses. Title production has been cut from 180 to 40 or 50 books a year. For the moment, reunited Germany continues to have two book markets — with free-market book distribution still lacking in the former East. In the past, some 85 percent of the Volk & Welt catalog was translated; in future the ratio will probably be 50–50. In another deal, Munich's K. G. Saur took over the mammoth *German Encyclopedia of Artists* from Leipzig's E. A. Seeman and has already issued the first five volumes.

Not everyone will appreciate news of the revival of the moribund Leipzig fair, thanks to new management that accepted help from the Frankfurt fair the old management had rejected. The new fair will target the eastern provinces but hopes to be an all-German fair for spring books, even a rights fair linking Germany and Eastern Europe; the dates are May 7–10, 1992. And then Roger Shashoua was busy with his own fairs, promoting not only a second Prague International Book Fair and Writers Festival but a first Bucharest International Book Fair and Writers Festival (May 14–17 and June 11–14, respectively) — even a first St. Petersburg International Book Fair (September 3–6).

The Business Picture: Not All Bleak

All these distractions were almost enough to make one forget that publishers had come to Frankfurt to do business. In his opening remarks to the press, fair chairman Ulrich Wechsler pointed to the decline in the number of copies published per title in almost all book markets. Yet it seemed clear that the trough was not as deep in some countries as in others (the others being the U.K., say, or France). Books weren't doing badly in Japan, according to Toshiyuki Hattori of Kodansha; the market was up 3 percent after inflation, and for the first time in quite a while big groups publishing both books and magazines were doing better with the former. In Germany, reunification has been a boon to publishers, especially those with cheaper lines more likely to be sold in former East Germany, although in the view of Fischer's Wolfgang Mertz the problem is not so much pricing as distribution. "We're much better off than other countries," noted Hans-Peter Ubleis of Heyne, Munich's mammoth paperback house, "but the forecast is for a slowdown."

The business year began well in Spain, without a Gulf war shock, but there was a summer slowdown and no autumn pickup. "We don't know what the next few months will bring," confessed Beatrix de Moura of Tusquets in Barcelona. "Perhaps we'll share the recession. After all, we're part of the European Community." Book turnover actually increased in the Netherlands in 1991, Meulenhoff's Maarten Asscher reports — a combination of higher prices *and* higher volume; Meulenhoff itself had a "record" year.

Italy's situation depended on whom one talked to. "We're still waiting for the tidal wave from America and Britain," Tiziano Barbieri of Sperling & Kupfer summed up. Agent Luigi Bernabò, however, thought his country might be protected by the small size of the market, its very inelasticity; without mass market paperbacks, for example, it's harder to have a boom followed by a bust.

The situation seemed bleak to many Swedish publishers, but in Denmark, after years of stagnation, things are moving, according to Kurt Fromberg of Copenhagen's Gyldendal. And European publishers swapped stories about market-driver *Scarlett;* at Spain's Ediciones B and France's Belfond, delighted publishers reported how fast they made back record-breaking advances.

The Bestsellers

Then there were the future bestsellers. London agent Andrew Nurnberg was again showing something from Boris Yeltsin; the still-unwritten *Three Days,* dealing with the August coup, is expected to bring $1 million, or about double what Gorbachev was getting for his (albeit brief) account of the event. Early sale of Yeltsin's book to London's Chapmans and Pan and Munich's Droemer was mentioned.

There was lively interest in the John Costello–KGB collaboration, *Deadly Illusion,* snapped up by Crown in New York, which promised to tell all on the Soviet Union's prewar master spy. Knopf had *How We Die* by Sherwin Nuland, billed as a close-up of how to cope with one's own or a loved one's death. Lisa Queen of Morrow was showing a completed manuscript—almost a first for this market of outlines and sample chapters—of *Head to Head: Coming Economic Battles Among Japan, Europe and America,* by MIT's Lester C. Thurow.

On the fiction side, Sam Lawrence at the Houghton Mifflin stand was selling Frank Conroy's *Body and Soul* around the world for good money, the excitement triggered by a *PW* report of a movie option.

Among foreign projects, some saw the Gallimard illustrated pocket travel guides as the fair's newest new thing, put together by the staff that does the Discovery nonfiction monographs soon to be launched by Abrams in the United States. Among early takers of the Gallimard line was the same Knopf-Everyman partnership that revived the Everyman classics line in both markets.

Those fortunate enough to operate out of the Agents and Scouts Center—located virtually at midpoint between U.S. and U.K. and other offshore publishers—seemed less affected by the new floor plan. "It's not quiet," affirmed scout Jutta Klein, "it's just that everybody is being careful." She could furnish evidence of a satisfactory level of acquisitions—better than in 1990—by some of her principals, which included Bertelsmann Munich trade imprints, Barcelona's Plaza y Janés (a Bertelsmann affiliate). She also represents some leading Bertelsmann clubs, including France Loisirs and Círculo de Lectores, neither of which likes to buy at the fair—although the Dutch club ECI did (for the first time) make a Frankfurt bid.

The coveted prize was Sultana, heroine of Jean Sasson's *Princess,* the life of a member of the Saudi royal family slightly disguised, in the words of the Morrow outline, "to ensure that the identity of the princess would not be obvious to the Saudi investigators." For Klein, the 1991 Frankfurt was a more interesting fair for shoppers, despite year-round travel and fax exchanges. "Expectations have changed—nobody is taken in by hype." She suspected that the reduction in staffing of many stands made the fair more personal.

Among the Americans

Agent Sandra Dijkstra had come all the way from Del Mar, California, for Amy Tan's *The Year of No Flood,* with two chapters written but not shown. Because she is far from the East Coast center of things most of the year, Dijkstra uses the fair as an opportunity to see American publishers. One of her best new authors was Susan Faludi, with *Backlash: The Undeclared War Against American Women.*

American publishers, despite their irritation with Hall 3, mostly found the fair useful – and the comparative quietness of the location even seemed a boon to some.

Morgan Entrekin of Atlantic Monthly Press stressed that "we just don't see as many people as we used to in Hall 4." He was insisting on world rights, which somewhat limited his opportunities, "but we're here more to sell than to buy" – like most U.S. visitors. "The Germans are the ones with the money," he noted, and he had already made a deal for a new Darcey Steinke novel, *Suicide Blonde.* He also found a great deal of interest in P. J. O'Rourke's new book, due in April, *Give War a Chance.*

As an art publisher, Paul Gottlieb at Abrams felt less affected than some by the general economic instabilities. Among his trading partners, "France and the U.K. are having a tough time, Germany and Spain are booming." On international co-editions, "people are cautious. You have to be prepared to show much more than you used to, which means you have to invest far more up front before you have a partner. It's more difficult than it used to be for foreign publishers to translate."

Frankfurt is also a time for introductions. One was by Donovan Publishing, a new house from California, whose president, Paul Sumner, described a program that involves handsomely produced books on war, on music, on recovery, and on the work of movie cartoon wizard Friz Freleng, accompanied by audiocassettes with narration, sound effects, and music. Initial plans call for six books by fall 1992, about ten a year thereafter.

Baker & Taylor was showing off its new B & T Link: The Title Source and BookFind-CD World Edition, born of its union with the U.K. firm Book Data, the former with more than a million title records, the latter with 1.6 million. Baker & Taylor's Mary Shapiro describes the union as "a response to the globalization of English-language sources." The relationship with Book Data, she said, is an equity interest, but both sides continue to develop their products independently. Already the two are linked in 45 countries and, with their combined marketing strength, plan to make the databases available worldwide.

Bob Miller of Hyperion, Disney's new publishing arm, was seizing the opportunity to show off his first list to British and foreign publishers, to what he called "a terrific response." He had made a number of sales – mostly of popular nonfiction, though even some fiction "traveled better than I expected" – and had bought three picture books from Britain.

At Warner, Olivia Blumer was busy, as always, around the clock, offering *Double Cross* by Sam and Chuck Giancana for reading in strictly supervised confidentiality. Laffont had already signed, others were "dallying." *Marilyn and Me: Sisters, Rivals, Friends* by Susan Strasberg went to Doubleday in London and was attracting much interest elsewhere.

For Houghton Mifflin's Joseph Kanon, the textbook operation was the more prominent at Frankfurt. "Trade you do by fax these days." He found the difficulties of Hall 3 overstated, but wondered aloud: "How much longer can Frankfurt exist? Do we really need it?"

Several religious publishers, located at the far end of Hall 6, found they were doing increased business with Eastern European countries. Tom Olson of Moody Press was looking at a new contract in Bulgaria, two in Poland. Attendance at Frankfurt didn't pay for itself, he found, "but we'd lose if we weren't here." David Toht of Lion Publishing already does a lot of business with Eastern Europe and finds it growing in "a broad range of spirituality." And Lion's David Alexander predicted that perhaps 300 or 400 deals would result from discussions at Frankfurt, for translations into 25 languages. Lion also bought religious fiction from France and Russia.

Sally Richardson of St. Martin's Press found that, although there might have been fewer editors than usual at the fair, they were working extra hard — and there was a great eagerness for new writers, especially of strong commercial fiction. "People are reading manuscripts overnight and talking them up the next day." Tom Dunne, of the same house, was pleased to notice that there was not as much editorial competition as usual, "and I'm taking home a lot of books to read."

Dan Harvey at Putnam was reveling in sales of Steven Rosenberg's *The Transformed Cell,* involving hope for cancer patients through a form of genetic engineering. Chapmans in London had paid a six-figure advance before the fair, a six-figure sale was made to Japan's Bungeishunju, and the book was shaping up to be one of the fair's biggest. Other Putnam winners were books by Patti Davis and David Bowie's ex-wife, Angela.

On the Party Circuit

After hours, one could pursue business over German *Sekt* or cocktails at a dizzying variety of parties, more foreign- than American-sponsored, some official, others (the best) strictly trade. A visitor might begin on the eve of the fair with the Fischer party held in the Verlag's attractive headquarters across the river. Then the regular Rowohlt fete on Wednesday (now challenged by John Wiley & Sons, mixing sci-tech and general trade guests) and Bertelsmann on Friday. Indeed, the Bertelsmann event had become so unmanageable that it was augmented at the 1991 fair by a Thursday reception sponsored by the worldwide Bertelsmann clubs. Saturday night was divided between the Reader's Digest sit-down dinner, mostly for Europeans, and the Heyne SRO buffet at the Frankfurter Hof.

One of the warmest parties was just a bunch of people sitting around the Lippizaner bar at the Frankfurter Hof: alumni of the Jerusalem Book Fair editorial fellows program, youngish, middle-management book people from around the world who keep in touch with each other, often working together. Another party introduced Turner Publishing, a subsidiary of the Turner Broadcasting System, whose Cable News Network kept fair-goers glued to the Clarence Thomas hearings.

Fair Miscellany

The Buchmesse, serving as spokesperson for the German book trade, again produced a catalog of "Books and Rights," listing 153 titles from 56 German imprints. (It sent copies in English to 800 editors and rights directors round the world.) With K. G.

Saur, the fair did another "Who's Who," listing everyone who had signed up, with their firms and responsibilities. The fair opened a pavilion to Book Trade Services, Remainder and Promotional Books, an alliance against nature that did not delight remainder dealers. It hopes to do better by them in 1992.

STM: Of Continuing Significance

Once again the fair cosponsored (with AAP) a "rights directors" meeting, this time devoted to "The Shifting Sands of International Publishing Economics." Perhaps the most significant single event at the fair was the general assembly of the International Group of Scientific, Technical and Medical Publishers, bringing together no fewer than 200 heads of houses in what may be considered the most lucrative, least vulnerable sectors of print and electronic publishing. The agenda dealt with growing challenges to copyright and innovations in marketing. According to speakers at the Tuesday morning meeting, within a few years STM publishers will be drawing covered wagons into a circle for a last stand against rip-off reprography. From the rostrum STM secretary Paul Nijhoff Asser issued an urgent invitation to a March 1992 Amsterdam seminar on "Electrocopying, Current Awareness and Document Delivery vs. STM Publishers' Marketing and Copyright Objectives." The emphasis, he said, was on the *versus*.

The Future of Frankfurt?

The 1991 theme—designed to help the German public grasp the book fair—was devoted to Spain. Some 80 separate exhibitions and other events had been scheduled on or off the fairgrounds. One could spend a pleasurable week sightseeing among things Spanish.

A quiet, working fair—that was the general verdict. "There is much less madness here, which doesn't mean that we're not doing business," said Mondadori editor Giancarlo Bonacina. For enthusiasm one had to talk to a small publisher like veteran Ian Chapman, of his and his wife's Chapmans of London, who was as excited as a young publisher. Or to veteran Roger Straus, who had a new Nobel winner (Gordimer) to line up alongside the old ones, or to a two-person operation called Peter Halban (U.K.), whose best money is made in foreign sales.

So is the fair on the way out? Agent Morton Janklow thought it might be. "A lot of foreign publishers tell me they do more business at ABA than at Frankfurt," said Janklow, who sees the transformation of the October event into a "sub rights fair."

"If ABA wants to kill Frankfurt," put in Sergio Machado of Brazil's Record, "all they have to do is hold it every year in New York." To see for yourself, tune in next year from September 30 to October 5.

Canadian Library Community

Gwynneth Evans

Director, External Relations
National Library of Canada

"Local libraries are facing serious compression as pressure continues to build on their services and resources fail to keep up." This quotation from "Giving Voice to a Quiet Majority," a report commissioned by public libraries in Alberta, reflects the situation in every province and territory in Canada and in all types of libraries. Several factors account for increased pressure in 1991. One is taxation.

On January 1, 1991, the government of Canada implemented the Goods and Services Tax (GST) as a replacement for its manufacturing tax. This 7 percent tax was applied to reading materials, which were previously exempt from tax. Some provinces also applied an additional 7 or 8 percent provincial sales tax (PST). An example of the impact was reported by the director of the Saskatoon Public Library, who found that 7,000 fewer books could be bought from the $1.4 million collections budget; yet with a 14 percent tax increase on books and periodicals, the general public was relying more on public libraries for reading materials.

Shrinking resources, human and financial, have also been a strong factor in prompting Canadian librarians to analyze their problems, to develop long-term plans, and to explore alternative sources of funding. Some plans have been prepared at the local level; others include networking and resource sharing strategies. For example, *One Place to Look: The Ontario Public Library Strategic Plan* (1990) is a provincial plan that stimulated meetings and discussion within the community and with potential partners during 1991. Another example comes from the academic community. The Royal Society of Canada was commissioned to study university research. One of its recommendations, based on extensive briefs and consultation, was to seek both short- and long-term strategies for Canadian university libraries. Unfortunately, an appropriate way to enhance the role of university libraries in research has not yet been found. In Manitoba, a group of libraries incorporated to establish a mechanism for resource sharing and for approaching outside bodies for support. A fourth, more specific, initiative for attracting support was the launching of the Friends of the National Library of Canada on November 4, 1991, when Robertson Davies read from his new novel *Murther and Walking Spirits*.

The climate of cutbacks has also directly affected library staff in many parts of Canada. In some provinces, public-sector wages were frozen. In the Public Service of Canada, a general strike in Fall 1991 curtailed delivery of many services. At the National Library, 73 percent of employees were on strike, leaving a skeleton staff to continue basic services such as the DOBIS Search Service and interlibrary loan and reference services. Some library staff at the University of Toronto were also involved in an extended strike in late Spring 1991.

Despite the political and economic changes within Canada, library staff have concentrated on professional concerns. Preservation programs have advanced through a number of initiatives: a concerted campaign at the federal level for the adoption of permanent paper for government publications; drafting of a national strategy and plan for preservation activities; a cooperative study on mass deacidification; development of cooperative provincial programs such as the Paper Heritage Group of Newfoundland; and the systematic development of disaster plans, staff training programs, and conservation/preservation programs in major research libraries.

Automation has also preoccupied many. The government of Canada granted the National Library $13.3 million over five years to upgrade its systems; Prince Edward Island and Newfoundland are engaged in their first automation projects for public libraries; and individual and groups of libraries are expanding their networking capacity. These activities — preservation, automation, networking — are increasing communication among different types of library within Canada and building a stronger, more unified voice within the Canadian library community. Library associations contribute to this development and to the formation of positions on such issues as copyright, "buying around" Canadian publishers and agents, and postal subsidies, which require continuing attention in the political arena.

Some major changes in personnel took place in the Canadian library community during 1991. Karen Adams was appointed executive director, Canadian Library Association, in January 1991. Margot Montgomery succeeded Elmer Smith as director general of the Canada Institute for Scientific and Technical Information. Maureen Cubberly became manager of Ontario Library Service/Public Library Service Unit, Libraries and Community Information Branch. Rosemary Kavanagh succeeded Helen Perry as executive director, Canadian National Institute for the Blind, Library Division. Neil Brearley was appointed university librarian, Carleton University, in January 1991, following the retirement of Geoffrey Briggs. Late in 1991, David Holmes was appointed university librarian, effective June 1992, on the retirement of Brearley.

John D. Teskey, formerly of the University of Alberta, succeeded Sheila Laidlaw as director of libraries, University of New Brunswick (Fredericton). Ron Clancy became chief librarian of New Westminster Public Library, British Columbia. Gerry Meek, former chief executive officer of Thunder Bay (Ontario) Public Library, was named director, Calgary Public Library, following the retirement of John Dutton. Karen Harrison succeeded Meek at Thunder Bay. Victor Desroches was named director, Agriculture Canada Library, following the retirement of Margaret (Peggy) Morton in June 1991.

The Canadian library community was saddened by the death of Margaret Elizabeth Miller in May 1991. At the time of her death Beth Miller was coordinator of the Cooperative Work/Study Program and placement officer, School of Library and Information Science, University of Western Ontario (London). She was president of the Canadian Library Association (CLA) in 1985–1986 and of the Ontario Library Association in 1982–1983 and she was the first recipient of the Ontario College and University Libraries Association Award of Merit, in 1985. She had also served as a member of the American Library Association/U.S. Department of Education Committee on Accreditation (1984–1986), as chairperson of the CLA Special President's Committee on Canadian Accreditation (1983–1986), as a member of the ALA Standards Revision Committee, and as secretary of the Continuing Professional Education Round Table of the International Federation of Library Associations and Institutions (IFLA).

Eastern Europe's Libraries: Emerging from Isolation

Rachel Roberts

International Affairs Officer
Library Association of the United Kingdom

Eastern Europe has a long library tradition, recognizably European in its history, development, and vocation. In keeping with much of Europe, its history can be traced to the Middle Ages and the emergence of monastic and university book collections. The library at the Benedictine Monastery in Pammonbalma is Hungary's oldest library still in use. Its records date as far back as 1090, a claim few libraries can make. In Poland, the medieval University of Cracow is rightly proud of its library, founded with the university in 1364. Subsequent library development until the end of World War II roughly followed Western European trends. For example, legal deposit in Czechoslovakia can be traced to not long after the British Library was granted the same privilege. In 1781, the National Library in Prague, known then as the Public Imperial and Royal University Library, became legally entitled to one copy of all material published in Prague.

Professional associations dedicated to library development sprang up throughout Europe at the beginning of this century. The Polish Library Association, for instance, held its first congress in 1928 and was among the founding members of the International Federation of Library Associations and Institutions (IFLA). After World War II, Eastern European librarianship was forced to follow a separate path, one shaped by socialist thinking and about which the outside world received only carefully censored and highly propagandist information. With the wind of change that has swept through Eastern Europe in the last few years, countless delegations of Western librarians have ventured east, to discover the fate of libraries behind the iron curtain during decades of isolation. Most have returned with reports of autocratic regimes, bureaucratic systems, severe underfunding, and cultural repression; slowly, a picture of the library scene in the Soviet bloc has emerged.

A striking feature of Eastern European librarianship is the importance it attaches to its cultural role. Libraries play a significant and prestigious part in cultural life and are objects of national pride. Romanian authors and poets, for example, traditionally donate manuscripts to the University Library of Bucharest. Libraries of all types are often housed in historic buildings of great beauty, which are not always practical. The Czech National Library is located in a former Jesuit monastery. The Baroque Room, the nucleus of the library, was the monastic library. In an attempt to preserve the room's character, installation of electricity has been prohibited. The primary objectives of libraries in many Eastern bloc countries have been preservation and conservation of their cultural heritage. Nowhere is this more noticeable than where the culture has been threatened. Poland's attitude toward its literary heritage is intrinsically linked to its historical struggle for survival. Even within living memory, the world has witnessed attempts to annihilate Poland's culture. During World War II, 2,500 incunabula, 40,000 manuscripts, and 50,000 early printed books of the National Library of Poland were deliberately destroyed by invading forces. That Polish librarianship has channeled much of its energy into the preservation, conservation, and painstaking recording of the nation's precious collections is hardly surprising. Since their loss of independence in 1940, the Baltic states have also suffered cultural repression. In an attempt to Russianize the region, books in native languages were forbidden. With the easing of Soviet rule and the regaining of independence, librarians in the Baltic states have seized the opportunity to become a vital element in the region's cultural renaissance. Libraries have been in the forefront of promoting native languages and culture.

Present library structures behind the former iron curtain reflect socialist political and economic ideology. After the war, libraries were restructured on the Soviet model into large, heavily centralized and bureaucratic systems. The Czechoslovakian postwar experience is typical of many countries within the Soviet bloc. In 1959, the Unified System of Libraries Act divided libraries into 12 networks and placed them in a hierarchical structure within each network under the direction of a central body. The State Library became responsible for public libraries, the Ministry of Education for high school libraries, the Central Trade Union Council for trade union libraries, and so forth. The problems created by these centralized structures are now being recognized and discussed. The system certainly has its critics. Since the "velvet revolution" in 1989, opposition to this management style has been growing, and major changes are likely in the near future. A disadvantage of the old system is that libraries have been geared to respond to central directives, to the detriment of users. The user is the first to suffer when major management decisions are taken off-site in a system where information mainly flows downward.

As these countries switch to a market economy, libraries will increasingly have to justify their existence and compete with other services for funds, a function for which they are ill-equipped. Moreover, a generation of professionals has been trained to accept and implement directives from above without question. Much retraining will be needed to develop a workforce capable of independent thought and initiative. The network system has also been criticized for its inflexible approach to subject specialization. Libraries with similar subject coverage are discouraged by this system from coordinating activities. Most accept reform as necessary but realize, unfortunately, that in the present climate of upheaval, libraries are near the bottom of the list of priorities. Censorship is another form of state control that was imposed on libraries. Czechoslovak libraries underwent two purges under Soviet rule. During the first, in the 1950s, destroyed material included works by Trotsky and Tito. The other followed the Soviet invasion in 1968.

Socialist isolationist policies have also had a great effect on library development. Tartu, Estonia's academic and cultural center, is an extreme example. Until a few years ago, the town was closed not only to foreigners but also to many Estonians. For the Tartu University Library to provide up-to-date service without outside help must have been a constant struggle. Restrictions on overseas travel and contact with the West were imposed on the vast majority of Eastern Europeans. Consequently, for librarians to attend overseas conferences and invite Western specialists was difficult, if not impossible.

Separated from the international exchange of ideas and information, some areas of Eastern European librarianship have remained stagnant, with attitudes and practices reminiscent of the 1950s. Others have established their own practices and developed separately. For example, Romanian public libraries developed an ingenious method of outreach using puppet theater. Government policies, however, are not solely to blame for restricted access to the West. The short supply of foreign currency has aggravated Eastern Europe's isolation. Without hard currency, libraries' access to foreign books and periodicals as well as their ability to purchase such equipment as computers has been severely curtailed. In the 15 years before the 1989 revolution, under the austere climate of the Ceauşescu regime, Romanian libraries acquired no new foreign literature. This problem was particularly acute for research libraries, which had no option but to collect and disseminate out-of-date information. Where possible, research libraries have relied on exchange programs to boost acquisition of foreign materials. The Bulgarian Academy of Science, for instance, has had an exchange program with the library of the University of California at Berkeley since 1908. Eastern European librarians have shown great resourcefulness in an adverse situation. To compensate for the shortfall in foreign material, they have produced their own, including indexing and abstracting publications.

During the last 20 years of Eastern European economic decline, libraries have been starved of resources. Underfunding has led to storage problems at the Czech National Library. The situation is so critical that the library has been described as "bursting at the seams." Hundreds of thousands of books are stored knee-high in crates and thus are practically inaccessible. The storage problem must contribute to the library's slow delivery service. It can take up to 14 days for a requested item to be found. Underfunding is responsible for impoverished collections, cramped and difficult working conditions, and shortages of up-to-date equipment.

Striking examples can be found in Romania. Few Romanian libraries were built for that purpose; the Romanian National Library is housed in the old stock exchange. At the time of the 1989 revolution, a new library designed as a monument to the glory of the Ceauşescus was half-built but was totally unsuited for library purposes. Romanian librarians have had to endure difficult working conditions. During the old regime, libraries were not heated in winter, as power was diverted to favored industries.

The poor state of library collections reflects the sad condition of the Romanian publishing industry. Book production has significantly decreased since 1945. In 1971, 5,000 books were produced; by 1989, the figure had fallen to a mere 1,000. Book quality has also deteriorated, and hardbacks became unavailable in the early 1980s. Moreover, librarians could not purchase book film to protect paperback stock. Poor paper quality is also to blame for the rapid deterioration of book collections. Library staff have had to carry out duties without the help of such basic equipment as typewriters and photocopying machines, let alone more advanced machines such as computers. In some libraries, catalog cards are still written by hand.

Library reformers recognize that only a well-trained and motivated workforce can bring about changes and have consequently focused on library education. In Romania, there has been no formal library education since the country's only library school was closed by the government around 1952. Most of its graduates have retired. Few among younger generations have taken library courses abroad, not even in other socialist countries. Training has been carried out at home as best as possible. The University of Cluj plans to start a school of librarianship, but no doubt will have difficulty recruiting professionally trained staff.

Library education in the Baltic states was not banned under Russian rule, but it was based on the Soviet model and was heavily politicized. Approximately one third of the program was devoted to the study of Marxism-Leninism and dialectical materialism. Major reforms to the curriculum are under way in the Baltic states.

In many Eastern European countries, professional associations have not been allowed to promote advancements in librarianship, to encourage good practices, or to raise the status of the profession. The Czechoslovak Library Association, for instance, was disbanded in 1969 by the Ministry of the Interior for involvement in the "Prague spring" and the association's leading figures were exiled to the provinces. The position of library associations that were allowed to exist under the socialist regime is unenviable. Polish library staff, for example, feel that the Polish Library Association collaborated with the government of martial law in the early 1980s. The stigma has eroded the association's influence. Under the old system, only those connected with the Communist Party could hope to attain important positions. Some old scores have been settled since the end of Soviet supremacy. In several instances, leading professionals have been replaced by inexperienced but politically untainted individuals.

Despite the odds, librarians in Eastern Europe have maintained library service. Since the lifting of travel restrictions, they have been eager to rejoin the international community. The world has greeted their return with enthusiasm and has been impressed by their eagerness to update services. But librarians still face major challenges, one of which will be to establish a fundamental role for libraries in the emerging democracies.

Library Developments in Western Europe

George Cunningham
Chief Executive
Library Association of the United Kingdom

In recent years, two developments have had far-reaching effects on European libraries: efforts to foster cooperation among libraries in the European Community and the revival of libraries in Eastern Europe following the collapse of communist regimes.

History of Library Cooperation

Cooperation among libraries in Europe is not a new phenomenon. National libraries have always had a great deal of contact with the principal special collections. From its inception, the Council of Europe, established in 1949 to foster European unity and overcome wartime antagonisms, promoted cooperation on cultural matters among its 21 full members; the European Cultural Convention was concluded as early as 1954. In 1971, the Ligue des Bibliothèques Européennes de Recherche (LIBER) was established with strong Council of Europe backing. With more than 200 members in nearly all member states of the Council of Europe, LIBER is the principal body regularly consulted by the council on matters concerning libraries. On occasion, LIBER assists the council financially.

Although the Council of Europe can be credited with some important contributions to library cooperation—notably the encouragement of retrospective cataloging in machine-readable form—the council has been eclipsed by the European Community in matters relating to the community's 12 member states because it is dependent on the voluntary cooperation of member states and is without significant financial resources. The council now focuses on one of its original objectives, cooperation between the countries of Western and Eastern Europe.

European Community

From its inception in 1957, the European Community has been a supranational organization, not just a mechanism for cooperation among sovereign states. The Treaty of Rome, along with its many amendments since 1957, provides that laws made by the community override national legislation of member states. In the early decades, the community concentrated on economic questions, and priorities were to establish a common external tariff, eradicate internal tariffs, and establish a common agricultural policy. But the intent always was to develop an entity with the characteristics of a single nation.

In recent years, the community has begun to take action in areas of policy generally regarded as proper to member states. One new area of activity is culture. But libraries had been the focus of attention long before this for other reasons. Concerned by the dominance of the United States and Japan in information technology, the community had taken steps to foster use and development of information technology within its borders. During the 1970s, the community adopted successive three- and five-year plans to promote a European information market. In September 1985, the ministers of culture of the member states adopted a resolution calling for closer cooperation among libraries in the community with particular reference to the use of new technology. Drawing attention to the vast treasure house of material in public and private libraries in the community, the resolution called for cooperative action to (1) define and set up a system based on existing systems and forms of collaboration that would enable computerized catalogs to be linked and (2) to prepare a work program designed to expedite development of libraries both culturally and as a major force for innovation and support in the information market.

European Library Action Plan

During the next few years, the so-called European Library Action Plan was designed to foster cooperation. The community would establish a fund to help finance library projects. After a long gestation period, libraries were invited in 1991 to submit proposals for use of the funds with precise guidelines regarding the areas in which the community wishes to offer help, all involving new technology in one way or another. In each member state, projects initiated by libraries are screened for "national focus" before they are considered by the community's institutions in Luxembourg. The plan will likely benefit research libraries in national libraries and higher academic institutions most, but public libraries are in no way excluded.

In accordance with its practice, the European Commission, the community's executive arm, has drawn up guidelines for areas to receive assistance. The guidelines specify four so-called action lines:

1 Computerized bibliographies
2 Projects that further international linking of systems holding source data for specific library functions
3 Projects that stimulate provision of innovative library services using information and communication technologies in smaller libraries
4 Projects that encourage development and production of prototypes of new technology-based products, services, and tools specifically for libraries.

All activities are designed to promote European performance in the development and application of information technology.

Issues of Cultural Identity

Meanwhile, developments in a different area of the community's cultural affairs have been the subject of controversy. Several member states, notably France, have always attached importance to the promotion of cultural identity with state assistance. These countries wish to foster a sense of identity within member states through community-based cultural activities, a move fiercely resisted by the British and to a lesser extent by the Danes and Germans. (Under the German constitution, responsibility for cultural matters rests with the provinces, not with the federal government.) After a long delay, member states adopted compromises to allow the community to undertake cultural activities.

Initially, members have focused on such activities as a European literary prize and limiting the proportion of non-community television on screens in member states. Unfortunately, little has been done to encourage exchange of skills and knowledge among librarians in different countries. The difference between the quality of services in Portugal and Great Britain or Greece and Denmark is vast. In due course, library services in less developed countries are expected to be brought to the level of the best libraries in the community.

Copyright

Besides activities related to culture and information technology, the European Community is involved in a variety of other matters. In 1989, the commission published a document setting out those aspects of copyright law on which harmonization throughout the community was desirable. The justification is that the European Community should be one single market, and providers of services, including authors and publishers, should not encounter different conditions in the different member states. The commission is particularly interested in audiovisual material and computer software. Laws protecting data have also attracted the community's attention. Draft directives are under consideration on all of these subjects. (A directive is an instruction adopted by the central institutions of the community requiring each member state to bring its law into conformity with the purposes stated in the directive.)

Retail Pricing and Lending Fees

Retail price control on books is another possible area for harmonization throughout the community. Most member states allow publishers to set minimum prices for publications, and the commission believes that distortions of trade can occur when a country that has such a system trades books with one that does not. Some member states have public lending rights systems (whereby a payment is made to authors whose books are borrowed from public libraries), and others do not. In such matters, member states can have different interests. On the whole, books and other materials in the English language are more commonly used by other members of the community than materials in other languages are in the United Kingdom. Although for British authors to be paid each time their books are borrowed from libraries in Denmark or Germany is in their interest, their books would certainly be borrowed many more times in those countries than Danish or German works would be in Britain.

Value-Added Tax

To harmonize taxation practices throughout the community, an attempt has been made to ensure that value-added tax (a sophisticated sales tax) should apply equally to books in all member states. This has elicited intense opposition, particularly in the United Kingdom, where there have been many historic battles in the last hundred years against "taxation of knowledge." When a proposal to apply value-added tax to books was being considered by the British government in 1984, the Library Association, the Publishers Association, and the Booksellers Association mounted a successful campaign to resist the attempt. The proposal reemerged, however, as part of efforts to harmonize fiscal practices throughout the community. After long and intense battles in the corridors of Brussels and Luxembourg, opponents of the proposal have succeeded in obtaining for those countries that currently apply no tax to books the right to continue that position at least for some years. The battle will be resumed in the mid-1990s when the pressure by European institutions to curb all variations in the community will no doubt be renewed.

Freedom of Establishment

One aspect of European unification of particular interest to professional librarians is "freedom of establishment." As stipulated in the original Treaty of Rome, which established the European Economic Community, in due course all persons should be able to move freely about the community and to pursue a profession in any member state. The community has taken a long time to draft law on this matter, but the Council of Ministers adopted a directive late in 1988 requiring member states to ensure that, subject to certain qualifications, persons who have obtained a professional designation in any member state should be able to practice in any other without restriction. The qualifications deal with cases where the length or depth of training in one member state is markedly different from that in the other, but, subject only to that, the requirement is absolute. This means that an organization like the Library Association of the United Kingdom, which in common with many other professional bodies awards professional status, will not be able to deny use of its postnominal letters ALA and FLA (Associate and Fellow of the Library Association) on the grounds that an applicant's training and experience were obtained in a country of the community other than the United Kingdom.

Future Cooperation

All these moves toward greater community involvement in library and information matters have made it necessary for library associations and their equivalents in the 12 member states to work together more closely. At a meeting in London in May 1991, delegates from organizations in all member countries agreed in principle to establish a small secretariat in or near Brussels to ensure that library organizations obtain up-to-date information on community developments in their field, to facilitate consultation among organizations on those and other matters, and, where agreement is sufficient, to channel the views of professional bodies to the community. It is hoped that the new secretariat, with the tentative title of European Bureau for Library and Information Services and Documentation, will be established before the end of 1992.

Federal Agency and Federal Library Reports

National Commission on Libraries and Information Science

1111 18th St. N.W., Suite 310, Washington, DC 20036
202-254-3100, FAX 202-254-3111

Charles E. Reid
Chairperson

The three major events in 1991 for the National Commission on Libraries and Information Science (NCLIS) were the commission's twentieth anniversary celebration in January, the second White House Conference on Library and Information Services (WHCLIS) in July, and the passage of technical amendments to the commission's enabling legislation in August. The White House conference dominated all other activities, but the commission pursued and made progress on other programs, too, despite a budget of $732,000 ($18,000 less than the previous fiscal year), staffing at only 6.5 full-time-equivalent positions (the level resulting from cutbacks during 1990), and vacant seats on the commission.

Charles Reid continued as commission chairperson, and Peter Young as executive director. In January Elinor Swaim was elected to a one-year term as vice chairperson and Daniel Casey to the executive committee, with Michael Farrell as alternate. Other members were Wanda Forbes, Jerald Newman, Julia Li Wu, and Winston Tabb, representing Librarian of Congress James Billington. Kay Riddle was confirmed as a commissioner in May 1991, and the terms of Carol DiPrete and Raymond Petersen expired in July 1991. In November the Senate confirmed DiPrete and Barbara Taylor for second terms and Norman Kelinson, Ben-Chieh Liu, and James Lyons as new commissioners.

Highlights of the Year

Twentieth Anniversary Celebration

On the evening of January 23, 1991, more than 250 current and former commissioners gathered with staff, associates, friends, and other distinguished guests in the Library of Congress for a reception to celebrate NCLIS's twentieth anniversary. The event was cosponsored by the Center for the Book, which also launched its "1991 – The Year of the Lifetime Reader" campaign. First Lady Barbara Bush was present to receive the Twentieth Anniversary Special Recognition Award for her work in support of literacy. The 1991 Annual Recognition Award went to the Girl Scouts of the U.S.A. for its "Right to Read" project.

White House Conference on Library and Information Services

The White House Conference on Library and Information Services (WHCLIS) was planned and conducted under the direction of NCLIS. NCLIS Chairperson Charles Reid and WHCLIS Advisory Committee Chairperson Richard Akeroyd were conference cochairpersons, and Joseph Fitzsimmons was vice chairperson. Commissioners served on committees dealing with delegates' credentials and conference rules and recommendations. At the last of several joint sessions on October 24–25, WHCLIS Advisory Committee members shared their observations and suggestions for actions with NCLIS representatives. [A special report on the conference, held July 9–13, 1991, in Washington, D.C., appears in the Special Reports section earlier in Part 1 – *Ed.*]

On November 21, NCLIS presented the WHCLIS summary report to President Bush. He had 90 days to transmit the report to Congress with the administration's recommendations. At year's end, NCLIS had begun identifying priorities and methods for coordinating efforts to implement the 95 recommendations passed at the conference.

Technical Amendments to NCLIS Statute

On August 14, President Bush signed into law (P.L. 102-95) amendments to the commission's enabling legislation (P.L. 91-345). The new law makes clear that NCLIS is to be involved in international cooperative activities and that it can receive monetary and other contributions. It also increases the commission's 20-year-old authorization level from $750,000 to $911,000 for FY 1992 and authorizes "such sums as may be necessary" for all subsequent years. (The actual appropriation for FY 1992 is $831,000.)

Library and Information Services to Native Americans

The Committee on Library and Information Services to Native Americans held its fourth and fifth regional hearings to obtain information on the status of tribal library and information services and to receive recommendations on the kinds of services needed by the tribes living in each region. (The first hearing, for the Southwest, was in Santa Fe, New Mexico, in January 1989. The second, for the Southeast, took place in Winter Park, Florida, in March 1990. The Northeast hearing was held in Hartford, Connecticut, on October 24, 1990.)

Twenty-three tribes participated in the fourth regional hearing in Seattle, Washington, on August 16, 1991, for the Pacific Northwest and the Mountain Plains. Before the hearing, site visits were conducted in California, Montana, and Washington. The fifth hearing, in Anchorage, Alaska, on October 16, 1991, was also preceded by site visits. At both hearings there was testimony in support of improved library facilities, professionally trained library staff, technical assistance, and additional and consistent funding for tribal libraries.

While the two hearings and the site visits were being planned and carried out, a strategic plan was being drafted to provide Native American tribes with adequate library and information services. The commission also helped plan and carry out the February 28–March 3 pre–White House Conference on Native American Library and

Information Services and the special May 23 hearing on Native Americans, called by Senator Daniel Inouye (D-Hawaii), chairperson of the Select Committee on Indian Affairs. A forum on library and information services to Native Americans on May 22 was cosponsored by NCLIS, the National Indian Policy Center, the American Indian Library Association, and the Society of American Archivists.

Library Statistics

NCLIS continued to work with the National Center for Education Statistics (NCES) on the cooperative library statistics program begun in 1988. In April 1991, NCES made available the first data from 8,699 public libraries in all 50 states and the District of Columbia, based on national standard data elements and definitions, in both printed and machine-readable form on floppy disks. By the end of September, all data for 1990 had been collected and were being analyzed for completeness and quality before publication in 1992. Development of the Public Library Universe File, with directory information on all public library service units in the United States, progressed much more rapidly in 1991 than expected.

NCLIS, NCES, and the American Library Association's Office for Research and Statistics took a major step forward in 1991 in their cooperative work on academic library statistics. Standard software was used to record the 1990 statistics submitted by the states. This could expedite publication of the data by nine to twelve months. Further improvements in the quality and usefulness of the data from the 1992 and 1994 biennial academic library surveys are planned.

A new questionnaire on school library media centers and specialists, developed by NCES in cooperation with NCLIS and the American Association of School Librarians, was field-tested in March 1991. The major NCES School and Staff Survey for 1990–1991 also contains several key questions on library media centers. Surveys being planned include a state library survey and a survey of federal libraries and information centers, which may be implemented in 1993. A survey of state-based networks is also under consideration.

Support for Executive and Legislative Branches

Working with the Legislative Reference Division of the Office of Management and Budget (OMB) — which coordinates and clears executive agencies' recommendations on proposed, pending, and enrolled legislation — NCLIS reviewed documents pertaining to the reauthorization of the Higher Education Act, the High Performance Computing Act (with a section on the National Research and Education Network), the American Technology Preeminence Act, and the National Literacy Act. The commission also conferred with OMB regarding the proposed revision to Circular A-130, "Management of Federal Information Resources."

NCLIS helped to arrange the joint congressional hearing during the White House Conference on Library and Information Services. NCLIS Chairperson Reid sent letters to the states encouraging them to adopt and implement policies similar to the congressional resolution on permanent paper and subsequently reported to Congress on their responses regarding use of permanent paper or plans to do so.

International Programs

Since FY 1986, NCLIS has cooperated with the Department of State to monitor and coordinate proposals for International Conventions and Scientific Organizations Contributions (ICSOC) grants and to disburse the funds. The six-year total is $1,055,500, of which $182,000 was awarded in FY 1991 to support a variety of international library, information, and archival activities. The technical amendments to the commission's enabling legislation that passed in late summer make it clear that NCLIS is to be involved in international cooperative activities (P.L. 102-95, sec. 4.).

In August 1991, Commissioner Daniel Casey represented NCLIS at the International Federation of Library Associations and Institutions (IFLA) conference in Moscow. During meetings with Casey, IFLA's president and secretary expressed interest in adapting the commission's Principles of Public Information for international use.

National Technical Information Service

Technology Administration
U.S. Department of Commerce, Springfield, VA 22161
703-487-4650

Dorothy Aukofer MacEoin
Fellow, Office of the Director

The National Technical Information Service (NTIS) is a self-supporting federal agency that actively collects and organizes scientific, technical, engineering, and business-related information generated by U.S. and foreign governments and makes it available for public sale. The volume and subject matter of the information have expanded dramatically since the service was established in 1945 as the Publications Board. The core collection now incorporates more than 2 million works covering current events, business and management, foreign and domestic trade, general statistics, environment and energy, health and the social sciences, and hundreds of other areas. The material is not limited to printed reports and documents. NTIS also provides access to electronic bulletin boards and carries computer software and computerized data files on tape, diskette, and optical disc. The NTIS Federal Computer Products Center carries more than 2,300 data files and 1,900 software programs.

In FY 1991, NTIS added 79,000 works to its collection and provided information to more than 500,000 individuals and organizations. Coverage is worldwide; nearly one third of new material comes from foreign sources.

All materials are permanently available. When government agencies, their contractors, and grantees forward reports and other items to NTIS, these items are cataloged, indexed, abstracted, and entered into the NTIS computerized bibliographic database. The database is available to the public through a number of commercial online vendors, which are listed in the free NTIS Products and Services catalog. (For a catalog, call 703-487-4650 and ask for PR-827.)

NTIS is unique among government agencies in that it operates independently of tax-supported congressional appropriations. By law, NTIS is required to recover the costs of updating and making its collection permanently available to the public through the sale of products and services.

The NTIS Collection

Information Sources

More than 200 federal agencies, including the National Aeronautics and Space Administration, the Environmental Protection Agency, the National Institute of Standards and Technology, the National Institutes of Health, and the departments of Agriculture, Defense, Energy, Commerce, Interior, Health and Human Services, and Transportation, contribute to the NTIS collection. The NTIS Office of International Affairs also has acquisition agreements with more than 60 countries, including Canada, India, Taiwan, China, Japan, and the countries of Western Europe.

Technology Transfer

NTIS operates the Center for the Utilization of Federal Technology (CUFT), established to keep industry and government informed of technological developments resulting from U.S. government research with potential commercial or practical applications. CUFT's Office of Federal Patent Licensing conducts the most active licensing program in the federal government. In 1991, NTIS granted licenses to 78 private firms and collected nearly $4 million in licensing revenues. (Licensable properties come primarily from the departments of Health and Human Services, Agriculture, Interior, and Commerce.)

In 1991, NTIS inaugurated the online Patent Licensing Bulletin Board, which lists government inventions available for licensing from NTIS. Customers receive vital information in electronic format as much as six weeks earlier than traditional paper formats. The free Bulletin Board started with more than 500 entries, and more are being added continuously. To access the Patent Licensing Bulletin Board directly, call 703-487-4061. For the *Users Guide*, call 703-487-4650 and ask for PR-903.

CUFT also issues catalogs and directories that publicize technologies and resources available from the federal government. The annual *Catalog of Government Inventions Available for Licensing* summarizes all inventions announced during the year. The *Directory of Federal Laboratory and Technology Resources* describes hundreds of federal laboratories willing to share expertise, equipment, and sometimes even facilities to aid U.S. research efforts (PB90-104480). NTIS also publishes the weekly newsletter *Government Inventions for Licensing*.

International Information

Worldwide

Tremendous changes throughout the world have drawn greater attention to the need for international current events information. Several NTIS publications report and analyze topical, international issues.

The Foreign Broadcast Information Service (FBIS) is a daily news service that features news reports, commentaries, and official government statements from foreign broadcasts, press agency transmissions, newspapers, and periodicals published within the previous 48 to 72 hours. FBIS covers political, military, economic, environmental, and sociological news as well as scientific and technical data and reports relating to Eastern Europe, China, East Asia, the Near East (including the Arabian peninsula and South Asia), Latin America, the former Soviet Union, Western Europe, and sub-Saharan Africa. The information is compiled by the Central Intelligence Agency, Washington, D.C.

The new, twice-weekly *Soviet Union Republic Affairs* subscription from FBIS covers current political, economic, military, and social affairs of all 15 former Soviet republics.

Dispatch, a weekly bulletin published by the Department of State, is a diverse compilation of major speeches, congressional testimony, policy statements, fact sheets, and other foreign policy information. Contents include profiles of countries in the news, lists of ambassadorial appointments, treaty actions, and updates on worldwide events and on public- and private-sector assistance to Eastern and Central Europe.

The *Foreign Technology Weekly Newsletter* carries topical news items and reports on foreign developments in science and technology. The information comes from science and technology counselors stationed at U.S. embassies, science officers of U.S. government agencies with overseas offices, and experts participating in overseas exchange programs and study tours. The newsletter is available in print from NTIS or online through Predicasts.

The Joint Publications Research Service's Worldwide series provides translations of scientific, technical, economic, political, and sociological reports that have appeared in foreign media. As many as 30 specialized reports are issued each year as information becomes available.

Europe

In cooperation with the Office of General Counsel of the Commerce Department, NTIS established the Central and Eastern European Legal Texts Service, which provides legal and regulatory information about these newly independent countries. Individual copies of texts and standing-order subscriptions covering particular areas can be requested. (For a free list of available reports, ask for PR-883.)

NTIS also distributes publications on conducting business in Eastern Europe, prepared in cooperation with the Commerce Department's Eastern Europe Business Information Center. Topics include the economic outlook, potential trade partners, investment regulations and incentives, and U.S. government programs that support private enterprise, trade, and investment.

The Eastern Europe Business Information Center (Tel. 202-377-2645) assists small and medium-size companies interested in exporting to or joint ventures in Eastern Europe. A list of publications produced by the center is available free from NTIS (ask for PR-882).

Japan

As a participant in the U.S./Japan Task Force on Access to Scientific and Technical Information, NTIS advised and assisted Japan in establishing the Japanese Reprographic Right Center in 1991. The center provides licensing programs and makes it possible for Japanese publishers to copyright their material and collect royalties, which will in turn help to increase the flow of technical literature between the United States and Japan.

A set of three NTIS reports forms a basic reference core of information about Japan: the *Directory of Japanese Technical Resources in the United States, 1990* (PB91-100958); the *Directory of Japanese Databases* (PB90-163080); and the *Directory of Japanese Technical Reports: 1989–1990* (PB90-163098). The three volumes are available separately or as a set (PB91-100941).

NTIS also provides access to the Japanese Online Information System, which consists of many technical databases in English and Japanese, mounted in Tokyo at the Japan Information Center for Science and Technology. The JICST/NTIS cooperative agreement allows U.S. residents access to the latest Japanese research results.

Customer Services

Improvements in Services

The NTIS total quality management program resulted in marked improvements in services throughout the agency during 1991. Most notable is a 38 percent reduction in customer complaints, attributed to several factors, including improvements in document delivery, quality, and fulfillment and in order turnaround time. Quality teams concentrated on projects specifically geared to customers' needs. NTIS has been experimenting with shipping methods to different parts of the country, using a variety of packaging.

Two-Day Rush Service

The new NTIS rush service provides customers with most publications in just two days for an additional fee (Tel. 800-553-NTIS).

Extended Hours

The Customer Services Division and Bookstore continue to offer extended hours. They are open from 8:30 A.M. to 5:30 P.M. Eastern Time.

NewsLine – Print and Online

NTIS NewsLine, a free quarterly publication that provides up-to-date general information about NTIS products and services, is now available through the online Patent Licensing Bulletin Board. To access *NTIS NewsLine OnLine*, dial 703-487-4061 To subscribe to the print version, call 703-487-4630.

Customized Collections

Copies of all reports in the NTIS collection on specialized subjects are available through the NTIS Selected Research in Microfiche service. Customers can choose from 350 preselected subject areas, or with help from an NTIS specialist they can custom-design a subject area to their needs. As reports enter the collection in the selected field, microfiche copies are automatically sent to subscribers. Customers often receive documents before NTIS officially announces their availability.

Electronic Formats

Through its Electronic Media Production Services, NTIS organizes and produces compact discs, magnetic tapes, diskettes, and digital tapes to assist other federal agencies in meeting their information dissemination missions. For example, NTIS reproduces a CD-ROM master for the National Trade Data Bank in the Department of Commerce's Economics and Statistics Administration and offers it as a monthly subscription item.

Defense

NTIS carries unrestricted publications from the U.S. Army, Air Force, and Navy. These include technical manuals, regulations, supply catalogs, administrative publications, and field manuals. Each branch sends different documents. Call 703-487-4684 for more information.

Environment

NTIS is the central distributor for Environmental Protection Agency Superfund program directives and guidelines. Customers with standing-order subscriptions automatically receive each directive or guideline as soon as it becomes available. The *Weekly Bulletins* and *Special Publications* produced by the Environmental and Energy Study Conference, a bipartisan congressional caucus that provides members of Congress with unbiased information, are also available from NTIS on a subscription basis. Call 703-487-4630 for details.

EPA's *Toxic Release Inventory* (TRI) is now available on CD-ROM, as well as magnetic tape and diskette. TRI lists facilities that release toxic emissions into the environment and the types of emissions they release. For a free brochure, ask for PR-859.

National Archives and Records Administration

Seventh St. and Pennsylvania Ave. N.W., Washington, DC 20408
202-501-5405

David R. Kepley
Chief, Program Analysis Branch
Office of Management and Administration

The National Archives and Records Administration (NARA) is responsible for identifying, preserving, and making available to the federal government and to the people of the United States all government records not restricted by law that have sufficient historical, informational, or evidential value to warrant preservation. All U.S. federal agencies are obliged by law to cooperate with the Archives and to transfer all historically valuable federal records more than 30 years old that are not needed for continuing agency business. In 1978, presidential records, formerly considered the private property of the president who created them, were declared government property and subject to NARA's authority. NARA inspects agency records, establishes standards for records retention, and guides and assists agencies in documenting government policies and transactions.

National Archives, 1934–Present

When the United States established a National Archives in 1934, it was the last major Western nation to do so. The act of establishment also created the National Historical Publications Commission, headed by the Archivist of the United States, and directed it to promote the publication of original source material. In 1975, the additional responsibility of providing aid to nonfederal records projects occasioned the name change to the National Historical Publications and Records Commission (NHPRC). The Federal Register was created as an office of the Archives in 1935. It provides official notice to the public through various publications of federal laws and administrative regulations, communicates the president's policies by publishing his official documents and papers, and provides indexes and other finding aids to ensure ready access to all its publications. The Federal Register also publishes annually *The United States Government Manual*, which provides comprehensive information on the agencies of the legislative, judicial, and executive branches and includes information on quasi-official agencies, on international organizations in which the United States participates, and on boards, committees, and commissions. The presidential libraries system was established in 1939 with the creation of the Franklin D. Roosevelt Library. There are now nine presidential libraries in addition to the Nixon and Bush Presidential Materials Staffs. [See related article, "The Nixon and Reagan Presidential Libraries," in the Special Reports section of Part 1 — *Ed.*]

The Federal Property and Administrative Services Act of 1949 transferred the National Archives to the newly created General Services Administration and changed the name to the National Archives and Records Service to reflect the agency's dual responsibilities for current records as well as permanently valuable archival materials. These responsibilities were clarified and expanded in the Federal Records Act of 1950. In the same year, the National Archives began establishing a series of records centers across the country to store semiactive federal records at low cost. These records are not needed for the daily business of the government, but federal law often requires that they be retained for a fixed period of time pending final disposition. Some are eventually transferred to the National Archives for permanent retention, but the majority are destroyed. During the late 1960s, a network of regional archives was created. These depositories, usually located in the same building as regional records centers, hold both microfilm and original federal records of particular significance to the geographic area in which they are located.

On April 1, 1985, the National Archives and Records Service became an independent agency in the executive branch of the federal government and was renamed the National Archives and Records Administration. This change, which marked a return to the status enjoyed by the National Archives from 1935 to 1949, had long been advocated by many users and by professional organizations associated with the Archives.

National Archives System

The National Archives occupies a massive classic structure on a site bounded by Pennsylvania and Constitution avenues and Seventh and Ninth streets, Northwest, exactly halfway between the White House and the Capitol in Washington, D.C. Designed by John Russell Pope, the building contains 21 levels of stack areas for records, which are controlled for temperature and humidity and equipped with smoke detection devices, sprinkler systems, and, in select areas, a Halon gas system to protect against fire. In addition to miles of stacks, the building contains research rooms, office and laboratory spaces, a theater, exhibit areas, and the 75-foot-high central rotunda in which the Declaration of Independence, the Constitution, and the Bill of Rights are on permanent display. A version of the Magna Carta from 1297 that is on indefinite loan can also be seen in the rotunda.

Several exhibits of Archives holdings will open in 1992 in the National Archives building. "Reeling Through History" (fourth floor lobby, from February 28, 1992 indefinitely) will help orient visitors and researchers unfamiliar with the National Archives and with microfilm records. The exhibit will debut in conjunction with the opening of microfilm records of the 1920 census. "Ties That Bind: Communities in American History" (rotunda, Spring 1992–March 1993) covers utopian settlements, suburbs, native groupings, and company towns, among others.

Several upcoming anniversaries will be commemorated in Archives exhibits. In recognition of the centennial of the Pledge of Allegiance, "I Pledge Allegiance" (rotunda lobby, late August 1992–February 1993) will show the origin and development of the pledge. A major exhibit in honor of the Columbus quincentennial will look westward: "Western Ways: Images of the American West" (circular gallery, October 1992–December 1993). Consisting of almost 200 photographic, cartographic, and other depictions of the history of the American West, the exhibit will be accompanied by a fully illustrated catalog.

The fiftieth anniversary of World War II (1991–1995) will be marked by numerous programs at the National Archives building. During the first week of December each year through 1995, the Archives-commissioned play *I Can't Come Home for Christmas* will be performed in the National Archives theater. This play is based on records relating to the United Services Organization (USO) and the Entertainment National Service Association (ENSA) in the custody of the National Archives. Throughout the anniversary period, the Archives will screen films related to World War II from its vast motion picture collections and will schedule lectures, workshops, and conferences on World War II topics.

The National Archives building reached its records storage capacity of approximately 800,000 cubic feet in the late 1960s. To alleviate the space shortage and to provide special facilities for nontextual material, such as photographs, film, and electronic records, NARA is constructing a new building, Archives II, adjacent to the University of Maryland campus in College Park. It will open in 1994. Current plans call for Archives II to house—along with nontextual records—modern military records (roughly since World War I) and most civilian records, including State Department records. Legislative and genealogical records, as well as permanent exhibits, will stay in the downtown Washington, D.C., building.

Archives II will provide state-of-the-art storage, reference, and laboratory facilities. Current standards established by the National Academy of Sciences will serve as the basis for the building's environmental controls. The design incorporates national and international guidance relating to reference service, building security, and classified records security. In addition to its archival functions, Archives II will provide space for offices and general facilities, including a theater, cafeteria, and conference rooms. Several NARA administrative offices and archival-holdings sites in the Washington metropolitan area will be moved to Archives II. These include the National

Audiovisual Center, which rents and sells to the public motion pictures, slides, and tapes created by many federal agencies; the Richard Nixon presidential materials; government cartographic and architectural records; and archival records stored temporarily at the Washington National Records Center in Suitland, Maryland.

NARA operates 25 additional facilities around the country. Two major facilities are the National Records Center in Suitland (housing inactive and semiactive records of federal agencies in the Washington, D.C., area) and the National Personnel Records Center in Saint Louis, Missouri (housing both military and civilian federal personnel records). Other facilities are located in or near Boston, New York, Philadelphia, Atlanta, Chicago, Dayton, Kansas City, Fort Worth, Denver, San Francisco, Los Angeles, Seattle, and Anchorage. Each has a regional archives and a federal records center (except for Dayton, which has no archives; Philadelphia, where the regional archives is at a separate downtown location; and Anchorage, which has only a regional archives). The ten other National Archives buildings are presidential libraries or museums: the Herbert Hoover Library in West Branch, Iowa; the Franklin D. Roosevelt Library in Hyde Park, New York; the Harry S. Truman Library in Independence, Missouri; the Dwight D. Eisenhower Library in Abilene, Kansas; the John F. Kennedy Library in Columbia Point, Massachusetts; the Lyndon B. Johnson Library in Austin, Texas; the Gerald R. Ford Library in Ann Arbor, Michigan; the Ford Museum in Grand Rapids, Michigan; the Jimmy Carter Library in Atlanta, Georgia; and the Ronald W. Reagan Library in Simi Valley, California. The Reagan Library is the largest presidential library, with approximately 62 million pages of text as well as photographs, videotapes, sound recordings, and museum objects. President Bush has selected Texas A & M University in College Station, Texas, as the site for the future George Bush Library.

The Archivist of the United States, appointed by the president with the advice and consent of the Senate, is assisted by a deputy and seven assistant archivists. Each assistant archivist has specific program or support function responsibilities, designated as an office. The major organizational elements are the Offices of Management and Administration, the National Archives, Federal Register, Federal Records Centers, Presidential Libraries, Records Administration, and Public Programs. The executive director of the National Historical Publications and Records Commission is also an assistant archivist. Special staff members reporting directly to the Archivist include the executive staff director (who directs public, congressional, and external-affairs and interagency liaison officers), the general counsel, the inspector general, and the archival research and evaluation staff.

The National Archives staff includes 2,000 full-time permanent employees and 1,000 part-time and intermittent employees, most of whom work in federal records centers, where they handle reference requests from federal agencies. For FY 1991, NARA's budget was $138 million, with $5 million supporting NHPRC programs.

A description of NARA's annual activities and finances can be found in the *Annual Report of the National Archives*, available from the agency's public information officer.

Holdings of the National Archives and Records Administration

NARA holdings are of two types: those in federal records centers waiting to be destroyed or transferred to the National Archives and those determined to have enduring value in the legal custody of the National Archives. The federal records centers hold more than 17.4 million cubic feet of noncurrent federal records. Although these records are in the physical custody of the National Archives, they remain under the legal control of the agency of origin. Most are from the Department of Defense, the Department of the Treasury (Internal Revenue Service), the Department of Health and Human Services (Social Security Administration), and the Veterans Administration. Although almost all records held by the Federal Records Centers, as well as those that remain in agency custody, will eventually be destroyed, the small portion determined to have enduring value is transferred each year to the Office of the National Archives and becomes part of the Archives of the United States. The National Archives also accepts some donated materials from private sources, most of which, except for donated film, is kept in the presidential libraries. All presidential materials made or received before 1981 are considered private property.

The current estimate of the holdings of the National Archives is 1.6 million cubic feet of records, including 4 billion paper documents; 100 million feet of motion pictures; 6.4 million still photographs and posters; 3.9 million maps, charts, and architectural drawings; more than 187,000 unique videotapes and sound recordings; 8.9 million aerial photographs; and more than 2,800 reels of computer tape containing nearly 7,000 discrete data sets. The records date from the papers of the Continental Congress to the recent past. The Office of Presidential Libraries estimates its holdings to be 212,173,163 pages of paper records; 13,467,961 feet of motion pictures; 3,445,284 photographs; more than 15,000 hours of videotape; 30,000 hours of audio recordings; 203,000 museum objects; and more than 190,000 pages of oral history interviews.

The National Archives building, the regional archives, and the presidential libraries also have among their holdings unique published items in addition to archival and manuscript materials. Of particular interest to librarians is the record set of the publications of the federal government, consisting of 1.8 million items, the core of which was formerly the Public Documents Library of the Government Printing Office. This is the most comprehensive set of federal publications in existence—dating from 1790 to 1979—but it is incomplete, especially for the years before 1895. The collection is among the holdings of the Center for Legislative Archives, located in the National Archives building.

Using the Archives

Researchers wishing to consult records in the National Archives building are issued a research card, which they must show when entering the Central Research Room. Those wishing to use only microfilm can sign in at the Microfilm Reading Room. Consultants are available to assist researchers; and numerous guides, lists, inventories, indexes, and other finding aids provide valuable information about the Archives' holdings. Among these sources are the *Guide to the National Archives of the United States* (1974), which is being revised; *Guide to Genealogical Research in the National Archives* (1985); *Guide to the Holdings of the Still Picture Branch of the National Archives* (1990); and the *Catalog of National Archives Microfilm Publications* (1990).

For more specific information on using records at the National Archives, researchers are encouraged to obtain a copy of General Information Leaflet No. 2 from the Reference Services Branch (NNRS), National Archives, Washington, DC 20408. Copies of documents or microfilm can be obtained at a modest price, and printed facsimiles of many historical documents are available for purchase. Microfilm of materials of interest primarily to genealogists can be rented for a modest fee from the National Archives Microfilm Rental Program, Box 30, Annapolis Junction, MD 20701-0030 (301-604-3699). The National Archives does not lend microfilm through interlibrary loan.

The National Archives building is open for research Monday through Friday from 8:45 A.M. to 10 P.M. and on Saturdays from 8:45 A.M. to 5 P.M.; it is closed Sundays and on federal holidays. Researchers are also welcome in the regional archives outside Washington and at the presidential libraries, all of which issue their own lists of holdings and maintain their own research rooms. Service hours of the regional archives and the presidential libraries vary; researchers should check with those facilities to determine the exact times. Up-to-date information on accessions and openings of records in all parts of the National Archives and Records Administration can be obtained by consulting lists published in the journal *Prologue: Quarterly of the National Archives*.

United States Information Agency

301 Fourth St. S.W., Washington, DC 20547

Don Hausrath and Mary Boone
Library Programs Division

The United States Information Agency (USIA), an independent organization within the executive branch, carries out the U.S. government's overseas information, educational exchange, and cultural programs. Overseas, the agency is known as the United States Information Service (USIS). The 928 foreign service officers assigned to the 208 offices in 131 countries work with 3,646 foreign national employees hired locally. A support staff of 4,210 is based in the United States, principally in Washington, D.C. Additional staff support English teaching and related activities in binational centers, independent national organizations partially funded by USIA. The agency's director, deputy director, and four associate directors (Voice of America, Educational and Cultural Affairs, Programs, and Management) are appointed by the president of the United States and are subject to confirmation by the Senate.

Office of Cultural Centers and Resources

Within the Bureau of Educational and Cultural Affairs, which oversees academic exchange and international visitor programs, the Office of Cultural Centers and Resources is responsible for USIA's book and library programs. Two of its divisions, Library Programs and Book Programs, are directly concerned with the use of American books and electronic media abroad. Through an international network of libraries and through the translation, promotion, and exhibition of American books, the Office of Cultural Centers and Resources provides foreign audiences with authoritative information about U.S. government policies as well as a greater understanding of American society and culture, past and present.

Library Programs

The Library Programs Division, established in 1938 as a division in the Department of State and later shifted to USIA, is part of the Bureau of Educational and Cultural Affairs. Its mandate is contained in the United States Information and Educational Exchange Act of 1961, commonly referred to as the Fulbright-Hays Act. Operating under the authority of this act, the bureau supports activities to increase mutual understanding between the people of the United States and other countries. Through these programs, the bureau seeks to promote the free exchange of ideas and information between U.S. citizens and people of other countries.

The oldest continuously operating library in the USIS system opened in Mexico City April 13, 1942. Its fiftieth anniversary celebration in 1992 will be followed by USIS library celebrations in Calcutta, Kinshasa, London, and New Delhi. The event will also be marked by various journal articles and a symposium at the Library of Congress. Libraries in Madrid and Montevideo will celebrate their fiftieth anniversaries in 1993, and those in Bombay, Cairo, Paris, Stockholm, Sydney, and Wellington in 1994. The agency library, originally the Voice of America library in New York, celebrated its fiftieth anniversary in 1991.

History of the USIA Library Program

Today's worldwide system of USIS libraries evolved from a matrix of programs. First, in Latin America, came libraries associated with President Franklin Roosevelt's "Good Neighbor" program. In 1941, the coordinator of Inter-American affairs, Nelson Rockefeller, contracted the American Library Association to establish and operate a library in Mexico City, the now-famous Biblioteca Benjamin Franklin. Under similar contracts, ALA opened and operated on behalf of the U.S. government two other libraries in Latin America: in Managua, Nicaragua (November 1942), and Montevideo, Uruguay (August 1943). These libraries came under Department of State supervision in 1947 and 1948.

Beginning in 1942, the Office of War Information (OWI) began to establish reference libraries as part of its overseas information program. These were separate and distinct from U.S. Embassy reference libraries at the outset. Later, parts of many embassy collections were turned over to USIS libraries. The American library in London started operations in December 1942 and officially opened in April 1943. The London library was the first overseas library directly under U.S. government control. Between 1942 and 1945, OWI started libraries in Ankara, Athens, Baghdad, Bangkok, Beirut, Belgrade, Berlin, Bern, Bombay, Brussels, Cairo, Calcutta, Copenhagen, Florence, Frankfurt, the Hague, Istanbul, Johannesburg, Kinshasa, Linz, Madrid, Manila, Melbourne, Milan, Munich, Naples, New Delhi, Novi Sad, Oslo, Palermo, Paris, Rome, Salzburg, Sofia, Stockholm, Sydney, Tokyo, Vienna, Wellington, and Wiesbaden. On January 1, 1945, OWI was abolished and the Department of State assumed responsibility for overseas libraries.

Shortly after World War II, the U.S. Military Government began opening Information Center (Amerika Häuser) libraries and reading rooms in Germany, throughout the American Zone and in the major cities of the British and French zones. In

1949, responsibility for these installations was transferred from the Army to the Department of State. In 1955, four Amerika Häuser were converted to binational operations, with the German government assuming financial responsibility for housing and local maintenance and the United States supplying an American director and program materials. Subsequently, additional Amerika Häuser were converted to binational operations. Also in 1945, Information Center libraries were started under the auspices of the United States Forces in Austria, the Supreme Commander for the Allied Powers in Japan, and the United States Armed Forces in Korea. The State Department assumed responsibility for these centers when civilian control was restored in each country. Nine centers came under the department's auspices in January 1949, and ten centers in Austria were added in 1950. In April 1952, with the ratification of the peace treaty in Japan, 23 information centers in that country were transferred to the State Department. On August 1, 1953, the United States Information Agency was established, and responsibility for overseas libraries and reading rooms was transferred to the new agency.

Present Status of the Program

The historic lack of a central "line item" appropriation for overseas libraries, in contrast with other major USIA programs (Voice of America, Worldnet, exhibits, cultural exchanges), has increasingly taxed the shrinking resources of overseas posts, and libraries have closed (or opened) with changes in the world's political map. In the past 20 years, the number of libraries has dropped from 253 to 153, with a concomitant reduction in worldwide book stock from 2.4 million to about 900,000 volumes. Since 1978, the number of libraries and collections with 5,000 to 10,000 books has dropped 72 percent, and the number of libraries with 1,000 to 5,000 books has doubled.

In 1991, libraries were opened in Windhoek, Namibia, and in Bratislava, Czechoslovakia. In 1992, libraries will be opened in Leipzig, Germany; Tallinn, Estonia; Vilnius, Lithuania; Riga, Latvia; and Tirana, Albania.

Even though many USIS libraries provide only reference services, USIS libraries are circulating more books and responding to more reference questions than they did ten years ago. This phenomenon is attributed to several factors: online full-text CD-ROM products published by the Library Programs Division; other automated services; and the effect of inflation and soft currencies in many countries, virtually sealing borders to U.S. publications. A May 21, 1990, *New York Times* editorial reinforced this point: "And even now, after political revolutions have demolished the ideological barriers (in Eastern Europe), hard currency remains scarce for all cultural institutions, and libraries and universities must survive on starvation budgets. . . . The hunger for books pervades their fragile new democracies." [For a report on library service in Eastern Europe, see the "International Reports" section of Part 1 — *Ed.*]

Although USIS libraries vary from country to country, all perform two mutually supportive functions: to provide the latest and most accurate information about U.S. government policies and to serve as a continuing source of informed commentary on the origin, growth, and development of American social, political, economic, and cultural life, while acting as a national focal point on these issues. Collections and services, which vary according to the location, can be grouped into five models.

Five Collection Models

Information-Rich Countries with Noncirculating Library Collections

In developed countries where access to information about the United States is available in most subject areas, universities are fully developed and have strong library collections. Major libraries provide access to information via electronic media. In this environment, the USIS library maintains 2,000 to 4,000 reference books but no circulating books, subscribes to approximately 100 air-shipped periodicals, and also provides specialized research and development studies and reports. The staff relies on online databases and CD-ROM products such as Public Diplomacy Query (PDQ), the Library Program Division's family of online and CD-ROM bibliographic and full-text databases. These libraries rank with other specialized libraries in the country and serve as a national referral center and focal point for U.S. information.

The 13 libraries of this type can be found in such cities as the Hague, London, Oslo, Ottawa, Paris, Stockholm, and Wellington. In London, British Broadcasting Corporation (BBC) News Information Research staff and House of Commons International Affairs Desk staff daily acquire USIS library materials, which during the gulf war included the texts of important briefings, news interviews, and related policy statements.

Information-Rich Countries without Strong Collections on the United States

In developed countries where access to information about the United States is available in many but not all subject areas, universities are fully developed but frequently lack strong collections to support the study of the United States. Access to modern information technology is available in many libraries. In this information environment, USIS libraries provide an American-style reference service and an open-access circulating book and document collection. Collections vary from 1,500 to 15,000 books, of which often 30 percent are reference books, with 100 to 300 magazines and a spectrum of online databases and CD-ROM products. The 25 libraries of this type are in such cities as Berlin, Brussels, Copenhagen, Madrid, Rome, Tel Aviv, Tokyo, and Vienna.

Newly Industrializing Countries

In newly industrializing countries, current information about the United States may be accessible but too expensive for the general population. Large universities exist, but textbooks and libraries are inadequate to support the curriculum. Development of and access to modern information technology are limited. In such an environment, the USIS library maintains 5,000 to 10,000 circulating books, 1,500 to 2,000 reference books, and 100 to 150 periodical subscriptions, and quite often has access to online databases and CD-ROM products. The 13 USIS libraries of this type are in such cities as Athens, Brasilia, Hong Kong, Kuala Lumpur, and Seoul. Four binational center libraries are also of this type.

Larger Libraries in Less Developed Countries

In large, densely populated, less developed countries, where access to information from and about the United States is limited, imported books tend to be too expensive for scholars and local libraries. There are large universities but inadequate textbooks and libraries and limited development of and access to modern information technology. Clients include members of parliament, government ministries, professors, students, and journalists. USIS libraries have between 13,000 and 30,000 books, with 2,000 to 4,000 reference books, and 150 to 350 periodicals. The 13 USIS and 5 binational center libraries of this kind are in such cities as Ankara, Buenos Aires, Cairo, Calcutta, Jakarta, Manila, Mexico City, and New Delhi.

Small Libraries in Less Developed Countries

In developing countries where access to information from and about the United States is limited and often only of a popular nature, imported books are expensive and not readily available. The country or province usually has at least one university, but textbooks and libraries are inadequate and development of and access to modern information technology are limited. In this environment, the USIS library maintains 3,000 to 12,000 books, 500 to 3,000 reference books, 50 to 200 periodical subscriptions, and often CD-ROM products, but seldom has access to online databases. In Latin America and the French-speaking countries in Africa, up to 40 percent of circulating collections are books by U.S. authors in Spanish or French translation.

The 81 USIS libraries and 42 binational center libraries of this type are in such cities as Belgrade, Bucharest, Harare, Katmandu, and Kingston.

Such libraries are struggling to cope with a flood of new visitors seeking information about democratic government, market-oriented economies, and technological change. An example is Daniel Daianu, a Romanian economist, now at the Soviet Studies Center at Harvard, who, during a conference in Athens, was asked by a colleague about his education in Romania. "I am self-educated," he replied, "with the help of the American Library in Bucharest." In January 1991, the USIS library in Bucharest set another attendance record with more than 9,300 patrons in a week. People waited in long lines to get into the library. A cable from the USIS offices in Bucharest explained: "What all this proves, we believe, is that the Romanians are desperate for information, for the opportunity to improve themselves, and for intellectual exchange with the outside world from which they were so long isolated."

Bookshelf "Libraries"

Eight posts maintain a bookshelf of 300 to 500 reference books and subscribe to 25 to 50 periodicals. These organized reference collections provide basic information on a limited number of subjects. Limitations in staff and training preclude these facilities from responding to reference questions that would be routinely fielded by personnel in the other models. Such collections are found in Bridgetown, Bern, and Suva, and were maintained in Kuwait and Baghdad before the gulf war.

Library Administration

With a staff of 48 in Washington and 550 foreign nationals worldwide, the Library Programs Division provides library services and support for staff in Washington and in USIS posts and USIA offices abroad. Sixteen foreign service field librarians work abroad.

USIS libraries field more than a million reference questions a year, providing support in areas where USIS does not even operate a library. For example, in Moscow, USIS supplied a court with texts of U.S. laws concerning freedom of the press and background information on the code of ethics for members of the U.S. Congress. Full-text databases and compact disc (CD-ROM) units are revolutionizing reference work abroad. More than 100 USIS and binational libraries routinely search on CD-ROM units. The units are invaluable in providing on call the texts of policy statements and data on the worldwide drug problem. These libraries receive a monthly updated compact disc, including official statements, documents, reports, and briefings.

The librarians and technicians of the USIA Library Programs Division staff one of the federal government's most dynamic special libraries, each year fielding 18,000 requests for information, half from USIA and Voice of America staff and half from overseas posts. The headquarters library maintains 50,000 books, 600 journals, and 1,000 online text sources, allowing staff to respond to a range of complex queries, achieving some of the shortest turnaround times of an American library. The headquarters library is increasingly involved in training overseas USIS librarians, either through internships of one to two months or during short visits of a week or less. The Library Programs Division also funds the prestigious USIA Library/Book Fellow program, allowing ten to fifteen American library and publishing professionals to carry out special projects abroad. The program is administered by the American Library Association.

For more information on the USIA library program, see the Winter 1990 issue of *Special Libraries.* For a listing of USIS libraries, write to the Office of Public Liaison, USIA, Washington, DC 20547.

Federal Library and Information Center Committee

Library of Congress, Washington, DC 20540
202-707-4800

Mary Berghaus Levering
Executive Director

The Federal Library and Information Center Committee (FLICC) officially celebrated its twenty-fifth anniversary in 1991. Established in 1965 as the Federal Library Committee by the Library of Congress (LC) to provide leadership and assistance to the nation's federal libraries and information centers, FLICC has developed as the focal point for cooperative efforts, a forum for considering issues and policies, and a promoter on behalf of its constituencies. The establishment of the FEDLINK network in 1978 provided for the delivery of cost-effective information services to federal agencies. FLICC now supports more than 2,400 federal libraries and information centers worldwide and almost 1,300 FEDLINK constituent agencies.

Highlights of 1991

In response to the rapid growth of FEDLINK and other recent developments, FLICC completed work to formalize and update its structure during FY 1991. The new FLICC bylaws and updated FLICC authorizing charter were completed under the leadership of FLICC Chairperson-Designate Donald Curran, associate librarian for constituent services at the Library of Congress, signed on July 16 by Librarian of

Congress James H. Billington, and published in the September 19 *Federal Register.* The bylaws formalize FLICC's operating rules and procedures and allow an expanded number of federal libraries to be involved in FLICC's activities.

In close cooperation with other federal agencies, FLICC and the federal libraries achieved several milestones in FY 1991. Nine of thirteen key federal library issues identified by federal delegates at the FLICC-sponsored federal Pre–White House Conference on Library and Information Services (November 26–27, 1990) were substantially approved at the Second White House Conference on Library and Information Services (July 9–13, 1991), demonstrating the federal delegates' effectiveness in carrying forward the federal library agenda and gaining national recognition and support for these issues. FLICC staff and volunteers continued to pursue opportunities to work with other professional groups that share its concerns, including the Coalition for Networked Information (CNI), the Confederation of Navy Scientific and Technical Libraries (CONSATL), the Military Librarians Division of the Special Libraries Association (SLA), and the Network Advisory Committee (NAC) of the Library of Congress.

Three new FLICC working groups were organized during FY 1991 to enable federal librarians to work collectively on preservation, federal library statistics, and implementation of the new FLICC bylaws. To support OCLC's new PRISM service, FEDLINK network librarians traveled to 29 regional locations nationwide to deliver on-site PRISM instruction. FEDLINK's network librarians taught a record 166 workshops during the year. As FY 1991 closed, FLICC secured new office space on Pennsylvania Avenue in Washington, D.C., thus consolidating two major operations formerly housed in separate locations.

FEDLINK personnel continued their efforts to ensure the program's scrupulous compliance with all federal regulations, cooperating fully with the General Services Administration (GSA) and the General Accounting Office (GAO) and continuing to forge strong working relationships with appropriate Library of Congress offices. The GAO report issued on August 22 on its first audit of the Library of Congress outlined the steps LC and FEDLINK have taken to strengthen and restructure the FEDLINK program in the past two and a half years. FLICC specialists designed, tested, and implemented a new automated networked fiscal accounting system for FEDLINK Fiscal Operations (FFO) to manage FEDLINK's complex fiscal accounts and improve accountability to LC and FEDLINK member federal agencies.

Membership Meetings

At their first quarterly meeting, on December 13, FLICC members were briefed by Harold Relyea, Congressional Research Service, on federal information policy issues confronting the 102d Congress. At the February 28 meeting, members approved FLICC's proposed draft revisions to Federal Classification Standards for 1410/1411 series positions. At the June 6 meeting, they heard a presentation by Stephen Perloff of the Office of Personnel Management (OPM) on federal librarian qualification standards and agreed in concept to FLICC's proposed draft revisions to Federal Qualification Standards for 1410 librarian positions. Michael Nelson of the Senate Committee on Commerce, Science, and Transportation briefed members on National Research and Education Network (NREN) legislation, and Maya Bernstein of the Office of Management and Budget (OMB) briefed them on OMB Circular A-130. On

September 26, at the fourth quarterly meeting, members received reports from the federal delegation on WHCLIS II and from Kurt Molholm, Defense Technical Information Center, and Gail Kohlhorst, General Services Administration Library, on proposed federal ethical standards.

Working Groups

During FY 1991, FLICC formed three new working groups: the Nominating Working Group, the Statistics Working Group, and the Preservation Working Group. Several others were already in operation. Highlights of working group accomplishments follow.

Members of the Binding Working Group worked closely with GPO representatives over several months to identify problems in the administration of the current GPO contract for library binding and to revise the technical specifications of the mandatory GPO B405 Binding Contract being rebid for FYs 1991–1994. GPO's proposed contract terms incorporated FLICC recommendations on behalf of federal libraries.

The more than forty professional librarians and information specialists from District of Columbia area agencies who make up the Cooperative Reference Working Group discussed ways in which libraries obtain materials published by federal agencies and, with the Education Working Group, coordinated an LC Reference Services orientation program for federal librarians. The Education Working Group continues to organize programs on topics of significance to federal librarians and information specialists in such areas as the changing federal procurement policy, NREN, and preservation strategies.

As a section of the Law Librarians Society of Washington, D.C., the Federal Law Librarians Working Group continues to sharpen its focus within FLICC. Members of the Membership and Governance Working Group, under the leadership of FLICC Chairperson-Designate Donald Curran, completed the proposed FLICC bylaws and forwarded them for review and approval.

The Nominating Working Group was established to implement the new bylaws by identifying and nominating candidates for election to FLICC and FEDLINK rotating memberships and other FLICC positions. During FY 1991, FEDLINK voting members elected 15 FEDLINK rotating members to FLICC. Nine rotating members are scheduled to take their seats in 1992.

Groundwork laid by members of the Personnel Working Group in cooperation with the LC Human Resources Directorate and several dedicated volunteers led to steady progress during FY 1991 on FLICC's proposed revisions to OPM's classification standards for the 1410/1411 series library positions and qualification standards for the 1410 series. OPM agreed to review the draft classification standards beginning in late FY 1991; the working group members are serving as a resource for OPM personnel. The Policy Working Group developed draft comments on the revision of OMB's Circular A-130, *Management of Federal Information Resources,* and responded on behalf of federal libraries and information centers to the proposed rules of the Office of Government Ethics on *Standards of Ethical Conduct of Employees of the Executive Branch.*

Organized in response to the recommendations of the federal Pre–White House Conference on Library and Information Services, the Preservation Working Group met several times during FY 1991 to address federal library preservation issues and needs. In August, members heard a presentation at the National Agricultural Library on practical applications of electronic imaging technologies.

During FY 1991, FLICC formed the Statistics Working Group to update the 1978 federal library statistics. The group will design the preliminary survey instrument to be used by FLICC and the National Center for Education Statistics in the sixth comprehensive statistics collection in the history of federal libraries.

Other Activities

Publications

The FLICC Publications/Education (FPE) Office publishes the monthly *FEDLINK Technical Notes* and the quarterly *FLICC Newsletter,* which included a special twelve-page twenty-fifth anniversary issue in 1991. Annual publications also include the *FEDLINK Services Directory,* the *FLICC Annual Report,* and the FEDLINK Services Registration and Amendment Forms Package.

Education Programs

In conjunction with the Education Working Group, FLICC planned and offered the monthly "brown-bag lunch" series on federal contract administration, the annual FLICC Forum on Federal Information Policies, its second Preservation Seminar, and seminars to educate agency employees about the FEDLINK program. FLICC also cosponsored educational events on issues affecting federal libraries with such groups as the District of Columbia Library Association (DCLA) for the Joint Spring Workshop, the D.C. Chapter of the Special Libraries Association for the annual Technology Update, the American Society for Information Science (ASIS), and Government Workplace. More than 1,200 members of the federal library and information center community attended ten daylong seminars and four brown-bag lunch programs.

Federal Pre-White House Conference on Library and Information Services

FLICC helped organize and advance the agenda of American libraries in general, and federal libraries and information centers in particular, with the successful staging of the federal Pre-White House Conference on Library and Information Services, held at the National Library of Medicine, Lister Hill Center, November 26-27, 1990. More than eighty delegates drafted resolutions stressing access, preservation, and networking and selected four voting delegates and four alternates to represent federal libraries and promote the federal resolutions at WHCLIS II. The main areas of federal concern were networking, funding, preservation, and access policies.

Members of the federal delegation were (information professional) Elisabeth Knauff, chief, Information Services Division, U.S. Department of the Treasury, and Doria Beachell Grimes (alternate), database product management specialist, National Technical Information Service; (government official) Gary North, assistant division chief, Information and Data Services, U.S. Geological Survey, and Kurt Molholm (alternate), administrator, Defense Technical Information System; (advisory boards) Bonnie Carroll, secretary director, CENDI, and president, Information International, and Egon Weiss (alternate), librarian emeritus, U.S. Military Academy; and (citizens) Davis McCarn, president, ONLINE, and Donald King (alternate), president, King Research.

FLICC's Twenty-Fifth Anniversary

On November 26, 1991, FLICC officially celebrated twenty-five years of service to the federal sector at a National Library of Medicine reception honoring those who helped found the original Federal Library Committee (FLC) and manage it through its transition to FLICC in 1984.

WHCLIS II

President Bush called the Second White House Conference on Library and Information Services to focus attention on productivity, literacy, and democracy. Coordinating FLICC's involvement was the FLAG Steering Committee. At WHCLIS II, held July 9-13, 1991, federal alternate Kurt Molholm devised an impromptu recommendation, eventually approved by all WHCLIS II delegates, calling for creation of the position of adviser on information policy to the president. Of the thirteen recommendations proposed by the federal preconference, nine were substantially approved at WHCLIS II. FLICC volunteers and staff and FEDLINK network librarians helped to plan, organize, and staff the WHCLIS II Resource Center. Federal delegates Doria Beachell Grimes and Davis McCarn were selected to serve on WHCLIS Taskforce II, formed to advance and monitor the implementation of the conference recommendations.

FEDLINK

FEDLINK (Federal Library and Information Network) is the national network of cooperating federal libraries and information centers that offers agencies the opportunity to procure information resources through a central source. Through FEDLINK almost 1,300 federal agencies, including 841 federal libraries, receive cost-effective access to a number of automated information retrieval services for online research, cataloging, and interlibrary loan. LC contracts with major vendors on behalf of FEDLINK members to enable them to procure publications, serials, and books through FEDLINK. FEDLINK network librarians provide training and serve as consultants on a variety of library-related issues.

The GAO report (GAO/AFMD-91-13) *First Audit of the Library of Congress Discloses Significant Problems,* published August 22, 1991, summarizes the legal and financial problems identified in the earlier management of the FEDLINK program. The report describes steps completed or undertaken by LC and FEDLINK to improve FEDLINK's financial and contracting activities since the FY 1988 period covered by the report. These include restricting FEDLINK services to designated purposes; adopting policies allowing procurement only of authorized automated data processing services; ensuring FEDLINK contract approval by authorized contracting officers; ensuring all obligations are based on proper documentation; documenting sole-source justifications for FEDLINK contracts over $25,000; ensuring amounts obligated and services provided do not exceed obligational authority; discontinuing carryover of expired funds to pay for a new year's FEDLINK services; ensuring accounts receivable and advances from other federal agencies are carefully tracked and determinable; and ensuring that invoice examination and payment follow regulations.

FEDLINK Network Operations

Nationwide Teaching Effort

During FY 1991, FEDLINK provided training in 12 key subject areas for 1,601 students in 166 scheduled classes—112 in the Washington, D.C., area and 54 in regional locations. Compared with FY 1990, 42 percent more classes were conducted and 33 percent more students trained in FY 1991. The increased effort was the measure of FEDLINK's response to major developments generated by bibliographic utilities. Following introduction in 1990 of the EPIC service to provide libraries with subject search capability for the national online union catalog and other reference databases, OCLC and the state/regional networks unveiled the new PRISM service to the nation's libraries. FEDLINK conducted two seminars on "OCLC's New Online System: An Introduction to PASSPORT Software and the PRISM Service" for approximately 300 federal librarians, then presented two three-hour televideo training conferences on PRISM service and PASSPORT software for 17 NASA libraries nationwide. FEDLINK staff crisscrossed the country to conduct PRISM and PASSPORT classes in 29 locations in 18 states.

Bibliographic Utilities

During FY 1991, FEDLINK network librarians conducted 160 specialized library training classes. From July 1990 to June 1991, FEDLINK members showed increases in interlibrary lending activity: Requests and referrals rose 7.1 percent to 294,073; holdings displays rose 5.1 percent to 555,551; and union list holdings displays rose 83.7 percent to 23,332. Activity on the cataloging subsystem also increased slightly (0.01 percent). Total first-time uses (FTUs) in cataloging, updates, reclassification, and retrospective conversion actions were 506,881 in 1991, compared with 504,331 in 1990. Original cataloging on OCLC rose 6.8 percent, to 66,925.

Library Automation Resource Service

Known for offering federal libraries expert counsel on application of automation to the library environment, the Library Automation Resource Service (LARS) focused in FY 1991 on the feasibility of FEDLINK becoming a node on Internet. The FEDLINK Internet Planning Group was established to determine the interest of federal libraries. Three new conferences were installed on ALIX, FEDLINK's electronic bulletin board operated from the LARS facility: News on OCLC, FEDLINK (to answer member questions), and Archives. ALIX is available on a 24-hour basis: 202-707-4888.

FEDLINK Fiscal Operations

New Networked Automated Fiscal Accounting System

The most significant project undertaken by FEDLINK Fiscal Operations (FFO) during FY 1991 was the implementation of the FEDLINK networked automated fiscal accounting system. With advice and assistance from technical experts at the Library of Congress, FLICC staff designed and installed a local area network (LAN) using Banyan Vines network software, IBM token ring network hardware, CompuAdd 316S workstations, and a Compaq SystemPro 386 fileserver. For the fiscal application on the LAN, the system development team designed, programmed, tested, and implemented a relational database system using Paradox software. All FY 1991 accounts-receivable and accounts-payable activities were processed in the new system.

Production Data

In support of the FEDLINK program during FY 1991, FFO processed hundreds of service registrations; 1,262 interagency agreements (IAGs), with 2,163 IAG amendments; and 3,961 individual service requests from federal agencies to the 73 FEDLINK vendors. The service requests were executed by delivery orders generated by FFO and issued to FEDLINK vendors by the library's Contracts and Logistics Services. Delivery orders issued to FEDLINK vendors in FY 1991 represented $60,707,848 in transfer-pay service dollars(for approximately 1,200 agencies) and $46,522,888 in direct-pay service dollars (for 480 agencies), for a total of $107,230,736 in FEDLINK service dollars for FY 1991. On behalf of transfer-pay agencies, FFO processed 86,173 invoices during FY 1991.

FEDLINK operating revenues are derived primarily from the FEDLINK transfer-pay fee of 6.75 percent of transferred service dollars and the direct-pay fee of $725 per direct-pay service. Revenue generated in FY 1991 was as follows: $4,400,130 from transfer-pay fees and $348,000 from direct-pay fees, for a total of $4,748,130 in FEDLINK operating revenue (see Figures 1–3).

Figure 1 / FEDLINK Service Requests FY 1991

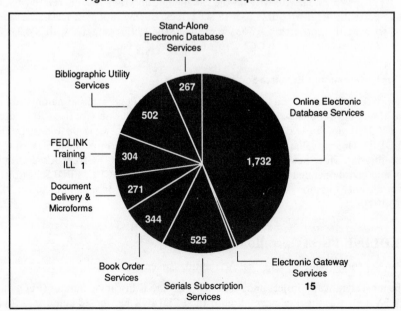

Figure 2 / FEDLINK Service Dollars
FYs 1981–1991
Transfer Pay* (In Millions)

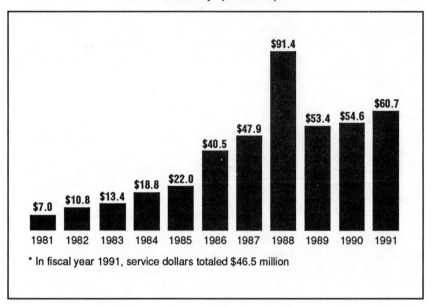

* In fiscal year 1991, service dollars totaled $46.5 million

Figure 3 / New Requests for FEDLINK Services
FYs 1981–1991

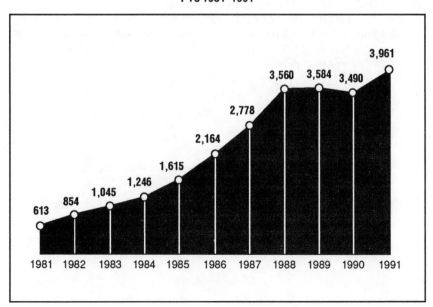

Fiscal Hot-Line Communications

In its second year of operation, the FEDLINK Fiscal Telephone Hotline recorded 12,286 calls, compared with nearly 9,000 calls in FY 1990. A variety of policies and procedures were instituted to improve communications with FEDLINK agencies. FFO continued to schedule special appointments with FEDLINK agencies and vendors to discuss complicated account problems and assign senior staff to concentrate on resolving complex situations.

Summary

Supported by a dedicated staff and the federal library community, FLICC officially celebrated its twenty-fifth anniversary in 1991, having strengthened and stabilized the FEDLINK program to ensure the delivery of services to its members and continuing the tradition of commitment to FLICC's founding principle of providing leadership and assistance to the nation's federal libraries and information centers.

During FY 1991, FLICC and its network components, FEDLINK Network Operations and FEDLINK Fiscal Operations, continued to work to improve the level of service to its members and to represent more effectively the interests of the federal library and information center community. GAO's audit confirmed that FLICC and the Library of Congress had made numerous changes to correct program deficiencies. FLICC staff specialists developed, tested, implemented, and refined a new networked automated fiscal accounting system, keyed to the special needs of FEDLINK's constituents.

The November federal Pre-White House Conference sponsored by FLICC brought together federal librarians and others to debate critical issues relating to federal libraries and information policies. The federal library delegation to WHCLIS II carried forward the federal sector's recommendations, winning national acceptance for nine of the thirteen. Dozens of federal librarians labored in FLICC working groups, three of them newly organized to focus on preservation, federal library statistics, and implementation of the new bylaws. FEDLINK network librarians undertook a nationwide program of specialized library training classes in addition to regularly scheduled workshops.

Library of Congress

Washington, DC 20540
202-707-5000

James W. McClung
Special Assistant to the Director of Communications

Milestones of 1991

Fiscal year 1991 was a year of anniversaries and beginnings for the Library of Congress, and it was also a year of progress on several fronts. After three and a half years, the Main Reading Room, splendidly restored, opened for business; the restoration of all the desks in the round room symbolized its coming full circle. No less significant was the first decrease in the backlog of unprocessed material (or "arrearages") in the library's collections in memory.

The Jefferson Decade was announced to encompass forthcoming library celebrations of the anniversary of Jefferson's birth, the completion of work on the Jefferson Building, and the library's bicentennial in 2000. Various celebrations in FY 1991 marked the seventy-fifth anniversary of the library's Judaic Section, the sixtieth anniversary of service to the blind and physically handicapped, the twenty-fifth anniversary of the Federal Library and Information Center Committee, and the twentieth anniversary of the Cataloging in Publication Program.

Automation, long a critical element in library operations, became a major theme in the budget request and the subject of long-range strategic planning to carry the library into the next century. Efforts to streamline processing through a reorganization of the cataloging directorate and to realize new economies through the sharing of cataloging resources moved ahead.

Reopening the Main Reading Room

When the Main Reading Room closed for renovation in December 1987, readers and reference librarians alike realized with both hope and trepidation that the room that was the heart and center of the library was about to change. With the reopening of this important space on June 3, the Main Reading Room emerged from the renovation process an architectural and technological triumph, integrating state-of-the-art information technology into a perfectly restored nineteenth-century room. The library published *Full Circle: Ninety Years of Service in the Main Reading Room* to mark the occasion.

Human Understanding, the figure central to the mural on the ceiling of the lantern of the dome, now presides over alcoves restored to the original terra cotta color, freshly washed marble, a new Wilton carpet, and refinished original furnishings as well as new work stations designed to accommodate wheelchairs. For the first time since 1900, when 44 readers' desks were displaced by the card catalog, the "full circle" of readers' desks is complete around the central desk. Each reader's station is now wired for power and data transmission. Patrons at the 236 desks can also access a CD-ROM–based information network of ten abstracting and indexing services.

The newly augmented Computer Catalog Center, located behind the Main Reading Room, now houses 58 terminals that can accommodate visually and physically handicapped readers. It also houses the newly developed PC-based ACCESS system, a user-oriented application that allows first-time or infrequent users of the library's information systems easy access to databases without training and with minimal assistance from reference librarians.

New photocopy "credit cards" are debited each time the reader uses the card, eliminating the need for change machines and coin boxes. Identification cards, designed for regular users of the reading room, facilitate collections security and, once bar-coded, will also expedite requesting materials. The library plans to link the user card and the photocopy card.

Processing the Arrearages

The number of items in the library's collections is now nearing 100 million. Unprocessed materials make up more than one third of the collections and were the focus of intense preparatory activity in 1990: a Special Project Team finding, a special report to Congress, and the theme of the library's FY 1991 budget request. The appropriations bill included 164 staff positions for this project. Thus, work toward solving this problem began in earnest. Numerous procedures were suggested and tested, including designating the third week of each month a production-only period. Staff from throughout the library lent time to this priority in other service units.

Although the arrearage total climbed even higher at the beginning of FY 1991 with the recording of additions to collections in 1990, arrearage workers accomplished a net decrease of 952,016 items (2.4 percent). The library's goal is a net reduction of 11.3 million items from the September 1989 benchmark of 38.6 million items during the pilot period, which ends December 1993. At the end of the fiscal year, the Librarian established an Arrearage Reduction Coordinating Group, directed by Michael Shelley, who also headed the Special Project Team, to develop and carry out an operations plan for the balance of the pilot project.

The highest arrearage reduction rates were in serials, pictorial materials, and microforms. Scores of collections previously unavailable to readers are now accessible. American Memory staff contributed significantly to this effort. (See information on the American Memory project later in this article.)

Sixty Years of Service to the Blind

On March 3, 1931, President Herbert Hoover signed the Pratt-Smoot Act authorizing the Library of Congress to produce embossed, or braille, books and to designate libraries around the country to distribute them to blind adults. Talking books, a radical concept in the 1930s, were added to the program two years later, and children's services were included in 1952, music services in 1962, and programs for physically handicapped individuals in 1966. Today, the National Library Service for the Blind and Physically Handicapped (NLS/BPH) administers this service.

In the past six decades, this program has enabled more than 14 million individuals who are unable to use standard print materials to enjoy the pleasures of reading books and magazines in braille and recorded formats.

Time, growth, and technology have decreed changes in the program. The original network of nineteen libraries has grown to almost 150. The $33\frac{1}{3}$-rpm disc of the 1930s has been replaced by a four-track, 15/16-ips cassette as the basic book format. Magazines are now distributed to patrons on flexible discs almost as soon as they are available to print subscribers. The original bulky talking-book machine has been replaced by the basic player and by easy-to-use cassette players, some designed especially for elderly or physically handicapped individuals. A machine that handles both discs and cassettes in a small space is under development.

NLS readership stands at nearly 700,000 out of an estimated eligible population of three million, two thirds of them visually impaired. This ratio of library users to nonusers is approximately the same as in the rest of the population. NLS patrons, however, read an average of thirty books a year—many more than sighted readers. Their reading interests are similar to those of the general public, although they are as a group older than the general population. Most patrons use one or more recorded formats for reading, and several thousand, most of them visually impaired from an early age, also use braille materials, including on-demand braille. Braille is an essential medium for lifetime readers of special-format materials.

Judaica at the Library

A major exhibition and publication in June, supported by the Project Judaica Foundation and devoted to the Judaic collections of the library, commemorated the seventy-fifth anniversary of the Hebraic Section, one of the world's foremost centers for the study of Hebrew and Yiddish materials. Abraham J. Karp—rabbi, author, and professor of history and religion at the University of Rochester—was guest curator of the exhibition as well as author of the illustrated volume accompanying it. Michael Grunberger, head of the Hebraic Section, was the library's curator for the exhibition.

Other activities in this observance included facsimile publication of the Washington Haggadah (named after the city where it is kept), an illuminated Hebrew manuscript copied and illustrated by Joel ben Simeon in 1478; the June symposium "The Hebrew Book," sponsored with the Meyerhoff Center for Jewish Studies, University of Maryland; and a lecture in July by Nobel Laureate Elie Wiesel on "Tolerance and Learning," sponsored with B'nai B'rith International. Other public lectures, special tours of the exhibition, and a screening of a series of Yiddish films from the library's collections were also part of this celebration of Jewish life and culture.

The Great British Picture Show

In cooperation with the British Academy of Film and Television Arts (BAFTA), the library organized a May festival of major British film and television productions. In addition to screenings, there were seminars, tutorials, and lectures by Sir Richard Attenborough, Martin Scorsese, Ken Adam, and David Francis. For the occasion, Queen Elizabeth II, on a state visit to Washington, D.C., attended a luncheon in her honor at the library on May 15 and toured the restored Main Reading Room, where she viewed a special exhibit of library treasures, including the L'Enfant plan for the capital, the 1531 Huejotzingo Codex (to be published in facsimile as part of the library's Columbus quincentenary program), and the April 29, 1865, letter of condolence from the queen's great-great-grandmother, Queen Victoria, to Mary Todd Lincoln.

At the luncheon, actress Angela Lansbury was presented BAFTA's Silver Mask award for her contributions to her craft in an Anglo-American environment. David Attenborough received the Benjamin Franklin Medal, awarded alternately to citizens of the United Kingdom and the United States, for promoting Anglo-American understanding.

A Global Library Project episode entitled "Thank You, Mr. Jefferson," focusing on the Main Reading Room and Jefferson's influence on the library, included footage of the queen's visit. The program was part of the "Liberty's Library" series telecast through Mind Extension University.

Special Initiatives

In addition to the Jefferson Decade, the library's initiative to build its science and technology collections and to enhance their availability shifted into the operational phase. New Special Project Teams will focus on the Jefferson Building, the library's data collection methods, and user evaluation of American Memory, which moved rapidly into expanded testing and production stages. Other new and continuing activities focused on the Columbus quincentenary, a proposed Japan Documentation Center, and the library's participation in the Decade of the Brain observance.

Jefferson Decade

A series of activities at the heart of the library's outreach efforts between 1992 and 2000 will mark several anniversaries that intersect simultaneously in the life of Jefferson and the history of the library. The celebration will allow the library to focus both on the relationship between the library and Jefferson and on the relationship between the library and a knowledge-based, democratic society.

An exhibition in 1993, the 250th anniversary of Jefferson's birth, will feature the books in the third president's personal library, which he sold to the nation in 1815 as a foundation for a library to replace the one destroyed in the War of 1812. "Thomas Jefferson, Reader" will examine how the ideas in Jefferson's library shaped his thinking.

In the mid-1990s, the library will reopen renovated exhibition halls and reading rooms in the Thomas Jefferson Building, the library's first home outside the U.S. Capitol and often considered its intellectual center. In 1997, there will be a celebration of the centenary of the completion of this building, itself a monument of American public architecture. A Special Project Team on Jefferson Building Reopenings under the leadership of John Y. Cole will coordinate this part of the Jefferson Decade observance.

In 2000, the library, so much a product of Jefferson's intellectual ideals, will celebrate its bicentennial. Jefferson's original dictum that "there is, in fact, no subject to which a member of Congress may not have occasion to refer" rings true as ever.

American Memory will create a multimedia collection on disc that will bring Jefferson and his ideas into schools and libraries across the nation. A 1993 Educators Institute for teachers and librarians will focus on Jefferson.

The Council of Scholars will organize a major conference on the future of knowledge to assess expectations for the twenty-first century in all major fields of knowledge. "Jefferson and the Education of Citizens in the New American Republic" will be the topic of a scholarly research conference organized by the Center for the Book.

Three new publications are envisioned: *Jefferson's Legacy* will be a brief, popular illustrated history of the library; *Great Collections in the Jefferson Building* will also appeal to a general audience; and a book-length, annotated bibliography will fill a void in scholarship on the institution.

Programs in the Jefferson Decade will be televised for cable transmission.

American Memory

In FY 1991, the library continued to evaluate a prototype delivery system for the American Memory program and began large-scale conversion of several Americana collections to electronic form preliminary to their distribution to U.S. libraries and schools. Selection and processing of collections, production and development, and user evaluation and response continued.

The American Memory project, which was able to lend support to the library's arrearage reduction efforts even before 1991, continued this support as staff selected and processed collections for inclusion in the program. For example, American Memory staff working in the Music Division almost completed processing the 24,000-item Edward and Marian MacDowell collection. Outside contractors also entered records for more than 1,000 Mathew Brady Civil War photographs, 3,000 early motion pictures, and at least 15,000 unpublished plays. In the next step, making electronic copies of the collections, the cataloging record will facilitate selection of materials for inclusion in American Memory and allow for production control over the items selected.

An American Memory by-product is a PC-based cataloging software program to create MARC (machine-readable cataloging) records. The program was used to catalog sound recordings, early motion pictures, and panoramic photographs as well as a folk music collection in the American Folklife Center. The center will also use the software to build a collection-level catalog of its holdings, previously accessible only through card files.

Production work continued, and in some instances was completed, on several collections, including African-American pamphlets, Civil War photographs, broadsides from the Continental Congress and Constitutional Convention, motion pictures of President William McKinley and the 1901 Pan-American Exposition, and the Nation's Forum (speeches by American political leaders). American Memory uses two kinds of automated system — disc-based personal computers and mainframe-based networked computers. For the former, three CD-ROMs represent stand-alone American Memory collections: congressional broadsides, Nation's Forum recordings, and Civil War photographs.

User evaluation of American Memory began in FY 1990 in three public school systems and one public library and continued in FY 1991 in six universities and the U.S. Naval Academy. Informal feedback has come from scores of visitors and others who have seen demonstrations of the prototype. Initial responses indicate that American Memory can be a valuable educational tool, but that only selected collections, such as local histories, will have success in public libraries. Secondary-school educators have shown great enthusiasm for the project.

The project will be further evaluated under the aegis of a Special Project Team created in January and headed by Susan Veccia of the Automation Office of the Congressional Research Service (CRS). The team invited other sites to apply to be part of the evaluation and, from 285 respondents, selected 37 applicants to participate in user evaluation in FY 1992. Scattered across the nation in a variety of settings, the sites reflect the distribution in the general population of media centers (13 sites), college and university libraries (14), public libraries (5), and others (5); testing also continued at 7 sites for evaluations begun earlier.

Congressional Research Service

In addition to participating in the Japan initiative, Congressional Research Service staff supported two special initiatives, the Seminar for New Members and assistance to the parliaments of Eastern Europe.

Seminar for New Members

Although in its fifth year, the Seminar for New Members in 1991 reflected both the immediacy of policy decisions facing Congress and the expanded scope of freshman participation. The three-day program, coordinated by CRS with the American Enterprise Institute and Brookings Institution, is designed to provide new members with facts, analytic resources, and perspectives on the critical and complex issues before Congress.

The program uses many approaches, from formal lectures to informal discussions to question-and-answer sessions, with emphasis on balanced, nonpartisan, analytic presentation in a setting away from Washington, D.C. The seminar includes events for members' families and sessions on the congressional family and the stresses to be encountered during congressional service. More than half of the forty-four new members of Congress attended the seminar.

Eastern Europe

The library's efforts on behalf of Congress to foster development of emerging democratic parliaments in Eastern Europe moved into operational phases in 1991. Through different House and Senate initiatives, CRS and other sections of the library are providing assistance to Bulgaria, the Czech and Slovak Federal Republic, Hungary, and Poland. Assistance to Poland, part of the Senate's Gift of Democracy, is in the form of computer, copying, and printing technology.

The House initiative, devoted to the other countries, focuses on four primary areas of assistance: development of an office automation program, establishment of parliamentary library collections, technical assistance in the creation of a research and analysis capability, and the development of parliamentary training programs and other technical assistance. House Information Systems is playing an important role in the equipment-related aspects of this program.

Although the library relies heavily on funds in the foreign operations appropriation for this initiative — transferred to the library through the Agency for International Development — assistance takes many forms. Library staff developed a core bibliography to use as a collections development and selection tool. Surplus reference books selected from the library's exchange collections were sent to Central and Eastern Europe. CRS has also encouraged coordination with other government agencies, private organizations and foundations, and the academic community in support of the initiative.

Science and Technology

A science and technology information initiative — under the direction of William W. Ellis, appointed to a one-year term as associate librarian for science and technology information in September — will enlarge the library's programs in this area, focusing on provision of scientific information and electronic publishing and copyright. The initiative was the primary product of a Special Project Team, formed in 1990 and headed by Prosser Gifford, director, Scholarly Programs, whose final report to the Management Team was delivered in March.

The team's recommendations included increasing the library's existing reference resources in science, technology, and business; achieving better bibliographic control and more rapid availability of foreign technical materials; and creating a new national directory, an Automated Reference Clearinghouse, as a pilot in 1992 to provide a foundation for a unique referral and reference service. The team also endorsed creating for researchers and educators electronic products combining both bibliographic and analytic materials and establishing a fee-based research service, initially to include information about engineering, for the business and industrial communities.

The Automated Reference Clearinghouse will give basic support for this initiative through a computer-based query-tracking system, substantive information from earlier library research, and, foremost, a large file of data on information sources. It will also provide a guide to the information resources available through Internet and the future National Research and Education Network (NREN). Through it, the library will begin seriously to participate in the new technology of electronic dissemination of information.

Special Project Teams

One other Special Project Team completed its work in FY 1991 with a report to Congress in January on interlibrary cooperative cataloging arrangements, especially as they may relate to the library's arrearage reduction efforts and other savings. This team was formed at the end of FY 1990 in response to a mandate from the House Committee on Appropriations.

The new Special Project Team on Key Indicators was established in January to analyze and validate the library's statistics collection activities. The team will develop and implement a system for reporting and publishing statistics. The first phase of its work, data gathering, was essentially completed by the end of FY 1991. In the next phase, the team will attempt to identify major indicators not currently tracked, to validate the indicators that have been identified, and to refine further the reporting system.

Other Programs

Japan Documentation Center

Negotiations continued in FY 1991 with the Japan Foundation and its Center for Global Partnership concerning the creation within the library of a documentation center that would house difficult-to-locate Japanese items on policy issues, social and economic materials, research reports, and draft legislation for the use of CRS and other U.S. research libraries. The process involved several meetings of the Japan Task Force, made up of CRS, the Asian Division, and other library staff, and a visit to the Center for Global Partnership. Electronic document delivery will be tested as one component of the center's operations, which are scheduled to get under way in mid-1992.

LC Direct

The LC Direct project to provide remote online access to the library's bibliographic databases began in January 1991. Thirty-three state library agencies are participating in the two-year experiment, conducted on a partial cost-recovery basis for the library.

Quincentenary

The library continued preparing for its celebration of the Columbus quincentenary in 1992. Project staff worked on the major exhibition "An Ongoing Voyage: 1492" and forwarded "The Hispanic World, 1492-1898" and "Keys to the Encounter" for publication. In addition to the 1531 Huejotzingo Codex, the library received funding for facsimiles of the 1540 Oztoicpac Lands Map and the 1562 Gutierrez Map of America.

The American Folklife Center completed field work in California, Washington, Nevada, Colorado, and Utah in its project to survey Italian-American contributions to the culture of the American West, generating a large quantity of photographs, sound recordings, videotapes, and manuscript materials. An exhibition based on this project, tentatively entitled "Ties and Attachments: Italian-Americans in the West," is scheduled to open in California in October 1992.

Among the programs produced by the Global Library Project in 1991 was "Christopher Columbus: The Ongoing Voyage," which offered a look at the Columbus materials in the library's rare book collections and an interview with the coordinator of the library's quincentenary observance, John Hébert. Historian Ida Altman, the curator for the library's upcoming Columbus exhibition, provided part of the commentary for a journey to the Bahamas retracing Columbus's route through some of the northern islands.

Educators Institute

An Educators Institute at the library in midsummer attracted some thirty elementary- and secondary-school teachers and librarians who examined the topic "The Bill of Rights and Beyond: Dialogue between Vision and Reality." Supported by the Commission on the Bicentennial of the United States Constitution and the History Teaching Alliance, the institute offered participants lectures by library staff and outside experts, discussion sessions, and opportunities for research in library collections. The institute, presented with the Catholic University of America, focused on rights in three areas: the First Congress and the Bill of Rights, the Civil War Amendments, and the Civil Rights Acts.

Civilization

The proposed new magazine of the Library of Congress passed its first hurdle, a marketing test, early in the calendar year. Despite recession and war, the response to the test was encouraging, with a better than 7 percent response rate compared to a normal response in such tests of 3-4 percent. The magazine, designed to make the public more aware of the library's collections and to create a constituency for the library and libraries in general, will be operated by a private company, LOC Corp., once financing is secured.

Decade of the Brain

In response to a presidential proclamation celebrating the 1990s, the library and the National Institute of Mental Health sponsored an all-day symposium in July as the first in the Decade of the Brain Lecture Series. The "Frontiers of Neuroscience" program and subsequent events are designed to alert Congress and the general public to the extraordinary advances in neuroscience and their relevance to public policy in such matters as artificial intelligence and Alzheimer's disease. Symposium participants included researchers, scientific leaders from several disciplines, government officials, and members of Congress.

Collections

The collections are the library's most fundamental mission. The challenge is to find new approaches to acquisition, cataloging and processing, preservation, and service of these collections in order to remain the preeminent source of knowledge and information for Congress, the nation's libraries, and the public. At the same time, the library must strive to extend its resources to new constituencies — to serve the public more broadly and more deeply, to serve libraries more comprehensively, to serve scholars more quickly and thoroughly, and to serve Congress more responsively.

Acquisitions

Library acquisitions are subject to many vagaries. One of the most common is economic fluctuations, both at home and abroad. But other trends and events that affect gifts, copyright deposits, and exchange arrangements also affect acquisitions. Abroad, acquisitions activity has also traditionally been subject to political unrest and civil upheaval, which certainly dominated headlines in 1991.

General acquisitions trends in 1991 showed an 18.4 percent increase in receipts of materials purchased for the collections, mostly in serials and microforms. Total law receipts increased 134 percent, the result of large microfiche purchases. Receipts of materials on exchange also increased, but most of the activity was in foreign materials. A single large gift of U.S. cartographic materials boosted U.S. receipts to an abnormally high figure of more than 136,000 items.

Acquisitions and Copyright

Acquisitions through copyright, now administratively part of Collections Services rather than the Copyright Office, continued through a second year without problems. The division, which still has statutory, fiscal, and workflow ties to the Copyright Office, also works closely with the administrative and custodial offices in its parent service unit to ensure the most efficient acquisition activity possible.

A revision in the copyright regulation to permit group registration of serials allows publishers to submit to the library two complimentary subscriptions of each title, which would potentially save the library a lot of money, and to deposit one copy later with the registration application. The change would also mean more timely receipts. By the end of the fiscal year, the library was receiving two subscriptions to 426 titles, valued at approximately $340,000. Unfortunately, lack of staff and space to process the complimentary and registered copies has inhibited the library from aggressively publicizing the change to publishers and has, therefore, prevented it from taking full advantage of the benefits.

Other acquisitions changes tied to copyright included transfer of the administration of the Motion Picture Agreement, under which producers may retain an expensive deposit copy for circulation to theaters on condition that a good copy come to the library later, from the Copyright Office to the Motion Picture, Broadcasting and Recorded Sound Division. Earlier regulations concerning deposits of CD-ROM products continued to help build acquisitions of these items, important both to the Machine-Readable Collections Reading Room and the science and technology collections.

Music Collections

A sad footnote to the history of the music collections was news of the deaths of two special library friends and benefactors, Lenore Gershwin, the widow of Ira, and Aaron Copland. Both enjoyed relationships with the library that extended back many decades, and the library certainly benefited from these friendships.

Before her death, Mrs. Gershwin gave the library four outstanding items relating to George Gershwin: a Gershwin *Tune Book,* a twenty-page sketchbook used by the composer from 1916 to 1922; four pages of Gershwin's sketches for *An American in Paris*; a signed holograph letter from Gershwin to Margaret Mower, written August 24, 1928; and a copy of Francis Poulenc's *Mouvements Perpétuels,* inscribed to Gershwin and signed by Poulenc. Two other Gershwin acquisitions were six letters from Gershwin to Selma Tamber, who worked for his publisher, and forty-two letters to Gershwin from Julia Van Norman, a friend and confidante. The latter are a complement to letters from Gershwin to Van Norman already in the library collection.

A collection of about 16,000 items belonging to pianist Arthur Rubinstein parallels similar collections of other twentieth-century performers, notably Henryk Szeryng and Jascha Heifetz. Important music manuscripts acquired were a rare holograph sketchbook of Franz Liszt, four unpublished works by composer Ernest Bloch given by his daughter Susan, and parts of Koussevitzky's own Concerto for double bass orchestra.

Monographs

Rare American works acquired in 1991 include an illustrated 1877 book entitled *Yellowstone National Park,* which contains chromolithographs of Thomas Moran's paintings of the Rocky Mountains during the period of their first exploration; a second known copy of *A Sketch of Bolivar in his Camp* (1834), an interview of the South American revolutionary by an anonymous American, and Robert Conner's *The Cabinet Maker's Assistant* (1842), the second Native American cabinet pattern book. Other rare books are William Herndon's *Life of Lincoln* (1889), the only known copy of the British edition of this controversial biography by Lincoln's former law partner; fourteen books that belonged to Jefferson's third library; and twelve political pamphlets in Jefferson's library that he sold to the United States in 1815, but which had strayed into the collections of the University of Alabama, Huntsville.

Cartography

Acquisition of twenty-two globes and seven maps from the Howard Welsh collection, all produced in the United States, makes the library's globe collection the preeminent resource for the study of early U.S. globes. Of particular note are the earliest dated globe, 1811, by the first U.S. commercial globe maker, James Wilson, and the earliest recorded U.S. lithographic globe, produced around 1830. Large collections include 69,621 maps from the Census Bureau's 1990 United States County Block Map series, of particular interest to congressional staff examining changing boundaries of congressional districts, and the National Wetlands Inventory of the U.S. Fish and Wildlife Service, the first shipment of some 18,974 of these maps. Mandated by Congress in 1986, these maps will be important in making environmental decisions. The library will receive one of the few complete sets of these maps.

Other Collections

The library's audiovisual collections were enhanced by the first sixty videotapes of classic Russian cinema and drama received from the Moscow State Theater Library, including many classic Soviet feature films such as *Chapayev, My Friend Ivan Lapshin,* and *Forgotten Melody for the Flute,* as well as *Uncle Vanya* performed by the Moscow Art Theater. The Berliner collection of early recorded materials was enriched by three very rare Berliner Gramophone Company discs.

The architectural collections were augmented by an important archive of nineteenth-century drawings by James Renwick and William Whitten Renwick, including the former's visionary scheme for a national gallery of science and art, his drawings for Saint Patrick's Cathedral in New York City, and a number of designs by the younger Renwick for ecclesiastical interiors and ornamentation.

Manuscript acquisitions came in large packages in 1991. Of the 1,163,000 items accessioned, nearly three fourths constituted additions to three collections: 300,000 new items for the papers of Raymond Loewy, America's foremost industrial designer; papers — 150,000 items — of former government official Donald Rumsfeld; and 326,000 items added to the records of the National Association for the Advancement of Colored People Legal Defense and Education Fund. The library also received the first installment of the papers of Justice Sandra Day O'Connor.

In photography, the AIDS Document Project neared completion of its first intensive phase with the acquisition of work by Jan Goldin and Brian Weil. This project, begun in 1989, was a first successful attempt by the library to document systematically, through a variety of the graphic arts, an important contemporary issue.

Through the Pennell Committee, the library focused on collecting the work of women and minority printmakers. In 1991, the committee recommended for purchase the work of Elizabeth Murray, Howardena Pindell, Emma Amos, Vincent Smith, Jacob Lawrence, Martin Puryear, Rafael Ferrer, and Yong Soon Min.

Electronic and Microform Acquisitions

Acquisition of CD-ROM products remains an important new collection activity. Additions in this medium in 1991 included important reference works in science and technology, indexes to French-language newspapers and periodicals, and (for the Machine-Readable Collections Reading Room) Congressional MasterFile, Statistical MasterFile, Global Access, *Collection of Notable Americans,* and *International Narcotics Information.*

More than 200,000 items were acquired and processed for the microform collections. New acquisitions covered such diverse subjects as FBI files on civil rights activity in the South, Patent Office gazettes, twentieth-century literature on the history of physics, and Shakespeariana.

The Library and the Nation

National Endeavors

Madison National Council

The James Madison National Council, established in FY 1990, grew by more than 50 percent in FY 1991 and now includes representatives from eighteen U.S. states, Mexico, and France. The council met at the library in March and October. The council's Steering Committee recommended support for such outreach projects as the Jefferson Decade and the Junior Fellows Program.

National Film Preservation Board

The National Film Preservation Board, which has advised the Librarian of Congress for the past three years on the annual selection of twenty-five films for the National Film Registry, met in November at the library's Motion Picture Conservation Center in Ohio, where members toured the facility's vaults and laboratory and attended a screening of *The Treasure of the Sierra Madre*. The print of the 1948 film, a 1990 registry selection, was made in the library's laboratory there. The board also met in Washington in June to review nominees for the 1991 registry. Legislation to reauthorize the board was introduced in the 101st Congress.

Public Programs and Outreach

Poetry Programs and Events

For the first time in many years, the library awarded a major prize in poetry when the Librarian presented the inaugural Rebekah Johnson Bobbitt National Prize for Poetry to poet, novelist, and playwright James Merrill. The prize honors the most distinguished book of poetry published by an American during the preceding two years, and the presentation was the year's major literary event. The $10,000 prize is given in memory of Rebekah Johnson Bobbitt of Austin, Texas, by her family.

Poet Laureate Consultant in Poetry Mark Strand presided over a year of increased literary activity for the library. In addition to the presentation of the Bobbitt Prize, there were readings by nineteen invited authors and a busy unofficial schedule for the laureate. In May, the Librarian named Joseph Brodsky the new laureate. A Russian-born poet who is now a U.S. citizen, Brodsky, a Nobel laureate, brings to the library's long tradition of consultants and laureates its first binational incumbent. Howard Nemerov, the 1989–1990 laureate, fell ill during his second term at the library and died during the summer of 1991. A memorial service was held at the library in October.

Arbuthnot Lecture

The library was host in 1991 to the prestigious May Hill Arbuthnot Lecture, established in 1969 to honor Arbuthnot, an authority on literature for children. It is presented each year in a different location by an outstanding author, critic, librarian, historian, or teacher of children's literature. The 1991 lecturer was Iona Opie, British folklorist, collector, and anthropologist of childhood. The event drew some 400 authors, illustrators, teachers, librarians, folklorists, and other bibliophiles from as far away as Utah and the Virgin Islands. The lecture is administered by the Association for Library Service to Children.

Center for the Book

In 1991, the library launched a new national reading promotion: "The Year of the Lifetime Reader." More than 105 organizations participated in the campaign, of which First Lady Barbara Bush was honorary chairperson. "Year of the Lifetime Reader" projects included a national photography contest with the American Library Association, a U.S. Postal Service poster on display in 40,000 post offices, and a Be a Lifetime Reader booth at the 1991 Easter-egg roll at the White House. In July, the library announced that "Explore New Worlds – READ!" will be the theme of its national reading promotion in 1992.

Three traveling exhibits were circulated to state Centers for the Book: "A Nation of Readers;" "The Bonfire of Liberties: Censorship of Humanities," which made its debut in Connecticut; and "Uncle Sam in the Oregon Country," which opened in Salem in October. The last, which examines the federal government's strong ties to the Pacific Northwest, was also the subject of a program in the Global Library Project's "Liberty's Library" series. A new Center for the Book in Alaska brought to twenty-four the number of state affiliates that promote the center's reading and literacy programs.

The Islamic Book

"The Book in the Islamic World," a two-day international conference in November, dealt with the development of the text of the Koran, the transition from manuscript to the age of printing, and related topics. An exhibit of Korans, manuscripts, early and modern printed books, and calligraphic sheets and bindings, representing a variety of styles as examples of Islamic calligraphy and book production, complemented the conference.

Global Library Project

Other productions not described elsewhere included shows in the 1990–1991 season on the theme "Treasures of the Library of Congress." Segments focused on the Whittall Stradivarius Collections, on items from the library's rare books collections and the curators who care for them, and on "Science, Adventure and the Entrepreneur," a look at the library's rich collections of materials on inventors and scientists, starting with Bell's designs for the telephone.

The 1991–1992 season, devoted to "Liberty's Library," included programs on libraries and democracy. Among them, "The Dreamkeepers: Oral Tradition, the Printed Word and Democracy" looks at early human efforts to collect and preserve knowledge through the oral tradition. "Library of Congress: Creativity, Culture and Democracy" explores the American tradition of artistic creativity and how it is protected and cherished at the library.

Funding for the 1991–1992 season was again provided by Jones Intercable. Programs are broadcast over Jones's Mind Extension University, estimated, by year's end, to reach 18 million cable TV households.

American Folklife Center

Among other outreach activities, the center launched the Maine Acadian Folklife Project, a collaborative effort between the center and the North Atlantic Regional Office of the National Park Service. Fieldwork along the Saint John Valley of northern Maine documented the Acadian cultural heritage. In another project with the National Park Service, the center assisted in the development of a cultural heritage center at New River Gorge in West Virginia.

Publications and Exhibitions

In addition to the new ways in which the library can share its rich collections with a larger audience, two traditional methods remain important parts of the outreach program: the traditional printed word and the visual display. The book is perhaps still the most portable means of sharing information and images, but the library's program of traveling exhibits and loans for exhibitions also brings to people around the nation material that otherwise would be inaccessible to them. A record twenty-two exhibitions and displays, including a major traveling exhibition, were mounted in 1991.

Publications

Full Circle: Ninety Years of Service in the Main Reading Room, by Josephus Nelson and Judith Farley, documents the history of the room and the reference librarians who have staffed it for nearly a century. Eighteen duotone illustrations document changes in fixtures and faces, culminating in the replacement of the card catalog with a Computer Catalog Center.

Living Traditions of Russian Faith: Books and Manuscripts of the Old Believers, by Abby Smith and Vladimir Budaragin, catalogs a 1990 exhibition at the library of rare books and manuscripts lovingly copied and illuminated by the faithful of the breakaway religious movement that began in the seventeenth century. Illustrations, twenty-two of them in color, show works by members of the Priestless Sect of Old Believers, books of liturgical music, and works from the nineteenth and twentieth centuries when the Old Belief came to be appreciated for its role in preserving traditional beliefs and reverence for books and icons.

Another work prepared in conjunction with an exhibition, *The Sister Republics: Switzerland and the United States from 1776 to the Present,* by James H. Hutson, explores historic ties between the two countries and the little-known constitutional borrowings of each republic from the other. The year marked the 700th anniversary of the creation of the federation that eventually became Switzerland.

The 400-page catalog to accompany the exhibition of the same title, *From the Ends of the Earth: Judaic Treasures of the Library of Congress,* includes a scholarly and informative text by Abraham J. Karp and more than 300 color and black-and-white illustrations depicting such treasures as Torah scrolls, illuminated Haggadoth, micrographic art, correspondence between early U.S. presidents and Jewish congregations, and the music of Irving Berlin and the Gershwins.

To mark the bicentennial of the nation's capital, which the library will celebrate with an exhibition in FY 1992, the library published both a full-color facsimile and a computer-assisted black-and-white reproduction entitled *L'Enfant's 1791 Manuscript Plan for the City of Washington.* The facsimile shows the original in its present poor condition, in which much detail is obscured by fading worsened by varnish that was wrongly applied in the mid-nineteenth century. The reproduction, done in cooperation with the U.S. Geological Survey, was created with a sophisticated computer graphics system that enhanced the original image to legibility. The National Geographic Society and the National Park Service also supported this project.

Technical publications included *CDMARC Bibliographic,* a six-disc CD-ROM that makes the library's USMARC database of more than four million records available to even the smallest library. The Cataloging Distribution Service published its first *Complete Catalog* and distributed 25,000 copies of it, 5,000 of them overseas.

The Federal Research Division produced twelve new titles in its series of country studies. Some books in the series are in their fourth, fifth, or sixth edition. Published under an agreement with the U.S. Department of the Army, the series consists of more than a hundred titles covering approximately 143 sovereign states and 15 dependencies.

The library also produced through Pomegranate Calendars and Books, one of the nation's leading specialty publishers, a selection of seven illustrated wall or desk calendars. The themes of the calendars ranged from the Columbus quincentenary to the Civil War, the birds of John Gould, and the law.

Exhibitions

The exhibition of Judaic treasures, "From the Ends of the Earth," which opened in June, included both the first Judaica the library acquired, part of the library of Thomas Jefferson purchased in 1815, and Judaic firsts since acquired by the library: the first Hebrew book printed by Gershom Soncino, the greatest of all Hebrew printers; one of the first seven printed Hebrew books; the first Hasidic publication; and the first books printed in Lisbon, on the African continent, and in the Holy Land. Early and rare printings of the Talmud and the Bible and materials dating from the first Jewish settlement in the New World in 1654 were also represented. The exhibition of some 240 items was made possible by the support of the Project Judaica Foundation in Washington, D.C.

In September, "Vision of a Collector," which celebrated the hundredth birthday of Lessing J. Rosenwald and coincided with a lecture and the dedication of the Rosenwald Room, paid tribute to the library's greatest donor of rare books. The Rosenwald Room re-creates the Alverthorpe Gallery from Rosenwald's home in Pennsylvania. The exhibition includes one hundred extraordinary books, drawings, prints, and bookbindings from the 2,600-piece collection, the focus of which is the illustrated book. The Rosenwald Collection, assembled over the bibliophile's lifetime, includes a 15,000-volume reference collection and several volumes presented to the library by Mrs. Rosenwald following her husband's death. Members of the Rosenwald family joined other guests and library officials for this occasion. The final event in the Rosenwald centennial anniversary will be publication of a volume of a hundred essays on the hundred works in the exhibition. The work was at press at year's end.

"Sister Republics: Switzerland and the United States from 1776 to the Present," on view during the summer months, focused on the development of Swiss democracy and its relationship to the American model of constitutional government. The political culture of Switzerland was used as an example by both federalists and antifederalists in the constitutional debates of 1787 and 1788, and the U.S. Constitution was a model for Switzerland's first federal constitution in 1848. More than a hundred manuscripts, broadsides, memorabilia, prints, paintings, and printed materials illustrated this binational influence. The exhibition was made possible by a grant from Ciba-Geigy and was mounted in cooperation with the Swiss Embassy. At a July 4 reception at the Swiss Embassy, Flavio Cotti, president of the Swiss Confederation, cited the exhibition as a special example of the deep ties that bind the two countries in friendship.

Several smaller exhibitions coincided with other special events. "Maps of the Persian Gulf," a selection of sixteen current and historical maps of the region, went on view in the newly named Current Events Corridor. The centerpiece of the exhibit was a large map of the Middle East that had become familiar to viewers of televised gulf war briefings at the Pentagon and in Saudi Arabia.

On view at the entrance to this display was the original yellow ribbon Mrs. Bruce Laingen tied around a tree in front of her house when her husband was a hostage in Iran and again when their son, a serviceman, was sent to the Persian Gulf. The Laingens presented the ribbon to the library in July at the invitation of the American Folklife Center, which has been documenting the yellow ribbon as a folk symbol in American society.

As part of the celebration of African American History Month (February) at the library, forty-two items from the Daniel A. P. Murray Collection were displayed. Murray, an African American historian and an employee of the library from 1871 to 1923, accumulated a large body of materials on slavery and the abolitionist movement. The preservation and processing work on the collection in FY 1990 was part of the American Memory project. The Office of Education Services, as part of its special outreach program for young people, developed a program of teacher and student materials to accompany this exhibit. Young people were given a sleuthing kit to encourage them to view the exhibit more carefully by searching for specific knowledge to answer questions in their packets.

At the time of the dedication of the Gibran Memorial Garden in northwest Washington, D.C., the library mounted a display of editions of Kahlil Gibran's work, original drawings from *The Prophet* and one of the memorial, and paintings. An evening of poetry readings also celebrated the dedication.

"Justice for the Benefit of All" marked the centennial of the enactment of the first international copyright law in 1891, which granted copyright for the first time to foreigners. The exhibition focused on such authors and composers as Dickens and Gilbert and Sullivan and their struggles here and abroad to gain copyright protection.

National Agricultural Library

U.S. Department of Agriculture, NAL Bldg., Beltsville, MD 20705

Brian Norris
Public Affairs Officer

Established in 1862 under legislation signed by President Lincoln, the National Agricultural Library (NAL), along with the Library of Congress and the National Library of Medicine, is one of three national libraries in the United States. It is the largest agricultural library in the world, with more than 2.3 million volumes on 48 miles of shelves. The collection includes books and journals, audiovisuals, reports, theses, patents, software, and laser discs. The library also receives 26,000 periodicals annually. Many print materials date back to the nineteenth century.

Preservation

The National Agricultural Library is battling a relentless adversary—time. Books such as a 1912 volume of the *American Cultivator* crumble like dried leaves when lifted from the shelves. Time, aided by the acid in the paper of books and materials, causes this calamity.

Identifying the Problem

Preservation of materials is a major concern of libraries. The problem can be traced to the development of wood pulp paper and its widespread use beginning around 1850. Due to general use of the highly acidic wood pulp paper well into the twentieth century, library materials are now deteriorating at an alarming pace.

Typically, about 25 percent of the collections of most large research libraries have become brittle, flaking to pieces despite the most careful handling. Agricultural publications may be even more susceptible to this malady. A large number of agricultural publications are published by societies and governments with the intent of free distribution. Agriculture is a chief concern of most governments, and spreading agricultural information quickly, broadly, and cheaply is often their aim. These sources frequently publish on poorer grades of paper, which are highly acidic and short-lived.

In the case of the NAL collection, more than 50 percent of the monographs and serials are disintegrating and about one fourth of NAL's 2.3 million volumes are brittle. The contents of brittle volumes need to be transferred to a format such as microform, photocopy, or optical disc to prevent loss to the scientific world.

After thoroughly reviewing the condition of the NAL collection, a task force headed by Les Kulp developed a plan to mitigate the effects of time and acid on these materials. The study, conducted with assistance from the Association of Research Libraries, was made public in Fall 1991.

Preservation Measures

Like most large research libraries faced with numerous demands and limited resources, NAL so far has been able to take only simple and inexpensive steps to preserve materials: storing materials flat rather than vertically to reduce the strain on old book bindings; using automatic timers to limit the amount of artificial irradiating light allowed to shine on materials stored in library stacks; and controlling temperature, moisture, and other environmental conditions under which materials are stored. Each year NAL binds many thousands of journals to extend their useful life, but much more needs to be done.

NAL began its program of full conservation of rare or historical items in 1971, contracting with a conservator to restore items of particular significance. To date, about 2,000 items — or about 4 percent of the estimated 50,000 titles in NAL's historic books and manuscripts collections — have been fully restored. The library also cooperates with land-grant university libraries, the Library of Congress, and commercial microform publishers to microfilm significant agricultural publications.

New Technologies

Perhaps most encouraging is the library's application of new technologies to preservation problems. These experimental projects need to be upgraded, however, to be of significant help to NAL's preservation program.

NAL has placed full-text, page images, photographs, and even audiovisual materials on CD-ROMs and laser discs. Working with the U.S. Department of Agriculture's Office of Public Affairs, NAL has developed a laser disc system containing 16,000 USDA photographs. The system allows searchers to find photographs in minutes instead of having to go through thousands of files manually, and it lessens wear and tear on photographs by reducing handling. In September 1991, more than 80 people from 14 countries attended an international symposium on information management technology, organized and hosted by NAL, for a week of expert lectures and technology demonstrations.

National Agricultural Text Digitizing Project

In a major experimental effort begun in 1987, the National Agricultural Text Digitizing Project (NATDP), the library has placed entire collections of materials on such critical subjects as acid rain, Agent Orange, and food irradiation on 5-inch, easy-to-use CD-ROMs. Each 5-inch disc contains thousands of pages of information, including diagrams, charts, and pictures. NAL makes these discs available to land-grant university libraries for use and evaluation.

Carver Collection

If alive today, George Washington Carver — one of the most famous agricultural scientists in American history and a man who reveled in experimentation and discovery — would no doubt be pleased that a microfilm collection of his papers, letters, records, and drawings of seeds, plants, and inventions at Tuskegee University is the focus of the next phase of NATDP. NAL is optically scanning the materials on 67 reels of microfilm to test the feasibility of converting microfilm to electronic page images that can be accessed by microcomputer. With Tuskegee's permission, NAL is placing the contents of three microfilm reels on CD-ROM along with bibliographic information for accessing the material. The CD-ROM, which will include the complete *Guide to the Microfilm Edition of the George Washington Carver Papers at Tus-*

kegee Institute, will be made available to agricultural and research libraries worldwide.

NAL Staff

An agency of USDA with an annual budget of approximately $16 million, the library reports to the assistant secretary for science and education. NAL Director Joseph H. Howard is supported by associate directors for automation, public services, and technical services, with a combined staff of approximately 200, including librarians, computer specialists, administrators, information specialists, and clerical personnel. Under the library's visiting scholar program, professors and librarians come from universities worldwide to work full time at the library on projects of mutual interest.

Library Services

As the chief U.S. resource and service for agricultural information, NAL has a mission to provide accurate and up-to-date agricultural information for researchers, educators, policymakers, farmers, consumers of agricultural products, and the public at large. Recently, the library expanded its international services.

NAL coordinates and is the primary resource for a nationwide network of state land-grant and USDA field libraries. Together, these libraries form a document delivery service offering agricultural materials through interlibrary loan. NAL supplies copies of agricultural materials not available elsewhere and also works with land-grant university libraries to improve access to and maintenance of U.S. agricultural knowledge.

NAL is also the departmental library for USDA, serving thousands of USDA employees worldwide. It is the keystone of the department's scientific and research activities, providing USDA scientists with the most current information available.

AGRICOLA (AGRICultural OnLine Access), NAL's bibliographic database, provides quick access to the NAL collection with its 2.6 million citations to agricultural literature. It is commercially available online or on computer disc. The ALF (Agricultural Library Forum) electronic bulletin board system is available 24 hours a day, 7 days a week (301-344-8510). The system provides a convenient tool for electronically accessing information about NAL products and services and for exchanging agricultural information and resources among libraries, information centers, and other information users.

NAL maintains specialized information centers in 11 areas of interest to the agricultural community: agricultural trade and marketing, alternative farming systems, animal welfare, aquaculture, biotechnology, food and nutrition, plant genome, rural information (including rural health), technology transfer, water quality, and youth development. Their custom services range from responding to reference requests and developing publications to coordinating outreach activities and establishing dissemination networks.

Since 1969, NAL has been located on the grounds of USDA's Beltsville Agricultural Research Center in Beltsville, Maryland. The library is open from 8 A.M. to 4:30 P.M., Monday through Friday, except on federal holidays.

National Library of Medicine

8600 Rockville Pike, Bethesda, MD 20894
301-496-6308

Robert Mehnert
Public Information Officer

The online information retrieval network of the National Library of Medicine (NLM) continues to grow both in number of users and breadth of services. Physicians, researchers, and health science educators are enrolling in record numbers; during summer 1991, NLM issued the fifty-thousandth user password. The number of searches done by network members also reached an all-time high (see Table 1). The most popular database, MEDLINE, covering journal literature since 1966, accounted for 77 percent of the searches.

The composition of the network has shifted radically since the user-friendly personal computer software Grateful Med was introduced five years ago. Where once the primary users were health science librarians and information specialists—those with the motivation to undergo detailed training on how to search NLM's databases—today the great majority of those joining the network are in the health field: physicians, scientists, nurses, instructors, and students.

NLM databases are available not only on the library's computers but also through such vendors as Dialog and BRS, on commercially produced CD-ROMs, and through foreign MEDLARS partners around the world.

New Network Features

Two new network capabilities were introduced in 1991. In January, the library unveiled the "clinical alert" service, designed to accelerate dissemination to the practicing community of potentially life-saving medical information from the National Institutes of Health. Prominent health communicators, medical editors, and government medical research administrators had repeatedly stressed the need for such a service at a January 15, 1991, meeting at NIH to discuss ways to make public highlights of important clinical trial findings before publication in medical journals.

Three days later NLM transmitted its first clinical alert over the online network, a 74-line statement regarding the efficacy of a drug used to treat HIV-infected chil-

Table 1 / Selected NLM Statistics*

Library Operation	Volume
Collection (book and nonbook)	4,821,000
Serial titles received	21,600
Articles indexed for MEDLINE	363,000
Titles cataloged	19,200
Circulation requests filled	385,000
For interlibrary loan	207,000
For on-site users	178,000
Computerized searches (all databases)	5,810,000

*For the year ending September 30, 1991.

dren. The alert remained on the network for 30 days. During the next few months, six more clinical alerts were placed on the network. Grateful Med users were taught how to retrieve the alerts using their software (at a cost of about 25 cents per alert).

In May 1991, Grateful Med users received the "Loansome Doc" floppy disk free. Loansome Doc allows users to place an online order for a copy of the full article for any reference retrieved from MEDLINE. This is only possible through the cooperation of health sciences libraries in hospitals and other institutions around the country, for the overwhelming majority of requests end up in such libraries, not at the National Library of Medicine. An electronic file (DOCLINE) "knows" which of some 2,000 libraries hold which journal titles; each Loansome Doc request is automatically routed to a library that holds the needed article.

Also noteworthy in 1991 was the release of an improved version of Grateful Med for Macintosh users. Version 1.5 (sent without charge to all registered 1.0 users) provides users with an array of new search features, four new databases, and direct access not only to MEDLINE but also, for the first time, to the National Cancer Institute's Physicians' Data Query service, to TOXNET (NLM's network of databases on toxicology, pharmacology, and hazardous materials), and to the Grateful Med Bulletin Board.

Outreach

On the theory that its information services are not fulfilling their potential unless they are serving the maximum number of health professionals, NLM continues to conduct a vigorous outreach program. Unfortunately, many American health professionals do not have easy access to computerized biomedical information — because of geographic isolation, nonaffiliation with a hospital or medical school library, or simply because they lack information about available services.

The outreach program intended to remedy this situation has been greatly aided by member institutions of the National Network of Libraries of Medicine (NN/LM). In 1991, five-year contracts were signed with the eight Regional Medical Libraries that, together with 130 Resource Libraries (primarily at medical schools) and 3,600 Local Libraries (primarily at hospitals), make up the NN/LM network. The new contracts emphasize Grateful Med training, demonstrations, exhibits, and other activities related to outreach.

Health science librarians and information specialists around the country have responded to NLM's appeal to help get the news to their clientele. At hospitals, universities, and schools of the health professions, medical librarians are holding Grateful Med workshops and training sessions and advising and counseling medical staff and students. Their outreach efforts have been especially valuable in small communities and rural areas, where the need is greatest.

NLM has targeted some 20 special efforts to reach health professionals who serve minority populations. Prominent among these is a collaboration with Meharry Medical College (Nashville) to develop an outreach demonstration project for health care practitioners (including family practice residents) in remote and professionally isolated settings. In another project, a "circuit rider" librarian is being evaluated as a method of bringing modern information services to geographically remote areas of south Texas. The circuit librarian makes weekly visits to nine hospitals in the region, performing

MEDLINE searches, arranging for speedy delivery of needed articles, and training health professionals to use Grateful Med so they can access MEDLINE themselves.

In another outreach effort, begun in 1991, medical and other health professional staff at historically black colleges and universities will receive training in the use of NLM's toxicological, environmental, and occupational information resources. This audience represents a group that would otherwise not receive exposure to these valuable information sources.

Communications Research

Two major components of the library are responsible for communications research and development: the Lister Hill National Center for Biomedical Communications and the National Center for Biotechnology Information.

Lister Hill Center research programs apply state-of-the-art computer and communications technologies to the management of biomedical knowledge. Such information can take the form of procedural rules found in expert systems, information in bibliographic and factual databases, as well as signals, images, and sound. Lister Hill Center programs create innovative methods for acquiring, storing, retrieving, analyzing, communicating, and presenting information to biomedical researchers and health care professionals.

Several years of research in electronic document storage and retrieval paid off in 1991 when NLM introduced the SAIL (System for Automated Interlibrary Loan) program. An optical disc has been created that contains the page images of articles from selected journals. If an article requested via NLM's electronic system is on the disc, a copy is automatically printed and mailed (or faxed) directly to the requester. Begun as a prototype system, SAIL has important implications for the future.

In 1991, NLM awarded a contract to the University of Colorado Health Sciences Center in Denver for the first phase of a project to create, in complete anatomical detail, three-dimensional representations of the male and female bodies. The images will be developed at the university's School of Medicine from material obtained through the combined resources of the State Anatomical Boards of Colorado and Texas. The "Visible Human Project" — building a digital image library of volumetric data representing a complete normal adult human male and female — will include digital representations derived from cross-sectional photographic images from cryosectioning, computerized tomography, and magnetic resonance imaging of cadavers.

Another new Lister Hill Center project that was successfully demonstrated in 1991 is "Coach," an expert searcher program to help Grateful Med users improve their retrieval skills. The first problem Coach tackles is null retrieval — searching a subject and finding nothing. The experimental program emulates the actions of an expert searcher in diagnosing problems and determining fixes. Coach has access to several knowledge sources (primarily the Unified Medical Language System Metathesaurus) to augment or replace the user's query terms. The program will be tested and refined before it is made available to Grateful Med users.

In 1991, the National Center for Biotechnology Information introduced "Entrez," a retrieval tool that searches nucleotide and protein sequence databases and MEDLINE citations in which the sequences were published. With Entrez and a database on CD-ROM or a local network, a user can rapidly search several hundred megabytes of sequence and literature data using fast, intuitive techniques. A key feature of the system is "neighboring," which permits a user to request all references or sequences that resemble a given paper or sequence. Neighbors and links provide a powerful yet intuitive way to traverse literature and molecular sequences to access data.

Another area of research is book and journal preservation. Changes in paper-making methods in the nineteenth century resulted in acid-based paper that begins to deteriorate rapidly and, within a few decades, crumbles at the touch. During the last five years, NLM has led a campaign to encourage medical publishers to use acid-free ("permanent") paper. On October 25, 1991, the library sponsored a conference to hear what progress had been made: In 1986, merely 2 percent of the 3,000 journals indexed by NLM were printed on acid-free paper; today, almost 50 percent are.

Administration

In the year ending September 30, 1991, NLM had a total budget of $91.4 million. The number of full-time staff remained at 550.

Educational Resources Information Center

ERIC Processing and Reference Facility
1301 Piccard Dr., Suite 300, Rockville, MD 20850-4305
301-258-5500

Ted Brandhorst
Director

In FYs 1990 and 1991, ERIC appropriated about $6.7 million annually. Roughly $5.2 million (78 percent) went to support the 16 clearinghouses (contract amounts ranged from $300,000 to $374,000). The remainder was used to fund the three support contractors (ERIC Facility, for database building; ERIC Document Reproduction Service (EDRS), for document delivery; ACCESS ERIC, for outreach) and the printing of ERIC publications by the Government Printing Office.

Adjunct Clearinghouses

Adjunct clearinghouses are independent organizations that acquire and process documents in specialized education-related subject areas without cost to ERIC and then forward the results to particular ERIC clearinghouses. They are part of a strategy to

Table 1 / Database Building, 1966-1991

File	No. of Records		
	1966–1990	1991	Total
Resources in Education (RIE) (1966–)	315,239	13,155	328,394
Current Index to Journals in Education (CIJE) (1969–)	412,631	18,119	430,750
Total	727,870	31,274	759,144

develop alternative funding sources for ERIC. By the end of 1991, the ERIC system had "commissioned" five adjunct clearinghouses. The Adjunct Clearinghouse on Consumer Education was added in 1991.

Adjunct Clearinghouse for Art Education (AR)

Indiana University, Social Studies Development Center, 2805 E. Tenth St., Suite 120, Bloomington, IN 47408-2373. Tel. 812-855-3838. FAX 812-855-7901.
Sponsor: Getty Foundation.
Adjunct to: ERIC Clearinghouse on Social Studies/Social Science Education (SO).

National Clearinghouse for United States–Japan Studies (JS)

Indiana University, Social Studies Development Center, 2805 E. Tenth St., Suite 120, Bloomington, IN 47408-2373. Tel. 812-855-3838. FAX 812-855-7901.
Sponsor: United States–Japan Foundation.
Adjunct to: ERIC Clearinghouse on Social Studies/Social Science Education (SO).

Adjunct Clearinghouse on Consumer Education (CN)

National Institute for Consumer Education, 207 Rackham Bldg., West Circle Dr., Eastern Michigan University, Ypsilanti, MI 48197. Tel. 313-487-2292. FAX 313-487-7153.
Sponsor: National Institute for Consumer Education.

Adjunct to: ERIC Clearinghouse on Adult, Career, and Vocational Education (CE).

Adjunct Clearinghouse on Literacy Education for Limited-English-Proficient Adults (LE)

Center for Applied Linguistics (CAL), 1118 22nd St. N.W., Washington, DC 20037. Tel. 202-429-9292; 202-429-9551. FAX 202-429-9766; 202-659-5641.
Sponsor: U.S. Department of Education, English Literacy Grants Program.
Adjunct to: ERIC Clearinghouse on Languages and Linguistics.

Adjunct Clearinghouse for Chapter 1 (Compensatory Education, CO)

Chapter 1 Technical Assistance Center (TAC), c/o Advanced Technology, Inc., 2601 Fortune Circle E., Suite 300-A, Indianapolis, IN 46241. Tel. 317-244-8160; 800-456-2380. FAX 317-244-7386.
Sponsor: U.S. Department of Education, Chapter 1 (Compensatory Education) Program.
Adjunct to: Documents and data transmitted directly to ERIC facility.

ERIC Products and Services

ERIC Document Reproduction Service

ERIC Document Reproduction Service (EDRS) is the document delivery arm of ERIC. In February 1991, the contract to operate EDRS was awarded to CBIS Federal, Inc., a wholly owned subsidiary of Cincinnati Bell Information Systems, Inc. EDRS is now located at 7420 Fullerton Rd., Suite 100, Springfield, VA 22153-2852 (Tel. 800-443-3742). This new state-of-the-art, high-volume micrographics production facility creates more than one million ERIC fiches per month and provides on-demand service by telephone, FAX, mail, online, and in person.

ERIC Clearinghouse Publications

During 1991, ERIC Clearinghouses issued 355 publications—an average of 22 per clearinghouse. They include monographs, research reviews, bibliographies, state-of-the-art studies, interpretive studies on topics of high interest, brief digests, and other publications designed to meet the information needs of ERIC users. These ERIC system products are listed in *ERIC Clearinghouse Publications,* an annual annotated bibliography prepared by and available from the ERIC Facility.

ERIC Digests

ERIC Digests are concentrated two-page treatments of education topics designed for the educator who needs information but has little time to search or to read. Through September 1991, ERIC had published 1,204 Digests (*see* ERIC Ready Reference 10A-B for a complete list). Most are available free from the producing clearinghouse. The full texts of 698 Digests (58 percent of the total) are now available online. In DIALOG, DT = 073 will retrieve the records and Format 9 will print the full text of each.

ERIC Ready References

In 1980, the ERIC Processing and Reference Facility began producing the ERIC Ready References series to provide maximum information on individual, well-defined ERIC database-related topics in a one-page reference sheet of the "Searchlight" type. Some have been expanded to several pages (for example, the list of ERIC Digests), but all can be readily attached to responses to public inquiries. Ideas for new topics are solicited both from within the network and externally and are regularly evaluated. ERIC Ready References are available from the ERIC Facility; duplication is discouraged. Those issued to date are listed in Table 2.

Table 2 / ERIC Ready References

Ready Reference Number	Title
1	ERIC Accession Number Ranges (By year)
2	ERIC Publication Types (All available types)
3	Sample Document Résumé *(RIE)*
4	How to Use the *Thesaurus of ERIC Descriptors* for an Effective ERIC Search
5	ERIC Price Codes (Used with ERIC document citations)
6	ERIC Clearinghouses (and other network components) (Addresses, telephone numbers, and brief scope notes)
7	ERIC Fact Sheet (Annual)
8	Target Audience (New data field added in 1984)
9	ERIC Digests (What they are and how to get them)
10A	ERIC Digests (A complete list of ERIC Digests to date, arranged by title)
10B	ERIC Digests (A complete list of ERIC Digests to date, arranged by clearinghouse)
11	ERIC Microfiche Statistics (1966 to date)
12	ERIC Telephone Directory
13	ERIC Search Aids (Annotated List)
14	Document Delivery (ED and EJ) (How to get ERIC documents and articles)
15	The Costs of Becoming an ERIC Information Service Provider (Three levels)
16	What Kinds of Documents are in the ERIC Database *(RIE)?* (A ranked list)

The Identifier Authority List

Identifiers are subject index terms that supplement the concept-related terms in the *Thesaurus of ERIC Descriptors*. Most are proper names of things, people, places, organizations, laws, equipment, and so on, but some descriptors are being "tried out" to determine their staying power. So far there are more than 40,000 ERIC Identifiers, but the number of possible subjects is infinite. The *Identifier Authority List* (*IAL*) has long been a tool for ERIC Clearinghouse indexers. Beginning in 1992, it will be published by Oryx Press and will sell for $55.

CD-ROM–Based Products

Several vendors have expressed interest in a product that stores the full text of all or selected ERIC accessions on optical media, such as CD-ROM discs. University Microfilms International (UMI) created and field-tested a prototype product with positive results, but its price is perceived as high. Current economic conditions have temporarily halted most plans for full-text products. Meanwhile, ERIC is retaining original copies of the documents it processes (with an eye to possible future interest in scanning these documents), and ERIC Clearinghouses continue to identify the ERIC accessions that are the best candidates for full-text products.

User Fees and Royalties

After several years of consideration, on November 22, 1991, the U.S. Department of Education formally decided to establish a system of fees for use of the ERIC database in machine-readable form. The system will be administered by the ERIC Processing and Reference Facility, the source of ERIC database tapes. Early in 1992, recipients of ERIC data will be asked to enter into contractual arrangements with the ERIC Facility. The fee will be about 10 percent of commercial vendor charges for ERIC. Academic institutions will be asked to pay an annual flat fee. Revenues will be used to support products to improve the ERIC system.

National Education Goals ("America 2000")

During 1990 and 1991, there was a major systemwide effort to develop and promote publications addressing the six National Education Goals established by the president and state governors and embodied in the America 2000 national strategy: readiness for school; high school completion; student achievement and citizenship; science and mathematics; adult literacy and lifelong learning; and safe, disciplined, and drug-free schools. The *ERIC Annual Report* for 1990/1991 identifies 21 ERIC publications directly tied to these goals.

Publications about ERIC

For the past three years, the central ERIC office within the Office of Educational Research and Improvement (OERI) has produced the *ERIC Annual Report,* the best single source summarizing ERIC's accomplishments. These reports are available on request from Central ERIC and are also entered into the ERIC database. The accession numbers follow:

Year	Accession No.
1987	ED-301 192
1988	ED-313 057
1989	ED-322 934
1990	In process

For a description of ERIC's priorities and future directions, see Robert M. Stonehill and Ted Brandhorst, "The Three Phases of ERIC," *Educational Researcher* (January 1992).

National Center for Education Statistics Library Statistics Program

U.S. Department of Education, Office of Educational Research and Improvement
555 New Jersey Ave. N.W., Washington, DC 20208-1404

Adrienne Chute
Library Statistics Program

The NCES mandate to collect library statistics is included in the Hawkins-Stafford Elementary and Secondary School Improvement Amendments of 1988 (PL 100-297). NCES collects and disseminates statistical information on public, academic, and elementary and secondary school libraries. These data provide the only current, national data on the status and rapid changes in libraries. They are used by federal, state, and local officials, professional associations, and local practitioners for planning, evaluation, and making policy. These data are also valuable to researchers and educators for developing valid and reliable conclusions concerning the state of the art of librarianship and to improve its practice.

Public Library Statistics

Nationwide public library statistics are collected and disseminated annually through the Federal-State Cooperative System for public library data (FSCS). FSCS completed its third data collection in July 1991. Descriptive statistics are produced for nearly 9,000 public libraries.

FSCS is an example of the synergy that can result from combining federal/state cooperation with state-of-the-art technology. FSCS was the first national NCES data collection in which the respondents supplied the data electronically and which was also edited and tabulated completely in machine-readable form. NCES developed a personal computer software tool, known as DECTOP (Data Entry, Conversion, Table, Output Program), for states to use in collecting and reporting their public library data. DECTOP also checks for missing data and errors. Potentially, DECTOP technology could be extremely cost-effective and improve statistical reliability.

Note: Jeff Williams, Library Statistics Program, contributed to this article.

The respondents are the 50 states and the District of Columbia, and 100 percent of these respondents participated in the data collection. At the state level, FSCS is administered by state data coordinators, appointed by each state's chief officer of the state library agency. FSCS has become a working network. An annual training conference is provided for the state data coordinators and a steering committee that represents them is active in the development and testing of FSCS instruments and software. Technical assistance to states is provided by phone and in person by state data coordinators and by NCES staff and contractors. NCES also works cooperatively with the National Commission on Libraries and Information Science (NCLIS), the Chief Officers of State Library Agencies (COSLA), the American Library Association (ALA), and the U.S. Department of Education's Library Programs Office.

Data are available on an individual library basis and are also aggregated to state and national levels. FSCS collects data on staffing; service outlets; operating income and expenditures; size of collection; and service measures such as reference transactions; interlibrary loans; circulation; and public service hours. The next FSCS survey is scheduled for July 1992, with release of these 1992 data scheduled for Spring 1993.

The following are highlights* from the E. D. TABS "Public Libraries: 1990," electronically released in March 1992.

- There were 8,978 public libraries reported in the 50 states and the District of Columbia in 1990.

- About 16 percent of public libraries reported one or more branch libraries, for a total of 6,562 branches. The total number of library buildings reported (central libraries and branches) was 15,438. Just over 10 percent of public libraries reported one or more bookmobiles. The total number of bookmobiles reported was 1,102.

- Public libraries reported a total of 108,246 paid full-time-equivalent (FTE) staff.

- Public library operating expenditures totaled about $4.1 billion in 1990. Of this, about 63 percent was expended for paid FTE staff and about 16 percent for library collections. The U.S. total per capita operating expenditure for library legal service area population was $16.28; the highest state reporting $31.58, the lowest, $6.44.

- About 45 percent of public libraries reported operating expenditures of less than $50,000 in 1990, about 36 percent expended between $50,000 and $399,000, and nearly 19 percent exceeded $400,000.

- Nationwide, public libraries reported over 613 million book and serial volumes in their collections or just over 2.5 volumes per capita of legal service area population; the highest state reporting 4.88 volumes, the lowest, 1.49.

- Reporting public libraries covering service areas of less than 1,000 averaged 11.82 volumes per capita, while those covering 1 million or more averaged 2.13 volumes per capita.

*The numbers and percentages in the highlights are based entirely on reporting public libraries. There was no imputation for public libraries that did not respond or for items left blank. The impact of nonresponse, especially on totals, can be significant.

- Nationwide, public libraries reported collections of over 18 million audio materials, just over 702,000 films, and nearly 3.8 million video materials, totaling just over 636 million physical units.
- Public libraries reported nationwide annual library visits of nearly 507 million, an average of 3.13 per capita of legal service area population. Reference transactions were over 201 million, an average of 0.92 per capita.
- Per capita library visits were 6.01 for public libraries covering service areas of less than 1,000 and 2.26 for those that covered 1 million or more.
- Total nationwide circulation of library materials was nearly 1.4 billion or 5.75 per capita of legal service area. Highest circulation per capita was 10.21; lowest was 2.98.
- Per capita circulation was 10.04 for public libraries covering service areas of less than 1,000; it was 3.52 for those that covered 1 million or more.
- Nationwide, library materials loaned by public libraries to other libraries totaled nearly 4.6 million.

To enhance FSCS, NCES has also developed the first comprehensive, public library universe file, PLUS (public library universe system). PLUS is automated. It includes identifying information on every public library (including outlets), all state libraries, and some library systems and cooperatives. This resource will be used to improve FSCS data quality and for drawing samples for special surveys on such topics as literacy, handicapped access, library construction, and networks and cooperatives. Prior to the development of PLUS, there was no national universe file of public and state libraries and their outlets. FSCS plans to merge DECTOP and PLUS in 1992.

Additional information on FSCS may be obtained from Carrol Kindel, Postsecondary Education Statistics Division, National Center for Education Statistics, Room 311A, 555 New Jersey Ave. N.W., Washington, DC 20208-5652 (202-219-1371).

Academic Libraries

NCES surveyed academic libraries on a three-year cycle between 1966 and 1988. Since 1988, the Academic Libraries Survey (ALS) has been a component of the Integrated Postsecondary Education Data System (IPEDS) and is on a two-year cycle. ALS provides data on 4,377 academic libraries. In aggregate, these data provide an overview of the status of academic libraries nationally and statewide.

The survey collects data on the libraries in the entire universe of accredited higher education institutions and on the libraries in nonaccredited institutions with a program of four years or more. ALS produces descriptive statistics on academic libraries in postsecondary institutions in the 50 states, the District of Columbia, and the outlying areas.

NCES has developed IDEALS, a software package for states to use in submitting ALS data to NCES. IDEALS was used by 40 states in 1990.

ALS, using FSCS as a model, has established an advisory committee. Its mission is to address the need for data editing at the state level by academic librarians, and to improve timeliness of data collection, processing, and release. This network of academic library professionals works closely with the state IPEDS coordinator. NCES also works cooperatively with ALA, NCLIS, the Association of Research Libraries, the Association of College and Research Libraries, and numerous academic libraries. ALS collects data on total operating expenditures, full-time-equivalent library staff, service outlets, total volumes held at the end of the fiscal year, circulation, interlibrary loans, public service hours, gate count, reference transactions per typical week, and online services. The next Academic Libraries Survey is scheduled for Fall 1992, with release of these 1992 data scheduled for Fall 1993.

Additional information on academic library statistics may be obtained from Jeffrey Williams, Postsecondary Education Statistics Division, National Center for Education Statistics, 320A, 555 New Jersey Ave. N.W., Washington, DC 20208-5652 (202-219-1362).

School Library Media Centers

The last national survey exclusively on school library media centers was conducted in school year 1985-1986.

In 1991, a small amount of data on school libraries was collected from a sample of public and private elementary and secondary schools in the 1990-1991 Schools and Staffing Survey (SASS). Data collected included number of students served; number of professional staff and aides; number of full-time-equivalent librarians/media specialists; vacant positions; positions abolished; approved positions; and amount of librarian input in establishing curriculum. NCES expects to release data from the 1990-1991 SASS in late 1992.

In 1991, NCES, as part of the Schools and Staffing Survey (SASS), field-tested two new more-comprehensive questionnaires for school libraries. One questionnaire covered the school library media center and the other covered the school library media specialist. A statistics committee has been established by the American Association of School Librarians to advise the federal government on the statistical needs and concerns of the school library media center community. The committee will evaluate the results of the field test and help revise questionnaires and procedures for the full-scale survey. NCES, with the assistance of the U.S. Bureau of the Census, will conduct this survey as part of the 1993 Schools and Staffing Survey (SASS). This survey will be repeated every four years. Release of these data is scheduled for early 1994. The school library media specialist questionnaire will provide a nationwide profile of the school library media specialist workforce. It is also expected that these data will provide a national picture of school library collections, expenditures, technology, and services. This survey will be used to assess the status of school library media centers, nationwide, and to assess the federal role in their support.

Additional information on school library media center statistics may be obtained from Jeffrey Williams, Postsecondary Education Statistics Division, National Center for Education Statistics, 320A, 555 New Jersey Ave. N.W., Washington, DC 20208-5652 (202-219-1362).

Plans for the Library Statistics Program

NCES plans to continue collecting public library data through FSCS and to update PLUS annually. Efforts will be made in both FSCS and PLUS to improve data quality, for example, by improving state and local training. In addition, data collection efficiency will be enhanced by collecting PLUS as part of the annual data collection of public libraries. NCES also hopes to do more analyses of the FSCS data, including measuring changes and making regional, size, and input/output comparisons. Improved dissemination of data is also planned.

The collection of academic library data through IPEDS will also be continued. NCES plans to improve the quality of the data by promoting the use of IDEALS software for data collection. New data elements focusing on electronic access and other new technologies may be added to the survey. The ALS reports will contain more detailed analyses of the data.

NCES will continue school library data collection through SASS. In addition, a follow-up survey of turnover and retention issues among school librarians may be conducted.

The first survey of topical interest in libraries, using the Postsecondary Education Quick Information System, is planned for FY 1993. NCES is also planning a survey of state library agencies for 1993 and has been working cooperatively with the staff of the Federal Library and Information Center Committee (Library of Congress) on preliminary plans for a federal libraries survey.

Selected Publications

- *Public Libraries in Forty-Four States and the District of Columbia: 1988; An NCES Working Paper* (November 1989).
- *E. D. TABS: Academic Libraries: 1988* (September 1990).
- *E. D. TABS: Public Libraries in Fifty States and the District of Columbia: 1989* (April 1991).

NCES publications are generally available through the Superintendent of Documents, Government Printing Office, Washington, DC 20402-9325. Tel. 202-783-3238.

Selected Data Files and Electronic Release

- Public Libraries in Forty-Four States and the District of Columbia: 1988 (March 1990).
- Public Libraries in Fifty States and the District of Columbia: 1989 (May 1990).
- Academic Libraries: 1988 (October 1990).
- E. D. TABS: Public Libraries: 1990 (March 1992). Electronically released through the OERI Toll-Free Electronic Bulletin Board System (EBBS). For more information, call Joyce Benton, 202-219-1547.

NCES data files are generally available on computer diskette through the U.S. Department of Education, Office of Educational Research and Improvement, Data Systems Branch, 555 New Jersey Ave. N.W., Washington, DC 20208-5725.

National Association Reports

American Library Association

50 E. Huron St., Chicago, IL 60611
312-944-6780, 800-545-2433

Patricia Glass Schuman
President

As budget cuts resulting from a sluggish economy took their toll on libraries and library users nationwide, the American Library Association (ALA) mobilized a campaign in 1991 to remind Americans of the need to support their libraries and librarians.

The Rally for America's Libraries was launched at the association's annual conference in June in Atlanta. Those speaking on behalf of libraries included the Reverend Jesse Jackson, shadow senator for the District of Columbia, and U.S. Representatives Newt Gingrich (R-Ga.), Major Owens (D-N.Y.), and Liz Patterson (D-S.C.). The campaign continued with the Rally on Wheels, which took the library support message to seven communities on the way to the final rally in Washington, D.C., before the opening of the second White House Conference on Library and Information Services. With media coverage by the Associated Press, *The New York Times,* CBS-TV "Sunday Morning," and the "Larry King Radio Show," the rally was a highly visible example of ALA's leadership in efforts to develop, promote, and improve library and information services and librarianship.

Founded in 1876, ALA is the world's oldest and largest library association, with 52,893 members (49,752 personal, 2,947 organizational, and 194 special members). Its priorities are access to information, legislation and funding, intellectual freedom, public awareness, personnel resources, and library services, development, and technology.

The association encompasses 11 divisions focused on various types of libraries and library services and 5 offices that deal with intellectual freedom, outreach services, personnel resources, public information, and research. In addition to its Chicago headquarters, ALA maintains a Washington, D.C., office and an editorial office for *Choice,* a review journal for academic libraries based in Middletown, Connecticut.

Conference Highlights

ALA sponsors two major membership meetings each year. The 110th Annual Conference, held June 29–July 4 in Atlanta, attracted 17,764 members, exhibitors, and

guests. The theme, selected by 1990-1991 ALA President Richard M. Dougherty, was "Kids Who Read Succeed." The Reverend Jesse Jackson was keynote speaker. Other speakers included Fred Rogers, Maya Angelou, Michael Blake, and Judy Blume. In her inaugural address, 1991-1992 ALA President Patricia Glass Schuman urged librarians across the nation to join her in fighting to protect "not just the future of libraries and librarians, but the future of the American people's Right to Know."

Highlights of the ALA Midwinter Meeting, held January 12-17, 1991, in Chicago, included remarks by Senator Albert Gore, Jr. (D-Tenn.) and presentation of a special ALA president's commendation to actress Glenn Close for her support of libraries and literacy. ALA's 1992 Annual Conference will be held June 25-July 2 in San Francisco; the Midwinter Meeting is set for January 22-28, 1993, in Denver. Divisions with upcoming conferences are the Association of College and Research Libraries, April 12-14, 1992, in Salt Lake City; the Library Information and Technology Association, September 13-17, 1992, in Denver; and the American Association of School Librarians, October 21-25, 1992, in Baltimore.

Issues

ALA addressed a range of issues during 1991, including the homeless, access to electronic information, and media censorship during the Persian Gulf war.

The association issued a legal brief urging library directors to review library access policies after a U.S. district court ruled that policies of the Morristown (N.J.) public library violated a homeless man's First Amendment right to receive information. A proposal for the federally funded Omnibus Children and Youth Literacy Through Libraries Act was the number one resolution passed by delegates at the White House Conference on Library and Information Services. The resolution was based on the position paper "Kids Need Libraries: School and Public Libraries Preparing the Youth of Today for the World of Tomorrow," prepared by ALA's three youth divisions.

ALA representatives urged that school and public libraries be included in any plan for measuring progress toward the National Educational Goals adopted by President Bush and the nation's governors. In testimony before five regional panels, they urged, among other things, that ownership of a library card be part of the assessment of school readiness.

ALA leadership went on record as supporting the Huntington Library's decision to allow unrestricted access to the California library's collection of Dead Sea Scrolls on film and as opposing proposed Department of Education rules that would prohibit basing college scholarships on race. An ALA Special Committee on Library School Closings recommended that the association focus on recasting the image of the profession as vital to society and influencing education programs to ensure that librarians are prepared to serve in the Information Age.

The ALA governing council passed the following resolutions:

- To adopt as policy Article 19 of the United Nations Universal Declaration of Human Rights supporting all peoples' right to freedom of opinion and expression.
- To oppose U.S. military intervention in the Persian Gulf and Pentagon censorship of the press.

- To call on the Soviet Union to restore library service to the citizens of Afghanistan.
- To oppose proposed changes in the ethical code for federal government employees that would exclude them from leadership in professional associations.

Washington Report

On ALA's seventeeth annual Legislative Day, held April 16 during National Library Week, some 550 library supporters from 48 states gathered on Capitol Hill to discuss library support issues with their senators and representatives.

ALA leaders testified before U.S. congressional committees on behalf of reauthorization of Title II of the Higher Education Act and funding of the Library Services and Construction Act and Department of Education library programs. They also testified in support of funding for the Government Printing Office to distribute electronic information through government depository libraries, which Congress passed. Legislation to establish the proposed National Research and Education Network (NREN), supported by ALA, was also passed and sent to the president for signature.

Intellectual Freedom

ALA was the leading plaintiff in a lawsuit challenging the Child Protection Restoration and Penalties Enhancement Act of 1990 on the grounds that the extensive record-keeping provisions, which purport to combat child pornography, in fact would place an onerous burden on distributors, such as libraries, of constitutionally protected material. The suit resulted in a restraining order delaying enforcement of the legislation.

Judith Krug, director of ALA's Office for Intellectual Freedom, testified before a Senate subcommittee on the First Amendment implications of the U.S. Supreme Court's *Rust* v. *Sullivan* decision. Krug said the ruling, which upheld new regulations barring federally funded family planning clinics from providing information on abortion, could open the door for the federal government to try to restrict libraries in the same way.

The ALA-led Coalition on Government Information honored Representative Don Edwards (D–Calif.) with its 1991 James Madison Award for leadership in protecting civil liberties and the right to privacy.

The seventh annual Banned Books Week, with the theme "Celebrating the Bicentennial of the Bill of Rights," was observed September 28–October 5, 1991. In 1992, Banned Books Week will be September 26–October 3. The event is cosponsored by ALA, the American Booksellers Association, the Association of American Publishers, the American Society of Journalists and Authors, and the National Association of College Stores.

Children's Book and Media Awards

Jerry Spinelli, author of *Maniac Magee* (Little, Brown), received the 1991 Newbery Medal for the most distinguished contribution to American literature for children published in 1990. David Macaulay, illustrator of *Black and White* (Houghton Mifflin), won the 1991 Caldecott Medal for the most distinguished American picture book for children. The awards are presented annually by the Association for Library Service to Children, a division of ALA.

The Coretta Scott King Award, given by ALA's Social Responsibilities Round Table to African American authors and illustrators, was awarded to Mildred D. Taylor, author of *The Road to Memphis* (Dial Books), and Leo and Diane Dillon, illustrators of *Aida* (Gulliver Books, Harcourt Brace Jovanovich). The Young Adult Library Services Association/*School Library Journal* Young Adult Author Achievement Award was presented to Robert Cormier for his body of work, which includes *The Chocolate Wars*. The first Andrew Carnegie Medal for excellence in children's video went to *Ralph S. Mouse,* produced by George McQuilkin and John Matthews (Churchill Films).

Public Awareness

ALA launches phase II of the Rally for America's Libraries on Freedom of Information Day, March 16, 1992, with ALA President Patricia Glass Schuman and other ALA leaders appearing on radio shows to rally support for libraries and librarians. Listeners will be able to call a 900 number to "Say Yes to Your Right to Know."

The Call for America's Libraries campaign runs through National Library Week, April 5-11, 1992, with the theme "Your Right to Know: Librarians Make It Happen." Participants include members of the ALA Speakers Network, established in 1991 with funding provided by a World Book–ALA Goals Award. Titled "A United Voice," the project provided media training and support materials for 60 leaders in the profession.

ALA again sponsors the nation's biggest pro-literacy event, the Great American Read Aloud/Night of a Thousand Stars, on April 8, 1992. More than 1,000 libraries participated in the 1991 event, held during National Library Week (April 14-20). Guest readers included TV host Kathie Lee Gifford, actor Charlton Heston, columnist Art Buchwald, the legendary disc jockey Wolfman Jack, and actress Ellen Burstyn. The theme was "Kids Who Read Succeed." In 1993, National Library Week will be April 18-24.

Well-known faces on ALA's 1991 celebrity "Read" posters included actors Harrison Ford and Denzel Washington and the band R.E.M. Some of the country's leading rap artists urged young people to read and support their libraries in radio public service announcements produced by the Brooklyn Public Library and distributed nationally by ALA. Children were encouraged to be Gold Medal Readers in a national reading program tied to the 1992 Olympic Games developed by ALA with *Sports Illustrated for Kids* magazine.

Special Projects

President Bush joined in honoring the Bell Atlantic/ALA Family Literacy Project, a winner in the American Business Press's first annual Points of Light competition. In 1991, 26 libraries in the Mid-Atlantic region received grants of $5,000 for projects to help low-literate parents share books with their children.

ALA's American Association of School Librarians helped launch the Technology for Teaching Project to develop high tech solutions to learning challenges in the

Information Age. Other participants are AT&T, IBM, US WEST Communications, the American Association of School Administrators, and the National Education Association. ALA's Library and Information Technology Association joined with IBM to award PALS in Libraries grants to enhance library literacy programs.

ALA's contribution to the nation's quincentennial observance of Columbus's voyages included the "Seeds of Change" exhibition developed with the Smithsonian Institution Traveling Exhibiting Service with $500,000 from the National Endowment for the Humanities (NEH). The exhibition will tour 60 public libraries beginning in January 1992. A second traveling exhibition, based on the New York Public Library's "New World, Ancient Texts" exhibit, is being developed with a $311,460 NEH grant.

ALA and the Modern Poetry Association are developing a program to revitalize reading and discussion of American poetry with support from NEH. The program will be offered at 20 public libraries in Spring 1992.

Through ALA's Books for Romania project, some 240,000 books and journals with an estimated value of more than $4 million were donated to the Central University Library in Bucharest after it was destroyed in the "Christmas Revolution" of 1990. In the fourth year of the Library/Book Fellows Program, supported by the U.S. Information Agency, ALA placed 11 librarians in positions abroad.

Officers and Staff

Patricia Glass Schuman, president of Neal-Schuman Publishers, took office as ALA 1991–1992 president at the Annual Conference in Atlanta. Marilyn Miller, chairperson of the University of North Carolina library school in Greensboro, was elected ALA vice president/president-elect for 1992–1993. Staff appointments at ALA headquarters included Delstene Atkinson, director of development; Prudence Dalrymple, director, Office for Accreditation; Eileen Fitzsimons, program officer for the Reference and Adult Services Division; Pamela Goodes, press officer, Public Information Office; Althea H. Jenkins, executive director of the Association of College and Research Libraries; Emily Melton, secretariat to the Executive Board; Mattye L. Nelson, director of the Office for Library Outreach Services; Carol S. Nielsen, program officer for the new Office of the President; and Linda Waddle, deputy executive director of the Young Adult Library Services Association.

Publishing Highlights

ALA Publishing, which published 51 titles in 1991, announced a historic agreement with Random House to distribute some of ALA's reference books for the general consumer during the next three years. Association publications include *Using the Public Library in the Computer Age: Present Patterns, Future Possibilities*; *Information Freedom and Censorship: World Report 1991*; *Library and Information Services Today: The Yearly Chronicle*; and *The Whole Library Handbook*.

Booklinks: Connecting Books, Libraries, and Classrooms, a magazine spin-off for educators from ALA's *Booklist* review journal, began regular bimonthly publication in September 1991. Circulation approached 20,000 by the end of the year.

Special Libraries Association

1700 18th St. N.W., Washington, DC 20009
202-234-4700

Mark S. Serepca
Director, Communications

More than 13,000 Special Libraries Association (SLA) members put knowledge to work in corporations, government agencies, universities, hospitals, museums, associations, and other organizations with specialized information needs. The 14-member board of directors establishes policy, and the professional staff carries out day-to-day operations. SLA has 55 chapters throughout the United States, Canada, and Europe; 28 subject area divisions; 4 caucuses; and 42 student groups.

Facilitating Professional Growth

Each year thousands of SLA members benefit from the association's educational programs and publications, which are carefully designed to meet members' needs. A premier annual event is the association conference. More than 5,000 people attended the eighty-second conference in San Antonio, Texas, in 1991. The program included myriad learning opportunities—workshops, exhibits, continuing education courses, field trips, and informal networking.

The November 1991 State-of-the-Art Institute had a timely theme: "Information in Eastern and Central Europe: Coming in from the Cold." The program provided practical information and insights for members of the information community with business interests in the region.

The 1991 Regional Continuing Education Program introduced "Management of Information Technologies" and brought back by popular demand "Mainstreaming the Special Library." Sessions were held in Ann Arbor, Baltimore, Kansas City, Knoxville, Los Angeles, Minneapolis, New York, Pittsburgh, San Francisco, and Vancouver.

Recognizing that special librarians' professional development needs depend on their experience and organizational level, SLA offers both a Middle Management Institute and the Executive Management Program. For members who prefer to develop themselves professionally at home, five cost-effective and convenient self-study programs are available. The most recent addition is "Database Design: An Introductory Guide to Creating a Database." Courses on budgeting, indexing, and presentation skills will follow.

In 1991, the nonserial publications program was streamlined to make more and better books available to members on a variety of topics. Publications range from introductory texts to focused research papers.

A major research project in 1991 was the Membership Needs Assessment Survey, or "Super Survey," covering member demographics and attitudes toward the organization and its programs. In Fall 1991, the association completed its most recent salary survey, as well as a special salary survey for the Private Law Libraries/Special Interest Section of the American Association of Law Libraries.

To encourage members to conduct research that will benefit the profession, the association awarded its first research grant to Joanne Marshall of Toronto, who will study "The Impact of the Special Librarian on Corporate Decision-Making." Marshall will present her findings at the 1992 SLA annual conference.

To support members with special needs and interests, the Solo Librarians Division and the Labor Issues and Diverse Issues Caucuses were formed in 1991. SLA also created six new student groups, bringing the total to 42.

Each year, SLA awards scholarships totaling more than $25,000 at both the master's and doctoral levels. In 1991, the association established the Mary Adeline Connor Scholarship for midcareer professionals.

To assist members having difficulty maintaining employment during the economic downturn, SLA published a booklet on job searches, streamlined the Employment Clearinghouse, and continued the Career Advisory Service and 24-hour jobline.

Enhancing the Profession's Image

A highlight of 1991 was the first International Special Librarians Day on April 18, during National Library Week. The event will be celebrated each year on Thursday of National Library Week.

To recognize outstanding public relations efforts by SLA members in conjunction with International Special Librarians Day, SLA created an award to be presented at the annual conference. Three other public relations awards were established to recognize individuals who have made significant contributions to the public relations goals of the profession, association unit (chapter, division, caucus), or organization for which they work.

The summer 1991 issue of *Special Libraries* featured a collection of articles on public relations offering tools and techniques for readers to use in their organizations.

Throughout the year, SLA's communications staff keeps the library and business press services informed of developments related to the profession, responds to their inquiries, and, with members' assistance, monitors media coverage to ensure that the profession is portrayed fairly and accurately. SLA staff members also assist chapters and divisions with public relations needs, including providing materials to be displayed at local conferences and meetings.

Serving as Government Relations Advocate

SLA actively participated in the second White House Conference on Library and Information Services and was an advocate for special libraries on diverse issues. A profile of the association and profession was distributed to all attendees, who included not only librarians and information professionals but also elected officials from federal, state, and local governments, corporate leaders, and other library advocates.

For Library Legislative Day, the association encouraged its members to visit members of Congress and urge them to support such legislation as bills providing library funding or increasing access to information. SLA representatives also worked with members of Congress and their staffs to ensure that libraries and information centers play an important role in the National Research and Education Network, a national information "superhighway" that will link users and computers and will speed transmission of data.

The association supported legislation to establish within the Government Printing Office a centralized location for accessing government information in electronic formats. The GPO Wide Information Network for Data Online (WINDO) would make it easier and less expensive for librarians and other interested parties to access government databases.

Among its other government relations activities, SLA

- Supported an amendment to the Copyright Act that would extend application of the fair use doctrine to unpublished works.
- Opposed proposed standards of conduct for employees of the executive branch of the federal government that would effectively prevent them from participating in an association's activities other than paying dues.
- Urged the U.S. Office of Personnel Management to revise its occupational standards for librarians and library technicians to reflect and provide compensation for the knowledge, skills, and abilities required for the profession.
- Published a paper on the need for national information policies that enhance the accessibility and usefulness of information across national borders.

Association of Research Libraries

1527 New Hampshire Ave. N.W., Washington, DC 20036

Pamela Bixby
Communications Specialist

The Association of Research Libraries (ARL), an organization of 119 major research libraries in the United States and Canada, is an advocate for research libraries in the library and scholarly communities, in government, and in the private sector. It conducts studies and serves as a forum for member institutions to consider issues and develop plans for coordinated, collective action as they adapt to changes in the world of scholarship and information, to technological developments, and to increasingly stringent economic conditions.

Statistics

ARL established the statistics program to collect and distribute data describing research libraries and to conduct research on new measures and interpretive approaches. In 1991, the program focused on three areas: government documents, access measures, and measures related to automation and electronic resources. In its decision to include government documents in counts of volumes, serial titles, and microforms, ARL collaborated with the American Library Association (ALA) and the U.S. National Center for Education Statistics (NCES). To measure access and services, ARL staff developed a group of core questions and a separate inventory of library services and facilities, to be updated every few years. ARL is also participating in a project with NCES, ALA, and the National Commission on Libraries and Information Science (NCLIS) to improve the academic library statistics collected by the NCES Integrated Postsecondary Education Data System (IPEDS), jointly moving toward national consistency in data gathering.

The 1990 *Salary Survey* shows trends in professional positions and salaries. Although more women were directors in 1990 than ever before, the ratio of men to women directors is nearly opposite that of the total professional library workforce, which is 35 percent men and 65 percent women. The 1989–1990 *ARL Statistics* reveals that rising material costs continue to threaten traditional acquisition levels. From 1986 to 1990, serials expenditures rose more than 50 percent; however, prices paid by libraries also rose more than 50 percent, to an average of $132.45 per subscription. Libraries are coping by canceling subscriptions, reducing monograph expenditures, and increasing interlibrary loan.

Communications and Scholarly Relations

The addition of a communications specialist, responsible for publication production, fulfillment, and press and general information, is credited with an increase in the association's productivity in 1991. Minutes of several membership meetings were published during the year: "Higher Education Reform in the 1990s," "Exploring the Future of Information Sciences," and "Is the Library a Place?" The staff also compiled and produced a comprehensive publications catalog.

ARL continues to build strategic alliances with other national organizations. Working closely with the Association of American Universities, ARL staff prepared a conceptual document on research library agendas based on ARL Strategic Program objectives. The association was represented at meetings with the National Humanities Alliance, the American Council on Education, the Society for Scholarly Publishing, and the American Council of Learned Societies, of which it is now an affiliate member.

Membership Meetings

The spring meeting, "Is the Library a Place?" held in conjunction with the Canadian Association of Research Libraries in Montreal, Quebec, focused on trends in library facilities. Guest speakers included architects, consultants, and library directors. The fall meeting, "Building a New Agenda: Economic Pressures, Technological Innovation, and Access to Information," sought to develop a consensus among the membership on strategies for action on major issues.

Governance

Standing committees in 1991 included Information Policies, Access to Information Resources, Research Collections, Preservation of Research Library Materials, the Management of Research Library Resources, and Scholarly Communication. The Advisory Committee on ARL Statistics, Task Force on Minority Recruitment, and Working Group on Future Online Library Information Systems complete the list of governing units. The standing Committee on Scholarly Communication was formed in 1991 to encourage electronic journal experiments, develop strategies, promote change in the management of intellectual property rights, and advance alliances with other higher education groups. The new Advisory Committee on the Office of Management Services (OMS) will advise OMS on program effectiveness and performance and review the OMS business plan. The new Task Force on a National Program for Scientific and Technical Information has recommended a strategy to address the needs of research libraries in this area; a review group will follow up on these issues.

Office of Management Services

The Office of Management Services provides consulting, training, and publishing services on managing human and material resources in libraries. The OMS Information Services Program gathers, analyzes, and distributes information on contemporary management techniques through the Systems and Procedures Exchange Center (SPEC). In 1991, SPEC kits were completed on the following topics: expert systems, staff recognition programs, library information desks, technical services training programs, scholarly information centers, library services for people with disabilities, and organizational charts of ARL libraries. Two new programs are Update I: Building Effective Performance and Update II: Managing Priorities and Making Decisions. Visiting program officer Susan Barnard from Kent State University is exploring the implications of applying total quality management to libraries.

Federal Relations

The House and Senate passed NREN (National Research and Education Network) legislation in 1991. ARL staff had reviewed and commented on multiple draft bills and provided language detailing the role of libraries and education in the emerging network. ARL staff continue to review National Technical Information Service (NTIS) operations, including proposed modernization measures and opportunities for disseminating scientific and technical information via NREN. Congress passed the resolution, which ARL had supported, calling for a national permanent paper policy: P.L. 101-423. The ARL board honored Senator Claiborne Pell (D-R.I.) for his support of critical research library issues including use of permanent paper and unrestricted reauthorization of the National Endowments for the Humanities and the Arts (NEH and NEA).

ARL recommended higher authorization levels and an emphasis on networking and access to information resources for Higher Education Act (HEA) Titles II and VI section 607. The full report and executive summary of *The Higher Education Act, Title II-C Program: Strengthening Research Library Resources — A Ten-Year Profile and an Assessment of the Program's Effects upon the Nation's Scholarship* were presented as evidence at a congressional hearing on HEA. Hiram Davis of Michigan State University testified on behalf of ARL.

Proposals to impose fees on users of government information led ARL to protest and to join a coalition to oppose such future measures. ARL's upcoming federal agenda includes the provision in the reauthorization of the Paperwork Reduction and Federal Resources Management Act of 1990 for a single point of access to government information via the Government Printing Office (GPO) and promotion of an Internet connection for GPO.

ARL is working to minimize the impact of the Supreme Court's ruling on *Rust* v. *Sullivan,* which upholds the legality of regulations that prohibit federally supported family planning clinics from providing information referral services or counseling related to abortion. The ruling could profoundly influence freedom of expression and federally funded programs. Other issues on ARL's government relations platform include the Regional Bell Operating Companies' bid to manufacture equipment and provide information services; privacy issues revolving around security in networking and federal monitoring of electronic, voice, and data communications; the granting of copyright to federal agencies, which might lead to restrictions on access and use; indirect costs of libraries; the roles and responsibilities of national libraries; and the disposition of federal records.

Collections Services

The Collections Services program addresses a range of collection management and preservation issues facing research libraries. ARL's collection development strategies include promoting federal and foundation support for collections of national importance; improving the structure of effective collection development programs, including the North American Collections Inventory Project (NCIP); providing collection management consulting services; and developing collection management training programs. The preservation program includes advocating broad-based participation in national preservation efforts in the United States and Canada, developing preservation programs in member libraries through the Preservation Planning Program, and monitoring the technological developments that influence preservation goals.

With support from the Andrew W. Mellon Foundation, ARL and the Northeast Document Conservation Center (NEDCC) jointly sponsored a roundtable on mass deacidification in September. Staff and committee members work closely with the Commission on Preservation and Access and the Division of Preservation and Access of the National Endowment for the Humanities. In 1991, the association published the 1989–1990 *ARL Preservation Statistics* and *Preservation Program Models,* which describes the major components of effective preservation programs and supersedes earlier minimum guidelines for preservation programs.

Access and Technology

ARL addresses issues related to scholarly information resources — bibliographic control, technology, and public service. The Committee on Access to Information Resources is investigating a distributed cataloging program that would link collection strengths to cataloging priorities, and it prepared a white paper on the "Evolution of Electronic Resource Sharing." The Task Force on Scientific and Technical Information (STI) recommended a stronger presence for ARL in efforts to define a national STI strategy. The Task Force on Telecommunications identified several needs, including a focal point for coordinated management of technology-related projects within ARL and an operating plan.

ARL joined the HEIRAlliance, an evolving umbrella organization to bring together the projects of ARL, CAUSE, and EDUCOM. Among its proposals are a joint newsletter and a closer working relationship between the Coalition for Networked Information (CNI) and the National Telecommunications and Networking Task Force.

Office of Scientific and Academic Publishing

With the objective of maintaining and improving scholars' access to information, the Office of Scientific and Academic Publishing (OSAP) works to influence the production, dissemination, and use of scholarly and scientific information. Following OSAP's investigation of the merger of Pergamon and Elsevier, the world's two largest scientific, technical, and medical (STM) publishers, ARL communicated its concern about the merger's effect on library acquisitions to the Justice Department and the Federal Trade Commission. U.S. regulatory agencies, however, ultimately approved the merger. The Scholarly Communication Committee issued a resolution to support and encourage diversity and competition in the scholarly publishing arena.

OSAP convened a meeting of representatives from learned societies and federal agencies to explore recent developments, consider their relationship to libraries and end users, and discuss possible collaboration among like-minded organizations. The information gathered from the Survey on Access to Full-Text Electronic Periodical Articles will form the basis for a more extensive report on the subject.

OSAP participated in the symposium "Cooperative Information Resources Development in the Sciences and Engineering." A critical issue surfacing at the meeting was academic ownership of intellectual creation. At the annual American Association of University Presses (AAUP) meeting, ARL speakers encouraged university presses to begin participating in the electronic academic medium. Midyear, OSAP released the first printed edition of its directory of networked academic serials, which generated much interest among member libraries as a tool for accessing and managing this serial information.

Office of Research and Development

"Meeting the Challenges of a Culturally Diverse Environment," a project awarded an H. W. Wilson Foundation grant in 1990, received a continuation grant from H. W. Wilson to complete Phase II—enhancing information services and training and consulting support. The goal of the project is to boost recruitment of a racially and culturally proportionate group of library professionals.

ARL received a $195,000 grant from the Andrew W. Mellon Foundation for a two-year project to increase understanding of the challenges in providing access to foreign materials: "Scholarship, Research Libraries, and Foreign Publishing in the 1990s." The project, undertaken in consultation with the Council of National Resource Centers and the American Academy of Arts and Sciences Midwest Center, will develop a broad consensus of priorities as well as structures and procedures for research library cooperation in maintaining foreign materials collections.

Ten ARL members participated in the Preservation Planning Program for the NEH-funded project "Supporting Collection Preservation Planning in Research Libraries." Preservation specialists served as consultants, and Margaret Child formally evaluated the program, underscoring the need to revise and expand its resources. With the support of another NEH grant, ARL will update the program's *Manual* and *Resources Notebook*.

As of September 1991, OCLC had processed some 151,800 records as part of the National Register of Microform Masters (NRMM) Recon Project, which is being jointly administered by ARL and the Library of Congress. The goal of the project is the conversion into machine-readable records of approximately 470,000 monographic reports in the NRMM Master File. ARL is seeking grant support to complete the conversion of NRMM.

Dan C. Hazen of Harvard College Library is ARL visiting program officer for the new Latin American Studies assessment project. Supported by Harvard College Library, the Research Libraries Group, and by several ARL libraries, the project will evaluate progress in providing machine-readable access to bibliographic records in Latin American studies in North American research libraries and the extent to which the needs of Latin American specialists have been met.

Coalition for Networked Information

Entering its second year of operation guided by its three parent organizations—ARL, CAUSE, and EDUCOM—the Coalition for Networked Information is working to promote creation of, and access to, information resources in networked environments to enrich scholarship and enhance intellectual productivity. The coalition grew from 118 to 151 institutions during 1991. Its priorities are modernization of scholarly publishing; provision of directories and resource information services; establishment of standards; promotion of legislation, codes, policies, and practices; and development of educational programs and packets for new users.

CNI held task force meetings in both the spring and fall and participated in the Research and Education Networking Conference and the Computers in Libraries Conference. A systems analyst jointly hired by ARL and CNI is configuring the newly installed DEC Ultrix server that will function as a node on Internet, supporting expanded electronic mail and information services.

American Society for Information Science

8720 Georgia Ave., Suite 501, Silver Spring, MD 20910
301-495-0900

Richard B. Hill
Executive Director

ASIS President Tefko Saracevic chose "The New ASIS" as the theme for his tenure, incorporating objectives for enhancing membership with increased learning opportunities and stressing continuity of leadership and direction for the association. In 1991, ASIS continued to work to bridge the gaps between the many issues and goals defined in the ASIS 2000 project for the ASIS constituency while taking an active role in developing information policy and ensuring equity of access to information. Other activities included drafting a code of ethics for information professionals and revising the ASIS educational objectives.

The 1991 annual meeting held in Washington, D.C., chaired by Nicholas Belkin of Rutgers University, featured presentations by more than 200 speakers from six continents. Among those speaking to standing-room-only crowds at plenary sessions were Kenneth Warren, science adviser to the late Robert Maxwell; Ben Shneiderman, University of Maryland; Donald A. B. Lindberg, director, National Library of Medicine; Mitchell D. Kapor, Electronic Frontier Foundation; and Frederick Weingarten, president, Computing Research Association. A highlight of the conference was a day-long symposium detailing the history, status, and prospects for full-text retrieval. Other sessions focused on areas for future research and policy development, including telecommunications, standards, and networking. Participants in more than 60 special-interest and contributed-paper sessions explored technical topics of domestic and international concern.

ASIS continues the tradition of exploring a major information science research topic at the annual midyear meeting. "Multimedia Information Systems" drew more than 600 attendees for an intensive look at research and applications with potential for redefining the work computers do for humans in both learning and work environments.

History of ASIS

When founded in 1937 as the American Documentation Institute (ADI), the society consisted of scientific and professional organizations, foundations, and government agencies oriented toward solving information-related problems using a promising new medium, microfilm. At that time, microfilm offered the first practical alternative to paper documentation and represented an exponential increase in the amount of information that could be stored and transmitted.

Over the years, the leaders of ADI recognized that the association could have greater impact on the burgeoning information profession by emphasizing the *science* of information rather than the *medium*. By the late 1960s, ADI had amended its by-laws to include individual members and had changed its name to the American Society for Information Science. Since then, ASIS has expanded its role within the information profession and today is active in the development and application of information technologies and techniques.

SIGs and Chapters

Since the early 1970s, many ASIS activities have been carried out under the auspices of chapters and Special Interest Groups (SIGs) created by the membership to represent their interests. More than 50 local and student chapters throughout the United States, Canada, Europe, and Asia serve the professional needs of members in specific geographic areas. Each chapter gears its program of activities to the needs of its membership. Special Interest Groups provide members with news and updates on the latest research in information science and technology, with special emphasis on the potential application of recent developments. An SIG exists for virtually every technology and subject area in information storage and retrieval.

1992 Initiatives

In 1992, ASIS President Ann Prentice (University of South Florida) will focus on marshaling resources to prepare for trends in the near future that will affect information professionals and their work environments. The 1992 midyear meeting in Albuquerque, New Mexico, May 27-30, will examine "Networks, Telecommunications, and the Networked Information Revolution." Brewster Kahle of Thinking Machines

Corporation, Vinton Cerf of the Corporation for National Research Initiatives, and Paul Peters of the Coalition for Networked Information will address members at plenary sessions. The 1992 annual meeting in Pittsburgh, Pennsylvania, October 26–29, will have as its theme "Celebrating Change: Information Management on the Move." Speakers will include Nobel laureate and National Medal of Science winner Herbert Simon and John Marous, chief executive officer of Westinghouse Corporation.

Awards

The 1991 Award of Merit, the association's highest honor, was presented to Roger K. Summit in recognition of his work as a researcher, educator, critic, businessman, and scholar and for his ongoing contribution to information science. Commemorating the founders of ASIS, the Watson Davis Award for outstanding and continuous contributions and dedicated service to the society was given to Mickie Voges. The ASIS Research Award for a systematic program of research that extends beyond a single area of study and has significant impact on information science went to Abraham Bookstein, University of Chicago. A special award, presented for only the seventh time, was given to Senator Albert Gore, Jr., for "his integrity, global vision, technological prescience, and continued leadership in the public policy debate on technology issues."

Other 1991 award winners were David C. Blair, University of Michigan, Best Information Science Book Award, for *Language and Representation in Information Retrieval;* Donna Harman and Gerald Candela, National Institute of Standards and Technology, Best JASIS Paper Award; and Diane H. Sonnenwald, Rutgers University, ISI Information Science Doctoral Dissertation Scholarship.

Publications

In 1991, ASIS published Volume 26 of the prestigious *Annual Review of Information Science and Technology (ARIST),* edited by Martha E. Williams; and Volume 27 of the *Proceedings of the ASIS Annual Meetings,* edited by José-Marie Griffith. Other publications included *Advances in Classification Research: Proceedings of the First SIG/CR Classification Research Workshop* and *Interfaces for Information Retrieval and Online Systems: The State of the Art,* edited by Martin Dillon.

In addition, ASIS continued publication of two leading information science periodicals. *The Journal of the American Society for Information Science,* published for ASIS by John Wiley and Sons, is a refereed scholarly and technical publication. The *Bulletin of the American Society for Information Science,* published by ASIS, is a newsmagazine covering information science issues, practical management topics, and news of people and events in the information community.

Summary

The activities of the American Society for Information Science emphasize providing services to information professionals in their rapidly changing work environments and increasing public awareness of their importance and value. Focusing on education, networking, and professional interaction, ASIS works to bridge the gaps between researchers and practitioners and serves as adviser to other organizations and government leaders on the value of information and of the information profession. Its programs are intended to broaden the impact of the profession and the members it represents and enhance their effectiveness.

Association of American Publishers

220 E. 23 St., New York, NY 10010
212-689-8920

1718 Connecticut Ave. N.W., Washington, DC 20009
202-232-3335

Judith Platt
Director of Communications

The Association of American Publishers (AAP), the principal trade association of the book publishing industry in the United States, was established in 1970 through the merger of the American Book Publishers Council and the American Educational Publishers Institute. The association has approximately 240 member firms located in every region of the United States. AAP members produce hardcover and paperback books in every field—general trade, textbooks and educational materials, reference works, and scientific, medical, technical, professional, and scholarly publications—as well as journals, loose-leaf services, and a range of educational and testing materials. In 1982, AAP broadened its membership base to include publishers of freestanding multimedia products, including computer software and online databases. The special nonvoting affiliate membership, created in 1987, is open to nonpublisher firms directly involved in the industry.

AAP works to expand the market for American books, journals, and software both at home and overseas. Association programs are directed toward promoting intellectual freedom at home and abroad; strengthening the U.S. copyright system; promoting literacy and expanding educational opportunities; fostering respect for U.S. copyrights in other parts of the world; helping member publishers manage their companies through practical educational programs; and providing members with up-to-date information on government policies, trade conditions, legislation, and other factors affecting the industry. AAP speaks for the publishing industry whenever its voice needs to be heard.

The association is structured to serve both the general and specific needs of its members. "Core" programs deal with such general-interest matters as copyright, postal issues, the First Amendment and international freedom to publish, tax and trade issues, education and library funding, and new technology. They are carried out with the guidance of standing "core" committees.

Each of the association's six divisions concerns itself with a specific market area: general trade, mass market paperbacks, elementary and secondary school publishing, publishing for the higher education market, professional and scholarly publishing, and the international marketplace. Each division has its own executive body to provide general direction within the framework of AAP's overall program.

Association policy is set by an eighteen-member board of directors elected for four-year terms. The chairperson serves for two years. Jerome Rubin (Times Mirror) began his second year as AAP chairperson on April 1, 1991. Ambassador Nicholas A. Veliotes, president of the association, manages the association within the guidelines set by the board.

AAP maintains offices in New York City and Washington, D.C., with approximately thirty-five professional and support staff members.

Highlights of 1991

- According to figures compiled by AAP, industry sales totaled $15.4 billion in 1990.
- A significant court victory was achieved in the copyright infringement suit against Kinko's.
- A major consumer market study of book buyers was undertaken with AAP support.
- Literacy promotion events included the annual Evening of Readings in New York City and the Little Flower reading awards.
- The AAP Reading Initiative sponsored its second Children and Books workshop.
- AAP extended the fight against international piracy to Japan and Puerto Rico.
- At a dinner on Capitol Hill cohosted by AAP on September 19, author Jonathan Kozol spoke to members of Congress and the Bush administration about inequities in the public education of poor children.
- The association held its twenty-first annual meeting in Naples, Florida. Jeremiah Kaplan, former president of Macmillan and Simon & Schuster, received the sixteenth Curtis Benjamin Award for creative publishing.
- Other AAP awards presented in 1991 included the following: Harold T. Miller, retired chairperson of Houghton Mifflin, received the School Division's Mary McNulty Award; Kenneth Zeigler (West) received the Higher Education Division's Achievement Award; Edward Booher, former chairperson of McGraw-Hill, received a special posthumous award for his distinguished contribution to college publishing. The Professional and Scholarly Publishing Division's Hawkins Award went to Harvard University Press for *The Ants*.

Divisions

General Publishing Division

The General Publishing Division (GPD) represents publishers of fiction, nonfiction, poetry, children's literature, and reference and religious books. Its programs, often carried out in conjunction with other AAP divisions, seek to broaden the audience for books. The division maintains close ties with the bookselling and library communities, wholesalers, and authors' groups through a series of joint liaison committees. It provides major support for literacy programs, the National Book Awards, and the reading promotion programs of the Center for the Book in the Library of Congress. Joseph Kanon (Houghton Mifflin) chaired the division during 1991.

The AAP Reading Initiative, a project of the Children's Publishing Committee to promote the integration of children's literature into the educational curriculum, sponsored its second Children and Books workshop on April 27, 1991. Publishers, reading professionals, educators, and researchers explored the use of children's books in the classroom. A survey of more than 5,000 elementary school principals in twenty-one states showed increasing use of children's trade books in the classroom. Under the Teachers as Readers Project, cosponsored by the Reading Initiative and the Virginia Reading Association, local school districts in Virginia received grants to set up teacher reading groups in 1991.

The division continued its informative series of Publishers Forum luncheon seminars. The 1991 programs covered such topics as special sales, marketing to retailers, and overseas sales. In cooperation with the Paperback Publishing Division, GPD again sponsored an Evening of Readings to benefit the Literacy Volunteers of New York City (LVNYC). The event featured First Lady Barbara Bush as guest of honor and raised more than $300,000 for LVNYC's literacy work. More than 350 people attended the symposium "The Coming Revolution in Bookselling," cosponsored by GPD and PEN American Center in observance of National Book Week.

Working with AAP's Postal Committee and the U.S. Postal Service, GPD developed a pilot program to use electronic scanning technology to return the more than 300,000 books (valued at some $9 million) that become separated from their shipping containers in the U.S. mail each year. The pilot program at the USPS Bulk Mail Center in Greensboro, North Carolina, was so successful that, with the support of the Postal Service, AAP announced its readiness to assist all bulk mail centers in installing scanning capability. AAP will regularly update an electronic database to provide the Postal Service with current information on corporate changes in the industry.

GPD hosted a second meeting with members of the American Wholesaler Booksellers Association in October to continue the publisher/wholesaler dialogue begun the previous year. Through its liaison committee with the American Booksellers Association, the division undertook a campaign to promote books as gifts during the 1991 holiday season.

Higher Education Division

The Higher Education Division (HED) is concerned with all aspects of marketing, production, and distribution of textbooks and related software materials for postsecondary education. The division maintains close ties with the National Association of College Stores, the American Association for Higher Education, and other groups concerned with the college publishing market. Carl Tyson (McGraw-Hill) was chairperson during 1991.

More than 135 publishers and guests attended the Ninth Annual Higher Education Division Meeting in Washington, D.C., May 20–22. Among the highlights was presentation of two awards for distinguished contributions to college publishing: Edward E. Booher, who brought McGraw-Hill's College Division to prominence during his four-decade career, received a posthumous award, and Kenneth Zeigler, who stepped down as division chairperson after two years, received the James F. Leisy Higher Education Division Achievement Award.

For the fifteenth year, the division sponsored its PUBCENTER at the annual meeting and exhibit of the National Association of College Stores, held in Indianapolis, Indiana, in April. HED also sponsored an exhibit at the annual meeting of the American Association for Higher Education in Washington, D.C., in March and participated in the fourth AAP/AAHE Roundtable at the meeting. The 1991 Roundtable focused on incentives for authoring textbooks.

A revised series of Study Skills booklets was published in 1991. The decision to revise the series stemmed from profound changes in the demographic makeup of high school and college students since the series was first published in 1975. The eight-booklet series, which is part of the division's student outreach program, covers such topics as improving reading skills, taking advantage of textbooks, dealing with technical material, test taking, and getting the most out of college, and includes guides for nontraditional students and students for whom English is a second language. Following publication of the new series, HED announced the donation of more than 100,000 booklets from the previous edition to schools and libraries in Eastern Europe.

Each year, HED sponsors the AAP/WEST seminars for publishers in the western United States. The Spring 1991 seminar, "The Electronic Pinata," was conducted by futurist Paul Saffo; the fall seminar examined interactive technologies. For the third year, HED and Apple Computer, Inc., cosponsored a seminar on emerging technologies. Held in New York on November 15, the conference offered a look at the latest technological developments and their application to the educational market.

In the wake of the recent court ruling against Kinko's Graphics Corporation for copyright infringement (see under "Copyright Committee" later in this report), HED established the Permissions Task Force to help the higher education community comply with U.S. copyright law. The task force's program includes development of the PUBNET Permissions System (see under "PUBNET" later in this report), a one-page guide for faculty members on how to request copyright permission, and the newly revised and updated *Questions and Answers on Copyright for the Campus Community*, published jointly by AAP and the National Association of College Stores and endorsed by the Association of American University Presses. A full-page ad in the *Chronicle of Higher Education* reassured the college community of the continued availability of "course packs" as teaching tools.

In Fall 1991, HED began disseminating the self-adhesive return mailers developed to aid college professors in returning unwanted complimentary or review copies of textbooks. The division also published the 1991 edition of the *College Textbook Publishers Greenbook*.

International Division

The membership of AAP's International Division (ID) reflects the full spectrum of the general AAP membership in market and size. The division is concerned with marketing American books and related products overseas through direct sales, copublishing ventures, sales of English-language and translation rights, and promotion of English as a second language. Richard Essig (Simon & Schuster) is chairperson.

ID offers a variety of educational programs to assist U.S. publishers in strengthening international operations and facilitates their participation at international book fairs. The division serves as liaison with the U.S. Information Agency, the State and Commerce Departments, the World Bank, and other agencies concerned with promoting American books overseas. Through its International Copyright Protection Committee, ID seeks to secure overseas markets for American books by putting foreign copyright pirates out of business. Damages received from pirates who are successfully prosecuted help to fund this program.

The division publishes *Inside Export,* a bimonthly newsletter announcing trade opportunities for American book and journal publishers in overseas markets. It contains export statistics, detailed market analyses, and information on projects funded by the World Bank and other global funding agencies. The newsletter is available to non–ID members on a subscription basis. In Fall 1991, the division issued *The Handbook of International Rights,* the first publication to deal comprehensively with principles and practices of international rights.

At a special ID-sponsored meeting in the AAP New York office on March 21, Canadian tax officials and U.S. publishers discussed the implications of the Canadian Goods and Services Tax and its effect on U.S. publishers doing business in Canada. The division was also involved in successful efforts to persuade the Indian government to rescind foreign exchange restrictions on book importers that required importers to post letters of credit in the amount of 200 percent of the value of each shipment.

The division's Export Statistics Committee continues to gather international sales data. The results of its first AAP International Rights survey will be released in 1992. As part of its educational program, ID sponsored a series of seminars and workshops during 1991, including "Buying a Book: Are You Getting the Most for Your Money?" and "Protecting Your Overseas Markets." "Publishing and Bookselling around the World" was a full-day program at the 1991 ABA Convention.

During 1991, the division kept the membership informed of efforts to amend the Australian copyright law. In direct communications and through an Australian representative, AAP expressed its concern over the erosion of the right of territorial exclusivity as an important component of copyright. The amendments went into effect December 23, 1991.

ID plans to invite several senior publishing executives from Eastern Europe to spend three to four weeks at U.S. publishing houses during 1992 to become familiar with marketing, finance, production, and distribution operations. The foreign visitors can then serve as contacts for their American hosts in future dealings with Eastern Europe.

Antipiracy: The International Copyright Protection Committee

The International Copyright Protection Committee operates under the administrative umbrella of the International Division. Its activities, however, are carried out in conjunction with AAP's domestic copyright activities. During 1991, AAP consolidated significant antipiracy enforcement successes in Taiwan, Korea, and Singapore; opened a new enforcement front in Puerto Rico; took action to end infringement by a Japanese-language school; and worked with other U.S. groups to achieve meaningful protection for intellectual property under the General Agreement on Tariffs and Trade (GATT).

Information provided by the International Intellectual Property Alliance (of which AAP is a founding member) resulted in the inauguration of "Special 301" investigations by the U.S. Trade Representative of copyright abuses in Thailand, India, and China. The investigations could result in retaliatory trade action against these countries. As a result of joint efforts by AAP and the British Publishers Association, four copy shops in Singapore were enjoined from infringing works of member publishers.

Three raids on Korean pirates during February 1991 netted four truckloads of pirated books. The pirates issued a statement of public apology to AAP and the publishers whose works they had infringed. In Taiwan, prison terms were imposed on pirates convicted of illegally printing and selling U.S. medical books. Civil damages and court costs were also levied against them. Other legal actions have almost eliminated book piracy from the country's major cities.

In July, AAP filed a copyright infringement suit against a commercial copy shop in Puerto Rico and moved to end piracy of AAP members' publications by a large Japanese-language school in Tokyo. Working through the International Intellectual Property Alliance, AAP sought extended "fast-track" negotiating authority for current GATT talks and the North American Free Trade Agreement and is seeking high-level intellectual property protection in both accords.

Paperback Publishing Division

The Paperback Publishing Division (PPD) focuses on issues of special concern to mass market paperback publishers. Along with the General Publishing Division, PPD is an active sponsor of literacy programs and cosponsors the annual Evening of Readings. Jack Hoeft (Bantam Doubleday Dell) is division chairperson.

Notwithstanding a successful litigation effort and the vigilance of the PPD Stripped Books Committee, stripped books continue to be a problem, in both U.S. and foreign markets. ("Stripped" paperbacks are books whose covers have been removed and returned to the publisher for credit. The coverless books are rendered unsalable.) During 1991, the division approached the problem on several fronts. The PASS ad campaign was developed to warn against the sale of stripped books, and formal investigations have been conducted at home and internationally. The division instituted the industrywide practice of printing a warning against the sale of stripped books in all paperback books. The American Wholesale Booksellers Association and the Council for Periodical Distributors Associations have cooperated in this effort.

The division again sponsored a Book Preview program at the 1991 NACS meeting and at a meeting of the National Council of Teachers of English. The program features a slide show previewing upcoming titles along with a printed bibliography. PPD also sponsors Bookstop, a cost-effective cooperative exhibits program that allows publishers to exhibit books at a fraction of the cost of an individual exhibit. With GPD, the division publishes the annual *Exhibits Directory* providing information on more than 500 meetings and exhibits of special interest to publishers.

PPD supported the Consumer Market Study carried out by the Book Industry Study Group. The results were to be announced in January 1992. In an effort to develop and support environmentally sound practices, the division inaugurated a survey of industry practices for disposing of paperback book remainders. Questionnaires were sent to wholesaler organizations to gather information on waste generation and methods used for recycling or disposal.

The division's Publicity Committee meets regularly with media representatives to raise the profile of paperback books. During 1991, the committee met with Roger Cohen (*New York Times*), Matthew Flam (*New York Post*), and others to encourage coverage of paperback books. The division also joined GPD and others in protesting the elimination of the *New York Times* Saturday book review. The division's Rack Clearance Center, now entering its fourteenth year of operation, acts as liaison between participating publishers and wholesalers, auditing reimbursement claims for mass market paperback book racks installed in retail locations.

Professional and Scholarly Publishing Division

The Professional and Scholarly Publishing Division (PSP) is concerned with technical, scientific, medical, and scholarly materials. Division members produce books, journals, computer software, loose-leaf services, databases, and CD-ROM products. Professional societies and university presses play a key role in the division's activities. Robert Bovenschulte (*New England Journal of Medicine*) was division chairperson during 1991.

The PSP annual meeting in Washington, D.C., drew a record number of participants. Featured speakers included Cokie Roberts, National Public Radio's congressional correspondent, and Timothy S. Healy, S.J., president of the New York Public Library. The outstanding professional and scholarly publications of the previous year were honored at an awards banquet on February 6. The R. R. Hawkins Award went to Harvard University Press for *The Ants* by Bert Holldobler and Edward O. Wilson. First-place book awards were made in thirteen subject categories, and awards were also presented in three categories for journals and for excellence in book and journal design and production. PSP will return to Washington, D.C., for its 1992 annual meeting.

The division publishes the quarterly newsletter *PSP Bulletin*. Its Electronic Information Committee monitors and participates in various electronic publishing projects. PSP-sponsored workshops in 1991 included "Orientation to PSP Marketing" and "Fundamentals of Copywriting." The division plans to offer its intensive journals-publishing course, cosponsored by International STM, again in Spring 1992.

School Division

The School Division is concerned with publishing for the elementary and secondary school (K–12) market. The division works to enhance the role of instructional materials in the education process, to secure increased funding for these materials, and to simplify the processes under which educational materials are "adopted" by various states. A bridge between the publishing industry and the educational community, the division represents educational causes at the state and local levels and maintains an effective lobbying network in key adoption states. Buzz Ellis (Macmillan/McGraw-Hill School Publishing) served as division chairperson in 1991.

The School Division's 1991 annual meeting was held in Boston January 14–15. Harold T. Miller, retired chairperson and chief executive officer of Houghton Mifflin and a pioneer in educational publishing, was awarded the eighth annual Mary McNulty Award.

The various committees of the School Division carried out a full agenda during 1991. Committees in the key adoption states of California, Florida, and Texas worked closely with legislative advocates in those states on specific legislation. The Critical Issues in Educational Publishing Committee sponsors programs on topics of immediate concern to educational publishers. A highlight of the year was a seminar in April on multicultural education and its impact in the classroom, on textbooks, and on families. The Research Committee sponsored the Visual Learning seminar. Other standing committees of the School Division include Statistics, Textbook Specifications, and the Depository Task Force.

At the national level, in addition to providing continued support for the Committee for Education Funding, division members met several times with Colorado Governor Roy Romer, chairperson of the Task Force on Implementing National Education Goals. They also met with staff members of the Office of Technology Assessment and the Office of Educational Research and Improvement and other government officials.

AAP Senior Vice President Donald Eklund, representing the School Division, participated in the National Summit on Mathematics Assessment sponsored by the National Academy of Science's National Research Council in Washington, D.C., in April 1991. Eklund also participated in the conference "Designing Textbooks for the Year 2001" at Stanford University.

Requests for the School Division's *Helping Your Child Succeed in School* continue to grow. The division has given the Southwire Company of Carrollton, Georgia, permission to print and distribute the booklet to its 5,000 employees.

PUBNET

The year 1991 was a banner year for PUBNET, AAP's electronic book-ordering service. A fifth birthday celebration was staged at the National Association of College Stores annual meeting and exhibit in Indianapolis in April, complete with a race car–decorated birthday cake. Reflecting the growing importance of PUBNET, at its meeting in December the AAP board approved the hiring of a full-time PUBNET managing director.

Originally established to serve the college publishing community, PUBNET has expanded in recent years to trade publishing. Several task forces have been established to explore the potential for serving other segments of the industry. The School Task Force will investigate the integration of school orders into the PUBNET system. The Printers and Manufacturers Systems Committee will review a possible PUBNET link between publishers and printers/binders. The MarketWatch Task Force will develop a store sales reporting network between publishers and bookstores. The Library Task Force will investigate a link between publishers and library book acquisition systems. And the PUBNET Permissions Task Force will facilitate obtaining permissions for college course packs.

Following are some highlights of 1991:

- Almost 750,000 documents (350,000 orders and 400,000 acknowledgments) were processed on the network, a 49 percent increase over 1990.
- PUBNET began the year with 1,300 participating stores and ended with 1,675.
- Seven publishers were added to the network during 1991, bringing the total to 35.
- Electronic Data Interchange (EDI) links were expanded between PUBNET publishers and their international operations offices: HarperCollins in Australia, the United Kingdom, and New Zealand; Houghton Mifflin in Canada; and Simon & Schuster in Canada.

• PUBNET began offering the Small Publishers Workstation communications package, which enables any publisher with an IBM-compatible PC and a modem to participate in the network.

PUBNET Permissions, an electronic system for requesting copyright permission, concluded its beta (preliminary) test phase in Summer 1991, and conducted a pilot program, open to PUBNET member college stores, for the remainder of the year. Following the pilot program, other college stores, campus copy centers, copy shops, and other organizations will be able to participate.

Core Committees

Affirmative Action Committee

The Affirmative Action Committee develops programs to aid publishers in meeting the challenges of an increasingly diverse workforce. The committee coordinates AAP support for the Howard University Press Book Publishing Institute and serves as liaison with such professional groups as Black Women in Publishing and the Minority Recruitment Committee of the American Newspaper Publishers Association. Cynthia Lawson (Addison-Wesley) is committee chairperson.

The committee sponsored the second Preparing for Workforce 2000 workshop on June 18. Looking at the social dynamics that often lead to misunderstandings among employees of diverse backgrounds, the workshop stimulated awareness of and sensitivity to cultural and gender differences.

The committee organized an industrywide advertising campaign to attract members of minority groups to careers in book publishing. The advertisement, which appeared in the magazines *Black Enterprise, Essence, Northstar,* and *Hispanic,* generated an excellent response. Participating publishers received hundreds of résumés from highly qualified applicants, and campus recruiters reported a heightened awareness of publishing career opportunities among minority students.

Copyright Committee

The Copyright Committee coordinates AAP efforts to protect and strengthen the proprietary rights of authors and publishers and to enhance public awareness of the importance of copyright. Edward Stanford (Simon & Schuster) chairs the committee.

The year's most significant copyright event was the federal court decision, handed down March 28, in *Basic Books, Inc. v. Kinko's Graphics Corporation.* The decision was a complete victory for AAP and the eight publishers who sued Kinko's for copyright infringement and a resounding affirmation of the rights of copyright holders.

Coordinated by AAP, the suit, brought in Spring 1989, charged that Kinko's widespread practice of photocopying portions of copyrighted works and assembling these materials into college course "anthologies" without permission was a clear violation of U.S. copyright law. The court agreed with the publishers in almost every respect and enjoined Kinko's from copying and anthologizing copyrighted materials without prior permission. Kinko's was ordered to pay $510,000 in statutory damages, one of the largest statutory damage awards ever made in a copyright case, and to pay attorney's fees.

On October 16, 1991, the eight plaintiff publishers, AAP, and Kinko's, signed an agreement ending the litigation. The agreement stipulated specific fees and damages (totaling $1,875,000) to be paid by Kinko's and set up guidelines to govern the future relationship between Kinko's copy shops in the United States and publishers both within and outside AAP. In turn, AAP and the plaintiff publishers agreed not to sue Kinko's for any infringing anthologies produced before the date of the federal court ruling.

In the wake of the Kinko's agreement, the AAP board approved an aggressive enforcement program to monitor compliance and to ensure that Kinko's and other copy shops that obey the copyright law are not forced to compete with shops producing illegal anthologies. The enforcement program is well under way, and AAP has collected and analyzed a large number of questionable anthologies to ascertain whether necessary permissions were sought and obtained. At year's end, AAP had begun contacting copy shops that have infringed copyrights of member publishers.

AAP's six-year campaign to end copyright violations by the British Library's Document Supply Center (DSC) came to a successful conclusion in 1991. DSC had been photocopying and supplying copyrighted materials to commercial document delivery services and for-profit corporations in the United States and elsewhere. Under an agreement that went into effect April 1, 1991, DSC will collect royalty fees. The British Copyright Licensing Agency will distribute them to domestic and foreign rights holders, and the U.S. Copyright Clearance Center will act as central recipient for royalties paid to U.S. rights holders.

The Copyright Committee coordinates AAP participation as a friend of the court in key copyright cases. AAP filed an amicus brief in the *Feist* case involving the copyrightability of white-pages telephone directories. On March 27, the Supreme Court ruled that such directories are not copyrightable, leaving the publishers of many directories and other compilations to consider alternative or additional means of protection.

AAP filed an amicus brief in *Wright* v. *Warner Books,* a case dealing with "fair use" of unpublished materials, in which it urged an appellate court to uphold a lower court ruling that use of Richard Wright's unpublished letters by his biographer did not constitute copyright infringement. A favorable ruling came down on November 25. In another case dealing with the copying of Cable News Network broadcasts, AAP joined a coalition of media and broadcast organizations asking the appellate court to rehear the case. The court has agreed, and the case was to be reheard in February 1992.

Use of copyrighted materials by commercial document delivery services and other copyright issues related to new technologies are matters of ongoing concern for the committee. During 1991, the Copyright Committee commissioned a study of the document delivery market in the United States. The Professional and Scholarly Publishing Division commissioned a parallel examination of the international document delivery market. The findings of both studies, along with an analysis of the copyright implications of recently passed legislation to establish a nationwide supercomputer network, were to be presented at the 1992 PSP annual meeting scheduled to be held in Washington, D.C., in February. The committee was active on a number of other legislative initiatives involving copyright. [For details, see the report "Legislation Affecting Book Publishing" in Part 2 — *Ed.*]

Freedom to Read Committee

The Freedom to Read Committee coordinates AAP's efforts to promote and protect First Amendment rights and intellectual freedom. These efforts include intervention in court cases, lobbying at the national and state levels, and educational programs and publications. The committee works closely with allied organizations — such as the American Library Association's Intellectual Freedom Committee and the American Booksellers Foundation for Intellectual Freedom — and coordinates AAP participation as a member of the Media Coalition, a group of trade associations formed to defend First Amendment rights. Betty Prashker (Crown) is committee chairperson.

The committee has focused much attention in recent years on New York's "Son of Sam" law, which required anyone committing a crime in the state to turn over profits from book and movie contracts to a Crime Victims Board. The money was to be held in escrow for distribution to victims (and certain creditors) who successfully sued for civil damages. AAP filed an amicus brief in the U.S. Supreme Court in support of Simon & Schuster's challenge to the law's constitutionality. On December 10, the Supreme Court struck down "Son of Sam," saying that by singling out certain types of expression based on content and imposing financial restrictions on that expression, the law is inconsistent with the First Amendment.

The committee was involved in a number of other cases with First Amendment implications. On January 15, the New York State Court of Appeals dismissed for the second time *Immuno AG* v. *J. Moor-Jankowski,* a libel case involving a letter to the editor of a scientific journal. AAP's amicus brief called the suit a "blatant . . . effort to use the libel laws to silence responsible criticism."

AAP also submitted an amicus brief to the Supreme Court in *Masson* v. *Malcolm,* a libel case involving "fabricated quotes." Although the Supreme Court decided that there was a cause of action for libel and sent the case back to the lower court, it did not, as had been feared, articulate such rigid guidelines for the accuracy of quotations that authors, publishers, and journalists could be sued for minor editorial changes.

In another friend-of-the-court brief, AAP joined a broad coalition of media groups asking the Supreme Court to rule unrestricted punitive damage awards unconstitutional. Although the case involved insurance fraud, media groups were concerned about the effects of such awards in libel cases. The Court, however, failed to impose limits on punitive damages.

On May 15, the committee sponsored "Can You Say That in 1991?" a workshop on libel, invasion of privacy, and the handling of confidential source material. Similar workshops were held in 1984 and 1989. During the year, the committee was concerned with a number of legislative issues with First Amendment implications. [For details, see the report "Legislation Affecting Book Publishing in Part 2.]

Observations marking the two-hundredth anniversary of ratification of the Bill of Rights took place throughout the year, and the Freedom to Read Committee participated in many. "The Freedom to Read Statement," originally issued by AAP and the American Library Association and subsequently endorsed by other groups, was reissued in poster format in celebration of the bicentennial. The statement outlines the obligations of publishers and librarians to make available the widest diversity of views and expression. The committee compiled and published "Read All about It," an extensive bibliography of recent books dealing with the Bill of Rights and the Constitution. The publication was made available to publishers, librarians, booksellers, and teachers.

AAP was well represented at many symposia and conferences marking the bicentennial: the First Amendment Congress held in Richmond, Virginia, October 27–29; "Protecting the First Amendment: Setting the Course for the 1990's," a symposium sponsored by the ALA Freedom to Read Foundation, November 7–10; a Caspar College/Wyoming Humanities Council symposium on the Bill of Rights in June; and "To Ourselves and Our Posterity," a conference on teaching the Bill of Rights, sponsored by the American Bar Association, in Washington, D.C.

International Freedom to Publish Committee

The International Freedom to Publish (IFTP) Committee is the only group formed by a major publishers' organization anywhere in the world for the specific purpose of defending and promoting the freedom of written communication internationally. The committee monitors human rights issues and provides moral support and practical assistance to publishers and authors outside the United States who are denied basic freedoms. IFTP works closely with other human rights groups, including Human Rights Watch and PEN International. Lisa Drew (William Morrow) is committee chairperson.

With the approval of the U.S. and Cuban governments, a mission sponsored by IFTP visited Cuba April 16–20 to make contact with the Cuban publishing community. The ten-member delegation included AAP Chairperson Jerome S. Rubin (Times Mirror), AAP President Nicholas Veliotes, IFTP Director Jeri Laber, and members of the Fund for Free Expression and Americas Watch. The mission's objectives were to examine the Cuban publishing scene with a view toward possible book trade, to establish contact with Cuban publishers and authors, to explore the feasibility of AAP participation at the Havana International Book Fair without Cuban censorship restrictions, and to make presentations on behalf of a number of Cuban prisoners of conscience.

In addition to an officially arranged program of meetings with Cuban government officials, the Cuban Institute of the Book, and Cuban publishers and authors, members of the delegation met with Cuban human rights activists. The delegation pressed Cuban authorities about restrictions on freedom of expression and presented a list of Cubans imprisoned for their views.

On November 11, the International Freedom to Publish Committee and the Fund for Free Expression formally protested the apparent resumption of "business as usual" with Iran as the one-thousandth day following the death sentence against author Salman Rushdie passed. The joint statement called on the U.S. government to speak out clearly and forcefully against the death threat and the violence that has resulted from it, including the murder of Rushdie's Japanese translator in Tokyo. AAP also supported publication by Article XIX, the international anticensorship organization headquartered in London, of a chronology of events since February 14, 1989, when the *fatwa* (death sentence) was pronounced against Rushdie.

During 1991, the committee made small grants to several beleaguered writers and publishers. One was to support the legal defense of three Indonesian students imprisoned for possession and distribution of literature; another provided start-up money for the Kenyan Documentation Center; a third was to help establish a literary journal in Kenya; and a fourth provided support for PIK, an independent publishing house in Moscow.

The committee continued protesting to governments about denials of freedom of expression to writers and publishers worldwide. A protest registered with the U.S. government took issue with the military censorship imposed on journalists covering the Persian Gulf war.

The committee received a number of distinguished visitors during 1991, including Argentinian author and publisher Jacobo Timmerman, a former political prisoner whose release came about as a result of strong pressure from the U.S. government and various human rights groups, among them AAP's International Freedom to Publish Committee, and Valentin Oskotsky, head of the independent Soviet publishing house PIK.

New Technology Committee

The New Technology Committee focuses on use of new technologies to produce print and electronic publications, channeling information to the AAP membership on the opportunities these technologies present both as publishing tools and products. Vane Lashua (Reader's Digest) and Paul Constantine (John Wiley) cochaired the committee in 1991.

A major 1991 committee project, undertaken with Northeast Consulting Resources, Inc. (NCRI), was the seminar series "Mapping the Future of Publishing." The seminars, held in New York in February and May, provided a framework for publishers to develop alternative scenarios of the future of the industry, broadening their perception of the corporate strategic planning process.

The committee invites industry representatives to make presentations on various developments. At an open meeting of the committee on May 29, representatives of Discis Knowledge Research demonstrated its new technology, capable of adding voices, sound effects, and graphic images to text to create multimedia electronic books. At a second open meeting on September 6, the executive director of the Optical Publishers Association discussed standardization of optical publishing media. A representative of Apple Computer demonstrated the new video compression architecture called Quicktime, and provided an advance look at Apple's notebook computer. The consumer-based multimedia product Compact Disk Interactive was highlighted at a third open meeting in December.

The committee monitors the work of the Electronic Publishing Special Interest Group (EPSIG), which promotes use of AAP's Electronic Manuscript Standard. The standard describes procedures for keying and marking up books, articles, and serials on computer. A special tutorial program was held in New York on December 10 to familiarize publishing personnel with the standard.

Postal Committee

The Postal Committee coordinates AAP initiatives on postal rates and regulations, monitoring the activities of the U.S. Postal Service and the independent Postal Rate Commission and intervening on publishers' behalf in formal proceedings before the commission. The committee directs AAP lobbying activities on postal legislation before Congress. Stephen Bair (Time-Life Books) chairs the committee.

On January 4, 1991, the U.S. Postal Service accepted under protest rate increases recommended by the Postal Rate Commission. The protest reflected the board of governors' concern that the new rates, which went into effect February 3, would not provide sufficient revenue for the Postal Service.

The overall rate increase for bound printed matter (the class most heavily used by book publishers) was 14 percent. A classification change strongly advocated by AAP permits bound printed matter to be mailed without advertising. The library rate increased 1.56 percent for the first pound and 4.35 percent for the next 2 to 7 pounds, with no increase for materials weighing more than 7 pounds. Of interest to publishers of journals and other periodicals eligible for second-class mail privileges is the fact that although rates increased overall, the existing rate design was not changed and editorial content is not subject to a zoned rate. On balance, book and journal publishers fared no worse than other mail users.

The Postal Committee was involved in developing the electronic scanning project for books lost in the mail (see earlier under "General Publishing Division") and the self-adhesive return mailer for review textbook copies (see earlier under "Higher Education Division").

The committee has worked strenuously (and, so far, successfully) to head off federal legislation that would allow states to impose state sales and use taxes on mail-order sales. The constitutionality of such taxes will be considered by the U.S. Supreme Court during its current term. The case involves a decision by the North Dakota Supreme Court holding that it is not unconstitutional for the state to force the Quill Corporation, an Illinois-based direct marketing company, to collect and remit taxes for purchases made by residents of North Dakota. The U.S. Supreme Court had ruled in an earlier case that a direct marketer is not required to collect such taxes if it has no business presence in the state. However, the North Dakota decision held that the earlier ruling was premised on an "economic and commercial landscape that no longer exists." AAP has joined the Magazine Publishers Association in an amicus brief urging the U.S. Supreme Court to find the North Dakota tax unconstitutional.

AAP actively worked to retain full funding for "revenue forgone" in the postal appropriations bill. These funds are used to subsidize nonprofit mailers (see the report "Legislation Affecting Book Publishers" in Part 2).

The consensus in Washington that the Postal Reorganization Act of 1971 needs an overhaul appears to be growing. The Postal Service commissioned a report by the Institute of Public Administration (IPA) on the postal rate-making process, which recommends changes and simplification of the process. The Postal Committee will continue to be active in this area in 1992.

Administrative Committees

Four administrative committees direct and coordinate AAP member services. Composed of both in-house and outside counsel of AAP member companies, the Lawyers Committee meets quarterly to consider legal issues affecting publishers in such areas as libel and invasion of privacy, the First Amendment, antitrust, and product liability. The Insurance Committee monitors the AAP-sponsored group insurance plan for member publishing companies. The Statistics Committee oversees preparation of monthly and annual statistical reports published by AAP. And the Compensation Survey Committee coordinates and oversees preparation of the *AAP Survey of Compensation and Personnel Practices in the Publishing Industry,* published every two years.

Public Information Program

Through its Public Information program, AAP keeps the trade press, the general press, and the membership informed about its activities and initiatives. The program includes regular mailings to press organizations, individual interviews with the media, press briefings, and coverage of AAP events. The AAP *Monthly Report* provides timely and comprehensive information on developments in Washington, in the committees, and in the divisions. The staff also issues the AAP *Annual Report* and informational brochures.

Political Action Committee

The AAP Political Action Committee (AAP/PAC) allows members to take an active part in the political process. The committee supports Senate and House candidates of both political parties who are responsive to and concerned about issues vital to American publishers. Although modest, AAP/PAC funds play an effective part in the association's work to promote and protect the interests of the industry in Washington, D.C.

American Booksellers Association

560 White Plains Road, Tarrytown, NY 10591
914-631-7800

Carol Miles
Director of Research

Overall, bookstores have proven remarkably resilient during the current recession. Their retail sales—reported monthly by the Current Retail Trade branch of the Bureau of the Census (U.S. Department of Commerce) and compiled since mid-1991 by the ABA Research Department for regular publication in *Newswire,* ABA's weekly newsletter—showed growth in every month of 1991, compared with the same month in 1990. Based on preliminary figures, retail sales in bookstores for the first 11 months of 1991 totaled approximately $6.83 billion, an 8.6 percent increase over the 1990 sales total of about $6.29 billion for the equivalent period. By contrast, total retail sales for the industry for the same period were essentially flat, rising only 0.7 percent over the 1990 figure.

Corroborating and complementing the Census Bureau data are the findings of two national surveys commissioned by ABA's Research Department and disseminated through the association's ongoing public relations program handled by the Allen Communications Group. First, a pre-Christmas Gallup survey revealed that approximately 113 million adult Americans (60 percent of those 18 or older) agreed that they would "like to receive a book as a gift," up from the 54 percent reported in an identical 1990 Gallup survey. A post-holiday survey conducted by the Wirthlin Group indicated that approximately 108 million Americans (58 percent of all adults 18 or older) gave and/or received a book during the 1991 holiday season, a 24 percent increase over the 1990 total of approximately 87 million adults, which in turn was a 21.5 percent increase over the 1989 total of about 72 million. Over the two-year period from 1989 to 1991, the increase is an impressive 50 percent. Of particular significance, nearly 90 million adults (48 percent) *gave* a book or books during the 1991 holiday season, an increase of about 43 percent over 1990.

The Annual Convention and Trade Exhibit

The 1991 ABA Convention and Trade Exhibit, held at New York City's Jacob K. Javits Center, was a resounding success. A total of 35,911 bookpeople registered, breaking the attendance record for the event. The show's theme was "Bookstore USA, Celebrate the Freedom to Read." Acclaimed author and artist Maurice Sendak created a limited-edition lithograph illustrating the theme of the show; it was also used to banner the exhibit hall. A number of seminars and speakers addressed current challenges to free expression, including Pulitzer Prize–winning author and journalist Anthony Lewis. The Book and Author breakfasts, once again sold out, featured such authors as Brock Cole, Gloria Steinem, Stephen King, and Alice Walker. Authors reading from their works on two evenings at the ABA Reading Room included Margaret Atwood, Norman Rush, Ethan Canin, and Jane Smiley.

Although the trade show is unquestionably the highlight of the annual convention, the popularity of the educational component continues to grow, as evidenced by the packed four-day schedule. Seminar, panel, and workshop topics ranged from "The Sales Rep's Role in the '90s" to "Community Outreach" and "Positioning African-American Books in Our Marketplace." In addition, there were roundtables for bookselling operations of various sizes and specialties, including feminist, mystery, travel, recovery, scientific-technical/professional/scholarly, and African-American, to name a few. Children's bookselling was featured in preconvention panels cosponsored by the ABA/CBC Joint Committee, and special sections on the trade floor for children's books (second year) and sci-tech/professional books (new in 1991) both drew heavy traffic.

One of the show's highlights was presentation of the first American Booksellers Book of the Year (ABBY) award, created by ABA's Honors and Awards Committee to honor the book that booksellers most enjoyed hand-selling during the previous year. The winning book, selected by ABA member bookstores, was Forrest Carter's *The Education of Little Tree,* which has subsequently enjoyed a long run on the *New York Times* paperback bestseller list. The four ABBY honor books were *The Civil War, Cold Sassy Tree, The Shell Seekers,* and *When I Am an Old Woman I Shall Wear Purple.* The ABBY award carries a $5,000 prize, in addition to a specially commissioned cast bronze statue.

A second undisputed highlight of the 1991 convention was the pre-opening Carnegie Hall gala sponsored by the American Booksellers Foundation for Free Expression (ABFFE). The event, which drew more than 1,800 people, was hosted by Garrison Keillor to benefit the foundation's ongoing fight against censorship. Entertainers included Marvin Hamlisch, Estelle Parsons, Sir Peter Ustinov, Mariette Hartley, Alan Dershowitz, William Warfield, Maurice Sendak, and the Boys Choir of Harlem. The first ABFFE Free Expression Award was presented to Czechoslovakian president and author Vaclav Havel, once imprisoned by the former Communist government for his plays. The award was accepted on his behalf by noted First Amendment attorney Martin Garbus. During the annual ABA gathering of bookpeople, ABFFE benefited from the sale of T-shirts, mugs, and books at the Good Foundations Store on the trade exhibit floor, as well as from the silent auction of Bantam Doubleday Dell's 6,500-title backlist.

First Amendment Initiatives

During 1991, ABFFE made great strides in promoting awareness and understanding of First Amendment issues to a wide audience through its quarterly newsletter, *Free*

Expression, as well as through the book *Censorship and First Amendment Rights: A Primer,* which ABFFE published as a guide to protecting First Amendment rights in the bookstore. ABFFE once again cosponsored Banned Books Week, during which thousands of booksellers nationwide featured in-store displays and/or activities highlighting the importance of free expression and First Amendment rights. In observance of the bicentennial of the Bill of Rights, the foundation cosponsored the rebroadcast of the original 1941 radio drama "We Hold These Truths." ABFFE continues to monitor First Amendment–related legislation on local, state, and national levels. In early May 1991, the ABFFE board voted to oppose the Pornography Victim's Compensation Act of 1991, which was before Congress, and later that month ABA President Joyce Meskis testified against the bill before the Senate Judiciary Committee.

The Publications Program

The year 1991 was one of the busiest ever for the ABA Publications Department. Besides publishing *ABACUS Expanded* (based on results of the annual financial and operations survey of member bookstores conducted by Ernst & Young under the direction of the Research Department), Booksellers Publishing, Inc. (BPI) began production on the first four titles in its new trade book publishing program under the Booksellers House imprint. These titles, the first of which is Christopher Morley's *Parnassus on Wheels,* are of particular interest to booksellers and others in the book industry. The updated and expanded 1991 ABA *Book Buyer's Handbook* features a new section listing more than 700 publishers, most of them newer and/or smaller companies than those in the main listings.

The *Daily ABA Program and Convention News* premiered at the 1991 Convention and Trade Exhibit, keeping attendees abreast of each day's events and activities with late-breaking reports from the exhibit floor and other book industry news, as well as a daily directory of exhibitors. A complete exhibitors directory for year-round reference was included in the July issue of *American Bookseller* magazine. *American Bookseller* continued its Research Reports, based on reader surveys and other research conducted by the ABA Research Department. The review board for "Pick of the Lists," the magazine's biannual review of children's books, was expanded to include experts on juvenile books from across the country. "Booksellers Choice" is a new monthly listing, by topic, of basic inventory recommended by booksellers for booksellers.

Professional Education

The association's educational programs continued to grow, with a new Booksellers School and an expanding lending library of educational videotapes. Nine booksellers schools were held at locations across the United States targeted to a variety of educational needs: prospective, basic professional, professional, advanced, children's, and staff of large stores. The graduate-level advanced business management school was held for the third consecutive year at the McIntire School of Commerce of the University of Virginia. The school for staff of large stores, based on a study of the educational needs of employees of large stores conducted by the Research Department for the ABA Education Committee, was offered for the first time in 1991. A one-day seminar in Atlanta devoted to financial management was also based on research conducted by the Research Department and is the prototype for other one-day seminars to follow.

Favorable financial results for fiscal 1991 have enabled ABA to inaugurate and continue numerous other programs for its diverse membership of some 8,000 in the book industry, more than 60 percent of which are bookstores. The association once again awarded Minority Bookseller Education Grants to cover tuition, accommodations, meals, and materials for specified booksellers schools. Recipients in 1991 were offered ten places at the Basic Professional Booksellers School held immediately before the New York Convention and five places at the other 1991 Professional Schools.

Membership Outreach

The association established two specialty membership segments during 1991 for members who sell African-American titles or science fiction titles or are interested in those fields. All ABA members received the premier issue of the two new quarterly newsletters, which ABA will continue to distribute to segment members. ABA will assist the specialty members in organizing meetings and plans to publish specialty directories in the near future. In 1992, ABA expects to expand into two other specialty areas: travel bookselling and gay and lesbian bookselling.

Other Activities

ABA joined with the Association of American Publishers and the Book Industry Study Group to sponsor a consumer-based benchmark study of book buying, the results of which appeared as the *Consumer Research Study on Book Purchasing.* As a bonus, a copy of the study was mailed to all bookseller members of the association. Continuing its program of generic book/bookstore advertising, ABA sponsored Garrison Keillor's "American Radio Company" for the third year. The weekly two-hour program — produced live during the 1991–1992 season from Manhattan's Symphony Space, as well as from other cities around the country — reaches approximately one million listeners over some 260 U.S. radio stations. Consumer research conducted by the NPD Group on behalf of the ABA Research Department and published in *American Bookseller* confirmed that the show's listeners are more predisposed toward books, reading, and bookstores than nonlisteners.

ABA *Newswire* began regular publication of a bestseller list rating the top fiction and nonfiction titles in hardcover and paperback by African-American authors or dealing with African-American subjects. Created by Faye Childs of Columbus, Ohio, and compiled monthly with the assistance of ABA's Research Department, "Blackboard" is composed of data collected from a number of general and specialty bookstores in 22 major urban markets nationwide.

Booksellers Order Service (BOS), a wholly owned subsidiary of ABA, continued to offer member stores the advantages of obtaining important bookstore merchandise shipped free-freight, with the increased purchasing power usually associated with bulk-rate orders. Besides offering various sizes of paper and photodegradable plastic bags, cotton tote bags, gift certificates, and gift wrapping paper, BOS's Book Shirt Program continues to provide cotton T-shirts imprinted with book-related quotes and, if desired, a store's name or logo. In Autumn 1991, BOS introduced the *American Spectrum Encyclopedia,* a one-volume family encyclopedia with 17,000 entries and 3,800 color illustrations designed to open a new market for bookstores. BOS also offered booksellers *Belle's Book of Books,* a premium tie-in to the blockbuster Walt Disney animated feature *Beauty and the Beast.*

Through the general legal information service initiated by ABA in 1991, member bookstores can fax queries regarding such topics as federal antitrust, trade regulation, and employment law to the service with the assurance of receiving general information in return within 48 hours. ABA's property, casualty, and workers' compensation insurance program entered its second year with steady growth in the number of participants and premium volume.

Together with the National Book Foundation, ABA compiled a list of the 213 winners of the National Book Award since its inception. The list was made available free to ABA member bookstores with a poster commemorating National Book Week. Finally, in 1991, the 3,000-plus-volume ABA Library and Resource Center, an integral part of the Research Department, was enhanced as an industry resource with the hiring of a professional librarian. The librarian has begun indexing ABA's extensive information resources and converting the library catalog to a computer database. The volume of telephone, mail, and fax inquiries handled by the center continued to expand during the year, as did the number of in-person visits to the facility, serving not only ABA members but also students and others in the book industry.

Book Industry Study Group, Inc.

160 Fifth Ave., New York, NY 10010
212-929-1393, FAX 212-989-7542

William G. Raggio
Assistant Managing Agent

The Book Industry Study Group is a membership-supported, not-for-profit research organization that provides the publishing industry throughout the world with accurate and up-to-date research information about the U.S. publishing industry. In 1976, its first year of operation, BISG undertook a study to determine the research needs of each sector of the industry. In 1991, in conjunction with the American Booksellers Association and the Association of American Publishers, BISG produced the *1990/1991 Consumer Research Study on Book Purchasing* prepared by the NPD Group, which updates the 1983 study.

BISG began FY 1991–1992 with a membership of 230 organizations from all sectors of the publishing industry, including publishers, wholesalers, book manufacturers, suppliers, retailers, libraries, and several trade organizations. The four 1991–1992 elected officers make up the executive committee: Laura Conley, John Wiley & Sons, chairperson; James Buick, Zondervan Corporation, vice chairperson; Seymour Turk, consultant, treasurer; and Robert W. Bell, Lehigh University Bookstore, secretary. The Board of Directors is made up of the elected officers and Paul

Alms, Rand McNally; DeWitt C. Baker, Natalis Press; Laraine Balk, Grolier Publishing Group; Robert Boyer, P. H. Glatfelter Company; John F. Boylan, Arcata Graphics Book Group; Robert Duncan, Macmillan/McGraw-Hill School Publishing; William Flavell, R. R. Donnelley and Sons; Albert N. Greco, Gallatin Division of New York University; W. Boyd Griffin, Hearst Books, Business Publishing Group; Richard S. Halsey, State University of New York; Paul McLaughlin, Time Inc. Book Company; Jean Reynolds, Millbrook Press; George Slowik, Jr., *Publishers Weekly*; Michael Strauss, Baker & Taylor; Kurt van Steemburg, S. D. Warren Company; Jon Wisotzkey, Little Professor Book Centers; and William Wright, Bantam Doubleday Dell.

Highlights of 1991

Publications

BISG issued its first annual *Book Industry Trends,* edited by John Dessauer, in 1977. *Trends 1991* provides a six-year history and a five-year projection of book sales, in dollars and units, by market segment. It also contains figures on consumer expenditures, library acquisitions, and manufacturing expenditures for the same 11-year period and an executive summary of economic and market factors affecting each segment of the industry.

Trends and *Trends Update* are edited by Statistical Service Center Executive Director Robert F. Winter. Data in the 1991 edition are based on the 1987 Census of Manufactures. A book industry resource panel prepared the five-year projections.

Meetings and Seminars

On April 3, 1991, in celebration of its fifteenth anniversary, BISG sponsored a symposium of 20 industry leaders to discuss issues facing the publishing industry. The participants overwhelmingly agreed that the book industry must confront the problem of inadequate educational programs in the United States and charged BISG to investigate an industrywide education program. Symposium participants will review the results and present them to the industry.

BISG conducts periodic seminars to keep the publishing community abreast of industry-related developments. Each year in June BISG cosponsors the Trends Seminar with *Publishers Weekly.* The 1991 seminar focused on educational publishing and bookselling in the 1990s, with a special presentation by Donald Lamm, chairperson of W. W. Norton. The 1992 Trends Seminar is scheduled for the third week of June.

On June 25, 1992, BISG will cosponsor its second American Library Association preconference on EDI (electronic data interchange) standards for library acquisitions.

Committees and Interest Groups

BISG continues to respond to the needs of its members and the industry through the work of individual committees. The BISG Distribution Committee sponsored two seminars at the September 1991 Book PubWorld, advocating the economic advantages of warehouse automation. Among the topics discussed was use of bar-coded shipping labels for book cartons. The information in the bar codes corresponds directly to that which vendors transmit electronically using BISAC's Advance Ship Notice to identify the books shipped in each carton.

The Juvenile Special Interest Group was established to investigate areas of research that will facilitate the continued growth of this segment of the industry. The new International Interest Group will provide a forum for U.S. agents of international publishing companies.

BISAC and SISAC

BISG is developing computer-to-computer and hard-copy formats for the book and serial industries through BISAC (Book Industry Systems Advisory Committee) and SISAC (Serials Industry Systems Advisory Committee). BISAC's industry-specific formats have been in place for more than 15 years. These include Order Acknowledgement, Invoice, Title Status, Payment Advice, Frontlist Diskette, Data Transmission Protocols, Royalty Statement, and Sales Reporting formats.

In response to a request by some of its members, BISAC is developing formats based on those developed by Accredited Standards Committee (ASC) X12 – Business Data Interchange. (ASC X12 formats are similar to those of EDIFACT – Electronic Data Interchange for Administration of Commerce and Transportation, which are administered by the United Nations and used internationally.) ASC X12 subsets have been completed for Purchase Order, Purchase Order Acknowledgement, and Invoice. BISAC has completed the Advance Ship Notice format and has established two subcommittees to develop other formats. The Returns Subcommittee will seek ways to use the Advance Ship Notice and Invoice formats for book returns and credit memos. The Publishers/Manufacturers Subcommittee is developing subsets for publishers and suppliers to use in orders, acknowledgments, invoices, and schedules. The Title Status format and several Publishers/Manufacturers formats are expected to be finalized by mid-1992.

BISAC has been instrumental in selecting and promoting Bookland EAN as the bar code of choice among U.S. and Canadian book publishers. It has also been a source of basic information on ISBN, Standard Address Number (SAN), and electronic data interchange formats for the book industry.

SISAC developed a Serial Item and Contribution Identifier (SICI) that is compatible with BIBLID, an ISO (International Organization for Standardization) standard. The new SISAC standard was approved as an American National Standard on July 15, 1991. John Wiley & Sons, Pergamon, Elsevier, and Kluwer are among the many publishers now committed to placing the identifier, in bar code symbology, on the cover of all their journals.

SISAC is developing ASC X12 subsets for the transmission of serials business transactions, including order, order acknowledgment, claims, invoice, and cancellations. Drafts should be available in early 1992.

Conclusion

BISG is a multifaceted organization. It continues to rely on publishing-related communities for information and cooperation to ensure that relevant data are available on a timely basis. For 16 years BISG has achieved this goal and the organization continues to flourish.

National Information Standards Organization

Kathleen Bales

Library Applications, Development Division, Research Libraries Group

Pat Ensor

Coordinator, Electronic Information Services, Indiana State University Libraries

In 1991, information standards developers focused on organizational development to facilitate the information standards process. The National Information Standards Organization (NISO) created a plan with the following goals: to strengthen the standards process; to strengthen NISO's financial base; to improve organizational support; to improve and expand communications; and to develop educational programs.

NISO Technical Plan

The NISO Technical Plan emphasizes activities in key study areas as well as improvement of the standards process. The plan sets out both short-term tactical goals for the first year and long-term strategic objectives. During the first year, the Standards Development Committee (SDC) focused on the most important standards activities and prioritized the steps in the standards process.

The committee evaluated standards development procedures in an attempt to streamline the process. Some procedures were improved; others will be refined and added to the revised NISO Operating Procedures. To give committees support and guidance, each SDC member is responsible for monitoring SDC activities. The revisions of the Technical Plan will reflect work accomplished as well as work planned for 1992.

Key Study Areas

Standards activities that will receive special attention in the next few years are organized in key study areas: Information Systems and Services, Telecommunications and Networking, Electronic Publishing, Abstracting and Indexing, Preservation of Library and Archival Materials, and Library Equipment and Supplies.

Improving the Standards Process

In the Information Systems and Services area, several groups worked on acquisitions and fulfillment standards. As publishers are beginning to use Accredited Standards Committee (ASC) X12 electronic data interchange standards for communicating with suppliers and book dealers, the Book Industry Systems Advisory Committee (BISAC) and the Serials Industry Systems Advisory Committee (SISAC) are mapping data elements from NISO standards to ASC X12 transaction sets; NISO members are reviewing the mapping.

Standards for Computerized Book Ordering, Serial Item Identifier, Identification Code for the Book Industry (SAN), and Record Format for Patron Records all advanced through the standards process in 1991. The charge for a committee to examine all acquisition and fulfillment standards was completed before the end of 1991. Common Command Language is out for balloting. Bibliographic Interchange and Extended Latin standards are being revised. The Serials and Non-serials Holdings Statements standards were combined into a draft standard, which will also be revised.

In Telecommunications and Networking, extensive activity centered on the Information Retrieval Service Definition and Protocol Specification for Library Applications (Z39.50), both for work by the maintenance agency (Library of Congress) and meetings of the Z39.50 Implementers Group (ZIG). A revision of Z39.50 is out for balloting.

In Electronic Publishing, Standard Committee TT worked on related standards for CD-ROM but concluded that interest and support for a standard are insufficient; the committee will issue a report to NISO. A committee has been appointed to create a standard for Interface-Independent Retrieval Protocol for CD-ROM. A Format for the Submission of Data for Multimedia CD-ROM Mastering was adopted and balloted as a draft standard.

Guidelines for Thesaurus Construction, Structure, and Maintenance was balloted and will be revised, and Basic Criteria for Indexes is being revised. Both standards are in the Abstracting and Indexing study area. Committee members met to plan the revision of Abbreviation of Titles of Publications, and the committee to develop the standard for guides to microform sets has been appointed.

Preservation was an active study area in 1991. The draft standard for Eye-Legible Information in Microfilm Leaders . . . is being revised after balloting, as is the draft standard for Durable Hard-Cover Binding for Books. Permanence of Paper for Printed Library Materials is being reballoted. Committees are preparing standards for Environmental Conditions, for Storage of Paper-Based Library and Archive Collections, as well as for Environmental Conditions for the Exhibition of Library and Archival Materials. New committees will work on standards for Information to be Included in Advertisements, Catalogs, Promotional Materials; Packaging for Products Used for the Storage, Binding, or Repair of Library Material; and Library Binding and Library Prebound Books. NISO preservation standards introduced to the international standards process include the Permanent Paper standard and Durable Hardcover Binding for Books.

For the Library Equipment and Supplies study area, revision of the standard for Permanent and Durable Library Catalog Cards awaited revision of the Permanent Paper standard, so that the paper requirements of the card standard could be aligned with the paper standard. American Library Association–sponsored library shelving tests will be the basis for the new NISO standard for library shelving.

Other NISO standards activities in 1991 included final editing of Periodicals: Format and Arrangement. A draft standard for Computer Software Description was balloted and is being revised. The standards for Compiling Book Publishing Statistics and International Standard Serial Numbering were both balloted and final comments will be incorporated. NISO's publisher, Transactions, published Z39.41-1990, Printed Information on Spines; Z39.56-1991, Serial Item and Contribution Indentifier; Z39.59-1988, Electronic Manuscript Preparation and Markup; and Z39.64-1989, East Asian Character Code for Bibliographic Use.

NISO Annual Meeting

On September 23, 1991, the National Information Standards Organization hosted more than 100 attendees at its annual meeting in Boston. The theme was "Controversies of the Information Age—Lessons for Standards Makers."

Linda Garcia, project director and senior analyst of Congress's Office of Technology Assessment, described the controversies in the U.S. standards-setting process. She concluded that librarians and publishers play an important role in dealing with technologies that may increase speed and use of resources.

Michael Spring, assistant professor of information science at the University of Pittsburgh, discussed "The Next Ten Years: The Candle and the Bushel," suggesting that in creating standards, we are lighting a candle and putting it under a bushel. He believes that there will be three issues in the future of information technology standardization—access, strategy, and technology—and concluded that NISO is well placed to lead the standards process in the 1990s. To do this, he urges a focus on who makes up NISO and not on the organization itself. Members must make the investment in NISO that will propel the standards process.

Jobe B. Morrison, president and general manager of Miami Mill, and Stephen Pekich, vice president and director of operations for school publishing at Houghton Mifflin, spoke at the session "Paper Permanence and the Environment." They discussed the conflicts in permanent paper standards and recycling, myths about paper recycling, and the future.

In the session "Computer Security: What's Possible? What's Fair?" David D. Clark, senior research scientist at the Massachusetts Institute of Technology, discussed his "Computers at Risk" study. The report recommends developing a comprehensive set of generally accepted system security principles, taking short-term action that would improve the current operating environment (requiring that everyone identify him- or herself before using the system), determining the level of threat and building security awareness, clarifying export control issues, stimulating research, and establishing an organization to pursue this agenda and work for more secure technology. Franklin Davis, project manager at Thinking Machines Corporation, ended the session by describing the Wide Area Information Server (WAIS) project and relating it to security concerns.

Rick Weingarten, executive director of the Computer Research Association, summed up his perspective on the controversies of the information age on NISO program day. He concluded that the burden is on all of us to build a connected infrastructure, and standards are the way to do this, to avoid a fragmented society.

NISO Organization

The board of directors has a new chairperson, James Rush, and a new vice chairperson/chairperson-elect, Michael J. Mellinger. Lois Granick (American Psychological Association) became director for information services. Directors include Karen Runyan (Houghton Mifflin), Peter J. Paulson (Forest Press/OCLC), and Connie Greaser (Honda), representing publishing; Susan Vita (Library of Congress), Shirley Kistler Baker (Washington University), and Lois Ann Coliani (National Library of Medicine), representing libraries; and Michael J. McGill (Ameritech) and Bill Bartenbach, representing information services. Officers are the chairperson and vice chair-

204 / National Association Reports

person; Paul Evan Peters, past chairperson; and Heike Kordish, treasurer. The number of voting members stands at 63, with 20 information associates. Executive Director Patricia Harris works at offices provided by the National Institute for Standards and Technology (NIST).

Information Standards Quarterly

The quarterly NISO newsletter covers NISO and other selected information standards activities as well as international news in which NISO has an interest. The most recent incarnation of the newsletter began with the January 1989 issue and continued under the editorship of Walt Crawford, with Lennie Stovel serving as associate editor, through the October 1991 issue (vol. 3, no. 4). Pat Ensor became editor, with Steve Hardin as associate editor, as of the January 1992 issue (vol. 4, no. 1). *ISQ* is distributed to NISO voting members and information associates and is available by subscription for $40 a year. Subscription and information requests should be sent to the National Information Standards Organization, Box 1956, Bethesda, MD 28027.

International Organization for Standards

The work of the International Organization for Standards (ISO) is accomplished by Technical Committees (TCs) and Joint Technical Committees (JTCs). TC 46, Information and Documentation, is responsible for libraries, publishing, and information services, and JTC 1, Information Processing Systems, develops standards for computer hardware and systems. NISO is the body within the American National Standards Institute (ANSI) responsible for tracking and participating in TC 46 activities.

More than 100 delegates representing 18 participating members of TC 46 met in Copenhagen, May 27–31. Four working documents were registered as Committee Drafts, six Committee Drafts were registered as Draft International Standards, and seven Draft International Standards were advanced to International Standard level. New International Standards included interlibrary loan service definition and protocol specification, search and retrieval service definition and protocol specification, Glagolitic script, mathematical coded character set for bibliographic information interchange, and presentation of catalogs of standards. Areas covered by new Draft International Standards include coded character sets such as Cyrillic, Hebrew, Armenian, Latin, and Georgian, and an international standard music number.

New Committee Drafts concern Arabic coded characters, bibliographic references for electronic documents, paper permanence, and a format for bibliographic information interchange on magnetic tape. Sixteen new work items covered such areas as requirements for document storage, recommendations for binding materials and practices, interlibrary loan, and various search and retrieval specifications.

Pat Harris presented a paper at the meeting of the International Federation of Library Associations and Institutions (IFLA) about the relationship between ISO and IFLA. "Exploring the ISO/IFLA Relationship" was published in *IFLA Journal* no. 4 (1991): 358–365.

USMARC Activities

USMARC formats are an implementation of NISO standard 239.2, Bibliographic Information Interchange, and are used extensively in the United States to communicate bibliographic and related data. The media of communication range from OSI computer to computer linkage, to floppy disks, CD-ROM, computer terminal transfer, and magnetic tape. The Library of Congress maintains the formats, and MARBI (Machine-Readable Bibliographic Information) is the ALA interdivisional committee responsible for channeling advice to LC on the formats.

In 1991, in relation to multiple formats, MARBI approved the addition of field 003 to the Bibliographic, Authority, Holdings, and Classification formats. Field 003 contains the NUC symbol of the system whose control number is in the 001 field. It also recommends that LC duplicate the LC control number from field 001 in field 010 for distribution.

In the authority format, two proposals originated from the Art and Architecture Program. One was referred to LC for revision, and the other was rejected. Discussions covered the kind of notes and the kind of tagging that should be used for public display, and whether separate tags were needed for history, scope, and application instruction information.

Addition of subfield 5 to 4XX/5XX fields in the authority format was approved. (Subfield 5 is the institution to which the field applies.) Libraries will now be able to indicate local cross-references. LC is investigating whether other fields should also have subfield 5 added. Alternate Graphic Representation in Authority Records, to support authority information in non-Roman scripts, was approved, using the technique present in the bibliographic format. MARBI also discussed linking authority records under different authority control.

In the bibliographic format, the addition of subfield 3 to field 050 was approved; subfield 3 enables identification of materials held at the location given in subfield "a." This should be particularly useful for identifying microform stored in different places. Additions and changes to leader/18 were also approved. The new code "u" is defined as "unknown," and the phrase "cataloging rules" was removed from the names of values blank, "a," and "i." The definitions of some of the values were cleaned. Finally, an addition/change to bibliographic field 074 was approved, defining subfield "z" (canceled/invalid GPO item number) and making field 074 repeatable. Other discussions concerning the bibliographic format related to the new USMARC field for related source of data, handling of relationship notes, enhancing USMARC records with a table of contents, and a dictionary of data elements for online resources.

In relation to the holdings format, a change to leader/06 was approved; it separates multipart items from serial items in the type of record leader byte. The approved change of subfield 6 to subfield 8 (link and sequence number) standardized holdings and bibliographic format practices for coding same-type intrarecord field linkages.

Two proposals related to the holdings format were discussed and rejected. The addition of 008/32 for type of unit called for the addition of a type of holdings designator, as described in the NISO holdings standards. A proposal for recording version information, based on the recommendations made at the Airlie House conference on multitype versions in December 1989, was also rejected.

The Airlie House two-tier approach fits well in the existing USMARC world, but some disagreed with its assumptions, including the CC:DA Task Force on Multiple Versions. Although the cataloger can use the multiple-tier approach recommended by the task force, communication by USMARC will probably remain two-tiered.

Finally, in relation to the holdings format, sequencing multiple holdings records was discussed. Other MARBI discussions covered item level information and the US-

MARC format for holdings data, and the proposed USMARC community information format.

The Library of Congress produced the following USMARC-related publications in 1991.

- *USMARC Diskette Label Specifications.* Washington: Network Development and MARC Standards Office, Library of Congress, 1991.
- *USMARC Format for Authority Data, Update No. 4.* Washington: Library of Congress, 1991.
- *USMARC Format for Bibliographic Data, Update No. 3.* Washington: Library of Congress, 1991.
- *USMARC Format for Classification Data.* Washington: Library of Congress, 1991.
- *USMARC Format for Holdings Data, Update No. 1.* Washington: Library of Congress, 1991.

USMARC standards are available from the Cataloging Distribution Service, Library of Congress, Washington, DC 20541.

NISO Standards

Book Production and Publications

Z39.4-1984*	Basic Criteria for Indexes
Z39.5	Abbreviation of Titles of Publications
Z39.6-1983*	Trade Catalogs
Z39.13-1979*	Describing Books in Advertisements, Catalogs, Promotional Materials, and Book Jackets
Z39.14-1987	Writing Abstracts
Z39.20-1983*	Criteria for Price Indexes for Library Materials
Z39.21-1988	Book Numbering (ISBN)
Z39.22-1989	Proof Corrections
Z39.30-1982*	Order Form for Single Titles of Library Materials in 3-Inch by 5-Inch Format
Z39.41-1990	Book Spine Formats
Z39.48-1984*	Permanence of Paper for Printed Library Materials
Z39.49-1985*	Computerized Book Ordering
Z39.52-1987*	Standard Order Form for Multiple Titles of Library Materials
Z39.59-1987	Electronic Manuscript Preparation and Markup

Codes and Numbering Systems

Z39.9-1979*	International Standard Serial Numbering (ISSN)
Z39.21-1980	Book Numbering (ISBN)
Z39.23-1990	Standard Technical Report Number (STRN), Format, and Creation
Z39.33-1988	Development of Identification Codes for Use by the Bibliographic Community

Z39.47-1985*	Extended Latin Alphabet Coded Character Set for Bibliographic Use
Z39.53-1987	Codes for the Representation of Languages for Information Interchange
Z39.56-198X	Serial Issue and Contribution Identifiers
Z39.64-1989	East Asian Character Code

Indexes, Thesauri, and Directories

Z39.4-1984*	Basic Criteria for Indexes

Microforms

Z39.26-1981*	Advertising of Micropublications
Z39.40-1987	Compiling U.S. Microform Publishing Statistics

Acquisitions and Ordering

Z39.30-1983*	Order Form for Single Titles of Library Materials in 3-Inch by 5-Inch Format
Z39.45-1983*	Claims for Missing Issues of Serials
Z39.49-1985*	Computerized Book Ordering
Z39.52-1987*	Standard Order Form for Multiple Titles of Library Materials

Romanization

Z39.11-1989	System for the Romanization of Japanese
Z39.12-1989	System for the Romanization of Arabic

Technical Reports and Papers

Z39.16-1979*	Preparation of Scientific Papers for Written or Oral Presentation
Z39.18-1987	Scientific and Technical Reports — Organization, Preparation, and Production
Z39.23-1983	Standard Technical Report Number (STRN), Format and Creation
Z39.31-1976*	Format for Scientific and Technical Translations
Z39.46-1983*	Identification of Bibliographic Data on and Relating to Patent Documents
Z39.61-1987	Recording, Use and Display of Patent Application Data in Printed and Computer-Readable Publications and Services

Serial Publications

Z39.5-1985*	Abbreviation of Titles of Publications
Z39.9-1979*	International Standard Serial Numbering (ISSN)
Z39.20-1983*	Criteria for Price Indexes for Library Materials
Z39.39-1988	Compiling Newspaper and Periodical Publishing Statistics
Z39.44-1986*	Serials Holding Statements
Z39.45-1983*	Claims for Missing Issues of Serials

Z39.46-1983*	Identification of Bibliographic Data on and Relating to Patent Documents
Z39.48-1984*	Permanence of Paper for Printed Library Materials
Z39.56-198X	Serial Issue and Contribution Identifiers
Z39.59-1987	Electronic Manuscript Preparation and Markup

Statistics

Z39.7-1983*	Library Statistics
Z39.39-1988	Compiling Newspaper and Periodical Publishing Statistics
Z39.40-1987	Compiling U.S. Microform Publishing Statistics

Automation

Z39.2-1985*	Bibliographic Information Interchange
Z39.44-1986*	Serials Holding Statements
Z39.45-1983*	Claims for Missing Issues of Serials
Z39.47-1985*	Extended Latin Alphabet Coded Character Set for Bibliographic Use
Z39.49-1985*	Computerized Book Ordering
Z39.50-1988*	Information Retrieval Service Definition and Protocol Specification for Library Applications
Z39.57-1989*	Holding Statements for Non-Serial Items
Z39.59-1987	Electronic Manuscript Preparation and Markup
Z39.63-1989	Interlibrary Loan Data Elements
ANSI/NISO/ ISO 9660	File Structure of CD-ROM for Information Interchange

Standards Not Yet Approved

Z39.58-198X	Common Command Language for Interactive Searching
Z39.62-199X	Eye-Legible Information on Microfilm Leaders and Trailers and on Containers of Processed Microfilm on Open Reels
Z39.66-199X	Durable Hard-Cover Binding for Books
Z39.67-198X	Computer Software Description
Z39.69-199X	Record Format for Patron Records
Z39.71-199X	Holdings Statements for Bibliographic Items

Overage Standards Administratively Withdrawn by ANSI

Z39.1-1977*	Periodicals: Format and Arrangement
Z39.8-1977	Compiling Book Publishing Statistics
Z39.10-1971*	Directories of Libraries and Information Centers
Z39.15-1980*	Title Leaves of a Book
Z39.19-1980*	Guidelines for Thesaurus Structure, Construction, and Use
Z39.24-1976	Romanization of Slavic Cyrillic Characters
Z39.25-1975	Romanization of Hebrew
Z39.29-1977*	Bibliographic References
Z39.32-1981*	Information on Microfiche Headings
Z39.35-1979	Romanization of Lao, Khmer, and Pali

Z39.37-1979	Romanization of Armenian
Z39.43-1980*	Identification Code for the Book Industry
Z85.1-1980*	Permanent and Durable Library Catalog Cards

Standards Committees

SC R	Environmental Conditions for Storage of Paper-Based Library and Archival Materials
SC LL	Exchange of Circulation Systems Data
SC MM	Environmental Conditions for the Exhibition of Library and Archival Materials
SC RR	Adhesives Used to Affix Labels to Library Materials
SC SS	Information to Be Included in Ads [etc.] for Products Used for the Storage, Binding, or Repair of Library Materials
SC XX	Abbreviations of Captions for Holdings Statements
SC ZZ	Library Binding and Library Prebound Books
SC AC	Guides to Microform Sets
SC AD	Interface-Independent Retrieval Protocol for CD-ROM
SC AF	Acquisitions Data Elements

*This standard is being reviewed by SDC or is under revision.

Part 2
Legislation, Funding, and Grants

Legislation

Legislation and Regulations
Affecting Libraries in 1991

Eileen D. Cooke
Director, Washington Office, American Library Association

Carol C. Henderson
Deputy Director, Washington Office, American Library Association

Congress once again continued funding for federal library programs, firmly rejecting the administration's request to cut the level by 75 percent and to block-grant the remaining funds. One program for library education fellowships was increased by an astounding 668 percent to a level not seen in more than 20 years. A program for acquisition of foreign journals received funds for the first time ever.

Both are part of the Higher Education Act (HEA), which received renewed attention through the reauthorization process still under way. Congressional education committees heard multiple library witnesses at a hearing on Legislative Day, and subsequent HEA reauthorization bills rejected the administration's proposal to eliminate HEA library programs and incorporated instead the combined recommendations of the library and higher education communities.

The National Literacy Act was signed into law, creating some new programs and opening others to new literacy service providers and to community partnerships, thereby offering opportunities for libraries. Legislation to establish the National Research and Education Network (NREN) was finally enacted after a crisis-prone legislative history. The inevitable compromises chipped away at library provisions, but library participation in NREN remained intact. A proposal for the Government Printing Office Wide Information Network for Data Online (GPO WINDO), which the American Library Association (ALA) helped to develop, was introduced by the new chairperson of the Joint Committee on Printing, and has since garnered 20 organizational endorsements.

Other government information policy issues continued to simmer, including still-pending bills to reauthorize the Paperwork Reduction Act, although a different approach, the Improvement of Information Access Act, was introduced in October by Representative Major Owens (D–N.Y.). Attempts to use government information (the Federal Maritime Commission tariff database) as a revenue source were blocked, but perhaps only temporarily. Library groups continued working to narrow and improve the pending fee-for-service legislation requested by the Library of Congress.

A milestone in 1991 was the July 9-13 White House Conference on Library and Information Services, which resulted in 95 policy recommendations by the delegates. Priorities for action include support for an omnibus children's and youth literacy initiative, for NREN with library participation, and for adequate funding of library and related programs.

Funding

FY 1991 Sequester

In April 1991, a minor adjustment was necessary in the federal funding totals for FY 1991. President Bush ordered a sequester or across-the-board cut of 0.0013 percent in all discretionary domestic programs. Although the cuts were too small to be reflected when program totals are rounded off, and the process of making the cuts may have cost more than was saved, the sequester highlighted the inflexibility of the caps on defense and domestic and international spending. The caps were imposed by the budget agreement forged by congressional leaders and the administration in Fall 1990 and the Budget Enforcement Act that implemented its provisions. Spending in each of the three areas was strictly limited, and neither funds nor savings could be shifted from one category to another.

This bizarre sequester was necessary because an $8 million pork barrel provision for a university was shifted from the Pentagon to the Department of Education, providing more flexibility in how the funds could be used, but exceeding the discretionary domestic cap. The bookkeeping shift caused a small reduction in everything else in that category to accommodate the grant without breaching the cap and breaking the law. The amount cut from the Department of Education library account (LSCA and HEA II) was $1,858.

FY 1992 Library Funding

President Bush submitted his FY 1992 budget to Congress on February 4 with only $35 million proposed for Department of Education library programs—75.5 percent less than the $143 million appropriated in FY 1991. The $35 million would be targeted to only one program—Library Services and Construction Act, Title I—and could be used for only one purpose—adult literacy activities—requiring legislative change in the LSCA statute. In addition, the $35 million program would be on a $20 billion list of possible programs to be consolidated and turned over to the states, a list that included the Chapter 2 school block grant. Higher Education Act, Title II, library programs were also proposed for zeroing out. However, the II-B library career training program would be included in a proposed graduate fellowship consolidation requiring new legislation.

Congressional appropriators were openly skeptical of the administration's budget for libraries. In the end, Department of Education LSCA and HEA library programs were increased 3.4 percent to $147,747,000. The only program funded at less than the 1991 level was LSCA II, which was decreased by $2.5 million. Table 1 lists funding levels for a wide group of library and related programs.

Congress firmly and impressively rejected the administration's proposal to consolidate the HEA II-B library career training program with other graduate assistance programs, increasing II-B training by $4,349,000 to $5 million, a 668 percent in-

Table 1 / Appropriations for Federal Library and Related Programs, FY 1992
(figures in thousands)

Library Programs	FY 1991 Appropriation	FY 1992 Bush Request	FY 1992 House	FY 1992 Senate	FY 1992 Appropriation
Elementary/Secondary Education Act I Chapter 2 (including school libraries)	$ 469,408	$ 462,577	$ 474,600	$ 474,600	$ 474,600
GPO Superintendent of Documents	26,500	27,371	26,327	26,327	26,327
Higher Education Act	10,735	0	15,584	17,584	18,084
Title II-A, College Libraries	0	0	0	0	0
II-B, Library Career Training	651	0	5,000	5,000	5,000
II-B, Research and Demonstrations	325	0	325	325	325
II-C, Research Libraries	5,855	0	5,855	5,855	5,855
II-D, College Library Technology	3,904	0	3,904	6,404	6,404
VI, Sec. 607 Foreign Journals	0	0	500	0	500
Library of Congress	305,071	359,962	327,456	323,819	322,228
Library Services and Construction Act	132,163	35,000	127,163	132,163	129,663
Title I, Public Library Services	83,898	35,000	83,898	83,898	83,898
II, Public Library Construction	19,218	0	14,218	19,218	16,718
III, Interlibrary Cooperation	19,908	0	19,908	19,908	19,908
IV, Indian Library Services*	–	–	–	–	–
V, Foreign Language Materials	976	0	976	976	976
VI, Library Literacy Programs	8,163	0	8,163	8,163	8,163
Medical Library Assistance Act	14,691	16,309	14,691	14,691	14,691
National Agricultural Library	16,798	17,453	17,253	17,149	17,715
National Commission on Libraries and Information Science	732	911	750	911	831
National Library of Medicine	76,717	84,205	84,874	85,858	85,612

Table 1 / Appropriations for Federal Library and Related Programs, FY 1992 (cont.)
(figures in thousands)

Library-Related Programs	FY 1991 Appropriation	FY 1992 Bush Request	FY 1992 House	FY 1992 Senate	FY 1992 Appropriation
Adult Education Act	$ 238,828	$ 250,727	$ 280,000	$ 280,510	$ 284,760
Bilingual, Immigrant, Refugee Education	198,014	200,789	249,000	201,814	225,407
ESEA Chapter 1 (Disadvantaged Children)	6,065,896	6,214,165	7,064,750	6,426,377	6,696,439
Education of Handicapped Children (state grants)	2,412,949	2,526,495	2,582,676	2,619,936	2,614,095
Educational Partnerships	4,233	4,233	4,233	4,233	4,233
Educational Research	64,714	74,296	71,000	71,500	71,000
Eisenhower Math and Science Education	202,011	239,011	240,000	240,000	240,000
HEA Title III, Developing Institutions	204,835	194,835	209,500	194,873	207,042
HEA Title IV-C, College Work-Study	594,689	396,615	595,000	618,476	615,000
HEA Title VI, International Education	28,670	28,670	34,000	34,170	34,000
National Archives and Records Administration	126,969	148,143	146,743	148,143	146,743
National Center for Education Statistics	63,523	80,060	78,000	64,313	77,213
National Endowment for the Arts	174,083	174,083	178,200	174,083	175,955
National Endowment for the Humanities	170,005	178,200	178,200	175,000	175,955
National Historical Publications and Records Commission	5,250	4,000	5,400	6,000	5,400
Postal revenue forgone subsidy	472,592	182,778†	649,301	383,000	470,000
Postsecondary Education Improvement Fund	14,639	14,639	15,000	15,000	15,000
Star Schools (ESEA IX)	14,417	10,000	0	18,404	18,417
VISTA Literacy Corps	4,621	4,930	4,621	4,930	4,776
Women's Educational Equity	1,995	500	2,000	500	500

*LSCA IV funded at 2 percent of appropriations for LSCA I, II, and III.
†USPS estimated $649,301,000 was needed to maintain preferred rates at current levels.

crease! The program had not been funded at that level for more than 20 years. The increase originated in the House L-HHS-ED Appropriations Subcommittee, and the Senate agreed. The House committee report (H. Rept. 102-121) explained that "because of information indicating a significant shortage of librarians in the late 1990s as a result of retirements, the committee has recommended a significant increase for this program."

Congress passed H.R. 3839, the FY 1992 Labor-HHS-Education Appropriations bill, on November 22 after failing to override the veto of an earlier bill. President Bush signed the bill into law (PL 102-170) on November 26, almost three months after the beginning of the fiscal year. Temporary continuing resolutions kept funds flowing at previous levels in the interim. H.R. 3839 was identical in every respect with the vetoed H.R. 2707, except that it omitted the prohibition on use of funds to promulgate regulations dealing with abortion information, which prompted the veto.

Arts and Humanities

The administration requested a 4.8 percent increase for the National Endowment for the Humanities, but Congress provided slightly less than that in the FY 1992 Interior Appropriations bill (H.R. 2686, PL 102-154). Table 2 shows amounts appropriated for selected NEH programs. The reduction proposed for Humanities Projects in Libraries and Archives was originally accepted by Congress, but the funds were restored in House-Senate conference thanks to Sidney Yates (D-Ill.), House subcommittee chairperson. All amounts agreed on by conferees were reduced across the board by 1.26 percent to make the bill conform to congressional budget allocations.

The issue of restricting the content of projects funded by the National Endowment for the Arts was raised again in 1991. The Senate adopted an amendment by Senator Jesse Helms (R-N.C.) with more restrictive language than the previous Congress had passed after much controversy during the reauthorization process. House-Senate conferees eventually dropped the Helms amendment and reiterated the earlier reauthorization language. As a weary senator noted after the final vote, it was the ninth time in two years the Senate had been asked to vote on the issue.

Table 2 / Selected NEH Programs, FY 1991
(figures in thousands)

Program	FY 1991 Appropriations	FY 1992 Administration Requests	FY 1992 House	FY 1992 Senate Committee	FY 1992 House-Senate Conferees*
NEH Total	$170,005	$178,200	$178,200	$175,000	$175,955
Humanities projects in libraries and archives	2,785	2,375	2,375	2,375	2,750
Office of Preservation	22,581	20,800	24,900	18,200	22,118
Research grants	18,503	19,900	19,500	19,900	19,254
Challenge grants	15,071	16,050	12,050	16,050	12,392

*Unofficial numbers incorporating 1.26 percent cut in each program imposed by conferees.

Copyright

Fair Use of Unpublished Materials

In September, the Senate passed S. 1035, a bill to clarify fair use of unpublished material. Recent decisions of the U.S. Court of Appeals for the Second Circuit, which has jurisdiction over many major publishing houses, make it legally difficult to quote even a limited amount of unpublished material without authorization.

S. 1035 represents a compromise between authors' organizations and the computer industry. The bill was not intended to broaden fair use of unpublished computer software but to make clear that the unpublished nature of a work should not create a per se bar to its use. S. 1035 would add a sentence to the end of Section 107 (the fair use section) of the copyright law:

> The fact that a work is unpublished is an important element which tends to weigh against a finding of fair use, but shall not diminish the importance traditionally accorded to any other consideration under this section, and shall not bar a finding of fair use, if such finding is made upon full consideration of all the above factors.

H.R. 2372, a House bill making miscellaneous amendments to the copyright law, originally contained a section clarifying fair use of unpublished material. However, the Intellectual Property Subcommittee deleted this section, and the House later passed H.R. 2372 without the provision. Subcommittee Chairperson William Hughes (D-N.J.) apparently thinks that the case for significant harm resulting from the current copyright law was inadequate. The subcommittee held hearings on H.R. 2372 on May 30 and June 6.

Five-Year Review

Both the House and the Senate passed legislation to repeal the requirement for a report to Congress every five years by the Register of Copyrights on the library photocopying provisions of Section 108 of the copyright law. The report was to set forth the extent to which Section 108 had achieved the intended statutory balancing of the rights of creators and the needs of users.

The House passed a separate bill, H.R. 1612, on this subject in November. The Judiciary Committee report (H. Rept. 102-196) on the bill noted "the consensus that Congress achieved a fair, workable accommodation in Section 108" and concluded: "Since the statutory balance has been achieved, Congress can dispense with further automatic reports and save the taxpayers' money."

The Senate passed a repeal of the reporting requirement in November in a package of copyright amendments. S. 756 also includes a provision for automatic copyright renewal in works first copyrighted between 1963 and 1977 and amendments to the National Film Registry and the National Film Preservation Board in the Library of Congress. The House passed another bill, H.R. 2372, with similar copyright renewal and film preservation provisions. H.R. 1612, S. 756, and H.R. 2372 must be reconciled in 1992.

Government Software

Library groups were active in a coalition with the information industry, publishers, and public interest groups opposing pending bills that would permit the government to copyright software developed as a result of cooperative research and development agreements. Section 105 of the copyright law prohibits government agencies or their employees from securing copyrights in such works. The groups oppose H.R. 191 and S. 1581 because of their precedent-setting erosion of the century-old prohibition on copyright in federal government works. The Commerce Department spearheaded the administration's support for H.R. 191 and S. 1581. House and Senate science committees approved revised versions of the bills in late November; judiciary committees are expected to take them up in 1992.

Federal Information Policy

GPO WINDO Bill

On June 26, Representative Charles Rose (D–N.C.), chairperson of the House Committee on Administration and the Joint Committee on Printing, introduced H.R. 2722, the GPO Wide Information Network for Data Online (GPO WINDO). The bill would establish online access to public government information through the Government Printing Office. GPO WINDO would be a single account, one-stop-shopping way to access and query federal databases, complementing, rather than supplanting, other agency efforts to disseminate information. Fees for information would approximate "the incremental cost of dissemination of the data" for most subscribers. The legislation would permit depository libraries to connect to, access, and query GPO WINDO databases without charge.

The proposal was the result of cooperation between ALA and other library associations and public interest organizations in developing legislation to encourage GPO to broaden its role as disseminator of electronic government databases to the public and to libraries. At year's end, 20 organizations had endorsed the concept.

OMB Circular A-130

In March, the Office of Management and Budget (OMB) announced plans (56 *Federal Register 9026–9028*) to revise its controversial OMB Circular A-130. In the advance notice (not a draft of the revised circular), OMB invited comments on the issues most requiring revision. Information dissemination policy was at the top of OMB's agenda, including guidance to federal agencies regarding depository libraries. For instance, OMB said it would encourage agencies to provide electronic information products (not both products and services) to depository libraries. This concerned the library community, because several government publications were being distributed through online services, and depositories were already participating in pilot projects for the dissemination of electronic services through GPO. OMB took no further action during 1991.

Paperwork Reduction Act

Bills to reauthorize the Paperwork Reduction Act were introduced in May in the Senate, and were still pending as the year ended. Senator John Glenn (D–Ohio) introduced S. 1044, the Federal Information Resources Management Act, reflecting the compromise reached (but not enacted) by the Senate, the House, and the administration at the end of the previous Congress.

Although S. 1044 includes provisions supporting dissemination of government information, it contains a list of restrictive factors that an agency would have to consider in determining how to carry out public information dissemination functions. Library groups objected to the list in previous versions. In particular, one factor, requiring consideration of "equivalent" public or private information products or services, would denigrate the role of the government agency and elevate the role of the private sector at the expense of the public. The bill would strengthen OMB's role in setting federal information policy.

Senator Sam Nunn (D-Ga.) introduced S. 1139, the Paperwork Reduction Act of 1991, with strong support from the small business community, to emphasize agency responsibility to minimize federal paperwork burdens on the public and to enhance OMB's role in setting governmentwide policies relating to management of the full spectrum of information resources. S. 1139 makes no mention of the Depository Library Program and contains a variation of the list of restrictive factors that library groups opposed.

Improvement of Information Access Act

Pending at year's end was H.R. 3459, introduced by Representative Major Owens (D-N.Y.) in October. Owens declared that the Improvement of Information Access Act was "based on the simple, irrefutable premise that government information belongs to the people." The bill would amend the Freedom of Information Act to direct federal agencies to disseminate government information through depository libraries, national computer networks, and other distribution channels that improve public access; include adequate documentation and useful features; use standardized record formats; charge no more than incremental dissemination costs; and solicit public comment on dissemination policies and practices.

Redissemination Fees

A bill (H.R. 534) still pending at year's end would repeal an unpopular recreational boat user fee and partially offset the loss of revenue by imposing a royalty-like fee of 35 cents per minute ($21 per hour) for public online access to the Federal Maritime Commission (FMC) Automated Tariff Filing and Information (ATFI) system. The bill would also require anyone who redisseminates information from ATFI to charge the customer (or user) an additional 35 cents per minute, to be paid directly to FMC. A similar fee was under consideration by a Senate committee.

Although Congress reauthorized the Coast Guard without imposing an FMC data user fee, the search for replacement revenues is likely to continue. Library organizations and the information industry opposed user fees for government information as a method of raising revenue.

Foreign Relations of the United States

History and library organizations have long been protesting omissions in the Foreign Relations of the United States series. Their efforts to resolve the problem culminated in enactment of a measure authorizing annual appropriations for the State Department (H.R. 1415, PL 102-138) to establish a systematic program for declassifying all but the most sensitive foreign-policy documents that are more than 31 years old.

Ethics for Government Employees

The Office of Government Ethics (OGE) published proposed standards of ethical conduct for employees of the executive branch in the July 23 *Federal Register* (56 FR 33778-815). The first substantial rewrite of the standards since 1965, the proposed changes address a range of conduct, including gifts, conflicts of interest, and bias. Of particular concern to employees active in professional associations was a section on "outside activities," which stipulated that federal employees could not spend time "to administer the internal affairs of any such organization or to carry out its business affairs."

ALA was among the nearly 1,000 groups that commented on the proposed standards, and the Office of Government Ethics later decided to delete the section concerning participation in professional associations when the final rules are issued early in 1992. In a December 9 letter to federal agencies, OGE Director Stephen Potts said the ethics office will revise the section on association participation and publish it later as a new proposed rule for comment.

The Ethics Reform Act of 1989, effective January 1, 1991, enacted an absolute ban against receipt of honoraria for "speeches, articles, or appearances" by all officers and employees of the federal government. As the intent of the original legislation was to ban honoraria for members of Congress and political appointees, efforts to amend this law began promptly. Bills were introduced and hearings were held, but no permanent solution was found by year's end.

Higher Education Act Reauthorization

Both House and Senate education committees developed and approved mammoth bills to reauthorize the Higher Education Act. Despite the administration's recommendation for repeal of all HEA library programs, recommendations developed by ALA and the Association of Research Libraries, and endorsed by 15 higher education and library organizations, were incorporated in both H.R. 3553 and S. 1150, although the Senate authorized lower levels than ALA had recommended. Congress will continue to work on these bills in 1992.

The library provisions in these bills include reauthorization of HEA Title II to reflect the new electronic networked environment and the changing roles of libraries and librarians in response to new ways of providing information. HEA Title II-A grants for college library resources (unfunded since FY 1983) would be replaced by an updated Title II-D technology assistance program. The Title II-B research and education program and Title II-C grants to major research libraries would be continued with minor amendments. Within HEA Title VI—foreign language and international education—Section 607 authorizing assistance for the acquisition of foreign periodicals would be expanded to include other kinds of research material.

H.R. 3553 also incorporated in Title II the new Strengthening Library and Information Science Programs in Historically Black Colleges and Universities, responding to a recommendation of the National Association for Equal Opportunity in Higher Education (NAFEO) endorsed by the White House Conference on Library and Information Services. S. 1150 included within Title VII the new Improvement of Academic and Library Facilities.

Library of Congress

Librarian of Congress James Billington requested an 18 percent increase for the Library of Congress (LC) for FY 1992. The total requested was $359,962,000, including authority to obligate $23,292,000 in receipts, compared with $304,997,000 available to LC in FY 1991. About half the increase ($27.3 million) was needed to maintain services, including work on the backlog of 40 million unprocessed items; the other half was for new initiatives. In the FY 1992 Legislative Branch Appropriation Bill (H.R. 2506, PL 102–90), LC received a 5.6 percent increase, or $322,228,000. Funding committees requested better long-range planning and setting of priorities by the library and warned in committee reports that "significant budgetary increases are not on the horizon."

On June 27, Senator Claiborne Pell (D–R.I.), chairperson of the joint committee on LC, introduced at the request of the Librarian of Congress S. 1416, a bill to authorize LC to provide fee-based library research and information products and services. No comparable House bill has been introduced. Although LC consulted the library community when drafting the legislation, the proposal has generated considerable controversy because of the scope of the services for which fees could be charged.

ALA and other library groups suggested revisions to the proposal, many of which LC accepted, but Senator Pell's version remained a cause of concern. At one point, the Senate Rules and Administration Committee scheduled a markup of the bill, then canceled it and scheduled a hearing for October. The hearing was canceled, however, and Pell requested that interested parties make suggestions to LC for clarifying or modifying the bill. At year's end, library groups had resumed discussions with LC officials concerning the legislation.

National Commission on Libraries and Information Science

Six appointees to the National Commission on Libraries and Information Science (NCLIS) were nominated by the president and confirmed by the Senate during 1991, giving NCLIS a full complement of commissioners for the first time in years.

S. 1593, making technical amendments to the 1970 statute authorizing NCLIS, was signed into law (PL 102–95) in August. The legislation permits NCLIS to obtain administrative support from any federal agency — not just the Department of Education, as was previously the case — to receive in-kind as well as monetary contributions and to become involved in international library and information activities and networks. It clarifies that a quorum is a majority of members and provides that commissioners serve until a successor is appointed (up to a year following expiration of their term).

The measure also lifts the former ceiling on appropriations of $750,000. Although the administration recommended a higher level in the four most recent budget requests, NCLIS has been funded at the $750,000 cap because congressional appropriators were unwilling to exceed the statutory authorization. For FY 1992, President Bush recommended $911,000, and the Senate agreed to that amount, but the House-passed level was $750,000. PL 102–95 authorized $911,000 for FY 1992 and such sums as necessary for each succeeding fiscal year making it possible for conferees to agree to $831,000, the highest amount NCLIS has ever received.

National Literacy Act

The National Literacy Act of 1991 (H.R. 751) was signed into law on July 25. The legislation, which originated in bills sponsored by Representative Thomas Sawyer (D-Ohio) and Senator Paul Simon (D-Ill.), became PL 102-73. The act defines literacy as "an individual's ability to read, write, and speak in English, and compute and solve problems at levels of proficiency necessary to function on the job and in society, to achieve one's goals, and develop one's knowledge and potential." The act authorizes programs for FYs 1991-1995, some of which are amendments to existing programs and some new programs, such as the National Institute for Literacy, State Literacy Resource Centers, National Workforce Literacy Strategies, Functional Literacy for State and Local Prisoners, and Life Skills for State and Local Prisoners.

The act requires that a state advisory council on adult education and literacy include a representative of the state library program. Under the state-administered adult education basic grant program, educational programs for criminal offenders in correctional institutions and for other institutionalized adults may include library development and library service programs. The act calls for collaboration and partnerships among literacy providers, thus providing opportunities for libraries both as applicants for adult education and other programs and as participants in grant projects.

The act also amended the LSCA Title VI library literacy program to give priority to literacy programs and services that are in areas of greatest need based on several factors and that coordinate with other organizations.

National Research and Education Network

On December 9, the president signed landmark legislation to establish the National Research and Education Network (NREN). The High-Performance Computing Act (S. 272, PL 102-194) — introduced by Senator Albert Gore, Jr. (D-Tenn.) in late 1988 and sponsored in the House by Representative George Brown (D-Calif.) — authorizes a five-year, two-part program. The National High-Performance Computing Program establishes goals and priorities for federal high-performance computing research, development, networking, and related activities, as well as providing for interagency coordination of such activities. The second part calls on several agencies to support the establishment of NREN by transmitting data at 1 gigabit per second or greater by 1996.

Compromises during the bill's three-year history resulted in departures from earlier versions. The National Science Foundation (responsible for the NSFNET backbone of Internet) was originally to be responsible for managing NREN. In the final version, no agency is designated to do so. Although the National Science Foundation still has a major role, the autonomy of agency networks has been strengthened. The director of the Office of Science and Technology Policy (OSTP) is to assist in interagency coordination, but the president has ultimate responsibility. The president is to establish a nonfederal advisory committee on high-performance computing, including representatives of the research, education, and library communities, network providers, and industry.

NREN is to link research institutions with educational institutions, government, and industry in every state. Federal agencies are to work with private network service providers, state and local agencies, libraries, educational institutions and organizations, and others to ensure that researchers, educators, and students have access to the network. NREN is to provide users with access to high-performance computing systems, electronic information resources, libraries, and other research facilities. It is also to provide access, to the extent practicable, to electronic information resources maintained by libraries, research facilities, publishers, and affiliated organizations.

The new law calls for development of NREN information services, including directories of users and services, federal databases, training of users, access to commercial information services, and technology to support computer-based collaboration. Federal agencies and departments are authorized to allow recipients of federal research grants to use grants to pay computer networking expenses.

The director of the Office of Science and Technology Policy is to submit an annual implementation report to Congress along with the president's budget request. Within a year, the OSTP director is to recommend ways to fund NREN (including user fees, industry support, and continued federal investment), charging mechanisms for commercial information service providers and users, ways to protect the copyright of material distributed over the network, and policies to ensure the security of resources and the privacy of users.

The National Science Foundation is to have primary responsibility for assisting colleges, universities, and libraries to connect to the network, with a late compromise proviso: "to the extent that colleges, universities, and libraries cannot connect to the network with the assistance of the private sector." Although language requiring privatization of the network within a certain period was dropped, industry involvement is expected to increase and is encouraged. NSF is also to serve as the primary source of information on access to and use of the network, to upgrade NSFNET, assist regional networks to upgrade capabilities, and provide other federal entities the opportunity to connect to NSFNET.

The purpose of the bill is to improve dissemination of federal agency data and electronic information and to educate and train more students in software engineering, computer science, library and information science, and computational science.

The $2.9 billion authorized over five years is spread among several agencies: National Science Foundation, National Aeronautics and Space Administration, Department of Energy, Commerce Department's National Institute of Standards and Technology and National Oceanic and Atmospheric Administration, Environmental Protection Agency, and Department of Education. The Defense Advanced Research Projects Agency is authorized in separate legislation. The NREN authorization is not specified.

The library, education, and research communities wanted broad participation in NREN, a strong voice in governance and policymaking for nonfederal entities to be served by the network, and heavy emphasis on interagency coordination, interoperability, and standards. The administration and certain mission agencies preferred maximum flexibility in the operation of the program and maximum autonomy for agency networks in carrying out their missions. During the measure's rocky history, some references to libraries and education, interoperability, and outside input were lost or qualified, but much was gained for the library and education communities.

Postal Issues

The FY 1992 Treasury-Postal Appropriations Bill (H.R. 2622, PL 102–141) provided $470 million for postal revenue forgone (revenue that the Postal Service forgoes when setting lower or preferred rates). The amount was $179.3 million less than was needed to maintain preferred postal rates at current levels, but considerably higher than the administration's request of $182,778,000. The immediate impact of the appropriations shortfall was felt only by mailers of nonprofit third-class, nonletter-sized mail, due to a legislative provision in the conference agreement.

The agreement provided that half the shortfall be made up by allowing the Postal Service to increase the rate for nonprofit third-class "flats" by an average 2.2 cents per piece; the increase was implemented in November. Another rate increase for nonprofit third-class flats averaging 2.2 cents per piece is expected to take effect in October 1992.

On November 5, the Board of Governors of the U.S. Postal Service unanimously rejected increases recommended a month earlier by the Postal Rate Commission. Thus, the 26.8 percent increase proposed for the fourth-class library rate—used by schools, colleges, and libraries for interlibrary loan, books-by-mail, film-sharing circuits, and receipt of new library and instructional materials—was not implemented. But a general rate increase for all classes of mail took effect February 3. For the fourth-class library rate, a 2-pound package increased 2.3 percent, to 89 cents from 87 cents.

White House Conference on Library and Information Services

On November 21, the summary report of the July 9–13 White House Conference on Library and Information Services (WHCLIS) was transmitted to the White House. *Information 2000: Library and Information Services for the 21st Century,* the full text of the 95 recommendations adopted by the delegates, is available for $6.00 (Stock No. 040-000-00564-1) from the U.S. Government Printing Office, Superintendent of Documents, Mail Stop: SSOP, Washington, DC 20402-9328 (202-783-3238). The president was to transmit the report to Congress with his recommendations within 90 days, or by February 19, 1992.

The summary report identifies 13 recommendations earmarked as priorities for action by an early vote of the conference delegates. In order of highest number of votes, the 13 recommendations are an omnibus children and youth literacy initiative, creation and funding of NREN with library participation, sufficient funding of library programs, creation of model library marketing programs, literacy initiatives to aid the disadvantaged, national policies for information preservation, networking equity for low-density areas, encouragement of multicultural and multilingual programs and staffs, amendment of copyright statutes for new technologies, ensuring access to government information resources, national information policies to ensure intellectual freedom and protect privacy and confidentiality, recognition of libraries as partners in lifelong education, and designation of libraries as educational agencies.

On July 11, during WHCLIS, the Senate Subcommittee on Education, Arts, and the Humanities and the House Subcommittee on Labor-Management Relations held a joint hearing on library and information services for literacy, productivity, and democracy, the three themes of WHCLIS. A diverse and eloquent group of 19 witnesses testified at the hearing chaired by Senator Pell, including ALA President Patricia Glass Schuman. Activity following the conference indicates that implementation of WHCLIS recommendations will be a high priority for the library community.

Table 3 indicates the status of legislation of interest to librarians.

Table 3 / Status of Legislation of Interest to Librarians

(102d Congress, 1st Session, Convened January 3, 1991, Adjourned November 27, 1991)

Legislation	House Introduced	House Hearings	House Reported by Subcommittee	House Committee Report No. — H. Rept. 102-	House Floor Action	Senate Introduced	Senate Hearings	Senate Reported by Subcommittee	Senate Committee Report No. — S. Rept. 102-	Senate Floor Action	Conference Report — H. Rept. 102-	Final Passage	Public Law — PL 102-
Abortion information	H.R. 392	*				S. 323	*		86	*			
AMERICA 2000 Excellence in Education Act	H.R. 2460					S. 1141							
American Technical Preeminence Act	H.R. 1989	*				S. 1034			none	*			
Civil rights bills	H.R. 1	*		40	*	S. 1745	*		none	*	none	*	166
Communications — Modernization Act	H.R. 2546					S. 1200			none				
Copyright — audio home recordings	H.R. 3204		*			S. 1623	*		254				
Copyright — federally funded software	H.R. 191	*		415		S. 1581	*						
Copyright — repeal five-year review	H.R. 1612				*	S. 756				*			
Copyright — unpublished materials, etc.	H.R. 2372	*	*	379	*	S. 1035	*		141	*			
Family and Medical Leave Act	H.R. 2		*	135	*	S. 5	*		68	*			
Federal ethics reform	H.R. 325	*				S. 242	*		29	*			
FMC database fee	H.R. 534												
FOIA amendments	H.R. 3877	*		182									
GPO WINDO	H.R. 2772					S. 1939, 1940							
Higher Education Act reauthorization	H.R. 3553	*	*		*	S. 1150	*	*	204				
Improvement of Information Access Act	H.R. 3459												
LC fee-for-service bill						S. 1416							
Medical Library Assistance Act reauthorization	H.R. 2507	*	*	136	*	S. 1523	*		43		none		
National Literacy Act	H.R. 751		*	23	*	S. 2, H.R. 751	*		57	*	none	*	73
National Research and Education Network	H.R. 656	*	*	66	*	S. 272	*			*	none	*	194
NCLIS amendments	S. 1593				*	S. 1593				*	none	*	95

Table 3 / Status of Legislation of Interest to Librarians (cont.)

(102d Congress, 1st Session, Convened January 3, 1991, Adjourned November 27, 1991)

Legislation	House					Senate					Final Action		
	Introduced	Hearings	Reported by Subcommittee	Committee Report No.— H. Rept. 102-	Floor Action	Introduced	Hearings	Reported by Subcommittee	Committee Report No.— S. Rept. 102-	Floor Action	Conference Report— H. Rept. 102-	Final Passage	Public Law— PL 102-
NREN—Dept. of Energy bill	H.R. 3446	*											
OERI reauthorization						S. 343	*		64				
Paperwork Reduction Act reauthorization						S. 1044, 1139	*						
PTO Reauthorization Act	H.R. 3531	*		382	*	S. 793	*		245	*	none	*	204
Regulatory review						S. 1942	*		*	*			
School reform bills	H.R. 3320	*		294		S. 2	*						
Taxation—extend expiring provisions	H.R. 3909					H.R. 3909							
Telecommunications, information services bills	H.R. 3515	*		none	*	S. 2112			none	*	none	*	227
Appropriations, FY 1992													
Agriculture	H.R. 2698	*		119	*	H.R. 2698	*	*	116	*	239	*	142
Commerce, State	H.R. 2608	*	*	106	*	H.R. 2608	*	*	106	*	233	*	140
Interior and related agencies	H.R. 2686	*	*	116	*	H.R. 2686	*	*	122	*	256	*	159
Labor-HHS-Education	H.R. 2707	*	*	121	*	H.R. 2707	*	*	104	*	282	*	veto
Labor-HHS-Education	H.R. 3839	*			*	H.R. 3839	*	*		*	none	*	170
Legislative branch	H.R. 2506	*	*	82	*	H.R. 2506	*	*	81	*	176	*	90
Treasury, Postal Service	H.R. 2622	*	*	109	*	H.R. 2622	*	*	95	*	234	*	141
VA, HUD, independent agencies	H.R. 2519	*	*	94	*	H.R. 2519	*	*	107	*	226	*	139

For free copies of bills, reports, and laws, write: House Document Rm., B-18 Annex No. 2, Washington, DC 20515; Senate Document Rm., B-04 Hart, Washington, DC 20510.

Legislation and Regulations Affecting Publishing in 1991

Judith Platt

Director of Communications
Association of American Publishers
and Members of the AAP Washington Staff*

Copyright

Fair Use of Unpublished Works

Legislation to clarify U.S. copyright law with respect to "fair use" of previously unpublished materials was approved by the Senate Judiciary Committee in June and passed by the Senate on September 27. However, wrangling over wording bogged the bill down in the House copyright subcommittee, ending any hope of passage during the first session. As Congress began its December recess, indication that consensus might be near raised hopes that the bill might be reported out of the Judiciary Committee and brought up for a vote on the House floor early in the second session.

Government Royalty Fees

Publishers were troubled by a proposal to allow the Federal Maritime Commission to collect a royalty fee for the use of tariff information it generates. Put forward to meet a revenue shortfall if a tax on recreational boating were repealed, the proposal was approved by the House Merchant Marine and Fisheries Committee. Publishers expressed concern that such a scheme would violate traditional and legal strictures against federal government copyright and would contravene long-standing policy to promote wide dissemination of government data. Congress failed to repeal the tax, eliminating the need to find another revenue source. However, the issue of government agencies licensing government data to meet budget shortfalls will probably surface again, and it bears watching.

Library of Congress Fee-Based Services

A legislative proposal to expand the authority of the Library of Congress to provide fee-based services and to charge for copying and document delivery was sent to Congress by the library. AAP advised the Senate Rules Committee that before Congress can move such legislation forward, extensive and broad-based hearings are needed to examine its possible impact on the publishing industry and other information providers. The proposed legislation was subsequently returned to the library with a request from Congress that its focus be sharpened and its intent clarified.

National Research and Education Network (NREN)

Senator Albert Gore (D–Tenn.) and Representative George Brown (D–Calif.) reintroduced legislation to establish a nationwide network of fiber-optic data highways and

*Contributors to this article include the following members of the AAP Washington staff:
Virginia Antos, Christine Callahan, Richard P. Kleeman, Diane Rennert, and Carol Risher.

digital libraries. Publishers' concerns centered on including information providers in planning and developing such a network, developing appropriate standards, and protecting the integrity of copyrighted material. The High-Performance Computing Act of 1991 received final congressional approval in November and was signed into law by President Bush on December 9, 1991. The new law contains provisions sought by AAP: an advisory committee representing various interests, including the private sector, and accounting mechanisms that will allow user charges for copyrighted material supplied over the network.

Automatic Copyright Renewal

Both the House and Senate passed legislation to provide for automatic renewal of works created between 1963 and 1978, when, for some reason, the author or the author's heirs have neglected to file formally for renewal. AAP is working with Congress to ensure that such a provision does not present potential problems for textbook publishers in cases where the copyright holder cannot be located.

First Amendment

"Pornography Victims" Bill

Legislation was introduced that would make producers and distributors of sexually explicit materials liable for civil damages if the victim of a sex crime could demonstrate that the crime was "caused" by the material. The bill was subsequently narrowed to apply only to commercial producers, distributors, and exhibitors of obscene material, but it remains troubling with respect to third-party liability and other constitutional and practical flaws. The legislation is likely to be revived in the second session.

National Endowment for the Arts

Funding for the National Endowment for the Arts again became embroiled in controversy as Senator Jesse Helms (R–N.C.) tried to push through language prohibiting funding of works containing "patently offensive" sexual material. The Helms amendment was passed by the Senate but dropped in conference. For the next year, the Endowment can continue to work within current flexible guidelines mandating that funded works meet "general standards of decency," but leaving determinations of obscenity to the courts. Helms is expected to continue his attempts to impose censorship restrictions on the Endowment.

Freedom of Information Act

Two bills were introduced late in the session to broaden the application of the Freedom of Information Act (FOIA) and to extend the definition of federal agency records to include data stored in electronic format. The Freedom of Information Improvement Act sponsored by Senator Patrick Leahy (D–Vt.) would extend the act to cover Congress and the Offices of the President and the Vice President. It would also narrow the scope of material that can be denied under FOIA requests because of national security considerations. The second bill, cosponsored by Leahy and Senator Hank Brown (R–Colo.), would allow FOIA requesters to decide whether they want paper or electronic format and would require agencies to make "reasonable efforts" to provide materials in the form requested. As an incentive to respond promptly to FOIA requests, the bill would allow a federal agency to keep a portion of the FOIA fees collected. (At present, all fees are sent to the Treasury.)

The "Gag Rule"

On July 20, the Senate Judiciary Committee's Subcommittee on the Constitution held a hearing on the First Amendment implications of the Supreme Court's ruling in *Rust* v. *Sullivan,* which upheld a ban on any mention of abortion in federally supported women's clinics. First Amendment advocates are deeply troubled by the implications of the *Rust* decision, and several roundly criticized the so-called gag rule in testimony presented by representatives of the American Library Association, the American Medical Association, People for the American Way, and a number of other groups. Late in the first session, both the House and Senate passed legislation to kill the gag rule, but Congress was unable to override President Bush's veto. The question of the government's right to attach ideological restrictions to federal funds promises to be of paramount concern to free-speech advocates.

Education and Literacy

Literacy

On July 25, President Bush signed into law the National Literacy Act of 1991 authorizing expenditure of $1.8 billion over the next four years for a range of federal literacy programs. Although funding levels will depend on specific appropriations bills, the new law authorizes expenditures of $60 million for Even Start over the next two fiscal years, $25 million for state literacy resource centers for FYs 1992–1996, $5 million to aid small and medium-sized businesses in providing literacy skills training, $2 million for the Corporation for Public Broadcasting for family literacy programming, $25 million to assist states in developing prison literacy programs, $15 million to establish a National Literacy Clearinghouse, and $260 million for basic state grants under the Adult Education Act.

Education Funding

Congress was generous in its treatment of Department of Education programs, appropriating more than $32 billion for FY 1992, an increase of $4.8 billion over FY 1991. The president signed the final version of the bill in early December.

The following programs are of interest to book publishers. The Even Start literacy program was funded at $70 million, $10 million over the authorization level and an increase of more than $20 million over FY 1991 appropriations; Chapter 2 Educational Improvement Program funding remained at $450 million; $10 million was allocated for the Inexpensive Book Distribution Program, a modest increase over the $9.3 million appropriated the previous year; the National Writing Project received $2.5 million, a $500,000 increase; and funding for bilingual and immigrant education was increased by $25 million to $225 million. Vocational and adult education programs, including various literacy initiatives, received $1.4 billion, an increase of $1 million; $263 million was allocated to programs carried out under the auspices of the Office of Educational Research and Improvement, $30 million more than in FY 1991; library programs received $148 million, an increase of approximately $5 million over FY 1991 and more than four times the amount recommended in the president's budget.

Telecommunications Policy: The RBOCs

The ban prohibiting the Regional Bell Operating Companies (RBOCs) from offering information services was lifted by a reluctant Judge Harold Greene in July. Judge Greene stayed his order pending completion of the appeals process, but that stay was subsequently overturned, leaving the RBOCs free to enter the information services market. Representative Jim Cooper (D–Tenn.) introduced legislation to encourage competition in the electronic information industry and to safeguard against anticompetitive behavior. Hearings were held on the Cooper bill (H.R. 3515), which has more than 40 cosponsors in the House, but no further action was taken prior to recess. Just before Congress recessed, Senator Daniel Inouye (D–Hawaii) introduced a similar bill in the Senate. AAP is working with a coalition of electronic publishers and industry groups to ensure that Congress enacts legislation containing reasonable and workable safeguards against anticompetitive behavior by the RBOCs.

Postal Funding

The House and Senate voted to provide less than full funding for revenue forgone in FY 1992, approving $470 million to fund the subsidy (down $3 million from the previous year). Congressional conferees decided that approximately half of the revenue shortfall should be made up by allowing the Postal Service to increase the rate for nonprofit third-class flats (non-letter-size pieces) by an average of 2.2 cents per piece, a move that will have a direct impact on mailing costs for journals. All other nonprofit rates, including the library rate, remain unchanged.

Tax Issues: Prepublication Expenses

Representative Thomas Downey (D–N.Y.) reintroduced his bill to allow publishers of classroom instructional materials to expense rather than capitalize research and development costs. No action was taken on the bill, and the AAP board has decided to reexamine the issue.

Legislation and Regulations Affecting the Information Industry in 1991

Steven J. Metalitz

Vice President and General Counsel
Information Industry Association

The earthshaking events of 1991 on the geopolitical scene found a faint echo in public policy developments affecting the information industry. The demise of the information services restriction on the Regional Bell Operating Companies (RBOCs), and the birth of the National Research and Education Network (NREN) certainly cannot compare in scale with upheavals such as the Persian Gulf war and the collapse of the Soviet Union. Yet many observers heralded the former developments with predictions and speculation nearly as grandiose as those that attended the latter. In less overheated moments, other significant public policy trends were discernable. If a common thread could be detected, it was the move toward greater government involvement in, and control over, how Americans acquire, use, and distribute information.

Telecommunications and NREN

Since April 1990, when a panel of the District of Columbia Circuit Court of Appeals overturned an order of U.S. District Court Judge Harold Greene, the handwriting was on the wall for the information services restriction of the Modification of Final Judgment (MFJ), the complex consent decree governing the breakup of AT&T and divestiture of the seven RBOCs, or so-called Baby Bells. Under this restriction, the RBOCs were barred from owning or controlling the information carried on the RBOC-controlled telecommunications network. When Judge Greene, on July 25, 1991, finally rendered his decision on remand from the Court of Appeals, he warned that the most probable consequence of eliminating this separation between information and the conduits that carry it would be "the elimination of competition from the market and the concentration of the sources of information of the American people in just a few dominant, collaborative conglomerates with the captive local telephone monopolies as their base." Nonetheless, viewing his options as foreclosed by the Court of Appeals, Judge Greene lifted the restrictions, but imposed a stay on this order in case he had misinterpreted the Court of Appeals' directive. The higher court did not take long to make clear that the judge's reading was right, even if he thought the result to be wrong: the Court of Appeals lifted the stay, and by year's end, the information services restriction was history — at least for now.

The immediate effect of the court decisions was minimal: Confounding some expectations, the RBOCs did not rush into the new opportunities open to them, but appeared to bide their time pending the outcome of redoubled legislative debate over their proper role in the information services marketplace. Congress, facing a judicial fait accompli, mulled several proposals to impose safeguards aimed at minimizing the RBOCs' ability to discriminate against, or to harm through cross-subsidy, potential competitors in the information services market. Some proposals included an entry test reimposing the information services restriction, at least in part, until the RBOCs faced real competition in providing local exchange telephone service. Although a rearguard action remains alive in the courts, clearly it is up to Congress to protect competition and the greater public interest by fashioning appropriate safeguards and conditions for RBOC participation in the information arena. That issue should demand considerable legislative attention in 1992.

As the sun set on the key information provisions of the MFJ, it rose on NREN, a national superhighway for high-speed, high-volume data flow. Here Congress led the way, with Senator Albert Gore (D–Tenn.) prodding a reluctant executive branch that thought legislation unnecessary. The final legislative product, signed into law by President Bush in December, called for a $3 billion High Performance Computing Initiative, of which NREN is a part. But passage of the bill only initiated a new phase in the debate over NREN's scope and significance.

NREN is clearly intended to be a superhighway, but the location and number of its exits remain in dispute, as do key rules of the road. Where some proponents see a network primarily designed to support scientists and researchers crunching large volumes of data, others see an almost ubiquitous network bringing new databases into every school and library. The legislation straddled most of these debates, even punting on such questions as who will make the decisions about who use NREN, for what, and under what financial and other conditions. The law does include some clear directives to design copyright protection and accounting mechanisms into the system, and the implementation of these directives will help determine whether the new network fully realizes its potential as a path-breaking new distribution system for information products and services. In the meantime, some skeptics have asked whether, during the four years it took to enact the NREN bill, the legislation was not overtaken by events: The real NREN, they assert, is the evolving Internet, the network of networks that is growing exponentially in scope and quality, and that uses federal dollars but rejects monolithic federal control. Stay tuned. . . .

Government Information Policy Developments

NREN was conceived as a distribution system for information, including government data, but the legislative history forswears any intention to set federal information dissemination policy, the rules governing federal agency decisions about how to ensure that public information is distributed to the public. Unfortunately, during 1991, no other initiatives materialized to fill that policy gap. Neither at the Office of Management and Budget (OMB), where work continued on a new draft of Circular A-130, nor on Capitol Hill, where information policy legislation, nearly enacted in 1990, remained hostage to partisan disputes over the regulatory activities of OMB, were the debates of earlier years publicly reopened. In the absence of an overall declaration of policy, Congress considered piecemeal the issues of access to, and dissemination of, government information.

Two proposals to restrict access advanced in Congress, although they ultimately fell short. The real aim of one bill, H.R. 534, was to eliminate an unpopular federal user fee on recreational boats, but the offsetting revenue raiser was to be an hourly fee on access to, and on downstream dissemination of, electronic tariff files of the Federal Maritime Commission. The legislation, quietly approved by the House Merchant Marine Committee in June, provoked an immediate response from information industry, library, and other interests, which viewed it as a dangerous precedent for selling government information to meet budgetary demands. The attempt to assert continuing government control over public data, even after it is made available to the public, also sparked opposition. The bill was sidetracked to the House Ways and Means Committee and was not voted on by either house of Congress before adjournment. However, the trail it blazed may prove attractive to Congress in the future, or to other agencies, at the federal or state level, confronted by mounting deficits and intrigued by government information as a bankable "asset."

Another measure with troubling access implications made even more progress. H.R. 191 and S. 1581 would erode the century-old prohibition on copyright on works of the federal government by authorizing government copyright claims on computer software developed collaboratively by federal laboratories and nonfederal parties. The ostensible goal was to promote technology transfer from the labs; but once again, fear of the precedent created by approving the federal government's copyright control over its own information led to creation of a broad industry-library-public interest coalition to raise the alarm about information access. Both the House Science and Senate Commerce committees approved the legislation, but it will have to undergo scrutiny by the Judiciary committees of both houses before advancing to the floor.

During its first session, the One hundred and second Congress also completed work on a bill directing the Patent and Trademark Office to establish a demonstration program for dissemination of selected patent information on CD-ROM as "estimated average marginal cost" of production and order processing. It also brought to the brink of enactment (and passed just after reconvening in January) legislation governing dissemination activities of the National Technical Information Service, including a study of the feasibility of creating an online inventory of government information products and services.

Several other bills introduced but not acted on during the first session could dominate information policy debate during the second session. S. 1416, to authorize the Library of Congress to sell information products and services and deposit the proceeds in a revolving fund apart from the regular appropriations process, was sent back to the drawing board after expressions of concern throughout the library and information communities, but may well be back with changes in 1992. H.R. 2772, the "GPO WINDO" bill, would establish the Government Printing Office as a single point of contact for public access to federal information in electronic form. And S. 1939 and 1940 would update the Freedom of Information Act to reflect the new realities of electronic access and dissemination.

Copyright Developments

The Supreme Court, not the Congress, was the dominant force on copyright issues affecting the information industry in 1991. In March, the Court for the first time interpreted the provisions of the 1976 Copyright Act on compilations. Although the specific case, *Feist Publications* v. *Rural Telephone Service Co.,* involved a white pages telephone directory, the same statutory provisions govern copyright claims in a range of databases composed of otherwise unprotectable information, such as scientific data, bibliographic material, and statutes and judicial case reports. The Court, in a unanimous decision written by Justice O'Connor, denied the claim of copyright in the white pages directory, but ruled that copyright is available to protect the original selection or arrangement of data in "the vast majority" of compilations. However, the Court affirmed that the scope of that protection is "inevitably thin" and does not extend to the facts themselves.

The practical guidance provided by the Court's decision is murky at best, and much attention has focused on subsequent decisions of lower federal courts in applying the *Feist* principles to other cases. These have held, among other things, that yellow pages directories, unlike the white pages, are copyrightable, and have begun to flesh out the question of "how much is too much" when some, but not all, of an original database is copied by a competitor.

Although *Feist* was an interpretation of the Copyright Act, the decision is couched in constitutional language that would make it difficult, although not impossible, to modify through legislation. Although the possibility of a bill to modify the post-*Feist* protections for databases was discussed in industry and academic circles, there was no consensus that such a response was necessary. Indeed, the first legislative response to *Feist* has come, not from Washington, but from Brussels, where the commission of the European Community (EC) in January 1992 unveiled its long-awaited proposal for a directive on legal protection of databases. Assuming that a significant number of commercially valuable databases would not meet European standards for copyright protection, the EC proposes a second tier of legal protection against "unfair extraction" of the contents of a database by competitors. This new form of protection would lack many of copyright's desirable features, including the prohibition on discrimination based on the nationality of the compiler. Reaction to the EC proposal is likely to dominate debate on copyright matters during 1992.

Important legislation on other copyright topics did advance in Congress during 1991. In what could be the climax of a decade-long struggle among the recording industry, music publishers and composers, and hardware manufacturers over home copying of recorded music, all the main protagonists united behind legislation (S. 1623) to impose royalties and technical limitations on digital home recording equipment and media (such as DAT, or digital audio tape). In return, the legislation would bar copyright lawsuits against home taping, thus accelerating introduction of these new copying technologies. The bill aims to avoid any effect on new information products (like multimedia productions) other than typical compact discs and similar sound recordings. It cleared the Senate Judiciary Committee during the first session and will get early attention in the House in 1992. There was also bicameral agreement on modifying the copyright renewal requirements of existing law. Both houses passed bills to ameliorate the effects of this anachronism on works created between 1963 and 1977 (no renewal is required for later works), although unresolved details prevented final passage before adjournment.

Information Regulation

Although some of the legislation summarized above threatens to increase government control over access to and use of information, that trend is most apparent and immediate in developments involving the use of the telephone to distribute information. In 1991, new federal regulations on audiotext went into effect, and even stronger legislation advanced toward final passage. Proposals to govern use of customer information obtained through the telecommunications network also advanced, as pressure grew for more comprehensive information regulations to protect personal privacy.

The audiotext regulations were a response to evidence that some unscrupulous operators were using new pay-per-call technologies and billing arrangements to bilk and mislead consumers. Unfortunately, the headlong rush to regulate also jeopardized legitimate information providers who view audiotext as a great equalizer, making Information Age services accessible to the millions of Americans who are unable or unwilling to invest in the home computer equipment necessary to participate in other electronic information networks. The final result, as announced in Federal Communications Commission regulations that went into effect in December, avoids some of the worst proposed regulatory excesses, such as a blanket ban on voice information services without prior subscriptions. The FCC rules did mandate a free preamble on nearly all pay-per-call services, and included valuable consumer protection features such as allowing customers to block their own access to such services. Many FCC requirements parallel provisions of the Senate-passed legislation, S. 1579, which also contained advertising disclosure requirements and a ban on some pay-per-call services directed at young children. Meanwhile, the House at adjournment was poised for action on a companion bill (H.R. 3490) that also set new rules for settling billing disputes on 900 services.

The continuing controversy over caller ID — the electronic peephole that reveals the telephone number of the calling party to the recipient of the call, even before the telephone rings — spilled over into debate about use of Automatic Number Identification (ANI), a less advanced but more commercially significant technology that allows operators of 800 and 900 services to identify the billing numbers of calling parties. Legislation approved by committees in both houses would codify the emerging consensus of state regulators on caller ID — that the technology, with its valuable privacy-enhancing features, should be permitted, as long as calling parties are given the opportunity to preserve their anonymity by preventing transmission of their numbers, on a call-by-call basis. But the bills (S. 652 and H.R. 1305) also include restrictions on use of ANI data, where the per-call blocking technology is not available. The details of those restrictions, and the requisites for obtaining the caller's consent for certain uses, could set powerful precedents for government regulation of data on customers obtained by businesses through other means. Privacy protection is a growing impetus for government to regulate information practices, a trend demonstrated by the swift enactment during 1991 of legislation to clamp down on abusive telephone marketing practices. The legislation includes a requirement for FCC recommendations on how best to allow consumers to "opt out" of telephone solicitations altogether, whether through creation of a national "do not call" database or through alternative means.

The most comprehensive governmental proposal to regulate information practices in the name of privacy remains the draft data protection directive offered by the European Commission in 1990. During 1991, European business opposition to this sweeping initiative grew and solidified, and at year's end the European Parliament was considering hundreds of proposed amendments. Although the European directive received a relatively muted response on Capitol Hill — the recurring proposal to establish a federal data protection agency was reintroduced by Representative Bob Wise (D-W.Va.), but no action was taken — it did seem to strike a chord in faraway Sacramento, where one house of the California Assembly once again passed legislation (A.B. 1168) requiring most database proprietors to notify subjects of the data and invite them to inspect and contest the files, even if based on public records.

On the international privacy front, renewed attention was focused on the privacy guidelines adopted in 1980 by the Organization for Economic Cooperation and Development (OECD), and later endorsed by hundreds of U.S. corporations and trade associations, as well as by the U.S. government. These voluntary principles, which stress self-regulation and a sector-by-sector approach, were reviewed at an OECD meeting in November, at which participants concluded that they needed no revision but offer a viable blueprint for balancing competing demands: protecting individual privacy while maximizing the social and economic benefits of a free flow of information, unimpeded by excessive government regulation. In the "New World Order" of 1992 and beyond, striking that balance remains the essential public policy challenge for the information industry, its customers, and policymakers in the United States and around the world.

Funding Programs and Grant-Making Agencies

National Endowment for the Humanities Support for Libraries, 1991

1100 Pennsylvania Ave. N.W., Washington, DC 20506
202-786-0438

The National Endowment for the Humanities (NEH), an independent federal grant-making agency created by Congress in 1965, supports research, education, and public understanding in the humanities through grants to organizations, institutions, and individuals. According to the legislation that established the endowment, the term "humanities" includes, but is not limited to, the study of archaeology, ethics, history, the history and criticism of the arts, the theory of the arts, jurisprudence, language (both modern and classical), linguistics, literature, philosophy, comparative religion, and those aspects of the social sciences that have humanities content and employ humanistic methods.

NEH's grant-making operations are conducted through six major divisions: (1) The Division of Research Programs supports the preparation for publication of editions and translations of significant work in the humanities; the preparation of reference materials; the conduct of large or complex interpretive studies; research conferences; and research opportunities offered through independent research centers and scholarly organizations. (2) The Division of Fellowships and Seminars, through several programs, provides stipends that enable individual scholars, teachers, and members of nonacademic professions to undertake study and research in the humanities that will enhance their capacity as teachers, scholars, or interpreters of the humanities and that will enable them to make significant contributions to thought and knowledge in the humanities. (3) The Division of Education Programs supports projects that promise to improve the substance and coherence of humanities education at all levels of instruction. (4) The Division of Public Programs endeavors to fulfill the endowment's mandate to foster public appreciation and understanding of the humanities. The division includes programs that assist institutions and organizations in developing humanities projects for presentation to general audiences, including adults and young adults. The division is composed of Museums and Historical Organizations, Media, Humanities Projects in Libraries and Archives, and the Public Humanities Program. Applications must meet published deadlines. (5) The Division of Preservation and Access makes grants to libraries and other repositories. And (6) The Division of State Programs makes grants to citizens' committees in each state to provide support for local humanities projects, primarily directed toward general audiences.

In addition to support through each of the six divisions, support is also available to libraries through the Office of Challenge Grants, which helps institutions to develop new and increased nonfederal, long-range sources of support in order to improve the quality of their humanities resources and activities and strengthen their financial stability.

Table 1 shows examples of grants made by the Office of Challenge Grants, the Division of Preservation and Access, the Division of Education Programs, the Division of Public Programs, and the Division of Research Programs that were in effect as of December 1991 and are wholly or partially for library support.

Categories of Support

NEH seeks to cooperate with libraries in strengthening the general public's knowledge and use of the humanities. A description of its various programs to accomplish this follows.

Division of Public Programs

The single program within the division that supports libraries directly is Humanities Projects in Libraries, though other programs offer indirect support. The program encourages public, academic, or special libraries to plan and present humanities programs. Cooperative projects between public, academic, or special libraries and between libraries, museums, historical societies, and other cultural institutions are also encouraged. Programs may take place at locations other than the library, but the primary objective of using library resources to enhance the understanding and appreciation of the humanities must be evident in the design of any project.

Among the many possible ways applicants to Humanities Projects in Libraries might fulfill the endowment's mandate to foster public understanding and appreciation of the humanities are the following: investigate the history of systems of thought; explore language as a reflection of culture; pose a philosophical debate concerning fundamental human rights; trace the development of the origins of social, political, or religious systems or institutions; or examine central themes such as love, war, family, or work through literature that illustrates such themes. A variety of methods and formats may be employed for the exploration of topics within the disciplines of the humanities. Some formats that have proven useful include reading and discussion groups; lecture series; conferences; film series accompanied by discussion groups and supplementary readings; exhibitions of library material or small exhibitions subordinate to other program formats; and such written materials as anthologies devoted to specific themes, essays illuminating specific topics, annotated bibliographies, or reading lists.

Applicants are urged to consider carefully the most appropriate means of implementing their projects and to discuss them with NEH staff. Projects should involve the active collaboration of scholars from the appropriate disciplines of the humanities during both the planning and presentation of programs. They should create an opportunity for thoughtful examination of scholarly work or dialogue between the scholarly community and the general public based on the existing collections of humanities resources of the library.

Table 1 / Examples of Current NEH Library Grants, December 1991

Recipient	Project Description	Amount
Office of Challenge Grants		
Cornell University Ithaca, NY	To support endowment of new faculty positions in pre-modern Chinese and Japanese literature, construction and equipment of the Asian Periodical Room and Media Center, integration of Asian collections, and conversion of records to machine-readable format.	$750,000
University of North Carolina Chapel Hill, NC	To support endowment of library acquisitions in Latin-American, Soviet, Eastern European, and African Studies; African-American and Women's Studies; and Southern Literature and History; and of needs in special collections and preservation programs.	$750,000
Hampshire College Amherst, MA	To support endowment of faculty development and library acquisitions in the humanities.	$285,000
Division of Preservation and Access		
New York Public Library New York, NY	To support the preservation of 40,000 endangered volumes on American history and culture.	$2,500,000
Hagley Museum and Library Wilmington, DE	To support the preservation on microfilm of the letter books of the Philadelphia and Reading Railroad Company, 1833 to 1900.	$51,583
Washington State Library Olympia, WA	To support the cataloging and preservation on microfilm of the state's newspaper holdings.	$436,388
Division of Education Programs		
Folger Shakespeare Library Washington, DC	To support a one-year program of activities for 15 college and university faculty members: an academic-year institute on "Shakespeare and the Languages of Performance," two weekend workshops, a semester-length seminar, and a series of lecture/discussion sessions on various aspects of Shakespeare studies.	$240,000
Newberry Library Chicago, IL	To support a summer institute for 20 and two workshops for 40 high school English teachers, school administrators, and American Indian community college instructors on the historical and cultural contexts of native American literature.	$308,294
Division of Public Programs		
Auburn University Auburn, AL	To support book and video discussions and a workshop about the influence of the Civil War in United States and Alabama history.	$150,000
Modern Poetry Association Chicago, IL	To support reading, listening, and discussion programs in libraries at 20 sites using the works of, taped interviews with, and readings by major contemporary American poets.	$211,980
Folger Shakespeare Library Washington, DC	To support an exhibition with an interpretive catalog, lectures, gallery tours, and curriculum materials about how Europeans in the 16th and 17th centuries formed their initial images of the New World.	$198,700
Division of Research Programs		
University of Iowa Iowa City, IA	To support the preparation of a guide to the manuscript records of the Court of Chancery in the 17th and 18th centuries.	$90,000
CUNY Research Foundation New York, NY	To support the conversion and editing of the database of the international bibliography of classical studies, *L'Année Philologique,* for production of a compact disc version containing 12 volumes of the bibliography, 1976–1987.	$200,000

The division also encourages libraries to design out-of-school projects for groups of young people of high school or junior high school age. By involving youth in projects, libraries can help them to acquire and apply new knowledge and skills in the disciplines of the humanities. Projects for this age group are intended to encourage a lifelong interest in the humanities on the part of young people by introducing them to the range of resources and activities in the humanities that are available to them outside school.

Division of Education Programs

Libraries may receive Division of Education Programs grants directly or may be part of a college or university effort to strengthen teaching in the humanities. Direct grants to libraries usually support humanities institutes at which elementary and secondary school teachers or college and university faculty use the library's resources as part of a program of study directed by recognized scholars. The John Carter Brown Library in Rhode Island and the public library of Selma, Alabama, are recent grantees. The division also encourages applications for projects to foster greater cooperation between libraries and humanities departments on individual college and university campuses.

Division of Fellowships and Seminars

The Division of Fellowships and Seminars' fellowship programs provide support for those who wish to work individually; the division's seminar programs enable individuals to pursue their work and to exchange ideas in the collegial atmosphere of a community of scholars.

NEH fellowships provide opportunities for individuals to pursue independent study and research that will enhance their capacity as teachers, scholars, or interpreters of the humanities and that will enable them to make significant contributions to thought and knowledge in the humanities. These 6- to 12-month fellowships free people from the day-to-day responsibilities of teaching and other work for extended periods of uninterrupted investigation, reflection, and often writing. The programs are designed to support a range of people from those who have made significant contributions to the humanities to those at the beginning of their careers. Projects also may cover a range of activities from general study to specialized research.

Fellowships for College Teachers and Independent Scholars are for faculty members of two-year, four-year, and five-year colleges; faculty members of departments and programs in universities that do not grant the Ph.D.; individuals employed by libraries, schools, museums, and the like; and scholars and writers working independently. The annual application deadline is June 1.

Fellowships for University Teachers are for faculty members of departments and programs that grant the Ph.D. and faculty members of postgraduate professional schools. The annual application deadline is June 1.

Summer Stipends provide support for faculty members in universities and two-year, four-year, and five-year colleges and for others working in the humanities, such as those employed by libraries, schools, museums, and so on, to pursue two consecutive months of full-time study or research. Applicants may propose projects that can be completed during the stipend period or that are part of a long-range endeavor. Each college and university in the United States may nominate three members of its faculty for the Summer Stipends competition. Nonfaculty college and university staff members and independent scholars are eligible for this program and may apply without nomination, provided that they have no teaching duties during the year of their application. The annual application deadline is October 1.

Summer Seminars for College Teachers provide opportunities to teachers in two-year, four-year, and five-year colleges and universities and to others who are qualified to do the work of the seminar and make a contribution to it. Participants, working under the direction of distinguished scholars and teachers at institutions with libraries suitable for advanced study, pursue research in their own fields or in fields related to their interests. The seminars last four to eight weeks, depending on the individual seminar, and are broadly distributed throughout the country. Seminars have been held at independent research libraries such as the Newberry and the Huntington. The annual application deadline for participants and directors is March 1.

Summer Seminars for School Teachers provide opportunities for teachers of grades K through 12 and other full-time or regular part-time school personnel to work in their areas of interest with accomplished teachers and active scholars studying significant works in the humanities systematically and thoroughly. The seminars last four, five, or six weeks, depending on the individual seminar, and are held at institutions broadly distributed throughout the country. The annual application deadline for participants is March 1 and for directors is April 1.

Graduate Study Fellowships for Faculty at Historically Black Colleges and Universities are intended to strengthen the teaching of the humanities at these colleges and universities by providing one year of support for teachers to work toward completion of a doctoral degree in one of the disciplines of the humanities. The annual application deadline is March 15.

The *Travel to Collections Program* offers small grants to scholars who must travel to use research collections of libraries, archives, museums, and other repositories. Awards are made to help defray the costs of transportation, subsistence and lodging, reproduction and photoduplication, and associated research. Annual application deadlines are January 15 and July 15.

Younger Scholars Awards provide for high school and college students to carry out projects of research and writing in the humanities during the summer. Recipients work under the close supervision of a humanities scholar, and no academic credit may be taken for this work. The annual application deadline is November 1.

The program of *Study Grants for College and University Teachers* offers support for college and university teachers to undertake six weeks of rigorous, full-time independent study in the humanities. These grants provide opportunities for faculty—especially those with heavy teaching responsibilities—to increase knowledge of their own disciplines and related disciplines, to enrich their understanding of the humanities, and to pursue intellectual projects that will inform their teaching. Grants will be made for intensive study rather than for research intended primarily for publication. The annual deadline for applications is August 15.

Division of Research Programs

The Editions Program supports various stages of the preparation of authoritative and annotated editions of works and documents of significant value to humanities scholars and general readers. The Translations Program supports individual or collaborative projects to translate into English works that provide insight into the history, literature, philosophy, and artistic achievements of other cultures and that make available to scholars, students, and the general public the thought and learning of those civilizations. Grants in the Publication Subvention Program support the publication of distinguished scholarly works in all fields of the humanities. Applications are particularly encouraged for projects that will be significant to general readers as well as to scholars and for projects of lasting value.

Grants in the Tools Program support the creation of dictionaries, historical or linguistic atlases, encyclopedias, concordances, linguistic grammars, databases, text bases, and other materials that codify information essential to research in the humanities. In the Guides Program, NEH supports projects that will assist scholars and researchers to locate information about humanities documentation or to determine the usefulness or relevance of specific materials for their research. The types of projects that are eligible for support include bibliographies, bibliographic databases, *catalogues raisonnés*, other descriptive catalogs, indexes, union lists, and guides. Libraries are also supported by many of the NEH challenge grants reviewed in the Division of Research Programs.

The Collaborative Projects Program supports major collaborative or coordinated projects having significant impact on scholarship in the humanities, especially projects that synthesize work on important scholarly and intellectual issues. Through this program, NEH supports projects that promise to strengthen understanding of history and culture by disseminating the results of archaeological fieldwork. In the Humanities, Science, and Technology Program, the endowment supports research that applies the theories and methods of humanities disciplines to science, technology, and medicine.

The Conferences Program supports conferences designed to advance the state of research in a field or topic of major importance in the humanities. Through grants in the Centers for Advanced Study Program, NEH supports interrelated research efforts in well-defined subject areas at independent research libraries and museums, U.S. research centers overseas, and centers for advanced study. Through the International Research Program, NEH provides funds to national organizations and learned societies to enable American scholars to pursue research abroad, to attend or participate in international conferences, and to engage in collaborative work with foreign colleagues.

Office of Challenge Grants

Libraries are eligible for support within the Challenge Grants Program, now (1992) in its sixteenth year of funding. By inviting libraries to appeal to a broader funding public, challenge grants assist them to increase long-term financial stability and capital support and thereby improve the quality of humanities activities and collections. To receive each federal dollar, a challenge grant recipient must raise $3 or $4 from new or increased nonfederal funding sources. Both federal and nonfederal funds may be used to support the costs of renovation and construction and the purchase of equipment. Funds may also be invested in interest-bearing accounts to ensure annual revenues to support programs in the humanities in perpetuity. Awards in this category are limited to two per institution; second awards require four-to-one matching.

Division of Preservation and Access

Grants are made to institutions for projects that will preserve and increase the availability of resources important for research, education, and public programming in the humanities. These may include books, journals, newspapers, manuscript and archival collections, maps, photographs, film, sound recordings, and objects of material culture held by libraries, archives, museums, historical organizations, and other repositories.

The division accepts applications that address problems of preservation and access from a variety of perspectives. Support may be sought for preservation microfilming projects conducted by individual libraries and archives or by institutions acting as a consortium; the conservation treatment of endangered materials, where conversion to a more stable medium is not appropriate; projects to preserve material culture collections; projects that will provide intellectual access to textual and nontextual collections; education and training projects on a regional or national level; the work of regional preservation services; the preparation of statewide preservation plans; research and demonstration projects to improve procedures and technology for preservation and access; and projects involving issues of national significance to the library and archives field. Proposals may combine preservation and access activities within a single project. Historically black colleges and universities with important institutional collections of primary source materials are encouraged to apply.

At the request of Congress, NEH has accelerated its activities to preserve brittle books and other deteriorating materials in the nation's research libraries. The endowment hopes to support projects that will cumulatively raise the annual rate of preservation microfilming across the country to a level that will permit in 20 years the preservation of the intellectual content of approximately three million volumes.

The division also administers the U.S. Newspaper Program, a national effort to locate, catalog, and preserve on microfilm the newspapers published in the United States since 1690. These projects are organized on a state-by-state basis. Awards are made for both planning and implementation.

In 1990, NEH established the National Heritage Preservation Program to support efforts to stabilize material culture collections important to the humanities through the appropriate housing and storage of objects, improved climate control, and the installation of security, lighting, and fire prevention systems. Grants are also available to establish regional or national training programs for the care and conservation of material culture collections, as well as for projects that will document collections significant to the humanities.

Support for access projects can involve the arrangement and description of archival and manuscript collections; archival surveys; the cataloging of graphic, film, sound, or artifact collections; the bibliographic control of printed works; the microfilming of collections in non-U.S. repositories; the preparation of oral histories; and the exploration of issues that have a national impact on the library and archives field.

Division of State Programs

NEH annually makes grants to state humanities councils in the 50 states, the District of Columbia, Puerto Rico, the U.S. Virgin Islands, Guam, and the Northern Marianas. The councils, in turn, award grants to institutions and organizations within each state or territory according to guidelines and application deadlines determined by each council. Most grants are for projects that promote public understanding and appreciation of the humanities. Guidelines and application deadlines may be obtained by contacting the appropriate state or territorial council directly.

State Humanities Councils

Alabama Humanities Foundation
Robert Stewart, Exec. Dir.
217 10th Ct. S.
Birmingham, AL 35205
205-930-0540

Alaska Humanities Forum
Steve Lindbeck, Exec. Dir.
430 W. Seventh Ave.
Anchorage, AK 99501
907-272-5341

Arizona Humanities Council
Dan Shilling, Exec. Dir.
The Ellis-Shackelford House
1242 N. Central Ave.
Phoenix, AZ 85004
602-257-0335

Arkansas Humanities Council
Robert E. Bailey, Exec. Dir.
10816 Executive Center Dr., Suite 310
Little Rock, AR 72211-4383
501-221-0091

California Council for the Humanities
James Quay, Exec. Dir.
312 Sutter St., Suite 601
San Francisco, CA 94108
415-391-1474

Colorado Endowment for the Humanities
James Pierce, Exec. Dir.
1623 Blake St., Rm. 200
Denver, CO 80202
303-573-7733

Connecticut Humanities Council
Bruce Fraser, Exec. Dir.
41 Lawn Ave., Wesleyan Sta.
Middletown, CT 06457
203-347-6888

Delaware Humanities Forum
Henry Hirschbiel, Exec. Dir.
2600 Pennsylvania Ave.
Wilmington, DE 19806
302-573-4410

D.C. Community Humanities Council
Francine Cary, Exec. Dir.
1331 H St. N.W., Suite 902
Washington, DC 20005
202-347-1732

Florida Humanities Council
Ann Henderson, Exec. Dir.
1718 E. Seventh Ave., Suite 301
Ybor City, Tampa, FL 33605
813-272-3473

Georgia Humanities Council
Ronald E. Benson, Exec. Dir.
1556 Clifton Rd. N.E.
Emory Univ.
Atlanta, GA 30322
404-727-7500

Hawaii Committee for the Humanities
Annette M. Lew, Exec. Dir.
First Hawaiian Bank Bldg.
3599 Waialae Ave., Rm. 23
Honolulu, HI 96816
808-732-5402

Idaho Humanities Council
Thomas H. McClanahan, Exec. Dir.
217 W. State St.
Boise, ID 83702
208-345-5346

Illinois Humanities Council
Frank Pettis, Exec. Dir.
618 S. Michigan Ave.
Chicago, IL 60605
312-939-5212

Indiana Humanities Council
Kenneth L. Gladish, Exec. Dir.
1500 N. Delaware St.
Indianapolis, IN 46202
317-638-1500

Iowa Humanities Board
Rick Knupfer, Exec. Dir.
Oakdale Campus N210 OH
Univ. of Iowa
Iowa City, IA 52242
319-335-4153

Kansas Committee for the Humanities
Marion Cott, Exec. Dir.
112 W. Sixth St., Suite 210
Topeka, KS 66603
913-357-0359

Kentucky Humanities Council, Inc.
Virginia Smith, Exec. Dir.
417 Clifton Ave.
Univ. of Kentucky

Lexington, KY 40508-3406
606-257-5932

Louisiana Endowment for the Humanities
Michael Sartisky, Exec. Dir.
1001 Howard Ave., Suite 3110
New Orleans, LA 70113
504-523-4352

Maine Humanities Council
Dorothy Schwartz, Exec. Dir.
Box 7202
Portland, ME 04112
207-773-5051

Maryland Humanities Council
Naomi F. Collins, Exec. Dir.
516 N. Charles St., Rm. 102
Baltimore, MD 21201
301-625-4830

**Massachusetts Foundation for the
    Humanities**
David Tebaldi, Exec. Dir.
One Woodbridge St.
South Hadley, MA 01075
413-536-1385

Michigan Council for the Humanities
Ronald Means, Exec. Dir.
Nisbet Bldg., Suite 30
1407 S. Harrison Rd.
East Lansing, MI 48823
517-355-0160

Minnesota Humanities Commission
Cheryl Dickson, Exec. Dir.
26 E. Exchange St., Lower Level S.
Saint Paul, MN 55101
612-224-5739

Mississippi Humanities Council
Cora Norman, Exec. Dir.
3825 Ridgewood Rd., Rm. 508
Jackson, MS 39211
601-982-6752

Missouri Humanities Council
Christine Reilly, Exec. Dir.
911 Washington Ave., Suite 215
Saint Louis, MO 63101-1208
314-621-7705

Montana Committee for the Humanities
Margaret Kingsland, Exec. Dir.
Box 8036, Hellgate Sta.
Missoula, MT 59807
406-243-6022

Nebraska Humanities Council
Jane Renner Hood, Exec. Dir.
Lincoln Center Bldg., Suite 225
215 Centennial Mall S.
Lincoln, NE 68508
402-474-2131

Nevada Humanities Committee
Judith K. Winzeler, Exec. Dir.
Box 8029
Reno, NV 89507
702-784-6587

New Hampshire Humanities Council
Charles G. Bickford, Exec. Dir.
19 Pillsbury St., Box 2228
Concord, NH 03302-2228
603-224-4071

New Jersey Committee for the Humanities
Miriam L. Murphy, Exec. Dir.
73 Easton Ave.
New Brunswick, NJ 08901
908-932-7726

New Mexico Endowment for the Humanities
John Lucas, Exec. Dir.
Onate Hall, Rm. 209
Univ. of New Mexico
Albuquerque, NM 87131
505-277-3705

New York Council for the Humanities
Jay Kaplan, Exec. Dir.
198 Broadway, 10th fl.
New York, NY 10038
212-233-1131

North Carolina Humanities Council
Alice Barkley, Exec. Dir.
425 Spring Garden St.
Greensboro, NC 27401
919-334-5325

North Dakota Humanities Council
Everett Albers, Exec. Dir.
Box 2191, Bismarck, ND 58502
701-255-3360

Ohio Humanities Council
Eleanor Kingsbury, Exec. Dir.
Box 06354
Columbus, OH 43206-0354
614-461-7802

Oklahoma Foundation for the Humanities
Anita May, Exec. Dir.
Festival Plaza

428 W. California, Suite 270
Oklahoma City, OK 73102
405-235-0280

Oregon Council for the Humanities
Richard Lewis, Exec. Dir.
812 S.W. Washington, Suite 225
Portland, OR 97205
503-241-0543

Pennsylvania Humanities Council
Craig Eisendrath, Exec. Dir.
320 Walnut St., Suite 305
Philadelphia, PA 19106
215-925-1005

Rhode Island Committee for the Humanities
Thomas H. Roberts, Exec. Dir.
60 Ship St.
Providence, RI 02903
401-273-2250

South Carolina Humanities Council
Randy L. Akers, Exec. Dir.
1610 Oak St.
Columbia, SC 29204
803-771-8864

South Dakota Humanities Council
John Whalen, Exec. Dir.
Box 7050, Univ. Sta.
Brookings, SD 57007
605-688-6113

Tennessee Humanities Council
Robert Cheatham, Exec. Dir.
1003 18th Ave. S.
Nashville, TN 37212
615-320-7001

Texas Committee for the Humanities
James Veninga, Exec. Dir.
Banister Place A
3809 S. Second St.
Austin, TX 78704
512-440-1991

Utah Humanities Council
Delmont Oswald, Exec. Dir.
Broadway Bldg., Suite 505
10 W. Broadway
Salt Lake City, UT 84101-2002
801-531-7868

Vermont Council on the Humanities
Victor R. Swenson, Exec. Dir.

Grant House, Box 58
Hyde Park, VT 05655
802-888-3183

Virginia Foundation for the Humanities
Robert C. Vaughan, Exec. Dir.
145 Ednam Dr.
Charlottesville, VA 22901-3207
804-924-3296

Washington Commission for the Humanities
Hidde Van Duym, Exec. Dir.
Lowman Bldg., Suite 312
107 Cherry St.
Seattle, WA 98104
206-682-1770

West Virginia Humanities Council
Charles Daugherty, Exec. Dir.
723 Kanawha Blvd. E., Suite 800
Charleston, WV 25301
304-346-8500

Wisconsin Humanities Committee
Patricia Anderson, Exec. Dir.
716 Langdon St.
Madison, WI 53706
608-262-0706

Wyoming Council for the Humanities
Robert Young, Exec. Dir.
Box 3643, Univ. Sta.
Laramie, WY 82071-3643
307-766-6496

Guam Humanities Council
Kathleen Roos, Exec. Dir.
House 6, Dean's Circle
University of Guam
UOG Sta.
Mangilao, GU 96923
671-734-1727

Fundación Puertorriqueña de las Humanidades
Juan M. Gonzalez Lamela, Exec. Dir.
Box S-4307
Old San Juan, PR 00904
809-721-2087

Virgin Islands Humanities Council
Magda Smith, Exec. Dir.
GERS Bldg., 3rd fl.
Kronprindsens Gade, Box 1829
Saint Thomas, VI 00803
809-776-4044

National Science Foundation Support for Research in Information Science and Technology, 1991

Laurence C. Rosenberg

Deputy Director
Information, Robotics, and Intelligent Systems Division
National Science Foundation
1800 G St. N.W., Washington, DC 20550
202-357-5000

The National Science Foundation (NSF), a federal agency established in 1950 to promote progress in science and engineering, provides financial and other support for research, education, and related activities in science, mathematics, and engineering. Information science and technology research is supported through the Information, Robotics, and Intelligent Systems Division of the Computer and Information Science and Engineering Directorate.

Division of Information, Robotics, and Intelligent Systems (IRIS)

Modern computer and communications technology is the foundation for dramatic transformations in the content and structure of societies. It allows us to gather, store, retrieve, and selectively disseminate vast amounts of data and facilitates conversion of these data into new information and knowledge. These capabilities are the touchstone of modern economic, social, governmental, and leisure activities. The IRIS Division responds to the continued challenges both to improve this technology and harness its power in the service of society by providing research support in areas of machine intelligence, database design, individual and group interfaces, and the comparative study of information processes in machines, individuals, and organizations. IRIS also supports research that will enhance the services available on scientific communications networks. This includes support for design of scientific databases, digital libraries and digital journals, remote interaction with scientific facilities and tools, and multimedia conferencing support for scientific collaboration.

Research Highlights

IRIS supports many areas of research. Recent areas of emphasis include

- Use of image, voice, and other sensory inputs to study human-machine partnerships and intelligent interfaces between perception and action.
- Theory and models of coordination mechanisms in organizations and machines, computer-supported cooperative work, and collaboration technology in distributed, networked computer systems.
- Study and design of large, heterogeneous, distributed databases, with an emphasis on scientific databases.
- Study and development of reasoning, planning, speech and language understanding, and other cognitive capabilities for computers in the face of imperfect information and changing environments.

- Development of robotics as the science of representing, recognizing, reasoning about, and manipulating objects in the physical environment or in the information space.

IRIS Division Programs

The IRIS Division organizes its research and education supporting activities in five highly interdisciplinary programs. Although the division concentrates its support on research that draws on computer science, mathematics, engineering, and behavioral and social sciences, applied research that is likely to increase general knowledge in a field of science is also considered.

Database and Expert Systems Program

The Database and Expert Systems Program supports research fundamental to the design, development, management, and use of databases and information retrieval and knowledge-based systems. The aim is to build "new generation" distributed, interoperable, multimedia, intelligent information systems capable of sophisticated and efficient information processing. Projects can be divided into four interrelated areas—information modeling, query processing, physical design, and system support—and include a wide range of subjects, from artificial intelligence methodologies to techniques for effective utilization of high-performance hardware technology. Special emphasis is placed on development of scientific databases and methods for analyzing scientific data, in collaboration with domain science directorates and related programs within IRIS and in the Division of Computer and Computation Research and the Directorate of Mathematical and Physical Sciences.

Information Technology and Organizations Program

The Information Technology and Organizations Program supports research to create knowledge about the integration of computer and communications technology into group activities and the social, organizational, and economic impact of computer and communications technology. The program funds research on computer-supported cooperative work, coordination, and collaboration. A major objective is to provide the knowledge base for development of the "collaboratory," a national resource that uses networking and computer technology to support scientific collaboration independent of distance by allowing robust, remote interchange of data and archival knowledge between colleagues and instruments.

The following are the three funding elements:

- Coordination theory—how people collaborate and coordinate work efficiently and productively in environments characterized by a high degree of decentralized computation and decision making.
- Collaboration technology—the design of multiuser interfaces and software systems, evaluation of collaboratory testbeds, empirical studies of existing coordination technologies and groupware, exploratory design of collaboratory-like systems that integrate invention and implementation, for the purpose of observing and evaluating effects of new technology.
- Information technology impacts and policy—the structure and output of organizations, industries, and markets that incorporate sophisticated, decentral-

ized information and communications technology as important components of their operations.

The results of the research are likely to contribute to an understanding of the impact of computer and communications technology and improve our ability to design systems and organizations.

Interactive Systems Program

The Interactive Systems Program sponsors fundamental research that assesses and enhances human interaction with computer systems. Research focuses on determining the scientific basis for the dynamic adaptation of systems to humans, interaction with virtual realities, interactive visualization, speech and language interfaces, and interaction via posture and sound. Research is supported in five areas:

- Adaptive systems—dynamic adaptation of computers to facilitate or enhance interactive tasks.
- Virtual systems—linear, nonlinear, and dynamic mapping of functional interaction with real or abstract objects or systems of objects, such as machines, robots, and physical or chemical objects.
- Interactive visualization—representing complex physical or abstract systems, models, or objects for interaction and understanding.
- Speech and language interfaces—speech recognition and understanding, language processing, and speech production in the context of human-computer interaction.
- Posture and sound—studies of human-controlled sounds and vibrations, tones, music, gestures, posture, body language, facial expression, tactile, and other motor channels to assess or influence human commands, intentions, and emotional or mental states (e.g., surprise, readiness, attention, fear, confusion, satisfaction) or their use to guide simulations or processes.

Knowledge Models and Cognitive Systems Program

The research focus of the Knowledge Models and Cognitive Systems Program spans computer science, chiefly artificial intelligence, and includes computational-based cognitive science. Major areas of research include

- Formal models of knowledge and information—support for work on formal models relating to knowledge, information, and imperfections in the two.
- Cognitive systems—knowledge representation and inference, highly parallel approaches, and computational characterization of human cognition.
- Machine learning—problems in automatic assimilation of information, including design of suitable knowledge structures, control paradigms, and dynamic change to embody the notion of learning.
- Natural language processing—computational aspects of syntax, semantics, and the lexicon; discourse, dialogue, and generation; and systems issues.

Robotics and Machine Intelligence Program

The Robotics and Machine Intelligence Program sponsors research in artificial intelligence applied to the physical world and in robotics, the science of machines that can perceive, reason about, and manipulate physical objects. The program supports research in the design of computational systems that can adapt to a perceived situation by planning and executing complex tasks. Building such systems requires a fundamental knowledge of machine vision, pattern recognition and speech understanding, planning of paths and trajectories, manipulation, locomotion, and sensor-based control. The program supports projects that seek to understand the computational, informational, design, and mechanical principles by which intelligent machines interact with their environments. The objective is to make machines and systems of all kinds operate more autonomously of human attention. Research topics include perception, recognition, and understanding of tactile and visual images representing two- and three-dimensional objects or scenes; pattern analysis; automated task planning; and robot reasoning for intelligent control and autonomous machine operation. The three program elements are

- Image understanding — reasoning about scenes that generate images and relating the images to machine tasks and to models of the physical world and/or objects.
- Pattern analysis — automatic extraction of meaning from sources of evidential data, with special consideration for robotic applications.
- Robotic perception and reasoning — tactile, visual, and range sensing for systems that move in their environment and/or manipulate objects.

Research Related to Library Science

Many research projects supported by IRIS are pertinent to modern library science and related activities. The division's interest in supporting research for scientific collaboration is particularly germane for the library of the future. Scientific reference services that operate on national networks and use sophisticated access to literature, references to human experts, and computer artificial intelligence are a realistic expectation for the 1990s. Also likely are digital journals, along with peer review, which would include electronic retrieval of journal material and logging of documents and comments on them. Digital journals and digital libraries will transform "collections" and the equipment and communications for collecting, maintaining, and using them. But the impact on the organization and physical form of the library will be even more profound. The distribution of electronic libraries among randomly located knowledge bases will affect the funding and meaning of a library. To deal with problems of search and retrieval and to protect the integrity of a collection, library science will need to evolve into a new discipline. Much of the subject matter of interest to this "new library science" is embodied in research projects funded by IRIS. A sampling of FY 1989–FY 1991 projects follows:

Bruce R. Schatz and Sam Ward (University of Arizona), "Systems Technology for Building a National Collaboratory," $360,631.

John B. Smith, F. Donelson Smith, Peter Calingaert, Kevin Jeffay, Dorothy Holland, John R. Hayes (University of North Carolina at Chapel Hill), "Building and Using a Collaboratory: A Foundation for Supporting and Studying Group Collaborations," $900,000.

Edward A. Fox, Lenwood S. Heath, and Deborah Hix (Virginia Polytechnic Institute and State University), "A User-Centered Database from the Computer Science Literature," $127,900.

Edward Sciore and Sharon C. Salveter (Boston University), "Deriving and Maintenance of Rules in an Intelligent DBMS," $158,002.

Vasant Dhar and Jarke Matthias (New York University), "REMAP: A New Approach for Large Systems Development and Maintenance," $61,613.

Jeffrey D. Ullman (Stanford University), "Research into the Design and Implementation of Knowledge-Based Systems," $205,443.

William M. Shaw and Judith B. Wood (University of North Carolina at Chapel Hill), "An Evaluation and Comparison of Term and Citation Indexing," $75,487.

Gary Marchionini (University of Maryland), "Mental Models for Adaptive Search Systems: A Theory for Information Seeking," $70,732.

Douglas P. Metzler (University of Pittsburgh), "An Expert System Approach to Syntactic Parsing and Information Retrieval," $76,122.

Donald W. Dearholt (New Mexico State University), "Properties of Networks Derived from Proximities," $62,730.

Gerard Salton (Cornell University), "Interface Tools and User-System Interaction in Automatic Information Retrieval," $139,553.

Vijay Raghavan and Jitender S. Deogun (University of Southwestern Louisiana), "Cluster-Based Adaptive Information Retrieval System," $69,013.

James H. Morris, David Kaufer, Christine M. Neuwirth, and Ravinder Chandok (Carnegie Mellon University), "The 'Work in Preparation' (PREP) Editor: Support for Co-Authoring and Commenting," $275,000.

Council on Library Resources, 1991

1785 Massachusetts Ave. N.W., Washington, D.C. 20036
202-483-7474

Mary Agnes Thompson
Secretary/Treasurer

The Council on Library Resources is a nonprofit foundation incorporated in the District of Columbia in 1956 for the general purpose of promoting library research. The Ford Foundation established the council with the charge to "aid in the solution of library problems; to conduct research in, develop and demonstrate new techniques and methods and to disseminate through any means the results thereof." Remarkable technological, economic, and social changes in the nation's educational and research environments occurred during the next decades. The processes by which users organize, retrieve, and disseminate information changed dramatically. Council-funded research has in many cases profoundly influenced the ways in which information is organized and put to use. Its projects have been carried out under the direction of the council's presidents and directors, but with the collaboration of many in the library, academic, and information services communities. The council's third president, Warren J. Haas, retired on December 31, 1990. W. David Penniman, former director of the Information Services Group at AT&T Bell Laboratories, became the new president on January 9, 1991.

The board of directors consists of 16 individuals from research libraries, academic institutions, the business community, and the professions. Council officers are Maximilian W. Kempner, chairperson; Charles D. Churchwell, vice chairperson; W. David Penniman, president; and Mary Agnes Thompson, secretary and treasurer. During the fiscal year ending June 30, 1991, the council received financial support from the AT&T Foundation, the J. Paul Getty Trust, the W. K. Kellogg Foundation, the Andrew W. Mellon Foundation, and the Pew Charitable Trusts.

Highlights of FY 1991

As a private operating foundation, the council conducts its work through directly administered projects as well as through grants and contracts with other organizations. The council made 30 new grants in FY 1991, and about 100 grants and projects were active during the year. New grants totaled $787,073 and ranged from $810 to $100,000.

Setting Library Policies and Priorities in Research Universities

Approximately half of the funds were allocated to the special program "Setting Library Policies and Priorities in Research Universities." The impetus for the new program came from the final statement of the Research Library Committee, established by the council with the cosponsorship of the American Council of Learned Societies, the Association of American Universities, and the Social Science Research Council. The committee concluded that the information base for teaching and learning was being rapidly transformed by integrated information technologies — computers, telecommunications, and text storage systems — but how libraries and faculties would deal with digitized information and virtually unbounded means of access was far from clear. Whether universities and their libraries would productively embrace information-age capabilities or be engulfed by them was also uncertain.

As a consequence, the committee statement concluded that universities had to fundamentally rethink library and information service objectives, including redefining the role of the research library. It further recommended that faculty and librarians should join forces to set realistic, forward-looking objectives for research resources and services and should actively promote collaboration among research libraries. Four awards of $100,000 each were made under the program.

Columbia University

As the first phase in a larger institutional planning effort focused on library acquisitions and information delivery, Columbia will study information strategies in three science departments that maintain libraries. Against a background of heavy reliance on serials whose prices are escalating, economic and organizational issues in providing access to electronic databases, and the likelihood of duplication in collections as well as staffing and service costs in a decentralized system, the project will seek a better understanding of scientists' information needs and preferences, including an examination of delivery time requirements and issues in replacing print formats with electronic ones.

Harvard University

Investigators will perform analytic studies to identify relevant characteristics of the Harvard College Library, as well as the expectations and future research and teaching needs of its users. Other studies will focus on making materials in remote or dispersed storage available through electronic record keeping, coupled with multichannel transfer through high-speed networks rather than by physical movement of volumes.

SUNY Consortium

The libraries at four State University of New York campuses (Albany, Binghamton, Buffalo, and Stony Brook) are formulating policies and plans to implement a program of cooperative collection development and resource sharing. The aim is to develop procedures for achieving institutional aspirations without needless duplication and within available resources.

Triangle Research Libraries Network

Duke University, the University of North Carolina, and North Carolina State University will explore extension of long-standing programs of collaboration in collection development in the social sciences and the humanities to electronic media and the natural sciences. Investigators will address issues of collaboration and communication among faculty, organizational and legal barriers to collaboration; overlap in collections and databases among campuses; budget models and funding mechanisms to support collaborative information resource delivery; and advisory group structures for interinstitutional collaboration.

Professional Education

The Academic Library Management Intern Program, offered biennially for librarians who have an interest in the management of large libraries, sponsored three interns for the academic year 1990–1991: Susan Klingberg interned at Princeton University, Margaret L. Morrison at the University of Chicago, and Virginia Steel at Brown University. The council announced a new project to ease the growing shortage of library science educators by helping graduate students in the field finish dissertations more rapidly than they would have without financial support and thus be available for faculty positions. The W. K. Kellogg Foundation sponsored the program on an experimental basis in 1991–1992. CLR/Kellogg Fellows were Ann P. Bishop, Philip Doty, and Herbert Snyder, Syracuse University; Tina Maragou Hovekamp, University of North Carolina at Chapel Hill; Dee Andy Michel, University of California at Los Angeles; and Sherry L. Vellucci, Columbia University.

The Advisory Committee on Library Education, a group of eleven library school deans, disbanded in November 1990. The text of its report, written by Warren J. Haas, was published as a program report and is available from the council.

Other grants and projects during the year were made in the program areas of bibliography, access to information, and library resources.

Major New Grants and Contracts, FY 1991

Columbia University, New York, N.Y.
For recasting scientific information delivery — $100,000
1991–1992 CLR/Kellogg Fellowship — $16,000

Drexel University, Philadelphia, Pa.
Invitational conference on public library effectiveness — $16,760

Harvard University, Cambridge, Mass.
Strategic planning process for libraries — $100,000

Indiana University of Pennsylvania, Indiana, Pa.
Further work on using hypermedia to improve subject access — $15,000

Library of Congress, Washington, D.C.
National Coordinated Cataloging Program — $16,299

SKP Associates, New York, N.Y.
Evaluation of the Cataloging in Publication program — $25,000

State University of New York, Buffalo, N.Y.
Developing an integrated acquisitions plan for several
SUNY campuses — $100,000

Syracuse University, Syracuse, N.Y.
Three CLR/Kellogg Fellowships — $48,000

University of California, Berkeley, Calif.
Development of collaborative relationships between humanities
researchers and librarians — $24,000

University of California, Los Angeles, Calif.
CLR/Kellogg Fellowship — $16,000

University of Illinois, Urbana, Ill.
Second Advanced Research Institute — $28,786

University of North Carolina, Chapel Hill, N.C.
Planning for collaborative collection development in
electronic media and the natural sciences — $100,000
CLR/Kellogg Fellowship — $16,000

University of Pittsburgh, Pittsburgh, Pa.
To study the effects of integrating information technology
on job classification and compensation systems — $18,560

White House Conference on Library and Information Services,
Washington, D.C. — $15,000

U.S. Department of Education Library Programs, 1991

555 New Jersey Ave. N.W., Washington, DC 20208-5571
202-219-2293

Ray M. Fry

Acting Director, Library Programs
Office of Educational Research and Improvement
U.S. Department of Education

The Library Programs Division in the U.S. Department of Education contributes to the improvement of the nation's libraries and library education by administering the 11 programs under the Library Services and Construction Act (LSCA) and the Higher Education Act, Title II (HEA II). The programs

- Promote resource sharing and cooperation among all types of libraries by facilitating development and access to information that permit individuals to find and use books and other materials from libraries across the country
- Assist state library agencies in improving local library services for all citizens, with a focus on underserved populations such as the handicapped and disadvantaged
- Support local and state efforts to construct new public library facilities and upgrade existing ones
- Improve library services to native populations — Indian tribes, Alaskan native villages, and Hawaiian natives — through basic and special projects
- Support acquisition of foreign-language materials by state and local public libraries
- Support adult literacy programs conducted by state library agencies and local public libraries
- Strengthen major research libraries, including those of postsecondary institutions, by helping them improve access to important collections, preserve deteriorating materials, and acquire unique, distinctive, and specialized materials
- Advance the education of librarians through fellowships and training institutes
- Encourage colleges and universities to promote and develop exemplary uses of technology for resource sharing and networking
- Fund research and demonstration projects on library and information science issues.

Besides administering LSCA and HEA II, Library Programs provides leadership to the library community by

Note: The following Library Programs staff assisted in writing and/or compiling data for this article: Yvonne Carter, Nancy Cavanaugh, Blane Dessy, Christina Dunn, Clarence Fogelstrom, Donald Fork, Barbara Humes, Neal Kaske, Dorothy Kittel, Robert Klassen, Linda Loeb, Carol Cameron Lyons, Evaline Neff, Jan Owens, Elizabeth Payer, Kathy Perkinson, Trish Skaptason, Sheryl Stein, Louise Sutherland, and Thea Wiggert.

- Planning for library development
- Implementing federal policies and programs
- Providing guidance and technical assistance to grant recipients
- Promoting the evaluation of library programs
- Recognizing exemplary library programs
- Conducting research to address national issues
- Interpreting federally funded library activities for library and nonlibrary audiences
- Integrating the contributions of libraries into the framework of the National Education Goals.

Higher Education Act (HEA, PL 99-498)

Title II of the Higher Education Act has been the backbone of federal financial assistance to college and university libraries for more than two decades. With the continuing expansion of information resources and increasing demand on higher education libraries, Title II has been a vital element in helping these libraries to preserve, acquire, and share resources; to train and retrain personnel; and to use new technologies to improve services. In 1986, HEA II was reauthorized and some parts rewritten to accommodate change, including establishment of the College Library Technology and Cooperation Grants program (HEA, Title II-D). In 1987, these amendments were implemented through revisions in the regulations and development of new regulations for the HEA II-D program.

College Library Resources Program (HEA, Title II-A)

During its reauthorization in Congress in 1986, Title II-A of the Higher Education Act was amended to award grants to institutions of higher education strictly on the basis of need. To date, no funds have been appropriated.

Library Career Training Program (HEA, Title II-B)

The Library Career Training Program (Title II-B of the Higher Education Act) authorizes a program of federal financial assistance to institutions of higher education and other library organizations and agencies to assist in training librarians and to establish, develop, and expand programs of library and information science. Grants are made for fellowships and traineeships in librarianship at the associate's, bachelor's, master's, post-master's, and doctoral levels. Grants may also be used to help cover the cost of institutes or courses to upgrade the skills of those serving in all types of libraries, information centers, and instructional materials centers offering library and information services, as well as the skills of educators.

In FY 1991, Congress appropriated $976,000 for the two programs under HEA II-B: the Library Career Training Program and the Library Research and Demonstration Program. Of this amount, $650,667 was allocated for the Library Career Training Program. Twenty-seven awards were made to support 50 fellowships (23 master's, 3 post-master's, and 24 doctoral) for a total of $644,000; there was no competition for institutes. Stipends were $5,400 for master's and $7,400 for post-master's and doctoral candidates. Institutions received an equal amount to cover the cost of training. Table 1 shows the Library Career Training grants awarded in FY 1991.

Between 1966 and 1991, institutions of higher education were awarded 4,386 grants — 1,135 doctoral, 253 post-master's, 2,852 master's, 16 bachelor's, and 53 associate's fellowships, and 77 traineeships. Table 2 reviews the fellowship program since it began in FY 1966.

Library Research and Demonstration Program (HEA, Title II-B)

The Library Research and Demonstration Program (Title II-B of the Higher Education Act) authorizes grants and contracts for research and demonstration projects related to the improvement of libraries, training in librarianship, and the dissemination of information derived from these projects. (Table 3 presents the funding history of the program.) Title II, Part B, of the Higher Education Act was amended by the Higher Education Amendments of 1986. In 1987, by statutory mandate, "information technology" was deleted from the list of authorized research and demonstration subjects. This amendment precludes research on or about information technology but allows use of technology to accomplish the goals of a research or demonstration project.

Table 1 / HEA, Title II-B, Library Career Training Program, FY 1991 Fellowships

	Fellowships	
Institution	No. and Level	Amount
University of Alabama	1 master's	$10,800
University of Alabama	3 master's	32,400
University of Alabama	1 doctoral	14,800
University of Central Arkansas	4 master's	43,200
University of California at Berkeley	1 doctoral	12,800
University of California at Los Angeles	4 doctoral	59,200
Florida State University	2 doctoral	29,600
University of Illinois	1 doctoral	14,800
Rosary College	1 master's	10,800
Indiana University	2 doctoral	29,600
Louisiana State University	2 master's	21,600
Louisiana State University	1 post-master's	12,800
University of Michigan	1 master's	10,800
University of Michigan	2 doctoral	29,600
Rutgers University	1 master's	10,800
Rutgers University	3 doctoral	44,400
Saint John's University	2 master's	21,600
SUNY at Albany	2 master's	21,600
University of North Carolina	2 doctoral	29,600
Kent State University	2 master's	21,600
Ohio University	1 master's	10,800
University of Oklahoma	2 master's	21,600
University of Oklahoma	2 post-master's	29,600
University of Pittsburgh	3 doctoral	44,400
Texas Woman's University	1 doctoral	14,800
University of Wisconsin at Madison	2 doctoral	29,600
University of Wisconsin at Milwaukee	1 master's	10,800
Subtotal	23 master's	
	24 doctoral	
	3 post-master's	
Total	50 fellowships	$644,000

Table 2 / HEA, Title II-B, Library Education
Fellowship/Trainee Program, Academic Years 1966-1992

Academic Year	Insti-tutions	Fellowship/Traineeship					Total	FY
		Doctoral	Post-Master's	Master's	Bachelor's	Associate's		
1966/67	24	52	25	62	–	–	139	1966
1967/68	38	116	58	327	–	–	501	1967
1968/69	51	168	47	494	–	–	709	1968
1969/70	56	193	30	379	–	–	602	1969
1970/71	48	171	15	200	20*	–	406	1970
1971/72	20	116	6	–	20*	–	142	1971
1972/73	15	39	3	20*	–	–	62	1972
1973/74	34	21	4	145+14*	–	20	204	1973
1974/75	50	21	3	168+3*	–	5	200	1974
1975/76	22	27	6	94	–	–	127	1975
1976/77	12	5	3	43	–	–	51	1976
1977/78	37	18	3	134	–	5	160	1977
1978/79	33	25	9	139	10	5	188	1978
1979/80	36	19	4	134	2	3	162	1979
1980/81	32	17	5	72	–	7	101	1980
1981/82	34	13	2	59	–	5	79	1981
1982/83	33	13	2	56	–	3	74	1982
1983/84	33	8	7	56	4	–	75	1983
1984/85	41	5	4	67	–	–	76	1984
1985/86	38	11	4	57	–	–	72	1985
1986/87	39	14	3	51	–	–	68	1986
1987/88	29	10	5	45	–	–	60	1987
1988/89	20	9	0	14	–	–	23	1988
1989/90	20	10	0	12	–	–	22	1989
1990/91	21	10	2	21	–	–	33	1990
1991/92	27	24	3	23	–	–	50	1991
Total	–	1,135	253	2,852+37*	16+40*	53	4,386	

*Indicates traineeships

In FY 1987, field-initiated applications were sought for the first time since 1980. In FY 1991, 43 proposals were submitted and 4 were selected for funding totaling $288,953. These projects are

Assessing Information on the Internet: Toward Providing Library Services for Computer-Mediated Communication (Online Computer Library Center. $48,675. *Chief investigator:* Martin Dillion). To investigate the nature of electronic information available on Internet and the problems associated with providing systematic access to it. By analyzing information resources, the project team will (1) locate and identify types of electronic information available on Internet; (2) produce 'a taxonomy of this information; and (3) assess the theoretical and applied problems that libraries face in acquiring, cataloging, indexing, storing, retrieving, and disseminating this information and in providing research and reference services.

Using the taxonomy, the project will develop methods to determine the value of electronic literature, devise techniques for preserving or enhancing its value, and determine the extent to which these tasks can be automated. Based on this evaluation, the project team will propose methods and levels of access to this information by type and develop a model system for libraries, information providers, and parties at Internet. Findings will be widely disseminated in printed and electronic formats as a catalyst for discussion and action to help ensure the value of Internet as a growing national information resource.

Table 3 / HEA, Title II-B, Library Research and Demonstration Program, Headline Years 1967-1991

Fiscal Year	Appropriation	Grants and Contracts Obligations	Number of Grants and Contracts
1967	$3,550,000	$3,381,052	38
1968	3,550,000	2,020,942	21
1969	3,000,000	2,986,264	39
1970	2,171,000	2,160,622	30
1971	2,171,000	2,170,274	18
1972	2,750,000	2,748,953	31
1973	1,785,000	1,784,741	24
1974	1,425,000	1,418,433	20
1975	1,000,000	999,338	19
1976	1,000,000	999,918	19
1977	1,000,000	995,193	18
1978	1,000,000	998,904	17
1979	1,000,000	980,563	12
1980	1,000,000*	319,046	4
1981	1,000,000*	239,954	12 (2 contracts, 10 commissioned papers)
1982	1,000,000*	243,438	1 contract
1983	1,000,000*	237,643	4 contracts
1984	1,000,000*	250,764	3 contracts
1985	1,000,000*	360,000	3 contracts
1986	1,000,000*	378,000	3 contracts
1987	1,000,000*	336,522	5 (3 grants, 2 contracts)
1988	718,000*	306,303	5 grants
1989	709,000*	297,325	5 grants
1990	855,000*	285,000	5 grants
1991	976,000*	320,753	4 grants 2 commissioned papers 1 contract

*Includes the II-B training appropriation

The Characteristics of Effective Literacy Programs: A Field Study (RMC Research Corporation. $62,949. *Chief investigator:* Andrew Seager). To examine the characteristics of effective library literacy programs. The objectives of the first stage of the project are (1) to synthesize relevant research and conceptual paradigms that can further understanding of library literacy programs; (2) to isolate and define those factors that research and experience indicate most determine their effectiveness; (3) to use this information to develop a series of research questions and data collection protocols to focus qualitative on-site data collection; and (4) to analyze the interview, observation, and archive data collection to describe the individual programs and identify common themes and issues.

In the second stage of the project, the information and knowledge gained from on-site study of library literacy programs will be disseminated to policymakers and practitioners through various channels, including a final report containing all the products created through the project; one or more papers in scholarly journals; presentations to library literacy groups; and materials and workshops developed for a variety of settings. One or more of the literacy programs may be included in the U.S. Department of Education's National Diffusion Network.

Assessment of the Public Library's Missions in Society (University of Minnesota, Center for Survey Research and the Carlson School of Management. $98,354. *Chief investigators:* William Craig and George D'Elia). To design and execute a national survey of households in the United States to assess public opinion concerning the public library's mission in society and the public's willingness to support public financing for library services; and to design and execute a national survey of public leaders concerning the mission of the public library in society and the level of public financial support for library services.

These data, broken down geographically and demographically, will assist public libraries throughout the nation in selecting missions (given the demographic characteristics of the communities they serve) and in tying these missions to resource acquisition and allocation.

Environment and Organizational Factors Associated with the Development of Family Literacy Programs in U.S. Public Libraries (University of Wisconsin. $78,975. *Chief investigator:* Debra Johnson). To assess the status of family literacy programs in public libraries and identify their characteristics. The investigator intends to develop a model for library involvement in such programs by identifying the variables influencing the library's decision to become involved. Libraries will be able to use the results in planning and carrying out family literacy services.

The study defines family literacy programs as programs targeted to adult new readers who are parents, relatives, or care-givers for children. Project staff will design and distribute a questionnaire for a sample of public libraries in the United States. An expert panel will then review the responses and the report, and an adult education consultant will evaluate the project. Besides the final report, the study will produce an invitational seminar, along with articles and presentations to disseminate results.

Library Programs also commissioned two papers for a publication celebrating the silver anniversary of the Adult Education Act:

- Beginnings: Public Libraries and Adult Education 1900 to 1966 by Margaret E. Monroe ($950) traces "the development of literacy education in the context of library adult education from the beginning of the twentieth century until 1966."
- The Developing Role of Public Libraries in Adult Education: 1966–1991 by Kathleen Heim ($950) picks up where *Beginnings* . . . ends, with discussions on federal support for library-based literacy projects, the coalition of professional library associations to increase awareness of illiteracy problems, and the future role of libraries and lifelong learning.

These papers were published as *Partners for Lifelong Learning: Public Libraries and Adult Education* (1991). Under the Small Business Innovation Research (SBIR) program in the U.S. Department of Education, COMSIS Corporation received $29,900 (*principal investigator:* John Ippolito) to research the feasibility of developing an electronic information system for literacy providers.

Strengthening Research Library Resources Program (HEA, Title II-C)

The Strengthening Research Library Resources Program, funded by Title II-C of the Higher Education Act, promotes quality research and education throughout the United States by providing grants to help major research libraries maintain and strengthen collections and make holdings available to other libraries and to outside researchers and scholars.

In authorizing the Strengthening Research Library Resources Program, Congress recognizes that expansion of educational and research programs, together with the rapid increase in the production of recorded knowledge, places unprecedented demands on major research libraries by requiring programs and services beyond their financial capability, individually or collectively. Further, the nation's major research libraries are defined as public or private nonprofit institutions that contribute significantly to higher education and research, with unique collections containing material that is not widely available but is in substantial demand by researchers and scholars not connected with the institution and of national or international significance for research.

The amendment regarding eligibility added in FY 1986 with the reauthorization of the Higher Education Act permits institutions that do not qualify under the criteria listed in the program regulations to provide information or documentation to demonstrate the national or international significance for scholarly research of the collection described in the grant application. The 1986 amendment allows the application to be evaluated on the quality of the proposed project.

During the 14 years of program operation, $81,506,188 has been awarded to acquire rare and unique materials; to augment special collections in demand by researchers and scholars; to preserve fragile and deteriorating materials not generally available elsewhere; and to provide access to research collections by converting bibliographic information into machine-readable form and entering the records into national databases. Overall, 1,239 applications have been received and 463 funded.

In FY 1991, 98 applications requesting more than $16 million were received. With an allotment of $5,854,924, 30 new and 6 continuation grants were awarded, supporting projects at 42 institutions. Bibliographic control again emerged as the major activity in FY 1991, accounting for 76 percent of the funds. Preservation was second, accounting for 15 percent, and collection development accounted for 9 percent.

Table 4 describes projects funded in FY 1991, Table 5 analyzes FY 1991 grant awards by major activity, and Table 6 summarizes Strengthening Research Library Resources Program grant activities since FY 1978.

Table 4 / Projects Funded under HEA, Title II-C, Strengthening Research Library Resources Program, FY 1991

Institution and Project Director	Grant Amount	Project Description
Amherst College Box 2256 Amherst, MA 01002 Daria D'Arienzo	$45,140	The personal papers of statesman, financier, and lawyer Dwight W. Morrow will be preserved by microfilming the collection of correspondence, speeches, reports, and scrapbooks.
Brandeis University Box 9110 Waltham, MA 02254 Bessie Hahn	$198,802	Brandeis will strengthen its Modern Jewish History, Modern History, and History and Politics of the Middle East collections by acquiring microfilm copies of the Chaim Weizmann Archives in Rehovot, Israel, creating an electronic index from the existing catalog using RLIN AMC format and adding collection level cataloging to OCLC and RLIN.
Columbia University 535 W. 114 St. New York, NY 10027 Carol Mandel and Marsha Wagner	$176,723	Columbia will catalog titles of Chinese gazetteers, genealogies, and Japanese Edo and Meiji period books using full standard cataloging and will make them

**Table 4 / Projects Funded under HEA, Title II-C,
Strengthening Research Library Resources Program, FY 1991** *(cont.)*

Institution and Project Director	Grant Amount	Project Description
		available through RLIN and Columbia's local online catalog, CLIO.
Columbia University Box 20, Low Memorial Library New York, NY 10027 Carol Mandel	$121,597	This project, continued from FY 1990, will provide widely accessible MARC records for rare and unique titles in the Avery Architectural and Fine Arts Library, as well as such preservation treatments as binding, microfilming, and rehousing for fragile items.
Columbia University Teachers College 525 W. 120 St. New York, NY 10027 Jennifer Whitten	$130,414	Works on the theory, methods, and institutional practices of mathematics education published since 1970 in Eastern and Western Europe and in Asia will be acquired and cataloged. Titles from the David Eugene Smith Collection, consisting primarily of nineteenth-century textbooks and pedagogical works, will also be cataloged. Older materials and items in poor condition will receive first-phase preservation treatment.
Cornell University A.R. Mann Library Ithaca, NY 14853 Samuel Demas	$125,237	Cornell will identify and preserve a heritage collection of entomological literature. The project will focus on non–North American serials. Bibliographic records will be upgraded and will reflect preservation in the RLIN database. Preservation activities will include microfilming, reformatting and replacement, photocopying, encapsulation, and appropriate new housings.
Cornell University Music Library 225 Lincoln Hall Ithaca, NY 14853 Lenore Coral	$591,723	Cornell, along with Eastman School of Music, Harvard College, Indiana University, and University of California at Berkeley, will convert manual bibliographic records for printed music and sound recordings to machine-readable records for entry into OCLC and RLIN.
Duke University 220 Perkins Library Durham, NC 27706 Jerry Campbell	$267,170	Duke, along with University of North Carolina at Chapel Hill and North Carolina State University, will continue a cooperative acquisition program by coordinating acquisition of Southern Americana. The three libraries will integrate collections in regional development, race and race relations, regional culture, and regional environment, filling in the retrospective lacunae and expanding into new formats.
Duke University 220 Perkins Library Durham, NC 27706 Jerry Campbell	$188,712	This project, a joint effort with Johns Hopkins University continuing from FY 1990, will create online cataloging records for all titles in the Harold Jantz Collection of German literature of the sixteenth, seventeenth, and early eighteenth centuries and enter them into OCLC and RLIN. It will also preserve items in the collection by encapsulation and protective rehousing.
Harvard University Holyoke Center Cambridge, MA 02138 Sidney Verba	$106,888	Manual card catalog records of monograph titles of the Andover-Harvard Theological Library will be converted to machine-readable form and, where neceesary,

**Table 4 / Projects Funded under HEA, Title II-C,
Strengthening Research Library Resources Program, FY 1991** *(cont.)*

Institution and Project Director	Grant Amount	Project Description
		enhanced and upgraded to current standards. Records will be contributed to RLIN and OCLC.
Huntington Library 1151 Oxford Rd. San Marino, CA 91108 William Moffett	$65,482	The Huntington will make its eighteenth-century books printed in English nationally accessible by entering machine-readable catalog records into the Eighteenth-Century Short Title Catalogue (ESTC), a special database in the Research Libraries Group computer system, RLIN.
Library Company of Philadelphia 1314 Locust St. Philadelphia, PA 19107 John Van Horne	$92,392	The Library Company will catalog into RLIN the imprints in its Afro-Americana Collection, which spans 400 years from the sixteenth century to the early years of the twentieth century, and will strengthen the collection through selective acquisition of pre-1900 imprints and scholarly monographs. At the conclusion of the project, the records will be tape-loaded into OCLC.
Miami University 271 King Library Oxford, OH 45056 Judith Sessions	$55,397	The A. W. Kuchler Vegetation Map Collection, containing both maps and books, will be cataloged and preserved by deacidification and encapsulation procedures and the records added to the OCLC and RLIN databases.
New York Public Library Fifth Ave. and 42 St. New York, NY 10018 Mary Bowling	$181,329	This project will preserve and expand RLIN-AMC bibliographic entries for noncommercial audiotapes, videotapes, phonodiscs, and motion pictures that are unique and historically significant. A state-of-the-art sound preservation laboratory will be established, and audio and video workstations will be provided for ready access to the collection. The collection includes oral history interviews with veterans of the Spanish Civil War.
New York Public Library Fifth Ave. and 42 St. New York, NY 10018 Edward Kasinec	$129,089	Original, enhanced cataloging and authority control in RLIN and OCLC for old and rare (pre-1860) Slavic and East European (and Slavica) manuscripts and printed books in NYPL's collection will form the basis for the first national union catalog in this subject area. Basic conservation and preservation microfilming will be performed, and the collection will be enhanced by acquiring relevant reference sources.
Ohio University Vernon Alden Library Athens, OH 45701 Hwa-Wei Lee	$145,506	Continued from FY 1990, this project will provide access, identification, and bibliographic control for Indonesian research materials in microfiche produced by the Netherlands Royal Institute of Linguistics and Anthropology. The records will be fully cataloged in OCLC as the Major Microforms Project, making possible the distribution of the major microform tapes to other libraries and bibliographic utilities nationwide.

**Table 4 / Projects Funded under HEA, Title II-C,
Strengthening Research Library Resources Program, FY 1991** *(cont.)*

Institution and Project Director	Grant Amount	Project Description
Princeton University Library Princeton, NJ 08544 Dorothy Pearson	$31,825	Brittle printed volumes in Arabic script will be preserved through microfilming, and scholarly access will be increased by creating bibliographic records with location information in the RLIN and OCLC databases. Film copies of all reproduced volumes will be made available to scholars and research libraries.
Stanford University Hoover Institution Stanford, CA 94305 Charles Palm	$349,551	In cooperation with Stanford University and the University of California at Berkeley, Hoover Institution will create machine-readable bibliographic records of Russian, Soviet, and Eastern European library materials in each institution's local card catalog. The automated records, representing the entire Slavic studies collections in the three libraries, will be added to RLIN and OCLC.
Stanford University Hoover Institution Stanford, CA 94305 Charles Palm	$93,379	Materials of the Russian and Polish Embassy Collections, many in an advanced state of deterioration, will be preserved on archival-quality microfilm. Access to the collections will be enhanced by updating the catalog records in RLIN to indicate the availability of the microfilm. The materials date from 1873 through 1945.
Tulane University 6823 Saint Charles Ave. New Orleans, LA 70118 Clifton Johnson	$79,644	Tulane will use basic conservation procedures and arrange and prepare a register with historical and biographical notes, scope notes, and container lists for its collection of the Federation of Southern Cooperatives and the Emergency Land Fund papers. Wide access will also be ensured by the entry of bibliographic records into OCLC and TULANET, the local online catalog. These documents relate to the condition of the rural black landowner in ten Southern states in the post–World War II era.
University of California at Berkeley Bancroft Library Berkeley, CA 94720 Joseph Rosenthal	$213,072	This retrospective project will convert catalog records to machine-readable form for manuscript collections and distribute them to OCLC, RLIN, the University of California's MELVYL, the Berkeley catalog GLADIS, and the National Union Catalog of Manuscript Collections. An automated survey to determine the preservation needs of the collections will also be performed.
University of California at Berkeley East Asiatic Library Berkeley, CA 94720 Donald Shively	$151,173	Rubbings of Chinese inscriptions to record or commemorate events and to establish and preserve officially approved texts of philosophical and religious canons will be cataloged, indexed, and input into a computer database. The rubbings will also be conserved by repairing items at greatest risk and by providing housing and storage boxes for the collection.

**Table 4 / Projects Funded under HEA, Title II-C,
Strengthening Research Library Resources Program, FY 1991** *(cont.)*

Institution and Project Director	Grant Amount	Project Description
University of California at Riverside Library Riverside, CA 92506 Henry Snyder	$231,792	This project, continued from FY 1989, will provide machine-readable catalog (MARC) records for and comprehensive access to units 1–48 of the 61-unit microfilm set Early English Books: Series I, 1475–1640 (EEBI), published by University Microfilms International.
University of California at Riverside Library Riverside, CA 92521 Henry Snyder	$85,331	In conjunction with the British Library and University Microfilms International, Riverside will create full bibliographic records for the microfilm set The Thomason Tracts. The records will be added to the Eighteenth-Century Short Title Catalog (ESTC), a special database in RLIN, as part of a plan to convert the ESTC file to a union catalog of English books through 1800.
University of California at San Diego La Jolla, CA 92093 Dorothy Gregor	$147,149	The papers of nine eminent scientists of the twentieth century, consisting of manuscripts critical to an understanding of the history of modern science and its impact on society, will be organized to nationally accepted archival standards, preserved by photocopy and encapsulation, and made available through national databases.
University of Hawaii 2444 Dole St. Honolulu, HI 96822 John Haak	$148,779	A digitized database of photographs from the Trust Territory (TT) Archives will be created and each image linked to cataloged records. The TT Photo Collection is a highly valuable archive of the U.S. administration of Micronesia, featuring individual Micronesians and Americans, cultural heritage, and social and political events.
University of Illinois 506 S. Wright St. Urbana, IL 61801 David Bishop	$337,155	The University of Illinois, along with Cornell, Duke, Indiana, and Yale universities, will create machine-readable bibliographic records for library materials on Latin America for selected areas represented in each institution's local card catalog. By contributing these records to OCLC and RLIN, a comprehensive national database of major Latin American holdings will be created.
University of Illinois 506 S. Wright St. Urbana, IL 61801 Carol Boast	$192,205	Major agricultural series from Agricultural Experiment Stations, land-grant universities in every state, and the U.S. Department of Agriculture will be made more accessible by providing subject, author, and title access to each item through series analytics in OCLC and the online catalogs of the University of Illinois and the National Agricultural Library (NAL) and through indexing in AGRICOLA, NAL's international database, and AGRIS, the United Nations food and agriculture database.

Table 4 / Projects Funded under HEA, Title II-C,
Strengthening Research Library Resources Program, FY 1991 *(cont.)*

Institution and Project Director	Grant Amount	Project Description
University of Kansas Spencer Research Library Lawrence, KS 66045 Alexandra Mason	$181,195	The books, serials, and ephemeral materials in the P. S. O'Hegarty Irish Library will be fully cataloged into OCLC, and fragile items will be preserved by microfilming. The collection covers such topics as revolutionary politics, Anglo-Irish literature, and Irish printing and publishing.
University of Maine 24 Coburn Hall Orono, ME 04469 Elaine Albright	$115,704	This project, begun with a FY 1990 grant, will identify, acquire, and catalog Canadian federal and provincial documents, Atlantic Provinces and Quebec nominal censuses, and back files of newspapers. The project will add holding symbols to the OCLC records for all titles in the collection and will load these data into the university's local online catalog.
University of Minnesota 1919 University Ave. Saint Paul, MN 55104 Mary Collins and Frank Immler	$81,693	The Tell G. Dahllof Collection of Swedish Americana contains monographs, periodicals, newspapers, and pamphlets about the history of Swedish immigration to America, Swedish culture in America, travel descriptions by Swedish visitors to America, and American history in general. These materials span more than 350 years of printing. Funds will be used to catalog them and to apply preservation treatment such as microfilming, restoration, and rehousing.
University of North Carolina Library Chapel Hill, NC 27599 Marcella Grendler	$116,868	The manuscript, sound recording, and pamphlet collections documenting the American South from the eighteenth century to the postwar era will be made more accessible by preparing MARC-AMC records and contributing them to OCLC, RLIN, and TRLN (Triangle Research Libraries Network serving the University of North Carolina at Chapel Hill, North Carolina State University, and Duke University).
University of Texas PCL 3.200 Austin, TX 78713 Harold Billings	$126,630	Manual catalog records for three groups of materials—southern U.S. history, Germanic literature, and linguistics—will be converted to machine-readable form and the bibliographic and holdings information disseminated via OCLC, RLIN, and UTCAT, the University of Texas at Austin online catalog.
University of Texas PCL 3.200 Austin, TX 78713 Harold Billings	$120,576	Catalog records related to the study of the history of the southern, southwestern, and Rocky Mountain regions of the United States will be converted into machine-readable form through OCLC. Records will also be disseminated via RLIN and UTCAT, the University of Texas at Austin online catalog.

Table 4 / Projects Funded under HEA, Title II-C,
Strengthening Research Library Resources Program, FY 1991 *(cont.)*

Institution and Project Director	Grant Amount	Project Description
University of Virginia Alderman Library Charlottesville, VA 22903 Carol Pfeiffer	$389,245	This project, continued from FY 1990, will complete the retrospective conversion of the holdings of the Rare Book Division consisting of twentieth-century American literature, including items from the Clifton Waller Barrett Library and the William Faulkner Collection. Records will be entered into OCLC.
Virginia Historical Society 428 North Blvd. Richmond, VA 23221 Paulette Thomas	$40,357	Fragile and brittle materials in the Historical Society's collection of rare Confederate imprints, dating from the time of each state's secession to the surrender of troops by a military commander, will be conserved and preserved by routine rehousing and encapsulation as well as more extensive treatments such as washing, deacidification, and mending.

College Library Technology and Cooperation Grants Program (HEA, Title II-D)

During reauthorization of the Higher Education Act in 1986, Title II-D was added to award grants to institutions of higher education for technological equipment to enhance resource-sharing activities among colleges and universities. In FY 1991, the fourth year of program funding, $3,903,949 was appropriated for Title II-D.

The College Library Technology and Cooperation Grants Program is designed to encourage resource-sharing projects among libraries of institutions of higher education and to conduct innovative research and demonstration projects that meet special needs in utilizing technology to enhance library services. Grants are awarded (1) to institutions of higher education that demonstrate a need for special assistance for planning, development, acquisition, installation, maintenance, or replacement of technological equipment (including computer hardware and software) necessary to participate in networks for sharing of library resources; (2) to combinations of institutions of higher education that demonstrate a need for special assistance in establishing and strengthening joint-use library facilities, resources, or equipment; (3) to other public and private nonprofit organizations that provide library services to institutions of higher education on a formal cooperative basis to establish, develop, or expand programs that improve their services to institutions of higher education; and (4) to institutions of higher education conducting research or demonstration projects to meet special national or regional needs by using technology to enhance library or information sciences.

In FY 1991, 238 applicants requested approximately $29 million. For the Networking Grant, 126 applications were received totaling approximately $10.5 million; for the Combination Grant, 56 applications totaled $10.6 million; for the Services to Institutions Grant, 11 applications totaled $1 million; and for the Research and Demonstration Grant, 45 applications totaled approximately $7 million. The average request ranged from $84,916 in Networking and $97,211 in

Table 5 / HEA, Title II-C, Strengthening Research Library Resources Program, Analysis of FY 1991 Grants, by Major Activity

Institution	Total	Program Activity		
		Bibliographic Control	Preservation	Collection Development
Amherst College	$45,140	$ —	$ 45,140	$ —
Brandeis University	198,802	62,474	—	136,328
Columbia University	176,723	176,723	—	—
Columbia University	121,597	110,893	10,704	—
Columbia University, Teachers College	130,414	63,618	11,485	55,311
Cornell University	125,237	2,618	95,589	27,030
Cornell University	591,723	591,723	—	—
Duke University	267,170	—	—	267,170
Duke University	188,712	181,517	7,195	—
Harvard University	106,888	106,888	—	—
Huntington Library	65,482	65,482	—	—
Library Company of Philadelphia	92,392	82,392	—	10,000
Miami University	55,397	55,397	—	—
New York Public Library	181,329	61,348	119,981	—
New York Public Library	129,089	7,297	121,792	—
Ohio University	145,506	145,506	—	—
Princeton University	31,825	—	31,825	—
Stanford University, Hoover Institution	349,551	349,551	—	—
Stanford University, Hoover Institution	93,379	—	93,379	—
Tulane University	79,644	—	79,644	—
University of California at Berkeley	213,072	213,072	—	—
University of California at Berkeley	151,173	120,203	30,970	—
University of California at Riverside	231,792	231,792	—	—
University of California at Riverside	85,331	85,331	—	—
University of California at San Diego	147,149	116,493	30,656	—
University of Hawaii	148,779	25,351	123,428	—
University of Illinois	337,155	337,155	—	—
University of Illinois	192,205	192,205	—	—
University of Kansas	181,195	181,195	—	—
University of Maine	115,704	56,318	—	59,386
University of Minnesota	81,693	74,658	7,035	—
University of North Carolina	116,868	114,268	2,600	—
University of Texas	126,630	126,630	—	—
University of Texas	120,576	120,576	—	—
University of Virginia	389,245	389,245	—	—
Virginia Historical Society	40,357	—	40,357	—
Total	$5,854,924	$4,447,919	$851,780	$555,225

Services to Institutions to $162,479 in Research and Demonstration and $189,525 in the Combination category.

Thirty-five grants totaling $3,903,949, the amount of the appropriation, went to institutions in 22 states and the District of Columbia. The following grants were awarded: 13 Networking Grants, averaging $65,504 each, for a total of $851,556; 7 Combination Grants, averaging $183,389 each, for a total of $1,283,724; 1 Services to Institutions Grant for $323,109; and 7 Research and Demonstration Grants, averaging $121,461 each, for a total of $850,226. Seven continuation awards, averaging $85,048 each, for a total of $595,334, were made for projects initially funded in FY 1990. Table 7 lists the projects funded, including the institution receiving the award, the amount, the expected duration of the project, the project director, and the project abstract. Table 8 summarizes the FY 1991 awards.

Table 6 / HEA, Title II-C, Strengthening Research Library Resources Program, Summary of Funding, by Major Activity, FYs 1978–1991

Fiscal Year	Total Funding	Bibliographic Control	Percent of Funding	Preservation	Percent of Funding	Collection Development	Percent of Funding
1978	$4,999,996	$2,864,339	57	$1,340,554	27	$795,103	16
1979	6,000,000	3,978,366	66	1,393,201	23	628,433	11
1980	5,992,268	4,345,765	73	805,383	13	841,120	14
1981	6,000,000	4,249,840	71	1,298,542	22	451,618	7
1982	5,760,000	4,042,549	70	1,521,258	27	196,193	3
1983	6,000,000	4,738,575	79	909,612	15	351,813	6
1984	6,000,000	4,526,772	76	1,044,973	17	428,255	7
1985	6,000,000	4,236,695	70	1,729,997	29	33,308	*
1986	5,742,000	4,429,374	77	1,122,409	20	190,217	3
1987	6,000,000	4,732,543	79	1,202,696	20	64,761	1
1988	5,744,000	4,804,408	84	850,570	15	89,022	1
1989	5,675,000	4,674,002	82	591,729	11	409,269	7
1990	5,738,000	5,141,888	90	510,255	9	85,857	1
1991	5,854,924	4,447,919	76	851,780	15	555,225	9
Total	$81,506,188	$61,213,035	75	$15,172,959	19	$5,120,194	6

*Less than 1 percent

Table 7 / Projects Funded under HEA, Title II-D: College Library Technology Grants to Support Networking and Resource-Sharing Activities, FY 1991

Networking Grants

Institution and Project Director	Grant Amount	Project Description
Arizona Western College Araby Rd., Box 929 Yuma, AZ 95366-0929 Eileen Shackelford	$51,105	The Arizona Western College (AWC) Networking Project will automate the circulation functions and the card catalog of the AWC Library, using the automated system of the Yuma County Library District. Dial-in ports will provide access to the La Paz Center in Parker, Arizona, by modem and telephone line and to anyone with a Personal computer and a modem. The automated AWC library will offer more efficient service and acquire extensive resource-sharing potential. The automation of AWC's holdings in the same database as the County Library District will initiate a regional network for southwestern Arizona.
Eastern Iowa Community College District 306 W. River Dr. Davenport, IA 52801-1221 David B. Canine	$67,909	The Eastern Iowa Community College District (EICCD) proposes to provide patron access to the 1.5 million holdings of the Quad-LINC library system, which networks 21 academic, special, and public libraries in the Quad Cities of Iowa and Illinois. EICCD will purchase and install terminals and compact disc technology at each of its three college libraries to give patrons access to the Quad-LINC database and public access software. This will allow patrons to search the holdings of the Quad-LINC consortium with minimum staff assistance.

Table 7 / Projects Funded under HEA, Title II-D: College Library Technology Grants to Support Networking and Resource-Sharing Activities, FY 1991 *(cont.)*

	Networking Grants	
Institution and Project Director	**Grant Amount**	**Project Description**
Central Maine Technical College 1250 Turner St. Auburn, ME 04210 Robert Kirchherr	$21,000	The Central Maine Technical College Networking Project will enable campus libraries to request and deliver information quickly for students, faculty, and staff members by way of fax machines installed in each library. The one-year project will involve procurement and installation of fax equipment in each library of the Maine Technical College System; development of fax protocol (policy and procedures governing use of the fax machines for interlibrary loan purposes); promotion of the service; and evaluation of the project. The resulting network will provide students, faculty, and staff members on all campuses rapid access to more than 600 unique periodicals as well as other information held at the six Maine Technical College campuses.
Ferris State University 901 S. State St. Big Rapids, MI 49307 Edwin Harris	$78,563	The Ferris State University (FSU) Library Networking Project will establish a prototype online library network along U.S. 131 in western Michigan. The service will be hosted on Ferris State University Library's mainframe and will initially serve Northwestern Michigan College at Traverse City (NMC) and Ferris State University at Big Rapids. When operational, it will be offered to other institutions on the northwestern lower peninsula, such as Grand Rapids Junior College. Specifically, the project will (1) establish a users' council to coordinate development and expansion of automated library services between FSU and community college libraries along the U.S. 131 corridor; (2) implement joint use of bibliographic resources by FSU and cooperating libraries; (3) provide local, online, systemwide access to the databases/catalogs of participating institutions; and (4) promote use of automated tools for resource sharing and collection development among these institutions using the FSU UNISYS 2200 mainframe.
University of Detroit–Mercy College Box 19900 Detroit, MI 48219-3599 Anne Sargent	$135,543	The University of Detroit will extend library automation and resource sharing to nontraditional students. The grant will be used to support network membership, OPAC, circulation, and serials implementation at the university's new, nontraditional adult student facility. It also will fund DALNET implementation, an automated library network system composed of 12 major Detroit area

Table 7 / Projects Funded under HEA, Title II-D: College Library Technology Grants to Support Networking and Resource-Sharing Activities, FY 1991 *(cont.)*

	Networking Grants	
Institution and Project Director	**Grant Amount**	**Project Description**
		libraries. The joint database displays the holdings of all member libraries. Each member institution installs telecommunication equipment for accessing the database and local site equipment for performing internal library operations, searching the central database, and manipulating information. Students, faculty, and independent researchers will have instant access to the resources of all member institutions.
Saint Louis College of Pharmacy 4588 Parkview Pl. Saint Louis, MO 63110 Judy Longstreth	$34,580	The innovative Bibliographic Access and Control System (BACS) developed by Washington University Medical School Library provides an excellent avenue for resource sharing for the libraries of Washington University Medical School, Barnes College of Nursing, Saint John's Mercy Medical Center, Saint Mary's Health Center, Children's Hospital, Jewish Hospital Medical, Mallinckrodt Institute of Radiology, Jewish Hospital School of Nursing, and the Saint Louis College of Pharmacy. BACS will provide the Saint Louis College of Pharmacy with an integrated online catalog and library management system as well as access to the collections of all BACS libraries. Direct reciprocal borrowing privileges and formal cooperative collection development policies will also increase resource sharing. MeSH authority tapes and MeSH-LCSH mapping tapes will be added to BACS, significantly enhancing subject searching.
University of Montana at Missoula Maureen and Mike Mansfield Library Missoula, MT 59812 William Elison	$97,500	The University of Montana will purchase 15 computer workstations with attendant file servers, compact disc players, printers, and retrieval software to establish a network of CD-ROM bibliographic databases. This local area network (LAN) will be tied to an online public access catalog (in progress) using Digital Equipment Corporation hardware and Dynix software, which will be part of a campus network and the statewide MUSENET system. MUSENET will enable the University of Montana to share resources and bibliographic search capabilities with a distant branch campus, Western Montana College, at Dillon, located in southwestern Montana some 170 miles from Missoula. Research efficiency will be greatly enhanced at these campuses as several students will be able to search a database simultane-

Table 7 / Projects Funded under HEA, Title II-D: College Library Technology Grants to Support Networking and Resource-Sharing Activities, FY 1991 *(cont.)*

Networking Grants

Institution and Project Director	Grant Amount	Project Description
		ously and faculty will be able to search the journal literature from their offices. Three workstations will be used in a library instruction lab to train students and faculty in methods of computer bibliographic instruction.
College of New Rochelle Castle Place New Rochelle, NY 10805 James T. Schleifer	$34,637	The grant will be used to enhance networking and resource sharing by expanding the MPALS college campus network to include the six campuses of the college's School of New Resources.
Saint John's University Grand Central and Utopia Pkwys. Jamaica, NY 11439 Teresa Edwards	$122,646	Saint John's University will enhance its academic programs and those of 23 other libraries by implementing within its libraries the PALS integrated library system, which will be out-sourced through Westchester County Information Services (WCIS) in White Plains, N.Y., acting on behalf of Westchester Community College. A strong, cost-effective telecommunications network is needed to connect the three libraries in Queens and Staten Island with WCIS, which maintains the database. WCIS staff will be a prime networked resource providing Multi-PALS (MPALS). The university's database will be available to the 23 members of the WALDO consortium; in turn, the university will have access to their databases. In addition to expert staff and databases, shared resources will include cataloging and collection development efforts of consortium members as well as third-party databases.
Immaculata College Immaculata, PA 19345 Sister Florence Marie, IHM	$73,003	Immaculata College Library proposes to accelerate retrospective conversion and bar-coding operations by purchasing two more OCLC-networked workstations and hiring extra part-time staff who will work during nonprime OCLC/ PALINET hours for three years. The project will maximize resource-sharing capability in a library that regularly fulfills requests from government agencies, business and industry, and other academic centers.
Aiken Technical College Box 696 Aiken, SC 29082 Charles H. Parker	$20,220	Aiken Technical College, a two-year community college, will complete the retrospective conversion of current holdings and those acquired in 1991–1992 from printed-card catalog records to full MARC format. The goal is to improve the higher education community's access to library resources through electronic networking. This

Table 7 / Projects Funded under HEA, Title II-D: College Library Technology Grants to Support Networking and Resource-Sharing Activities, FY 1991 *(cont.)*

Networking Grants

Institution and Project Director	Grant Amount	Project Description
		project combines off-line searches with online OCLC database searching to improve the college's capability to access and share information with other networked libraries and agencies. This project, to be accomplished by both in-house professional staff and a temporary part-time professional library staff person, will also enhance information access for South Carolina and Georgia residents of the Central Savannah River Area.
Columbia College J. Drake Edens Library 1301 Columbia College Dr. Columbia, SC 29203 Mary Robinson Cross	$31,709	Columbia College, one of the few liberal arts colleges for women in the Southeast, will participate fully in national, regional, and local resource sharing. The Edens Library has developed a collection that emphasizes women in all disciplines. These resources are not easily accessible and are not widely known outside the state as less than 4 percent of the library's collection is in the OCLC database. By using the SOLINET CD-ROM Data Conversion System, the library will convert 82,055 bibliographic records to machine-readable format. This project will increase student and faculty access to outside resources, make available to other libraries the interdisciplinary women's collection, and create a database for a future online catalog.
Voorhees College Voorhees Rd. Denmark, SC 29042 Thomas J. Donahue, Jr.	$83,141	The Voorhees College Networking Project will enable the Wright/Potts Library to participate in the Southeastern Library Network (SOLINET), a regional affiliate of OCLC. Membership in the online bibliographic network will enhance efficiency in cataloging and interlibrary loan.

Combination Grants

Institution and Project Director	Grant Amount	Project Description
University of Arkansas 120 Ozark Hall Fayetteville, AR 72701 John A. Harrison and Robert Zimmerman	$213,115	The University of Arkansas Library Technology Project will link academic libraries in Arkansas by means of the telecommunications infrastructure of the ARKnet academic/research network. More than 90 percent of the state's higher education students attend the 20 colleges and universities in the ARKnet Confederation. Although ARKnet was designed to extend a spectrum of services to each school using the TCP/IP standard network protocol and 56-kilobit-per-second leased lines, the full benefit of ARKnet cannot be realized until the state's academic libraries become

Table 7 / Projects Funded under HEA, Title II-D: College Library Technology Grants to Support Networking and Resource-Sharing Activities, FY 1991 *(cont.)*

Combination Grants		

Institution and Project Director	Grant Amount	Project Description
		fully integrated users of the network. The goal of the project is to ensure that each academic library has the equipment and software necessary to achieve this end, including a high-end workstation configured with peripheral equipment to support document scanning and telefacsimile transmission, access to a graphic user interface that will direct librarians (and patrons) to available resources and maintain utilization statistics, and access to joint-use CD-ROM resources.
Carl Sandburg College 2232 S. Lake Storey Rd. Galesburg, IL 61401 Frederick Visel	$84,660	Carl Sandburg College, Spoon River College, and Black Hawk College, East Campus, serve 250,780 people in an area covering 5,463 square miles of west central Illinois. The participating colleges will complete the conversion of their records to machine-readable format, develop a common database on CD-ROM to share their resources, and establish the capability to participate in future regional, state, and nationwide resource-sharing projects predicated on library records in MARC format.
Indiana Vocational Technical College Library Resource Center One W. 26 St., Box 1763 Indianapolis, IN 46206-1763 Susan Mannan	$266,810	The Ivy Tech Library Automation Project will place personal computers at campus sites throughout Indiana so that students and faculty can access the online catalogs of the State University Library Automation Network (SULAN). An online union catalog will be created for the Ivy Tech libraries and mounted with NOTIS on the college's mainframe computer. Procedures for interlibrary loan and document delivery among the Ivy Tech campuses and between those campuses and other institutions will be established, with training to emphasize the fullest possible use of the expanded resource-sharing capabilities made available through the college and SULAN networks.
University of Maine System Raymond H. Fogler Library Orono, ME 04469-0139 Marilyn Lutz	$150,718	The libraries of the University of Maine System and Bates, Bowdoin, and Colby colleges have installed integrated systems that are being linked electronically and designed to promote maximum sharing of library resources, thereby enhancing the teaching and research capabilities of each institution. The institutions propose to take a new direction in information sharing among libraries via computer by jointly acquiring two standard periodical databases and sharing them electronically. The University of Maine System will provide access

Table 7 / Projects Funded under HEA, Title II-D: College Library Technology Grants to Support Networking and Resource-Sharing Activities, FY 1991 *(cont.)*

		Combination Grants

Institution and Project Director	Grant Amount	Project Description
		to periodical subject indexes by means of linked systems and regional and national access to the serial holdings of the principal libraries. They will purchase software and software licenses to load and index two online periodical indexes on the University of Maine System library computer and software to create an online Maine Union List of serial holdings information indexed by the databases from these and other Maine libraries.
Webster University 470 E. Lockwood Ave. Saint Louis, MO 63119 Susan Wartzak	$92,504	Eden-Webster Libraries' Joint-Use Automation Project will acquire equipment to establish and support an online public access catalog and circulation system at Eden-Webster's main library and complete retrospective conversion of the library's catalog to machine-readable form. This initial step toward an integrated library system will provide dial access links between the main library and Webster University's 46 extended-campus libraries. Besides strengthening library services to 10,498 students and faculty of Webster University and Eden Theological Seminary, they will enhance local and national resource sharing among libraries by contributing holdings information to OCLC and MCAT (Missouri State Catalog on CD-ROM) during retrospective conversion. This project will strengthen library services to the underserved members of the U.S. Armed Forces who attend Webster University's extended campuses on military bases.
Montana State University Bozeman, MT 59717-0332 Elaine Peterson	$245,000	Montana State University (MSU) seeks to improve access to MSU Libraries by faculty and students at Montana's seven tribally controlled Native American colleges by expanding the capacity and enhancing the response of the online public access catalog (OPAC) to users. At present, all Montana tribal colleges can determine MSU holdings by connecting with MSU's OPAC, CatTrac, via CatLink. MSU libraries will purchase electronic versions of commercially available bibliographic databases and concomitant software to be mounted on the hardware that drives the CatTrac system. This project will allow and encourage access to bibliographic databases (initially, ERIC, General Science Index, Social Science Index, and AGRICOLA), enabling users to find references to articles. The off-campus

Table 7 / Projects Funded under HEA, Title II-D: College Library Technology Grants to Support Networking and Resource-Sharing Activities, FY 1991 *(cont.)*

Combination Grants

Institution and Project Director	Grant Amount	Project Description
		clientele who will be able to search CatTrac and these databases directly using the 800 line are the students and faculty at the tribal colleges, MSU faculty who serve as county extension agents throughout the state and at the three extended-campus nursing sites, as well as by junior high school students throughout the state who are gifted in mathematics and science and who participate by computer in MSU's Young Scholars Program (funded by the National Science Foundation). The MSU Libraries will install and maintain a toll-free WATS telephone line for MSU dial-in access to CatTrac and the bibliographic databases. The libraries will also accept telefaxed interlibrary loan requests that would include printouts of CatTrac data or database citations for journals, thereby eliminating the need for verification and greatly expediting delivery of information. The indexes mounted on the MSU OPAC will provide students and faculty at tribal colleges with information that would not otherwise be available to them. MSU Libraries hold approximately 85 percent of the indexed material on the four tapes to be mounted on the system. The requested hardware, software, and expert support will enhance MSU libraries' capability to meet the growing demand of the diverse groups of Montana residents for information through OPAC, CatTrac, and the remote-access component, CatLink.
University of Nevada Computing Services 2601 Enterprise Rd. Reno, NV 89512 Donald Zitter	$230,917	The University of Nevada System (UNS) Libraries and UNS Computing Services will establish a statewide information system that provides single-point menu-type access to a broad range of resources. This project will enhance the ability of Nevada's academic libraries to serve the information needs of students, faculty, and the general public and to promote increased resource sharing. Building on statewide telecommunications networks already in place, the proposed project will provide ready access, regardless of location, to UNS library online catalogs, electronic journal indexes, and a major government publications catalog, and will serve as a gateway to other major resources.

Table 7 / Projects Funded under HEA, Title II-D: College Library Technology Grants to Support Networking and Resource-Sharing Activities, FY 1991 (cont.)

Services to Institutions Grants

Institution and Project Director	Grant Amount	Project Description
Forest Trail Library Consortium LeTourneau University Box 7001 Longview, TX 75607 Joycelyn Claer	$323,109	By signing reciprocal borrowing agreements, East Texas libraries banded together for mutual support and resource sharing as the Forest Trail Library Consortium. In a two-year planning process, the multitype member institutions agreed that their first priority was conversion of the remaining 450,000 card catalog records into MARC format. They discovered that this could most efficiently and economically be achieved using a combination of BiblioFile and OCLC workstations. This project will promote resource sharing and cooperative collection development by connecting member libraries with the national network and making possible sharing of local catalogs and clienteles. It will make available to scholars everywhere unique resources on aviation, engineering, inventors, artists, politicians, and historical material of the early Texas oil industry and minority groups.

Research and Demonstration Grants

San Francisco State University 1600 Holloway Ave. San Francisco, CA 94132 Harriet Talan	$89,363	San Francisco State University will develop an integrated set of multimedia, interactive, self-paced, computer-assisted tutorials to teach basic library research skills, using HyperCard. The tutorials are designed primarily for academic libraries, but because they are generic, they may be adapted by other types of libraries. The flexible modules can be used in a variety of settings, including home computers. Computer-assisted instructional design and human interface principles will be integrated into the learning modules with sophisticated graphics to enhance interactivity and interest.
University of California at Berkeley Information Systems and Technology 299 Evans Hall Berkeley, CA 94720 Barbara Morgan	$60,000	The University of California at Berkeley is developing access to image-oriented databases using computer workstations connected to the campus data communications network. Feasibility of on-line access to visual and object collections using high-resolution digital images of maps, slides, paintings, photographs, rare manuscripts, museum artifacts, botanical specimens, and other visual materials has been demonstrated with prototype databases. The proposed research and demonstration

Table 7 / Projects Funded under HEA, Title II-D: College Library Technology Grants to Support Networking and Resource-Sharing Activities, FY 1991 *(cont.)*

Research and Demonstration Grants

Institution and Project Director	Grant Amount	Project Description
		project will use read/write optical disc storage technology to store a large number of images from the Berkeley Architecture Slide Library collection. Use of this technology will enhance the services of the Slide Library, allow software developers to investigate image compression and speed of query response over networks, and demonstrate the feasibility of wide-area network access to image collections of reasonable size.
Georgetown University Biomedical Information Resources Center and Medical Center Library 37 and O Sts. N.W. Washington, DC 20057 Naomi C. Broering	$178,859	The Dahlgren Memorial Library at Georgetown University will launch a three-year study to design a prototype digital full-text biotechnology system that provides users with complete journal articles including illustrations. The grant will enable the library to investigate new technical methods of storing and transmitting documents and to demonstrate this capability in biotechnology with a small test base in cancer and genetics. The goals are to improve knowledge management and library services by using advanced technologies and to accelerate development of the library's capability to deliver full-text documents electronically. The objectives of the system are (1) to design and maintain a digital full-text database of articles with illustrations; (2) to develop, test, and modify the storage/retrieval system and transmission technology; and (3) to provide selected users with access to the full-text system and evaluate its usefulness and applicability.
University of Michigan School of Information and Library Studies 550 E. University Ave. Ann Arbor, MI 48109-1092 Karen Markey Drabenstott	$95,500	After a decade of online catalog research and development, many of the same problems that the earliest online catalog searchers experienced still plague subject searchers. The University of Michigan will test a new subject access design in which search trees control system responses and determine subject searching approaches to user queries. If the performance of search trees is superior to the performance of subject searching approaches chosen at random, then online catalogs can be programmed to respond to user queries with the most sensible approach to subject searching. Search trees place the responsibility of determining which approach is most likely to succeed on the system.

Table 7 / Projects Funded under HEA, Title II-D: College Library Technology Grants to Support Networking and Resource-Sharing Activities, FY 1991 (cont.)

Research and Demonstration Grants

Institution and Project Director	Grant Amount	Project Description
Rutgers University School of Communication, Information and Library Studies 4 Huntington St. New Brunswick, NJ 08903 Paul B. Kantor	$106,444	Rutgers University will construct and study a new interface to the online catalog in libraries, based on pointers from book to book supplied by users of the catalog and managed by the new interface. The Adaptive Network Library Interface (ANLI) will be installed at four libraries and studied over three years. This approach to library access is related to the concept of neural-net computation. Research objectives include the study of adoption patterns, the impact of ANLI on its users, the relation of the ANLI network to other networks, and the relation of the network to other schemes for classifying and cataloging library materials. The project team includes information scientists and communications scientists.
University of Texas at Austin General Libraries PCL 3.200 Austin, TX 78713-7330 Harold W. Billings	$100,664	In this project, four workstations and a multiple CD-ROM player equipped with several CD-ROM manifestations of depository government documents—to be located in a special microcomputer center in the University of Texas at Austin main library (the Perry-Castaneda Library—PCL)—will be networked on an Ethernet local area network so that multiple users can access information simultaneously. Direct telephone lines will be established from the user workstations to the workstations for reference and government documents librarians. Should patrons have difficulty using the information on the CD-ROMs, they can call the reference librarian for assistance. To provide a higher level of service, experts specially trained in the use of access software and the data on the CD-ROMs will answer the telephone during designated hours. Reference workstations will be equipped with special software that will enable reference librarians to intervene directly in user search sessions. Librarians will be able to manipulate data or view the user's activities in real time on the screen to determine the problem and help the user gain the desired information. When this first phase of the project is running, the networked CD-ROMs will be connected to the campus broadband Ethernet network via a Cisco System Router. In the Public Affairs Library, several blocks from the Perry-Castaneda Library, one more user work-

Table 7 / Projects Funded under HEA, Title II-D: College Library Technology Grants to Support Networking and Resource-Sharing Activities, FY 1991 *(cont.)*

Research and Demonstration Grants		
Institution and Project Director	**Grant Amount**	**Project Description**
		station and one workstation for the reference librarian will be networked so that staff at both locations can provide reference assistance. These workstations will also be connected to the campus broadband network by a Cisco System Router so that users in a remote building will be able to avail themselves of the same intervention services as users in the PCL reference area and in the physically separated microcomputer center. No matter where they are located, other users connected to the campus broadband can take advantage of the same services.
University of Wisconsin at Milwaukee Department of Geography Box 413 Milwaukee, WI 53201 John Grozik and Sona Karentz Andrews	$219,396	Two basic objectives of the University of Wisconsin project are to enable international access to the American Geographical Society Collection by creating a visual archive of more than 30,000 images coupled with a powerful, flexible database; and to create an interactive videodisc that illustrates the broad and diverse topic of mapping and how maps are used to understand the physical and human geography of our planet. Maps and images from the internationally renowned American Geographical Society Collection at the University of Wisconsin at Milwaukee will form the core of the images on the videodisc. Linear video segments will highlight and explain the mapping process and various map elements, and thousands of video still frames of maps, charts, globes, and photographs will display a range of spatial images covering different parts of the world from earliest times to automated satellite imagery. The University of Wisconsin at Milwaukee will design index software and a database that researchers, archivists, instructors, and students can use interactively to access data and related images. Experts in cartography and geography will evaluate the videodisc and software before duplication for distribution. This comprehensive multimedia cartobibliography will be marketed internationally and the program will be distributed to libraries and museums, as well as for use in courses on cartography, geography, and related disciplines.

Table 7 / Projects Funded under HEA, Title II-D: College Library Technology Grants to Support Networking and Resource-Sharing Activities, FY 1991 *(cont.)*

Noncompeting Continuations

Institution and Project Director	Grant Amount	Project Description
University of Florida Florida Center for Library Automation 2002 N.W. 13 St., Suite 320 Gainesville, FL 36209 James F. Corey	$91,971	The Florida Center for Library Automation (FCLA), charged with automating the libraries at all nine universities of the State University System (SUS), will continue to develop the capability of linking the SUS shared-NOTIS system to other automated library systems via the NISO Z39.50 Information Retrieval protocol, using the Open Systems Interconnect (OSI) standard. This project would enable FCLA to support a standard interface with other library systems in and outside Florida, specifically the Florida community college system.
University of Minnesota University of Minnesota Libraries 180 Wilson Library Minneapolis, MN 55455 James A. Cogswell	$179,243	In the final year of this three-year project, the University of Minnesota will permanently establish a full-service information center dedicated to providing end users with direct access to machine-readable data files produced by the federal government. The Machine-Readable Data Center (MRDC) will provide space, staff, equipment, and services needed to identify, acquire, organize, and access numeric and statistical data sets produced and distributed by the U.S. government. The project is developing an innovative approach to provide users, both on- and off-site, with direct access to primary data files, whether on magnetic tape, in microcomputer storage devices, or through online searching.
University of Minnesota Information and Decision Sciences Department Saint Paul, MN 55101 Joseph Branin and George D'Elia	$55,914	The University of Minnesota Libraries, in collaboration with the Carlson School of Management and the Hubert H. Humphrey Institute of Public Affairs, will continue to implement the Integrated Information Center to serve the scholarly and administrative information requirements of the two schools. The project will demonstrate and evaluate a model for delivering information services.
Mississippi University for Women John Clayton Fant Memorial Library W-Box 1625 Columbus, MS 39701 David L. Payne	$36,910	The Mississippi CLSI Library Network and Resource-Sharing Project will continue to increase significantly the Mississippi University for Women's contribution to regional, state, and national library networks by entering its monographic records into the OCLC and the Computerized Library Services, Inc. (CLSI) databases. The project will also evaluate the CLSI/OCLC database and other new technologies used to participate in the Mississippi CLSI Network.

Table 7 / Projects Funded under HEA, Title II-D: College Library Technology Grants to Support Networking and Resource-Sharing Activities, FY 1991 *(cont.)*

Noncompeting Continuations		
Institution and Project Director	**Grant Amount**	**Project Description**
North Carolina State University Campus Box 7111 Raleigh, NC 27695-7111 Susan K. Nutter	$71,690	The North Carolina State University (NCSU) Libraries will continue to evaluate a system to improve access to agricultural research information by direct delivery of digitized research materials to desktop computers through the national NSFnet-Internet. The NCSU Libraries will install off-the-shelf, graphics-capable, networked hardware platforms, along with off-the-shelf and other software, at 14 land-grant campuses. They will thereby test and evaluate a full-scale, digitized text delivery system among a representative subset of the land-grant library community. The project builds on a demonstration study on the transmission of digitized images conducted jointly by the National Agricultural Library, the NCSU Libraries, and the NCSU Computing Center and completed in September 1990.
Oglala Lakota College Learning Resources Center Box 490 Kyle, SD 57752 Ted Hamilton	$67,355	The Oglala Lakota College Networking Project will continue to install an automated system to improve library services, access to resources, and delivery of documents to college faculty and students, patrons of Pine Ridge Reservation, and members of the American Indian Higher Education Consortium (AIHEC).
Milwaukee Area Technical College 700 W. State St. Milwaukee, WI 53233 Richard Meerdink	$92,251	The faculty and library staff of Milwaukee Area Technical College will continue the pilot project to develop a curriculum-based collection, evaluation, and selection system and AC-CESS library model for community colleges.

Library Services and Construction Act

Library Services for Indian Tribes and Hawaiian Natives Program (LSCA, Title IV)

LSCA Title IV discretionary grants awarded in FY 1991 will improve public library services to 183 Indian tribes and 170,000 Hawaiian natives. Funds are supporting a variety of activities in 27 states, including salaries and training of library staff, purchase of library materials, and renovation or construction of library facilities.

Since FY 1985, 2 percent of the appropriations for LSCA Titles I, II, and III has been set aside for LSCA Title IV (1.5 percent for Indian tribes and 0.5 percent for Hawaiian natives). Only federally recognized Indian tribes and Alaska native villages and organizations serving Hawaiian natives that are recognized by the governor of Hawaii are eligible to participate in the program. For the past seven years, Alu Like,

Table 8 / Projects Funded under HEA, Title II-D, College Library Technology and Cooperation Grants Program, Summary Listing for FY 1991

Institution	City	State	Funding Granted
Networking			
Arizona Western College	Yuma	AZ	$51,105
Eastern Iowa Community College District	Davenport	IA	67,909
Central Maine Technical College	Auburn	ME	21,000
Ferris State University	Big Rapids	MI	78,563
University of Detroit—Mercy College	Detroit	MI	135,543
Saint Louis College of Pharmacy	Saint Louis	MO	34,580
University of Montana	Missoula	MT	97,500
College of New Rochelle	New Rochelle	NY	34,637
Saint John's University	Jamaica	NY	122,646
Immaculata College	Immaculata	PA	73,003
Aiken Technical College	Aiken	SC	20,220
Columbia College	Columbia	SC	31,709
Voorhees College	Denmark	SC	83,141
(Mean award: $65,504)		Subtotal	$851,556
Combination			
University of Arkansas	Fayetteville	AR	$213,115
Carl Sandburg College	Galesburg	IL	84,660
Indiana Vo-Tech College	Indianapolis	IN	266,810
University of Maine	Orono	ME	150,718
Webster University	Saint Louis	MO	92,504
Montana State University	Bozeman	MT	245,000
University of Nevada	Reno	NV	230,917
(Mean award: $183,389)		Subtotal	$1,283,724
Services to Institutions			
Forest Trail Library Consortium	Longview	TX	$323,109
Research and Demonstration			
San Francisco State University	San Francisco	CA	$89,363
University of California	Berkeley	CA	60,000
Georgetown University	Washington	DC	178,859
University of Michigan	Ann Arbor	MI	95,500
Rutgers University*	New Brunswick	NJ	106,444
University of Texas	Austin	TX	100,664
University of Wisconsin*	Milwaukee	WI	219,396
(Mean award: $121,461)		Subtotal	$850,226
Noncompetitive Continuations			
University of Florida	Gainesville	FL	$91,971
University of Minnesota	Minneapolis	MN	179,243
University of Minnesota	Saint Paul	MN	55,914
Mississippi University for Women	Columbus	MS	36,910
North Carolina State University	Raleigh	NC	71,690
Oglala Lakota College	Kyle	SD	67,355
Milwaukee Area Technical College	Milwaukee	WI	92,251
(Mean award: $85,048)		Subtotal	$595,334
		Total Awards	$3,903,949

*Recommended noncompeting continuation awards in FY 1992

Inc. has been the only organization recognized to apply for the Hawaiian native set-aside.

Two types of grant are awarded, Basic Grants and Special Projects Grants. The Basic Grant is noncompetitive, and if an Indian tribe or Alaska native village is eligible and pursues authorized activities, funding is guaranteed. In FY 1991, each Indian tribe's Basic Grant was $5,123. Alu Like, Inc. applied for the entire Hawaiian native set-aside of $615,120 under the Basic Grant Program. These funds are being used to support eight projects emphasizing outreach, collection development, and training.

Indian tribes are using the majority of the 1991 Basic Grant funds to support library personnel and purchase library materials. For example, the Standing Rock Sioux tribe of North Dakota is using most of its Basic Grant to pay the salary of a library employee who will work during evening and weekend hours. The remaining funds will be used to purchase supplies like catalog cards and materials to repair loan items. The Tunica-Biloxi Indians of Louisiana will use the entire Basic Grant to purchase Native American materials for the Tribal Library. The Lummi tribe of Washington is using its Basic Grant to provide library cultural programs for children, conducted by Lummi elders and storytellers with the intent of passing on traditional knowledge. The Nenana Native Council of Alaska will support the salary of a library page who will learn the various aspects of library work. It will also fund the librarian's travel expenses to research the archival and Alaskana collections at the University of Alaska at Fairbanks. With the remainder of its grant, the council will develop its collection in areas of native interest, such as wildlife, hunting, crafts, and culture; purchase reference materials; and upgrade its computers and software.

The Native Hawaiian Library Project is using its $615,120 Basic Grant to support several projects that target Hawaiian natives, including a library resource van that travels by boat to four islands to circulate books, artifacts, brochures, and videotapes; a Books-by-Mail program for remote areas; workshops to encourage parents to read to children; homework centers to improve students' study habits; public service announcements, posters, and bookmarks to inform the Hawaiian native community of the importance of lifelong learning and the public library; and two fellowships for Hawaiian natives to pursue graduate degrees in library science.

Although a Basic Grant is reserved for each eligible Indian tribe and Alaska native village, only one third of those eligible applied for and received Basic Grants. More than $930,000 was awarded under the Basic Grant Program (see Table 9); the remaining $922,734 was used for special projects.

The Special Projects Program supports the same activities as the Basic Grant Program, but the programs are very different. All Special Projects proposals are reviewed for quality of project, scored, and ranked on a competitive basis. Each grantee is required to have a librarian and a long-range program of three to five years and to contribute a minimum of 20 percent of the project's total cost. Fifteen Indian tribes successfully competed for Special Projects funds, with grants ranging from more than $16,000 to the Oneida tribe in Wisconsin, which will fund the salary of a library trainee who will help expand services, to more then $157,000 to the Blackfeet tribe of Montana for the construction of an addition to the library facility. Table 10 lists the grants made under the Special Projects Program in FY 1991 with a breakdown of the federal (F) and nonfederal (NF) funds awarded.

With its Special Projects award of $42,331, the Red Lake Band of Chippewa, Minnesota, will hire a consulting librarian to help expand its innovative programming. Grant funds will also maintain the salaries of two tribal members who serve as library technicians and will help to expand existing circulation and reference collections.

The Miami tribe of Oklahoma supports a library for Native American elders. Grant monies of $61,340 will fund the purchase of computer equipment, software, and supplies for this library. The grant will also support travel expenses for selected speakers, dissemination of materials, and the salaries of a librarian, a library assistant, and a bookkeeper.

**Table 9 / Library Services and Construction Act, Title IV,
Library Services for Indian Tribes and Hawaiian Natives Program,
Basic Grant Awards, FY 1991**

State	No. of Awards	Amount
Alabama	1	$3,750
Alaska	41	218,543
Arizona	8	38,824
California	27	136,698
Connecticut	1	5,123
Florida	2	10,246
Hawaii	1	615,120
Idaho	2	10,246
Iowa	1	5,123
Louisiana	2	10,246
Maine	1	5,123
Michigan	4	20,492
Minnesota	2	10,246
Mississippi	1	5,123
Missouri	1	5,123
Montana	7	34,315
Nebraska	2	10,246
Nevada	5	24,119
New Mexico	12	61,476
New York	2	10,246
North Carolina	1	4,000
North Dakota	4	20,492
Oklahoma	18	95,843
Oregon	4	20,492
South Dakota	6	28,392
Washington	19	97,337
Wisconsin	6	30,738
Total	181*	$1,537,722

*Two awards serve more than one Indian tribe, and 15 tribes requested amounts under the established Basic Grant of $5,123. A total of 183 tribes and one Hawaiian native organization received the Basic Grant.

**Table 10 / Library Services and Construction Act, Title IV, Library Services for
Indian Tribes Program, Special Projects Awards, FY 1991**

Project and Director	Grant Amount	Project Description
California		
Morongo Band of Mission Indians Banning, CA 92220 Katherine Wiener	(F) $23,776 (NF) 6,175 $29,951	The Morongo Band of Mission Indians will use its Special Projects Grant to help support the salary of a librarian and in-service training and supervision for the library clerk, a tribal member. The tribe will also purchase fiction and nonfiction books for adults and juveniles for the library's core collection.
Rincon, San Luiseno Band of Mission Indians Valley Center, CA 92082 James Fletcher	(F) $49,071 (NF) 32,057 $81,128	The Rincon, San Luiseno Band of Mission Indians will use its grant for library renovation, including the installation of a doorway, an entrance for the handicapped, outside steps, a walkway, lighting, and shelving. The tribe will also hire and train a library assistant; support part of the library

Table 10 / Library Services and Construction Act, Title IV, Library Services for Indian Tribes Program, Special Projects Awards, FY 1991 *(cont.)*

Project and Director	Grant Amount	Project Description
		manager's salary; and purchase books and computer terminals.
Minnesota		
Red Lake Band of Chippewa Red Lake, MN 56671 Kathryn Beaulieu	(F) $42,331 (NF) 60,049 $102,380	The Red Lake Band of Chippewa will hire a consulting librarian to help expand its innovative programming. Grant funds will also maintain the salaries of two tribal members who serve as library technicians and will expand circulation and reference collections.
Montana		
Blackfeet Tribe Blackfoot Community College Browning, MT 59417 Rosemary Austin	(F) $157,851 (NF) 167,002 $324,853	Through an agreement with the Blackfoot Community College, the Blackfeet tribe will construct a 6,281-square-foot library building. This will triple the space available for library services.
New Mexico		
Santa Clara Indian Pueblo Espanola, NM 87532 Teresa Naranjo	(F) $66,368 (NF) 20,471 $86,839	The Santa Clara Pueblo will use its award to fund part of the salary of a librarian and clerk. The award will also support the staff's travel expenses to classes and to a conference; special programs; an evaluation of library services; delivery of books to homebound individuals; and purchase of library furniture and resources (including, but not limited to, a circulation desk, a laser printer, shelving, a book drop, computer software, books, and educational videos).
North Dakota		
Standing Rock Sioux Tribe Standing Rock Community College Fort Yates, ND 58538 Greta Knudsen	(F) $38,249 (NF) 11,644 $49,893	The Standing Rock Sioux Tribe will use its grant to support the salaries and travel expenses of eight reading assistants who will work with children in the eight communities on the reservation. The tribe will also purchase library books and materials.
Three Affiliated Tribes Fort Berthold Reservation Library New Town, ND 58763 Quincee Baker-Gwin	(F) $64,325 (NF) 81,068 $145,393	The Three Affiliated Tribes will purchase computer software and equipment and pay travel expenses for staff to attend a computer training course. The grant will support the salaries of a library technical assistant and personnel to provide special services and children's programming and will pay staff's travel expenses to a statewide library conference. Funds will also support a continuing evaluation and needs assessment.

Table 10 / Library Services and Construction Act, Title IV, Library Services for Indian Tribes Program, Special Projects Awards, FY 1991 *(cont.)*

Project and Director	Grant Amount	Project Description
Turtle Mountain Band of Chippewa Indians Turtle Mountain Community College Belcourt, ND 58316 Margaret Kroll	(F) $58,622 (NF) 30,170 $88,792	The Turtle Mountain Band of Chippewa Indians will use its grant to support public library services at the tribally controlled community college, including the salary of a library assistant; travel expenses for staff training; and purchase of a computer system, software, and library materials.

Oklahoma

Project and Director	Grant Amount	Project Description
Cherokee Nation of Oklahoma Tahlequah, OK 74464 Mary Jo Cole	(F) $41,514 (NF) 41,699 $83,213	The Cherokee Nation of Oklahoma will use its award to pay the salaries of the library assistant and the library clerk and part of the library coordinator's salary. The award will also support adult education classes and staff travel expenses to the state library conference. The tribe also plans to purchase library books, supplies, and materials.
Miami Tribe of Oklahoma Miami, OK 74354 Karen Alexander	(F) $61,340 (NF) 53,737 $115,077	The Miami tribe supports a library for Native American elders. Grant monies will fund the purchase of computer equipment, software, and supplies for the library; travel expenses for selected speakers; dissemination of materials, and the salaries of a librarian, a library assistant, and a bookkeeper.

Washington

Project and Director	Grant Amount	Project Description
Lummi Nation Northwest Indian College Bellingham, WA 98227 Pauline Hanson	(F) $94,016 (NF) 23,514 $117,530	The Lummi nation will complete the renovation of its library building by remodeling 2,370 square feet of space. The grant will support part of the library director's salary. Further, it will enable the tribe to hire a special-collection technician, who will develop and manage the special tribal collection for research in culturally relevant subjects while protecting rare and fragile materials.
Nisqually Indian Tribe Olympia, WA 98501 Maria Fletter	(F) $106,400 (NF) 24,100 $130,500	The Nisqually tribe will build an 864-square-foot addition to its library to provide more space for special library activities, resource materials, and tribal archival activities. The grant will also support the salaries of the librarian and library technician.

Wisconsin

Project and Director	Grant Amount	Project Description
Bad River Band of Lake Superior Chippewa Norma Soulier	(F) $48,443 (NF) 12,701 $61,144	The Bad River Band of Lake Superior Chippewa plans to renovate and remodel an existing building to accommodate tribal library collections. Access ramps, doors, and bathrooms for the handicapped will be added to the structure, as well as equipment to control temperature and humidity.

Table 10 / Library Services and Construction Act, Title IV, Library Services for Indian Tribes Program, Special Projects Awards, FY 1991 (cont.)

Project and Director	Grant Amount		Project Description
			The grant will also partially support the salaries of some staff members.
Lac Courte Oreilles Tribe Lac Courte Oreilles/Ojibwa Community College Hayward, WI 54843 Caryl Pfaff	(F) (NF)	$53,642 32,300 $85,942	The Lac Courte Oreilles Tribe will purchase much-needed library books and tapes; a dedicated line for an online network; children's software, books, and magazines; and large-print materials. It will also acquire an IBM PC, furniture, and book shelving for both the children and adult sections.
Oneida Tribe of Indians of Wisconsin Oneida, WI 54155 Judy M. Cornelius	(F) (NF)	$16,786 4,623 $21,409	The Oneida Community Library will hire a full-time trainee to expand the hours of operation of the main library and its satellite. The tribe estimates that 16 to 25 percent more patrons will be served.
Total funds awarded		$922,734	

Foreign-Language Materials Acquisition Program (LSCA, Title V)

Title V of the Library Services and Construction Act authorizes discretionary grants to state and local public libraries for acquisition of foreign-language materials to meet the needs of the communities they serve. Although the Foreign-Language Materials Acquisition Program was established in 1984, Congress did not appropriate funds until FY 1991, in the amount of $976,000. By law, 30 percent of the funds are for large requests, ranging from $35,000 to $125,000; the remainder is for requests of $35,000 or less. Grants may be used to acquire library materials, including books, periodicals, newspapers, documents, pamphlets, photographs, reproductions, microforms, pictorial and graphic works, musical scores, maps, charts, globes, sound recordings, slides, films, filmstrips, videotapes, computer software, and materials designed for the handicapped.

During the first year of the program, 204 applications were received from urban, suburban, and rural libraries. By September 30, 1991, 31 grants totaling $976,000 were awarded to public libraries in 13 states. A panel of 72 foreign-language experts representing local and state libraries, schools, and institutions of higher education reviewed the growth, which ranged from $3,951 to more than $75,000 and included projects in more than 20 languages. Funds are being used to expand and improve foreign-language collections, to develop language services at new locations, and to increase the number and types of materials available.

Table 11 lists the grants made under the Foreign-Language Materials Acquisition Program in FY 1991, giving the name of the library, its location and funding level, and the language(s) to be collected. Activities supported by the Foreign-Language Materials Acquisition Program in FY 1991 include (1) establishing life skills collections; (2) initiating collections for newly arrived immigrants; (3) developing basic collections of instructional and reference materials to support the library as an

Table 11 / Projects Funded under LSCA Title V,
Foreign-Language Materials Acquisition Program, FY 1991

Library	City/State	Funding	Language
Huntsville Madison County Public Library	Huntsville, AL	$35,000	Multi
Akiachak Community Library	Akiachak, AK	3,951	Yupik
Fairbanks Public Library	Fairbanks, AK	32,890	Multi
Chandler Public Library	Chandler, AZ	31,964	Spanish
Tucson-Pima Library	Tucson, AZ	35,000	Spanish
Alhambra Public Library	Alhambra, CA	12,695	Chinese
Fresno Public Library	Fresno, CA	35,000	Multi
Hayward Public Library	Hayward, CA	23,410	Multi
Los Angeles Public Library	Los Angeles, CA	72,289	Multi
Monterey County Free Libraries	Monterey, CA	35,000	Spanish
Bruggemeyer Memorial Library	Monterey Park, CA	30,000	Asian, Spanish
National City Public Library	National City, CA	32,800	Spanish
Oakland Public Library	Oakland, CA	35,000	Multi
Redwood City Public Library	Redwood City, CA	29,850	Spanish
San Bernardino Public Library	San Bernardino, CA	35,000	Spanish
Stockton San Joaquin County	Stockton, CA	30,000	Multi
Miami Dade Public Library	Miami, FL	72,289	French, Spanish
Volusia County Public Library	Volusia, FL	35,000	Spanish
Rolling Meadows Public Library	Rolling Meadows, IL	10,320	Spanish
Skokie Public Library	Skokie, IL	10,000	Russian
Assumption Parish Library System	Assumption, LA	20,000	French
Cambridge Public Library	Cambridge, MA	16,620	Chinese, French, Russian
New Bedford Free Public Library	New Bedford, MA	35,000	Portuguese
Harrison County Public Library	Harrison, MS	10,000	Vietnamese
Brooklyn Public Library	Brooklyn, NY	73,063	French, Chinese, Russian
New York Public Library	New York, NY	75,155	Multi
Queens Public Library	Queens, NY	12,772	Korean
Yonkers Public Library	Yonkers, NY	27,998	Spanish
Eugene Public Library	Eugene, OR	20,149	Spanish
Harris County Public Library	Harris Co., TX	12,772	Spanish
Seattle Public Library	Seattle, WA	35,000	Chinese, Spanish, Vietnamese, Russian

independent learning center; (4) enhancing language collections at branches to meet the diverse needs of multiethnic, multicultural communities; (5) developing and strengthening collections of audio and video materials and computer software; and (6) collecting materials to support and promote family literacy and use of the library.

Library Literacy Program (LSCA, Title VI)

Title VI of the Library Services and Construction Act authorizes a discretionary grant program to support literacy programs of state and local public libraries. The program received an appropriation of $8,162,894 for FY 1991.

Under the Library Literacy Program, state and local public libraries may apply directly to the U.S. Department of Education for grants of up to $35,000. State libraries may use grants to coordinate and plan library literacy programs and to train librarians and volunteers to carry out such programs. Local public libraries may use grants to promote use of voluntary services of individuals, agencies, and organizations in literacy programs and to acquire library materials, use library facilities, and train volunteers for the programs.

By August 1991, 263 grants totaling $8.16 million were awarded to 246 local public libraries and 17 state libraries. The grants were reviewed by a panel of 90 literacy experts representing local and state libraries, literacy councils, state departments of education, institutions of higher education, and private or other literacy efforts. Grants ranged from $6,000 to $35,000. The average amount was $31,038. Grantees planned and coordinated literacy activities with literacy councils, schools, private agencies, or other literacy providers in the state or community. They were also encouraged to coordinate literacy activities with recipients of grants under Title I of the Library Services and Construction Act.

The Library Literacy Program supported training of volunteers as tutors, recruiting students to participate in the projects, and purchasing books, videocassettes, and other teaching materials. Examples of library literacy activities in FY 1991 include (1) helping adult new readers use public libraries for consumer education, job searching, reading for pleasure, and to help their children learn; (2) enlisting adults for literacy programs through library outreach sites at homeless shelters, Salvation Army facilities, and food distribution centers; (3) recruiting current and former Hispanic inmates to enroll as tutors in correctional institutions with significant Hispanic populations; and (4) training leaders of book discussion groups for new adult readers. Specific projects funded in FY 1991 follow.

The Houston Public Library in Texas received $27,418 to help 90 Spanish-speaking adults become literate in their first language to help them transfer their skills to English more easily. The program was conducted at two library branches in Hispanic neighborhoods. Classes included literacy in Spanish; a parent-child reading program to enhance Spanish literacy, reinforce basic learning concepts, and introduce English; and English as a second language to transfer literacy skills in Spanish to the English language.

The Elizabeth Jones Library in Grenada, Mississippi, received $35,000 to conduct a workplace literacy program. The program was designed with three options in order to serve every business regardless of size and every worker regardless of literacy skills. Each option features a model program that a company can use or adapt to its needs. Model 1 is a skills refresher course, a literacy-only program that helps employees improve basic skills on-site. Companies with employee development plans can incorporate this model into their plans easily. Model 2 is the Vocational Improvement Program, designed for companies with no employee development program. Employees are placed in educational programs in the library or other agencies in the community. Some companies and employees also established peer tutoring programs. Model 3, Volunteers Involved with People, was developed for companies that did not have a literacy problem. These companies worked with the library to encourage employees to become tutors. For all the models, the library's literacy coordinator helped companies recruit tutors and students, arrange training for tutors, match students with tutors, or place them in appropriate educational programs.

The Joliet (IL) Public Library received $35,000 to establish an adult literacy center dedicated solely to literacy tutoring and computer instruction. The library will explore use of CD-ROM interactive software combined with a hypermedia format to produce self-directed instructional materials. With the help of sound, video, and a mouse, students will learn to read using the methods employed in the basic one-on-one tutorials. The library will produce a user-friendly, hypermedia tour of the library with maps and other graphic aids printed out on command to help adult new readers locate materials and become oriented to the library.

New Haven (CT) Free Public Library received $33,081 to recruit and train volunteers to tutor people in the community who wish to improve their basic literacy skills. Volunteers will be recruited from among Yale University students to work with young adult learners and recent dropouts from high school. The Yale tutors, who are experienced in software use, will be able to train other tutors to use the computer as a tutoring tool. See Table 12 for a complete list of FY 1991 grantees under the Library Literacy Program.

Table 12 / LSCA, Title VI, Library Literacy Program Grants, FY 1991

State	Grantee	Amount
Alabama	Anniston & Calhoun County Library, Anniston	$30,650
	Clyde Nix Public Library, Hamilton	35,000
		65,650
Alaska	Fairbanks North Star Borough Public Library, Fairbanks	31,994
	Skagway Public Library, Skagway	12,275
		44,269
Arizona	Camp Verde Public Library, Camp Verde	17,500
	Casa Grande City Library, Casa Grande	31,300
	Nogales/Santa Cruz County Public Library, Nogales	33,870
	Yuma County Library District, Yuma	29,937
		112,607
Arkansas	Arkansas State Library, Little Rock	35,000
	Gravette Public Library, Gravette	16,510
	Pine Bluff/Jefferson County Library, Pine Bluff	34,994
	Stuttgart/N. Arkansas County Public Library, Stuttgart	35,000
		121,504
California	Alameda County Library, Writing Literature Program, Fremont	34,403
	Alameda County Library, Multicultural Program, Fremont	34,871
	Auburn/Placer County Library, Auburn	34,650
	Blanchard Community Library, Santa Paula	35,000
	California State Library, Sacramento	35,000
	Colton Public Library, Colton	24,956
	Contra Costa County Library, Computer-Assisted Learning Center, Pleasant Hill	19,104
	Contra Costa County Library, Detention Literacy Program, Pleasant Hill	29,550
	Contra Costa County Library, Job Development Program, Pleasant Hill	22,550
	Coyote Valley Tribal Council, Community Library, Redwood Valley	35,000
	Del Norte County Library District, Crescent City	30,000
	Huntington Beach Library, Huntington Beach	34,461
	Livermore Public Library, Livermore	33,310
	Long Beach Public Library, Long Beach	20,747
	Los Angeles Public Library, Los Angeles	34,046
	Marin County Free Library, San Rafael	34,965
	Menlo Park Public Library, Menlo Park	34,997
	Merced County Library, Merced	35,000
	Monterey County Free Library, Salinas	27,375
	Napa City-County Library, Napa	35,000
	National City Public Library, National City	30,582
	Oakland Public Library, Oakland	28,400
	Orange Public Library, Orange	35,000
	Salinas Public Library, Salinas	28,822
	San Francisco Public Library, Project READ–Learner Support, San Francisco	25,447

Table 12 / LSCA, Title VI, Library Literacy Program Grants, FY 1991 (cont.)

State	Grantee	Amount
	San Francisco Public Library, Project READ–Tutor Support, San Francisco	$34,530
	Santa Clara County Library, CAL and other projects, San Jose	120,500
	Santa Clara County Library, Reading Program, San Jose	34,785
		963,051
Colorado	Clear Creek County District Library, Georgetown	33,993
	Colorado State Library, Assessment Training Project, Denver	26,525
	Colorado State Library/Library Literacy Development Project, Denver	34,859
	Durango Public Library, Durango	34,790
	Eagle County Public Library, Eagle	30,731
	Fort Collins Public Library, Adult Literacy Network, Fort Collins	35,000
	Fort Collins Public Library/LIFE, Fort Collins	34,515
	Garfield County Public Library, New Castle	32,204
	Mesa County Public Library, Grand Junction	35,000
		297,617
Connecticut	Bugbee Memorial Library, Danielson	35,000
	Groton Public Library, Groton	27,519
	New Britain Public Library, New Britain	35,000
	New Haven Free Public Library, New Haven	33,081
	Stratford Library Association. Stratford	7,685
		138,285
Delaware	Corbit Calloway Library, Odessa	6,000
	Kent County Department of Library Services, Dover	25,350
	Sussex County Department of Libraries, Georgetown	35,000
	Wilmington Institute Library, Wilmington	35,000
		101,350
District of Columbia	District of Columbia Public Library, Washington	28,780
		28,780
Florida	Bay County Public Library Association, Panama City	25,000
	Calhoun County Public Library, Blountstown	210,000
	Central Regional Library of Florida, Ocala	18,417
	Gadsen County Public Library, Quincy	34,868
	Jefferson County Public Library, Monticello	33,100
	Miami/Dade Public Library System, Miami	35,000
	New Port Richey Public Library, New Port Richey	34,198
		390,583
Georgia	Athens Regional Library System, Athens	34,749
	Brooks County Public Library, Quitman	26,980
	Clayton County Library System, Jonesboro	11,500
	DeKalb County Public Library, Decatur	32,479
	Oconee Regional Library, Dublin	32,014
	Sara Hightower Regional Library, Rome	34,338
		172,060
Idaho	Boise Public Library, Boise	28,466
	Clearwater Memorial Public Library, Orofino	16,899
	Idaho State Library, Boise	34,838
	Shelley Public Library, Shelley	25,858
		106,061
Illinois	Champaign Public Library, Champaign	35,000
	Chicago Public Library, Adult Education, Chicago	35,000
	Chicago Public Library, Altgeld Branch, Chicago	35,000
	Chicago Public Library, Blackstone Branch, Chicago	35,000
	Chicago Public Library, Humboldt Branch, Chicago	35,000

Table 12 / LSCA, Title VI, Library Literacy Program Grants, FY 1991 *(cont.)*

State	Grantee	Amount
	Joliet Public Library, Joliet	$35,000
	Saint Charles Public Library District, Saint Charles	19,395
	Schaumburg Township District Library, Schaumburg	15,300
	Western Illinois Library System, Galesburg	30,844
		275,539
Indiana	Anderson/Story Creek, Union Township, Anderson	34,003
	Hammond Public Library, Hammond	34,842
	Indiana/Marion County Public Library, Indianapolis	35,000
	Indiana State Library, Indianapolis	35,000
	Lake County Public Library, Merrillville	34,969
	Lowell Public Library, Lowell	34,826
	Michigan City Public Library, Michigan City	6,000
	Vigo County Public Library, Terre Haute	33,925
	Wayne Township/Morrison Reeves, Richmond	35,000
		283,565
Kansas	Kansas City Public Library, Kansas City	11,500
		11,500
Kentucky	Bath County Memorial Library, Owingsville	25,000
	Breathitt County Public Library, Jackson	34,956
	Grayson County Public Library, Leitchfield	23,960
	Hopkinsville Christian County, Hopkinsville	25,000
	Laurel County Public Library, London	34,992
	Lexington Public Library, Lexington	35,000
	Marshall County Public Library, Benton	23,347
	Owsley County Public Library, Booneville	34,961
	Perry County Public Library District, Hazard	34,421
	Withers Memorial Public Library, Nicholasville	20,816
		292,453
Louisiana	Calcasieu Parish Library, Lake Charles	28,000
	Evangeline Parish Library, Ville Platte	35,000
	Franklin Parish Library, Winnsboro	35,000
	Louisiana State Library, Baton Rouge	34,850
	New Orleans Public Library, New Orleans	35,000
	Ouachita Parish Public Library, Monroe	35,000
	Saint Mary's Parish Library, Franklin	35,000
	Shreve Memorial Library, Shreveport	10,500
	Terrebonne Parish Library/City, Houma	21,077
	Terrebonne Parish Library/North, Houma	19,840
	Terrebonne Parish Library/South, Houma	19,840
		309,107
Maine	Fort Kent Public Library and two other libraries, Fort Kent	27,371
	Sanford Library Association, Sanford	34,999
		62,370
Maryland	Eastern Shore Regional Library, Salisbury	30,785
	Enoch Pratt Free Library, Baltimore	35,000
	Ruth Enlow Library, Oakland	35,000
		100,785
Massachusetts	Brookline Public Library, Brookline	35,000
	Cary Memorial Library, Lexington	23,750
	Chicopee Public Library, Chicopee	34,800
	Haverhill Public Library, Haverhill	32,773
	Holyoke Public Library, Holyoke	34,600
	Plymouth Public Library, Plymouth	29,386
	Sawyer Free Library, Gloucester	30,000
	Springfield Library/Museum Association, Springfield	29,504
	Thomas Crane Public Library, Quincy	30,190
	Watertown Free Public Library, Watertown	35,000

Table 12 / **LSCA, Title VI, Library Literacy Program Grants, FY 1991** *(cont.)*

State	Grantee	Amount
	West Tisbury Free Public Library, West Tisbury	$8,831
		323,834
Michigan	Adrian Public Library, Adrian	35,000
	Bay County Library System, Bay City	19,124
	Blue Water Library Federation, Port Huron	32,670
	Branch County Library System, Coldwater	27,408
	Capital Library Cooperative, Mason	35,000
	Grand Rapids Public Library, Grand Rapids	30,226
	Greenville Public Library, Greenville	28,136
	Hastings Public Library, Hastings	25,652
	Kalamazoo Public Library, Kalamazoo	34,940
	Jackson District Library, Jackson	35,000
	Library Cooperative of Macomb, Mount Clemens	35,000
	Ypsilanti District Library, Ypsilanti	33,451
		371,607
Minnesota	Duluth Public Library, Duluth	34,917
		34,917
Mississippi	Carnegie Public Library, Clarksdale	19,639
	Elizabeth Jones Library, Grenada	35,000
	Madison County/Canton Public Library, Canton	34,367
	Mid-Mississippi Regional Library System, Kosciusko	35,000
	Sunflower County Library, Indianola	35,000
		159,006
Missouri	Rolla Free Public Library, Rolla	16,443
	Saint Louis Public Library, Saint Louis	35,000
		51,443
Montana	Bitterroot Public Library, Hamilton	19,800
	Bozeman Public Library, Bozeman	34,912
	Lewiston City Library, Lewiston	20,942
	Melstone Public Library, Melstone	31,598
	Missoula Public Library, Missoula	35,000
	Sidney Public Library, Sidney	24,475
		166,727
Nebraska	Broken Bow Public Library, Custer	30,595
	Columbus Public Library, Columbus	33,675
	Hastings Public Library, Hastings	28,902
		93,172
Nevada	Nevada State Library/Archives, Carson City	35,000
	Washoe County Library, Reno	35,000
		70,000
New Hampshire	Howe Public Library, Hanover	20,069
	Keene Public Library, Keene	34,533
	New Hampshire State Library/ACTION, Concord	35,000
	New Hampshire State Library, Family Literacy, Concord	32,530
	New Hampshire State Library/VITAL, Concord	35,000
		157,132
New Jersey	Burlington County Public Library, Mount Holly	35,000
	Camden County Library, with Camden Free Library, Voorhees	56,934
	Elizabeth Public Library, Elizabeth	18,000
	Jersey City Public Library, Jersey City	13,800
	Joint Free Public Library, Morristown	28,850
	Newark Public Library, Newark	35,000
	Old Bridge Public Library, with 23 other libraries, Old Bridge	35,000

Table 12 / LSCA, Title VI, Library Literacy Program Grants, FY 1991 *(cont.)*

State	Grantee	Amount
	Westwood Free Public Library, Westwood	$27,150
		249,734
New Mexico	Harwood Public Library, Taos	33,379
	Jemez Community Library, Jemez Pueblo	17,754
		51,133
New York	Amsterdam Free Library, Amsterdam	27,000
	Chemung/Southern Tier Library System, Corning	27,635
	Huntington Memorial Library, Oneonta	34,920
	Mas-Mor/Shirley Community Library, Shirley	35,000
	Mid-York Library System, Utica	32,000
	Nassau Library System, Uniondale	35,000
	New York Public Library, New York	35,000
	Queens Borough Public Library, Jamaica	35,000
	Riverhead Free Library, Riverhead	26,639
	Schenectady County Public Library, Schenectady	35,000
	Suffolk Cooperative Library System, Bellport	35,000
	Westchester Library System, Elmsford	35,000
		393,194
North Carolina	Ashe County Public Library, West Jefferson	35,000
	Charlotte/Mecklenburg County Public Library, Charlotte	35,000
	Rowan Public Library, Salisbury	35,000
	Watauga County Public Library, Boone	34,625
		139,625
Ohio	Clark County Public Library, Springfield	26,750
	Clermont County Public Library, with Mary P. Shelton Public Library, Clermont	26,574
		53,324
Oklahoma	Ada Public Library, Ada	31,853
	Anadarko Community Library, Anadarko	30,465
	Blackwell Public Library, Blackwell	25,838
	Buckley Public Library, Poteau	23,766
	Choctaw County Library, Hugo	22,205
	Lawton Public Library, Lawton	30,000
	Metropolitan Library System, Oklahoma City	25,000
	Oklahoma Department of Libraries, Oklahoma City	32,695
	Southern Prairie Library System, Altus	34,890
	Tulsa City-County Library, Tulsa	35,000
		291,712
Oregon	Eugene Public Library, Eugene	33,438
		33,438
Pennsylvania	Buhl-Henderson Community Library, Sharon	24,437
	Centre County Library/History Museum, with Schlow Memorial Library, Bellefonte	61,132
	Free Library of Philadelphia, Philadelphia	34,200
	Indiana Free Library, Indiana	31,253
	J. Lewis Crozer Library, Chester	33,000
	Juniata County Library, Mifflintown	28,059
	State Library of Pennsylvania, Harrisburg	35,000
		247,081
Rhode Island	Coventry Public Library, Coventry	15,700
	Pawtucket Public Library, Pawtucket	21,640
	Providence Public Library, Providence	34,885
	Rhode Island Department of State Library Services, Providence	26,014
		98,239
South Carolina	South Carolina State Library, Columbia	35,000
		35,000

Table 12 / LSCA, Title VI, Library Literacy Program Grants, FY 1991 *(cont.)*

State	Grantee	Amount
South Dakota	Smee School District, Standing Rock Sioux Tribal Library, Wakpala	$32,775
		32,775
Tennessee	Brownsville/Haywood County Library, Brownsville	8,000
		8,000
Texas	Andrews County Library, Andrews	33,020
	Corpus Christi Public Library, Corpus Christi	34,874
	Decatur Public Library, Decatur	34,287
	Delta County Public Library, Cooper	35,000
	Emily Fowler Public Library, Project REAL, Denton	27,533
	Emily Fowler Public Library, Project REAL Expansion, Denton	9,507
	Fort Bend County Library System, Richmond	28,081
	Franklin County Public Library, Mount Vernon	35,000
	Harris County Public Library, Houston	29,467
	Houston Public Library, Houston	27,418
	Kountze Public Library, Kountze	34,580
	Lubbock City-County Library, Lubbock	34,935
	Plano Public Library System, Plano	35,000
	Smithville Public Library, Smithville	34,942
	Speer Memorial Library, Mission	24,500
	Sterling Municipal Library, Baytown	29,639
	Tom Green County Library System, San Angelo	28,400
	Unger Memorial Library, Plainview	16,893
	Victoria Public Library, Victoria	35,000
	Ward County Library, Monahan	10,000
	Weslaco Public Library, Weslaco	24,500
		602,576
Utah	Brigham City Library, Brigham City	10,135
	Payson City Library, Payson	35,000
	Provo City Public Library, Provo	24,600
		69,735
Virginia	Botetourt County Library, Roanoke	15,876
	Caroline Library, Inc., Bowling Green	18,541
	Charlotte County Public Library, Charlotte Court House	24,045
	Jefferson/Madison Regional Library, Charlottesville	32,976
	Lonesome Pine Regional Library, Wise	35,000
	Smyth-Bland Regional Library/SCALE, Marion	35,000
	Southside Regional Library, Kenbridge	20,136
		181,574
Washington	Lummi Reservation Library System, Bellingham	22,119
	Longview Public Library, Longview	29,997
	Nisqually Indian Tribal Library, Olympia	35,000
	Seattle Public Library, Seattle	32,974
		120,090
West Virginia	Fayette County Public Library, Oak Hill	35,000
	Martinsburg/Berkeley County Public Library, Martinsburg	35,000
	Mason County Library, Point Pleasant	11,811
	Monroe County Library, with Peterson Public Library, Union	68,231
	Summers County Public Library, Hinton	34,880
	West Virginia Library Commission, Charleston	35,000
		219,922
Wisconsin	Dane County Library Service, Madison	30,768
		30,768
Total Grants		263
Total Awarded		$8,162,894

LSCA State-Administered Programs

In FY 1991, the first year of the administration of the new five-year reauthorization of the Library Services and Construction Act (LSCA) signed into law March 15, 1990, programs in technology, intergenerational library services, child-care library outreach, library literacy centers, drug abuse prevention, and preservation received new emphasis. Several technical amendments were added to increase the flexibility of program operation. Table 13 gives a state-by-state breakdown of FY 1991 funding for LSCA, Titles I, II, and III.

Public Library Services (LSCA, Title I)

The state library agencies made Title I subgrants in 14 legislated service categories, ranging from library-based literacy efforts to strengthening state library agencies to meet the needs of the people. The most recent state reports (1989) reflect the following ranking for funding categories:

1 Areas with inadequate library services
2 Strengthening state library agencies to meet the library and information needs of the people of the state
3 Strengthening the national resources of major urban libraries
4 Library services to the blind and physically handicapped
5 Library services to the disadvantaged
6 LSCA administration
7 Library services to the limited English-speaking
8 Areas without library services
9 Literacy
10 State institutional library services
11 Strengthening the regional library resources of metropolitan public libraries
12 Library services to the elderly
13 Community information referral
14 Other library services to the handicapped

[An article entitled "Library Services for Special User Groups" appears in the Special Reports section of Part I — *Ed.*]
The office is also attempting to identify selected LSCA subgrants that link with the National Education Goals and the America 2000 educational reform effort. The goals for the year 2000 follow:

1 All children in the United States will start school ready to learn.
2 The high school graduation rate will increase to at least 90 percent.
3 U.S. students will leave grades 4, 8, and 12 having demonstrated competency in challenging subject matter including English.
4 U.S. students will be first in the world in science and mathematics achievement.
5 Every adult American will be literate and will possess the knowledge and skills necessary to compete in a global economy and to exercise the rights and responsibilities of citizenship.

Table 13 / Funding for LSCA Titles I, II, and III, FY 1991

State	Title I	Title II	Title III
Alabama	$1,371,830	$321,615	$324,370
Alaska	349,965	128,360	76,392
Arizona	1,211,907	291,370	285,561
Arkansas	884,659	229,482	206,148
California	8,470,260	1,664,066	2,046,952
Colorado	1,143,896	278,509	269,057
Connecticut	1,121,700	274,311	263,671
Delaware	391,511	136,218	86,475
District of Columbia	371,876	132,505	81,709
Florida	3,805,700	781,908	914,998
Georgia	2,031,449	446,362	484,440
Hawaii	516,434	159,844	116,789
Idaho	488,547	154,570	110,022
Illinois	3,517,438	727,392	845,046
Indiana	1,791,562	400,995	426,226
Iowa	1,008,159	252,839	236,117
Kansas	915,107	235,241	213,536
Kentucky	1,260,567	300,574	297,369
Louisiana	1,446,956	335,824	342,600
Maine	547,736	165,764	124,385
Maryland	1,535,740	352,614	364,145
Massachusetts	1,882,622	418,216	448,324
Michigan	2,838,754	599,040	680,349
Minnesota	1,438,704	334,263	340,597
Mississippi	945,840	241,053	220,994
Missouri	1,668,061	377,639	396,256
Montana	429,358	143,376	95,659
Nebraska	658,431	186,698	151,248
Nevada	516,150	159,790	116,720
New Hampshire	515,011	159,575	116,444
New Jersey	2,401,381	516,324	574,211
New Mexico	634,813	182,231	145,516
New York	5,307,909	1,066,005	1,279,541
North Carolina	2,069,865	453,628	493,762
North Dakota	387,812	135,519	85,576
Ohio	3,303,731	686,976	793,185
Oklahoma	1,117,432	273,504	262,634
Oregon	1,002,468	251,762	234,736
Pennsylvania	3,626,141	747,950	871,425
Rhode Island	483,994	153,709	108,917
South Carolina	1,199,386	289,003	282,522
South Dakota	403,463	138,479	89,374
Tennessee	1,605,742	365,853	381,133
Texas	5,035,013	1,014,395	1,213,317
Utah	685,749	191,865	157,877
Vermont	361,347	130,514	79,154
Virginia	1,935,266	428,172	461,099
Washington	1,554,805	356,220	368,772
West Virginia	728,434	199,937	168,236
Wisconsin	1,584,969	361,924	376,092
Wyoming	335,168	125,563	72,801
American Samoa	50,045	21,900	12,438
Guam	74,091	26,447	18,273
Puerto Rico	1,130,522	275,980	265,811
Virgin Islands	70,591	25,785	17,423
Northern Mariana Islands	45,293	21,001	11,284
Palau	7,612	2,736	1,878
Total	$82,218,972	$18,833,395	$19,509,586

6 Every school in the United States will be free of drugs and violence and will offer a disciplined environment conducive to learning.

Random examples from the state LSCA reports indicate that public libraries support these goals:

Goal 1: Readiness for School

Baby Talk (Decatur Public Library, Decatur, Illinois). "Baby Talk" was developed in an effort to educate parents of newborns about the importance of reading, talking, and playing with their babies and to make them aware of the library and other community agencies that can help them succeed as parents. Program staff visited Decatur hospitals to talk with new mothers about using books and the library with their babies. At the same time, they developed and distributed a booklet entitled *Babies and Books: A Joyous Beginning* and gave each newborn a book; 2,088 books were distributed. Besides the information provided during the hospital visit, new parents received quarterly newsletters during their baby's first year. Each participating library received 70 baby books and a copy of a videotape on baby books to support parent interest.

To further publicize library services for parents with young children, a notebook with information on participating libraries was placed in each Decatur hospital. Schools and local organizations were also given information about the project. Quarterly meetings of participating libraries were an important part of the project, encouraging cooperation and providing better service to the target group.

Partners: Parents, Child Care Providers, the Library (L. E. Phillips Public Library, Eau Claire, Wisconsin). The L. E. Phillips Public Library designed a program to attract parents of preschoolers to the library, especially parents who had preschoolers enrolled with child care providers or Head Start programs; families of preschoolers receiving public financial assistance; and families with one or both parents enrolled in the Literacy Volunteers of America adult literacy program. The library issued coupons through local child-care and literacy agencies entitling parents and their children to a "red-carpet tour" of the library and a free kit containing a paperback picture book, bookmarks, reading-tip brochures, and library promotional material. Funding also supported a workshop on reading-readiness activities, a quarterly newsletter aimed at child-care providers, and a collection of reading-readiness materials. The workshop evaluation revealed that 87 percent of the participants learned of the workshop through the newsletter; 87 percent also reported that they had checked out library materials to use in their work with children.

Goal 2: High School Completion

Target Teens (Plainville Public Library, Plainville, Massachusetts). This library purchased materials for young adults in such high-interest areas as career guidance, coping skills, literary criticism, health, sports, and world issues. It also provided special programming, including a baby-sitting workshop, career and college workshops, and a tutoring program run by young adults. The Youth Advisory Board suggested books and other materials and program topics.

Southeast Asian Young Adult Literacy Skills (Milwaukee Public Library, Milwaukee, Wisconsin). Project staff developed a collection of materials for Southeast Asian young adults, enabling them to enhance their literacy in both English and their native language, to learn more successfully in school and at home, to integrate into

American culture with greater ease, and to develop an appreciation of their own cultural heritage. The grant also supported a cooperative program with the Milwaukee public school system to share materials.

Goal 3: Student Achievement and Citizenship

Helping Hand Homework Assistance Program (Enoch Pratt Free Library, Baltimore, Maryland). The library provided a quiet place for Baltimore's homeless children to study and receive assistance with homework and other school assignments.

Mark Twain Program (Long Beach Public Library, Long Beach, California). The library opened an after-school study center that includes homework assistance, to improve young Cambodians' chances of succeeding in school. Participants also received assistance through science projects and library skills workshops.

Increasing Library Service to the Disadvantaged (South Georgia Regional Library, Valdosta, Georgia). Children in the Head Start program were provided with programs, books, and films every month. The library also supported a "study hall" for children needing extra help with school assignments. The library staff provided the Southside Recreation Center with a book collection, films, and study hall and maintained a permanent library at the Boys and Girls Club of Valdosta.

Goal 4: Science and Mathematics

Collection Management/Science and Technology (Monroe County Public Library, Stroudsburg, Pennsylvania). Following a demonstration of natural and scientific phenomena at the library, staff prepared a list of books on science and technology. The library also purchased materials on science and technology and distributed a bibliography of new materials to science faculty in county schools.

Computer Literacy for Children Project (Hubbard Public Library, Hubbard, Ohio). Computer equipment, including four Apple II-GS microcomputers, two Apple Image Writers, and 68 software titles were provided for use by children ages 3–10. Computer literacy training was also provided.

Oregon Library Exhibits Network (Oregon Museum of Science and Industry). Contemporary interactive science and technology exhibits were combined with books and multimedia in the public libraries of five area counties. Research has shown that such exhibits are particularly successful in motivating physically handicapped, mentally disabled, and learning-disabled individuals with literacy barriers resulting from limited education, as well as individuals with foreign-language limitations.

Goal 5: Adult Literacy and Lifelong Learning

Learn for Life (Delta City Library, Delta, Utah). Two types of literacy class for adult learners—English as a second language and reading improvement—were held at the Delta City Library. Materials purchased to support the project included approximately 70 high-interest/low-vocabulary books; computer programs on history, math, reading, and geography; videos on American history; and print materials on literacy.

Services to the Elderly (District of Columbia Public Library, Washington, D.C.). The Mobile Service to Seniors (bookmobile) brought programs and books to 15 senior centers. The Washington Lifelong Learning Center, headquartered at the Martin Luther King Memorial Library, also sponsored programs and seminars at various branch library locations.

Programs to Achieve Job Success (Marshall County Cooperative Library, Arab, Alabama). This library assisted disadvantaged young people and adults in job planning through workshops on such topics as résumé writing, planning for a job interview, using study skills, and understanding career fields. Videotapes and talks by community leaders were incorporated into the programs.

Goal 6: Disciplined Environment and Drug-Free Schools

Project LEAD (Summit Public Library, Summit, Illinois). The Librarians and Educators Against Drugs (LEAD) project focused on creating drug awareness among the elementary school children of the village of Summit. The MacNeal Health Sciences Resource Center furnished the Summit Public Library with catalogs and sample pamphlets on the topic. Librarians distributed pamphlets, bookmarks, buttons, and bags to local elementary school children on community awareness day. The materials were popular with the other exhibitors as well as with the approximately 1,000 children present. A professional speaker was retained to discuss drug abuse prevention at area schools and to distribute materials on drug abuse. Programs were also offered in the library and, as time and money permitted, in schools and public libraries in two adjacent communities. The various activities of the project reached approximately 1,200 children.

Public Library Services to Areas with Inadequate Services (Cedar Rapids Public Library, Cedar Rapids, Iowa). The number of requests received by the Iowa Substance Abuse Information Center, in the Cedar Rapids Public Library, indicated that many people in the area were not aware of the center. To publicize its services, the center set up a display at the Iowa Library Association Conference where many library staff members picked up materials that they in turn would make available to the public. The center also mailed information about its services and materials to all public libraries in Iowa. During the year following the dissemination project, the center received 348 requests for information from public libraries. In earlier years, it only received an estimated 50–75 requests.

To provide a more focused perspective on Title I Public Library Service projects, the Public Library Support Staff reviewed state library reports for FY 1989 and, when available, for FY 1990 to look for trends in LSCA service areas. Their analyses follow.

Library Services to Special Populations: The Illiterate

In FY 1989, public libraries spent $12,677,555 for literacy projects, $2,886,654 of which came from LSCA, Title I; $9,686,702 from state funds; and $104,199 from localities (see Table 14). According to state reports, 401 projects involved more than 800 tutors and approximately 700 students. The projects encompassed such activities as the training of tutors and librarians; English as a second language (ESL), family literacy, and workplace literacy programs; literacy projects in institutions; computer-assisted learning; and the purchase of reading and viewing materials to facilitate learning to read. Activities were sponsored either by one public library or through the cooperation of a public library with a variety of other educational agencies.

A sampling of LSCA Title I–funded literacy projects illustrates some innovative programs and their beneficial effects on participants:

Alaska: Haines Borough Public Library. Through the Chilkat Valley Reads Around the World project, public and school libraries combined efforts to encourage

Table 14 / LSCA Title I Expenditures for Literacy, FY 1989

State	Federal	State	Local	Total	Population Served
Alabama	$2,225	$0	$1,039	$3,264	100
Alaska	13,221	0	0	13,221	300
Arizona	3,500	0	0	3,500	0
Arkansas	6,201	0	0	6,201	1,500
California	89,060	5,635,000	0	5,724,060	67,500
Colorado	51,610	0	0	51,610	413
Connecticut	42,260	0	0	42,260	1,240
Delaware	9,848	325	0	10,173	171
District of Columbia	32,938	3,000	0	35,938	75,000
Florida	212,537	0	46,336	258,873	11,986
Georgia	56,091	0	7,004	63,095	1,843
Hawaii	0	0	0	0	0
Idaho	27,316	0	0	27,316	*
Illinois	36,396	3,965,915	0	4,002,311	*
Indiana	12,000	0	0	12,000	9,494
Iowa	2,495	0	0	2,495	*
Kansas	8,294	0	0	8,294	650
Kentucky	85,518	0	0	85,518	1,801
Louisiana	11,374	11,172	0	22,546	0
Maine	0	0	0	0	0
Maryland	102,274	0	0	102,274	8,516
Massachusetts	126,466	0	0	126,466	1,207
Michigan	134,504	0	0	134,504	1,312
Minnesota	0	0	0	0	0
Mississippi	0	0	0	0	0
Missouri	65,979	0	9,820	75,799	333
Montana	0	0	0	0	0
Nebraska	3,929	0	0	3,929	*
Nevada	5,000	0	0	5,000	*
New Hampshire	9,474	0	0	9,474	*
New Jersey	234,242	43,411	0	277,653	1,111
New Mexico	0	0	0	0	0
New York	344,455	0	0	344,455	20,777
North Carolina	87,632	10,000	10,000	107,632	145
North Dakota	5,000	0	0	5,000	500
Ohio	76,641	11,093	30,000	117,734	4,337
Oklahoma	40,015	0	0	40,015	*
Oregon	0	0	0	0	0
Pennsylvania	28,000	0	0	28,000	225
Rhode Island	44,126	0	0	44,126	2,773
South Carolina	97,991	3,597	0	101,588	5,725
South Dakota	685	115	0	800	331
Tennessee	101,106	0	0	101,106	69,885
Texas	221,954	0	0	221,954	54,896
Utah	47,454	0	0	47,454	1,451
Vermont	0	0	0	0	0
Virginia	292,666	0	0	292,666	1,572
Washington	38,183	0	0	38,183	*
West Virginia	0	0	0	0	0
Wisconsin	61,935	0	0	61,935	957
Wyoming	3,986	3,074	0	7,060	*
Guam	0	0	0	0	0
Puerto Rico	10,073	0	0	10,073	283
Virgin Islands	0	0	0	0	0
Total	$2,886,654	$9,686,702	$104,199	$12,677,555	348,334

*Population figures either not given or unusable

good reading habits for all ages, promote critical TV/video viewing, and increase each participant's knowledge of the world. Preschoolers to senior citizens joined in the program by completing "travel logs" as they read (or were read) books of their choice, by attending monthly programs that focused on various areas of the world, or by creating posters or displays for the library. Although many who read books did not complete a travel log, more than 400 individuals turned them in. On eight occasions between November 25 and April 15, more than 600 adults and children gathered for programs on Russia, Australia, Christmas Around the World, and Africa.

Kentucky: Owsley County. Initially, the library purchased 780 low-level reading books and cassettes and 10 portable cassette players to support outreach efforts to the rural population. The books included classics, thrillers, mysteries, and 15 read-along sets for parents and children. These new materials and portable cassette players were delivered by bookmobile to families throughout the small, rural county. For many, the bookmobile is the only resource for reading materials. As one patron commented, "Since we don't have television, these read-alongs are our entertainment." The project helped the library become a resource for a section of the population that had not been reached before. As a result of a number of publicity activities, the library reached more than 1,500 people, well over the projected 570.

Kentucky: State Library. The Statewide Literacy Program planned and developed literacy activities for adults and school dropouts in local public libraries in coordination with other agencies, organizations, and groups. The program fostered development and maintenance or expansion of literacy activities and provided education for public librarians in literacy programming.

In preparation for the program and to determine the involvement of public libraries in literacy activities, a questionnaire was mailed to all local public libraries in the state. Responses from 86 libraries indicated that the majority of public libraries provided some support for literacy programs and a lesser number provided office or tutoring space for the General Equivalency Diploma (G.E.D.) program.

This project involved extensive interagency cooperation among the State Library, the Literacy Commission, the Louisville Education and Employment Partnership, Jefferson County School System, Kentucky Educational Television, and United Way, as well as local librarians, literacy coordinators, and adult educators. The organizations were instrumental in bringing the Adult Literacy and Technology Conference to Kentucky and in organizing the statewide Partners in Adult Learning Conference. Their efforts laid a strong foundation for future cooperation.

In a project conducted by the Kentucky Humanities Council, Kentucky scholars wrote five books for adult new readers: *Why Work?, Women Who Made a Difference, Choices, History Mysteries,* and *Kentucky Folklore.* The State Library supported the project by purchasing 800 sets of the five books and distributing them to local public libraries, bookmobiles, and institutional libraries in the state.

Massachusetts: Brookline Public Library's Publishing for Literacy project provided a vehicle for publishing the writing of students participating in adult literacy programs in the Greater Boston area. A retreat that brought together adult learners, their families, and tutors for an intensive writing session was an important aspect of the program. The result was the two-volume anthology of their writings, *Need I Say More.* The project improved their writing skills and had a significant effect on their lives and families.

The project was featured on the cover of World Education's international newsletter *Focus on Basics* and was the lead article in the U.S. Department of Education's

ESL Notes in May 1989. Teachers in adult learning centers have commented on the improvement in participants' writing skills. As a result of this activity, a similar pilot project is being conducted in the western part of the state. The project demonstrated the growing interest in writing and community publishing among adult learners and the libraries that serve them.

New Jersey: Trenton Public Library. Once the Literacy for the Family project was under way, it took nearly a year to gain the trust and confidence of participants in the Head Start Program. In time, library representatives developed an excellent working relationship with them, speaking at staff meetings and attending monthly parent involvement meetings at the nine centers (average parent attendance is 8 to 10). These meetings with parents are intended to help young children become readers. To strengthen links with Head Start, the library also became involved with the Head Start substitute teacher training program, introducing teachers to library services and helping them improve their reading skills.

The library also cosponsored a Reading Jamboree with the Greater Trenton Dropout Prevention Planning Collaborative. The purpose of the jamboree was to acquaint children and their parents with the public library and its services; to register children for library cards and involve them in learning activities; and to introduce the library to all as a place to enjoy. The more than 150 children and parents who attended received gift books donated by a publishing company and listened to professional storytellers. Nearly 40 children registered for library cards, and many registered for the summer reading program at the library. The jamboree was such a success that it will be an annual event.

The library also donated children's books withdrawn from its collection to the Austin Health Center for use in the center's waiting rooms. Because the children can take the books home, the library staff placed a notice in each book, "Adult Reading and Writing Help," anticipating that the advertisement might prompt adults in the family to seek tutoring help. More than 110 volunteers were trained during seven sessions to assist adult new learners. The program also arranged for tutor training at the New Jersey Department of Transportation, which, for the first time, gives release time to employees involved in tutoring activities. ESL tutoring has begun; the library plans to add computers and software to supplement the one-on-one tutoring program.

New York: Nassau Library System. As part of the Literacy Volunteers Support Services project, the Nassau Library System contracted with the Literacy Volunteers of America Nassau County affiliate to provide four one-day training workshops for tutors. More than 300 new students were tested and matched with a trained tutor, and more than 42 high-interest, low-level books for new readers were purchased. For this project the Nassau Literacy Volunteers affiliate won its second Connie Haendle Affiliate of the Year Award, an honor no other affiliate could then claim. The award was for sound program management.

Queens Borough Public Library. The goal of the library's Adult Literacy program was to provide pre-ABE (Adult Basic Education) classes to help students reluctant to leave one-on-one tutoring make the transition to a classroom. The project also proposed to help the students attain a median reading level gain of 1.5. To support the project, the library purchased 124 titles for student use. The materials were organized numerically according to the sequence of presentation in class to ensure that students returning to class after temporary absences did not have to face the large sequential gap in instruction that so often discourages returning students. The system also addressed the variety in students' learning styles—students can advance at their own pace. Students participating in the program achieved a median reading level of 1.7. For a unit on letter writing, one elderly student who noted several discrepancies in her bank statement, wrote several letters to the bank asking for a review of her records. An investigation ensued, and $400 was restored to her account.

Upper Hudson Library System. One goal of the Literacy Services to Adults project was to encourage family reading with students participating in the Literacy Volunteers adult education program. Library staff also worked with groups of Head Start and other "at-risk" illiterate parents, encouraging them to begin reading to their children.

South Carolina: Chester County Library. The library purchased software for its literacy computer lab. The software ranged from dictionary skills reinforcement to introduction of basic math skills to career/job skills such as *Resume Writer* and *Typing Made Easy.* Of 55 tutors who worked with the 80 students, 19 received computer training. With several tutors' help, students made excellent use of the math software. Two of the "star" students, who are brothers, dramatically improved their math competency by making a competition out of the drills and exercises, using the computer as a reinforcement tool.

Utah: Logan Public Library coordinated its literacy effort with the two school districts in its service area. It recruited and trained volunteers as tutors, matching them with 70 of the 82 functionally illiterate adults who enrolled in the program. By the end of the project, 57 students were still active and 11 completed the curriculum, testing at a 5th- to 8th-grade proficiency level.

One success story involved a 10th grade dropout reading at a 1st-grade level. The student, a house painter, suffered an accidental fall that prevented him from working. He needed to learn a new trade and to read. Four months after he entered the program, he had completed the four-level course, which usually takes nine months. The culmination of his efforts came when he was awarded the Outstanding Adult Learners Certificate by the American Association for Adult Continuing Education "in recognition of extraordinary initiative and dedication in the pursuit of learning that gives inspiration to others."

Library Services to Special Populations: The Handicapped

Nearly all states and most outlying areas provide services for the blind and the physically handicapped through "regional" libraries. Regional libraries for the blind and the physically handicapped act as service and distribution centers for audio-recorded materials and playback equipment from the National Library Service (NLS) of the Library of Congress. Many states also use LSCA funds for local projects to reach people whose disabilities prevent them from coming to the library.

Statewide services include books and magazines recorded on disc, cassette, and magnetic tape, along with playback equipment, and materials in braille. Area and community projects focus on outreach activities, such as visits to shut-ins, programs for the deaf and the hearing-impaired, and radio reading services.

Major trends include (1) automation of records on users, materials, equipment, and circulation, enabling libraries to serve more users with the same or less staff; (2) greater use of such assistive devices as print-to-voice; print-to-braille; and text on computer screen to either large print, voice, or braille for the visually impaired, telecommunication devices for the deaf (TDDs); and closed-captioned video/television programs for the hearing-impaired; and (3) radio reading programs for the blind and physically handicapped.

In FY 1989, $22,135,600 in federal, state, and local funds were expended for services to the handicapped. $5,377,832 in federal funds, $16,697,693 in state funds, and $60,075 from local sources supported services to 444,871 persons (see Table 15). A sampling of LSCA-funded projects for the handicapped follows:

Illinois: Chicago Public Library. The three goals of the Lift Up Your Hearts, Open Your Doors project were to expand public libraries' awareness of the needs of handicapped children unable to read printed matter, to promote the services of the Illinois network of libraries serving the blind and the physically handicapped, and to lay the groundwork for a statewide Summer Reading Program for print-handicapped children in cooperation with the Illinois Library Association, the first such effort in Illinois. Children's author Jean Little, who is blind, was selected to speak at programs and workshops on library services to the disabled. Many of her works are published in braille and on audiotape. Touring the state with her guide dog, Zepher, Little made 14 stops for programs and workshops that attracted 937 people.

Tours by storytellers also encouraged support for the Summer Reading Program. The storytellers conducted 11 programs and workshops for more than 1,200 at 16 locations around the state to inform the public about the talking-book program. At the end of the grant year, two blind storytellers toured the state for a week, drawing many from the audience that attended the first round of programs. The strongest support and attendance were in rural communities where people came from miles around.

New York: Chemung–Southern Tier Library System. The purpose of the Special Spaces disabled project was to foster design awareness and provide advice through the library to employers, housing providers, and people with physical disabilities, regarding the legal requirements and architectural solutions for adapting living and work spaces for people with physical disabilities. Two conferences were conducted. Living and Working Spaces for People with Physical Disabilities concentrated on the legal requirements and design solutions for "reasonable accommodation" within the workplace for employees with physical disabilities. Living and Working with a Visual Disability provided design solutions for home and "reasonable accommodation" within the workplace for employees with visual disabilities. Information was also disseminated at various activities for the general public, for citizens with disabilities, those who serve citizens with disabilities, and area public library trustees. Pamphlets on disabilities were distributed to system libraries.

Pennsylvania: Free Library of Philadelphia, Library for the Blind and Physically Handicapped. The highlight of this project was the upgrading of the online circulation and inventory control system to a new VAX computer with a new software system. The new programs were the result of networking with the Library for the Blind and Physically Handicapped at the Carnegie Library of Pittsburgh and the New Jersey Regional Library for the Blind and Physically Handicapped. The three organizations formed the Consortium of User Libraries (CUL), a nonprofit legal entity to protect ownership, use, and further development of the software. The primary goal of CUL was to share the future cost and development of the automated system. As other Regional Libraries for the Blind and Physically Handicapped joined CUL, their software license and other members' fees were used for software enhancements and maintenance to benefit all members.

South Carolina: State Library, Blind and Physically Handicapped Services. The purpose of this project was to provide service for the blind and the physically handicapped in cooperation with the Library of Congress National Library Service for the

Table 15 / LSCA Title I Expenditures for the Handicapped, FY 1989

State	Federal	State	Local	Total	Population Served
Alabama	$26,527	$240,073	$1,858	$268,458	2,735
Alaska	0	61,000	0	61,000	505
Arizona	24,516	354,351	0	378,867	11,170
Arkansas	98,863	69,140	0	168,003	7,000
California	0	1,851,000	0	1,851,000	24,100
Colorado	74,000	190,912	0	264,912	7,475
Connecticut	257,898	6,500	0	264,398	9,000
Delaware	30,558	70,105	0	100,663	1,176
District of Columbia	13,873	120,529	0	134,402	9,000
Florida	181,049	586,844	47,548	815,441	2,429
Georgia	101,069	721,338	563	822,970	15,000
Hawaii	0	319,054	0	319,054	1,571
Idaho	1,798	171,015	0	172,813	2,763
Illinois	343,247	1,974,720	0	2,317,967	28,829
Indiana	312,537	162,905	0	475,442	9,089
Iowa	29,693	29,327	0	59,020	13,936
Kansas	122,500	175,000	0	297,500	7,417
Kentucky	6,200	158,900	0	165,100	7,618
Louisiana	141,121	150,099	0	291,220	4,042
Maine	216,927	50,045	0	266,972	3,000
Maryland	62,813	466,621	0	529,434	6,000
Massachusetts	0	126,473	0	126,473	18,000
Michigan	540,767	118,291	0	659,058	13,435
Minnesota	12,633	249,224	0	261,857	14,437
Mississippi	28,418	130,947	0	159,365	3,109
Missouri	105,162	209,145	6,000	320,307	12,000
Montana	106,694	41,340	0	148,034	2,517
Nebraska	75,346	339,785	0	415,131	4,007
Nevada	37,599	0	0	37,599	2,000
New Hampshire	43,131	48,793	0	91,924	2,373
New Jersey	385,519	72,928	0	458,447	12,500
New Mexico	771	139,120	0	139,891	2,474
New York	407,804	1,135,638	0	1,543,442	28,052
North Carolina	22,694	709,794	0	732,488	6,617
North Dakota	121,409	0	0	121,409	2,480
Ohio	413,057	903,136	4,106	1,320,299	32,725
Oklahoma	25,179	0	0	25,179	4,300
Oregon	43,726	235,794	0	279,520	7,227
Pennsylvania	166,090	0	0	166,090	9,662
Rhode Island	95,801	184,337	0	280,138	2,600
South Carolina	89,884	546,019	0	635,903	7,013
South Dakota	159,354	40,387	0	199,741	2,740
Tennessee	157,569	334,509	0	492,078	4,917
Texas	0	1,117,121	0	1,117,121	21,182
Utah	109,100	189,410	0	298,510	5,716
Vermont	23,210	23,801	0	47,011	2,335
Virginia	0	138,090	0	138,090	9,293
Washington	54,000	997,457	0	1,051,457	20,000
West Virginia	19,319	179,646	0	198,965	4,571
Wisconsin	0	430,000	0	430,000	10,577
Wyoming	34,050	21,333	0	55,383	973
Guam	3,000	16,170	0	19,170	129
Puerto Rico	36,906	40,818	0	77,724	705
Virgin Islands	14,451	48,709	0	63,160	350
Total	$5,377,832	$16,697,693	$60,075	$22,135,600	444,871

Blind and Physically Handicapped. The Library of Congress provided recordings of books and magazines on discs and cassettes, the required playback equipment, and books in braille. The state library provided staff, facilities, operating costs, a supplemental collection of books in large print, and contracts with the North Carolina State Library for braille service. The highlight of the fiscal year was receipt of state funding and the subsequent employment of the volunteer coordinator, who was credited with more than $25,000 in donated services. The 61 volunteers, 27 of whom were new recruits, donated 2,417 hours to the project. Telephone Pioneers who repair playback machines contributed 1,416 of those hours.

Brochures, posters, and easels advertised the services in public libraries throughout South Carolina and were distributed to other agencies. Results of a patron survey showed a high degree of satisfaction attributed to a good communication system. In one year, staff responded to 9,417 calls on the In-WATS line and placed 1,909 long-distance calls. Most outgoing calls were to new patrons to determine their needs and reading preferences. Walk-in visitors averaged 125 a month.

South Dakota: State Library Services for the Blind and Physically Handicapped. This project served blind and physically handicapped patrons in both North and South Dakota. The outstanding event of the fiscal year was the Summer Reading Program, which involved the cooperation of the Governor's Office, the State Fair Board, special education teachers and parents across the state, and the North Dakota State Library. Based on the Year of the Young Reader theme, the program was designed to introduce visually handicapped youngsters to the concept that reading for fun is desirable. Readers grouped according to age competed in both the braille and recorded-book categories. The 105 participating students checked out more than 1,000 books and returned more than 500 written book reports.

Winners were invited to a ceremony at the State Fair in Huron where they received their awards from the governor. Each prize winner was given the opportunity to read his or her plaque (overprinted in braille). The winner of the young braille reader division read a poem to the audience and then presented the poem to the governor. The program was continued into the school year.

Tennessee: Public Library of Nashville and Davidson County. Library Service for Hearing Impaired (LSHI): An Information Resource Center offered services for hearing-impaired patrons: 24-hour automated TDD News Service, information and referral services, a special media collection, TDDs and Television Telecaption Decoders for loan, and special programs to encourage deaf people to use library services. The center also offered services for hearing patrons about hearing impairment: information and referral services, the most comprehensive book collection on hearing impairment in the Southeast, an extensive media collection, awareness literature, presentations to groups, in-service training programs for staff, display materials, and mailings with current information about the program.

After information on TDDs was sent to his office, the governor had a TDD installed there to make him more accessible to persons with hearing impairments. In conjunction with the lip-reading instructor at the League for the Hearing Impaired in Nashville, LSHI produced a series of speech-reading lessons that were open-captioned with a set of accompanying worksheets. Preliminary reaction to the series was encouraging. The project served people from 40 counties across the state and 10 cities outside Tennessee.

Library Services to Special Populations: The Elderly

Since 1971, library services to the elderly have been a priority under Title I of LSCA. The amendments to the act that took effect in FY 1991 added Intergenerational Services to the eligible services. The elderly, in conjunction with children, are the primary focus of intergenerational services projects. In the past, these projects involved older children, who, under the sponsorship of the library, visited nursing homes and either read to residents or provided other entertainment, such as plays and sing-alongs. Recently, more projects have been designed to encourage the elderly to provide services to children instead. Many intergenerational projects involve the elderly in teaching preschoolers the skills necessary to learn to read. Such projects include "lap sitting" (reading to a child, one-on-one, while he or she sits in the lap of an elderly "grandma") or services to latchkey, elementary school children after school. The primary aim of both programs is to improve the literacy skills of children as well as to fill social and emotional needs of both the children and the elderly.

These projects give many elderly, who may live far from young relatives, an opportunity for a rewarding relationship with children. The experience also gives the mobile elderly an outlet in meaningful voluntary work. The children, especially those of disadvantaged parents with poor reading skills, receive the opportunity to learn the skills they need to be successful readers. With many children spending the day in preschool or with other child-care providers, intergenerational activities give both the children and the elderly opportunities for desirable physical contact and individual attention. The Grandparents and Books project at the Los Angeles Public Library provides such opportunities. It has proved extremely popular, having completed its second year in 30 branches. Some 76 public libraries in the state plan to continue the project for a third year. As further evidence of its popularity, more than 150 public libraries applied to the state library for grants to fund such programs.

Developing special collections, primarily large-print books, is the most frequent federally funded activity for the elderly; however, other special materials for the elderly, such as videos and cassette and picture books, are common. For example, although the Brooks County (Georgia) Public Library found that the majority of elderly patrons preferred large-print books, it also found that a significant number had good vision and preferred paperbacks because they were easier to hold for long periods of time.

Library projects that added special materials for the elderly, such as at the Thomas Ford Memorial Library (Western Springs, Illinois), showed that as holdings of special materials increased, circulation of the materials to the elderly also increased. For example, a 17.5 percent increase in large-print holdings resulted in a 41 percent increase in their circulation. The Pottsville (Pennsylvania) Free Library found that with only a 35 percent increase in the materials in the rotating collection, use of the materials increased 60 percent.

The Austin (Texas) Public Library produced a large-print catalog of holdings for its *Project Walking Books;* and the Flint (Massachusetts) Memorial Library published another, *Aging Well—Living Well.* The Fort Smith (Arkansas) Public Library made available for check-out magnifiers and kits containing collections of low-vision aids for trial use by patrons. Many elderly were not aware of the kits, which contain check-writing and signature guides, low-vision pens, and enlarged phone dials. The library reported that "there are many magnifying aids on the market, but they must be available for a person to try out over a period of time and in their own setting in order to find one that really helps." The Brookline (Massachusetts) Public Library found that new vision aids circulated on the average of twice a week.

Occasionally, a collection development project started for other reasons unexpectedly fills a need of the elderly population, often resulting in an increase in elderly users of the library. An example is La Biblioteca Outreach Project in Wilmington, Delaware. Adding Spanish-language books to the collection resulted in a noticeable increase in older adults and senior citizens visiting the library.

Sharing collections is common and is usually coordinated by a regional library system, the state library, or a designated statewide center. Rural Western states, where populations are scattered, find such a policy one of the few economic ways to get materials to users. In South Dakota, almost 60 percent of the aging population (65 +) live in rural communities where services are limited, making bulk loans by the state library to local libraries necessary. As the state audiovisual center, the Wichita (Kansas) Public Library rotates collections of films and videocassettes to 87 nursing homes throughout the state. Other projects, such as the one at the Citrus County (Florida) Library System, stock special rotating libraries at nursing homes.

The Milwaukee County (Wisconsin) Federated Library System's Alzheimer's Materials Development project produced *Moments*, a six-volume set of picture books, reflecting life experiences, that could be used by librarians and other caregivers with Alzheimer's patients and dementia victims. These books were sent to every Wisconsin public library system. The Collier County (Florida) Public Library produced a bibliography of its health-related materials, increasing use of these materials and visits to the library by senior citizens.

Title I funds were also used to support special programs for elderly library patrons, nursing home residents, and those who meet at various sites, including multisensory programs and life review kits. Such projects were the second most commonly funded type. "Fun" items, such as games for those with physical or visual limitations, are a new trend. Bags or baskets of large-print or otherwise-adapted games that can be checked out to nursing homes, including games for stroke patients, were cited in reports of the Atchison (Kansas) Public Library. The Westchester (New York) Library System used older volunteers to tell stories in nursing homes and at the library. Volunteers were trained in storytelling techniques. The program was so popular that it was extended to the local jail and became intergenerational when it was taken to children's units in several hospitals.

Projects such as the Consumer Rights Workshops for the Elderly at the Public Library organized by the Tinley Park (Illinois) Public Library for ten libraries in the Suburban Library System sought to provide information important to the life of the senior citizen, as well as to increase library use by this age group. The Lexington (Kentucky) Public Library sponsored workshops on programming for older adults. The workshops, given in three locations in the state, promoted similar projects for senior citizens. For the Rocking Chair Reminiscences project at the DeSoto (Louisiana) Parish Library, older citizens were invited to sit in a rocking chair and tell stories of childhood experiences, folktales, or other stories that they wanted to share with the next generation.

The Anderson (Indiana) Public Library's Outreach Services Enhancement project used Retired Senior Volunteer Program (RSVP) members to deliver materials. Like many library projects, this one relied on other agencies, primarily Meals-on-Wheels, to help identify potential clients. Books-by-mail projects are still being supported, as postal service to the visually impaired is free. However, when the Richland

County (South Carolina) Public Library project offered the choice between delivery of books by a person or through the mail, the participants all rejected delivery by mail. The implication was that a personal visit was preferred.

Promotion of library services to the elderly was cited in many project reports. The Tinley Park Public Library had to promote its special programs "by contacting government agencies that deal with senior citizens at the township level, by reaching out to church groups, and by old-fashioned glad-handing at the circulation desk!" The Kent (Ohio) Free Library found that "the most effective promotion was the one-on-one discussion."

Several public libraries funded activities to upgrade services to the elderly and reassessed program needs. In the first category was the well-documented reworking of the Ypsilanti (Michigan) District Library's Services to the Elderly. In assessing the previous program, a library official stated, "the effort has not been as forceful, as funded, or as staffed as it should be." After upgrading the deposit collections, adding Books-on-Wheels delivery to shut-ins, and introducing a Read-Aloud program, the library has successfully expanded and refined its senior outreach program. The Multnomah County (Oregon) Library funded a state survey of informational needs of senior citizens to the year 2000. A Washington State Library survey found that of the 71 local libraries in the state, only 17 offered services to the aging, even though those over age 65 composed almost 12 percent of the state's population.

For FY 1989, $2,010,200 of Title I funds was used for library projects to serve the elderly. This amount was matched by $871,161 in state funds and $6,049,859 in local funds for a total of $8,931,220. Preliminary data for FY 1990 show $1,598,163 in federal LSCA Title I funds being matched by $355,910 in state and $126,577 in local funds for a total of $2,080,650. A breakdown of expenditures by state for FY 1989 and the preliminary data for FY 1990 are in Tables 16 and 17.

The FY 1989 and 1990 reports indicate a reduction in spending for these services similar to that seen during the last economic downturn in the early 1980s. The increases and decreases do not relate to the funds available under Title I; rather they correspond to the two recessions in the last 20 years. In economic hard times, expensive services, such as those to the elderly and other outreach efforts, suffer.

Library Services Through Major Urban Resource Libraries

Legislation requires that when the total appropriation for the Library Services and Construction Act (LSCA), Title I exceeds $60,000,000, each state must reserve a percentage of these funds under the Major Urban Resource Libraries (MURLs) Program for urban libraries whose collections and services are used beyond their local jurisdiction. In FY 1989, 161 cities in 41 states and Puerto Rico served as MURLs under the requirements of LSCA, Section 3(14). These provisions define a major urban resource library as "any public library located in a city having a population of 100,000 or more individuals, as determined by the Secretary."

Before a city of 100,000 or more can serve as a MURL, it must agree to meet the requirements of Section 102(a)(3) of LSCA, that the city will provide services to users throughout the region in which it is located. For example, in Texas, 20 cities had a population of more than 100,000 in FY 1989. Public libraries in 18 of the cities met the following criteria established by the Texas State Library:

Table 16 / LSCA Title I Expenditures for the Aging, FY 1989

State	Federal	State	Local	Total
Alabama	$21,100	$0	$30,576	$51,676
Alaska	0	0	0	0
Arizona	5,879	0	0	5,879
Arkansas	1,923	0	0	1,923
California	696,746	0	0	696,746
Colorado	3,070	0	0	3,070
Connecticut	80,775	0	0	80,775
Delaware	2,571	14,008	0	16,579
District of Columbia	253	42,230	0	42,483
Florida	128,811	0	44,830	173,641
Georgia	32,348	33,997	20,222	86,567
Hawaii	0	0	0	0
Idaho	3,909	0	0	3,909
Illinois	108,074	0	0	108,074
Indiana	23,391	0	0	23,391
Iowa	21,126	0	0	21,126
Kansas	41,473	0	0	41,473
Kentucky	58,196	0	0	58,196
Louisiana	6,499	6,384	0	12,883
Maine	0	41,535	0	41,535
Maryland	22,517	0	0	22,517
Massachusetts	37,411	0	0	37,411
Michigan	0	0	0	0
Minnesota	4,368	0	0	4,368
Mississippi	0	0	0	0
Missouri	58,415	0	0	58,415
Montana	0	0	0	0
Nebraska	0	0	0	0
Nevada	0	0	0	0
New Hampshire	4,000	0	0	4,000
New Jersey	56,150	538,991	5,875,768	6,470,909
New Mexico	4,600	0	0	4,600
New York	24,191	0	0	24,191
North Carolina	0	40,413	0	40,413
North Dakota	2,500	0	0	2,500
Ohio	45,620	14,740	66,958	127,318
Oklahoma	112,656	0	0	112,656
Oregon	18,664	0	0	18,664
Pennsylvania	5,000	0	0	5,000
Rhode Island	26,465	29,545	0	56,010
South Carolina	15,000	0	11,505	26,505
South Dakota	17,272	5,371	0	22,643
Tennessee	16,666	16,666	0	33,332
Texas	98,553	56,283	0	154,836
Utah	0	0	0	0
Vermont	37,074	20,000	0	57,074
Virginia	59,375	0	0	59,375
Washington	21,092	0	0	21,092
West Virginia	0	0	0	0
Wisconsin	77,842	0	0	77,842
Wyoming	0	0	0	0
Guam	2,000	2,000	0	4,000
Puerto Rico	6,625	8,998	0	15,623
Virgin Islands	0	0	0	0
Total	$2,010,200	$871,161	$6,049,859	$8,931,220

Table 17 / LSCA Title I Expenditures for the Aging (Preliminary Data), FY 1990

State	Federal	State	Local	Total
Alabama	$6,867	$0	$376	$7,243
Alaska	0	0	0	0
Arizona	28,800	0	0	28,800
Arkansas	9,427	0	0	9,427
California	106,463	0	0	106,463
Colorado	0	0	0	0
Connecticut	14,636	0	0	14,636
Delaware	12,991	14,695	0	27,686
District of Columbia	15,000	75,000	0	90,000
Florida	100,837	0	29,000	129,837
Georgia	18,000	29,000	16,153	63,153
Hawaii	0	0	0	0
Idaho	1,986	0	0	1,986
Illinois	14,860	0	0	14,860
Indiana	23,250	0	0	23,250
Iowa	24,293	0	0	24,293
Kansas	31,300	0	0	31,300
Kentucky	67,954	0	0	67,954
Louisiana	2,970	2,512	0	5,482
Maine	0	41,009	0	41,009
Maryland	15,597	0	0	15,597
Massachusetts	39,275	0	0	39,275
Michigan	199,615	0	0	199,615
Minnesota	6,415	160,689	0	167,104
Mississippi	0	0	0	0
Missouri	51,151	0	0	51,151
Montana	0	0	0	0
Nebraska	0	0	0	0
Nevada	0	0	0	0
New Hampshire	2,000	0	0	2,000
New Jersey	20,000	0	0	20,000
New Mexico	0	0	0	0
New York	161,859	0	0	161,859
North Carolina	51,746	0	0	51,746
North Dakota	0	0	0	0
Ohio	12,281	7,890	14,153	34,324
Oklahoma	0	0	0	0
Oregon	17,076	0	0	17,076
Pennsylvania	45,530	0	0	45,530
Rhode Island	14,776	0	0	14,776
South Carolina	73,900	0	66,895	140,795
South Dakota	14,367	14,107	0	28,474
Tennessee	50,125	0	0	50,125
Texas	187,916	0	0	187,916
Utah	0	0	0	0
Vermont	0	0	0	0
Virginia	15,305	0	0	15,305
Washington	29,684	0	0	29,684
West Virginia	0	0	0	0
Wisconsin	107,911	0	0	107,911
Wyoming	0	0	0	0
Guam	2,000	0	0	2,000
Puerto Rico	0	11,008	0	11,008
Virgin Islands	0	0	0	0
Total	$1,598,163	$355,910	$126,577	$2,080,650

1 The library collection has at least 100,000 book volumes

2 The library provides reference services and on-site use of the collection to nonresidents without charge

3 Verification of on-site collection use is required

4 The geographic area served by the library is the entire state

5 The population served by each MURL is outside the city and county that financially support it and may include residents in other regions (10 regional systems) of the state.

The Texas state report for FY 1989 indicates that $501,520 of the $512,603 was expended. Eighteen public libraries participated in the Major Urban Resource Libraries Grant Program. Plano Public Library System, Plano, and Arnulfo L. Oliveira Memorial Library, Brownsville, were in the grant program for the first time in FY 1989. MURL libraries received grants totaling $512,603 to purchase library materials, equipment, and services that would improve their ability to serve without charge the residents outside their tax-supporting political subdivisions. The evaluation reports received from subgrantees at the end of the project year indicate that 22,637 library materials were purchased with MURL grant funds.

The Texas State Library requires each MURL library to set one or more objectives for service to nonresidents during the grant year. Tables 18 and 19 summarize the free services received by nonresidents. Because every nonresident patron using the library cannot always be identified, the number served is undoubtedly higher than shown.

From FY 1984 to FY 1989, Texas MURLs spent $2,439,863; in FY 1990, $558,737 was obligated for MURL purposes (see Table 20).

Arizona is the one state where cities with more than 100,000 residents represent 56.5 percent of the state's population and is required to program at least 50 percent of "excess" funds for its six MURLs. The other states and Puerto Rico are required to reserve a percentage of the allocation equal to the ratio of the combined population of cities with more than 100,000 residents to the state's total population. States with no cities with more than 100,000 residents include Delaware, Maine, Montana, New Hampshire, North Dakota, South Carolina, South Dakota, Vermont, West Virginia, and Wyoming. Each received a proportionate share of the "excess" to use for other activities under Title I.

Since 1979, MURLs have spent the following amounts: $1,666,225 in FY 1979; $1,722,990 in FY 1980; $1,776,609 in FY 1981; $2,142,102 in FY 1984; $4,256,151 in FY 1985; $4,231,144 in FY 1986; $4,921,172 in FY 1987; $4,857,391 in FY 1988;

Table 18 / Services Received by Nonresidents in Texas MURLs, by Service Objective, FY 1991

Service Objective	Libraries Setting Objective	Nonresidents Served
Use by nonresidents of collections and services in the library	17	634,172
Nonresident use of reference services	9	76,106
Circulation to nonresidents	7	147,532

Table 19 / Services Received by Nonresidents in Texas MURLs,
by Service Category, FY 1991

MURL	In-Library Users	Reference Questions	Circulation	In-Library Circulation	Materials Purchased
Abilene	820	–	4,106	–	733
Amarillo	2,381	3,559	928	33,235	1,548
Arlington	–	3,458	–	–	1,213
Austin	–	17,657	–	–	509
Beaumont	1,767	14,480	–	–	344
Brownsville	8,590	1,584	1,236	–	2
Corpus Christi	843	–	–	–	1,179
Dallas	406,811	–	–	–	6,303
El Paso	23,231	3,311	–	–	410
Fort Worth	6,671	–	–	–	2,576
Garland	12,476	–	79,802	–	109
Houston	70,000	30,750	–	–	2,874
Irving	150	555	–	–	658
Lubbock	1,611	–	4,229	–	863
Oasadeba	–	–	53,776	50,881	1,058
Plano	10,078	–	–	–	133
San Antonio	–	–	3,455	3,322	1,800
Waco	1,854	712	–	1,451	325

and $5,086,800 in FY 1989. In FYs 1982 and 1983, the Title I appropriation was $60,000,000. The FY 1990 obligation was $5,637,256.

Examples of how MURLs used Title I funds in FY 1989 follow:

Alaska: The Anchorage Municipal Library (AML) serves as the regional resource library for all south central Alaska, providing collection backup for small community libraries through interlibrary loan (ILL) and direct-mail services to rural residents for the region unserved by a local library. The local Anchorage population with direct access to materials purchased with MURL funds is estimated at 218,979. The Kenai and Mat-Su boroughs, along with other major towns in the region, add another 88,000 people, bringing the total served to at least 307,000. Because all new titles are added to the Western Library Network (WLN), the potential benefit extends to the entire state of Alaska and to WLN users throughout the Pacific Northwest.

The objectives of the MURL Grant ($17,101) were to assist the library in building a collection of 3.5 volumes per capita and to enable it to fill at least 90 percent of interlibrary loan requests for monographs. With the grant, the library added 717 English-language monographs to its collection on science, technology, medicine, law, political science, psychology, fiction, photography, and literature. They account for 2 percent of the volumes added in FY 1989. Although the present 1.74 volumes per capita is only half of the targeted 3.5 volumes per capita, the library increased its monographic collection by 8 percent during FY 1989. It also filled 4,321 ILL requests, 10.4 percent more than in FY 1988. The fill rate for FY 1989 was 74 percent, down from 76 percent the previous year.

Colorado: The purpose of the project ($39,136) at the Pueblo Library District was to strengthen the adult and juvenile collections and to improve access to materials in the library. The library purchased books on economics, business, and biography. The library also purchased and installed three computer workstations, one of which was an OCLC workstation, and trained staff to use them. All materials were cataloged and entered into the library's database, which can be accessed on the local, re-

Table 20 / Major Urban Resource Libraries (MURLs),
Expenditures for FY 1989 and Funds Obligated and
Reserved for FY 1990

State	FY 1989	Obligation for FY 1990
Alabama	$88,681	$62,948
Alaska	17,101	16,639
Arizona	104,072	174,951
Arkansas	18,900	19,392
California	758,319	839,258
Colorado	195,682	195,683
Connecticut	47,880	47,880
Delaware	n/a	n/a
District of Columbia	n/a	n/a
Florida	164,235	364,101
Georgia	65,299	71,602
Hawaii	76,548	2,900
Idaho	18,190	18,190
Illinois	266,395	266,395
Indiana	99,832	106,711
Iowa	27,358	27,507
Kansas	46,634	56,671
Kentucky	39,192	42,390
Louisiana	184,262	184,262
Maine	n/a	n/a
Maryland	58,308	59,789
Massachusetts	69,381	74,367
Michigan	153,700	158,810
Minnesota	48,982	50,427
Mississippi	15,923	16,480
Missouri	85,436	87,560
Montana	n/a	n/a
Nebraska	39,226	41,655
Nevada	23,226	25,265
New Hampshire	n/a	n/a
New Jersey	61,411	64,570
New Mexico	29,075	31,634
New York	642,067	687,460
North Carolina	74,200	80,530
North Dakota	n/a	n/a
Ohio	234,072	233,721
Oklahoma	92,636	100,649
Oregon	39,084	44,032
Pennsylvania	202,809	202,807
Rhode Island	11,972	12,458
South Carolina	n/a	n/a
South Dakota	n/a	n/a
Tennessee	120,000	120,000
Texas	501,520	558,737
Utah	25,000	25,000
Vermont	n/a	n/a
Virginia	117,005	156,020
Washington	75,536	121,388
West Virginia	n/a	n/a
Wisconsin	71,016	100,723
Wyoming	n/a	n/a
Puerto Rico	76,635	85,694
Total	$5,086,800	$5,637,256

gional, state, and national levels through the Pueblo Library Network, Microlink, and OCLC.

Illinois: Chicago Public Library used its FY 1989 MURL Grant of $237,652 to strengthen the research collections of the Central Library, preserve African-American resources housed at the Woodson Regional Library, and develop new collections throughout the system to serve a special user group. The Business, Science and Technology Division made major additions to its collection of patents on microfilm, and staff of the Vivian G. Harsh Research Collection organized and preserved the Horace Cayton and Ben Burns collections. Print and nonprint materials related to deafness and hearing impairment were identified and acquired for all 84 branches, the two regional libraries, and the Central Library.

The Cayton Collection contains more than 12,500 items, including clippings, financial records, scrapbooks, and photographs belonging to Horace Revels Cayton (1903-1970), a University of Chicago sociologist and the author of *Black Metropolis.* Staff prepared a finding aid that lists items in the collection; sent out 100 pictures for preservation and had master negatives made; and sent 20 letters for encapsulation. Fireproof file cabinets were purchased for storage.

The Burns Collection contains more than 42,500 items, including newspaper extracts, photographs, photographic negatives, and pamphlets belonging to Ben Burns, a prominent journalist. The preservation project, completed with FY 1989 funds, will enable the library to honor requests for access to these collections. The staff produced a container list for holdings, assessed and assigned numbers to each item in the collection, and prepared a finding aid. Acid-free folders and fireproof filing cabinets were purchased.

In light of the growing awareness of hearing impairment, the most prevalent chronic disability in the United States, and the plan to distribute TDDs to all deaf people in Illinois, the Chicago Public Library (one of only two public libraries in the Chicago area serving the hearing-impaired) anticipated an increase in demand for related materials. The library used $150,000 of MURL funds to build collections of related materials, including books and videos on deafness, deaf culture and history, deaf psychology, and sign language. Also included were high-interest/low-vocabulary, or simplified-English, books for use by the deaf. The library acquired a core collection of materials for every branch, the two regional libraries, and the Central Library. Designated agencies received additional funds to enhance core collections with titles selected from lists developed by the library's deaf services coordinator. The MURL funds have enabled the library to respond to changing public demand, enhance areas of the collection for which resources were not readily available, and address the needs of a special user group. An added benefit has been the augmentation of the library's high-interest/low-vocabulary collections. These collections promote reading motivation not only among the hearing-impaired, but among all those with reading difficulties.

To enhance its collection of historical materials, the library allocated $51,746 for back files (1891-1965) of patents on cartridge microfilm. The Chicago Public Library is one of the nation's oldest patent depository libraries, but many patents are in fragile condition. Microfilm maximizes access to the collection and enables the library to satisfy interlibrary loan requests. The MURL grant allowed the library to make its research collections more accessible and to enhance services to a new, previously underserved group.

Louisiana: With $91,492 in MURL funds, New Orleans Public Library purchased audiovisual materials for the Central Library and three regional branches; Black History Month materials; high-demand books on school reading lists; and easy books for preschool children. The library also stocked the collection of three mini-libraries used as homework centers for area children. The increase in purchasing power resulting from the grant is credited with the rise in circulation in 1989.

Maryland: The MURL project at Enoch Pratt Library ($58,308) enhanced its resources and the state's ability to respond to the needs of special clients by concentrating on five areas:

1 The library micrographically reproduced local Maryland newspapers from the late 19th and early 20th centuries, focusing on six housed at the library that were in the most danger of disintegration. Beginning in February 1989, an outside contractor filmed the newspapers, producing 55,537 images in five months. This project facilitated public access to holdings at Enoch Pratt and other selected state libraries.

2 Pratt Library collects heavily in African-American materials and maintains a staff specialist in the field. Many of its African-American holdings are reference materials that do not circulate. The library augmented the collection with archival materials and increased the number of duplicate copies. The first priority was to purchase duplicate titles to service heavy interlibrary loan demand. The library purchased 192 volumes that are bibliographically accessible via the Maryland Interlibrary Loan Network (MILNET).

3 To support G.E.D. and adult literacy efforts, the library purchased 15 educational videos; approximately one third were duplicates of already held items that are in great demand because of the limited number of quality titles available.

4 The library increased the number of educational videos with captioning for the deaf and/or hearing-impaired.

5 Six days a week, 52 weeks a year, the Audiovisual Department tapes Maryland news programs off the air. These tapes are forwarded to the University of Baltimore, where they are indexed and stored in environmentally safe containers.

New York: With its grant of $223,184, New York Public Library acquired materials to enrich the special collections and services offered by the Central Library and the Branch Library System and provided bibliographic information about these holdings in print and online. Units of Central Library Services purchased materials for each area of specialization, including 3,365 books, 28 periodicals, 17 CD-ROMs, and 654 audiovisual/computer materials.

The grant continued to help the library meet the demands of a highly diverse and sophisticated population for specialized print and nonprint materials. Users whose needs were met by MURL-purchased materials included a partially deaf young woman who came to Mid-Manhattan's Project ACCESS for two or three hours each week to learn sign language from *Joy of Signing* videotapes; the daughter of an Alzheimer's victim who was able to find much needed information on this disease; and an artist using the Mid-Manhattan Art collection who was so pleased to see exhibition catalogs of his work that he donated several others.

Library Services Through Metropolitan Public Libraries
That Serve as National or Regional Resource Centers

Since FY 1972, under Section 102 (a)(2)(c) of LSCA, states must strengthen metropolitan public libraries that serve as national or regional resource centers. This provision allows states to determine the metropolitan public libraries that have the capacity to serve as resource centers without meeting the MURL requirement that the city have a population of more than 100,000. The following amounts were expended for this activity between FY 1984 and FY 1989 and obligated in FY 1990: $2,726,236 in FY 1984, $3,571,713 in FY 1985, $3,514,961 in FY 1986, $2,959,216 in FY 1987, $2,972,531 in FY 1988, $2,892,955 in FY 1989, and $2,879,610 in FY 1990, for a total of $21,517,222. (See Table 21 for a state-by-state listing of expenditures in FY 1989 and funds obligated for FY 1990.) Examples of activities carried out under this provision follow:

California: FY 1989 was a year of transition for the Southern California Answering Network (SCAN) ($503,673), from serving only the Southern California library systems to reference referral statewide and from temporary quarters at UCLA into the new Los Angeles Central Library. A series of meetings planned by the State Library were held throughout the state to introduce system reference staff to SCAN staff and to discuss new procedures. Information files from the Bay Area Reference Center (BARC) in San Francisco were made available to SCAN; a monthly news publication was launched; and a new computer software program, SCANLOG, was developed with State Library staff assistance to aid in reference question record-keeping. During FY 1989, staff answered 2,586 questions and completed 741 database searches.

Since the Bay Area Reference Center merged with the Southern California Answering Network, San Francisco Public Library used $285,679 in LSCA Title I funds to establish a municipal reference service that provided 75 city departments with answers to more than 600 work-related reference and research questions. To support this project, three databases were created — Bay Area Publishers Directory, Business Resource File, and City Government File — and an electronic bulletin board with the minutes and agendas of 20 city boards and commissions was established for dial-up access. More than 250 log-ons were reported in the first six months. The San Francisco Board of Supervisors funded the municipal reference service for a second year to continue to provide information and research assistance to city government employees. The library is seeking funding from the private sector to continue database development.

Minnesota: The primary objective of the Metropolitan Library Service Agency (MELSA) project ($330,209) was to support public library cooperation in the metropolitan area of Minneapolis and Saint Paul by reimbursing member libraries for serving patrons from outside the primary funding jurisdiction (city or county). The seven county libraries and two city libraries that are members of MELSA began by extending reciprocity to each other and then to patrons of Minnesota libraries that participate in an eligible regional public library system. During the year, 2,279,122 items circulated and staff handled 749,928 reference questions and 250,198 directional questions, many more than were estimated because of the extension of reciprocity beyond the system.

Tennessee: The Chattanooga–Hamilton County Bicentennial Library; Knox County Public Library, Knoxville; Memphis–Shelby County Public Library and Information Center; and the Public Library of Nashville and Davidson County were designated as single-county metropolitan library regions and became part of the Tennessee Regional Library System, as authorized by *Tennessee Code Annotated 10-5*. The four single-county regions are administered by library boards composed of representatives of all types of library user from throughout the region. These library boards enter into a contractual relationship with the state, which allows them to re-

Table 21 / Metropolitan Public Libraries Serving as
National/Regional Resource Centers, Expenditures for FY 1989
and Funds Obligated and Reserved in FY 1990

State	FY 1989	Obligation for FY 1990
Alabama	$126,691	$0
Alaska	0	0
Arizona	82,676	39,772
Arkansas	0	0
California	789,352	778,287
Colorado	0	0
Connecticut	0	0
Delaware	—	—
District of Columbia	—	—
Florida	302,500	605,000
Georgia	222,611	179,850
Hawaii	0	0
Idaho	0	0
Illinois	0	0
Indiana	0	0
Iowa	0	0
Kansas	15,507	15,507
Kentucky	0	0
Louisiana	0	0
Maine	—	—
Maryland	0	0
Massachusetts	0	0
Michigan	99,723	96,627
Minnesota	330,209	306,723
Mississippi	0	0
Missouri	75,432	0
Montana	—	—
Nebraska	0	0
Nevada	154,097	149,669
New Hampshire	—	—
New Jersey	39,602	0
New Mexico	0	0
New York	0	0
North Carolina	393,185	493,085
North Dakota	0	0
Ohio	0	0
Oklahoma	0	0
Oregon	0	0
Pennsylvania	0	0
Rhode Island	0	0
South Carolina	0	0
South Dakota	0	0
Tennessee	247,090	215,090
Texas	0	0
Utah	0	0
Vermont	0	0
Virginia	0	0
Washington	0	0
West Virginia	0	0
Wisconsin	0	0
Wyoming	0	0
Puerto Rico	11,280	0
Total	$2,889,955	$2,879,610

ceive and expend state and federal funds as a supplement to locally authorized funds. In FY 1989, the library boards of the four single-county metropolitan library regions received a MURL grant of $247,090.

During 1989, the single-county regional libraries provided materials and services to all residents of their metropolitan areas. They also provided resources to public libraries statewide, through the Area Resource Center (ARC) housed at each metropolitan library. ARCs provided reference and interlibrary loan services to designated multicounty regional library systems. The Memphis ARC served 20 county libraries in the Forked Deer, Reelfoot, and Shiloh regions. The Nashville ARC served 26 counties in the Blue Grass, Highland Rim, and Warioto regions. The Chattanooga ARC served 26 counties in the Caney Fork, Fort Loudoun, and Upper Cumberland regions, and the Knoxville ARC served 19 counties in the Clinch-Powell, Nolichucky, and Watauga regions.

ARCs are not designed to supplant local public library services, but rather to ensure that all library users have access to all of Tennessee's public library resources. This project enhanced the metropolitan libraries' ability to meet the needs of metropolitan and rural residents of the counties within each ARC service area. All four metropolitan libraries used project funds exclusively to purchase library materials.

Tennessee Area Resource Centers were established by the Tennessee State Library and Archives to ensure that residents of rural areas in Tennessee had access to the same library materials and services available to residents of metropolitan areas. ARCs provide the following services to library users within their service area: They locate and lend fiction and nonfiction books and other materials; provide photocopies of materials, including magazine and newspaper articles; answer reference questions that require materials not available at the local public library; and provide information and referral services to identify local, state, and national agencies and organizations.

Public Library Construction (LSCA, Title II)

During FY 1989, more than $26.8 million in federal funds was obligated by the states for public library construction projects. This included more than $15.4 million in LSCA, Title II funds from the FY 1989 allotment and $11.4 million carried over from previous years. Some $6.4 million from the FY 1989 allotment and more than $2.2 million in carryover funds were available for approved projects in FY 1990.

During FY 1989, 33 states completed 150 public library construction projects, 13 less than in FY 1988. Combined (state, local, and federal) funding for completed public library construction projects that received LSCA, Title II assistance during FY 1988 was $46 million. Of this amount, slightly more than 24 percent of the construction costs of federally assisted public library projects completed in FY 1989 was from LSCA, Title II. Comparison of FY 1989 figures with those for FY 1988 reveals a decrease of approximately 21 percent in LSCA funds used for Title II projects. State support for public library construction decreased almost 15 percent, and local support increased less than half of 1 percent during the same period.

Combined matching funds from state and local sources in FY 1989 amounted to more than $36.2 million and supported more than 78 percent of the total cost of completed public library construction projects. Of this amount, the largest percentage was from local contributions (74 percent). Table 22 is a partial listing of LSCA, Title II projects completed during FY 1989.

Table 22 / LSCA Title II, Public Library Construction Projects Completed in FY 1989

State	Project	Federal	State	Local	Total
Alabama	Eufaula	$36,508	$0	$46,748	$83,256
	Fairhope	40,000	0	40,019	80,019
	Helena	75,000	0	120,643	195,643
	Montgomery	51,405	0	60,058	111,463
Alaska		0	0	0	0
Arizona	Benson	126,250	0	131,323	257,573
	Black Canyon City	117,760	0	117,760	235,520
	Royall	100,000	0	113,887	213,887
Arkansas	Arkansas River	58,000	0	58,896	116,896
	Columbia-Lafayette	107,000	0	140,628	247,628
	North Logan	81,812	0	114,686	196,498
	Randolph	38,274	0	77,246	115,520
	Central Arkansas	143,530	0	314,470	458,000
California		0	0	0	0
Colorado	Dolores	7,695	0	9,405	17,100
	Pueblo (A)	73,321	0	89,614	162,935
	Pueblo (B)	18,540	0	26,059	44,599
	Bud Werner	5,321	0	6,754	12,075
Connecticut	Levi E. Coe	12,847	8,564	18,568	39,979
	Preston	100,000	222,112	367,113	689,225
Delaware		0	0	0	0
District of Columbia		0	0	0	0
Florida	Lynn Haven	199,204	200,000	156,669	555,873
Georgia		0	0	0	0
Hawaii		0	0	0	0
Idaho	Council Valley	400	0	399	799
	Salmon	39,868	0	88,412	128,280
Illinois	Chicago	140,964	0	211,446	352,410
	Glenwood/Lynwood	209,682	40,318	419,579	669,579
	Waukegan	50,000	0	50,000	100,000
Indiana	Hammond	12,500	0	12,652	25,152
	Peru	24,750	0	39,050	63,800
	Thorntown	3,100	0	9,306	12,406
Iowa	Norelius	16,000	0	20,401	36,401
	Ottumwa (A)	16,284	0	16,284	32,568
	Ottumwa (B)	16,284	0	16,284	32,568
	Sioux Center	75,000	0	226,146	301,146
	Westcliffe	43,200	0	52,800	96,000
Kansas		0	0	0	0
Kentucky		0	0	0	0
Louisiana		0	0	0	0
Maine	Shaw (A)	2,765	0	7,581	10,346
	Shaw (B)	235	0	235	470
Maryland		0	0	0	0
Massachusetts		0	0	0	0
Michigan	Fowlerville	20,392	0	43,440	63,832
	Taylor	118,800	0	999,706	1,118,506
Minnesota	Pelican Rapids	84,810	0	172,604	257,414
Mississippi		0	0	0	0
Missouri		0	0	0	0
Montana		0	0	0	0
Nebraska	Beaver City	35,000	0	35,000	70,000
	Bruno	23,050	0	34,154	57,204

Table 22 / LSCA Title II, Public Library Construction Projects Completed in FY 1989 *(cont.)*

State	Project	Funding			
		Federal	State	Local	Total
	Lyman	4,850	0	14,403	19,253
	Woods	10,650	0	14,923	25,573
Nevada	Beatty	1,200	0	1,590	2,790
	Henderson (A)	8,441	11,189	0	19,630
	Henderson (B)	48,160	63,840	0	112,000
	Lyon Co. Fernley	34,212	191,749	79,000	304,961
	Lyon Co. Silver Springs	22,633	74,646	30,721	128,000
New Hampshire	Laconia	26,500	0	26,500	53,000
	State Library (Admin.)	2,774	4,361	0	7,135
	North Conway	45,044	0	59,825	104,869
	Orford	36,500	0	36,500	73,000
	Whitefield	6,000	0	6,000	12,000
	Wilton	41,500	0	45,000	86,500
New Jersey	Clark	19,000	0	19,000	38,000
	Elizabeth	63,235	0	63,236	126,471
	Hamilton	94,945	0	119,771	214,716
	Ho-Ho-Kus	67,936	0	248,518	316,454
	Piscataway	85,808	154,692	500,000	740,500
	Newark	65,000	0	1,053,907	1,118,907
	Red Bank (A)	10,000	0	12,663	22,663
	Red Bank (B)	10,000	0	1,000	11,000
New Mexico	Bayard	20,750	0	24,455	45,205
New York	Avon	242	0	543	785
	Baldwin	267,955	31,672	805,604	1,105,231
	Brooklyn	700,000	0	3,653,000	4,353,000
	Byron-Bergen	25,466	0	71,526	96,992
	Copiague	15,013	0	65,480	80,493
	Croton	82,298	20,591	432,295	535,184
	Cutchogue	6,745	0	13,196	19,941
	East Syracuse	43,851	0	213,851	257,702
	Field	645	0	1,569	2,214
	Finklestein	28,489	8,000	58,083	94,572
	Corneila Greene	444	0	861	1,305
	Irondequoit	97,756	55,270	202,056	355,082
	Mohawk Valley	46,662	0	86,658	133,320
	NYPL–Aguilar	108,500	0	201,500	310,000
	NYPL–Countee Cullen	139,281	0	258,666	397,947
	Nioga	5,600	1,342	9,142	16,084
	North Castle	35,173	0	100,557	135,730
	North County	9,422	17,722	0	27,144
	North Tonawanda	1,184	0	11,661	12,845
	Onondaga	180,582	0	933,952	1,114,534
	Oriskany	43,724	17,199	242,402	303,325
	Patchogue	43,750	53,369	37,622	134,741
	Queens–Rego Park	49,700	0	168,940	218,640
	Ransomville	26,067	37,500	32,412	95,979
	Rochester	35,000	0	72,318	107,318
	Rochester–South Aven	127,050	0	269,151	396,201
	Sanford	143,841	0	403,028	546,869
	Schenectady	62,650	0	116,850	179,500
	Stevens	568	0	1,507	2,075
	Suffern	1,191	0	20,509	21,700
	Voorheesville	172,341	0	749,418	921,759
	Wantagh	120,194	0	389,838	510,032
	Warsaw	83,072	0	410,337	493,409
	Wead	1,666	0	4,490	6,156
	Albert Wisner	8,380	0	21,970	30,350
	Woodward	57,844	0	208,500	266,344

Table 22 / LSCA Title II, Public Library Construction Projects Completed in FY 1989 *(cont.)*

State	Project	Federal	State	Local	Total
North Carolina	Ashe Co.	153,000	0	189,188	342,188
	Harnett Co.	270,976	0	626,524	897,500
	Valdese	80,000	0	255,483	335,483
North Dakota	Minot	39,000	0	129,682	168,682
Ohio	Coshocton	170,603	0	207,999	378,602
Oklahoma	Grove	100,000	0	190,322	290,322
	Hominy	50,000	0	52,000	102,000
	Yale	50,000	0	50,031	100,031
Oregon	North Bend	95,544	0	1,682,968	1,778,512
	Sandy	95,544	0	414,768	510,312
Pennsylvania		0	0	0	0
Rhode Island		0	0	0	0
South Carolina	Great Falls	40,000	0	54,529	94,529
	Lake Wylie	52,000	0	447,465	499,465
	Laurens	200,000	0	1,392,474	1,592,474
	Marlboro	4,304	0	4,305	8,609
South Dakota	Canton	132,600	0	306,142	438,742
	Clear Lake	1,717	0	1,717	3,434
	Deadwood	1,144	0	1,663	2,807
	Deubrook	1,038	0	1,221	2,259
	Dewey	49,015	2,000	54,872	105,887
	Hyde	2,370	0	2,549	4,919
	Sioux Falls	18,600	0	27,835	46,435
Tennessee	Argie Cooper	70,420	0	86,562	156,982
	Harvey Freeman	48,475	0	53,175	101,650
	Lannom	100,000	0	187,011	287,011
	Loretto	50,359	0	62,864	113,223
	Manchester	100,000	0	144,715	244,715
Texas	Allen	200,000	0	2,355,000	2,555,000
	Atlanta	100,000	0	442,260	542,260
	Decatur	200,000	0	741,489	941,489
	El Paso	100,000	0	518,633	618,633
	Smithville	50,000	0	84,781	134,781
Utah	Davis Co.	200,000	0	1,363,321	1,563,321
	Millard Fillmore	950	0	1,000	1,950
	Lehi	100,000	0	124,739	224,739
	Milford	950	0	1,030	1,980
	Mount Pleasant	950	0	1,028	1,978
	Park	111,449	0	786,879	898,328
	Provo	207,892	0	2,105,212	2,313,104
	Salina	950	0	1,049	1,999
	Smithfield	550	0	682	1,232
Vermont	Bradford	20,500	0	26,493	46,993
	Burnham (A)	93,500	0	519,745	613,245
	Burnham (B)	6,500	0	6,500	13,000
Virginia		0	0	0	0
Washington		0	0	0	0
West Virginia	Gilmer	25,000	0	57,332	82,332
	Hurricane	56,000	20,000	60,333	136,333
	Pioneer	16,000	0	28,126	44,126
Wisconsin	Cross Plains	23,103	0	238,518	261,621
	Dodgeville	125,000	0	534,215	659,215
	Galesville	48,600	0	147,698	196,298
	Verona	125,000	0	291,834	416,834

Table 22 / LSCA Title II, Public Library Construction Projects Completed in FY 1989 *(cont.)*

State	Project	Federal	State	Local	Total
				Funding	
Wyoming	Encampment	115,219	0	337,000	452,219
	Johnson Co.	98,480	250,000	178,599	527,079
	Platte Co.	36,956	0	55,434	92,390
Guam		0	0	0	0
Puerto Rico		0	0	0	0
Virgin Islands		0	0	0	0
Total		$9,863,293	$1,486,136	$34,729,523	$46,078,952

Interlibrary Cooperation and Resource Sharing (LSCA, Title III)

In FY 1989, the Title III appropriation was $18,719,960. Expenditures reported by all but three states amounted to $15,749,179. Funds were from FY 1988 and FY 1989 appropriations, with some FY 1989 funds reserved for expenditure in FY 1990.

The LSCA, Title III program provides limited financial support for networking and other cooperative programs throughout the nation. Because no matching state or other funds are required, states report only expenditures from Title III funds, providing an incomplete record of expenditures for networking and cooperative programs.

The purpose of Title III is to assist states to develop and extend library services through networking and other cooperative activities among all types of library within a state and across state lines. With the advice and assistance of the LSCA-mandated State Advisory Council on Libraries, state library agencies continue to identify current and long-range needs and to develop library programs to meet those needs. Activities in FY 1989, as in previous years, may be categorized as follows:

1 Establishing, expanding, and operating networks
2 Automating circulation/resource-sharing systems
3 Converting bibliographic holdings to machine-readable records
4 Improving interlibrary loan and document delivery services
5 Continuing education and staff development
6 Preservation of library materials

In the 1990 reauthorization of LSCA, Congress added the provision that Title III grants will be used for "developing the technological capacity of libraries for interlibrary cooperation and resource sharing." Thus, states are encouraged to support new technological developments. Some states have already done so. For example, Louisiana and Mississippi are using the laser disc to record MARC bibliographic holdings, and several states are using telefacsimile transmission for interlibrary loan and document delivery services.

Another new Title III emphasis allows states to plan for preservation cooperation in annual and long-range programs. Connecticut, Massachusetts, and South Carolina are among the few that have used Title III funds to develop such a plan. However, the overall impact of the new focus on state programs will not be known until the FY 1991 and 1992 state reports are received.

LSCA report forms do not request data on the number of different types of library participating in Title III projects. In part, this is because defining "participation" is difficult. Is a library that only uses the statewide interlibrary loan and reference referral online network a "participant?" Is a library that contributes bibliographic records to the statewide database a "participant?" Although no data are available on the number of libraries by type (or, for that matter, on the total number of libraries) involved in Title III activities, the narrative evaluations of the projects provide important information. Table 23 is based on an analysis of the annual reports from each state, the District of Columbia, and U.S. territories for FY 1989 and 1990. The number of libraries of each type involved in each type of project was tallied, but because reporting methods vary among the states, results should not be considered exact. Some reports are detailed, identifying each library or type of library involved in each project; others provide either estimates or no specific information regarding participating libraries.

Among states providing a breakdown by type of library, the largest number of libraries are involved in cooperative resource-sharing projects and networking. Of special interest is the significant number of elementary and secondary school systems converting bibliographic records to machine-readable form, which will enable them to participate more effectively in networking and resource sharing. More multitype cooperatives are involved in resource sharing and networking projects than any other type of library (though their members *are* "other" types of library).

Although their information is incomplete, state library reports show that all types of library are using LSCA, Title III funds to some extent for interlibrary cooperation and resource-sharing activities. Excerpts from a few FY 1989 reports follow:

North Carolina: Federal funds enabled the state library to run the North Carolina Information Network (NCIN). More than 60,000 monographic records from three multitype libraries were tape-loaded into the NCIN database. This is less than was projected due to the way OCLC loaded the data. More than 7,000 serial records from 18 libraries were also tape-loaded into the database. The state library concentrated on loading public library holdings.

NCIN has become a link between widespread sources of information and local libraries of all types. By using the latest computer/communication technologies, 235 NCIN users were able to expand library services efficiently and effectively.

Minnesota: The Central Minnesota Libraries Exchange (CMLE) coordinated activities for 112 member libraries of all types. The principal program of this cooperative is resource sharing. During the year, CMLE received 10,872 requests for interlibrary loans and 222 for reference assistance compared with the estimated 9,500. CMLE filled 97 percent of the requests. Of the interlibrary loan requests, 60 percent were filled the same day; 75 percent were filled within two days. The number of borrowing libraries grew from 109 to 120; and the number of lenders grew from 58 to 61, surpassing the estimate by more than 50 percent. These statistics reflect borrowing transactions through the CMLE office but do not include direct borrowing between libraries under the CMLE umbrella.

Delivery is largely achieved through a contract with the Central Minnesota Educational Research and Development Council. Its vans connect the CMLE office with the Great River Regional Library every work day; deliveries reach schools twice a week. In a year, 2,024 packages were sent from the CMLE office, 69 percent more than estimated.

Table 23 / Library Services and Construction Act, Title III Projects
FYs 1989 and 1990

Type of Library	Networking*	Automation*	Conversion*	Resource Sharing	Staff Training	User Training	Preservation	Research	Total
Elementary	7	2	38	5	1	—	—	—	53
Secondary	11	2	44	9	—	2	—	—	68
Jr./Comm. College	5	—	8	8	1	—	—	—	22
Higher Education	32	—	38	57	—	1	1	1	130
Research	2	—	1	—	—	—	1	—	4
Public	48	2	22	37	3	4	3	5	124
Health Science	10	—	1	9	—	—	—	—	20
Law	12	—	2	3	—	—	—	—	17
Multitype	75	1	14	92	18	2	4	9	215
Other	2	—	1	3	—	—	—	1	7
Total	204	7	169	223	23	9	9	16	660

*Networking includes interlibrary loan and referral services. Automation refers to automated circulation systems. Conversion refers to conversion of card catalogs to computerized catalogs.

To assist smaller libraries in converting catalog records to MARC format, CMLE administered the Laser Quest project with the CD-ROM system funded by the Central Minnesota Educational Research and Development Council. Holdings of 14 libraries were combined in a regional catalog.

Indiana: Title III funds supported Objective 3.1 of the Indiana Long Range Plan for Library Services and Development by providing continuing support for the basic cooperative services of the Area Library Services Authorities (ALSA) and the Indiana Cooperative Library Services Authority, as defined in the most recent standards (1988–1993). The long-range plan makes ALSAs a major part of the framework for the Indiana Library Information Services Network (ILISN). Through the ALSA network, Hoosiers even have access to resources that are not owned by the local public library.

Besides the basic services of interlibrary loan, reference/referral, and consultation/staff development, the following statewide objectives were reached in FY 1989: The minimum fill rate of reference referrals in each ALSA increased to 85 percent; the number of ALSAs approved by the Indiana Council of Approval of Providers (ICAP) for staff development/continuing education increased to 6 (out of 9 ALSAs); and ALSAs completed new five-year plans by September 30, 1989. Each ALSA had to prepare an annual service plan, budget, and report, containing statistical and narrative information. A site visit was made to each ALSA and member libraries evaluated the effectiveness of activities and services. Staff of the Extension Division also evaluated each ALSA on attainment of goals and objectives of the LSCA grant, the Indiana Long Range Plan, the ALSA long-range plan, and state standards for public libraries and library service authorities. Area program goals and objectives were compared with actual performance.

Hawaii: The resource-sharing project in Hawaii included the following activities:

1 Production and distribution of a microfiche catalog of the Hawaii State Public Library System. The bimonthly catalog was sent to 164 libraries, including academic, special, and school libraries.

2 Subgrants for resource-sharing projects. The Hawaii Medical Library was awarded a contract to develop a HealthFax network.

3 The Hawaii State Library indexing project continued for a second year. Its most notable product was an index to Hawaiian legends in both book and diskette formats.

Texas: One objective of the Texas State Library's long-range plan is "to encourage provision of regional and local cooperative services for meeting common user needs through joint planning, informal cooperation, and contractual arrangements among public, academic, school, and special libraries." To implement this objective in FY 1989, the LSCA, Title III grant supported interlibrary cooperation at the following sites: Brazoria County Library System ($52,100), Corpus Christi Public Libraries ($20,364), Stephen F. Austin State University ($90,306), University of Houston at Victoria ($127,547), and Wellington Independent School District ($52,308), for a total of $342,625. A sampling of reports follows:

Stephen F. Austin State University, representing the University and Nacogdoches Public Library, converted more than 36,000 public library holdings and more than

5,000 public library patron records to machine-readable form and added them to the university's NOTIS system, creating a common online database available at both locations. Automated circulation was also instituted at the public library. One feature of the project was the assistance received from volunteers who applied OCR labels and input bibliographic and patron records. By the end of the grant period, more than 1,100 hours had been donated. Reciprocal borrowing and courier service between the two institutions began September 11, 1989. Requests for 87 items were filled during the month, 24 for university material, 63 for public library material.

Wellington Independent School District, representing the Collingsworth Public Library (a new school/county library), linked the library to the Harrington Library Consortium's automated system, providing it with a public access catalog and automated circulation. Approximately 18,000 records were converted to machine-readable form. Other automated services available from the consortium included external database searching, newspaper indexes, information and referral, union lists, inventory control, material booking, and cataloging. Completion of the project has allowed the library to participate more fully in area resource-sharing activities.

The University of Houston at Victoria, representing three library consortia, conducted Phase I of a two-year project by creating a CD-ROM union catalog containing 713,141 unique records and 1,067,125 holdings from 31 public, academic, school, and special libraries. The project included all available machine-readable records from the participants, authority control, and CD-ROM workstations and printers for all locations. Several administrative challenges involved negotiations with OCLC about including the PAISANO Union List of Serials, receipt of workstations not in compliance with contract specifications, and a CD-ROM catalog that did not, in some instances, accurately reflect holdings and had other problems. An evaluation is under way, and a supplemental report is expected by the end of December 1992. In Phase II, which will be privately funded, the university will add records not currently in machine-readable form, more libraries, and possibly an interlibrary loan communications subsystem for resource sharing.

Part 3
Library/Information Science Education, Placement, and Salaries

Guide to Employment Sources in the Library and Information Professions

Margaret Myers

Director, Office for Library Personnel Resources
American Library Association

This guide updates the listing in the 1991 *Bowker Annual* with information on new services and changes in contact information for previously listed groups. The sources given primarily assist professionals in obtaining positions, although a few assist paraprofessionals, who tend, however, to be recruited through local sources.

General Sources of Library and Information Jobs

Library Literature

Many national, regional, and state library journals and newsletters carry classified ads of library job vacancies and positions wanted. Association members can sometimes list a position-wanted ad free in association publications. *American Libraries, Chronicle of Higher Education, College & Research Libraries News, Library Journal,* and *Library Hotline* regularly carry listings of available positions. State and regional library association newsletters, state library journals, foreign library periodicals, and other types of periodicals that carry such ads are listed in later sections of this guide.

Newspapers

In addition to the regular classifieds, the *New York Times* Sunday Week in Review includes a special section of jobs for librarians. Local newspapers—particularly the larger city Sunday editions, such as the *Washington Post, Los Angeles Times,* and *Chicago Tribune*—often carry listings for both professional and paraprofessional positions in libraries.

Library Joblines

Library joblines, or job hotlines, provide a quick, up-to-date listing of job openings in a specific geographic area in a recorded telephone message. Most tapes are changed once a week, although a listing may sometimes be carried for several weeks. The information is brief, and the job seeker pays for the call.

Note: The author wishes to thank Maxine Moore, OLPR administrative assistant, for her help in gathering and compiling updated information.

Most joblines only carry listings for their state or region, although some occasionally accept out-of-state positions if there is room on the tape. A few list technician and other paraprofessional positions, but the majority include only professional jobs. Callers sometimes find that the jobline doesn't answer; this usually means that the tape is being changed or that there are no new jobs for that period. The classified section of *American Libraries* carries jobline numbers in each issue.

The following joblines are in operation:

Jobline Sponsor	Job Seekers (To Hear Job Listings)	Employers (To Place Job Listings)
American Association of Law Libraries	312-939-7877	53 W. Jackson Blvd., Suite 940, Chicago, IL 60604. FAX 312-431-1097
American Library Association Jobline (staff positions only)	312-280-2464	50 E. Huron St., Chicago, IL 60611
Arizona Department of Library, Archives and Public Records (Arizona libraries only)	602-275-2325	Research Div., 1700 Washington, Rm. 300, Phoenix, AZ 85007. FAX 602-255-4312
Association of College and Research Libraries	312-944-6795	ALA/ACRL, 50 E. Huron St., Chicago, IL 60611. 312-280-2513
British Columbia Library Association (B.C. listings only)	604-430-6411	Jobline, 110-6545 Bonsor Ave., BC V51 1H3, Burnaby, Canada
California Library Association (identical listings)	916-443-1222 818-797-4602	717 K St., No. 301, Sacramento, CA 95814-3477. 916-447-8541
California Media and Library Educators Association	415-697-8832	1575 Old Bayshore Hwy., Suite 204, Burlingame, CA 94010. 415-692-2350
Colorado State Library (Colorado listings only; includes paraprofessional)[1]	303-866-6741	Jobline, 201 E. Colfax, 3rd fl., Denver, CO 80203. 303-866-6910
Connecticut Library Association	203-645-8090	638 Prospect Ave., Hartford, CT 06105
Delaware Division of Libraries	800-282-8696 (in-state) 302-739-4748	43 S. Dupont Hwy., Dover, DE 19901
Drexel University College of Information Studies	215-895-1672	College of Information Studies, Philadelphia, PA 19104
State Library of Florida	904-488-5232 (in-state)	R. A. Gray Bldg., Tallahassee, FL 32399-0251. 904-487-2651
Library Jobline of Illinois[2]	312-828-0930 (professional) 312-828-9198 (support staff)	Illinois Library Assn., 33 W. Grand, Suite 301, Chicago, IL 60610. 312-644-1896 ($20 fee/two weeks)

Jobline Sponsor	Job Seekers (To Hear Job Listings)	Employers (To Place Job Listings)
Indiana Statewide Library Jobline	317-924-9584	Indiana ALSA, 1100 W. 42 St., Indianapolis, IN 46208. 317-926-6561
Kansas State Library Jobline (includes paraprofessional and out-of-state positions)	913-296-3296	c/o Jana Renfro, 3rd fl., State Capitol, Topeka, KS 66612
Maryland Library Association	301-685-5760	115 W. Franklin St., Baltimore, MD 21201. 301-727-7422. (Mon.–Fri., 9:30 A.M.–2:30 P.M.)
Metropolitan Washington Council of Governments Library Council (D.C.)	202-962-3712	1875 I St. N.W., No. 200, Washington, DC 20006. 202-223-6800, Ext. 458
Michigan Library Association	517-694-7440	1000 Long Blvd., No. 1, Lansing, MI 48911 517-694-6615 ($20/week)
Missouri Library Association Jobline	314-442-6590	1015 E. Broadway, Suite 215, Columbia, MO 65201. 314-449-4627
Mountain Plains Library Association	605-677-5757[3]	c/o I. D. Weeks Library, University of South Dakota, Vermillion, SD 57069
Nebraska Job Hotline (business hours)	402-471-2045	Library Commission, 1420 P St., Lincoln, NE 68508
New England Library Jobline (New England jobs only)	617-738-3148	GSLIS, Simmons College, 300 The Fenway, Boston, MA 02115
New Jersey Library Association	609-695-2121	Box 1534, Trenton, NJ 08607
New York Library Association	518-432-6952 (NY 800-232-6952)	252 Hudson Ave., Albany, NY 12210-1802. 518-432-6952 (members $25/week, $40/two weeks)
North Carolina State Library (professional jobs in N.C. only)	919-733-6410	Div. of State Library, 109 E. Jones St., Raleigh, NC 27611. 919-733-2570
Oklahoma Jobline (5 P.M.–8 A.M., Monday–Friday and all weekend)	405-521-4202	Oklahoma Dept. of Libraries, 200 N.E. 18 St., Oklahoma City, OK 73105. 405-521-2502
Oregon Library Association Jobline (Northwest listings only)	503-585-2232	Oregon State Library, State Library Bldg., Salem, OR 97310. 503-378-4243
Pacific Northwest Library Association[4] (professional, paraprofessional, and other library-related jobs)	206-543-2890	c/o Graduate School of Library and Information Sciences, University of Washington, FM-30, Seattle, WA 98195. 206-543-1794
Pennsylvania Jobline[5] (also accepts paraprofessional out-of-state listings)	717-234-4646	Pennsylvania Library Association, 3107 N. Front St., Harrisburg, PA 17110. 717- 233-3113 (weekly fee for nonmembers).
Pratt Institute GLIS Job Hotline	718-636-3742	GLIS Dept., Brooklyn, NY 11205
Special Libraries Association	202-234-3632	1700 18th St. N.W., Washington, DC 20009. 202-234-4700

Jobline Sponsor	Job Seekers (To Hear Job Listings)	Employers (To Place Job Listings)
Special Libraries Association, New York Chapter	212-214-4226	Nan Schubel, Ernst & Young, 277 Park Ave., New York, NY 10172
Special Libraries Association, San Andreas-San Francisco Bay Chapter	408-378-8854 or 415-391-7441	415-620-4919
Special Libraries Association, Southern California Chapter	818-795-2145	818-356-6704
Texas Library Association Job Hotline (5:30 P.M. Friday–8 A.M. Monday)	512-328-1518	3355 Bee Cave Rd., Suite 603, Austin, TX 78746
Texas State Library Jobline (Texas listings only)	512-463-5470	Library Development, Box 12927, Austin, TX 78711. 512-463-5447
University of South Carolina College of Library and Information Science (no geographic restrictions)	803-777-8443	Admissions & Placement Coordinator, Columbia, SC 29208
Virginia Library Association Jobline (Virginia libraries only)	703-519-8027	669 S. Washington St., Alexandria, VA 22314
University of Western Ontario School of Library and Information Science	519-661-3543	London, ON N6G 1H1, Canada. 519-661-3542

1. Biweekly printed listing sent on receipt of SASE.
2. Cosponsored by the Special Libraries Association, Illinois Chapter, and Illinois Library Association.
3. 800-356-7820 available from all MPLA states, 10 P.M.–8 A.M., Sunday–Thursday; 5 P.M. Friday–5 P.M. Sunday (includes listings for Arizona, Colorado, Kansas, Montana, Nebraska, Nevada, Oklahoma, North and South Dakota, Utah and Wyoming; $10/week for other states).
4. Alaska, Alberta, British Columbia, Idaho, Montana, Oregon, and Washington.
5. Sponsored by the Pennsylvania Library Association.

Specialized Library Associations and Groups

The National Registry for Librarians, formerly housed in the Illinois State Job Service at 40 W. Adams St., Chicago, IL 60603, is no longer in operation. Referral service is still available, however, through state and local Job Service offices.

Advanced Information Management

444 Castro St., Suite 320, Mountain View, CA 94041 (415-965-7799). This placement agency, with offices in Southern California (310-799-5538) as well as in the San Francisco Bay area, specializes in library and information personnel. It offers professional librarians and paraprofessionals work on a temporary, permanent, or contract basis in special, public, and academic libraries. It also places consultants on special projects in libraries or as managers of library development projects.

American Association of Law Libraries Career Hotline

53 W. Jackson Blvd., Suite 940, Chicago, IL 60604 (312-939-7877). The hotline is a 24-hour-a-day recording updated each Friday at noon and available as an index in

geographic order of positions currently available in full text in the AALL Job Data Base. AALL members receive the complete Job Data Base free on request. Others must send a written request with $5 to AALL, Dept. 77-6021. To list a position, contact AALL, Placement Assistant, 312-939-4764, FAX 312-431-1097.

American Libraries "Career LEADS"

c/o *American Libraries,* 50 E. Huron St., Chicago, IL 60611. Classified job listings are published in each monthly issue of *American Libraries.* Some 100 job openings are grouped by type, and "Late Job Notices" are added near press time. Subsections are Positions Wanted, Professional Exchange, Requests for Proposals, Librarians' Classified, joblines, and regional salary scales. "ConsultantBase" (see below) appears four times a year.

American Libraries "Career LEADS EXPRESS"

c/o Jon Kartman, 50 E. Huron St., Chicago, IL 60611. Advance galleys (3–4 weeks) of classified job listings with approximately 100 "Positions Open" to be published in the next issue of *American Libraries* are sent about the 17th of each month. Galleys do not include editorial corrections and late changes, but they do include some "Late Job Notices." For each month, send a $1 check made out to AL EXPRESS and a self-addressed, standard business-size envelope (4 x 9) with 52 cents postage.

American Libraries ConsultantBase (CBase)

This *AL* service helps match professionals offering library/information expertise with institutions. Published quarterly, CBase appears in the "Career LEADS" section of *AL's* January, April, June, and October issues. Rates: $4.50/line (classified); $45/inch (display). Inquiries should be made to Jon Kartman, LEADS Editor, *American Libraries,* 50 E. Huron St., Chicago, IL 60611 (312-280-4211).

American Library Association, Association of College and Research Libraries

50 E. Huron St., Chicago, IL 60611-2795 (312-280-2513). In addition to classified advertising in *College & Research Libraries News* each month, the ACRL Jobline updates a recorded telephone message each Friday. Call 312-944-6795 to hear the recording or 312-280-2513 to place a listing for two weeks.

American Library Association, ASCLA/SLAS State Library Consultants to Institutional Libraries Discussion Group

This group compiles a list of job openings in institutional libraries throughout the United States and its territories. Send self-addressed, stamped envelope(s) to Institutional Library Mailed Jobline, c/o S. Carlson, Rhode Island Department of State Library Services, 300 Richmond St., Providence, RI 02903. Send job listings to the same address, or call 401-277-2726. Listings appear for one month unless resubmitted.

American Library Association, Office for Library Personnel Resources

50 E. Huron St., Chicago, IL 60611 (312-280-4277). A placement service is provided at each annual conference (June or July) and midwinter meeting (January). Request job seeker or employer registration forms before the conference. Those unable to at-

tend a conference can register with the service and have job or applicant listings sent directly to them from the conference site for a fee. Handouts on interviewing, preparing a résumé, and other job-seeking information are available from the ALA Office for Library Personnel Resources.

ALA divisions also usually have a placement service at national conferences. See *American Libraries* "Datebook" for dates of upcoming divisional conferences (not held every year).

American Society for Information Science

8720 Georgia Ave., No. 501, Silver Spring, MD 20910-3602 (301-495-0900). ASIS operates an active placement service at annual (usually October) and midyear (usually May) meetings. Locales change. All conference attendees (both ASIS members and nonmembers), as well as ASIS members who cannot attend the conference, are eligible to use the service to list or find jobs. The service accepts listings from employers who cannot attend the conference, arranges interviews, and sponsors special seminars. Throughout the year, job openings are listed in *ASIS JOBLINE,* a monthly publication sent to all members and available to nonmembers on request.

Art Libraries Society/North America (ARLIS/NA)

c/o Executive Director, 3900 E. Timrod St., Tucson, AZ 85711 (602-881-8479, FAX 602-322-6778). *ARLIS/NA UPDATE* (6 issues a year) lists jobs for art librarians and slide curators, and the society maintains a job registry at its headquarters. Any employer may list a job with the registry, but only members may request job information.

Asian/Pacific American Libraries Newsletter

c/o Jack Tsukamota, Ball State University Library, 4000 University Ave., Muncie, IN 47306 (317-285-5722). This quarterly newsletter includes some job ads. It is free to members of the association.

Association for Educational Communications and Technology

Placement and Referral Service, 1025 Vermont Ave. N.W., Suite 820, Washington, DC 20005 (202-347-7834, FAX 202-347-7839). A referral service is available free to AECT members. The placement center at the annual conference is free to all conference registrants. Members also receive a free monthly newsletter of job vacancies.

Association for Information Management

c/o David Kahn, Managing Director, Box 374, McLean, VA 22101 (703-790-0403). Each month, *AIM Career Exchange Clearinghouse* lists positions open and wanted in conjunction with the *AIM Network.* Applicants send résumé and cover letter to AIM for forwarding to employers. Employers may list their organization name, contact person, and telephone number or use AIM as the clearinghouse. AIM assigns a reference number to each listing. The Career Exchange Clearinghouse distribution is open only to AIM members, but nonmembers may list job vacancies.

Association for Library and Information Science Education

c/o Olson Management Group, Inc., 4101 Lake Boone Trail, Raleigh, NC 27606 (919-787-5181). ALISE provides a placement service for library education faculty and administrative positions at its annual conference in January.

C. Berger and Company

327 E. Gundersen Dr., Carol Stream, IL 60188 (708-653-1115). CBC conducts nation-wide executive searches to fill permanent management, supervisory, and director positions in libraries, information centers, and related firms. It also supplies special, academic, and public libraries in Illinois, Wisconsin, Indiana, and Texas with temporary professional personnel and clerks to work under contract or for short- or long-term assignments. In addition, CBC offers library and records management consultant services and provides staff to manage projects for clients.

Black Caucus Newsletter

c/o George C. Grant, Ed., Rollins College, Campus Box 2654, Winter Park, FL 32789 (407-646-2676, FAX 407-646-1515). Published bimonthly by Four-G Publishers, this newsletter lists paid advertisements for job vacancies and complementary brief summaries of others, as well as news reports, biographies, essays, and book reviews of interest to members. Free to members; $7.50/year to others.

Theresa M. Burke Employment Agency

60 E. 42 St., Suite 1333, New York, NY 10165-1333 (212-986-4050). The first employment service for information personnel, this New York City-based agency with an international reputation was founded in 1949. The majority of library openings are in special libraries in the New York City metropolitan area. Records management positions are available in law firms, corporations, and government agencies. Ask for Catherine Kenny. The employer pays all fees.

Canadian Association of Special Libraries and Information Services/Ottawa Chapter Job Bank

c/o CASLIS Job Bank Coordinator, 266 Sherwood Dr., Ottawa, ON K1Y 3W4, Canada. Job seekers should send a résumé; employers who want to list a job should call 613-237-3688.

Canadian Library Association

200 Elgin St., Suite 602, Ottawa, ON K2P 1L5, Canada (613-232-9625). This national association operates a Jobmart at its annual conference in June and publishes classified job ads in *Feliciter* (11 issues/year).

Catholic Library Association

461 W. Lancaster Ave., Haverford, PA 19041 (215-649-5250). Personal and institutional members can advertise for jobs or list job openings (up to 35 words) free in *Catholic Library World* (6/year). The rate for others is $15/printed line (36 characters).

Center for the Study of Rural Librarianship

Department of Library Science, Clarion University, Clarion, PA 16214 (814-226-2383). For a monthly listing in *Rural Libraries Jobline,* send $1.

Chinese-American Librarians Association Newsletter

c/o Ingrid Hsieh-Yee, SLIS, Catholic University of America, 620 Michigan Ave. N.E., Washington, DC 20064 (202-319-5085, FAX 202-319-5574). The association newsletter issued in February, June, and October includes job listings. Free to members.

Council on Library/Media Technicians

c/o Ruth A. Tolbert, Membership Chairperson, Central Indiana ALSA, 1100 W. 42 St., No. 305, Indianapolis, IN 46208. *COLT Newsletter* appears bimonthly in *Library Mosaics.* Personal dues: $25; students: $20; institutions, U.S.: $40; foreign: $55.

Gossage Regan Associates

25 W. 43 St., New York, NY 10036 (212-869-3348, FAX 212-997-1127). Gossage Regan Associates is a full-service library personnel and consulting firm that places librarians and information managers in permanent positions nationwide. The emphasis, however, is on the New York metropolitan area, where the agency is the leading provider of temporary professional support personnel to libraries. Other services include executive search for library directors, division heads, and information vice presidents and managers, and information management consultation.

HBW Library Recruiters Associates

419 S. Carroll, Denton, TX 76201-5928 (817-566-0417). A firm of professional librarians, HBW assists library boards, county administrators, city managers, faculty search committees, library directors, and personnel officers with the selection of key administrative and managerial staff. HBW also assists libraries and information centers to develop guidelines and requirements for positions; compile candidate lists; screen, check, and verify credentials; and do preliminary interviews through final selections. There is no obligation for an exploratory discussion.

Indiana Jobline, Central Indiana Area Library Services Authority

c/o Publications Coordinator, 1100 W. 42 St., Suite 305, Indianapolis, IN 46208 (317-926-6561). Libraries may access this computer-based listing of job openings in all types of libraries in Indiana through telex or another electronic communication system by calling 317-924-9584. A printed listing is available on request.

Information Exchange System for Minority Personnel

Box 90216, Washington, DC 20090. This nonprofit organization recruits minority librarians for Equal Employment Opportunity/Affirmative Action employers. Its quarterly newsletter is *Informer.* Write for membership categories, services, and fees.

Labat-Anderson, Inc.

2200 Clarendon Blvd., Suite 900, Arlington, VA 22201 (703-525-9400). This federal government contractor specializes in library and information services.

Library Associates

8845 W. Olympic Blvd., Suite 205, Beverly Hills, CA 90211 (213-289-1067). Owned and managed by librarians, this consulting firm provides personnel on a permanent, temporary, or contract basis to fill vacancies, provide project support, and substitute for regular staff. Pacific Automation Group, the cataloging division, provides FAST-CAT—USMARC and customized cataloging records on a per-title basis for English, Asian, and European languages. FASTCAT also includes retrospective conversions. Consulting services include automation development, database creation, records management, indexing/abstracting, research and document retrieval, and development of marketing plans and strategies for vendors who sell information products to libraries.

Library Co-Op

3840 Park Ave., Suite 107, Edison, NJ 08820 (201-906-1777, 800-654-6275). This employment agency supplies permanent and temporary personnel and consultants to work in a variety of information settings, from library moving to database management, catalog maintenance, reference, and more. The agency recently formed a new division, ABCD Filing Services, and hired two specialists in space planning.

Library Management Systems

4730 Woodman Ave., Suite 330, Sherman Oaks, CA 91423 (818-789-3141); and 1300 Dove St., Suite 200, Newport Beach, CA 92660 (714-251-1020). Established in 1983 to provide contract library services and personnel to public and special libraries and businesses, Library Management Systems organizes and manages small- to medium-sized special libraries and designs and implements major projects such as retrospective data conversions, automation studies, reference services, and records management. LMS has 75 librarians and library assistants on call for long- and short-term projects and provides permanent placement at all levels.

Library Mosaics

Box 5171, Culver City, CA 90231 (310-410-1573). This bimonthly accepts job listings for library/media technicians but does not handle correspondence relating to advertised jobs.

Medical Library Association

6 N. Michigan Ave., Suite 300, Chicago, IL 60602 (312-419-9094). *MLA News* (10 issues/year, June/July and November/December combined issues) lists positions wanted and available in its "Employment Opportunities" column. The position-available rate is $13.50/line for nonmembers and for advertisements received through an employment or advertising agency or other third party. Up to 10 lines are free for MLA members; each additional line is $12. Both members and nonmembers may re-run ads once in the next consecutive issue for $25. Positions-available advertisements

must list a salary range. Positions-wanted rates are $8.50/line for nonmembers; 20 free lines for members and $7.50 for each additional line. Advance mailing of "Employment Opportunities" is available for six months for a prepaid fee: MLA members, $15; nonmembers, $25. MLA also offers a placement service and job market sessions at its annual conference each spring. Job advertisements received for publication in *MLA News* are posted to the Information Network-MLA Jobline the week of receipt. The jobline can be accessed 9 A.M. to 5 P.M. Central Time by calling 312-419-9094, Ext. 401; for 24-hour access, call 312-553-4636, Ext. 4646. In the MLA jobline, positions are categorized by type, salary range, and regional area.

Online, Inc.

c/o June Thompson, 11 Tannery Lane, Weston, CT 06883 (203-227-8466; Electronic Mail-CompuServe 76077, 1320, CLASS.ONLINE [ONTYME]). Positions sought and available in the online/library field can be listed free through the Online Chronicle (File 170) on DIALOG, attention Tasha Heinnrichs, ed., Jobline.

Pro Libra Associates

6 Inwood Place, Maplewood, NJ 07040 (201-762-0070, 800-262-0070). A multiservice agency, Pro Libra specializes in consulting, personnel, and project support for libraries and information centers.

REFORMA, National Association to Promote Library Service to the Spanish-Speaking

The REFORMA jobline publication is no longer issued. Employers wishing to send direct mailings to the REFORMA membership (500+) may obtain mailing labels arranged by zip code for $125 per set from REFORMA, Box 832, Anaheim, CA 92815-0832. For those who want to mail job fliers to REFORMA Executive Board members (20–25), a set of mailing labels is available for $5, or contact Al Milo, 714-738-6383.

Rhode Island Library Association Bulletin Jobline

c/o Pamela Stoddard, Government Publications Office, University of Rhode Island Library, Kingston, RI 02881 (401-792-2606). The jobline in the monthly *RILA Bulletin* lists positions in southeast New England, including paraprofessional and part-time jobs. For a copy of the most recent jobline, send a self-addressed, stamped envelope. (Groups of envelopes may also be sent.) To post a notice, contact Pamela Stoddard.

School Library Career Awareness Network (SCAN)

School of Information Studies, Syracuse, NY 13244 (315-443-2740). In coordination with the New York Library Association, School Library Media Section, Syracuse University operates a clearinghouse for recruitment and placement of school library media specialists in New York State. *SCANsheet* is mailed biweekly from April to September and monthly from October to March to members of the NYLA School Library Media Section for a $10 fee ($15 for nonmembers). *SCANfolio* gives school administrators information from the database directory of participating library media specialists seeking positions. *SCANline* is a 24-hour hotline. Employers are not charged to list jobs; a *SCANfolio* search costs $25. Payment of $10/year ($15 for nonmembers) entitles registrants to all SCAN services.

Society of American Archivists

600 S. Federal, Suite 504, Chicago, IL 60605 (312-922-0140). The bimonthly *SAA Newsletter* (sent only to members) contains features about the archival profession and other timely topics, such as courses in archival administration, meetings, and professional opportunities (job listings). The "Employment Bulletin" is a bimonthly listing of job opportunities available to members by subscription for $24/year and to nonmembers for $10/issue. Prepayment is required.

Special Libraries Association

1700 18th St. N.W., Washington, DC 20009-2508 (202-234-4700). SLA operates the Resume Referral Service for information professionals and employers and a telephone jobline called SpeciaLine, 202-234-3632, available 24 hours a day, seven days a week. Most SLA chapters have employment chairpersons who provide referral services for employers and job seekers. Several SLA chapters have joblines. The association's monthly newsletter, *The SpeciaList,* carries classified advertising, and SLA offers an employment clearinghouse at the annual conference in June.

State Library Agencies

Some state library agencies issue lists of job openings within their area. These include Colorado (biweekly, sent on receipt of SASE); Indiana (monthly on request); Iowa (*Joblist,* monthly on request); Massachusetts (*Massachusetts Position Vacancies,* monthly, sent to all state public libraries and to interested individuals on a one-time basis); Mississippi (*Job Vacancy List,* monthly); and Ohio (*Library Opportunities in Ohio,* sent monthly to accredited library education programs and to interested individuals on request).

The North Carolina and South Carolina state libraries have an electronic bulletin board service that lists job openings in each state. North Carolina can be accessed nationally by Western Union Easylink system users (use NCJOBS). South Carolina can be accessed in-state by users of the South Carolina Library Network.

On occasion, state library newsletters or journals list vacancies. These include Alabama (*Cottonboll,* quarterly); Arizona (*Libraries News Week*); Indiana (*Focus on Indiana Libraries,* 11/year); Iowa (*Joblist*); Kansas (*Kansas Libraries,* bimonthly); Louisiana (*Library Communique,* monthly); Missouri (*Show-Me Libraries,* quarterly); Nebraska (*Overtones,* quarterly); New Hampshire (*Granite State Libraries,* bimonthly); New Mexico (*Hitchhiker,* weekly); North Carolina (*NEWS FLASH,* monthly, public libraries only); Utah (*Directions for Utah Libraries,* monthly); and Wyoming (*Outrider,* monthly).

Many state library agencies do not have formal placement services but refer applicants informally when they know of vacancies. The following states primarily make referrals to public libraries: Alabama, Arizona, Arkansas, California, Georgia, Idaho, Louisiana, Pennsylvania, South Carolina (institutional also), Tennessee, Utah, Vermont, and Virginia. Those that refer applicants to all types of libraries are Alaska, Delaware, Florida, Illinois, Kansas, Maine, Maryland, Massachusetts, Mississippi, Montana, Nebraska, Nevada (largely public and academic), New Hampshire (public, school, and academic), New Mexico, North Carolina, North Dakota, Ohio, Pennsylvania, Rhode Island, South Dakota, West Virginia (on Pennsylvania Jobline, public, academic, and special), and Wyoming.

The following state libraries post job notices for all types of libraries on a bulletin board: California, Connecticut, Florida, Georgia, Illinois, Indiana, Iowa, Maine, Michigan, Montana, Nevada, New Jersey, New York, Ohio, Pennsylvania, South Dakota, Utah, and Washington. [For the addresses of state agencies, see Part 6 of the *Bowker Annual—Ed.*]

State and Regional Library Associations

State and regional library associations often make referrals, run ads in association newsletters, or operate a placement service at annual conferences. Some also sponsor joblines. The following associations refer applicants when they know of jobs: Alabama, Arkansas, Delaware, Hawaii, Louisiana, Michigan, Nevada, Pennsylvania, South Dakota, Tennessee, Texas, and Wisconsin. (Alabama's job database matches job announcements with résumés; open to all who send in résumé or job announcement; there is a $4 search charge; contact Job Placement Database, Box 87052, Tuscaloosa, AL 35487-0252.)

Although listings are infrequent, the following association newsletters and journals do announce job vacancies: Alabama (*Alabama Librarian,* 7/year); Alaska (*Newspoke,* bimonthly); Arizona (*Newsletter,* 10/year); Arkansas (*Arkansas Libraries,* 6/year); Connecticut (*Connecticut Libraries,* 11/year); Delaware (*Delaware Library Association Bulletin,* 3/year); District of Columbia (*Intercom,* 11/year); Florida (*Florida Libraries,* 10/year); Indiana (*Focus on Indiana Libraries,* 11/year); Iowa (*Catalyst,* 6/year); Kansas (*KLA Newsletter,* 6/year); Minnesota (*MLA Newsletter,* 10/year); Missouri (bimonthly); Mountain Plains (*MPLA Newsletter,* bimonthly, lists vacancies and positions wanted for individual and institutional members and area library school students); Nebraska (*NLAQ,* 4/year); Nevada (*Highroller,* 4/year); New Hampshire (*NHLA Newsletter,* 6/year); New Jersey (*NJLA Newsletter,* 10/year); New Mexico (shares notices via State Library's *Hitchhiker,* weekly); New York (*NYLA Bulletin,* 10/year; free for institutional members; $25/week, $40/2 weeks for others); Oklahoma (*Oklahoma Librarian,* 6/year); Rhode Island (*RILA Bulletin,* 9/year); South Dakota (*Bookmarks,* bimonthly); Tennessee (*Tennessee Librarian,* 4/year); Vermont (*VLA News,* 10/year); and Virginia (*Virginia Librarian,* quarterly).

At their annual conference, the following associations have some type of placement service, although it may only consist of bulletin board postings: Alabama, California, Connecticut, Georgia, Idaho, Illinois, Indiana, Kansas, Louisiana, Maryland, Massachusetts, Mountain Plains, New England, New Jersey, New York, North Carolina (biennial), Oregon, Pacific Northwest, Pennsylvania, South Dakota, Southeastern, Tennessee, Texas, Vermont, and Wyoming.

The following associations have no placement service at this time: Kentucky, Middle Atlantic Regional Library Federation, Midwest Federation, Minnesota, Mississippi, Montana, Nebraska, Nevada, New Mexico, North Dakota, and Utah. [State and regional association addresses are listed in Part 6 of the *Bowker Annual—Ed.*]

Library Education Programs

Library education programs offer some type of service for current students as well as alumni. Most schools provide job-hunting and résumé-writing seminars. Many invite outside speakers who represent different types of library or recent graduates who relate career experiences. Faculty members or a designated placement officer offer individual advisory services or résumé critiques.

Of the ALA-accredited programs, the following handle placement activities through the library school: Alabama (job database matches job announcements with résumés; open to all who send a résumé or job announcement; $4 search charge); Albany, Alberta, British Columbia, Columbia, Dalhousie, Drexel, Hawaii, Illinois, Louisiana, McGill, Michigan, Missouri, Pittsburgh (Department of Library Science only), Pratt, Puerto Rico, Queens, Rhode Island, Rosary, Rutgers, Saint John's, South Carolina, Syracuse, Tennessee, Texas–Austin, Toronto, UCLA, Western Ontario, Wisconsin–Madison, and Wisconsin–Milwaukee.

Although the central university placement center handles placement activities for California–Berkeley and Emporia, in both cases faculty in the library school still counsel job seekers informally. Some schools handle placement services in a cooperative manner; in most cases, the university placement center sends out credentials and the library school posts or compiles the job listings. Such schools include Alabama, Albany, Arizona, Brigham Young, Buffalo, Catholic, Clarion, Florida State, Indiana, Iowa, Kent State, Kentucky, Maryland, Montreal, North Carolina–Chapel Hill, North Carolina–Greensboro, North Carolina Central, North Texas, Northern Illinois, Oklahoma, Pittsburgh, Pratt, Queens, Saint John's, San Jose, Simmons, South Florida, Southern Connecticut, Southern Mississippi, Syracuse, Tennessee, Texas Woman's, Washington, Wayne State, and Wisconsin–Milwaukee.

Schools vary as to whether they distribute placement credentials free, charge a general registration fee, or request a fee for each file or set of credentials sent out.

Schools that post job notices for review but do not issue printed lists include Alabama, Alberta, Arizona, British Columbia, Buffalo, Catholic, Clark–Atlanta, Columbia, Dalhousie, Drexel, Florida State, Hawaii, Kent State, Kentucky, Louisiana, Maryland, McGill, Montreal, North Carolina–Chapel Hill, North Carolina–Greensboro, North Carolina Central, Northern Illinois, Oklahoma, Puerto Rico, Queens, Rutgers, Saint John's, San Jose, Simmons, South Carolina, South Florida, Southern Mississippi, Syracuse (general postings), Tennessee, Texas Woman's, Toronto, UCLA, Washington, Wayne State, Western Ontario, and Wisconsin–Milwaukee.

In addition to posting job vacancies, some schools offer printed listings, joblines, or database services:

- Alabama (matches job announcements with résumés; anyone can send a résumé or position announcement free of charge; the charge to search the database is $4)
- Albany (free to School of Information Science and Policy students and for one year following graduation; $10/year for others)
- Brigham Young
- British Columbia (uses British Columbia Library Association Jobline, 604-430-6411)

- California–Berkeley (weekly out-of-state job list and jobline free to students and graduates for six months after graduation; $55 annual fee for University of California alumni; call 415-642-3283)
- Clarion (free with SASE to alumni)
- Drexel (job hotline listing local jobs only, changed each Monday, 215-895-1672)
- Emporia (weekly bulletin of school, university, and public jobs; separate bulletin for special libraries positions; $15.71/6 months for Emporia graduates; $30 plus tax/6 months for others)
- Florida State
- Illinois (8 issues by mail for $4 and 8 No. 10 SASEs to alumni, $8 and 8 SASEs to nonalumni; also free online placement database on campus and via dial access through Internet)
- Indiana (free for one year following graduation; alumni and others may send SASEs)
- Iowa ($15/year for registered students and alumni)
- Michigan (free for one year following graduation; all other graduates, $15/year for 24 issues; $20 for others)
- Missouri (Library Vacancy Roster, monthly printout, $1/issue, with minimum of 6 issues, to anyone)
- North Texas ($5/6 months, students and alumni)
- Pittsburgh (free online placement to alumni)
- Pratt (free to students and alumni for full-time professional positions only)
- Rhode Island (monthly, $5/year)
- Rosary (*Placement News* every 2 weeks, free for 6 months following graduation, $15/year for students and alumni, $25 to others; *Placement News* is also on Lincolnet and can be accessed by telephone)
- Simmons operates the New England Jobline, which announces professional vacancies in New England, 617-738-3148
- Southern Connecticut (printed listing twice a month, free in office, mailed to students and alumni free)
- Syracuse (lists selected jobs online through electronic mail to students; School Media–New York State Listings, $10 for NYLA members, $15 for nonmembers)
- Texas–Austin (bimonthly *Placement Bulletin* free to students and alumni for one year following graduation, $15/6 months and $26/year thereafter; Austin Area Job-Hunters' List—full job descriptions are sent as often as notices are received—$14/6 months, $24/year thereafter, free to students and alumni for one year following graduation; job announcements are sent to students and graduates registered for this service if qualifications match the job type and location of their interest)
- Wisconsin–Madison (subscription $22/year for 12 issues plus $1.25 tax for Wisconsin residents; free in the office)

- Western Ontario operates the SLIS (School of Library and Information Science) Jobline, which announces openings for professionals, 519-661-3543; to list positions, 519-661-2111, Ext. 8495.

Employers often list jobs only with schools in their geographic area; some library schools give nonalumni information in person regarding specific locales, but are not staffed to handle mail requests. Schools that allow librarians in the area to view listings are Alabama, Albany, Alberta, Arizona, Brigham Young, British Columbia, Buffalo, California–Berkeley, Catholic, Clarion, Columbia, Dalhousie, Drexel, Emporia, Florida State, Hawaii, Illinois, Indiana, Iowa, Kent State, Kentucky, Louisiana, Maryland, McGill, Michigan, Missouri, Montreal, North Carolina–Chapel Hill, North Carolina–Greensboro, North Carolina Central, North Texas, Northern Illinois, Oklahoma, Pittsburgh, Pratt, Puerto Rico, Queens, Rhode Island, Rutgers, Saint John's, San Jose, Simmons, South Carolina, Southern California, Southern Connecticut, Southern Mississippi, Syracuse, Tennessee, Texas–Austin, Texas Woman's, Toronto, UCLA, Washington, Wayne State, Western Ontario, Wisconsin–Madison, and Wisconsin–Milwaukee. [For a list of accredited library schools, see later in Part 3 of the *Bowker Annual*. For information on the placement services of other library education programs, contact the school directly.]

Federal Library Jobs

To be considered for employment in many federal libraries, an applicant must establish civil service eligibility and be placed on the Office of Personnel Management (OPM) register in the appropriate geographic area. As of November 1987, OPM terminated its nationwide register and each office in the OPM network became responsible for hiring librarians in its area.

Eligibility can be established by meeting education and/or experience requirements and submitting appropriate forms to OPM during designated "open" periods. Interested applicants should contact their local Federal Job Information/Testing Center (FJI/TC) periodically to find out when the next open period will be and to obtain the proper forms. FJI/TCs are listed under "U.S. Government" in metropolitan telephone directories. A list of FJI/TCs is also available from the ALA Office for Library Personnel Resources. When the Washington, D.C., area register is open, the librarian packet can be obtained from the OPM Washington Area Service Center, Rm. 1447, 1900 E St. N.W., Washington, DC 20415 (202-606-2700; press 1, 1, 280). The packet includes an SF171 form, a supplemental qualifications form, and a computer-generated form. Job openings in libraries are on a recorded message with other federal jobs (202-606-2700; press 1, 2, 406).

Applications are evaluated by the grade(s) for which applicants are qualified. Information on beginning salary levels can be obtained from FJI/TC. To qualify for librarian positions, applicants must possess a master's degree in library science, a fifth-year bachelor's degree in library science, or 30 semester hours of graduate study in library science. (Candidates who have a combination of education and/or experience may qualify to take the written subject-matter test, which is administered in the Washington, D.C., metropolitan area. To be considered for librarian positions and testing outside the D.C. metropolitan area, contact the nearest FJI/TC.)

The OPM office that maintains the register refers candidates but does not hire and therefore is unaware of a vacancy until an agency requests candidates to fill it. Applications are evaluated according to the agency's requirements. OPM refers only the most qualified candidates.

In addition to filing the appropriate forms, applicants can contact federal agencies directly. More than half the vacancies occur in the Washington, D.C., area. Most positions are in three agencies: the Army, Navy, and Veterans Administration.

The Department of Veterans Affairs (VA) employs more than 350 professional librarians at 176 health care facilities throughout the United States and Puerto Rico. Although most VA positions require training in medical librarianship, many entry-level GS-9 positions require no previous experience; each GS-11/13 position requires specific experience. The VA has examining authority for library positions throughout the agency. This register is open continuously. To receive information and application forms, contact the VA Special Examining Unit, Box 24269, Richmond, VA 23224, or call 800-368-6008 (in Virginia, 800-552-3045). For a copy of the current job vacancy list, call 202-233-2820 Monday–Friday, 8:00 A.M.–4:30 P.M. (Eastern Time).

Some "excepted" agencies are not required to hire through usual OPM channels. Although these agencies may require the standard forms, they maintain their own employee selection policies and procedures. Agencies with positions outside the competitive civil service include the Board of Governors of the Federal Reserve System, Central Intelligence Agency, Defense Intelligence Agency, Department of Medicine and Surgery, Federal Bureau of Investigation, Foreign Service of the United States, General Accounting Office, Library of Congress, National Science Foundation, National Security Agency, Tennessee Valley Authority, U.S. Nuclear Regulatory Commission, U.S. Postal Service, judicial branch of the government, legislative branch of the government, U.S. Mission to the United Nations, World Bank, International Finance Corporation, International Monetary Fund, Organization of American States, Pan American Health Organization, and United Nations Secretariat.

The Library of Congress (LC), the world's largest and most comprehensive library, administers its own merit selection system. Job classifications, pay, and benefits are the same as in other federal agencies, and job qualifications generally correspond to those required of the U.S. Office of Personnel Management. LC does not use registers but announces vacancies as they become available. A separate application must be submitted for each position. Announcements for most professional positions stating required qualifications and ranking criteria are widely distributed and remain posted for a minimum of 30 days. The Library of Congress Human Resources Operations Office is located in the James Madison Memorial Bldg., 101 Independence Ave. S.E., Washington, DC 20540 (202-707-5620).

Additional Sources: General and Specialized Jobs

Affirmative Action Register

8356 Olive Blvd., Saint Louis, MO 63132. The goal of the register is to "provide female, minority, handicapped, and veteran candidates with an opportunity to learn of professional and managerial positions throughout the nation and to assist employers in implementing their Equal Opportunity Employment programs." The monthly bulletin is distributed free to leading businesses, industrial and academic institutions, and more than 4,000 agencies that recruit qualified minorities and women, as well as to all known professional organizations for women, minorities, and the handicapped; placement offices; newspapers; magazines; rehabilitation facilities; and more than 8,000 federal, state, and local governmental employment units. The bulletin's total readership is more than 3.5 million (audited). Individual mail subscriptions are available for $15 a year (free to libraries on request). Almost every issue has library job listings.

Chronicle of Higher Education

1255 23rd St. N.W., Suite 700, Washington, DC 20037 (202-466-1000). Forty-eight issues a year with breaks in August and December. This publication lists a variety of library positions each week, including administrative and faculty jobs.

Education Information Service

4523 Andes Dr., Fairfax, VA 22030. For $45, Instant Alert Service will send individual notices of domestic or overseas openings meeting your criteria on the same day EIS learns of the opening. EIS also publishes a monthly list of education openings worldwide, a small number of which are for librarians. Each list costs $8.

National Faculty Exchange

4656 W. Jefferson, Suite 140, Fort Wayne, IN 46804. This program brokers the exchange of faculty and staff at U.S. institutions. Librarians interested in participating should ascertain whether their academic institution is a member.

Additional Sources: School Libraries

School librarians often find that the channels for locating positions in education, such as contacting county or city school superintendent offices, are of more value than the usual library channels. The Fall 1982 issue of *School Library Media Quarterly* (11:63–65) offers strategies for seeking a position in a school library media center in the "Readers' Queries" column. Primary sources include university placement offices, which carry listings for a variety of school system jobs, and local information networks of teachers and library media specialists. A list of teachers' agencies may be obtained from the National Association of Teachers' Agencies, Sandra R. Alexander, CPC, Secy.-Treas., c/o G. A. Agency, 104 S. Central Ave., Valley Stream, NY 11580-5442 (516-568-8871).

Overseas

Opportunities for employment in foreign countries are limited, and interested candidates should investigate the immigration policies of individual countries. Employment for Americans is virtually limited to U.S. government libraries, libraries of U.S. firms doing worldwide business, and American schools abroad. Library journals from other countries sometimes list job vacancies. Some individuals have obtained jobs by contacting foreign publishers or vendors directly. Non–U.S. government jobs usually call for foreign-language fluency. "Job-Hunting in the UK" by Diane Brooks, *Canadian Library Journal,* 45:374–378 (December 1988), offers advice for those interested in the United Kingdom.

Council for International Exchange of Scholars (CIES)

3007 Tilden St. N.W., Suite 5M, Washington, DC 20008-3097 (202-686-7877). CIES administers U.S. government Fulbright awards for those wishing to lecture at universities or do advanced research abroad; usually 10 to 15 awards are made to specialists in library science each year. In addition, many countries offer research or lecture awards for which specialists in library and information science may apply. Open to U.S. citizens with university or college teaching experience. Several opportunities exist for professional librarians as well. Applications and information may be obtained, beginning each year in March, directly from CIES.

Department of Defense, Dependents Schools

2461 Eisenhower Ave., Alexandria, VA 22331-1100 (703-325-0885). With overall management and operational responsibilities for the education of dependent children of active-duty U.S. military personnel and DOD civilians stationed in foreign areas, this agency is responsible for teacher recruitment. Write for the complete application brochure. The latest edition of *Overseas Opportunities for Educators* provides information on employment opportunities in more than 250 schools worldwide operated for the children of U.S. military and civilian personnel stationed overseas.

Education Information Service

4523 Andes Dr., Fairfax, VA 22030. A monthly update on overseas job openings in education includes positions for librarians, media center directors, and audiovisual personnel. A sister publication provides the same information for U.S. schools, colleges, and universities.

Instant Alert

4523 Andes Dr., Fairfax, VA 22030. This service notifies clients of library job openings in U.S. schools overseas, international schools, and colleges and universities. As soon as the service learns of a position that meets an applicant's requirements, it mails the applicant a personal notice.

International Association of School Librarianship

Box 1486, Kalamazoo, MI 49005. Informal contacts can be established through this group.

International Schools Services

Box 5910, Princeton, NJ 08543 (609-452-0990). This private, not-for-profit organization, founded in 1955, serves U.S. schools, other than Department of Defense schools, overseas — international elementary and secondary schools that enroll children of businessmen and -women and diplomats living abroad. ISS services to overseas schools include recruitment and recommendation of personnel, curricular and administrative guidance, purchasing, and facility planning. ISS also publishes a comprehensive directory of overseas schools and a bimonthly newsletter, *NewsLinks,* for those interested in the intercultural educational community. Write for information regarding these publications and other services.

Library/Book Fellows Program

c/o Robert P. Doyle, American Library Association, 50 E. Huron St., Chicago, IL 60611 (312-280-3200). ALA administers a grant from the U.S. Information Agency for a program that places American library and book service professionals in institutions overseas for several months to one year. Assignments vary depending on the projects requested by host countries. Candidates should have foreign-language skills, technical expertise, and international interests or expertise. Positions are announced in January, interviews are held in May, and fellows start assignments in mid-September.

Peace Corps

1990 K St. N.W., 9th fl., Washington, DC 20526. The Peace Corps needs several professionals with experience in medicine, agriculture, automated systems, cataloging, and technical services. Write for a brochure and application form, or call 800-424-8580, Ext. 2293.

U.S. Information Agency (USIA)

Special Services Branch, USIA, 301 Fourth St. S.W., Washington, DC 20547. USIA, known as the U.S. Information Service (USIS) overseas, seeks librarians with an MLS and at least four years' experience for regional library officer positions. Candidates must have a master's degree in librarianship from an ALA-accredited graduate library program, proven administrative ability, and the skills to coordinate the overseas USIS library program with other USIS information functions in various cities worldwide. Practical experience in at least one of the major functional areas of adult library services is required. Other relevant experience could include cooperative library program development, community outreach, public affairs, project management, and personnel training. USIA maintains 153 libraries in 100 countries, with 900,000 books and about 450 local library staff. Libraries provide reference service and publications about the United States for foreign audiences. U.S. citizenship is required. Benefits include overseas allowances and differentials where applicable, vacation, term life insurance, and medical and retirement programs. To apply, send the standard U.S. government application (SF171).

Overseas Exchange Programs

Most exchanges are handled by direct negotiation between interested parties. A few libraries have established exchange programs for their own staff. To facilitate exchange arrangements, the *IFLA Journal* (issued February, May, August, and November) lists individuals wishing to exchange their position for one outside their country. Listings must include the following information: full name, address, present position, qualifications (with year obtained), language abilities, and preferred country, city, library, and type of position. Send to International Federation of Library Associations and Institutions Secretariat, Box 95312, 2509 CH The Hague, Netherlands.

The two-page "Checklist for Preparing for an International Exchange," prepared by the ALA International Relations Committee/International Relations Round Table (IRC/IRRT), is available from the ALA Office for Library Personnel Resources or the ALA International Relations Committee. Under the auspices of the IRC/IRRT Joint Committee on International Exchange of Librarians and Information Professionals, Linda E. Williamson wrote *Going International: Librarians' Preparation Guide for a Work Experience/Job Exchange Abroad* (1988, 74 pp., ISBN 0-8389-7268-3, $15 from ALA Order Services, 50 E. Huron St., Chicago, IL 60611).

LIBEX Bureau for International Staff Exchange

c/o A. J. Clark, Information and Library Studies Library, University College of Wales, Aberystwyth (formerly College of Librarianship Wales Library), Llanbadarn Fawr, Aberystwyth, Dyfed SY23 3AS, Wales (Tel. 0970-622417, Telecom Cold/LA-NET 79:2039, FAX 0970-622190, JANET e mail AJC@UK.AC.ABER). LIBEX assists in two-way exchanges for British librarians wishing to work abroad and for librarians from the United States, Canada, the European Community, the Commonwealth, and many other countries who wish to work in Britain.

Using Information Skills in Nonlibrary Settings

Information professionals have shown a great deal of interest in "alternative careers" and in using information skills in a variety of settings. These jobs are not usually found through regular library placement channels, although many library schools are trying to generate such listings for students and alumni. Listings for jobs that require information management skills may not specifically call for librarians, so job seekers may need to use ingenuity to find them. Some librarians offer their services on a free-lance basis to businesses, alternative schools, community agencies, legislators, and the like; these opportunities are usually not advertised but are found through contacts developed over time. A number of businesses that broker information have developed from individual free-lance experiences. Small companies or other organizations often need a one-time service for organizing files or collections, bibliographic research for special projects, indexing or abstracting, compiling directories, or consulting work. Bibliographic networks and online database companies are using librarians as information managers, trainers, researchers, systems and database analysts, and online services managers. Jobs are sometimes advertised in library network newsletters or data-processing journals. Librarians can be found working in law firms as litigation case supervisors (organizing and analyzing records for legal cases); in publishing companies as sales representatives, marketing directors, editors, and computer services experts; in community agencies as adult education coordinators, volunteer administrators, and grant writers. The three-page handout "Alternative Career Directions for Librarians," available from OLPR/ALA (50 E. Huron St., Chicago, IL 60611), provides a list of job titles.

The classifieds in *Publishers Weekly* and *National Business Employment Weekly* may lead to information-related positions. One might also consider reading the Sunday classified sections in metropolitan newspapers to locate job descriptions under a variety of job titles calling for information skills.

The *Burwell Directory of Information Brokers* is an annual publication that lists information brokers, free-lance librarians, independent information specialists, and institutions that provide services for a fee. Individuals do not need to pay to be listed; the 1991 directory is available for $59.50 plus $5 postage and handling (foreign postage, $10) from Burwell Enterprises, 3724 FM 1960 West, Suite 214, Houston, TX 77068 (713-537-9051). It is supplemented by *The Information Broker* ($35; foreign postage, $10), which includes articles by, for, and about individuals and companies in the fee-based information field, book reviews, a calendar of events, issue-oriented articles, and new listings for companies that will appear in subsequent editions of the *Directory.*

The Independent Librarians Exchange Round Table is a unit within the American Library Association that serves as a networking source for owners of information businesses, consultants, and those who work for a company that provides support services to libraries or other information services outside traditional library settings. The membership fee is $8, in addition to ALA dues, and includes the newsletter *ILERT Alert.* The Association of Independent Information Professionals, not affiliated with ALA, was formed in 1987 for individuals who own and operate for-profit information companies. Contact Marilyn Levine, 2266 N. Prospect, Suite 314, Milwaukee, WI 53202.

A growing number of publications describe opportunities for librarians in the broader information arena. "Information Brokering: The State of Art" by Alice Sizer Warner, *Wilson Library Bulletin,* April 1989, pp. 55–57, and "The Information Broker: A Modern Profile" by Mick O'Leary, *Online,* November 1987, pp. 24–30, provide an overview of information brokerage. *Mind Your Own Business: A Guide for the Information Entrepreneur* by Alice Sizer Warner (New York: Neal-Schuman, 1987, 165 pp., ISBN 1-55570-014-4, $24.95) describes planning for and managing an information business, including marketing, sales, and record keeping.

New Options for Librarians: Finding a Job in a Related Field, edited by Betty-Carol Sellen and Dimity S. Berkner (New York: Neal-Schuman, 1984, 300 pp., ISBN 0-918212-73-1, $27.95), covers how to prepare for and initiate a job search and examines career possibilities in publishing, public relations, abstracting and indexing, association work, contract service companies, information management, and more. Also included is a survey of librarians working in related fields and an annotated bibliography. The survey results are summarized in "Librarians in Alternative Work Places," *Library Journal* 110 (February 15, 1985): pp. 108–110.

Careers in Information, edited by Jane F. Spivack (White Plains, N.Y.: Knowledge Industries, 1982, ISBN 0-914236-70-9, $37.50), includes chapters on the work of information specialists, entrepreneurship in the information industry, and information professionals in the federal government, as well as guidance on finding a job and information on placements and salaries for the broader information field as well as librarianship. "Atypical Careers and Innovative Services in Library and Information Science," edited by Walter C. Allen and Lawrence W. S. Auld, composes the entire issue of *Library Trends* 32 (Winter 1984): pp. 251–358. It focuses on new directions with potential employment opportunities for librarians and some of the implications for the changing role of the information professional.

Information Broking: A New Career in Information Work by Marshall Jean Crawford (London: Library Association, 1988, 36 pp.) is available through ALA Order Services for $14 (ISBN 0-85365-718-1).

Infomediary, an international, professional quarterly journal, edited by an international board of experts and published since 1985, focuses on information brokerage, consulting, and the entrepreneurial aspects of the library and information field. Since 1989 (vol. 3), the journal has been published by IOS Press, Van Diemenstr. 94, 1013 CN Amsterdam, Netherlands. The subscription price for 1992 (vol. 6) is $165. A personal subscription costs $60.

Other publications include *What Else You Can Do with a Library Degree,* edited by Betty-Carol Sellen (New York: Neal-Schuman and Gaylord Brothers, 1979); *The*

Information Brokers: How to Start and Operate Your Own Fee-Based Service by Kelly Warnken (New York: Bowker, 1981); *Abstracting & Indexing Career Guide* (1986, 63 pp.), available for $18.50 ($13.50 for ten or more copies) and *Guide to Careers in Abstracting and Indexing* by Wendy Wicks and Ann Marie Cunningham (1991, 100 pp.), available for $25 from the National Federation of Abstracting and Information Services, 1429 Walnut St., Philadelphia, PA 19102.

Careers in Other Fields for Librarians . . . Successful Strategies for Finding the Job by Rhoda Garoogian and Andrew Garoogian, published by ALA in 1985, is a useful source but is now out of print. Chapters include bridging traditional and nontraditional employment; opportunities in business, government, education, and entrepreneurship; and employment techniques (where to look for jobs, résumés and letters, and interviewing). Of particular interest is the chapter describing the process of translating traditional library tasks and skills into new types of job responsibility. Scattered throughout are sample job descriptions in other fields that incorporate information functions.

Temporary/Part-Time Positions

Working as a substitute librarian or in temporary positions may be an alternative career path or interim step while looking for a regular job. This type of work can provide valuable contacts and experience. Organizations that hire library workers for part-time or temporary jobs include Pro Libra Associates, Inc., 6 Inwood Place, Maplewood, NJ 07040 (201-762-0070); C. Berger and Co., 327 E. Gundersen Dr., Carol Stream, IL 60188 (708-653-1115), in the Chicago area; Gossage Regan Associates, Inc., 25 W. 43 St., New York, NY 10036 (212-869-3348); Library Associates, 8845 W. Olympic Blvd., Suite 205, Beverly Hills, CA 90211 (213-289-1067); The Library Co-op, Inc., 3840 Park Ave., Suite 107, Edison, NJ 08820 (201-906-1777, 800-654-6275); Library Management Systems, 4730 Woodman Ave., Suite 330, Sherman Oaks, CA 91423 (818-789-3141) or 1300 Dove St., Suite 200, Newport Beach, CA 92660 (714-251-1020); and Advanced Information Management, 444 Castro St., Suite 320, Mountain View, CA 94041 (415-965-7799).

Part-time jobs are not always advertised, and they are often found by canvassing local libraries and leaving applications.

Job Hunting in General

Wherever information needs to be organized and presented to patrons in an effective, efficient, and service-oriented fashion, professional librarians can apply their skills. However, one must be prepared to invest considerable time, energy, imagination, and money to create or obtain a satisfying position in a conventional library or other type of information service. Usually, one job-hunting method or source is not enough.

"How to Find a Job Online" by Ann J. Van Camp, *Online* 12 (July 1988): pp. 26–34, offers guidance on databases that might lead to library or information-related positions.

Public and school library certification requirements often vary from state to state; contact the state library agency for such information. Certification requirements are summarized in *Certification of Public Librarians in the United States* (4th ed., 1991), available from the ALA Office for Library Personnel Resources. A summary of school library/media certification requirements by state is included in *Requirements for Certification* edited by Mary P. Burks and published annually by the University of Chicago Press. "School Library Media Certification Requirements: 1990 Update" by Patsy H. Perritt also provides this information (*School Library Journal* 36 [June 1990], pp. 41-60). For information on a specific state, contact the state supervisors of school library media services. [For a list of the state supervisors, see Part 6 of the *Bowker Annual — Ed.*]

Civil service requirements — be they on the local, county, or state level — can add another layer of procedures to the job search. Some require written and/or oral examinations; others assign a ranking based on a review of credentials. Jobs are usually filled from a list of qualified candidates. As the exams are held only at certain times and a variety of jobs can be filled from a single list of applicants (e.g., all Librarian I positions, regardless of type of function), candidates should be certain that the library of interest falls under civil service regulations.

For a position in a specific specialty or geographic area, remember those reference skills to ferret information from directories and other tools regarding local industries, schools, subject collections, and the like. Directories such as the *American Library Directory, Subject Collections, Directory of Special Libraries and Information Centers,* and *Directory of Federal Libraries,* as well as state directories and directories for other special subject areas, can provide a wealth of information for job seekers. Some students have pooled resources to hire a clipping service for a specific period to get classified ads for a particular geographic area.

For information on other job-hunting and personnel matters, request a checklist of materials from the ALA Office for Library Personnel Resources, 50 E. Huron St., Chicago, IL 60611.

Placements and Salaries, 1990: Losing Ground in the Recession

Fay Zipkowitz
Associate Professor, Graduate School of Library and Information Studies
University of Rhode Island, Kingston

This fortieth annual report of placements and salaries of graduates of American Library Association–accredited library school programs includes information from 42 of the 52 eligible institutions. The study was undertaken in May 1991, and schools did not receive survey forms until June. Consequently, some institutions found participation difficult or impossible, and others could only supply partial information in the short time frame. Four northeastern, two southeastern, one midwestern, one southwestern, and two western schools did not contribute data.

Due to time constraints, the organization and style of this report closely follow those of the 1989 report, but several tables with data on high and low salaries and the effect of experience on salaries prepared by Carol Learmont and Stephen Van Houten have been omitted. (See Tables 1-8.)

Note: Adapted from *Library Journal,* November 1, 1991.

Table 1 / Status of 1990 U.S. Graduates, Spring 1991*

	Graduates			Not in Lib. Positions			Empl. Not Known			Perm. Prof. Placements			Temp. Prof. Placements			Nonprof. Lib. Placements			Total in Lib. Positions		
	Women	Men	Total	Women	Men	Total	Women	Men	Total	Women	Men	Total	Women	Men	Total	Women	Men	Total	Women	Men	Total
Northeast	784	216	1,000	24	4	29	109	36	206	366	83	464	27	3	31	14	4	18	407	90	513
Southeast	561	118	679	20	12	32	133	32	242	262	52	314	12	2	16	6	0	6	280	54	336
Midwest	826	253	1,079	10	3	13	163	58	221	443	117	561	40	8	48	28	11	39	511	136	648
Southwest	359	64	423	7	4	11	36	10	46	150	33	183	25	12	37	8	0	8	183	45	228
West	264	77	341	7	1	8	32	18	55	141	41	182	14	4	18	7	2	9	162	47	209
All schools	2,794	728	3,522	68	24	93	473	154	770	1,362	326	1,704	118	29	150	63	17	80	1,543	372	1,934

*Includes placements undifferentiated by sex.

Table 2A / Placements and Full-Time Salaries of 1990 U.S. Graduates: Summary by Region*

		Salaries			Low Salary			High Salary			Average Salary			Median Salary		
	Placements	Women	Men	Total	Women	Men	Total	Women	Men	Total	Women	Men	Total	Women	Men	Total
Northeast	529	318	65	398	12,000	12,000	12,000	56,850	68,000	68,000	26,981	27,326	27,147	25,500	25,000	25,590
Southeast	363	233	49	282	10,500	16,000	10,500	38,000	42,666	42,666	23,512	25,000	23,776	23,000	24,000	23,121
Midwest	645	358	108	467	12,000	11,440	11,440	51,125	56,000	56,000	24,077	24,674	24,215	23,816	23,000	23,288
Southwest	213	131	29	160	12,100	18,000	12,100	37,500	57,047	57,047	24,015	25,995	24,374	23,025	23,700	23,500
West	233	120	35	155	18,000	20,300	18,000	40,000	49,230	49,230	27,853	26,797	27,615	27,000	26,000	27,000
All Schools	1,983	1,160	286	1,462	10,500	11,440	10,500	56,850	68,000	68,000	25,204	25,724	25,306	24,000	24,700	24,200

*Includes placements undifferentiated by sex.

Table 2B / Placements and Full-Time Salaries of 1990 U.S. Graduates by School*

School	Placements	Salaries			Low Salary			High Salary			Average Salary			Median Salary		
		Women	Men	Total	Women	Men	Total	Women	Men	Total	Women	Men	Total	Women	Men	Total
Alabama	36	21	5	26	$14,300	$20,088	$14,300	$28,900	$31,500	$31,500	$22,015	$23,666	$22,374	$21,130	$21,500	$21,500
Calif., Berkeley	53	35	13	48	21,035	20,300	20,300	40,000	37,000	40,000	28,871	26,385	28,119	28,000	25,000	27,595
Calif., Los Angeles	81	34	14	49	22,500	17,000	17,000	40,000	31,692	40,000	28,988	26,187	28,135	28,733	27,240	28,000
Catholic	29	22	4	26	13,300	21,600	13,300	35,000	68,000	68,000	26,069	42,667	27,984	25,500	30,000	25,750
Columbia	37	11	8	19	23,691	20,000	20,000	38,000	40,000	40,000	27,891	28,563	28,174	25,500	28,000	26,500
Drexel	57	44	10	54	11,000	12,000	11,000	40,000	37,400	40,000	24,497	26,640	24,894	24,000	26,500	25,267
Florida State	52	40	8	48	18,000	18,000	18,000	40,000	33,000	40,000	24,770	25,492	24,890	23,991	24,500	24,000
Hawaii	36	28	4	32	12,000	24,000	12,000	49,230	29,000	49,230	27,480	26,000	27,301	26,000	25,500	26,000
Illinois	53	31	17	48	17,250	12,500	12,500	30,000	30,000	30,000	22,853	23,075	22,932	22,750	23,000	23,000
Indiana	88	65	13	78	11,400	12,000	11,400	44,000	56,000	56,000	23,388	24,800	23,623	22,800	22,000	22,650
Iowa	40	22	10	32	19,000	19,000	19,000	46,000	28,200	46,000	24,977	23,512	24,519	23,500	23,750	23,750
Kent State	89	43	11	54	15,000	19,500	15,000	42,500	29,000	42,500	22,816	23,014	22,856	23,300	23,500	23,500
Louisiana State	46	26	14	40	15,000	18,500	15,000	36,000	50,000	50,000	22,148	25,367	23,275	21,300	22,000	21,800
Michigan	75	50	16	66	12,400	13,500	12,400	51,125	36,000	51,125	26,959	26,169	26,768	25,000	25,896	25,150
Missouri	64	37	7	44	14,000	16,800	14,000	35,000	33,500	35,000	20,832	24,123	21,355	21,023	23,000	21,500
N.Y., Albany	63	44	8	52	19,000	20,000	19,000	45,000	34,500	45,000	28,858	27,150	28,600	28,750	26,600	28,750
N.Y., Buffalo	59	44	1	45	19,500	21,425	19,500	42,092	21,425	42,092	25,583	21,425	25,490	24,250	21,425	24,000
North Carolina	48	24	10	34	20,111	22,000	20,111	35,140	29,760	35,140	25,837	25,651	25,782	25,250	26,500	26,000
N.C., Central	15	11	2	13	12,000	32,000	12,000	30,000	32,500	32,500	23,463	32,125	24,815	24,000	32,125	25,500
N.C., Greensboro	29	24	2	26	19,000	22,000	19,000	29,484	25,392	29,484	23,315	23,696	23,347	24,450	23,696	22,578
North Texas	143	57	11	68	12,100	20,500	12,100	40,000	30,000	40,000	22,996	24,047	23,166	22,000	24,000	22,250
Northern Illinois	40	29	4	33	14,634	21,000	14,634	33,000	43,000	43,000	22,450	27,500	23,045	23,000	23,000	23,000

(cont.)

Table 2B / Placements and Full-Time Salaries of 1990 U.S. Graduates by School* (cont.)

School	Placements	Salaries			Low Salary			High Salary			Average Salary			Median Salary		
		Women	Men	Total	Women	Men	Total	Women	Men	Total	Women	Men	Total	Women	Men	Total
Pratt	14	14			25,000			45,000	47,500	45,000			30,289			29,125
Rhode Island	33	23	5	28	17,000	22,000	17,000	40,000	26,000	40,000	26,375	23,400	25,844	24,562	23,000	24,000
Rosary	95	49	12	61	17,000	18,200	17,000	56,850	28,000	56,850	23,707	23,732	23,712	22,661	24,144	23,000
Rutgers	113	79	16	95	20,000	23,400	20,000	48,000	50,000	50,000	28,657	27,788	28,510	27,000	25,000	27,000
Saint John's	14	7	4	11	19,999	22,000	19,999	48,000	30,000	48,000	30,500	23,750	28,045	28,500	23,500	27,250
Simmons	120	78	17	95	15,000	18,700	15,000	41,800	35,000	41,800	25,338	26,124	25,479	24,150	25,700	25,000
South Carolina	69	58	7	65	17,000	20,000	17,000	38,000	42,666	42,666	24,894	27,238	25,151	24,250	24,000	24,100
South Florida	29	24	3	27	18,000	20,000	18,000	37,000	28,900	37,000	23,669	23,633	23,665	23,579	22,000	23,547
Southern Mississippi	24	17	3	20	10,500	16,000	10,500	36,000	26,000	36,000	19,359	21,667	19,705	19,800	23,000	19,900
Tennessee	21	17	4	21	18,500	23,000	18,500	35,000	27,300	35,000	23,720	25,200	24,002	23,076	25,250	23,076
Texas, Austin	64	44	17	61	18,720	20,000	18,720	37,107	57,047	57,047	24,860	27,920	25,713	24,863	25,717	25,000
Texas Woman's	64	46	4	50	16,000	18,000	16,000	37,500	32,000	37,500	24,004	24,750	24,064	23,013	24,500	25,013
Washington	65	41	8	49	18,000	21,200	18,000	33,500	40,000	40,000	25,660	27,748	26,001	25,000	26,649	25,500
Wayne State	82	44	13	57	12,000	21,000	12,000	38,000	42,000	42,000	23,308	25,620	23,835	22,759	25,000	23,818
Wisconsin, Madison	58	24	12	36	19,560	18,720	18,720	32,000	38,000	38,000	24,031	24,524	24,327	23,998	24,000	24,000
Wisconsin, Milwaukee	28	15	5	20	16,000	18,500	16,000	24,000	32,000	32,000	20,225	23,449	21,039	20,000	23,246	22,273

*Includes placements undifferentiated by sex.

Table 3 / Placements by Type of Library of 1990 U.S. Graduates by School*

School	Public			Elementary & Secondary			Colleges & Universities			Special			Other			Total		
	Women	Men	Total	Women	Men	Total	Women	Men	Total	Women	Men	Total	Women	Men	Total	Women	Men	Total
Alabama	9	0	9	11	2	13	10	3	13	1	0	1	0	0	0	31	5	36
Calif., Berkeley	14	4	18	0	0	0	10	9	19	11	1	12	3	1	4	38	15	53
Calif., Los Angeles	16	8	24	0	1	1	21	10	31	14	5	19	4	0	4	55	24	79
Catholic	7	0	7	2	0	2	4	0	4	7	3	10	3	0	3	23	3	26
Columbia	4	5	9	2	0	2	6	7	13	5	3	8	3	0	3	20	15	35
Drexel	11	2	13	8	0	8	6	3	9	12	3	15	9	3	12	46	11	57
Florida State	14	4	18	9	1	10	8	2	10	5	0	5	6	1	7	42	8	50
Hawaii	10	2	12	13	1	14	4	2	6	4	0	4	0	0	0	31	5	36
Illinois	31	17	48	16	4	20	3	2	5	10	10	20	5	2	7	65	35	100
Indiana	27	8	35	11	0	11	22	5	27	11	2	13	0	0	0	71	15	86
Iowa	8	4	12	6	0	6	8	7	15	2	1	3	3	1	4	27	13	40
Kent State	31	12	43	11	1	11	17	6	23	9	0	9	2	1	3	70	19	89
Louisiana State	9	4	13	5	1	6	5	9	14	8	2	10	1	0	1	28	16	44
Michigan	18	6	24	12	0	12	18	7	25	11	2	13	0	1	1	59	16	75
Missouri	11	2	13	10	0	10	9	4	13	9	1	10	0	0	0	39	7	46
N.Y., Albany	10	0	10	18	1	19	5	3	8	10	5	15	6	0	6	49	9	60
N.Y., Buffalo	15	0	15	16	1	17	17	0	17	7	0	7	0	1	1	55	2	57
North Carolina	9	2	11	7	0	7	8	9	17	2	0	2	7	4	11	33	15	48
N.C., Central	2	0	2	10	1	11	1	1	2	0	0	0	0	0	0	13	2	15
N.C., Greensboro	7	2	9	8	0	8	3	1	4	6	0	6	1	0	1	25	3	28
North Texas	24	1	25	17	1	18	21	11	32	6	2	8	2	0	2	70	15	85
Northern Illinois	18	3	21	7	0	7	5	0	5	1	1	2	2	0	2	33	4	38

(cont.)

Table 3 / Placements by Type of Library of 1990 U.S. Graduates by School* (cont.)

School	Public Women	Public Men	Public Total	Elem. & Sec. Women	Elem. & Sec. Men	Elem. & Sec. Total	Colleges & Univ. Women	Colleges & Univ. Men	Colleges & Univ. Total	Special Women	Special Men	Special Total	Other Women	Other Men	Other Total	Total Women	Total Men	Total Total
Pratt			2			1			3			7			1			14
Rhode Island	9	2	11	11	1	12	4	1	5	3	2	5	0	0	0	27	6	33
Rosary	21	2	23	18	1	19	14	5	19	13	5	18	0	0	0	66	13	79
Rutgers	38	5	44	16	3	19	12	8	20	24	3	27	3	0	3	93	19	113
Saint John's	4	0	4	1	0	1	1	2	3	2	2	4	0	0	0	8	4	12
Simmons	45	3	48	10	0	10	21	9	30	24	8	32	0	0	0	100	20	120
South Carolina	11	3	14	39	2	41	5	2	7	6	0	6	1	0	1	62	7	69
South Florida	8	2	10	9	0	9	6	1	7	2	0	2	1	0	1	26	3	29
Southern Mississippi	7	2	9	7	0	7	1	1	2	2	0	2	2	0	2	19	3	22
Tennessee	4	0	4	3	1	4	5	0	5	0	0	0	5	3	8	17	4	21
Texas, Austin	8	2	10	7	1	8	18	5	23	9	7	16	4	3	7	46	18	64
Texas Woman's	14	1	15	22	1	23	9	3	12	11	0	11	1	1	2	57	6	63
Washington	21	1	22	1	0	1	16	6	22	16	4	20	0	0	0	54	11	65
Wayne State	28	7	35	16	1	17	13	4	17	8	5	13	0	0	0	65	17	82
Wisconsin, Madison	7	3	10	7	0	7	20	9	29	5	4	9	2	0	2	41	16	57
Wisconsin, Milwaukee	1	5	6	4	7	11	0	1	1	0	2	2	0	1	1	5	16	21
Totals	533	124	661	370	31	403	356	157	517	275	84	366	75	24	100	1,609	420	2,047

*Includes placements undifferentiated by sex.

Table 4 / Placements by Type of Library, 1980–1990

Year	Public		School		Colleges & Universities		Other Lib. Agencies*		Total
1980	659	27.1%	473	19.5%	610	25.1%	687	28.3%	2,429
1981	642	27.3%	451	19.2%	556	23.6%	704	29.9%	2,353
1982	588	28.5%	358	17.4%	505	24.5%	612	29.7%	2,063
1983	501	28.1%	308	17.3%	424	23.8%	552	30.9%	1,785
1984	548	27.9%	284	14.4%	551	28.0%	583	29.7%	1,966
1985	565	29.4%	300	15.6%	522	27.2%	533	27.8%	1,920
1986	576	30.3%	288	15.2%	488	25.7%	548	28.8%	1,900
1987	610	30.5%	355	17.7%	434	21.7%	602	30.1%	2,001
1988	624	31.4%	386	19.4%	464	23.4%	511	25.7%	1,985
1989	587	31.9%	330	17.9%	460	25.0%	462	25.1%	1,839
1990	651	32.0%	403	19.8%	517	25.4%	466	22.9%	2,037

*From 1951 through 1966, "special and other placements" in all kinds of libraries were included in this category. The figures for 1967–1979 include only placements in library agencies that do not clearly belong to one of the other three groups. The figures for 1980–1990 reflect placements in special libraries and in other information specialties. For figures for earlier years, see earlier reports in this series.

In 1990, the average (mean) beginning salary was $25,306, based on 1,462 known, full-time, permanent, professional salaries, a modest increase over the 1989 figure of $24,581. The average beginning salary for women was $25,204, a 2.7 percent increase over 1989; for men, $25,724, a 4.3 percent increase. The median salary was $24,200 for all graduates; $24,000 for women; $24,700 for men.

Some 150 temporary professional placements were reported in 1990, compared with 198 in 1989 and 201 in 1988. The category "Other Placements" includes a variety of nontraditional positions, but because of a change in the form of the questionnaire, some "specialties" overlap traditional categories, e.g., school libraries. Split or combined positions, such as cataloging/reference, are not reflected in the "Other Placements" listing. For future reports, this category will be redesigned to reflect changes in library position titles.

Placements

First professional degrees were awarded to 3,522 graduates of the 42 schools reporting in 1990. In 1989, 43 reporting schools awarded 3,356 first professional degrees; in 1988, 51 reporting schools awarded 3,691 first professional degrees. In 1990, the average number of graduates of schools reporting was 84; in 1989, it was 78; in 1988, it was 72.

Table 1 shows permanent and temporary professional placements, as well as nonprofessional library placements, and the totals for the three. These are library or information-related positions. Table 1 also shows the number of graduates in nonlibrary positions or whose employment status was unknown in Summer 1991. Less than 1 percent were in nonlibrary positions, compared with 9 percent in 1990 and 8 percent in 1989. In Summer 1991, the employment status of 21 percent of the graduates was unknown, compared with 26 percent in 1990 and 27 percent in 1989.

Of the 1990 graduates, 55 percent were employed either in professional or nonprofessional positions in libraries or information-related work, as were 65 percent of 1989 graduates and 64 percent of 1988 graduates. Of the 1990 graduates, 48 percent were employed in permanent professional positions, compared with 56 percent in both 1989 and 1988. (Some schools reported only the total number of graduates, with no placement breakdown.)

Table 5 / Special Placements, 1990*

	Women	Men	Total
Government jurisdictions (U.S.)			
State libraries	13	5	18
Other government agencies (except USVA hospitals)	9	1	10
National libraries	2	0	2
Armed Services libraries (domestic)	2	0	2
Overseas agencies (incl. Armed Services)	3	0	3
Library science			
Advanced study	2	1	3
Other			
Children's services (school libraries)	20	0	20
Children's services (public libraries)	13	2	15
Youth services (school libraries)	14	4	18
Youth services (public libraries)	50	0	50
Law	62	17	79
Business (finance, industrial, corporate, banking, insurance, oil, etc.)	24	14	41
Medicine (incl. nursing schools)	27	6	33
Science and technology	18	12	30
Systems analysis, automation	14	7	21
Audiovisual and media centers	13	1	14
Hospitals (incl. USVA hospitals)	7	0	7
Rare books, manuscripts, archives	20	5	26
Research and development	6	2	8
Government documents	9	6	15
Information services (nonlibrary)	7	1	8
Historical agencies and archives	4	4	8
Religion (seminaries, theological schools)	4	5	9
Art and museums	12	1	13
Databases (publishing, servicing)	5	1	6
Outreach activities and services	7	1	8
Social sciences	7	1	8
Indexing	5	1	6
Records management	5	2	7
Networks and consortia	2	0	2
Free-lance	0	1	1
Pharmaceutical	8	1	9
Professional associations	5	0	5
Maps	0	1	1
Bookstores	3	1	4
Genealogical	1	0	1
Services to the handicapped	2	0	2
Theater, film, dance, music	1	1	2
Correctional institutions	0	1	1
Spanish-speaking centers	1	0	1
Total special placements reported	407	106	517

*Includes special placements reported in all types of libraries. Also includes placements undifferentiated by sex.

Employment distribution by type of library is shown in Tables 3 and 4. Table 4 is an 11-year listing of placements by type of library and information-related agencies (see footnote to Table 4).

Openings and Applicants

Thirty-six schools received a total of 46,836 listings of open library positions, with the number received ranging from 100 to 3,000. Listings were for positions at all

Table 6 / Salary Data Summarized, 1990

	Women	Men	Total
Average (mean) salary	$25,204	$25,724	$25,306
Median salary	24,000	24,700	24,200
Individual salary range	10,500–56,850	11,440–68,000	10,500–68,000

levels, and no doubt many were duplicated in several places. In 1989, 35 schools reported 52,564 listings; and in 1988, 38 schools reported 62,230 listings. Eleven schools reported an increase of from 3 percent to 50 percent in the number of position listings in 1990 over 1989. The median was 8 percent. Seven schools reported no significant change from 1989; 12 reported a decrease ranging from 2 percent to 60 percent.

Most institutions reported no significant difficulty in placing 1990 graduates, and several emphasized the specializations for which they are having difficulty in referring qualified candidates: children's services, both public and school; computer science, information science, and automation; medicine and the sciences, both life sciences and physical sciences; and cataloging.

The Bottom Line

The salary statistics in this report reflect only full-time annual salaries. Variables such as vacations and other fringe benefits, which may be part of the total compensation, are excluded. Salaries do not reflect differences in hours worked per week. While such information might provide for more precise comparability of compensation, the salary data in this analysis are consistent with those collected for this survey since 1951.

Not all of the 42 reporting schools provided salary data, nor could all schools provide all the information requested for all employed graduates. Data for graduates in irregular placements — such as those from abroad returning to a post in their homeland; appointments in religious orders or elsewhere where remuneration is some combination of salary plus living expenses; and all part-time employees — were excluded.

Another unexplored group, graduates staying in a position or organization with which they were affiliated while attending school, might account for high salaries for first professional degree recipients in some placements.

Table 7 / Average Salary Index:
Starting Library Positions, 1985–1990*

Year	Library Schools	Average Beginning Salary	Dollar Increase in Average Salary	Beginning Index	BLS-CPI
1985	58	$19,753	$ 962	111.6	109.3
1986	54	20,874	1,121	118.0	110.5
1987	55	22,247	1,373	125.7	115.4
1988	51	23,491	1,244	132.8	120.5
1989	43	24,581	1,090	138.9	124.0
1990	38	25,306	725	143.0	130.7

*Bureau of Labor Statistics Consumer Price Index based on 1982–1984 = 100. Average beginning salary for 1982–1984 was $17,693.

Table 8 / Comparisons of Salaries by Type of Library, 1990*

School	Placements	Salaries			Low Salary			High Salary			Average Salary			Median Salary		
		Women	Men	Total	Women	Men	Total	Women	Men	Total	Women	Men	Total	Women	Men	Total
Public libraries																
Northeast	165	113	14	130	$13,300	$20,200	$13,300	$30,000	$30,000	$30,000	$23,732	$25,429	$23,940	$24,000	$25,000	$24,200
Southeast	99	75	16	91	14,700	12,250	12,250	30,000	26,000	30,000	21,945	21,681	21,899	22,000	22,576	22,500
Midwest	237	138	45	184	11,783	18,000	11,783	32,252	43,000	43,000	22,464	23,909	22,809	22,273	23,275	22,500
Southwest	50	34	4	48	13,000	20,300	13,000	36,435	31,000	36,435	22,409	25,020	22,684	22,000	21,790	22,000
West	76	46	12	58	14,000	20,300	14,000	38,700	31,080	38,700	27,247	26,367	27,065	25,444	26,699	26,500
All schools	627	406	91	511	11,783	18,000	11,783	38,700	43,000	43,000	23,528	24,124	23,420	23,200	24,000	34,500
School libraries																
Northeast	91	79	4	85	11,400	21,425	11,400	56,850	50,000	56,850	27,994	31,856	28,223	26,500	28,000	26,500
Southeast	117	93	7	100	10,500	20,088	10,500	38,000	32,236	38,000	24,703	28,475	24,967	24,040	31,500	24,850
Midwest	105	85	3	88	12,000	21,600	12,000	51,125	42,000	51,125	25,873	29,400	25,994	25,000	24,600	25,000
Southwest	49	38	1	39	12,100	32,000	12,100	37,500	32,000	37,500	25,770	32,000	25,929	26,500	32,000	26,000
West	16	14	2	16	12,000	17,000	12,000	49,230	26,000	49,230	29,484	22,500	28,486	26,500	22,500	25,000
All schools	378	309	17	328	10,500	17,000	10,500	56,850	50,000	56,850	26,214	28,821	26,372	24,300	26,000	25,000
College/Univ. libraries																
Northeast	112	58	24	85	10,500	11,250	10,500	40,000	41,000	41,000	25,262	24,829	25,248	25,160	23,750	25,000
Southeast	78	44	24	68	17,000	20,000	17,000	33,000	42,666	42,666	22,344	25,415	23,428	22,000	23,370	22,350
Midwest	193	98	45	143	12,400	11,440	11,440	39,882	38,000	39,882	22,708	23,737	23,032	21,500	23,288	23,000
Southwest	67	41	15	56	13,500	18,000	13,500	33,000	36,000	36,000	23,035	23,293	23,104	22,800	22,000	22,500
West	78	36	17	53	13,500	12,500	12,500	34,000	40,000	40,000	26,528	26,862	26,635	28,000	26,400	27,360
All schools	528	277	125	405	10,500	11,250	10,500	40,000	42,666	42,666	23,730	24,641	24,045	23,500	23,700	23,600

Table 8 / Comparisons of Salaries by Type of Library, 1990* (cont.)

School	Salaries				Low Salary			High Salary			Average Salary			Median Salary		
	Placements	Women	Men	Total	Women	Men	Total	Women	Men	Total	Women	Men	Total	Women	Men	Total
Special libraries																
Northeast	132	82	27	116	15,000	12,000	12,000	48,000	68,000	68,000	29,788	28,596	29,686	30,000	27,000	30,000
Southeast	34	27	3	30	12,480	22,000	12,480	30,000	33,000	33,000	23,732	27,013	24,061	24,000	26,040	24,500
Midwest	94	57	21	78	14,000	12,480	12,480	40,000	56,000	56,000	25,496	25,553	25,511	24,000	25,000	24,513
Southwest	35	24	9	33	16,000	20,000	16,000	36,000	57,047	57,047	24,265	30,264	25,901	23,600	28,000	25,000
West	55	31	7	38	18,000	21,500	18,000	40,000	37,000	40,000	26,987	26,672	26,920	26,780	24,000	24,960
All schools	350	221	67	295	12,480	12,000	12,000	48,000	68,000	68,000	26,757	27,589	27,081	22,824	26,400	26,000
Other libraries																
Northeast	29	21	3	25	19,000	32,000	19,000	40,000	37,400	40,000	29,881	35,133	30,516	29,400	36,000	30,000
Southeast	32	17	8	25	18,000	22,000	18,000	39,000	50,000	50,000	27,726	29,123	28,463	26,400	25,000	26,000
Midwest	13	9	3	12	20,000	19,500	19,500	46,000	35,000	46,000	26,835	26,840	26,836	25,000	26,000	25,358
Southwest	11	7	3	10	21,800	20,300	20,300	40,000	33,000	40,000	28,563	28,100	28,424	27,100	31,000	28,050
West	8	6	1	7	26,000	33,200	26,000	31,000	33,200	33,200	28,583	33,200	29,243	28,000	33,200	28,000
All schools	93	60	18	79	18,000	19,500	18,000	46,000	50,000	50,000	28,530	29,257	28,698	27,300	28,100	27,500

* Includes placements undifferentiated by sex.

Average (Mean) and Median Salaries

The average (mean) salary for all 1990 graduates was $25,306, an increase of $725 over the 1989 average of $24,581. The average salary for women was $25,204, and the average for men was $25,724, a difference of $520 (Table 6). Table 7 shows the Bureau of Labor Statistics base determined by averaging beginning salaries for 1982, 1983, and 1984. The consumer price index (CPI) for 1990 was 130.7, a gain of 5.4 percent over 1989. The beginning salary index was 143.0, an increase of 3 percent over 1989. Library school graduates appear to have lost ground here.

In Table 8, the average salary is higher for men in three categories (the difference ranges from $1,697 to $5,322). The median salary for all graduates in 1990 was $24,200, an increase of $522 (only 2.2 percent) over 1989. The median for women was $24,000; for men, $24,700. Of the 37 schools reporting on both men and women, the median salary was higher for women in 12 schools; for men in 24 schools; and the same in one.

Accredited Library Schools

This list of graduate schools accredited by the American Library Association was issued in October 1991. A list of more than 300 institutions offering both accredited and nonaccredited programs in librarianship appears in the forty-fourth edition of the *American Library Directory* (R. R. Bowker, 1991).

Northeast: Conn., D.C., Md., Mass., N.J., N.Y., Pa., R.I.

Catholic University of America, School of Lib. and Info. Science, Washington, DC 20064. Deanna B. Marcum, Dean. 202-319-5085.

Clarion University of Pennsylvania, College of Communication, Computer Info. Science, and Lib. Science, Clarion, PA 16214. Ahmad Gamaluddin, Dir. 814-226-2271.

Columbia University, School of Lib. Service, New York, NY 10027. Robert Wedgeworth, Dean. 212-854-2292. (In 1990, Columbia announced it would close the library school in 1992. As of March 1992, the school was still seeking a new home.)

Drexel University, College of Info. Studies, Philadelphia, PA 19104. Richard H. Lytle, Dean. 215-895-2474.

Pratt Institute, School of Info. and Lib. Science, Brooklyn, NY 11205. S. M. Matta, Acting Dean. 718-636-3702.

Queens College, City University of New York, Grad. School of Lib. and Info. Stud-ies, Rosenthal Hall, Rm. 254, Flushing, NY 11367. Marianne Cooper, Dir. 718-520-7194.

Rutgers University, School of Communication, Info., and Lib. Studies, 41 Huntington St., New Brunswick, NJ 08903. Betty J. Turock, Chpn. and Program Dir. 201-932-7917.

Saint John's University, Div. of Lib. and Info. Science, Jamaica, NY 11439. Emmett Corry, Dir. 718-990-6200.

Simmons College, Grad. School of Lib. and Info. Science, Boston, MA 02115-5898. Robert D. Stueart, Dean. 617-738-2225.

Southern Connecticut State University, School of Lib. Science and Instructional Technology, New Haven, CT 06515. Emanuel T. Prostano, Dean. 203-397-4532.

State University of New York at Albany, School of Info. Science and Policy, Albany, NY 12222. Richard S. Halsey, Dean. 518-442-5115.

State University of New York at Buffalo, School of Info. and Lib. Studies, Buffalo,

NY 14260. George S. Bobinski, Dean. 716-636-2412.

Syracuse University, School of Info. Studies, 4-206 Center for Science and Technology, Syracuse, NY 13244-2340. Donald A. Marchand, Dean. 315-443-2736.

University of Maryland, College of Lib. and Info. Services, College Park, MD 20742. Claude E. Walston, Dean. 301-405-2033.

University of Pittsburgh, School of Lib. and Info. Science, Pittsburgh, PA 15260. Toni Carbo Bearman, Dean. 412-624-5230.

University of Rhode Island, Grad. School of Lib. and Info. Studies, Rodman Hall, Kingston, RI 02881. Elizabeth Futas, Dir. 401-792-2947.

University of South Carolina, College of Lib. and Info. Science, Columbia, SC 29208. Fred W. Roper, Dean. 803-777-3858.

University of South Florida, School of Lib. and Info. Science, Tampa, FL 33620-8300. John A. McCrossan, Interim Dir. 813-974-3520.

University of Southern Mississippi, School of Lib. Science, Hattiesburg, MS 39406. Joy Greiner, Dir. 601-266-4228.

University of Tennessee, Knoxville, Grad. School of Lib. and Info. Science, Knoxville, TN 37996-4330. Glenn E. Estes, Dir. 615-974-2148.

Southeast: Ala., Fla., Ga., Ky., La., Miss., N.C., S.C., Tenn., P.R.

Clark Atlanta University, School of Lib. and Info. Studies, Atlanta, GA 30314. Charles D. Churchwell, Dean. 404-880-8698.

Florida State University, School of Lib. and Info. Studies, R 106, Tallahassee, FL 32306-2048. F. William Summers, Dean. 904-644-5775.

Louisiana State University, School of Lib. and Info. Science, Baton Rouge, LA 70803. Bert R. Boyce, Dean. 504-388-3158.

North Carolina Central University, School of Lib. and Info. Sciences, Durham, NC 27707. Benjamin F. Speller, Jr., Dean. 919-560-6485.

University of Alabama, School of Lib. and Info. Studies, Tuscaloosa, AL 35487-0252. Philip M. Turner, Dean. 205-348-4610.

University of Kentucky, College of Lib. and Info. Science, Lexington, KY 40506-0039. Thomas J. Waldhart, Dean. 606-257-8876.

University of North Carolina, School of Info. and Lib. Science, Chapel Hill, NC 27599-3360. Barbara B. Moran, Dean. 919-962-8366.

University of North Carolina at Greensboro, Dept. of Lib. and Info. Studies, Greensboro, NC 27412. Marilyn L. Miller, Chair. 919-334-5100.

University of Puerto Rico, Escuela Graduada de Bibliotecologia y Ciencias de la Información, Rio Piedras, PR 00931. Annie F. Thompson, Dir. 809-763-6199.

Midwest: Ill., Ind., Iowa, Kan., Mich., Mo., Ohio, Wis.

Emporia State University, School of Lib. and Info. Management, Emporia, KS 66801. Martha L. Hale, Dean. 316-343-5203.

Indiana University, School of Lib. and Info. Science, Bloomington, IN 47405. Blaise Cronin, Dean. 812-855-2848.

Kent State University, School of Lib. Science, Kent, OH 44242. Rosemary R. Dumont, Dean. 216-672-2782.

Northern Illinois University, Dept. of Lib. and Info. Studies, DeKalb, IL 60115. Cosette N. Kies, Chpn. 815-753-1733.

Rosary College, Grad. School of Lib. and Info. Science, River Forest, IL 60305. Michael E. D. Koenig, Dean. 708-366-2490.

University of Illinois, Grad. School of Lib. and Info. Science, 1407 W. Gregory, 410 DKH, Urbana, IL 61801-3680. Leigh Estabrook, Dean. 217-333-3280.

University of Iowa, School of Lib. and Info. Science, Iowa City, IA 52242. Carl F. Orgren, Dir. 319-335-5707.

University of Michigan, School of Info. and Lib. Studies, Ann Arbor, MI 48109-1092. Robert M. Warner, Dean. 313-764-9376.

University of Missouri, Columbia, School of Lib. and Info. Science, Columbia, MO 65211. Mary F. Lenox, Dean. 314-882-4546.

University of Wisconsin–Madison, School of Lib. and Info. Studies, Madison, WI 53706. Jane B. Robbins, Dir. 608-263-2900.

University of Wisconsin–Milwaukee, School of Lib. and Info. Science, Milwaukee, WI

53201. Mohammed M. Aman, Dean. 414-229-4707.

Wayne State University, Lib. Science Program, Detroit, MI 48202. Joseph J. Mika, Dir. 313-577-1825.

Southwest: Ariz., Okla., Tex.

Texas Woman's University, School of Lib. and Info. Studies, Denton, TX 76204-0905. Keith Swigger, Interim Dean. 817-898-2602.

University of Arizona, Grad. Lib. School, Tucson, AZ 85719. Charles D. Hurt, Dir. 602-621-3565.

University of North Texas, School of Lib. and Info. Sciences, Denton, TX 76203. Raymond F. Vondran, Dean. 817-565-2445.

University of Oklahoma, School of Lib. and Info. Studies, Norman, OK 73019. Robert D. Swisher, Dir. 405-325-3921.

University of Texas at Austin, Grad. School of Lib. and Info. Science, Austin, TX 78712-1276. Brooke E. Sheldon, Dean. 512-471-3821.

West: Calif., Hawaii, Utah, Wash.

Brigham Young University, School of Lib. and Info. Sciences, Provo, UT 84602. Nathan M. Smith, Dir. 801-378-2977.

San Jose State University, Div. of Lib. and Info. Science, San Jose, CA 95192-0029. James S. Healey, Dir. 408-924-2490.

University of California at Berkeley, School of Lib. and Info. Studies, Berkeley, CA

94720. Nancy Van House, Acting Dean. 510-642-1464.

University of California, Los Angeles, Grad. School of Lib. and Info. Science, Los Angeles, CA 90024-1520. Beverly P. Lynch, Dean. 213-825-8799.

University of Hawaii, School of Lib. and Info. Studies, Honolulu, HI 96822. Miles M. Jackson, Dean. 808-948-7321.

University of Washington, Grad. School of Lib. and Info. Science, Seattle, WA 98195. Margaret Chisholm, Dir. 206-543-1794.

Canada

Dalhousie University, School of Lib. and Info. Studies, Halifax, NS B3H 4H8. Mary Dykstra, Dir. 902-494-3656.

McGill University, Grad. School of Lib. and Info. Studies, Montreal, PQ H3A 1Y1. J. Andrew Large, Dir. 514-398-4204.

Université de Montréal, Ecole de bibliothèconomie et des sciences de l'information, Montreal, PQ H3C 3J7. Marcel Lajeunesse, Dir. 514-343-6044.

University of Alberta, School of Lib. and Info. Studies, Edmonton, AB T6G 2J4. Sheila Bertram, Dir. 403-492-4578.

University of British Columbia, School of Lib., Archival, and Info. Studies, Vancouver, BC V6T 1Z1. Peter Simmons, Acting Dir. 604-822-2404.

University of Toronto, Faculty of Lib. and Info. Science, Toronto, ON M5S 1A1. Adele M. Fasick, Dean. 416-978-3202.

University of Western Ontario, School of Lib. and Info. Science, London, ON N6G 1H1. Catherine Ross, Acting Dean. 519-661-3542.

Library Scholarship Sources

For a more complete list of scholarships, fellowships, and assistantships offered for library study, see *Financial Assistance for Library Education,* published annually by the American Library Association.

American Association of Law Libraries. (1) A varying number of scholarships of a minimum of $1,000 for graduates of an accredited law school who are degree candidates in an accredited library school; (2) a varying number of scholarships of varying amounts for library school graduates working on a law degree, nonlaw graduates enrolled in an accredited library school, and law librarians taking a course related to law librarianship; (3) a stipend of $3,500 for an experienced minority librarian working toward an advanced degree to further a law library career. For information, write to: Scholarship Committee, AALL, 53 W. Jackson Blvd., Suite 940, Chicago, IL 60604.

American Library Association. (1) The David H. Clift Scholarships of $3,000 for U.S. or Canadian citizens who have been admitted to accredited library schools. For information, write to: Staff Liaison, David H. Clift Scholarship Jury, ALA, 50 E. Huron St., Chicago, IL 60611; (2) the Louise Giles Minority Scholarship of $3,000 for a varying number of minority students who are U.S. or Canadian citizens and have been admitted to accredited library schools. For information, write to: Staff Liaison, Louise Giles Minority Scholarship Jury, ALA, 50 E. Huron St., Chicago, IL 60611; (3) the AASL School Librarians Workshop Scholarship of $2,500 for a candidate admitted to a full-time ALA-accredited or school library media program. For information, write to: AASL/ALA, 50 E. Huron St., Chicago, IL 60611; (4) the ACRL Doctoral Dissertation Fellowship of $1,000 for a student who has completed all coursework in the area of academic librarianship. For information, write to: ACRL/ALA, 50 E. Huron St., Chicago, IL 60611; (5) the Samuel Lazerow Fellowship of $1,000 for a librarian currently working in acquisitions or technical services in an academic or research library. For information, write to: ACRL/ALA, 50 E. Huron St., Chicago, IL 60611; (6) the Nijhoff International West European Specialist Study Grant pays travel expenses, room, and board for a ten-day trip to The Netherlands and two other European countries for an ALA member. Selection based on proposal outlining purpose of trip. For information, write to: ACRL/ALA, 50 E. Huron St., Chicago, IL 60611; (7) Bound to Stay Bound Books Scholarship of $3,500 for two students admitted to an ALA-accredited program who will work with children in a library for one year after graduation. For information, write to: Exec. Dir., ALSC/ALA, 50 E. Huron St., Chicago, IL 60611; (8) NMRT/EBSCO Scholarship of $1,000 for a U.S. or Canadian citizen and member of the ALA New Members Round Table. Based on financial need and professional goals. For information, write to: ALA Programs Office, 50 E. Huron St., Chicago, IL 60611; (9) two LITA Scholarships in Library and Information Technology of $2,500 each for students (one of whom is a minority student) who may not have completed more than 12 hours toward a degree in library science before June 1, 1992. Foreign students may apply. For information, write to: LITA/ALA, 50 E. Huron St., Chicago, IL 60611; (10) Bogle International Library Travel Fund grant of $500 for a varying number of ALA members to attend a first international conference. For information, write to: Robert P. Doyle, ALA, 50 E. Huron St., Chicago, IL 60611; (11) PLA/CLSI International Study Award of up to $5,000 for a PLA member with five years' experience in public libraries. For information, write to: PLA/ALA, 50 E. Huron St., Chicago, IL 60611.

American-Scandinavian Foundation. Fellowships and grants for 25 to 30 students, in amounts from $2,500 to $15,000, for advanced study in Denmark, Finland, Iceland, Norway, or Sweden. For information, write to: Exchange Div., American-Scandinavian Foundation, 725 Park Ave., New York, NY 10021.

Association for Library and Information Science Education. A varying number of research grants of up to $2,500 for members of ALISE and the Jane Hannigan Research Award of $500 for an untenured faculty member or doctoral student. For information, write to: Joan Durrance, Awards Committee, ALISE, School of Info. and Lib. Studies, Univ. of Michigan, 550 E. University, 304 West Engineering, Ann Arbor, MI 48109-1092.

Association of Jewish Libraries. A varying number of scholarships of $500 and up for candidates with an MLS who plan to work as a Judaica librarian. For information, write to: Ralph Simon, Assn. of Jewish Libs., 2200 S. Green Rd., Cleveland, OH 44121.

Beta Phi Mu. (1) The Sarah Rebecca Reed Scholarship of $1,500 for a person accepted in an ALA-accredited library program; (2) the Frank B. Sessa Scholarship of $750 for a Beta Phi Mu member for continuing education; (3) the Harold Lancour Scholarship of $1,000 for graduate study in a foreign country related to the applicant's work or schooling. For information, write to: Exec. Secy., Beta Phi Mu, School of Lib. and Info. Science, Univ. of Pittsburgh, Pittsburgh, PA 15260.

Canadian Library Association. (1) The Howard V. Phalin–World Book Graduate Scholarship in Library Science of $2,500; (2) the H. W. Wilson Foundation Scholarship of $2,000; and (3) the CLA Dafoe Scholarship of $1,750 are given to a Canadian citizen or landed immigrant to attend an accredited Canadian library school. For information, write to: CLA Membership Services Dept., Scholarships and Awards Committee, Canadian Lib. Assn., 200 Elgin St., Suite 602, Ottawa, ON K2P 1L5, Canada.

Catholic Library Association. (1) Rev. Andrew L. Bouwhuis Scholarship of $1,500 for a person with a B.A. degree who has been accepted in an accredited library school; (2) World Book, Inc., Grant: up to four scholarships for a total of $1,500 for continuing education. Open to CLA members only. For information, write to: Scholarship Committee, Catholic Lib. Assn., 461 W. Lancaster Ave., Haverford, PA 19401.

Chinese American Librarians Association. Sheila Suen Lai Scholarship of $500 for a Chinese descendant who has been accepted in an ALA-accredited program. For information, write to: Suzanne Lo, Chpn., Scholarship Committee, c/o Asian Community Lib., 449 Ninth St., Oakland, CA 94610.

Church and Synagogue Library Association. Muriel Fuller Memorial Scholarship of $75 for a correspondence course offered by the Univ. of Utah Continuing Education Div. For information, write to: Lorraine Burson, CSLA, Box 19357, Portland, OR 97280-0357.

Information Exchange System for Minority Personnel. Scholarship of $500, intended for minority students, for graduate study. For information, write to: Dorothy M. Haith, Chpn., Clara Stanton Jones School, Box 90216, Washington, DC 20090.

Massachusetts Black Librarians' Network Scholarship of at least $500 for a minority student entering an accredited master's program in library science with no more than 12 semester hours toward a degree. For information, write to: Pearl Mosley, Chpn., MBLN, 27 Beech Glen St., Roxbury, MA 02119.

Medical Library Association. (1) A scholarship of $2,000 for graduate study in medical librarianship, with at least one half of the program yet to be completed; (2) a scholarship of $2,000 for a minority student for graduate study; (3) a varying number of Research, Demonstration and Development Project grants of $100–$500 for U.S. or Canadian citizens who are ALA members; (4) continuing education awards of $100–$500 for U.S. or Canadian citizens who are ALA members; (5) Cunningham Memorial International Fellowship of $3,000 plus travel expenses for a foreign student for postgraduate study in the United States; (6) MLA Doctoral Fellowship of $1,000 for postgraduate work in medical librarianship or information science. For information, write to: Professional Service Area, Medical Lib. Assn., Suite 300, 6 N. Michigan Ave., Chicago, IL 60602.

Frederic G. Melcher Scholarship (administered by the Association for Library Service to Children, ALA). Two scholarships of $5,000 each for a U.S. or Canadian citizen admitted to an accredited library school who plans to work with children in school or public libraries. For information, write to: Exec. Dir., Assn. for Lib. Service to Children, ALA, 50 E. Huron St., Chicago, IL 60611.

Mountain Plains Library Association. (1) A varying number of grants of up to $500 each; and (2) a varying number of grants of $100 each for residents of the association area who are MPLA members with at least two years of membership for continuing education. For information, write to: Joseph R. Edelen, Jr., MPLA Exec. Secy., Univ. of South Dakota Lib., Vermillion, SD 57069.

Natural Sciences and Engineering Research Council of Canada. (1) A varying number of scholarships and fellowships of $15,000 per year; and (2) a varying number of scholarships of varying amounts for postgraduate study in science librarianship and documentation for a Canadian citizen or landed immigrant with a bachelor's degree in science or engineering. For information, write to: Scholarships and Fellowships, Natural Sciences and Engineering Research Council, 200 Kent St., Ottawa, ON K1A 1H5, Canada.

REFORMA, the National Association to Promote Library Services to the Spanish-Speaking. Three scholarships of at least $1,000 each to attend an ALA-accredited program. For information, write to: Camila Alire, Auraria Lib., Univ. of Colorado, Lawrence at 11 St., Denver, CO 80204.

Society of American Archivists. Two continuing education grants of $900 each for specific types of repositories and collections. For information, write to: Society of American Archivists, 600 S. Federal, Suite 504, Chicago, IL 60605.

Southern Regional Education Board. (1) A varying number of grants of varying amounts to cover in-state tuition for West Virginia residents for undergraduate, graduate, or postgraduate study in an accredited library school; and (2) a varying number of grants of varying amounts to cover in-state tuition for residents of Arkansas, Georgia, Kentucky, Louisiana, Mississippi, Oklahoma, South Carolina, Tennessee, Texas, Virginia, or West Virginia, for postgraduate study in an accredited library school. For information, write to: SREB, 592 Tenth St. N.W., Atlanta, GA 30318-5790.

Special Libraries Association. (1) Two $6,000 scholarships for U.S. or Canadian citizens, accepted by an ALA-accredited library education program, who show an aptitude for and interest in special libraries; (2) two $1,000 scholarships for U.S. or Canadian citizens with an MLS and an interest in special libraries who have been accepted in an ALA-accredited Ph.D. program; (3) two scholarships of $6,000 each for minority students with an interest in special libraries. Open to U.S. or Canadian citizens only. For information, write to: Manager of Membership Development, Special Libs. Assn., 1700 18th St. N.W., Washington, DC 20009.

Library Scholarship and Award Recipients, 1991

AALL Scholarships. *Offered by:* American Association of Law Libraries. *Winners:* Type I (Library Degree for Law School Graduates): Wendy S. Cohen, Vicente Ernesto Graces, Linda Rae Kawaguchi, Bruce Lee Kleinschmidt, Jack Edward Kotvas, Melissa Margaret Serfass, Jeffrey Robert Stickle, Feng Wang, Heidi J. Weston, John Clinton Shafer; Type II (Law Degree for Library School Graduates): Frances Schmid Holland, Chandini Shireen Kumar; Type III (Library Degree for Non–Law School Graduates): Trisha Bradbury Fabugais, M. Constance Fleischer, Linda Baltrusch Freeman, Eric C. Kennedy, Sharon Margaret-Marie McNally, Lauren Renee Meader, Juliane Anastasia Novak, Lynda J. Warmath, Elizabeth Jean Wetzel, Joan Monica Weyhe, Linda Louise Wood; Type IV (Special Course in Law Librarianship and Meira Pimsleur Scholarship):

Sandra Ann Hyclak; Type V (George A. Strait Minority Stipend): Jill L. Feldman.

AASL/ABC-Clio Leadership Development Award. *Offered by:* ALA American Association of School Librarians and ABC-Clio Company. *Winner:* South Dakota School Library Media Association, Pierre, SD.

AASL/Baker & Taylor Distinguished Service Award — $2,000. For outstanding contributions to librarianship and school library development. *Offered by:* ALA American Association of School Librarians and Baker & Taylor. *Winner:* Barbara Spriestersbach, Oklahoma City, OK.

AASL/Encyclopaedia Britannica National School Library Media Program of the Year Award. *Offered by:* ALA American Association of School Librarians and Encyclopaedia Britannica Companies. *Winners:* (single school) Beecher Road School, Woodbridge, CT, Bernice L. Yesner; (small school district) not awarded in 1991; (large school district) Irving Independent School, Irving, TX, Mary D. Lankford.

AASL/Follett Microcomputer in the Media Center Award. *Offered by:* ALA American Association of School Librarians and Follett Software Company. *Winners:* David Henderson, Roosevelt Elementary School, Leonard, MI; Bonnie Lynn Fish, Cameron High School, Cameron, MO.

AASL/SIRS Distinguished Library Service Award for School Administrators. *Offered by:* ALA American Association of School Librarians and Social Issues Resources Series, Inc. *Winner:* Marilyn Blakely, Vigo County School Corporation, Terre Haute, IN.

AASL/SIRS Intellectual Freedom Award — $1,000. For a school library media specialist who has upheld principles of intellectual freedom. *Offered by:* ALA American Association of School Librarians and Social Issues Resources Series, Inc. *Winner:* Neva Thompson, Dewey, AZ.

AASL Emergency Librarian Publication Award. For an outstanding publication in the field of school librarianship. *Offered by:* ALA American Association of School Librarians and *Emergency Librarian. Winner: Florida Media Quarterly,* Nell Brown, ed., Bunnell, FL.

AASL School Librarians Workshop Scholarship. *Offered by:* ALA American Association of School Librarians and Library Learning Resources Company. *Winner:* Brian Paul Stafford, Jenkintown, PA.

ACRL Academic/Research Librarian of the Year Award — $2,000. For an outstanding national or international contribution to academic and research librarianship and library development. *Offered by:* ALA Association of College and Research Libraries. *Donor:* Baker & Taylor. *Winner:* Richard DeGennaro.

ACRL Community College Learning Resources Achievement Awards. *Offered by:* ALA Association of College and Research Libraries. *Winners:* Jimmie Anne Nourse and Rudy Widman; James O. Wallace.

ACRL Doctoral Dissertation Fellowship. For research in academic librarianship. *Offered by:* ALA Association of College and Research Libraries. *Winner:* Kamala Balaraman.

AIA/ALA-LAMA Library Buildings Awards. *Offered by:* ALA Library Administration and Management Association. *Winners:* Las Vegas-Clark County (NV) Library and Discovery Museum; Bucks County (PA) Free Library and District Center; Stillwater (MN) Public Library; Humboldt Library, Berlin, Germany; Headquarters Library of the Clayton County Library System, Jonesboro, GA; Buckhead Branch Library, Atlanta, GA.

ALA Armed Forces Library Achievement Citation. *Offered by:* ALA Armed Forces Library Round Table. *Winner:* Norman E. Dakan.

ALA Armed Forces Library Certificate of Merit. *Offered by:* ALA Armed Forces Library Round Table. *Winner:* Eugene L. Stong.

ALA Armed Forces Library Section Newsbank Scholarship Award. *Offered by:* ALA Armed Forces Library Round Table. *Winner:* Carolyn Covington.

ALA Equality Award — $500. For an outstanding contribution toward promoting equality between women and men in the library profession. *Donor:* Scarecrow Press. *Offered by:* American Library Association. *Winner:* E. J. Josey.

ALA Honorary Membership Award. *Offered by:* ALA Awards Committee. *Winners:* Robert Frasc, Miriam Hornback.

ALA Map and Geography Honor Award. *Offered by:* ALA Map and Geography Round Table. *Winner:* Donna Koepp.

ALCTS Resources Section/Blackwell North America Scholarship Award. Presented to the author(s) of an outstanding monograph, published article, or original paper on acquisitions pertaining to college or university libraries. *Offered by:* ALA Association for Library Collections and Technical Services, Resources Section. *Donor:* Blackwell North America. *Winner:* Gary D. Bird.

ALISE Award for Professional Contribution to Library and Information Science Education. *Offered by:* Association for Library and Information Science Education. *Winner:* Herman Totten.

ALISE Doctoral Students Dissertation Awards — $400. To promote the exchange of research ideas between doctoral students and established researchers. *Offered by:*

A Reed Reference Publishing Company

Thank you for purchasing this vital resource from R.R. Bowker.

We want to make sure that you can take advantage of the full range of reference products and services available from Bowker and Reed Reference Publishing. That's why we've provided the postage-paid Product Information Request cards at right to make it easy for you to learn about everything from Bowker's bibliographic and serials references to Marquis Who's Who biographical resources.

Simply check-off the product lines you're interested in, fill in your name and address, and drop the card in the mail. We'll get your information to you as soon as we can!

Key Titles available from Bowker and Reed Reference Publishing

- *Books in Print*
- *Ulrich's*
- *Magazines for Librarie*
- *Literary Market Place*
- *The Bowker Annual*
- *Bowker's Complete Video Directory*
- *A to Zoo*
- *Library Reference Plus*
- *Broadcasting and Cabl Market Place*
- *Yearbook of International Organizations*
- *Martindale-Hubbell Law Directory*
- *Who's Who in America*
- *Standard Directory of Advertisers*

BOWAN

Please send me more information on the many products and services available through R.R. Bowker and Reed Reference Publishing. I've checked my selections below:

○ Bibliographic References
○ Serials References
○ Professional Directories
○ Library and Book Trade Administration References
○ Entertainment and Performing Arts References
○ A&I References
○ Children's and Young Adult References

○ CD-ROM Databases/Online Services
○ K.G. Saur International References
○ Martindale-Hubbell Legal References
○ Marquis Who's Who Biographical References
○ National Register Publishing Company Directories

○ *Please send me my personal copy of Reed Reference Publishing's latest catalog.*
○ *I'd like a Sales Representative to call at the number below.*

Name _____
Title _____
Institution _____
Address _____
City/State/Zip _____ *Telephone* _____

R.R.BOWKER

Product Information Request

R.R.BOWKER
A Reed Reference Publishing Company

Association for Library and Information Science Education. *Winners*: Ruth Palmquist (University of Tennessee) for a Study of Word Associations in the Natural Language Expression of Information Needs in an Information Retrieval Setting; and Nancy Everhart (Florida State University) for Analysis of the Work Activities of High School Media Specialists in Automated and Non-automated Library Media Centers Using Work Sampling.

ALISE Research Award—$2,500. For a project that reflects ALISE goals and objectives. *Offered by:* Association for Library and Information Science Education. *Winner:* Patricia Reeling (Rutgers University) for Doctorate Recipients: How They Compare with Doctorate Recipients in Other Disciplines.

ALISE Research Paper Competition—$500. For a research paper concerning any aspect of librarianship or information studies by a member of ALISE. *Offered by:* Association for Library and Information Science Education. *Winner:* John Richardson (University of California at Los Angeles) for The Logic of Ready-Reference Work: Basic and Subordinate Level Knowledge.

ALISE Service Award. For outstanding contributions to the association. *Offered by:* Association for Library and Information Science Education. *Winner:* Not awarded in 1991.

ALTA/Gale Outstanding Trustee Conference Grant Award. *Offered by:* ALA American Library Trustee Association. *Winner:* Suzan G. Allen.

ALTA Literacy Award. For an outstanding contribution to the extirpation of illiteracy. *Offered by:* ALA American Library Trustee Association. *Winner:* Helen S. Kohlman.

ALTA Major Benefactors Honor Awards. *Offered by:* ALA American Library Trustee Association. *Winners:* The Colt Family; Charles W. Barber and the Rapides Bank & Trust Company; Sioux City Public Library Foundation; Estate of Alvin F. and Gertrude M. Schroeder.

ALTA Trustee Citations. *Offered by:* ALA American Library Trustee Association. *Winners:* Roslyn S. Kurland, Renee Becker Swartz.

ARMA International Scholarships. *Offered by:* Association of Records Managers and Administrators, Inc. *Winners:* Cynthia Caballero ($750), Alycia Hicks ($1,500), Ting Lim ($1,500), Susan M. Lucci ($750).

ASCLA Exceptional Achievement Award. For recognition of leadership and achievement in the areas of library cooperation and state library development. *Offered by:* ALA Association of Specialized and Cooperative Library Agencies. *Winners:* William G. Asp, Barratt Wilkins.

ASCLA Exceptional Service Award. For exceptional service to ASCLA or any of its component areas of service, namely, services to patients, the homebound, medical, nursing, and other professional staff in hospitals, and inmates; demonstrating professional leadership, effective interpretation of program, pioneering activity, or significant research or experimental projects. *Offered by:* ALA Association of Specialized and Cooperative Library Agencies. *Winner:* Kathleen Mayo.

ASCLA National Organization on Disability Award for Library Service for Persons with Disabilities. *Offered by:* ALA Association of Specialized and Cooperative Library Agencies. *Winners:* King County Library System, Seattle, WA; Seattle (WA) Public Library.

ASIS Award of Merit. For an outstanding contribution to the field of information science. *Offered by:* American Society for Information Science. *Winner:* Roger K. Summit.

ASIS Best Information Science Book. *Offered by:* American Society for Information Science. *Winner:* David C. Blair, for *Language and Representation in Information Retrieval* (Elsevier Scientific).

ASIS Best Information Science Teacher Award—$500. *Offered by:* American Society for Information Science. *Winner:* Not awarded in 1991.

ASIS Best Student Paper Award. *Offered by:* American Society for Information Science. *Winner:* Not awarded in 1991.

ASIS Doctoral Dissertation Scholarship. *Offered by:* American Society for Information Science. *Winner:* Diane H. Sonnenwald.

ASIS Doctoral Forum Award. *Offered by:* American Society for Information Science. *Winners:* Louise Su, for An Investigation to Find Appropriate Measures for Evaluating Interactive Information Retrieval;

Thomas E. Pinelli for The Relationship Between the Use of U.S. Government Technical Reports by U.S. Aerospace Engineers and Scientists and Selected Institutional and Sociometric Variables.

ASIS Research Award. For an outstanding research contribution in the field of information science that consists of a systematic program of research in a single study. *Offered by:* American Society for Information Science. *Winner:* Abraham Bookstein.

ASIS Special Award. For contributions outside the everyday activities of information professionals. *Offered by:* American Society for Information Science. *Winner:* Senator Albert Gore (D–Tenn.).

Advancement of Literacy Award. *Offered by:* ALA Public Library Association. *Winner:* Baker & Taylor Books.

May Hill Arbuthnot Lecturer for 1991. *Offered by:* ALA Association for Library Service to Children. *Winner:* Iona Opie.

Hugh C. Atkinson Memorial Award. *Offered by:* ALA divisions. *Winner:* Donald E. Riggs.

(Carroll Preston) Baber Research Grant— $7,500. *Offered by:* American Library Association. *Winner:* Delia Neuman.

Baker & Taylor Conference Grants. *Offered by:* ALA Young Adult Library Services Association. *Winners:* Nancy E. Strong, Miriam Temsky.

Mildred L. Batchelder Award. *Offered by:* ALA Association for Library Service to Children. *Winner:* Dutton Children's Books for *A Handful of Stars* by Rafik Schami, translated by Rika Lesser.

The Best of LRTS Award. *Offered by:* ALA Association for Library collections and Technical Services. *Winners:* Beth M. Paskoff, Anna H. Perrault.

Beta Phi Mu Award— $500. For distinguished service to education for librarianship. *Offered by:* ALA Awards Committee. *Donor:* Beta Phi Mu Library Science Honorary Association. *Winner:* Edward G. Holley.

Bogle International Library Travel Fund. *Offered by:* ALA International Relations Committee. *Winner:* Connie Wu.

Bound to Stay Bound Books Scholarship. *Offered by:* ALA Association for Library Service to Children. *Winners:* Anna Stephens Watkins, Chance Andrews Hunt.

R. R. Bowker/Ulrich's Serials Librarianship Award. *Offered by:* ALA Association for Library Collections and Technical Services. *Winners:* Deana L. Astic, Charles A. Hamaker.

Estelle Brodman Award. To honor both significant achievement and the potential for leadership and continuing excellence at midcareer in the area of academic health sciences librarianship. *Offered by:* Medical Library Association. *Winner:* Richard E. Lucier.

CACUL Distinguished Academic Librarian Award. *Offered by:* Canadian Association of College and University Libraries. *Winner:* Nancy Williamson, Toronto, ON.

CACUL Innovative Achievement Award— $1,500. *Offered by:* Canadian Association of College and University Libraries. *Winner:* University of Saskatchewan, Saskatoon.

CACUL Micromedia Award of Merit—$500. *Offered by:* Canadian Association of College and University Libraries and Micromedia. *Winner:* Ross Carter, Vancouver, BC.

CALA Distinguished Service Award. *Offered by:* Chinese-American Librarians Association. *Winner:* Norma Yueh.

CALA President's Award. *Offered by:* Chinese-American Librarians Association. *Winner:* Agnes M. Griffin.

CAPL Outstanding Public Library Service Award. *Offered by:* Canadian Association of Public Libraries. *Winner:* John Dutton, Calgary, AB.

CASLIS Award for Special Librarianship in Canada. *Offered by:* Canadian Association of Special Libraries and Information Services. *Winner:* Brian Land.

CIS/GODORT/ALA Documents to the People Award— $1,000. For effectively encouraging the use of federal documents in support of library services. *Offered by:* ALA Government Documents Round Table. *Donor:* Congressional Information Service, Inc. *Winner:* Mary Redmond.

CLA Dafoe Scholarship—$1,750. For a Canadian citizen or landed immigrant to attend an accredited Canadian library school. *Offered by:* Canadian Library Association. *Winner:* Caroline Daniel.

CLA Outstanding Service to Librarianship Award. *Offered by:* Canadian Library Association. *Winner:* Ken Haycock.

CLR Grants. For a list of the recipients of CLR grants for the 1990–1991 academic year, see the report from the Council on Library Resources, in Part 2.

CLTA Achievement in Literacy Award. For an innovative literacy program by a public library board. *Offered by:* Canadian Library Trustee Association. *Winner:* Saint John Regional Library Board, NB.

CLTA Merit Award. For outstanding leadership in the advancement of public library trusteeship and public library service in Canada. *Offered by:* Canadian Library Trustees Association. *Winner:* Ian MacDonald, New Brunswick.

CSLA Award for Outstanding Congregational Librarian. For distinguished service to the congregation and/or community through devotion to the congregational library. *Offered by:* Church and Synagogue Library Association. *Winner:* Helen Sheets.

CSLA Award for Outstanding Congregational Library. For responding in creative and innovative ways to the library's mission of reaching and serving the congregation and/or the wider community. *Offered by:* Church and Synagogue Library Association. *Winner:* Not awarded in 1991.

CSLA Award for Outstanding Contribution to Congregational Libraries. For providing inspiration, guidance, leadership, or resources to enrich the field of church or synagogue librarianship. *Offered by:* Church and Synagogue Library Association. *Winner:* Claudia Hannaford.

Francis Joseph Campbell Citation and Award. For an outstanding contribution to the advancement of library service to the blind. *Offered by:* Section on Library Service to the Blind and Physically Handicapped of ALA's Association of Specialized and Cooperative Library Agencies. *Winner:* Stuart Carothers.

Canadian School Executive Distinguished Service Award for School Administrators. *Offered by:* Canadian School Library Association. *Winner:* Not awarded in 1991.

Canebsco School Library Media Periodical Award. *Offered by:* Canadian School Library Association. *Winner: The Alberta Learning Resources Council Newsletter,* Teddy Moline and Sylvia Ewanchuk, eds.

Andrew Carnegie Medal. For excellence in children's video. *Offered by:* Carnegie Corporation of New York. *Winner: Ralph S. Mouse,* produced by George McQuilkin and John Matthews (Churchill Films).

Carnegie Reading List Awards — $1,800. *Offered by:* ALA Publishing Committee. *Winners:* Coretta Scott King Award Task Force of the SSRT; ALA Association for Library Service to Children, for How to Raise a Reader.

James Bennett Childs Award. For a distinguished contribution to documents librarianship. *Offered by:* ALA Government Documents Round Table. *Winner:* Not awarded in 1991.

David H. Clift Scholarship — $3,000. For a worthy student to begin a program of library education at the graduate level. *Offered by:* ALA Awards Committee, Standing Committee on Library Education. *Winners:* Anne Marie Hudson, Margaret M. Kulis.

C. F. W. Coker Prize. *Offered by:* Society of American Archivists. *Winner:* Historical Documents Inventory of the New York Historical Resources Center at Cornell University for outstanding finding aids and innovative development in archival descriptive tools.

Colonial Dames Scholarship. *Offered by:* Society of American Archivists. *Winners:* Mary Lee Perona, Mary Frances Heathwaite.

Cunningham Memorial International Fellowship — $3,500. A six-month grant and travel expenses in the United States and Canada for a foreign librarian. *Offered by:* Medical Library Association. *Winner:* Ruitong Zhang (China).

John Cotton Dana Award. For exceptional support and encouragement of special librarianship. *Offered by:* Special Libraries Association. *Winner:* Dorothy McGarry.

John Cotton Dana Library Public Relations Award. *Offered by:* ALA Library Administration and Management Association with the H. W. Wilson Company. *Winners: College or University Library Category:* Friends of Louisiana State University Libraries; *Library Associations Category:* British Columbia Library Association; *Public Library Category:* Atlanta-Fulton County (GA) Public Library; Cumberland County (NC) Public Library and Information Center; George County (MS) Library; Multnomah County (OR) Library; Nappanee (IN) Public Library; Pikes Peak Library District, Colorado Springs, CO; Prince Georges County Memorial Library System, Hyattsville, MD; Spokane (WA) Public Library; Coronado (CA) Public Library; *School Library Category:* Harry Spence Elementary School, LaCrosse, WI; Holloway Middle School Library, Whitehouse, TX; Metropolitan School District, Washington Township Media Services, Indianapolis, IN; *Special Library Category:* Animal Welfare Information Center, National Agriculture Library/USDA, Beltsville, MD; *State Library Category:* Illinois State Library, Springfield, IL.

Louise Darling Medal. For significant contributions to health sciences librarianship. *Offered by:* Medical Library Association. *Winner:* Dottie Eakin.

Dartmouth Medal. For achievement in creating reference works of outstanding quality and significance. *Offered by:* ALA Reference and Adult Services Division. *Winner: Encyclopedia of the Holocaust* (Macmillan); *Honor Certificate: Art Across America* (Abbeville).

Watson Davis Award. For a significant long-term contribution to the American Society for Information Science. *Offered by:* American Society for Information Science. *Winner:* Mickie Voges.

Denali Press Award. *Offered by:* ALA Reference and Adult Services Division. *Winner: Harlem Renaissance and Beyond: Literary Biographies of 100 Black Women Writers, 1900-1945* by Lorraine Roses and Ruth Randolph (G. K. Hall).

Melvil Dewey Medal. For recent creative professional achievement, particularly in library management, library training, cataloging and classification, and the tools and techniques of librarianship. *Offered by:* ALA Awards Committee. *Winner:* Lucia J. Rather.

Janet Doe Lectureship — $250. *Offered by:* Medical Library Association. *Winner:* Lois Ann Colaianni.

Robert B. Downs Intellectual Freedom Award. For significant contributions by a professional librarian in defense of the First Amendment. *Offered by:* Greenwood Press and Graduate School of Library Science,

University of Illinois at Urbana-Champaign. *Winner:* C. James Schmidt.

Vincent H. Duckles Award — $500. For the best book-length bibliography or music reference work. *Offered by:* Music Library Association. *Winners:* Hans Joachim Schulze and Christoff Wolff, for *Bach Compendium: Analytisch-bibliographisches Repertorium der Werke Johann Sebastian Bachs* (Leipzig: Edition Peters; Frankfurt, N.Y.: C. F. Peters, 1985-1989).

Miriam Dudley Bibliographic Instruction Award. For leadership in academic library instruction. *Offered by:* ALA Association of College and Research Librarians and Mountainside Publishing. *Winner:* Carla Stoffle.

ECONO-CLAD Literature Program Award. *Offered by:* ALA Association for Library Service to Children and ALA Young Adult Library Services Association. *Winners:* Ellen Fader, Constance Johnson.

Margaret A. Edwards Award. *Offered by:* ALA Young Adult Library Services Association. *Winner:* Robert Cormier.

Ida and George Eliot Prize — $100. For an essay published in any journal in the preceding calendar year that has been judged most effective in furthering medical librarianship. *Offered by:* Medical Library Association. *Donor:* Login Brothers Books. *Winner:* Not awarded in 1991.

FLRT Achievement Award. For leadership or achievement in the promotion of library and information service and the information profession in the federal community. *Offered by:* ALA Federal Librarians Round Table. *Winner:* Elizabeth S. Knauff.

Facts on File Grant — $1,000. For a librarian who has made current affairs more meaningful to adults. *Offered by:* ALA Reference and Adult Services Division. *Winner:* Gale Borden Public Library District, Elgin, IL.

Fellows' Posner Prize. For the best article in the *American Archivist Journal. Offered by:* Society of American Archivists. *Winner:* James O'Toole.

Muriel Fuller Scholarship. *Offered by:* Church and Synagogue Library Association. *Winner:* Joyce D. Philpott.

Gale Research Award for Excellence in Business Librarianship. *Offered by:* ALA Reference and Adult Services Division. *Winner:* Gerald L. Gill.

Gale Research Award for Excellence in Reference and Adult Services. *Offered by:* ALA Reference and Adult Services Division. *Winner:* University of Arkansas Library, Fayetteville, for its *Arkansas Periodical Index.*

Gale Research Company Financial Development Award—$2,500. *Offered by:* American Library Association. *Donor:* Gale Research Company. *Winner:* Bud Werner Memorial Library, Steamboat Springs, CO.

Walter Gerboth Award—$500. To support research in the first five years as a music librarian. *Offered by:* Music Library Association. *Winner:* Alan A. Green.

Louise Giles Minority Scholarship—$3,000. For a worthy student who is a U.S. or Canadian citizen and is also a member of a principal minority group. *Offered by:* ALA Awards Committee, Office for Library Personnel Resources Advisory Committee. *Winners:* Judith Ann Bruce, Ngoc-My Guidarelli.

Murray Gottlieb Prize—$100. For the best unpublished essay submitted by a medical librarian on the history of some aspect of health sciences or a detailed description of a library exhibit. *Offered by:* Medical Library Association. *Donor:* Ralph and Jo Grimes. *Winner:* Mary Rhinelander McCarl.

Grolier Award for Research in School Librarianship in Canada—$1,000. For theoretical or applied research that advances the field of school librarianship. *Offered by:* Canadian School Library Association. *Winner:* Larry Amey.

Grolier Foundation Award—$1,000. For an unusual contribution to the stimulation and guidance of reading by children and young people through high school age, for continuing service, or one particular contribution of lasting value. *Offered by:* ALA Awards Committee. *Donor:* Grolier Foundation. *Winner:* Dorothy M. Broderick.

Grolier National Library Week Grant. *Offered by:* ALA National Library Week Committee. *Winner:* Not awarded in 1991.

G. K. Hall Award for Library Literature. *Offered by:* American Library Association. *Winner:* Wayne A. Wiegand.

Philip M. Hamer–Elizabeth Hamer Kegan Award. For increasing public awareness of a specific body of documents. *Offered by:* Society of American Archivists. *Winners:* James D. Folts, Larry Hackman, Judy Hohmann.

Jane Anne Hannigan Research Award—$500. *Offered by:* Association for Library and Information Science Education. *Winner:* Holly Willett.

Frances Henne Award. For a school library media specialist with five years' or less experience who demonstrates leadership qualities. *Offered by:* ALA American Association of School Librarians and R. R. Bowker Company. *Winner:* David Wayne Calender, Wickersham Elementary School, Lancaster, PA.

Richard S. Hill Award. For the best article-length bibliography or article on music librarianship—$250. *Offered by:* Music Library Association. *Winner:* Gillian B. Anderson, for "Putting the Experience of the World at the Nation's Command: Music at the Library of Congress, 1800-1917" *Journal of the American Musicological Society* Vol. 42 (1989), pp. 108-149.

Oliver Wendell Holmes Award. *Offered by:* Society of American Archivists. *Winner:* Julie Stacker.

(John Ames) Humphrey/Forest Press Award. *Offered by:* ALA International Relations Committee. *Winner:* Hwa-wei Lee.

ISI Information Science Doctoral Dissertation Scholarship. *Offered by:* American Society for Information Science. *Donor:* Institute for Scientific Information. *Winner:* Diane H. Sonnenwald, Rutgers Univ.

ISI Scholarship—$1,000. For beginning doctoral candidates in library/information science. *Offered by:* Special Libraries Association. *Donor:* Institute for Scientific Information. *Winner:* Not awarded in 1991.

John Phillip Imroth Memorial Award for Intellectual Freedom—$500. For a notable contribution to intellectual freedom and remarkable personal courage. *Offered by:* ALA Intellectual Freedom Round Table. *Winner:* Christopher Merrett.

Information Plus Continuing Education Scholarship. For a school library media specialist to attend an ALA or AASL preconference or regional workshop. *Offered by:* ALA American Association of School Librarians and Information Plus. *Winner:* Elinor "Maureen" White, Johnston Elementary School, Abilene, TX.

Intellectual Freedom Round Table State Program Award. *Offered by:* ALA Intellectual Freedom Round Table. *Donor:* Social Issues Resources Series, Inc. (SIRS). *Winner:* Oregon Intellectual Freedom Clearinghouse.

JASIS Paper Award. For the outstanding paper published in the *Journal of the American Society for Information Science. Offered by:* American Society for Information Science. *Winners:* Donna Harman and Gerald Candela, for Retrieving Records from a Gigabyte of Text on a Minicomputer Using Statistical Ranking.

J. Franklin Jameson Award. For archival advocacy. *Offered by:* Society of American Archivists. *Winners:* Andrew W. Mellon Foundation, N.Y. Assemblyman William B. Hoyt (D-Buffalo).

J. Morris Jones-World Book Encyclopedia-ALA Goal Award. *See* World Book-ALA Goal Awards.

Coretta Scott King Awards. *Offered by:* ALA Social Responsibilities Round Table. *Winners:* Mildred D. Taylor for *The Road to Memphis;* Leo and Diane Dillon for illustrations in *Aida.*

LITA/Gaylord Award for Achievement in Library and Information Technology. For distinguished leadership, notable development or application of technology, superior accomplishments in research or education, or original contributions to the literature of the field. *Offered by:* ALA Library and Information Technology Association. *Winner:* Clifford Lynch.

LITA/OCLC Minority Scholarship in Library Information Technology. *Offered by:* ALA Library and Information Technology Association. *Winner:* Alvaro Victor Simon.

Sheila Suen Lai Scholarship – $500. *Offered by:* Chinese-American Librarians Association. *Winner:* Wu Chen Chen.

Harold Lancour Scholarship – $1,000. For graduate study in a foreign country related to the applicant's work or schooling. *Offered by:* Beta Phi Mu. *Winner:* Lori D. Foulke.

Sister M. Claude Lane Award. For a significant contribution to the field of religious archives. *Offered by:* Society of American Archivists. *Winner:* Elizabeth Yakel.

Samuel Lazerow Fellowship – $1,000. For outstanding contributions to acquisitions or technical services in an academic or research library. *Offered by:* ALA Association of College and Research Libraries and the Institute for Scientific Information. *Winner:* Not awarded in 1991.

Katharine Kyes Leab and Daniel J. Leab *American Book Prices Current* Award. *Offered by:* ALA Association of College and Research Libraries. *Winners: Expensive:* Stephen Harvard: A Life in Letters, Harvard University Library; *Moderate:* The Face of the Moon: Galileo to Apollo, Linda Hall Library; *Inexpensive:* Fifteenth Century Italian Woodcuts from the Biblioteca Classense, Ravenna, University of Toronto, Thomas Fisher Rare Book Library.

Joseph Leiter Lectureship. *Offered by:* Medical Library Association. *Winner:* Joshua Lederberg.

Waldo Gifford Leland Prize. For writing of superior excellence and usefulness in the field of archival history, theory, or practice. *Offered by:* Society of American Archivists. *Winners:* Richard J. Cox, for American Archival Analysis: The Recent Development of the Archival Profession in the United States; Marie B. Allen and Michael Miller, for The Intergovernmental Records Project Phase 1 Report.

Joseph W. Lippincott Award – $1,000. For distinguished service to the profession of librarianship, such service to include outstanding participation in the activities of professional library associations, notable published professional writing, or other significant activity on behalf of the profession and its aims. *Offered by:* ALA Awards Committee. *Donor:* Joseph W. Lippincott. *Winner:* Peggy Sullivan.

MLA Award for Distinguished Public Service. *Offered by:* Medical Library Association. *Winner:* Senator Dale Bumpers (D-Ark.)

MLA Award for Excellence and Achievement in Hospital Librarianship. *Offered by:* Medical Library Association. *Winner:* Pamela Jean Jajko.

MLA Citation. For distinguished service to music librarianship. *Offered by:* Music Library Association. *Winner:* Lenore Coral.

MLA Continuing Education Award. *Offered by:* Medical Library Association. *Winner:* Patricia J. Hamilton.

MLA Doctoral Fellowship—$1,000. *Offered by:* Medical Library Association. *Donor:* Institute for Scientific Information. *Winner:* Not awarded in 1991.

MLA President's Award. For an outstanding contribution to medical librarianship. *Offered by:* Medical Library Association. *Winner:* Not awarded in 1991.

MLA Research, Development, and Demonstration Projects Grants. *Offered by:* Medical Library Association. *Winners:* Joanne G. Marshall; Barbara Carlson and Robert Poyer.

MLA Scholarship—$2,000. For graduate study in medical librarianship at an ALA-accredited library school. *Offered by:* Medical Library Association. *Winner:* Joyce Condon.

MLA Scholarship for Minority Students—$2,000. *Offered by:* Medical Library Association. *Winner:* Louis Lik-Fu Tong.

John P. McGovern Award Lectureship—$500. *Offered by:* Medical Library Association. *Winners:* George D. Lundberg II, Stephen P. Lock.

Maclean Hunter Teacher-Librarian of the Year Award. *Offered by:* Canadian Library Association. *Winner:* Iris Spurrell.

Margaret Mann Citation. For outstanding professional achievement in the area of cataloging and classification. *Offered by:* ALA Association for Library Collections and Technical Services. *Winner:* Margaret F. Maxwell.

Allie Beth Martin Award—$2,000. For an outstanding librarian. *Offered by:* ALA Public Library Association. *Donor:* Baker & Taylor. *Winner:* Sandra M. Neerman.

Frederic G. Melcher Scholarship—$4,000. For young people who wish to enter the field of library service to children. *Offered by:* ALA Association for Library Service to Children. *Winners:* Molly K. McConnell, Elizabeth Beaumont Lee.

Margaret E. Monroe Library Adult Services Award. *Offered by:* ALA Reference and Adult Services Division. *Winner:* Kathleen M. Heim.

Bessie Boehm Moore Award. *Offered by:* American Library Association. *Winner:* Rochester Hills (MI) Public Library.

Isadore Gilbert Mudge Citation. For a distinguished contribution to reference librarianship. *Offered by:* ALA Reference and Adult Services Division. *Winner:* Peter Watson-Boone.

Gerd Muehsam Memorial Award. For the best paper on a subject related to art or visual resources curatorship. *Offered by:* Art Libraries Society of North America. *Winner:* Not awarded in 1991.

NMRT/EBSCO Scholarship. *Offered by:* ALA New Members Round Table. *Winner:* Margaret M. Kulis.

NMRT Professional Development Grant. *See* 3M/NMRT Professional Development Grant.

Martinus Nijhoff International West European Specialist Study Grant. *Offered by:* ALA Association of College and Research Libraries. *Winner:* Nancy S. Reinhardt.

Marcia C. Noyes Award. For an outstanding contribution to medical librarianship. *Offered by:* Medical Library Association. *Winner:* Irwin H. Pizer.

Oberly Award. For bibliography in the agricultural sciences. *Offered by:* ALA Association of College and Research Libraries. *Winner: Useful Palms of the World: A Synoptic Bibliography* by Michael J. Balick and Hans T. Beck.

Eli M. Oboler Memorial Award. *Offered by:* ALA Intellectual Freedom Round Table. *Winner:* Not awarded in 1991.

Shirley Olofson Memorial Award. For individuals to attend their second annual conference of ALA. *Offered by:* ALA New Members Round Table. *Winner:* Deb Tuma Church.

Eva Judd O'Meara Award. For the best book or score review published in *MLA Notes*. *Offered by:* Music Library Association. *Winner:* William Kraft, for his review of Stravinsky's *L'Histoire du Soldat* ed. by Johann Carewe and James Blades (*MLA Notes*, 46, no. 1, pp. 212–216).

Helen Keating Ott Award. *Offered by:* Church and Synagogue Library Association. *Winner:* Miriam Johnson.

PLA Library Video Award. *Offered by:* ALA Public Library Association. *Winner:* Dixon (IL) Public Library.

Pease Award. For superior writing achievement by a student of archival administration. *Offered by:* Society of American Archivists. Not awarded in 1991.

Howard V. Phalin-World Book Graduate Scholarship in Library Science—$2,500 (maximum). For a Canadian citizen or landed immigrant to attend an accredited library school in Canada or the United States. *Offered by:* Canadian Library Association. *Winner:* Joy McGregor.

Esther J. Piercy Award. For contributions to librarianship in the field of technical services by younger members of the profession. *Offered by:* ALA Resources and Technical Services Division. *Winner:* Carol Pitts Hawks.

Plenum Scholarship—$1,000. For graduate study leading to a doctorate in library and information science. *Offered by:* Special Libraries Association. *Winner:* Yvonne Chandler.

Herbert W. Putnam Honor Award—$500. A grant-in-aid for an American librarian of outstanding ability for travel, writing, or any other use that might improve his or her service to the profession. *Offered by:* American Library Association. *Winner:* Not awarded in 1991.

Putnam Grosset Group Awards. To attend the ALA annual conference. *Offered by:* ALA Association for Library Service to Children. *Winners:* Eleanor A. Brust, Karen Quinn-Wisniewski, Sara Wright Ashworth, Cathleen A. Towey.

RTSD/Blackwell North America Scholarship. *See* ALCTS/Blackwell North America Resources Section Scholarship.

Readex/GODORT/ALA Catherine J. Reynolds Award. *Offered by:* ALA Government Documents Round Table. *Winners:* Suzanne Clark, John Shuler, Laura Lee Carter.

Sarah Rebecca Reed Scholarship. For study at an ALA-accredited library school. *Offered by:* Beta Phi Mu. *Winner:* Ann B. Kratz.

Reference Service Press Award. *Offered by:* ALA Reference and Adult Services Division. *Winner:* In-house Databases: An Opportunity for Progressive Librarians, by A. Annell Ahtola *(RQ,* 29, Fall 1989).

Rittenhouse Award—$200. For the best unpublished paper on medical librarianship submitted by a student enrolled in, or having been enrolled in, a course for credit in an ALA-accredited library school, or a trainee in an internship program in medical librarianship. *Offered by:* Medical Library Association. *Donor:* Rittenhouse Medical Bookstore. *Winner:* Not awarded in 1991.

Frank Bradway Rogers Information Advancement Award—$500. For an outstanding contribution to knowledge of health science information delivery. *Offered by:* Medical Library Association. *Donor:* Institute for Scientific Information. *Winners:* Jack G. Goellner, Charles Goldstein, Richard E. Lucier, Victor A. McKusick.

SAA Distinguished Service Award. *Offered by:* Society of American Archivists. *Winner:* Billy Graham Center Archives.

SAA Fellows. *Offered by:* Society of American Archivists. *Winners:* Timothy L. Ericson, Steven L. Hensen, Charles G. Palm, Mary Lynn Ritzenthaler.

SLA Affirmative Action Scholarship—$6,000. *Offered by:* Special Libraries Association. *Winner:* Ada Pagan.

SLA Fellows. *Offered by:* Special Libraries Association. *Winners:* Anne P. Mintz, Emily Mobley, James B. Tchobanoff.

SLA Hall of Fame Award. *Offered by:* Special Libraries Association. *Winners:* Efren W. Gonzalez, Dorothy Kasman, Charles D. Missar, Mary Vasilakis.

SLA Honorary Member. *Offered by:* Special Libraries Association. *Winner:* Joseph Becker.

SLA Meckler Award for Innovations in Technology. *Offered by:* Special Libraries Association. *Winner:* Susan Ardis.

SLA Member Recognition for Excellence in Public Relations. *Offered by:* Special Libraries Association. *Winner:* Carol Ginsburg.

SLA President's Award. *Offered by:* Special Libraries Association. *Winner:* Barbara S. Mattscheck.

SLA Professional Award. *Offered by:* Special Libraries Association. *Winners:* James M. Matarazzo, Laurence Prusak.

SLA Public Relations Award—$1,000. For an outstanding article on special librarianship. *Offered by:* Special Libraries Association. *Winner:* Gloria Stashower, for Checking Out Library Automation.

SLA Research Grant. *Offered by:* Special Libraries Association. *Winner:* Joanne G. Marshall.

SLA Scholarships—$6,000. For students with financial need who show potential for special librarianship. *Offered by:* Special Libraries Association. *Winners:* Meredith Eliassen, Kathryn Ellis, Anita Szafran.

SLA H. W. Wilson Award. For the most outstanding article in the past year's *Special Libraries*. *Offered by:* Special Libraries Association. *Winners:* James Matarazzo and Laurence Prusak, for Valuing Corporate Libraries.

SRRT/Gay and Lesbian Task Force, Gay and Lesbian Book Awards. *Offered by:* ALA Social Responsibilities Round Table. *Winners: Crime Against Nature* by Minnie Bruce Pratt (fiction); *Encyclopedia of Homosexuality,* ed. Wayne Dynes (nonfiction).

K. G. Saur Award for Best *College and Research Libraries* Article. *Offered by:* ALA Association of College and Research Libraries. *Winner:* The Electronic Revolution in Libraries: Microfilm Déjà Vu, by Susan A. Cady (July 1990).

Margaret B. Scott Award of Merit—$400. For the development of school libraries in Canada. *Offered by:* Canadian School Library Association and Ontario Library Association. *Winner:* John Tooth.

Frank B. Sessa Scholarship. For continuing education for a Beta Phi Mu member. *Offered by:* Beta Phi Mu. *Winner:* Lauretta McCusker.

John Sessions Memorial Award. For significant efforts to work with the labor community. *Offered by:* ALA Reference and Adult Services Division. *Winner:* Department of Archives and Special Collections, Ohio University Libraries, Athens.

Jesse H. Shera Award for Research. *Offered by:* ALA Library Research Round Table. *Winners:* Patricia Dewdney, Roma M. Harris.

(Louis) Shores—Oryx Press Award. *Offered by:* ALA Reference and Adult Services Division. *Winner:* Helen K. Wright.

May K. Simon Scholarship—$500. For a student who intends to become a Judaica librarian. *Offered by:* Association of Jewish Libraries. *Winner:* Sharona Wachs.

Social Issues Resources Series, Inc., Peace Award. *Offered by:* ALA Social Responsibilities Round Table. *Winner:* Faye A. Lander.

Pat Tabler Memorial Award. *Offered by:* Church and Synagogue Library Association. *Winner:* Leila Sehesta.

3M/NMRT Professional Development Grant. To encourage professional development and participation of new librarians in ALA and NMRT activities. To cover expenses for recipients to attend ALA conferences. *Offered by:* ALA New Members Round Table. *Winners:* Joni Gomez, Glendora Johnson-Cooper, Ann L. Pinnack.

(Leonard) Wertheimer Multilingual Award. *Offered by:* ALA Public Library Association. *Winner:* Adriana Acauan Tandler.

Whitney-Carnegie Awards. *Offered by:* ALA Publishing Committee. *Winners:* Julia Rholes, for Water Resources: A Sourcebook; J. Gormly Miller, for A Guide to the Literature and Sources of Information on Employment Relations in the U.S.; David Pfeiffer, for An Annotated Bibliography of Disability Studies; Sharon Rush, Betty Taylor, and Robert J. Munro, for Bibliographic Research Guide on Feminist Jurisprudence; Helaine Selin, for Comparative Scientific Traditions: A Bibliography; Anne Dickason, for Continuing Education for the Professions: A Selective Annotated Bibliography, 1985-1990; Nancy O'Brien, for Alice, Jerry, Dick and Jane: Catalog of Historical Curriculum Materials at the University of Illinois, 1821-1940; Ellen Mazur Thomson, for American Graphic Arts Design: A Bibliography of Visual Communications; Barbara Baskin and Karen Harris, for Interdisciplinary Books for Children; Suzanne D. Gyeszly, for Eastern Europe: A Resource Guide; Susan Duffy, for The Political Left in American Theatre During the 1920s and 1930s: A Bibliographic Sourcebook; Alan M. Greenberg, for Gay/Lesbian Periodicals Index; Connie Wu and James E. Young, for Information Guides to Engineering Journals.

Laura Ingalls Wilder Medal. *Offered by:* ALA Association for Library Service to Children. *Winner:* Not awarded in 1991.

H. W. Wilson Company. Scholarship—$2,000. Available to a Canadian citizen or landed immigrant for pursuit of studies at an accredited Canadian library school. *Offered by:* Canadian Library Association. *Winner:* Beth Tompkins.

H. W. Wilson Library Periodical Award—$500. To a periodical published by a local, state, or regional library, library group, or library association in the United States or Canada that has made an outstanding contribution to librarianship. *Offered by:* ALA Awards Committee. *Donor:* H. W. Wilson

Company. *Winner: Mississippi Libraries,* Jackson, MS.

H. W. Wilson Library Staff Development Grant—$2,500. *Offered by:* ALA Awards Committee. *Winner:* South Central Research Library Council, Ithaca, NY.

Justin Winsor Prize Essay. *Offered by:* ALA Library History Round Table. *Winner:* Margaret F. Stieg, for Post-War Purge of German Public Libraries, Democracy, and the American Reaction.

World Book-ALA Goal Awards—$5,000. To support programs that recognize, advance, and implement the goals and objectives of the American Library Association. *Offered by:* American Library Association. *Donor:* World Book-Childcraft International, Inc. *Winners:* ALA Public Information Office; ALA Chapter Relations Office; ALA President-Elect, The Right to Know.

YALSA/*SLJ* Young Adult Author Achievement Award. *Offered by:* ALA Young Adult Library Services Association and *School Library Journal. Winner:* Robert Cormier, for works including *The Chocolate Wars.*

YALSA/VOYA Research Grant. *Offered by:* ALA Young Adult Library Services Association. *Winner:* Not awarded in 1991.

Part 4
Research and Statistics

Library Research and Statistics

Research on Libraries and Librarianship in 1991

Mary Jo Lynch
Director, ALA Office for Research and Statistics

In 1991, the library and information science community, dismayed by the recent closing of prestigious schools, began to face seriously the cataclysmic changes taking
place in the field. The editor of the *Journal of the American Society for Information
Science (JASIS)* expressed the problem succinctly:

> The library community, plodding along at what they may think has been a fairly furious
> pace, is being overtaken by waves of scientists, technologists, and entrepreneurs who are
> moving even faster. To retain their identity as a community, library and information
> scientists must change. But how; and by how much?

The *JASIS* editor offered one guide to the future by reprinting an article originally published in 1980, Laurence Heilprin's "The Library Community at Technological and Philosophical Crossroads: Necessary and Sufficient Conditions for
Survival." Heilprin argues that "In order to attain control over its own destiny the library community must keep its own members up to date educationally; and beyond
this, itself perform the research that alone creates and keeps leadership in its field."

The importance of research to the survival of the field was a prominent theme in
the June 1991 report of the ALA Special Committee on Library School Closings,
otherwise known as the "Shank Report," after its chairperson, Russell Shank of
UCLA. Despite its title, the committee recommended that ALA *not* focus on library
school closings but instead "establish a future-oriented activity aimed at recasting the
image of the functions of libraries in the information age and specifying the educational and research needs for the future."

As one component, the committee recommended inquiry into five areas:

- Information providers in the twenty-first century
- Libraries among the information agencies
- The workforce
- The educational system
- Research

Regarding the last, the Shank Report lists the following questions as essential:

In what general areas is research needed to advance the profession? Which disciplines are likely to be vital in the performance of relevant research? How is research best related to the development and operation of libraries and their information services and their response to the needs of a changing society?

W. David Penniman, president of the Council on Library Resources, offered some possible answers to those questions in the Lazerow Lecture at Simmons College in September 1991. In "Libraries and the Future: Critical Research Needs," Penniman stressed his proactive vision of libraries as information delivery systems and the need for major change. He identified four general areas where CLR will focus its research dollars:

- Human resources—"the end-to-end issues of attracting, educating, maintaining, and advancing individuals in the information services profession."
- Economics of information services—"the full range of economic issues associated with libraries and related information services, including both micro- and macroeconomic issues."
- Infrastructure—"the systems, services, and facilities that are drawn upon to help libraries and other information services operate more efficiently and effectively. Included . . . are communication networks, bibliographic utilities, software and hardware vendor communities, and publishers."
- Processing and access—"*All* processing undertaken by an information service should be for the purpose of access. . . . [but] if we look carefully at today's libraries, we find that much of the resource is consumed to support internal processes [and] it is often unclear how these processes directly (or indirectly) benefit the user."

Under each topic, Penniman listed questions that need answers and pledged that "the council stands ready to help those who are willing to undertake the necessary (and painful) effort of redesigning the information systems we call libraries."

Council on Library Resources

The 1991 Annual Report of the Council on Library Resources (CLR) describes four projects mentioned in Penniman's speech. The funding program was developed in response to the recent "Statement from the Research Library Committee." As summarized in the 1991 Annual Report, the committee stated that the information base for teaching and learning is being rapidly transformed by integrated information technologies—computers, telecommunications, and text storage systems—but that the way in which libraries and faculties will deal with digitized information and virtually unbounded means of access is far from clear. Whether universities and their libraries will productively embrace information age capabilities or be engulfed by them is also uncertain. In response, CLR invited research universities to submit proposals to undertake "policy studies and implementation planning related to future library resources and services."

Four $100,000 grants were made for projects at Columbia University, Harvard, SUNY, and Triangle Research Libraries Network. [For further information, see the Council on Library Resources article in Part 2—*Ed.*]

In addition to these major grants, the 1991 Annual Report describes a number of smaller ones:

- Columbia University ($4,500). To study by qualitative and quantitative analysis the information needs of members of the academic community at a research university. The investigators will examine the relationships among characteristics of the information seeker, specific kinds of information need, the information environment as perceived by the information seeker, sources used to satisfy the need, and the factors involved in satisfying it. *Principal investigator:* Maxine H. Reneker, School of Library Service.

- Indiana University of Pennsylvania ($5,000). To develop an intelligent system that will narrow or expand the set of citations found in subject searches of online catalogs to make the online catalog an effective reference tool. *Principal investigator:* Mary Micco, professor, Department of Computer Science.

- Long Island University ($18,060). To study similarities between jobs in libraries and computing centers. The researcher will develop and test a methodology to analyze and evaluate the tasks of librarians and computer specialists in colleges that have integrated their information technology. The methodology will be used in college and university personnel systems in classifying jobs and compensating workers. *Principal investigator:* Anne Woodsworth, associate professor, Palmer School of Library and Information Science.

- Ohio State University ($3,100). To study innovative library projects that apply cutting-edge technology to library operations. The researcher will focus on the criteria that have made these projects successful. *Principal investigator:* Virginia Tiefel, director, Library User Education, University Libraries.

- State University of New York at Buffalo ($3,000). To determine the extent to which library resources are being used to provide access to nonbibliographic computer files. *Principal investigators:* Renee B. Bush, senior assistant librarian, Science and Engineering Library, and William E. McGrath, professor, School of Information and Library Studies.

- Texas A&M University ($2,245). To establish guidelines, procedures, and methodology for automated collection analysis and development based on the business collections of the Sterling C. Evans Library at Texas A&M. *Principal investigator:* Suzanne D. Gyeszly, coordinator, Social Sciences and Preservation, Sterling C. Evans Library.

- Texas A&M University ($3,000). To examine through statistical means use of periodicals housed in the Current Periodicals Department and back volumes in both paper and microformat. By defining and comparing use with such factors as subscription cost, impact, and relative value as reported by faculty, this study is to provide a model for use in making objective decisions concerning serials control. *Principal investigators:* Marifran Bustion, head, Serials Department, Sterling C. Evans Library, and John L. Eltinge, assistant professor, Statistics Department.

- University of California at Los Angeles ($810). To explore problems associated with discrepancies in the assignment of Library of Congress subject headings. *Principal investigators:* Elaine Svenonius, professor, Graduate School of Library and Information Science, and Dorothy McGarry, head of cataloging, Physical Sciences and Technology Libraries.

* University of California at Los Angeles ($4,600). To compare the impact of technology on the structure of functional departments in three research libraries. *Principal investigator:* Beverly Lynch, dean, Graduate School of Library and Information Science.
* University of California at Santa Cruz ($2,367). To study detailed statistics on remote use of the Melvyl Library System, a pioneering public access catalog system whose use has dramatically increased over the past few years. *Principal investigators:* Terry Ellen Ferl and Larry Millsap, librarians, University Library.
* University of Illinois at Urbana-Champaign ($4,000). To describe the history of Argentina's National Library under the directorship of Hugo Wast, 1931–1955. *Principal investigator:* Allan Metz, assistant professor, Latin American Library Services Unit.
* Yale University ($9,000). To establish a rapid alternative electronic distribution system for mathematics preprints and to explore how the electronic distribution of documents affects their use. *Project coordinators:* Katherine Branch, head, Science Libraries, and Ronald Coifman, professor, Mathematics Department.

CLR also provided support for meetings at two institutions that should lead to research:

* Drexel University ($16,760). To fund an invitational conference of leading public library researchers and managers designed to develop an agenda for advancing the state of measurement and evaluation in public libraries. The conference focused on the critical areas of research and development in evaluation of public library performance.
* University of Illinois at Urbana-Champaign ($28,786). To fund the second Advanced Research Institute to enhance the quality of research by some of the most promising and capable researchers on the library in transition.

Allerton Institute

The University of Illinois Graduate School of Library and Information Science sponsored a conference for practitioners interested in applied research, the thirty-third annual Allerton Institute in October 1991. "Applying Research to Practice: How to Use Data Collection and Research to Improve Library Management Decision-Making" was designed for librarians with responsibility for planning and analyzing library operations and services. Participants focused on when to conduct research as well as what questions to ask.

In the keynote address, Glenn Holt, executive director of the Saint Louis Public Library, spoke about "Research for Change: Creating Strategic Futures for Public Libraries." The conference combined presentations by experts with work in small groups. The topics and speakers were:

Use of Statistics for Management Decisions, Keith Lance (Colorado State Library) and Katy Sherlock (Library Research Center)

Evaluation Strategies, Nancy Van House (University of California at Berkeley)

Perils and Pitfalls in Survey Research, Joe Spaeth (Survey Research Lab, University of Illinois)

Communication and Dissemination of Research, Jane Robbins (University of Wisconsin at Madison)

The Ivory Tower or the Temple of Doom? Some Questions on Applying Research, Margaret Kimmel (University of Pittsburgh)

How Much Do You Really Need to Know about Research Methods, Jana Bradley (University of Illinois)

When Is a Problem a Research Problem? Blaise Cronin (Indiana University)

Identifying Roles in the Research Process, Debra Johnson (University of Wisconsin at Madison)

The proceedings of the conference will be published late in 1992.

Research at OCLC

The *Annual Review of OCLC Research, June 1990–June 1991* has the same four major sections as earlier editions: (1) OCLC Project Reports, (2) External and Collaborative Research, (3) Library and Information Science Research Grant Program, and (4) Distinguished Seminar Series. The 1990–1991 edition also includes a thoughtful and succinct summary, by Office of Research Director Martin Dillon, of the work completed and in progress in four strategic areas.

"Strategic Areas and Associated Projects" includes seven projects under way to enhance "Effective Use of the Online Union Catalog." Dillon notes that "after careful analysis and testing, computer processes are now in place to detect and resolve potentially duplicate records." Another problem is erroneous headings. In this area, "previous research has led to algorithms that detect and correct headings with common tagging, style, or typographical errors. . . . [And] more recent research focuses on identifying obsolete Library of Congress subject headings and matching them with headings currently in use." Several projects "explore how to streamline the cataloging task through applied technology."

The Electronic Library is the second strategic area, and several OCLC projects investigate how one might look. The CORE (Chemical Online Retrieval Experiment) project—a joint effort with the American Chemical Society (including Chemical Abstracts Service), Bellcore, Cornell University, and OCLC—is purportedly building the largest database of its kind. Consisting of the full text and images from seven years of back issues of 20 chemical journals, the CORE system will deliver information online to scientists and students in the chemical sciences as part of their everyday work routine. The Internet Resources project, funded by the U.S. Department of Education, Office of Library Programs, examines the nature of electronic information available on Internet and the problems of describing, locating, and accessing this information.

The third strategic area, Image Processing, involves capturing and preserving the world's knowledge on optical media. OCLC's subsidiary MAPS (the MicrogrAphics

Preservation Service) has mounted a large-scale effort to microfilm threatened materials. To gain a fundamental understanding of the nature and condition of such materials, OCLC is collaborating with the State Library of Ohio to sample and study books from Ohio Libraries. OCLC is also exploring the capabilities and applications of digital scanning and optical character recognition (OCR) either as an alternative or as a complement to microfilming.

Central to success in these three areas is work in the fourth strategic area, Interface Design. OCLC's Usability Laboratory, put into service for the first time in Summer 1990 to evaluate the ease of learning and using a product, continues to function. Significant progress can be achieved in a short time through iterative testing and user feedback.

Dillon summarizes the output of his office in four categories of research product. "Much of our effort is directly related to enhancing existing products and services, developing prototype systems, devising reusable software tools, or seeking fundamental knowledge and insight." Speaking of the fourth category, he says, "In traditional terms, we do very little basic research. It is all applied — to solving the problems that our members are having or anticipating the problems they have as the technological landscape evolves."

U.S. Department of Education

Research and demonstration grants were awarded by this agency under two titles of the Higher Education Act administered by the Office of Library Programs within the Office for Educational Research and Improvement. Title II-B supported four projects, for a total of $288,953.

Two of the projects will focus on literacy:

- The Characteristics of Effective Literacy Programs: A Field Study. RMC Research Corporation. $62,949. *Principal investigator:* Andrew Seager.
- Environment and Organizational Factors Associated with the Development of Family Literacy Programs in U.S. Public Libraries. University of Wisconsin. $78,975. *Principal investigator:* Debra Johnson.

The third project builds on the work done to identify the public library's mission in PLA's *Planning and Role Setting for Public Libraries* (ALA, 1987).

- Assessment of the Public Library's Missions in Society. University of Minnesota. Center for Survey Research and the Carlson School of Management. $98,354. *Principal investigators:* William Craig and George D'Elia.

The fourth grant should provide libraries with information they need to operate effectively when the proposed National Research and Education Network becomes a reality.

- Assessing Information on the Internet: Toward Providing Library Services for Computer-Mediated Communication. Online Computer Library Center. $48,675. *Principal investigator:* Martin Dillon.

[Additional information on these and other grants can be found in the U.S. Department of Education Library Programs article in Part 2, under the heading "Library Research and Demonstration Programs" — *Ed.*]

Title II-D of the Higher Education Act, the College Library Technology and Cooperation Grants Program, awards grants in four categories: Networking, Combination (joint-use facilities, resources, equipment), Service to Institutions, and Research and Demonstration. In the last category, grants support research or demonstration projects to meet specialized national or regional needs in using technology to enhance library and information services. Seven awards were made in 1991 for a total of $850,226, all on the demonstration end of the research and demonstration continuum.

Two of the projects deal with improving online catalogs:

- Testing a New Design for Subject Access to Online Catalogs. University of Michigan. $95,500. *Principal investigator:* Karen Markey Drabenstott.
- Adaptive Network Library Interface. Rutgers University. $106,444. *Principal investigator:* Paul B. Kantor.

The following two projects are developing ways to store and share visual images:

- Architecture Slide Library Image Database. University of California at Berkeley. $60,000. *Principal investigator:* Barbara Morgan.
- Geography and Mapping Interactive Videodisc and Database. University of Wisconsin at Milwaukee. $219,396. *Principal investigators:* John Grozik, associate director, Educational Communications Division, and Sona Karentz Andrews, professor, Department of Geography.

Two projects are exploring new ways to make text available:

- A Digital Full-Text Biotechnology System. Georgetown University. $178,859. *Principal investigator:* Naomi C. Broering.
- Remote Reference Assistance for Electronic Information Resources over Networked Workstations. University of Texas at Austin. $100,664. *Principal investigator:* Harold W. Billings.

The seventh project uses new technology to teach basic library skills:

- Teaching Core Library Skills Through Multimedia and Computer-Assisted Design. San Francisco State University. $89,363. *Principal investigator:* Harriet Talan.

[Additional information on these grants can be found in the U.S. Department of Education Library Programs article in Part 2, under the heading "College Library Technology and Cooperation Grants Program" — *Ed.*]

Public Libraries

An important tool for public library research became available in April 1991, the first annual report of the Federal-State Cooperative System for Public Library Data (FSCS). *Public Libraries in 50 States and the District of Columbia: 1989,* published by the National Center for Education Statistics (NCES), contains 30 tables of basic descriptive statistics about collections, services, staffing, income, and expenditures from the more than 8,900 public libraries in the United States. Data are shown for the nation as a whole and by state.

In addition to the paper report, data are available in machine-readable form. NCES is also completing work on a universe file for FSCS. This computerized directory of public libraries will include branches and bookmobiles and will also contain major variables for sample selection.

NCES, NCLIS, and ALA organized an invitational seminar in November where ten leading researchers from the library community met with federal and state officials to discuss uses of the data and universe files for research and policy analysis. Researchers participating in the seminar included Thomas Childers, Drexel University; Phillip Clark, Saint John's University; Joan Durrance, University of Michigan; Charles McClure, Syracuse University; Verna Pungitore, Indiana University; Jane Robbins, University of Wisconsin; Bernard Vavrek, Clarion State University; Howard White, Drexel University; Robert Williams, University of South Carolina; and Douglas Zweizig, University of Wisconsin.

Another meeting in November 1991 focused on the people most likely to use public libraries: readers. The Library of Congress symposium "Developing the Lifetime Reading Habit: Libraries, Youth and Elders" was the occasion for unveiling the "Survey of Lifetime Readers" sponsored by the Library of Congress Center for the Book and the Book of the Month Club (BOMC). The purpose of this joint project was to learn more about the development of lifetime reading habits, including the socialization of readers in childhood, changes in reading habits during the lifespan, and the influence of childhood circumstances on subsequent reading habits. Information Analysis Systems Corporation of Mansfield Center, Connecticut, gathered data through a questionnaire mailed to a random sample of 5,000 BOMC subscribers.

Data from 2,032 of those sampled are not generalizable to a wider population, but they do describe lifetime readers who are interested in the topic of reading experiences. With that caveat in mind, the following conclusions are of interest:

- Children who read extensively become lifetime readers.
- Children will be helped in developing the reading habit if they see adult role models incorporating reading into their own lives.
- It is important that children have books available to them in the home and someone to read to them if they are to become lifelong readers.
- Even among these committed and well-educated readers, television plays a major role in their lives. In fact, on average, they spend more time watching television than reading.
- Major time commitments to schooling, work, and child rearing keep people from reading during periods in their lives.

The Coalition for Public Library Research — a group of public libraries that pay annual membership fees to support research and dissemination activities by the University of Illinois Graduate School of Library and Information Science (GSLIS) — received a report from Brett Sutton of the GSLIS faculty, who assessed the last ten years of long-range planning in public libraries. Focusing on staff, Sutton investigated their awareness of the planning process, level of participation, and degree of satisfaction with results. Sutton's work will soon be generally available through several articles and a monograph.

Another Coalition research project will study the impact of technology on work in public libraries. A pilot study in early 1992 will refine research methodologies for the larger study, using surveys and focus groups as well as logs of staff activity prompted by a randomly programmed beeper.

Research Staff in Library Associations

Several library organizations made staff changes in the area of research. At the Association of Research Libraries (ARL), Jaia Barrett replaced Jeffrey Gardner as director of the Office of Research and Development, and at the Special Libraries Association (SLA), Ann Thompson replaced Tobi Brimsek as research director.

At ALA, the name of the Office for Research (OFR) was changed to Office for Research and Statistics (ORS) on the recommendation of the ALA Executive Board Subcommittee. The subcommittee also recommended modifying the charge for the Office to read:

1 To collect and interpret data to support and inform decision-making at ALA;
2 to collect or facilitate the collection of consistent and pertinent statistical data and other research results related to libraries and librarians;
3 to monitor ongoing research related to libraries and disseminate information about such studies within and outside the profession;
4 to facilitate quality research design in the studies and collection of data initiated by the ALA Executive Board, Council, Offices, Committees, Divisions, Round Tables, and other ALA units and to provide technical assistance.

Researchers on BITNET

Researchers and interested others began using BITNET listservers to communicate in 1991. At the ALA Annual Conference, the Research Committee of the Association of College and Research Libraries (ACRL) sponsored "Mentoring and Academic Research: Using BITNET Conferencing to Encourage Research," a program that introduced ACRL's Pilot Project in Electronic Mentoring. Attendees heard several speeches about mentoring and about using electronic mail. They also received a handbook of information about the project, which will be updated electronically.

The Library and Information Science Research List on BITNET is a "closed, unmoderated, unarchived list" managed by "list owner" Tom Peters of Mankato State University (TAPETERS@MSUS1). Mentors and protégés are organized into eight subgroups on the following topics: Bibliographical Control (two groups), Library Effectiveness (two groups), Collection Management, Expert Systems, Scholarly Communication, and Understanding the User.

ACRL Research Committee Chairperson Vicki Gregory (University of South Florida School of Library and Information Science) conducted an informal survey of project participants in November 1991. She concluded that some subgroups were more productive than others but the project as a whole was not as successful as had been hoped.

Another attempt to use BITNET was initiated in 1991 by Charles Seavey and Gretchen Whitney at the University of Arizona Graduate School of Library and Information Science. Open to anyone, ELEASAI@ARIZVM1 is an unmoderated, unedited forum for discussion of research topics in library and information science of interest to researchers, practitioners, and others. To subscribe, send a message to: "LISTSERV@ARIZVM1.BITNET". The message should read: SUBSCRIBE ELEASAI YOUR PERSONAL NAME.

Electronic Records

The increasing use of electronic records in all areas of life in recent years presents librarians and archivists with new preservation problems. In January 1991, the Minnesota Historical Society sponsored the Working Meeting on Research Issues in Electronic Records, funded by a grant from the National Historical Publications and Records Commission. Individuals from a variety of disciplines met to examine issues related to identification, preservation, and long-term use of electronic records. Working in task groups, participants developed questions for the research agenda, which was published in the October/November 1991 issue of the *Bulletin of the American Society for Information Science:*

1 What functions and data are required to manage electronic records in order to meet archival requirements? Do data requirements and functions vary for different types of automated applications?

2 What are the technological, conceptual, and economic implications of capturing and retaining data, descriptive information, and contextual information in electronic form from a variety of applications?

3 How can software-dependent data objects be retained for future use?

4 How can data dictionaries, information resource directory systems, and other metadata systems be used to support electronic records management and archival requirements?

5 What archival requirements have been addressed in major systems development projects, and why?

6 What policies best address archival concerns for the identification, retention, preservation, and research use of electronic records?

7 What functions and activities should be present in electronic records programs, and how should they be evaluated?

8 What incentives can contribute to creator and user support for electronic records management concerns?

9 What barriers have prevented archivists from developing and implementing archival electronic records programs?

10 What do archivists need to know about electronic records?

Awards

The first library and information science awards of 1991 were presented in January at the annual meeting of the Association for Library and Information Science Education (ALISE), which preceded the 1991 ALA midwinter meeting in Chicago. Daniel Barron (University of South Carolina) described "Part-time and Distance Students in Library and Information Science Education Programs," a study completed with support from the 1990 Research Grant Award. In his survey of deans and directors of graduate library education programs accredited by ALA and their faculties, Barron found that "there is a generally positive view of these students on the part of both deans and faculty; however, there is also a strong concern for quality experiences, especially as related to access to resources and socialization." Based on his data, Barron will propose a series of in-depth studies of the topic.

Patricia Reeling (Rutgers), winner of the $2,500 Research Grant Award for 1991, described her project, "Doctorate Recipients in Library Science: How They Compare with Doctorate Recipients in Other Disciplines." Reeling will use several sources, including (1) a special tabulation of data resulting from the National Research Council's annual Survey of Earned Doctorates; (2) other secondary sources, including ALISE reports and U.S. Department of Education statistics; and (3) interviews with those faculty and administrators responsible for directing library and information science doctoral programs.

The two recipients of ALISE Doctoral Students Dissertation Awards were Ruth Palmquist (University of Tennessee), for her Ph.D. dissertation at Syracuse, "A Study of Word Associations in the Natural Language Expression of Information Needs in an Information Retrieval Setting," and Nancy Everhart (University of Georgia), for her dissertation at Florida State, "An Analysis of the Work Activities of High School Media Specialists in Automated and Non-Automated Library Media Centers Using Work Sampling."

John Richardson (UCLA) won the 1991 Research Paper Award ($500) for "The Logic of Ready-Reference Work: Basic and Subordinate Level Knowledge." The first winner of the Jane Anne Hannigan Research Award ($500), Holly Willet, presented plans to develop "Environment Rating Scales for Public Library Services to Children" based on those used for day care centers, which she will then test in several public library settings.

At the 1991 annual conference in Atlanta, ALA's Library Research Round Table (LRRT) presented the Jesse H. Shera Award for Research to Patricia Dewdney and Roma Harris for "Community Information Needs: The Case of Wife Assault," a study funded by the Social Sciences and Humanities Research Council of Canada. Both researchers are faculty members at the School of Library and Information Science, University of Western Ontario. At the joint awards program with LHRT, the Library History Round Table presented its Justin Winsor Prize to Margaret F. Stieg of the University of Alabama, School of Library and Information Studies for "Post-War Purge of German Public Libraries, Democracy, and the American Reaction."

In Chicago, the Association of College and Research Libraries presented its ACRL Doctoral Dissertation Fellowship ($1,000) to Kamala Balaraman, a student at the University of Hawaii in the Interdisciplinary Doctoral Program in Communication and Information Sciences. Balaraman's proposed dissertation is "Study of Individual Differences in the Use of CD-ROM Databases by Undergraduate Students at the University of Hawaii."

The 1991 Martinus Nijhoff International West European Study Grant was awarded to Nancy S. Reinhardt, rare books cataloger/bibliographer at Harvard University. She will trace the book-buying journey of Henry Wadsworth Longfellow to Stockholm, Copenhagen, Amsterdam, and Rotterdam from April to December 1835, covering both book dealers and the list of titles acquired. While in the Netherlands, Reinhardt will try to reconstruct the content of a shipment of Dutch books lost at sea. Based on her research, Reinhardt plans to write a monograph on Longfellow's role as a book selector for modern European languages and as an advocate for curriculum reform.

ALA's largest award for research, the Carroll Preston Baber Grant, was given to Delia Neuman of the University of Maryland at College Park for "High School Students' Use of Databases: Implications from Instructional Systems Design." The $10,000 grant will enable Neuman to examine several issues related to electronic database use by high school students: the design of databases and their interfaces, the instructional needs that must be met for students to use the materials effectively, and the curricular and policy questions emanating from these two areas. The proposed project will build on Neuman's earlier work and will result in empirically based suggestions for improvements in database design, in the content and conduct of instructions in using databases, and in policies for implementing database curricula.

Two ALA awards were not made in 1991 for lack of a suitable winner: the YALSA/VOYA Research Grant and the Samuel Lazerow Fellowship for Research in Acquisitions or Technical Services.

The Special Libraries Association announced in June the first recipient of its Research Grant. Joanne G. Marshall of Toronto, Canada, will receive nearly $15,000 to examine "The Impact of the Special Librarian on Corporate Decision-Making." Marshall will study evaluations by randomly selected library users at several large organizations.

In late October 1991, four awards for research were announced at the fifty-fourth annual meeting of the American Society for Information Science (ASIS) in Washington, D.C. The $1,000 ISI Information Science Doctoral Dissertation Scholarship was awarded to Diane H. Sonnenwald of Rutgers University for "Communications in Design." Two Doctoral Forum Awards were given for outstanding doctoral research. Winners were Louise Su, Rutgers University, for "An Investigation to Find Appropriate Measures for Evaluating Interactive Information Retrieval" and Thomas E. Pinelli, Indiana University, for "The Relationship Between the Use of U.S. Government Technical Reports by the U.S. Aerospace Engineers and Scientists and Selected Institutional and Sociometric Variables." The ASIS Research Award for outstanding research in information science was presented to Abraham Bookstein of the University of Chicago.

In 1991, the prestigious ASIS Award of Merit went to Roger K. Summit, president and chief executive officer of Dialog Information Services. Summit was cited for his work as a researcher, educator, innovator, scholar, and industry leader. He is widely recognized as the guiding force behind the online information industry through his work at Dialog.

The year was almost over when *Library Acquisitions: Practice and Theory* magazine announced a $1,000 award to fund research on acquisitions, serials, publishing, and collection management. The award, to be presented for the first time at the American Library Association Annual Conference in San Francisco in June 1992, will be administered in two parts: $500 when the proposal is selected and $500 when the manuscript is submitted for publication in the magazine. The project must be completed one year from proposal, and the magazine has the right of first refusal on the manuscript.

Selected Characteristics of the U.S. Population

W. Vance Grant

Specialist in Education Statistics, Education Information Branch
Office of Educational Research and Improvement
U.S. Department of Education

Item	Number	Percent
Total U.S. population (July 1, 1991)[1]	252,626,000	100.0
Resident population, 50 states and D.C.	252,120,000	99.8
Armed forces overseas	506,000	0.2
Resident population, outlying areas of the U.S.		
(July 1, 1988)[2]	3,588,000	—
U.S. population, 5 years old and over, including		
armed forces overseas (July 1, 1991)[3]	234,117,000	100.0
5 to 9 years	18,490,000	7.9
10 to 14 years	17,757,000	7.6
15 to 19 years	16,869,000	7.2
20 to 24 years	18,745,000	8.0
25 to 64 years	130,211,000	55.6
65 years and over	32,045,000	13.7
Public and private school enrollment (Fall 1990)[4]	60,131,000	100.0
Elementary and secondary schools	46,419,000	77.2
Public	41,224,000	68.6
Private	5,195,000	8.6
Institutions of higher education	13,712,000	22.8
Public	10,742,000	17.9
Private	2,970,000	4.9
Estimated enrollment and teaching staff (Fall 1991)[5]	64,737,000	100.0
Elementary and secondary schools	49,818,000	77.0
Enrollment	47,032,000	72.7
Teachers	2,786,000	4.3
Institutions of higher education	14,919,000	23.0
Enrollment	14,157,000	21.9
Senior instructional staff[6]	762,000	1.2

Item	Number	Percent
Educational attainment of the population 25 years old		
and over (March 1989)[7]	154,155,000	100.0
With 4 or more years of college	32,565,000	21.1
With 1 to 3 years of college	26,614,000	17.3
With 4 years of high school or more	118,515,000	76.9
With less than 4 years of high school	35,641,000	23.1
Population residing in and outside metropolitan		
areas (April 1, 1990)[8]	248,710,000	100.0
Metropolitan areas	192,726,000	77.5
Nonmetropolitan areas	55,984,000	22.5
Employment status[9]		
Total noninstitutional population 16 years old		
and over (November 1990)	192,057,000	—
Civilian labor force[10]	125,257,000	100.0
Employed[10]	116,758,000	93.2
Unemployed[10]	8,499,000	6.8

Note: Because of rounding, details may not add to totals.

[1]Estimates of the Bureau of the Census, *Current Population Reports,* Series P-25, No. 1080.

[2]Estimates of the Bureau of the Census, *Current Population Reports,* Series P-25, No. 1049.

[3]Estimates of the Bureau of the Census, *Current Population Reports,* Series P-25, No. 1018.

[4]Data are from the National Center for Education Statistics. The figure for private elementary and secondary schools is an estimate.

[5]Data derived from early estimates of the National Center for Education Statistics and from the *Digest of Education Statistics,* 1991 edition.

[6]Includes instructional staff with the rank of instructor or above. Excludes graduate and teaching assistants.

[7]Data from the Bureau of the Census, *Current Population Reports,* Series P-20, No. 451.

[8]Data from the Bureau of the Census, *Statistical Abstract of the United States,* 1991 edition.

[9]Data from the Bureau of Labor Statistics, published in *Economic Indicators,* December 1991.

[10]Data are seasonally adjusted.

Number of Libraries in the United States and Canada

Statistics are from the forty-fourth edition of the *American Library Directory (ALD)* (R. R. Bowker, 1991). Data are exclusive of elementary and secondary school libraries. The directory does not list public libraries with holdings of fewer than 500 volumes. Law libraries with fewer than 10,000 volumes are included only if they specialize in a specific field.

Note: Numbers followed by an asterisk are added to find "Total libraries counted" for each of the three geographic areas (United States, U.S.-administered regions, and Canada). The sum of the three totals is the "Grand total of libraries listed" in *ALD.* For details on the count of libraries, see the preface to the forty-fourth edition of *ALD*—Ed.

Libraries in the United States

Public Libraries	14,948*
Public libraries, excluding branches	9,075
Main public libraries that have branches	1,277
Public library branches	5,873
Academic Libraries	4,613*
Junior college libraries	1,237
Departmental	78
Medical	7
Religious	3
University and college	3,376
Departmental	1,472
Law	178
Medical	212
Religious	105
Armed Forces Libraries	485*
Air Force	137
Medical	18
Army	194
Law	1
Medical	37
Navy	154
Medical	20
Government Libraries	1,773*
Law	421
Medical	228
Special Libraries (excluding public, academic, armed forces, and government)	9,348*
Law	665
Medical	1,861
Religious	955
Total Special Libraries (including public, academic, armed forces, and government)	10,345
Total law	1,276
Total medical	2,418
Total religious	1,064
Total Libraries Counted (*)	31,167

Libraries in Regions Administered by the United States

Public Libraries	29*
Public libraries, excluding branches	12
Main public libraries that have branches	3
Public library branches	17

Academic Libraries	52*
Junior college libraries	7
University and college	45
Departmental	21
Law	2
Armed Forces Libraries	3*
Air Force	1
Army	1
Navy	1
Government Libraries	9*
Law	1
Medical	2
Special Libraries (excluding public, academic, armed forces, and government)	14*
Law	1
Medical	5
Religious	1
Total Special Libraries (including public, academic, armed forces, and government)	18
Total law	4
Total medical	7
Total religious	1
Total Libraries Counted (*)	107

Libraries in Canada

Public Libraries	1,771*
Public libraries, excluding branches	756
Main public libraries that have branches	145
Public library branches	1,015
Academic Libraries	505*
Junior college libraries	139
Departmental	42
Medical	2
Religious	3
University and college	365
Departmental	176
Law	21
Medical	24
Religious	22
Government Libraries	368*
Law	20
Medical	3

Special Libraries (excluding public, academic, armed forces, and government)	1,212*
Law	86
Medical	240
Religious	77
Total Special Libraries (including public, academic, and government)	1,305
Total law	121
Total medical	270
Total religious	102
Total Libraries Counted (*)	3,856

Summary

Total U.S. Libraries	31,167
Total Libraries Administered by the United States	107
Total Canadian Libraries	3,856
Grand Total of Libraries Listed	35,130

Library Acquisition Expenditures, 1990–1991: Public, Academic, Special, and Government Libraries

For more than two decades, the R. R. Bowker Company has compiled statistics on public and academic library acquisition expenditures (Tables 1 and 2) from information reported in the *American Library Directory (ALD)*. Since 1987, statistics also have been compiled for special and government libraries (Tables 3 and 4). The information in these tables is taken from the forty-fourth edition of the directory (1991) and in most cases reflects expenditures for the 1990–1991 period. The total number of libraries listed in the forty-fourth edition of *ALD* is 31,167, including 9,075 public libraries, 4,613 academic libraries, 9,348 special libraries, and 1,773 government libraries.

Understanding the Tables

Number of libraries includes only those libraries in *ALD* that reported annual acquisition expenditures (6,425 public libraries, 3,142 academic libraries, 2,736 special libraries, 727 government libraries). Libraries that reported annual income but not expenditures are not included in the count. Academic libraries include university, college, and junior college libraries. Special academic libraries, such as law and medical libraries, that reported acquisition expenditures separately from the institution's main library are counted as independent libraries.

The amount in the *total acquisition expenditures* column for a given state is generally greater than the sum of the categories of expenditures. This is because the total

Table 1 / Public Library Acquisition Expenditures

State	Number of Libraries	Total Acquisition Expenditures	Books	Other Print Materials	Periodicals	Manuscripts & Archives	AV Materials	AV Equipment	Microform	Machine-Readable Materials	Preservation	Database Fees	Unspecified
Alabama	82	5,226,759	3,160,471	19,528	305,581	85	306,964	14,651	448,857	6,871	14,042	13,573	190,610
Alaska	22	1,968,986	519,596	23,478	100,948	—	182,370	19,882	12,207	4,516	9,845	182,315	283
Arizona	62	10,395,007	5,785,194	96,712	913,622	—	348,455	30,268	95,550	62,234	127,710	84,915	682,890
Arkansas	31	2,677,550	1,486,940	6,531	146,554	5,500	41,260	10,654	40,328	1,925	12,841	57,717	22,606
California	183	77,242,913	45,825,475	537,693	7,567,292	32,953	4,750,734	61,043	1,202,794	378,645	620,268	992,710	1,653,195
Colorado	82	10,862,174	7,409,517	11,960	1,108,867	11,337	416,744	22,389	92,262	7,337	41,366	198,497	90,905
Connecticut	137	12,038,571	6,585,763	31,646	914,007	726	851,595	80,186	162,598	80,212	57,739	324,136	84,307
Delaware	22	2,028,589	676,133	1,000	91,857	—	51,004	11,828	15,700	67,524	—	20,167	—
District of Columbia	2	36,777,700	1,359,428	—	255,572	—	46,000	—	—	—	—	—	—
Florida	110	34,602,191	16,110,583	209,881	2,282,222	5,000	1,857,177	95,563	779,430	65,875	169,951	438,237	211,414
Georgia	54	10,824,583	5,232,837	77,184	562,489	—	398,591	56,313	182,889	6,965	23,348	7,147	7,264
Hawaii	2	4,035,920	2,099,826	—	679,483	—	259,075	803,664	193,872	—	—	—	—
Idaho	66	1,906,374	1,065,554	43,150	166,732	—	117,122	8,027	12,527	10,798	9,966	67,560	4,136
Illinois	425	43,155,224	22,784,852	304,992	3,170,285	630	2,904,207	218,409	642,241	100,698	115,644	532,608	637,795
Indiana	181	19,820,004	12,379,055	133,704	1,863,496	8,000	2,254,234	129,053	417,427	154,789	137,442	225,121	365,150
Iowa	286	6,801,503	4,219,929	32,837	666,989	120	436,678	66,240	67,775	95,472	35,278	49,312	50,972
Kansas	195	8,062,545	5,075,834	48,204	771,839	—	366,607	55,382	101,420	36,397	25,865	144,211	270,663
Kentucky	90	5,350,568	2,071,909	16,209	276,009	79	260,727	85,310	35,242	5,003	14,366	99,988	171,575
Louisiana	55	9,885,042	4,545,618	7,981	808,614	—	229,569	30,069	97,720	11,664	51,195	61,835	669,537
Maine	110	2,511,048	1,429,398	13,324	203,503	2,200	79,014	2,729	26,841	4,215	25,626	30,567	20,480
Maryland	31	18,597,137	13,224,803	320,240	845,825	62,300	2,539,789	29,634	141,145	90,653	98,263	217,365	143,521
Massachusetts	283	26,248,422	15,158,907	31,573	1,933,051	1,000	1,052,043	77,415	452,445	59,355	58,097	218,101	597,018
Michigan	251	26,254,961	10,992,769	147,833	1,592,396	377	1,758,358	81,429	186,754	116,945	150,673	377,283	799,851
Minnesota	93	13,111,804	7,674,790	89,939	907,734	—	897,174	21,053	60,813	472,457	51,380	289,077	24,216
Mississippi	46	3,663,529	1,962,970	24,382	300,505	—	180,974	25,490	32,536	10,419	23,634	13,755	36,513
Missouri	86	13,517,766	7,925,019	17,216	1,057,171	—	745,501	42,168	445,166	38,669	308,030	84,130	265,991
Montana	48	1,861,415	1,026,129	7,713	104,110	—	24,687	4,415	8,182	19,005	6,818	75,800	87,510
Nebraska	106	3,217,522	1,732,716	5,826	342,089	—	115,132	4,396	39,940	4,403	19,025	38,022	103,894
Nevada	16	4,198,253	2,362,856	35,127	501,563	—	27,445	5,585	31,274	78,500	3,225	19,000	5,500
New Hampshire	134	2,873,106	1,494,453	7,978	186,318	621	99,599	5,750	63,250	6,977	20,028	1,331	37,143
New Jersey	249	47,838,974	15,583,726	93,122	2,522,001	13,273	1,400,591	78,272	555,685	304,359	166,858	476,928	17,385,596
New Mexico	40	3,710,151	2,351,365	1,928	347,273	550	60,123	23,329	11,296	23,720	6,871	141,040	175

New York	493	481,179,371	1,014,749	7,173,053	24,937	4,231,437	277,876	915,386	168,038	842,867	383,935	392,891,555
North Carolina	100	14,579,524	50,221	1,402,872	2,000	1,160,898	101,618	217,318	262,008	98,411	39,623	219,956
North Dakota	35	2,633,012	19,206	109,162	—	48,261	7,395	27,150	7,100	6,000	19,300	3,772
Ohio	214	59,436,832	712,411	5,135,976	3,784	5,936,029	229,304	1,320,937	334,626	797,286	344,126	727,755
Oklahoma	58	6,483,819	27,221	839,977	—	213,861	35,144	79,198	8,698	43,209	186,271	152,131
Oregon	87	7,347,762	9,841	615,958	—	311,727	10,385	56,663	19,460	50,536	84,484	23,530
Pennsylvania	328	23,851,308	70,225	2,404,443	4,293	1,202,939	88,856	866,539	114,894	220,689	259,664	1,180,458
Rhode Island	39	2,278,512	500	230,639	5,157	132,634	—	22,368	124,940	29,337	63,127	4,730
South Carolina	39	7,986,876	3,873	626,863	3,100	332,727	65,140	68,698	58,606	45,331	46,156	45,831
South Dakota	44	1,896,116	6,431	129,325	—	108,565	2,820	62,354	1,063	2,520	337,431	5,729
Tennessee	80	9,356,788	58,097	929,271	—	692,196	32,801	204,053	13,205	72,847	208,098	1,912,036
Texas	292	28,953,955	108,780	3,203,402	1,112	1,474,239	197,866	399,230	133,226	142,415	257,571	806,340
Utah	34	4,097,214	31,680	250,156	—	338,648	77,152	65,499	10	38,858	91,973	147,761
Vermont	102	1,843,232	6,315	153,986	9,200	49,727	200	66,022	2,018	9,337	1,959	10,908
Virginia	76	19,630,622	17,262	1,712,237	—	950,496	56,595	318,007	77,936	78,632	72,189	392,238
Washington	58	16,580,027	53,702	2,288,501	100	422,386	5,207	84,853	8,877	81,121	145,730	844,633
West Virginia	63	2,881,328	612	238,641	—	233,422	17,658	2,892	1,075	21,312	20,217	129,572
Wisconsin	261	14,458,359	57,456	1,379,756	3,345	1,023,656	59,260	133,323	139,022	72,505	334,366	882,435
Wyoming	22	1,601,640	26,310	103,881	500	81,046	10,500	29,524	2,441	13,582	2,966	29,752
Pacific Islands	1	180,000	2,500	—	—	—	—	—	—	—	—	—
Puerto Rico	1	6,200	2,000	1,000	—	—	—	—	200	—	—	—
Alberta	60	9,142,308	36,179	394,357	—	596,268	5,177	12,669	2,050	16,909	39,103	79,287
British Columbia	38	11,476,269	280,632	1,180,573	—	505,248	8,800	57,084	5,000	43,580	450	348,643
Manitoba	27	6,968,090	1,197	158,666	7,800	99,675	500	25,500	610	1,372	127,000	3,371,679
New Brunswick	6	1,058,324	—	189,669	—	68,924	—	10,651	—	4,764	—	—
Newfoundland	11	1,702,257	—	313,550	—	8,968	—	—	—	—	—	147
Northwest Terr.	4	337,700	1,280	29,453	—	39,894	5,000	—	3,800	—	750	—
Nova Scotia	12	2,771,821	8,291	170,889	—	225,654	10,670	7,084	—	67,424	8,300	4,000
Ontario	184	10,232,311	334,929	2,615,313	11,552	2,939,266	201,573	322,047	16,208	259,759	303,754	1,391,413
Prince Edward Is.	3	574,276	—	44,500	—	49,886	—	59,000	—	—	5,000	139,226
Quebec	61	16,817,589	106,800	1,094,770	89,500	679,190	184,616	66,462	20,711	1,353,982	161,927	574,148
Saskatchewan	11	4,579,413	500	313,078	—	456,219	5,932	67,078	—	51,737	96,950	64,300
Yukon Terr.	1	144,700	—	15,700	—	25,000	15,000	500	5,000	—	1,500	—
Total U.S. & Canada	6,425	1,274,333,846	5,448,091	68,945,614	311,131	49,698,629	3,913,641	12,224,255	3,857,424	6,871,716	9,126,368	431,004,675
Estimated % of Acquisition Expenditures		44.01	0.52	6.53	0.03	4.70	0.37	1.16	0.37	0.65	0.86	40.80

Table 2 / Academic Library Acquisition Expenditures

State	Number of Libraries	Total Acquisition Expenditures	Categories of Expenditures										
			Books	Other Print Materials	Periodicals	Manuscripts & Archives	AV Materials	AV Equipment	Microform	Machine-Readable Materials	Preservation	Database Fees	Unspecified
Alabama	48	16,009,018	5,795,909	81,784	6,845,433	8,353	213,044	150,521	224,466	21,762	486,325	115,474	215,757
Alaska	6	2,544,748	1,061,764	4,901	1,035,030	1,500	25,313	27,389	15,165	10,246	90,912	132,211	139,993
Arizona	29	14,163,582	5,870,691	15,400	5,870,119		271,429	82,114	139,131	84,497	643,531	143,859	453,781
Arkansas	32	9,023,851	2,314,506	3,545	4,026,609	48,681	128,408	34,047	237,254	55,331	177,883	207,891	72,701
California	222	120,688,114	41,726,058	1,264,815	47,104,879	25,273	1,754,638	1,327,624	2,339,329	715,341	4,874,389	1,190,935	6,209,575
Colorado	39	16,913,166	4,005,120	903	6,295,444	4,920	243,627	81,049	367,723	254,915	362,500	115,951	73,453
Connecticut	65	31,789,731	10,115,383	1,758,624	12,692,953	1,395,600	164,538	107,291	2,346,479	152,305	1,625,072	246,127	272,512
Delaware	8	5,713,727	2,684,977	11,718	2,379,036	50	17,342	33,450	52,800	29,500	17,100	45,170	149,465
District of Columbia	34	19,696,426	5,343,367	116,763	10,990,212	16,600	82,962	20,886	280,845	51,518	349,021	345,105	49,500
Florida	90	50,465,456	16,348,643	2,750,102	15,513,917	8,366	1,173,409	271,153	2,822,536	945,110	1,067,938	666,772	670,420
Georgia	67	24,681,868	6,920,969	112,571	12,534,247	27,200	337,446	172,513	1,128,608	336,205	447,878	340,520	756,697
Hawaii	11	5,266,716	1,590,940	230	2,502,463		64,297	25,000	108,597	15,150	254,489	11,785	163,825
Idaho	9	4,210,338	651,350		1,428,134		132	1,546	8,833	11,440	37,186	32,838	420,060
Illinois	116	55,824,030	16,178,818	207,963	19,516,979	31,788	927,181	832,632	492,689	441,014	1,727,853	970,927	799,394
Indiana	58	24,669,558	7,591,559	241,515	11,502,623	242,420	295,733	192,836	329,880	100,993	880,429	347,396	127,136
Iowa	51	24,051,558	3,767,320	20,989	5,584,126	57,193	234,376	169,704	61,431	110,014	179,175	164,023	182,372
Kansas	49	15,475,566	2,751,974	7,571	3,669,752	27,679	160,853	65,499	141,237	30,242	177,345	91,734	60,563
Kentucky	54	15,970,509	3,371,337	598,890	5,391,952	3,500	247,811	77,053	174,646	45,093	291,009	245,687	31,685
Louisiana	32	15,217,410	3,347,553	3,333	6,428,643	6,485	85,035	45,500	167,389	70,402	587,355	283,184	41,454
Maine	25	5,729,378	2,214,187	179,730	2,602,223	9,000	63,332	37,834	94,616	25,004	131,163	120,778	38,820
Maryland	51	21,805,359	7,004,529	92,935	10,050,424	5,500	378,231	198,995	306,336	162,517	355,877	378,500	1,316,042
Massachusetts	111	99,227,696	22,298,759	835,677	24,362,477	10,112	675,086	275,147	1,675,510	507,415	2,687,112	1,189,560	824,507
Michigan	86	38,931,034	10,547,507	242,849	16,017,606	33,234	338,366	452,344	539,586	297,204	918,610	591,512	548,977
Minnesota	56	23,013,643	7,534,903	734,380	9,317,711	5,371	427,964	241,996	232,992	88,913	1,115,582	211,318	792,835
Mississippi	37	9,575,198	2,270,567	139,180	4,711,075		209,047	268,475	181,752	118,564	216,926	220,815	339,484
Missouri	78	25,583,291	6,521,095	365,941	11,311,401	2,451	289,415	271,027	546,083	214,189	410,207	279,101	2,930,246
Montana	13	3,089,832	659,324	43,732	1,478,839	1,600	49,521	22,865	17,040	11,082	56,606	165,751	—
Nebraska	29	7,777,725	2,121,933	15,842	3,825,251		126,733	135,739	59,625	2,914	100,182	167,808	50,332
Nevada	9	4,105,955	1,362,639	190	1,704,516		91,002	30,743	118,361	71,789	145,212	11,720	84,963
New Hampshire	22	6,561,477	1,872,918	9,210	3,693,483	4,100	41,248	38,413	112,306	20,800	118,811	22,086	72,409
New Jersey	56	19,180,519	6,056,955	499,846	7,816,373		239,038	115,613	331,969	210,001	544,329	212,222	308,407
New Mexico	21	7,498,228	2,061,600	455,635	3,613,101		113,991	43,936	39,719	7,670	151,127	77,020	3,500

	Count											
New York	212	255,572,607	2,357,852	36,855,468	30,151	1,140,400	556,904	1,850,426	850,961	2,660,039	1,472,238	155,056,030
North Carolina	103	37,140,838	185,369	17,164,045	1,894	694,888	666,384	757,910	263,177	908,409	616,164	310,246
North Dakota	15	3,812,861	13,368	2,006,848	–	48,246	83,350	88,525	15,478	84,028	35,402	23,532
Ohio	130	46,562,666	98,726	23,908,349	3,415	732,720	338,629	502,115	103,619	1,205,181	559,851	630,166
Oklahoma	39	13,445,804	49,866	5,188,556	750	98,843	120,965	163,600	85,098	183,140	132,517	1,314,772
Oregon	40	13,366,153	61,660	6,809,419	3,500	205,066	98,473	209,213	137,897	312,353	229,006	167,435
Pennsylvania	163	66,293,437	258,701	21,081,755	28,554	771,075	397,863	949,863	707,406	1,491,260	751,117	784,573
Rhode Island	13	14,761,076	–	2,254,485	5,000	66,600	33,428	78,821	12,590	118,467	175,632	191,743
South Carolina	53	16,692,696	330,874	5,550,720	2,140	315,679	116,758	277,469	144,449	352,835	205,423	106,053
South Dakota	18	3,444,122	–	1,925,103	1,250	48,876	42,459	22,927	26,900	82,922	114,454	77,348
Tennessee	66	22,012,601	106,927	9,555,437	5,646	537,303	193,973	450,268	158,109	450,774	298,616	90,054
Texas	156	70,936,493	874,932	25,498,959	319,159	1,285,353	639,502	1,280,071	568,430	1,038,955	1,113,880	1,445,453
Utah	14	9,077,776	3,250	3,622,185	–	83,821	11,695	38,396	35,674	133,760	123,155	1,323,875
Vermont	23	5,525,100	21,633	2,501,700	450	120,380	37,592	138,801	31,348	133,065	128,859	10,772
Virginia	69	33,194,332	452,836	14,176,442	6,879	651,256	124,144	1,200,615	100,517	535,634	449,817	946,964
Washington	45	21,293,202	187,221	10,287,573	31,967	391,840	429,431	219,262	163,292	248,435	332,336	203,907
West Virginia	27	5,900,452	60,445	1,026,505	217	54,083	184,019	104,168	69,896	21,349	130,573	271,108
Wisconsin	71	21,320,134	84,422	9,027,761	13,597	754,759	392,023	883,253	148,119	347,854	298,376	988,556
Wyoming	6	3,486,591	–	1,720,325	–	82,382	–	13,192	3,246	–	37,212	190,553
Pacific Islands	3	252,408	400	86,506	–	31,000	1,850	25,800	–	–	5,000	3,000
Puerto Rico	33	5,307,920	4,000	2,550,785	–	201,004	193,402	56,392	4,200	97,736	27,280	69,153
Virgin Islands	2	268,584	2,288	92,600	–	500	–	14,413	2,000	2,464	18,574	81,404
Alberta	31	17,225,253	27,600	6,723,005	–	92,332	92,532	14,798	62,323	78,167	49,361	17,808
British Columbia	25	14,230,854	72,852	4,252,570	–	185,086	160,140	39,650	25,495	388,850	208,063	43,800
Manitoba	11	4,347,700	–	2,319,584	100	500	500	–	–	189,436	41,971	30,090
New Brunswick	11	3,595,218	500	625,428	–	2,600	8,000	1,000	46,500	39,641	19,369	58,467
Newfoundland	6	873,124	–	434,928	–	61,547	23,602	500	6,934	16,023	1,388	35,500
Northwest Terr.	–	–	–	–	–	–	–	–	–	–	–	–
Nova Scotia	17	5,481,080	–	2,256,723	500	50,445	1,135	18,550	7,559	79,583	85,400	235,636
Ontario	75	56,527,796	157,994	20,444,266	66	413,483	129,341	40,940	35,466	1,558,027	235,459	4,104,516
Prince Edward Is.	1	554,959	–	331,249	–	–	–	6,449	–	24,346	–	–
Quebec	41	24,409,449	106,523	8,455,612	100	234,566	194,150	271,200	53,122	557,573	368,395	340,374
Saskatchewan	8	5,628,613	115	3,094,175	11,200	30,162	25	1,790	–	181,369	73,109	47,720
Yukon Terr.	1	83,900	–	27,000	–	–	6,500	–	500	–	1,200	–
Total U.S. & Canada	3,142	1,547,080,506	16,337,118	533,673,097	2,443,511	18,856,843	11,129,703	25,415,310	9,089,445	34,822,079	17,684,977	187,401,473
Estimated % of Acquisition Expenditures		31.53	1.31	42.65	0.20	1.51	0.89	2.03	0.73	2.78	1.41	14.98

Table 3 / Special Library Acquisition Expenditures

State	Number of Libraries	Total Acquisition Expenditures	Books	Other Print Materials	Periodicals	Manuscripts & Archives	AV Materials	AV Equipment	Microform	Machine-Readable Materials	Preservation	Database Fees	Unspecified
Alabama	9	611,150	118,950	–	224,500	–	5,000	–	14,000	13,000	8,200	38,500	–
Alaska	6	72,700	11,200	3,000	10,500	800	–	1,700	–	14,500	4,000	17,000	–
Arizona	30	2,034,607	341,036	9,240	217,171	500	13,982	13,667	21,400	6,761	11,611	772,715	186,375
Arkansas	2	22,670	4,500	–	4,150	–	10,200	–	250	–	–	–	–
California	229	20,465,000	3,544,189	309,770	6,460,237	55,395	86,654	297,850	131,708	753,956	306,278	1,800,597	940,683
Colorado	50	2,431,105	548,700	15,000	966,735	6,300	73,275	13,997	12,900	11,015	29,350	289,457	143,085
Connecticut	55	2,600,341	433,849	41,116	530,946	16,960	99,957	28,306	49,563	7,650	37,956	215,854	27,971
Delaware	12	1,224,948	269,273	–	133,585	4,000	4,600	5,400	7,200	–	17,430	76,260	14,000
District of Columbia	63	7,332,663	2,376,751	6,850	2,359,126	3,800	8,380	5,911	56,877	83,740	230,679	662,891	34,048
Florida	62	2,332,328	738,959	76,749	803,219	3,370	42,595	16,878	24,575	33,359	22,255	278,901	36,097
Georgia	30	1,114,688	451,943	6,071	236,400	6,429	54,622	13,995	12,767	9,136	55,214	44,963	23,309
Hawaii	13	603,007	119,119	1,260	318,247	1,500	4,761	7,500	1,000	1,100	9,020	19,775	–
Idaho	5	76,920	14,500	–	21,500	–	–	–	–	2,500	–	6,420	–
Illinois	140	8,700,292	1,636,228	257,804	2,521,928	63,250	82,288	43,041	346,906	82,360	220,027	362,001	46,267
Indiana	56	2,156,610	584,491	98,848	756,905	1,002	36,812	20,518	14,344	42,955	11,112	86,970	63,298
Iowa	38	1,251,710	307,728	6,220	320,490	5,400	25,835	9,000	11,550	3,640	163,630	168,626	20,310
Kansas	26	764,977	242,009	22,018	146,812	–	4,106	11,695	23,050	5,603	4,564	14,293	1,552
Kentucky	18	723,729	225,502	5,190	108,257	20,000	14,387	8,096	22,200	52,500	5,531	43,550	756
Louisiana	13	343,116	38,150	1,025	68,687	–	4,251	2,480	500	87	4,830	5,560	1,000
Maine	24	769,416	113,623	1,800	280,409	5,015	25,338	3,079	26,000	750	7,780	82,066	10,165
Maryland	63	3,348,639	900,443	70,105	966,036	3,150	59,563	33,575	87,286	51,043	48,282	467,041	687
Massachusetts	124	10,341,734	3,141,545	70,720	2,293,498	21,820	73,568	128,497	59,900	23,993	141,669	774,041	118,016
Michigan	68	5,204,109	1,355,717	50,312	1,279,436	100	77,011	34,890	102,340	155,269	30,693	296,514	79,392
Minnesota	46	2,808,181	893,816	207,296	383,933	15,900	19,583	28,806	87,331	61,096	13,577	206,507	100,642
Mississippi	4	32,034	5,500	1,000	4,070	–	800	1,500	2,494	–	1,670	–	–
Missouri	47	4,509,173	654,760	63,665	1,896,608	4,065	56,324	8,987	64,047	13,720	159,730	553,668	86,328
Montana	14	152,631	38,329	1,061	35,998	300	1,557	18,558	13,715	218	5,231	11,322	–
Nebraska	11	161,540	72,010	2,100	50,980	–	700	1,530	3,350	2,925	5,830	7,015	2,435
Nevada	9	202,974	45,534	–	57,194	500	5,400	45,698	19,254	200	6,378	3,525	10,710
New Hampshire	13	845,172	89,950	500	410,341	3,300	5,000	8,831	12,000	34,500	22,800	25,100	10,300
New Jersey	74	6,655,619	1,955,124	40,475	2,199,327	2,050	66,793	48,368	103,350	176,450	35,725	508,685	53,170
New Mexico	19	3,596,861	1,132,626	20,300	1,990,500	400	54,569	2,100	700	742	35,059	88,250	2,161

New York	265	29,549,808	4,963,747	989,370	4,551,641	520,625	168,112	2,060,852	613,590	148,690	339,222	4,047,966	779,787
North Carolina	35	1,352,114	337,460	25,450	439,746	–	27,107	17,300	9,777	54,730	11,071	37,008	1,500
North Dakota	9	202,960	44,219	1,027	73,259	–	4,686	5,573	–	20,833	28,267	7,390	400
Ohio	116	7,238,554	1,791,273	323,055	1,468,754	6,100	79,351	37,565	92,527	34,260	101,080	459,754	149,769
Oklahoma	18	389,277	68,548	456	169,862	410	6,055	20,000	37,932	5,300	532	7,758	1,733
Oregon	27	755,071	89,677	5,316	153,235	–	9,100	6,300	4,800	624	2,818	29,900	8,872
Pennsylvania	168	7,881,217	1,477,002	602,282	2,061,522	42,894	84,073	83,680	223,220	93,625	516,528	709,656	103,166
Rhode Island	11	114,060	15,223	75	37,651	1,400	1,348	1,500	1,000	5,692	5,845	7,128	–
South Carolina	19	814,272	162,111	1,415	341,636	5,500	13,417	10,275	26,800	20	12,214	27,150	425
South Dakota	9	234,654	75,758	2,200	85,540	–	1,613	1,731	4,000	10,800	–	16,723	8,653
Tennessee	35	2,613,820	727,425	30,914	1,474,628	–	43,857	5,783	26,418	26,430	29,184	78,289	74,439
Texas	99	5,039,904	1,215,362	177,448	1,044,759	24,250	60,567	27,991	124,359	88,342	81,411	877,920	51,201
Utah	6	485,070	29,120	16,750	62,000	15,000	2,000	6,000	178,400	–	5,000	2,770	64,000
Vermont	13	115,506	55,100	1,600	29,400	2,000	2,400	1,000	7,190	–	4,400	2,455	480
Virginia	74	4,870,147	570,120	66,314	863,454	22,660	38,961	16,175	165,150	75,000	80,833	238,034	79,035
Washington	36	2,025,390	364,571	5,529	848,414	3,462	31,197	4,800	31,905	6,000	35,371	150,050	5,736
West Virginia	11	194,852	36,036	500	139,735	–	4,975	2,600	100	3,000	945	1,000	5,436
Wisconsin	50	1,382,197	396,566	14,315	373,363	3,550	24,575	21,145	11,209	14,230	17,252	83,348	72,449
Wyoming	7	84,272	23,600	1,085	10,800	300	23	–	3,200	50	1,487	6,132	50
Pacific Islands	1	108,037	104,329	–	2,247	–	–	–	1,415	–	–	46	–
Puerto Rico	1	50,889	40,083	–	8,331	–	–	–	–	–	2,475	–	–
Alberta	47	2,983,332	411,724	162,950	861,190	5,000	28,662	2,600	24,500	12,700	34,160	137,644	14,819
British Columbia	46	1,733,435	448,432	72,500	559,901	4,100	47,030	28,700	13,300	24,300	11,072	74,300	19,300
Manitoba	17	799,537	204,388	4,500	366,858	–	22,170	–	4,100	6,000	3,900	102,050	5,900
New Brunswick	8	661,735	36,180	3,000	79,200	5,000	3,160	500	19,000	500	61,500	12,000	1,000
Newfoundland	1	95,073	14,166	–	76,207	–	–	–	–	–	2,000	–	–
Northwest Terr.	1	2,000	1,500	–	250	–	–	–	–	–	–	–	–
Nova Scotia	5	88,665	41,500	–	22,300	–	–	–	10,000	–	–	2,665	–
Ontario	141	23,111,557	1,992,159	107,262	4,327,174	40,550	102,596	34,969	63,709	95,495	132,863	827,672	133,631
Prince Edward Is.	2	24,800	5,000	–	13,300	–	–	–	–	–	1,000	3,000	1,900
Quebec	66	5,312,469	1,359,319	81,700	2,247,608	3,000	20,514	64,900	190,550	80,512	36,778	330,284	120,638
Saskatchewan	19	741,236	197,812	29,650	75,698	–	30,850	15,140	47,000	1,800	9,190	6,446	33,450
Total U.S. & Canada	2,736	194,546,554	39,705,564	4,116,158	50,927,388	951,107	1,876,310	3,341,532	3,260,518	2,461,491	3,224,509	16,214,199	3,753,226
Estimated % of Acquisition Expenditures			30.58	3.17	39.23	0.73	1.45	2.57	2.51	1.90	2.48	12.49	2.89

Table 4 / Government Library Acquisition Expenditures

State	Number of Libraries	Total Acquisition Expenditures	Books	Other Print Materials	Periodicals	Manuscripts & Archives	AV Materials	AV Equipment	Microform	Machine-Readable Materials	Preservation	Database Fees	Unspecified
Alabama	4	98,230	76,015	103	3,161	—	—	—	3,000	—	2,838	7,718	394
Alaska	10	919,334	71,173	200	806,779	350	50	—	7,843	2,775	8,000	10,000	1,138
Arizona	12	864,854	255,600	391,774	58,325	1,000	5,000	500	58,855	4,000	4,500	16,000	66,300
Arkansas	5	203,560	71,110	4,506	87,014	—	23,475	—	1,250	—	—	9,084	—
California	58	7,928,704	1,727,370	611,714	1,987,714	—	126,450	18,850	67,605	1,150	68,749	138,761	138,075
Colorado	15	819,518	234,896	1,400	420,841	250	16,681	5,993	6,102	2,500	800	120,033	6,623
Connecticut	4	104,700	10,600	400	71,900	200	400	4,400	1,100	200	1,800	13,500	—
Delaware	3	173,998	83,788	1,000	47,000	—	1,000	2,000	7,310	—	900	—	—
District of Columbia	32	9,718,378	2,760,040	48,200	1,823,700	200	4,100	800	141,700	178,988	60,450	1,346,400	231,100
Florida	31	2,461,571	720,332	6,788	760,675	7,000	41,611	9,020	38,705	22,431	14,958	147,013	14,627
Georgia	5	138,720	54,200	5,800	56,600	—	3,406	1,099	20	1,500	2,000	3,500	6,750
Hawaii	4	640,300	24,900	—	9,200	1,000	200	—	—	—	—	3,000	—
Idaho	1	29,000	4,700	—	17,900	—	40	—	300	—	—	3,200	2,240
Illinois	10	4,210,651	835,498	1,100	573,771	—	11,700	3,550	49,958	2,600	14,500	34,280	8,600
Indiana	9	430,279	96,009	—	52,682	—	12,860	—	4,600	—	500	2,846	3,345
Iowa	7	169,265	33,785	1,654	98,146	20	2,000	—	3,000	—	2,000	6,500	3,285
Kansas	6	609,163	154,746	122,958	140,508	—	3,100	—	100	—	23,927	16,258	7,466
Kentucky	5	556,748	40,019	5,000	105,229	—	4,150	—	15,000	1,000	6,500	10,000	14,200
Louisiana	6	232,184	18,350	—	89,700	—	1,954	—	6,000	—	1,000	3,000	1,000
Maine	4	369,515	41,552	—	203,306	—	4,143	20,000	14,584	20,000	4,968	41,751	19,111
Maryland	15	17,372,408	1,959,730	37,000	4,850,793	6,500	238,600	9,500	134,500	80,025	2,050,791	954,231	536,600
Massachusetts	14	2,676,878	2,077,887	—	173,936	—	9,934	14,000	17,682	9,120	16,500	40,537	26,000
Michigan	11	764,622	161,429	12,600	98,143	—	13,718	—	15,024	7,534	2,050	4,709	—
Minnesota	8	574,300	63,600	210,000	164,000	3,000	4,700	13,400	11,000	8,000	1,500	73,000	9,675
Mississippi	5	492,365	255,300	—	72,052	—	9,495	1,200	14,500	—	3,594	4,924	2,500
Missouri	3	134,575	9,600	—	36,000	—	6,400	—	750	—	—	—	—
Montana	7	439,828	29,800	500	147,100	—	1,800	60	4,700	9,000	8,330	7,400	3,100
Nebraska	6	216,718	17,226	—	42,702	—	53,127	8,000	10,263	50	—	45,133	4,000
Nevada	4	675,290	355,959	—	12,930	—	—	181	15,577	644	2,666	36,333	1,000
New Hampshire	1	49,500	—	—	—	—	—	—	29,500	—	20,000	—	—
New Jersey	12	779,127	300,712	15,000	67,227	3,000	5,000	3,000	7,000	200	9,500	104,000	12,512
New Mexico	6	396,077	101,900	136,250	90,402	—	1,000	3,000	23,000	2,700	10,000	25	—

New York	52	5,131,916	2,072,986	7,755	567,709	–	44,820	9,156	119,948	75,730	30,862	61,545	50,356
North Carolina	9	1,204,221	431,154	5,000	449,583	–	–	5,000	16,722	–	10,567	149,000	3,195
North Dakota	3	78,005	29,271	500	44,204	280	735	–	1,695	–	–	1,600	–
Ohio	18	1,695,554	428,640	15,430	155,862	–	18,950	800	15,450	3,000	700	26,513	29,539
Oklahoma	8	388,165	52,958	6,300	77,148	–	13,237	1,200	500	10,100	7,148	9,634	2,694
Oregon	7	654,848	311,738	60	197,396	–	11,828	–	500	–	2,000	130,326	–
Pennsylvania	33	2,247,044	927,748	1,175	156,634	–	20,456	10,758	12,500	14,500	12,546	46,951	90,000
Rhode Island	3	384,296	35,882	–	36,614	–	8,000	–	300	500	4,000	26,000	–
South Carolina	6	203,455	49,700	–	17,300	–	12,500	5,600	–	–	–	63,355	–
South Dakota	7	133,873	39,186	–	61,958	–	8,290	8,301	8,500	378	750	2,700	2,410
Tennessee	5	152,571	55,900	500	62,150	–	8,000	10,300	–	2,200	5,421	4,400	–
Texas	12	552,686	160,014	211,160	89,458	1,100	10,026	3,000	9,684	–	15,818	29,112	963
Utah	5	159,886	23,438	–	82,800	–	9,585	–	59	3,355	15,500	14,109	–
Vermont	3	99,568	19,000	1,500	100	–	–	–	3,000	–	5,000	200	–
Virginia	19	5,142,567	208,335	13,500	696,597	–	13,200	–	51,818	177,204	9,320	491,629	350
Washington	10	1,276,584	152,433	100	111,605	10,000	5,000	–	1,000	–	21,540	6,231	3,872
West Virginia	5	730,930	259,729	300	224,201	600	–	1,600	1,000	30,500	13,000	31,500	2,000
Wisconsin	17	404,425	88,245	150	62,890	–	5,300	1,800	8,453	3,200	300	14,650	7,287
Wyoming	7	243,521	154,868	1,000	20,953	–	900	10,000	2,000	2,500	3,800	3,057	–
Puerto Rico	3	755,846	246,565	104,643	367,313	–	2,000	–	10,000	–	7,000	18,000	–
Alberta	22	3,601,946	274,069	1,180,000	702,781	4,000	8,800	2,000	57,150	18,400	10,880	130,775	50,711
British Columbia	10	989,212	109,600	10,000	282,000	10,000	1,500	–	17,000	20,000	–	22,500	–
Manitoba	11	1,404,900	106,712	11,050	150,904	–	218,500	26,600	1,710	15,200	20,000	17,000	–
New Brunswick	2	119,000	58,000	–	52,000	–	–	–	8,000	–	1,000	–	–
Newfoundland	4	414,440	16,093	–	20,515	–	120,000	18,540	–	–	1,300	7,000	–
Northwest Terr.	2	30,200	21,000	–	9,200	–	–	–	–	–	–	–	–
Nova Scotia	9	333,983	118,968	1,300	125,765	–	17,700	–	21,500	–	700	5,350	–
Ontario	68	26,679,838	2,713,980	368,842	5,711,598	16,556	49,290	15,000	1,010,319	114,322	98,060	804,254	12,380,564
Prince Edward Is.	1	18,000	5,000	–	12,000	–	–	–	–	–	1,000	–	–
Quebec	30	2,152,870	387,450	4,000	786,770	2,250	7,600	25,210	27,800	800	29,450	146,200	17,600
Saskatchewan	12	525,245	167,050	5,600	220,200	–	15,000	–	1,800	11,000	4,600	38,995	6,200
Yukon Terr.	1	39,000	–	–	39,000	–	–	–	–	–	–	–	–
Total U.S. & Canada	727	113,198,955	22,373,538	3,563,812	24,764,644	67,306	1,237,311	273,418	2,118,936	857,306	2,675,583	5,505,722	13,767,382
Estimated % of Acquisition Expenditures			28.98	4.62	32.08	0.09	1.60	0.35	2.74	1.11	3.47	7.13	17.83

acquisition expenditures amount also includes the expenditures of libraries that did not itemize by category.

Figures in *categories of expenditure* columns represent only those libraries that itemized expenditures. Libraries that reported a total acquisition expenditure amount but did not itemize are only represented in the total acquisition expenditures column.

Unspecified includes monies reported as not specifically for books, periodicals, audiovisual materials and equipment, microforms, preservation, other print materials, manuscripts and archives, machine-readable materials, or database fees (e.g., library materials). This column also includes monies reported for categories in combination — for example, audiovisual *and* microform. When libraries report only total acquisition expenditures without itemizing by category, the total amount is not reflected as unspecified.

Library Price Indexes for Colleges and Schools

Kent Halstead

Research Associates of Washington, 2605 Klingle Rd. N.W., Washington, DC 20008

A rise in prices with the gradual loss of the dollar's buying power has been a continuing phenomenon in the U.S. economy. Libraries have been especially affected by the higher prices of books and periodicals. Price indexes are useful in documenting the impact of inflation. A measure of composite yearly price changes in the items libraries purchase, they can be projected to determine the additional funding required to maintain buying power. Price indexes can also be used to ascertain if spending has kept pace with inflation. A decline in constant dollars per user means a loss in real investment.

A price index compares the aggregate price level of a fixed market basket of goods and services in a given year with the price in the base year. To measure price change accurately, the *quality* and *quantity* of the items purchased must remain constant as defined in the base year. Weights attached to the importance of each item in the budget are changed infrequently — only when the relative *amount* of the various items purchased clearly shifts or when new items are introduced.

The indexes in Tables 1 through 6 are calculated with FY 1983 as the base year. This means that current prices are expressed as a percentage of prices for 1983. (Prices for library materials are generally quoted for the calendar year. They are reported here for the corresponding *fiscal year* — for example, calendar year 1985 prices are reported for FY 1985–1986.) An index of 110 means that prices have increased 10 percent since the base year. The indexes may be converted to any desired base period by dividing each index number by the value of the index for the selected base year.

Tables 1 through 6 show library price indexes for colleges and schools and their component subindexes for 1976–1990. (Subsequent data are currently available from Research Associates of Washington.[1]) The first measures inflation affecting the *total operating budget* of college and university libraries; the second measures relative price levels for *new acquisitions* of elementary-secondary school libraries.

Table 1 / Budget Composition of College and University Library Operations by Object Category, FY 1983 Estimate

Category	Percent	Distribution
Personnel Compensation		
1.0 Salaries and wages		50.0
1.1 Administrators	15.0	
1.2 Librarians	30.0	
1.3 Other professionals	5.0	
1.4 Nonprofessional staff	40.0	
1.5 Students	10.0	
	100.0	
2.0 Fringe benefits		10.0
Acquisitions		
3.0 Books and periodicals		26.0
3.1a U.S. college books	20.0	
3.1b North American academic books	20.0	
3.2 Foreign books	10.0	
3.3 U.S. periodicals for academic libraries	40.0	
3.4 Foreign periodicals	10.0	
	100.0	
4.0 Other materials		2.0
4.1 Microfilm	60.0	
4.2 16-mm film	5.0	
4.3 Videocassettes	15.0	
4.4 Filmstrip	10.0	
4.5 Cassette tape	10.0	
	100.0	
Contracted Services, Supplies, Equipment		
5.0 Binding		1.2
6.0 Contracted services		5.4
7.0 Supplies and materials		3.0
8.0 Equipment		2.4
		100.0

Source: Derived from the National Center for Education Statistics, U.S. Department of Education, library budget data for 1985 and earlier years.

Library Price Index

The Academic Library Current Operations and Acquisitions Price Index (LPI), together with its various subcomponents, is reported in Tables 2 through 5. The LPI reflects the relative year-to-year price level of the goods and services purchased by college and university libraries for their current operations. Table 1 shows the composition of the library budget for pricing purposes and the 1982–1983 estimated national weighting structure. The priced components are organized in three major categories — personnel compensation; acquisitions; and contracted services, supplies, and materials. Because the size, responsibilities, and collections of academic libraries vary widely within the higher education community, individual libraries may want to compile the price index for their own operations, using the price series in Tables 2 through 5 weighted by the composition of their local library budget. The tailoring procedure using a computer disc is outlined in *Inflation Measures for Schools & Colleges: 1991 Update.*

The LPI reports inflation affecting a fixed market basket of goods and services and hence measures only the added funding necessary to buy the equivalent of last year's purchases. But library operations are seldom "business as usual." The collection acquisitions component in particular requires special attention.

Table 2 / Library Price Indexes for Major Components, FYs 1976–1990*

1983 = 100 Fiscal Year	Personnel Compensation		Acquisitions			Contracted Services, Supplies, and Materials			Library Price Index† LPI
	Salaries and Wages (L1.0)	Fringe Benefits (L2.0)	Books and Periodicals (L3.0)	Other Acquisitions (L4.0)	Binding (L5.0)	Contract Services (L6.0)	Supplies and Materials (L7.0)	Eqipment (L8.0)	
1976	61.0	47.8	52.7	69.0	60.7	60.0	64.6	61.7	57.8
1977	64.2	52.8	57.8	70.9	64.7	63.5	67.8	64.8	61.6
1978	67.9	58.4	63.4	78.4	69.4	67.0	70.7	69.3	66.1
1979	73.1	64.5	70.9	79.5	75.2	71.0	75.2	74.7	71.8
1980	79.5	72.6	79.2	85.0	83.3	76.5	85.0	81.6	78.9
1981	86.5	81.8	89.7	83.7	89.7	85.3	92.9	89.6	87.0
1982	94.1	91.5	95.1	102.5	97.9	94.8	99.8	96.4	94.6
1983	100.0	100.0	100.0	100.0	100.0	100.0	100.0	100.0	100.0
1984	105.0	108.3	103.8	103.6	105.2	104.7	105.9	102.2	104.9
1985	110.4	117.7	108.7	104.8	106.8	109.2	112.1	104.8	110.4
1986	115.2	127.7	117.7	110.5	107.9	114.3	112.5	106.9	116.6
1987	118.9	137.5	131.5	101.2	111.6	117.8	118.8	108.8	123.3
1988	123.0	147.2	141.4	97.4	116.1	122.1	125.3	110.9	129.3
1989	129.2	159.0	153.1	99.8	124.0	129.0	137.9	115.8	137.7
1990*	135.2	171.6	167.8	97.4	125.1	134.2	138.4	120.8	146.1

*Data for 1991 are available from Research Associates of Washington.

†1983 weights: LPI = 50.0% salaries and wages + 10% fringe benefits + 26.0% books and periodicals + 2.0% other materials + 1.2% binding + 5.4% contracted services + 3.0% supplies and materials + 2.4% equipment.

Sources: Personnel compensation, see Table 3; acquisitions, see Tables 4 and 5; binding, Bureau of Labor Statistics (BLS), earnings in the printing and publishing industry; contracted services, see *Higher Education Price Indexes 1990 Update, Elementary-Secondary School Price Indexes, 1990,* and *Inflation Measures for Schools & Colleges: 1991 Update* (Research Associates of Washington); supplies and equipment, Producer Price Index components, BLS.

Table 3 / Library Price Indexes for Personnel Compensation, FYs 1976–1990

1983 = 100 Fiscal Year	Salaries and Wages						Fringe Benefits (L2.0)
	Administrators (L1.1)	Librarians (L1.2)	Other Professionals (L1.3)	Non-Professionals (L1.4)	Students (L1.5)	Total* (L1.0)	
1976	62.7	62.7	63.9	59.0	60.0	61.0	47.8
1977	65.1	65.1	66.9	62.9	64.4	64.2	52.8
1978	67.6	67.6	70.4	67.7	69.2	67.9	58.4
1979	73.0	73.0	74.5	72.7	74.7	73.1	64.5
1980	78.6	78.6	79.8	79.6	82.2	79.5	72.6
1981	85.4	85.4	86.7	87.0	89.4	86.5	81.8
1982	93.7	93.7	93.9	94.3	95.5	94.1	91.5
1983	100.0	100.0	100.0	100.0	100.0	100.0	100.0
1984	104.9	104.9	104.7	105.6	103.6	105.0	108.3
1985	111.3	111.3	111.6	109.9	107.4	110.4	117.7
1986	116.8	116.8	118.4	114.2	110.3	115.2	127.7
1987	120.2	120.2	125.4	118.3	112.1	118.9	137.5
1988	123.1	123.1	131.6	123.5	116.5	123.0	147.2
1989	130.6	130.6	139.2	128.7	119.9	129.2	159.0
1990	136.8	136.8	147.7	134.5	124.5	135.2	171.6

*1983 weights: total salaries = 15% administrators + 30% librarians + 5% other professional + 40% nonprofessionals + 10% students.
Sources: Colleges and University Personnel Association, American Association of Colleges and University Professors, and U.S. Bureau of Labor Statistics.

Table 4 / Library Price Indexes for Books and Periodicals, FYs 1976–1990

| 1983 = 100 Fiscal Year | Hardcover Books | | | | | | Periodicals | | | Books and Periodicals |
| | U.S. College Books | | North American Academic Books | | Library of Congress Foreign Books | | U.S. Academic | | Foreign (7 countries) | |
	Price	Index (L3.1a)	Price	Index (L3.1b)	Price	Index (L3.2)	Price	Index (L3.3)	Index (L3.4)	Index* (L3.0)
1976	$13.20	52.8	$14.00	47.2	$7.91	65.4	$38.94	49.9	62.0	52.7
1977	14.80	59.2	15.50	52.3	8.89	73.5	41.85	53.6	67.0	57.8
1978	16.50	66.0	17.60	59.4	9.41	77.8	45.14	57.8	74.0	63.4
1979	18.02	72.1	19.60	66.1	11.52	95.3	50.11	64.2	80.0	70.9
1980	19.70	78.8	21.98	74.2	13.05	107.9	57.23	73.3	84.5	79.2
1981	21.50	86.0	25.00	84.4	13.84	114.5	67.81	86.9	93.8	89.7
1982	23.10	92.4	27.87	94.1	11.91	98.5	73.89	94.7	100.8	95.1
1983	25.00	100.0	29.63	100.0	12.09	100.0	78.04	100.0	100.0	100.0
1984	27.00	108.0	30.34	102.4	11.78	97.4	82.47	105.7	97.0	103.8
1985	29.00	116.0	31.77	107.2	11.66	96.4	86.10	110.3	102.9	108.7
1986	31.00	124.0	33.60	113.4	13.52	111.8	92.32	118.3	116.9	117.7
1987	33.40	133.6	36.93	124.6	15.94	131.8	104.69	134.1	132.1	131.7
1988	35.07	140.3	39.14	132.1	14.59	120.7	117.75	150.9	144.6	141.4
1989	38.14	152.6	41.21	139.1	17.97	148.6	125.87	161.3	153.4	153.1
1990	40.52	162.1	44.19	149.1	20.15	166.7	139.75	179.1	172.7	167.8

Note: Prices of library materials are generally quoted for the calendar year, but they are reported here for the corresponding *fiscal year*, e.g., calendar year 1985 prices are reported for FY 1985–1986.

* 1983 weights: books and periodicals = 20% U.S. college books + 20% North American academic books + 10% foreign books + 40% U.S. periodicals for academic libraries + 10% foreign periodicals.

Sources: U.S. College Books compiled by Kathrine Soupiset, Trinity University. North American Academic Books compiled by Stephen Bosch, University of Arizona. Foreign book prices compiled by Linda Pletzke, U.S. Library of Congress. U.S. Periodicals for Academic Libraries average subscription price, the Faxon Institute. Foreign periodical price indexes compiled from the Faxon Institute price data for Canada, Germany, France, Italy, Japan, the Netherlands, and the United Kingdom.

Table 5 / Library Price Index for Other Acquisitions Components, FYs 1976–1990

1983 = 100 Fiscal Year	Microfilm		16-mm Film		Videocassettes		Filmstrip		Prerecorded Cassette Tape		Other Acquisitions
	Price	Index (L4.1)	Price	Index (L4.2)	Price	Index (L4.3)	Price	Index (L4.4)	Price	Index (L4.5)	Index* (L4.0)
1976	$0.1190	54.5	$12.85	85.6	$—	—	$73.91	90.6	$10.32	96.1	69.0
1977	0.1335	61.1	12.93	86.1	—	—	58.41	71.6	12.08	112.5	70.9
1978	0.1475	67.5	13.95	92.9	—	—	76.26	93.4	10.63	99.0	78.4
1979	0.1612	73.8	12.56	83.7	—	—	62.31	76.3	12.47	116.1	79.5
1980	0.1750	80.1	13.62	90.7	—	—	65.97	80.8	12.58	117.1	85.0
1981	0.1890	86.5	12.03	80.1	7.58	72.4	67.39	82.6	9.34	87.0	83.7
1982	0.2021	92.5	16.09	107.2	14.87	142.0	71.12	87.1	12.48	116.2	82.5
1983	0.2184	100.0	15.01	100.0	10.47	100.0	81.62	100.0	10.74	100.0	100.0
1984	0.2274	104.1	15.47	103.1	11.04	105.4	79.57	97.5	11.23	104.6	100.0
1985	0.2450	112.2	16.93	112.8	8.44	80.6	85.76	105.1	9.99	93.0	103.6
1986	0.2612	119.6	16.50	109.9	10.24	97.8	83.50	102.3	8.99	83.7	104.8
1987	0.2350	107.6	16.85	112.3	7.44	71.1	85.33	104.5	10.61	98.8	110.5
1988	0.2198	100.6	17.00	113.3	6.79	64.9	112.15	137.4	8.50	79.1	101.2
1989	0.2352	107.7	18.96	126.3	7.21	68.9	74.45	91.2	10.12	94.2	97.4
1990	0.2244	102.7	20.63	137.4	5.67	54.2	89.14	109.2	10.58	98.5	99.8

*1983 weights: other acquisition materials = 60% microfilm + 5% 16-mm film + 15% videocassettes + 10% filmstrip + 10% prerecorded cassette tape.

Sources: Microfilm compiled by Imre Jarmy, U.S. Library of Congress. 16-mm film, videocassettes, filmstrip, and prerecorded cassette tape compiled by David Walch, California Polytechnic State University.

Table 6 / School Library Acquisitions Price Indexes, FYs 1976–1990*

1983 = 100 Fiscal Year	Hardcover Books					Mass Market Paperback Books				
	Elementary†		Secondary		Total Index§	Elementary		Secondary		Total Index‖
	Average Price	Index	Average Price	Index		Average Price	Index	Average Price	Index	
1976	$5.82	65.6	$16.19	52.9	59.0	$1.07	53.0	$1.46	49.5	51.2
1977	5.87	66.2	17.20	56.2	61.0	1.22	60.4	1.60	54.2	57.3
1978	6.64	74.9	18.03	58.9	66.6	1.41	69.8	1.71	58.0	63.9
1979	6.59	74.3	20.10	65.7	69.8	1.47	72.8	1.91	64.7	68.8
1980	7.13	80.4	22.80	74.5	77.3	1.48	73.3	2.06	69.8	71.6
1981	8.21	92.6	23.57	77.1	84.5	1.65	81.7	2.50	84.7	83.2
1982	8.29	93.5	25.48	83.3	88.2	1.79	88.6	2.65	89.8	89.2
1983	8.87	100.0	30.59	100.0	100.0	2.02	100.0	2.95	100.0	100.0
1984	9.70	109.4	31.19	102.0	105.5	2.24	110.9	3.13	106.1	108.5
1985	10.11	114.0	29.82	97.5	105.4	2.28	112.9	3.38	114.6	113.7
1986	9.95	111.5	31.46	102.8	107.0	2.71	132.2	3.62	121.7	127.0
1987	10.64	118.5	32.43	105.9	112.0	2.71	134.2	3.86	131.2	132.7
1988	11.48	127.8	36.28	118.5	123.0	2.80	138.6	4.00	135.9	137.3
1989	11.79	131.3	39.00	127.4	129.3	3.18	157.4	4.55	154.6	156.0
1990	13.01	144.9	40.61	132.7	138.5	3.19	157.9	4.32	146.8	152.4

* Data for 1991 are available from Research Associates of Washington.

† Juvenile books (age 8 or younger), fiction.

§ Hardcover books total = 47.9% elementary + 52.1% secondary.

‖ Mass market paperback books total = 50.2% elementary + 49.8% secondary.

Note: Prices for library materials are generally quoted for the calendar year. They are reported here for the corresponding fiscal year, e.g., calendar year 1985 prices are reported for FY 1985–1986.

Table 6 / School Library Acquisitions Price Indexes, FYs 1976–1990 (cont.)

| | U.S. Periodicals | | | | | | Microfilm | | Audiovisual Materials | | | | | |
| 1983 = 100 Fiscal Year | Elementary | | Secondary | | Total Index# | | | | 16-mm Film | | Videocassette | | Filmstrip | |
	Average Price	Index	Average Price	Index		Average Price	Index		Average Price	Index	Average Price	Index	Average Price	Index
1976	$4.69	47.4	$14.36	60.0	54.0	$0.1190	54.5	$12.85	85.6	$–	—	$73.91	90.6	
1977	5.32	53.7	15.24	63.7	58.9	0.1335	61.1	12.93	86.1	–	—	58.41	71.6	
1978	5.82	58.8	16.19	67.7	63.4	0.1475	67.5	13.95	92.9	–	—	76.26	93.4	
1979	6.34	64.0	17.26	72.1	68.3	0.1612	73.8	12.56	83.7	–	—	62.31	76.3	
1980	6.70	67.7	18.28	76.4	72.2	0.1750	80.1	13.62	90.7	–	—	65.97	80.8	
1981	7.85	79.3	19.87	83.0	81.2	0.1890	86.5	12.03	80.1	7.58	72.4	67.39	82.6	
1982	8.56	86.5	21.83	91.2	88.9	0.2021	92.5	16.09	107.2	14.87	142.0	71.12	87.1	
1983	9.90	100.0	23.93	100.0	100.0	0.2184	100.0	15.01	100.0	10.47	100.0	81.62	100.0	
1984	11.49	116.1	26.43	110.4	113.1	0.2274	104.1	15.47	103.1	11.04	105.4	79.57	97.5	
1985	12.21	123.3	27.90	116.6	119.8	0.2450	112.2	16.93	112.8	8.44	80.6	85.76	105.1	
1986	13.31	134.4	26.41	110.4	121.9	0.2612	119.6	16.50	109.9	10.24	97.8	83.50	102.3	
1987	13.76	139.0	26.95	112.6	125.3	0.2350	125.9	16.85	112.3	7.44	71.1	85.33	104.5	
1988	15.19	153.4	27.79	116.1	134.0	0.2198	117.8	17.00	113.3	6.79	64.9	112.15	137.4	
1989	16.39	165.6	28.29	118.2	140.9	0.2352	126.0	18.96	126.3	7.21	68.9	74.45	91.2	
1990	16.95	171.2	29.69	124.1	146.7	0.2244	120.2	20.63	137.4	5.67	54.2	89.14	109.2	

#U.S. periodicals total = 47.9% elementary + 52.1% secondary.

Table 6 / School Library Acquisitions Price Indexes, FYs 1976-1990 *(cont.)*

1983 = 100 Fiscal Year	Audiovisual Materials (cont.)						Free Textbooks to Students					Library Materials and Textbooks
	Prerecorded Cassette Tape		Multimedia Kits		Audiovisual	Library Materials	Hardbound		Paperbound			
	Average Price	Index	Average Price	Index	Total Index**	Index‡ (7.1)	Average Price	Index	Average Price	Index	Total Index§§ (7.2)	Index‖ ‖ (7.0)
1976	$10.32	96.1	$140.25	n/a	89.5	64.5	$4.10	57.7	$2.08	58.4	57.8	60.6
1977	12.08	112.5	93.63	n/a	76.1	63.8	4.67	65.5	2.27	63.8	65.3	64.7
1978	10.63	99.0	93.65	n/a	93.0	71.7	5.23	73.6	2.40	67.4	72.4	72.1
1979	12.57	117.0	117.38	n/a	79.9	71.8	5.78	81.3	2.70	75.8	80.2	76.7
1980	12.58	117.1	85.70	n/a	84.3	78.1	6.12	86.1	2.87	80.6	85.0	82.1
1981	9.34	87.0	92.71	n/a	81.9	83.6	6.42	90.3	3.05	85.7	89.4	86.9
1982	12.48	116.2	46.99	n/a	95.4	89.9	6.64	93.4	3.23	90.7	92.9	91.6
1983	10.74	100.0	57.52	n/a	100.0	100.0	7.11	100.0	3.56	100.0	100.0	100.0
1984	11.23	104.6	Discontinued		99.2	105.1	7.80	109.7	3.75	105.3	108.9	107.3
1985	9.99	93.0			103.3	107.1	8.40	118.1	4.05	113.8	117.3	113.0
1986	8.99	83.7			101.7	108.6	9.12	128.1	4.98	139.9	130.4	121.2
1987	10.61	98.8			102.5	112.6	9.71	136.4	5.73	161.0	141.2	129.1
1988	8.50	79.1			125.0	125.1	11.82	156.1	5.62##	175.0	159.8	145.2
1989	10.12	94.2			94.0	124.0	13.47	177.9	6.25	194.6	181.2	157.0
1990	10.58	98.5			107.7	133.0	15.18	200.5	6.95	216.4	203.6	173.8

**Total audiovisual = 12.3% 16-mm film + 7.9% videocassettes + 73.5% filmstrips + 6.3% prerecorded tapes.

‡Library materials index = 61.2% hardcover books + 3.6% paperback books + 11.7% periodicals + 2.3% microfilm + 21.2% audiovisual.

§§Textbook index = 80.5% hardbound + 19.5% paperbound.

‖ ‖ Library materials and textbook index = 42.2% library materials + 57.8% textbooks.

##Price source changed in FY 1988 and linked to previous series.

Sources: The following prices are published in Part 4 of the *Bowker Annual:* hardcover and paperback books, Dennis E. Smith and Sue Plezia, University of California; U.S. periodicals, Kathryn Hammell Carpenter and Adrian W. Alexander; 16-mm film, videocassettes, filmstrip, and prerecorded cassette tape, David Walch, California Polytechnic State University; and free textbooks compiled from prices reported by the Association of American Publishers.

The acquisition budget should consist of three parts, each of which must be separately defended:

1 The basic acquisition budget is the amount required to maintain and update the collection; that is, sufficient funds to purchase annually the number of volumes that equals 5 percent of the collection (discounting older materials). The L3.0 and L4.0 components of the LPI preserve the purchasing power of this basic acquisition budget.

2 Additional acquisition funding is the amount required annually to *extend* the collection in breadth and/or depth to satisfy changes in curriculum and other educational programs, changes in institutional level, or in faculty needs. The LPI does not account for this funding.

3 Additional acquisition funding is the amount required annually to *upgrade* the overall rating of the collection by extending the quantity and price range of new acquisitions. This quality change is not accounted for by the LPI. In the event that additional funding becomes a permanent part of the basic funding requirement, the purchasing power of the enlarged basic acquisition budget may be maintained by using the L3.0 and L4.0 price series as deflators.

L1.0 Salaries and Wages

For pricing purposes, library personnel are organized in five divisions. *Administrators (L1.1)* consists of the chief, deputy, associate, and assistant chief librarian—that is, staff members having administrative responsibilities for management of the library. L1.1 is based on the head librarian salary series reported by the College and University Personnel Association (CUPA). *Librarians (L1.2)* are all other professional library staff. Since 1984–1985, the L1.2 price series is based on the average median salary for circulation, acquisition, technical service, and public service librarians reported by CUPA. *Other Professionals (L1.3)* includes personnel who are not librarians in positions normally requiring at least a bachelor's degree, including curators, archivists, computer specialists, budget officers, information and system specialists, subject bibliographers, and media specialists. The Higher Education Price Index (HEPI) faculty salary price series is used as a proxy. *Nonprofessional staff (L1.4)* includes technical assistants, secretaries, clerical, shipping, and storage personnel specifically assigned to the library and covered by the library budget, but excludes general custodial and maintenance workers and student employees. As the category is dominated by office workers, its wages are based on the HEPI clerical workers price series reported by the BLS (Bureau of Labor Statistics) Employment Cost Index. *Students (L1.5)* are usually employed part time for nearly minimum hourly wages. In some instances, wages are set by work-study program requirements of the institution's student financial aid office. The proxy price series used for student wages is the Employment Cost Index series for nonfarm laborers reported by the Bureau of Labor Statistics.

L2.0 Fringe Benefits

The price of fringe benefits is based on the HEPI fringe benefit price series for all college and university personnel.

L3.0 Books and Periodical Acquisitions

The price of U.S. book acquisitions for smaller college libraries (L3.1a) is based on the U.S. College Books price series, which is derived from the prices of approximately 6,000 titles reviewed in *Choice* during the calendar year. The prices of books acquired by larger university libraries (L3.1b) are based on the North American Academic Books price series, which is derived from data on approximately 85,000 titles in approval plans. (In this national LPI the college and university price series have equal weight; however, in tailoring the LPI to its own needs, a library should use the more suitable series.) The price of *foreign books (L3.2)* is based on Library of Congress data on appropriated funds for foreign books and titles purchased.[2] The price of *U.S. periodicals (L3.3)* is based on the U.S. Periodicals for Academic Libraries price series compiled by the Faxon Institute. *Foreign periodical (L3.4)* prices are based on a fixed weighted index of unit prices for seven major countries from data provided by the Faxon Institute.[3]

L4.0 Other Materials

The five other materials — microfilm, 16-mm film, videocassettes, filmstrip, and prerecorded cassette tape — are representative of all collected library material other than books and periodicals. The largest estimated weight is assigned to microform used in the collection of government documents, newspapers, and preservation works. (Only the microfilm price is given; no price series for microfiche is available.) For the price sources, see Table 5. Note the absence of certain new items in this category, such as CD-ROM discs and other machine-readable software products, for which no price series is published.

L5.0 Binding

Binding is increasingly being contracted out at all but the largest libraries. As no wage series focuses exclusively on binding, L5.0 is based on the average weekly earnings of production or nonsupervisory workers in the printing and publishing industry (BLS, Employment and Earnings series).

L6.0 Contracted Services

Services contracted by libraries include communications, postal service, data processing, and printing and duplication. The L6.0 price is based on the HEPI contracted services subcomponent. (In this instance the data processing component generally represents the library's payment for use of a central campus computer service.) Libraries may also contract out such specialized activities as ongoing public access cataloging (OPAC), which are not given separate prices in the L6.0 component.

L7.0 Supplies and Materials

Prices of office supplies, which constitute the bulk of library supplies and materials, are based on the BLS Producer Price Indexes.

L8.0 Equipment

Equipment is limited to small, easily movable, relatively inexpensive and short-lived items, such as hand calculators, projectors, fans, cameras, tape recorders, and small televisions, which are not regarded as depreciable capital equipment. Prices are based on the HEPI equipment price series.

School Library Acquisitions Price Index

The School Library Acquisitions Price Index measures year-to-year price changes for a typical fixed market basket of books, periodicals, and other materials purchased by elementary-secondary school libraries. Table 6 shows the index and its subcomponents as well as prices paid by schools for students' textbooks. See the footnotes to Table 6 for a brief description of the various price series and sources.

Notes

1. *Inflation Measures for Schools & Colleges: 1991 Update* (Research Associates of Washington, Washington, D.C., 1991) includes overall inflation measures for the higher education and school communities for 1976 through 1991.
2. The Library of Congress acquires much standard foreign material through exchange programs. Purchased foreign materials include exceptional monographs that would not normally be acquired by academic libraries.
3. Canada, Germany (FRG), France, Italy, Japan, the Netherlands, and the United Kingdom.

Expenditures for Resources in School Library Media Centers FY 1989–1990

Marilyn L. Miller and Marilyn Shontz

This is the fifth in a series of *School Library Journal* reports summarizing expenditures for public and private school library resources in the United States. The purpose of this series has been to provide readers of *SLJ* with an up-to-date account of national trends in expenditures for program development dependent on funding. This report covers the school year 1989–1990; previous reports were published in the October 1983, May 1985, June/July 1987, and June 1989 issues of *SLJ.* All of the articles have focused attention on the status of school library resources, expenditures for those collections, media center staffing, instructional involvement, and the steady escalation of the use of microcomputers for management and program development in library media centers (LMCs).

Each *SLJ* report outlining expenditures for resources has provided additional, current data on one or more aspects of library media programs. This current report broadens the description of LMC involvement in resource sharing networks, which

Note: Reprinted from *School Library Journal,* August 1991

was introduced in the last report. Information is provided about the extent of the use of external sources made by library media specialists to obtain information for students and teachers. Readers also will find more information about the role of library media specialists in planning with other school staff both for decision-making and instructional development.

All references to LMCs and staff in this report refer *only* to those schools that subscribe to *SLJ*. In addition to the public schools surveyed, responses were received from 69 private schools. Although this is an increase of 30 over the 39 private school responses received for the last report, this response level is still not high enough to report valid private school data separately. Table 15 does provide information on private school collection sizes and expenditures so that media specialists in the reporting schools can have access to what was collected.

The data are presented in a total of 24 charts and tables, offering readers several ways to compare their own LMC expenditures, services, and programs with a national norm. The series of surveys have filled a need for up-to-date information about school library media program development. Since the publication in 1960 of *Standards for School Library Programs* (American Association of School Librarians/ALA), the landmark national standards that introduced the concept of the library as a program of multimedia services, only four comprehensive national surveys have been conducted by the federal government on the status of school library media programs. The most recent was published in 1985 by the U.S. Department of Education [National Center for Education Statistics. *Statistics of Public and Private School Library Media Centers, 1985-86 (with historical comparisons from 1958-1985)*. U.S. Department of Education, 1987].

Methodology

In mid-September of 1990, a questionnaire was mailed to 1,508 school library media centers in the 50 states. These were chosen by systematic random sampling from the approximately 33,000 school-based subscribers to *SLJ*. (Questionnaires were mailed only to subscribers who indicated either the name of a school, or some form of the title "school library media specialist" included in the address.) Two subsequent mailings were sent to non-respondents. Eight hundred and fifty responses had been received by February 1, 1991. The usable response rate was 55.03 percent, two percentage points higher than that of the last report.

Each response was checked for accuracy, then coded and entered into the computer. Data analysis was done using the Statistical Package for the Social Sciences (SPSS-x). Measures of central tendency (means and medians) were produced for all of the budget items listed on the survey. Chi Square and ANOVA tests were used in statistical analysis of data presented in Tables 22-24. (For purposes of this study, both means and medians are reported, wherever appropriate, to give a more accurate description of the data. The means provide comparability with earlier studies that have used this measure; the medians indicate accurately the expenditures reported by most LMCs.)

Although the mean (or average) is the descriptive statistic most commonly used in studies of this type, analysis of the data showed that much of it was positively skewed because a few respondents reported spending extremely high amounts for various kinds of library materials. With data distribution like this, the few large scores make the mean a less desirable measure of central tendency because those scores cause the mean to be unrealistically large.

In instances where the data were skewed, simply to report the mean would be misleading. For example, one high school specialist reported spending $24 on books in 1989-1990. At least one other media specialist reported spending $59,999. This is a range of $59,975 resulting in a mean of $6,589 but a more realistic median of $4,475.

As in previous surveys, each school library media specialist was asked to describe the LMC staff and note the size of the media collection and the specific amounts expended for a variety of materials, including audiovisual rental fees and leasing costs, and audiovisual and microcomputer equipment purchases and maintenance costs. Respondents were asked if the district employed a system media coordinator.

Other questions, also asked in previous surveys, concerned the availability of online bibliographic and technical services and the availability and use of microcomputers, both by students and library media specialists. For this report, we sought expanded information on networking by asking library media specialists to identify the external sources they use for borrowing materials for teachers and students. We also extended the information we sought on planning by asking media specialists to describe their roles in all school planning, policy development, and curriculum implementation.

There is no foolproof method for ascertaining all of the possible funding sources for the LMC program in a relatively short questionnaire. In this survey we continue to concentrate on local, federal, and gift monies, including those from fundraisers. Local is defined as money allocated by local school boards, states, and/or counties that fund all or part of local school expenses and are administered through the local education agency (LEA). Federal funding continues to decline, but there were some federal funds available in the school year 1989-1990 from the Education Consolidation and Improvement Act of 1981 (ECIA), commonly known as block grants.

Tables 4 through 7 summarize (public and private school) expenditures of local funds for materials reported categorically in fiscal year 1989-1990 and provide comparisons with the four previous studies. Tables 8 and 9 report the use of federal funds. Table 4 reports mean and median amounts spent per school from local funds on books, AV, periodicals, microform, and software. Table 5 shows a comparison of the median expenditures from all five *SLJ* reports; Table 6 summarizes per pupil expenditures of local funds for materials in the same categories.

Table 7 shows a *decrease* in median expenditures from local sources in FY 1989-1990. As shown in Table 7, *less* local money was spent for books, AV materials, and periodicals in 1989-1990 than in the previous years of the study. Table 8 describes the use of federal funds for library resources in 1989. As noted in Table 9, middle and high school media specialists received the highest allocations and spent slightly over $5.80 per pupil in federal funds. Seventy-five percent of those respondents who had federal funds spent an average of $2,172 on books for school collections. Computer-related resources accounted for the majority of the remainder of federal funds expended on resources. The amounts of federal funds expended in 1989 are comparable to those spent in 1987.

The median per pupil expenditure for books in 1989-1990 was $5.48 (Table 7). The inflation rate for 1990 was 6 percent. The average price for a children's book was $13.98 in 1990. The average price for an adult hardcover novel was $20.01. This means that the average elementary library media specialist could purchase a little over one-half of a book per child; the average secondary library media specialist could purchase one novel for every four students. In each report we have noted that book collections have to be deteriorating because of the inability of library media specialists to purchase one book per child per year. We are now talking about serious problems confronting school media staffs in their ability to support instructional and developmental reading programs.

In all of these tables the funds reported for AV materials include expenditures for new materials, videos, rentals, and leasing. Amounts expended for microcomputer resources include hardware and maintenance, as well as software, online fees, and technical processing charges. The amount reported for periodicals includes money spent for magazines, journals, and newspapers for both student and professional use. The amount expended for books includes titles designated for the reference collection and all preprocessing costs.

Many library media specialists have yet to establish an accounting method for their expenditures that permits them to retrieve specific amounts spent by category of resource. Those respondents did estimate by category, which is helpful. Other respondents just provided lump sums for materials such as print items, AV and computer software, and services.

Respondents

Respondents were asked to identify their gender and to describe themselves in terms of certification, educational background, employment status, years of experience in the field of education as well as in the field of librarianship, and salary. Table 16 presents a summary of some of these data. Tables 1 to 3 describe demographic characteristics of the respondents.

In comparison to the last survey, the responses to the 1989 survey reflect a 2 percent sample gain in both the Northeast and South and a loss of 4 percent in the North Central region sample. The distribution also reflects 3 percent fewer schools in the 1,000–1,999 enrollment range and 2 percent more in the 300–499 range. The "other" category includes combinations that do not fit traditional grade groupings, for example K–9 and 3–9. Over one-third of the units in this category are private schools.

Collections and Expenditures

Data about collections and expenditures are organized in Tables 10 to 15. Data on size of collections and expenditures reported categorically from local funds and organized by geographic region, school level, and enrollment are shown in Tables 10 to 12. In order to display the total amounts reported, whether categorically or in a lump sum, from all sources—local, federal, gifts, and fundraising, Total Material Expenditures (TME) are reported at the bottom of each table for purposes of comparison. TME reflects *all* expenditures for resources including audiovisual equipment, computer hardware, rentals, leasing, and maintenance, but excluding salaries.

Library media specialists in the Northeast continue to spend more of their money on print materials (Table 11). The LMCs in the Northeast also have the largest book, periodical, and microform collections as well as the smallest audiovisual and software collections. School library media centers in the Southern schools continue

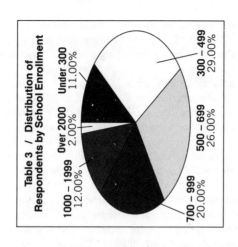

Table 3 / Distribution of
Respondents by School Enrollment

Over 2000 2.00%
Under 300 11.00%
1000 – 1999 12.00%
300 – 499 29.00%
700 – 999 20.00%
500 – 699 26.00%

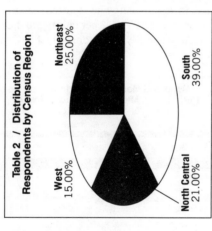

Table 2 / Distribution of
Respondents by Census Region

West 15.00%
Northeast 25.00%
North Central 21.00%
South 39.00%

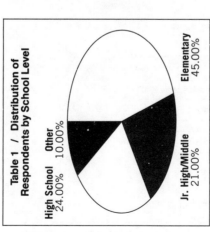

Table 1 / Distribution of
Respondents by School Level

High School 24.00%
Other 10.00%
Jr. High/Middle 21.00%
Elementary 45.00%

427

to have the smallest book collections and the largest audiovisual collections. As shown in Table 12, library media specialists in small schools with under 300 students spent $25 per pupil on resources, which is significantly more than any of the larger schools.

No matter how the data are organized, it is obvious that although the microform and microcomputer software collections are still relatively small, most library media specialists are spending more money each year on those collections. In the 1989 report, we displayed a table of total expenditures and collection sizes for the high school respondents. In this report, Table 13 presents total local expenditures and holdings for elementary schools. The data are a dramatic presentation of inequities of resources in elementary schools of all sizes. Readers should note particularly the budget ranges for books, audiovisual resources, and computer resources in schools with under 600 students enrolled. In these schools, according to the data, staff is spending more money for audiovisual resources than for books. In some schools, the data indicate, staff is spending more for computer software per pupil than for books and audiovisual materials combined. Table 14 summarizes median expenditures for microcomputer resources by respondents who reported spending money in these categories from any funding source. The $1,448 per unit figure shows an increase of $300 over the previous report. As previously noted, only 69 school library media specialists

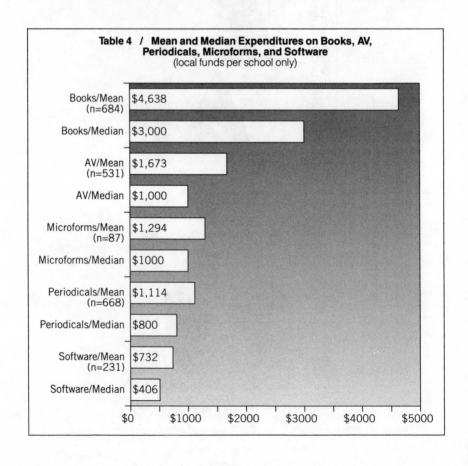

Table 4 / Mean and Median Expenditures on Books, AV, Periodicals, Microforms, and Software
(local funds per school only)

Books/Mean (n=684)	$4,638
Books/Median	$3,000
AV/Mean (n=531)	$1,673
AV/Median	$1,000
Microforms/Mean (n=87)	$1,294
Microforms/Median	$1000
Periodicals/Mean (n=668)	$1,114
Periodicals/Median	$800
Software/Mean (n=231)	$732
Software/Median	$406

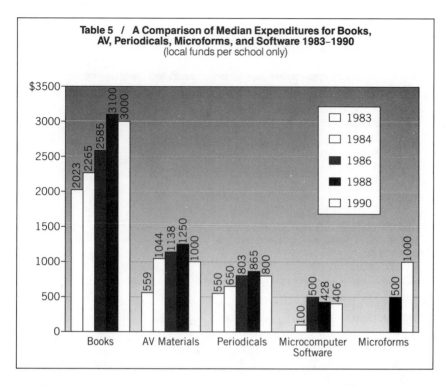

Table 5 / A Comparison of Median Expenditures for Books, AV, Periodicals, Microforms, and Software 1983-1990 (local funds per school only)

working in private schools responded to the questionnaire. We are presenting Table 15 showing private school data so that private school media specialists can see what was collected for whatever comparison purposes might be interesting and helpful.

According to our survey, salaries for professional library media specialists, reported in Table 16, continued to rise. The largest increase, $3,000, went to specialists working in middle schools. The lowest salary increase was the average $250 awarded to library media specialists working in schools in the "other" category. Respondents to the 1989 survey were more experienced than those who participated in the 1987 survey, with the greatest difference apparent in the elementary schools. Current respondents report a median number of 17 years of experience with 12 of those years being in a library media program. The mean and median figures are almost identical for these data supporting the contention that we are not recruiting young people into the school library media field. Library media specialists who are in the *SLJ* sample have managed to retain their support staff, but they still do not report wide use of adult volunteers.

Technology in LMCs

Tables 17 and 18 show a wide range of responses to questions about the use of technology in LMCs. In Table 17 data show that 59 percent of the respondents reported using cable TV, which makes this resource the most highly used of the electronic technologies. The data on use of databases and CD-ROM show a marginal increase over the data reported two years ago. Responses to a new question about LMC access to

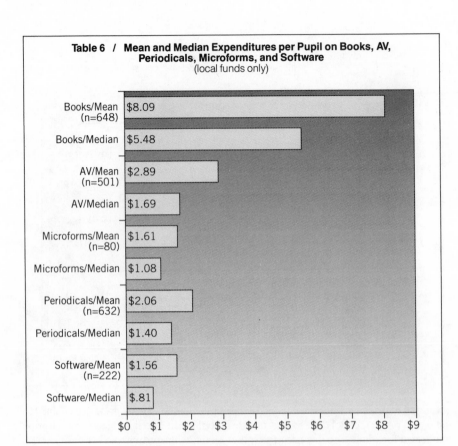

Table 6 / Mean and Median Expenditures per Pupil on Books, AV, Periodicals, Microforms, and Software
(local funds only)

Books/Mean (n=648)	$8.09
Books/Median	$5.48
AV/Mean (n=501)	$2.89
AV/Median	$1.69
Microforms/Mean (n=80)	$1.61
Microforms/Median	$1.08
Periodicals/Mean (n=632)	$2.06
Periodicals/Median	$1.40
Software/Mean (n=222)	$1.56
Software/Median	$.81

FAX machines reveal that a small number of media specialists have access to FAX machines either in the LMC or its building. The data show a steady increase in installations of online public access catalogs (OPACs) and circulation systems as well as plans to install both. In 1989, 29 percent of the respondents reported planning for online catalogs. In 1991, the number of media specialists planning for OPACs has increased to 40 percent of the respondents.

Library media specialists' use of microcomputers for management tasks is still increasing as displayed in Table 18; however, the huge growth in management uses that was reported in previous studies has leveled off. The biggest increase in microcomputer use for management functions has been 7 percent for circulation; 6 percent for acquisition; 5 percent for cataloging; and 4 percent for overdues. It is heartening to note that nearly 50 percent of those who use micros for management use them for those labor-intensive tasks.

Network Participation

The 1991 study continued to collect information on the extent of school library media center specialists' participation in resource sharing. Table 19 reports the percentage of all schools reporting participation in networking. Incredibly, fewer than 50 percent of

Table 7 / A Comparison of Median Expenditures per Pupil for Books, AV, Periodicals, Microforms, and Software 1983-1990
(local funds per school only)

Legend:
- ☐ 1983
- ☐ 1984
- ■ 1986
- ■ 1988
- ■ 1990

Books: 3.71, 4.10, 4.45, 5.55, 5.48
AV Materials: 1.00, 1.90, 1.96, 2.00, 1.69
Periodicals: .96, 1.14, 1.31, 1.43, 1.40
Microcomputer Software: .18, .88, .78, .81
Microforms: .66, 1.08

Table 8 / Use of Federal Funds for Resources
(expenditures in specific categories)

	Number Responding	Mean Amount
Books	222	$2,172
Periodicals	15	734
Microform	10	1,019
Total audiovisual resources	123	1,986
Microcomputer software	45	793
Online services, including CD-ROM	11	893
Microcomputer hardware	38	2,738
Technical processing	2	3,250
Total microcomputer resources	73	2,956
Total federal funds—all categories	297	$3,396

Table 9 / Use of Federal Funds by School Level

	Elementary n = 128		Middle/Jr. High n = 47		Senior High n = 83		Other n = 35	
	median	mean	median	mean	median	mean	median	mean
Total federal funds	$1,906	$2,281	$2,631	$4,011	$3,000	$4,752	$2,800	$3,559
Federal funds per pupil	3.52	4.45	5.83	7.42	5.82	6.30	5.75	17.67

Table 10 / Collection Size and Local Expenditures in LMCs by School Level

	Elementary n = 367		Middle/Jr. High n = 173		Senior High n = 191		Other n = 83	
	median	mean	median	mean	median	mean	median	mean
Size of book collection	8,678	8,806	10,226	10,732	12,100	14,309	9,000	10,650
Volumes added, 1989–1990	328	450	300	464	368	527	340	438
Number of books per pupil	16	18	17	18	16	24	22	26
Volumes discarded, 1989–1990	150	367	158	314	151	384	100	247
Size of AV collection	980	1,223	695	1,231	976	2,137	538	1,192
Number of AV items added, 1989–1990	25	48	25	41	25	54	25	34
Number of AV items per pupil	2	3	1	2	1	3	1	3
AV items discarded, 1989–1990	5	28	3	28	3	34	1	44
Size of microcomputer software collection	100	152	31	91	10	45	25	120
Microcomputer software added, 1989–1990	10	25	5	15	1	10	2	9
Microcomputer software per pupil	0	0	0	0	0	0	0	0
Microcomputer software discarded, 1989–1990	0	3	0	1	0	1	0	1
Expenditures								
Books	$2,500.00	$3,562.00	$3,458.00	$4,587.00	$4,475.00	$6,589.00	$3,000.00	$5,416.00
Books per pupil	5.38	7.25	5.00	7.39	5.90	8.97	7.32	12.34
Periodicals	453.00	531.00	1,000.00	1,203.00	1,820.00	2,112.00	950.00	1,295.00
Periodicals per pupil	0.98	1.11	1.61	2.11	2.49	3.62	2.47	2.73
Microform	500.00	400.00	998.00	988.00	1,158.00	1,449.00	605.00	907.00
Microform per pupil	1.17	1.17	1.77	1.93	1.06	1.62	0.79	1.07
Audiovisual materials	1,000.00	1,394.00	880.00	1,470.00	1,175.00	2,464.00	650.00	1,557.00
Audiovisual materials per pupil	1.78	2.66	1.04	2.83	1.61	3.18	1.97	3.43
Microcomputer software	500.00	736.00	356.00	785.00	342.00	623.00	500.00	939.00
Microcomputer software per pupil	0.99	1.66	0.72	1.66	0.33	0.95	1.20	2.50
*Total materials expenditures (TME)	$6,712.00	$11,937.00	$8,666.00	$11,408.00	$12,675.00	$17,324.00	$6,573.00	$11,264.00
TME per pupil	$12.63	$24.73	$14.07	$19.63	$17.95	$23.37	$17.34	$29.96

*See narrative for explanation of TME

Table 11 / Collection Size and Local Expenditures in LMCs by Region

	Northeast n = 205		South n = 317		North Central n = 177		West n = 120	
	median	mean	median	mean	median	mean	median	mean
Size of book collection	11,000	11,725	9,074	10,080	9,965	10,888	9,799	10,313
Volumes added, 1989–1990	343	422	350	527	300	374	430	552
Number of books per pupil	20	24	14	16	21	25	16	18
Volumes discarded, 1989–1990	150	371	153	389	110	258	150	333
Size of AV collection	800	1,931	1,000	1,395	753	1,337	425	775
Number of AV items added, 1989–1990	24	41	37	59	18	41	20	26
Number of AV items per pupil	1	3	2	2	2	3	1	2
AV items discarded, 1989–1990	4	22	4	36	3	43	1	17
Size of microcomputer software collection	25	104	50	120	87	132	35	75
Microcomputer software added, 1989–1990	3	17	5	20	9	20	3	10
Microcomputer software per pupil	0	0	0	0	0	0	0	0
Microcomputer software discarded, 1989–1990	0	2	0	2	0	3	0	1
Expenditures								
Books	$4,000.00	$6,122.00	$2,705.00	$4,289.00	$3,000.00	$3,529.00	$3,050.00	$4,760.00
Books per pupil	8.48	12.13	4.33	5.88	5.87	7.35	5.43	8.28
Periodicals	937.00	1,377.00	700.00	1,016.00	800.00	1,020.00	800.00	1,104.00
Periodicals per pupil	1.80	2.89	1.07	1.51	1.66	2.20	1.31	1.92
Microform	1,109.00	1,570.00	1,087.00	1,259.00	428.00	429.00	1,505.00	1,462.00
Microform per pupil	1.53	2.49	1.11	12.70	0.57	0.79	1.01	1.32
Audiovisual materials	1,036.00	1,998.00	1,000.00	1,754.00	846.00	1,400.00	941.00	1,418.00
Audiovisual materials per pupil	2.50	3.86	1.54	2.19	1.94	3.09	1.40	2.98
Microcomputer software	700.00	1,029.00	300.00	508.00	580.00	815.00	350.00	599.00
Microcomputer software per pupil	1.51	2.43	0.46	0.80	1.13	2.00	0.78	1.09
*Total materials expenditures (TME)	$8,548.00	$12,773.00	$8,173.00	$12,077.00	$7,800.00	$15,870.00	$7,700.00	$11,731.00
TME per pupil	$16.45	$26.83	$12.02	$17.58	$17.35	$34.21	$14.46	$20.73

*See narrative for explanation of TME

433

Table 12 / Collection Size and Local Expenditures in LMCs by School Enrollment

	Under 300 Students n = 87		300–499 n = 224		500–699 n = 198		700–999 n = 157		1000–1999 n = 96		2000 and up n = 15	
	median	mean	median	mean	median	mean	median	mean	median	mean	median	mean
Size of book collection	6,000	7,719	8,000	8,717	9,843	9,945	11,000	11,905	14,238	15,908	22,000	22,601
Volumes added, 1989–1990	238	293	300	363	327	479	419	526	500	583	1,100	1,811
Number of books per pupil	29	43	21	22	16	17	13	15	11	12	9	10
Volumes discarded, 1989–1990	75	175	110	263	150	403	180	354	230	538	300	638
Size of AV collection	350	574	671	1,262	800	1,232	1,160	1,602	1,377	1,918	1,763	7,775
Number of AV items added, 1989–1990	20	32	20	37	25	43	40	64	37	55	71	135
Number of AV items per pupil	2	3	2	3	1	2	1	2	1	1	1	3
AV items discarded, 1989–1990	0	10	5	23	3	29	8	32	1	48	13	60
Size of microcomputer software collection	30	94	50	107	50	131	70	136	47	94	4	52
Microcomputer software added, 1989–1990	4	11	7	15	3	21	7	27	6	14	0	9
Microcomputer software per pupil	0	0	0	0	0	0	0	0	0	0	0	0
Microcomputer software discarded, 1989–1990	0	2	0	3	0	2	0	2	0	1	0	0
Expenditures												
Books	$2,001.00	$2,434.00	$2,470.00	$3,277.00	$3,179.00	$4,589.00	$3,822.00	$5,805.00	$4,785.00	$6,088.00	$11,000.00	$18,751.00
Books per pupil	10.27	14.23	6.25	8.24	5.48	7.92	4.55	7.09	3.54	4.67	4.89	7.92
Periodicals	638.00	805.00	555.00	783.00	750.00	1,003.00	935.00	1,148.00	1,728.00	2,119.00	2,330.00	2,431.00
Periodicals per pupil	2.84	4.95	1.50	1.95	1.24	1.73	1.07	1.39	1.28	1.64	1.01	1.02
Microform	304.00	276.00	830.00	1,003.00	700.00	1,181.00	1,087.00	1,579.00	1,158.00	1,356.00	1,550.00	1,935.00
Microform per pupil	1.67	1.67	2.10	2.59	1.39	2.05	1.42	1.92	0.69	0.94	0.65	0.82
Audiovisual materials	520.00	1,100.00	620.00	1,127.00	1,000.00	1,462.00	1,295.00	2,048.00	1,622.00	2,379.00	4,550.00	7,431.00
Audiovisual materials per pupil	2.23	5.62	1.73	2.81	1.67	2.49	1.59	2.48	1.21	1.87	1.88	3.13
Microcomputer software	389.00	623.00	490.00	769.00	500.00	791.00	500.00	749.00	390.00	760.00	300.00	592.00
Microcomputer software per pupil	2.62	4.08	1.19	1.90	0.80	1.40	0.56	0.92	0.32	0.59	0.14	0.24
Total materials expenditures (TME)*	$4,860.00	$6,567.00	$6,325.00	$13,308.00	$8,174.00	$11,383.00	$9,847.00	$13,053.00	$13,600.00	$18,687.00	$32,474.00	$40,809.00
TME per pupil	25.00	39.18	16.56	31.26	13.79	19.31	12.15	16.06	9.91	14.33	13.83	17.20

*See narrative for explanation of TME

Table 13 / Total Budget, Total Book Budget, Total AV Budget, Total Microcomputer Budget and Book Collection Size by Elementary School Enrollment
(local funds only)

	Under 300 Students	300–499 Students	500–699 Students	700–999 Students	1000–1999 Students
Expenditures					
Total budget (median)					
per school	$2,792.00	$4,265.00	$5,380.00	$6,458.00	$6,636.00
per student	12.88	11.21	9.33	8.43	5.85
Total budget range					
per school	500–23,600.00	50–51,707.00	350–45,001.00	393–56,770.00	5,000–22,393.00
per student	1.92–80.00	.14–164.00	.67–68.39	.40–66.55	3.94–19.14
Book budget (median)					
per school	1,432.00	2,267.00	2,798.00	3,167.00	4,797.00
per student	6.00	5.84	5.06	4.09	3.81
Book budget range					
per school	241–3,635.00	56–42,000.00	150–40,000.00	292–23,700.00	1,900–10,957.00
per student	1.60–23.82	.15–140.00	.26–69.93	.29–27.78	1.68–9.37
AV resources budget (median)					
per school	900.00	1,475.00	1,626.00	2,100.00	2,000.00
per student	3.72	3.55	2.84	2.68	1.68
AV resources budget range					
per school	250–9,300.00	75–50,550.00	15–11,000.00	100–30,900.00	300–10,700.00
per student	1.42–31.52	.22–113.60	.03–20.00	.10–36.23	.29–9.68
Computer resources budget (median)					
per school	431.00	1,000.00	1,077.00	695.00	800.00
per student	2.20	2.29	1.85	0.97	0.51
Computer resources budget range					
per school	50–10,500.00	30–20,750.00	20–35,170.00	50–32,700.00	200–2,100.00
per student	.19–42.35	.07–43.23	.04–53.45	.06–45.42	.20–1.75
Collections					
Size of book collection (median)	5,390	8,000	8,931	10,000	10,620
Range of book collection (median)	1,000–19,350	1,000–20,000	1,600–22,260	3,000–22,000	9,200–17,693

the LMCs in the study have telephones at hand. Although more than 50 percent of the respondents report being involved in some form of resource sharing, many still participate without the necessary telephone in the center. Elementary media specialists participating in interlibrary loan reported that they loaned more materials than they borrowed; this is the reverse of all other levels of schools. Table 19 also shows the small number of resources being loaned or borrowed by those schools reporting such activity.

Table 20 describes the extent to which the media center staff borrowed materials for students and teachers from a variety of external sources ranging from the public library and district and regional materials centers to academic and special libraries and specialized information agencies including commercial sources for rentals and online services. Regardless of the source, library media specialists borrow more resources for teachers than they do for students.

Planning and Decision Making

Seventy-nine percent of all of the respondents reported that they regularly plan curricular content with teachers so that instruction in information use and communica-

Table 14 / Median Expenditures for Microcomputer Resources
(all funding sources)

	Elementary	Middle/Jr. High	Senior High	Other	Total
Expenditures					
Microcomputer software					
Local	$500	$356	$342	$500	$406
Federal	364	899	1,000	1,193	500
Gift	200	275	185	104	200
Total	500	500	375	780	480
Online resources					
Local	450	400	1,000	1,000	944
Federal	0	475	1,000	0	500
Gift	0	150	375	0	350
Total	450	400	1,000	1,000	600
Technical processing					
Local	2,120	206	713	200	550
Federal	0	0	3,250	0	3,250
Gift	100	0	0	0	100
Total	2,000	206	863	200	600
Equipment					
Local	2,000	2,100	2,000	1,850	2,000
Federal	1,383	2,000	2,168	1,295	1,876
Gift	2,250	900	2,308	1,455	1,985
Total	2,100	2,523	2,400	2,698	2,398
Maintenance					
Local	200	200	450	263	225
Federal	0	100	0	0	100
Gift	125	100	0	0	100
Total	200	200	450	263	200
All microcomputer resources					
Local	1,000	725	1,000	1,287	1,000
Federal	694	1,609	1,900	1,147	1,295
Gift	900	525	1,438	600	800
Total	1,250	1,464	1,600	2,000	1,448

Table 15 / Collection Size and Local Expenditures in LMCs for Private Schools

	Elementary n=10		Senior High n=26		Other n=33	
	median	mean	median	mean	median	mean
Size of book collection	6,355	6,943	10,000	12,663	10,000	12,446
Volumes added, 1989–1990	363	479	250	393	300	498
Number of books per pupil	24	25	23	44	25	30
Volumes discarded, 1989–1990	88	211	135	406	100	202
Size of AV collection	380	446	800	2,746	699	1,149
Number of AV items added, 1989–1990	8	106	20	26	25	37
Number of AV items per pupil	1	2	3	8	1	3
AV items discarded, 1989–1990	1	4	1	11	0	97
Size of microcomputer software collection	0	52	15	33	3	139
Microcomputer software added, 1989–1990	0	10	1	10	0	7
Microcomputer software per pupil	0	0	0	1	0	1
Microcomputer software discarded, 1989–1990	0	0	0	0	0	2
Expenditures						
Books	$3,500.00	$3,563.00	$3,000.00	$3,496.00	$2,000.00	$4,079.00
Books per pupil	7.96	10.89	5.51	11.92	9.53	10.49
Periodicals	400.00	565.00	1,575.00	1,769.00	750.00	1,620.00
Periodicals per pupil	1.42	1.72	3.36	7.54	2.66	2.96
Microform	0.00	0.00	829.00	955.00	950.00	1,178.00
Microform per pupil	0.00	0.00	0.73	1.66	1.41	1.35
Audiovisual materials	290.00	932.00	600.00	831.00	600.00	1,814.00
Audiovisual materials per pupil	1.09	3.07	0.91	2.52	2.06	3.88
Microcomputer software	397.00	1,166.00	300.00	308.00	1,244.00	989.00
Microcomputer software per pupil	2.63	4.40	0.36	0.88	1.20	4.51
*Total material expenditures (TME)	$3,445.00	$7,696.00	$10,121.00	$12,842.00	$5,915.00	$12,286.00
TME per pupil	$18.28	$25.39	$19.17	$33.90	$21.09	$43.31

* See narrative for explanation of TME

Table 16 / School Library Media Specialists Experience, Salary, and Supporting Staff

	Elementary		Middle/Jr. High		Senior High		Other	
	median	mean	median	mean	median	mean	median	mean
No. media specialists in school	1.00	0.98	1.00	1.04	1.00	1.36	1.00	1.13
Years experience in K–12 schools	17	16	17	17	18	17	13	14
Years experience library/media	12	12	13	13	15	15	10	11
Salary of head media specialist	$30,000	$31,477	$32,000	$31,969	$31,100	$31,696	$25,000	$25,549
Student assistants	0.00	4.52	7.68	5.00	4.00	6.52	1.00	3.95
Support staff/paid clerks	1.00	0.77	1.00	0.81	1.00	1.11	1.00	0.68
Adult volunteers	1.00	3.84	0.00	0.83	0.00	1.06	1.00	3.53

tion skills is integrated into the curriculum. Table 21 characterizes the kind of planning that takes place between teachers and media specialists and the length of time specialists spend in planning. Formal planning is defined as planned meetings scheduled in advance of a specific instructional unit while informal planning is defined as spur-of-the-moment planning with no advance notice. At all school levels, library media specialists do more informal, or spur-of-the-moment, planning than they do formal planning.

For the current study, library media specialists were asked to indicate their level of participation in 13 schoolwide decision-making activities. These are listed in Table 22. We compared the 13 decision-making activities and the availability of a telephone in the media center. For whatever reason, library media specialists who have tele-

Table 17 / LMCs and Technology

	Number Responding	Percent
Additional funds provided for		
Microcomputer software	180	24
Online bibliographic services	41	6
CD-ROM	67	9
Technical processing services	39	5
LMC uses satellite transmissions	133	17
LMC uses cable TV transmissions	473	59
LMC has automated card catalog on-site	59	7
LMC plans to develop automated card cataloging	282	40
LMC has automated circulation system on-site	240	30
LMC plans to develop automated circulation	231	45
Student access to electronic database searching		
On-site online access to databases	94	12
Off-site online access to databases	30	4
On-site CD-ROM	93	12
Off-site CD-ROM	18	2
LMC has access to fax machine		
Yes, in center	20	2
Yes, in school	78	10
Yes, elsewhere	18	2
No access	691	86

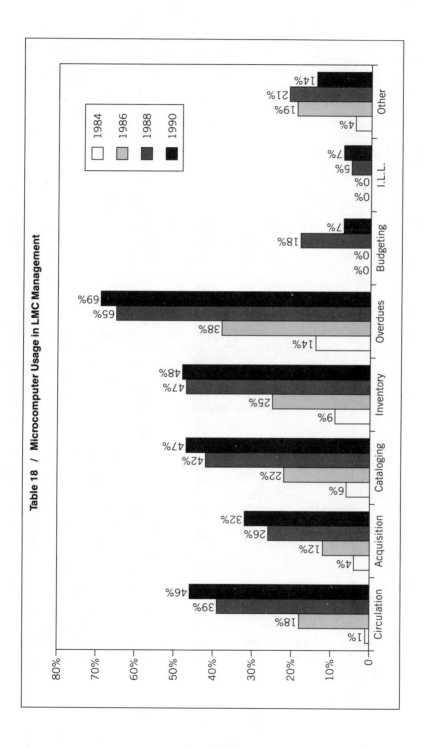

Table 18 / Microcomputer Usage in LMC Management

Legend:
- 1984
- 1986
- 1988
- 1990

Circulation
- 1984: 1%
- 1986: 18%
- 1988: 39%
- 1990: 46%

Acquisition
- 1984: 4%
- 1986: 12%
- 1988: 26%
- 1990: 32%

Cataloging
- 1984: 6%
- 1986: 22%
- 1988: 42%
- 1990: 47%

Inventory
- 1984: 9%
- 1986: 25%
- 1988: 47%
- 1990: 48%

Overdues
- 1984: 14%
- 1986: 38%
- 1988: 65%
- 1990: 69%

Budgeting
- 1984: 0%
- 1986: 0%
- 1988: 18%
- 1990: 7%

I.L.L.
- 1984: 0%
- 1986: 0%
- 1988: 5%
- 1990: 7%

Other
- 1984: 4%
- 1986: 19%
- 1988: 21%
- 1990: 14%

439

Table 19 / LMC and Network Participation

	Elementary	Middle/Jr. High	Senior High	Other
LMC member of network	53%	64%	68%	68%
LMC has telephone	36%	54%	70%	51%
Added funds for interlibrary loan	5%	3%	12%	6%
Interlibrary loan status				
Net lender	42%	30%	31%	15%
Net borrower	36%	50%	59%	72%
Even	5%	5%	3%	0%
No transactions	17%	15%	7%	13%
Median print items loaned	20	23	20	10
Median print items borrowed	20	20	38	30
Median nonprint items loaned	5	5	8	6
Median nonprint Items borrowed	7	10	15	30

phones in the LMC are more likely to participate in schoolwide policy development, planning for facilities, staff development, and curriculum. They are also more involved in evaluating LMC staff, budgeting, developing school goals and objectives, and scheduling LMC use.

District Coordination

Forty-seven percent of the respondents work with district level media coordinators, at least part-time. This is a larger number than reported in 1989 that they had access to a district consultant. In the previous four studies, the data never supported statistically significant positive relationships between access to district level media coordinators and collections/expenditures. However, in the current study, with the addition of microcomputer resources in the analysis, several factors are statistically significant at the .05 level or below.

These factors included size of school, number of AV items added, size of the microcomputer software collection including additions and discards, salary of the library media specialist, availability of clerical assistance, and use of adult volunteers. In districts without coordinators, TME, number of books per pupil, and number of books added, are still slightly higher. Regardless of the availability of district media leadership, media specialists do little formal planning with teachers. It seems apparent that library media specialists have not yet adjusted their concept of integration of library resources into the curriculum to include the need for formal planning with teacher colleagues.

The value of the district coordinator is emphasized when we examine the data in Table 22. These data compare administrative functions and services in districts with and without district level media coordinators. Media specialists who have access to district leadership are more likely to have a library media advisory committee, a selection policy, cable TV capacity in the media center, and plans for OPACs and automated circulation systems. Indeed, Table 23 indicates a statistically significant positive relationship between all of the above variables and access to a district level media coordinator.

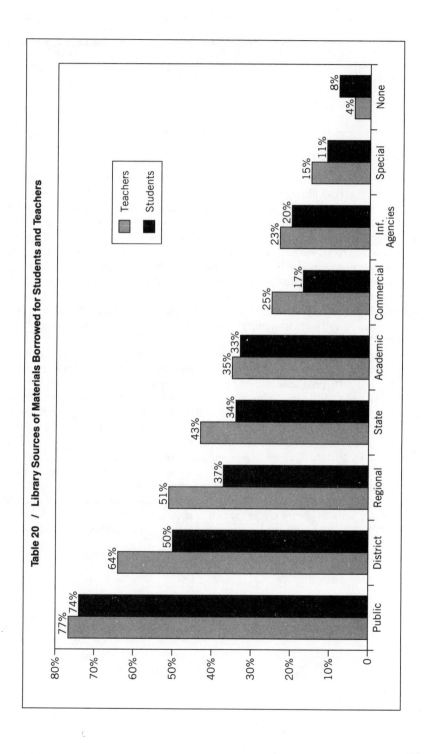

Table 20 / Library Sources of Materials Borrowed for Students and Teachers

Legend:
☐ Teachers
■ Students

Source	Teachers	Students
Public	77%	74%
District	64%	50%
Regional	51%	37%
State	43%	34%
Academic	35%	33%
Commercial	25%	17%
Inf. Agencies	23%	20%
Special	15%	11%
None	4%	8%

Table 21 / Library Media Specialist/Teacher Instructional Planning by Grade Levels

	Mean No. Hours Formal Instructional Planning	Mean No. Hours Informal Instructional Planning
Elementary	1.02	2.26
Middle/Jr. High	1.68	3.28
Senior High	1.78	2.85
Other	1.22	2.64
Total	1.35	2.65

A Ten-Year Picture

This report, together with the previous reports, presents a ten-year picture of the development of school library media centers during the 1980s, a view that is both sweet and sour. It is disappointing to have to document the continued erosion of school library resource collections. It is disappointing to note that library media specialists do not do serious planning with teachers and to find that so few are reaching out beyond their buildings to network. It is sweet to note the progress of those pioneers who are leading their programs into the Information Age by laying the groundwork for effective networking and creating bridges for users to the world of information outside their school buildings. If we consider the 1945 publication of *School Libraries for Today and Tomorrow* (ALA) as the origin of our philosophy that the school library media program is intrinsic to quality education, then these data show remarkable progress.

However, it also shows we must move forward more rapidly in asserting to our administrators and to our communities that library media centers are not fixed assets and that adequate programs cannot be developed unless resources are regularly replaced and updated. We must also move forward more aggressively in our roles as advocates for instructional programs that will guarantee student access to the wide variety of resources and skills that will enable them to become lifelong learners. In order to make these moves we must use research findings intelligently. We need to keep our own records of expenditures and acquisitions so that we can quickly gain access to the data that will support our requests for funding and program development. We must do our own local research with teachers and students and communicate those findings to support our arguments for better collections and services. The value of our work as library media specialists should be measured not by the quality of our efforts in running a media center but rather by the quality of our efforts in getting students and teachers to use resources.

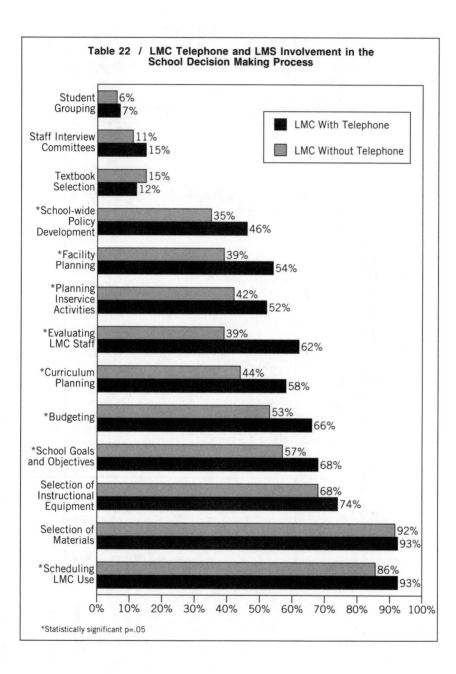

Table 22 / LMC Telephone and LMS Involvement in the School Decision Making Process

Legend:
- LMC With Telephone
- LMC Without Telephone

Category	LMC Without Telephone	LMC With Telephone
Student Grouping	6%	7%
Staff Interview Committees	11%	15%
Textbook Selection	15%	12%
*School-wide Policy Development	35%	46%
*Facility Planning	39%	54%
*Planning Inservice Activities	42%	52%
*Evaluating LMC Staff	39%	62%
*Curriculum Planning	44%	58%
*Budgeting	53%	66%
*School Goals and Objectives	57%	68%
Selection of Instructional Equipment	68%	74%
Selection of Materials	92%	93%
*Scheduling LMC Use	86%	93%

*Statistically significant p=.05

Table 23 / Comparison of Schools with and without District Level Media Coordinators: Collection, Expenditures, and Planning Time

	With Full-Time n = 296		With Part-Time n = 93		Without n = 397	
	median	mean	median	mean	median	mean
Enrollment	625	730	559	676	516	613
Total materials expenditures (TME)	$8,019	$15,232	$8,759	$11,918	$8,007	$11,756
Total materials expenditure (TME) per pupil	$13.24	$25.27	$14.40	$19.03	$15.14	$23.52
Size of book collection	10,000	10,704	10,230	10,859	9,229	10,556
Number of books per pupil	15.39	17.15	16.50	18.54	17.71	21.30
Volumes added, 1989–1990	350	514	350	399	300	453
Volumes discarded, 1989–1990	175	388	173	366	108	309
Size of AV collection	1,102	1,556	1,000	1,965	500	1,197
Number of AV items per pupil	1.84	2.47	1.63	3.73	1.03	1.97
Number of AV items added, 1989–1990*	33	57	25	56	20	36
Number of AV items discarded, 1989–1990	5	46	9	28	2	22
Size of software collection*	75	147	73	118	25	85
Microcomputer software per pupil	0.00	0.00	0.00	0.00	0.00	0.00
Microcomputer software added, 1989–1990*	9	26	9	14	2	12
Microcomputer software discarded, 1989–1990*	0	2	0	3	0	1
Microcomputer software local funds per pupil	$0.70	$1.04	$0.89	$1.22	$0.99	$2.14
Library media specialist salary*	$32,000	$32,227	$32,000	$33,126	$29,010	$29,672
Clerical assistance*	1.00	0.82	1.00	1.03	1.00	0.83
Adult volunteers*	0.00	3.07	0.00	2.42	0.00	2.03
Weekly time of formal planning with teachers (hrs.)	1.00	1.39	1.00	1.41	1.00	1.32
Weekly time of informal planning with teachers (hrs.)	2.00	2.83	2.00	2.51	2.00	2.52

Statistically significant relationship p = .05

Table 24 / Comparison of Schools with and without District Level
Media Coordinators: Administrators and Services

	Percent with Full-Time District Coordinator n = 296	Percent with Part-Time District Coordinator n = 93	Percent without District Coordinator n = 397
Use of library media advisory committee*	40	27	13
Availability of selection policy*	88	86	73
Planning with teachers for integrated instruction	78	76	80
Added funds for microcomputer software	26	21	23
Added funds for online searching	4	7	6
Added funds for technical processing	6	5	6
Added funds for CD-ROM	8	8	10
LMC member of network	56	66	63
Added funds for interlibrary loan	7	3	7
Telephone in LMC	48	58	48
LMC uses cable TV*	67	56	54
LMC uses satellite transmissions	16	14	18
Automated card catalog on-site	6	7	8
Plans for automated card catalog*	49	41	35
Automated circulation system on-site	33	27	28
Plans for automated circulation system*	58	46	37
Online access on-site	9	12	14
CD-ROM access on-site	10	14	13
Fax machine in school or library**	9	7	15

*Statistically significant p = .05, positive relationship

**Statistically significant p = .05, negative relationship

Library Buildings, 1991:
Between a Recession and a Hard Place

Bette-Lee Fox
Managing Editor, *Library Journal*

Michael Rogers
Assistant News Editor, *Library Journal*

Ann Burns
Staff Editor, *Library Journal*

Keith R. A. DeCandido
Assistant Editor/Keyboard, *Library Journal*

Despite the dismal outlook for library budgets, salaries, and hours, libraries are still being built. However, most of the money for the projects featured in Tables 1–9 was appropriated years ago, through public referenda and community planning, or from the private sector. Perhaps the real question is whether some of the 948 buildings in progress will be allowed to wither and die in various stages of wishful thinking. In the meantime, how are we going to stock and staff the newly finished libraries?

The outcome is not clear. Nor is it necessarily bleak. But library growth must be watched carefully, and *Library Journal* will continue to monitor the capital improvement activity of academic and public libraries as long as it persists.

From July 1, 1990, to June 30, 1991, 120 new public buildings and 108 addition and renovation projects were completed. Some 36 academic projects were completed during that same period. The largest new academic project is the University of California–San Francisco Library ($40.4 million, 120,000 square feet). The largest new public project is the Alachua County Library District building in Gainesville, Florida ($10.9 million, 85,000 square feet).

The number of buildings in progress (projects not yet completed by June 30, 1991) is growing once again. With 948 projects, we've almost matched the all-time high of 949 reached in 1989. The 1991 list contains 847 public buildings from 45 states and 101 academic buildings from 39 states, the District of Columbia, and Guam. The list of individual projects submitted is contained in Tables 8 and 9, with the stage(s) of progress checked accordingly.

An obvious concession to the stringent economic environment is the multipurpose building at the center of several new projects. Libraries are sharing space and costs with police departments, community centers, senior citizens centers, and healthcare facilities to get the most use from limited funds.

What will the future hold for libraries hoping to expand or improve services by undertaking a capital improvement project? Will patrons come to the rescue of libraries by voting funds and donating money as government participation continues to recede? Or will libraries be abandoned by the public and private sectors alike? This report offers some answers.

Note: Adapted from *Library Journal,* December 1991

Table 1 / New Public Library Buildings, 1991

Community	Pop. in M	Code	Project Cost	Const. Cost	Gross Sq. Ft.	Sq. Ft. Cost	Equip. Cost	Site Cost	Other Costs	Volumes	Reader Seats	Federal Funds	State Funds	Local Funds	Gift Funds	Architect
Arizona																
Phoenix	150	MS	$6,399,940	$4,653,830	66,000	$70.51	$1,200,000	Owned	$546,110	250,000	471	0	0	$6,399,940	0	Anderson DeBartolo Pan
California																
Covina	13	B	59,080	24,300	2,600	9.35	34,780	Leased	0	20,000	22	0	0	53,380	$5,700	none
El Cajon	89	B	4,013,015	3,515,608	30,166	116.54	202,407	Owned	295,000	200,000	170	$570,889	0	3,392,626	151,264	Decker & Associates
Roseville	10	B	1,610,673	1,249,683	10,300	121.33	151,009	Owned	209,981	30,000	61	0	$138,029	1,472,644	0	Barnum & Folsom
Stratford	46	B	445,286	310,923	3,400	91.45	67,826	$28,421	38,116	15,000	50	228,698	0	228,698	0	Donald Christensen
Colorado																
Estes Park[1]	11	M	1,374,773	867,127	13,652	63.52	227,738	Leased	279,908	40,000	109	0	0	1,354,773	20,000	Thorp Associates
Florida																
Brandon	93	B	2,538,000	2,300,000	30,000	76.67	75,000	n/a	163,000	120,000	175	0	0	2,538,000	n/a	James A. Jennewein
Daytona Beach	370	S	664,346	498,346	10,000	49.83	120,000	Owned	46,000	0	0	0	200,000	464,346	0	Dana Smith
Fort Myers	349	B	1,072,069	642,021	7,000	91.72	228,142	Owned	201,906	35,000	55	0	0	1,047,279	24,790	Gora/McGahey/Lee
Gainesville	187	MS	10,877,951	7,820,500	85,000	92.01	502,611	200,000	2,354,840	400,000	240	0	0	10,853,951	24,000	Hunter-McKellips; Turnbull
Indiantown	5	B	610,528	474,528	5,009	94.74	104,212	221,636	31,787	10,000	44	0	216,980	314,989	78,559	John M. Foster
Jacksonville	40	B	4,725,000	2,364,964	23,000	102.83	392,710	Leased	1,745,690	100,000	116	0	200,000	4,525,000	0	Bhide & Hall
Miami[2]	250	B	2,150,000	1,340,000	41,400	32.37	650,000	Leased	160,000	175,000	350	0	0	2,150,000	0	H.J. Ross
New Port Richey	14	M	1,979,721	1,496,376	15,230	98.25	0	421,345	62,000	50,000	100	400,000	0	1,158,376	421,345	Gee & Jensen
New Port Richey	60	B	1,316,353	907,555	11,181	81.17	175,000	219,385	14,413	40,000	111	0	0	1,316,353	0	Fletcher, Valenti . . .
Tallahassee	195	M	10,362,391	8,231,627	88,300	93.22	514,900	525,000	1,090,864	382,000	312	200,000	0	9,980,391	182,000	Jim Roberson
Georgia																
Atlanta	5	B	908,560	446,618	4,000	111.65	122,190	250,000	89,752	10,000	40	0	0	908,560	0	Leo A. Daly
Atlanta	15	B	766,495	353,253	5,000	70.65	157,428	197,500	58,314	10,000	40	0	0	766,495	0	Leo A. Daly
Buena Vista	6	B	437,259	297,627	4,300	69.22	104,705	Owned	34,927	18,000	30	0	393,533	43,726	0	Mike Parker
Chamblee	15	B	740,580	388,809	4,000	97.20	125,161	125,000	101,610	18,000	40	0	0	740,580	0	Leo A. Daly
Clarkston	38	B	1,447,155	954,664	10,000	95.47	293,585	108,900	90,006	45,000	78	0	0	1,447,155	0	Stevens/Wilkinson; Brown
Decatur	38	B	1,576,246	1,125,460	10,000	112.55	331,510	227,000	119,276	25,000	72	0	0	1,576,246	0	Stevens/Wilkinson; Brown
Decatur	26	B	1,693,980	1,086,020	10,000	108.60	290,703	227,000	90,257	45,000	78	0	0	1,693,980	0	Stevens/Wilkinson; Brown
Decatur[3]	n/a	B	99,711	86,500	300	288.33	n/a	Leased	13,211	5,000	8	0	0	99,711	0	Porta-Structures
Decatur	50	BS	2,978,735	1,888,100	21,500	87.82	696,821	149,475	244,339	85,000	121	0	1,900,649	1,078,086	41,050	Stevens Wilkinson; Brown
Helen	3	B	393,108	269,440	4,200	64.15	48,844	40,000	34,824	14,000	44	0	282,754	69,304	20,077	Walden, Ashworth
Hogansville	7	B	420,434	252,403	3,500	72.12	75,723	20,000	72,308	14,000	29	0	343,300	57,057	0	James W. Buckley
Lithonia	15	B	767,554	482,913	4,000	120.73	122,190	99,884	62,567	20,000	40	0	0	767,554	0	Leo A. Daly
Montezuma	9	B	552,372	363,429	6,500	55.91	142,767	Owned	46,176	22,270	106	0	480,245	53,223	18,904	Brittain, Thompson, Bray
Oakwood	32	B	1,204,357	898,750	12,970	69.29	245,069	Owned	60,538	82,000	135	0	919,571	284,786	0	Garland Reynolds
Redan	70	B	3,228,242	1,848,310	21,500	85.97	696,821	515,160	167,951	85,000	121	0	1,853,160	1,375,082	0	Stevens/Wilkinson; Brown
Stone Mountain	15	B	1,103,109	411,794	4,000	102.95	122,190	510,998	58,127	85,000	40	0	0	1,103,109	0	Leo A. Daly
Tallapoosa	6	B	455,256	333,012	4,000	83.25	81,199	Owned	41,045	16,520	42	0	403,236	52,020	0	Alex Roush
Tucker	20	B	1,879,561	1,078,540	10,000	107.85	258,340	391,475	151,206	45,000	63	0	0	1,879,561	0	Stevens/Wilkinson; Brown

Symbol Code: B—Branch Library; BS—Branch & System Headquarters; M—Main Library; MS—Main & System Headquarters; S—System Headquarters; n/a—not available

Table 1 / New Public Library Buildings, 1991 (cont.)

Community	Pop. in M	Code	Project Cost	Const. Cost	Gross Sq. Ft.	Sq. Ft. Cost	Equip. Cost	Site Cost	Other Costs	Volumes	Reader Seats	Federal Funds	State Funds	Local Funds	Gift Funds	Architect
Illinois																
Chicago	5	B	630,273	340,951	12,000	28.41	270,000	Leased	19,322	65,000	82	0	0	630,273	0	Andrew S. Jaworksi
Chicago	40	B	3,000,000	2,065,000	12,600	163.89	175,000	400,000	360,000	50,000	96	0	1,250,000	1,750,000	0	Kendall Fleming
Elk Grove Village	33	M	6,610,371	4,915,745	63,000	78.03	1,168,865	Owned	525,761	275,000	377		250,000	6,360,371	0	Wendt, Cedarholm . . .
Fairview Heights	14	M	1,816,642	1,656,642	20,000	82.83	60,000	Owned	100,000	35,000	57	200,000		1,493,095	123,547	EWR & Associates
Girard	3	M	345,589	273,932	5,787	47.34	9,474	1	62,182	22,000	33		132,000	17,000	223,269	Stanton J. Grainick
Maquon	2	M	138,867	118,120	1,960	60.27	0	10,500	10,247	13,000	13		50,937	62,579	25,351	Laverdere Construction
Morrisonville	1	M	121,000	116,000	2,100	55.24	0	5,000		5,000	10		40,000	54,000	30,000	Morton Bldgs.
Richmond[4]	5	M	831,000	634,000	9,000	70.44	62,000	28,000	107,000	35,000	35	250,000		581,000	.	David L. Jenkins
Seneca	3	M	1,350,000	987,000	9,480	104.11	150,495	72,852	139,653	27,000	46			1,350,000		Frye Gillan Molinaro
Indiana																
Bicknell	8	M	211,897	182,500	4,536	40.23	24,690	4,432	275	100,000	25	0	0	1,212	210,685	Ridgeview Homes
Ellettsville	15	B	1,622,762	1,002,093	10,460	95.80	157,391	312,450	150,828	40,000	85	199,206	0	1,421,556	2,000	Pecsok, Jelliffe . . .
Iowa																
Earlville	1	M	85,016	69,000	1,800	38.33	10,016	Owned	6,000	12,000	16	0	0	75,000	10,016	Craig D. Schwerdtfeger
Nevada	12	M	947,085	724,345	11,000	65.85	122,475	Owned	100,265	45,000	68	0	3,000	792,000	152,085	Rudi-Lee-Dreyer
Kansas																
Gridley[5]	3	B	427,762	331,858	4,300	77.18	43,205	14,950	37,749	20,000	22	0	0	427,762	0	David G. Emig
Waverly	3	B	410,451	313,429	4,200	74.63	48,039	15,000	33,983	20,000	22	0	0	408,751	1,700	David G. Emig
Maryland																
Savage[6]	28	B	3,488,000	2,464,000	20,500	120.20	501,000	244,000	279,000	50,000	80	0	0	3,488,000	0	Greenman-Pedersen
Massachusetts																
W. Bridgewater	8	M	1,306,037	1,195,037	12,074	98.98	50,000	Owned	61,000	60,000	75	0	0	1,236,037	70,000	Robert Therrien
Norton	15	M	2,000,000	1,570,175	15,175	103.47	165,870	Owned	263,955	60,000	80	0	0	1,500,000	500,000	Richard ONeil
Wareham	20	M	2,693,515	2,261,116	20,450	110.57	263,112	Owned	169,287	85,000	140	115,160	1,142,570	1,277,730	158,055	Amsler Woodhouse . . .
Michigan																
Schoolcraft	5	M	170,309	131,150	3,000	43.72	11,000	25,000	3,159	15,000	34	0	0	22,000	148,309	Norm Hamann
Minnesota																
Apple Valley	56	B	3,794,510	3,027,510	28,500	106.23	432,000	335,000	n/a	100,000	n/a	200,000		3,594,510	0	Leonard Parker
Duluth	9	B	2,365,386	1,591,615	16,636	95.67	109,024	183,978	480,769	25,000	69	1,560,000	292,500	452,913	59,973	Schaefer; Meyer . . .
Melrose	6	B	252,268	197,719	2,850	69.38	38,518	Owned	16,031	15,000	37	0		252,268		Boarman & Associates
Mahtomedi	10	B	1,379,629	1,093,140	9,003	121.42	65,298	146,826	74,365	25,000	33	0		1,379,629		SKD Architects
Mounds View	19	B	1,816,230	824,617	8,000	103.08	156,644	493,908	341,061	46,000	46	0		1,816,230		Buetow & Associates
Mississippi																
Pelahatchie	2	B	111,500	80,000	1,680	47.62	8,800	18,000	4,700	8,500	14	0	0	111,500	0	Robb Farr
Missouri																
Independence	50	B	962,700	700,634	17,887	39.17	108,083	124,500	29,483	170,000	132	0	0	962,700	0	Tognascioli, Gross . . .
Kansas City	56	B	922,525	615,066	15,580	39.48	136,497	147,219	23,743	115,000	110	0	0	922,525	0	Tognascioli, Gross . . .

Symbol Code: B – Branch Library; BS – Branch & System Headquarters; M – Main Library; MS – Main & System Headquarters; S – System Headquarters; n/a – not available

Lee's Summit	70	B	1,049,111	677,938	17,500	38.74	187,329	157,500	26,344	173,000	124	0	0	1,049,111	0	Tognascioli, Gross . . .
Union	15	MS	958,310	731,079	10,696	68.35	33,074	130,000	64,157	90,000	55	298,378	0	0	659,932	Robert A. Horn
Nebraska																
Clarkson	1	M	178,320	142,810	3,000	47.60	9,870	10,900	14,740	10,000	10	62,500	0	0	115,820	Krhounek & Povondra
Nevada																
Round Mountain	2	M	594,000	474,000	5,020	94.42	56,900	30,000	33,100	30,000	42	56,900	0	507,100	30,000	Scott Willison
New Jersey																
Brick	66	B	2,760,965	2,460,533	18,691	131.64	250,311	Owned	50,121	65,000	100	0	0	2,760,965	0	James W. Hyres
Hillsborough	30	B	2,303,094	1,817,640	17,820	102.00	399,329	Owned	86,125	99,800	134	0	208,000	2,094,086	1,008	Robert W. Russell
New York																
Brooklyn	40	B	3,521,000	2,278,000	7,800	292.05	65,000	Owned	1,178,000	30,000	100	200,467	0	3,320,533	0	Perkins Geddes . . .
Clifton Springs[7]	2	M	n/a	n/a	6,500	n/a	61,884	n/a	n/a	n/a	50	0	0	0	n/a	Bern Associates
Lewiston	11	M	1,782,552	1,493,759	11,687	127.81	118,120	24,432	146,241	52,000	70	251,096	109,880	1,413,536	8,040	August S. Jubulis
North Carolina																
Charlotte	100	B	5,218,036	2,058,216	24,400	84.35	248,885	2,600,000	310,935	90,000	137	0	0	2,618,036	2,600,000	Clark, Tribble . . .
Fayetteville	59	B	2,071,881	1,141,878	18,000	63.44	239,242	112,500	578,261	60,000	58	0	100,000	1,971,881	0	Walter Vick
Lowell	5	B	382,123	300,156	3,604	83.28	7,508	44,000	30,459	15,000	16	0	0	382,123	0	Beam & Yeargin
Thomasville	16	B	1,561,409	1,210,260	19,360	62.51	120,309	125,000	105,840	70,000	95	0	125,000	349,409	1,087,000	Newman & Jones
North Dakota																
Harvey	5	M	406,641	316,728	5,000	63.35	5,708	18,000	66,205	23,000	18	124,500	390	121,624	160,127	Robert Anderson
Ohio																
Akron	35	B	1,566,192	1,184,886	11,950	99.15	171,306	100,000	110,000	50,000	62	0	0	1,566,192	0	T.C. Architects
Brecksville	24	B	2,594,198	1,526,000	15,600	97.82	321,600	Owned	746,598	73,000	100	0	0	2,594,198	0	van Dijk, Johnson
Columbus	23	B	1,460,000	729,000	7,500	97.20	144,900	475,000	111,100	36,000	49	0	0	1,460,000	0	Moody/Nolan
Columbus	20	B	1,185,000	678,500	7,500	90.47	149,058	250,000	107,442	36,000	49	0	0	1,185,000	0	Moody/Nolan
Gahanna	24	B	1,870,000	1,130,000	12,000	94.17	203,374	350,000	186,626	65,000	95	0	0	1,870,000	0	Design Group, Inc.
New Lexington	34	MS	1,382,766	1,036,356	11,994	86.41	186,632	87,000	72,778	70,000	60	385,396	0	987,370	10,000	Mark Denny
Ostrander	1	B	351,653	269,827	2,500	107.93	54,919	5,000	21,907	10,000	24	0	0	346,653	5,000	Alexander-Seckel
Toronto	15	B	597,723	510,586	5,000	102.12	44,085	Owned	43,052	18,000	35	185,989	0	405,234	6,500	Michael Tabeling
Oklahoma																
Konawa	2	M	206,191	153,191	5,243	29.22	45,500	Owned	7,500	20,000	75	0	0	0	206,555	Locke-Wright
Oklahoma City[8]	5	M	2,580,000	2,424,738	39,000	62.17	35,262	Owned	120,000	n/a	12	0	2,500,000	0	0	Robison Boeck
Owasso	14	B	625,555	383,325	5,800	66.09	48,735	164,880	28,615	25,000	30	0	0	625,555	0	Olsen-Coffey
Tulsa	36	B	1,091,415	698,205	9,800	71.25	108,135	196,050	89,025	35,000	33	0	0	1,051,415	40,000	Wallace & Bates
Oregon																
Dallas	12	M	786,644	516,258	10,540	49.40	69,990	n/a	200,396	39,000	54	90,428	0	690,916	5,300	Carl Sherwood
Florence	10	M	1,600,000	990,000	14,800	66.89	350,000	145,000	115,000	60,000	50	135,000	0	1,150,000	315,000	Richard P. Turi
Pennsylvania																
Bradford	25	M	2,026,255	1,747,280	18,000	97.07	34,600	110,000	134,375	80,000	100	400,000	10,000	35,000	1,581,255	Robert K. Hendryx
Freedom	2	M	320,000	259,000	5,856	44.23	20,000	15,000	26,000	n/a	20	150,000	50,000	85,000	35,000	John Regney
Jefferson Boro	10	M	3,075,000	n/a	33,000	n/a	90,676	Owned	180,000	40,000	40	0	0	3,230,000	0	Don Gmitter

Symbol Code: B—Branch Library; BS—Branch & System Headquarters; M—Main Library; MS—Main & System Headquarters; S—System Headquarters; n/a—not available

Table 1 / New Public Library Buildings, 1991 (cont.)

Community	Pop. in M	Code	Project Cost	Const. Cost	Gross Sq. Ft.	Sq. Ft. Cost	Equip. Cost	Site Cost	Other Costs	Volumes	Reader Seats	Federal Funds	State Funds	Local Funds	Gift Funds	Architect
Johnstown	16	M	663,000	500,000	6,550	76.34	38,000	100,000	25,000	40,000	44	0	500,000	63,000	100,000	Milton Shaulis
Pittsburgh	11	M	949,000	800,000	14,021	57.06	112,000	Owned	37,000	60,000	65	0	0	837,000	112,000	Don Stanish
South Carolina																
Goose Creek	25	B	1,525,595	1,023,962	15,000	68.26	147,040	206,678	147,915	50,000	80	0	0	1,525,595	0	Vito Pascullis
Greenville	22	B	1,361,709	937,526	12,050	77.80	117,268	220,000	86,915	65,000	68	100,000	0	1,111,709	150,000	F. Earle Gaulden
Inman	12	B	663,204	453,146	7,765	58.36	97,000	40,000	73,058	55,000	53	75,000	0	438,204	150,000	C. Wayne Crocker
South Dakota																
Faith	1	M	187,141	159,872	2,880	55.51	13,000	Leased	14,269	18,000	80	83,541	0	75,581	28,019	Bill Thomas
Tennessee																
Erin	7	M	239,000	192,700	2,800	68.82	8,000	25,000	13,300	15,000	15	100,000	35,784	103,266	0	Rufus Johnson Associates
Gleason	2	M	50,000	410,000	1,440	27.78	10,000	Owned	0	8,700	26	0	0	0	50,000	none
Lake City	3	M	270,000	185,000	3,660	50.55	41,000	30,000	14,000	15,000	36	100,000	35,784	93,216	41,000	Barge, Waggoner . . .
Westmoreland	2	M	n/a	130,000	2,400	54.17	n/a	Owned	0	5,000	12	65,000	35,000	30,000	0	Gingles & Gingles
Texas																
Bridge City	81	M	82,963	54,517	2,500	21.81	3,446	25,000	0	12,000	12	0	0	56,908	26,055	none
Hawkins	5	M	306,208	227,061	5,300	42.84	52,100	8,000	19,047	17,000	47	100,000	0	125,000	81,208	Gohmert Associates
Kaufman	40	M	611,000	520,000	9,500	54.74	59,000	Owned	32,000	53,000	65	200,000	0	0	411,000	Joseph F. Gordon
Mason	4	M	410,750	328,968	5,550	59.27	51,920	Owned	29,862	20,000	24	100,000	0	0	310,750	Jack E. Meek
Sachse	5	M	333,152	269,000	5,000	53.80	12,352	8,100	43,700	16,000	21	100,000	0	128,100	105,052	Black & Veatch
Willis	14	B	224,957	135,853	6,000	22.64	20,284	62,220	6,600	30,000	n/a	100,000	0	70,307	54,650	Edward D. Campbell
Utah																
Sandy	80	B	3,272,852	1,788,775	26,600	67.25	353,931	986,000	144,146	300,000	251	0	0	2,336,852	936,000	Scott, Louie . . .
Vermont																
Proctorsville	1	M	225,000	191,000	2,176	87.78	0	Owned	34,000	12,000	25	0	67,500	0	157,500	Kasser; Cavendish
Virginia																
Stuart	18	B	1,262,757	1,090,079	13,200	82.58	28,578	49,000	95,100	45,000	70	0	0	112,818	1,149,939	Williams, Tazewell
Washington	6	M	747,900	571,846	6,000	95.31	56,689	75,000	44,365	25,000	30	140,998	0	0	606,902	McClintock, Modiset
Washington																
Spokane	25	BS	1,883,295	1,347,284	18,000	74.85	170,625	221,215	144,171	40,000	84	0	0	1,863,295	20,000	Integrus Architecture
West Virginia																
Huntington	15	MS	492,290	355,569	5,000	71.11	47,740	60,750	28,231	25,000	30	175,000	0	112,000	205,290	Jerry Goff
Petersburg	10	M	651,507	461,081	7,780	59.26	53,435	105,000	31,991	80,000	24	310,000	80,000	25,000	236,507	J. D. King
Wisconsin																
Black Earth	1	M	238,441	132,574	2,560	51.79	26,000	50,000	29,867	13,700	24	0	0	216,441	22,000	K. Brink & Associates
Phillips	5	M	416,588	343,282	5,800	59.19	37,856	Owned	35,450	17,500	48	125,000	0	199,013	92,575	Devin Mogck
Stetsonville	1	M	317,275	249,065	3,990	62.42	36,534	14,865	16,811	18,000	32	0	0		317,275	Nelson & Jorgensen
Whitewater	17	M	1,972,306	1,311,016	15,872	82.60	218,571	234,854	207,865	75,000	72	0	0	1,095,093	877,213	HSR Associates

Symbol Code: B — Branch Library; BS — Branch & System Headquarters; M — Main Library; MS — Main & System Headquarters; S — System Headquarters; n/a — not available

Table 2 / Public Library Buildings: Additions and Renovations, 1991

Community	Pop. in M	Code	Project Cost	Const. Cost	Gross Sq. Ft.	Sq. Ft. Cost	Equip. Cost	Site Cost	Other Costs	Volumes	Reader Seats	Federal Funds	State Funds	Local Funds	Gift Funds	Architect
Alabama																
Notasulga	1	B	$27,500	$13,513	1,890	$7.15	$1,500	$12,487	0	375	50	0	0	0	$27,500	Broach & Sons
Alaska																
Skagway	1	M	211,938	n/a	1,288	n/a	n/a	Owned	n/a	20,000	30	0	$190,745	$21,193	0	Minch Ritter Forrest...
Arizona																
Scottsdale	40	B	343,582	200,610	2,000	100.30	114,205	Owned	$28,767	75,000	250	0	0	343,582	0	Roberts/Dinsmore Associates
Arkansas																
Newport	21	M	476,200	427,800	9,000	47.53	14,000	Owned	34,400	72,000	53	$134,227	0	77,000	264,973	Polk Stanley Saunders...
California																
Beverly Hills	36	M	20,963,568	n/a	92,000	n/a	n/a	Owned	n/a	300,000	330	0	0	20,963,568	0	Moore/Martin & Associates
Los Angeles[9]	41	B	1,402,636	1,193,175	5,000	238.64	28,034	Owned	181,427	24,000	40	800,000	0	602,636	0	Martinez Hirsch Associates
Ramona	25	B	129,000	103,500	800	129.37	0	Owned	25,500	n/a	n/a	120,000	0	9,000	0	Alfredo Larin
Rancho Santa Fe	8	B	489,000	344,000	2,400	143.33	40,000	80,000	25,000	5,000	30	0	0	129,000	360,000	Howard Spector
Colorado																
Louisville	15	M	929,262	189,381	9,100	20.81	89,000	620,881	30,000	30,000	60	79,000	5,000	845,262	0	Midgette/Seirroe & Associates
Connecticut																
Greenwich	58	M	778,288	431,085	7,000	61.58	156,883	Owned	190,320	n/a	n/a	0	216,133	65,000	497,155	Richard Foster Associates
New Canaan[10]	19	M	992,760	874,355	8,000	109.29	0	Owned	118,405	32,400	48	0	315,000	0	677,760	SMS Architects PC
New Haven	130	MS	17,300,000	13,000,000	103,000	126.21	2,042,594	Owned	2,257,406	450,000	275	100,000	350,000	16,850,000	0	Hardy Holzman...
Florida																
Bonita Springs	349	B	860,258	659,083	11,900	55.39	107,719	Owned	93,456	60,000	78	0	0	774,258	86,000	Gee & Jenson
Largo	140	M	304,494	287,814	22,082	13.03	0	Owned	16,680	200,000	175	0	0	293,915	10,579	Theodore J. Williamson
Miami[11]	23	B	710,000	494,000	5,500	89.81	40,000	60,000	116,000	22,000	44	0	0	710,000	0	Jerome Filer
Miami Beach	75	B	150,000	100,000	25,000	4.00	50,000	Owned	0	100,000	70	0	0	150,000	0	none
Miami Beach	30	B	265,000	219,000	1,500	146.00	25,000	Owned	21,000	25,000	46	0	0	265,000	0	Filer & Hammond
Ormond Beach	45	B	1,853,100	1,342,800	31,000	43.31	414,000	Owned	96,300	150,000	150	200,000	200,000	1,268,100	185,000	Spillis, Candela & Partners
Sebring	18	MS	594,800	480,076	10,776	44.55	42,900	Owned	71,824	54,096	88	222,400	150,000	77,400	145,000	Stottler, Stagg & Associates
Yankeetown	5	B	70,259	61,450	1,500	40.96	4,416	Owned	4,393	8,000	30	0	0	0	70,259	Davies & Fleeger
Georgia																
Atlanta	15	B	538,595	385,428	6,835	56.39	99,221	Owned	53,946	36,000	32	0	0	538,595	0	Leo A. Daly
Dallas	45	B	665,541	512,495	13,000	39.42	106,392	Owned	46,654	61,500	187	0	550,476	115,065	0	Southern Engineering
Decatur	20	B	275,837	169,670	8,670	19.57	91,779	Owned	14,388	44,000	66	0	0	275,837	0	Leo A. Daly

Symbol Code: B – Branch Library; BS – Branch & System Headquarters; M – Main Library; MS – Main & System Headquarters; S – System Headquarters; n/a – not available

Table 2 / Public Library Buildings: Additions and Renovations, 1991 (cont.)

Community	Pop. in M	Code	Project Cost	Const. Cost	Gross Sq. Ft.	Sq. Ft. Cost	Equip. Cost	Site Cost	Other Costs	Volumes	Reader Seats	Federal Funds	State Funds	Local Funds	Gift Funds	Architect
Idaho																
Twin Falls	28	M	2,748,882	2,251,440	41,000	54.91	100,888	265,436	131,118	165,000	215	256,089	0	2,322,290	170,503	Richardson Design...
Illinois																
Ashland[12]	6	M	50,000	34,291	3,300	10.39	0	Owned	15,709	12,000	23	0	40,000	10,000	0	Graham O'Shea & Hyde
Chester	8	M	765,456	688,353	5,208	132.17	21,959	Owned	55,144	45,000	100	200,000	0	565,456	0	McLaughlin & Associates
Chicago	86	B	500,000	330,000	1,500	220.00	36,000	Owned	134,000	80	12	0	500,000	0	0	Kendall Fleming
Dwight[13]	4	M	405,456	320,880	4,500	71.31	0	31,484	53,092	16,000	28	0	123,514	222,863	59,079	Kenyon & Associates
Lake Zurich	25	M	3,750,000	2,600,000	33,000	79.00	710,025	Owned	439,975	120,000	120	250,000	0	3,500,000	0	Hunter & Hammond...
Prospect Heights	12	M	3,150,000	2,551,204	26,000	98.12	287,973	20,000	290,823	85,000	110	250,000	0	2,900,000	0	Carow Architects
Indiana																
Delphi	8	M	830,000	660,000	10,750	61.40	135,000	Owned	35,000	60,000	48	271,116	0	433,619	125,265	H. L. Mohler & Associates
Kokomo	81	M	771,000	491,000	54,878	8.95	154,365	Owned	125,635	250,000	180	200,000	0	571,000	0	Parke Randall
Muncie	119	B	321,656	199,089	11,000	18.09	79,324	Owned	43,243	70,210	87	0	0	321,656	0	Cooler Group
Oakland City	4	M	495,000	405,616	4,731	85.74	41,565	Owned	47,819	45,000	38	495,000	0	0	0	Key Construction Company
South Whitley	3	M	135,500	112,000	2,800	40.00	10,500	Owned	13,000	5,270	20	0	0	10,500	125,000	Searce & Associates
Iowa																
Colo[14]	1	M	55,000	27,500	2,400	11.45	25,000	Owned	2,500	13,000	28	0	0	7,000	48,000	Charles Johnston...
Cresco[15]	3	M	625,997	497,997	7,800	63.85	60,000	18,000	50,000	35,000	60	150,000	0	275,997	200,000	Schute-Larson
Spirit Lake	5	M	375,000	95,000	9,000	10.55	80,000	200,000	0	25,000	60	0	0	200,000	175,000	none
Waukee	5	M	92,483	10,000	2,700	3.70	12,483	70,000	0	8,000	n/a	0	0	38,313	54,170	not reported
Kansas																
Haysville	26	M	324,965	238,000	9,491	25.07	66,346	Owned	20,619	21,885	44	10,000	0	222,465	92,500	Joe W. Carmichael
Inman	2	M	166,000	137,000	3,570	38.37	7,000	Owned	22,000	15,400	19	40,000	0	90,000	36,000	Mike Decker
South Haven	1	M	9,500	9,000	1,250	7.20	500		0	4,928	14	4,065	0	5,435	0	Dennis Johnson
Louisiana																
Breaux Bridge	6	B	200,600	171,262	5,537	30.93	10,251	Owned	19,087	40,000	52	100,000	0	99,600	1,000	Glenn Angelle
Duson[16]	1	B	24,213	16,663	1,600	10.41	7,550	Owned	0	5,000	12	0	0	24,213	0	none
Maine																
Bucksport	7	M	194,860	179,381	1,120	160.16	837	Owned	14,642	18,000	15	93,160	0	49,894	51,806	WBRC Architects...
Ellsworth	8	M	1,075,000	849,300	12,840	66.14	88,000	Owned	137,700	28,000	97	75,000	0	1,000,000	0	Bingham & Woodward
Old Town[17]	13	M	1,260,000	961,200	10,300	93.32	140,000	Owned	158,800	54,000	30	0	0	90,000	1,170,000	Stephen B. Rich
Maryland																
New Carrollton	146	B	418,450	127,022	58,500	2.17	291,428	Owned	0	200,000	60	0	0	418,450	0	none
Towson	54	BS	4,176,123	3,372,356	37,000	91.14	410,000	Owned	393,767	n/a	39	0	4,176,123	0	0	Desman Associates
Massachusetts																
Marblehead	20	M	3,329,325	2,817,521	26,000	108.37	234,386	Owned	277,418	120,000	120	0	0	3,171,490	157,835	Architects Design II

Symbol Code: B – Branch Library; BS – Branch & System Headquarters; M – Main Library; MS – Main & System Headquarters; S – System Headquarters; n/a – not available

Location	No.	Code	(1)	(2)	(3)	(4)	(5)	(6)	(7)	(8)	(9)	(10)	(11)	(12)	(13)	Architect
North Attleboro	24	M	743,000	661,270	10,000	66.13	0	Owned	81,730	45,000	65	0	0	743,000	0	Stopfell Miller
Woburn	35	M	313,500	144,000	n/a	n/a	135,000	Owned	34,500	n/a	n/a	0	0	313,500	0	Berg/Howland Associates
Michigan																
Howell	32	M	5,056,876	3,787,061	31,000	122.16	800,000	Owned	469,815	90,000	112	95,000	0	4,895,876	66,000	Osler/Miller Architects
Minnesota																
Blaine	40	M	2,594,070	1,943,539	38,000	51.15	351,104	Owned	299,247	400,000	207	0	0	2,594,070	0	Sirnay Architects
North Branch	9	B	188,666	0	4,312	0	63,666	125,000	0	10,000	36	0	0	188,666	0	none
Mississippi																
Yazoo City	27	M	139,818	71,020	3,459	20.64	44,537	Owned	24,261	18,500	33	65,000	0	55,106	19,712	Canaizaro Trigianai
Missouri																
Saint Peters	50	B	689,524	585,867	22,440	26.11	32,000	60,418	11,239	110,000	136	0	0	689,524	0	Rataj Architects
New Hampshire																
Brentwood	2	M	70,000	69,500	750	93.33	0	Owned	500	16,000	12	0	0	0	70,000	Gilbert & Beard
New London	3	M	1,344,567	1,047,390	13,633	89.70	175,000	Owned	121,637	60,000	122	0	0	786,497	558,070	Ingram/Wallace
New York																
Fredonia	15	M	21,327	16,944	273	62.07	0	Owned	4,387	60,000	150	7,464	0	0	13,863	Habiterra Associates
Greenport	6	M	22,220	19,475	n/a	n/a	0	Owned	2,744	n/a	n/a	7,000	0	15,220	0	Ward Associates
Hamburg	53	M	85,689	78,088	701	111.39	748	Owned	6,853	50,000	91	67,817	0	17,872	0	Robert J. Sartini
Milton	1	M	204,794	188,684	3,924	48.08	16,110	Owned	n/a	12,000	20	44,356	0	28,758	121,680	Frank J. Taylor
New York	60	B	2,100,000	1,575,000	13,615	115.68	300,000	Owned	225,000	30,500	84	121,541	0	1,978,459	0	Samuel J. Desanato
North Bellmore	27	M	1,318,098	1,140,906	14,800	77.09	49,036	Owned	128,156	101,000	64	39,096	0	1,279,002	0	Roy McCutcheon
Staten Island	70	B	390,000	225,000	6,306	35.68	145,000	Leased	20,000	47,300	72	0	10,000	390,000	0	Margaret Fitzpatrick
North Carolina																
Bakersville	7	M	115,700	68,200	2,400	28.42	7,500	35,000	5,000	15,000	40	0	49,500	20,000	64,200	John P. Stevens
Bethel	2	B	187,000	169,000	2,700	62.59	14,000	Owned	4,000	14,000	20	85,000	0	102,000	0	Hite Associates
Winterville	2	B	109,639	67,834	1,455	46.62	10,323	26,500	4,892	12,000	16	0	50,000	0	59,639	Hite Associates
Ohio																
Columbus	31	B	650,000	440,650	6,000	73.44	114,350	31,000	64,000	36,000	47	0	0	650,000	0	Spencer & Spencer
Dublin	16	B	1,703,000	1,351,000	20,000	67.55	271,250	Owned	80,750	100,000	146	0	0	1,703,000	0	Myers/NBD
Gallipolis	30	M	818,947	656,981	14,300	45.93	60,295	42,000	59,671	85,000	104	295,745	0	483,702	39,500	McDonald, Cassell …
Kingsville	5	M	168,682	141,535	2,151	65.80	24,923	Owned	2,224	50,000	50	0	0	44,664	124,018	Van Allen & Payne
Mentor	60	M	4,101,404	3,064,116	41,188	73.60	532,659	Owned	504,629	172,400	216	0	0	4,095,412	5,992	Beck & Tabeling
Oxford	18	B	1,093,586	782,361	15,368	50.90	239,037	Owned	72,188	35,000	88	0	0	1,076,336	17,250	Steed Hammond Paul
Toledo	463	B	2,529,628	1,848,171	21,125	87.48	215,798	235,693	229,966	72,800	232	0	2,529,628	0	0	Munger Munger
Oklahoma																
Anadarko	7	M	604,016	404,268	11,000	36.75	66,423	97,500	35,825	50,000	100	125,000	20,000	125,000	334,016	Beck Associates
Harrah	5	B	152,287	88,394	1,800	49.11	4,624	52,000	7,269	10,000	15	0	0	95,287	57,000	Elliott & Associates
Oregon																
Salem	150	M	6,679,351	5,600,000	82,720	30.65	400,000	Owned	679,351	325,000	350	0	235,863	6,297,752	145,736	Settecase Smith Doss

Symbol Code: B – Branch Library; BS – Branch & System Headquarters; M – Main Library; MS – Main & System Headquarters; S – System Headquarters; n/a – not available

Table 2 / Public Library Buildings: Additions and Renovations, 1991 (cont.)

Community	Pop. in M	Code	Project Cost	Const. Cost	Gross Sq. Ft.	Sq. Ft. Cost	Equip. Cost	Site Cost	Other Costs	Volumes	Reader Seats	Federal Funds	State Funds	Local Funds	Gift Funds	Architect
Pennsylvania																
Annville	12	M	359,390	313,877	3,980	78.86	24,721	Owned	20,792	35,000	40	0	0	113,653	245,737	Robert L. Beers
Elizabethville	10	B	355,000	295,000	6,000	49.16	34,500	Owned	25,500	25,000	32	0	35,000	0	320,000	Crabtree Rohrbaugh
Mars	15	M	752,374	291,300	11,000	26.48	110,424	328,150	22,500	55,000	88	200,000		441,950	110,424	Ross Schonder …
Richland	4	M	400,000	270,000	5,000	54.00	40,000	Owned	90,000	30,000	30	0	10,000	14,000	376,000	Rich Walter
Spring City	8	M	45,956	38,464	660	58.28	6,722	Owned	770	2,000	12	0	0	6,204	39,752	none
Rhode Island																
Greenville	25	M	2,044,073	1,353,222	15,000	90.22	209,251	182,712	298,888	80,000	92	71,093	894,316	522,600	556,064	David Presbrey
Hope Valley	6	M	11,458	9,820	676	14.54	1,638	Owned	0	4,600	15	0	0	11,458	0	not reported
Portsmouth	17	M	1,395,417	1,178,670	9,516	123.86	97,681	Owned	119,066	55,000	65	0	627,000	399,973	368,444	Donald Prout Associates
Tennessee																
Chattanooga	286	M	769,903	449,655	67,255	7.43	199,792	50,000	70,456	400,000	458	100,000	35,784	634,119	0	Derthick, Henley …
Paris	28	B	282,178	253,708	3,450	73.54	8,914	Owned	19,556	40,000	91	100,000	35,784	76,394	70,000	TLM Associates
Texas																
Austin 18	24	B	136,000	60,000	5,000	12.00	25,000	35,000	16,000	33,000	40	0	0	15,000	121,000	John W. Gillum
Austin 19	26	B	137,850	66,750	5,100	13.09	26,000	25,600	19,500	30,000	25	0	0	18,500	119,350	Robert James Riba
Beaumont	118	B	1,600,000	1,350,000	15,000	90.00	60,000	Owned	190,000	25,000	100	0	0	1,350,000	250,000	David Hoffman
Brenham	27	B	370,250	311,605	5,000	62.32	28,346	Owned	30,299	58,000	75	0	0	72,000	298,250	Hidell Architects
Freeport	13	B	728,000	579,000	9,100	63.63	101,000	Owned	48,000	80,000	58	0	0	728,000	0	Hamilton & Associates
Lake Jackson	25	B	994,501	747,533	21,000	35.60	169,837	Owned	77,131	85,000	128	0	0	994,501	0	Hall/Merriman
Weatherford	50	M	770,605	601,500	17,048	35.28	127,000	Owned	42,105	92,000	120	0	0	668,663	101,942	Jackson & Ayers
Utah																
American Fork	16	M	95,000	40,000	5,000	8.00	50,000	Owned	5,000	25,000	30	47,000	0	47,000	5,000	Nelsen-Howden
Virginia																
Fredericksburg	155	M	4,071,894	2,490,084	37,500	66.40	505,748	Owned	1,076,062	150,000	120	200,000	0	3,791,894	80,000	Lukemire Partnership
Kilmarnock	12	M	737,000	674,000	10,200	66.08	25,000	Owned	38,000	45,000	68	196,000	0	26,000	515,000	not reported
Salem	24	M	952,049	757,244	16,542	45.78	123,703	Owned	71,102	90,000	124	200,000	0	752,049	0	Glenn Reynolds
Washington																
Bellingham	75	S	845,000	724,000	15,000	48.27	63,000	Owned	58,000	30,000	20	0	0	845,000	0	Ernst Associates
Lynwood	29	B	798,224	654,772	14,400	45.47	73,604	Owned	69,848	76,000	82	0	0	798,224	0	Lewis-Nelson Associates
Wisconsin																
Bangor	3	M	136,775	120,675	4,800	25.14	5,600	10,500		n/a	18	0	0	62,500	92,155	La Crosse Investments
Brookfield	38	M	4,405,546	3,612,325	49,288	73.29	417,727	Owned	375,494	165,000	274	0	0	4,356,456	49,090	Engberg Anderson
Delavan	11	M	755,389	694,800	12,500	55.58	20,000	Owned	40,589	50,900	70	125,000	0	320,000	310,389	DePietro Design Associates
Kenosha	80	B	777,673	698,673	3,800	183.86	63,000	Owned	16,000	23,000	65	0	0	714,673	63,000	Herbst, Eppstein …
Racine	140	B	5,305,000	4,488,000	62,500	71.81	429,000	Owned	388,000	250,000	192	125,000	0	4,713,000	467,000	Carow Architects

Symbol Code: B – Branch Library; BS – Branch & System Headquarters; M – Main Library; MS – Main & System Headquarters; S – System Headquarters; n/a – not available

| Wyoming | | | | | | | | | | | | | | | | |
| Sundance | 3 | M | 472,921 | 256,979 | 5,733 | 44.82 | 2,441 | 196,651 | 16,850 | 30,000 | 36 | 166,550 | 90,000 | 15,267 | 201,104 | Rundquist & Hard |

Symbol Code: B — Branch Library; BS — Branch & System Headquarters; M — Main Library; MS — Main & System Headquarters; S — System Headquarters; n/a — not available

Notes (Tables 1 and 2):

1. Located at entrance to Rocky Mountain National Park; windows offer view of mountainsides and cliffs.
2. Anchor of new strip shopping center, built on lease-purchase arrangement with mall developers.
3. Kiosk in suburban shopping mall.
4. Winner of Northern Illinois chapter, American Institute of Architects 1991 Excellence in Architecture award.
5. Town's first new library building.
6. Multipurpose building shares space with Health Center.
7. Historic railroad depot converted to library; most of funds from anonymous benefactor.
8. Oklahoma Library for the Blind and Physically Handicapped.
9. Renovation and seismic reinforcement of a 1926 building of variegated brick; tile roof.
10. Synthesis of original 1913 building with three additions from the 1930s to late 1970s.
11. First library in the system to open with an online public-access catalog.
12. Former bank building donated to library.
13. Restoration of a historic building.
14. Remodeled fire station.
15. Remodeled 75-year-old Carnegie building.
16. Building previously used as a fire department.
17. Restored 1904 Carnegie Foundation structure.
18. Owner paid for $120,000 of renovations.
19. Owner paid for $118,350 of renovations.

Table 3 / Public Library Buildings: Six-Year Cost Summary, 1986–1991

	Fiscal 1986	Fiscal 1987	Fiscal 1988	Fiscal 1989	Fiscal 1990	Fiscal 1991
Number of new buildings	71	101	101	111	127	120
Number of ARRs*	120	150	142	124	123	108
Sq. ft. new buildings	1,141,957	1,370,479	1,449,397	1,760,743	1,592,389	1,520,121
Sq. ft. ARRs	1,189,319	1,582,106	1,280,321	1,612,495	1,707,313	1,689,484
New buildings						
Construction cost	$73,092,317	$101,016,870	$100,984,847	$160,937,343	$128,175,181	$121,884,749
Equipment cost	9,799,996	17,958,318	20,489,527	19,450,410	16,922,110	18,603,687
Site cost	4,211,461	5,047,659	10,403,705	14,191,713	13,147,809	14,504,740
Other costs	10,869,097	12,096,087	12,349,755	16,693,362	13,357,985	18,521,472
Total—project cost	97,972,871	136,952,501	144,237,174	211,716,128	176,628,983	176,127,088
ARRs—project cost	59,634,921	80,534,403	104,179,480	135,015,044	113,769,695	141,262,919
New & ARR project cost	$157,607,792	$217,486,904	$248,416,654	$346,731,172	$290,398,678	$317,390,007
Fund sources						
Federal, new buildings	$6,367,559	$5,757,098	$7,352,110	$8,140,109	$10,593,149	$8,139,146
Federal, ARRs	4,753,052	4,677,400	7,321,967	8,264,044	6,984,747	6,533,719
Federal, total	$11,120,611	$10,434,498	$14,674,077	$16,404,153	$17,577,896	$14,672,865
State, new buildings	$1,863,277	$7,710,681	$13,849,248	$48,714,905	$29,450,257	$14,349,412
State, ARRs	7,054,676	5,310,877	6,922,165	6,997,782	7,315,892	11,439,866
State, total	$8,917,953	$13,021,558	$20,771,413	$55,712,687	$36,766,149	$25,789,278
Local, new buildings	$73,997,971	$117,135,870	$112,230,599	$137,650,121	$124,136,070	$138,176,957
Local, ARRs	42,971,936	64,050,359	79,197,138	108,753,024	84,323,211	111,788,933
Local, total	$116,969,907	$181,186,229	$191,427,737	$246,403,145	$208,459,281	$249,965,890
Gift, new buildings	$15,771,620	$7,182,656	$11,084,832	$17,428,326	$13,094,262	$15,810,151
Gift, ARRs	4,982,621	6,734,422	10,805,194	11,219,980	15,928,366	11,561,261
Gift, total	$20,754,241	$13,917,078	$21,890,026	$28,648,306	$29,022,628	$27,371,412
Total funds used	$157,762,712	$218,559,363	$248,763,253	$347,168,291	$291,825,954	$317,799,445

*Additions, remodelings, and renovations.

Table 4 / New Academic Library Buildings, 1991

Institution	Project Cost	Gross Sq. Ft.	Sq. Ft. Cost	Construction Cost	Equipment Cost	Book Capacity	Seating Capacity	Architect
University of California, San Francisco, CA	$40,379,829	120,000	$305.51	$36,661,444	$3,400,660	600,000	904	Esherick Homsey Dodge & Davis
University of California Science Library, Santa Cruz, CA	13,111,000	74,138	151.46	11,228,950	497,000	275,000	860	Esherick Homsey Dodge & Davis
Salve Regina University, Newport, RI	8,600,000	71,000	112.68	8,000,000	600,000	235,000	450	Robinson Green Beretta
Shawnee State University, Portsmouth, OH	7,500,000	72,000	77.75	5,597,650	800,000	145,000	600	Hayes, Tanner, & Stone
Roger Williams College, Bristol, RI	7,348,000	55,928	121.01	6,768,000	580,000	154,000	425	Robinson Green Beretta
Longwood College, Farmville, VA	6,683,500	71,000	80.99	5,750,500	993,000	410,366	900	Odell Associates
David Lipscomb University, Nashville, TN	5,250,000	55,852	85.94	4,800,000	450,000	204,400	559	Tuck Hinton Everton
Martin Library of the Sciences & Computer Center, Franklin & Marshall College, Lancaster, PA	5,050,000	34,700	131.98	4,579,625	200,000	80,000	126	Shepley Bulfinch . . .
Young Science Library, Smith College, Northampton, MA	4,300,000	22,376	143.01	3,200,000	1,100,000	135,000	115	Shepley Bulfinch . . .
Cornell Library, Vermont Law School, South Royalton, VT	3,663,000	34,000	84.94	2,888,000	n/a	300,000	350	Truex deGroot Cullins
Edgewood College, Madison, WI	3,100,000	41,000	n/a	n/a	n/a	100,000	200	Durrant Group
Miramar College Library/ Learning Resources Center San Diego, CA	1,424,764	10,600	118.66	1,257,764	167,000	15,000	118	Blurock Partnership
Burlington Textiles Library, North Carolina State University, Raleigh, NC*	n/a	12,700	102.36	1,300,000	75,000	35,000	150	Walter, Robbs . . .
Atlanta Christian College, East Point, GA	1,200,000	20,000	60.00	1,200,000	0	100,000	125	Thomas F. Williams

*Library part of 300,000-sq.-ft., $30 million building complex.

Table 5 / Academic Library Buildings: Additions and Renovations, 1991

Institution	Status	Project Cost	Gross Sq. Ft.	Sq. Ft. Cost	Construction Cost	Equipment Cost	Book Capacity	Seating Capacity	Architect
Allen & Suzallo Libraries, University of Washington, Seattle, WA	Total	$38,000,000	274,929	$88.75	$24,400,000	$3,400,000	1,056,000	592	Edward Larrabee Barnes; John M. V. Lee
	New	36,200,000	215,000	106.97	23,000,000	3,000,000	1,056,000	592	
	Renovated	1,800,000	59,929	23.36	1,400,000	400,000	0	0	
Western Michigan University, Kalamazoo, MI	Total	19,200,000	258,595	62.65	16,200,000	3,000,000	1,400,000	1,800	WBDC Group
	New	n/a	104,672	n/a	n/a	n/a	n/a	n/a	
	Renovated	n/a	153,923	n/a	n/a	n/a	n/a	n/a	
California State University, Northridge, CA	Total	18,542,000	128,196	131.62	6,873,000	933,000	1,082,750	1,079	Leo A. Daly
	New	n/a	110,732	n/a	n/a	n/a	n/a	n/a	
	Renovated	n/a	17,464	n/a	n/a	n/a	n/a	n/a	
Hamon Arts Library, Southern Methodist University, Dallas, TX	Total	10,400,000	86,974	72.48	6,304,000	1,930,000	140,000	300	Milton Powell
	New	5,408,000	45,520	72.01	3,278,080	1,207,000	140,000	300	
	Renovated	4,992,000	41,454	72.99	3,025,920	723,000	0	0	
Rotch Library of Architecture, Planning & Art, Massachusetts Institute of Technology, Cambridge, MA	Total	7,500,000	26,666	193.09	5,148,998	450,000	180,000	157	Schwartz/Silver
	New	n/a	17,483	n/a	n/a	n/a	170,000	67	
	Renovated	n/a	9,183	n/a	n/a	n/a	10,000	90	

Institution		Total	Sq. Ft.	Cost/Sq. Ft.	Construction	Equipment	Other	Book Capacity	Architect
Roanoke College, Salem, VA	Total	7,041,075	76,000	85.21	6,475,908	538,167	300,000	430	Horner & Associates
	New	n/a	47,000	n/a	n/a	n/a	n/a	n/a	
	Renovated	n/a	29,000	n/a	n/a	n/a	n/a	n/a	
Jason Library–Learning Center, Delaware State College, Dover, DE	Total	5,266,353	96,637	43.38	4,674,976	591,377	300,000	970	Martin F. Shannon
	New	n/a	42,305	n/a	n/a	n/a	n/a	n/a	
	Renovated	n/a	54,332	n/a	n/a	n/a	n/a	n/a	
University of Missouri—Kansas City, MO	Total	5,132,124	119,352	33.92	4,048,000	470,000	730,000	1,729	Peckham Guyton . . .
	New	4,333,992	66,920	51.40	3,440,000	470,000	180,000	1,029	
	Renovated	798,132	52,432	11.60	608,000	0	550,000	700	
Wabash College, Crawfordsville, IN	Total	4,816,500	61,428	66.75	4,100,115	454,661	276,000	281	Browning Day . . .
	New	n/a	19,750	121.52	2,400,115	n/a	n/a	n/a	
	Renovated	n/a	41,678	40.79	1,700,000	n/a	n/a	n/a	
Harding University, Searcy, AR	Total	2,300,000	44,450	44.99	2,000,000	300,000	235,000	475	Horace A. Piazza
	New	n/a	7,168	n/a	n/a	n/a	n/a	n/a	
	Renovated	n/a	37,282	n/a	n/a	n/a	n/a	n/a	
York College of Pennsylvania, York, PA	Total	922,000	42,928	21.48	922,000	0	130,800	410	Associated Architects
	New	n/a	3,728	80.00	298,240	0	10,800	108	
	Renovated	n/a	39,200	15.91	623,760	0	120,000	302	
Embry-Riddle Aeronautical University, Prescott Campus Library, Prescott, AZ	Total	456,800	16,080	24.66	396,524	60,275	25,000	280	Reilly, Zucker
	New	449,523	6,240	62.38	389,247	60,275	0	197	
	Renovated	7,277	9,840	00.74	7,277	0	25,000	83	

Table 6 / Academic Library Buildings: Additions Only, 1991

Institution	Project Cost	Gross Sq. Ft.	Sq. Ft. Cost	Construction Cost	Equipment Cost	Book Capacity	Seating Capacity	Architect
Hill Library, North Carolina State University, Raleigh, NC	$9,325,000	106,642	$84.54	$9,015,000	$310,000	487,250	977	ENG/Six Associates

Table 7 / Academic Library Buildings: Renovations Only, 1991

Institution	Project Cost	Gross Sq. Ft.	Sq. Ft. Cost	Construction Cost	Equipment Cost	Book Capacity	Seating Capacity	Architect
Fine Arts Library, University of Pennsylvania, Philadelphia, PA	$8,500,000	26,800	n/a	n/a	$435,000	108,000	335	Venturi, Scott, Brown
Morse Library, Beloit College, Beloit, WI	3,500,000	53,000	$56.11	$2,974,000	526,000	380,000	306	DeStefano/Goettsch
Viterbo College, La Crosse, WI	1,421,090	27,504	32.32	888,866	145,000	101,120	254	Schute-Larson
Library West, University of Florida, Gainesville, FL	398,000	12,000	33.17	398,000	0	570,000	100	Gene Davis
Lesley College, Cambridge, MA	350,000	16,550	21.15	350,000	0	120,000	101	Dennis J. Carlone
Ringling School of Art & Design, Sarasota, FL	130,717	6,800	17.65	120,000	10,717	20,000	52	Don Lawson
D'Youville College, Buffalo, NY	n/a	3,450	14.06	48,500	n/a	n/a	n/a	D'Youville College
Hartford Graduate Center Library, Hartford, CT	15,621	672	23.25	15,621	0	n/a	n/a	none
Pennsylvania State University, Altoona Campus, University Park, PA	6,000	12,000	0.23	2,800	3,200	45,000	180	none

Table 8 / Public Library Projects in Progress, 1991

Library	1	2	3	4	5	6	7	8
Alabama								
Washington Cty., Chatom [1991]								X
Elba [1992]			X	X	X			
Enterprise [1993]	X		X	X	X			
Greene Cty., Eutaw [1993]	X	X	X					
Greenville-Butler Cty. [1992]	X	X	X	X		X	X	
Guntersville [1992]	X	X	X	X	X			
Mobile [1992]	X	X	X	X	X	X	X	
Prichard [1991]				X	X			
Rainbow City [1991]	X	X	X	X	X	X	X	X
Rainsville [1992]	X	X	X	X	X	X	X	X
Annie L. Awbrey, Roanoke [?]	X							
Arizona								
Chandler [1994]	X	X	X	X	X	X		
Velma Teague Branch Lib., Glendale [1991]	X	X	X					X
Mohave Cty. Lib., Kingman [1991]	X	X	X	X	X	X	X	X
Peoria [1993]				X				X
Ironwood Branch Lib., Phoenix [1991]	X	X	X	X	X	X	X	X
Phoenix Central Lib. [1994]	X	X	X	X	X			
Prescott [1992]	X	X	X	X	X	X	X	X
Scottsdale Civic Ctr. Lib. [1993]	X	X	X	X	X			
Sedona [1993]	X	X		X	X	X		
Arkansas								
Fayetteville [1992]								X
Perry Cty. Lib., Little Rock [1992]	X	X	X	X	X			
Polk Cty. Lib., Mena [1992]					X			
Stone Cty. Lib., Mountain View [1992]	X	X	X	X	X	X		
Perry Cty. Lib., Perryville [1992]	X	X	X	X	X			
California								
Alameda Free Lib. [1994]	X	X		X	X			
Albany Branch Lib. [1992]	X	X	X	X	X			
Arvin Branch Lib. [1994]	X	X						
Baker Branch Lib., Bakersfield [1991]						X	X	X
Benicia [1993]	X	X	X	X	X	X		
Platt Branch, Canoga Park [1993]	X	X	X	X	X			
Carlsbad City Lib. [1992]	X	X	X	X	X	X		
Cathedral City Lib. [1993]	X	X		X	X			
Chowchilla Branch Lib. [1993]	X	X						
Chula Vista [1994]	X	X	X		X			
Coachella Lib. [1993]	X	X		X	X			
Yolo Cty. Lib., Davis [1993]	X	X	X	X	X			
Del Mar Branch Lib. [?]	X	X		X	X			
Descanso Branch Lib. [1992]	X		X	X	X			
Escalon Lib. [1991]	X	X	X	X	X	X	X	X
Humboldt Cty. Main Lib., Eureka [1994]	X	X	X	X	X			
Fountain Valley Branch Lib. [1991]	X	X	X	X	X	X	X	X
Frazier Park Branch Lib. [1994]	X							
Granite Bay Branch Lib. [1994]	X	X						
Greenfield Community Lib. [1993]		X		X	X			
Hacienda Heights [1993]	X	X		X				
Humboldt Cty. Lib. [1991]	X	X	X	X	X	X	X	X
Huntington Beach [1993]	X	X	X	X	X	X		
La Quinta Lib. [1993]	X	X		X	X			
Lakeside Lib. [1993]	X	X		X	X	X		
Lancaster [1994]	X	X		X	X	X		
Lawndale [1993]	X	X		X	X			

Predesign Stages: (1) preliminary investigation, (2) program filed, (3) project funded, (4) architect selected; *Design Stages:* (5) design stage in progress, (6) construction documents completed, (7) bidding completed, (8) contracts awarded. The date following the library name represents the estimated year of completion.

Table 8 / Public Library Projects in Progress, 1991 *(cont.)*

Library	Stages							
	1	2	3	4	5	6	7	8
Livermore [1992]	X	X	X	X	X	X	X	X
Los Altos Lib. [1992]	X	X	X	X	X	X	X	
Angeles Mesa Branch, Los Angeles [1994]	X	X	X	X				
Brentwood Branch, Los Angeles [1993]	X	X	X	X	X			
Cahuenga Branch, Los Angeles [1995]	X	X	X	X	X			
Felipe de Neve Branch, Los Angeles [1995]	X	X	X	X				
John C. Fremont Branch Lib., Los Angeles [1995]	X		X	X				
Lincoln Heights Branch, Los Angeles [1994]	X	X	X	X	X			
Malabar Branch, Los Angeles [1992]	X	X	X	X	X	X	X	X
Memorial Branch, Los Angeles [1994]	X	X	X					
John Muir Branch, Los Angeles [1994]	X	X		X	X			
Robertson Branch, Los Angeles [1995]	X		X	X				
Venice Branch Lib., Los Angeles [1993]	X	X	X	X	X	X		
Vermont Square Branch, Los Angeles [1994]	X	X	X	X	X			
Watts Branch, Los Angeles [1995]	X	X	X	X				
Wilshire Branch, Los Angeles [1994]	X	X	X	X	X			
Los Gatos [?]	X	X						
McFarland Branch Lib. [1994]	X	X						
Marina Del Rey [?]	X	X		X				
Menlo Park Lib. [1992]								X
Hanshaw Branch Lib., Modesto [1991]	X	X	X	X	X	X	X	X
Nevada Cty. Lib., Nevada City [1991]	X	X	X	X	X	X	X	X
Newport Beach [1993]	X	X	X	X	X			
Mid Valley Regional Branch, Northridge [1993]	X	X	X	X	X			
Porter Ranch Branch, Northridge [1994]	X	X	X	X				
Oakhurst Branch Lib. [1992]	X	X	X	X	X			
Asian Branch Lib., Oakland [1992]	X	X	X	X	X	X		
Brookfield Village Branch, Oakland [1992]	X	X	X	X	X	X	X	X
Oxnard [1991]	X	X	X	X				X
Pacific Grove [1994]	X			X	X			
Palm Desert Lib. [1993]	X	X	X	X	X			
Palos Verdes Lib. [1994]	X	X	X	X	X			
Paso Robles [1993]	X	X		X	X			
Perris Lib. [1993]	X	X	X	X	X			
El Dorado Cty. Lib., Placerville [1993]	X	X	X	X	X			
Danville Branch, Pleasant Hill [1993]	X	X	X	X	X			
Poway Branch Lib. [1993]	X	X	X	X				
Plumas Cty. Lib., Quincy [1992]	X	X	X	X	X			
Redondo Beach [1994]	X	X	X	X	X			
Ripon Lib. [1993]	X	X						
Rosamond Branch Lib. [1994]	X							
Arden Lib., Sacramento [1998]	X							
Carmichael Lib., Sacramento [1995]	X							
Central Lib., Sacramento [1991]	X	X	X	X	X	X	X	X
Cooledge Lib., Sacramento [1992]	X	X		X	X			
Elk Grove Lib., Sacramento [1993]	X			X	X			
Folsom Lib., Sacramento [2000]	X							
Franklin-Laguna Lib., Sacramento [2000]	X							
McKinley Lib., Sacramento [1996]	X							
N. Highlands/Antelope Lib., Sacramento [1993]	X							
N. Natomas Lib., Sacramento [2010]	X							
N. Sacramento/Hagginwood Lib., Sacramento [2005]	X							
Sacramento [1991]	X	X	X	X	X	X	X	X
S. Natomas Lib., Sacramento [1995]	X							

Predesign Stages: (1) preliminary investigation, (2) program filed, (3) project funded, (4) architect selected; *Design Stages:* (5) design stage in progress, (6) construction documents completed, (7) bidding completed, (8) contracts awarded. The date following the library name represents the estimated year of completion.

Table 8 / Public Library Projects in Progress, 1991 *(cont.)*

Library	Stages							
	1	2	3	4	5	6	7	8
State Lib. & Courts Bldg. Lib., Sacramento [1993]	X	X	X	X	X			
Valley-Hi Lib., Sacramento [2000]	X							
Calaveras Cty. Lib., San Andreas [1994]	X	X			X			
Carmel Valley Lib., San Diego [1992]	X	X	X	X	X	X		
Mira Mesa Lib., San Diego [1993]	X	X	X	X	X			
Point Loma Lib., San Diego [?]	X	X		X				
Rancho Bernardo Lib., San Diego [?]	X	X						
Rancho Penasquitos Lib., San Diego [1992]	X	X	X	X	X	X	X	X
Rancho San Diego Branch Lib., San Diego [?]	X	X	X	X	X	X		
Scripps Ranch Lib., San Diego [1992]	X	X	X	X	X	X	X	X
Earl & Birdie Taylor Lib., San Diego [?]	X	X		X	X			
Valencia Park Lib., San Diego [?]	X	X		X				
Chinatown Branch Lib., San Francisco [1993]	X	X	X	X	X			
Park Branch Lib., San Francisco [1991]	X	X	X	X		X	X	X
Presidio Branch Lib., San Francisco [1991]	X	X	X	X		X	X	X
San Francisco [1995]	X	X	X	X	X			
Sunset Branch Lib., San Francisco [1992]	X	X	X	X	X	X		
San Marcos Branch [1992]	X	X	X	X	X			
Sonoma Cty. Lib., Santa Rosa [1993]					X			
Bear Mountain Lib., Squaw Valley [1993]	X	X						
N.W. Lib., Stockton [1994]	X	X						
S.E. Lib., Stockton [1993]	X	X	X					
Suisun City Lib. [1991]	X	X	X	X	X	X	X	X
Temecula Lib. [1992]	X	X	X	X	X	X	X	X
Sunland-Tujunga Branch, Tujunga [1994]	X	X	X	X	X			
Vacaville [1992]	X	X	X	X	X	X	X	X
Vista Lib. [?]	X	X			X			
Yolo Cty. Lib., Woodland [1991]	X	X	X	X	X			
Yorba Linda [1992]								X
Colorado								
Denver [1992–1994]	X	X	X	X	X			
Denver [1992–1994]	X	X	X	X	X			
Denver [1992–1994]	X	X	X	X	X			
Denver [1992–1994]	X	X	X	X	X			
Denver [1992–1994]	X	X	X	X	X			
Denver [1992–1994]	X	X	X	X	X			
Denver [1992–1994]	X	X	X	X	X			
Denver [1992–1994]	X	X	X	X	X			
Denver [1992–1994]	X	X	X	X				
Denver [1992–1994]	X	X	X					
Denver [1992–1994]	X	X	X					
Denver [1992–1994]	X	X	X					
Denver [1992–1994]	X	X	X					
Denver [1992–1994]	X	X	X					
Denver [1992–1994]	X	X	X					
Denver [1992–1994]	X	X	X					
Denver [1992–1994]	X	X	X					
Denver [1992–1994]	X	X	X					
Denver [1992–1994]	X	X	X					
Denver [1995]	X	X	X	X	X			
Fowler [1993]	X							
Arapahoe Main Lib., Littleton	X	X	X	X	X	X	X	X
Longmont [1993]	X	X		X	X			
Connecticut								
Bridgeport [1991]	X	X	X	X	X	X	X	X

Predesign Stages: (1) preliminary investigation, (2) program filed, (3) project funded, (4) architect selected; *Design Stages:* (5) design stage in progress, (6) construction documents completed, (7) bidding completed, (8) contracts awarded. The date following the library name represents the estimated year of completion.

Table 8 / Public Library Projects in Progress, 1991 *(cont.)*

Library	1	2	3	4	5	6	7	8
Bridgeport [1991]	X	X	X	X	X	X	X	X
Bridgeport [1993]			X	X	X			
Bridgeport Community Ctr. [1993]	X	X	X	X	X			
Burlington [?]	X	X		X				
Cheshire [1994]	X	X						
Derby [1993]		X		X	X			
Hall Memorial Lib., Ellington [1992]	X	X	X	X	X	X	X	X
Fairfield Woods Branch Lib. [1991]	X	X	X	X		X	X	X
Greenwich Lib. [1991]	X	X	X	X	X		X	X
Manchester [1992]	X	X	X	X	X			
Mystic & Noank Lib. [1991]	X	X	X	X	X		X	X
Wheeler Lib., North Stonington [?]	X	X	X	X	X			
Ridgefield Lib. & Historical Assn. [1992]	X	X			X	X	X	
Minor Memorial Lib., Roxbury [1993]					X	X		
Seymour [?]	X	X				X	X	
Fairchild-Nichols Memorial Lib., Trumbull [1991]	X	X	X	X	X	X	X	X
Gunn Memorial Lib., Washington [1993]	X	X			X	X		
Silas Bronson Lib., Waterbury [1998]	X							
Weston [1991]	X	X	X	X	X	X		
Delaware								
S. Coastal Lib., Bethany Beach [1992]	X	X			X	X		
Bridgeville [1991]			X					X
Florida								
Bartow [?]	X							
Hernando Cty. System, Brooksville [1992]	X	X	X	X	X			
Cocoa Beach [1991]					X	X	X	X
N. Regional Lib., Coconut Creek [1992]	X	X	X	X	X	X	X	X
Hugh Embry Lib., Dade City [1991]	X	X	X	X	X	X	X	X
Deerfield Beach Branch [1992]	X	X	X	X	X	X	X	X
Dunnellon Branch Lib. [1991]	X	X	X	X	X	X	X	X
Eustis Memorial Lib. [1991]		X	X	X	X			
Zora Neale Hurston Branch, Fort Pierce [1991]	X	X	X	X	X		X	X
N.W. Branch Lib., Gainesville [1992]	X	X	X	X			X	X
S.W. Branch Lib., Gainesville [1992]	X	X	X	X			X	X
S. Holiday Branch Lib., Holiday [1991]	X	X	X	X		X	X	X
Columbia Cty., Lake City [1991]	X	X	X	X	X	X	X	X
Lake Wales [1991]	X	X	X	X	X	X	X	X
Land O' Lakes Branch Lib. [1991]	X	X	X	X	X	X	X	X
Mary Esther [1991]	X	X	X	X	X	X	X	X
Eau Gallie, Melbourne [1991]	X	X	X	X	X	X	X	X
Micanopy Branch Lib. [1991]	X		X				X	X
Mount Dora [1993]	X		X		X	X		
Collier Cty., Naples [1991]	X	X	X	X	X	X	X	X
Golden Gate Branch Lib., Naples [1992]	X		X	X	X			
North Fort Myers Branch Lib. [1993]	X	X	X	X	X			
DeGroodt Memorial Lib., Palm Bay [1992]	X	X	X	X	X	X	X	X
Palm City Lib. [1993]		X		X	X			
Pembroke Pines Branch Lib. [1994]	X							
N.W. Branch, Ponte Vedra Beach [1992]	X	X	X	X	X	X		
Morningside Branch Lib., Port St. Lucie [1992]	X	X	X	X	X	X	X	
Satellite Beach [1991]	X	X	X	X	X	X	X	X
Seminole Lib. [1992]	X	X	X	X	X	X	X	X
Sunrise Branch Lib. [1993]	X	X	X	X	X	X		
Tampa–Hillsborough Cty. System [1993]	X	X	X	X	X			
Anthony Branch, West Palm Beach [1992]	X	X	X	X	X	X	X	X
Central Lib., West Palm Beach [1994]	X	X	X					

Predesign Stages: (1) preliminary investigation, (2) program filed, (3) project funded, (4) architect selected; *Design Stages:* (5) design stage in progress, (6) construction documents completed, (7) bidding completed, (8) contracts awarded. The date following the library name represents the estimated year of completion.

Table 8 / Public Library Projects in Progress, 1991 *(cont.)*

Library	Stages							
	1	2	3	4	5	6	7	8
Greenacres Branch Lib., West Palm Beach [1991]	X	X	X	X	X	X	X	X
Jupiter Branch Lib., West Palm Beach [1991]	X	X	X	X	X	X	X	X
N. Cty. Branch Lib., West Palm Beach [1993]	X	X	X	X	X			
Okeechobee Blvd. Branch, West Palm Beach [1992]	X	X	X	X	X	X		
Palm Beach Gardens Reg., West Palm Beach [1993]	X	X	X	X	X			
S.W. Cty. Regional, West Palm Beach [1991]	X	X	X	X	X	X	X	X
Wellington Branch Lib., West Palm Beach [?]	X	X	X	X				
W. Atlantic Ave. Branch, West Palm Beach [1994]	X	X	X					
W. Boynton Beach Branch, West Palm Beach [1993]	X	X	X	X	X			
New River Branch Lib., Zephyrhills [1991]	X	X	X	X	X	X	X	X
Georgia								
Dougherty Cty., Albany [1992]	X	X	X	X	X			
Athens Regional Lib. [1992]	X	X	X	X	X	X	X	X
Auburn Ave. Lib., Atlanta [1993]	X	X	X	X	X	X	X	
Central Lib., Atlanta [1992]	X	X	X	X				
Cleveland Ave. Lib., Atlanta [1992]	X	X	X	X		X	X	X
Dogwood Lib., Atlanta [1992]	X	X	X	X	X	X	X	X
West End Lib., Atlanta [1992]	X	X	X	X	X			
W. Hunter Lib., Atlanta [1992]	X	X	X	X	X	X		X
S.W. Georgia Regional Lib., Bainbridge [1994]	X	X	X	X	X			
Butler [1993]		X						
Neva Lomason Memorial Lib., Carrollton [1993]	X	X	X	X	X			
Adairsville Lib., Cartersville [1993]	X	X						
Chickamauga [1992]	X	X	X	X	X			
S. Fulton Lib., College Park [1992]	X	X	X	X	X	X	X	X
Forsyth Cty. Lib., Cumming [1992]	X	X	X	X	X	X	X	X
Decatur Lib. [1992]	X	X	X	X		X	X	X
Greenville [1993]		X						
Harris Cty. Lib., Hamilton [1991]	X	X	X	X	X	X	X	X
Banks Cty. Lib., Homer [1992]	X	X	X	X	X	X		
Jefferson [1992]	X	X	X	X	X	X		
Cherokee Regional Lib., LaFayette [1992]	X	X	X	X	X	X	X	X
Lee Cty. Lib., Leesburg [1994]	X	X	X	X				
Lithonia Lib. [1992]	X	X	X	X	X	X	X	
Louisville [1993]	X	X	X	X	X			
Maysville [1992]	X	X	X	X	X	X		
Jenkins Cty. Memorial Lib., Millen [1993]	X	X	X	X	X			
Morrow Branch Lib. [1991]	X	X	X	X	X	X	X	X
Brooks Cty., Quitman [1993]	X	X	X	X				
Reynolds [1993]		X						
Echols Cty. Lib., Statenville [1992]	X	X	X	X	X	X		
Thomas Cty. System, Thomasville [1992]	X	X	X	X	X			
Trion [1991]	X	X	X	X	X	X	X	X
McMullen Memorial Lib., Valdosta [1992]	X	X	X	X	X	X	X	X
S. Georgia Regional Lib., Valdosta [1993]	X	X	X	X	X			
Villa Rica [1991]	X	X	X	X		X	X	X
Bedingfield-Pritchard, Wadley [1992]	X	X	X	X	X	X	X	X
McCollum, Wrens [1992]	X	X	X	X	X	X	X	X
Idaho								
Buhl [1993]		X		X	X			
Kootenai Cty. Libs., Hayden [1992]	X	X	X	X	X			

Predesign Stages: (1) preliminary investigation, (2) program filed, (3) project funded, (4) architect selected; *Design Stages:* (5) design stage in progress, (6) construction documents completed, (7) bidding completed, (8) contracts awarded. The date following the library name represents the estimated year of completion.

Table 8 / Public Library Projects in Progress, 1991 *(cont.)*

Library	1	2	3	4	5	6	7	8
					Stages			
Mullan [1992]		X	X	X	X			
Illinois								
Addison [1993]	X	X	X	X	X	X		
Arthur [1991]	X	X	X	X	X	X	X	X
Astoria District [1991]	X	X	X	X	X	X	X	X
Aurora [1992]	X	X	X	X	X	X		
Barrington District [1993]			X		X		X	X
Berwyn [1994]	X	X			X			
Breese [1991]	X	X	X		X		X	X
Cambridge District [1993]	X	X	X	X	X			
Auburn/Hamilton Park Branch, Chicago [1993]	X	X	X	X	X			
Clearing Branch Lib., Chicago [1993]	X	X	X	X	X			
Hegewisch Branch, Chicago [1991]	X	X	X	X	X	X	X	X
Legler Branch Lib., Chicago [1992]	X	X	X	X	X	X	X	
McKinley Park Branch Lib., Chicago [1993]	X	X	X	X	X			
Near W. Side Branch Lib., Chicago [1993]	X	X	X	X	X			
N. Austin Branch Lib., Chicago [1993]	X	X	X	X	X			
N. Pulaski/Humboldt Park Lib., Chicago [1993]	X	X	X	X	X			
Pullman Branch Lib., Chicago [1993]	X	X	X	X	X			
S. Chicago Branch Lib. [1993]	X	X	X	X	X			
Uptown Branch Lib., Chicago [1992]	X	X	X	X	X	X	X	X
Walker Branch Lib., Chicago [1993]	X	X	X	X	X			
Woodlawn/Washington Park, Chicago [1992]	X	X	X	X	X	X	X	X
Coal City District [1991]	X	X	X	X	X	X	X	X
Eldorado Memorial District [1991]								X
Evanston [1995]		X	X	X	X			
Flora [1992]	X	X	X	X	X	X	X	X
Jacksonville [?]	X			X	X			
Joliet [1991]	X	X	X	X	X	X	X	X
Midlothian [1991]	X	X	X	X	X	X	X	X
Morris Area [1992]	X	X	X	X	X	X	X	X
Naperville [1992]	X	X	X	X	X	X	X	X
Palatine [1993]	X	X	X	X	X			
Green Hills District, Palos Hills [1991]	X	X	X	X	X	X	X	X
Paris Carnegie [1992]	X	X	X	X	X	X	X	X
Park Forest [1991]						X		
Paxton Carnegie [1991]								X
Plainfield District [1991]	X	X	X	X	X	X	X	X
Vernon Area District, Prairie View [1993]	X	X	X	X	X			
Quincy [1991]	X	X	X	X	X	X	X	X
Schaumburg Twp. District Lib. [1992]	X	X	X	X	X	X	X	X
Westmont [1991]				X	X	X	X	X
Indiana								
Austin Lib. [1991]						X	X	X
Bloomfield–Eastern Greene Cty. [1991]	X	X	X	X	X	X	X	X
Bluffton–Wells Cty. [1991]		X	X	X	X	X	X	X
Bremen [1991]	X	X	X	X	X	X	X	X
Lincoln Heritage, Dale [1991]	X	X	X	X	X	X	X	X
Demotte Branch Lib. [1993]	X	X	X			X	X	X
Crawford Cty. Lib., English [?]	X							
Evansville–Vanderburgh Cty. [1991]	X	X	X	X	X	X	X	X
Frankfort Community [1992]			X		X			
W. E. B. DuBois Branch Lib., Gary [1992]	X	X	X	X	X			
Gary [1992]	X	X	X	X	X			
Ora L. Wildermuth Branch Lib., Gary [1991]	X	X	X	X	X		X	X
Greensburg [1993]	X			X	X			

Predesign Stages: (1) preliminary investigation, (2) program filed, (3) project funded, (4) architect selected; *Design Stages:* (5) design stage in progress, (6) construction documents completed, (7) bidding completed, (8) contracts awarded. The date following the library name represents the estimated year of completion.

Table 8 / Public Library Projects in Progress, 1991 *(cont.)*

Library	Stages							
	1	2	3	4	5	6	7	8
Greenwood [1991]	X	X	X	X	X	X	X	X
Lib. Services Ctr., Indianapolis [1992]	X	X	X	X	X			
Jeffersonville Twp. [1992]	X	X	X	X	X			
Lebanon [1991]	X	X	X	X	X	X	X	X
Lowell [1993]	X	X	X	X	X			
Marion [1991]	X	X	X	X	X	X	X	X
Monticello–Union Twp. [1992]	X	X	X	X	X	X	X	X
Montpelier–Harrison Twp. [1991]								X
Noblesville-Southeastern [1993]	X			X				
Pendleton Community Lib. [1991]	X	X	X	X	X	X	X	X
Pike Cty., Petersburg [?]	X							
Jasper Cty., Rensselaer [1992]	X	X	X	X		X	X	X
Rockville [1991]	X		X	X		X	X	X
St. Joseph Cty. [1991]								X
Crothersville Branch, Seymour [1991]	X	X	X	X	X	X	X	X
Jackson Cty., Seymour [1992]	X	X	X	X	X	X	X	X
Medora Branch, Seymour [1991]	X	X	X	X	X	X	X	X
Shelbyville–Shelby Cty. [1996]	X			X				
Speedway [1991]	X	X	X	X		X	X	X
Syracuse–Turkey Creek Twp. [1991]	X	X	X	X	X	X	X	X
Switzerland Cty., Vevay [1992]	X	X	X	X	X	X	X	X
Warsaw Community [1993]	X			X	X			
Iowa								
Audubon [?]	X	X	X	X	X			
Bettendorf & Info. Ctr. [1991]	X	X	X	X	X	X	X	X
Ericson, Boone [1993]								X
Free, Chariton [1991]	X	X	X	X	X	X	X	X
Chelsea [1992]	X							
Clermont [?]	X				X			
Correctionville [1991]								X
Decorah [1995]				X	X			
Edgewood [1992]	X	X	X	X	X	X		
Estherville [?]	X							
Fairfax [1991]								X
Fairfield [?]	X	X		X	X			
Guthrie Center [?]	X			X				
Wilson Memorial Lib., Keota [1992]				X	X			
Little Rock [1992]	X	X	X	X	X	X	X	X
Maquoketa [1994]	X			X	X			
Newton [1992]	X	X	X	X		X	X	X
Field-Carnegie Lib., Odebolt [?]	X			X	X			
Oskaloosa [?]	X							
Perry [?]	X			X				
Reinbeck [1991]				X				X
Urbandale [1991]	X	X	X	X	X	X	X	X
Vinton [?]				X	X			
Kendall Young Lib., Webster City [1994]	X	X		X	X			
Kansas								
Burlington Branch [1994]	X	X		X	X			
Chanute [1992]	X	X	X	X		X	X	X
Haven [1992]	X	X	X	X	X	X		
Hesston [1992]	X	X	X	X	X	X		
Morrill, Hiawatha [1992]	X	X	X	X	X	X	X	X
Lebo Branch [1992]	X	X	X	X		X	X	X
LeRoy Branch [1992]	X	X	X	X	X			
Lindsborg Community Lib. [1992]	X	X	X	X	X	X	X	X

Predesign Stages: (1) preliminary investigation, (2) program filed, (3) project funded, (4) architect selected; *Design Stages:* (5) design stage in progress, (6) construction documents completed, (7) bidding completed, (8) contracts awarded. The date following the library name represents the estimated year of completion.

Table 8 / Public Library Projects in Progress, 1991 *(cont.)*

Library	\-Stages\- 1	2	3	4	5	6	7	8
Johnson Cty. Lib., Shawnee Mission [1996]	X	X		X				
Lackman Lib., Shawnee Mission [1995]	X							
Leawood Pioneer Lib., Shawnee Mission [1992]	X	X	X					
Shawnee Lib., Shawnee Mission [1991]	X	X	X	X	X	X	X	X
Wellsville City Lib. [1992]					X			
Kentucky								
Eagle Creek Branch, Lexington [1992]	X	X	X	X	X	X	X	X
Lexington [1992]								X
Casey Cty., Liberty [1991]	X	X	X	X	X	X	X	X
Louisiana								
Bell City Branch [1992]	X	X	X	X	X			
Cameron Parish Lib. [1991]	X					X	X	X
DeQuincy Branch [1992]	X	X	X	X	X			
Hayes Branch [1992]	X	X	X	X	X			
Iowa Branch [1992]	X	X	X	X	X			
Carnegie Memorial Branch, Lake Charles [1992]	X	X	X	X	X			
Central Lib., Lake Charles [1993]	X	X	X	X	X			
Epps Memorial Branch, Lake Charles [1992]	X	X	X	X	X	X		
Vernon Parish Lib., Leesville [?]	X			X				
Moss Bluff Branch [1993]	X	X	X	X	X			
Cecilia Branch Lib., St. Martinvile [?]	X	X	X	X				
St. Martin Parish Lib., St. Martinville [1992]	X	X	X	X				
Stephensville Branch Lib., St. Martinville [?]	X	X	X	X				
Starks Branch [1992]	X	X	X	X	X			
Maplewood Branch, Sulphur [1992]	X	X	X	X	X			
Sulphur Regional Branch [1992]	X	X	X	X	X			
Fontenot Memorial Branch, Vinton [1992]	X	X	X	X	X			
Westlake Branch [1993]	X	X	X	X	X			
Winn Parish Lib. [1992]	X							
Maryland								
Loch Raven Branch, Baltimore [1992]			X	X	X			
E. Columbia Major Branch Lib. [1993]	X	X	X	X	X	X		
Elkridge Branch Lib. [1993]	X	X	X	X	X			
Laurel Branch [1992]	X	X	X	X			X	X
Whiteford Branch Lib. [1991]								X
Massachusetts								
Jones Lib., Amherst [1992]	X	X	X	X	X	X	X	X
Robbins Lib., Arlington [1993]						X		
Attleboro [1993]	X	X	X	X	X			
Bedford [?]	X	X		X				
Boston [1995]	X	X		X	X	X	X	X
Duxbury Free Lib. [1996]	X	X						
Parlin Memorial Lib., Everett [1991]	X	X		X	X	X	X	X
Holmes, Halifax [?]	X	X	X	X	X	X		
Frederic C. Adams, Kingston [1992]		X	X	X				
Lynnfield [1991]	X	X	X	X	X		X	X
Middleboro [1992]	X	X	X	X	X	X	X	X
Newton Free Lib. [1991]	X	X	X	X	X	X	X	X
Flint Memorial Lib., North Reading [1991]	X	X	X	X	X	X	X	X
Forbes Lib., Northampton [1992]	X	X	X	X	X	X	X	X
Snow Lib., Orleans [1991]								X
Plympton [1991]			X	X		X	X	X
Rockland Memorial Lib. [1992]	X	X	X	X	X	X	X	X
Southwick [?]				X				
Richard Sugden Lib., Spencer [?]	X	X	X	X	X			
Springfield City Lib. [1991]	X	X	X	X	X	X	X	X

Predesign Stages: (1) preliminary investigation, (2) program filed, (3) project funded, (4) architect selected; *Design Stages:* (5) design stage in progress, (6) construction documents completed, (7) bidding completed, (8) contracts awarded. The date following the library name represents the estimated year of completion.

Table 8 / Public Library Projects in Progress, 1991 *(cont.)*

Library	Stages							
	1	2	3	4	5	6	7	8
Waltham [1992]	X	X	X	X	X	X	X	
West Springfield [1991]	X	X	X	X	X	X		
West Tisbury Free [?]	X	X	X	X	X			
Weston [1993]	X	X	X	X	X			
Williamstown [1993]	X							
Woburn [1991]	X	X	X	X	X	X	X	X
Michigan								
Ann Arbor [1991]								X
Fred C. Fischer, Belleville [1992]	X	X	X	X		X	X	X
Independence Twp., Clarkston [1991]	X	X	X	X		X	X	X
Marlette District Lib. [1991]	X	X	X	X	X	X	X	X
Oscoda Cty. Lib., Mio [?]	X							
Veterans Memorial Lib., Mt. Pleasant [?]					X			
Egelston Branch, Muskegon [1991]	X	X	X	X	X	X	X	X
Paw Paw District Lib. [1991]	X	X	X	X	X	X	X	X
Petoskey [1992]	X	X		X	X			
Plymouth District Lib. [1994]	X			X				
Rochester Hills [1992]	X	X	X		X	X	X	X
Hoyt Lib., Saginaw [1992]					X	X	X	
Dalton Twp. Branch Lib., Twin Lake [1991]	X	X	X	X	X	X	X	X
Webberville Branch [1991]	X	X	X	X	X	X	X	X
Wixom [1991]	X	X	X	X	X	X		
Minnesota								
Ada [1992]				X		X	X	X
Aitkin [?]	X	X		X	X			
Douglas Cty. Lib., Alexandria [?]	X			X	X			
Benson [1992]			X	X	X			
Dakota Cty. Lib., Eagan [1992]								X
Southdale-Hennepin Area Lib., Edina [1994]			X	X	X	X		X
Foley [1992]	X	X	X	X				X
Hector [1991]	X	X	X	X	X	X	X	X
Hinckley [1991]	X	X	X	X	X	X	X	X
Hoyt Lakes [1992]								X
Washburn Community Lib., Minneapolis [1991]	X	X	X	X	X	X	X	X
Princeton Community Lib. [?]	X			X				
St. Paul [1992]						X		
Sandstone [1991]	X	X	X	X	X	X	X	X
Mississippi								
Batesville [1991]	X	X	X	X	X			
N.W. Point Reservoir Lib., Brandon [?]	X							
Itawamba Cty. Lib., Fulton [1992]	X	X	X	X	X	X		
Magee [?]			X	X	X			
Morton [1991]	X	X	X	X	X	X	X	X
Moss Point City Lib. [1992]	X		X	X	X	X	X	X
Armstrong Lib., Natchez [1991]	X	X	X	X	X	X	X	X
Pass Christian [1991]	X	X	X	X	X	X	X	X
Richland [1992]	X			X	X	X		
Richland [1992]						X		
Ridgeland [1991]	X	X	X	X	X	X	X	X
Missouri								
Blue Ridge Branch Lib. [1991]	X	X	X	X		X	X	X
Parkville Branch Lib., Kansas City [1992]	X	X	X	X				
Riverside Branch Lib., Kansas City [1991]	X	X	X	X		X	X	X
Liberty Branch Lib. [1991]	X	X	X	X		X	X	X

Predesign Stages: (1) preliminary investigation, (2) program filed, (3) project funded, (4) architect selected; *Design Stages:* (5) design stage in progress, (6) construction documents completed, (7) bidding completed, (8) contracts awarded. The date following the library name represents the estimated year of completion.

Table 8 / Public Library Projects in Progress, 1991 *(cont.)*

Library	Stages							
	1	2	3	4	5	6	7	8
Nebraska								
Beatrice [1991]	X	X	X	X	X	X	X	X
Central City [1991]	X	X	X	X	X	X	X	X
Franklin [1991]	X	X	X	X		X	X	X
Gretna [1991]	X	X	X	X	X			
Nevada								
Nevada State Lib. & Archives, Carson City [1992]								X
Clark Cty. Lib., Las Vegas [1994]	X	X	X	X	X			
E. Las Vegas Lib., Las Vegas [1994]	X	X	X					
Enterprise Lib., Las Vegas [1995]	X		X					
Rainbow Lib., Las Vegas [1993]	X	X	X	X	X			
Sahara W. Lib., Las Vegas [1995]	X	X	X	X	X			
Summerlin Lib., Las Vegas [1994]	X	X	X	X	X			
W. Charleston Lib., Las Vegas [1993]	X	X	X	X	X			
W. Las Vegas Lib., Las Vegas [1993]	X		X					
Laughlin Lib. [1994]	X		X					
Lake Tahoe Branch Lib., Minden [1991]	X	X	X	X	X	X	X	X
Wells Branch Lib. [1991]	X	X	X	X	X	X	X	X
New Hampshire								
Griffin Free & Museum, Auburn [1991]	X							X
Brookline [?]	X							
Smyth, Candia [1993]	X							
Chesterfield [1995]	X							
Fiske Free Lib., Claremont [2000]	X							
Philbrick-James Lib., Deerfield [?]	X							
Gorham [?]	X							
Fuller, Hillsborough [?]	X							
Keene [1992]	X	X	X	X	X	X	X	X
Kensington Social [?]	X							
Laconia [1991]	X	X	X	X	X	X		
Weeks Memorial Lib., Lancaster [?]	X							
Lincoln [?]	X		X					
Madison Lib. [1993]	X							
Ronham Memorial Lib., Nelson [?]	X			X	X			
Philip Read Memorial Lib., Plainfield [?]	X							
Dudley-Tucker Lib., Raymond [?]	X			X	X			
Rye [1992]			X	X	X			
Sandown [1991]			X	X	X	X	X	X
Brown Lib., Seabrook [?]	X	X						
Somersworth [?]	X							
Cass Memorial Lib., Springfield [1992]	X			X	X			
Thornton [1991]	X	X	X	X	X	X	X	X
Wilton [1991]	X	X	X	X	X	X	X	X
Conant, Winchester [1992]		X	X	X	X	X		
New Jersey								
Berkeley Branch, Bayville [1991]	X	X	X	X	X	X	X	X
Clifton [1991]	X	X	X	X	X	X	X	X
Elizabeth [1992]					X			
Ft. Lee [1993]	X			X				
Rohrer Memorial Lib., Haddon [1992]	X	X	X	X	X			
Highland Park [1993]	X	X		X	X			
Madison [1991]	X	X	X	X		X	X	X
Old Bridge [1991]	X	X	X	X	X	X	X	X
Paterson Free [1992]	X	X	X	X	X			
Plainsboro Free [1992]							X	

Predesign Stages: (1) preliminary investigation, (2) program filed, (3) project funded, (4) architect selected; *Design Stages:* (5) design stage in progress, (6) construction documents completed, (7) bidding completed, (8) contracts awarded. The date following the library name represents the estimated year of completion.

Table 8 / Public Library Projects in Progress, 1991 *(cont.)*

Library	Stages							
	1	2	3	4	5	6	7	8
Dowdell Lib., South Amboy [1994]	X			X				
New Mexico								
Thomas Branigan Lib., Las Cruces [1991]	X	X	X	X	X	X	X	X
Mesa [1994]	X	X	X	X	X			
New York								
Guilderland, Albany [1992]	X	X	X	X	X	X	X	X
Bethpage [?]	X	X		X				
Broome Cty., Binghamton [?]	X	X						
Bayport–Blue Point, Blue Point [1992]	X	X		X	X	X	X	X
Brewster [?]	X	X	X	X		X		
Sedgwick Branch, Bronx [1992]	X	X	X	X	X	X	X	
W. Farms Branch, Bronx [1992]	X	X	X	X	X	X	X	
Brighton Beach Branch, Brooklyn [1991]	X	X	X	X	X	X	X	X
Brooklyn Heights/Business Lib. [1993]	X	X	X	X	X	X	X	X
Cypress Hills Branch, Brooklyn [1993]	X	X	X	X	X	X		
McKinley Park Branch, Brooklyn [1993]	X	X	X	X	X			
Midwood Branch Lib., Brooklyn [1993]	X	X	X					
Kent, Carmel [1992]	X	X	X		X	X	X	
Lyme Free Lib., Chaumont [1995]	X			X	X			
Village Lib. of Cooperstown [1993]	X							
Eden Lib. [1991]	X	X	X	X	X	X	X	X
Farmingdale Lib. [1994]	X	X	X	X	X			
Floral Park [1991]	X	X	X	X	X	X	X	X
Geneva Free Lib. [1993]	X	X	X	X	X			
Guilderland [1992]					X	X		
Haverstraw King's Daughters [1993]	X							
Hicksville [1991]	X	X	X	X	X	X	X	X
Tompkins Cty., Ithaca [1991]		X	X	X		X	X	X
Katonah Village Lib. [1991]	X	X	X	X	X	X		
Peninsula, Lawrence [?]	X	X		X				
Lindenhurst Memorial Lib. [1991]								X
Liverpool [1994]	X							
Lynbrook [1991]	X	X	X	X	X	X	X	X
Massapequa [1994]	X			X	X			
Massapequa, Massapequa Park [?]	X	X		X				
Massena [1992]	X	X	X	X	X			
Merrick [?]	X	X		X				
Thrall Lib., Middletown [?]	X							
Moffat Lib. [1992]	X	X	X	X		X		
Montauk Lib. [1991]	X	X	X	X		X	X	X
Mt. Kisco [1991]	X	X	X	X		X	X	X
Aguilar Branch, New York [1993]	X	X	X	X	X	X		
Library for the Blind & Physically Handicapped, New York [1992]	X	X	X	X	X	X	X	X
Riverside Branch, New York [1992]	X	X	X	X	X	X	X	X
Tompkins Sq. Branch, New York [1992]	X	X	X	X	X	X		
Washington Heights Branch, New York [1993]	X	X	X	X	X	X	X	
Newfield [1994]	X							
Platt Cady Lib., Nichols [1992]	X	X	X	X	X	X	X	X
Oyster Bay–East Norwich [1992]	X	X	X			X	X	X
Palisades Free Lib. [?]				X				
Pearl River [1991]	X	X	X	X	X	X	X	X
Town of Pelham [1993]	X			X	X			
Phoenix [1991]	X	X	X	X	X	X	X	
Piermont [1994]	X							
Port Jervis Free Lib. [1992]	X			X				

Predesign Stages: (1) preliminary investigation, (2) program filed, (3) project funded, (4) architect selected; *Design Stages:* (5) design stage in progress, (6) construction documents completed, (7) bidding completed, (8) contracts awarded. The date following the library name represents the estimated year of completion.

Table 8 / Public Library Projects in Progress, 1991 *(cont.)*

	Stages							
Library	1	2	3	4	5	6	7	8
Brighton Memorial Lib., Rochester [1994]	X							
Rockville Centre [1991]	X	X	X	X	X	X	X	X
Roosevelt [1992]	X	X	X	X			X	X
Seaford [1992]	X	X	X	X	X	X		
Mastic-Moriches-Shirley, Shirley [1993]	X	X		X	X			
Sidney Memorial [1993]	X			X	X			
Spencer Lib. [1991]				X		X		
Great Kills Branch, Staten Island [1993]	X	X	X	X	X			
Tottenville Branch, Staten Island [1992]	X	X	X	X	X	X	X	X
Tappan Lib. [1993]	X	X		X	X			
Ulysses Philomasthic Lib., Trumansburg [1992]	X							
Tuxedo Park Lib. [1992]				X	X			
Uniondale [1992]	X	X	X	X				X
Valley Cottage Lib. [1993]	X			X	X			
Ogden Free Lib., Walton [1992]	X			X	X	X		
Walworth-Seely [1992]	X	X	X	X	X	X	X	
Waterloo Lib. [1992]					X			
Westbury Memorial [1992]	X	X	X	X	X	X	X	X
Western Town Lib., Westernville [1992]	X	X	X	X	X			
White Plains [1991]	X	X	X	X	X	X	X	X
North Carolina								
Chapel Hill [1994]	X	X	X	X	X			
Univ. City Branch Lib., Charlotte [1992]	X	X	X	X	X	X		
Denton [1992]	X	X	X	X	X	X	X	X
S.W. Branch Lib., Durham [1992]		X	X	X		X		
Cumberland Cty. & Info. Center, Fayetteville [1992]	X	X	X	X	X	X	X	X
Chavis Lifelong Learning Branch, Greensboro [1992]				X				
Greensboro Branch Lib. [1993]				X				
Greensboro Main Lib. [1994]				X				
Henderson Cty., Hendersonville [1991]	X	X	X	X	X	X	X	X
High Point [1991]	X	X	X	X	X	X	X	X
North Dakota								
Hebron [1991]				X	X		X	X
Minot [1991]	X	X	X	X	X	X	X	X
Ft. Berthold Reservation, New Town [1992]	X	X	X	X	X	X	X	X
Ohio								
Andover [1992]	X	X	X	X	X	X	X	X
Ashtabula Cty. District Lib. [1991]	X	X	X	X	X	X	X	X
Seneca East, Attica [1992]	X			X	X			
Aurora Memorial Lib. [1991]	X	X	X	X		X	X	X
Clermont Cty. Lib., Batavia [?]				X		X		
Bedford Branch Lib. [1991]	X	X	X	X	X	X	X	X
Logan Cty. District Lib., Bellefontaine [?]	X			X	X			
Bexley [1992]								X
Brooklyn Branch Lib. [1992]	X	X	X	X	X	X	X	X
Canal Fulton [1992]	X	X	X	X	X	X	X	X
Smith Lib., Cleveland [1991]	X	X	X	X		X	X	X
Columbiana [1991]	X	X	X	X	X	X	X	X
Livingston Branch, Columbus [1992]	X	X	X	X	X	X	X	X
Northern Lights Branch, Columbus [1993]	X	X	X	X	X			
S. High Branch, Columbus	X	X	X	X	X	X	X	X
Westland Area Lib., Columbus [1991]	X	X	X	X	X	X	X	X
Conneaut Carnegie Lib. [?]	X							
Viets Memorial Lib., Cortland [1991]	X	X	X	X	X	X	X	X

Predesign Stages: (1) preliminary investigation, (2) program filed, (3) project funded, (4) architect selected; *Design Stages:* (5) design stage in progress, (6) construction documents completed, (7) bidding completed, (8) contracts awarded. The date following the library name represents the estimated year of completion.

Table 8 / Public Library Projects in Progress, 1991 *(cont.)*

Library	Stages							
	1	2	3	4	5	6	7	8
Crestline [1993]				X	X			
Creston Branch Lib. [1991]								X
Wright Memorial, Dayton [1991]	X	X	X	X				X
Delaware Cty. District Branch Lib. [1992]	X	X	X	X	X			
Delaware Cty. District Main Lib. [1992]	X	X	X	X	X			
East Cleveland [1991]	X	X	X	X		X	X	X
Carnegie, East Liverpool [1992]						X		
East Palestine Memorial [1992]	X	X	X	X	X	X	X	X
Eastlake Lib. [1992]	X	X	X	X	X			
Fairborn Community Lib. [1991]	X	X	X	X	X	X	X	X
Findlay–Hancock Cty., Findlay [1991]	X	X	X	X	X	X	X	X
Garfield Heights Branch [1991]	X	X	X	X	X	X	X	X
Hubbard [?]	X							
Independence Branch Lib. [1992]	X	X	X	X	X	X	X	X
Kirtland [1992]	X	X	X	X	X	X		
Fairfield Cty. District Lib. [1992]	X	X	X	X	X	X		
Wagnalls Memorial Lib., Lithopolis [1992]	X	X	X	X				X
Wescoat Memorial Lib., McArthur [1991]	X	X	X	X	X	X	X	X
Washington Cty. [1992]						X		
Medina Cty. District Lib. [1992]	X			X	X			
Sylvester Lib., Medina [1992]	X	X	X	X	X			
New Madison [1991]						X		
Tuscarawas Cty., New Philadelphia [1991]	X	X	X	X	X	X	X	X
Cuyahoga Cty. [1991]	X	X	X	X	X	X	X	X
Parma–Snow Branch, Parma [1991]	X	X	X	X	X	X	X	X
Rupp, Port Clinton [1991]	X	X	X	X	X	X	X	X
Rocky River [1993]	X	X		X	X			
Shaker Heights Branch Lib. [1991]	X	X	X	X	X	X	X	X
Shaker Heights Main Lib. [1992]	X	X	X	X	X			
Marvin Memorial Lib., Shelby [1991]	X	X	X	X	X	X	X	X
Schiappa Branch, Steubenville [1992]	X	X	X	X	X			
Community Lib., Sunbury [1993]		X		X	X			
Tipp City [1991]	X	X	X	X	X	X	X	X
Trotwood Branch [1991]	X	X	X	X	X	X	X	X
Twinsburg [?]			X	X				
Ritter, Vermilion [?]	X	X		X				
Westerville [1993]	X	X		X	X			
Willoughby Lib. [1994]	X	X	X	X	X			
Willoughby Hills Community Ctr. & Lib. [1992]	X	X	X	X	X			
Willowick Lib. [1993]	X	X	X	X	X			
Green Cty., Xenia [1991]	X	X	X	X	X	X	X	X
Youngstown & Mahoning Cty. [1992]	X	X	X	X	X	X	X	X
Oklahoma								
Healdton Community Lib., Ardmore [1992]			X	X	X			
Bartlesville [1991]	X	X	X	X	X	X	X	X
Chandler Lib. [1992]	X	X	X	X				
Jim Lucas, Checotah [1991]								X
Slief Memorial Lib., Cheyenne [1992]	X	X		X				
Will Rogers Lib., Claremore [1991]	X	X	X	X	X			
Clinton [1991]	X	X		X				
Glenpool Lib. [1992]	X	X	X	X	X	X	X	X
Carnegie Lib., Guthrie [1991]	X	X	X	X	X	X	X	X
Perry Carnegie Lib. [1991]	X	X	X	X	X	X	X	X
Sallisaw Lib. [1992]	X	X	X	X	X			
Tubbs Memorial Lib., Sallisaw [1991]	X	X	X	X	X	X	X	X
Pratt Lib., Sand Springs [1991]	X	X	X	X	X	X	X	X

Predesign Stages: (1) preliminary investigation, (2) program filed, (3) project funded, (4) architect selected; *Design Stages:* (5) design stage in progress, (6) construction documents completed, (7) bidding completed, (8) contracts awarded. The date following the library name represents the estimated year of completion.

Table 8 / Public Library Projects in Progress, 1991 *(cont.)*

Library	1	2	3	4	5	6	7	8
Stillwater [1993]	X	X	X	X	X			
Hardesty S. Regional Lib., Tulsa [1991]	X	X	X	X	X	X	X	X
S. Tulsa Lib., Tulsa [1991]	X	X	X	X	X	X	X	X
Waurika [1990]	X	X	X	X	X	X	X	X
Weatherford [1991]	X	X	X	X	X		X	X
Wewoka [1991]							X	X
Oregon								
Corvallis–Benton Cty. [1992]	X	X	X	X	X	X	X	X
Philomath Branch, Corvallis [1992]	X	X		X				
Eugene [?]	X	X		X	X			
Driftwood Lib., Lincoln City [1992]			X					
Douglas Cty. Lib. System, Roseburg [?]		X		X	X			
Toledo [?]						X		
Pennsylvania								
Brownsville Free [?]	X							
Abington Community Lib., Clarks Summit [1992]								X
East Berlin Community Lib. [1991]			X					X
Ephrata [1993]	X	X		X	X			
Adams Cty. Lib. System, Gettysburg [1991]	X	X	X	X	X	X	X	X
Magill Lib., Haverford [1992]						X		X
Huntingdon Valley Lib. [1992]	X	X		X	X			
Peoples Lib., New Kensington [1992]	X	X	X	X	X	X		
Pottstown [1993]	X	X	X	X	X		X	X
Franco Lib./Learning Ctr., Reading [1991]								X
Saxton Community Lib. [1992]	X	X	X	X				
Spring Grove Area [1991]	X	X	X	X			X	X
Citizens Lib., Washington [1992]			X			X	X	X
Wyalusing [1991]								X
Rhode Island								
Glocester Manton Lib., Chepachet [1992]	X			X	X			
Smith Memorial Lib., Harrisville [1991]	X	X	X	X	X	X	X	X
Jamestown Philomenian Lib. [1993]	X	X		X	X	X		
Brownell Lib., Little Compton [?]		X			X			
North Kingstown Free Lib. [?]	X							
Rochambeau Branch, Providence [?]	X				X			
Hale Branch Lib., Wakefield [1991]	X	X	X	X	X	X	X	X
West Warwick System [1991]	X	X	X	X	X	X	X	X
South Carolina								
Midland Valley Lib., Bath [1991]	X	X	X	X	X	X	X	X
Beaufort Cty. Lib. [1992]	X	X	X	X	X	X	X	
Blythewood Branch Lib. [1992]	X	X	X	X	X			
James Island Branch, Charleston [1992]	X	X	X	X	X	X		
Main Lib., Charleston [1993]	X	X		X	X			
St. Andrews Regional Branch, Charleston [1992]	X	X	X	X	X	X	X	X
Cooper Branch, Columbia [1991]	X	X	X	X	X	X	X	X
Richland Cty., Columbia [1992]	X	X	X	X	X	X	X	X
South Carolina State Lib., Columbia [?]	X	X	X	X	X			
S.E. Regional Branch, Columbia [1991]	X	X	X	X	X	X	X	X
Horry Cty., Conway [1992]			X					X
Iva Branch Lib. [1992]	X	X	X	X	X	X	X	X
McClellanville Branch [1992]	X	X	X	X	X	X		
Mt. Pleasant Regional Branch [1991]	X	X	X	X	X	X	X	X
Village Branch, Mt. Pleasant [1991]	X		X					
Dorchester Rd. Regional, North Charleston [1991]	X	X	X	X	X	X	X	X
Otranto Rd. Regional, North Charleston [1991]	X	X	X	X	X	X	X	X

Predesign Stages: (1) preliminary investigation, (2) program filed, (3) project funded, (4) architect selected; *Design Stages:* (5) design stage in progress, (6) construction documents completed, (7) bidding completed, (8) contracts awarded. The date following the library name represents the estimated year of completion.

Table 8 / Public Library Projects in Progress, 1991 *(cont.)*

Library	1	2	3	4	5	6	7	8
Edgar Allan Poe Branch, Sullivans Island [1992]	X	X	X	X	X	X		
West Columbia/Cayce Lib. [1992]						X		
Tennessee								
S.E. Branch Lib., Antioch [1991]	X	X	X	X		X	X	X
Brownsville–Haywood Cty. Lib. [1991]	X	X	X	X	X	X	X	X
Bicentennial Lib., Chattanooga [1992]			X	X	X			
Ooltewah/Collegedale Branch Lib. [1992]			X	X		X		
Sequatchie Cty., Dunlap [1992]	X	X		X	X			
Martin Curtis, Hendersonville [1992]	X	X	X	X	X	X	X	
Jasper [?]	X	X		X	X			
Washington Cty.–Gray Lib., Jonesborough [1992]	X	X	X	X	X			
Kingston Lib. [1992]	X	X	X	X	X	X		
Macon Cty. Lib., Lafayette [1992]		X	X	X	X			
Magness Lib., McMinnville [?]	X	X		X	X			
North Memphis Branch, Memphis [1993]	X	X	X	X	X			
Pkwy. Village/Fox Meadows Reg., Memphis [1993]	X	X	X	X	X	X		
Bledsoe Cty., Pikeville [1991]	X	X	X	X				
Elmer Hinton Lib., Portland [1992]			X	X				
Texas								
N. Loop Area Branch, Austin [1991]	X	X	X	X	X	X	X	X
Kinney Cty., Brackettville [1992]		X	X	X	X			
Moreau Memorial Lib., Buda [1992]	X	X	X	X	X			
Van Zandt Cty. Lib., Canton [?]				X	X			
Delta Cty., Cooper [1992]	X			X	X			
William T. Cozby, Coppell [1993]					X			
DeSoto [1992]	X	X	X	X	X	X	X	X
Duncanville [1994]	X				X			
Armijo Branch, El Paso [1992]	X	X	X	X	X	X		
Irving Schwartz Branch, El Paso [1991]						X	X	X
Graham [1993]	X	X	X	X	X			
Grand Prairie Memorial Lib. [1993]	X							
Robinson-Westchase Lib., Houston [1991]		X	X	X	X	X	X	X
Lampasas [1992]	X	X	X	X	X			
Marble Falls Lib. [?]	X							
Plano System [1993]	X	X	X	X				
Tawakoni Area, Quinlan [1992]	X		X	X	X			
Rockwall Cty. Lib. [1991]	X	X	X	X	X	X	X	X
San Marcos [1994]	X			X	X			
Tatum Branch Lib. [1992]	X			X	X	X		
Cameron–J. Jarvis Municipal Lib., Troup [1991]					X			X
Van Alstyne [?]	X							
Utah								
Uintah Cty. Lib., Vernal [1991]	X	X	X	X	X	X	X	X
Vermont								
Richmond Free Lib. [1991]	X	X	X	X	X	X	X	X
Virginia								
Alexandria Lib. [1993]	X	X		X	X			
Burke Branch, Alexandria [1998]	X							
Community Lib., Alexandria [2000]	X							
Duncan Branch, Alexandria [1991]	X							
Sherwood Regional, Alexandria [1991]	X	X	X	X	X	X	X	X
Amherst Cty. [1991]	X	X	X	X	X	X	X	X
G. Mason Regional Lib., Annandale [1995]	X	X	X	X	X			

Predesign Stages: (1) preliminary investigation, (2) program filed, (3) project funded, (4) architect selected; *Design Stages:* (5) design stage in progress, (6) construction documents completed, (7) bidding completed, (8) contracts awarded. The date following the library name represents the estimated year of completion.

Table 8 / Public Library Projects in Progress, 1991 *(cont.)*

Library		Stages						
	1	2	3	4	5	6	7	8
Jamerson Memorial Lib., Appomattox [1991]	X	X	X	X	X	X	X	X
Arlington Cty. Central Lib. [1992]	X	X	X	X	X	X	X	X
Bedford [1994]				X	X			
Clarksville Area Lib. Branch, Boydton [1991]	X	X	X	X	X	X		X
Kings Park Community Lib., Burke [1993]	X	X	X	X	X	X	X	X
Centreville Regional Lib. [1991]	X	X	X	X	X	X	X	X
Chantilly Regional Lib. [1993]	X	X	X	X	X	X	X	
Jefferson-Madison Regional, Charlottesville [1991]	X	X	X	X	X	X	X	X
Chesapeake Central Lib. [1992]	X	X	X	X	X	X	X	X
Greenbrier Lib., Chesapeake [1992]	X	X	X	X	X	X	X	X
Russell Memorial Lib., Chesapeake [1992]	X	X	X	X	X	X	X	X
Central Lib., Chesterfield [1993]	X	X	X	X	X			
Enon Branch, Chesterfield [1992]	X	X	X	X	X			
W. Branch Lib., Chesterfield [1993]	X	X	X	X	X			
Govt. Lib. & Info. Ctr., Fairfax [1992]	X	X						
Mary Riley Styles, Falls Church [1993]					X			
Central Rappahannock Regional, Fredericksburg [1994]	X		X					
N. Stafford Branch, Fredericksburg [1992]	X	X	X	X	X	X		
Great Falls Lib. [?]	X	X	X	X	X			
Rockingham, Harrisonburg [1991]	X	X	X	X	X	X	X	X
Herndon Community Lib. [1995]	X	X	X	X	X			
Leesburg Lib. [1991]	X	X	X	X	X		X	X
Thomas Balch Lib., Leesburg [1995]	X							
Bull Run Regional Lib., Manassas [1993]	X	X	X	X	X			
Midlothian Branch Lib. [1993]	X	X	X	X	X			
Orange Cty. Branch Lib. [1995]	X							
Orange Cty. Main Lib. [1998]	X							
Bull Run Regional Lib., Prince William [1993]	X	X	X	X	X			
Chinn Park Regional Lib., Prince William [1991]	X	X	X	X	X	X	X	X
Purcellville Lib. [1992]		X	X	X	X	X	X	X
Bon Air Branch, Richmond [1992]	X	X	X	X	X	X	X	X
Staunton [1993]				X	X			
Eastern Loudoun Regional Lib., Sterling [1991]	X	X	X	X	X		X	X
Patrick Henry Community Lib., Vienna [1995]	X	X	X	X	X			
Princess Anne Lib., Virginia Beach [?]	X	X	X	X				
Fauquier Cty. Lib., Warrenton [1991]	X	X	X	X	X			
Washington								
Bothell Regional Lib. [1993]	X	X	X	X	X			
Burien Lib. [1993]			X	X	X			
Deming Lib. [1991]	X	X	X	X	X	X	X	X
Federal Way Lib. [1991]	X	X	X	X	X	X	X	X
N. Federal Way Lib. [1995]	X	X	X					
Ferndale Lib. [1992]	X	X	X		X	X	X	
Covington Resource Lib., Kent [1993]	X	X	X	X	X			
Maple Valley Lib. [1995]	X	X	X					
Medical Lake Lib. [1991]	X	X	X	X	X	X	X	X
Sammamish Lib., Redmond [1995]	X	X	X					
Richmond Beach Community Lib. [1993]			X	X				
Shoreline Lib., Seattle [1993]	X	X	X	X	X	X		
Downtown Lib., Spokane [1993]	X	X	X	X	X			
E. Side Branch, Spokane [1993]	X		X					
Hillyard Branch, Spokane [1993]	X		X					
N. Side Lib., Spokane [1994]	X							
Otis Orchard Lib., Spokane [1991]	X	X	X	X	X	X	X	X

Predesign Stages: (1) preliminary investigation, (2) program filed, (3) project funded, (4) architect selected; *Design Stages:* (5) design stage in progress, (6) construction documents completed, (7) bidding completed, (8) contracts awarded. The date following the library name represents the estimated year of completion.

Table 8 / Public Library Projects in Progress, 1991 *(cont.)*

Library	1	2	3	4	5	6	7	8
Shadle Branch, Spokane [1994]			X					
S. Hill Lib., Spokane [1994]			X					
Woodinville Lib. [1993]	X	X	X	X	X			
West Virginia								
Bolivar–Harpers Ferry [1991]	X	X	X	X	X	X	X	
Philippi [1991]	X	X	X	X	X	X	X	X
Stephenson Memorial Lib., Summersville [1992]	X	X	X	X	X			
Wisconsin								
Clintonville [1991]							X	X
Columbus [1991]	X		X	X	X	X	X	X
L. E. Phillips Memorial, Eau Claire [1992]					X			
Horicon [1992]	X	X	X	X	X	X		
Johnson Creek [1991]	X	X	X	X	X	X	X	X
Kenosha [1993]	X	X	X	X	X			
Mazomanie Free Lib. [1992]	X			X				
Llewellyn Neighborhood Lib., Milwaukee [1993]	X	X	X	X	X			
Cook Memorial Lib., Oconto Falls [1991]	X	X	X	X	X	X	X	X
Plover Branch Lib. [1991]	X	X	X	X	X	X	X	X
Muehl, Seymour [1992]		X	X	X	X			
Shell Lake [1992]	X	X	X	X	X	X	X	X
Portage Cty., Stevens Point [1992]		X	X	X		X	X	X
Superior [1991]								X
Waupaca [1993]	X			X	X			
Weyauwega [1991]	X	X	X	X	X	X	X	X
Wyoming								
Big Piney Branch Lib. [1991]							X	X

Predesign Stages: (1) preliminary investigation, (2) program filed, (3) project funded, (4) architect selected; *Design Stages:* (5) design stage in progress, (6) construction documents completed, (7) bidding completed, (8) contracts awarded. The date following the library name represents the estimated year of completion.

Table 9 / Academic Library Projects in Progress, 1991

Library	1	2	3	4	5	6	7	8
Alabama								
Univ. of Alabama Busn. Lib., Tuscaloosa [1994]	X	X	X					
Univ. of Alabama Hoole Special Collections, Tuscaloosa [1993]	X	X	X	X	X			
Arizona								
Northern Arizona Univ., Flagstaff [1992]	X	X	X	X	X	X	X	X
Arkansas								
Univ. of Arkansas, Fayetteville [1994]	X		X	X	X			
Arkansas State Univ., State University [1993]					X	X		
California								
California State–Hayward, Concord [1992]	X	X	X	X	X	X	X	X
Univ. of California, Davis [1992]	X	X	X	X	X	X		
Univ. of California–San Diego, La Jolla [1993]	X	X	X	X	X	X	X	X
Naval Postgraduate School, Monterey [1992]								X
Pfau Lib., California State Univ., San Bernardino [1993]	X	X	X	X		X		

Predesign Stages: (1) preliminary investigation, (2) program filed, (3) project funded, (4) architect selected; *Design Stages:* (5) design stage in progress, (6) construction documents completed, (7) bidding completed, (8) contracts awarded. The date following the library name represents the estimated year of completion.

Table 9 / **Academic Library Projects in Progress, 1991** *(cont.)*

Library	Stages							
	1	2	3	4	5	6	7	8
City Coll. of San Francisco [1994]	X	X		X	X			
Cal. State Univ., San Marcos [1992]								X
Stanford Univ. Lib. [1994]	X	X		X	X			
Colorado								
Eng. Lib., Univ. of Colorado–Boulder [1992]	X	X	X	X	X	X	X	X
District of Columbia								
Georgetown Univ. [1991]	X	X	X	X	X	X	X	X
Georgetown Univ. [1995]	X							
Florida								
Univ. of Florida, Gainesville [1993]		X	X					
Florida International Univ. Atheneum, Miami [1993]	X	X	X	X	X			
Florida International Univ. Lib. Ext., Miami [1994]	X	X	X	X	X			
Polk Community Coll., Winter Haven [1991]	X	X	X	X	X	X	X	X
Georgia								
Piedmont Coll., Demorest [1992]								X
Idaho								
Boise State Univ. [1993]	X	X	X	X	X			
North Idaho Coll., Coeur d'Alene [1991]	X	X	X	X	X	X	X	X
Univ. of Idaho, Moscow [1993]		X	X	X	X	X	X	
Indiana								
Anderson Univ. [1992]	X	X		X				
Earlham Coll., Richmond [1993]								X
Iowa								
Mount Mercy Coll., Cedar Rapids [1992]						X	X	X
St. Ambrose Univ., Davenport [1995]	X	X		X				
Grand View Coll., Des Moines [1993]	X	X	X	X	X	X		
Kansas								
Washburn Univ., Topeka [1991]	X	X	X	X	X	X	X	X
Kentucky								
Berea Coll. [1991]	X	X	X	X	X	X	X	X
Northern Kentucky Univ., Highland Heights [1994]		X	X	X	X			
Eastern Kentucky Univ., Richmond [1994]	X	X	X	X	X			
Louisiana								
Xavier Univ., New Orleans [1992]	X	X	X	X		X	X	X
Maine								
Univ. of Southern Maine, Portland [1993]	X	X	X	X	X	X		
Maryland								
Univ. of Maryland–Baltimore Cty. [1994]	X	X	X	X	X			
Western Maryland Coll., Westminster [1991]	X	X	X	X	X	X	X	X
Massachusetts								
Eastern Nazarene Coll., Wollaston [1991]	X	X	X	X	X	X	X	X
Michigan								
Ferris State Univ., Big Rapids [1991]	X	X	X	X	X	X	X	X
Cooley Law Lib., Lansing [1991]	X	X	X	X	X	X	X	X
Olivet Coll. [1992]	X	X	X	X	X	X	X	X
Minnesota								
Univ. of Minnesota Archives Center, Minneapolis [1998]	X							
Univ. of Minnesota Walter Lib., Minneapolis [1997]	X							

Predesign Stages: (1) preliminary investigation, (2) program filed, (3) project funded, (4) architect selected; *Design Stages:* (5) design stage in progress, (6) construction documents completed, (7) bidding completed, (8) contracts awarded. The date following the library name represents the estimated year of completion.

Table 9 / Academic Library Projects in Progress, 1991 *(cont.)*

Library	1	2	3	4	5	6	7	8
Univ. of Minnesota Wilson Lib., Minneapolis [1992]				X	X			
Mississippi								
Univ. of Southern Mississippi, Hattiesburg [1994]	X	X	X	X	X			
Missouri								
Southwest Baptist Univ., Bolivar [?]	X	X		X	X			
Hannibal–La Grange Coll. [?]	X							
Nevada								
Univ. of Nevada, Reno [1993]				X	X			X
New Hampshire								
St. Anselm Coll., Manchester [1992]		X	X	X	X			
New Jersey								
Caldwell Coll. [1991]	X	X	X	X	X	X	X	X
Georgian Court Coll., Lakewood [1993]	X	X		X	X			
Seton Hall Univ., South Orange [1993]	X	X						
New Mexico								
NM Inst. of Mining & Technology, Socorro [1991]	X	X	X	X	X	X	X	X
New York								
SUNY–Albany [1995]	X	X	X	X	X			
Fordham Univ., Bronx [1994]	X	X	X	X	X			
Polytechnic Univ., Brooklyn [1991]			X	X				X
Queens Coll., Flushing [1991]								X
Cornell Univ., Ithaca [1992]	X	X	X	X	X	X	X	X
Nazareth Coll. of Rochester [1994]	X	X		X				
Rochester Inst. of Technology [1991]	X	X	X	X	X	X	X	X
SUNY Health Science Center at Syracuse [1995]					X			
Pace Univ. Law Lib., White Plains [1991]	X	X	X	X	X	X	X	X
North Carolina								
East Carolina Univ., Greenville [1993]	X	X	X	X	X			
Wake Forest Univ., Winston-Salem [1991]	X	X	X	X	X	X	X	X
North Dakota								
Standing Rock Coll., Fort Yates [1992]					X	X		
Ohio								
Design, Architecture, Art & Planning Lib., Univ. of Cincinnati [1994]	X	X	X	X	X			
Coll. of Law, Ohio State Univ., Columbus [1992]								X
Miami Univ., Oxford [1993]	X	X	X	X	X			
Coll. of Wooster [1993]	X	X						
Oklahoma								
Oklahoma State Univ., Stillwater [?]	X							
Oregon								
Northwest Christian Coll., Eugene [1995]	X							
Oregon Health Sciences Univ., Portland [1991]	X	X	X	X	X	X	X	X
Willamette Coll. of Law, Salem [1992]	X	X	X	X	X	X	X	X
Pennsylvania								
Moravian Coll., Bethlehem [1992]	X	X	X	X	X	X	X	X
Bloomsburg Univ. of Pennsylvania [?]	X	X						
Univ. of Pittsburgh at Greensburg [1993]	X	X	X	X	X			
Immaculata Coll. [1993]	X	X	X	X	X	X		
Mansfield Univ. of Pennsylvania [?]	X	X	X	X	X	X		
Mansfield Univ. of Pennsylvania [1994]	X	X	X	X	X	X		
Philadelphia Coll. of Textiles & Science [1992]	X	X	X	X	X	X	X	X
Pennsylvania State, Schuylkill Haven [1993]	X	X	X	X	X	X		

Predesign Stages: (1) preliminary investigation, (2) program filed, (3) project funded, (4) architect selected; *Design Stages:* (5) design stage in progress, (6) construction documents completed, (7) bidding completed, (8) contracts awarded. The date following the library name represents the estimated year of completion.

Table 9 / Academic Library Projects in Progress, 1991 *(cont.)*

Library	1	2	3	4	5	6	7	8
Univ. of Scranton [1992]	X	X	X	X	X	X	X	X
Rhode Island								
Univ. of Rhode Island, Kingston [1992]	X	X	X	X	X	X	X	X
South Dakota								
Univ. of South Dakota, Vermillion [1994]			X	X	X			
Texas								
Univ. of Texas at Austin [1992]	X	X	X	X	X			
Southern Methodist Univ., Dallas [1994]			X					
South Texas Coll. of Law, Houston [1991]	X	X	X	X	X	X	X	X
Vermont								
Middlebury Coll. [1992]	X	X	X	X	X	X	X	X
Norwich Univ., Northfield [1992]	X	X	X	X	X	X	X	X
Virginia								
Washington & Lee Univ., Lexington [1991]	X	X	X	X	X	X	X	X
Christopher Newport Coll., Newport News [?]						X		
Shenandoah Univ., Winchester [1992]	X	X	X	X	X	X	X	X
Washington								
Music Lib., Western Washington Univ., Bellingham [1991]					X	X	X	X
Washington State Univ., Pullman [?]	X	X	X	X		X		
Seattle Pacific Univ. [1993]	X	X		X	X			
Center for Info. and Tech., Gonzaga Univ., Spokane [1992]	X	X	X	X	X	X	X	X
Crosby Lib., Gonzaga Univ., Spokane [1992]								X
Whitworth Coll., Spokane [1993]	X	X	X	X		X	X	X
West Virginia								
Davis & Elkins Coll., Elkins [1992]								X
Wisconsin								
Univ. of Wisconsin—Eau Claire [1993]	X	X	X	X	X			
Guam								
Univ. of Guam, Mangilao [1992]	X	X	X	X	X	X	X	X

Predesign Stages: (1) preliminary investigation, (2) program filed, (3) project funded, (4) architect selected; *Design Stages:* (5) design stage in progress, (6) construction documents completed, (7) bidding completed, (8) contracts awarded. The date following the library name represents the estimated year of completion.

Book Trade Research and Statistics

Prices of U.S. and Foreign Published Materials

John Haar

Chair, ALA ALCTS Library Materials Price Index Committee

Prices of library materials once again increased at a rate considerably higher than the consumer price index in 1991. While consumer prices rose a moderate 3.1 percent from 1990, the average price of U.S. periodicals increased 11.7 percent and U.S. serial services averaged 9.3 percent higher. Materials in both these categories experienced their highest rate of increase in three years. Other average price increases, while less severe, were still higher than the CPI. As the following table illustrates, price increases in excess of the CPI have been the norm for most materials from 1989 through 1991:

		Percent Change	
Index	1989	1990	1991
Consumer Price Index	4.6	6.1	3.1
Periodicals	9.5	9.5	11.7
Serial Services	6.4	3.9	9.3
Hardcover Books	4.1	3.7	3.3*
Academic Books	5.3	7.2	5.3
College Books	6.2	3.7	6.0
Mass Market Paperbacks	–4.8	5.8	6.1*
Trade Paperbacks	14.3	1.7	3.4*

preliminary

U.S. Published Materials

Tables 1 through 8 report average prices and price indexes for U.S. materials. Categories include periodicals (Table 1), serial services (Table 2), hardcover books (Table 3), North American academic books (Table 4), college books (Table 5), mass market paperback books (Table 6), trade paperback books (Table 7), and nonprint media (Table 8).

Periodical and Serial Prices

The U.S. periodical price index for 1991 is a collaborative effort of the ALA ALCTS Library Materials Price Index Committee and the Faxon Company. Subscription prices cited are list prices obtained directly from publishers and do not include cus-

Table 1 / U.S. Periodicals: Average Prices and Price Indexes, 1988–1991*
(Index Base: 1977 = 100)

Subject Area	1977 Average Price	1988 Average Price	1988 Index	1989 Average Price	1989 Index	1990 Average Price	1990 Index	1991 Average Price	1991 Index
U.S. periodicals Excluding Soviet translations**	$24.59	$77.93	316.9	$85.37	347.2	$93.45	380.0	$104.36	424.4
U.S. periodicals Including Soviet translations									
Agriculture	33.42	105.45	315.5	114.07	341.3	124.74	373.2	138.53	414.5
Business and economics	11.58	33.56	289.8	36.62	316.2	42.43	366.4	42.36	365.8
	18.62	53.89	289.4	57.93	311.1	63.25	339.7	70.87	380.6
Chemistry and physics	93.76	329.99	352.0	367.99	392.5	412.66	440.1	472.84	504.3
Children's periodicals	5.82	16.39	281.6	16.95	291.2	17.51	300.9	18.38	315.8
Education	17.54	47.95	273.4	51.43	293.2	56.33	321.2	62.43	355.9
Engineering	35.77	114.83	321.0	128.37	358.9	138.84	388.1	160.13	447.7
Fine and applied arts	13.72	32.43	236.4	35.07	255.6	36.89	268.9	38.61	281.4
General interest periodicals	16.19	28.29	174.7	29.69	183.4	31.24	193.0	32.25	199.2
History	12.64	30.16	238.6	32.27	255.3	35.51	280.9	38.35	303.4
Home economics	18.73	54.73	292.2	60.92	325.3	64.49	344.3	74.11	395.7
Industrial arts	14.37	44.20	307.6	48.68	338.8	54.69	380.6	60.96	424.2
Journalism and communications	16.97	53.39	314.6	58.13	342.5	60.85	358.6	62.81	370.1
Labor and industrial relations	11.24	44.06	392.0	50.65	450.6	52.74	469.2	57.59	512.4
Law	17.36	43.33	249.6	46.01	265.0	50.32	289.9	53.30	307.0

Library and information sciences	16.97	51.61	304.1	54.45	320.9	57.34	337.9	62.73	369.7
Literature and language	11.82	28.04	237.2	29.41	248.8	30.63	259.1	32.99	279.1
Mathematics, botany, geology, and general science	47.13	159.33	338.1	173.21	367.5	188.19	399.3	209.55	444.6
Medicine	51.31	180.67	352.1	199.22	388.3	217.87	424.6	249.94	487.1
Philosophy and religion	10.89	27.09	248.8	28.62	262.8	30.76	282.5	32.91	302.2
Physical education and recreation	10.00	28.60	286.0	30.16	301.6	32.20	322.0	34.64	346.4
Political science	14.83	41.55	280.2	45.03	303.6	49.67	334.9	52.81	356.1
Psychology	31.74	100.57	316.9	114.52	360.8	125.31	394.8	135.40	426.6
Sociology and anthropology	19.68	64.27	326.6	66.73	339.1	77.61	394.4	88.69	450.7
Soviet translations**	175.41	592.22	337.6	621.70	354.4	678.09	386.6	742.80	423.5
Zoology	33.69	127.33	377.9	142.13	421.9	153.78	456.5	172.56	512.2
Total number of periodicals								
Excluding Soviet translations	3,218	3,731		3,731		3,731		3,731	
Including Soviet translations	3,418	3,942		3,942		3,942		3,942	

*Compiled by Kathryn Hammell Carpenter and Adrian W. Alexander. For further comments see *Library Journal*, April 15, 1991, "Price Index for U.S. Periodicals." The price index is based on subscription price information supplied, compiled, and analyzed by the Faxon Company, and follows guidelines, definitions, and criteria established by the American National Standards Institute in *American National Standard for Library and Information Services and Related Publishing Practices—Library Materials—Criteria for Price Indexes* (ANSI Z39.20—1983).

**The Soviet translations category was added in 1986.

Table 2 / U.S. Serial Services: Average Prices and Price Indexes, 1988-1991*

(Index Base: 1977 = 100)

Subject Area	1977 Average Price per Title	1988 Average Price per Title	1988 Index	1989 Average Price per Title	1989 Percent Increase	1989 Index	1990 Average Price per Title	1990 Percent Increase	1990 Index	1991 Average Price per Title	1991 Percent Increase	1991 Index
U.S. serial services**	$142.27	$341.32	239.9	$363.20	6.4	255.3	$377.24	3.9	265.2	$412.38	9.3	289.9
Business	216.28	$458.33	211.9	493.23	7.6	228.1	523.79	6.2	242.2	584.93	11.7	270.5
General and humanities	90.44	225.95	249.8	255.27	13.0	282.3	274.39	7.5	303.4	292.23	6.5	323.1
Law	126.74	338.13	266.8	354.32	4.8	279.6	390.98	10.3	308.5	424.68	8.6	335.1
Science and technology	141.16	378.37	268.0	420.19	11.1	297.7	443.36	5.5	314.1	483.90	9.1	342.8
Social sciences***	145.50	441.67	303.6	418.14	-5.3	287.4	370.40	-11.4	254.6	398.76	7.7	274.1
U.S. documents	62.88	101.88	162.0	110.79	8.7	176.2	101.45	-8.4	161.3	107.74	6.2	171.3
Wilson Index	87.51	212.17	242.5	225.21	6.1	257.4	237.99	5.7	272.0	262.97	10.5	300.5
Total number of services	1,432	1,310		1,308			1,308			1,307		

*Compiled by Andrew Shroyer, University of California, Santa Barbara, from data supplied by the Faxon Company, publishers' price lists, and library acquisition records. The definition of a serial service has been taken from *American National Standard for Library and Information Services and Related Publishing Practice — Library Materials — Criteria for Price Indexes* (ANSI Z39.20 – 1983).

**Excludes "Wilson Index"; excludes Soviet translations as of 1988.

***The 1988 average price includes two expensive titles: "Leading National Advertiser Multi-Media Report Service" (LNAMMRS), \$8,750, and "LNA-PIB Magazine Service," \$7,300. The two Leading National Advertiser titles are "LNAMMRS," \$4,200, and "LNA-PIB," \$7,885. The 1989 average price includes "LNAMMRS," \$4,200, and "LNA-PIB," \$7,885. The two Leading National Advertiser titles were dropped in 1990 because they are no longer sold to libraries. Without these, average prices would be: 1988 — \$343.18 (index 235.9); 1989 — \$345.10 (index 237.2).

484

Table 3 / U.S. Hardcover Books: Average Prices and Price Indexes, 1988–1991*
(Index Base: 1977 = 100)

Category	1977 Average Price	1988 (Final) Volumes	1988 (Final) Average Price	1988 (Final) Index	1989 (Final) Volumes	1989 (Final) Average Price	1989 (Final) Index	1990 (Final) Volumes	1990 (Final) Average Price	1990 (Final) Index	1991 (Preliminary) Volumes	1991 (Preliminary) Average Price	1991 (Preliminary) Index
Agriculture	$16.24	438	$49.36	303.9	387	$51.17	315.1	359	$54.24	334.0	331	$58.97	363.1
Art	21.24	958	39.96	188.1	941	50.30	236.8	759	42.18	198.6	624	44.85	211.2
Biography	15.34	1,538	25.99	169.4	1,485	27.34	178.2	1,337	29.58	192.8	1,279	27.54	179.5
Business	18.00	1,120	37.51	208.4	922	37.94	210.8	748	45.48	252.7	724	43.14	239.7
Education	12.95	620	33.55	259.1	534	37.62	290.5	562	38.72	299.0	490	41.05	317.0
Fiction	10.09	2,258	17.63	174.7	2,236	18.69	185.2	1,962	19.83	196.5	1,831	21.88	216.8
General works	30.99	1,448	50.35	162.5	1,257	49.73	160.5	1,035	54.77	176.7	974	50.37	162.5
History	17.12	1,992	33.44	195.3	1,747	37.95	221.7	1,450	36.43	212.8	1,315	39.76	232.2
Home economics	11.16	474	21.38	191.6	458	22.17	198.7	357	23.80	213.3	320	24.30	217.7
Juvenile	6.65	3,603	11.79	177.3	4,040	13.01	195.6	3,675	13.01	195.6	3,367	16.64	250.2
Language	14.96	339	40.42	270.2	297	47.35	316.5	312	42.98	287.3	221	52.18	348.8
Law	25.04	957	50.85	203.1	767	58.62	234.1	596	60.78	242.7	606	59.73	238.5
Literature	15.78	1,465	30.85	195.5	1,421	32.74	207.5	1,312	35.80	226.9	1,157	35.86	227.2
Medicine	24.00	2,914	66.59	277.5	2,455	69.87	291.1	2,215	72.24	301.0	1,842	70.43	293.5
Music	20.13	217	36.95	183.6	254	41.73	207.3	184	41.86	207.9	164	40.72	202.3
Philosophy and psychology	14.43	1,120	34.75	240.8	1,158	36.55	253.3	963	40.58	281.2	879	42.68	295.8
Poetry and drama	13.63	649	28.02	205.6	574	31.12	228.3	486	32.19	236.2	473	32.37	237.5
Religion	12.26	1,163	26.73	218.0	1,082	28.12	229.4	977	31.31	255.4	846	32.97	268.9
Science	24.88	2,904	66.91	268.9	2,341	68.90	276.9	2,028	74.39	299.0	1,626	79.73	320.5
Sociology and economics	29.88	5,430	37.25	124.7	4,987	41.26	138.1	4,504	42.10	140.9	3,907	47.86	160.2
Sports and recreation	12.28	518	27.33	222.6	476	29.42	239.6	403	30.52	248.5	387	31.44	256.0
Technology	23.61	1,992	65.26	276.4	1,902	71.04	300.9	1,521	76.80	325.3	1,398	74.89	317.2
Travel	18.44	215	26.22	142.2	239	31.37	170.1	181	30.41	164.9	133	32.08	174.0
Total	$19.22	34,332	$39.00	202.9	31,960	$40.61	211.3	27,926	$42.12	219.1	24,894	$43.52	226.4

*Compiled by Sue Plezia, University of California, from data supplied by the R. R. Bowker Company. Price indexes on Tables 3 and 7 are based on books recorded in the R. R. Bowker Company's *Weekly Record* (cumulated in *American Book Publishing Record*). The 1991 preliminary figures include items listed during 1991 with an imprint date of 1991. Final data for previous years include items listed between January of that year and June of the following year with an imprint date of the specified year.

Table 4 / North American Academic Books: Average Prices and Price Indexes, 1988–89 to 1990–91*
(Index Base: 1979-80 = 100)

Subject	LC Class	1979-80		1988-89			1989-90				1990-91			
		Number of Titles	Average Price	Number of Titles	Average Price	Index	Number of Titles	Average Price	Percent Increase	Index	Number of Titles	Average Price	Percent Increase	Index
Agriculture	S	1,275	$22.80	1,811	$46.33	203.2	1,518	$52.59	13.5	230.7	1,640	$56.09	6.7	246.0
Anthropology	GN	688	18.23	765	33.30	182.7	845	34.54	3.7	189.5	914	37.45	8.4	205.4
Botany	QK	428	30.06	452	68.80	228.9	385	75.99	10.5	252.8	411	81.45	7.2	271.0
Business and economics	H	6,980	18.92	10,934	37.92	200.4	10,174	40.97	8.0	216.5	10,778	42.90	4.7	226.7
Chemistry	QD	950	43.44	1,057	91.96	211.7	1,064	95.94	4.3	220.9	1,035	104.50	8.9	240.6
Education	L	2,682	14.37	3,022	30.23	210.4	2,926	32.76	8.4	228.0	3,197	34.39	5.0	239.3
Engineering and technology	T	5,277	28.83	7,533	60.30	209.2	7,417	65.15	8.0	226.0	7,979	67.55	3.7	234.3
Fiction and children's literature	PZ	572	11.47	1,576	17.94	156.4	1,441	19.11	6.5	166.6	1,791	20.07	5.0	175.0
Fine and applied arts	M,N	4,846	21.82	5,214	38.69	177.3	4,678	42.26	9.2	193.7	5,238	43.81	3.7	200.8
General works	A	322	22.71	346	67.18	295.8	297	63.21	-5.9	278.3	345	73.14	15.7	322.1
Geography	G	554	23.22	671	39.25	169.0	584	50.64	29.0	218.1	665	54.54	7.7	234.9
Geology	QE	475	31.59	533	65.10	206.1	537	68.99	6.0	218.4	507	70.69	2.5	223.8
History	C,D,E,F	5,713	18.95	8,169	31.15	164.4	8,137	33.65	8.0	177.6	8,571	36.25	7.7	191.3
Home economics	TX	492	16.71	679	28.49	170.5	596	30.33	6.5	181.5	656	30.06	-0.9	179.9
Industrial arts	TT	111	16.14	173	24.95	154.6	175	26.98	8.1	167.2	232	23.98	-11.1	148.6
Law	K	1,122	19.82	1,668	45.35	228.8	1,613	49.40	8.9	249.2	1,804	49.56	0.3	250.1
Library and information science	Z	774	21.82	1,167	39.64	181.7	1,448	49.37	24.5	226.3	1,734	49.70	0.7	227.8
Literature and language	P	8,823	15.43	13,965	27.98	181.3	14,282	28.73	2.7	186.2	15,091	31.39	9.3	203.4

Subject	Class												
Mathematics and computer science	QA	2,281	24.62	5,543	43.64	177.3	5,473	46.46	6.5	188.7	5,427	49.33	6.2	200.4
Medicine	R	6,636	26.02	9,493	57.61	221.4	9,651	61.17	6.2	235.1	9,472	65.29	6.7	250.9
Military and naval science	U,V	599	18.14	1,315	31.96	176.2	1,360	38.40	20.2	211.7	1,144	37.19	-3.2	205.0
Philosophy and religion	B	3,319	15.63	5,791	29.61	189.4	5,860	33.36	12.7	213.4	6,042	35.71	7.0	228.5
Physical education and recreation	GV	1,391	12.43	1,207	20.20	162.5	1,030	21.88	8.3	176.0	1,034	23.22	6.1	186.8
Physics and astronomy	QB	1,114	35.63	2,128	68.13	191.2	2,324	67.74	-0.6	190.1	2,313	71.74	5.9	201.3
Political science	J	2,861	17.25	3,445	33.34	193.3	3,430	36.45	9.3	211.3	3,703	39.92	9.5	231.4
Psychology	BF	1,752	18.84	1,531	35.63	189.1	1,615	38.44	7.9	204.0	1,746	39.14	1.8	207.7
Science (general)	Q	313	22.85	504	46.33	202.8	590	49.76	7.4	217.8	636	47.78	-4.0	209.1
Sociology	HM	4,851	16.87	4,846	31.22	185.1	4,880	33.36	6.9	197.7	5,356	36.10	8.2	214.0
Zoology	QH,QL,QP,QR	2,982	32.70	3,934	71.39	218.3	3,669	74.64	4.6	228.3	3,773	79.91	7.1	244.4
Average for all subjects		70,183	$21.98	99,472	$41.21	187.5	97,999	$44.19	7.2	201.0	103,234	$46.53	5.3	211.7
Canadian history		348	$9.17	260	$25.63	279.5	327	$16.40	-36.0	178.8	332	$24.57	49.8	267.9
Canadian literature		540	5.37	558	13.36	248.8	678	9.41	-29.6	175.2	795	13.69	45.5	254.9

*Compiled by Stephen Bosch, University of Arizona, from data collected from approval plan statistics supplied by Baker & Taylor, Coutts Library Services, and Blackwell/North America. Baker & Taylor and Blackwell/North America used a fiscal year from July 1 to June 30. Coutts Library Services used a fiscal year from June 1 to May 31 from 1979–80 to 1982–83; in 1983–84 Coutts changed its fiscal year to February 1 to January 31. This table covers titles published or distributed in the United States and Canada. Baker & Taylor data include continuations (series, serials, and sets) and paperbacks of 48 pages or less. "General Supplementary" and "Extracurricular" (non-academic) categories are included by Baker & Taylor in 1979–80 but excluded beginning with 1980–81.

Table 5 / U.S. College Books: Average Prices and Prices Indexes, 1989-1991*
(Index Base for all years: 1978 = 100. 1990 also indexed to 1989; 1991 also indexed to 1990)

Choice Subject Categories	1978 Number of Titles	1978 Average Price per Title	1989 Number of Titles	1989 Average Price per Title	1989 Prices Indexed to 1978	1990 Number of Titles	1990 Average Price per Title	1990 Prices Indexed to 1978	1990 Prices Indexed to 1989	1991 Number of Titles	1991 Average Price per Title	1991 Prices Indexed to 1978	1991 Prices Indexed to 1990
General	47	$15.25	19	$40.19	263.5	25	$45.28	296.9	112.7	13	$42.85	281.0	94.6
Humanities	92	$16.14	21	$32.33	200.3	33	$35.67	221.0	110.3	18	$43.30	268.3	121.4
Art and architecture	315	26.60	276	55.56	208.9	304	51.72	194.4	93.1	296	55.62	209.1	107.5
Photography [a]	–	–	24	44.11	–	17	44.77	–	101.5	15	47.85	–	106.9
Communication	71	14.03	42	32.70	233.1	48	33.80	240.9	103.4	42	36.82	262.4	108.9
Classical studies [b]	–	–	75	43.07	–	–	–	–	0.0	–	–	–	–
Language and literature	97	13.38	110	35.17	262.9	83	35.47	265.1	100.9	84	36.71	274.4	103.5
Linguistics [c]	22	15.07	–	–	–	–	–	–	–	–	–	–	–
Classical [d]	18	13.41	–	–	–	–	–	–	–	–	–	–	–
English and American	834	12.42	547	30.27	243.7	571	31.49	253.5	104.0	565	31.22	251.4	99.1
Germanic	51	12.35	38	32.18	260.6	26	28.92	234.2	89.9	37	28.79	233.1	99.6
Romance	101	12.27	97	30.30	246.9	104	29.56	240.9	97.6	114	30.11	245.4	101.9
Slavic	46	13.22	41	27.92	211.2	33	32.93	249.1	117.9	27	26.50	200.5	80.5
Other	67	13.03	63	25.09	192.6	88	34.30	263.2	136.7	68	35.62	273.4	103.8
Performing arts	16	15.07	20	29.41	195.2	26	29.71	197.1	101.0	20	33.49	222.2	112.7
Dance	21	12.95	12	30.97	239.2	12	29.89	230.8	96.5	14	52.20	403.1	174.6
Film	80	15.70	82	33.00	210.2	70	35.89	228.6	108.8	66	39.11	249.1	109.0
Music	138	15.10	156	35.34	234.0	130	37.19	246.3	105.2	144	42.92	284.2	115.4
Theatre	34	13.84	46	35.01	253.0	60	38.14	275.6	108.9	40	44.44	321.1	116.5
Philosophy	197	14.21	185	37.25	262.1	232	38.83	273.3	104.2	253	41.30	290.6	106.4
Religion	300	11.98	174	33.49	279.5	169	36.49	304.6	109.0	126	34.68	289.5	95.0
Total humanities	2,500	$14.86	2,009	$36.09	242.9	2,006	$36.93	248.5	102.3	1,929	$38.69	260.4	104.8
Science and technology	102	21.31	99	46.90	220.1	79	36.83	172.8	78.5	97	39.46	185.2	107.1
History of science and technology	85	17.37	74	40.56	233.5	61	46.09	265.3	113.6	73	38.19	219.9	82.9
Astronautics and astronomy	22	23.78	22	50.56	212.6	25	48.36	203.4	95.6	37	39.41	165.7	81.5
Biology	231	23.67	97	51.01	215.5	89	56.41	238.3	110.6	70	68.97	291.4	122.3
Botany [a]	–	–	29	63.91	–	53	55.17	–	86.3	54	54.74	–	99.2
Zoology [a]	–	–	53	49.21	–	34	57.03	–	115.9	43	51.25	–	89.9
Chemistry	95	28.59	21	70.76	247.5	44	87.52	306.1	123.7	44	76.24	266.7	87.1

Earth science	84	29.99	264.9	79.44	34	51	70.56	235.3	88.8	58	64.02	213.5	90.7
Engineering	241	25.75	259.2	66.74	87	70	57.35	222.7	85.9	85	66.86	259.7	116.6
Health sciences	92	14.88	234.6	34.91	94	100	40.31	270.9	115.5	111	44.93	301.9	111.5
Information and computer science	53	20.37	198.1	40.35	70	102	47.71	234.2	118.2	74	44.73	219.6	93.8
Mathematics	70	22.54	215.3	48.53	60	66	54.00	239.6	111.3	62	50.48	224.0	93.5
Physics	47	28.77	152.7	43.94	22	37	51.05	177.4	116.2	38	52.04	180.9	101.9
Sports and physical education	73	10.32	266.1	27.46	18	26	26.74	259.1	97.4	24	34.87	337.9	130.4
Total sciences	1,195	$22.77	217.6	$49.54	780	837	$51.76	227.3	104.5	870	$51.79	227.4	100.1
Social and behavioral sciences	156	16.37	226.6	37.09	92	47	35.50	216.9	95.7	55	34.58	211.2	97.4
Anthropology	102	16.97	235.4	39.94	96	154	36.67	216.1	91.8	143	39.56	233.1	107.9
Business, management, and labor	136	14.36	248.7	35.72	145	124	36.73	255.8	102.8	127	39.84	277.4	108.5
Economics	242	17.65	230.9	40.75	332	334	41.15	233.1	101.0	321	44.32	251.1	107.7
Education	129	12.48	276.4	34.50	71	119	34.86	279.3	101.0	163	40.38	323.6	115.8
History, geography, and area studies	116	16.26	258.9	42.10	59	45	36.56	224.8	86.8	59	43.08	264.9	117.8
Ancient (including archaeology) [d]	67	21.79	—	—	—	—	—	—	—	—	—	—	—
Africa	38	16.34	213.3	34.85	44	33	35.20	215.4	101.0	35	36.18	221.4	102.8
Asia and Oceania	78	19.03	182.6	34.75	76	80	40.96	215.2	117.9	58	39.50	207.6	96.4
Europe	308	16.52	254.7	42.08	287	353	42.59	257.8	101.2	355	44.59	269.9	104.7
Latin America and the Caribbean	47	15.82	235.3	37.23	42	44	36.64	231.6	98.4	42	53.42	337.7	145.8
Middle East and North Africa	40	16.80	216.2	36.32	30	33	41.27	245.7	113.6	37	47.62	283.5	115.4
North America	275	16.08	190.0	30.56	349	362	32.46	201.9	106.2	350	33.98	211.3	104.7
Political science	281	14.74	227.7	33.56	28	27	32.97	223.7	98.2	19	38.51	261.3	116.8
Comparative politics [e]	—	—	—	37.82	236	208	38.02	—	100.5	227	40.75	—	107.2
International relations [e]	—	—	—	35.74	207	199	38.59	—	108.0	160	40.32	—	104.5
Political theory [e]	—	—	—	37.76	59	61	34.83	—	92.2	62	37.12	—	106.6
U. S. politics [e]	—	—	—	29.37	212	167	33.96	—	115.6	184	35.97	—	105.9
Psychology	142	15.39	236.3	36.36	179	220	38.55	250.5	106.0	178	36.47	237.0	94.6
Sociology	280	14.69	247.5	36.36	178	181	37.85	257.7	104.1	210	37.07	252.3	97.9
Total social and behavioral sciences	2,437	$15.98	228.0	$36.43	2,722	2,791	$37.69	235.9	103.5	2,785	$39.81	249.1	105.6
Total (excluding reference)	6,179	$16.83	226.7	$38.16	5,530	5,659	$39.54	234.9	103.6	5,597	$41.29	245.3	104.4
Reference	453	$34.15	178.7	$61.02	636	663	$63.15	184.9	103.5	660	$72.20	211.4	114.3
Grand total	6,632	$18.02	224.9	$40.52	6,166	6,322	$42.01	233.1	103.7	6,257	$44.55	247.2	106.0

*Compiled by Kathryn A. Soupiset, Trinity University, from book reviews appearing in Choice during the calendar year indicated. The cooperation of the Choice editorial staff is gratefully acknowledged. Additional information about these data appears in the March 1992 issue of Choice.

a. Began appearing as a separate section in September 1983.
b. Began appearing as a separate section in December 1985, and ceased in November 1989.
c. Incorporated into Language and Literature in December 1985.
d. Incorporated into Classical Studies in December 1985.
e. Began appearing as a separate section in March 1988.

tomer discounts or service charges. The complete report, including subject break-downs, multiyear comparisons, and rankings by rate of increase and average prices, is published annually in the April 15 issue of *Library Journal*. The 1991 average price for U.S. periodicals, excluding Soviet translations, was $104.36, an 11.7 percent increase over the 1990 average price of $93.45 (Table 1). The average price increased 9.5 percent in each of the two previous years. When Soviet translations are included in the total, the 1991 average price was $138.53, an 11.1 percent increase over the 1990 average of $124.74. Consistent with the past several years, the subjects with the highest average prices were chemistry and physics, medicine, mathematics, and zoology. Subjects with the highest increases in average price from 1990 to 1991 were engineering (15.3 percent), home economics (14.9 percent), medicine (14.7 percent), chemistry and physics (14.6 percent), and sociology and anthropology (14.3 percent).

The average price for U.S. serial services (Table 2) was $412.38, an increase of 9.3 percent over the 1990 average price of $377.24. The highest average price increases by subject were in business (11.7 percent) and science and technology (9.1 percent).

Book Prices

Preliminary figures show that U.S. hardcover book prices for 1991 increased on average by only 3.3 percent over those of 1990 (Table 3). The 1991 average price was $43.52. Juvenile works saw the largest increase (27.9 percent), followed by language (21.4 percent) and sociology and economics (13.7 percent). Works of fiction increased by 10.3 percent. Data for this index is supplied by the R. R. Bowker Company.

Prices for North American academic books (titles published or distributed in the United States and Canada) rose by an average of 5.3 percent in 1990–91, a somewhat slower rate of increase than the 7.2 percent recorded in 1989–90 (Table 4). The 1990–91 average price for these materials was $46.53. Aside from general works, the highest rate of 1990–91 increases occurred in political science, literature and language, and chemistry. Over the last decade, however, the sciences have generally witnessed the greatest increases. Baker & Taylor, Coutts Library Services, and Blackwell North America provide the data for this index.

The U.S. college books price index (Table 5) is compiled from book reviews appearing in *Choice*. Books in this category increased by 6 percent in 1991, a significant change from the 3.7 percent increase in 1990. Reference book prices, which rose by 14.3 percent, accounted for most of the higher rate of increase. Surprisingly, books in the sciences increased in price by less than 0.1 percent over the last year and have in fact increased at a lower rate than works in the humanities and social and behavioral sciences since the base year of 1978. Additional data are published in the March issue of *Choice*. The R. R. Bowker Company provides data for paperback prices. The preliminary 1991 average price for mass market paperbacks (Table 6) was $4.85, a 6.1 percent increase over the 1990 average of $4.57. In categories with the largest number of titles, the price of fiction works increased 5.9 percent on average, while juvenile works cost 8.4 percent less. Trade (higher priced) paperbacks rose a more modest 3.4 percent to a preliminary average price of $18.05 (Table 7). General works saw the highest increase (19.6 percent); these titles have increased almost 500 percent since the 1977 base year.

TABLE 6 / U.S. Mass Market Paperback Books: Average Prices and Price Indexes, 1988–1991*
(Index Base: 1981 = 100)

Category	1981 Average Price	1988 (Final) Total Volumes	1988 (Final) Average Price	1988 (Final) Index	1989 (Final) Total Volumes	1989 (Final) Average Price	1989 (Final) Index	1990 (Final) Total Volumes	1990 (Final) Average Price	1990 (Final) Index	1991 (Preliminary) Total Volumes	1991 (Preliminary) Average Price	1991 (Preliminary) Index
Agriculture	$2.54	3	$4.32	170.1	4	$8.45	332.7	1	$3.95	155.5	2	$3.45	135.8
Art	5.49	15	10.35	188.5	9	11.84	215.7	11	13.40	244.1	1	19.95	363.4
Biography	3.82	67	6.20	162.3	77	6.44	168.6	58	7.24	189.5	43	6.13	160.5
Business	4.63	11	7.55	163.1	20	8.93	192.9	16	7.86	169.8	7	8.03	173.4
Education	3.96	15	7.19	181.6	19	8.42	212.6	15	8.08	204.0	3	7.30	184.3
Fiction	2.47	1,956	3.99	161.5	2,628	3.78	153.0	2,855	4.06	164.4	1,600	4.30	174.1
General works	3.63	54	6.92	190.6	64	7.04	193.9	44	6.87	189.3	31	7.39	203.6
History	3.53	19	6.56	185.8	32	6.37	180.5	28	6.25	177.1	15	7.15	202.5
Home economics	4.35	73	6.27	144.1	48	7.20	165.5	44	6.75	155.2	39	7.78	178.9
Juvenile	1.79	297	3.18	177.7	376	3.19	178.2	433	3.56	198.9	301	3.26	182.1
Language	3.42	11	6.01	175.7	14	5.49	160.5	17	5.36	156.7	8	8.16	238.6
Law	3.09	4	4.59	148.5	2	6.95	224.9	3	6.62	214.2	2	9.95	322.0
Literature	3.42	31	5.44	159.1	29	6.10	178.4	28	6.45	188.6	13	5.59	163.5
Medicine	3.66	34	6.72	183.6	29	8.11	221.6	31	8.24	225.1	20	6.10	166.7
Music**	5.68	1	2.95	51.9	2	6.73	118.5	7	14.66	258.1	1	2.75	48.4
Philosophy and psychology	2.84	89	6.11	215.1	108	5.09	179.2	121	6.82	240.1	43	8.04	283.1
Poetry and drama	3.22	46	3.29	102.2	11	5.44	168.9	4	6.09	189.1	7	6.82	211.8
Religion	2.70	17	4.76	176.3	11	6.33	234.4	13	6.96	257.8	5	9.76	361.5
Science	4.45	9	5.46	122.7	16	9.99	224.5	9	9.17	206.1	12	9.43	211.9
Sociology and economics	3.43	63	5.82	169.7	59	6.25	182.2	50	6.89	200.9	26	7.88	229.7
Sports and recreation	3.05	126	5.87	192.5	134	5.66	185.6	136	5.29	173.4	74	6.77	222.0
Technology	4.20	26	18.16	432.4	17	20.95	498.8	14	24.16	575.2	15	28.42	676.7
Travel	3.23	17	10.95	339.0	13	9.95	308.0	29	11.23	347.7	23	11.56	357.9
Total	$2.65	2,984	$4.54	171.3	3,722	$4.32	163.0	3,967	$4.57	172.5	2,291	$4.85	183.0

*Compiled by Sue Plezia, University of California, from data supplied by the R. R. Bowker Company. Average prices of mass market titles in *Paperbound Books in Print.*

**1982 is used as the index base for Music.

TABLE 7 / U.S. Trade (Higher Priced) Paperbook Books: Average Prices and Price Indexes, 1988–1991*

(Index Base: 1977 = 100)

	1977 Average Price	1988 (Final)			1989 (Final)			1990 (Final)			1991 (Preliminary)		
		Number of Books	Average Price	Index	Number of Books	Average Price	Index	Number of Books	Average Price	Index	Number of Books	Average Price	Index
Agriculture	$5.01	194	$17.14	342.1	155	$16.49	329.1	142	$16.42	327.7	117	$14.60	291.4
Art	6.27	602	15.65	249.6	585	17.07	272.2	462	17.90	285.5	444	19.26	307.2
Biography	4.91	609	11.12	226.5	601	11.42	232.6	520	13.05	265.8	480	13.34	271.7
Business	7.09	470	19.43	274.0	533	21.29	300.3	398	19.61	276.6	428	21.34	301.0
Education	5.72	451	15.64	273.4	461	18.80	328.7	436	19.20	335.7	390	20.36	355.9
Fiction	4.20	1,338	10.07	239.8	1,026	9.87	235.0	885	11.32	269.5	723	11.29	268.8
General works	6.18	904	23.85	385.9	912	26.94	435.9	629	29.67	480.1	568	35.50	574.4
History	5.81	891	13.88	238.9	791	15.69	270.1	701	17.39	299.3	637	16.51	284.2
Home economics	4.77	493	11.61	243.4	422	12.10	253.7	351	12.97	271.9	345	12.88	270.0
Juvenile	2.68	959	6.13	228.7	941	6.64	247.8	938	6.79	253.4	744	7.53	281.0
Language	7.79	246	15.50	199.0	231	18.02	231.3	292	16.67	214.0	228	16.92	217.2
Law	10.66	348	24.73	232.0	291	23.81	223.4	269	25.15	235.9	268	21.31	199.9
Literature	5.18	712	13.33	257.3	726	14.83	286.3	671	15.54	300.0	591	15.22	293.8
Medicine	7.63	882	19.74	258.7	841	22.25	291.6	696	22.82	299.1	638	23.96	314.0
Music	6.36	104	14.54	228.6	110	18.45	290.1	92	19.17	301.4	99	17.48	274.8
Philosophy and psychology	5.57	688	13.72	246.3	723	15.06	270.4	563	15.29	274.5	593	16.43	295.0
Poetry and drama	4.71	551	10.36	220.0	518	10.98	233.1	368	12.43	263.9	313	11.73	249.0
Religion	3.68	1,527	9.99	271.5	1,434	11.06	300.5	1,248	12.12	329.3	1,135	12.66	344.0
Science	8.81	736	23.76	269.7	744	27.14	308.1	621	28.01	317.9	488	27.31	310.0
Sociology and economics	6.03	2,545	16.69	276.8	2,584	20.33	337.1	2,333	19.60	325.0	2,001	19.07	316.3
Sports and recreation	4.87	437	12.26	251.7	446	13.36	274.3	422	13.67	280.7	401	14.82	304.3
Technology	7.97	624	23.93	300.3	678	28.64	359.3	509	30.06	377.2	497	33.21	416.7
Travel	5.21	429	11.73	225.1	442	15.71	301.5	280	13.32	255.7	259	14.08	270.2
Total	$5.93	16,740	$15.01	253.1	16,195	$17.16	289.4	13,826	$17.45	294.3	12,387	$18.05	304.4

*Compiled by Sue Plezia, University of California, from data supplied by the R. R. Bowker Company. Price indexes on Tables 3 and 7 are based on books recorded in the R. R. Bowker Company's *Weekly Record* (cumulated in *American Book Publishing Record*). The 1991 preliminary figures include items listed during 1991 with an imprint date of 1991. Final data for previous years include items listed between January of that year and June of the following year with an imprint date of the specified year.

Table 8 / U.S. Nonprint Media: Average Prices and Price Indexes, 1986–1991*
(Index Base: 1980 = 100)

Category	1980 Average Price	1986 Average Price	1986 Index	1987 Average Price	1987 Index	1988 Average Price	1988 Index	1989 Average Price	1989 Index	1990 Average Price	1990 Index	1991 Average Price	1991 Index
16mm films													
Rental cost per minute	$1.41	$2.00	141.8	$1.86	131.9	$2.54	180.1	$2.87	203.5	$2.02	143.3	$2.46	174.5
Purchase cost per minute	12.03	16.85	140.1	17.00	141.3	18.96	157.6	20.63	171.5	18.40	153.0	20.08	166.9
Cost of film	279.09	507.19	181.7	515.78	184.8	499.22	178.9	421.00	150.8	517.72	185.5	525.50	188.3
Length per film (min.)	23.20	30.10	—	30.30	—	26.33	—	20.41	—	28.14	—	26.17	—
Videocassettes													
Purchase cost per minute	7.58	7.44	98.2	6.79	89.6	7.21	95.1	5.67	74.8	5.60	73.9	4.81	63.5
Cost of video	271.93	274.54	101.0	240.16	88.3	262.08	96.4	169.21	62.2	215.34	79.2	199.67	73.4
Length per video (min.)	—	36.90	—	35.40	—	36.35	—	29.86	—	35.91	—	41.51	—
Filmstrips													
Cost of filmstrip	21.74	34.13	157.0	39.49	181.6	37.54	172.7	33.14	152.4	37.38	171.9	36.90	169.7
Cost of filmstrip set	67.39	85.33	126.6	112.15	166.4	74.45	110.5	89.14	132.3	121.76	180.7	97.90	145.3
Number of filmstrips per set	3.10	2.50	—	2.80	—	2.00	—	2.69	—	3.26	—	2.65	—
Number of frames per filmstrip	67.90	65.90	—	65.10	—	66.10	—	55.90	—	46.50	—	56.60	—
Sound recordings													
Average cost per cassette	9.34	10.61	113.6	8.50	91.0	10.12	108.4	10.58	113.3	10.47	112.1	12.18	130.4

*Compiled by David B. Walch, Rosalyn Harding, and Lynda Alamo, California Polytechnic State University, from selected issues of *Choice, School Library Journal,* and *Booklist.*

Prices of Other Media

The U.S. nonprint media index (Table 8) is compiled from data in *Choice, School Library Journal,* and *Booklist* and includes 16mm films, videocassettes, filmstrips, and audio cassettes. Rental and purchase costs per minute for films continued to increase steadily (a 21.8 percent increase for rental and 9.1 percent increase for purchase in 1991). By contrast, video costs continued to decrease in 1991; total video costs dropped 7.3 percent. Compiler David Walch notes that, measured in purchase cost per minute, 16mm films now cost more than four times as much as videos. In addition, production of films and filmstrips continues to decline as videocassette production increases; there were over six videos produced for every 16mm film in 1991. Audio cassette prices rose 16.3 percent during the year.

The inventory of CD-ROM prices from 1989–1991 (Table 9) surveys titles appropriate for library purchase separated into serials and monographs. Prices are based on highest level of service, meaning the most frequent interval (plus all available archival discs) for serials and the most complete version of monographs. The inventory includes only prices for discs on single workstations and does not report additional charges for networking. The average price of all CD-ROMs declined 16.7 percent from 1990 to 1991. This decline is entirely attributable to new, comparatively inexpensive products produced in the past two years. Prices of titles produced continuously since 1989 have held steady. The inventory illustrates that the CD-ROM output continues to grow rapidly.

Foreign Prices

Indexes are included for British academic books (Table 10), German academic books (Table 11), and Latin American books (Table 12).

British Prices

B. H. Blackwell supplies the information used to compile the British academic books index (Table 10). The 1991 average price for British books was £32.06, a 9.8 percent increase over the 1990 average of £29.21 (1990 prices increased 6.6 percent over those of 1989). Compiler Curt Holleman calculates that the inflationary cost for U.S. libraries to keep pace with British book production in 1991 was approximately 9.1 percent. This inflationary cost resulted from the combination of a slight decrease in the average value of the pound compared with the dollar from 1990–1991 and a slight decrease in the total output of British books.

German Prices

German academic book prices (Table 11) are compiled from data furnished by Otto Harrassowitz, Wiesbaden, Germany. The data pertain to books published in Germany and supplied to North American approval plan customers. All prices are in deutsche marks. Compilers revised the index beginning with 1989 data; thus 1989 serves as the base year. German books rose in average price to DM57.48 in 1991, an increase of only 2.8 percent over the 1990 average. This small rate of increase does not necessarily reflect increases experienced by American libraries resulting from wide fluctuations in the dollar's value against the mark during the past year.

Table 9 / CD-ROM Price Inventory 1989–1991: Average Costs by Classification and Material Type (Serials and Monographs)*

Classification	LC Class	Number of Titles 1989 Serials	Number of Titles 1989 Monographs	Number of Titles 1990 Ser.	Number of Titles 1990 Mono.	Number of Titles 1991 Ser.	Number of Titles 1991 Mono.	Average Price 1989 Ser.	Average Price 1989 Mono.	Average Price 1990 Ser.	Average Price 1990 Mono.	Average Price 1991 Ser.	Average Price 1991 Mono.	Percent Increase 1989–90 Ser.	Percent Increase 1989–90 Mono.	Percent Increase 1990–91 Ser.	Percent Increase 1990–91 Mono.
General works	A	28	10	34	11	43	21	$1,908	$642	$2,187	$630	$1,839	$460	14.6	-1.9	-15.9	-27.0
Philosophy, psychology, and religion	B	2	2	2	5	2	6	2,395	545	2,395	1,336	2,395	1,060	0.0	145.1**	0.0	-20.7**
Auxiliary sciences of history	C	1	0	1	0	1	0	1,095	–	1,095	–	1,095	–	0.0	–	0.0	–
History: general & Old World	D	0	1	0	1	0	1	–	350	–	350	–	350	–	0.0	–	0.0
History: America	E-F	1	2	1	2	1	7	295	100	295	100	295	113	0.0	0.0	0.0	13.0
Geography, anthropology, and recreation	G	5	12	6	16	6	29	5,480	662	5,646	544	5,646	484	3.0	-17.8	0.0	-11.0
Social sciences	H	50	32	59	30	60	38	4,281	1,553	3,933	1,671	3,084	1,462	-8.1	7.6	-21.6	-12.5
Political science	J	0	0	0	0	0	0	–	–	–	–	–	–	–	–	–	–
Law	K	5	2	7	2	7	2	2,089	2,400	2,052	2,048	2,695	2,048	-1.8	-14.7	31.3	0.0
Education	L	12	1	13	1	13	2	971	1,950	938	1,950	896	1,015	-3.4	0.0	-4.5	-47.9**
Music	M	0	0	3	4	4	7	–	–	535	70	575	74	–	–	7.5	5.7
Fine arts	N	3	15	3	17	5	29	881	668	881	630	624	453	0.0	-5.7	-29.2	-28.1
Language and literature	P	4	8	4	20	4	24	1,081	419	1,081	261	1,081	275	0.0	-37.7	0.0	5.4
Science	Q	56	23	67	32	68	43	1,485	484	1,824	415	1,807	393	22.8	-14.3	-0.9	-5.3
Medicine	R	40	4	47	3	52	9	1,472	1,496	1,676	798	1,619	676	13.9	-46.7**	-3.4	-15.3**
Agriculture	S	10	5	13	8	14	8	1,891	319	1,718	255	1,688	253	-9.1	-20.1	-1.7	-0.8
Technology	T	6	4	8	7	9	7	1,761	1,090	2,620	985	2,718	985	48.8	-9.6	3.7	0.0
Military science	U-V	2	1	2	1	2	1	1,000	149	1,000	149	1,000	149	0.0	0.0	0.0	0.0
Bibliography, library science	Z	41	5	47	6	47	6	1,247	4,010	1,202	3,518	1,202	3,518	-3.6	-12.3	0.0	0.0
Totals: serials & monographs		266	127	317	166	338	240	2,086	1,016	2,159	852	1,942	693	3.5	-16.1	-10.1	-18.7
Combined totals		1989: 393		1990: 483		1991: 578		1989 Comb. $1,740		1990 Comb. $1,710		1991 Comb. $1,424		1989–90: -1.7		1990–91: -16.7	

*Compiled by Pamela R. Mason, National Agricultural Library. Note that the average prices used here are for the current subscription or current edition, received at the "highest level of service," i.e., (if a serial) at the most frequent level of service, and including all archival discs.
**Distorted by small sample.

Table 10 / British Academic Books: Average Prices and Price Indexes, 1989-1991*
(Index Base: 1985 = 100)

Subject Category	1985 Number of Titles	1985 Average Price	1989 Number of Titles	1989 Average Price	1989 Index	1990 Number of Titles	1990 Average Price	1990 Index	1991 Number of Titles	1991 Average Price	1991 Index
General works	29	£30.54	37	£28.95	94.8	41	£27.09	88.7	44	£38.12	124.8
Fine arts	329	21.70	403	26.04	120.0	479	26.33	121.3	436	32.00	147.5
Architecture	97	20.68	106	25.47	123.2	151	24.03	116.2	119	30.35	146.8
Music	136	17.01	103	20.85	122.6	144	24.29	142.8	166	25.84	151.9
Performing arts except music	110	13.30	131	17.49	131.5	121	20.44	153.7	92	25.06	188.4
Archaeology	146	18.80	209	23.87	127.0	154	31.85	169.4	151	28.75	152.9
Geography	60	22.74	77	41.55	182.7	58	28.78	126.6	72	30.91	135.9
History	1,123	16.92	1,305	23.17	136.9	1,312	25.42	150.2	1,321	26.85	158.7
Philosophy	127	18.41	161	27.73	150.6	161	27.94	151.8	180	33.06	179.6
Religion	328	10.40	330	17.17	165.1	367	18.25	175.5	368	19.72	189.6
Language	135	19.37	116	24.75	127.8	142	25.42	131.2	144	30.44	157.2
Miscellaneous humanities	59	21.71	58	29.35	135.2	67	29.48	135.8	62	34.57	159.2
Literary texts (excluding fiction)	570	9.31	437	11.94	128.2	578	12.25	131.6	461	12.96	139.2
Literary criticism	438	14.82	595	22.23	150.0	581	25.96	175.2	494	28.58	192.8
Law	188	24.64	203	36.70	148.9	265	38.10	154.6	239	41.68	169.2
Library science and book trade	78	18.69	110	35.17	188.2	94	28.08	150.2	102	27.61	147.7
Mass communications	38	14.20	65	18.73	131.9	88	22.78	160.4	82	29.71	209.2
Anthropology and ethnology	42	20.71	51	25.42	122.7	61	28.04	135.4	66	31.45	151.9
Sociology	136	15.24	175	26.10	171.3	193	29.54	193.8	156	35.71	234.3
Psychology	107	19.25	123	25.62	133.1	135	28.17	146.3	126	34.88	181.2
Economics	334	20.48	470	31.02	151.5	515	37.44	182.8	520	41.29	201.6
Political science and international relations	314	15.54	484	24.48	157.5	504	27.38	176.2	440	31.08	200.0
Miscellaneous social sciences	20	26.84	8	30.32	113.0	15	32.41	120.8	10	36.61	136.4
Military science	83	17.69	105	28.34	160.2	113	30.00	169.6	72	24.72	139.7
Sports and recreation	44	11.23	54	13.80	122.9	50	16.26	144.8	69	16.79	149.5
Social service	56	12.17	70	18.60	152.8	67	21.39	175.8	47	23.28	191.3
Education	295	12.22	381	19.56	160.1	385	20.82	170.4	300	25.38	207.7
Management and business administration	427	19.55	459	35.19	180.0	475	35.14	179.7	416	35.48	181.5
Miscellaneous applied social sciences	13	9.58	16	78.31	817.4	15	30.16	314.8	14	40.90	426.9

	No.	Price	No.	Price	Index	No.	Price	Index	No.	Price	Index
Criminology	45	11.45	65	18.71	163.4	58	21.66	189.2	68	23.16	202.3
Applied interdisciplinary social studies	254	14.17	350	22.69	160.1	404	25.06	176.9	370	25.44	179.5
General science	43	13.73	50	34.91	254.3	50	31.97	232.8	45	35.13	255.9
Botany	55	30.54	46	33.08	108.3	48	43.11	141.2	51	42.24	138.3
Zoology	85	25.67	88	29.94	116.6	86	32.53	126.7	110	37.39	145.7
Human biology	35	28.91	29	38.94	134.7	24	41.63	144.0	25	42.62	147.4
Biochemistry	26	33.57	35	35.73	106.4	34	39.20	116.8	28	43.64	130.0
Miscellaneous biological sciences	152	26.64	154	38.17	143.3	154	38.16	143.2	164	36.51	137.0
Chemistry	109	48.84	98	63.56	130.1	100	59.60	122.0	98	77.00	157.7
Earth sciences	87	28.94	93	43.30	149.6	108	47.94	165.7	102	54.73	189.1
Astronomy	43	20.36	34	32.68	160.5	43	35.00	171.9	35	32.36	158.9
Physics	76	26.58	102	42.73	160.8	101	43.86	165.0	94	45.72	172.0
Mathematics	123	20.20	146	27.82	137.7	155	30.90	153.0	139	30.71	152.0
Computer sciences	150	20.14	255	31.45	156.2	271	27.43	136.2	259	31.25	155.2
Interdisciplinary technical fields	38	26.14	82	31.30	119.7	74	31.13	119.1	66	35.26	134.9
Civil engineering	134	28.68	146	42.81	149.3	165	49.87	173.9	167	51.99	181.3
Mechanical engineering	27	31.73	46	40.64	128.1	48	50.07	157.8	45	47.12	148.5
Electrical and electronic engineering	100	33.12	99	42.62	128.7	130	46.91	141.6	115	49.34	149.0
Materials science	54	37.93	114	64.52	170.1	116	58.50	154.2	103	71.86	189.5
Chemical engineering	24	40.48	37	45.06	111.3	35	52.19	128.9	46	53.66	132.6
Miscellaneous technology	217	36.33	260	40.58	111.7	289	45.58	125.5	222	51.54	141.9
Food and domestic science	38	23.75	61	35.05	147.6	63	46.63	196.3	54	44.61	187.8
Non-clinical medicine	97	18.19	105	21.73	119.5	103	24.87	136.7	99	31.46	173.0
General medicine	73	21.03	78	33.57	159.6	87	33.13	157.5	59	38.44	182.8
Internal medicine	163	27.30	189	35.65	130.6	162	36.72	134.5	168	40.18	147.2
Psychiatry and mental disorders	71	17.97	90	26.73	148.7	78	24.89	138.5	113	30.47	169.6
Surgery	50	29.37	48	48.73	165.9	39	49.22	167.6	39	50.14	170.7
Miscellaneous medicine	292	22.08	289	33.50	151.7	251	34.00	154.0	287	37.73	170.9
Dentistry	20	19.39	31	23.76	122.5	28	36.21	186.7	23	26.41	136.2
Nursing	71	8.00	65	10.59	132.4	81	11.36	142.0	48	13.53	169.1
Agriculture and forestry	78	23.69	89	28.94	122.2	109	35.05	148.0	82	37.85	159.8
Animal husbandry and veterinary medicine	34	20.92	34	32.80	156.8	48	32.25	154.2	47	34.30	164.0
Natural resources and conservation	58	22.88	54	26.17	114.4	57	28.94	126.5	54	31.20	136.4
Total, all books**	9,049	£19.07	10,678	£27.40	143.7	11,276	£29.21	153.2	10,561	£32.06	168.1

*Compiled by Curt Holleman, Southern Methodist University, from data supplied by Chris Tyzack of B. H. Blackwell and Alan F. MacDougall of Loughborough University of Technology. The committee uses 1985 as the base year because that is the first year that the BHB database was used as the source of prices.

**Includes other small categories not listed in this table.

Table 11 / German Academic Books: Average Prices and Price Indexes, 1989–91*

(Index Base: 1989 = 100)

Subject	LC Class	1989		1990				1991			
		Number of Titles	Average Price	Number of Titles	Average Price	Percent Increase	Index	Number of Titles	Average Price	Percent Increase	Index
Agriculture	S	240	DM50.06	262	DM46.42	-7.3	92.7	192	DM62.46	34.6	124.8
Anthropology	GN	86	83.17	88	68.27	-17.9	82.1	48	76.98	12.8	92.6
Botany	QK	70	88.44	68	92.00	4.0	104.0	76	98.59	7.2	111.5
Business and economics	H-HJ	1,152	51.21	1,582	53.54	4.5	104.5	1,443	56.98	6.4	111.3
Chemistry	QD	65	100.61	90	93.48	-7.1	92.9	80	95.39	2.0	94.8
Education	L	243	45.10	308	40.05	-11.2	88.8	273	39.39	-1.6	87.3
Engineering and technology	T	593	84.44	597	76.24	-9.7	90.3	505	89.28	17.1	105.7
Fine and applied arts	M-N	2,131	52.35	2,269	57.02	8.9	108.9	1,762	56.24	-1.4	107.4
General works	A	45	47.68	48	55.93	17.3	117.3	47	47.21	-15.6	99.0
Geography	G	332	51.29	241	55.14	7.5	107.5	212	58.55	6.2	114.2
Geology	QE	41	75.91	60	83.14	9.5	109.5	41	110.41	32.8	145.4
History	C,D,E,F	1,281	53.29	1,764	51.36	-3.6	96.4	1,583	47.13	-8.2	88.4
Home economics	TX	40	55.79	32	47.39	-15.1	84.9	13	44.88	-5.3	80.4
Industrial arts	TT	11	49.92	7	68.36	36.9	136.9	6	72.17	5.6	144.6
Law	K	613	83.11	986	72.63	-12.6	87.4	1,091	67.85	-6.6	81.6
Library and information science	Z	137	77.88	162	65.39	-16.0	84.0	151	94.77	44.9	121.7

Subject	LC Class	Count	Price	Count	Price	% Change	Index	Count	Price	% Change	Index
Literature and language	P	3,535	47.45	3,948	45.43	-4.3	95.7	2,878	46.83	3.1	98.7
Mathematics and computer science	QA	212	79.92	270	79.22	-0.9	99.1	300	76.21	-3.8	95.4
Medicine	R	1,289	72.47	1,830	64.83	-10.5	89.5	1,431	73.64	13.6	101.6
Military and naval science	U-V	99	50.50	74	49.39	-2.2	97.8	69	48.99	-0.8	97.0
Natural history	QH	91	89.25	123	73.11	-18.1	81.9	132	77.09	5.4	86.4
Philosophy and religion	B	1,109	59.27	1,416	62.76	5.9	105.9	1,097	53.67	-14.5	90.6
Physical education and recreation	GV	104	36.56	77	32.52	-11.1	88.9	79	35.95	10.5	98.3
Physics and astronomy	QB-QC	148	81.45	170	77.93	-4.3	95.7	177	85.37	9.5	104.8
Physiology	QM-QR	144	99.59	168	109.32	9.8	109.8	140	102.52	-6.2	102.9
Political science	J	622	40.87	706	46.57	13.9	113.9	487	44.71	-4.0	109.4
Psychology	BF	135	54.13	225	43.42	-19.8	80.2	193	46.17	6.3	85.3
Science (general)	Q	86	56.47	95	53.54	-5.2	94.8	114	59.16	10.5	104.8
Sociology	HM-HX	838	39.50	1,026	39.81	0.8	100.8	959	38.86	-2.4	98.4
Zoology	QL	52	124.77	68	74.58	-40.2	59.8	48	99.24	33.1	79.5
Total		15,544	DM56.79	18,760	DM55.93	-1.5	98.5	15,627	DM57.48	2.8	101.2

*Compiled by John Haar, Virginia Commonwealth University, and Steven E. Thompson, Brown University, from approval plan data supplied by Otto Harrassowitz. Data represent a selection of materials relevant to research and documentation published in Germany (see text for more information regarding the nature of the data).

Unclassified material has been removed from the data. Prices quoted in deutsche marks.

The index is not adjusted for high-priced titles.

Latin American Prices

Data reported for books published in over 25 Latin American countries (Table 12) are compiled from acquisitions records of seven large research libraries; they are not, therefore, a true price index based on the total publishing output of these nations. The reported prices are dependent in part upon each library's purchasing pattern. Prices may also be affected by the state of the book trade in each country, the lack of meaningful list prices for many countries, varying rates of inflation, currency revaluations, changes in the scope of dealer coverage, and other inconsistencies in reporting practice. The combined average 1991 book price for the region was $14.64, a 15.8 percent increase over 1990. The three major Latin American publishing countries — Argentina, Brazil, and Mexico — recorded increases of 53.5 percent, 23.5 percent, and 21 percent respectively. Average prices ranged from $6.72 in Honduras to $29.16 in Jamaica.

U.S. Purchasing Power Abroad

The dollar's value against most major foreign currencies in December 1991 reflected little change from its value in December 1990 (the yen was the only exception). A comparison of these two months is misleading, however, because 1991 was in fact a rather volatile year for exchange rates. During the first half of the year, the dollar rose steadily only to fall sharply in the second half. Thus, libraries witnessed sharp fluctuations in their buying power during the course of the year. Over the two-year period since January 1990, the dollar has declined significantly in value. The following chart reports rates in currency per U.S. dollar based on quotations in the *Wall Street Journal*. Readers interested in quotations for earlier years may examine earlier volumes of the *Bowker Annual*.

	1/31/90	6/29/90	12/31/90	1/31/91	6/28/91	12/31/91
Canada	1.1865	1.1637	1.1600	1.1623	1.1420	1.1555
France	5.7195	5.5820	5.0900	5.0155	6.1375	5.1800
U.K.	0.5956	0.5718	0.5181	0.5083	0.6158	0.5349
Germany	1.6842	1.6607	1.4945	1.4745	1.8115	1.5150
Japan	144.40	152.05	135.80	131.17	137.65	124.80
Netherlands	1.8990	1.8700	1.6860	1.6625	2.0410	1.7070

Using the Price Indexes

Librarians are encouraged to monitor trends in the publishing industry as well as changes in economic conditions when preparing budget projections. To make these data on publishing trends readily available, the ALA ALCTS Library Materials Price Index Committee sponsors the annual compilation and publication of price data contained in Tables 1 through 12. The price indexes for different categories of library materials document the rate of price change at the national level of newly published materials against those of earlier years. They are useful benchmarks against which local costs may be compared, but because they reflect retail prices in the aggregate, they are not a substitute for price data that reflect the collecting patterns of individual libraries.

TABLE 12 / Number of Copies and Average Cost of Latin American Books
Purchased by Seven Selected U.S. Libraries in FYs 1990 and 1991*

	Number of Books		Average Cost**		Percent increase/ Decrease in Cost over 1990
	FY 1990	FY 1991	FY 1990	FY 1991	
Argentina	7,657	4,876	$9.79	$15.02	53.49
Bolivia	1,847	1,934	9.52	9.39	-1.39
Brazil	7,810	6,400	12.53	15.48	23.48
Chile	1,801	2,128	15.85	15.50	-2.16
Colombia	3,069	3,663	11.74	11.21	-4.56
Costa Rica	1,432	772	12.14	15.18	24.97
Cuba	406	249	13.18	15.40	16.78
Dominican Republic	315	264	18.45	17.89	-3.04
Ecuador	1,876	2,011	8.79	8.50	-3.32
El Salvador	284	285	10.51	11.00	4.71
Guatemala	256	671	13.91	15.31	10.06
Guyana	5	7	8.80	8.75	-0.58
Haiti	43	129	17.44	20.47	17.38
Honduras	324	248	11.92	6.72	-43.58
Jamaica	62	96	18.32	29.16	59.16
Mexico	8,334	8,744	15.52	18.78	21.03
Nicaragua	482	387	11.61	12.16	4.72
Panama	310	215	12.60	14.14	12.24
Paraguay	638	525	13.69	11.19	-18.26
Peru	2,832	2,746	12.04	13.10	8.85
Puerto Rico	116	63	18.70	26.00	39.07
Suriname	11	11	28.18	27.88	-1.07
Trinidad	91	7	18.02	28.86	60.15
Uruguay	2,480	1,758	14.55	15.47	6.30
Venezuela	2,432	2,298	13.98	11.17	-20.10
Other Caribbean	994	726	11.80	16.35	38.57
Total	45,907	41,213	$12.63	$14.64	15.84

*Compiled by David Block, Seminar on the Acquisition of Latin American Library Materials (SALALM)
Acquisition Committee, from reports on the number and cost of current monographs purchased by the
libraries of Cornell University, Library of Congress, New York Public Library, University of Arizona, University
of Illinois, University of Texas, and University of Wisconsin.
**Some figures include binding costs.

Differences arise because of the inclusion of discounts, service charges, or shipping and handling fees in library price indexes that are not included in the national
indexes. Discrepancies may also be related to subject focus, mix of current and retrospective materials, and the portion of total library acquisitions composed by foreign
imprints. Such variables can affect the average price paid by a particular library, although the library's rate of price increase may not significantly differ from national
price indexes. The Library Materials Price Index Committee is interested in pursuing
studies correlating a particular library's prices with national prices and would appreciate being informed of any planned or ongoing studies. The committee is also investigating the compilation of price indexes for foreign periodicals and would like to
review any library studies of prices for these materials. The committee welcomes interested parties to its meetings at the American Library Association annual and midwinter conferences.

Current members of the Library Materials Price Index Committee are John
Haar (chairperson), Dana Alessi, Adrian Alexander, Donna Alsbury, Bernard Basch,
Stella Bentley, Stephen Bosch, Dana D'Andraia, Cynthia Hepfer, Curtis Holleman,
Genevieve Owens, Mark Sandler, and Wilba Swearingen. Consultants and others

who contributed to the preparation of indexes are David Block, Kathryn Hammell Carpenter, Mary E. Clack, Frederick Lyndon, Pamela Mason, Sue Plezia, Dennis Smith, Kathryn Soupiset, Sharon Sullivan, Steven Thompson, David Walch, and Sally Williams.

Book Title Output and Average Prices: 1991 Preliminary Figures

Chandler B. Grannis
Contributing Editor, *Publishers Weekly*

American book title production in 1991 should total about 47,000, judging from preliminary figures prepared for *Publishers Weekly* by R. R. Bowker data services. This estimate suggests little change from a newly updated and revised "final" total for 1990 of 46,738 (see Table 1). Both years mark a sharp decline from the record output of 56,027 in 1987.

Average prices, comparing preliminary 1991 data with new final 1990 figures, indicate moderate overall changes with many fluctuations in specific areas.

Data for all books except mass market paperbacks are compiled from the bibliographical entries in Bowker's monthly *American Book Publishing Record (ABPR)*. The *ABPR* database is produced from listings supplied by the Library of Congress (LC). The need for new 1990 computations stems from a change in LC procedure. In 1989, to deal with increased demand, LC began a program of early "abbreviated cataloging." Complete details (Dewey numbers, for instance) are now not available for *ABPR* use in some cases until the year following actual publication. Accordingly, it has been necessary to revise—in effect to update—the final 1990 totals. The 1990 tabulations in *PW* of September 20, 1991, are therefore superseded by those appearing here. About 2,000 titles are affected.

These revisions do not apply to the mass market paperback figures presented here. These are derived from the new entries in Bowker's *Paperbound Books in Print* (Tables 3 and B). Here, preliminary title figures suggest a large title drop in 1991, but overall changes in average prices are not dramatic. The average mass market per-volume price in 1990 was $4.57. The preliminary average for 1991 is $4.85. Mass market fiction in 1990 was $4.05 per volume and $4.30 in the preliminary report for 1991.

Table A-1 (hardcover books under $81 per volume) shows an overall price average (except mass market) of $31.60 per volume in 1990 and a $31.86 price per volume, preliminary, for 1991. Fiction in the two years shows average per-volume prices of $19.27 and $19.91, respectively.

For paperbacks other than mass market (Table C), overall averages are $17.45 for 1990 and $18.04 for 1991 preliminary.

Each of the 23 standard subject groups used here represents one or more specific Dewey Decimal Classification numbers, as follows:

Note: Adapted from *Publishers Weekly*, April 6, 1992.

Table 1 / American Book Title Production, 1989–1991

Category	1989 All Hard and Paper*	1990 Final Hard and Trade Paper			1990 Final All Hard and Paper	1991 Preliminary Hard and Trade Paper			1991 Preliminary All Hard and Paper
		Books	Editions	Totals		Books	Editions	Totals	
Agriculture	562	428	85	513	514	368	98	466	468
Art	1,569	1,113	137	1,250	1,262	991	127	1,118	1,119
Biography	2,193	1,674	225	1,899	1,957	1,665	182	1,847	1,890
Business	1,569	880	295	1,175	1,191	962	329	1,291	1,298
Education	1,054	867	157	1,024	1,039	832	138	970	973
Fiction	5,941	2,725	184	2,909	5,764	2,414	185	2,599	4,199
General works	2,332	1,456	260	1,716	1,760	1,412	241	1,653	1,684
History	2,563	1,840	375	2,215	2,243	1,719	373	2,092	2,107
Home economics	949	595	119	714	758	566	116	682	721
Juveniles	5,413	4,496	243	4,739	5,172	4,000	254	4,254	4,555
Language	586	487	145	632	649	409	104	513	521
Law	1,096	649	244	893	896	670	289	959	967
Literature	2,298	1,802	219	2,021	2,049	1,664	226	1,890	1,903
Medicine	3,447	2,438	545	2,983	3,014	2,154	536	2,690	2,710
Music	375	223	59	282	289	222	52	274	275
Philosophy, psychology	2,058	1,350	212	1,562	1,683	1,320	248	1,568	1,611
Poetry, drama	1,128	826	44	870	874	770	44	814	821
Religion	2,586	2,005	267	2,272	2,285	1,738	316	2,054	2,059
Science	3,288	2,276	457	2,733	2,742	1,930	485	2,415	2,427
Sociology, economics	7,971	6,146	846	6,992	7,042	5,564	918	6,482	5,508
Sports, recreation	1,077	721	116	837	973	708	111	819	893
Technology	2,690	1,687	391	2,078	2,092	1,633	441	2,074	2,089
Travel	701	365	101	466	495	291	111	402	425
Total	53,446	37,049	5,726	42,775	46,743	34,002	5,924	39,926	41,223

*Revised.

Note: Except for mass market, all 1990 figures in tables 1–5 and A–C replace the "1990 Final" figures shown in *Publishers Weekly,* September 20, 1991.

Table 2 / Paperbacks (Excluding Mass Market), 1989-1991

Category	1989 Totals	1990 Final			1991 Preliminary		
		New Books	New Editions	Totals	New Books	New Editions	Totals
Fiction	558	286	116	402	360	117	477
Nonfiction	16,055	11,234	2,525	13,759	10,154	2,638	12,792
Total	16,613	11,520	2,641	14,161	10,514	2,755	13,269

Agriculture, 630–639, 712–719; Art, 700–711, 720–779; Biography, 920–929; Business, 650–659; Education, 370–379; Fiction, General Works, 000–099; History, 900–909, 930–999; Home Economics, 640–649; Juveniles; Language, 400–499; Law, 340–349; Literature, 800–810, 813–820, 823–899; Medicine, 610–619; Music, 780–789; Philosophy, Psychology, 100–199; Poetry, Drama, 811, 812, 821, 822; Religion, 200–299; Science, 500–599; Sociology, Economics, 300–339, 350–369, 380–399; Sports, Recreation, 790–799; Technology, 600–609, 620–629, 660–699; Travel, 910–919.

Table 3 / Mass Market Paperbacks, 1989-1991

Category	1989 Final	1990 Final	1991 Preliminary
Agriculture	4	1	2
Art	9	12	1
Biography	77	58	43
Business	20	16	7
Education	19	15	3
Fiction	2,678	2,855	1,600
General works	64	44	31
History	32	28	15
Home economics	48	44	39
Juveniles	376	433	301
Language	14	17	8
Law	2	3	2
Literature	29	28	13
Medicine	29	31	20
Music	2	7	1
Philosophy, psychology	108	121	43
Poetry, drama	11	4	7
Religion	11	13	5
Science	16	9	12
Sociology, economics	59	50	26
Sports, recreation	134	136	74
Technology	17	14	15
Travel	13	29	23
Total	3,772	3,968	2,291

Table 4 / Imported Titles, 1989–1991
(Hard and Trade Paper Only)

Category	1989 Totals	1990 Final			1991 Preliminary		
		Books	Editions	Totals	Books	Editions	Totals
Agriculture	104	68	18	86	59	13	72
Art	128	80	14	94	61	8	69
Biography	144	108	7	115	98	6	104
Business	152	111	23	134	117	9	126
Education	233	220	14	234	142	11	153
Fiction	119	139	27	166	50	2	52
General works	322	237	29	266	192	19	211
History	376	285	44	329	223	51	274
Home economics	31	14	5	19	14	4	18
Juveniles	101	97	6	103	54	1	55
Language	182	176	26	202	137	21	158
Law	156	109	29	138	128	14	142
Literature	275	223	19	242	156	14	170
Medicine	712	524	64	588	330	49	379
Music	78	41	11	52	63	3	66
Philosophy, psychology	348	270	14	284	211	18	229
Poetry, drama	147	104	15	119	93	6	99
Religion	173	153	23	176	97	14	111
Science	1,187	910	120	1,030	609	79	688
Sociology, economics	1,575	1,276	92	1,368	1,105	80	1,185
Sports, recreation	94	69	6	75	58	6	64
Technology	638	480	66	546	377	43	420
Travel	39	45	3	48	34	8	42
Total	7,314	5,739	675	6,414	4,408	479	4,887

Table 5 / Translations into English Hard and Trade Paper Only

	1987 Final	1988 Final	1989 Final	1990 Final	1991 Prelim.
Arabic	33	27	45	26	18
Chinese	39	34	26	45	33
Danish	24	23	49	24	18
Dutch	45	49	33	40	28
Finnish	5	3	3	10	0
French	580	570	442	389	340
German	486	501	453	252	362
Hebrew	45	45	56	35	38
Italian	115	129	142	79	80
Japanese	65	95	84	82	77
Latin	38	43	38	51	45
Norwegian	16	12	12	7	6
Russian	245	256	251	185	150
Spanish	130	162	121	120	116
Swedish	36	47	36	30	24
Yiddish	9	14	12	5	11
Total	1,909	2,012	1,803	1,380	1,346

Note: "Total" covers only the languages listed here.

Table A / Hardcover Average Per-Volume Prices, 1989–1991

Category	1977 Prices	1989 Prices	1990 Final Vols.	1990 Final $ Total	1990 Final Prices	1991 Preliminary Vols.	1991 Preliminary $ Total	1991 Preliminary Prices
Agriculture	$16.24	$51.05	359	$19,472.60	$54.24	331	$19,518.32	$58.96
Art	21.24	50.30	759	32,014.30	42.18	624	27,989.22	44.85
Biography	15.34	27.34	1,337	39,547.10	29.58	1,279	35,220.09	27.53
Business	18.00	37.94	748	34,017.46	45.48	724	31,232.86	43.13
Education	12.95	37.62	562	21,759.75	38.72	490	20,116.91	41.05
Fiction	10.09	18.69	1,962	38,915.69	19.83	1,831	40,067.07	21.88
General works	30.99	49.73	1,035	56,685.05	54.77	974	49,062.26	50.37
History	17.12	37.95	1,450	52,829.98	36.43	1,315	52,279.60	39.75
Home economics	11.16	22.17	357	8,498.26	23.80	320	7,775.95	24.29
Juveniles	6.65	13.01	3,675	47,817.98	13.01	3,367	56,033.03	16.64
Language	14.96	47.35	312	13,408.80	42.98	221	11,530.85	52.17
Law	25.04	58.62	596	36,227.32	60.78	606	36,197.94	59.73
Literature	15.78	32.74	1,312	46,975.79	35.80	1,157	41,489.95	35.85
Medicine	24.00	69.87	2,215	160,019.61	72.24	1,842	129,735.75	70.43
Music	20.13	41.73	184	7,702.20	41.86	164	6,677.48	40.71
Philosophy, psychology	14.43	36.55	963	39,079.83	40.58	879	37,514.94	42.67
Poetry, drama	13.63	31.12	486	15,642.71	32.19	473	15,310.23	32.36
Religion	12.26	28.12	977	30,585.32	31.31	846	27,894.72	32.97
Science	24.88	68.90	2,028	150,855.34	74.39	1,626	129,636.97	79.72
Sociology, economics	29.88	41.26	4,504	189,623.83	42.10	3,907	187,005.07	47.86
Sports, recreation	12.28	29.46	403	12,300.49	30.52	387	12,167.25	31.43
Technology	23.61	71.04	1,521	116,808.11	76.8	1,398	104,699.76	74.89
Travel	18.44	31.37	181	5,504.18	30.41	133	4,267.00	32.08
Total	$19.22	$40.61	27,926	$1,176,291.70	$42.12	24,894	$1,083,423.22	$43.52

Table A-1 / Hardcover Average Per-Volume Prices—Less Than $81, 1989–1991

Category	1987 Prices	1989 Prices	1990 Final Vols.	1990 Final $ Total	1990 Final Prices	1991 Preliminary Vols.	1991 Preliminary $ Total	1991 Preliminary Prices
Agriculture	$32.44	$34.06	288	$9,764.18	$33.90	256	$8,219.82	$32.10
Art	33.07	37.74	714	26,637.75	37.31	579	21,989.06	37.97
Biography	22.75	23.49	1,305	33,238.15	25.47	1,251	31,673.24	25.31
Business	30.48	34.01	705	25,681.61	36.43	676	25,723.14	38.05
Education	29.37	36.33	549	19,955.80	36.35	475	17,562.41	36.97
Fiction	17.02	18.50	1,952	37,622.79	19.27	1,823	36,307.07	19.91
General works	34.22	37.93	896	36,373.45	40.60	868	34,604.16	39.86
History	29.58	31.96	1,407	47,516.47	33.77	1,270	44,476.64	35.02
Home economics	19.23	21.60	353	7,919.76	22.44	317	7,588.44	23.93
Juveniles	11.29	12.19	3,671	47,297.40	12.88	3,361	44,765.71	13.31
Language	33.26	34.76	276	9,587.12	34.74	184	7,497.85	40.74
Law	37.40	38.70	464	18,756.47	40.42	462	18,835.89	40.77
Literature	28.97	30.77	1,283	42,979.29	33.50	1,136	37,994.10	33.44
Medicine	38.33	40.22	1,474	61,221.05	41.53	1,223	48,460.05	39.62
Music	31.92	35.50	174	6,646.25	38.20	155	5,894.58	38.02
Philosophy, psychology	31.48	33.40	898	32,115.17	35.76	833	30,447.04	36.55
Poetry, drama	24.99	27.83	476	14,247.71	29.93	465	14,371.73	30.90
Religion	23.09	26.75	950	27,832.62	29.30	823	24,819.37	30.15
Science	43.02	36.80	1,341	60,954.03	45.45	1,056	47,983.25	45.43
Sociology, economics	31.65	35.50	4,301	162,497.08	37.78	3,693	144,755.76	39.19
Sports, recreation	23.32	27.40	400	11,872.99	30.00	381	11,435.50	30.01
Technology	41.68	44.19	1,004	45,913.61	45.73	969	44,146.73	45.55
Travel	24.45	26.65	178	5,184.18	29.12	127	3,634.50	28.61
Total	$28.96	$30.08	25,059	$791,814.93	$31.60	222,383	$713,186.04	$31.86

Table B / Mass Market Paperbacks Average Per-Volume Prices, 1989–1991

Category	1989 Prices	1990 Final			1991 Preliminary		
		Vols.	$ Total	Prices	Vols.	$ Total	Prices
Agriculture	$8.45	1	$3.95	$3.95	2	$6.90	$3.45
Art	11.83	11	147.45	13.40	1	19.95	19.95
Biography	6.44	58	420.00	7.24	43	263.48	6.13
Business	8.93	16	125.75	7.85	7	56.20	8.02
Education	8.42	15	121.25	8.08	3	21.90	7.30
Fiction	3.78	2,855	11,579.99	4.05	1,600	6,887.66	4.30
General works	7.04	44	302.45	6.87	31	229.09	7.39
History	6.37	28	174.90	6.24	15	107.20	7.14
Home economics	7.20	44	297.04	6.75	39	303.38	7.77
Juveniles	3.19	433	1,543.25	3.56	301	982.61	3.26
Language	5.49	17	91.85	5.36	8	65.25	8.15
Law	6.95	3	19.85	6.61	2	19.90	9.95
Literature	6.10	28	180.60	7.09	13	72.61	5.58
Medicine	8.11	31	255.55	8.24	20	121.91	6.09
Music	6.73	7	102.65	14.66	1	2.75	2.75
Philosophy, psychology	5.09	121	824.95	6.81	43	345.77	8.04
Poetry, drama	5.44	4	24.35	6.08	7	47.74	6.82
Religion	6.96	13	90.45	6.95	5	48.80	9.76
Science	9.99	9	82.55	9.17	12	113.10	9.42
Sociology, economics	6.24	50	344.45	6.88	26	204.97	7.88
Sports, recreation	5.66	136	719.55	5.29	74	501.03	6.77
Technology	20.95	14	338.30	24.16	15	426.25	28.42
Travel	9.95	29	325.55	11.22	23	265.85	11.55
Total	$4.32	3,967	$18,116.68	$4.57	2,291	$11,114.30	$4.85

Table C / Trade Paperbacks Average Per-Volume Prices, 1989–1991

Category	1977 Prices	1989 Prices	1990 Final			1991 Preliminary		
			Vols.	$ Total	Prices	Vols.	$ Total	Prices
Agriculture	$5.01	$16.49	142	$2,331.93	$16.42	117	$1,707.90	$14.59
Art	6.27	17.07	462	8,268.35	17.90	444	8,549.37	19.25
Biography	4.91	11.42	520	6,783.68	13.05	480	6,401.69	13.33
Business	7.09	21.29	398	7,804.57	19.61	428	9,134.41	21.34
Education	5.72	18.80	436	8,371.05	19.20	390	7,941.96	20.36
Fiction	4.20	9.87	885	10,018.63	11.32	723	8,160.34	11.28
General works	6.18	26.94	629	18,660.16	29.67	568	20,162.66	35.49
History	5.81	15.69	701	12,189.53	17.39	637	10,517.46	16.51
Home economics	4.77	12.10	351	4,552.99	12.97	345	4,444.99	12.88
Juveniles	2.68	6.64	938	6,366.75	6.78	744	5,603.67	7.53
Language	7.79	18.02	292	4,867.58	16.67	228	3,857.52	16.91
Law	10.66	23.81	269	6,765.37	25.15	268	5,711.06	21.30
Literature	5.18	14.83	671	10,427.58	15.54	591	8,995.13	15.22
Medicine	7.63	22.25	696	15,879.68	22.82	638	15,287.36	23.96
Music	6.36	18.45	92	1,764.05	19.17	99	1,730.23	17.47
Philosophy, psychology	5.57	15.06	563	8,609.10	15.29	593	9,740.25	16.42
Poetry, drama	4.71	10.98	368	4,573.23	12.43	313	3,672.94	11.73
Religion	3.68	11.06	1,248	15,123.35	12.12	1,135	14,364.91	12.65
Science	8.81	27.14	621	17,397.25	28.01	488	13,328.78	27.31
Sociology, economics	6.03	20.33	2,333	45,716.77	19.60	2,001	38,157.88	19.06
Sports, recreation	4.87	13.36	422	5,770.34	13.67	401	5,941.26	14.81
Technology	7.97	28.64	509	15,300.67	30.06	497	16,506.22	33.21
Travel	5.21	15.71	280	3,730.35	13.32	259	3,647.15	14.08
Total	$5.93	$17.16	13,826	$241,272.96	$17.45	12,387	$223,565.14	$18.04

Table D / Three Cloth Categories—*PW* Announcement Fall Ads

	Average Price	Median Price
Novels*		
1991—148 vols./43 pubs.	$20.99	$19.95
1990—136 vols./35 pubs.	19.84	19.95
1989—187 vols./20 pubs.	15.88	18.95
1988—209 vols./39 pubs.	18.48	18.95
1987—198 vols./42 pubs.	17.90	16.95
1986—305 vols./53 pubs.	17.13	16.95
1985—219 vols./49 pubs.	16.53	16.95
Biography†		
1991—129 vols./63 pubs.	25.83	22.95
1990—135 vols./62 pubs.	26.04	24.95
1989—133 vols./61 pubs.	22.64	19.95
1988—132 vols./55 pubs.	25.29	22.50
1987—115 vols./64 pubs.	25.30	19.95
1986—125 vols./53 pubs.	22.28	19.95
1985—137 vols./60 pubs.	22.09	19.50
History‡		
1991—114 vols./43 pubs.	30.84	24.95
1990—153 vols./62 pubs.	28.79	25.00
1989—151 vols./71 pubs.	28.92	22.50
1988—154 vols./68 pubs.	27.17	24.95
1987—182 vols./66 pubs.	27.05	24.95
1986—73 vols./24 pubs.	28.99	24.95
1985—179 vols./70 pubs.	24.25	25.00

*Not mystery, Western, science fiction, light romances
†Includes letters, diaries, memoirs
‡Not art books

Book Sales Statistics, 1990 and 1991: Highlights from the AAP Annual Survey

Chandler B. Grannis

Contributing Editor, *Publishers Weekly*

American book publishers' sales income passed the $16 billion mark in 1991, according to estimates released by the Association of American Publishers (AAP) in March 1992. The total, subject to moderate correction later in the year, was $16.145 billion, compared with a final figure for 1990 of $15.438 billion—an increase of only 4.6 percent. The 1990 increase was 5.3 percent over that of 1989, which, in contrast, had been 10.9 percent above 1988 results.

The healthiest segments of book sales in 1991 were general trade books, with a 9.1 percent increase (including a jump of over 13 percent in children's books); Bibles and related materials, up 10.8 percent (including important new translations); mass market rack-size paperbacks, up 9.6 percent; and university press books, up 8 percent (see Table 1). The important professional books group had an aggregate increase of only 2.2 percent, according to the estimates. Textbook and reference sales increases were as low or lower.

Table 1 / Estimated Book Publishing Industry Sales 1982, 1985, 1989–1991
(Millions of Dollars)

	1982 $	1985 $	1989 $	1990 $	1990 % Change from 1989	1991 (Prelim.) $	1991 % Change from 1990	Compound Growth Rate (%) 1982–1991	1985–1991	1989–1991
Trade (total)	1,513.0	2,210.9	3,623.5	3,892.8	7.4	4,248.5	9.1	12.2	11.5	8.3
Adult hardbound	770.8	1,113.0	1,745.4	1,808.2	3.6	1,961.9	8.5	10.9	9.9	6.0
Adult paperbound	458.2	622.3	976.6	1,063.5	8.9	1,128.4	6.1	10.5	10.4	7.5
Juvenile hardbound	206.9	358.7	665.1	761.5	14.5	862.8	13.3	17.2	15.8	13.9
Juvenile paperbound	77.1	116.9	236.4	259.6	9.8	295.4	13.8	16.1	16.7	11.8
Religious (total)	425.5	536.7	737.1	788.0	6.9	838.5	6.4	7.8	7.7	6.7
Bibles, testaments, hymnals, and prayer books	149.1	156.3	201.0	229.9	14.4	254.7	10.8	6.1	8.5	12.6
Other religious	276.4	380.4	536.1	558.1	4.1	583.8	4.6	8.7	7.4	4.4
Professional (total)	1,536.4	1,928.0	2,592.8	2,765.9	6.7	2,826.7	2.2	7.0	6.6	4.4
Business	224.2	321.3	481.7	527.9	9.6	—	—	—	—	—
Law	560.9	685.8	883.0	947.5	7.3	—	—	—	—	—
Medical	287.2	363.6	490.5	526.3	7.3	—	—	—	—	—
Technical, scientific, and other professional	464.1	557.3	737.6	764.2	3.6	—	—	—	—	—
Book clubs	522.9	598.0	704.0	725.1	3.0	753.4	3.9	4.1	3.9	3.4
Mail order publications	568.6	629.6	796.8	731.4	-8.2	733.6	0.3	2.9	2.6	-4.0
Mass market paperback rack-sized	703.4	803.7	1,094.5	1,148.6	4.9	1,258.9	9.6	6.7	7.8	7.2
University presses	125.4	146.8	227.0	245.8	8.3	265.5	8.0	8.7	10.4	8.1
Elementary and secondary text	1,108.2	1,472.9	1,983.6	2,025.8	2.1	2,060.2	1.7	7.1	5.8	1.9
College text	1,206.1	1,358.4	1,842.1	1,991.3	8.1	1,997.3	0.3	5.8	6.6	4.1
Standardized tests	70.4	90.6	119.4	127.6	6.9	133.5	4.6	7.4	6.7	5.7
Subscription reference	306.9	390.2	509.4	540.5	6.1	552.4	2.2	6.7	6.0	4.1
AV and other media (total)	148.0	199.5	223.7	237.2	6.0	—	—	—	—	—
El-hi	130.1	173.9	178.6	186.1	4.2	—	—	—	—	—
College	7.9	9.9	17.4	20.0	14.9	—	—	—	—	—
Other	10.0	15.7	27.7	31.1	12.3	—	—	—	—	—
Other sales	162.1	187.8	211.3	217.6	3.0	—	—	—	—	—
Total	8,396.9	10,553.1	14,665.2	15,437.6	5.3	16,144.9	4.6	7.5	7.3	4.9

Source: Association of American Publishers.

AAP's industry estimates are based on the five-year U.S. Census of Manufactures figures (1987 being the most recent), which are "brought forward" by AAP between censuses by using the percentage changes indicated in AAP's own monthly sales reports and other sources.

Final figures appear as Table S-1 in the *AAP Industry Statistics,* usually issued in the Spring.

AAP covers certain data not included in the Census reports: most university presses; other institutionally sponsored and not-for-profit publishing activities; and audiovisual and other materials. On the other hand, AAP excludes Sunday school materials and some pamphlets, which the Census does cover.

At the retail level, sales of books in 1991 showed very moderate increases on the average, helped by a brief spurt in the last days before Christmas, according to a survey by *Publishers Weekly.* The magazine queried representative booksellers of various sizes around the country. Among reported trends: Extra promotional effort was needed to keep sales from falling off; wholesalers' service to retailers showed improvement; price resistance continued, as did the dealers' use of bargain tables and selected price discounting; nonfiction sold better than most fiction and, as one bookseller put it, "the huge, huge bestseller sales aren't what they used to be."

U.S. Book Exports and Imports, 1990

Chandler B. Grannis

Contributing Editor, *Publishers Weekly*

U.S. book exports amounted to $1.43 billion in 1990, according to data extracted by *Publishers Weekly* from U.S. Department of Commerce (USDC) reports. Imports came to more than $902 million. The 1990 export-to-import ratio for books was therefore about 61 to 39 (see Tables 1–4).

USDC book export and import figures are always incomplete because, among other reasons, they do not include low-value shipments. Currently, export shipments valued at less than $2,500 and import shipments valued below $1,250 are excluded. With industry cooperation, USDC attempts to improve the accuracy of the statistics each year. According to William S. Lofquist, printing and publishing specialist at USDC's International Trade Association, for 1990, the United States and Canada used each other's import data to enhance their own export data. Lofquist made the following statement on the matter:

> "In an attempt to get better trade data between the United States and Canada, both countries agreed in January 1990 to an exchange of import data. The purpose of this exchange was to use each country's imports as a 'proxy' for each country's exports: hence, to ostensibly obtain more complete and meaningful trade statistics. With regard to the 1990 trade data, the result is better detail at the aggregate level (i.e., books) but little or no detail at the individual category level (textbooks). This inadvertent result came about

Note: Adapted from "Balancing the Books, 1990," *Publishers Weekly,* July 5, 1991.

Table 1 / U.S. Book Exports, 1990
(Shipments Valued at $2,500 or More)
(Dollars and Units in Thousands)

	1990 $	% Chg. 1989–1990	1990 Units	% Chg. 1989–1990
Dictionaries	4,659.0	+.001	1,231.9	+6
Encyclopedias	39,369.0	+26.0	6,694.9	+18
Textbooks	128,431.0	–35.3	24,720.7	–30
Bibles & other religious books	55,341.0	–9.4	38,308.1	–24
Technical, scientific, & professional books	322,647.0	–15.8	46,218.8	–19
Art & pictorial books	12,242.0	–27.6	7,062.1	+5
Hardbound books not elsewhere indicated	42,194.0	–61.1	15,535.2	–61
Rack-size paperbound	49,956.0	–70.6	34,118.3	–63
Other books not elsewhere indicated	736,063.0	+468.4	1,092,877.9	+180
Children's picture, coloring, drawing	12,875.0	+26.6	–	–
Music books	17,502.0	+112.8	–	–
Atlases	6,725.0	+619.3	–	–
Total Exports	$1,428,004.0	+27.1	–	–

Table 2 / U.S. Book Imports, 1989–1990
(Shipments Valued at $1,250 or More)
(Dollars and Units in Thousands)

	1990 $	% Chg. 1989–1990	1990 Units	% Chg. 1989–1990
Dictionaries, thesauruses	7,040.0	+52.2	4,728.3	+256.3
Encyclopedias (incl. installments)	7,143.0	+35.2	956.3	+9.9
Textbooks	87,040.0	+9.8	17,913.9	+7.9
Bibles & other religious books	33,636.0	+9.6	40,599.9	+34.9
Technical, scientific, & professional	112,713.0	+19.7	24,608.1	+26.7
Art, pictorial:				
under $5 each	17,559.0	+6.2	12,020.9	–32.2
$5 and up each	28,925.0	+45.8	2,578.6	+46.6
Hardbound books not elsewhere specified	314,803.0	+10.2	95,317.2	+6.5
Rack-size paperbound	41,574.0	+53.7	34,078.7	+65.3
Other, not over 4 pp.	4,245.0	+7.1	16,707.1	–9.8
5–48 pp.	52,574.0	+6.7	120,820.5	+.001
49 pp. or more	136,473.0	+.001	70,729.8	–7.6
Children's picture, coloring, drawing	50,565.0	+26.9	–	–
Music books	3,600.0	22.2	–	–
Maps, atlases	4,311.0	–	–	–
Totals	$902,201.0	+12.8	441,059.3	–

Table 3 / Book Export-Import Ratios, 1975–1990
(Millions of Dollars)

	Exports	Imports	Approx. Ratio
1990	1,428.0	902.2	61–39
1985	591.2	564.3	51–49
1980	518.9	511.6	50.1–49.9
1975	269.3	147.6	60–40

Table 4 / U.S. Book Exports Compared to
Total U.S. Book Sales, 1970–1990
(in Thousands of dollars)

	Exports	Total sales	Exports as % of total sales
1990	1,428.0	15,365.1	9.4
1985	591.2	10,156.0	5.8
1980	518.9	6,411.0	8.1
1975	269.3	3,789.3	7.1
1970	174.9	2,677.0	6.5

because both countries have significantly different categories covering their trade in books, as well as some other commodities. This problem of adequate coverage of individual categories is expected to be corrected beginning with the 1991 trade data."

Tables 1 and 2 break down U.S. exports and imports according to specific categories, including textbooks, Bibles, and professional books, but many miscellaneous books are still being grouped in the immense, catch-all "not elsewhere specified or indicated." Tables 5 and 6 show dollars and quantities for transactions between the United States and its major book trade partners.

Table 5 / U.S. Book Exports to Principal Countries, 1989–1990
(Shipments Valued at $2,500 or More)
(Ranked by 1990 Dollar Amounts, in Thousands)

	1990 $	1989 $	1990 Units	1989 Units
Canada	664,448	394,189	935,424.3	168,523.6
United Kingdom	171,391	167,138	64,943.9	63,578.6
Australia	106,274	112,683	50,651.8	50,377.2
Japan	87,562	79,159	39,113.4	31,377.2
Germany, West	42,244	39,873	15,856.3	12,290.1
Netherlands	33,715	32,735	13,321.7	12,610.9
Mexico	32,337	26,339	11,064.9	10,542.3
Singapore	31,321	21,715	15,467.2	11,541.8
France	20,144	21,448	8,091.4	6,649.8
India	17,576	15,615	5,213.3	4,344.3
Taiwan	15,304	12,648	6,004.2	6,420.3
Hong Kong	12,853	10,987	5,517.7	4,400.0
Brazil	12,451	14,910	4,724.0	4,839.1
South Africa	11,378	14,752	7,993.2	9,203.1
Philippines	10,560	11,949	5,369.5	7,203.1
Switzerland	9,854	6,922	4,083.6	2,814.7
Italy	9,799	8,815	3,172.4	3,537.1
Spain	9,687	7,208	3,916.0	2,613.7
New Zealand	9,600	8,007	4,807.0	4,884.1
Korea, South	8,245	7,764	3,054.1	3,143.9
Ireland	7,946	9,782	1,826.7	2,521.7
Sweden	6,597	6,403	1,864.1	2,303.4
Argentina	5,746	3,440	4,987.1	2,938.3
Finland	5,095	3,020	2,796.0	1,485.0
Venezuela	4,772	4,999	5,275.2	5,618.9
Israel	4,321	4,232	1,826.5	1,633.5
Denmark	4,012	3,031	1,354.6	1,133.5
Malaysia	3,998	3,386	1,483.6	1,209.3
Portugal	3,881	4,836	1,918.8	1,757.8
All Countries	$1,428,003	$1,123,155	1,266,767.9	477,465.5

Table 6 / U.S. Book Imports from Principal Countries, 1989-1990
(Shipments Valued at $1,250 or More)
(Ranked by 1990 Dollar Amounts, in Thousands)

	1990 $	1989 $	1990 Units	1989 Units
United Kingdom	216,420	189,482	59,412.7	59,430.2
Hong Kong	136,701	102,504	61,110.5	49,378.5
Japan	123,351	120,694	61,048.7	54,980.4
Italy	81,731	62,409	53,740.3	49,378.3
Canada	61,584	61,896	92,332.3	104,902.3
Singapore	55,604	44,774	19,757.6	19,573.7
Germany, West	38,952	37,438	11,490.9	11,167.7
Spain	38,906	43,947	12,844.0	14,369.1
Netherlands	14,188	14,648	5,448.6	4,436.1
Korea, South	14,064	12,618	7,658.7	6,893.7
France	11,235	10,638	5,248.5	4,524.2
Belgium	10,797	12,396	4,864.9	4,854.7
Taiwan	10,668	9,983	3,303.2	7,572.5
Colombia	10,489	9,355	5,883.9	5,450.5
Switzerland	10,369	8,640	2,348.9	2,173.7
Mexico	8,028	7,100	5,800.9	3,275.4
Yugoslavia	7,609	5,815	4,506.4	4,428.3
Australia	6,964	5,314	2,097.8	1,587.1
Denmark	6,657	6,521	2,289.9	1,402.9
Israel	5,847	6,004	1,249.0	1,651.6
Sweden	5,359	3,133	1,369.5	1,573.4
China	3,595	4,887	1,351.4	2,480.8
World Totals	902,201	799,932	441,059.2	408,642.9

A completely different universe of data is represented in Tables A, B, and C, which *PW* derived mainly from the *UNESCO Statistical Yearbook*. They show trends in the number of titles translated from major languages and by selected countries, and title output as reported — somewhat unevenly — by nations around the world.

Table A / Translation Publishing by Principal Countries, 1982-1984

	1982	1983	1984
Brazil	519	1,433	1,331
Czechoslovakia	1,673	1,161	1,272
Denmark	1,387	1,503	1,659
Finland	1,425	1,250	1,421
France	1,894	3,436	3,821
Germany, West	8,168	7,600	6,868
Hungary	1,227	1,397	1,238
Italy	2,034	2,939	2,289
Japan	2,479	2,498	2,698
Norway	1,000	1,004	1,251
Poland	1,009	704	615
Spain	7,381	7,447	7,741
Sweden	2,128	1,996	1,916
Switzerland	1,002	1,106	1,084
Turkey	811	808	1,152
USSR	7,196	7,443	7,758
United Kingdom	1,070	1,143	1,153
United States	1,319	969	1,439
Yugoslavia	1,599	1,297	1,280
All Reporting Countries	52,198	55,618	52,405

Table B / World Translation Publications, 1982–1984
(From Selected Languages)

	1982	1983	1984
English	22,208	24,468	22,724
French	6,205	6,084	4,422
German	4,501	4,818	5,311
Russian	6,238	6,370	6,230
Italian	1,433	1,645	1,544
Scandinavian*	1,957	2,176	2,192
Spanish	715	847	839
Classical, Greek, Latin	839	1,116	1,035
Hungarian	703	665	679
Arabic	298	322	536
Japanese	208	222	204
Chinese	159	148	163
World Totals	52,198	55,618	52,405

Source: UNESCO Statistical Yearbook, 1990 (partial data).
*Swedish, Danish, Norwegian, Icelandic

**Table C / World Book Title Output, 1986–1988:
Principal Publishing Countries**

	1986	1987	1988
Africa			
Egypt	1,416	1,276	1,451
Nigeria	—	2,352	1,424
Tunisia	—	1,160	293
North America			
Canada	6,623	7,263	7,550
Cuba	2,174	2,315	2,069
Mexico	4,897	7,725	4,826
United States	52,637	56,027	52,069
South America			
Argentina	—	4,818	4,826
Chile	1,499	1,654	1,840
Venezuela	—	1,202	—
Asia			
Bangladesh	1,806	1,709	1,209
India	12,543	14,965	14,408
Indonesia	2,480	2,052	1,687
Iran	—	2,996	3,401
Japan	44,686	36,346	—
Korea, South	41,543	44,288	42,942
Malaysia	3,397	—	—
Philippines	804	1,768	1,072
Sri Lanka	2,368	—	—
Thailand	7,728	—	—
Europe			
Austria	9,560	8,910	8,360
Belgium	—	7,091	—
Bulgaria	4,924	4,583	4,379
Czechoslovakia	10,020	10,565	9,558
Denmark	10,957	11,129	—
Finland	8,694	9,106	10,386
France	32,934	43,505	39,026
Germany, East	6,486	6,515	6,526
Germany, West	63,724	65,670	68,611
Hungary	9,857	9,111	8,621
Iceland	—	1,231	—
Italy	16,297	17,109	19,820
Netherlands	13,368	13,329	13,845
Norway	3,284	6,757	4,894
Poland	9,881	10,416	10,728
Portugal	10,782	7,733	—
Spain	38,405	38,302	35,426
Sweden	10,587	11,516	11,794
Switzerland	11,626	12,410	12,696
United Kingdom	57,845	59,839	62,069
Yugoslavia	10,734	10,619	12,100
Oceania			
Australia	7,460	—	—
U.S.S.R			
U.S.S.R	83,472	83,011	—
Byelorussia	3,182	—	2,962
Ukraine	8,155	8,134	8,311

Source: UNESCO Statistical Yearbook, 1990, except U.S. figures derived by *Publishers Weekly* from R. R. Bowker Data Services; U.K. figures from *The Bookseller,* London; Canadian figures from *Statistics Canada* (Michel Frve, Book Publishing Survey manager), Ottawa. U.S. figures do not include publications of state and local governments, some institutions, company reports, proceedings, lab manuals, yearbooks, U.S. Government Printing Office output, and university theses. However, the books of university presses, religious organizations, and other nonprofit publishers are included.

Number of Book Outlets in the United States and Canada

The *American Book Trade Directory* has been published by R. R. Bowker since 1915. Revised annually, it features lists of booksellers, wholesalers, periodicals, reference tools, and other information about the U.S. and Canadian book markets. The data shown in Tables 1 and 2, the most current available, are from the 1991-1992 edition of the directory.

The 27,953 stores of various types shown in Table 1 are located throughout the United States, Canada, and regions administered by the United States. "General" bookstores stock trade books and children's books in a general variety of subjects. "College" stores carry college-level textbooks. "Educational" outlets handle school textbooks up to and including the high school level. "Mail order" outlets sell general trade books by mail and are not book clubs; all others operating by mail are classified according to the kinds of books carried. "Antiquarian" dealers sell old and rare books. Stores handling secondhand books are classified as "used." "Paperback"

Table 1 / Bookstores in the United States and Canada, 1991

Category	United States	Canada
Antiquarian general	1,033	75
Antiquarian mail order	566	20
Antiquarian specialized	250	7
Art supply store	84	1
College general	3,127	152
College specialized	166	12
Department store	2,626	94
Drugstore	22	8
Educational*	167	56
Exporter-importer	13	1
Federal sites†	284	n/a
Foreign language*	123	30
General	6,694	1,066
Gift shop	196	24
Juvenile*	433	55
Law*	40	2
Mail order general	418	21
Mail order specialized	157	11
Medical*	35	1
Museum store and art gallery	463	29
Newsdealer	139	6
Office supply	84	16
Other§	2,504	302
Paperback‡	611	29
Religious*	3,817	253
Remainders	23	5
Science-technology*	37	5
Stationer	94	32
Used*	1,323	111
Total	25,529	2,424

*Includes mail order shops for this topic, which are not counted elsewhere in this survey.

†National historic sites, national monuments, and national parks.

‡Includes mail order. Excludes used paperback bookstores, stationers, drugstores, or wholesalers handling paperbacks.

§Stores specializing in subjects or services other than those covered in this survey.

Table 2 / Retailers and Wholesalers in the United States and Canada, 1991

Category	United States	Canada	Totals
Retailers			
Bookstore chain headquarters	1,076	129	1,205
Bookstore chain branches	10,000	889	10,889
Independent bookstores	15,703	1,594	17,297
Total retailers	26,779	2,612	29,391
Wholesalers			
General wholesalers	888	138	1,026
Paperback wholesalers*	361	50	411
Total wholesalers	1,249	188	1,437

*Paperback sales account for at least 51 percent of the total title volume of these wholesalers.

stores have more than 80 percent of their stock in paperbound books. Stores with paperback departments are listed under the appropriate major classification ("general," "department store," "stationer," etc.). Bookstores with at least 50 percent of their stock on a particular subject are classified by subject.

Book Review Media Statistics

Number of Books Reviewed by Major Book-Reviewing Publications, 1990–1991

	Adult		Juvenile		Young Adult		Total	
	1990	1991	1990	1991	1990	1991	1990	1991
Booklist[1]	4,883	3,933	2,148	2,628	2,186	1,199	9,217	8,254
Bulletin of the Center for Children's Books	—	—	770	768	—	—	770	768
Chicago Sun Times[2]	1,040	1,050	280	275	—	—	1,320	1,325
Chicago Tribune	1,100	1,100	150*	150	—	—	1,250	1,250
Choice[3]	6,737	6,592	—	—	—	—	6,737	6,592
Horn Book Magazine	13	20	404	400	68	75	485	495
Horn Book Guide	—	—	2,689	2,700	597	600	3,286	3,300
Kirkus Services[4]	4,000	4,000	—	—	—	—	4,000	4,000
Library Journal[5]	4,470	5,063	—	—	—	—	4,470	5,063
Los Angeles Times	1,700	1,700	300	300	—	—	2,000	2,000
New York Review of Books	347	489	—	—	—	—	347	489
New York Times Sunday Book Review[6]	2,000	2,000	300	300	—	—	2,300	2,300
Publishers Weekly[7]	4,261	4,046	1,100	1,200	—	—	5,361	5,246
School Library Journal[8]	—	—	2,963	2,873	—	433	3,233	3,306
Washington Post Book World[9]	1,813	1,820	84	110	22	—	1,959	1,930
West Coast Review of Books	1,080	750	—	—	—	—	1,080	750

[1] All figures are for a 12-month period from September 1 to August 31; 1991 figures are for September 1, 1990–August 31, 1991. Totals include reference and subscription books. In addition, *Booklist* publishes reviews of nonprint materials—1,124 in 1990 and 939 in 1991—and of special bibliographies—about 6,000 each year.
[2] Includes books mentioned in columns.

[3] All figures are for a 12-month period beginning September and ending July/August; 1991 figures are for September 1990–August 1991. Total for 1990 includes 308 nonprint materials and 130 periodicals; total for 1991 includes 276 nonprint materials.

[4] Adult figures include both adult and juvenile books.

[5] In addition, *LJ* reviewed 119 magazines and 785 nonprint (audio/visual) materials in 1990, and 107 magazines and 983 nonprint materials in 1991.

[6] Juvenile figures include books reviewed in "Bookshelf" column.

[7] Includes reviews of paperback originals and reprints.

[8] *SLJ* also reviewed about 1,000 audiovisual materials each year.

[9] The 1991 total includes 39 recorded books.

*Revised

Part 5
Reference Information

Ready Reference

Publishers' Toll-Free Telephone Numbers

Publishers' toll-free numbers continue to play an important role in ordering, verification, and customer service. This year's list comes from *Literary Market Place* (R. R. Bowker) and includes distributors and regional toll-free numbers, where applicable. The list is not comprehensive and toll-free numbers are subject to change. Readers may want to call for toll-free directory assistance (800-555-1212).

Publisher/Distributor	Toll-Free No.
ABBA Publishing, San Antonio, TX	800-445-6754
Abbeville Press, New York, NY	800-227-7210
Abbot, Foster & Hauserman Co., Spokane, WA	800-562-0025
ABC-CLIO, Santa Barbara, CA	800-422-2546
Aberdeen Group, Addison, IL	800-323-3550
Abingdon Press, Nashville, TN	800-251-3320
Harry N. Abrams Inc., New York, NY	800-345-1359
ACA Books, New York, NY	800-321-4510
Academic Press, San Diego, CA	800-321-5068
Academic Therapy Publications, Novato, CA	800-422-7249
Academy Chicago Publishers, Chicago, IL	800-248-7323
Academy of Producer Insurance Studies, Austin, TX	800-526-2777
Accelerated Development Inc., Muncie, IN	800-222-1166
Accounting Publications, Gainesville, FL	800-874-5346
Acropolis Books, Reston, VA	800-451-7771
ACS Publications, San Diego, CA	800-888-9983
ACTA Publications, Chicago, IL	800-397-2282
ACU Press, Abilene, TX	800-444-4228
Bob Adams, Inc., Holbrook, MA	800-872-5627
Addison-Wesley Publishing, Reading, MA	800-447-2226
AEI Press, Washington, DC	800-223-2336
Aerofax Inc., Arlington, TX	800-733-2329
Agora Inc., Baltimore, MD	800-433-1528
Alaska Northwest Books, Bothell, WA	800-331-3510
Alba House, Staten Island, NY	800-343-2522
Alban Institute Inc., Washington DC	800-457-2674
Alfred Publishing Co., Van Nuys, CA	800-292-6122

Publisher/Distributor	Toll-Free No.
Alpine Publications, Loveland, CO	800-777-7257
Frank Amato Publications, Portland, OR	800-541-9498
America West Pubs., Tehachapi, CA	800-729-4131
American Academy of Orthopaedic Surgeons, Park Ridge, IL	800-626-6726
American Academy of Pediatrics, Elk Grove Village, IL	800-433-9016
American & World Geographic Publishing, Helena, MT	800-654-1105
American Assn. for Counseling & Development, Alexandria, VA	800-545-2223; 800-347-6647
American Assn. for Vocational Instructional Materials, Athens, GA	800-228-4689
American Assn. of Cereal Chemists, St. Paul, MN	800-328-7560
American Assn. of Community & Junior Colleges, Washington, DC	800-336-4776
American Assn. of Engineering Societies, Washington, DC	800-658-8897
American Bible Society, New York, NY	800-543-8000
American Chemical Society, Washington, DC	800-227-5558
American Correctional Assn., Laurel, MD	800-825-2665
American Diabetes Assn., Alexandria, VA	800-232-3472
American Guidance Service Inc., Circle Pines, MN	800-328-2560
American Hazmat Inc., San Diego, CA	800-448-4023
American Health Publishing, Dallas, TX	800-736-7323
American Hospital Publishing, Chicago, IL	800-621-6902
American Institute of Architects Press, Washington, DC	800-457-3239
American Institute of Physics, New York, NY	800-247-7497
American Law Institute, Philadelphia, PA	800-253-6397
American Library Assn., Chicago, IL	800-545-2433
American Map Corp., Maspeth, NY	800-432-6277
American Mathematical Society, Providence, RI	800-321-4267
American Psychiatric Press, Washington, DC	800-368-5777
American Society for Nondestructive Testing, Columbus, OH	800-222-2768
American Society of Civil Engineers, New York, NY	NY 800-548-2723, 800-628-0041
American Society of Mechanical Engineers, New York, NY	800-843-2763
American Standard Text Corp., New York, NY	800-533-4027
American Technical Publishers, Homewood, IL	800-323-3471
Analytic Press, Hillsdale, NJ	800-926-6579
Ancestry Inc., Salt Lake City, UT	800-531-1790
Anchor Publishing, Landover Hills, MD	800-448-6280
Anderson Publishing, Cincinnati, OH	800-543-0883; 800-582-7295
Andover Medical Publishers, Reading, MA	800-366-2665
Andrews & McMeel, Kansas City, MO	800-826-4216
Annabooks, San Diego, CA	800-462-1042
Annual Reviews, Inc., Palo Alto, CA	800-523-8635
Antioch Publishing, Yellow Springs, OH	800-543-2397
Antique Publications, Marietta, OH	800-533-3433
Apollo Book, Poughkeepsie, NY	800-431-5003; NY 800-942-8222
Appleton & Lange, East Norwalk, CT	800-423-1359
Archives Press, Los Altos, CA	800-338-4454
Ariel Press, Canal Winchester, OH	800-336-7769

Publisher/Distributor	Toll-Free No.
Jason Aronson Inc., Northvale, NJ	800-782-0015
Arrow Mapp Inc., Taunton, MA	800-343-7500
Art Institute of Chicago, Chicago, IL	800-621-2736
Artabras Inc., New York, NY	800-227-7210
Artech House Inc., Norwood, MA	800-225-9977
ASCP Press, Chicago, IL	800-621-4142
Aslan Publishing, Boulder Creek, CA	800-372-3100
Aspen Publishers Inc., Gaithersburg, MD	800-638-8437
Association for Research & Enlightenment Inc., Virginia Beach, VA	800-368-2727
ATLA Press, Washington, DC	800-424-2727
Auerbach Publishers, New York, NY	800-922-0066
Augsburg Fortress Publishers, Minneapolis, MN	800-328-4648
August House Publishers, Little Rock, AR	800-284-8784
Avalon Books, New York, NY	800-223-5251
Ave Maria Press, Notre Dame, IN	800-282-1865
Avery Publishing Group, Wayne, NJ	800-548-5757
Aviation Supplies & Academics, Renton, WA	800-426-8338
Avon Books, New York, NY	800-238-0658
Back to the Bible Broadcast, Lincoln, NE	800-759-2425
Baha'i Publishing Trust, Wilmette, IL	800-999-9019
Baker Book House, Grand Rapids, MI	800-877-2665
Balcony Publishing, Austin, TX	800-777-7949
Ballantine/Del Rey/Fawcett/Ivy Books, New York, NY	800-638-6460
Bancroft-Sage Publishing, Marco, FL	800-942-1745
Banks-Baldwin Law Publishing, Cleveland, OH AZ, OH & PA	800-362-4500;
	KY 800-221-2630
Bantam Books, New York, NY	800-223-6834
Bantam Doubleday Dell Publishing Group, New York, NY	800-223-6834
Baptist Spanish Publishing House, El Paso, TX	800-755-5958
Barbour & Co, Westwood, NJ	800-221-2648
Barclay Press, Newberg, OR	800-962-4014
Barron's Educational Series Inc., Hauppauge, NY	800-645-3476
Basic Books, New York, NY	800-242-7737
Battelle Press, Columbus, OH	800-451-3543
BDD Promotional Book Co., New York, NY	800-223-6834
Beacon Hill Press of Kansas City, Kansas City, MO	800-877-0700
Bear & Co., Santa Fe, NM	800-932-3277
Beautiful America Publishing, Wilsonville, OR	800-874-1233
Peter Bedrick Books, New York, NY	800-365-3453
Behrman House, West Orange, NJ	800-221-2755
Matthew Bender & Co., New York, NY Outside NY 800-223-1940;	800-422-2022
Benjamin-Cummings Publishing, Redwood City, CA	800-950-2665
Robert Bentley Inc., Cambridge, MA	800-423-2595
Benziger Publishing, Mission Hills, CA	800-423-9534
Berkley Publishing, New York, NY	800-223-0510
Berkshire House Publishers, Stockbridge, MA	800-321-8526

Publisher/Distributor	Toll-Free No.
Best Publishing, Flagstaff, AZ	800-328-6109
Betterway Publications, Crozet, VA	800-522-2782
Betz Publishing Co., Potomac, MD	800-634-4365
Beverage Marketing Corp., Mingo Junction, OH	800-332-6222
Beyond Words Publishing, Hillsboro, OR	800-284-9673
Birkhauser Boston, Cambridge, MA	800-777-4643
Blackwell Publishers, Cambridge, MA	800-445-6638
John F. Blair, Publisher, Winston-Salem, NC	800-222-9796
Blue Bird Publishing, Tempe, AZ	800-654-1993
Blue Mountain Press, Boulder, CO	800-525-0642
Blue Note Publications, Melbourne Beach, FL	800-624-0401
Clark Boardman Co., New York, NY	800-221-9428
Bob Jones University Press, Greenville, SC	800-845-5731
Bonus Books, Chicago, IL	800-225-3775
Book Lures Inc., O'Fallon, MO	800-444-9450
Book Peddlers, Deephaven, MN	800-255-3379
Thomas Bouregy & Co., New York, NY	800-223-5251
R. R. Bowker, New Providence, NJ	800-521-8100
Boyd & Fraser Publishing, Boston, MA	800-225-3782
Boynton/Cook Publishers, Portsmouth, NH	800-541-2086
Branden Publishing, Boston, MA	800-537-7335
Breakthrough Publications, Ossining, NY	800-824-5000
Brethren Press, Elgin, IL	800-323-8039
Brick House Publishing, New Boston, NH	800-446-8642
Bridge Publications, Los Angeles, CA	800-722-1733; CA 900-843-7389
E. J. Brill USA Inc., Kinderhook, NY	800-962-4406
Bristol Publishing Enterprises Inc., San Leandro, CA	800-346-4889
Broadman Press, Nashville, TN	800-251-3225
Paul H. Brookes Publishing Co., Baltimore, MD	800-638-3775
Brookings Institution, Washington, DC	800-275-1447
Brookline Books, Cambridge, MA	800-666-2665
Brooks/Cole Publishing, Pacific Grove, CA	800-354-9706
Wm. C. Brown Group, Dubuque, IA	800-338-5578
Brunner/Mazel Inc., New York, NY	800-825-3089
Buckingham Mint Inc./Derrydale Press, Lyon, MS	800-443-6753
Business & Legal Reports Inc., Madison, CT	800-727-5257
Business News Publishing, Troy, MI	800-837-1037
Business One Irwin, Homewood, IL	800-634-3961
Business Research Services Inc., Washington, DC	800-845-8420
Butterworth-Heinemann, Stoneham, MA	800-366-2665; 800-544-1013
Butterworth Legal Publishers, Austin, TX	800-749-3888
C & T Publishing, Martinez, CA	800-284-1114
C Q Press, Washington, DC	800-543-7793
CAB International North America, Tucson, AZ	800-528-4841
Caddylak Systems Inc., Brentwood, NY	800-523-8060
Calgre Press, Antioch, CA	800-397-8423

Publisher/Distributor	Toll-Free No.
California College Publishing, National City, CA	800-221-7374
Callaghan & Co., Deerfield, IL	800-323-8067
Cambridge Career Products, Charleston, WV	800-221-4227
Cambridge University Press, New York, NY	800-221-4512
Camden House Publishing, Charlotte, VT	800-344-3350
Camelot Books, New York, NY	800-238-0658
Career Press, Hawthorne, NJ	800-227-3371
Career Publishing, Orange, CA	800-854-4041
William Carey Library, Pasadena, CA	800-777-6371
Carlson Publishing, Brooklyn, NY	800-336-7460
Carolina Biological Supply Co., Burlington, NC	800-334-5551
Carolrhoda Books, Minneapolis, MN	800-328-4929
Carroll & Graf Publishers, New York, NY	800-365-3453
Cassell Communications, Fort Lauderdale, FL	800-351-9278
Castle Books, Secaucus, NJ	800-526-7257
CAT Publishing, Redding, CA	800-767-0511
Caxton Printers, Caldwell, ID	800-451-8791
CEF Press, Warrenton, MO	800-748-7710
Celestial Arts, Berkeley, CA	800-841-2665
Center for Career Development Inc., Cincinnati, OH	800-992-4226
Chadwyck-Healey Inc., Alexandria, VA	800-752-0515
Chalice Press, St. Louis, MO	800-366-3383
Charlesbridge Publishing, Watertown, MA	800-225-3214
Chartwell Books, Secaucus, NJ	800-526-7257
Chelsea Green Publishing, Post Mills, VT	800-445-6638
Cherokee Publishing, Marietta, GA	800-548-8778
Chicago Review Press, Chicago, Il	800-888-4741
Childrens Press, Chicago, IL	800-621-1115
Child's Play, New York, NY	800-472-0999
Child's World Inc., Mankato, MN	800-445-6209
Chilton Book, Radnor, PA	800-695-1214
Christian Books Publishing House, Auburn, ME	800-228-2665
Christian Brothers Publications, Romeoville, IL	800-433-7593
Christian Classics Inc., Westminster, MD	800-888-3065
Christian Schools International, Grand Rapids, MI	US 800-635-8288; Canada 800-637-8288
Chronicle Books, San Francisco, CA	800-722-6657; CA 800-445-7577
Chronicle Guidance Publications, Moravia, NY	800-622-7284
Churchill Livingstone Inc., New York, NY	IL only 800-553-5426
Clark City Press, Livingston, MT	800-835-0814
Clearlight Publishers, Santa Fe, NM	800-253-2747
Cliffs Notes, Lincoln, NE	800-228-4078
Cold Spring Harbor Laboratory Press, Cold Spring Harbor, NY	800-349-1946
Collector Books, Paducah, KY	800-626-5420
College Press Publishing, Joplin, MO	800-289-3300
Colorado School of Mines Press, Golden, CO	800-446-9488
Colormore Inc., Carrollton, TX	800-545-2005

Publisher/Distributor	Toll-Free No.
Columba Publishing, Akron, OH	800-999-7491
Columbia Publishing, Baltimore, MD	800-544-0042
Comex Systems Inc., Mendham, NJ	800-543-2862
Commerce Clearing House Inc., Chicago, IL	800-248-3248
Communication Publications & Resources, Blackwood, NJ	800-888-2086
Community Intervention Inc., Minneapolis, MN	800-328-0417
Compact Books, Hollywood, FL	800-771-3355
CompCare Publishers, Minneapolis, MN	Outside MN 800-328-3330
Computer Publishing Enterprises, San Diego, CA	800-544-5541
Concept Management, Mesa, AZ	800-258-0877
Concordia Publishing House, St. Louis, MO	800-325-3040
Conference Board Inc., New York, NY	800-872-6273
Congressional Information Service, Bethesda, MD	800-638-8380
Congressional Quarterly Books, Washington, DC	800-543-7793
Consulting Psychologists Press Inc, Palo Alto, CA	800-624-1765
Contemporary Books, Chicago, IL	800-691-1918
David C. Cook Publishing, Elgin, IL	800-323-7543
Copley Publishing Group, Acton, MA	800-562-2147
Cornell Maritime Press, Centreville, MD	800-638-7641
Cornell University Press, Ithaca, NY	Outside NY 800-666-2211
Cornerstone Large Print Books, Santa Barbara, CA	800-422-2546
Corporate Technology Information Services Inc., Woburn, MA	800-333-8036
Council Oak Publishing, Tulsa, OK	800-247-8850
Countryman Press, Woodstock, VT	800-245-4151
Covenant Publications, Chicago, IL	800-621-1250
Cowley Publications, Boston, MA	800-225-1534
Crabtree Publishing, New York, NY	800-387-7650
Craftsman Book, Carlsbad, CA	800-829-8123
CRC Publications, Grand Rapids, MI	800-333-8300
Creation House, Altamonte Springs, FL	800-451-4598
Creative Education Inc., Mankato, MN	800-445-6209
Creative Homeowner Press, Upper Saddle River, NJ	800-631-7795
Creative Teaching Press Inc., Cypress, CA	800-732-1548
Cross Group, Boston, MA	800-682-5759
Crossing Press, Freedom, CA	800-777-1048
Crossroad/Continuum Publishing Group, New York, NY	800-937-5557
Crossway Books, Wheaton, IL	800-323-3890
Crowne Publications Inc., Southbridge, MA	800-345-0795
Crystal Clarity Publishers, Nevada City, CA	800-424-1055
Curley Publishing, South Yarmouth, MA	800-621-0182
D G C Associates Inc., Cedarhurst, NY	800-442-2342
Da Capo Press, New York, NY	800-221-9369
Dale Seymour Publications, Palo Alto, CA	800-872-1100
Dance Horizons, Pennington, NJ	800-326-7149
John Daniel & Co., Publishers, Santa Barbara, CA	800-662-8351
Daring Publishing Group, Canton, OH	800-445-6321

Publisher/Distributor	Toll-Free No.
Dartnell Corp., Chicago, IL	800-621-5463
DATA Business Publishing, Englewood, CO	800-447-4666
Data Research Inc., Eagan, MN	800-365-4900
Database Publishing, Newport Beach, CA	800-888-8434
DataTrends Publications, Vienna, VA	800-766-8130
Daughters of St. Paul, Boston, MA	800-876-4463
F. A. Davis Co., Philadelphia, PA	800-523-4049
Davis Publications, Worcester, MA	800-533-2847
Davis Publishing Co./Law Enforcement Division, Montgomery, AL	800-221-2040
DAW Books, New York, NY	800-526-0275
Dawbert Press, Duxbury, MA	800-933-2923
DBI Books, Northbrook, IL	800-767-6310
DCI Publishing, Minnetonka, MN	800-444-5951
Cy De Cosse Inc., Minnetonka, MN	800-328-0590
De Vorss & Co., Marina Del Rey, CA CA 800-331-4719; Outside CA	800-843-5743
Dearborn Financial Publishing, Chicago, IL	800-621-9621
Ivan R. Dee Inc., Chicago, IL	800-634-0226
Marcel Dekker Inc., New York, NY	800-228-1160
Dell Publishing, New York, NY	800-223-6834
Delmar Publishers, Albany, NY	NY 800-347-7707
Delta Books, New York, NY	Outside NY 800-223-6834
S. Denison & Co., Minneapolis, MN	800-328-3831
Deseret Book, Salt Lake City, UT	800-453-3876
Destiny Image, Shippensburg, PA	800-722-6774
Paul M. Deutsch Publishing Inc., Orlando, FL	800-999-8773
Devyn Press, Louisville, KY	800-274-2221
Dharma Publishing, Berkeley, CA	800-873-4276
Dictation Disc Co., New York, NY	800-528-3897
Digital Press, Bedford, MA 800-922-0579 (Prentice Hall);	800-223-1360
Discovery Enterprises Ltd., Lowell, MA	800-729-1720
Discovery House Publishers, Grand Rapids, MI	800-283-8333
Distinctive Publishing, Plantation, FL	800-683-3722
DLM, Allen, TX	800-527-4747
F. W. Dodge Residential Statistical Services, Lexington, MA	800-541-9913
DOK Publishers, Cheektowaga, NY	800-458-7900
Don Bosco Multimedia, New Rochelle, NY	800-342-5850
Donning Co./Publishers, Virginia Beach, VA	800-446-8572
Doral Publishing, Wilsonville, OR	800-876-5197
Dorset House Publishing, New York, NY	800-342-6657
Doubleday, New York, NY	800-223-6834
Douglas Charles Press, North Attleboro, MA	800-752-3769
Dover Publications, Mineola, NY	800-223-3130
Down East Books, Camden, ME	800-432-1670
Duquesne University Press, Pittsburgh, PA	800-666-2211
Durkin Hayes Publishing, Niagara Falls, NY	800-962-5200
Dustbooks, Paradise, CA	800-477-6110

Publisher/Distributor	Toll-Free No.
Eagle's View Publishing, Liberty, UT	800-547-3364
Earthbooks, Denver, CO	800-423-0395
Eclipse Books, Forestville, CA	800-468-6828
ECS Learning Systems Inc., San Antonio, TX	800-688-3224
EDC Publishing, Tulsa, OK	800-331-4418
Ediciones del Norte, Hanover, NH	800-782-5422
Editorial Caribe, Miami, FL	800-633-6248
EDL, Columbia, SC	800-227-1606
Educational Assessment Publishing, San Diego, CA	800-888-5111
Educational Impressions, Hawthorne, NJ	800-451-7450
Educational Insights Inc., Dominguez Hills, CA	800-933-3277
Educational Ministries Inc., Brea, CA	800-221-0910
Educators Publishing Service, Cambridge, MA	800-225-5750
Wm. B. Eerdmans Publishing, Grand Rapids, MI	800-253-7521; 800-633-9326
Effective Learning Ad Infinitum Press, Mount Vernon, NY	800-424-0634
EMC Corp., St. Paul, MN	800-328-1452
Encyclopaedia Britannica Educational Corp., Chicago, IL	800-554-9862
Encyclopaedia Brittanica Inc., Chicago, IL	800-554-9862
Engineering Information Inc., New York, NY	800-221-1044
Enterprise Publishing, Wilmington, DE	800-533-2665
EPM Publications, McLean, VA	800-289-2339
Robert Erdmann Publishing, San Marcos, CA	800-833-0720
Lawrence Erlbaum Associates Inc., Hillsdale, NJ	800-926-6579
Essential Medical Information Systems Inc., Durant, OK	800-225-0694
Evanston Publishing, Evanston, IL	800-594-5190
Everton Publishers, Logan, UT	800-443-6325
Executive Enterprises Publications, New York, NY	800-332-1105
Faber & Faber, Winchester, MA	800-445-6638
Fables Inc., Littleton, CO	800-782-8072
Facts on File, New York, NY	800-322-8755
Fairchild Books & Visuals, New York, NY	800-247-6622
Falcon Press Publishing, Helena, MT	800-582-2665
W. D. Farmer Residence Designer Inc., Atlanta, GA	800-225-7526; GA 800-221-7526
Farrar, Straus & Giroux, New York, NY	800-631-8571
Fearon Education, Belmont, CA	800-877-4283
Fearon/Janus, Belmont, CA	800-877-4283
Fearon Teacher Aids, Carthage, IL	800-242-7272
Philip Feldheim Inc., Spring Valley, NY	800-237-7149
Fell Publishers, Hollywood, FL	800-771-3355
Fireside Books, St. Louis, MO	800-537-0655
Fisher Books, Tucson, AZ	800-255-1514
Fliptrack Learning Systems, Glen Ellyn, IL	800-222-3547
Focus Information Group, Newburyport, MA	800-848-7236
Focus on the Family Publishing, Pomona, CA	800-232-6459
Fodor's Travel Publications, New York, NY	800-327-4801

Publisher/Distributor	Toll-Free No.
Foghorn Press, San Francisco, CA	CA 800-842-7477
Fortress Press, Minneapolis, MN	800-328-4648
Foundation Center, New York, NY	800-424-9836
Franciscan University Press, Steubenville, OH	800-783-6357
Burt Franklin & Co., New York, NY	800-223-0766
Friends United Press, Richmond, IN	800-537-8838
Fulcrum Publishing, Golden, CO	800-992-2908
Futura Publishing, Mount Kisco, NY	800-877-8761
Gale Research, Detroit, MI	800-877-4253
Gallaudet University Press, Washington, DC	800-451-1073
Gareth Stevens Inc., Milwaukee, WI	800-341-3569
Garland Publishing, New York, NY	800-627-6273
Garrett Educational Corp., Ada, OK	800-654-9366
Gaslight Publications, Bloomington, IN	800-243-1895
Wm. W. Gaunt & Sons, Holmes Beach, FL	800-942-8683
GemStone Press, Woodstock, VT	800-962-4544
Genealogical Publishing, Baltimore, MD	800-727-6687
Genun Publishers, Orem, UT	800-666-4363
Geological Society of America, Boulder, CO	800-472-1988
C. R. Gibson Co., Norwalk, CT	800-243-6004
Ginn Press, Needham, MA	800-428-4466
Michael Glazier Inc., Wilmington, DE	800-541-4420
Glen Abbey Books, Seattle, WA	800-782-2239
Glencoe, Westerville, OH	800-848-1567
Peter Glenn Publications, New York, NY	800-223-1254
Golf Gifts Inc., Lombard, IL	800-552-4430
Good Apple, Carthage, IL	800-435-7234
Good Books, Intercourse, PA	PA 800-762-7171
Goodheart-Willcox Co., South Holland, IL	800-323-0440
Gordon & Breach, Science Publishers, New York, NY	800-545-8398
Gospel Publishing House, Springfield, MO	800-641-4310
Gould Publications, Binghamton, NY	800-847-6502
Government Research Service, Topeka, KS	800-346-6898
Gower Medical Publishing, New York, NY	800-638-3030
Grapevine Publications, Corvallis, OR	800-338-4331
Graphic Arts Center Publishing, Portland, OR	800-452-3032
Great Quotations Inc., Lombard, IL	800-621-1432
Green Hill Publishers, Ottawa, IL	800-426-1357
Warren H. Green Inc., St. Louis, MO	800-537-0655
Greenhaven Press, San Diego, CA	800-231-5163
Greenwillow Books, New York, NY	800-631-1199
Grove Weidenfeld, New York, NY	800-521-0178
Grove's Dictionaries of Music, New York, NY	800-221-2123
Gryphon Editions, New York, NY	800-633-8911
Gryphon House, Mount Rainier, MD	800-638-0928
Guilford Press, New York, NY	800-365-7006

Publisher/Distributor	Toll-Free No.
Gulf Publishing, Book Division, Houston, TX	TX 800-392-4390; all other except AK & HI 800-231-6275
Hagstrom Map, Maspeth, NY	800-432-6277
Alexander Hamilton Institute, Maywood, NJ	800-879-2441
Hammond Inc., Maplewood, NJ	800-526-4953
Hampton-Brown Co., Carmel, CA	800-933-3510
Hampton House Publishing, Placerville, CA	800-248-3555
Hanley & Belfus Inc., Philadelphia, PA	800-962-1892
Harbinger House, Tucson, AZ	800-447-9945
Harbor House (West) Publishers, Rancho Mirage, CA	800-423-8811
Harcourt Brace Jovanovich, Orlando, FL	800-225-5425
HarperCollins Publishers, New York, NY	800-242-7737; PA 800-982-4377
Harrington Park Press, Binghamton, NY	800-342-9678
Harris Publishing, Twinsburg, OH	800-888-5900
Harrison House Publishers, Tulsa, OK	800-888-4126
Hartley & Marks Inc., Point Roberts, WA	800-283-3572
Harvest House Publishers, Eugene, OR	800-547-8979
Haworth Press, Binghamton, NY	800-342-9678
Hawthorne Educational Services, Columbia, MO	800-542-1673
Hay House, Carson, CA	800-654-5126
Haynes Publications, Newbury Park, CA	800-442-9637
Hazelden Publishing Group, Center City, MN	800-328-9000
Health Communications, Deerfield Beach, FL	800-851-9100
Health for Life, Los Angeles, CA	800-874-5339
Health Press, Santa Fe, NM	800-288-0718
D. C. Heath & Co., Lexington, MA	800-235-3565
William S. Hein & Co., Buffalo, NY	800-828-7571
Heinemann Educational Books, Portsmouth, NH	800-541-2086
Heinle & Heinle Publishers, Boston, MA	800-237-0053
Hemisphere Publishing, Bristol, PA	800-821-8312
Hendrickson Publishers, Peabody, MA	800-358-3111
Virgil W. Hensley Inc., Tulsa, OK	800-288-8520
Herald House, Independence, MO	800-767-8181
Herald Press, Scottdale, PA	800-245-7894
Here's Life Publishers, San Bernardino, CA	800-950-4457
Heritage Quest Inc., Orting, WA	800-442-2029
Hero Games, Charlottesville, VA	800-457-4263
Hi-Time Publishing, Milwaukee, WI	800-558-2292
Hi Willow Research & Publishing, Englewood, CO	800-237-6124
Hill & Wang, New York, NY	800-631-8571
Lawrence Hill Books, Brooklyn, NY	800-888-4741
Hillsdale College Press, Hillsdale, MI	800-437-2268
Hilmar Publishing, Louisville, CO	800-786-4098
Himalayan Publishers, Honesdale, PA	800-444-5772
Hogrefe & Huber Publishers, Lewiston, NY	800-228-3749
Holman Bible Publishers, Nashville, TN	800-251-3225; TN 800-342-0021

Publisher/Distributor	Toll-Free No.
Henry Holt & Co., New York, NY	800-247-3912
Holt, Rinehart and Winston Inc., Orlando, FL	800-782-4479
Holt, Rinehart and Winston School Division, Austin, TX	800-782-4479
Los Hombres Press, San Diego, CA	800-729-3559
Home Builder Press, Washington, DC	800-223-2665
Home Planners Inc., Tucson, AZ	800-521-6797
Homestyles Publishing & Marketing Inc., Minneapolis, MN	800-547-5570
Hope Publishing Co., Carol Stream, IL	800-323-1049
Hope Publishing House, Pasadena, CA	800-326-2671
Horizon Publishers & Distributors Inc., Bountiful, UT	800-453-0812
Houghton Mifflin, Boston, MA	
Trade books	800-225-3362
Textbooks	800-257-9107
College texts	800-225-1464
Howell Press, Charlottesville, VA	800-868-4512
Human Kinetics Publishers, Champaign, IL	800-747-4457
Human Resources Development Press, Amherst, MA	800-822-2801
Humanics Ltd., Atlanta, GA	800-874-8844
Huntington House Publishers, Lafayette, LA	800-749-4009
Hyperion, New York, NY	800-343-9204
I Do Publishing, Colorado Springs, CO	800-888-0385
IAP Inc., Casper, WY	800-443-9250
IBC USA (Publications) Inc., Holliston, MA	800-343-5413
ICP, Indianapolis, IN	800-428-6179
ICS Books, Merrillville, IN	800-541-7323
Ideals Publishing, Nashville, TN	800-558-4383
IEEE Computer Society Press, Los Alamitos, CA	800-272-6657
IFSTA/Fire Protection Publications, Stillwater, OK	800-654-4055
Igaku-Shoin Medical Publishers, New York, NY	800-765-0800
Ignatius Press, San Francisco, CA	800-322-1531
InBook, East Haven, CT	800-253-3605
Incentive Publications, Nashville, TN	800-421-2830
Indiana University Press, Bloomington, IN	800-842-6796
Infinity Impressions Ltd., Mendham, NJ	800-926-7696
Information Guides, Hermosa Beach, CA	800-347-3257
Information Resources Press, Arlington, VA	800-451-7363
Initiatives Publishing, Knoxville, TN	800-873-6463
Inner Traditions International Ltd., Rochester, VT	800-445-6638;
	VT call collect 802-878-0315
Institute for International Economics, Washington, DC	800-229-3226
Institute for Palestine Studies, Washington, DC	800-874-3614
Instrument Society of America, Research Triangle Park, NC	800-334-6391
Insurance Information Institute Press, New York, NY	800-331-9146
Intercultural Press, Yarmouth, ME	800-359-5488
International Center for Creative Thinking, Mamaroneck, NY	800-328-4465
International Library-Book Publishers Inc., Gaithersburg, MD	800-359-3349

Publisher/Distributor	Toll-Free No.
International Linguistics Corp., Kansas City, MO	800-237-1830
International Marine Publishing, Rockport, ME	800-822-8138
International Wealth Success, Merrick, NY	800-323-0548
Interpersonal Communication Programs Inc., Littleton, CO	800-328-5099
Interstate Publishers, Danville, IL	800-843-4774
Interurban Press, Glendale, CA	800-899-8722
InterVarsity Press, Downers Grove, IL	800-843-7225
Iron Crown Enterprises Inc., Charlottesville, CA	800-457-4263
Richard D. Irwin Inc., Homewood, IL	Continental US 800-634-3961
Ishiyaku EuroAmerica Inc., St. Louis, MO	800-633-1921
Island Press, Washington, DC	800-828-1302
Ivory Tower Publishing, Watertown, MA	800-322-5016
J-Mart Press, Virginia Beach, VA	800-487-4060
Jalmar Press, Rolling Hills Estates, CA	800-662-9662
Jameson Books, Ottawa, IL	800-426-1357
Jamestown Publishers, Providence, RI	800-872-7323
Jane's Information Group, Alexandria, CA	800-243-3852
Janson Publications, Providence, RI	800-322-6284
January Productions, Hawthorne, NJ	800-451-7450
Jewish Lights Publishing, Woodstock, VT	800-962-4544
Jewish Publication Society, Philadelphia, PA	800-234-3151
Jist Works Inc., Indianapolis, IN	800-648-5478
Johnson Books, Boulder, CO	800-662-2665
Johnson Institute, Minneapolis, MN	800-231-5165; MN 800-247-0484; Canada 800-447-6660
Jones & Bartlett Publishers, Boston, MA	800-832-0034
Joy Publishing, San Juan Capistrano, CA	800-783-6265
Judson Press, Valley Forge, PA	800-331-1053
K Dimension Publishers/Kingdom Publishers, Decatur, GA	800-241-4702
Kalmbach Publishing, Waukesha, WI	800-558-1544
Kaplan Press, Lewisville, NC	800-334-2014
Kar-Ben Copies Inc., Rockville, MD	800-452-7236
KC Publications, Las Vegas, NV	800-626-9673
Kendall/Hunt Publishing, Dubuque, IA	800-338-5578
Kent State University Press, Kent, OH	800-666-2211
Key Computer Publications, Louisville, KY	800-752-6083
Key Curriculum Press, Berkeley, CA	800-338-7638
Kirkbride Bible Co., Indianapolis, IN	800-428-4385
Neil A. Kjos Music Co., San Diego, CA	800-854-1592
Knightsbridge Publishing, New York, NY	800-243-4151
Alfred A. Knopf, New York, NY	800-638-6460
Knowledge Industry Publications, White Plains, NY	800-800-5474
Kodansha America Inc., New York, NY	Except NJ 800-631-8571
Kraus International Publications, Millwood, NY	800-223-8323
Kraus Reprint, Millwood, NY	800-223-8323

Publisher/Distributor	Toll-Free No.
Kregel Publications, Grand Rapids, MI	800-733-2607
Ladybird Books, Auburn, ME	800-523-9247
Lake Publishing, Belmont, CA	800-877-4283
Lakewood Publications, Minneapolis, MN	800-328-4329
Lambert Gann Publishing, Pomeroy, WA	800-228-0324
Langenscheidt Publishers, Maspeth, NY	800-432-6277
Lawyers Co-Operative Publishing, Rochester, NY	800-527-0430
Lea & Febiger, Malvern, PA	800-444-1785
Learning Publications, Holmes Beach, FL	800-222-1525
Learning Resources Network, Manhattan, KS	800-678-5376
Learning Works, Santa Barbara, CA	800-235-5767
J. Hardy Lewin, Newton Centre, MA	800-334-7510
Lerner Publications, Minneapolis, MN	800-328-4929
Lewis Publishers/CRC Press, Chelsea, MI	800-272-7737
Libraries Unlimited, Englewood, CO	800-237-6124
Life Action Press, Los Angeles, CA	800-367-2246
Liguori Publications, Liguori, MO	800-325-9521
Lincoln Institute of Land Policy, Cambridge, MA	800-848-7236
LinguiSystems Inc., East Moline, IL	800-776-4332
Linton Day Publishing, Stone Mountain, GA	800-927-0409
Lion Publishing, Batavia, IL	800-447-5466
J. B. Lippincott, Philadelphia, PA	MA 800-638-3030; PA 800-242-7737
Little, Brown & Co., Boston, MA	800-343-9204
Liturgical Publications, New Berlin, WI	800-876-4574
Liturgy Training Publications, Chicago, IL	800-933-1800
Llewellyn Publications, St. Paul, MN	800-843-6666
Lloyd's of London Press, New York, NY	800-955-6937
Loizeaux Brothers, Neptune, NJ	800-526-2796
Lone Eagle Publishing, Los Angeles, CA	800-345-6257
Lonely Planet Publications, Oakland, CA	800-229-0122
Rey Longhurst, West Jordan, UT	800-347-5163
Longman Publishing Group, White Plains, NY	800-447-2226
Longriver Books/Truck Press, East Haven, CT	800-243-0138
Longstreet Press, Marietta, GA	800-927-1488
Lothrop, Lee & Shepard Books, New York, NY	800-843-9389
Lotus Light Publications, Wilmot, WI	800-548-3824
Loyola University Press, Chicago, IL	800-621-1008
Lucent Books, San Diego, CA	800-231-5163
LuraMedia Inc., San Diego, CA	800-367-5872
M & H Publishing, LaGrange, TX	800-521-9950
M & T Books, Redwood City, CA	800-533-4372; CA 800-356-2002
McCutchan Publishing, Berkeley, CA	800-227-1540
Mage Publishers, Washington, DC	800-962-0922
Magna Publications, Madison, WI	800-433-0499
Manning, St. Louis, MO	800-878-8093

Publisher/Distributor	Toll-Free No.
Mariposa Publishing, St. Paul, MN	800-735-3001
Market Data Retrieval, Shelton, CT	800-333-8802
Marketcom, Fenton, MO	800-325-3884
Marlor Press, St. Paul, MN	800-669-4908
Marquis Who's Who, Wilmette, IL	800-621-9669
Master Books, El Cajon, CA	800-999-3777
MasterMedia Ltd., New York, NY	800-334-8232
Masters Press, Grand Rapids, MI	800-722-2677
Mathematical Assn. of America, Washington, DC	800-331-1622
Maverick Publications, Bend, OR	800-627-7932
Mayfair Games, Niles, IL	800-432-4376
Mayfield Publishing, Mountain View, CA	800-433-1279
Meadowbrook Press, Deephaven, MN	800-338-2232
R. S. Means Co., Kingston, MA	800-448-8182
Meckler Publishing, Westport, CT	800-635-5537
Media & Methods, Philadelphia, PA	800-523-4540
Media Publishing, Lincoln, NE	800-366-3342
Melius Publishing, Aberdeen, SD	800-882-5171
Menasha Ridge Press, Birmingham, AL	800-247-9437
Mercer Inc., New York, NY	800-348-7583
Mercer University Press, Macon, GA	800-637-2378; 800-342-0841
Mercury House, San Francisco, CA	800-926-9292
Merriam-Webster, Springfield, MA	800-828-1880
Mesorah Publications, Brooklyn, NY	800-637-6724
Metal Bulletin, New York, NY	800-638-2525
Metamorphous Press, Portland, OR	800-937-7771
Michelin Travel Publications, Greenville, SC	800-423-0485; 800-223-0987
Michie Co., Charlottesville, VA	800-446-3410
Microsoft Press, Redmond, WA	800-677-7377
Midwest Plan Service, Ames, IA	800-562-3618
Milady Publishing, Albany, NY	800-836-5239
HBJ Miller Accounting Publications, San Diego, CA	800-543-1918
Milliken Publishing, St. Louis, MO	800-325-4136; MO 800-333-7323
Mills & Sanderson Publishers, Bedford, MA	800-441-6224
Minerva Books, New York, NY	800-345-5946
Minnesota Historical Society Press, St. Paul, MN	800-647-7827
MIT Press, Cambridge, MA	800-356-0343
Mitchell Publishing, Watsonville, CA	800-435-2665
Monday Morning Books, Palo Alto, CA	800-435-7234
Moody Press, Chicago, IL	800-678-8812
Moon Publications, Chico, CA	800-345-5473
Moonbeam Publications, Grosse Pointe, MI	800-445-2391
More Than a Card Inc., New Orleans, LA	800-635-9672
Thomas More Press, Chicago, IL	800-835-8965
Morehouse Publishing, Ridgefield, CT	800-877-0012
Morgan-Rand, Philadelphia, PA	800-441-3839
Morrow Junior Books, New York, NY	800-843-9389

Publisher/Distributor	Toll-Free No.
William Morrow & Co., New York, NY	800-843-9389
Mosby-Year Book, St. Louis, MO	800-325-4177
Motorbooks International Publishers & Wholesalers, Osceola, WI	800-826-6600; 800-458-0454
Mountain Press Publishing, Missoula, MT	800-234-5308
Mountaineers Books, Seattle, WA	800-553-4453
Moyer Bell Ltd., Mount Kisco, NY	800-759-4100
John Muir Publications, Santa Fe, NM	800-888-7504
Multnomah Press, Portland, OR	800-547-5890
Munchkin Publications Etcetera, Lynbrook, NY	800-247-6553
Municipal Analysis Services, Austin, TX	800-488-3932
Mike Murach & Associates, Fresno, CA	800-221-5528
MUSA Video Publishing, Dallas, TX	800-421-5355
Music Sales Corp., New York, NY	800-431-7187
Naiad Press, Tallahassee, FL	800-533-1973
National Academy Press, Washington, DC	800-624-6242
National Assn. of Broadcasters, Washington, DC	800-368-5644
National Assn. of Social Workers, Silver Spring, MD	800-638-8799
National Council on Radiation Protection & Measurements, Bethesda, MD	800-229-2652
National Geographic Society, Washington, DC	800-638-4077
National Health Publishing, Baltimore, MD	800-446-2221
National Information Center for Educational Media, Albuquerque, NM	800-468-3453
National Institute for Trial Advocacy, Notre Dame, IN	800-225-6482
National Learning Corp., Syosset, NY	800-645-6337
National Practice Institute, Minneapolis, MN	800-328-4444
National Press, Bethesda, MD	800-622-6657
National Publishing, Philadelphia, PA	800-631-1970
National Reference Press, Wilmette, IL	800-621-9669
National Textbook Co., Lincolnwood, IL	800-323-4900
Naval Institute Press, Annapolis, MD	800-233-8764
NavPress, Colorado Springs, CO	800-366-7788
Nelson Publications, Port Chester, NY	800-333-6357
Thomas Nelson Inc., Nashville, TN	800-251-4000
Network Publications, Santa Cruz, CA	800-321-4407
New City Press, Brooklyn, NY	800-462-5980
New Creation Publishing Group, Stone Ridge, NY	800-875-4325
New Dimensions in Education Inc., Waterford, CT	800-227-9120
New Directions Publishing, New York, NY	PA 800-233-4830
New Harbinger Publications, Oakland, CA	800-748-6273
New Horizon Press, Far Hills, NJ	800-533-7978
New Leaf Press, Green Forest, AR	800-643-9535
New Readers Press, Syracuse, NY	800-448-8878
New Society Publishers, Philadelphia, PA	800-333-9093
New World Library, San Rafael, CA	800-227-3900; CA 800-632-2122

Publisher/Distributor	Toll-Free No.
New York Academy of Sciences, New York, NY	800-843-6927
New York Zoetrope, New York, NY	800-242-7546
Noble Press, Chicago, IL	800-486-7737
Nolo Press, Berkeley, CA	800-992-6656; CA 800-640-6656
Norman Publishing, San Francisco, CA	800-544-9359
North Light Books, Cincinnati, OH	800-289-0963
North-South Books, New York, NY	800-282-8257
Northland Publishing, Flagstaff, AZ	800-346-3257
NorthWord Press, Minocqua, WI	800-336-6398
Jeffrey Norton Publishers, Guilford, CT	800-243-1234
W. W. Norton & Co., New York, NY	800-233-4830
Nucleus Publications, Willow Springs, MO	800-762-6595
Oakwood Publications, Torrance, CA	800-326-2671
Ocean Sport Fishing, Point Pleasant, NJ	800-553-4745
Ohara Publications Inc, Santa Clarita, CA	800-423-2874
Ohio University Press, Athens, OH	800-666-2211
Oliver-Nelson Books, Nashville, TN	800-251-4000
Oliver Wight Ltd. Publications, Essex Junction, VT	800-343-0625
OMF Books, Robesonia, PA	800-422-5330
Omnigraphics Inc., Detroit, MI	800-234-1340
Open Court Publishing, Peru, IL	800-435-6850; IL 800-892-6831
Open Horizons Publishing, Fairfield, IA	800-669-0773
Orbis Books, Maryknoll, NY	800-258-5838
Orchard Books, New York, NY	800-433-3411
Orchard House, Concord, MA	800-423-1303
O'Reilly & Associates, Sebastopol, CA	800-338-6887
Orion Research Corp., Durango, CO	800-748-1984
Oryx Press, Phoenix, AZ	800-279-6799
Our Sunday Visitor Publishing, Huntington, IN	800-348-2440
Outlet Book, New York, NY	800-526-4264
Overmountain Press, Johnson City, TN	800-992-2691
Richard C. Owen Publishers, Katonah, NY	800-336-5588
Oxbridge Communications, New York, NY	800-955-0231
Oxford University Press, New York, NY	800-451-7556
Oxmoor House, Birmingham, AL	800-366-4712
Pacific Press Publishing, Boise, ID	800-447-7377
Paladin Press, Boulder, CO	800-392-2400
Palindrome Press, Washington, DC	800-843-5990
Panoptic Enterprises, Woodbridge, VA	800-594-4766
Pantheon Books/Schocken Books, New York, NY	800-638-6460
PAR Publishers, Homewood, IL	800-634-3961
Para Publishing, Santa Barbara, CA	800-727-2782
Paragon House, New York, NY	800-727-2466
Parenting Press, Seattle, WA	800-922-6657
Parker & Son Publications, Carlsbad, CA	800-452-9873

Publisher/Distributor	Toll-Free No.
Parkside Publishing, Park Ridge, IL	800-221-6364
Pathway Press, Cleveland, TN	800-553-8506
Patrice Press, St. Louis, MO	800-367-9242
Patrick's Press, Columbus, GA	800-654-1052
Neil Patterson Publishers, Burlington, NC	800-227-1150
PBC International Inc., Glen Cove, NY	800-527-2826
Peachpit Press, Berkeley, CA	800-283-9444
Peachtree Publishers, Atlanta, GA	800-241-0113
Pelican Publishing, Gretna, LA	800-843-4558
PennWell Publishing, Tulsa, OK	800-752-9764
Per Annum Inc., New York, NY	800-548-1108
Perfection Form Co., Des Moines, IA	800-762-2999
Pergamon Press, Elmsford, NY	800-257-5755
Perma Bound Books, Jacksonville, IL	800-637-6581
Personal Selling Power Inc., Fredericksburg, VA	800-752-7355
Peter Pauper Press, White Plains, NY	800-833-2311
Peterson's Guides, Princeton, NJ	800-338-3282
Phanes Press, Grand Rapids, MI	800-678-0392
Pharos Books, New York, NY	800-221-4816
Phi Delta Kappa Educational Foundation, Bloomington, IN	800-766-1156
Philosophical Library, New York, NY	800-336-6050
PIA Press, Summit, NJ	800-526-4494 ext 9191
Picture Book Studio, Saxonville, MA	800-462-1252
Pierian Press, Ann Arbor, MI	800-678-2435
Planning Communications, River Forest, IL	800-829-5220
Pleasant Co., Middleton, WI	800-233-0264
Plenum Publishing, New York, NY	800-221-9369
PMA Publishing, Costa Mesa, CA	800-654-4425
Popular Culture Ink, Ann Arbor, MI	800-678-8828
Positive Parenting Inc., Phoenix, AZ	800-334-3143
Clarkson N. Potter Publishers, New York, NY	800-526-4264
Powerhouse Publishing, Fawnskin, CA	800-366-3119
Prairie House, Fargo, ND	800-866-2665
Prakken Publications, Ann Arbor, MI	800-530-9673
Precept Press, Chicago, IL	800-225-3775
Presbyterian & Reformed Publishing, Phillipsburg, NJ	800-631-0094
Preservation Press, Washington, DC	800-677-6847
Presidio Press, Novato, CA	800-966-5179
Price Stern Sloan Inc., Los Angeles, CA	800-421-0892
Princeton Architectural Press, New York, NY	800-458-1131
Princeton Book Co. Publishers, Pennington, NJ	800-326-7149
Princeton University Press, Princeton, NJ	800-777-4726
Printers Shopper, Chula Vista, CA	800-854-2911
Pro Lingua Associates, Brattleboro, VT	800-366-4775
Probus Publishing, Chicago, IL	800-776-2871
Productivity Press, Cambridge, MA	800-274-9911
Professional Publications, Belmont, CA	800-426-1178

Publisher/Distributor	Toll-Free No.
Professional Resource Exchange, Sarasota, FL	800-443-3364
Programs for Education, Rosemont, NJ	800-627-5867
Prometheus Books, Buffalo, NY	800-421-0351
Pruett Publishing, Boulder, CO	800-247-8224
Psychological Assessment Resources Inc., Lutz, FL	800-331-8378
The Psychological Corp., San Antonio, TX	800-228-0752
Purple Mountain Press, Fleischmanns, NY	800-325-2665
Putnam Berkley Group, New York, NY	800-631-8571
PWS-Kent Publishing, Boston, MA	800-343-2204
QED Technical Publishing Group, Wellesley, MA	800-343-4848
Quail Ridge Press, Brandon, MS	800-343-1583
Quality Medical Publishing, St. Louis, MO	800-423-6865
Quality Press, Milwaukee, WI	800-248-1946
Quality Resources, White Plains, NY	800-247-8519
Quantum Books, Mill Valley, CA	800-441-4372
Questar Publishers, Sisters, OR	800-933-7526
Quintessence Publishing, Carol Stream, IL	800-621-0387
Rainbow Books, Moore Haven, FL	800-356-9315
Raintree/Steck-Vaughn Publishers, Milwaukee, WI	800-558-7264
RAM Research Publishing, Frederick, MD	800-344-7714
Rand McNally, Skokie, IL	800-323-4070
Random House, New York, NY	800-726-0600
Rapha Publishing, Houston, TX	800-542-1550
Reader's Digest, Pleasantville, NY	800-431-1726
Recovery Publications, San Diego, CA	800-873-8384
Recruiting & Search Report, Panama City Beach, FL	800-634-4548
Regal Books, Ventura, CA	800-235-3415
Regnery Gateway Inc., Washington, DC	800-462-6420
Regular Baptist Press, Schaumburg, IL	800-727-4440
Research Books, Madison, CT	800-445-7359
Research Publications, Woodbridge, CT	800-444-0799
Resource Media, Philadelphia, PA	800-441-3839
Retail Reporting Corp., New York, NY	800-251-4545
Retail Strategies & Publishing, Overland Park, KS	800-733-6160
Fleming H. Revell Co., Tarrytown, NY	800-631-1970
Review & Herald Publishing Association, Hagerstown, MD	800-234-7630
Riverside Publishing, Chicago, IL	800-323-9540
Rizzoli International Publications, New York, NY	800-433-1238
Rockwell Publishing, Redmond, WA	800-221-9347
Rodale Press, Emmaus, PA	800-441-7761
Roper Press, Dallas, TX	800-284-0158
Rosen Publishing Group, New York, NY	800-237-9932
Ross Books, Berkeley, CA	800-367-0930
Norman Ross Publishing, New York, NY	800-648-8850
Roth Publishing, Great Neck, NY	800-327-0295

Publisher/Distributor	Toll-Free No.
Fred B. Rothman & Co., Littleton, CO	800-457-1986
Roundtable Publishing, Malibu, CA	800-222-5322
Running Press Book Publishers, Philadelphia, PA	800-345-5359
Russell Meerdink Co., Menasha, WI	800-635-6499
Russell Sage Foundation, New York, NY	800-666-2211
Rutgers University Press, New Brunswick, NJ	800-446-9323
Rutledge Hill Press, Nashville, TN	800-234-4234
William H. Sadlier Inc., New York, NY	800-221-5175
Sagamore Publishing, Champaign, IL	800-327-5557
St. Anthony Messenger Press, Cincinnati, OH	800-488-0488
St. James Press, Chicago, IL	800-345-0392
St. Martin's Press, New York, NY	800-221-7945
St. Mary's Press, Winona, MN	800-533-8095
Salem Press, Englewood Cliffs, NJ	800-221-1592
Salesman's Guide, New Providence, NJ	800-223-1797
Sams, Carmel, IN	800-628-7460
Sania Publishing Corp. & CompuPress, Albuquerque, NM	800-873-2363
Santillana Publishing, Compton, CA	800-245-8584
W. B. Saunders Co., Philadelphia, PA	800-545-2522
K. G. Saur, New Providence, NJ	800-521-8110
Scarecrow Press, Metuchen, NJ	800-537-7107
Scholarly Resources Inc., Wilmington, DE	800-772-8937
Scholars Press, Atlanta, GA	800-437-6692
Scholastic Inc., New York, NY	800-392-2179
Scholastic Professional Books, New York, NY	800-325-6149
School Zone Publishing, Grand Haven, MI	800-253-0564
Scientific Press, San Francisco, CA	800-451-5409
Scott, Foresman & Co., Glenview, IL	800-782-2665
Scott Publications, Livonia, MI	800-458-8237
Scott Publishing, Sidney, OH	800-448-3611; OH 800-327-1259
Scripture Press Publications, Wheaton, IL	800-323-9409
Self-Counsel Press, Bellingham, WA	800-663-3007
Selous Foundation Press, Washington, DC	800-255-1906
Sentinel Books, Orlando, FL	800-347-6868
Serif Publishing, El Segundo, CA	800-762-4496
Servant Publications, Ann Arbor, MI	800-458-8505; MI 800-533-8505
Seven Locks Press, Cabin John, MD	800-537-9359
Shambhala Publications, Boston, MA	800-638-6460
Shapolsky Publishers, New York, NY	800-288-8889
M. E. Sharpe Inc., Armonk, NY	800-541-6563
Harold Shaw Publishers, Wheaton, IL	800-742-9782
Sheed & Ward, Kansas City, MO	800-333-7373; 800-444-8910
Signature Books, Salt Lake City, UT	800-356-5687
Silver Burdett Press, Englewood Cliffs, NJ	800-843-3464
Simon & Schuster, New York, NY	800-223-2348; 800-223-2336
Skidmore-Roth Publishing, El Paso, TX	800-825-3150

Publisher/Distributor	Toll-Free No.
Skillpath Publications, Mission, KS	800-873-7545
Slack Inc., Thorofare, NJ	800-257-8290
Slawson Communications, San Marcos, CA	800-752-9766
Gibbs Smith Publisher, Layton, UT	800-421-8714
Smithmark Publishers, New York, NY	800-645-9990
Smithsonian Institution Press, Washington, DC	800-678-2675
Snow Lion Publications, Ithaca, NY	800-950-0313
Society for Industrial & Applied Mathematics, Philadelphia, PA	800-447-7426
Society of Manufacturing Engineers, Dearborn, MI	800-733-4763
Solitaire Publishing, Tampa, FL	800-226-0286
Sophia Institute Press, Manchester, NH	800-888-9344
Soundprints Corp., Norwalk, CT	800-228-7839
South Carolina Bar, Columbia, SC	800-768-7787
South-Western Publishing, Cincinnati, OH	800-543-0487
Southern Illinois University Press, Carbondale, IL	Prepaid orders only 800-848-4270 Ext. 950
Southern Institute Press, Indian Rocks Beach, FL	800-633-4891
Specialty Press, Stillwater, MN	800-888-9653
Spoken Arts Inc., Pinellas Park, FL	800-726-8090
Springer-Verlag New York Inc., New York, NY	800-777-4643
Springhouse Corp., Springhouse, PA	800-346-7844
SPSS Inc., Chicago, IL	800-543-9263
SRA (Science Research Associates), Chicago, IL	School 800-621-0476 ISED orders 800-772-1277
ST Publications Book Division, Cincinnati, OH	800-543-1925
Stackpole Books, Harrisburg, PA	800-732-3669
Standard Publishing, Cincinnati, OH	800-543-1301
Star Books, Wilson, NC	800-476-1591
Starburst Publishers, Lancaster, PA	800-441-1456
State University of New York Press, Albany, NY	800-666-2211
Statesman Examiner Inc., Colville, WA	800-488-5676
Steck-Vaughn Co., Austin, TX	800-531-5015
Sterling Publishing, New York, NY	800-367-9692
Steven J. Nash Publishing, Highland Park, IL	800-843-8545
Stewart, Tabori & Chang, Publishers, New York, NY	800-722-7202
Stillpoint Publishing International, Walpole, NH	800-847-4014
Stockton Press, New York, NY	800-221-2123
Stoeger Publishing, South Hackensack, NJ	800-631-0722
Strang Communications Co./Creation House, Altamonte Springs, FL	800-451-4598
Lyle Stuart, New York, NY	800-572-6657
Studio Press, Soulsbyville, CA	800-445-7160
Sulzburger & Graham Publishing, New York, NY	800-366-7086
Summit University Press, Livingston, MT	800-323-5228
Sunset Books, Menlo Park, CA	800-227-7346
Sunstone Publications, Cooperstown, NY	800-327-0306
Surrey Books, Chicago, IL	800-326-4430
SYBEX Inc, Alameda, CA	800-227-2346

Publisher/Distributor	Toll-Free No.
Syracuse University Press, Syracuse, NY	800-365-8929
TAB Books, Blue Ridge Summit, PA	800-233-1128
Tabor Publishing, Allen, TX	800-527-4747
Taft Group, Rockville, MD	800-877-8238
Tambourine Books, New York, NY	800-843-9389
Taterhill Press, Santa Cruz, CA	800-366-5163
Taunton Press, Newtown, CT	800-283-7252; 800-888-8286
Taylor Publishing, Dallas, TX	Voice & FAX 800-677-2800
Teach Me Tapes Inc., Minneapolis, MN	800-456-4656
Teacher Ideas Press, Englewood, CO	800-237-6124
Teachers College Press, New York, NY	800-445-6638
Teachers Friend Publications, Riverside, CA	800-343-9680
Technical Association of the Pulp and Paper Industry, Atlanta, GA	800-332-8686
Technomic Publishing, Lancaster, PA	800-233-9936
Telecom Library Inc., New York, NY	800-542-7279
Templegate Publishers, Springfield, IL	800-367-4844
Ten Speed Press, Berkeley, CA	800-841-2665
Texas A & M University Press, College Station, TX	800-826-8911
Texas Tech University Press, Lubbock, TX	800-832-4042
TFH Publications, Neptune, NJ	800-631-2188
Thames & Hudson Inc., New York, NY	800-233-4830
That Patchwork Place Inc., Bothell, WA	800-426-3126
Theosophical Publishing House, Wheaton, IL	800-669-9425
Thieme Medical Publishers, New York, NY	800-782-3488
Thinkers Press, Davenport, IA	800-397-7117
Thinking Publications, Eau Claire, WI	800-225-4769
Third World Press, Chicago, IL	800-527-8340
Thomasson-Grant Publishers, Charlottesville, VA	800-999-1780
Thomson Financial Publishing, Skokie, IL	800-444-0064
Thomson Professional Publishing, Englewood Cliffs, NJ	800-562-0245
Tidewater Publishers, Centreville, MD	800-638-7641
Time Life Inc., Alexandria, VA	800-621-7026
Times Books, New York, NY	800-733-3000
Tiny Thought Press, Louisville, KY	800-456-3208
Tor Books, New York, NY	800-221-7945
Torah Aura Productions, Los Angeles, CA	800-238-6724
Tower Publishing, Portland, ME	800-287-7323
Toys N Things Press, St. Paul, MN	800-423-8309
Traders Press, Greenville, SC	800-927-8222
Trails Illustrated, Evergreen, CO	800-962-1643
Trakker Maps Inc., Miami, FL	800-432-1730
Travel Keys, Sacramento, CA	800-872-5627
Treasure Chest Publications, Tucson, AZ	800-627-0048
Triad Publishing, Gainesville, FL	800-525-6902
Trinity Press International, Philadelphia, PA	800-523-1631
Triumph Books, Tarrytown, NY	800-631-1970

Publisher/Distributor	Toll-Free No.
Troll Associates, Mahwah, NJ	800-526-5289
TSR Inc., Lake Geneva, WI	800-372-4667
Charles E. Tuttle Co., Rutland, VT	800-526-2778
21st Century Education Inc., New York, NY	800-866-5559
Twenty-Third Publications, Mystic, CT	800-321-0411
Tyndale House Publishers, Wheaton, IL	800-323-9400
ULI-The Urban Land Institute, Washington, DC	800-462-1254
Ulverscroft Large Print Books, Guilford, CT	800-955-9659
UMI Publications, Charlotte, NC	800-462-5831
Unique Publications, Burbank, CA	800-332-3330
United Nations, New York, NY	800-253-9646
United States Pharmacopeial Convention Inc., Rockville, MD	800-227-8772
United States Tennis Assn., Princeton, NJ	800-223-0456
University Microfilms International, Ann Arbor, MI	800-521-0600; Canada 800-343-5299
University of Arizona Press, Tucson, AZ	800-426-3797
University of Arkansas Press, Fayetteville, AR	800-525-1823
University of California Press, Berkeley, CA	800-822-6657
University of Chicago Press, Chicago, IL	800-621-2736
University of Illinois Press, Champaign, IL	800-545-4703
University of Iowa Press, Iowa City, IA	800-235-2665
University of Minnesota Press, Minneapolis, MN	800-388-3863
University of Missouri Press, Columbia, MO	800-828-1894
University of Nebraska at Omaha Center for Public Affairs Research, Omaha, NE	800-227-4533
University of Nebraska Press, Lincoln, NE	800-755-1105
University of North Carolina Press, Chapel Hill, NC	800-848-6224
University of Oklahoma Press, Norman, OK	800-627-7377
University of Pennsylvania Press, Philadelphia, PA	800-445-9880
University of Pittsburgh Press, Pittsburgh, PA	800-666-2211
University of South Carolina Press, Columbia, SC	800-762-0089
University of Tennessee Press, Knoxville, TN	800-621-2736
University of Utah Press, Salt Lake City, UT	800-444-8638 Ext. 6771
University of Washington Press, Seattle, WA	800-441-4115
University Press of America, Lanham, MD	800-462-6420
University Press of Kentucky, Lexington, KY	800-666-2211
University Press of New England, Hanover, NH	800-421-1561
University Publications of America, Bethesda, MD	800-692-6300
University Publishing Group, Frederick, MD	800-654-8188
Upstart Publishing, Dover, NH	800-235-8866
US Games Systems Inc., Stamford, CT	800-544-2637
Useable Portable Publications, Winchester, MA	800-648-3166
Van Nostrand Reinhold, New York, NY	800-555-1212
VanDam Inc., New York, NY	800-321-6277
Vanderbilt University Press, Nashville, TN	800-545-4703

Publisher/Distributor	Toll-Free No.
Vantage Press, New York, NY	800-882-3273
VCH Publishers, New York, NY	800-422-8824
Victor Books, Wheaton, IL	800-323-9409
Vitesse Press, Brattleboro, VT	800-848-3747
Voyageur Press, Stillwater, MN	800-888-9653
J. Weston Walch Publisher, Portland, ME	800-341-6094
Walker & Co., New York, NY	800-289-2553
Walker Western Research Co., San Mateo, CA	800-258-5737
Wallace Homestead Book, Radnor, PA	800-695-1214
Warren, Gorham & Lamont Inc., New York, NY	800-922-0066
Waterfront Books, Burlington, VT	800-639-6063
WaterMark Inc., Homewood, AL	800-676-6371
Watson-Guptill Publications, New York, NY	800-451-1741
Franklin Watts Inc., New York, NY	800-672-6672; 800-843-3749
Weatherhill Inc., New York, NY	800-788-7323
Webster International Inc., Brentwood, TN	800-727-6833
Samuel Weiser Inc., York Beach, ME	800-423-7087
Wesleyan University Press, Middletown, CT	800-421-1561
West Publishing, St. Paul, MN	800-328-9352
Westcliffe Publishers, Englewood, CO	800-523-3692
Western Marine Enterprises Inc., Los Angeles, CA	800-292-6657
Western Psychological Services, Los Angeles, CA	800-648-8857
Western Publishing, Racine, WI	800-558-5972
Westminster Press/John Knox Press, Louisville, KY	800-523-1631
Westport Publishers, Kansas City, MO	800-347-2665
Whitaker House, Springdale, PA	800-444-4484
White Cliffs Media Co., Crown Point, IN	800-359-3210
Whitehorse Press, Boston, MA	800-842-7077
Albert Whitman & Co., Morton Grove, IL	800-255-7675
Whitney Library of Design, New York, NY	800-526-3641
Wilderness Adventure Books, Fowlerville, MI	800-852-8652
Wilderness Press, Berkeley, CA	800-443-7227
Williams & Wilkins, Baltimore, MD	800-638-0672
Williamson Publishing, Charlotte, VT	800-234-8791
H. W. Wilson Co., Bronx, NY	800-367-6770
Windsor Publications, Chatsworth, CA	800-678-2574
Windward Publishing, Miami, FL	FL 800-330-6232
Wine Appreciation Guild, San Francisco, CA	800-242-9462
Winston-Derek Publishers, Nashville, TN	800-826-1888
Wisdom Publications, Boston, MA	800-272-4050
Woldt Publishing, Sarasota, FL	800-768-4738
Wolfe Publishing, Prescott, AZ	800-899-7810
Kaye Wood Publishing, West Branch, MI	800-248-5293
Woodbine House, Rockville, MD	800-843-7323
Woodbridge Press Publishing, Santa Barbara, CA	800-237-6053
Woodland Books, Provo, UT	800-777-2665

Publisher/Distributor	Toll-Free No.
Word Inc., Irving, TX	800-433-3340
Wordware Publishing, Plano, TX	800-229-4949
Workman Publishing, New York, NY	800-722-7202
World Bible Publishers, Iowa Falls, IA	800-247-5111
World Book, Chicago, IL	800-621-8202
World Eagle Inc., Wellesley, MA	800-634-3805
World Scientific Publishing, River Edge, NJ	800-227-7562
Wright Group, Bothell, WA	800-523-2371; 800-345-6073
Write Source Educational Publishing House, Burlington, WI	800-445-8613
Writer's Digest Books, Cincinnati, OH	800-289-0963
Wynwood Press, Tarrytown, NY	800-631-1970
Wyrick & Co., Charleston, SC	800-227-5898
Yankee Books, Camden, ME	800-955-0933
Ye Galleon Press, Fairfield, WA	800-621-1504
YMAA Publication Center, Jamaica Plan, MA	800-669-8892
Young Discovery Library, Ossining, NY	800-343-7854
Zaner-Bloser Inc., Columbus, OH	800-421-3018
Zebra Books, New York, NY	800-221-2647
Ziff-Davis Press, Emeryville, CA	800-688-0448
Zondervan Publishing House, Grand Rapids, MI	800-727-1309

How to Obtain an ISBN

Emery Koltay

Director
United States ISBN Agency

The International Standard Book Numbering (ISBN) system was introduced into the United Kingdom by J. Whitaker & Sons, Ltd., in 1967 and into the United States in 1968 by R. R. Bowker Company. The Technical Committee on Documentation of the International Organization for Standardization (ISO TC 46) defines the scope of the standard as follows:

. . . the purpose of this standard is to coordinate and standardize the use of identifying numbers so that each ISBN is unique to a title, edition of a book, or monographic publication published, or produced, by a specific publisher, or producer. Also, the standard specifies the construction of the ISBN and the location of the printing on the publication.

Books and other monographic publications may include printed books and pamphlets (in various bindings), mixed media publications, other similar media including educational films/videos and transparencies, books on cassettes, microcomputer software, electronic publications, microform publications, braille publications and maps. Serial publications and music sound recordings are specifically excluded, as they are covered by other identification systems. [ISO Standard 2108]

The ISBN is used by publishers, distributors, wholesalers, bookstores, and libraries, among others, in 77 countries to expedite such operations as order fulfillment, electronic point-of-sale checkout, inventory control, returns processing, circulation/location control, file maintenance and update, library union lists, and royalty payments.

Construction of an ISBN

An ISBN consists of 10 digits separated into the following parts:

1 Group identifier: national, geographic, language, or other convenient group
2 Publisher or producer identifier
3 Title identifier
4 Check digit

When an ISBN is written or printed, it should be preceded by the letters *ISBN*, and each part should be separated by a space or hyphen. In the United States, the hyphen is used for separation, as in the following example: ISBN 1-879500-01-9. In this example, 1 is the group identifier, 879500 is the publisher identifier, 01 is the title identifier, and 9 is the check digit. The group of English-speaking countries, which includes the United States, Australia, Canada, New Zealand, and the United Kingdom, uses the group identifiers 0 and 1.

The ISBN Organization

The administration of the ISBN system is carried out at three levels—through the International ISBN Agency in Berlin, Germany; the national agencies; and the publishing houses themselves. Responsible for assigning country prefixes and for coordinating the worldwide implementation of the system, the International ISBN Agency in Berlin has an advisory panel that represents the International Organization for Standardization (ISO), publishers, and libraries. The International ISBN Agency publishes the *ISBN System User's Manual*—the basic guide for all national agencies—and the *Publishers International ISBN Directory*, which is distributed in the United States by R. R. Bowker. As the publisher of *Books in Print*, with its extensive and varied database of publishers' addresses, R. R. Bowker was the obvious place to initiate the ISBN system and from which to provide the service to the U.S. publishing industry. To date, the U.S. ISBN Agency has entered more than 60,000 publishers into the system.

ISBN Assignment Procedure

Assignment of ISBNs is a shared endeavor between the U.S. ISBN Agency and the publisher. The publisher is provided with an application form, an Advanced Book Information (ABI) form, and an instruction sheet. After an application is received and verified by the agency, an ISBN publisher prefix is assigned, along with a computer-generated block of ISBNs. The publisher then has the responsibility to assign an ISBN to each title, to keep an accurate record of the numbers assigned by entering each title in the ISBN Log Book, and to report each title to the *Books in Print* database. One of the responsibilities of the ISBN Agency is to validate assigned ISBNs and to retain a record of all ISBNs in circulation.

ISBN implementation is very much market driven. Wholesalers and distributors, such as Baker & Taylor, Brodart, and Ingram, as well as such large retail chains as Waldenbooks and B. Dalton, recognize and enforce the ISBN system by requiring all new publishers to register with the ISBN Agency before accepting their books for sale. Also, the ISBN is a mandatory bibliographic element in the International Standard Bibliographical Description (ISBD). The Library of Congress Cataloging in Publication (CIP) Division directs publishers to the agency to obtain their ISBN prefixes.

Location and Display of the ISBN

On books, pamphlets, and other printed material, the ISBN shall be on the verso of the title leaf or, if this is not possible, at the foot of the title leaf itself. It should also appear at the foot of the outside back cover if practicable and at the foot of the back of the jacket if the book has one (the lower right-hand corner is recommended). If neither of these alternatives is possible, then the number shall be printed in some other prominent position on the outside. The ISBN shall also appear on any accompanying promotional materials following the provisions for location according to the format of the material.

On other monographic publications, the ISBN shall appear on the title or credit frames and any labels permanently affixed to the publication. If the publication is issued in a container that is an integral part of the publication, such as a cassette or microcomputer software, the ISBN shall be displayed on the label. If it is not possible to place the ISBN on the item or its label, then the number should be displayed on the bottom or the back of the container, box, sleeve, or frame. It should also appear on any accompanying material, including each component of a multitype publication.

Printing of ISBN in Machine-Readable Coding

In the last few years, much work has been done on machine-readable representations of the ISBN, and now all books should carry ISBNs in bar code. The rapid worldwide extension of bar code scanning has brought into prominence the 1980 agreement between the International Article Numbering, formerly the European Article Numbering (EAN), Association and the International ISBN Agency, which allows the ISBN to be translated into an EAN bar code.

All EAN bar codes start with a national identifier (00–09 representing the United States), *except* those on books and periodicals. The agreement replaces the usual national identifier with a special "Bookland" identifier represented by the digits 978 for books (see example) and 977 for periodicals. The 978 Bookland/EAN prefix is followed by the first nine digits of the ISBN. The check digit of the ISBN is dropped and replaced by a check digit calculated according to the EAN rules (see Figure 1).

Figure 1 / Printing the ISBN in Bookland/EAN Symbology

The following is an example of the conversion of the ISBN to ISBN Bookland/EAN:

ISBN	1-879500-01-9
ISBN without check digit	1-879500-01
Adding EAN flag	978187950001
EAN with EAN check digit	9781879500013

Five-Digit Add-On Code

In the United States, a five-digit add-on code is used for additional information. In the publishing industry, this code can be used for price information or some other specific coding. The lead digit of the five-digit add-on has been designated a currency identifier, when the add-on is used for price. Number 5 is the code for the U.S. dollar; number 6 is for the Canadian dollar. Currency identifiers for other English-speaking countries will be determined in the future. Publishers that do not want to indicate price in the add-on should print the code 90000 (see Figure 2).

Figure 2 / Printing the ISBN Bookland/EAN Number in Bar Code with the Five-Digit Add-On Code

978 = ISBN Bookland/EAN prefix
5 = Code for U.S. $
0995 = $9.95

90000 means no information
in the add-on code

Reporting the Title and the ISBN

After the publisher reports a title to the ISBN Agency, the number is validated and the title is listed in the many R. R. Bowker hard-copy and electronic publications, including *Books in Print, Forthcoming Books, Paperbound Books in Print, Books in Print Supplement, Books Out of Print, Books in Print Online, Books in Print Plus-CD ROM, Children's Books in Print, Subject Guide to Children's Books in Print, On*

Cassette: A Comprehensive Bibliography of Spoken Word Audiocassettes, Variety's Complete Home Video Directory, Software Encyclopedia, Software for Schools, and other specialized publications.

For an ISBN application form and additional information, write to United States ISBN Agency, R. R. Bowker Company, 121 Chanlon Rd., New Providence, NJ 07974, or call 908-665-6770.

How to Obtain an ISSN

Julia C. Blixrud

Head, National Serials Data Program,
Library of Congress

Two decades ago, the rapid increase in the production and dissemination of information and an intensified desire to exchange information about serials in computerized form among different systems and organizations made it increasingly clear that a means to identify serial publications at an international level was needed. The International Standard Serial Number (ISSN) was developed and has become the internationally accepted code for identifying serial publications. The number itself has no significance other than as a brief, unique, and unambiguous identifier. It is an international standard, ISO 3297, as well as a U.S. standard, ANSI/NISO Z39.9. The ISSN consists of eight digits in arabic numerals 0 to 9, except for the last, or check, digit, which can be an X. The numbers appear as two groups of four digits separated by a hyphen and preceded by the letters ISSN—for example, ISSN 1234-5679.

The ISSN is not self-assigned by publishers. Administration of the ISSN is coordinated through the International Serials Data System (ISDS), an intergovernmental organization within the UNESCO/UNISIST program. ISDS is a network of national and regional centers, coordinated by an international center. Centers have the responsibility to register serials published in their respective countries.

Because serials are generally known and cited by title, assignment of the ISSN is inseparably linked to the key title, a standardized form of the title derived from information in the serial issue. Only one ISSN can be assigned to a title; if the title changes, a new ISSN must be assigned. Centers responsible for assigning ISSNs also construct the key title and create an associated bibliographic record.

The ISDS International Center handles ISSN assignments for international organizations and for countries that do not have a national center. It also maintains and distributes the collective ISDS database that contains bibliographic records corresponding to each ISSN assignment as reported by the rest of the ISDS network. The ISDS database contains more than 600,000 ISSNs.

In the United States, the National Serials Data Program at the Library of Congress is responsible for assigning and maintaining the ISSN to all U.S. serial titles. Publishers wishing to have an ISSN assigned can either request an application form from or send a current issue of the publication to the program and ask for an assignment. Assignment of the ISSN is free, and there is no charge for its use.

The ISSN is used all over the world by serial publishers to distinguish similar titles from each other. It is used by subscription services and libraries to manage files for orders, claims, and back issues. It is used in automated check-in systems by libraries that wish to process receipts more quickly. Copyright centers use the ISSN as a means to collect and disseminate royalties. It is also used as an identification code by postal services and legal deposit services. The ISSN is included as a verification element in interlibrary lending activities and for union catalogs as a collocating device. In recent years, the ISSN has been incorporated into bar codes for optical recognition of serial publications and into the standards for the identification of issues and articles in serial publications.

For further information about the ISSN or the ISDS network, U.S. libraries and publishers should contact the National Serials Data Program, Library of Congress, Washington, DC 20540 (202-707-6452). Non-U.S. parties should contact the ISDS International Center, 20 rue Bachaumont, 75002 Paris, France (1) 42.36.73.81.

Distinguished Books

Notable Books of 1991

This is the forty-fifth year in which this list of distinguished books has been issued by the Notable Books Council of the Reference and Adult Services Division of the American Library Association.

Fiction

Alvarez, Julia. *How the Garcia Girls Lost Their Accents.* Algonquin. $16.95.

Banks, Russell. *The Sweet Hereafter.* HarperCollins. $19.95.

Bly, Carol. *The Tomcat's Wife and Other Stories.* HarperCollins. $19.95.

Brown, Larry. *Joe.* Algonquin. $19.95.

Griffith, Patricia. *The World Around Midnight.* Putnam. $21.95.

Lucas, Russell. *Evenings at Mongini's and Other Stories.* Summit. $18.95.

Malone, Michael. *Foolscap.* Little Brown. $19.95.

Morris, Mary M. *A Dangerous Woman.* Viking. $19.95.

Nordan, Lewis. *Music of the Swamp.* Algonquin. $15.95.

Parks, Jim. *Goodness.* Grove Weidenfeld. $18.95.

Porter, Connie. *All-Bright Court.* Houghton. $19.95.

Tan, Amy. *The Kitchen God's Wife.* Putnam. $21.95.

Poetry

Levine, Philip. *What Work Is.* Knopf. $18.50.

Nonfiction

Campbell, Edward. *Before Freedom Came: African American Life in the Ante-Bellum South.* Univ. Press of Virginia. pap. $19.95.

Carles, Emilie. *A Life of Her Own: A Country-Woman in 20th-Century France.* Rutgers Univ. Press. $19.95.

Cary, Lorene. *Black Ice.* Knopf. $20.

Dubus, Andre. *Broken Vessels.* David Godine. pap. $19.95.

Faludi, Susan. *Backlash: The Undeclared War Against American Women.* Crown. $24.

Greene, Melissa. *Praying for Sheetrock.* Addison-Wesley. $21.95.

Klinkenberg, Verlyn. *The Last Fine Time.* Knopf. $19.95.

Kotlowitz, Alex. *There Are No Children Here.* Doubleday. $21.95.

Kozol, Jonathan. *Savage Inequalities.* Crown. $20.

Lemann, Nicholas. *The Promised Land: The Great Black Migration and How It Changed America.* Knopf. $24.95.

Lewis, R. W. B. *The Jameses: A Family Narrative.* Farrar. $35.

Radetsky, Peter. *Invisible Invaders.* Little Brown. $22.95.

Roth, Philip. *Patrimony: A True Story.* Simon & Schuster. $19.95.

Best Young Adult Books of 1991

Each year, a committee of the Young Adult Services Division of the American Library Association compiles a list of best books for young adults, selected on the basis of young adult appeal. These titles must meet acceptable standards of literary merit and provide a variety of subjects for different tastes and a broad range of reading levels. *School Library Journal (SLJ)* also provides a list of best books for young adults. The 1991 list was compiled by the Adult Books for Young Adults Committee, made up of public and school librarians, and was published in the December 1991 issue of the journal. The following list combines the titles selected for both lists. The notation "ALA" or *"SLJ"* following the price indicates the source of each selection.

Aaron, Henry. *I Had a Hammer.* HarperCollins. $21.95. ALA.

Adams, Douglas. *Last Chance to See.* Harmony. $20. ALA.

Alexander, Lloyd. *The Remarkable Journey of Prince Jen.* Dutton. $14.95. *SLJ.*

Anastos, Phillip, and Chris French. *Seeking the American Dream.* Rizzoli. pap. $19.95. ALA.

Arter, Jim. *Gruel and Unusual Punishment.* Delacorte. $13.95. ALA.

Avi. *Nothing but the Truth: A Documentary Novel.* Orchard. $14.95. ALA, *SLJ.*

Bing, Leon. *Do or Die.* HarperCollins. $19.95. ALA.

Block, Francesca Lia. *Witch Baby.* HarperCollins. $13.95. *SLJ.*

Blumberg, Rhoda. *The Remarkable Voyages of Captain Cook.* Bradbury. $18.95. *SLJ.*

Bode, Janet. *Beating the Odds: Stories of Unexpected Achievers.* Watts. $13.95. ALA.

Brooks, Bruce. *Predator.* Farrar, Straus. $13.95. ALA.

Buss, Fran Leeper. *Journey of the Sparrows.* Lodestar/Dutton. $14.95. ALA.

Cannon, A. E. *Amazing Gracie.* Delacorte. $15. ALA.

Card, Orson S. *Xenocide.* Tor. $21.95. *SLJ.*

Cary, Lorene. *Black Ice.* Knopf. $20. ALA, *SLJ.*

Choi, Sook Nyul. *Year of Impossible Goodbyes.* Houghton Mifflin. $13.95. ALA.

Cooper, J. California. *Family.* Doubleday. $18.95. ALA.

Corman, Avery. *Prized Possessions.* Simon & Schuster. $19.95. ALA.

Cormier, Robert. *We All Fall Down.* Delacorte. $16. ALA.

Counter, S. Allen. *North Pole Legacy: Black, White, and Eskimo.* Univ. of Massachusetts. $24.95. ALA.

Crichton, Michael. *Jurassic Park.* Knopf. $19.95. ALA, *SLJ.*

Crutcher, Chris. *Athletic Shorts.* Greenwillow. $13.95. ALA, *SLJ.*

Davis, Jenny. *Checking on the Moon.* Orchard. $14.95. ALA, *SLJ.*

Durham, Michael S. *Powerful Days: The Civil Rights Photography of Charles Moore.* Stewart, Tabori. pap. $24.95. ALA.

Fleischman, Paul. *The Borning Room.* HarperCollins. $13.95. ALA, *SLJ.*

Fluek, Toby Knobel. *Memories of My Life in a Polish Village: 1930–1949.* Knopf. $19.95. ALA.

Fox, Paula. *Monkey Island.* Orchard. $14.95. ALA.

Freedman, Russell. *The Wright Brothers: How They Invented the Airplane.* Photos by Wilbur Wright, Orville Wright, and others. Holiday. $16.95. ALA, *SLJ.*

Fritz, Jean. *Bully for You, Teddy Roosevelt.* Illus. by Mike Wimmer. Putnam. $15.95. *SLJ.*

Fussell, Samuel. *Muscle: Confessions of an Unlikely Bodybuilder.* Poseidon. $18.95. ALA, *SLJ.*

Gaiman, Neil, and Terry Prachett. *Good Omens: The Nice and Accurate Prophecies of Agnes Nutter, Witch.* Workman. $18.95. ALA.

Giblin, James Cross. *The Truth about Unicorns.* Illus. by Michael McDermott. HarperCollins. $14.95. *SLJ.*

Glenn, Mel. *My Friend's Got This Problem, Mr. Candler.* Clarion. $14.95. ALA.

Greenberg, Jan, and Sandra Jordan. *The Painter's Eye: Learning to Look at Contemporary American Art.* Delacorte. $20. *SLJ.*

Hall, Lynn. *Flying Changes.* Harcourt Brace Jovanovich. $13.95. ALA.

Halsey, David, and Diana Landau. *Magnetic North: A Trek Across Canada.* Sierra Club. $19.95. *SLJ.*

Harmon, William, ed. *The Concise Columbia Book of Poetry.* Columbia Univ. $27.50. *SLJ.*

Hathorn, Libby. *Thunderwith.* Little, Brown. $15.95. ALA.

Hayden, Torey. *Ghost Girl.* Little, Brown. $19.95. ALA.

Hayes, Daniel. *The Trouble With Lemons.* Godine. $14.95. ALA.

Henry, Sue. *Murder on the Iditarod Trail.* Atlantic. $17.95. ALA.

Hermes, Patricia. *Mama, Let's Dance.* Little, Brown. $14.95. *SLJ.*

Higa, Tomiko. *The Girl with the White Flag.* Kodansha. $16.95. ALA.

Hobbs, Will. *Downriver.* Macmillan. $13.95. ALA.

Hoffman, Mary. *Amazing Grace.* Illus. by Caroline Binch. Dial. $13.95. *SLJ.*

Honeycutt, Natalie. *Ask Me Something Easy.* Orchard. $13.95. ALA.

Jones, Diana Wynne. *Castle in the Air.* Greenwillow. $13.95. ALA.

Kay, Susan. *Phantom.* Delacorte. $19.95. *SLJ.*

Kingsolver, Barbara. *Animal Dreams.* HarperCollins. $21.95. ALA.

Kotlowitz, Alex. *There Are No Children Here: The Story of Two Boys Growing Up in the Other America.* Doubleday. $21.95. ALA.

Kuklin, Susan. *What Do I Do Now? Talking about Teenage Pregnancy.* Putnam. $15.95. ALA.

Landrey, Tom, and Greg Lewis. *Tom Landry: The Man under the Hat.* Zondervan. $18.95. *SLJ.*

Lauber, Patricia. *Summer of Fire: Yellowstone, 1988.* Orchard. $17.95. ALA, *SLJ.*

Lee, Tanith. *Black Unicorn.* Atheneum. $14.95. ALA.

Lewington, Anna. *Plants for People.* Oxford Univ. $39.95. *SLJ.*

Lipsyte, Robert. *The Brave.* HarperCollins. $14.95. ALA.

Lisle, Janet Taylor. *The Lampfish of Twill.* Illus. by Wendy Anderson Halperin. Orchard. $15.95. *SLJ.*

Lyons, Mary E. *Sorrow's Kitchen: The Life and Folklore of Zora Neale Hurston.* Scribner. $13.95. ALA.

McCaffrey, Anne. *Pegasus in Flight.* Del Rey. $19.95. ALA, *SLJ.*

McCammon, Robert. *Boy's Life.* Pocket. pap. $5.99. ALA.

McCorkle, Jill. *Ferris Beach.* Algonquin. $18.95. *SLJ.*

MacLachlan, Patricia. *Journey.* Delacorte. $13.50. ALA, *SLJ.*

McPherson, James M. *Abraham Lincoln and the Second American Revolution.* Oxford Univ. $17.95. *SLJ.*

Marino, Jan. *The Day that Elvis Came to Town.* Little, Brown. $14.95. *SLJ.*

Meltzer, Milton. *Thomas Jefferson: The Revolutionary Aristocrat.* Watts. $15.95. *SLJ.*

Montgomery, Sy. *Walking with the Great Apes.* Houghton Mifflin. $19.45, pap. $9.70. ALA.

Morpurgo, Michael. *Waiting for Anya.* Viking. $12.95. ALA, *SLJ.*

Murphy, Jim. *The Boys' War: Confederate and Union Soldiers Talk About the Civil War.* Clarion. $15.95. ALA.

Myers, Walter Dean. *Now Is Your Time!: The African-American Struggle for Freedom.* HarperCollins. $17.95. ALA.

Naylor, Phyllis Reynolds. *Reluctantly Alice.* Atheneum. $13.95. *SLJ.*

O'Brien, Tim. *The Things They Carried.* Houghton Mifflin. $19.95. *SLJ.*

Orlev, Uri. *The Man from the Other Side.* Houghton Mifflin. $13.95. ALA.

Osius, Alison. *Second Ascent: The Story of Hugh Herr.* Stackpole. $19.95. *SLJ.*

Paterson, Katherine. *Lyddie.* Lodestar/Dutton. $14.95. ALA, *SLJ.*

Paulsen, Gary. *The Cookcamp.* Orchard. $13.95. ALA, *SLJ.*

———. *The Monument.* Delacorte. $15. ALA.

Pelta, Kathy. *Discovering Christopher Columbus: How History Is Invented.* Lerner. $14.95. *SLJ.*

Plummer, Louise. *My Name Is Sus5an. The 5 Is Silent.* Delacorte. $14.95. ALA, *SLJ.*

Rappaport, Doreen. *American Women: Their Lives in Their Words*. Crowell. $16.95. ALA.

Riley, Judith Merkle. *In Pursuit of the Green Lion*. Delacorte. $19.95. *SLJ.*

Rinaldi, Ann. *Wolf by the Ears*. Scholastic. $13.95. ALA.

Savage, Georgia. *House Tibet*. Graywolf. pap. $12.95. ALA.

Schusterman, Neal. *What Daddy Did*. Little, Brown. $15.45. ALA.

Speigelman, Art. *Maus: A Survivor's Tale, II: And Here My Troubles Began*. Pantheon. $18. ALA.

Spinelli, Jerry. *There's a Girl in My Hammerlock*. Simon & Schuster. $13. ALA.

Sullivan, Charles. *Children of Promise: African-American Literature and Art for Young People*. Abrams. $24.95. ALA.

Sutter, Barton. *My Father's War and Other Stories*. Viking. $19.95. *SLJ.*

Talbert, Marc. *Pillow of Clouds*. Dial. $14.95. *SLJ.*

Tan, Amy. *Kitchen God's Wife*. Putnam. $21.95. *SLJ.*

Tepper, Sheri. *Beauty*. Doubleday. $20. ALA.

Thesman, Jean. *The Rain Catchers*. Houghton Mifflin. $13.95. ALA, *SLJ.*

Westall, Robert. *The Kingdom by the Sea*. Farrar, Straus. $13.95. ALA.

White, Ryan, and Ann M. Cunningham. *Ryan White: My Own Story*. Dial. $14.95. ALA.

Williams-Garcia, Rita. *Fast Talk on a Slow Track*. Lodestar/Dutton. $14.95. ALA.

Wisler, G. Clifton. *Red Cap*. Lodestar/Dutton. $14.95. ALA.

Wolff, Virginia E. *The Mozart Season*. Holt. $15.95. ALA.

Yolen, Jane. *Vampires*. HarperCollins. $14.95. ALA.

Young, Carrie. *Nothing to Do but Stay: My Pioneer Mother*. Univ. of Iowa. $22.50, pap. $8.50. *SLJ.*

Best Children's Books of 1991

A list of notable children's books is selected each year by the Notable Children's Books Committee of the Association for Library Service to Children of the American Library Association (ALA). The committee is aided by suggestions from school and public children's librarians throughout the United States. The book review editors of *School Library Journal (SLJ)* also compile a list each year, with full notations, of best books for children. The following list is a combination of ALA's Notable Children's Books of 1991 and *SLJ*'s "Best Books of the Year 1991," published in the December 1991 issue of *SLJ.* The source of each selection is indicated by the Notation "ALA" or "*SLJ*" following each entry. [See "Literary Prizes, 1991" later in Part 5 for Newbery, Caldecott, and other award winners — *Ed.*].

Aardema, Verna, reteller. *Borreguita and the Coyote*. Illus. by Petra Mathers. Knopf. $15. *SLJ.*

————. *Traveling to Tondo: A Tale of the Nkundo of Zaire*. Illus. by Will Hillenbrand. Knopf. $13.95. ALA.

Alexander, Lloyd. *The Remarkable Journey of Prince Jen*. Dutton. $14.95. *SLJ.*

Anno, Mitsumasa. *Anno's Math Games, III*. Philomel/Putnam. $19.95. ALA.

Avi. *Nothing but the Truth: A Documentary Novel*. Orchard. $14.95. ALA, *SLJ.*

Baker, Jeannie. *Window*. Greenwillow. $13.95. ALA.

Bergman, Tamar. *Along the Tracks*. Trans. by Michael Swirsky. Houghton Mifflin. $14.95. ALA.

Block, Francesca Lia. *Witch Baby*. HarperCollins. $13.95. *SLJ.*

Blumberg, Rhoda. *The Remarkable Voyages of Captain Cook*. Bradbury. $18.95. ALA, *SLJ.*

Browne, Anthony. *Changes*. Knopf. $14.95. ALA.

Bunting, Eve. *Fly Away Home*. Illus. by Ronald Himler. Clarion. $13.95. ALA, *SLJ.*

Burleigh, Robert. *Flight: The Journey of Charles Lindbergh*. Illus. by Mike Wimmer. Philomel/Putnam. $14.95. ALA.

Byars, Betsy. *Wanted . . . Mud Blossom*. Illus. by Jacqueline Rogers. Delacorte. $14. ALA, *SLJ.*

Calhoun, Mary. *High-Wire Henry*. Illus. by Erick Ingraham. Morrow. $13.95. *SLJ.*

Carter, Anne, sel. *Birds, Beasts, and Fishes: A Selection of Animal Poems*. Illus. by Reg Cartwright. Macmillan. $16.95. *SLJ.*

Chang, Ina. *A Separate Battle: Women and the Civil War*. Lodestar/Dutton. $15.95. ALA.

Choi, Sook Nyul. *Year of Impossible Goodbyes*. Houghton Mifflin. $13.95. ALA.

Cowcher, Helen. *Tigress*. Farrar, Straus. $14.95. *SLJ.*

Crew, Linda. *Nekomah Creek*. Illus. by Charles Robinson. Delacorte. $14. ALA.

Crews, Donald. *Bigmama's*. Greenwillow. $13.95. ALA.

Crutcher, Chris. *Athletic Shorts*. Greenwillow. $13.95. *SLJ.*

Davis, Jenny. *Checking on the Moon*. Orchard. $14.95. *SLJ.*

Dorros, Arthur. *Abuela*. Illus. by Elisa Kleven. Dutton. $13.95. ALA.

Esbensen, Barbara Juster. *Tiger with Wings: The Great Horned Owl*. Illus. by Mary Barrett Brown. Orchard. $14.95. ALA.

Fleischman, Paul. *The Borning Room*. HarperCollins. $13.95. ALA, *SLJ.*

———. *Time Train*. Illus. by Claire Ewart. HarperCollins. $14.95. *SLJ.*

Fleming, Denise. *In the Tall, Tall Grass*. Holt. $15.95. ALA, *SLJ.*

Foreman, Michael. *Michael Foreman's Mother Goose*. Harcourt Brace Jovanovich. $19.95. ALA.

Fox, Paula. *Monkey Island*. Orchard. $14.95. ALA.

Freedman, Russell. *The Wright Brothers: How They Invented the Airplane*. Photos by Wilbur Wright, Orville Wright, and others. Holiday. $16.95. ALA, *SLJ.*

Fritz, Jean. *Bully for You, Teddy Roosevelt*. Illus. by Mike Wimmer. Putnam. $15.95. ALA, *SLJ.*

Giblin, James Cross. *The Truth about Unicorns*. Illus. by Michael McDermott. HarperCollins. $14.95. ALA, *SLJ.*

Greenberg, Jan, and Sandra Jordan. *The Painter's Eye: Learning to Look at Contemporary American Art*. Delacorte. $20. ALA, *SLJ.*

Greenfield, Eloise. *Night on Neighborhood Street*. Illus. by Jan Spivey Gilchrist. Dial. $13.95. ALA.

Hahn, Mary Downing. *Stepping on the Cracks*. Clarion. $13.95. ALA, *SLJ.*

Henkes, Kevin. *Chrysanthemum*. Greenwillow. $13.95. ALA, *SLJ.*

Hermes, Patricia. *Mama, Let's Dance*. Little, Brown. $14.95. *SLJ.*

Hodges, Margaret, reteller. *St. Jerome and the Lion*. Illus. by Barry Moser. Orchard. $14.95. ALA.

Hoffman, Mary. *Amazing Grace*. Illus. by Caroline Binch. Dial. $13.95. ALA, *SLJ.*

Hughes, Ted. *Tales of the Early World*. Illus. by Andrew Davidson. Farrar, Straus. $13.95. ALA.

Isadora, Rachel. *At the Crossroads*. Greenwillow. $13.95. ALA.

Johnston, Ginny, and Judy Cutchins. *Slippery Babies: Young Frogs, Toads, and Salamanders*. Morrow. $13.95. *SLJ.*

Jones, Diana Wynne. *Castle in the Air*. Greenwillow. $13.95. ALA.

Joseph, Lynn. *A Wave in Her Pocket: Stories from Trinidad*. Illus. by Brian Pinkney. Clarion. $13.95. ALA.

Kellogg, Steven, adapt. *Jack and the Beanstalk*. Morrow. $14.95. ALA.

Lauber, Patricia. *Living with Dinosaurs*. Illus. by Douglas Henderson. Bradbury. $15.95. ALA, *SLJ.*

———. *Summer of Fire: Yellowstone, 1988*. Orchard. $17.95. ALA.

Lear, Edward. *The Owl and the Pussycat*. Illus. by Jan Brett. Putnam. $14.95. ALA, *SLJ.*

Lewis, Richard. *All of You Was Singing*. Illus. by Ed Young. Atheneum. $13.95. ALA.

Lisle, Janet Taylor. *The Lampfish of Twill*. Illus. by Wendy Anderson Halperin. Orchard. $15.95. *SLJ.*

Little, Jean. *Stars Come Out Within*. Viking. $14.95. ALA.

Livingston, Myra Cohn. *Poem-Making: Ways to Begin Writing Poetry.* HarperCollins. $15.95. ALA.

McClintock, Barbara, adapt. and illus. *Animal Fables from Aesop.* Godine. $17.95. ALA.

MacLachlan, Patricia. *Journey.* Delacorte. $13.50. ALA, *SLJ.*

McMillan, Bruce. *Eating Fractions.* Scholastic. $13.95. ALA.

Maestro, Betsy. *The Discovery of the Americas.* Illus. by Giulio Maestro. Lothrop, Lee & Shepard. $14.95. ALA, *SLJ.*

Marino, Jan. *The Day that Elvis Came to Town.* Little, Brown. $14.95. *SLJ.*

Marshall, James. *Old Mother Hubbard and Her Wonderful Dog.* Farrar, Straus. $13.95. ALA.

———. *Rats on the Roof: And Other Stories.* Dial. $12.95. *SLJ.*

Martin, Bill. *Polar Bear, Polar Bear, What Do You Hear?* Illus. by Eric Carle. Holt. $13.95. *SLJ.*

Martin, James. *Chameleons: Dragons in the Trees.* Photos by Art Wolfe. Crown. $13. ALA.

Martinez, Alejandro Cruz. *The Woman Who Outshone the Sun: The Legend of Lucia Zentano.* Illus. by Fernando Olivera. Trans. and adapt. by Rosalma Zubizarreta and others. Children's Book. $13.95. ALA.

Meltzer, Milton. *Thomas Jefferson: The Revolutionary Aristocrat.* Watts. $15.95. ALA, *SLJ.*

Metropolitan Museum of Art. *Songs of the Wild West.* Simon & Schuster. $19.95. ALA.

Mollel, Tololwa M., adapt. *The Orphan Boy: A Maasai Story.* Illus. by Paul Morin. Clarion. $14.95. ALA.

Morpurgo, Michael. *Waiting for Anya.* Viking. $12.95. *SLJ.*

Myers, Walter Dean. *Now Is Your Time!: The African-American Struggle for Freedom.* HarperCollins. $17.95. ALA.

Nash, Ogden. *The Adventures of Isabel.* Illus. by James Marshall. Little, Brown. $14.45. ALA.

Naylor, Phyllis Reynolds. *Reluctantly Alice.* Atheneum. $13.95. *SLJ.*

———. *Shiloh.* Atheneum. $12.95. ALA.

Orlev, Uri. *The Man from the Other Side.* Houghton Mifflin. $13.95. ALA.

Osborne, Mary Pope. *American Tall Tales.* Illus. by Michael McCurdy. Knopf. $18. *SLJ.*

Paterson, Katherine. *Lyddie.* Lodestar/Dutton. $14.95. ALA, *SLJ.*

Paulsen, Gary. *The Cookcamp.* Orchard. $13.95. *SLJ.*

Pelta, Kathy. *Discovering Christopher Columbus: How History Is Invented.* Lerner. $14.95. ALA, *SLJ.*

Plummer, Louise. *My Name Is Sus5an. The 5 Is Silent.* Delacorte. $14.95. *SLJ.*

Prelutsky, Jack, sel. *For Laughing Out Loud: Poems to Tickle Your Funnybone.* Illus. by Marjorie Priceman. Knopf. $14.95. *SLJ.*

Rankin, Laura. *The Handmade Alphabet.* Dial. $13.95. ALA, *SLJ.*

Ray, Jane, illus. *The Story of Christmas.* Dutton. $15.95. ALA.

Ringgold, Faith. *Tar Beach.* Crown. $15.99. ALA, *SLJ.*

Rylant, Cynthia. *Appalachia.* Illus. by Barry Moser. Harcourt Brace Jovanovich. $14.95. ALA.

———. *Henry and Mudge and the Bedtime Thumps.* Illus. by Suçie Stevenson. Bradbury. $11.95. *SLJ.*

Say, Allen. *Tree of Cranes.* Houghton Mifflin. $16.95. ALA.

Schertle, Alice. *Witch Hazel.* Illus. by Margot Tomes. HarperCollins. $14.95. *SLJ.*

Schoenherr, John. *Bear.* Philomel/Putnam. $14.95. *SLJ.*

Schwartz, Howard, and Barbara Rush, adapts. *The Diamond Tree: Jewish Tales from Around the World.* Illus. by Uri Schulevitz. HarperCollins. $16.95. ALA.

Scieszka, Jon. *The Frog Prince, Continued.* Illus. by Steve Johnson. Viking. $14.95. ALA.

———. *Knights of the Kitchen Table.* Illus. by Lane Smith. Viking. $10.95. *SLJ.*

Segal, Jerry. *The Place Where Nobody Stopped.* Illus. by Dav Pilkey. Orchard. $14.95. ALA.

Shaw, Nancy. *Sheep in a Shop.* Illus. by Margot Apple. Houghton Mifflin. $12.95. *SLJ.*

Sis, Peter. *Follow the Dream: The Story of Christopher Columbus.* Knopf. $15. *SLJ.*

Smith, Doris Buchanan. *The Pennywhistle Tree.* Putnam. $14.95. ALA, *SLJ.*

Smith, Lane. *Glasses—Who Needs 'Em?* Viking. $13.95. ALA.

Stanley, Fay. *The Last Princess: The Story of Princess Ka'iolani of Hawai'i.* Illus. by

Diane Stanley. Four Winds/Macmillan. $15.95. ALA.

Talbert, Marc. *Pillow of Clouds*. Dial. $14.95. *SLJ.*

Thesman, Jean. *The Rain Catchers*. Houghton Mifflin. $13.95. *SLJ.*

Tryon, Leslie. *Albert's Alphabet*. Atheneum. $13.95. ALA.

Turner, Ann. *Rosemary's Witch*. HarperCollins. $13.95. *SLJ.*

Walsh, Ellen Stoll. *Mouse Count*. Harcourt Brace Jovanovich. $11.95. ALA.

Wells, Rosemary. *Max's Dragon Shirt*. Dial. $10.95. ALA.

Wiesner, David. *Tuesday*. Clarion. $15.95. ALA, *SLJ.*

Willard, Nancy. *Pish, Posh, Said Hieronymus Bosch*. Illus. by the Dillons. Harcourt Brace Jovanovich. $18.95. ALA.

Wolff, Virginia E. *The Mozart Season*. Holt. $15.95. ALA.

Wood, Audrey, and Don Wood. *Piggies*. Illus. by Don Wood. Harcourt Brace Jovanovich. $13.95. ALA, *SLJ.*

Wrede, Patricia. *Searching for Dragons, Vol. II: The Enchanted Forest Chronicles*. Harcourt Brace Jovanovich. $16.95. ALA.

Zhensun, Zheng, and Alice Low. *A Young Painter*. Scholastic. $17.95. ALA.

Bestsellers of 1991:
Hardcover Fiction and Nonfiction

Daisy Maryles
Executive Editor, *Publishers Weekly*

FICTION

1. *Scarlett: The Sequel to Margaret Mitchell's Gone With the Wind* by Alexandra Ripley (Warner, 9/25/91; *2,148,225*)
2. *The Sum of All Fears* by Tom Clancy (Putnam, 11/7/91; *1,783,399*)
3. *Needful Things: The Last Castle Rock Story* by Stephen King (Viking Penguin, 10/15/91; *1,508,732*)
4. *No Greater Love* by Danielle Steel (Delacorte, 11/22/91; *1,406,643*)
5. *Heartbeat* by Danielle Steel (Delacorte, 3/11/91; *1,074,340*)
6. *The Doomsday Conspiracy* by Sidney Sheldon (Morrow, 9/91)
7. *The Firm* by John Grisham (Doubleday, 4/91; *544,079*)
8. *Night Over Water* by Ken Follett (Morrow, 9/91)
9. *Remember* by Barbara Taylor Bradford (Random House, 11/5/91; *445,564*)
10. *Loves Music, Loves to Dance* by Mary Higgins Clark (Simon & Schuster, 5/6/91)
11. *Cold Fire* by Dean R. Koontz (Morrow, 1/16/91; *410,334*)
12. *The Kitchen God's Wife* by Amy Tan (Morrow, 6/17/91; *385,373*)
13. *Sleeping Beauty* by Judith Michael (Poseidon, 10/29/91)
14. *Star Wars: Heir to the Empire, Vol. I* by Timothy Zahn (Spectra/Bantam, 11/91)
15. *WLT: A Radio Romance* by Garrison Keillor (Viking Penguin, 11/12/91; *292,366*)

Note: Excerpted from *Publishers Weekly*, April 6, 1992.

16. *The Deceiver* by Frederic Forsyth (Bantam, 10/91; *280,000*)
17. *Flowers in the Rain: And Other Stories* by Rosamunde Pilcher (St. Martin's; *265,715*)
18. *The Seeress of Kell* by David Eddings (Del Rey; *265,000*)
19. *Forgiving* by LaVyrle Spencer (Morrow; *254,216*)
20. *Comeback* by Dick Francis (Morrow; *251,106*)
21. *As the Crow Flies* by Jeffrey Archer (HarperCollins; *250,014*)
22. *The Seventh Commandment* by Lawrence Sanders (Morrow; *227,510*)
23. *Blindsight* by Robin Cook (Putnam; *224,070*)
24. *Battleground* by W. E. B. Griffin (Putnam; *214,056*)
25. *Vortex* by Larry Bond (Warner; *212,117*)
26. *Saint Maybe* by Anne Tyler (Knopf; *200,000*)
27. *The Druid of Shannara* by Terry Brooks (Del Rey; *220,000*)
28. *Paradise* by Judith McNaught (Pocket Books; *200,000*)
29. *The Duchess* by Jude Deveraux (Pocket Books; *175,000*)
30. *All the Weyrs of Pern* by Anne McCaffrey (Del Rey; *170,000*)
31. *Reunion: Star Trek: The Next Generation* by Michael Jan Friedman (Pocket Books)
32. *The Rustlers of Westfork* by Louis L'Amour (Bantam)
33. *Bright Captivity* by Eugenia Price (Doubleday)
34. *The Grass Crown* by Colleen McCullough (Morrow)
35. *The Novel* by James Michener (Random House)
36. *Lila: An Inquiry into Morals* by Robert M. Pirsig (Bantam)
37. *Beast* by Peter Benchley (Random House)
38. *Darkness* by John Saul (Bantam)
39. *Skymasters* by Dale Brown (Donald I. Fine/Putnam)
40. *The Eagle Has Flown* by Jack Higgins (Simon & Schuster)
41. *Russka* by Edward Rutherfurd (Crown)
42. *"H" Is for Homicide* by Sue Grafton (Holt)
43. *The Secret Pilgrim* by John Le Carré (Knopf)
44. *Harlot's Ghost* by Norman Mailer (Random House)
45. *Aspen Gold* by Janet Dailey (Little, Brown)
46. *Curtain* by Michael Korda (Simon & Schuster)
47. *Griffin & Sabine* by Nick Bantock (Chronicle)
48. *Pastime* by Robert B. Parker (Morrow)
49. *For All Their Lives* by Fern Michaels (Ballantine)
50. *Angel Eyes* by Eric Lustbader (Fawcett)
51. *Imajica* by Clive Barker (HarperCollins)
52. *The Dragon Reborn* by Robert Jordan (St. Martin's)
53. *The Piranhas* by Harold Robbins (Simon & Schuster)
54. *Magic Hour* by Susan Isaacs (HarperCollins)
55. *Outer Banks* by Anne Rivers Siddons (HarperCollins)
56. *Maximum Bob* by Elmore Leonard (Delacorte)
57. *Daughter of Deceit* by Victoria Holt (Doubleday)
58. *Love and Desire and Hate* by Joan Collins (Simon & Schuster)

NONFICTION

1. *Me: Stories of My Life* by Katharine Hepburn (Knopf, 9/24/91; *800,000*)
2. *Nancy Reagan: The Unauthorized Biography* by Kitty Kelley (Simon & Schuster, 4/17/91)
3. *Uh-Oh: Some Observations from Both Sides of the Refrigerator Door* by Robert Fulghum (Villard Books, 8/26/91; *550,403*)
4. *Under Fire: An American Story* by Oliver North with William Novak (Harper-Collins, 10/24/91; *547,633*)
5. *Final Exit: The Practicalities of Self-Deliverance and Assisted Suicide for the Dying* by Derek Humphry (Hemlock/Carol, 4/91; *456,634*)
6. *When You Look Like Your Passport Photo, It's Time to Go Home* by Erma Bombeck (HarperCollins, 8/1/91; *411,541*)
7. *More Wealth Without Risk* by Charles J. Givens (Simon & Schuster, 11/15/91)
8. *Den of Thieves* by James B. Stewart (Simon & Schuster, 11/15/91)
9. *Childhood* by Bill Cosby (Putnam, 10/25/91; *384,840*)
10. *Financial Self-Defense* by Charles J. Givens (Simon & Schuster; 11/16/90)
11. *The Frugal Gourmet Celebrates Christmas* by Jeff Smith (Morrow; 11/91)
12. *Iron John: A Book About Men* by Robert Bly (Addison-Wesley, 11/12/90; *319,195*)
13. *The Commanders* by Bob Woodward (Simon & Schuster, 5/20/91)
14. *The Best Treatment* by Isadore Rosenfeld, M.D. (Simon & Schuster, 11/4/91)
15. *Do It! Let's Get Off Our Buts* by Peter McWilliams and John-Roger (Prelude Press, 6/91; *285,918*)
16. *Awaken the Giant Within* by Anthony Robbins (Simon & Schuster; *286,000*)
17. *Cruel Doubt* by Joe McGinnis (Simon & Schuster; *286,000*)
18. *The Jordan Rules* by Sam Smith (Simon & Schuster; *236,000*)
19. *Parliament of Whores* by P.J. O'Rourke (Atlantic Monthly Press; *225,000*)
20. *Dance While You Can* by Shirley MacLaine (Bantam; *225,000*)
21. *Chutzpah* by Allan Dershowitz (Little, Brown; *217,000*)
22. *Memories: The Autobiography of Ralph Emery* by Ralph Emery with Tom Carter (Macmillan; *200,740*)
23. *LaToya: Growing Up in the Jackson Family* by LaToya Jackson with Patricia Romanowski (Dutton; *195,693*)
24. *Fire in the Belly: On Being a Man* by Sam Keen (Bantam; *196,000*)
25. *You'll Never Eat Lunch in this Town Again* by Julia Phillips (Random House; *193,452*)
26. *Chef Paul Prudhomme's Seasoned America* by Paul Prudhomme (Morrow; *192,039*)
27. *The World Is My Home: A Memoir* by James Michener (Random House; *189,823*)
28. *Wisdom of the 90s* by George Burns (Morrow; *183,491*)
29. *My Favorite Summer* by Mickey Mantle (Doubleday; *181,238*)
30. *The Carbohydrate Addict's Diet* by Richard and Rachael Heller (Dutton; *175,730*)
31. *PrairyErth* by William Least Heat-Moon (Houghton Mifflin)
32. *The Civil War: An Illustrated History* by Geoffrey C. Ward with Ric and Ken Burns (Knopf)
33. *Dave Barry's Only Travel Guide You'll Ever Need* by Dave Barry (Fawcett)

34. *French for Cats: All the French Your Cat Will Ever Need* by Henri De La Barbe/ Henry Beard (Villard Books)
35. *Zapp: The Lightning of Empowerment* by William C. Byham (Harmony)
36. *The Prize: The Epic Quest for Oil, Money, and Power* by Daniel Yergin (Simon & Schuster)
37. *Martha Stewart's Gardening: Month by Month* by Martha Stewart (Clarkson Potter)
38. *Madonna Unauthorized* by Christopher Anderson (Simon & Schuster)
39. *Exposing Myself* by Geraldo Rivera with Daniel Paisner (Bantam)
40. *Graham Kerr's Smart Cooking* by Graham Kerr (Doubleday)
41. *Making the Most of Your Money* by Jane Bryant Quinn (Simon & Schuster)
42. *Still Talking* by Joan Rivers (Turtle Bay/Simon & Schuster)
43. *Paul Harvey's for What It's Worth* edited by Paul Harvey Jr. (Bantam)
44. *Suddenly: The American Idea Abroad and at Home, 1986–1990* by George F. Will (Free Press)
45. *If You Really Loved Me* by Ann Rule (Simon & Schuster)
46. *Toujours Provence* by Peter Mayle (Knopf)
47. *History of the Arab Peoples* by Albert Hourani (Harvard University Press)
48. *Forever Fit* by Cher and Dr. Robert Hass (Bantam)
49. *J. Edgar Hoover* by Curt Gentry (Norton)
50. *There Are No Children Here* by Alex Kotlowitz (Doubleday)
51. *Silent Coup: The Removal of a President* by Len Colodny and Robert Gettlin (St. Martin's)
52. *Real Ponies Don't Go Oink!* by Patrick F. McManus (Henry Holt)
53. *Principle-Centered Leadership* by Stephen R. Covey (Simon & Schuster)
54. *Dave Barry Talks Back* by Dave Barry (Crown)
55. *Boss of Bosses: The Fall of the Godfather: The FBI and Paul Castellano* by Joseph F. O'Brien and Andris Kurins (Simon & Schuster)
56. *The Money Culture* by Michael Lewis (Norton)
57. *And the Sea Will Tell* by Vincent Bugliosi (Norton)
58. *Christmas Cats* by Lesley A. Ivory (Crown)
59. *Backlash: The Undeclared War Against American Women* by Susan Faludi (Crown)
60. *Photographs of Annie Leibovitz* by Annie Leibovitz (HarperCollins)
61. *Muhammad Ali: His Life and Times* by Thomas Hauser (Simon & Schuster)
62. *A Question of Character: A Biography of John F. Kennedy* by Thomas C. Reeves (Free Press)

Literary Prizes, 1991

Gary Ink
Research Librarian, *Publishers Weekly*

ABBY Award. *Offered by:* American Booksellers Association. To honor the title that members have most enjoyed hand-selling in the past year. *Winner:* Forrest Carter for *The Education of Little Tree* (Univ. of New Mexico).

Academy of American Poets Fellowship Award. For distinguished poetic achievement. *Winner:* J. D. McClatchy.

Jane Addams Children's Book Award. For a book promoting the cause of peace, social justice, and world community. *Offered by:* Women's International League for Peace and Freedom and the Jane Addams Peace Association. *Winner:* Ann Durell and Marilyn Sachs for *The Big Book for Peace* (Dutton).

Martha Albrand Award for Nonfiction. *Offered by:* PEN American Center. *Winner:* Gerald Marzorati for *A Painter of Darkness: Leon Golub and Our Times* (Viking).

Nelson Algren Award. For a previously unpublished short story. *Offered by: Chicago Tribune. Winner:* Thomas Barbash for "Howling at the Moon."

American Academy and Institute of Arts and Letters Awards in Literature. *Winners:* Edgar Bowers, Christopher Davis, Jaimy Gordon, Rachel Ingalls, Harry Matthews, J. D. McClatchy, Albert F. Moritz, James Schevil; (Gold Medal for Poetry) Richard Wilbur.

American Academy in Rome Fellowship in Literature. *Offered by:* American Academy and Institute of Arts and Letters. *Winner:* Mary Caponegro.

Association of Jewish Libraries Children's Book Award. For the most outstanding contribution in the field of Jewish literature for children and young people. *Winners:* (younger readers) Eric A. Kimmel for *Chanukkah Guest,* illus. by Carmi Giora (Holiday House); (older readers) Adele Geras for *My Grandmother's Stories: A Collection of Jewish Folktales,* illus. by Jael Jordan (Knopf).

Caroline Bancroft History Prize. For nonfiction works dealing with the history of the trans-Mississippi West. *Offered by:* Denver Public Library. *Winner:* Harlan Hague and David J. Langum for *Thomas O. Larkin: A Life of Patriotism and Profit in Old California* (Univ. of Oklahoma).

Bancroft Prizes — $4,000 each. For books of exceptional merit and distinction in American history, American diplomacy, and the international relations of the United States. *Offered by:* Columbia University. *Winners:* Lizabeth Cohen for *Making a New Deal: Industrial Workers in Chicago, 1919–1939* (Cambridge Univ.); Laurel Thatcher Ulrich for *A Midwife's Tale: The Life of Martha Ballard Based on Her Diary, 1785–1812* (Knopf).

Mildred L. Batchelder Award. For an American publisher of a children's book originally published in a foreign language in a foreign country and subsequently published in English in the United States. *Offered by:* ALA Association for Library Service to Children. *Winner:* Dutton for *A Hand Full of Stars* by Rafik Schami, trans. from German by Rika Lesser.

Bay Area Book Reviewers Association. *Winners:* (fiction) Ella Lefland for *The Knight, Death and the Devil* (Morrow); (nonfiction) Linda Niemann for *Boomer: Railroad Memoirs* (Univ. of California); (poetry) Thomas Centolella for *Terra Firma* (Copper Canyon); (children's literature) Ellen Kindt McKenzie for *Stargone John* (Holt); (publishing citation) North Point Press.

Before Columbus Foundation American Book Awards. For literary achievements by people of various ethnic backgrounds. *Winners:* Lucia Berlin for *Homesick: New and Selected Stories* (Black Sparrow); Thomas Centolella for *Terra Firma* (Copper Canyon); Mary Crow Dog with Richard Erdoes for *Lakota Woman* (Grove Weidenfeld); Nora Marks Dauenhauer and Richard Dauenhauer for *Haa Tuwunaagu Yis, for Healing Our Spirit: Tlingit Oratory* (Univ. of Washington); Jessica Hagedorn for *Dogeaters* (Pantheon); Joy Harjo for *In Mad Love and War* (Wesleyan Univ.); Bell

Books for *Yearning: Race, Gender, and Cultural Politics* (South End); Deborah Keenan and Roseann Lloyd for *Looking for Home: Women Writing About Exile* (Milkweed Editions); Meridel Le Sueur for *Harvest Song* (West End); D. H. Melhem for *Heroism in the New Black Poetry* (Univ. Press of Kentucky); The Mill Hunk Herald for *Overtime: Punchin' Out with the Mill Hunk Herald* (West End); R. Baxter Miller for *The Art and Imagination of Langston Hughes* (Univ. Press of Kentucky); Alejandro Murguia for *Southern Front* (Bilingual Review/Press); Charley Trujillo for *Soldados: Chicanos in Vietnam* (Chusma House); Karen Tei Yamashita for *Through the Arc of the Rain Forest* (Coffee House); John Edgar Wideman for *Philadelphia Fire* (Holt); Bruce Wright for *Black Robes, White Justice* (Lyle Stuart); (lifetime achievement award) Ernesto Cardenal; (editor/publisher award) Haki R. Madhubuti, Third World Press.

Curtis G. Benjamin Award for Creative Publishing. *Offered by:* Association of American Publishers. *Winner:* Jeremiah Kaplan.

Helen B. Bernstein Award for Excellence in Journalism: *Offered by:* New York Public Library. *Winner:* Nicholas Lemann for *The Promised Land: The Great Black Migration and How It Changed America* (Knopf).

Irma Simonton Black Award. For unified excellence of a story line, language, and illustration in a published work for young children. *Offered by:* Bank Street College of Education. *Winner:* Barbara Abercrombie for *Charlie Anderson,* illus. by Mark Graham (Macmillan).

James Tait Black Memorial Prizes (Great Britain). For the best biography and the best novel of the year. *Offered by:* University of Edinburgh. *Winners:* (biography) Claire Tomalin for *The Invisible Woman: The Story of Nelly Ternan and Charles Dickens* (Viking); (novel) William Boyd for *Brazzaville Beach* (Sinclair-Stevenson).

Elmer Holmes Bobst Awards in Arts and Letters. *Offered by:* New York University. *Winners:* (lifetime achievement) Gwendolyn Brooks, Stanley Elkin, Bill Moyers, V. S. Pritchett; (emerging writers) Laura Kasischke for poetry; Robert Schirmer for fiction.

Bollingen Prize in Poetry. *Offered by:* Yale University. *Winners:* Laura Riding Jackson; Donald Justice.

Book-of-the-Month Club Translation Award. *Offered by:* PEN American Center. *Winner:* Richard Pevear and Larissa Volokhonsky for *The Brothers Karamazov* by Fyodor Dostoyevsky (North Point).

Booker Prize for Fiction (Great Britain). *Offered by:* Book Trust. *Winner:* Ben Okri for *The Famished Road* (Jonathan Cape).

Boston Globe–Horn Book Awards. For excellence in text and illustration. *Winners:* (fiction) Avi for *The True Confessions of Charlotte Doyle* (Orchard); (nonfiction) Cynthia Rylant for *Appalachia: The Voices of Sleeping Birds,* illus. by Barry Moser (Harcourt Brace Jovanovich); (picture book) Katherine Paterson for *The Tale of the Mandarin Ducks,* illus. by Leo and Diane Dillon (Harcourt Brace Jovanovich).

Michael Braude Award for Light Verse. *Offered by:* American Academy and Institute of Arts and Letters. *Winner:* Gavin Ewart.

Bumbershoot/Weyerhaeuser Publication Award. To a small press located in Washington, Oregon, Alaska, Montana, or British Columbia for a particularly outstanding publishing project. *Offered by:* Weyerhaeuser Company Foundation. *Winner:* Arrowood Books for *Sorrowful Mysteries and Other Stories* by Normandi Ellis.

Witter Bynner Foundation Prize for Poetry. *Offered by:* American Academy and Institute of Arts and Letters. *Winner:* Thylias Moss.

Caldecott Medal. For the artist of the most distinguished picture book. *Offered by:* R. R. Bowker Company. *Winner:* David Macaulay for *Black and White* (Houghton Mifflin).

Italo Calvino Award. *Offered by:* Columbia University Translation Center. *Winner:* Estelle Gilson for *The Lost World of Umberto Saba* by Umberto Saba (Carcanet).

John W. Campbell Memorial Award. For outstanding science fiction writing. *Offered by:* Center for the Study of Science Fiction. *Winner:* Julia Ecklar.

Canada-Australia Literary Prize. To familiarize Australians and Canadians with each other's writers and writings. *Offered by:* the Canada Council and the Australia Council. *Winner:* Audrey Thomas.

Canada Council Governor General's Literary Awards. *Winners: English Language Titles:* (translation) Albert W. Halsall for *A Dictionary of Literary Devices: Gradus, A–Z* (Univ. of Toronto) trans. of Bernard Dupriez's *Les procédés littéraires*; (nonfiction) Robert Hunter and Robert Calihoo for *Occupied Canada: A Young White Man Discovers His Unsuspected Past* (McClelland & Stewart); (poetry) Don McKay for *Night Field* (McClelland & Stewart); (drama) Joan MacLeod for *Amigo's Blue Guitar* (Blizzard); (fiction) Rohinton Mistry for *Such a Long Journey* (McClelland & Stewart); (children's illustration) Joanne Fitzgerald for *Doctor Kiss Says Yes,* text by Teddy Jam (Groundwood); (children's text) Sarah Ellis for *Pick-Up Sticks* (Groundwood). *French-Language Books:* (translation) Jean-Paul Sainte-Marie and Brigitte Chabert Hacikyan for *Les Enfants d'Aataentsic: l'histoire du peuple huron* (Editions Libre Expression), trans. of *Children of Aataentsic* by Bruce G. Trigger; (nonfiction) Bernard Arcand for *Le Jaguar et le Tamanoir* (Editions du Boréal); (poetry) Madeleine Gagnon for *Chant pour un Quebec lointain* (VLB Editeur/Table rase); (drama) Gilbert Dupuis for *Mon oncle Marcel qui vague vague près du métro Berri* (Editions de l'Hexagone); (fiction) André Brochu for *La Croix du Nord* (XYZ Editeur); (children's illustration) Sheldon Cohen for *Un Champion,* text by Roch Carrier (Livres Toundra/Grandir); (children's text) François Gravel for *Deux heures et demie avant Jasmine* (Editions du Boréal).

Canada-Japan Book Award. *Winner:* E. Patricia Tsurumi for *Factory Girls: Women in the Thread Mills of Meiji Japan* (Princeton Univ.).

Melville Cane Award. For a critical work on poetry, a poet, or poets. *Offered by:* Poetry Society of America. *Winner:* J. D. McClatchy for *White Paper* (Columbia Univ.).

Carnegie Medal (Great Britain). *Offered by:* The Library Association. *Winner:* Gillian Cross for *Wolf* (Oxford Univ.).

Children's Book Award (Great Britain). To recognize the achievement of authors and illustrators. *Offered by:* Federation of Children's Book Groups. *Winner:* Mick Inkpen for *Threadbear* (Hodder).

Cholmondeley Award (Great Britain). For contributions to poetry. *Offered by:* Society of Authors. *Winners:* James Berry, Sujata Bhatt, Michael Hulse, Derek Mahon.

Christopher Book Awards. For books that affirm the highest values of the human spirit. *Winners:* (adult) Bernard Gotfryd for *Anton the Dove Fancier: And Other Tales of the Holocaust* (Washington Square); Robert Marion for *The Boy Who Felt No Pain* (Addison-Wesley); Mary Oliver for *House of Light* (Beacon); Paul Wilkes for *In Mysterious Ways: The Death and Life of a Parish Priest* (Random House); Nechama Tec for *In the Lion's Den: The Life of Oswald Rufeisen* (Oxford Univ.); Pierre Raphael for *Inside Rikers Island: A Chaplain's Search for God* (Orbis); Kathleen O'Connell Chesto for *Risking Hope: Fragile Faith in the Healing Process* (Sheed & Ward); Natalie Kusz for *Road Song* (Farrar, Straus & Giroux); Robert Coles for *The Spiritual Life of Children* (Houghton Mifflin); (children's) Mildred D. Taylor for *Mississippi Bridge,* illus. by Max Ginsburg (Dial); Ted Rand for *Paul Revere's Ride* (Dutton).

Arthur C. Clarke Award (Great Britain). For best science fiction novel of the year. *Winner:* Colin Greenland for *Take Back Plenty* (Unwin Hyman).

Fred Cody Memorial Award. *Offered by:* Bay Area Book Reviewers Association. *Winner:* William Everson.

Carr P. Collins Award for Nonfiction. *Offered by:* Texas Institute of Letters. *Winner:* Virginia Stem Owens for *If You Do Love Old Men* (Eerdmans).

Commonwealth Club of California Book Awards. For books of exceptional literary merit by authors who are legal residents of California. *Winners: Gold Medals:* (fiction) Michelle Latiolais for *Even Now* (Farrar, Straus & Giroux); (nonfiction) Edwin Bernbaum for *Sacred Mountains of the World* (Sierra Club). *Silver Medals:* (notable contribution to publishing) Stephen Vincent for *O California!* (Bedford Arts); (Californiana) Caroline A. Jones for *Bay Area Figurative Art, 1950–1965* (Univ. of California); (juvenile, ages 11–16) Morton Grosser for *The Fabulous Fifty* (Atheneum); (juvenile, 10 and under) Patricia Polacco for *Babushka's Doll* (Simon &

Schuster); (unclassified) Rick Hillis for *Limbo River* (Univ. of Pittsburgh); Carol Field for *Celebrating Italy* (Morrow); Kenneth M. Stampp for *America in 1857: A Nation on the Brink* (Oxford Univ.); Ella Leffland for *The Knight, Death and the Devil* (Morrow).

Commonwealth Writers Prize (Great Britain). *Winners:* David Malouf for *The Great World* (Chatto); (first work) Pauline Melville for *Shape-Shifter* (Women's Press).

Thomas Cook Travel and Guide Book Awards. *Winners:* (travel) Jonathan Raban for *Hunting Mister Heartbreak* (Collins Harvill); (guide book) Ben Box and Sarah Cameron for *The Caribbean Islands Handbook* (Trade & Travel).

Crime Writers' Association/Agatha Christie Dagger Awards (Great Britain). *Winners:* (Gold Dagger) Ruth Rendell for *King Solomon's Carpet* (Viking); (Silver Dagger) Frances Fyfield for *Deep Sleep* (Heinemann); (Diamond Dagger for outstanding achievements) Ruth Rendell.

De la Torre Bueno Prize. For the most distinguished book of dance scholarship. *Offered by:* Dance Perspectives Foundation. *Winner:* Elizabeth Souritz for *Soviet Choreographers in the 1920's* (Duke Univ.).

Deo Gloria Award (Great Britain). For a work of fiction written from a Christian standpoint. *Offered by:* Deo Gloria Trust. *Winner:* Elizabeth Gibson for *Old Photographs* (Lion).

John Dos Passos Prize for Literature. To a writer who has a substantial body of significant publication, and whose work demonstrates an intense and original exploration of American themes. *Offered by:* Longwood College. *Winner:* Larry Woiwode.

Geoffrey Faber Memorial Prize (Great Britain). For a volume of verse or a volume of prose fiction of great literary merit. *Offered by:* Faber & Faber. *Winner:* Carol Birch for *The Fog Line* (Bloomsbury).

Norma Farber First Book Award. For a first book of poetry. *Offered by:* Poetry Society of America. *Winner:* Karl Kirchwey for *A Wandering Island* (Princeton Univ.).

Faulkner Award for Fiction. *Offered by:* PEN American Center. *Winner:* John Edgar Wideman for *Philadelphia Fire* (Holt).

Richard F. Fenno Prize. For the outstanding legislative studies book on any American,

foreign, or cross-national topic. *Offered by:* American Political Science Association. *Winner:* R. Douglas Arnold for *The Logic of Congressional Action* (Yale Univ.).

Robert L. Fish Memorial Award. *Offered by:* Mystery Writers of America. *Winner:* Jerry F. Skarky.

John Florio Prize (Great Britain). For recognition of the best translation from Italian into English of a twentieth-century Italian work of literary merit and general interest. *Offered by:* Society of Authors and the Translators Association. *Winner:* Patrick Creagh for *Danube* by Claudio Magris (Harvill).

Food and Beverage Book Awards. *Offered by:* International Association of Culinary Professionals. *Winners:* (book of the year) Deborah Madison for *The Savory Way* (Bantam); (bread, baking and sweets) Alice Meredith for *Cocolat: Extraordinary Chocolate Desserts* (Warner); (ethnic/regional) Carol Field for *Celebrating Italy* (Morrow); (reference/technical) Jill Norman for *The Complete Book of Spices* (Dorling Kindersley); (general) Deborah Madison for *The Savory Way* (Bantam); (health and diet) Sunset Editors for *Light and Healthy Cook Book* (Sunset); (illustrated/photography) Phillip Stephen Schulz for *America The Beautiful Cookbook: Authentic Recipes from the United States of America* (Collins); (literary food writing) Jennifer Brennan for *Curries and Bugles: A Memoir and a Cookbook of the British Raj* (HarperCollins); (single subject) Bruce Aidells and Denis Kelly for *Hot Links and Country Flavors: Sausages in American Regional Cooking* (Knopf); (wine, beer, and spirits) Burton Anderson for *The Wine Atlas and Traveller's Guide to the Vineyards* (Simon & Schuster); (Julia Child Award) Alice Meredith for *Cocolat: Extraordinary Chocolate Desserts* (Warner).

E. M. Forster Award. *Offered by:* American Academy and Institute of Arts and Letters. *Winner:* Alan Hollinghurst for *The Swimming Pool Library* (Random House).

Miles Franklin Award (Australia). For a novel or play that portrays an aspect of Australian life. *Offered by:* Arts Management Ltd. *Winner:* David Malouf for *The Great World* (Chatto).

Soeurette Diehl Fraser Award. For the best translation of a book-length work. *Offered by:* Texas Institute of Letters. *Winner:* Frances Lopez-Morillas for *Behind the Curtains,* by Carmen Martin Gaite (Columbia Univ.)

Friends of the Dallas Public Library Award. *Offered by:* Texas Institute of Letters. *Winner:* Nicolas Kanellos for *A History of Hispanic Theatre in the United States: Origins to 1940* (Univ. of Texas).

Frost Silver Medal. To a person who has shown lifelong dedication and achievement in poetry. *Offered by:* Poetry Society of America. *Winner:* Donald Hall.

Ralph J. Gleason Music Book Awards. To honor outstanding books about music and musicians in all areas of popular music. *Offered by: Rolling Stone,* BMI, and New York University. *Winners:* (first prize) Laurence Bergreen for *As Thousands Cheer: The Life of Irving Berlin* (Viking); (second prize) Fredric Dannen for *Hit Men: Power Brokers and Fast Money Inside the Music Business* (Random House); (third prize) Charles Shaar Murray for *Crosstown Traffic: Jimi Hendrix and the Rock 'N' Roll Revolution* (St. Martin's).

Tony Godwin Award. For an American or British editor (in alternate years) to spend six weeks working at a publishing house in the other's country. *Offered by:* Harcourt Brace Jovanovich. *Winner:* George Hodgman, Simon & Schuster.

Golden Kite Awards. *Offered by:* Society of Children's Book Writers. *Winners:* (fiction) Avi for *The True Confessions of Charlotte Doyle* (Orchard/Jackson); (nonfiction) Jim Murphy for *The Boys' War* (Clarion); (picture/illustration) Jerry Pinkney for *Home Place,* by Crescent Dragonwagon (Macmillan). *Honor Awards:* (fiction) Bruce Brooks for *Everywhere* (HarperCollins); (nonfiction) Russell Freedman for *Franklin Delano Roosevelt* (Clarion); (picture/illustration) Dennis Nolan for *Dinosaur Dream* (Macmillan).

Grand Prix de la Littérature Policière (France). *Winner:* Thomas Harris for *Silence of the Lambs* (Albin Michel).

Charles Grawemeyer Awards. For outstanding achievement in music, education, religion, and improving world peace. *Offered by:* University of Louisville. *Winners:* (reli-

gion) John Harwood Hick for *An Interpretation of Religion: Human Responses to the Transcendent* (Yale Univ.); (education) Kieran Egan for *Primary Understanding: Education in Early Childhood* (Routledge).

Kate Greenaway Medal (Great Britain). *Offered by:* The Library Association. *Winner:* Gary Blythe for *The Whale's Song* (Hutchinson).

Eric Gregory Trust Awards (Great Britain). For poets under the age of 30. *Offered by:* Society of Authors. *Winners:* Glyn Maxwell, Stephen Smith.

R. R. Hawkins Award. *Offered by:* American Association of Publishers Professional and Scholarly Publishing Division. *Winner:* *The Ants* by Bert Holldobler and Edward O. Wilson.

Heartland Prizes. *Offered by: Chicago Tribune. Winners:* (fiction) Kaye Gibbons for *A Cure for Dreams* (Algonquin Books); (nonfiction) William Cronon for *Nature's Metropolis: Chicago and the Great West* (Norton).

W. H. Heinemann Prize (Great Britain). *Offered by:* Royal Society of Literature. *Winner:* Alan Judd for *Ford Madox Ford* (HarperCollins).

Drue Heinz Literature Prize. For an outstanding collection of unpublished fiction. *Offered by:* University of Pittsburgh Press and the Howard Heinz Endowment. *Winner:* Elizabeth Graver for *Have You Seen Me?* (Univ. of Pittsburgh).

Peggy V. Helmerich Distinguished Author Award. To give formal recognition to nationally acclaimed writers who have created a distinguished body of work. *Offered by:* Tulsa Library Trust. *Winner:* Eudora Welty.

Ernest Hemingway Foundation Award. *Offered by:* PEN American Center. For a work of first fiction by an American. *Winner:* Bernard Cooper for *Maps to Anywhere* (Univ. of Georgia).

David Higham Prize for Fiction (Great Britain). For recognition of a first novel or book of short stories written in English. *Offered by:* Book Trust. *Winner:* Elspeth Barker for *O Caledonia* (Hamish Hamilton).

Winifred Holtby Prize (Great Britain). For the best regional novel of the year. *Offered by:* Royal Society of Literature. *Winner:* Nino

Ricci for *Lives of the Saints* (Allison & Busby).

Langston Hughes Award. To individuals who, in the tradition of Langston Hughes, have made a distinguished contribution to arts and letters. *Offered by:* Modern Poetry Association. *Winner:* Maya Angelou.

Ingersoll Prizes in Literature and Humanities. *Offered by:* Ingersoll Foundation. *Winners:* (T. S. Eliot Award) Mario Vargas Llosa; (Richard M. Weaver Award) John Lukacs.

International Reading Association Children's Book Awards. For an author's first or second work for a juvenile audience. *Winners:* (younger readers) Megan McDonald for *Is This a House for Hermit Crab?* illus. by F. D. Schindler (Orchard); (older readers) Mariata Conlon-McKenna for *Under the Hawthorn Tree,* illus. by Donald Teskey (Holiday House).

Irish Literature Prize for a First Book (Ireland). *Winner:* Nina Fitz-Patrick for *Fables of the Irish Intelligentsia* (Fourth Estate).

Irish Literature Prize for Nonfiction (Ireland). *Winner:* J. J. Lee for *Ireland 1912–1985* (Cambridge Univ.).

*Irish Times/*Aer Lingus International Fiction Prize (Ireland). *Winner:* Louis Begley for *Wartime Lies* (Macmillan).

Jerard Fund Award. For an emerging woman writer of nonfiction with work in progress. *Offered by:* PEN American Center. *Winner:* Lydia Yuri Minatoya for *Talking to High Monks in the Snow* (in progress).

Jerusalem Prize (Israel). *Winner:* Zbigniew Herbert.

Jesse H. Jones Award for Fiction. *Offered by:* Texas Institute of Letters. *Winner:* Lionel G. Garcia for *Hardscrub* (Arte Publico).

Juniper Prize. For an outstanding manuscript of original English poetry. *Offered by:* University of Massachusetts Press. *Winner:* Mark Halliday for *Tasker Street* (Univ. of Massachusetts).

Janet Heidinger Kafka Prize. To an American woman for a work of fiction. *Offered by:* Susan B. Anthony Center, University of Rochester. *Winner:* Marianne Wiggins for *John Dollar* (HarperCollins).

Sue Kaufman Prize. For a first work of fiction. *Offered by:* American Academy and Institute of Arts and Letters. *Winner:*

Charles Palliser for *The Quincunx* (Ballantine).

Sir Peter Kent Conservation Prize (Great Britain). *Winner:* Jonathan Kingdon for *Island Africa* (Collins).

Aga Khan Fiction Prize. *Offered by:* Paris Review. *Winner:* Larry Woiwode for *Summer* (Addison-Wesley).

Coretta Scott King Award. For a work that promotes the cause of peace and brotherhood. *Offered by:* American Library Association Social Responsibilities Round Table. *Winners:* Mildred D. Taylor for *The Road to Memphis* (Dial); Leo and Diane Dillon, illustrators, for *Aida,* as told by Leontyne Price (Harcourt Brace Jovanovich).

Norma Klein Award. To recognize an emerging voice of literary merit among American writers of children's fiction. *Offered by:* PEN American Center. *Winner:* Cynthia Grant.

Gregory Kolovakos Award. For AIDS writing. *Offered by:* Words Project for AIDS. *Winner:* Kenny Fries for *The Healing Notebooks* (Open Books).

Lamont Poetry Prize. *Offered by:* Academy of American Poets. *Winner:* Susan Wood for *Campo Santo* (Louisiana State Univ.).

Harold Morton Landon Translation Award. *Offered by:* American Academy of Poets. *Winner:* Robert Fagles for *The Iliad* by Homer (Viking).

Lannan Literary Awards. *Offered by:* Lannan Foundation. *Winners:* (fiction) Alexander Theroux; (nonfiction) Christopher Hitchens; (poetry) William Bronk.

Ruth Lilly Poetry Prize. *Offered by:* American Council for the Arts. *Winner:* David Wagoner.

Locus Awards. *Offered by:* Locus Publications. *Winners:* (science fiction novel) Dan Simmons for *The Fall of Hyperion* (Doubleday); (fantasy novel) Ursula K. Le Guin for *Tehanu: The Last Book of Earthsea* (Atheneum); (horror novel) Anne Rice for *The Witching Hour* (Knopf); (first novel) Michael Flynn for *In the Country of the Blind* (Baen); (nonfiction) *SFWA Handbook: The Professional Writer's Guide to Writing Professionally* (Writers Notebook); (anthology) Gardner Dozois, ed., *The Year's Best SF: Seventh Annual Collection* (St. Martin's).

Los Angeles Times Book Prizes. To honor literary excellence. *Winners:* (fiction) Allan Gurganus for *White People: Stories and Novellas* (Knopf); (poetry) Philip Levine for *What Work Is* (Knopf); (history) Nicholas Lemann for *The Promised Land: The Great Black Migration and How It Changed America* (Knopf); (biography) T. H. Watkins for *Righteous Pilgrim: The Life and Times of Harold L. Ickes, 1874–1952* (Holt); (science and technology) Grigori Medvedev for *The Truth About Chernobyl* (Basic Books); (current interest) E. J. Dionne, Jr. for *Why Americans Hate Politics* (Simon & Schuster); (Art Seidenbaum Award for First Fiction) David Wong Louie for *Pangs of Love* (Knopf); (Robert Kirsch Award) Ken Kesey.

Barbara McCombs/Lon Tinkle Award. For continuing excellence in Texas letters. *Offered by:* Texas Institute of Letters. *Winner:* Marshall Terry.

McKitterick Prize (Great Britain). For a first novel by a writer over the age of 40. *Offered by:* Society of Authors. *Winner:* John Loveday for *A Summer to Halo* (unpublished).

Mary McNulty Award. *Offered by:* Association of American Publishers School Division. *Winner:* Harold T. Miller.

Bernard Malamud Memorial Award. To honor the work of distinguished short story writers. *Offered by:* PEN American Center. *Winners:* Frederick Busch, André Dubus.

Lenore Marshall/*The Nation* Poetry Prize. For an outstanding book of poems published in the United States. *Offered by: The Nation* and New Hope Foundation. *Winner:* John Haines for *New Poems: 1980–88* (Story Line).

Kurt Maschler Award (Great Britain). For a children's book in which text and illustration are both excellent and perfectly harmonious. *Winner:* Colin McNaughton for *Have You Seen Who's Just Moved in Next Door to Us?* (Walker).

Somerset Maugham Awards (Great Britain). For young British authors to gain experience in foreign countries. *Offered by:* Society of Authors. *Winners:* Helen Simpson for *Four Bare Legs in a Bed* (Heinemann); Peter Benson for *The Other Occupant* (Macmillan); Lesley Glaister for *Honour Thy Father* (Secker & Warburg).

Vicky Metcalf Award (Canada). *Offered by:* Canadian Authors Association. *Winner:* Brian Doyle.

Scott Moncrieff Prize (Great Britain). For the best translation of a French book into English. *Winner:* Beryl and John Fletcher for *The Georgics* by Claude Simon (John Calder).

Mother Goose Award (Great Britain). To recognize the most exciting newcomer to the field of children's book illustration. *Offered by:* Books for Children Book Club. *Winner:* Amanda Harvey for *A Close Call* (Macmillan).

Frank Luther Mott–Kappa Tau Alpha Award. For the best-researched book dealing with the media. *Offered by:* National Journalism Scholarship Society. *Winner:* Peter Kurth for *American Cassandra* (Little, Brown).

NCR Book Award (Great Britain). For nonfiction. *Winner:* Claire Tomalin for *The Invisible Woman: The Story of Nelly Ternan and Charles Dickens* (Viking).

National Arts Club Medal of Honor for Literature. *Winner:* Philip Roth.

National Book Awards. *Winners:* (fiction) Norman Rush for *Mating* (Knopf); (nonfiction) Orlando Patterson for *Freedom* (Basic Books); (poetry) Philip Levine for *What Work Is* (Knopf).

National Book Critics Circle Awards. *Winners:* (fiction) John Updike for *Rabbit at Rest* (Knopf); (general nonfiction) Shelby Steele for *The Content of Our Character* (St. Martin's); (biography/autobiography) Robert A. Caro for *Means of Ascent* (Knopf); (criticism) Arthur C. Danto for *Encounters and Reflections* (Farrar, Straus & Giroux); (poetry) Amy Gerstler for *Bitter Angel* (North Point).

National Book Foundation Medal for Distinguished Contribution to American Letters. *Winner:* Eudora Welty.

National Jewish Book Awards. *Winners:* (autobiography/memoir) Irving Louis Horowitz for *Daydreams and Nightmares: Reflections of a Harlem Childhood* (Univ. Press of Mississippi); (contemporary Jewish life) Daniel J. Elazar and Harold M. Waller for *Maintaining Consensus: The Canadian Jewish Polity in the Postwar World* (Jerusalem Center for Public Affairs/Univ. Presses of America); (fiction) Chaim Potok for *The Gift of Asher Lev* (Knopf); (Holocaust) Lani Yahil for *The Holocaust: The Fate of European Jewry, 1932-1945* (Oxford Univ.); (Israel) Sergio I. Minerbi for *The Vatican and Zionism: Conflict in the Holy Land, 1895-1925* (Oxford Univ.); (Jewish history) Elisheva Carlebach for *The Pursuit of Heresy: Rabbi Moses Hagiz and the Sabbatian Controversies* (Columbia Univ.); (Jewish thought) Neil Gillman for *Sacred Fragments: Recovering Theology for the Modern Jew* (Jewish Publication Society); (scholarship) Gavin Langmuir for *History, Religion and Antisemitism* (Univ. of California); (visual arts) Shalom Sabar for *Ketubbah: Jewish Marriage Contracts of Hebrew Union College Skirball Museum and Klau Library* (Jewish Publication Society); (children's literature) Nava Semel for *Becoming Gershona* (Viking Penguin); (children's picture book) Roni Schotter for *Hanukkah!* illus. by Marilyn Hafner (Little, Brown).

Native American Literature Prize. To honor an author who has published outstanding literature about Native American Indians. *Offered by:* University of Oklahoma. *Winner:* James Welch.

Nebula Awards. *Offered by:* Science Fiction Writers of America. *Winners:* (novel) Ursula K. Le Guin for *Tehanu: The Last Book of Earthsea* (Atheneum); (grand master award) Lester del Rey.

Nero Award for Detective Fiction. *Offered by:* The Wolfe Pack. *Winner:* Tony Hillerman for *Coyote Waits* (HarperCollins).

Richard Neustadt Book Award. For the best scholarly book addressing the presidency. *Offered by:* American Political Science Association. *Winner:* Harold Hongju Koh for *The National Security Constitution: Sharing Power Since the Iran-Contra Affair* (Yale Univ.).

John Newbery Medal. For the most distinguished contribution to literature for children. *Donor:* ALA Association for Library Service to Children. *Medal contributed by:* Daniel Melcher. *Winner:* Jerry Spinelli for *Maniac Magee* (Little, Brown).

Charles H. and N. Mildred Nilon Excellence in Minority Fiction Award. *Offered by:* University of Colorado. *Winner:* Yvonne Veronica Sapia for *Valentino's Hair* (Univ. of Colorado/Fiction Collective Two).

Nobel Prize in Literature. For the total literary output of a distinguished writer. *Offered by:* Swedish Academy. *Winner:* Nadine Gordimer.

Noma Award for Publishing in Africa (Japan). *Winner:* Niya Osundare for *Waiting Laughters* (Malthouse Press, Lagos).

North American Indian Prose Award. For the best new work by an American Indian writer. *Offered by:* University of Nebraska Press. *Winner:* Diane Glancy for *Claiming Breath* (Univ. of Nebraska).

Odd Fellows MU Social Concern Book Award (Great Britain). *Offered by:* Odd Fellows Manchester Unity Friendly Society. *Winner:* Oliver Sacks for *Seeing Voices* (Picador).

Scott O'Dell Award for Historical Fiction. *Winner:* James Duffy for *A Time for Troubles* (Scribner).

Natalie Ornish Award. For the best book of poetry. *Offered by:* Texas Institute of Letters. *Winner:* Daryl Jones for *Someone Going Home Late* (Texas Tech Univ.).

PEN Center USA West Annual Literary Awards. For outstanding literary achievement by writers living west of the Mississippi. *Winners:* (fiction) Barbara Kingsolver for *Animal Dreams* (HarperCollins); (nonfiction) Richard Misrach and Myriam Weisang Misrach for *Bravo 20: The Bombing of the American West* (Johns Hopkins Univ.); (poetry) Donald Revell for *New Dark Ages* (Wesleyan Univ.); (children's literature) Deborah Nourse Lattimore for *The Dragon's Robe* (HarperCollins); (Elinor D. Randall Translation Award) Tiina Nunnally for *Niels Lyhne* by Jens Peter Jacobsen (Fjord).

PEN Medal for Translation. To one whose career as a translator has been distinguished by a commitment to excellence. *Offered by:* PEN American Center. *Winner:* William Weaver.

Edgar Allan Poe Awards. For outstanding mystery, crime, and suspense writing. *Offered by:* Mystery Writers of America. *Winners:* (novel) Julie Smith for *New Orleans Mourning* (St. Martin's); (first novel) Patricia Cornwell for *Post Mortem* (Scribner); (original paperback) David Handler for *The Man Who Would Be F. Scott Fitzgerald* (Bantam); (fact crime) Peter Maas for *In a Child's Name* (Simon & Schuster); (critical/

biographical) John Conquest for *Trouble Is Their Business: Private Eyes in Fiction, Film, and Television, 1927–1988* (Garland); (young adult) Chap Reaver for *Mote* (Delacorte); (juvenile) Pam Conrad for *Stonewords* (HarperCollins); (special) Jay Robert Nash for *The Encyclopedia of World Crime* (Crime Books); (Grandmaster) Tony Hillerman.

Poets' Prize. For the best book of verse published by a United States poet in the preceding year. *Offered by:* Poets' Prize Foundation. *Winner:* Miller Williams for *Living on the Surface: New and Selected Poems* (Louisiana State Univ.).

Renato Poggioli Translation Award. For an outstanding translation. *Offered by:* PEN American Center. *Winner:* Lynne Sharon Schwartz for *Smoke over Birkenau* by Liana Millu (Jewish Publication Society).

Prix Goncourt (France). For a work of imagination in prose, preferably a novel, exemplifying youth, originality, esprit, and form. *Winner:* Pierre Combescot for *Les Filles du Calvaire* (Grasset).

Prix Mystère (France). *Winner:* Thomas Harris for *Silence of the Lambs* (Albin Michel).

Pulitzer Prizes in Letters. To honor distinguished works by American writers, dealing preferably with American themes. *Winners:* (biography) Steven Naifeh and Gregory White Smith for *Jackson Pollock: An American Saga* (Clarkson Potter); (fiction) John Updike for *Rabbit at Rest* (Knopf); (general nonfiction) Bert Holldobler and Edward O. Wilson for *The Ants* (Belknap/Harvard Univ.); (history) Laurel Thatcher Ulrich for *A Midwife's Tale: The Life of Martha Ballard* (Knopf); (poetry) Mona Van Duyn for *Near Changes* (Knopf).

QPB New Visions Award. For the most distinctive and promising work of nonfiction offered by the Quality Paperback Club. *Winner:* Rian Malan for *My Traitor's Heart* (Atlantic Monthly).

QPB New Voices Award. For the most distinctive and promising work of fiction offered by the Quality Paperback Club. *Winner:* David Foster Wallace for *Girl with Curious Hair* (Norton).

Rea Award. For an outstanding short story. *Winner:* Paul Bowles.

Regina Medal. For excellence in the writing of literature for children. *Offered by:* Catholic Library Association. *Winner:* Leonard Everett Fisher.

Revson Foundation Fellowship. For a poet aged 35 or under, to recognize a young writer whose published work or work in progress shows exceptional promise. *Offered by:* PEN American Center. *Winner:* Lucia Maria Perillo.

John Llewellyn Rhys Memorial Award (Great Britain). *Offered by: Mail on Sunday. Winner:* Ray Monk for *Wittgenstein: The Duty of Genius* (Jonathan Cape).

Romance Writers of American RITA Awards. *Winners:* (romance of the year) Laura Kinsale for *Prince of Midnight* (Avon); (traditional novel) Christine Fiorotto for *Song of the Lorelei* (Silhouette); (short contemporary) Janece Hudson for *Step into My Parlor* (Bantam); (long contemporary) Cheryl Reavis for *Patrick Gallagher's Widow* (Silhouette); (single title contemporary) Nora Roberts for *Public Secrets* (Bantam); (Regency) Loretta Chekani for *The Sandalwood Princess* (Walker); (romantic suspense) Sandra Canfield for *Night Spice* (Silhouette); (series historical) Penelope Williamson for *A Wild Yearning* (Avon); (single title historical) Elizabeth Awbrey Beach for *Where Love Dwells* (St. Martin's); (first novel) Nancy Harwood Bulk for *Black Horse Island* (Silhouette); (lifetime achievement) Barbara Mertz.

Richard and Hilda Rosenthal Foundation Award. For a work of fiction that is a considerable literary achievement though not necessarily a commercial success. *Offered by:* American Academy and Institute of Arts and Letters. *Winner:* Joanna Scott for *Arrogance* (Simon & Schuster).

Runciman Award (Great Britain). For a book about Greece. *Offered by:* Anglo-Hellenic League. *Winner:* Hugh Lloyd-Jones for *Greek Epic, Lyric, and Tragedy* (Clarendon).

Félix-Antoine Savard Award. *Offered by:* Columbia University Translation Center. *Winner:* Susanne De Lotbiniere Harwood for *Letters from Another* by Lise Gauvin (Woman's Press).

Delmore Schwartz Memorial Poetry Award. *Offered by:* New York University College of Arts and Sciences. *Winner:* Joy Harjo.

Shamus Awards. *Offered by:* Private Eye Writers of America. *Winners:* (fiction) Sue Grafton for *G Is for Gumshoe* (Holt); (first novel) Walter Mosely for *Devil with a Blue Dress On* (Norton); (paperback original) W. Glenn Duncan for *Rafferty: Fatal Sister* (Fawcett); (lifetime achievement) Roy Huggins.

Shelley Memorial Award. To a poet living in the United States who is chosen on the basis of genius and need. *Offered by:* Poetry Society of America. *Winner:* Shirley Kaufman.

Smarties Book Prizes (Great Britain). *Winners:* (Grand Prix and under age 5) Martin Waddell for *Farmer Duck*, illus. by Helen Oxenbury (Walker); (6 to 8) Magdalen Nabb for *Josie Smith and Eileen*, illus. by Pirkko Vainio (HarperCollins); (9 to 11) Philip Ridley for *Krindlekrax* (Jonathan Cape).

W. H. Smith Illustration Award (Great Britain). *Winner:* Angela Barrett for *The Hidden House* by Martin Waddell (Walker).

W. H. Smith Literary Award (Great Britain). For a significant contribution to literature. *Winner:* Derek Walcott for *Omeros* (Faber).

Spielvogel-Diamonstein Award. For a collection of essays by an American writer. *Offered by:* PEN American Center. *Winner:* Martha C. Nussbaum for *Love's Knowledge: Essays on Philosophy and Literature* (Oxford Univ.).

Elaine and David Spitz Book Prize. For the best English-language book published on liberal and/or democratic theory. *Offered by:* Conference for the Study of Political Thought. *Winner:* Robert A. Dahl for *Democracy and Its Critics* (Yale Univ.).

Spur Awards. To promote excellence in writing about the West. *Offered by:* Western Writers of America. *Winners:* (Owen Wister Award) Glendon Swarthout; (Stirrup Award) Elmer Kelton; (Medicine Pipe Bearer's Award) Tim MacCurdy; (novel) Jeanne Williams for *Home Mountain* (St. Martin's); (nonfiction) Valerie Sherer Mathes for *Helen Hunt Jackson and Her Indian Reform Legacy* (Univ. of Texas); (paperback original) Don Coldsmith for *The Changing Wind* (Bantam); (Western novel) Gary Svee for *Sanctuary* (Walker); (juvenile fiction) Madge Harrah for *Honey Girl*

(Avon/Camelot); (juvenile nonfiction) Gary Paulsen for *Woodsong* (Bradbury).

Agnes Lynch Starrett Poetry Prize. *Offered by:* University of Pittsburgh Press. *Winner:* Julia Kasdorf for *Sleeping Preacher* (Univ. of Pittsburgh).

Sunday Express Book of the Year Award (Great Britain). *Winner:* Michael Frayn for *A Landing on the Sun* (Viking).

Sunday Times Small Publishers Award (Great Britain). *Offered by: Sunday Times Books Supplement*. *Winner:* Verso.

Sunday Times Young Writer of the Year Award (Great Britain). *Winner:* Helen Simpson for *Four Bare Legs in a Bed* (Heinemann).

Aiken Taylor Award for Modern American Poetry. To a writer of poetry who has had a substantial and distinguished career. *Offered by: Sewanee Review*. *Winner:* John Frederick Nims.

Betty Trask Awards (Great Britain). *Offered by:* Society of Authors. *Winners:* Amit Chaudhuri for *A Strange and Sublime Address* (Heinemann); Mark Swallow for *Teaching Little Fang* (Macmillan); Suzannah Dunn for *Quite Contrary* (Sinclair-Stevenson); Nino Ricci for *Lives of the Saints* (Allison & Busby); Simon Mason for *The Great English Nude* (Constable).

Frederick Jackson Turner Award. For a book on a significant phase of American history, by an author who has not previously published a book-length study of history. *Offered by:* Organization of American Historians. *Winner:* Christopher Clark for *The Roots of Rural Capitalism: Western Massachusetts, 1780–1860* (Cornell Univ.).

Turner Tomorrow Award. For the best work of fiction set in the near future with the theme of insuring the survival and prosperity of life on the planet. *Offered by:* Turner Publishing. *Winner:* Daniel Quinn for *Ishmael* (Turner).

Harold D. Vursell Memorial Award. *Offered by:* American Academy and Institute of Arts and Letters. *Winner:* Ursula K. Le Guin.

Whitbread Literary Awards (Great Britain). For literature of merit that is readable on a wide scale. *Offered by:* Booksellers Association of Great Britain. *Winners:* (novel) Jane Gardam for *The Queen of the Tambourine* (Sinclair-Stevenson); (first novel)

Gordon Burn for *Alma Cogan* (Secker & Warburg); (biography) John Richardson for *Life of Picasso: Volume I, 1881–1906* (Jonathan Cape); (poetry) Michael Longley for *Gorse Fires* (Secker & Warburg); (children's) Diana Hendry for *Harvey Angell* (Julia MacRae).

William Allen White Children's Book Award. *Winner:* Bill Wallace for *Beauty* (Holiday House).

Bill Whitehead Award. For lifetime achievement in gay and lesbian literature. *Offered by:* Publishing Triangle. *Winner:* James Purdy.

Whiting Writers Awards. *Offered by:* Mrs. Giles Whiting Foundation. *Winners:* Stanley Crouch, Rebecca Goldstein, Allegra Goodman, John Holman, Cynthia Kadohata, Scott McPherson, Thylias Moss, Rick Rofihe, Anton Shammas, Franz Wright.

Walt Whitman Award. *Offered by:* Academy of American Poets. *Winner:* Greg Glazner for *From the Iron Chair* (Norton).

Thornton Niven Wilder Prize. *Offered by:* Columbia University Translation Center. *Winners:* (Arabic) Jabra Ibrahim Jabra; (Czech) Luba and Rudolf Pellar; (Korean) Wang-rok Chang.

William Carlos Williams Award. For the best book of poetry published by a small, nonprofit, or university press. *Offered by:* Poetry Society of America. *Winners:* Joy Harjo for *In Mad Love and War* (Wesleyan Univ.); Safiya Henderson-Holmes for *Madness and a Bit of Hope* (Harlem River).

Woodrow Wilson Award. For the best book on government, politics, or international affairs. *Offered by:* American Political Science Association. *Winner:* Charles E. Londblom for *Inquiry and Change: The Troubled Attempt to Understand and Shape Society* (Yale Univ./Russell Sage).

Robert H. Winner Memorial Award. For a poem or sequence of poems characterized by a delight in language and the possibilities of ordinary life. *Offered by:* Poetry Society of America. *Winner:* James Richardson.

Laurence L. Winship Book Award. For a book having some relation to New England. *Offered by: Boston Globe. Winner:* Mary Oliver for *House of Light* (Beacon).

George Wittenborn Memorial Book Awards. *Offered by:* Art Libraries Society of North America. *Winners:* Abbeville Press for *Art Across America: Two Centuries of Regional Painting* by William Gerdts; Bedford Arts and the Corcoran Gallery of Art for *Facing History: The Black Image in American Art, 1710–1940* by Guy McElroy; Graphics Press for *Envisioning Information* by Edward Tufte; National Gallery of Canada for *Lisette Model* by Ann Thomas; Yale University Press for *Greek Sculpture: An Exploration* by Andrew Stewart.

Wolfson History Prize (Great Britain). *Offered by:* Wolfson Foundation. *Winner:* Colin Platt for *The Architecture of Medieval Britain* (Yale Univ.).

World Fantasy Convention Awards. *Winners:* (novel) James Morrow for *Only Begotten Daughter* (Morrow) and Ellen Kushner for *Thomas the Rhymer* (Morrow); (short story collection) Carol Emshwiller for *The Start of the End of It All* (Mercury House); (anthology) Stephen Jones and Ramsey Campbell, eds., for *Best New Horror* (Carroll & Graf); (life achievement) Rau Russell.

World Mystery Convention Anthony Awards. For outstanding mystery writing. *Winners:* (fiction) Sue Grafton for *G Is for Gumshoe* (Holt); (first novel) Patricia Daniels Cornwell for *Postmortem* (Scribners); (paperback original) Rochelle Krich for *Where's Mommy Now?* (Windsor) and James McCahery for *Grave Undertaking* (Knightsbridge); (critical work) Jon L. Breen and Martin H. Greenberg, eds., for *Synod of Sleuths* (Scarecrow).

World Science Fiction Convention Hugo Awards. For outstanding science fiction writing. *Winners:* (fiction) Lois McMaster Bujold for *The Vor Game* (Baen); (nonfiction) Orson Scott Card for *How to Write Science Fiction and Fantasy* (Writer's Digest).

Morton Dauwen Zabel Award for Criticism. *Offered by:* American Academy and Institute of Arts and Letters. *Winner:* Gordon Rogoff.

Part 6
Directory of Organizations

Directory of Library and Related Organizations

Networks, Consortia, and Other Cooperative Library Organizations

United States

Alabama

Jefferson County Hospital Librarians Association, Medical Lib., AMI, Brookwood Medical Center, 2010 Brookwood Dr., Birmingham 35209. SAN 371-2168. Tel. 205-877-1131. *Coord.* Lucy Moor.

Library Management Network, Inc., 915 Monroe St., Box 443, Huntsville 35804. SAN 322-3906. Tel. 205-532-5963. FAX 205-532-5967. *Pres.* Donna Schremser; *System Coord.* Charlotte Moncrief.

Marine Environmental Sciences Consortium, Dauphin Island Sea Lab, Box 369-370, Dauphin Island 36528. SAN 322-0001. Tel. 205-861-2141. FAX 205-861-4646. *Libn.* Connie Mallon; *Dir.* Judy Stout.

Network of Alabama Academic Libraries, c/o Alabama Commission on Higher Education, One Court Sq., Suite 221, Montgomery 36104-3584. SAN 322-4570. FAX 205-240-3349. *Dir.* Sue O. Medina.

Alaska

Alaska Library Network, c/o Alaska State Lib., Box G, Juneau 99811. SAN 371-0688. Tel. 907-465-2910. *Coord.* Judy Monroe.

Alaska State Library, Media Services, 650 W. International Airport Rd., Anchorage 99518-1393. SAN 300-2411. Tel. 907-561-1132. FAX 907-561-4683. *Supv.* Mary Jennings.

Arizona

Arizona Resources Consortium, c/o Northland Pioneer College, 1200 E. Hermosa Dr., Box 610, Holbrook 86025-0610. SAN 329-5176. Tel. 602-524-6111, Ext. 265. FAX 602-524-2772. *Head Libn.* Allen P. Rothlisberg; *Co-Dir.* Glen Tiller.

Central Arizona Biomedical Librarians, c/o Health Sciences Lib., 10450 N. 92 St., Scottsdale 85258-4514. SAN 370-7598. Tel. 602-860-3870. *Chpn.* Mary Lou Goldstein; *Program Chpn., Chpn.-Elect.* Susan Harker.

Maricopa County Community College District, Library Technical Services, 2325 E. McDowell Rd., Phoenix 85006. SAN 322-0060. Tel. 602-275-3301, 275-0474, 275-3588. FAX 602-220-9041. *Dir.* Laurita Moore de Diaz; *Bibliog. Coord.* Kathy A. Lynch.

Navajo County Library Consortium, c/o Northland Pioneer College, Box 610, Holbrook 86025. SAN 323-9896. Tel. 602-524-6111, Ext. 202. FAX 602-524-2772. *Admin.* Ronald J. Kupper; *Asst. Admin.* Allen P. Rothlisberg.

Arkansas

Arkansas Area Health Education Center Consortium (AHEC), Sparks Regional Medical Center, 1311 S. I St., Box 17006, Fort Smith 72917-7006. SAN 329-3734. Tel. 501-441-5337. FAX 501-441-5339. *Regional Health Science Libn.* Grace Anderson.

Independent College Fund of Arkansas, Twin City Bank Bldg., Suite 610, One Riverfront Place, North Little Rock 72114. SAN 322-0079. Tel. 501-378-0843. *Pres.* E. Kearney Dietz.

Northeast Arkansas Hospital Library Consortium, 223 E. Jackson, Jonesboro 72401. SAN 329-529X. Tel. 501-972-1290. FAX 501-931-0839. *Dir.* Peggy Blair.

South Arkansas Film Coop, Ash and E. Third, Malvern 72104. SAN 321-5938. Tel. 501-332-5442. FAX 501-332-6679. *Coord.* Mary Ann Griggs; *Project Dir.* Mary Cheatham.

California

Area Wide Library Network (AWLNET), 2420 Mariposa St., Fresno 93721. SAN 322-0087. Tel. 209-488-3229. *Dir. Info. Services* Sharon Vandercook.

Bay Area Library and Information Network (BAYNET), California Academy of Science, M. W. Malliard Jr. Lib., Golden Gate Park, San Francisco 94111. SAN 371-0610. Tel. 415-750-7101. *Pres.* Tom Moritz; *Treas.* Ann Patterson.

Central Association of Libraries, 605 N. El Dorado, Stockton 95202. SAN 322-0125. Tel. 209-944-8649. FAX 209-944-8292. *Pres.* Dennis Ward; *Dir.* Janet Kase.

Chiropractic Library Consortium (CLIB-CON), Los Angeles College of Chiropractic, 16200 E. Amber Valley Dr., Whittier 90604. SAN 370-078X. Tel. 213-947-8755, Ext. 235. *Pres.* Nahmat Saab.

CHLIC (Coastal Health Library Information Consortium), California Polytechnic State Univ., Kennedy Lib. Reference Dept., San Luis Obispo 93407. SAN 329-5427. Tel. 805-756-2649. *Chpn. of the Bd.* Eileen Pritchard.

Cooperating Libraries in Claremont (CLIC), c/o Honnold Lib., Claremont Colleges, 800 Dartmouth Ave., Claremont 91711. SAN 322-3949. Tel. 714-621-8045. *Dir.* Bonnie J. Clemens.

Cooperative Library Agency for Systems and Services (CLASS), 2225 W. Commonwealth Ave., Suite 313, Alhambra 91803-1332. SAN 322-0117. Tel. 408-453-0444. FAX 408-453-5379 (San Jose), 818-284-1475 (Alhambra). *Exec. Dir.* Robert A. Drescher; *Chpn.* Thomas E. Alford.

Dialog Information Services, Inc., 3460 Hillview Ave., Palo Alto 94304. SAN 322-0176. Tel. 415-858-3785. WATS 800-334-2564. FAX 415-858-7069. *Pres.* Patrick Tierney.

Health Information to Community Hospitals (HITCH), c/o Univ. of Southern California, Norris Medical Lib., 2003 Zonal Ave., Los Angeles 90033. SAN 322-4066. Tel. 213-342-1967. FAX 213-221-1235. *Dir.* Nelson J. Gilman; *Coord. and Libn.* Alice Karasick.

Inland Empire Academic Libraries Cooperative, c/o Univ. of California, Univ. Lib., Box 5900, Riverside 92517. SAN 322-015X. Tel. 714-787-3220. FAX 714-787-3285. *Chpn.* Doris Weingart.

Learning Resources Cooperative, c/o County Office of Education, 6401 Linda Vista Rd., San Diego 92111. SAN 371-0785. Tel. 619-693-6800. *Dir.* Marvin Barbula.

Los Angeles County Health Sciences Library Consortium, c/o Rancho Los Amigos Medical Center, Health Sciences Lib., 7601 E. Imperial Hwy., Downey 90242. SAN 322-4317. Tel. 213-940-7696. *Coord.* Evelyn Marks.

Medical Library and Information Consortium, c/o Planetree at San Jose Medical Center, 98 N. 17 St., San Jose 95112. SAN 371-0513. Tel. 408-998-3212, Ext. 4137. *Chpn.* Candace Ford.

Medical Library Consortium of Santa Clara Valley, Milton J. Chatton Medical Lib., 751 S. Bascom Ave., San Jose 95128. SAN 322-0184. Tel. 408-299-5650. FAX 408-299-8859. *Acting Medical Libn.* Shirley Kinoshita.

Mendocino-Lake Regional Library Consortium, c/o Ukiah Valley Medical Center, 275 Hospital Dr., Ukiah 95482. SAN 322-4090. Tel. 707-462-3111, ext. 177. *Libn.* Anna Sims.

Merced County Health Information Consortium, 301 E. 13 St., Merced 95240. SAN 329-4072. Tel. 209-385-7058. *Dir.* Betty Maddalena.

North Valley Health Science Library Consortium, 1540 Spruce, Chico 95926. SAN 329-5273. Tel. 916-894-8780. *Lib. Consultant.* Roger Brudno.

Northern California and Nevada Medical Library Group, 2140 Shattuck Ave., Box

2105, Berkeley 94704. SAN 329-4617. Tel. 415-266-1037. *Pres.* Terri L. Malmgren.

Northern California Association of Law Libraries (NOCALL), 1800 Market St., Box 109, San Francisco 94102. SAN 323-5777. Tel. 415-763-2070, Ext. 3495. FAX 415-273-8898. *Pres.* Nora Skrukrud; *V.P./Pres.-Elect.* Judy James.

Northern California Telecommunications Consortium, 2211 Park Towne Circle, No. 4, Sacramento 95825. SAN 329-4412. Tel. 916-483-2496. FAX 916-483-2497. *Exec. Dir.* Robert Wynian.

OCLC Pacific Network (PACNET), 9227 Haven Ave., Suite 260, Rancho Cucamonga 91730. SAN 370-0747. Tel. 714-941-4220. FAX 714-948-9803. *Dir.* Bruce Preslan.

Pacific Southwest Regional Medical Library Service, c/o Louise Darling Biomedical Lib., 10833 Le Conte Ave., Los Angeles 90024-1798. SAN 322-0192. Tel. 213-825-1200. ONTYME code: PSRMLS. *Dir.* Alison Bunting; *Assoc. Dir.* Beryl Glitz.

Psychological Studies Librarians, c/o Virginia Allan Detloff Lib., C. G. Jung Institute of San Francisco, 2040 Gough St., San Francisco 94109. SAN 329-4544. Tel. 415-771-8055. *Dir.* Joan Alpert.

Research Libraries Group, Inc., 1200 Villa St., Mountain View 94041-1100. SAN 322-0206. Tel. 415-962-9951. FAX 415-964-0943. *Pres.* James Michalko.

Sacramento Area Health Sciences Librarians, Guttman Lib. and Info. Center, Sacramento–El Dorado Medical Society, 5380 Elvas Ave., Sacramento, 95819. SAN 322-4007. Tel. 916-456-2687. FAX 916-456-2904. *Chpn.* Kathleen Rainey.

San Bernardino, Inyo, Riverside Counties United Library Services, 312 W. 20 St., Suite 2, San Bernardino 92405. SAN 322-0222. Tel. 714-882-7577. FAX 714-882-6871. *Dir.* Vaughn L. Simon.

San Francisco Biomedical Library Group, Northern California Health Center, Medical Lib., San Francisco 94115. SAN 371-2125. Tel. 415-750-6072. *Coord.* Peggy Tahir.

San Francisco Consortium, 513 Parnassus Ave., Box 0400, San Francisco 94143. SAN 322-0249. Tel. 415-476-9155. *Exec. Dir.* Malcolm S. M. Watts.

The SMERC Library, San Mateo County Office of Education, 333 Main St., Redwood City 94063. SAN 322-0265. Tel. 415-363-5470, Ext. 200. *Dir.* Karol Thomas; *Ref. Coord.* Mary Moray.

SOUTHNET, c/o South Bay Cooperative Lib. System, 180 W. San Carlos St., San Jose 95113. SAN 322-4260. Tel. 408-294-2345. FAX 408-295-7388. *Systems Dir.* Susan Holmer.

State of California Answering Network (SCAN), c/o Los Angeles Public Lib., 630 W. Fifth St., Los Angeles 90071-2097. SAN 322-029X. Tel. 213-612-3216. FAX 213-612-0546. *Dir.* Evelyn Greenwald.

Total Interlibrary Exchange (TIE), 5574 Everglades St., Suite A, Ventura 93003. SAN 322-0311. Tel. 805-650-7732, Ext. 25. ONTYME Code: AHNCL. FAX 805-643-8316. *Pres.* Benjamin E. Talley.

Colorado

Bibliographical Center for Research, Rocky Mountain Region, Inc., 4500 Cherry Creek Dr. S., Suite 206, Denver 80222-4310. SAN 322-0338. Tel. 303-691-0550. FAX 303-691-0112. *Exec. Dir.* David H. Brunell.

Colorado Alliance of Research Libraries, 777 Grant, Suite 304, Denver 80203. SAN 322-3760. Tel. 303-861-5319.

Colorado Association of Law Libraries, Box 13363, Denver 80201. SAN 322-4325. Tel. 303-492-4544. *Pres.* Richard Jost.

Colorado Council of Medical Librarians, c/o VA Medical Center, Lib. Service, 1055 Clermont St., Suite 142D, Denver 80220. SAN 370-0755. Tel. 303-393-2821. FAX 303-333-4935. *Pres.* Deborah A. Thompson; *Pres.-Elect.* Martha Burroughs.

Colorado Resource Sharing Network, c/o Colorado State Lib., 201 E. Colfax, Denver 80203-1799. SAN 322-3868. Tel. 303-866-6900. FAX 303-830-0793. *Coord.* Susan Fayad.

High Plains Regional Library Service System, 800 Eighth Ave., Suite 341, Greeley 80631. SAN 371-0505. Tel. 303-356-4357. *Dir.* Nancy Knepel; *Chpn.* Susan Wisner.

Irving Library Network, c/o Central Colorado Lib. System, 43 50 Wadsworth Blvd., Suite 340, Wheat Ridge 80033. SAN 325-321X. Tel. 303-422-1150. FAX 303-431-9752. *Network Mgr.* Gordon C. Barhydt.

Peaks and Plains Library Consortium, c/o Arkansas Valley Regional Lib. Service System, 635 W. Corona Ave., Suite 113, Pueblo 81004. SAN 328-8684. Tel. 719-542-2156. *Pres.* Jean Entze.

Pueblo Library System Software Users' Group, 100 E. Abriendo Ave., Pueblo 81004. SAN 322-4635. Tel. 719-543-9607. FAX 719-543-9610. *Dir.* Charles E. Bates.

Southwest Regional Library Service System, 736 Main Ave., Suite 200, Drawer B, Durango 81302. SAN 371-0815. Tel. 303-247-4782. *Technical Services Consultant.* Judith M. Griffiths.

Connecticut

Capitol Area Health Consortium, 183 E. Cedar St., Newington 06111. SAN 322-0370. Tel. 203-666-3304, Ext. 302. *Dir.* Robert Boardman.

Capitol Region Library Council, 599 Matianuck Ave., Windsor 06095-3567. SAN 322-0389. Tel. 203-549-0404. *Exec. Dir.* Dency Sargent; *Asst. Exec. Dir.* Elizabeth Wilkens; *Asst. Dir. for Automated User Services* Robert Connell; *Asst. Dir. for Automated Systems* Joan Graep.

Connecticut Association of Health Sciences Libraries, Waterbury Hospital, Health Sciences Lib., 64 Robbins St., Waterbury 06721. SAN 322-0397. Tel. 203-573-6148. FAX 203-573-7324. *Pres.* Joan Ruszkowski.

Council of State Library Agencies in the Northeast (COSLINE), Connecticut State Lib., 231 Capitol Ave., Hartford 06106. SAN 322-0451. Tel. 203-566-4301. FAX 203-566-8940. *Pres.* Richard G. Akeroyd, Jr.

CTW Library Consortium, Olin Memorial Lib., Wesleyan Univ., Middletown 06457-6065. SAN 329-4587. Tel. 203-347-9411, Ext. 3143. FAX 203-344-7969. *Dir.* Alan E. Hagyard; *Applications Programmer* Mary Wilson; *Systems Programmer* Bu Yang.

Eastern Connecticut Library Association, 15 Wilson St., Willimantic 06226-1920. SAN 322-0427. Tel. 203-456-4343. FAX 203-423-1839. *Exec. Dir.* Marietta Johnson.

Film Cooperative of Connecticut, Inc., Wilson Public Lib., 365 Windsor Ave., Windsor 06095. SAN 322-0435. Tel. 203-285-1931, 247-8960. *In Charge* Gay Rizzo.

Hartford Consortium for Higher Education, 260 Girard Ave., Hartford 06105. SAN 322-0443. Tel. 203-236-1203. *Dir.* Ruth Billyou.

LEAP (Library Exchange Aids Patrons), 2901 Dixwell Ave., Hamden 06518. SAN 322-4082. Tel. 203-281-7498. FAX 203-248-8431. *Exec. Dir.* Richard Dionne; *Chpn.* Lois Baldini.

Libraries Online Inc. (LION), 123 Broad St., Middletown 06457. SAN 322-3922. Tel. 203-347-1704. *Pres.* Sandra Ruoff; *Exec. Dir.* William F. Edge, Jr.

North Atlantic Health Science Libraries, c/o Univ. of Connecticut Health Center Lib., Box 4003, Farmington 06034-4003. SAN 371-0599. Tel. 203-679-3323. *Chpn.* Marion Holena Levine; *Chpn.-Elect.* Darryl Hamson.

Northwestern Connecticut Health Science Libraries, 50 Hospital Hill Rd., Sharon 06069. SAN 329-5257. Tel. 203-364-4095. *Libn.* Michael Schott; *Coord.* Jackie Rourke.

Region One Cooperating Library Service Unit, Inc., 267 Grand St., Waterbury 06702-1981. SAN 322-046X. Tel. 203-756-6149. FAX 203-757-1117. *Coord.* Tom Laurence; *Admin. Asst.* Vanessa Vowe.

Southeastern Connecticut Library Association (SECLA), 1084 Shennecossett Rd., Groton 06340-9998. SAN 322-0478. Tel. 203-445-5577. *Dirs.* Patricia Holloway, Joan Schneider.

Southern Connecticut Library Council, 60 N. Main St., Wallingford 06492-3712. SAN 322-0486. Tel. 203-284-3641. FAX 203-269-8359. *Dir.* Susan Carlquist Muro.

Southwestern Connecticut Library Council, Inc., 925 Broad St., Bridgeport 06604. SAN 322-0494. Tel. 203-367-6439. FAX 203-367-2521. *Admin.* Ann Neary.

Delaware

Central Delaware Library Consortium, Dover Public Lib., 45 S. State St., Dover 19901. SAN 329-3696. Tel. 302-736-7030. *Dir.* Robert S. Wetherall.

Delaware Library Consortium, Delaware Academy of Medicine, 1925 Lovering Ave., Wilmington 19806. SAN 329-3718. Tel. 302-656-6398. FAX 302-656-0470. *Contact* Gail P. Gill.

Kent Library Network, Dover High School Lib., 625 Walker Rd., Dover 19901. SAN 371-2214. Tel. 302-739-5578. *Pres.* Ralph B. Hinzman.

Libraries in the New Castle County System (LINCS), Delaware Academy of Medicine, 1925 Lovering Ave., Wilmington 19806. SAN 329-4889. Tel. 302-656-6398. *Pres.* Louise Tabasso; *Treas.* Dee Dee Dodd.

Sussex Help Organization for Resources Exchange (SHORE), Laurel and Railroad Ave., Georgetown 19947-1442. SAN 322-4333. Tel. 302-227-8044. *Pres.* Margaret Lafond.

Wilmington Area Biomedical Library Consortium, 1925 Lovering Ave., Wilmington 19806. SAN 322-0508. Tel. 302-656-6398. *Pres.* Gail P. Gill.

District of Columbia

CAPCON Library Network, 1717 Massachusetts Ave. N.W., Suite 101, Washington 20036. SAN 321-5954. Tel. 202-745-7722. *Exec. Dir.* Dennis Reynolds.

Christian College Coalition, 329 Eighth St. N.E., Washington 20002. SAN 322-0524. Tel. 202-546-8713. FAX 202-546-8913. *Pres.* Myron S. Augsburger.

Cluster of Independent Theological Schools, 391 Michigan Ave. N.E., Washington 20017. SAN 322-0532. Tel. 202-529-5244. *Pres.* Richard Murphy.

District of Columbia Health Sciences Information Network, 409 12th St. S.W., Washington 20024. SAN 323-9918. Tel. 202-863-2548. *Pres.* Cathie DeGeorges; *V.P. & Program Chpn.* Kathie Meikamp.

Division of Information and Library Services, Dept. of the Interior, 18 and C Sts. N.W., Mail Stop 2249, Washington, 20240. SAN 322-080X. Tel. 202-208-5821. *Chpn.* Philip Haymond.

EDUCOM, c/o 1112 16th St. N.W., Suite 600, Washington 20036. SAN 371-487X. Tel. 202-872-4200. *Pres.* Kenneth King; *Mgr. of Membership* Kathy Schaible.

ERIC (Educational Resources Information Center), U.S. Dept. of Educ., 555 New Jersey Ave. N.W., Washington 20208-5720. SAN 322-0567. Tel. 202-219-2289. FAX 202-219-1817. *Dir.* Robert Stonehill.

ERIC Clearinghouses
—ERIC Clearinghouse for Junior Colleges, Mathematical Sciences Bldg., Rm. 8118, Univ. of California, 405 Hilgard Ave., Los Angeles, CA 90024-1564. SAN 322-0648. Tel. 213-825-3931. FAX 213-206-8095. *Dir.* Art Cohen.
—ERIC Clearinghouse for Science, Mathematics and Environmental Education, Ohio State Univ., 1200 Chambers Rd., Rm. 310, Columbus, OH 43212-1792. SAN 322-0680. Tel. 614-292-6717. FAX 614-292-0263. *Dir.* Patricia Blosser.
—ERIC Clearinghouse for Social Studies–Social Science Education, Indiana Univ., Social Studies Development Center, 2805 E. Tenth St., Bloomington, IN 47408-2373. SAN 322-0699. Tel. 812-885-3838. FAX 812-855-7901. *Dir.* John Patrick.
—ERIC Clearinghouse on Adult, Career, and Vocational Education, Center on Education and Training for Employment, 1900 Kenny Rd., Columbus, OH 43210-1090. SAN 322-0575. Tel. 614-292-4353. WATS 800-848-4815. FAX 614-292-1260. *Dir.* Susan Imel.
—ERIC Clearinghouse on Counseling and Personnel Services, Univ. of Michigan, School of Education, Rm. 2108, 610 E. University St., Ann Arbor, MI 48109-1259. SAN 322-0583. Tel. 313-764-9492. FAX 312-247-2425. *Dir.* Garry Walz.
—ERIC Clearinghouse on Educational Management, Univ. of Oregon, 1787 Agate St., Eugene, OR 97403-5207. SAN 322-0605. Tel. 503-686-5043. *Dir.* Phil Piele.
—ERIC Clearinghouse on Elementary and Early Childhood Education, College of Education, Univ. of Illinois, 805 W. Pennsylvania Ave., Urbana, IL 61801-4897. SAN 322-0591. Tel. 217-333-1386. *Dir.* Lilian Katz.
—ERIC Clearinghouse on Handicapped and Gifted Children, Council for Exceptional Children, 1920 Association Dr., Reston, VA 22091-1589. SAN 322-0613. Tel. 703-620-3660. FAX 703-264-9494. *Dir.* Fred Weintraub.
—ERIC Clearinghouse on Higher Education, George Washington Univ., One Dupont Circle, Suite 630, Washington, DC 20036-1183. SAN 322-0621. Tel. 202-296-2597. FAX 202-296-8379. *Dir.* Jon Fife.

—ERIC Clearinghouse on Information Resources, Syracuse Univ., School of Education, Huntington Hall, Rm. 030, Syracuse, NY 13244-2340. SAN 322-063X. Tel. 315-443-3640. FAX 315-443-5732. *Dir.* Michael Eisenberg.

—ERIC Clearinghouse on Languages and Linguistics, Center for Applied Linguistics, 1118 22nd St. N.W., Washington, DC 20037-0037. SAN 322-0656. Tel. 202-429-9551. FAX 202-429-9766. *Dir.* Charles Stansfield.

—ERIC Clearinghouse on Reading and Communication Skills, Indiana Univ., Smith Research Center, Bloomington, IN 47405-2373. SAN 322-0664. Tel. 812-855-5847. FAX 812-855-7901. *Dir.* Carl Smith.

—ERIC Clearinghouse on Rural Education and Small Schools, Appalachia Educational Laboratory, 1031 Quarrier St., Box 1348, Charleston, WV 25325-1348. SAN 322-0672. Tel. 304-347-0400. WATS 800-624-9120. FAX 304-347-0487. *Dirs.* Todd Strohmenger, Craig Howley.

—ERIC Clearinghouse on Teacher Education, American Association of Colleges for Teacher Education, One Dupont Circle N.W., Suite 610, Washington, DC 20036-2412. SAN 322-0702. Tel. 202-293-2450. FAX 202-457-8095. *Dir.* Mary Dilworth.

—ERIC Clearinghouse on Tests, Measurement and Evaluation, American Institutes for Research, Washington Research Center, 3333 K St. N.W., Washington, DC 20007. SAN 322-0710. Tel. 202-342-5600. FAX 202-342-5033. *Dir.* Lawrence Rudner.

—ERIC Clearinghouse on Urban Education, Teachers College, Columbia Univ., 525 W. 120 St., Box 40, New York, NY 10027-9998. SAN 322-0729. Tel. 212-678-3433. FAX 212-678-4048. *Dir.* Erwin Flaxman.

FEDLINK (Federal Library and Information Network), c/o Federal Lib. and Info. Center Committee, Lib. of Congress, Washington 20540. SAN 322-0761. Tel. 202-707-6454. *Network Dir.* Mary B. Levering; *Network Coord.* Milton Megee.

Forest Service Information Network, USDA Forest Service, Box 96090, Washington 20090-6090. SAN 322-032X. Tel. 703-235-1042. *Mgr.* Seung Ja Sinatra; *Libn.* Hope Stanton.

NASA Library Network, ARIN (Aerospace Research Information Network), NASA Headquarters, Code NTT-1, Washington 20546. SAN 322-0788. Tel. 703-271-5626. FAX 703-271-5669. *Admin. Libn.* Adelaide DelFrate.

National Library Service for the Blind and Physically Handicapped, 1291 Taylor St. N.W., Washington 20542. SAN 370-5870. Tel. 202-707-5100. FAX 202-707-0712. *Dir.* Frank Kurt Cylke; *Asst. to the Dir.* Marvine R. Wanamaker.

Transportation Research Information Services, 2101 Constitution Ave. N.W., TRB, GR322, Washington 20418. SAN 370-582X. Tel. 202-334-2995. *Mgr.* Jerome T. Maddock.

Veterans Affairs Library Network (VALNET), VA Lib. Div. (143D), 810 Vermont Ave. N.W., Washington 20420. SAN 322-0834. Tel. 202-233-2711. FAX 202-535-7539. *Asst. Dir.* Karen Renninger.

Washington Theological Consortium, 487 Michigan Ave. N.E., Washington 20017-1585. SAN 322-0842. Tel. 202-832-2675. *Exec. Dir.* David Trickett.

Florida

Florida Library Information Network, c/o Bureau of Lib. Development, State Lib. of Florida, R. A. Gray Bldg., Tallahassee 32399-0250. SAN 322-0869. Tel. 904-487-2651. *State Libn.* Barratt Wilkins; *Chief, Lib. Development* Sandra Cooper.

Library Affairs Committee of the Associated Mid-Florida Colleges, c/o Merl Kelce Lib., Univ. of Tampa, Tampa 33606. SAN 322-0877. Tel. 813-253-6231. FAX 813-251-0016. *Dir.* Lydia Acosta.

Miami Health Sciences Library Consortium, c/o South Miami Hospital, Health Sciences Lib., 7400 S.W. 62 Ave., Miami 33143. SAN 371-0734. Tel. 305-661-4611, Ext. 8219. *Contact* Celia Steinberg.

Palm Beach Health Sciences Library Consortium, c/o Good Samaritan Health Systems Medical Lib., Box 3166, West Palm Beach 33402. SAN 370-0380. Tel. 407-650-6315. FAX 407-650-6239. *Chpn.* Linda Kressal.

Panhandle Library Access Network, 25 W. Government St., Caller Box 2625, Panama City 32401. SAN 370-047X. Tel. 904-785-3457. *Chpn.* George W. Vickery.

Southeast Florida Library Information Network, Inc. (SEFLIN), 100 S. Andrews Ave.,

Fort Lauderdale 33301. SAN 370-0666. Tel. 305-357-7318. FAX 305-357-6998. *Exec. Dir.* Richard Luce; *Pres.* Carol Roehrenback.

Tampa Bay Library Consortium, Inc., 10002 Princess Palm Ave., Suite 126, Tampa 33619. SAN 322-371X. Tel. 813-622-8252. FAX 813-628-4425. *Pres.* Barbara Ponce; *Acting Exec. Dir.* Deborah Fritz.

Tampa Bay Medical Library Network (TABAMLN), VA Medical Center Lib., Box 527, Bay Pines 33504. SAN 322-0885. Tel. 813-462-7889.

South Georgia Associated Libraries, 208 Gloucester St., Brunswick 31523-0901. SAN 322-0966. Tel. 912-267-1212. FAX 912-267-9597. *Secy.-Treas.* Jim Darby.

Southeastern Library Network (SOLINET), 400 Colony Sq., Plaza Level, Atlanta 30361-6301. SAN 322-0974. Tel. 404-892-0943. FAX 404-892-7879. *Exec. Dir.* Frank P. Grisham.

University Center in Georgia, Inc., 50 Hurt Plaza, Suite 465, Atlanta 30303-2923. SAN 322-0990. Tel. 404-651-2668. FAX 404-656-0757. *Exec. Dir.* Charles B. Bedford.

Georgia

Atlanta Health Science Libraries Consortium, Saint Joseph's Hospital, 5665 Peachtree Dunwoody Rd., Atlanta 30342. SAN 322-0893. Tel. 404-851-7040. FAX 404-851-7869. *Pres.* Beth Poisson.

Central Georgia Associated Libraries, c/o Wesleyan College, Willet Memorial Lib., 4760 Forsyth Rd., Macon 31297. SAN 322-0907. Tel. 912-477-1110, Ext. 200.

Consortium of Southern Biomedical Libraries (CONBLS), c/o Mercer Univ., Macon 31207. SAN 370-7717. Tel. 912-752-2515. *Pres.* Jocelyn Rankin; *Pres.-Elect.* Janet Fisher.

Cooperative College Library Center, Inc., Suite 602, 159 Ralph McGill Blvd., Atlanta 30308. SAN 322-0915. Tel. 404-659-6886. FAX 404-577-0131. *Dir.* Christopher Keene.

Emory Medical Television Network, 1440 Clifton Rd. N.E., Rm. 110, Atlanta 30322. SAN 322-0931. Tel. 404-688-8736. FAX 404-523-4706. *Dir.* Dan Joiner; *Business Mgr. & Producer* Julie S. Budnik.

Georgia Interactive Network for Medical Information (GaIN), c/o Medical Lib., School of Medicine, Mercer Univ., 1550 College St., Macon 31207. SAN 370-0577. Tel. 912-752-2515. FAX 912-752-2051. *Dir.* Jocelyn A. Rankin.

Georgia Online Database (formerly Georgia Library Information Network), c/o Div. of Public Lib. Services, 156 Trinity Ave. S.W., 1st fl., Atlanta 30303-3692. SAN 322-094X. Tel. 404-656-2461. FAX 404-656-7297. *Dir.* Joe Forsee; *Consultant* Jo Ellen Ostendorf.

Idaho

Boise Valley Health Sciences Library Consortium, Health Sciences Lib., Saint Alphonsus Regional Medical Center, Boise 83706. SAN 371-0807. Tel. 208-378-2271. *Contact* Judy Bakerzak.

CLSI Consortium, 715 S. Capitol Blvd., Boise 83702. SAN 323-7710. Tel. 208-384-4466. *Contact* Marilyn Taylor.

Cooperative Information Network, 5920 Government Way, Coeur d'Alene 83814. SAN 323-7656. Tel. 208-772-7648. *Contact* John Hartung.

Eastern Idaho System, 457 Broadway, Idaho Falls 83402. SAN 323-7699. Tel. 208-529-1450. FAX 208-529-1148. *Contact* Paul Holland.

Health Information Retrieval Center, Saint Luke's Regional Medical Center, 190 E. Bannock St., Boise 83712. SAN 322-1008. Tel. 208-386-2277. FAX 208-384-0254. *Dir.* Pamela Spickelmier.

Southeast Idaho Health Information Consortium, Bannock Regional Medical Center, Medical Lib., Pocatello 83201. SAN 322-4341. Tel. 208-232-6150, Ext. 1170. FAX 208-232-6441. *Lib. Technician* Lynda Greenwood.

VALNET, Eighth Ave. and Sixth St., Lewiston 83501. SAN 323-7672. Tel. 208-799-2395. FAX 208-799-2831. *Contact* Ann Harris.

Illinois

Areawide Hospital Library Consortium of Southwestern Illinois (AHLC), c/o Memorial Hospital, 4501 N. Park Dr., Belleville

62223. SAN 322-1016. Tel. 618-233-7750, Ext. 5343. *Coord.* Barbara Grout.

Association of Chicago Theological Schools, 5757 S. University Ave., Chicago 60637. SAN 370-0658. Tel. 312-752-5757. *Pres.* Mark Sisk; *Pres.-Elect.* Don Senior.

Capital Area Consortium, Passavant Area Hospital Lib., 1600 W. Walnut, Jacksonville 62650. SAN 322-1024. FAX 217-245-9341. *Coord.* Dorothy Knight.

Center for Research Libraries, 5721 Cottage Grove Ave. and 6050 S. Kenwood, Chicago 60637. SAN 322-1032. Tel. 312-955-4545. FAX 312-955-4339. *Pres.* Donald B. Simpson.

Chicago and South Consortium, c/o Good Samaritan Hospital, Medical Lib., 3815 Highland Ave., Downers Grove 60575. SAN 322-1067. Tel. 708-963-5900, Ext. 1070. *Coord.* Susan Marshall.

Council of Directors of State University Librarians of Illinois, Western Illinois Univ. Lib., Macomb 61455-1391. SAN 322-1083. Tel. 309-298-2762 (voice and FAX). *Chpn.* Donna Goehner.

East Central Illinois Consortium, Medical Lib., Sarah Bush Lincoln H.C., Box 372, Mattoon 61938. SAN 322-1040. Tel. 217-258-2262. FAX 217-258-2111. *Coord.* Nina Pals.

Fox Valley Health Science Library Consortium, Marianjoy Rehabilitation Center, Medical Lib., Box 795, Wheaton 60189. SAN 329-3831. Tel. 708-462-4104. *Coord.* Nalini Mahajan.

Greater Midwest Regional Medical Library Network — Region 3, c/o Lib. of the Health Sciences, Univ. of Illinois at Chicago, 1750 W. Polk St., Box 7509, Chicago 60680. SAN 322-1202. Tel. 312-996-2464. *Regional Medical Lib. Dir.* Frieda O. Weise; *Assoc. Regional Medical Lib. Dir.* Ruby S. May.

Heart of Illinois Library Consortium, c/o Health Sciences Lib., Bromenn Health Care, 807 N. Main St., Bloomington 61702. SAN 322-1113. Tel. 309-827-4321. FAX 309-829-0707. *Dir.* Toni Tucker.

Illinois Department of Mental Health and Developmental Disabilities Library Services Network (LISN), c/o ISPI, 1601 W. Taylor, Chicago 60612. SAN 322-1121. Tel. 312-413-1320. FAX 312-413-1010. *Chpn.* Margo McClelland.

Illinois Health Libraries Consortium, c/o Meat Industry Info. Center, National Livestock and Meat Board, 444 N. Michigan Ave., Chicago 60611. SAN 322-113X. Tel. 312-467-5520, Ext. 272. *Dir.* William D. Siarny, Jr.

Illinois Library and Information Network (ILLINET), c/o Illinois State Lib., Springfield 62701-1796. SAN 322-1148. Tel. 217-782-2994. FAX 217-785-4326. *Dir.* Bridget L. Lamont; *Asst. Dir.* Preston Levi.

Illinois Library Computer Systems Organization, Univ. of Illinois, 205 Johnstowne Centre, 502 E. John St., Champaign 61820. SAN 322-3736. Tel. 217-244-7593. FAX 217-244-7596. *Dir.* Bernard G. Sloan; *Assoc. Dir.* Kristine Hammerstrand; *Lib. Systems Coord.* Mary Ellen Farrell.

Illinois Valley Library System, 845 Brenkman Dr., Peekman 61554. SAN 371-0637. Tel. 309-353-4110. *Exec. Dir.* Valerie J. Wilford.

Judaica Library Network of Metropolitan Chicago, c/o Asher Lib., Spertus College of Judaica, 618 S. Michigan Ave., Chicago 60605. SAN 370-0615. Tel. 312-922-9012, Ext. 252. *Pres.* Robin Katzin.

Libras Inc., Barat College, 700 E. Westleigh Rd., Lake Forest 60045. SAN 322-1172. Tel. 708-295-4488, Ext. 617. *Pres.* Alan Barney.

Metropolitan Consortium of Chicago, Illinois College of Optometry Lib., 3241 S. Michigan, Chicago 60616. SAN 322-1180. Tel. 312-225-1700, Ext. 691. FAX 312-791-1971. *Coord.* Gerald Dujsik.

Northern Illinois Learning Resources Cooperative, 91 Sugar Lane, Suite 4, Box 509, Sugar Grove 60554. SAN 329-5583. Tel. 708-466-4848. FAX 708-466-4895. *Exec. Dir.* Donald E. Drake.

Private Academic Libraries of Illinois, c/o North Park College Lib., 3225 W. Foster Ave., Chicago 60625. SAN 370-050X. Tel. 312-583-2700, Ext. 4081. FAX 312-463-0570.

River Bend Library System, Box 125, Coal Valley 61240. SAN 371-0653. Tel. 309-799-3155. *Coord.* Mary Root.

Sangamon Valley Academic Library Consortium, Box 19231, Springfield 62794-9231. SAN 322-4406. Tel. 217-782-2658. FAX 217-782-0988. *Chpn.* Roger Guard.

Shabbona Consortium, c/o Illinois Valley Community Hospital, 925 West St., Peru

61354. SAN 329-5133. Tel. 815-223-3300, Ext. 494. *Dir.* Karen Miller.

Upstate Consortium of Illinois, Saint Anthony College of Nursing Lib., 5666 E. State St., Rockford 61108. SAN 329-3793. Tel. 815-395-5097. *Coord.* Mary Pat Pryor.

USA Toy Library Association, 2719 Broadway, Evanston 60201. SAN 371-215X. Tel. 708-864-8240. *Exec. Dir.* Judith Q. Iacuzzi.

Indiana

Area Library Services Authority Region 2, 209 Lincolnway E., Mishawaka 46544-2084. SAN 322-1210. Tel. 219-255-5262. FAX 219-255-8489. *Exec. Dir.* James D. Cline.

Area 3 Library Services Authority (TRI-ALSA), 900 Webster St., Box 2270, Fort Wayne 46801-2270. SAN 322-1229. Tel. 219-424-6664. FAX 219-422-9688. *Coord.* Jane Raifsnider; *Reference Center Dir.* Marla Baden.

Central Indiana Area Library Services Authority, 1100 W. 42 St., Suite 305, Indianapolis 46208. SAN 322-1237. Tel. 317-926-6561. FAX 317-923-3658. *Exec. Dir.* Judith Ellyn.

Central Indiana Health Science Libraries Consortium, 1701 N. Senate Blvd., Methodist Hospital Lib., Box 1367, Indianapolis 46206. SAN 322-1245. Tel. 317-929-8021. *Coord.* Dorothy Jobe.

Collegiate Consortium Western Indiana, c/o Cunningham Memorial Lib., Indiana State Univ., Terre Haute 47809. SAN 329-4439. Tel. 812-237-3700. FAX 812-237-2567. *Dean* Ronald G. Leech.

Eastern Indiana Area Library Services Authority, 111 E. 12 St., Anderson 46016. SAN 322-1253. Tel. 317-641-2471. FAX 317-641-2468, 747-8221. *Admin.* Harold W. Boyce.

Evansville Area Library Consortium, 3700 Washington Ave., Evansville 47750. SAN 322-1261. Tel. 812-479-4151. *Coord.* E. Jane Saltzman.

Four Rivers Area Library Services Authority, Rm. 5, Old Vanderburgh County Court House, Evansville 47708-1355. SAN 322-127X. Tel. 812-425-1946. FAX 812-425-1969. *Exec. Dir.* Ida L. McDowell.

Indiana Cooperative Library Services Authority (INCOLSA), 5929 Lakeside Blvd., Indi-

anapolis 46278-1996. SAN 322-1296. Tel. 317-298-6570. FAX 317-328-2380. *Exec. Dir.* Barbara Evans Markuson; *Asst. Exec. Dir.* Jan Cox.

– INCOLSA Processing Center, 5929 Lakeside Blvd., Indianapolis 46278-1996. SAN 322-130X. Tel. 317-298-6570. *Head* Nancy Davey.

Indiana State Data Center, Indiana State Lib., 140 N. Senate Ave., Indianapolis 46204-2296. SAN 322-1318. Tel. 317-232-3733. *Coord.* Roberta Eads.

La Porte, Porter, Starke Health Science Library Consortium, Moellering Lib., Valparaiso Univ., Valparaiso 46383-9978. SAN 322-1334. Tel. 219-464-5366, Ext. 7177. *Coord.* Judith Miller.

Northwest Indiana Area Library Services Authority, 1919 W. 81 Ave., Merrillville 46410. SAN 322-1342. Tel. 219-736-0631. WATS 800-552-8950. FAX 219-736-0633. *Pres.* Philip Baugher; *Admin.* Barbara Topp.

Northwest Indiana Health Science Library Consortium, c/o Northwest Center for Medical Education, Indiana Univ. School of Medicine, 3400 Broadway, Gary 46408-1197. SAN 322-1350. Tel. 219-980-6852. FAX 219-980-6566. *Coord.* Rachel Feldman.

Society of Indiana Archivists, c/o Indiana Historical Society, 315 W. Ohio St., Indianapolis 46202. SAN 329-5508. Tel. 317-232-1882. FAX 317-233-3109. *Pres.* F. Gerald Handfield; *Secy.-Treas.* Thomas Krasean.

Southeastern Indiana Area Library Services Authority, 128 W. Spring St., New Albany 47150-3639. SAN 322-1369. Tel. 812-948-8639. FAX 812-948-0293. *Exec. Dir.* Sue Stultz.

Stone Hills Area Library Services Authority, 112 N. Walnut, Suite 500, Bloomington 47408. SAN 322-1377. Tel. 812-334-8347. FAX 812-323-4352. *Coord.* Sara G. Laughlin.

Wabash Valley Library Network, 629 South St., Lafayette 47901. SAN 322-1385. Tel. 317-429-0250. *Admin.* Dennis Lawson; *Reference Libn.* Becky Marthey.

Iowa

Bi-State Academic Libraries (BI-SAL), c/o Marycrest College, Davenport 52804. SAN 322-1393. Tel. 319-326-9254. *Chpn.* Sister Joan Sheil.

Chiropractic Library Consortium (CLIB-CON), c/o Palmer College Lib., 1000 Brady St., Davenport 52803. SAN 328-8218. Tel. 319-326-9894. FAX 319-326-9897. *Chpn.* Nehmat Saab.

Dubuque (Iowa) Area Library Information Consortium, c/o Carnegie-Stout Lib., 360 11th St., Dubuque 52001. SAN 322-1407. *Pres.* Carolynne Lathrop, Univ. of Dubuque Lib. Tel. 319-589-3100; *Lib. Mgr.* James H. Lander.

Iowa Computer Assisted Network, State Lib. of Iowa, E. 12 and Grand Ave., Des Moines 50319. SAN 322-1415. Tel. 515-281-4118. *State Libn.* Shirley George.

Iowa Online Users Group, Iowa Dept. of Educ., Grimes State Office Bldg., Des Moines 50319-0146. SAN 322-3728. Tel. 515-281-5286. *Chpn.* Mary Jo Bruett.

Iowa Private Academic Library Consortium (IPAL), Central College Lib. Center, 812 University, Pella 50219. SAN 329-5311. Tel. 515-628-9000. *Dir.* Julie Hansen; *Reference Libn.* Christie Lindemann.

Linn County Library Consortium, Box 125, Cedar Rapids 52406. SAN 322-4597. Tel. 319-395-6581. *Pres.* Jo Ann Pearson; *V.P.* Margaret White.

Polk County Biomedical Consortium, c/o State Medical Lib., E. 12 and Grand Ave., Des Moines 50319. SAN 322-1431. Tel. 515-281-5772. *Coord.* Tricia Downey.

Quad City Area Biomedical Consortium, United Medical Center, School of Nursing Lib., 501 Tenth Ave., Moline 61265. SAN 322-435X. Tel. 309-757-2912. *Coord.* Jeanne Gittings.

Sioux City Library Cooperative, c/o Sioux City Public Lib., 529 Pierce St., Sioux City 51101-1203. SAN 329-4722. Tel. 712-252-5669. *Agent* George H. Scheetz.

Tri-College Cooperative Effort, Loras College, c/o Wahlert Memorial Lib., 1450 Alta Vista, Dubuque 52004-0178. SAN 322-1466. Tel. 319-588-7125. FAX 319-588-7292. *Dirs.* Paul Roberts, Joel Samuels, Robert Klein.

Kansas

Associated Colleges of Central Kansas, 105 E. Kansas, McPherson 67460. SAN 322-1474. Tel. 316-241-5150. *Libn.* Donna Zerger.

Dodge City Library Consortium, 1001 Second Ave., Dodge City 67801. SAN 322-4368. Tel. 316-225-0248. *Chpn.* Cathy Reeves.

Kansas City Regional Council for Higher Education, 8016 State Line Rd., Suite 205, Leawood 66208-3710. SAN 322-211X. Tel. 913-341-4141. FAX 913-341-5768. *Dir.* D. Stanley Love; *Pres.* Larry Rose.

Kansas Library Network Board, State Capitol, 3rd fl., Topeka 66612. SAN 329-5621. Tel. 913-296-3296. FAX 913-296-6650. *Exec. Dir.* Michael Piper.

Kansas State Audiovisual Center, 223 S. Main, Wichita 67202. SAN 322-1482. Tel. 316-262-0611. FAX 316-262-2552. *Dir.* Sondra B. Koontz.

UTLAS International US Inc., 8300 College Blvd., Overland Park 66210. SAN 322-3701. Tel. 913-451-3111. FAX 913-451-2551. *Pres. and Chief Exec. Officer* Richard W. Newman; *Sr. V.P. Marketing and Planning* Ken Harris.

Kentucky

Council of Independent Kentucky Colleges and Universities, Box 668, Danville 40423-0668. SAN 322-1490. Tel. 606-236-3533. FAX 606-236-3534. *Exec. Dir.* John W. Frazer; *Dir. Lib. Consortium* Christy Robinson.

Eastern Kentucky Health Science Information Network, c/o Camden-Carroll Lib., Morehead State Univ., Morehead 40351. SAN 370-0631. Tel. 606-783-2610. FAX 606-784-3788. *Consortium Coord.* William DeBord.

Kentuckiana Metroversity Inc., 3113 Lexington Rd., Louisville 40206. SAN 322-1504. Tel. 502-897-3374. FAX 502-895-1647. *Exec. Dir.* Thomas Diener.

Kentucky Health Science Libraries Consortium, Methodist Evangelical Hospital, 211 E. Jacob St., Louisville 40203-2341. SAN 370-0623. Tel. 502-897-8183. *Libn.* Garry Block Johnson; *Pres.* Leslie Pancratz.

Kentucky Library Information Center, c/o Western Kentucky Univ., Helm Lib., Office 101, Bowling Green 42101-3576. SAN 322-1512. Tel. 502-745-4011. FAX 502-745-5943. *Dir.* Michael Binder.

Kentucky Library Network Inc., 300 Coffee Tree Rd., Box 537, Frankfort 40602. SAN

371-2184. Tel. 502-875-7000. *Pres.* Sally Livingston.

Northern Kentucky Regional Library Consortia, c/o Northern Kentucky Regional Lib., Covington 41011. SAN 329-5079. Tel. 606-431-1043. FAX 606-491-2860. *Regional Libn.* Martha Rankin.

State Assisted Academic Library Council of Kentucky, c/o Eastern Kentucky Univ., Crab Lib., Richmond 40575. SAN 371-2222. Tel. 602-622-1778. *Chpn. and Pres.* Ernest E. Weyhrauch.

Theological Education Association of Mid America (TEAM-A), c/o Southern Baptist Theological Seminary, 2825 Lexington Rd., Louisville 40280-0294. SAN 322-1547. Tel. 502-897-4807. *Dir.* Ronald F. Deering.

Louisiana

Baton Rouge Hospital Library Consortium, Our Lady of the Lake Regional Medical Center, 5000 Hennessy Blvd., Baton Rouge 70808. SAN 329-4714. Tel. 504-765-8756. *Dir.* Diane Whited.

Louisiana Government Information Network (LaGIN), c/o State Lib. of Louisiana, Box 131, Baton Rouge 70821. SAN 329-5036. Tel. 504-342-4918. *Coord., User Services* Blanche Cretini.

New Orleans Educational Telecommunications Consortium, 501 City Park Ave., Bldg. 7, New Orleans 70118. SAN 329-5214. Tel. 504-865-3092. *Chpn.* Gordon Mueller; *Exec. Dir.* Robert J. Lucas.

Maine

Health Science Library Information Consortium, Box 3395, Togus 04330. SAN 322-1601. Tel. 207-795-2560. *Chpn.* Robin Rand; *Dir. of Libs.* Cora Damon.

Maryland

Cooperating Libraries of Central Maryland, 115 W. Franklin St., Baltimore 21201-4484. SAN 322-3914. Tel. 301-396-3921. FAX 301-396-5856. *Exec. Dir.* Cecy Keller.

Criminal Justice Information Exchange Group, c/o National Institute of Justice/NCJRS, 1600 Research Blvd., Rockville 20850. SAN 322-580X. Tel. 301-251-5101. FAX 301-251-5212. *Coord.* Jennifer Lusk.

ERIC Processing and Reference Facility, 2440 Research Blvd., Rockville 20850. SAN 322-161X. Tel. 301-258-5500. FAX 301-948-3695. *Dir.* Ted Brandhorst.

Interlibrary Users Association, c/o Logistics Management Institute, 640 Goldsboro Rd., Bethesda 20817-5886. SAN 371-0548. Tel. 301-320-7249. *Pres.* Nancy E. Venator; *V.P.* Charles Gallagher.

Maryland Interlibrary Organization (MILO), c/o Enoch Pratt Free Lib., 400 Cathedral St., Baltimore 21201-4484. SAN 343-8600. Tel. 301-396-5328. FAX 301-396-5837.

Metropolitan Area Collection Development Consortium (MCDAC), c/o Montgomery County Dept. of Public Libs., 99 Maryland Ave., Rockville 20850. SAN 323-9748. Tel. 301-217-3834. FAX 301-217-3895.

Mid-America Law School Library Consortium, Univ. of Missouri, School of Law Lib., Hulston Hall, Columbia 65211. SAN 370-0429. Tel. 314-882-2025. *Chpn.* Susan Csaky.

National Library of Medicine, Medical Literature Analysis and Retrieval System (MEDLARS), 8600 Rockville Pike, Bethesda 20894. SAN 322-1652. Tel. 301-496-6193. *Head MEDLARS Mgt. Section* Carolyn Tilley.

−AIDSDRUGS. SAN 323-7427.

−AIDSLINE. SAN 323-7443.

−AIDSTRIALS. SAN 323-746X.

−AVLINE. SAN 326-7180.

−BIOETHICSLINE. SAN 326-7202.

−CANCERLIT. SAN 326-7229.

−CATLINE. SAN 326-7261.

−CCRIS (Chemical Carcinogenesis Information System). SAN 328-8560.

−ChemID. SAN 371-4772.

−CHEMLINE. SAN 322-1679.

−DART (Development and Reproduction Toxicology). SAN 371-4780.

−DBIR (Directory of Biotechnology Information Resources). SAN 323-7486.

−DENTALPROJ. SAN 323-7508.

−DIRLINE. SAN 326-730X.

−DOCUSER. SAN 323-7524.

−EMICBACK (Environmental Mutagen Information BACKfile). SAN 371-4799.

−ETICBACK (Environmental Teratology Information Center BACKfile). SAN 371-4802.

−GENETOX. SAN 371-4756.

— Health Planning and Administration. SAN 326-7326.
— HISTLINE. SAN 326-6796.
— HSDB (Hazardous Substances Data Bank). SAN 326-6818.
— IRIS (Integrated Risk Information System). SAN 371-4764.
— MEDLINE. SAN 322-1695.
— MESH Vocabulary File. SAN 326-6893.
— Name Authority File. SAN 326-6915.
— PDQ (Physician Data Query). SAN 326-6931.
— POPLINE. SAN 326-6958.
— Registry of Toxic Effects of Chemical Substances (RTECS). SAN 322-1709.
— SDILINE. SAN 326-6974.
— SERLINE. SAN 326-6990.
— TOXLINE. SAN 322-1660.
— TOXLIT. SAN 323-7540.
— TRI (Toxic Chemical Release Inventory). SAN 323-7567.
Southeastern-Atlantic Regional Medical Library Services (RML 2), Univ. of Maryland, Health Sciences Lib., 111 S. Greene St., Baltimore 21201-1583. SAN 322-1644. Tel. 301-328-2855. WATS 800-638-6093. FAX 301-328-8403. *RML Dir.* Open; *Exec. Dir.* Faith A. Meakin.
Washington Research Library Consortium, 4207 Forbes Blvd., Lanham 20706. SAN 322-0540. Tel. 301-731-1000. FAX 301-731-1012. *Exec. Dir.* Paul Vassallo.

Massachusetts

Association of Visual Science Librarians, c/o New England College of Optometry Lib., Boston 02115. SAN 370-0569. Tel. 617-266-2030, Ext. 120. *Chpn.* Lynne Epstein.
Boston Area Music Libraries, c/o Creative Arts Section, Farber Lib., Brandeis Univ., Waltham 02254-9110. SAN 322-4392. Tel. 617-736-4681. *Coord. and Dir.* Brad Short.
Boston Biomedical Library Consortium, Beth Israel Hospital Medical Lib., 330 Brookline Ave., Boston 02215. SAN 322-1725. Tel. 617-735-4225. *Pres.* Dan DeStefano.
Boston Library Consortium, c/o Boston Public Lib., Rm. 339, 666 Boylston St., Boston 02117. SAN 322-1733. Tel. 617-262-0380. *Pres.* Richard Talbot; *Exec. Dir.* Marianne Burke.
Boston Theological Institute Library Program, 45 Francis Ave., Cambridge 02138.

SAN 322-1741. Tel. 617-482-5800. *Asst. Lib. Coord.* Clifford Putney.
Cape Libraries Automated Materials Sharing (CLAMS), Box 2788, Hyannis 02601. SAN 370-579X. Tel. 508-790-4399. *Pres.* Cynthia Mills.
Central Massachusetts Consortium of Health Related Libraries, Harrington Memorial, 100 S. St., Southbridge 01550. SAN 371-2133. Tel. 508-765-9771, Ext. 2753. *Chpn.* Joan Boyer.
Consortium for Information Resources, Emerson Hospital, 133 Old Rd. to Nine Acre Center, Concord 01742. SAN 322-4503. Tel. 508-369-1400, Ext. 1141. FAX 508-369-7655. *Dir.* Nancy Callender.
Cooperating Libraries of Greater Springfield, c/o Alumnae Lib., 291 Springfield, Chicopee 01013. SAN 322-1768. Tel. 413-594-2761. *Chpn.* Mary Brennan.
C W Mars (Central Western Massachusetts Automated Resource Sharing), One Sunset Lane, Paxton 01612-1197. SAN 322-3973. Tel. 508-755-3323. FAX 508-755-3721. *Mgr.* David T. Sheehan; *Supv. User Services* Gale E. Eckerson.
Digital Library Network, 111 Powder Mill Rd., Maynard 01754. SAN 370-0534. *Mgr.* Howard Williams.
Essex County Cooperating Libraries, c/o Gordon College, 255 Grape Vine Rd., Wenham 01984. SAN 322-1776. Tel. 508-927-2300, Ext. 4339. *Chpn.* Suzanne Nicholson.
Fenway Library Consortium, Brookline Public Lib., 361 Washington St., Brookline 02146. SAN 327-9766. Tel. 617-730-2360. FAX 617-232-7146. *Coord.* Michael Steinfeld.
HILC, Inc. (Hampshire Interlibrary Center), Box 740, Amherst 01004. SAN 322-1806. Tel. 413-256-8316. *Admin. Asst.* Dora Tudryn; *Business Mgr.* Jean Stabell.
Libraries and Information for Nursing Consortium, c/o School of Nursing Lib., Saint Elizabeth's Hospital, 159 Washington St., Brighton 02135. SAN 371-0580. Tel. 617-789-2304. *Coord.* Robert L. Loud.
Merrimac Interlibrary Cooperative, Hemingway Lib., Bradford College, 320 S. Main St., Haverhill 01835. SAN 329-4234. Tel. 508-372-7161, Ext. 387. *Chpn.* Ruth Hooten.

Merrimack Valley Library Consortium, c/o Memorial Hall Lib., Elm Sq., Andover 01810. SAN 322-4384. Tel. 508-475-6960. *Chpn.* Joseph Dionne; *Dir.* Evelyn Kuo.

Minuteman Library Network, 49 Lexington St., Framingham 01701. SAN 322-4252. Tel. 508-879-8575. FAX 508-879-5470. *Exec. Dir.* Joan Kuklinski.

NELINET, Inc., 2 Newton Executive Park, Newton 02162. SAN 322-1822. Tel. 617-969-0400. FAX 617-332-9634. *Exec. Dir.* Marshall Keys.

New England Deposit Library, 135 Western Ave., Allston 02134. SAN 322-1830. Tel. 617-782-8441. *Dir.* Morris I. Hyman; *Asst. Mgr.* Michael J. O'Neil.

New England Law Library Consortium, Inc., Harvard Law School Lib., Langdell Hall, Cambridge 02138. SAN 322-4244. Tel. 617-495-9918. *Coord.* Martha Berglund Crane.

North of Boston Library Exchange, Inc. (NOBLE), 112 Sohier Rd., Suite 117, Beverly 01915. SAN 322-4023. Tel. 508-927-5050. *Network Admin.* Ronald A. Gagnon; *Database Mgr.* Elizabeth B. Thomsen.

Northeast Consortium of Colleges and Universities in Massachusetts (NECCUM), 51 Lawrence St., Lawrence 01841. SAN 371-0602. Tel. 508-686-3183. *Dir.* Mary Ellen Smith.

Northeastern Consortium for Health Information (NECHI), Lawrence Memorial, 170 Governors Ave., Medford 02155. SAN 322-1857. Tel. 617-396-9250. FAX 617-391-2235. *Chpn.* John C. Harris.

Southeastern Massachusetts Consortium of Health Science Libraries (SEMCO), Quincy City Hospital, 114 Whitwell St., Quincy 02169. SAN 322-1873. Tel. 617-773-6100, Ext. 4094. *Chpn.* Sandra Chiller; *Pres.* Carolyn Rubenstein.

Southeastern Massachusetts Cooperating Libraries, c/o Bridgewater State College Lib., Clement C. Maxwell Lib., Shore Rd., Bridgewater 02325. SAN 322-1865. Tel. 508-230-1111. *Chpn.* Janet Freedman; *Coord.* William E. Boyle.

Wellesley–Lexington Area Cooperative Libraries (WELEXACOL), c/o Horn Lib., Babson College, Babson Park 02157. SAN 370-5978. Tel. 617-239-4473. *Pres.* Sherman Hayes; *Treas.* Marion Slack.

Western Massachusetts Health Information Consortium, Mercy Hospital, 271 Carew St., Springfield 01104. SAN 329-5443. Tel. 413-787-9100. *Dir.* Roger Manhan.

Worcester Area Cooperating Libraries, c/o Worcester State College, Learning Resources Center, Rm. 301, 486 Chandler St., Worcester 01602-2597. SAN 322-1881. Tel. 508-754-3964, 793-8000, Ext. 8544. *Coord.* Gladys Wood.

Michigan

Berrien Library Consortium, Andrews Campus, Berrien Springs 49104. SAN 322-4678. Tel. 616-982-3691, 471-3379. FAX 616-982-3710. *Pres.* Carol Wojcikiewicz.

Capital Area Library Network (CALNET), 407 N. Cedar St., Mason 48854. SAN 370-5927. Tel. 517-676-2008. *Contact* Kathleen M. Vera; *Chpn.* Catherine A. Smith.

Cloverland Processing Center, c/o Bay de Noc Community College, Learning Resource Center, 2001 N. Lincoln Rd., Escanaba 49829-2511. SAN 322-189X. Tel. 906-786-5802, Ext. 122. FAX 906-786-5802, Ext. 244. *Dean* Christian Holmes.

Detroit Area Consortium of Catholic Colleges, c/o Marygrove College, 8425 W. McNichols Rd., Detroit 48221-2599. SAN 329-482X. Tel. 313-862-8000. FAX 313-864-6670. *Coord.* John Shay.

Detroit Associated Libraries Region of Cooperative (DALROC), c/o James Lawrence, Detroit Public Lib., 5201 Woodward Ave., Detroit 48202. SAN 371-0831. Tel. 313-833-4036. *Contact* Lesley C. Loke; *Chpn.* Joseph Oldenburg.

Flint Area Health Science Libraries Network, c/o Flint Osteopathic Hospital, Medical Lib., 3921 Beecher Rd., Flint 48532-3699. SAN 329-4757. Tel. 313-762-4587. *Chpn. of the Consortium* Ria Lukes; *Dir. of Lib.* Doris Blauet.

Kalamazoo Consortium for Higher Education, Western Michigan Univ., Admin. Bldg. 3052, Kalamazoo 49008-3899. SAN 329-4994. Tel. 616-387-2351. *Chpn.* Andrew Rivers.

Lakeland Area Library Network (LAKENET), 60 Library Plaza N.E., Grand Rapids 49503. SAN 371-0696. Tel. 616-454-0272. *Coord.* Harriet Field.

Michigan Health Sciences Libraries Association, Wyandotte Hospital and Medical Center Lib., 2333 Biddle, Wyandotte

48192. SAN 323-987X. Tel. 313-284-2400. *Pres.* Diana O'Keefe.

Michigan Library Consortium, Suite 8, 6810 S. Cedar St., Lansing 48911. SAN 322-192X. Tel. 517-694-4242. WATS 800-292-1359 (Mich. only). FAX 517-694-9303. *Exec. Dir.* Kevin C. Flaherty.

Northern Interlibrary System, 316 E. Chisholm St., Alpena 49707. SAN 329-4773. Tel. 517-356-1622. *Dir.* Rebecca E. Cawley.

Sault Area International Library Association, c/o Lake Superior State Univ. Lib., Sault Sainte Marie 49783. SAN 322-1946. Tel. 906-635-2402. FAX 906-635-2193. *Chpns.* Ruth Neveu, Brian Ingram.

Southeastern Michigan League of Libraries (SEMLOL), c/o Schoolcraft College Lib., 18600 Haggerty Rd., Livonia 48152-2696. SAN 322-4481. Tel. 313-462-4440. FAX 313-462-4495. *Chpn.* Roy Nuffer.

State Council of Michigan Health Science Libraries, 401 W. Greenlawn Ave., Lansing 48910-2819. SAN 329-4633. Tel. 517-334-2270. FAX 517-334-2551. *Pres.* Barbara Kormelink; *Mid-West Rep.* David Keddle.

Upper Peninsula of Michigan Health Science Library Consortium, c/o Marquette General Hospital, 420 W. Magnetic, Marquette 49855. SAN 329-4803. Tel. 906-225-3429. FAX 906-225-3524. *Chpn.* Mildred Kingsbury.

Upper Peninsula Region Library Cooperation, Inc., 1615 Presque Isle Ave., Marquette 49855. SAN 329-5540. Tel. 906-228-7697. *Chpn.* Janet Benson.

Wayne Oakland Library Federation, 33030 Van Born Rd., Wayne 48184. SAN 370-596X. Tel. 313-326-8910. *Dir.* Malcolm K. Hill; *Deputy Dir.* Douglas A. Whitaker.

Minnesota

Arrowhead Professional Libraries Association, Hilding Medical and Health Sciences Lib., Saint Luke's Hospital, 915 E. First St., Duluth 55805. SAN 322-1954. Tel. 218-726-5320. *Coord.* Doreen Roberts.

Central Minnesota Libraries Exchange, c/o Learning Resources, Rm. 61, Saint Cloud State Univ., Saint Cloud 56301. SAN 322-3779. Tel. 612-255-2950. *Dir.* Patricia E. Peterson.

Community Health Science Library, c/o Saint Francis Medical Center, 415 Oak St., Breckenridge 56520. SAN 370-0585. Tel. 218-643-7507. *Dir.* Geralyn Terfehr.

Cooperating Libraries in Consortium (CLIC), 1457 Grand Ave., Suite N, Saint Paul 55105. SAN 322-1970. Tel. 612-699-9300. *Consortium Mgr.* Terrance J. Metz.

Honeywell Information Network, Honey Well Plaza MN12-2162, Minneapolis 55408. SAN 371-2141. Tel. 612-870-2377. *Coord.* Kathy Knaver.

METRONET, 226 Metro Sq. Bldg., Seventh and Robert Sts., Saint Paul 55101. SAN 322-1989. Tel. 612-224-4801. FAX 612-224-4827. *Dir.* Mary Treacy Birmingham.

MINITEX Library Information Network, c/o S-33 Wilson Lib., Univ. of Minnesota, 309 19th Ave. S., Minneapolis 55455-0414. SAN 322-1997. Tel. 612-624-4002. WATS 800-328-5534, 800-462-5348 (Minn.). FAX 612-624-4508. *Dir.* William DeJohn; *Asst. Dir. Doc. Delivery & MULS* Anita Branin; *Asst. Dir. OCLC & Reference Services* M. J. Rossman; *OCLC Services Coords.* Mary Miller, Marlene Forney; *Admin. Dir.* Anne Stagg.

Minnesota Department of Human Services Library Consortium (DHS Learning Consortium), Oak Terrace Nursing Home, 14500 County Rd. 62, Minnetonka 55345. SAN 370-0682. Tel. 612-934-4100, Ext. 238. *Lib. Dir.* Colleen Spadaccini.

Minnesota Theological Library Association, c/o Luther Northwestern Theological Seminary, 2375 Como Ave., Saint Paul 55108. SAN 322-1962. Tel. 612-641-3224. *Database Admin.* Tom Walker.

North Country Library Cooperative, Olcott Plaza, Suite 110, 820 Ninth St. N., Virginia 55792-2298. SAN 322-3795. Tel. 218-741-1907. FAX 218-741-1907. *Dir.* Sandra Isaacson.

Northern Lights Library Network, Box 845, Alexandria 56308-0845. SAN 322-2004. Tel. 218-762-1032. *Dir.* Joan B. Larson.

SMILE (Southcentral Minnesota Inter-Library Exchange), Box 3031, Mankato 56001. SAN 321-3358. Tel. 507-389-5108. FAX 507-389-1772. *Dir.* Lucy Lowry; *Smiline I & R Dir.* Kate Tohal.

Southeast Library System (SELS), 107 W. Frontage Rd., Hwy. 52 N., Rochester

55901. SAN 322-3981. Tel. 507-288-5513. *Multitype Libn.* Roger Leachman.

Southwest Area Multi-County Multi-Type Interlibrary Exchange (SAMMIE), Southwest State Univ. Lib., Marshall 56258. SAN 322-2039. Tel. 507-532-9013. *Coord.* William W. Pollard.

Twin Cities Biomedical Consortium, Midway Hospital, Health Sciences Lib., 1700 University Ave., Saint Paul 55104. SAN 322-2055. Tel. 612-641-5607. *Chpn.* Carol Windham.

Waseca Interlibrary Resource Exchange (WIRE), Waseca-LeSueur Regional Lib., 408 N. State St., Waseca 56093. SAN 370-0593. Tel. 507-835-2910. FAX 507-835-3700.

Westlaw, c/o West Publishing Co., 50 W. Kellogg Blvd., Box 64526, Saint Paul 55164-0526. SAN 322-4031. Tel. 612-688-3654. WATS 800-328-0109. *Mgr.* Thomas McLeod.

Mississippi

Gulf Coast Biomedical Library Consortium, Learning Resources Service (142D), VA Medical Center, Biloxi 39531. SAN 322-2063. Tel. 601-388-5541. *Chpn.* Connie Keel.

Mississippi Biomedical Library Consortium, Forrest General Hospital, Hattiesburg 39531. SAN 322-4422. Tel. 601-388-5541, Ext. 221. *Pres.* Betty Duncan.

Missouri

Higher Education Center of Saint Louis, 8420 Belmar, Suite 504, Saint Louis 63124. SAN 322-208X. Tel. 314-991-2700. *Pres.* Samuel E. Wood.

Kansas City Library Network, Inc., Univ. of Missouri Health Sciences Lib., 2411 Holmes, Kansas City 64108. SAN 322-2098. Tel. 913-676-2101. *Pres.* Naomi R. Adelman.

Kansas City Metropolitan Library Network, 15624 E. 24 Hwy., Independence 64050. SAN 322-2101. Tel. 816-836-5200, Ext. 257. *Office Mgr.* Sharon Jennings.

Mid-Missouri Library Network, 111 N. Fourth, Moberly 65270. SAN 322-2136. Tel. 816-263-4426.

Missouri Library Network Corporation, 10332 Old Olive St. Rd., Saint Louis 63141. SAN 322-466X. Tel. 314-567-3799. WATS 800-444-8096. *Dir.* Mary Ann Mercante.

Municipal Library Cooperative, 140 E. Jefferson, Kirkwood 63122. SAN 322-2152. Tel. 314-966-5568. *ILL.* Vera H. Moeller.

PHILSOM-PHILNET-BACS Network, c/o Washington Univ., 660 S. Euclid Ave., Saint Louis 63110. SAN 322-2187. Tel. 314-362-2788. *Dir.* Loretta Stucki.

Saint Louis Regional Library Network, 9425 Big Bend, Saint Louis 63119. SAN 322-2209. Tel. 314-965-1305. *Admin.* Bernyce Christiansen; *Dir.* Maggie Huxhold.

Montana

Helena Area Health Science Libraries Consortium, Corette Lib., Carroll College, Helena 59625. SAN 371-2192. Tel. 406-442-1295. *Chpn.* Lois Fitzpatrick.

Montana Information Network and Exchange (MINE), c/o Montana State Lib., 1515 E. Sixth Ave., Helena 59620. SAN 322-2241. Tel. 406-444-3004. FAX 406-444-5612. *Dir.* Richard Miller.

Nebraska

Lincoln Health Sciences Library Group, c/o Saint Elizabeth Community Health Center, Medical Lib., 555 S. 70 St., Lincoln 68510. SAN 329-5001. Tel. 402-486-7307. *Pres.* Beth Goble.

Meridian Library System, Kearney Reference Interloan Center, 1811 W. Second St., Suite 340, Grand Island 68801. SAN 325-3554. Tel. 308-348-8113. *Pres.* John Mayeski; *Admin.* Sharon Osenga.

Midcontinental Regional Medical Library Program (RML4), c/o McGoogan Lib. of Medicine, Univ. of Nebraska Medical Center, 600 S. 42 St., Omaha 68198-6706. SAN 322-225X. Tel. 402-559-4326. WATS 800-MED-RML4. FAX 402-559-5498. *Dir.* Nancy N. Woelfl.

NEBASE, c/o Nebraska Lib. Commission, 1420 P St., Lincoln 68508-1683. SAN 322-2268. Tel. 402-471-2045. FAX 402-471-2083. *Dir.* Jacqueline Mundell; *Coord.* Paul Seth Hoffman.

Northeast Library System, 2504 14th St., Columbus 68601. SAN 329-5524. Tel. 402-564-7116. *Admin.* Carol Speicher.

Southeast Nebraska Library System, Union College Lib., 3800 S. 48 St., Lincoln 68506. SAN 322-4732. Tel. 402-486-2555. *Admin.* Kate Marek; *Admin. Asst.* Connie Holland.

Nevada

Information Nevada, Interlibrary Loan Dept., Nevada State Lib., Capitol Complex, Carson City 89710-0001. SAN 322-2276. Tel. 702-887-2619. FAX 702-887-2630. *Contact* Millie L. Syring.

Nevada Cooperative Medical Library, 2040 W. Charleston Blvd., Suite 500, Las Vegas 89102. SAN 321-5962. Tel. 702-383-2368. *Dir. Lib. Services* Aldona Jonynas.

Nevada Medical Library Group, Lahonton Basin Medical Lib., Box 2168, Carson City 89702. SAN 370-0445. Tel. 702-882-1361, Ext. 358. *Chpn.* Elaine Laessle.

New Hampshire

Merri-Hill-Rock Library Cooperative, Hampstead Public Lib., Box 190, Hampstead 03841. SAN 329-5338. Tel. 603-329-6411. *Chpn.* Elizabeth B. Rooney.

New Hampshire College and University Council, Lib. Committee, 2321 Elm St., Manchester 03104. SAN 322-2322. Tel. 603-669-3432. *Exec. Dir.* John W. Ryan.

North Country Consortium, Gale Medical Lib., Littleton Hospital, 107 Cottage St., Littleton 03580. SAN 370-0410. Tel. 603-444-7731, Ext. 164. *Coord.* Linda L. Ford.

Nubanusit Library Cooperative, c/o Peterborough Town Lib., Main St., Peterborough 03458. SAN 322-4600. Tel. 603-924-6401.

Scrooge and Marley Cooperative, 310 Central St., Franklin 03235. SAN 329-515X. Tel. 603-934-2911. *Chpn.* Randy Brough.

Seacoast Coop Libraries, Weeks Public Lib., Box 430, Greenland 03840. SAN 322-4619. Tel. 603-436-8548.

New Jersey

AT&T Library Network, 600 Mountain Ave., Rm. 6A-412, Murray Hill 07974. SAN 329-5400. Tel. 908-582-4361. FAX 908-582-2255. *Mgr.* Ronnye Schreiber.

Bergen Passaic Health Sciences Library Consortium, c/o Chilton Memorial Hospital Medical Lib., Pompton Plains 07444. SAN 371-0904. Tel. 201-831-5058. *Pres.* Janice Sweeton; *Secy.* Ron Rizio.

Central Jersey Health Science Libraries Association, Saint Francis Medical Center Medical Lib., 601 Hamilton Ave., Trenton 08629. SAN 370-0712. Tel. 609-599-5068. *Dir.* Donna Barlow; *Technical Info. Specialist* Eileen Monroe.

Central Jersey Regional Library Cooperatives—Area V, 55 Schanck Rd., Suite B-15, Freehold 07728-2942. SAN 370-5102. Tel. 908-409-6484. FAX 908-409-6492. *Exec. Dir.* Dottie Hiebing.

Cosmopolitan Biomedical Library Consortium, United Hospital Medical Center, 15 S. Ninth St., Newark 07107. SAN 322-4414. Tel. 201-268-8776. *Chpn.* Linda Demuro.

County of Essex Cooperating Libraries System, 57 Kendal Ave., Maplewood 07040. SAN 322-4562. Tel. 201-763-9006. *Admin.* Karen Lee.

Dow Jones News Retrieval, Box 300, Princeton 08543-0300. SAN 322-404X. Tel. 609-452-1511. WATS 800-257-5114. *Sr. Marketing Coord.* Carla Gaffney.

Essex-Hudson Regional Library Cooperative—Region Three, 250 Scotland Rd., Suite 201, Orange 07050. SAN 329-5117. Tel. 201-673-6373. FAX 201-673-6121. *Exec. Dir.* Gladys Odette.

Health Sciences Library Association of New Jersey, c/o J. Harold Johnston Memorial Lib., Health Research and Educational Trust of New Jersey, 760 Alexander Rd., CN-1, Princeton 08543-0001. SAN 370-0488. Tel. 609-275-4230. *Pres.* James G. Delo; *V.P.* Duressa Pujat.

LMX Automation Consortium, c/o MCC Lib., 155 Mill Rd., Edison 08818-3050. SAN 329-448X. Tel. 201-548-7113. *Database Mgr.* Ann MacDonald.

Medical Resources Consortium of Central New Jersey (MEDCORE), 253 Witherspoon St., Princeton 08540. SAN 322-2349. Tel. 609-497-4488. *Libn.* Louise M. Yorke.

Monmouth-Ocean Biomedical Information Consortium, Community Medical Center, 99 Hwy. No. 37 W., Toms River 08755.

SAN 329-5389. Tel. 908-240-8117. FAX 908-341-8093. *Dir.* Reina Reisler.

Morris Automated Information Network, 30 E. Hanover Ave., Whippany 07981. SAN 322-4058. Tel. 201-285-6955. FAX 201-285-6965. *Supv. Libn.* Kathleen Jones Harris.

Morris-Union Federation, 214 Main St., Chatham 07928. SAN 310-2629. Tel. 201-635-0603. *Contact* Diane O'Brien.

New Jersey Academic Library Network, c/o Kean College, Nancy Thompson Lib., Union 07083. SAN 329-4927. Tel. 908-527-2017. *Chpn.* Barbara Simpson.

New Jersey Health Sciences Library Network, c/o Health Sciences Lib., Mountainside Hospital, Montclair 07042. SAN 371-4829. Tel. 201-429-6462. *Chpn.* Patricia Regenberg.

Northwest Regional Library Cooperative, 31 Fairmount Ave., Box 486, Chester 07930. SAN 329-4609. Tel. 908-879-2442. FAX 908-879-8812. *Exec. Dir.* Keith Michael Feils; *Prog. Coord.* Diane Solomon.

Pinelands Consortium for Health Information, c/o Kennedy Memorial Hospital, Washington Township Div., Huffville-Cross Keys Rds., Turnersville 08012. SAN 370-4874. Tel. 609-582-2675. *Coord.* William Dobkowski.

Society for Cooperative Healthcare and Related Education, Union County College, 1033 Springfield Ave., Cranford 07016. SAN 371-0718. Tel. 201-276-5710. *Contact* Carol Dreyer; *Coord.* Anne Calhoun; *Chpn.* Elaine Przepadlo.

South Jersey Regional Library Cooperative, c/o Midway Professional Center, Suite 102, 8 N. Whitehorse Pike, Hammonton 08037. SAN 329-4625. Tel. 609-561-4646. FAX 609-561-4950. *Exec. Dir.* Karen Hyman; *Prog. Devt. Coord.* Jeanne Robbana.

New Mexico

New Mexico Consortium of Biomedical and Hospital Libraries, c/o Lovelace Medical Lib., 5400 Gibson Blvd. S.E., Albuquerque 87108. SAN 322-449X. Tel. 505-262-7158. *Permanent Contact* Sarah Morley.

New York

Academic Libraries of Brooklyn, Box 40-0949, Brooklyn 11240. SAN 322-2411. Tel. 718-636-3545. FAX 718-622-6174. *Pres.* Tad Kumatz.

Associated Colleges of the Saint Lawrence Valley, Satterlee Hall, State Univ. of New York, Potsdam 13676-2299. SAN 322-242X. Tel. 315-265-2790. *Exec. Dir.* Judy C. Chittenden.

Brooklyn–Queens–Staten Island Health Sciences Librarians (BQSI), 355 Bard Ave., Staten Island 10310. SAN 370-0828. Tel. 718-876-3117. FAX 718-727-2456. *Pres.* Lucy A. DiMatteo; *V.P.* George Wahlert.

BRS Information Technologies, Div. of Maxwell ONLINE, 8000 Westpark Dr., McLean 22102. SAN 322-2438. Tel. 703-442-0900. WATS 800-345-4277. FAX 703-893-4632. *Pres.* James Terragno.

Capital District Library Council for Reference and Research Resources, 2255 Story Ave., Schenectady 12309. SAN 322-2446. Tel. 518-382-2001. Dataphone 785-0787. FAX 518-382-3826. *Exec. Dir.* Charles D. Custer; *Admin. Secy.* Mary L. Schatke.

Central New York Library Resources Council, 763 Butternut, Syracuse 13208. SAN 322-2454. Tel. 315-478-6080. WATS 800-848-8448 (N.Y. only). FAX 315-478-0512. *Exec. Dir.* Keith E. Washburn; *Asst. Dir.* Jeannette Smithee.

Consortium of Foundation Libraries, c/o Rockefeller Foundation, 1133 Ave. of the Americas, New York 10036. SAN 322-2462. Tel. 212-869-8500. FAX 212-986-0414. *Pres.* Meredith S. Averill.

Council of Archives and Research Libraries in Jewish Studies, 330 Seventh Ave., 21st fl., New York 10001. SAN 371-053X. Tel. 212-490-2280. *Contact* Abraham Atik; *Pres.* Herbert Zafren.

Educational Film Library Association, c/o AV Resource Center, Cornell Univ., Business and Technology Park, Ithaca 14850. SAN 371-0874. Tel. 607-255-2090. *AV Coord.* Rich Gray; *AV Sales* Holly Ouderkirk; *AV Technology* Gerry Kalk.

Health Information Libraries of Westchester, c/o New York Medical College, Medical Lib., Basic Sciences Bldg., Valhalla 10595. SAN 371-0823. Tel. 914-993-4204. *Pres.* Chris Hunter.

Library Consortium of Health Institutions in Buffalo, Office of the Consortium, c/o Info. Dissemination Service, Health Sciences Lib., State Univ. of New York,

Buffalo 14214. SAN 329-367X. Tel. 716-831-3351. *Dir.* Cindy Bertuca.

Library Exchange and Resources Network, Saint Elizabeth Hospital Medical Staff Lib., Utica 13502. SAN 371-4853. Tel. 315-798-8143. *Secy.* Sister Ellen Burke.

Long Island Library Resources Council, Melville Lib. Bldg., Suite E5310, Stony Brook 11794-3399. SAN 322-2489. Tel. 516-632-6650. FAX 516-632-6662. *Dir.* Herbert Biblo; *Asst. Dir.* Judith Neufeld.

Manhattan-Bronx Health Sciences Libraries Group, c/o Our Lady of Mercy Medical Center, 600 E. 233 St., Bronx 10466. SAN 322-4465. Tel. 212-920-9869. *Pres.* Sister Jeanne Atkinson.

Medical and Scientific Libraries of Long Island (MEDLI), c/o C. W. Post Campus, Long Island Univ., Palmer School of Lib. and Info. Science, Brookville 11548. SAN 322-4309. Tel. 516-299-2178. *Chpn.* Deborah Sler.

Medical Library Center of New York, 5 E. 102 St., New York 10029. SAN 322-3957. Tel. 212-427-1630. FAX 212-860-3496. *Dir.* Lois Weinstein.

Middle Atlantic Regional Medical Library Program (formerly Greater Northeastern Regional Medical Library Program), New York Academy of Medicine, 2 E. 103 St., New York 10029-5293. SAN 322-2497. Tel. 212-876-8763. FAX 212-722-7650. *Assoc. Dir.* Mary Mylenki.

New York Metropolitan Reference and Research Library Agency (METRO), 57 E. 11 St., New York 10003. SAN 322-2500. Tel. 212-228-2320. FAX 212-228-2598. *Dir.* Joan Neumann; *Assoc. Dir. & Coord. of Programs and Services* Alar Kruus.

New York State Interlibrary Loan Network (NYSILL), c/o New York State Lib., Albany 12230. SAN 322-2519. Tel. 518-474-5383; Easylink: 710-441-8770. *State Libn.* Joseph F. Shubert; *Dir.* Jerome Yavarkovsky; *Principal Libn.* J. Van der veer Judd.

North Country Reference and Research Resources Council, Box 568, Canton 13617-0568. SAN 322-2527. Tel. 315-386-4569. *Exec. Dir.* John J. Hammond; *Head of Bibliog. Service* Tom Blauvelt; *Regional Service Coord.* Bridget Doyle; *Business Mgr.* Joan Anderson.

Rochester Regional Library Council, 302 N. Goodman St., Rochester 14607. SAN 322-2535. Tel. 716-461-5440. *Dir.* Janet M. Welch.

South Central Research Library Council, 215 N. Cayuga St., Ithaca 14850. SAN 322-2543. Tel. 607-273-9106. *Exec. Dir.* Janet E. Steiner; *Special Projects Dir.* Jean Currie.

Southeastern New York Library Resources Council, 220 Rte. 299, Box 879, Highland 12528. SAN 322-2551. Tel. 914-691-2734. WATS 800-251-1131. *Exec. Dir.* Ellen A. Parravano; *Special Project Coord.* Sarah P. Browne; *Bibliog. Services Coord.* Christine Crawford-Oppenheimer; *Health Info. Coord.* Ronald Crovisier.

State University of New York–OCLC Library Network (SUNY–OCLC), Central Administration, State Univ. of New York, State University Plaza, Albany 12246. SAN 322-256X. Tel. 518-443-5444. WATS 800-342-3353 (N.Y. only). FAX 518-432-4346. *Dir.* Glyn T. Evans; *Assoc. Dir.* David Forsythe; *Business Officer* Chuck Yandell; *Sr. Network Asst.* Penny Wilson.

Western New York Library Resources Council, 180 Oak St., Buffalo 14203. SAN 322-2578. Tel. 716-852-3844. FAX 716-852-0276. *Exec. Dir.* Mary W. Ghikas.

North Carolina

Cape Fear Health Sciences Information Consortium, Fayetteville State Univ., Charles W. Chestnutt Lib., 1200 Murchison Rd., Newbold Sta., Fayetteville 28301-4298. SAN 322-3930. Tel. 919-486-1111, Ext. 1233. *Dir. Lib. Services* Bobby Wynn.

Microcomputer Users Group for Librarians in North Carolina, c/o Susan Speer, Health Sciences Lib., East Carolina Univ., Greenville 27858-4354. SAN 322-4449. Tel. 919-551-2231. FAX 919-551-2224. *Pres.* Jim Coble.

NC Area Health Education Centers, Health Sciences Lib., CB 7585, Univ. of North Carolina, Chapel Hill 27599-7585. SAN 323-9950. Tel. 919-962-0700. *Network Coord.* Diane C. McDuffee.

North Carolina Department of Community Colleges, Institutional Services, 200 W. Jones St., Raleigh 27603-1337. SAN 322-2594. Tel. 919-733-7051. *Dir.* Major Boyd; *Coord. Lib. Tech. Assistance* Pamela B.

Doyle; *Coord. Lib. Acquisitions* Azalee B. Sain; *Coord. Lib. Cataloguing* Ortha B. Allen.

North Carolina Information Network, 109 E. Jones St., Raleigh 27601-2807. SAN 329-3092. Tel. 919-733-2570. FAX 919-733-8748. *Dir.* Diana Young.

Northwest AHEC Library at Salisbury, c/o Rowan Memorial Hospital, 612 Mocksville Ave., Salisbury 28144. SAN 322-4589. Tel. 704-638-1081. *Dir.* Connie Schardt.

Northwest AHEC Library Information Network, Northwest Area Health Education Center, Bowman Gray School of Medicine, 300 S. Hawthorne Rd., Winston-Salem 27103. SAN 322-4716. Tel. 919-777-3020. FTS 704-322-0662. *Coord.* Phyllis Gillikin.

Resources for Health Information Consortium (ReHI), Box 14465, Raleigh 27620-4465. SAN 329-3777. Tel. 919-250-8529. *Dir.* Karen Grandage.

Science and Technology Research Center, 2 Davis Dr., Box 12235, Research Triangle Park 27709-2235. SAN 322-2608. Tel. 919-549-0671. *Dir.* H. L. Reese.

Triangle Research Libraries Network, Wilson Lib., CB 3940, Chapel Hill 27599-3940. SAN 329-5362. Tel. 919-962-8022. FAX 919-962-0484. *Exec. Dir.* David Carlson.

Unifour Consortium of Health Care and Educational Institutions, c/o Northwest AHEC Lib. at Hickory, Catawba Memorial Hospital, 810 Fair Grove Church, Hickory 28602-9463. SAN 322-4708. Tel. 704-322-0662. FAX 704-322-2921. *Dir.* Phyllis Gillikin; *Asst. Dir.* Judy Wojcik.

North Dakota

North Dakota Network for Knowledge, c/o North Dakota State Lib., Liberty Memorial Bldg., Capitol Grounds, 604 E. Blvd. Ave., Bismarck 58505. SAN 322-2616. Tel. 701-224-2492. FAX 701-224-2040. *Dir. and State Libn.* Patricia L. Harris.

Prairie Library Network, c/o VA Medical Lib., 142D Dept. of VA, 2101 Elm St., Fargo 58102. SAN 371-4837. Tel. 701-293-4155. *Coord.* Jane Borland.

Tri-College University Libraries Consortium, c/o North Dakota State Univ., 306 Ceres Hall, Fargo 58105. SAN 322-2047. Tel. 701-237-8170. *Coord.* Darrel M. Meinke; *Provost, Tri-College Univ.* William Jones.

Valley Medical Network, 1720 S. University Dr., Box 6014, Fargo 58108-6014. SAN 329-4730. Tel. 701-280-4187. *Pres.* Artis Haaland.

Ohio

Central Ohio Hospital Library Consortium, Medical Lib., Riverside Methodist Hospital, 3535 Olentangy River Rd., Columbus 43214. SAN 371-084X. Tel. 614-261-5230. *Archival Records* Jo Yeoh.

Cleveland Area Metropolitan Library System, 3645 Warrensville Center Rd., Suite 116, Shaker Heights 44122-5210. SAN 322-2632. Tel. 216-921-3900. *Dir.* Tory Gangloff.

Cleveland Consortium, Medical Lib., 18101 Lorain Ave., Cleveland 44111. SAN 329-420X. Tel. 216-476-7118. *Dir.* Susan Favorite.

Consortium of College and University Media Centers, Media Res., Iowa State Univ., 121 Pearson Hall, Ames 50011. SAN 322-1091. Tel. 515-294-8022. FAX 515-294-0907. *Exec. Dir.* Don A. Rieck.

Consortium of Popular Culture Collections in the Midwest, c/o Popular Culture Lib., Bowling Green State Univ., Bowling Green 43403. SAN 370-5811. Tel. 419-372-2450. FAX 614-292-7859. *Curator* Lucy S. Caswell.

Greater Cincinnati Library Consortium, Suite 605, 3333 Vine St., Cincinnati 45220-2214. SAN 322-2675. Tel. 513-751-4422. *Exec. Dir.* Martha J. McDonald.

Miami Valley Libraries, c/o Amos Memorial Public Lib., 230 E. North St., Sidney 45365. SAN 322-2691. Tel. 513-492-8354. *Pres.* Scott Parsons.

Mideastern Ohio Library Organization, 403 N. Mill St., Louisville 44641-1428. SAN 322-2705. Tel. 216-875-4269. *Dir.* Jane Biehl.

NEOUCOM Council of Associated Hospital Librarians, Ocasek Regional Medical Info. Center, Rootstown 44272. SAN 370-0526. Tel. 216-325-2511, Ext. 542. FAX 216-325-0522. *Dir.* Jean Williams Sayre.

NOLA Regional Library System, Ohio One Bldg., 25 E. Boardman St., Youngstown 44503-1802. SAN 322-2713. Tel. 216-746-7042. FAX 216-746-7426. *Dir.* Holly C. Carroll.

North Central Library Cooperative, 27 N. Main St., Mansfield 44902-1703. SAN 322-2683. Tel. 419-526-1337. FAX 419-526-2145. *Dir.* Cathy Caine; *Media Specialist* Stephen Fought; *Members Service Coord.* Jennifer Davis.

Northeastern Ohio Major Academic and Research Libraries (NEOMARL), Cleveland State Univ. Lib., 1860 E. 22 St., Cleveland 44115. SAN 322-4236. Tel. 216-687-2475. FAX 216-687-9380. *Dir.* Hannelore B. Rader.

Northern Ohio Film Circuit, c/o Rodman Public Lib., 215 E. Broadway St., Alliance 44601-2694. SAN 322-2721. Tel. 216-821-2665. *Admin.* George W. S. Hays.

Northwest Library District (NORWELD), 251 N. Main St., Bowling Green 43402. SAN 322-273X. Tel. 419-352-2903. FAX 419-354-0405. *Dir.* Allan Gray.

OCLC (Online Computer Library Center), 6565 Frantz Rd., Dublin 43017-0702. SAN 322-2748. Tel. 614-764-6000. WATS 800-848-5878. FAX 614-764-6096. *Pres.* K. Wayne Smith.

Ohio-Kentucky Coop Libraries, c/o Serials Dept., Univ. Lib., Wright State Univ., Dayton 45435. SAN 325-3570. Tel. 513-873-3034. *Managing Ed.* Madeleine Marchesseault.

Ohio Network of American History Research Centers, Archives Lib. Div., Ohio Historical Society, 1982 Velma Ave., Columbus 43211. SAN 323-9624. Tel. 614-297-2510. FAX 614-297-2411. *Archivist* George Parkinson.

Ohio Valley Area Libraries, 252 W. 13 St., Wellston 45692-2299. SAN 322-2756. Tel. 614-384-2103. *Dir.* Eric S. Anderson; *Consultant* Leah Griffith.

OHIONET, 1500 W. Lane Ave., Columbus 43221-3975. SAN 322-2764. Tel. 614-486-2966. WATS 800-686-8975. FAX 614-486-1527. *Exec. Dir.* Joel S. Kent; *Computer Operation Asst. Dir.* Robert Busick; *Asst. Dir. for Member Services* Gregory Pronevitz.

Southwest Ohio Regional Library System (SWORL), 505 Kathryn Dr., Wilmington 45177-2274. SAN 322-2780. Tel. 513-382-2503. FAX 513-382-2504. *Dir.* Corinne Johnson.

Southwestern Ohio Council for Higher Education, 2900 Acosta St., Suite 141, Dayton 45420-3467. SAN 322-2659. Tel. 513-297-3150. FAX 513-297-3163. *Pres.* Pressley C. McCoy; *Chpn. Lib. Div.* John Montag.

Western Ohio Video Circuit, c/o Lima Public Lib., 650 W. Market St., Lima 45801. SAN 322-2799. Tel. 419-228-5113. *Admin.* James Bouchard; *Coord.* Barbara Baker.

Oklahoma

Greater Oklahoma City Area Health Sciences Library Consortium, Box 60918, Oklahoma City 73146. SAN 329-3858. Tel. 405-270-0501. *Pres.* Verlean Delaney.

Midwest Curriculum Coordination Center, 1500 W. Seventh Ave., Stillwater 74074-4364. SAN 329-3874. Tel. 405-377-2000. FAX 405-743-5541. *Dir.* Richard Makin; *Asst. Project Dir.* Tina Sturgess.

Oklahoma Telecommunications Interlibrary System, 200 N.E. 18 St., Oklahoma City 73105-3298. SAN 322-2810. Tel. 405-521-2502. FAX 405-525-7804. *Head* Mary Hardin.

Tulsa Area Library Cooperative, 400 Civic Center, Tulsa 74103. SAN 321-6489. Tel. 918-596-7893. *Coord.* Cheryl Wells.

Oregon

Chemeketa Cooperative Regional Library Service, c/o Chemeketa Community College, Box 14007, Salem 97309-7070. SAN 322-2837. Tel. 503-399-5105. FAX 503-399-2514. *Coord.* Linda Cochrane.

Coos Cooperative Library Service, c/o Southwestern Oregon Community College, Coos Bay 97420. SAN 322-4279. Tel. 503-888-7260. *Ext. Services Coord.* Dianne Hall.

Economic Information Network, Oregon State Lib., State Lib. Bldg., Salem 97310-0640. SAN 329-5230. Tel. 503-378-4367. *State Libn.* Wesley Doak.

Library Information Network of Clackamas County, 16201 S.E. McLoughlin Blvd., Oak Grove 97267. SAN 322-2845. Tel. 503-655-8550. FAX 503-655-8555. *Network Admin.* Joanna Rood.

Marine Valley Health Information Network, Linn Benton Community College Lib., 6500 S.W. Pacific Blvd., Albany 97321. SAN 329-3890. Tel. 503-757-5007. *Coord.* Arleen Libertini.

Oregon Health Information Network, Oregon Health Sciences Univ. Lib., Box 573, Portland 97207-0573. SAN 322-4287. Tel. 503-494-8026. *Coord.* Steve Teich.

Oregon Health Sciences Libraries Association, Oregon Health Sciences Univ. Lib., Box 573, Portland 97207-0573. SAN 371-2176. Tel. 503-494-8026. *Chpn.* Patrice O'Donavan.

Southern Oregon Library Federation, 1250 Siskiyou Blvd., Ashland 97520. SAN 322-2861. Tel. 503-552-6442. *Pres.* Ruth Monical.

Washington County Cooperative Library Services, 17880 S.W. Blanton St., Box 5129, Aloha 97006. SAN 322-287X. Tel. 503-642-1544. *Coord.* Peggy Forcier; *Automation Specialist* Eva Calcagno; *Outreach Services* Diane Barry; *Branches* Mary Lee Gregg.

Pennsylvania

Associated College Libraries of Central Pennsylvania, c/o Dickinson College, Carlisle 10713. SAN 322-2888. Tel. 717-245-1396. *Chpn.* John Stachacz.

Basic Health Sciences Library Network, c/o Abington Memorial Medical Center, Abington 19001. SAN 371-4888. Tel. 215-572-2096. *Pres.* Marion Chayes.

Berks County Library Association, Box 13566, Reading 19612-3566. SAN 371-0866. Tel. 215-921-7517, Ext. 7202. *Pres.* Rosemary Deegan; *Treas.* Cathy Boyer.

Central Pennsylvania Consortium, c/o Gettysburg College, Box 421, Gettysburg 17325. SAN 322-2896. Tel. 717-337-6140. FAX 717-337-6596. *Dir.* Janet M. Powers.

Confederation of State and State Related Institutions, Somerset State Hospital, Staff Lib., Box 631, Somerset 15501. SAN 323-9829. Tel. 814-443-0216. FAX 814-443-0217. *Dir. Lib. Services* Eve Kline.

Consortium for Health Information and Library Services, One Medical Center Blvd., Upland 19013-3995. SAN 322-290X. Tel. 215-447-6163. FAX 215-447-6164. *Exec. Dir.* Kathleen Vick Kell.

Cooperating Hospital Libraries of the Lehigh Valley Area, Allentown Osteopathic Medical Center, 1736 W. Hamilton St., Allentown 18104. SAN 371-0858. Tel. 215-770-8355. *Libn.* Linda Schwartz.

Delaware Valley Information Consortium, Abington Memorial Hospital, 1200 York Rd., Abington 19001. SAN 329-3912. Tel. 215-576-2096. *Coord.* Marion Chayes.

Film Library Intercollege Cooperative of Pennsylvania (FLIC), c/o Bucks County Community College, Swamp Rd., Newtown 18940. SAN 322-2926. Tel. 215-968-8004. FAX 215-968-8005. *Dir.* John Bradley.

Health Information Library Network of Northeastern Pennsylvania, VA Medical Center Medical Lib., Wilkes-Barre 18711. SAN 322-2934. Tel. 717-824-3521, Ext. 7420. *Chpn.* Bruce Reid.

Health Sciences Libraries Consortium, 3600 Market St., Suite 550, Philadelphia 19104. SAN 323-9780. Tel. 215-222-1532. FAX 215-222-0416. *Exec. Dir.* Joseph C. Scorza; *Assoc. Dir.* Alan C. Simon.

Interlibrary Delivery Service of Pennsylvania, 471 Park Lane, State College 16803-3208. SAN 322-2942. Tel. 814-238-0254. FAX 814-238-9686. *Admin. Dir.* Janet C. Phillips.

Laurel Highlands Health Sciences Library Consortium, Univ. Lib., Rm. 209, Univ. of Pittsburgh at Johnstown, Johnstown 15904. SAN 322-2950. Tel. 814-266-9661, Ext. 305. *Dir.* Heather W. Brice.

Lehigh Valley Association of Independent Colleges, Inc., Moravian College, Bethlehem 18018. SAN 322-2969. Tel. 215-691-6131. *Dir.* Galen C. Godbey.

Mid-Atlantic Law Library Cooperative (MALLCO), c/o Law Lib., Duquesne Univ., 900 Locust St., Pittsburgh 15282. SAN 371-0645. Tel. 412-434-5018. *Dir.* Jenni Parish; *Coord.* Frank Liu.

Northeastern Pennsylvania Bibliographic Center, c/o D. Leonard Corgan Lib., King's College, Wilkes-Barre 18711-0850. SAN 322-2993. Tel. 717-826-5900, Ext. 643. *Dir.* Terrence Mech.

Northwest Interlibrary Cooperative of Pennsylvania, c/o David Pinto, Mercyhurst College, 501 E. 38 St., Erie 16546. SAN 370-5862. Tel. 814-825-0232. *Chpn.* David E. Pinto; *V.Chpn.* Jean Tavber.

Oakland Library Consortium, Carnegie Mellon Univ., Hunt Lib., Rm. 302, Pittsburgh 15213-3890. SAN 370-5803. Tel. 412-268-2890. *Exec. Dir.* Sylverna Ford.

PALINET and Union Library Catalogue of Pennsylvania, 3401 Market St., Suite 262, Philadelphia 19104. SAN 322-3000. Tel. 215-382-7031. FAX 215-382-0022. *Exec. Dir.* James E. Rush; *Mgr. OCLC Services* Meryl Cinnamon; *Mgr. Microcomputer Services* Clifford Coughlin; *Mgr. Admin. Services* Donna Wright.

Pennsylvania Community College Library Consortium, Northampton Community College, 3835 Green Pond Rd., Bethlehem 18017. SAN 329-3939. Tel. 215-861-5358. *Dir.* Sarah B. Jubinski.

Philadelphia Area Consortium of Special Collections Libraries, c/o Academy of Natural Sciences, 19 and Parkway, Philadelphia 19103. SAN 370-7504. Tel. 215-299-1040. *Chpn. Exec. Committee* Carol M. Spawn.

Pittsburgh Council on Higher Education, 3814 Forbes Ave., Pittsburgh 15213-3506. SAN 322-3019. Tel. 412-683-7905. *Exec. Dir.* Betty K. Hunter.

Pittsburgh-East Hospital Library Cooperative, c/o Forbes Center for Gerontology, Frankstown Ave. at Washington Blvd., Pittsburgh 15206. SAN 322-3027. Tel. 412-665-3050. *Libn.* Susan Reeber.

Pittsburgh Regional Library Center, 103 Yost Blvd., Pittsburgh 15221-4833. SAN 322-3035. Tel. 412-825-0600. FAX 412-825-0762. *Exec. Dir.* H. E. Broadbent III.

Somerset–Bedford County Medical Library Consortium, Box 631, Somerset 15501-0631. SAN 322-3043. Tel. 814-445-6501, Ext. 216. FAX 814-443-0217. *Dir.* Eve Kline; *Libn.* Kathy Plaso.

Southeastern Pennsylvania Theological Library Association (SEPTLA), c/o Mary Immaculate Seminary, 300 Cherryville Rd., Northampton 18067. SAN 371-0793. Tel. 215-262-7866. *Pres.* Cait Kokolus.

State System of Higher Education Libraries Council, c/o Shippensburg Univ., Ezra Lehman Memorial Lib., Shippensburg 17257. SAN 322-2918. Tel. 717-532-1463. *Chpn.* Virginia M. Crowe.

Susquehanna Library Cooperative, J. V. Brown Lib., 19 E. Fourth St., Williamsport 17701. SAN 322-3051. Tel. 717-326-0536. FAX 717-323-6938. *Chpn.* Janice Trapp; *Treas.* Betsy Driebelbies.

Tri-State College Library Cooperative, c/o Kistler Memorial Lib., Rosemont College, Rosemont 19010-1699. SAN 322-3078. Tel. 215-525-0796. FAX 215-525-1939. *Pres.* Helen Hayes.

Rhode Island

Association of Rhode Island Health Sciences Librarians, c/o Health Sciences Lib., Our Lady of Providence Unit, Saint Joseph Hospital, 21 Peace St., Providence 02907. SAN 371-0742. Tel. 401-456-4035, 456-3035. *Pres.* Mary Zammarelli; *Pres.-Elect.* Mary Ann Slocomb.

Consortium of Rhode Island Academic and Research Libraries, Box 40041, Providence 02940-0041. SAN 322-3086. Tel. 401-253-1040. *Pres.* Carol K. DiPrete.

Cooperating Libraries Automated Network, c/o Providence Public Lib., 225 Washington St., Providence, 02903. SAN 329-4560. Tel. 401-455-8044, 455-8085. FAX 401-455-8080. *Chpn.* Christopher LaRoux.

Rhode Island Library Film Cooperative, 600 Sandy Lane, Warwick, 02886-3998. SAN 322-3116. Tel. 401-739-2278. *Coord.* Sonita Cummings.

South Carolina

Catawba-Wateree Health Education Consortium, 1020 W. Meeting St., Box 1045, Lancaster 29720. SAN 329-3971. Tel. 803-286-4121. *Libn.* Eric Lease Morgan.

Charleston Academic Libraries Consortium, College of Charleston, Robert Scott Small Lib., Charleston 29424. SAN 371-0769. Tel. 803-792-5530. *Chpn.* Richard Wood; *Pres.* David Cohen.

South Carolina Consortium (AHEC), 171 Ashley Ave., Charleston, 29425. SAN 329-3998. Tel. 803-792-4430. *Dir.* Dean Cleghorn.

South Carolina Health Information Network, Medical Univ. of South Carolina Lib., 171 Ashley Ave., Charleston 29425. SAN 370-0542. Tel. 803-792-7672. FAX 803-792-7947. *Exec. Dir.* Nancy C. McKeehan; *Chpn. SCHIN Users Group* Mary Ann Camp.

South Carolina State Library, South Carolina Library Network, 1500 Senate St., Box 11469, Columbia 29211-1469. SAN 322-4198. Tel. 803-734-8666. FAX 803-734-8676. *State Libn.* James B. Johnson, Jr.

Upper Savannah Area Health Education Medical Library (AHEC), Self Memorial Hospital, 1325 Spring St., Greenwood 29646. SAN 329-4110. Tel. 803-227-4851. FAX 803-227-4205. *Dir.* Jane Powers.

South Dakota

American Indian Higher Education Consortium, Box 490, Rosebud 57570. SAN 329-4056. Tel. 605-747-2263. *Pres.* Lionel Bordeaux.

Colleges of Mid-America, Inc., c/o Mount Mary College, 1105 W. Eighth St., Yankton 57058. SAN 322-3132. Tel. 605-668-1555. *Pres.* Mary C. Miller; *Secy.* Aileen Maddox.

South Dakota Library Network, 800 Governor's Dr., Pierre 57501-2294. SAN 371-2117. Tel. 605-773-3131. *Coord.* Jane Kobe.

Tennessee

Association of Memphis Area Health Science Libraries, c/o Univ. of Tennessee, Health Science Lib., 877 Madison Ave., Memphis 38163. SAN 323-9802. Tel. 901-528-5634. *Pres.* Jane Mertzlufft; *V.P.* Deb Lawless.

Jackson Area Colleges, c/o Jackson State Community College Lib., Jackson 38301-3797. SAN 322-3175. Tel. 901-424-3520. FAX 901-425-2615. *Dir.* Van Veatch.

Knoxville Area Health Sciences Library Consortium, c/o College of Nursing, Univ. of Tennessee, 1200 Volunteer Blvd., Knoxville 37996. SAN 371-0556. Tel. 615-974-7632. *Pres.* Beth Barret.

Mid-Tennessee Health Science Librarians Consortium, c/o Vanderbilt Univ. Medical Center Lib., Nashville 37232-2340. SAN 329-5028. Tel. 615-322-2299. FAX 615-343-6454. *Pres.* Mattie McHollin.

Tennessee Health Science Library Association, Vanderbilt Univ. Medical Center Lib., A-1300 MCN, Nashville 37232-2340. SAN 371-0726. Tel. 615-322-2291. *Pres.* Evelyn Forbes.

Tri-Cities Area Health Sciences Libraries Consortium, East Tennessee State Univ., James H. Quillen College of Medicine, Medical Lib., Box 23290A, Johnson City 37614-0002. SAN 329-4099. Tel. 615-929-6252. FAX 615-461-7025. *Dir.* Janet S. Fisher.

Texas

Abilene Library Consortium, Abilene Christian Univ. Lib., 1600 Campus Ct., Abilene 79699. SAN 322-4694. Tel. 915-674-2344. FAX 915-674-2202.

Amigos Bibliographic Council, Inc., 11300 N. Central Expressway, Suite 321, Dallas 75243. SAN 322-3191. Tel. 214-750-6130. WATS 800-843-8482 (national). FAX 214-750-7921. *Exec. Dir.* Bonnie Juergens.

APLIC International Census Network, c/o Population Research Center, 1800 Main Bldg., Univ. of Texas, Austin 78713. SAN 370-0690. Tel. 512-471-5514. FAX 512-471-4886. *Dir.* Gera Draaijer; *Libn.* Doreen Goyer.

Association for Higher Education, 17811 Waterview Pkwy., Suite 125, Dallas 75252-8016. SAN 322-3337. Tel. 214-231-7211. FAX 214-231-4031. *Dir. Lib. Programs and Services* Katherine Pearson Jagoe.

Coastal Bend Health Sciences Library Consortium, 2606 Hospital Blvd., Box 5280, Corpus Christi 78465-5280. SAN 322-3205. Tel. 512-881-4197. FAX 512-881-1198. *Coord.* Angie Hinojosa.

Council of Research and Academic Libraries, Box 290236, San Antonio 78280-1636. SAN 322-3213. Tel. 512-245-2133. *Pres.* Joan Theath.

— Automation Emerging Technologies, Southwest Texas State Univ. Lib., J. C. Kellam Bldg., San Marcus 78666-4606. SAN 329-6997. Tel. 512-245-2288. *Chpn.* Sam Knosh-khui.

— Circulation and Interlibrary Loan Group (CIRCILL), c/o Interlibrary Loan Dept., San Antonio Area Lib. System, 203 S. Saint Mary's, San Antonio 78205. SAN 322-323X. Tel. 512-299-7803. *Chpn.* Basil Aivaliotis.

— Coral Periodicals-Serials Librarians Group (CORPSE), San Antonio College, 1001 Howard St., Brooks AFB 78284. SAN 322-3248. Tel. 512-733-2480. *Chpn.* John Conyers.

— Documents Users Group (DOCS), San Antonio College Lib., 1001 Howard St., San Antonio 78284. SAN 322-3256. Tel. 512-733-2598. *Chpn.* Norma Carmack.

— Instructional Media Services Group (IMS), Univ. of Texas Health Science Center, 7703 Floyd Curl Dr., San Antonio 78284. SAN

322-3221. Tel. 512-567-2485. *Pres.* Mario Ramirez.
—Reference and Instructional Services Interest Group, Univ. of Texas Health Center Lib., 7703 Floyd Curl Dr., San Antonio 78285. SAN 328-753X. Tel. 512-567-2460. *Chpn.* Judy Larson.
—San Antonio Area Online Users Group (SOLUG), Univ. of Texas at San Antonio, San Antonio 78285. SAN 322-3264. Tel. 512-691-4573. *Chpn.* Pat Donegan.
—Special Collections Interest Group, Univ. of Texas at San Antonio, San Antonio 78285. SAN 324-2986. Tel. 512-691-4570. *Pres.* Craig Likness.
—Technical Services Interest Group, Our Lady of the Lake Univ. Lib., 411 S.W. 24 St., San Antonio 78284. SAN 322-3272. Tel. 512-434-6711, Ext. 328. *Pres.* Sue Tyner.

Del Norte Biosciences Library Consortium, c/o Reference Dept. Lib., Univ. of Texas at El Paso, El Paso 79968-0582. SAN 322-3302. Tel. 915-747-5643. *Pres.* Esperanza A. Moreno.

Harrington Library Consortium, Box 447, Amarillo 79178. SAN 329-546X. Tel. 806-371-5135. *Mgr.* Judabeth Floyd.

Health Library Information Network, c/o Baylor School of Nursing, Learning Resource Center, 3700 Worth St., Dallas 75246. SAN 322-3299. Tel. 214-820-2100. *Chpn.* Jody Guenther.

Houston Area Research Library Consortium (HARLiC), Texas Southern Univ. Lib., 3201 Wheeler Ave., Houston 77004. SAN 322-3329. Tel. 713-527-7121. *Pres.* Adele Dendy.

Northeast Texas Library System, 625 Austin, Garland 75040-6365. SAN 370-5943. Tel. 214-205-2566. *Dir.* Lowell Lindsey; *Coord.* Elizabeth Crabb.

Piasano Consortium, Victoria College, Univ. of Houston at Victoria, 2602 N. Ben Jordan, Victoria 77901-5699. SAN 329-4943. Tel. 512-573-3291, 576-3151. FAX 512-573-4401. *Dir.* Joe F. Dahlstrom.

Regional Information and Communication Exchange, Fondren Lib., Rice Univ., Box 1892, Houston 77251-1892. SAN 322-3345. Tel. 713-528-3553. FAX 713-523-4117. *Dir.* Una Gourlay.

South Central Regional Medical Library Program (TALON), 5323 Harry Hines Blvd.,

Dallas 75235-9049. SAN 322-3353. Tel. 214-688-2085. FAX 214-688-3277. *Dir.* Kathy Hoffman; *Assoc. Dir.* Regina Lee.

Texas Council of State University Librarians, Texas Woman's Univ., Box 23715, Denton 76204. SAN 322-337X. Tel. 817-898-2665. FAX 817-898-3726. *Chpn.* Elizabeth Snapp.

TEXNET, Box 12927, Austin 78711. SAN 322-3396. Tel. 512-463-5465. FAX 512-463-5436. *Mgr.* Rebecca Linton.

USDA Southwest Regional Document Delivery System, c/o Texas A&M Univ. Lib., Interlib. Loan Service, College Station 77843-5000. SAN 322-340X. Tel. 409-845-5641. FAX 409-845-4512. *ILL Head* Rachel Robbins.

Utah

Utah College Library Council, c/o Brigham Young Univ., 1354 HBLL, Provo 84602. SAN 322-3418. Tel. 801-378-4482. *Secy.* Terry Dahlin.

Utah Health Sciences Library Consortium, Eccles Health Sciences Lib., Bldg. 589, 10 N. Medical Dr., Salt Lake City 84112. SAN 370-5900. Tel. 801-581-8771. *Chpn.* Joan M. Stoddart.

Western Council of State Libraries, Inc., Utah State Lib., 2150 S. 300 W., Suite 16, Salt Lake City 84115. SAN 322-2314. Tel. 801-466-5888. *Pres.* Jane Kolbe.

Vermont

Vermont Resource Sharing Network, c/o Vermont Dept. of Libraries, Pavilion Office Bldg., 109 State St., Montpelier 05609-0601. SAN 322-3426. Tel. 802-828-3261. FAX 802-828-2199.

Virginia

American Gas Association Library Services, 1515 Wilson Blvd., Arlington 22219. SAN 371-0890. Tel. 703-841-8400. *Dir.* Steven Dorner.

Association of Southeastern Research Libraries, E. G. Swem Lib., College of William and Mary, Williamsburg 23185. SAN 322-1555. Tel. 804-221-3055. FAX 804-221-3088. *Chpn.* Nancy Marshall.

Consortium for Continuing Higher Education in Northern Virginia, 4400 University Dr., George Mason Univ., Fairfax 22030. SAN 322-3434. Tel. 703-323-2341. *Admin.* Sally Reithlingshoefer.

Defense Technical Information Center, Cameron Station, Bldg. 5, Alexandria 22304-6145. SAN 322-3442. Tel. 703-274-6800. *Admin.* Kurt N. Molholm.

Interlibrary Users Association, Center for Naval Analyses, 4401 Ford Ave., Alexandria 22302. SAN 322-1628. Tel. 703-824-2096. FAX 703-824-2949. *Mgr.* Pamela Charles.

Lynchburg Area Library Cooperative, Mary Helen Cochran Lib., Sweet Briar College, Sweet Briar 24595. SAN 322-3450. Tel. 804-381-6139. *Pres.* David Barnett.

Maxwell Online Inc., 8000 Westpark Dr., Suite 500, McLean 22102. SAN 322-0273. Tel. 703-442-0900. FAX 703-893-4632. *Pres.* James Terragno.

Richmond Academic Library Consortium, Univ. of Richmond, Richmond 23173. SAN 371-2230. Tel. 804-289-8456. *Acting Pres.* James Gwin.

Richmond Area Film-Video Cooperative, c/o Virginia Commonwealth Univ., James Branch Cabell Learning Resource Center, Richmond 23284-2033. SAN 322-3469. Tel. 804-367-1088. *Assoc. Dir.* Richard Winant.

Southwestern Virginia Health Information Librarians (SWVAHILI), Memorial Hospital of Danville Lib., 142 S. Main St., Danville 24541. SAN 323-9527. Tel. 804-799-4418. *Chpn.* Ann Sasser; *Secy.-Treas.* Lucy Glenn.

Tidewater Health Sciences Libraries, c/o Eastern Virginia Medical School Lib., Box 1980, Norfolk 23501. SAN 317-3658. Tel. 804-446-5840. *Chpn.* Joan Taylor.

U.S. Army Training and Doctrine Command (TRADOC), Lib. and Info. Network (TRALINET) Center, ATBO-N, Bldg. 117, Fort Monroe 23651-5117. SAN 322-418X. Tel. 804-727-4491. FAX 804-727-2750. *Dir.* James H. Byrn; *Systems Libn.* Edwin Burgess.

Virginia Tidewater Consortium, Health Science Bldg., Rm. 129, 5215 Hampton Blvd., Norfolk 23529-0293. SAN 329-5486. Tel. 804-683-3183. FAX 804-683-4515. *Dir.* Lawrence G. Dotolo.

Washington

Central Washington Hospital Consortium, Box 1887, Wenatchee 98807. SAN 329-3750. Tel. 509-662-1511. *Libn.* Jane Belt.

Consortium for Automated Library Services, Evergreen State College Lib. L2300, Olympia 98505. SAN 329-4528. Tel. 206-866-6000, Ext. 6260. *Systems Mgr.* Steven A. Metcalf.

Council on Botanical Horticultural Libraries, Pierce Lib., Rhododendron Species Federation, 2525 S. 336 St., Box 3798, Federal Way 98063-3798. SAN 371-0521. Tel. 206-927-6960. *Chpn.* Mrs. George Harrison.

Inland Northwest Health Sciences Libraries, Box 854, W. 800 Fifth Ave., Spokane 99210-0854. SAN 370-5099. Tel. 509-328-4220, Ext. 3125. *Chpn.* Lewis Miller; *Chpn.-Elect.* Gail Fielding.

Northwest Consortium of Law Libraries (NWCLL), Univ. of Puget Sound Law Lib., 950 Broadway Plaza, Tacoma 98402. SAN 370-081X. Tel. 206-591-2204. FAX 206-591-6313. *Registered Agent* Anita M. Steele; *Chpn.* Judith Meadows.

Pacific Northwest Regional Health Sciences Library Service, Univ. of Washington, SB-55, Seattle 98195. SAN 322-3485. Tel. 206-543-8262. FAX 206-543-8066. *Dir.* Sherrilynne S. Fuller.

Seattle Area Hospital Library Consortium, Health Info. Network Services, Everett 98206. SAN 329-3815. Tel. 206-258-7558. *Dir.* Rhe Jain; *Pres.* Cheryl Noble.

Spokane Cooperative Library Information System (SCOLIS), c/o Spokane County Lib. Dist., N4322 Argonne Rd., Spokane 99212-2101. SAN 322-3892. Tel. 509-924-4122. FAX 509-926-7139. *Admin.* Michael J. Wirt; *Mgr.* Linda Dunham.

WLN (formerly Western Library Network), Box 3888, Lacey 98503-0888. SAN 322-3507. Tel. 206-459-6518. FAX 206-459-6341. *Exec. Dir.* Ronald F. Miller.

West Virginia

East Central Colleges, c/o Bethany College, Bethany 26032. SAN 322-2667. Tel. 304-829-7812. FAX 304-829-7546. *Exec. Dir.* Nancy Siferd; *Dir.* Dennis Landon.

Huntington Health Science Library Consortium, Marshall Univ., Health Science Libs.,

Huntington 25701. SAN 322-4295. Tel. 304-696-3170. *Chpn.* Edward Dzierzak.

Mountain States Consortium, c/o West Virginia Wesleyan College, Buckhannon 26201. SAN 329-4765. Tel. 304-473-8000. *Treas.* J. David Thomas.

Southern West Virginia Library Automation Corporation, 221 N. Kanawha St., Box 1876, Beckley 25802. SAN 322-421X. Tel. 304-255-0511, Ext. 19. *Systems Mgr.* Maria Moon.

Wisconsin

Council of Wisconsin Libraries, Inc. (COWL), 728 State St., Rm. 464, Madison 53706-1494. SAN 322-3523. Tel. 608-263-4962. *Dir.* Kathryn Schneider Michaelis.

Fox River Valley Area Library Consortium, c/o Saint Nicholas, 1601 N. Taylor Dr., Sheboygan 53081. SAN 322-3531. Tel. 414-433-3693. *Coord.* Kathleen Blaser.

Fox Valley Library Council, 225 N. Oneida St., Appleton 54911. SAN 323-9640. *Pres.* Mary Brown; *V.P.* Joan Mueller.

Library Council of Metropolitan Milwaukee, Inc., 814 W. Wisconsin Ave., Milwaukee 53233. SAN 322-354X. Tel. 414-271-8470. FAX 414-278-2137. *Exec. Dir.* Corliss Rice.

North East Wisconsin Intertype Libraries, Inc., c/o Nicolet Federated Lib. System, 515 Pine St., Green Bay 54301. SAN 371-0777. Tel. 414-497-3468. *Coord.* Mary Schmidt.

Northwestern Wisconsin Hospital Library Consortium, c/o Health Sciences Lib., Saint Michael's Hospital, 900 Illinois Ave., Stevens Point 54481. SAN 322-3604. Tel. 715-346-5091. FAX 715-341-7429. *Dir.* Jan Kraus.

South Central Wisconsin Health Science Library Cooperative, Meriter Hospital, Park Medical Lib., 202 S. Park St., Madison 53715. SAN 322-4686. Tel. 608-267-6234. FAX 608-267-6016. *Coord.* Joanne Muellenbach.

Southeastern Wisconsin Health Science Library Consortium, c/o Curative Rehabilitation Center, 1000 N. 92 St., Wauwatosa 53226. SAN 322-3582. Tel. 414-259-1414, Ext. 394. *Libn.* Terry Bochte.

Wisconsin Interlibrary Services, 728 State St., Rm. 464, Madison 53706-1494. SAN 322-3612. Tel. 608-263-4962, 263-5051. FAX

608-263-3684. *Dir.* Kathryn Schneider Michaelis; *Asst. Dir.* Mary Williamson.

Wyoming

Health Sciences Information Network, c/o Science and Technology Lib., Univ. of Wyoming, University Sta., Box 3262, Laramie 82071. SAN 371-4861. Tel. 307-766-4263.

Northeastern Wyoming Medical Library Consortium, Campbell County Memorial Hospital, Box 3011, Gillette 82801-0683. SAN 370-484X. Tel. 307-682-8811, Ext. 183. FAX 307-672-7273. *Chpn.* Dorothy O'Brien.

Wyoming Library Network, c/o Wyoming State Lib., Supreme Court and State Lib. Bldg., Cheyenne 82002. SAN 371-0661. Tel. 307-777-7281. *State Libn.* Suzanne LeBarron.

Virgin Islands

VILINET (Virgin Islands Library and Information Network), c/o Division of Libs., Archives and Museums, 23 Dronningens Gade, Saint Thomas 00802. SAN 322-3639. Tel. 809-774-3407 (DLMAS), 774-3725. *Chpn.* David Oettinger.

Canada

Alberta

Alberta Association of College Librarians, c/o Medicine Hat College, 299 College Dr. S.E., Medicine Hat T1A 3Y6. SAN 370-0763. Tel. 403-529-3867. *Chpn.* Keith Walker.

Alberta Government Libraries Council, Cooperative Govt. Lib. Services Section, 9718 107th St., Edmonton T5K 1E4. SAN 370-0372. Tel. 403-427-3837. FAX 403-427-1623. *Chpn.* Heather Gordon; *V.Chpn.* Susan Carlisle.

Alberta Occupational Health and Safety, Alberta Community and Occupational Health Lib. Services, 10709 Jasper Ave., Edmonton T5J 3N3. SAN 370-0801. Tel. 403-427-3530. *Acting Mgr.* W. Keith McLaughlin; *Public Services Libn.* J. Lavulich.

Calgary Online Users Group (COLUG), c/o Lib., Alberta and Southern Gas Co. Ltd.,

425 First St. S.W., Calgary T2P 3L8. SAN 370-0453. Tel. 403-260-9919. *Treas.* Abe Cohen.

Northern Alberta Health Libraries Association, c/o Misericordia Hospital, Weinlos Lib., 16940 87th Ave., Edmonton T5R 4H5. SAN 370-5951. Tel. 403-486-8708. *Pres.* John Back.

British Columbia

British Columbia College and Institute Library Services, Clearinghouse for the Print Impaired (CILS), Vancouver Community College, Langara Campus Lib., 100 W. 49 Ave., Vancouver V5Y 2Z6. SAN 329-6970. Tel. 604-324-5237. FAX 604-324-5875. *Coord.* Mary Anne Epp.

British Columbia Post-Secondary Interlibrary Loan Network (NET), Univ. of British Columbia, Box 2139, Vancouver V6B 3T1. SAN 322-4724. Tel. 604-228-4430. FAX 604-228-6465. *Head ILL* Margaret Friesen.

Central Vancouver Librarian Group, c/o Lib. Processing Centre–Serials, Univ. of British Columbia, 2206 E. Mall, Vancouver V6T 1Z8. SAN 323-9543. Tel. 604-228-5038. *Chpn.* Kat McGrath.

Media Exchange Cooperative, 1266 72nd Ave., Box 9030, Surrey V3W 2M8. SAN 329-6954. Tel. 604-588-4411, 599-2299. FAX 604-591-6398. *Pres.* Janice Friesen.

New Brunswick

LINK–Library Information Network, c/o Ward Chipman Lib., Univ. of New Brunswick, Box 5050, Saint John E2L 4L5. SAN 370-0798. Tel. 506-648-5704. *Coord.* Susan Collins.

Maritimes Health Libraries Association (MHLA/ABSM), Bibliothèque des Sciences et de la Santé, Hôpital Dr. G. L. Dumont, 330 rue Archibald, Moncton E1C 2Z3. SAN 370-0836. Tel. 902-858-3247. *Pres.* Martha Brideau.

Nova Scotia

Council of Metropolitan University Librarians, Technical Univ. of Nova Scotia, Box 1000, Halifax B3J 2X4. SAN 370-0704. Tel. 902-420-7700. FAX 902-420-7551. *Chpn.* M. Riaz Hussain.

Ontario

Bibliocentre, 80 Cowdray Ct., Scarborough M1S 4N1. SAN 322-3663. Tel. 416-754-6600. FAX 416-299-0902. *Dir.* Doug Wentzel.

Canadian Association of Research Libraries (CARLABRC), Univ. of Ottawa, Morisset Hall, Rm. 602, 65 University St., Ottawa K1N 9A5. SAN 323-9721. Tel. 613-564-5864. FAX 613-564-5871.

Canadian Health Libraries Association (CHLA/ABSC), Office of Secretariat, Box 434, Sta. K, Toronto M4P 2G9. SAN 370-0720. Tel. 416-485-0377. *Pres.* Catherine A. Quinlan; *V.P.* Susan Hendricks.

Canadian Heritage Information Network, Journal Tower S., 12th fl., 365 Laurier Ave. W., Ottawa K1A 0C8. SAN 329-3076. Tel. 613-992-3333. FAX 613-952-2318. *Dir.* P. Homulos; *Document Researcher* Deborah F. Jewett.

County and Regional Municipal Library, c/o Haliburton County Public Lib., Box 119, Haliburton K0M 1S0. SAN 323-9705. Tel. 705-457-2241. *Chpn.* Janet Booth.

Disability Resource Library Network, G. Allan Roeher Institute, Kinsmen Bldg., York Univ. Campus, 4700 Keele St., Toronto M3J 1P3. SAN 323-9837. Tel. 416-661-9611. *Chpn.* Miriam Ticoll.

Education Libraries Sharing of Resources – A Network (ELSOR), Metro Toronto School Bd., 45 York Mills Rd., Willowdale M2P 1B6. SAN 370-0399. Tel. 416-397-2523. FAX 416-397-2640. *Chpn.* Martha E. Murphy.

Hamilton Wentworth Health Library Network, c/o Health Science Lib., McMaster Univ., 1200 Main St. W., Hamilton L8N 3Z5. SAN 370-5846. Tel. 416-525-9140, Ext. 2322. *Network Coord.* Linda Panton.

Health Science Information Consortium of Toronto, Univ. of Toronto, 7 King's College Circle, Toronto M5S 1A5. SAN 370-5080. Tel. 416-978-6359. FAX 416-978-7666. *Exec. Dir.* Joan L. Leishman.

Hi-Tech Libraries Network, c/o Cal Corp., 1050 Morrison Dr., Ottawa K2H 8K7. SAN 323-9586. Tel. 613-820-8280. FAX 613-820-8314. *Contact* Marjorie Whalen.

Kingston Area Health Libraries Association, c/o Kingston General Hospital Lib., 76 Stuart St., Kingston K7L 2V7. SAN 370-0674.

Tel. 613-548-3232. *Pres.* Margaret Darling; *Pres.-Elect.* Barbara Carr.

Ontario Hospital Association Region No. 9 Hospital Libraries Group (OHAHLG9), c/o Rhodes Chalke Lib., Royal Ottawa, 1145 Carling Ave., Ottawa K1Z 7K4. SAN 370-0550. Tel. 613-722-6521, Ext. 6268. FAX 613-722-5048. *Chpn.* Janet Joyce.

Ontario Hospital Libraries Association, 150 Ferrand Dr., Don Mills M3C 1H6. SAN 370-0739. Tel. 416-429-2661. *Pres.* Linda Panton; *Pres.-Elect.* Mary Gillies.

Ontario Public Library Information Network, Ministry of Culture & Communications Libs. and Community Info. Branch, 77 Bloor St. W., 3rd fl., Toronto M7A 2R9. SAN 329-5605. Tel. 416-965-2696. FAX 416-965-5883. *Dir.* Barbara Clubb.

Ottawa Hull Health Libraries Association, c/o Canadian Dental Association Lib., 1815 Alta Vista Dr., Ottawa K1G 3Y6. SAN 370-0844. Tel. 613-523-1770, Ext. 223. FAX 613-523-7736. *Pres.* Martha Vaughan; *Secy.-Treas.* Judith Bosschart.

QL Systems Limited, One Gore St., Box 2080, Kingston K7L 5J8. SAN 322-368X. Tel. 613-549-4611. *Pres.* Hugh Lawford.

— Calgary Branch, 505 Third St. S.W., Suite 1010, Calgary, AB T2P 3E6. SAN 322-3817. Tel. 403-262-6505. *Marketing Mgr.* Anita Manley.

— Halifax Branch, 1819 Granville St., Suite 300, Halifax, NS B3J 1X8. SAN 325-4194. Tel. 902-420-1666. *Mgr.* Ruth Rintoul.

— Ottawa Branch, 901 Saint Andrew Towers, 275 Sparks, Ottawa, ON K1R 7X9. SAN 322-3825. Tel. 613-238-3499. *V.P. Marketing* Adrienne Herron; *Mgr.* Alan Dingle.

— Toronto Branch, 411 Richmond St. E., Suite 101, Toronto, ON M5A 3S5. SAN 322-3833. Tel. 416-862-7656. *Mgr.* Angela Moutoulas.

— Vancouver Branch, 355 Burrard St., Suite 920, Vancouver, BC V6C 2G8. SAN 322-3841. Tel. 604-684-1462. *Mgr.* Tim Outhit.

Shared Library Services, South Huron Hospital Shared Lib. Services, 24 Huron St. W., Exeter N0M 1S2. SAN 323-9500. Tel. 519-235-2700. FAX 519-235-2700. *Dir.* Linda Wilcox.

Sheridan Park Association Library and Information Science Committee (SPA LISC), Sheridan Park Association, 2275 Speakman Dr., Mississauga L5K 1B1. SAN 370-

0437. Tel. 416-823-6160. *Chpn.* Linda Pauloske; *V.Chpn.* Laurie Scott.

Toronto Health Libraries Association, Univ. of Toronto, Science and Medicine Lib., Reference Dept., Seven King's College Circle, Toronto M5S 1A5. SAN 323-9853. Tel. 416-978-8617. FAX 416-978-7666. *Pres.* Eva Gulbinowicz; *Pres.-Elect.* Rosemary Ullyot.

Toronto School of Theology, 75 Queen's Park Crescent E., Toronto M5S 1K7. SAN 322-452X. Tel. 416-585-4551. FAX 416-978-7821. *Coord.* R. Grant Bracewell.

Waterloo-Wellington Museum Computer Network, Doon Heritage Crossroads, RR 2, Kitchener N2G 3W5. SAN 329-4862. Tel. 519-748-1914. *Coord.* Liz Macnaughton.

Wellington Waterloo Dufferin (WWD) Health Library Network, Cambridge Memorial Hospital, 700 Coronation Blvd., Cambridge N1R 3G2. SAN 370-0496. Tel. 519-623-3758, Ext. 2308. *Coord.* Nancy Pal.

Quebec

Association des Bibliothèques de la Santé Affiliées à l'Université de Montréal (ABSAUM), c/o Health Lib., Univ. of Montreal, Montreal H3C 3J7. SAN 370-5838. *Secy.* Bernard Bedard.

Canadian Agriculture Library Network of Library Services (QSFAG), c/o Agriculture Canada Research Sta., 2560 Hochelaga Blvd., Sainte Foy G1V 2J3. SAN 370-5889. Tel. 418-657-7980, Ext. 211. *Lib. Coord.* Paul R. Venne; *Lib. Clerk* Suzanne Cote.

Montreal Health Libraries Association, c/o DSC Montreal General Hospital, 980 Guy, Suite 300A, Montreal H3H 2K3. SAN 323-9608. Tel. 514-932-3055. FAX 514-932-1502. *Pres.* Nora Stamboulieh.

Montreal Medical Online Users Group, McGill Health Sciences Lib., 3655 Drummond St., Montreal H3G 1Y6. SAN 370-0771. Tel. 514-398-4757. FAX 514-398-3890. *Coord.* Angella Lambrou.

Saskatchewan

Saskatchewan Government Library Council, c/o Saskatchewan Education Resource Centre, 2220 College Ave., Regina S4P 3V7. SAN 323-956X. Tel. 306-787-5977. *Chpn.* Rebecca Landau.

National Library and Information-Industry Associations, United States and Canada

American Association of Law Libraries

Executive Director, Judith Genesen
53 W. Jackson Blvd., Chicago, IL 60604
312-939-4764

Object

"To promote librarianship, to develop and increase the usefulness of law libraries, to cultivate the science of law librarianship, and to foster a spirit of cooperation among members of the profession." Established 1906. Memb. 4,700. Dues (Indiv.) $115; (Inst.) two or fewer professional libns., $230; more than two, $115 times the number of professionals; (Indiv. Assoc.) $115; (Inst. Assoc.) $220 times the number of members; (Retired) $32.50; (Student) $25; (SIS Memb.) $12 each per year. Year. July 1 to June 30.

Membership

Persons officially connected with a law library or with a law section of a state or general library, separately maintained. Associate membership available for others.

Officers (July 1991–July 1992)

Pres. Carolyn P. Ahearn, Shaw Pittman Potts and Trowbridge, 2300 N St. N.W., Washington, DC 20037. Tel. 202-663-8500, FAX 202-663-8007; *V.P./Pres.-Elect.* Mark E. Estes, Holme Roberts and Owen, 1700 Lincoln St., Suite 4100, Denver, CO 80203. Tel. 303-861-7000, FAX 303-866-0200; *Past Pres.* Penny Hazelton, Univ. of Washington, Gallagher Law Lib., Condon Hall JB-20, 1100 N.E. Campus Pkwy., Seattle, WA 98105. Tel. 206-543-4086, FAX 206-685-2165; *Secy.* Paul Fu, Supreme Court of Ohio Law Lib., 30 E. Broad St., 4th fl., Columbus, OH 43266. Tel. 614-466-2044, FAX 614-466-1559; *Treas.* Claire Engel, Kilpatrick & Cody, 100 Peachtree St., Suite 3100, Atlanta, GA 30303. Tel. 404-572-6397, FAX 404-572-6555.

Executive Board (1991–1992)

Carol D. Billings, Shirley David, James Hambleton, Sandy Peterson, Mary Lu Linnane, Robert L. Oakley.

Committee Chairpersons

Awards. James S. Heller, College of William & Mary, Marshall-Wythe Law Lib., S. Henry St., Williamsburg, VA 23185. 804-221-3252.

Call for Papers. Rita T. Reusch, Univ. of Utah Law Lib., Salt Lake City, UT 84112. 801-581-6594.

CONELL. Hazel L. Johnson, 3408 Bonaparte Way, Durham, NC 27707. 919-493-1347; Donna Purvis, Baker & McKenzie, 2 Embarcadero Center, Suite 2400, San Francisco, CA 94111. 415-576-3066.

Constitution and Bylaws. Joyce Manna Janto, Univ. of Richmond School of Law Lib., Richmond, VA 23173. 804-289-8223.

Copyright. Kathleen Vanden Heuvel, Univ. of California School of Law Lib., Boalt Hall, Berkeley, CA 94720. 415-643-9147.

Education. Patrick E. Kehoe (Chpn.), American Univ., Washington College of Law Lib., Myers 11 Bldg., 4400 Massachusetts Ave. N.W., Washington, DC 20016-8087. 202-885-2674; Lei Seeger (V.Chpn.) Univ. of Idaho Law Lib., College of Law, Moscow, ID 83843. 208-885-6521.

Financial Advisory. Cornelia Trubey, Ropes & Gray, Lib., 41st fl., One International Place, Boston, MA 02110. 617-951-7713.

Government Relations. Tim Coggins, Univ. of North Carolina at Chapel Hill Law Lib., Van Hecke-Wettach Bldg., CB 3385, Chapel Hill, NC 27599. 919-962-6202.

Grants. Thomas L. Hanley, Univ. of Dayton Law Lib., 300 College Park, Dayton, OH 45469. 513-229-2444.

Index to Foreign Legal Periodicals. Lorraine A. Kulpa, Baker & McKenzie, One Prudential Plaza, Suite 2800, 130 E. Randolph St., Chicago, IL 60601. 312-861-2915.

Indexing Periodical Literature. Lawrence Cheeseman, Connecticut Judicial Dept. Law Lib. at Harvard, Court House, 95 Washington St., Hartford, CT 06106. 203-566-3900.

Law Library Journal and Newsletter. Frank G. Houdek, Southern Illinois Univ. School of Law Lib., Lesar Law Bldg., Carbondale, IL 62901. 618-453-8788.

Minorities. Allyson Withers, 2 E. Eighth St., Apt. 703, Chicago, IL 60605. 312-853-7475.

National Legal Resources. Claire Germain, Duke Univ. School of Law Lib., Durham, NC 27706. 919-684-6182.

Nominations. Maria Sekula, Social Law Lib., 1200 Court House, Boston, MA 02108. 617-742-0956.

Placement. Rosalie Sanderson, 4104 N.W. 70 Terr., Gainesville, FL 32606. 904-392-0417.

Preservation. Margaret Leary, Univ. of Michigan, Law Lib., Legal Research Bldg., Ann Arbor, MI 48109. 313-764-9322.

Public Relations. Edgar J. Bellefontaine, Social Law Lib., 1200 Court House, Boston, MA 02108. 617-742-0956.

Publications Policy. Maria E. Protti, Univ. of Oklahoma Law Lib., 300 Timberdell Rd., Norman, OK 73019. 405-325-4311.

Publications Review. Barbara Greenspahn, Univ. of Denver College of Law, Westminster Law Lib., 1900 Olive St. LTLB, Denver, CO 80220. 303-871-6200.

Recruitment. Gail Daly, Southern Methodist Univ., Underwood Law Lib., Dallas, TX 75275-0354.

Relations with Information Vendors. Edmund Edmonds, Loyola Univ. Law School Lib., 7214 Saint Charles Ave., New Orleans, LA 70118. 504-861-5543.

Scholarships. Katherine Malmquist, Cleveland State Univ., Cleveland Marshall College of Law Lib., 1801 Euclid Ave., Cleveland, OH 44115. 216-687-2253.

Statistics. Pamela Gregory, Circuit Court for Prince George's County Law Lib., Court House Box 580, 14735 Main St., Rm. 118, Upper Marlboro, MD 29772. 301-952-3436.

Special-Interest Section Chairpersons

Academic Law Libraries. Bruce Johnson, Univ. of South Carolina, Coleman Karesh Law Lib., Main and Greene St., Columbia, SC 29208. 803-777-5944.

Automation and Scientific Development. Nuchine Nobari, Lib. Alliance, 264 Lexington Ave., Suite 4C, New York, NY 10016-4182. 212-685-5297.

Contemporary Social Problems. Rebecca S. Trammell, Univ. of Nebraska College of Law Lib., Lincoln, NE 68583-0902. 402-472-3547.

Foreign, Comparative, and International Law. Amber Lee Smith, Los Angeles County Law Lib., 301 W. First St., Los Angeles, CA 90012. 213-629-3531.

Government Documents. Susan Dow, State Univ. of New York at Buffalo, Charles B. Sears Law Lib., John Lord O'Brian Hall, Amherst Campus, Buffalo, NY 14260. 716-636-2041.

Legal History and Rare Books. Nicholas Triffin, Pace Univ. School of Law Lib., 78 N. Broadway, White Plains, NY 10603. 914-422-4273.

Legal Information Services to the Public. R. Kathy Garner, Southern Illinois Univ. School of Law Lib., Lesar Law Bldg., Carbondale, IL 62901. 618-536-7711.

Micrographics/Audiovisual. Merle J. Slyhoff, Univ. of Pennsylvania, 3400 Chestnut St., Philadelphia, PA 19104-6279. 215-898-7478.

Online Bibliographic Services. Alva T. Stone, Florida State Univ., College of Law Lib., Tallahassee, FL 32306-1043. 904-644-4578.

Private Law Libraries. Janet Zagorin, Baker & McKenzie, 805 Third Ave., New York, NY 10022. 212-891-3968.

Reader Services. Joan Shear, Boston College Law School Lib., 885 Centre St., Newton Centre, MA 02159-1161. 617-552-4405.

State, Court, and County Law Libraries. Judith Meadows, State Law Lib. of Montana, Justice Bldg., 215 N. Sanders, Helena, MT 59620-3004. 406-444-3660.

Technical Services. Janis L. Johnston, Notre Dame Law School, Kresge Lib., Notre Dame, IN 46556. 219-239-7024.

American Film and Video Association

8050 Milwaukee Ave., Box 48659, Niles, IL 60648
708-698-6440

Object

"To promote the production, distribution, and utilization of educational films and videos and other audiovisual materials." Incorporated 1943. Memb. 1,500. Dues (Inst.) $210; (Commercial organizations) $315; (Indiv.) $55; (Students and Retirees) $35. Floating membership year.

Officers (1991-1992)

Pres. Anthony Marshalek, Northeast Ohio IMC, 347 N. Park, Warren, OH 44481; *Pres.-Elect.* Roberto Esteves, San Francisco Public Lib., Civic Center, San Francisco, CA 94102; *Past Pres.* Beverly Teach, Indiana Univ., AV Center, Bloomington, IN 47405-5901; *Treas.* Kathryn Elder, Film Lib., York Univ. Libs., 4700 Keele St., North York, ON M3J 1P3, Canada; *Secy.* Maria Johns, Montgomery County Intermediate Unit, Montgomery Ave. and Paper Mill Rd., Erdenheim, PA 19118.

Board of Directors

Officers; Kevin Conner, Robert Gurn, Nora McMartin, John Rowe, Karen Sayer, Irene Wood; *Acting Exec. Dir.* Kathryn Lamont Osen; *Managing Dir.* Lawrence J. Skaja.

Publications

AFVA Bulletin (6 per year).
AFVA Evaluations (2 per year).
Festival Guide (ann.).
Sightlines (q.). *Ed.* Ray Rolff.

American Library Association

Executive Director, Linda Crismond
50 E. Huron St., Chicago, IL 60611
312-944-6780; 800-545-2433

Object

The mission of the American Library Association is to provide leadership for the development, promotion, and improvement of library and information services and the profession of librarianship in order to enhance learning and ensure access to information for all. Memb. (Indiv.) 49,752; (Inst.) 3,141; (Total) 52,893. Dues (Indiv.) 1st year, $38; renewing memb., $75; (Nonsalaried Libn.) $26; (Trustee and Assoc. Membs.) $34; (Student) $19; (Foreign Indiv.) $45; (Inst.) $70 and up, depending on operating expenses of institution.

Membership

Any person, library, or other organization interested in library service and librarians.

Officers

Pres. Patricia Glass Schuman, Pres., Neal-Schuman Publishers, Inc., 100 Varick St., New York, NY 10013; *Treas.* Carla J. Stoffle, Univ. of Arizona Lib., Tucson, AZ 85721; *Exec. Dir.* Linda F. Crismond, ALA Headquarters, 50 E. Huron St., Chicago, IL 60611.

Executive Board

Officers; *Past Pres.* Richard M. Dougherty, School of Info. and Lib. Studies, Univ. of Michigan, Ann Arbor, MI 48109; Betty J. Blackman, Betty J. Turock (1995); Nancy M. Bolt, Judith A. Sessions (1994); Agnes M. Griffen, Ann K. Symons (1993); J. Dennis Day, Sharon A. Hogan (1992).

Endowment Trustees

Eric Moon (1994), Richard A. Olsen (1993), Bernard A. Margolis (1992); *Exec. Board Liaison*. Carla J. Stoffle; *Staff Liaison*. Linda F. Crismond.

Divisions

See the separate entries that follow: American Assn. of School Libns.; American Lib. Trustee Assn.; Assn. for Lib. Collections and Technical Services; Assn. for Lib. Service to Children; Assn. of College and Research Libs.; Assn. of Specialized and Cooperative Lib. Agencies; Lib. Admin. and Management Assn.; Lib. and Info. Technology Assn.; Public Lib. Assn.; Reference and Adult Services Div.; Young Adult Lib. Services Assn.

Publications

ALA Handbook of Organization and Membership Directory 1991–1992 (ann.).
American Libraries (11 per year; free to membs.; organizations $60/year; foreign $70; single copy $6).
Booklist (22 issues; U.S. and possessions $60/year; foreign $75; single copy $4.50).
Choice (11 issues; U.S. $148; foreign $165).

Round Table Chairpersons

(ALA staff liaison is given in parentheses.)
Armed Forces Libraries Round Table. James F. Aylward, 95 Echo Lane, Portsmouth, RI 02871 (Patricia A. Muir).
Continuing Library Education Network and Exchange. Darlene E. Weingand, Univ. of Wisconsin—Madison, School of Lib. and Info. Studies, Helen C. White Hall, 600 N. Park St., Madison, WI 53706 (Margaret Myers).
Ethnic Materials and Information Exchange. Patricia F. Beilke, Ball State Univ., Dept. of Secondary Education, TC-811, Muncie, IN 47306 (Mattye L. Nelson).
Exhibits. Mary Schwartz, H. W. Wilson Co., 950 Univ. Ave., Bronx, NY 10452 (Barbara Macikas).
Federal Librarians. Sami W. Klein, 11041 Wood Elves Way, Columbia, MD 21044 (Anne A. Heanue).

Government Documents. Linda M. Kennedy, 2319 Cezanne Ct., Davis, CA 95616 (Patricia A. Muir).
Independent Librarians Exchange. Carol A. Berger, C. Berger & Co., 327 E. Gundersen Dr., Carol Stream, IL 60188 (Margaret Myers).
Intellectual Freedom. Frances M. McDonald, R.R. 1, Box 173, Kasota, MN 56050 (Anne Levinson).
International Relations. Hannelore B. Rader, Cleveland State Univ. Lib., 1860 E. 22 St., Cleveland, OH 44115 (Robert Doyle).
Library History. Mary Niles Maack, 2872 Nicada Dr., Los Angeles, CA 90077 (Charles T. Harmon).
Library Instruction. Dianne C. Langlois, 13 Woodlot Lane, Middletown, CT 06457 (Jeniece Guy).
Library Research. Wayne A. Wiegand, Univ. of Wisconsin—Madison, 600 N. Park St., Madison, WI 53706 (Mary Jo Lynch).
Map and Geography Round Table. Jim Walsh, 161 Boutelle St., Fitchburg, MA 01420 (JoAn Segal).
New Members. James R. Mouw, 929 Belleforte, Oak Park, IL 60302 (JoAn Segal).
Social Responsibilities. Sherre Dryden, Vanderbilt Univ. Central Lib., 419 21st Ave. S., Nashville, TN 37240-0007 (Mattye Nelson).
Staff Organizations. Donna Epps Ramsey, Box 6769, El Paso, TX 79906 (Jeniece Guy).
Video Round Table. Mary Patricia Lora, 3411 Scarborough Rd., Toledo, OH 43615 (JoAn Segal).

Committee Chairpersons

Accreditation (Standing). Charles A. Bunge, Univ. of Wisconsin—Madison, School of Lib. and Info. Science, Helen C. White Hall, Madison, WI 53706.
American Libraries (Advisory). Salvador Guerena, Univ. of California, UCSB Lib., Santa Barbara, CA 93106 (Thomas M. Gaughan).
Appointments (Advisory). Marilyn L. Miller, Dept. of Lib. and Info. Studies, Univ. of North Carolina, Greensboro, NC 27412.
Awards. Diane Gordon Kadanoff, Norwell Public Lib., 64 South St., Norwell, MA 02061 (JoAn Segal).

Chapter Relations (Standing). Carol K. Di-Prete, 26 Slater Ave., Providence, RI 02906 (Gerald G. Hodges).

Committee on Committees (Elected Council Committee). Marilyn L. Miller, Univ. of North Carolina, Dept. of Lib. and Info. Studies, Greensboro, NC 27412-5001.

Conference Planning (Standing), New Orleans (1993). Marilyn L. Miller, Univ. of North Carolina, Dept. of Lib. and Info. Studies, Greensboro, NC 27412-5001.

Conference Program (Standing), San Francisco (1992). Patricia Glass Schuman, Neal-Schuman Publishers, Inc., 100 Varick St., New York, NY 10013 (Peggy Barber, JoAn Segal).

Constitution and Bylaws (Standing). John W. Berry, Univ. of Illinois at Chicago, Univ. Lib., Box 8198/MC 234, Chicago, IL 60680.

Council Orientation (Special). Elizabeth Futas, Univ. of Rhode Island, Graduate School of Lib. and Info. Studies, Rodman Hall, Kingston, RI 02881.

Intellectual Freedom (Standing, Council). Arthur Curley, Boston Public Lib., Copley Sq., Boston, MA 02117-0286 (Judith F. Krug).

International Relations (Standing, Council). Robert D. Stueart, Simmons College Graduate School of Lib. and Info. Science, 300 The Fenway, Boston, MA 02115 (Robert P. Doyle).

Legislation (Standing, Council). E. J. Josey, 5 Bayard Rd., Apt. 505, Pittsburgh, PA 15213 (Eileen D. Cooke).

Library Education (Standing, Council). F. William Summers, Florida State Univ., School of Lib. and Info. Science, Tallahassee, FL 32306 (Margaret Myers).

Library Outreach Services, Office for (Standing, Advisory). Virginia H. Mathews, 412 Horse Pond Rd., Madison, CT 06443 (Mattye L. Nelson).

Library Personnel Resources, Office for (Standing, Advisory). Maureen Sullivan, 34 Autumn St., New Haven, CT 06511 (Margaret Myers).

Membership (Standing). Kay A. Cassell, New York Public Lib., Programs and Services, 455 Fifth Ave., New York, NY 10016.

Minority Concerns (Standing, Council). Herman L. Totten, Univ. of North Texas, School of Lib. and Info. Sciences, Box 13796 NT Sta., Denton, TX 76203.

Nominating, 1992 Election (Special). Estelle M. Black, Rockford Public Lib., 215 N. Wyman St., Rockford, IL 61101-1061.

Organization (Standing, Council). Suzanne J. LeBarron, Wyoming State Lib., Supreme Court Bldg., Cheyenne, WY 82002-0650 (Roger H. Parent).

Pay Equity (Standing, Council). Lourdes Y. Collantes, State Univ. of New York College at Old Westbury Lib., Box 229, Old Westbury, NY 11568 (Margaret Myers).

Planning (Standing, Council). Patricia W. Berger, National Institute of Standards and Technology, Bldg. 101, Rm. E-106, Gaithersburg, MD 20899 (Linda F. Crismond).

Policy Monitoring (Council). Norman Horrocks, Scarecrow Press, Box 4167, Metuchen, NJ 08840.

Professional Ethics (Standing, Council). Neel Parikh, San Francisco Public Lib., Civic Center, San Francisco, CA 94102 (Judith Krug).

Program Evaluation and Support (Standing, Council). Mary W. Ghikas, Western New York Lib. Resources Council, 180 Oak St., Buffalo, NY 14203 (Roger H. Parent).

Public Information (Standing, Advisory). Elizabeth Futas, 11 Misty River Terr., Saunderstown, RI 02874 (Linda K. Wallace).

Publishing (Standing, Council). Sharon J. Rogers, George Washington Univ., Gelman Lib., Suite 201, 2130 H St. N.W., Washington, DC 20052 (Edgar S. McLarin).

Research and Statistics (Standing). Barbara F. Immroth, Univ. of Texas at Austin, Graduate School of Lib. and Info. Science, EDB 564, Austin, TX 78712 (Mary Jo Lynch).

Resolutions (Standing, Council). Bernard A. Margolis, Pikes Peak Lib. Dist., 5550 N. Union Blvd., Box 1579, Colorado Springs, CO 80901 (Miriam L. Hornback).

Review, Inquiry, and Mediation (Standing). Anne Grodzins Lipow, 2135 Oregon St., Berkeley, CA 94705 (Roger H. Parent, JoAn Segal, Jeniece Guy).

Standards (Standing). Keith C. Wright, Univ. of North Carolina, Dept. of Lib. and Info. Studies, School of Education, 349 Curry Bldg., Greensboro, NC 27412-5001 (Mary Jo Lynch).

User Instruction for Information Literacy (Standing). John C. Tyson, Virginia State Lib. and Archive, 11 St. at Capitol Sq., Richmond, VA 23219 (Andrew M. Hansen).

Women in Librarianship, Status of (Standing, Council). Estelle M. Black, Rockford Public Lib., 215 N. Wyman St., Rockford, IL 61101-1061 (Margaret Myers).

Joint Committee Chairpersons

American Association of Law Libraries/ American Correctional Association– ASCLA Committee on Institution Libraries (joint). Thea Chesley, 301 E. Walnut, Dawson, IL 62520-0216 (ACA); Martin Monahan, 1925 Melrose, Apt. 22, Walla Walla, WA 99362 (AALL); Jay Ihrig, Corrections Dept. of New Mexico, 1422 Paseo de Peralta, Santa Fe, NM 87503 (ALA/ ASCLA).

American Federation of Labor/Congress of Industrial Organizations–ALA, Library Service to Labor Groups, RASD. Leslie S. Hough, Georgia State Univ., Pullen Lib., Southern Labor Archives, 100 Decatur St. S.E., Atlanta, GA 30303-3081 (ALA); Anthony Sarmiento, AFL/CIO, Dept. of Education, 815 16th St. N.W., Rm. 407, Washington, DC 20006 (AFL/CIO).

Anglo-American Cataloguing Rules Common Revision Fund. Edgar S. McLarin, Assoc. Exec. Dir. for Publishing, ALA Headquarters, 50 E. Huron St., Chicago, IL 60611 (ALA); Barbara Zatlokal, Canadian Lib. Assn., 200 Elgin St., Suite 602, Ottawa, ON K2P 1L5, Canada (CLA); George Cunningham, Lib. Assn. Publishing, 7 Ridgmount St., London WC1E 7AE, England (British Lib. Assn.).

Anglo-American Cataloguing Rules, Joint Steering Committee for Revision of. Janet Swan Hill, Univ. of Colorado, Norlin Lib., Boulder, CO 80309-0184 (ALA).

Association for Educational Communications and Technology–AASL. Kay Bland, 4 Oakbrooke Dr., Sherwood, AR 72120.

Association for Educational Communications and Technology–ACRL. Marilyn McDonald, Foothill College Lib., 12345 El Monte Rd., Los Altos Hills, CA 94022-4599.

Association of American Publishers–ALA. Patricia Glass Schuman, Neal-Schuman Publishers, Inc., 100 Varick St., New York, NY 10013 (ALA); To be appointed (AAP).

Association of American Publishers– ALCTS. Peter McCallion, 232 E. Fifth St., New York, NY 10003 (ALCTS); Peter Simon, 759 Hawthorne St., Lynbrook, NY 11563 (AAP).

Children's Book Council–ALA. Judith Rovenger, Westchester Lib. System, 8 Westchester Plaza, Elmsford, NY 10523 (ALA); James Giblin, Clarion Books, 215 Park Ave., New York, NY 10003 (CBC).

Society of American Archivists–ALA (Joint Committee on Library-Archives Relationships). Robert M. Warner, Univ. of Michigan School of Info. and Lib. Studies, 304 W. Engineering, 550 E. University, Ann Arbor, MI 48109-1092 (ALA); Lewis Bellardo, Georgia Historical Society, 501 Whitaker St., Savannah, GA 31499 (SAA).

American Library Association
American Association of School Librarians

Executive Director, Ann Carlson Weeks
50 E. Huron St., Chicago, IL 60611
312-944-6780; 800-545-2433

Object

The American Association of School Librarians is interested in the general improvement and extension of library media services for children and young people. AASL has specific responsibility for: planning of program of study and service for the improvement and extension of library media services in elementary and secondary schools as a means of strengthening the educational program; evaluation, selection, interpretation, and utilization of media as it is used in the context of the school program; stimulation of continuous study and research in the library field and to establish criteria of evaluation; synthesis of the activities of all units of the American Library Association in areas of mutual concern; representation and interpretation of the need for the function of school libraries to other educational and lay groups; stimulation of professional growth, improvement of the status of school librarians, and encouragement of participation by members in appropriate type-of-activity divisions; conducting activities and projects for improvement and extension of service in the school library when such projects are beyond the scope of type-of-activity divisions, after specific approval by the ALA Council. Established in 1951 as a separate division of ALA. Memb. 7,000.

Membership

Open to all libraries, school library media specialists, interested individuals, and business firms with requisite membership in ALA.

Officers

Pres. Dawn Hansen Heller, 516 S. Ashland, LaGrange, IL 60525; *V.P./Pres.-Elect.* Ruth Toor, 61 Greenbriar, Berkeley, NJ 07922; *Secy.* Pamela Parman, 2312 Island Blvd., Sevierville, TN 27862; *Past Pres.* Winona Jones, 911 Manning Rd., Palm Harbor, FL 34683.

Board of Directors

Officers; *Regional Dirs.* Harriet Selverstone, M. Ellen Jay, Helen R. Adams, Clara G. Hoover, Philip Turner, Mary D. Lankford, Jody Gehrig; *Affiliate Assembly Delegates.* Cecile H. Dorr, James F. Bennett, Lorrie M. Monprode-Holt; *Sec. Dirs. ELMSS.* Selvin Royal; *NPSS.* Mary (Meb) Norton; *SPVS.* Charles R. White; *Ex officio.* Jane C. Terwillegar, Ann Carlson Weeks.

Publications

AASL Presidential Hotline (s. ann.; memb.).
School Library Media Quarterly (q.; memb.; nonmemb. $40). *Eds.* Mary Kay Biagini, Margaret Mary Kimmel, Blanche Wooll;

SLIS, Univ. of Pittsburgh, 135 N. Bellefield Ave., Pittsburgh, PA 15260.

Committee Chairpersons

Unit I: Organizational Maintenance

Unit Head. Phyllis Heroy, 5768 Hyacinth Ave., Baton Rouge, LA 70808.
Budget. Barbara Nemer.
Bylaws and Organizations. Emily Boyce.
Financial Planning and Fund Raising (Special). Barbara Nemer and Bernadette Winter.
Identification of Future Sites (Special). Jerry Wicks.
Leadership Enhancement. Jody Gehrig.
Long-Range Planning. Hilda K. Weisburg.
Membership. Gail Dickinson.
Nominating, 1992 Election. Merrilyn Ridgeway.

Unit II: Organizational Relationships

Unit Head. Marian Karpisek, 57 San Rafael Ct., West Jordan, UT 84088.
AECT/AASL Joint Committee. Drucilla Raines.
American University Press Services Publication Selection. Betty Bankhead.
International Relations. Jean Lowrie.
Legislation. Thomas L. Hart.
National Council for the Accreditation of Teacher Education. Marilyn Shontz.
School Library Statistics Program. Jacqueline Morris.

Unit III: Library Media Personnel Development

Unit Head. Jacqueline Morris, 5225 Leone Place, Indianapolis, IN 46226.
Annual Conference Local Arrangements. Barbara Jeffus, John McGinnis.
Annual Conference Program Planning. Valerie Wilford.
Certification Model Revision (Task Force). Selvin Royal.
General Conference, Baltimore. Linda L. Cornwell.
Professional Development Coordinating. Betty Marcoux.
Publications Advisory. Betty Kulleseid.
Publications Coordinating. Betty Kulleseid.

Recruitment (Special). Rita Adams.
SLMQ Editorial Board. Mart Kat Biagini.

Unit IV: Library Media Program Development

Unit Head. Drucilla Raines, 101 Remington Pl., Goose Creek, SC 29445.
Cultural Diversity (Special). Antoinette Negro.
Information Skills (Special). Paula Kay Montgomery.
Intellectual Freedom. Ginny Moore Kruse.
Research. Michael B. Eisenberg and Carol Truett.
Site-Based Management. Bettie Estes Rickner.
Technology. Catherine Murphy.
Whole Language (Special). Sharon A. Coatney.

Unit V: Public Information

Unit Head. Joanne Troutner, Tippecanoe School Corp., 21 Elston Rd., Lafayette, IN 47905.
Awards. Rocco Staino; ABC/CLIO, Pamela Kramer; Distinguished School Administrator's Award, AASL/SIRS, Cecile H. Dorr; Distinguished Service Award, AASL/Baker & Taylor, Blanche Woolls; Emergency Librarian Periodical Award, Carol L. Diehl; Frances Henne Award, Kay Maynard; Information Plus Continuing Educa-

tion Award, Yvonne B. Carter; Intellectual Freedom Award, AASL/SIRS, Rebecca S. Poole; Microcomputer in the Media Center Award Selection, AASL/Follett, Linda Hartman; National School Library Media Program of the Year Award Selection, AASL/Encyclopaedia Britannica Companies, Karen Winsor; School Librarians Workshop Award, Linda Bartone; National School Library Month, Sara Stubbins; Public Awareness, Doris Epler.

Section Chairpersons

Educators of Library Media Specialists (ELMSS). Savam Wilson.
Non-Public Schools (NPSS). Mary Lou Treat.
Supervisors (SPVS). Joyce Carpenter Wallach.

Representatives

ALA Appointments Committee. To be appointed.
ALA Legislation Assembly. Thomas L. Hart.
ALA Planning and Budget Assembly. Bernadette Winter.
ALTCA-CCS Cataloging of Children's Materials Committee. Frances Corcoran.
Freedom to Read Foundation. To be appointed.
Library Education Assembly. Betty Marcoux.

American Library Association
American Library Trustee Association

Executive Director, Susan Roman
50 E. Huron St., Chicago, IL 60611-2795
312-280-2161, 800-545-2433, FAX 312-280-3257

Object

The development of effective library service for all people in all types of communities and in all types of libraries; it follows that its members are concerned as policymakers with organizational patterns of service, with the development of competent personnel, the provision of adequate financing, the passage of suitable legislation, and the encouragement of citizen support for libraries. Open to all interested persons and organizations. Organized 1890. Became an

ALA division in 1961. Memb. 1,734. (For dues and membership year, see ALA entry.)

Officers (1991–1992)

Pres. Mary Arney, 3646 Charlotte, Kansas City, MO 64109; *1st V.P./Pres.-Elect.* Aileen R. Schrader, 275 Promontory Dr. W., Newport Beach, CA 92660; *2nd V.P.* Ann L. Donoghue, 15411 Betty Ann Lane, Oak Forest, IL 60452; *Immediate Past Pres.* Wayne Moss, 5329 Boulevard Pl., Indianapolis, IN 46208; *Secy.* Lillian Broad, 2210 Jackson Pl., North Bellmore, NY 11710.

Board of Directors

ALTA Councillor. Terri C. Jacobs, 1335 N. Astor, No. 14A, Chicago, IL 60610; *PLA Rep.* Carolyn Anthony, Skokie Public Lib., 5215 Oakton St., Skokie, IL 60077; *ALTA Newsletter Ed.* Sharon Saulmon, 12228 High Meadow Ct., Oklahoma City, OK 73170; *Parliamentarian.* Ira Harkavy, 1784 E. 29 St., Brooklyn, NY 11229; *Council Administrators.* Judith M. Baker, Cheryl Cooper, Gloria Dinerman, Esther W. Lopato, Holley Wilkinson; *Regional V.P.s.* Susan Churchill, Robert G. Gaylor, Danny Lee, Virginia M. McCurdy, Rochelle S. Reagan, Thomas F. Schlafly, Ramonda Wertz (1992); Wayne L. Coco, Jack Cole, Ira Harkavy, Colleen Minson, Patricia F. Turner (1993).

Publication

ALTA Newsletter (6 per year; memb.). *Ed.* Sharon Saulmon, 12228 High Meadow Ct., Oklahoma City, OK 73170.

Committee Chairpersons

Action Development. Paulette Holahan, 6417 Fleur de Lis Dr., New Orleans, LA 70124.

ALTA/ALSC Interdivisional. Ruth Newell, 380 Ingleside Dr., Bolingbrook, IL 60440.

ALTA/PLA Committee on Common Concerns. Wayne Moss, 5329 Boulevard Pl., Indianapolis, IN 46208; Carolyn Anthony, Skokie Public Lib., 5215 Oakton St., Skokie, IL 60077.

ALTA Will Task Force. Minnie-Lou Lynch, 404 E. Sixth Ave., Oakdale, LA 71463; Virginia G. Young, 10 E. Parkway Dr., Columbia, MO 65203.

Budget. Aileen R. Schrader, 275 Promontory Dr. W., Newport Beach, CA 92660.

Conference Program and Evaluation. Carol K. Vogelman, 894 Iris Dr., North Bellmore, NY 11710; Bonnie Bellany, 309 Lafayette Ave., Brooklyn, NY 11238.

Education of Trustees. Gloria F. Aguilar, 3647 Morningstar Circle, Farmers Branch, TX 75234; Denise E. Botto, 26 Farnham Ave., New Haven, CT 06515.

Financial Development. Norman Kelinson, 1228 Coffelt Ave., Bettendorf, IA 52722.

Intellectual Freedom. Judith E. Petrou, 9100 W. 129 Pl., Cedar Lake, IN 46303.

Legislation. Dorris D. Holmes, 3927 Glencrest Ct., Atlanta, GA 30319.

Liability Exemption for Trustees (Ad Hoc). Glen R. Dunlap, 500 Country Club Dr., Ozark, AL 36360.

Membership. Leroy D. Williams, Box 468, Reserve, LA 70084-0468.

Nominating. Norman Kelinson, 1228 Coffelt Ave., Bettendorf, IA 52722.

Pre-Conference. Cheryl Cooper, 112 Main St., Franklin, LA 70538.

President's Program. Catherine S. Wallace, 444 W. 44 St., Indianapolis, IN 46208.

Publications. Sharon Saulmon, 12228 High Meadow Ct., Oklahoma City, OK 73170.

Resolutions. John Parsons, Country Club Hills, Plymouth, IN 46563.

Speakers Bureau. Sharon Saulmon, 12228 High Meadow Ct., Oklahoma City, OK 73170.

Special Functions. Ruth Newell, 380 Ingleside Dr., Bolingbrook, IL 60440.

Specialized Outreach Services. Floy W. Johnson, 161 Greenhill Rd., Dayton, OH 45405.

Trustee Citations, Jury on. Gloria T. Glaser, 60 Sutton Pl. S., No. 8CD-S., New York, NY 10022.

White House Conference Subcommittee. Cynthia W. Everett, 704 Buena Vista St., Pascagoula, MS 39567.

Representatives

ALA Committee on Organizations. Ramonda Wertz.

ALA Committee on Professional Ethics. Aileen R. Schrader.

ALA Legislative Assembly. Dorris D. Holmes.

ALA Literacy Assembly. Floy W. Johnson.

ALA Membership Committee. Barbara D. Cooper.

ALA Membership Promotion Task Force. Leroy D. Williams.

ALA Planning and Budget Assembly. Aileen R. Schrader.

ALA Public Relations Assembly. Bonnie Bellamy.

ALA Standing Committee on Library Education. Gloria F. Aguilar.
ASCLA Decade of Disabled Persons. Ann L. Donoghue.

FOLUSA Liaison. Virginia G. Young.
Freedom to Read Foundation. Judith E. Petrou.
PLA Board of Directors. Deborah Miller.

American Library Association
Association for Library Collections and Technical Services

Executive Director, Karen Muller
Deputy Executive Director, Alex Bloss
50 E. Huron St., Chicago, IL 60611
312-280-5036, 800-545-2433

Object

The Association for Library Collections and Technical Services is responsible for the following activities: acquisition, identification, cataloging, classification, and preservation of library materials; the development and coordination of the country's library resources; and those areas of selection and evaluation involved in the acquisition of library materials and pertinent to the development of library resources. Any member of the American Library Association may elect membership in this division according to the provisions of the bylaws. Established 1957, renamed 1988. Memb. 5,854. (For information on dues, see ALA entry.)

Officers (July 1991–July 1992)

Pres. Arnold Hirshon, Dir., Wright State Univ. Lib., Dayton, OH 45435; *V.P.* Lizbeth Bishoff, OCLC, 6565 Frantz Rd., Dublin, OH 45385.

Address correspondence to the executive director.

Directors

Officers; *Council of Regional Groups Chpn.* Joan W. Hayes, Huron Valley Lib. System, Box 8645, Ann Arbor, MI 48107; *ALCTS Councillor.* Jean Farrington (1995); *Exec. Dir.* Karen Muller; *Past Pres.* Ruth Carter; *Dirs.-at-Large.* Sharon Bonk (1992); Katha Massey (1994); *Council of Regional Groups V.Chpn.* Jean A. Wright; *LRTS Ed.* Richard Smiraglia; *ALCTS Newsletter Ed.* Ann Swartzell; *ALCTS Planning Committee Chpn.* John Webb (1992); *LC Liaison.* Henriette D. Avram; *Parliamentarian.* Walter High; *Section Chairpersons.*

Publications

ALCTS Network News (irreg.; free). *Ed.* Karen Muller. Available on Bitnet. Subscribe via LISTSERV@UICVM.
ALCTS Newsletter (6 per year; memb.; nonmemb. $25). *Ed.* Ann Swartzell, Univ. of California—Berkeley, Conservation Dept., 416 Lib., Berkeley, CA 94720.
Library Resources and Technical Services (q.; memb.; nonmemb. $45). *Ed.* Richard Smiraglia, Columbia Univ. School of Lib. Service, 516 Butler, New York, NY 10027.

Section Chairpersons

Acquisition of Library Materials (ALMS). Carol Chamberlain, 545 W. Ridge Ave., State College, PA 16803.
Cataloging and Classification (CCS). F. Kathleen Bales, Research Libs. Group, 1255 Sherman Ave., Menlo Park, CA 94025.
Collection Management and Development (CMDS). Carolyn Bucknall, 808 West Ave., Austin, TX 78701.
Preservation of Library Materials (PLMS). Lisa L. Fox, SOLINET, 400 Colony Sq., Plaza Level, Atlanta, GA 30361-6301.
Reproduction of Library Materials (RLMS). Debra McKern, Emory Univ., Woodruff Lib. G-23, Atlanta, GA 30322.
Serials (SS). Suzanne Thomas, 309 Center Ave., Aspinwall, PA 15215.

Committee Chairpersons

Association of American Publishers/ALCTS Joint Committee. Peter McCallion, 232 E. Fifth St., New York, NY 10003; Audrey

Melkin, John Wiley & Sons, 605 Third Ave., New York, NY 10158.

Audiovisual. Joan Swanekamp, Eastman School of Music, Sibley Music Lib., 27 Gibbs St., Rochester, NY 14604.

Best of LRTS. Jasper Schad, Wichita State Univ., Box 68, Wichita, KS 67208-1595.

Blackwell North American Scholarship Award. Ellen Zyroff, San Diego County Public Lib., 5555 Overland Ave., Bldg. 15, San Diego, CA 92123.

Budget and Finance. Robert P. Holley, Assoc. Dean of Libs., 134 Purdy Lib., Wayne State Univ., Detroit, MI 48202.

Catalog Form and Function. Suzanne Striedieck, North Carolina State Univ. Libs., Box 7111, Raleigh, NC 27695.

Commercial Technical Services. Rexford Bross, Jr., Univ. of Toledo Libs., 2801 W. Bancroft St., Toledo, OH 43606.

Conference Program, New Orleans (1993). Lizbeth Bishoff, OCLC, 6565 Frantz Rd., Dublin, OH 45385.

Conference Program, San Francisco (1992). Arnold Hirshon, Wright State Univ. Lib., Dayton, OH 45435.

Duplicates Exchange Union. Jane Johnson, 210 Merrywood Dr., Statesboro, GA 30458.

Education. Sally Rausch, 3715 Fenway Pl., Bloomington, IN 47405.

International Relations. D. Whitney Coe, 34 Franklin Corner Rd., Box 6292, Lawrenceville, NJ 08648.

Legislative. Jon Eldredge, Chief, Collection and Information Resource Development, Univ. of New Mexico, North Campus, Albuquerque, NM 87131.

Library Materials Price Index. John Haar, III, 1505 Westshire Lane, Richmond, VA 23233.

LRTS Editorial Board. Richard Smiraglia, Columbia Univ. School of Lib. Service, 516 Butler, New York, NY 10027.

MARBI. Ann L. Highsmith, Texas A&M Univ., Sterling C. Evans Lib., College Sta., TX 77843-5000.

Membership. Barry Baker, Univ. of Georgia Libs., Main Lib., Athens, GA 30602.

Nominating. Walter High, North Carolina State Univ. Libs., Box 7111, Raleigh, NC 27695-2603.

Organization and Bylaws. Ruth Carter, 121 Pikemont Dr., Wexford, PA 15090.

Esther J. Piercy Award Jury. George Gibbs, 1304 Inverness Dr., Lawrence, KS 66049.

Planning. John Webb, Oregon State Lib., Salem, OR 97310.

Preservation Microfilming. Marjorie Bloss, 2827 W. Gregory St., Chicago, IL 60625.

Program Initiatives. Dorothy Keeton McKowen, 7625 Summit Lane, Lafayette, IN 47905.

Publications. Carolyn J. Mueller, 825 Park Ave., Arcata, CA 95521.

Publisher/Vendor–Library Relations. Richard P. Jasper, 818 Medlock Rd., Decatur, GA 30033.

Research and Statistics. Joe Hewitt, Univ. of North Carolina, Davis Lib., CB 3906, Chapel Hill, NC 27599-3906.

Scholarly Communication. To be appointed.

Technical Services Costs. Kathleen Brown, North Carolina State Univ. Libs., Box 7111, Raleigh, NC 27695-7111.

Representatives

ALA Committee on Research and Statistics. Joe Hewitt.

ALA Conference Program Representative, New Orleans (1993). Lizbeth Bishoff.

ALA Conference Program Representative, San Francisco (1992). Arnold Hirshon.

ALA Freedom to Read Foundation. John Hostage.

ALA Legislation Assembly. Jon Eldredge.

ALA Library Education Assembly. Sally Rausch.

ALA Membership Promotion Task Force. Barry Baker.

ALA Planning and Budget Assembly. Arnold Hirshon; Lizbeth Bishoff.

American Institute for Conservation of Historic and Artistic Works. Constance L. Brooks.

Hugh Atkinson Memorial Award. Thomas W. Leonhardt.

Joint Advisory Committee on Nonbook Materials. Katha D. Massey; Janice DeSirey.

Joint Steering Committee for Revision of AACR. Janet Swan Hill.

National Information Standards Organization (NISO) Standards Committee Z39 on Library Work, Documentation, and Related Publishing Practices. Myron Chace; Alternate. Glenn B. Patton.

National Institute for Conservation. Margaret Child.

American Library Association
Association for Library Service to Children

Executive Director, Susan Roman
50 E. Huron St., Chicago, IL 60611
312-944-6780, 800-545-2433

Object

Interested in the improvement and extension of library services to children in all types of libraries. Responsible for the evaluation and selection of book and nonbook material for, and the improvement of techniques of, library services to children from preschool through the eighth grade or junior high school age, when such materials or techniques are intended for use in more than one type of library. Founded 1901. Memb. 3,550. (For information on dues, see ALA entry.)

Membership

Open to anyone interested in library services to children.

Officers

Pres. Linda A. Perkins; *Pres.-Elect.* Kathy Ann East; *Past Pres.* Barbara M. Barstow.
Address correspondence to the executive director.

Directors

Therese G. Bigelow, Gayle Cole, Carla D. Hayden, Steven L. Herb, Elizabeth F. Howard, Phyllis K. Kennemer, Penny S. Markey, Elizabeth S. Watson; *Councillor.* Elizabeth M. Greggs; *Staff Liaison.* Susan Roman.

Publications

ALSC Newsletter (s. ann.; memb.). *Ed.* Anitra T. Steele, ALSC/ALA, 50 E. Huron St., Chicago, IL 60611.
Journal of Youth Services in Libraries (q.; memb.; nonmemb. $40; foreign $50). *Eds.* Donald J. Kenney and Linda J. Wilson, Box 90001, Virginia Polytechnic Institute, Blacksburg, VA 24062-9001.

Committee Chairpersons

Priority Group I: Child Advocacy

Consultant. Ann Kalkoff, 220 Berkley Pl., Brooklyn, NY 11217.
Boy Scouts of America (Advisory).
Legislation.
Liaison with Mass Media.
Liaison with National Organizations Serving the Child.

Priority Group II: Evaluation of Media

Consultant. Margaret A. Bush.
Computer Software Evaluation.
Film and Video Evaluation.
Filmstrip Evaluation.
Notable Children's Books.
Recording Evaluation.
Selection of Children's Books from Various Cultures.

Priority Group III: Professional Development

Consultant. Clara Bohrer, 4886 School Bell Lane, Birmingham, MI 48010.
ALSC/Econo-Clad Literature Program Award.
Arbuthnot Honor Lecture.
Education.
Managing Children's Services (Committee and Discussion Group). Putnam and Grosset Group Awards.
Scholarships: Melcher and Bound to Stay Bound.
State and Regional Leadership (Discussion Group).
Teachers of Children's Literature (Discussion Group).

Priority Group IV: Social Responsibilities

Consultant. Eliza T. Dresang.
Intellectual Freedom.
International Relations.

Library Service to Children with Special Needs.

Preschool Services and Parent Education.

Preschool Services (Discussion Group).

Social Issues in Relation to Materials and Services for Children (Discussion Group).

Priority Group V: Planning and Research

Consultant. Therese G. Bigelow.

Budget and Finance.

Caldecott Medal Calendar.

Collections of Children's Books for Adult Research (Discussion Group).

Grants.

Local Arrangements.

Membership.

National Planning of Special Collections.

National Reading Program.

Nominating.

Organization and Bylaws.

Publications.

Research and Development.

Storytelling (Discussion Group).

Priority Group VI: Award Committees

Consultant. Ruth I. Gordon.

Mildred L. Batchelder Award Selection.

Caldecott Award.

Newbery Award.

Wilder Award.

Representatives

ALA Appointments Committee. To be appointed.

ALA Budget Assembly. Elizabeth S. Watson.

ALA Conference Program (San Francisco, 1992). Linda A. Perkins.

ALA Legislative Assembly. To be appointed.

ALA Library Education Assembly. Melody Allen.

ALA Literacy Assembly. Helen Mae Mullen.

ALA Membership Promotion Task Force. Susan Knorr.

ALCTS/CCS Cataloging of Children's Materials. Jane Marton; Jennifer Abramson.

ASCLA Decade of Disabled Persons Committee. Leslie Edmonds.

RASD Reference Services for Children and Young Adults. June Schlessinger.

Liaison with Other National Organizations

American Association for Gifted Children. To be appointed.

Association for Childhood Education International. To be appointed.

Association for Children and Adults with Learning Disabilities. Clara Bohrer.

Association for the Care of Children's Health. Maria Salvadore.

Big Brothers and Big Sisters of America. Helen Mullen.

Boy Scouts of America. Caroline Parr.

Boys Clubs of America. To be appointed.

Camp Fire Inc. Anitra T. Steele.

Child Welfare League of America. Ethel Ambrose.

Children's Defense Fund. Effie Lee Morris.

Four-H Programs, Extension Service. Elizabeth Simmons.

Freedom to Read Foundation. Marcella Bina.

Girl Scouts of America. To be appointed.

Girls Club of America. To be appointed.

International Reading Association. Steven Herb.

National Association for the Education of Young Children. Toni Bernardi.

National Association for the Perpetuation and Preservation of Storytelling. Elizabeth Simmons.

National Committee for the Prevention of Child Abuse. Melanie Myers.

National Multiple Sclerosis Society. Melanie Myers.

Parent Cooperative Preschool International. Blair Christolon.

Parents without Partners. Lucy Marx.

Puppeteers of America. Frances J. McCurdy.

Reading Is Fundamental. To be appointed.

Salvation Army. To be appointed.

American Library Association
Association of College and Research Libraries

Executive Director, Althea Jenkins
50 E. Huron St., Chicago, IL 60611
312-944-6780, 800-545-2433

Object

The mission of the Association of College and Research Libraries (ACRL) is to foster the profession of academic and research librarianship and to enhance the ability of academic and research libraries to serve effectively the library and information needs of current and potential library users. This includes all types of academic libraries—-community and junior college, college, and university—as well as comprehensive and specialized research libraries and their professional staffs. Founded 1938. Memb. 10,170. (For information on dues, see ALA entry.)

Officers (June 1991–1992)

Pres. Anne K. Beaubien, Univ. of Michigan Libs., 106 Harlan Hatcher Lib., Ann Arbor, MI 48109-1205. Tel. 313-763-5060; *Pres.-Elect.* Jacquelyn M. McCoy, Dir., Occidental College Lib., 1600 Campus Rd., Los Angeles, CA 90041. Tel. 213-259-2640; *Past Pres.* Barbara J. Ford, Virginia Commonwealth Univ., James Branch Cabell Lib., 901 Park Ave., Richmond, VA 23284-2033; *Councillor.* Rochelle Sager, Dir., Lib. and Media Services, Fashion Institute of Technology Lib., Seventh Ave. at 27 St., New York, NY 10001; *Committee Rep.* Leslie A. Manning, Lib. Dir., Univ. of Colorado Lib., Box 7150, Colorado Springs, CO 80933-7150; *Ex officio.* Althea Jenkins, ACRL Exec. Dir., ALA, 50 E. Huron St., Chicago, IL 60611.

Board of Directors

Officers; *Membs.* Karin E. Begg, Eileen Dubin, Evan Ira Farber, Ray E. Metz, Linda L. Phillips, Shelley E. Phipps; Barbara J. Wittkopf.

Publications

ACRL Publications in Librarianship (formerly ACRL Monograph Series) (irreg.). *Ed.* Jonathan A. Lindsey, Baylor Univ., Waco, TX 76793.
Choice (11 per year; $148; foreign $165). *Choice Reviews-on-Cards* ($225; foreign $245). *Ed.* Patricia E. Sabosik, 100 Riverview Center, Middletown, CT 06457.
College & Research Libraries (6 per year; memb.; nonmemb. $45). *Ed.* Gloriana St. Clair, Pennsylvania State Univ., University Park, PA 16802.
College & Research Libraries News (11 per year; memb.; nonmemb. $20). *Ed.* Mary Ellen Kyger Davis, ACRL, 50 E. Huron St., Chicago, IL 60611.
Rare Books and Manuscripts Librarianship (2 per year; $30). *Ed.* Alice D. Schreyer, Univ. of Delaware Lib., Newark, DE 19717-5267.

Committees and Advisory Boards

Academic Library Statistics. Richard W. Meyer, Lib. Dir., Trinity Univ., 715 Stadium Dr., San Antonio, TX 78212.
Academic or Research Librarian of the Year Award. Karin Wittenborg, Assoc. Univ. Libn., Univ. of California, 405 Hilgard Ave., Los Angeles, CA 90024-1450. Tel. 213-825-1202.
Academic Status. Larry R. Oberg, Dir. of Libs., Albion College, 602 E. Cass St., Albion, MI 49224. Tel. 517-629-0285.
Access Policy Guidelines (Task Force). Kathleen Gunning, Asst. Dir., Univ. of Houston Libs., 4800 Calhoun Blvd., Houston, TX 77204-2091. Tel. 713-749-4241.
Accreditation Advisory Board. David B. Walch, California Polytechnic State Univ., Robert F. Kennedy Lib., San Luis Obispo, CA 93407. Tel. 805-746-2345.
ACRL/AECT Joint Committee. Marilyn M. McDonald, Foothill College Lib., 12345 El

Monte Rd., Los Altos Hills, CA 94022-4599. Tel. 415-960-4390.

Appointments (1991) and Nominations (1992). Marion T. Reid, Dir. of Lib. Services, California State Univ., 820 W. Los Vallecitos, San Marcos, CA 92096. Tel. 619-471-4184.

Appointments (1992) and Nominations (1993). Hiram L. Davis, Dir. of Libs., Michigan State Univ., East Lansing, MI 48824-1048. Tel. 517-355-2344.

Hugh C. Atkinson Memorial Award. Michele I. Dalehite, Asst. Dir. for Lib. Services, Florida Center for Lib. Automation, 2002 N.W. 13 St., No. 320, Gainesville, FL 32609. Tel. 904-392-9020.

Audiovisual. Richard N. Shaw, Dir., Technical College of the Low Country, Box 1288, 100 S. Ribaut Rd., Beaufort, SC 29902. Tel. 803-525-8324.

Budget and Finance. Leslie A. Manning, Dir., Univ. of Colorado Lib., Box 7150, Colorado Springs, CO 80933-7150. Tel. 719-593-3296.

Conference Program Planning, New Orleans (1993). Jacquelyn M. McCoy, Dir., Occidental College Lib., 1600 Campus Rd., Los Angeles, CA 90041. Tel. 213-259-2640.

Conference Program Planning, San Francisco (1992). Anne K. Beaubien, Univ. of Michigan Libs., 106 Harlan Hatcher Lib., Ann Arbor, MI 48109-1205. Tel. 313-763-5060.

Constitution and Bylaws. J. Daniel Vann III, Dean of Lib. Services, Bloomsburg Univ., Bloomsburg, PA 17815. Tel. 717-638-2197.

Copyright. Kristine R. Brancolini, Indiana Univ., Univ. Libs., Rm. W101A, Tenth St. and Jordan Ave., Bloomington, IN 47405. Tel. 812-855-3710.

Doctoral Dissertation Fellowship. Roger W. Durbin, Assoc. Dir., Univ. Lib. and Learning Resource Center, Akron, OH 44325-1707. Tel. 216-972-7497.

Government Relations. Hiram L. Davis, Dir. of Libs., Michigan State Univ., East Lansing, MI 48824-1048. Tel. 517-355-2344.

Information Literacy Advisory Board. Hannelore B. Rader, Cleveland State Univ. Lib., 1860 E. 22 St., Cleveland, OH 44115. Tel. 216-987-2085.

International Relations. Maureen D. Pastine, Dir., Central Univ. Lib., Southern Methodist Univ., Dallas, TX 75275. Tel. 214-692-2400.

Samuel Lazerow Fellowship. Betty Landesman, George Washington Univ., Gelman Lib., 2130 H St. N.W., Washington, DC 20052. Tel. 202-994-6455.

Managing Academic Libraries Advisory Board. Mary J. Cronin, Boston College Libs., Chestnut Hill, MA 02167. Tel. 617-552-3195.

Membership. Andrea C. Hoffman, Dir., Wheelock College Lib., 132 Riverway, Boston, MA 02215. Tel. 617-734-5200.

MLA Bibliography Scope and Overlap. Elaine A. Franco, Univ. of California, Shields Lib., Davis, CA 95616. Tel. 916-752-1126.

National Conference Executive Committee, Salt Lake (1992). Joseph A. Boisse, Dir., UCSB Lib., Univ. of California, Santa Barbara, CA 93106-9010. Tel. 805-961-2741.

New Publications (Advisory). Damaris A. Schmitt, Reference Libn., Saint Louis Community College, 11333 Big Bend Blvd., Saint Louis, MO 63122. Tel. 314-966-7623.

Organizational Member (Task Force). Maxine H. Reneker, 437 College Ave., Palo Alto, CA 94306. Tel. 415-324-4197.

Orientation. Barbara J. Ford., Dir., Univ. Lib. Services, Virginia Commonwealth Univ., 901 Park Ave., Richmond, VA 23284-2033. Tel. 804-257-1116.

Planning. Mary Sue Ferrell, Exec. Dir., California Lib. Assn., 717 K St., Suite 300, Sacramento, CA 95814. Tel. 916-447-8541.

President's Program Planning, San Francisco (1992). Mary W. George, General and Humanities Reference Div., Firestone Lib., Princeton Univ., Princeton, NJ 08544. Tel. 609-258-3180.

Professional Development (Task Force). Meredith A. Butler, Dir. of Libs., State Univ. of New York, 1400 Washington Ave., Albany, NY 12222. Tel. 518-442-3568.

Professional Education. Keith Swigger, Texas Woman's Univ., School of Lib. and Info. Studies, Box 22905, TWU Sta., Denton, TX 76204. Tel. 817-898-2621.

Professional Liaison. Melvin R. George, Dir., Oregon State Univ. Lib., Corvallis, OR 97331-4501. Tel. 503-737-3411.

Publications. Pamela Snelson, Drew Univ., Rose Memorial Lib., Madison, NJ 07940-4007. Tel. 201-408-3125.

Racial and Ethnic Diversity. Susana A. Hinojosa, Univ. of California Lib., Berkeley, CA 94720. Tel. 415-642-3773.

Research. Vicki Gregory, Univ. of South Florida, School of Lib. and Info. Science, Tampa, FL 33620. Tel. 813-974-3520.

K. G. Saur Award for Best College and Research Libraries Article. Anne Woodsworth, Univ. of Pittsburgh, School of Lib. and Info. Science, 626 LIS Bldg., Pittsburgh, PA 15260. Tel. 412-648-7710.

Social Issues (Task Force). Cerise Oberman, Feinberg Lib., State Univ. of New York, Plattsburgh, NY 12901. Tel. 518-564-5180.

Standards and Accreditation. John S. Page, Jr., Learning Resources Div., Univ. of the District of Columbia, 4200 Connecticut Ave. N.W., Washington, DC 20008. Tel. 202-282-7536.

White House Conference (Ad hoc). Patricia A. Wand, Libn., American Univ. Lib., 4400 Massachusetts Ave. N.W., Washington, DC 20016-8046. Tel. 202-885-3238.

Discussion Groups

Academic Librarians' Associations. Roberta J. Kovac.

Australian Studies. Murray Martin.

Canadian Studies. Albert H. Joy.

Electronic Library Development in Academic Libraries. Cynthia Rhine.

English and American Literature. Candace R. Benefiel.

Exhibits and Displays. Michael M. Miller.

Fee-Based Information Service Centers in Academic Libraries. Lee Anne George.

Fundraising and Development. Barbara Irene Dewey.

Heads of Public/Readers Services. Joanne M. Bessler.

Home Economics/Human Ecology Librarians. Judy M. Nixon.

Journal Costs in Academic and Research Libraries. Robert L. Houbeck, Jr.

Librarians of Library Science Collections. Patsy Haley Stann.

Performance/Output Measures for Academic Libraries. Patricia M. Kelley.

Personnel Administrators and Staff Development Officers. Barbara J. Doyle; Darlene M. Ziolkowski.

Philosophical, Religious, and Theological Studies. Barbara E. Beaton.

Popular Culture and Libraries. Douglas B. Highsmith.

Public Relations in Academic Libraries. Katharina J. Blackstead.

Research. Darrell L. Jenkins.

Undergraduate Librarians. Paula M. Walker.

Representatives

ALA Committee on Appointments. Jacquelyn M. McCoy.

ALA Committee on Professional Ethics. Lorene B. Brown.

ALA Conference Program Planning Committee, New Orleans (1993). Jacquelyn M. McCoy.

ALA Conference Program Planning Committee, San Francisco (1992). Anne K. Beaubien.

ALA Legislation Assembly. Hiram L. Davis.

ALA Literacy Assembly. Trish Ridgeway.

ALA Membership Promotion Task Force. Andrea C. Hoffman.

ALA Planning and Budget Assembly. Anne K. Beaubien.

ALA Standing Committee on Library Education. Larry R. Oberg; Patsy Haley Stann; Keith Swigger.

ALCTS Committee on Cataloging: Description and Access. Colby M. Riggs.

American Association for Higher Education. To be appointed.

American Association for the Advancement of Science. Martin A. Kesselman.

American Association of University Professors. To be appointed.

American Chemical Society. Arleen N. Somerville.

American Council on Education. Ann K. Randall.

Association for Asian Studies, Committee on East Asian Libraries. Margaret W. Wang.

Association of American Colleges. To be appointed.

Consortium of Affiliates for International Programs. Martin A. Kesselman.

Freedom to Read Foundation. Noreen S. Alldredge.

LC Cataloging in Publication Advisory Group. Robert P. Holley.

Modern Language Association. To be appointed.

National Forum on Information Literacy. Barbara J. Ford.

Sections

Afro-American Studies. Stanton F. Biddle, Baruch College, 17 Lexington Ave., New York, NY 10010. Tel. 212-447-3881.

Anthropology and Sociology. Robert B. Marks Ridinger, Northern Illinois Univ., 303 Founders Lib., DeKalb, IL 60115-2868. Tel. 815-753-1094.

Arts. Kim N. Fisher, Box 461, Lemont, PA 16851-0461. Tel. 814-865-1858.

Asian and African. Merry L. Burlingham, Univ. of Texas Libs., PCL5.108, Box P, Austin, TX 78713-7330. Tel. 512-471-3811.

Bibliographic Instruction. Mary Ellen Litzinger, Pennsylvania State Univ., Pattee Lib., University Park, PA 16802. Tel. 814-865-3064.

College Libraries. Mary Lee Sweat, Loyola Univ. Lib., 6363 Saint Charles Ave., New Orleans, LA 70118. Tel. 504-865-3346.

Community and Junior College Libraries. Paul E. Dumont, Dallas County Community College Dist., 4343 N. Hwy. 67, Mesquite, TX 75150-2095. Tel. 214-324-7785.

Education and Behavioral Sciences. Barbara Kemp, Columbia Univ. Lib., New York, NY 10027. Tel. 212-854-7602.

Extended Campus Library Services. Barton M. Lessin, Asst. Dean, Wayne State Univ. Lib., Detroit, MI 48202. Tel. 313-577-4195.

Law and Political Science. Patricia A. McCandless, Ohio State Univ. Libs., 1858 Neil Ave. Mall, Columbus, OH 43210-1286. Tel. 614-292-6151.

Rare Books and Manuscripts. Cathy Henderson, Univ. of Texas Lib., Box 7219, Austin, TX 78713. Tel. 512-471-9119.

Science and Technology. Beverlee A. French, Univ. of California Lib., Davis, CA 95616. Tel. 916-752-2110.

Slavic and East European. Tatjana Lorkovic, Yale Univ., Sterling Memorial Lib., Box 1603A, Yale Sta., New Haven, CT 06511. Tel. 203-432-1762.

University Libraries. Joseph J. Branin, Univ. of Minnesota, 170 O. Meredith Wilson Lib., 309 19th Ave. S., Minneapolis, MN 55455-0414. Tel. 612-624-4520.

Western European Specialists. John R. Kaiser, State Univ. Lib., University Park, PA 16802.

Women's Studies. Jacquelyn Marie, Univ. of California Lib., Santa Cruz, CA 95064. Tel. 408-459-2076.

American Library Association
Association of Specialized and Cooperative Library Agencies

Deputy Executive Director, Joanne Crispen
50 E. Huron St., Chicago, IL 60611
312-944-6780, 800-545-2433

Object

To represent state library agencies, specialized library agencies, and multitype library cooperatives. Within the interest of these types of library organizations, the Association of Specialized and Cooperative Library Agencies has specific responsibility for

1. Development and evaluation of goals and plans for state library agencies, specialized library agencies, and multitype library cooperatives to facilitate the implementation, improvement, and extension of library activities designed to foster improved user services, coordinating such activities with other appropriate ALA units.

2. Representation and interpretation of the role, functions, and services of state library agencies, specialized library agencies, and multitype library cooperatives within and outside the profession, including contact with national organizations and government agencies.

3. Development of policies, studies, and activities in matters affecting state library agencies, specialized library agencies, and multitype library cooperatives relating to (a) state and local library legislation, (b) state grants-in-aid and appropriations, and (c) relationships among state, federal, regional, and local governments, coordinating such activities with other appropriate ALA units.

4. Establishment, evaluation, and promotion of standards and service guidelines relating to the concerns of this association.
5. Identifying the interests and needs of all persons, encouraging the creation of services to meet these needs within the areas of concern of the association, and promoting the use of these services provided by state library agencies, specialized library agencies, and multitype library cooperatives.
6. Stimulating the professional growth and promoting the specialized training and continuing education of library personnel at all levels of concern of this association and encouraging membership participation in appropriate type-of-activity divisions within ALA.
7. Assisting in the coordination of activities of other units within ALA that have a bearing on the concerns of this association.
8. Granting recognition for outstanding library service within the areas of concern of this association.
9. Acting as a clearinghouse for the exchange of information and encouraging the development of materials, publications, and research within the areas of concern of this association.

Memb. 1,420.

Board of Directors

Pres. Duane F. Johnson, Kansas State Lib., State Capitol, 3rd fl., Topeka, KS 66612. Tel. 913-296-3296; *V.P.* Janice Beck-Ison, Lincoln Trail Libs. System, 1704 W. Interstate Dr., Champaign, IL 61821-1068. Tel. 217-352-0047; *Past Pres.* Clarence R. Walters, OCLC, 6565 Frantz Rd., Dublin, OH 43017-0702. Tel. 614-764-4399; *Dirs.-at-Large.* Linda D. Crowe, Alan D. Lewis, Richard T. Miller, Jr.; *Div. Councillor.* Suzanne Le Barron; *Sec. Reps. Libraries Serving Special Populations (LSSPS).* John M. Day; *Multitype Library Networks and Cooperatives (Multi-LINCS).* Martha J. McDonald; *State Library Agencies (SLAS).* J. Gary Nichols; *Ex officio. "Interface" Ed.* Thomas J. Dorst; *Organization and Bylaws Committee Chpn.* Steven Prine; *ASCLA Exec. Dir.* Andrew M. Hansen; *ASCLA Deputy Exec. Dir.* Joanne Crispen.

Publications

Interface (q.; memb.; nonmemb. $15). *Ed.* Jeannette Smithee, Asst. Dir., Central New York Lib. Resources Council, 763 Butternut St., Syracuse, NY 13208. Tel. 315-478-6080.

Committees

American Correctional Association/ASCLA Joint Committee on Institution Libraries. Jay Ihrig, Thea Chesley.
Awards. Alphonse F. Trezza.
Budget and Finance. Clarence Walters.
Conference Program Coordination. Leslie Burger.
Interface Advisory. Michelle M. Gardner.
Legislation. Bruce Daniels.
Library Personnel and Education. Donna Pontau.
Membership Promotion. Barbara Mates.
Nominating (1991). Timothy Lynch.
Organization and Bylaws. Stephen Prine, Jr.
Planning. William G. Asp.
Publications. Bill Crowley.
Research. Jeannette Smithee.
Standards Review. Lorraine S. Summers; Library Standards for Adult Correctional Institutions (Ad hoc). Ann L. Piascik; Standards for Juvenile Correctional Institutions (Ad hoc). Myra F. Albert.

Representatives

ALA Conference Program, San Francisco (1992). Duane F. Johnson.
ALA Government Documents Round Table (GODORT). To be appointed.
ALA Legislation Assembly. Sara Ann Parker.
ALA Library Education Assembly. Steven A. Baugham.
ALA Membership Promotion (Task Force). Nancy L. Zussy.
ALA/ALCTS/CCS Cataloging: Description and Access Committee. To be appointed.
ALA/RASD Interlibrary Loan Committee. Helen Morgan.
American Correctional Association. To be appointed.
Association of Radio Reading Services. To be appointed.

Freedom to Read Foundation. To be appointed.

Interagency Council on Library Resources for Nursing. Frederic C. Pachman.

Library of Congress/NLS Cost Study Committee. Donna O. Dziedzic.

American Library Association
Library Administration and Management Association

Executive Director, Karen Muller
50 E. Huron St., Chicago, IL 60611
800-545-2433, Ext. 5038

Object

"The Library Administration and Management Association provides an organizational framework for encouraging the study of administrative theory, for improving the practice of administration in libraries, and for identifying and fostering administrative skill. Toward these ends, the division is responsible for all elements of general administration which are common to more than one type of library. These may include organizational structure, financial administration, personnel management and training, buildings and equipment, and public relations. LAMA meets this responsibility in the following ways:

1. Study and review of activities assigned to the division with due regard for changing developments in these activities.
2. Initiating and overseeing activities and projects appropriate to the division, including activities involving bibliography compilation, publication, study, and review of professional literature within the scope of the division.
3. Synthesis of those activities of other ALA units which have a bearing upon the responsibilities or work of the division.
4. Representation and interpretation of library administrative activities in contacts outside the library profession.
5. Aiding the professional development of librarians engaged in administration and encouragement of their participation in appropriate type-of-library divisions.
6. Planning and development of those programs of study and research in library administrative problems which are most needed by the profession."

Established 1957. Memb. 5,278.

Officers

Pres. Sue E. Stroyan; *V.P./Pres.-Elect.* James G. Neal; *Past Pres.* Susanne Henderson; *Councillor.* Rodney Hersberger.

Address correspondence to the executive director.

Board of Directors

Dirs. Suellyn Hunt, Vicki R. Kreimeyer, Harold D. Neikirk, Julie D. Pringle, Mary E. Raphael, Charlotte Rubens, Jeanne M. Thorsen; *Dirs.-at-Large.* Carol F. L. Liu, Anders Dahlgren; *Ex officio.* Christian Esquevin, Elizabeth K. Gay, Paul M. Gherman, Keith Curry Lance, Judith Paquette, Sandra A. Scherba, J. Linda Williams.

Publication

Library Administration and Management (q.; memb.; nonmemb. $45; foreign $55). *Ed.* Fred M. Heath, Dir., Texas Christian Univ. Lib., Box 32904, Fort Worth, TX 76129.

Committee Chairpersons

Budget and Finance. O. Dallas Baillio, Jr., Dir., Mobile Public Lib., Mobile, AL 36618. Tel. 205-438-7073.

Editorial Advisory. Anders C. Dahlgren, 5814 Dorsett Dr., Madison, WI 53711. Tel. 608-266-3874.

Governmental Affairs. Robert A. Daugherty, Univ. of Illinois Lib., Box 8198, Chicago, IL 60680. Tel. 312-996-2734.

Membership. Robert A. Almony, Univ. of Missouri Libs., 104 Ellis Lib., Columbia, MO 65201-5149. Tel. 314-882-4701.

Nominating, 1992 Election. Kay Runge, Dir., Davenport Public Lib., 321 Main St., Davenport, IA 52801. Tel. 319-326-7841.

Organization. Gerard B. McCabe, Clarion Univ., Carlson Lib., Clarion, PA. Tel. 814-226-2343.

Orientation. Sharon L. Stewart, McLure Education Lib., 511 Reston Dr., Tuscaloosa, AL 35406. Tel. 205-348-1506.

Program. Richard M. Parker, Tulsa City-County Lib., 400 Civic Center, Tulsa, OK 74103. Tel. 981-596-7897.

Publications. Carol F. L. Liu, Queens Borough Public Lib., 162-20 Ninth Ave., No. 9C, Whitestone, NY 11357. Tel. 718-990-0890.

Recognition of Achievement. Dale S. Montanelli, Univ. of Illinois Lib., 1408 W. Gregory Dr., Urbana, IL 61801. Tel. 217-333-0791.

Small Libraries Publications. Marcia L. Thomas, Eureka Public Lib. Dist., 202 S. Main, Eureka, IL 61530. Tel. 309-467-2922.

Special Conferences and Programs. Katherine A. Branch, Kline Science Lib., 77 Livingston St., New Haven, CT 06511. Tel. 203-432-3439.

Discussion Group Chairpersons

Assistant-to-the-Director. Steven H. Hagstrom, Tarrant Co. Jr. College Lib., N.E.

Campus, 828 Harwood Rd., Hurst, TX 76054. Tel. 817-656-6637.

Middle Management. Margaret Gordon, Univ. of California Lib., Santa Cruz, CA 95064. Tel. 408-459-2076.

Women Administrators. Eileen B. Longsworth, Salt Lake County Lib. System, 2197 E. 7000 S., Salt Lake City, UT 84121-3188. Tel. 801-943-4636.

Section Chairpersons

Buildings and Equipment. Elizabeth K. Gay, Los Angeles Public Lib., 800 W. First St., No. 806, Los Angeles, CA 90012. Tel. 213-612-3338.

Fund Raising and Financial Development. Christian Esquevin, Coronado Public Lib., 640 Orange Ave., Coronado, CA 92118.

Library Organization and Management. Paul M. Gherman, Dir.'s Suite, Box 90001, Blacksburg, VA 24062-9001. Tel. 703-231-5593.

Personnel Administration. J. Linda Williams, Div. of Lib. Development and Services, 200 W. Baltimore St., Baltimore, MD 21201. Tel. 301-333-2133.

Public Relations. Sandra A. Scherba, Cromain Lib., 3688 N. Hartland Rd., Hartland, MI 48353. Tel. 313-632-5200.

Statistics. Keith Curry Lance, Colorado State Lib., 201 E. Colfax, Denver, CO 80203. Tel. 303-866-6737.

Systems and Services. Judith Paquette, Univ. of California, McHenry Lib., Santa Cruz, CA 95064. Tel. 408-459-2970.

American Library Association
Library and Information Technology Association

Executive Director, Linda J. Knutson
50 E. Huron St., Chicago, IL 60611
312-280-4270, 800-545-2433

Object

The Library and Information Technology Association provides its members, other ALA divisions, and the library and information science field as a whole with a forum for discussion, an environment for learning, and a program for action on the design, development, and implementation of automated and techno-

logical systems in the library and information science fields. Since its activities and interests are derived as responses to the needs and demands of its members, its program is flexible, varied, and encompasses many aspects of the information technology field. Within that general precept, the interests of the division include such varied activities as systems development, electronic data processing, mechanized information retrieval, operations research, technical standards development, telecommunications, networks and collaborative efforts, management techniques, information technology, information aspects of audiovisual and video cable communications activities, and hardware applications related to all of these areas. LITA attempts to encourage its members to undertake research through support of grant applications and other efforts to identify funding for research projects.

Information about all of these activities is disseminated through the division's publishing program, institutes, exhibits, conference programs, committee work, and interest groups. The division provides an advisory and consultative function when called upon to do so.

LITA regards continuing education as one of its major responsibilities, and through the above channels it attempts to inform its members of current activities and trends. It provides retrospective information for those new to the field. Memb. 5,130.

Officers

Pres. Paul Evan Peters; *V.P.* Paul Crawford; *Past Pres.* Jo-Ann Michalak.

Directors

Officers; Katharina Klemperer, Linda D. Miller, Nolan F. Pope (1994); Ching-chih Chen, Gail M. Persky (1993); James F. Corey, R. Bruce Miller (1992); *Councillor.* Donald E. Riggs (1993); *Ex officio.* John Popko; *Exec. Dir.* Linda J. Knutson.

Publications

Information Technology and Libraries (q.; memb.; nonmemb. $45; single copy $15). *Ed.* Thomas W. Leonhardt, Dean of Ls, Univ. of the Pacific, Stockton, CA 95211. For information or to send manuscripts, contact the editor.

LITA Newsletter (q.; memb.; nonmemb. $25; single copy $8). *Ed.* Walt Crawford, Research Libs. Group, Inc., 1200 Villa St., Mountain View, CA 94041-1100.

Committee Chairpersons

Budget Review. Jo-Ann Michalak.
Bylaws and Organization. John Popko.
Education. To be appointed.
Financial Development. Louella V. Wetherbee.
Gaylord Award. To be appointed.
International Relations. Michael J. Gorman.
ITAL Editorial Board. Thomas W. Leonhardt.
Leader Development. Elizabeth S. Lane.
Legislation and Regulation. Elaine M. Albright.
Membership. Jeanne M. Somers.
National Conference Steering. Betty G. Bengtson.
Nominating. David R. McDonald.
Program Planning. To be appointed.
Publications. William Gray Potter.
Silver Celebration. Stephen R. Salmon.
Technical Standards for Library Automation. Sylvia M. Carson.
Technology and Access. Carolyn M. Gray.
Ten Days to 2000. Paul Evan Peters.

Interest Group Chairpersons

Adaptive Technologies. Joan Maier McKean.
Artificial Intelligence/Expert Systems. Denise A. D. Bedford.
Authority Control in the Online Environment LITA/ALCTS/CCS (Interdivisional). Deborah J. Husted.
Customized Applications for Library Microcomputers. Dan Marmion; Norman Howden.
Desktop Publishing. John A. Lima.
Distributed Systems. Charles Forrest.
Electronic Mail/Electronic Bulletin Boards. Dawn E. Talbot; Gregory J. Zuck.
Emerging Technologies. Colby M. Riggs.
Human/Machine Interface. Mary G. McMahon.
Hypertext. Judy E. Myers.
Imagineering. Milton T. Wolf.
Innovative Microcomputer Support of Cataloging. Stephen A. Marine.
Library Consortia/Automated Systems. Michele I. Dalehite.
MARC Holdings. Edward S. Weissmann.
Microcomputer Users. Richard E. Gates.
Online Catalog. Elizabeth Patterson.
Optical Information Systems. Ka-Neng Au.

Programmer/Analyst. Jennie L. McKee.
Retrospective Conversion, LITA/ALCTS. Daphne Hsueh (ALCTS); Mitchell Turitz (LITA).
Serial Automation, LITA/ALCTS. Marcia Anderson.

Small Integrated Library Systems. Gregory Zuck.
Telecommunications. Charles J. D. Blair.
Vendor/User. Elizabeth D. Nichols.

American Library Association
Public Library Association

Executive Director, Eleanor J. Rodger
50 E. Huron St., Chicago, IL 60611
800-545-2433, Ext. 5752, FAX 312-280-5029

Object

The Public Library Association will advance the development and effectiveness of public library service and public librarians.

The Public Library Association has specific responsibility for

1. Conducting and sponsoring research about how the public library can respond to changing social needs and technical developments.
2. Developing and disseminating materials useful to public libraries in interpreting public library services and needs.
3. Conducting continuing education for public librarians by programming at national and regional conferences, by publications such as the newsletter, and by other delivery means.
4. Establishing, evaluating, and promoting goals, guidelines, and standards for public libraries.
5. Maintaining liaison with relevant national agencies and organizations engaged in public administration and human services such at the National Association of Counties, Municipal League, Commission on Post-Secondary Education.
6. Maintaining liaison with other divisions and units of ALA and other library organizations such as the Association of American Library Schools and the Urban Libraries Council.
7. Defining the role of the public library in service to a wide range of user and potential user groups.
8. Promoting and interpreting the public library to a changing society through legislative programs and other appropriate means.

9. identifying legislation to improve and to equalize support of public libraries.

PLA exists to provide a diverse program of communication, publication, advocacy, and continuing education. The program priorities are determined by PLA members and may include some areas or concerns also identified as priorities by ALA. The primary staff program responsibility is to facilitate members' activities and initiatives by providing coordination and support.

As a division, we are effective when we

1. Provide leadership for the improvement of public libraries.
2. Provide an effective forum for discussing issues of concern to public librarians.
3. Provide relevant, high-quality continuing education through publications, workshops, and programs.
4. Provide opportunities for developing and enhancing individual professional networks.
5. Develop and disseminate policy statements on matters affecting public libraries.
6. Communicate effectively with the non-library world about matters impacting public library service.
7. Maintain a stable membership and financial base.

PLA's priority concerns are adequate funding for public libraries; improved management of public libraries; recognition of the importance of all library staff in providing quality public service; recruitment, education, training, and compensation of public librarians; effective use of technology; intellectual freedom; improved access to library resources; and effective communication with the non-library world.

Organized 1944. Memb. 7,000 + .

Membership

Open to all ALA members interested in the improvement and expansion of public library services to all ages in various types of communities.

Officers (1991-1992)

Pres. June M. Garcia, Phoenix Public Lib., 12 E. McDowell Rd., Phoenix, AZ 85004; *V.P./Pres.-Elect.* Elliot Shelkrot, Free Lib. of Philadelphia, Logan Sq., Philadelphia, PA 19103; *Past Pres.* Charles M. Brown, Arlington County Public Lib., One Courthouse Plaza, Suite 402, 2100 Clarendon Blvd., Arlington, VA 22203.

Board of Directors (1991-1992)

Dirs.-at-Large. Ginnie Cooper, Fran C. Freimarck, Martin J. Gomez, Victor Frank Kralisz, Kay K. Runge, Barbara A. Webb; *Sec. Reps. ALLS Pres.* Marianne C. Fairfield; *CIS Past Pres.* Mary L. Cass; *MLS Pres.* Marilyn L. Hinshaw; *MPLSS Pres.* Roberta A. E. Cairns; *PLSS Pres.* Donna L. Riegel; *SMLS Rep.* John A. Moorman; *Ex officio: ALTA Past Pres.* Deborah Miller; *"Public Libraries" Feature Ed.* Gerald R. Shields; *ALA/ PLA Councillor.* Linda Mielke; *PLA/ALA Memb. Rep.* Carole Dickerson; *PLA Budget and Finance Rep.* Ronald A. Dubberly; *PLA Affiliates Network Rep.* Christine L. Hage; *PLA Exec. Dir.* Eleanor J. Rodger.

Publication

Public Libraries (bi-mo.; memb.; nonmemb. $45; foreign $55; single copy $10). *Feature Ed.* Gerald R. Shields, 105 Short St., Leland, IL 60531; *Managing Ed.* Sandra Causey Garrison, PLA, 50 E. Huron St., Chicago, IL 60611.

Section Presidents

Adult Lifelong Learning. Marianne C. Fairfield.
Community Information. C. Amoes Hunt.
Marketing of Public Library Services. Roberta A. E. Cairns.
Metropolitan Libraries. Marilyn L. Hinshaw.
Public Library Systems. Donna L. Riegel.
Small and Medium-Sized Libraries. Annette M. Milliron.

Committee Chairpersons

Audiovisual. James E. Massey, One N. Atwood Rd., Bel Air, MD 21014.
Awards. Honore L. Francois, Prince George's County Memorial Lib., 6532 Adelphi Rd., Hyattsville, MD 20782.
Baker & Taylor Video. Phyllis Y. Massar, Arts and Media Dept., Ferguson Lib., One Public Lib. Plaza, Stamford, CT 06904.
Budget and Finance. Ronald A. Dubberly, Atlanta Fulton Public Lib., One Margaret Mitchell Sq. N.W., Atlanta, GA 30303-1089.
Business Council. Michael J. Wirt, Spokane County Lib. Dist., 4322 N. Argonne Rd., Spokane, WA 99212.
Bylaws and Organization. Jane S. Eickhoff, Pikesville Public Lib., 1301 Pikesville Rd., Pikesville, MD 21208.
Cataloging Needs of Public Libraries. Catherine A. Dixon, Fort Worth Public Lib., 300 Taylor, Fort Worth, TX 76102.
Certification, PLA/LAMA. F. William Summers, Florida State Univ., School of Lib. and Info. Studies, Tallahassee, FL 32306.
Children, Service to. Gretchen M. Wronka, Hennepin County Lib., 12601 Ridgedale Dr., Minnetonka, MN 55343.
CLSI International Study Grant. Louise A. Sevold, Cuyahoga County Public Lib., 4510 Memphis Ave., Cleveland, OH 44144.
Common Concerns, ALSC/PLA. June M. Garcia (PLA), Phoenix Public Lib., 12 E. McDowell Rd., Phoenix, AZ 85004; Linda A. Perkins (ALSC), Berkeley Public Lib., Berkeley, CA 94704.
Common Concerns, ALTA/PLA. Carolyn Anthony (PLA), Skokie Public Lib., 5215 Oakton St., Skokie, IL 60077; Wayne Moss (ALTA), Indianapolis-Marion County Public Lib., Box 211, Indianapolis, IN 46206.
Conference Program Coordinating. Sandra S. Nelson, Tennessee State Lib., 403 Seventh Ave. N., Nashville, TN 37219.
Education of Public Librarians. June Lester, School of Lib. and Info. Sciences, Univ. of North Texas, Denton, TX 76203.

Executive Assembly. Charles M. Brown, Arlington County Public Lib., One Courthouse Plaza, Suite 402, 2100 Clarendon Blvd., Arlington, VA 22203.

Fund Raising. Clyde S. Scoles, Toledo-Lucas County Public Lib., 325 Michigan St., Toledo, OH 43624.

Goals, Guidelines, and Standards for Public Libraries. Karen J. Krueger, Janesville Public Lib., 316 S. Main St., Janesville, WI 53545.

Hot Topics. Mary K. Chelton, Montgomery County Dept. of Public Libs., 99 Maryland Ave., Rockville, MD 20850.

Institute for Public Library Development, PLA/ASCLA. Sandra S. Nelson, Tennessee State Lib., 403 Seventh Ave. N., Nashville, TN 37219.

Intellectual Freedom. Candace D. Morgan, Fort Vancouver Regional Lib., 1007 E. Mill Plain Blvd., Vancouver, WA 98663.

International Relations. Gordon M. Conable, Monroe County Lib. System, 3700 S. Custer Rd., Monroe, MI 48161.

IRS Tax Form Distribution Program. To be appointed.

Leadership Development. Victor Frank Kralisz, 2928 Wildflower Dr., Dallas, TX 75229.

Legislation. Sarah A. Long, North Suburban Lib. System, 200 Dundee Rd., Wheeling, IL 60090.

Liaison with National Organizations. John D. Christenson, Box 67, Good Thunder, MN 56037.

Library Camp Advisory. Elaine E. Meyers, Phoenix Public Lib., 12 E. McDowell Rd., Phoenix, AZ 85004.

Allie Beth Martin (1991) Award. Samuel F. Morrison, Broward County Lib., 100 S. Andrews Ave., Fort Lauderdale, FL 33301.

Membership. Carole Dickerson, Lake Oswego Public Lib., 706 Fourth St., Lake Oswego, OR 97034.

Multilingual Materials and Library Service. Pat C. Kelker, Free Lib. of Philadelphia, Logan Sq., Philadelphia, PA 19103.

National Achievement Citation. Dorothy S. Puryear, Nassau Lib. System, 900 Jerusalem Ave., Uniondale, NY 11553.

National Conference, 1994. Susan S. Goldberg, 110 First Ave. N.E., Apt. 1103, Minneapolis, MN 55413.

National Conference Exhibitors Advisory. Fred A. Philipp, Blackwell North America, 6024 S.W. Jean Rd., Bldg. G, Lake Oswego, OR 97035.

National Conference Local Arrangements. William Sannwald, San Diego Public Lib., 820 E St., San Diego, CA 92101; and Catherine E. Lucas, San Diego County Lib., 5555 Overland Ave. No. 15, San Diego, CA 92123.

National Conference Program. Sandra S. Nelson, Tennessee State Lib., 403 Seventh Ave. N., Nashville, TN 37219.

National Conference, 1997. To be appointed.

National Library Card. James LaRue, Douglas Public Lib. Dist., 961 S. Plum Creek Blvd., Castle Rock, CO 80104.

Nominating, 1992. Judith A. Drescher, Memphis–Shelby County Public Lib., 1850 Peabody Ave., Memphis, TN 38104.

Nominating, 1993. To be appointed.

Output Measures for Children's Services (ALSC/PLA). Kathleen S. Reif, Baltimore County Public Lib., 7802 Elmhurst Ave., Baltimore, MD 21234.

Personal Networking. K. Lynn Schule, Baltimore County Public Lib., 320 York Rd., Towson, MD 21204.

PLA Partners. LaDonna T. Kienitz, Newport Beach Public Lib., 856 San Clemente Dr., Newport Beach, CA 92660.

Policy Manual (Advisory). Jo Ann Pinder, Lake Lanier Regional Lib., 1001 Hwy. 29 S., Lawrenceville, GA 30245.

Political Effectiveness. Daniel J. Bradbury, Kansas City Public Lib., 311 E. 12 St., Kansas City, MO 64106.

President's Program, 1992. Laura G. Johnson, Indianapolis–Marion County Public Lib., Box 211, Indianapolis, IN 46206.

Public Libraries Advisory Board. William Sannwald, San Diego Public Lib., 820 E St., San Diego, CA 92101.

Public Library Advocates. Cecil P. Beach, Broward County Florida, Government Center 433, 115 S. Andrews Ave., Fort Lauderdale, FL 33301.

Public Library Data Service. Janice Feye-Stukas, Office Lib. Development Services, 440 Capitol Sq., 550 Cedar St., Saint Paul, MN 55101.

Public Library Services to the Homeless. Jane S. Salisbury, 1625 S.E. Pine, Portland, OR 97214.

Publications. Christine L. Hage, Rochester Hills Public Lib., 210 W. Univ. Dr., Rochester, MI 48063.

Recognition. Kathleen Mehaffey Balcom, Arlington Heights Memorial Lib., 50 N. Dunton Ave., Arlington Heights, IL 60004.

Research. Reginald P. Coady, Dearborn Dept. of Libs., 16301 Michigan Ave., Dearborn, MI 48126.

Retail Outlets in Public Libraries. A. Michael Deller, Livonia Civic Center Lib., 32777 Five Mile Rd., Livonia, MI 48154.

Service Clubs, Liaison with. Fay Clow, Bettendorf Public Lib. and Info. Center, Box 1326, Bettendorf, IA 52722.

Small and Rural Libraries. Donald B. Reynolds, Jr., Central Kansas Lib. System, 1409 Williams St., Grand Bend, KS 67530-4090.

Strategic Issues and Directions. Charles W. Robinson, Baltimore County Public Lib., 320 York Rd., Towson, MD 21204.

Technology in Public Libraries. Laura J. Isenstein, 4110 Colonial Rd., Baltimore, MD 21208.

Urban Public Library Issues. David M. Henington, 6225 San Felipe Rd., Houston, TX 77057.

Leonard Wertheimer Multilingual Award. Carmen L. Martinez, Orange County Public Lib., 14361 Yale Ave., Irvine, CA 92714.

White House Conference Planning. To be appointed.

Young Adult Services in Public Libraries (YASD/PLA). Mary K. Chelton, Montgomery County Dept. of Public Libs., 99 Maryland Ave., Rockville, MD 20814.

Discussion Group Chairpersons

Adult Services Coordinators in Public Libraries. Gayle E. Koster, Free Lib. of Philadelphia, Logan Sq., Philadelphia, PA 19103.

Bookmobile Service. Ellen G. Hellard, Dept. for Libs. and Archives, Box 537, Frankfort, KY 40602.

Cost Finding. Catherine J. Caine, Public Lib. of Columbus, 96 S. Grant, Columbus, OH 43215.

Humanities Programming. Marianne K. Cassell, Vermont Dept. of Libs., Pavilion Office Bldg., Montpelier, VT 05602.

Popular Materials Library. Karen B. Douglas, Newark Public Lib., 259 Eastern Pkwy., Newark, NJ 07106.

Preschoolers' Door to Learning. Kathleen S. Reif, Baltimore County Public Lib., 7802 Elmhurst Ave., Baltimore, MD 21234.

Public Library Service Evaluation. Karen J. Krueger, Janesville Public Lib., 316 S. Main St., Janesville, WI 53545.

American Library Association
Reference and Adult Services Division

Executive Director, Andrew M. Hansen
50 E. Huron St., Chicago, IL 60611
312-944-6780, 800-545-2433

Object

The Reference and Adult Services Division is responsible for stimulating and supporting in every type of library the delivery of reference/information services to all groups, regardless of age, and of general library services and materials to adults. This involves facilitating the development and conduct of direct service to library users, the development of programs and guidelines for service to meet the needs of these users, and assisting libraries in reaching potential users.

The specific responsibilities of RASD are

1. Conduct of activities and projects within the division's areas of responsibility.

2. Encouragement of the development of librarians engaged in these activities, and stimulation of participation by members of appropriate type-of-library divisions.

3. Synthesis of the activities of all units within the American Library Association that have a bearing on the type of activities represented by the division.

4. Representation and interpretation of the division's activities in contacts outside the profession.

5. Planning and development of programs of study and research in these areas for the total profession.
6. Continuous study and review of the division's activities.

Memb. 5,483. (For more information on dues, see ALA entry).

Officers (1991-1992)

Pres. Susan DiMattia; *Pres.-Elect.* James R. Rettig; *Secy.* Sandra Leach.

Directors and Other Members

Anita Evans, Sally Kalin, Judith Reid, Susan M. Riehm, Nancy H. Sherwin, Steven Zink; *Councillor.* Rebecca Watson-Boone; *Past Pres.* James Sweetland; *Ed. RASD Update.* Jane Kleiner; *Eds. RQ.* Connie Van Fleet, Danny Wallace; *Exec. Dir.* Andrew M. Hansen.

Address correspondence to the executive director.

Publications

RASD Occasional Papers (irreg.). David Hovde, Purdue Univ., HSSE Lib., Stewart Center, West Lafayette, IN 47906.
RASD Update (memb.; nonmemb. $15). *Ed.* Jane Kleiner, Louisiana State Univ., Middleton Lib., Baton Rouge, LA 70803-7010.
RQ (q.; memb; nonmemb. $42). *Eds.* Connie Van Fleet and Danny Wallace, Louisiana State Univ., 267 Coates, Baton Rouge, LA 70803-3290.

Section Chairpersons

Business Reference and Services. Priscilla Geahigan.
Collection Development. William Galaway.
History. Nancy Huling.
Machine-Assisted Reference. Jane Kleiner.
Management and Operation of Public Services. Emily Batista.
Services to User Populations. Allan Kleiman.

Committee Chairpersons

Access to Information. William R. Kinyon.
AFL/CID Joint Committee on Library Services to Labor Groups. Leslie Hough.
Awards Coordinating. Peter McCallion.
Conference Program Coordinating. Theodora Haynes.
Conference Program, 1992.
Dartmouth Medal. Mary Goulding.
Denali Press Award. Patrick J. Dawson.
Executive. Susan DiMattia.
Facts on File Grant. Gary Claxton.
Finance. James R. Rettig.
Gale Research Award for Excellence in Reference and Adult Services. Merle Jacob.
Legislation. Charles L. Gilreath.
Memberbship. Jacqueline B. Hambric.
Margaret E. Monroe Library Adult Services Award. Larayne J. Dallas.
Isadore Gilbert Mudge Citation. To be appointed.
Nominating. Danuta Nitecki.
Organization. Judith Reid.
Planning. To be appointed.
Publications. David M. Hovde.
Reference Service Press Award. Celia C. Gibson.
John Sessions Memorial Award. Mary Hicks.
Louis Shores/Oryx Press Awards. To be appointed.
Speakers and Consultants Directory (Ad hoc). Ronald Blazek.
Standards and Guidelines. Mary E. Jackson.
White House Conference (Ad hoc). Allen Kleiman.

Representatives

ALA Legislation (Copyright Subcommittee; Ad hoc). Allison Cowgill.
ALA Membership Promotion Task Force. Mary U. Hardin.
ALCTS Cataloging and Classification. Noelle Van Pulis.
ASCLA Decade of Disabled. Philip Wong-Cross.
Coalition of Adult Education. Andrew M. Hansen.
Freedom to Read Foundation. To be appointed.
Library of Congress. Arthur Meyers.
LIRT. Christine G. Hannon.

American Library Association
Young Adult Library Services Association

Executive Director, Ann C. Weeks
50 E. Huron St., Chicago, IL 60611
312-944-6780, 800-545-2433

Object

The goal . . . is to advocate, promote, and strengthen service to young adults as part of the continuum of total library service. The following concerns and activities are interdependent in fulfilling the goal of YALSA. The Young Adult Library Services Association

1. Advocates the young adult's right to free and equal access to materials and services, and assists librarians in handling problems of such access.

2. Evaluates and promotes materials of interest to adolescents through special services, programs, and publications, except for those materials designed specifically for curriculum use.

3. Identifies research needs related to young adult service and communicates those needs to the library academic community in order to activate research projects.

4. Stimulates and promotes the development of librarians and other staff working with young adults through formal and continuing education.

5. Stimulates and promotes the expansion of young adult service among professional associates and agencies at all levels.

6. Represents the interests of librarians and staff working with young adults to all relevant agencies, government or private, and to industries that serve young adults as clients or consumers.

7. Creates and maintains communication links with other units of ALA whose developments affect service to young adults.

Established 1957. Memb. 2,284. (For information on dues, see ALA entry.)

Membership

Open to anyone interested in library services and materials to young adults.

Officers (July 1991–July 1992)

Pres. Mary Elizabeth Wendt, New York Public Lib., 2556 Bainbridge Ave., Bronx, NY 10458. Tel. 212-220-6560; *V.P./Pres.-Elect.* Elizabeth M. O'Donnell, Manchester City Lib., 405 Pine St., Manchester, NH 03104. Tel. 603-624-6550; *Past Pres.* Christy Tyson, Southwest Lib., 9010 35th Ave. S.W., Seattle, WA 98126. Tel. 206-684-7455; *Councillor.* Pamela R. Klipsch, Hayner Public Lib. Dist., 401 State St., Alton, IL 62002. Tel. 618-462-0651.

Directors

Officers; Betty Carter, Judith Druse, Constance P. Lawson, Barbara Lynn, Pamela G. Spencer, Helen Tallman; *Ex Officio Chpn., Organization and Bylaws.* Doris C. Losey; *Ex Officio Chpn., Budget and Finance.* Beth Wheeler Dean; *Exec. Dir.* Ann Carlson Weeks.

Publication

Journal of Youth Services in Libraries (q.; memb.; nonmemb. $40, foreign $50). *Eds.* Donald J. Kenney and Linda J. Wilson, Director's Office, Virginia Polytechnic Institute, Box 90001, Blacksburg, VA 24062-9001.

Committee Chairpersons

Adolescent Health (Task Force). Susan Rosenzweig.
Baker & Taylor Conference Grant. Ranae Pierce.
Best Books for Young Adults. Frances Bradburn.
Best Books for Young Adults Policies and Procedures (Task Force). Judy Nelson.
Computer Applications. Frances Jacobson.

Directions for Library Service to Young Adults (Revision Task Force). Marilee Foglesong.

Division Promotion. Stephen L. Gallant.

Econo-Clad Program Literature Award. Susan F. Tait.

Education. Carolyn S. Brodie.

Margaret A. Edwards Award, 1992. Betty Carter.

Margaret A. Edwards Award, 1993. Marion Hargrove.

Executive. Mary Elizabeth Wendt.

Genre List Coordinator. Karlan Sick.

Genre List, Historical Fiction. Barbara Lynn.

Genre List, Humor. Judy Sasges.

Genre List, Mystery. Bunni Union.

Genre List, Science Fiction. Elizabeth E. Elam.

Intellectual Freedom. Frances M. McDonald.

Interdivisional Committee on Youth Services in Public Libraries. Mary K. Chelton.

Journal of Youth Services Editorial. Donald J. Kenney, Linda J. Wilson.

Leadership. Mary Elizabeth Wendt.

Legislation. Deirdre O'Hagan.

Library of Congress (Advisory). Jody Stefansson.

Local Arrangements. Caryn Gail Sipos.

Media Selection and Usage. Lesley S. J. Farmer.

Membership Recruitment. Judith Brill.

National Organizations Serving the Young Adult (Liaison). Lily Helwig.

Nominating. Ellen Ramsay.

Organization and Bylaws. Doris C. Losey.

Program Planning. S. Kay Brunton Covode.

Public Relations. Chapple Langemack

Publications. Jana R. Fine.

Publishers' Liaison. Catherine M. G. Macrae.

Recommended Books. Nel Ward.

Research. Kathy Latrobe.

Selected Films. Ralph Huntzinger.

Special Needs. John W. Callahan.

Youth Participation. Candace V. Conklin.

American Merchant Marine Library Association

(Affiliated with United Seamen's Service)
Executive Director, Ernest H. Pigott
One World Trade Center, Suite 2161, New York, NY 10048
212-775-1038

Object

Provides ship and shore library service for American-flag merchant vessels, the Military Sealift Command, the U.S. Coast Guard, and other waterborne operations of the U.S. government.

Officers

Honorary Chpn. Warren G. Leback; *Pres.* Talmage E. Simpkins; *Treas.* William G. Croly; *Secy.* Ellen Craft Dammond.

Board of Directors

F. Lee Betz, Paul D. Butcher, Bruce Carlton, William G. Croly, Ellen Craft Dammond, Vando Dell'Amico, Paul Dempster, John I. Dugan, Stanford Erickson, Florence R. Fleming, Arthur W. Friedberg, Thomas Harper, Robert E. Hart, James J. Hayes, Edward Honor, Thomas A. King, Paul L. Krinsky, Lillian C. Liburdi, Robert McKeon, Edward R. Morgan, Thomas Murphy, Milton G. Nottingham, Jr., Louis Parise, Lillian Rabins, Franklin K. Riley, Ronald Rothman, R. F. Schamann, Allen Scott, Talmage E. Simpkins, Richard A. Simpson, Kenneth Standard, A. Faulkner Watts, Vice Admiral Paul A. Welling, James R. Whittemore, Kenneth Young.

Committee Chairperson

AMMLA. Milton G. Nottingham, Jr.

American Society for Information Science

Executive Director, Richard B. Hill
8720 Georgia Ave., Suite 501, Silver Spring, MD 20910
301-495-0900

Object

The American Society for Information Science provides a forum for the discussion, publication, and critical analysis of work dealing with the design, management, and use of information, information systems, and information technology. Memb. (Indiv.) 3,700; (Student) 600; (Inst.) 115. Dues (Indiv.) $85; (Student) $20; (Inst.) $350 and $550.

Officers

Pres. Ann Prentice, ADM 226, Univ. of S. Florida, Tampa, FL 33620-6100; *Pres.-Elect.* José-Marie Griffith, King Research/Univ. of Tennessee, 804 Volunteer Blvd., Knoxville, TN 37996; *Treas.* N. Bernard Basch, 860 N. Lake Shore Dr., Apt. 71, Chicago, IL 60611; *Past Pres.* Tefko Saracevic, Rutgers Univ., 4 Huntington St., New Brunswick, NJ 08876.

Address correspondence to the executive director.

Board of Directors

Chapter Assembly Dir. Jane Banks; *SIG Cabinet Dir.* Karla Peterson; *Dirs.-at-Large.* Harold Borko, Clifford Lynch, Nancy Roderer, Debora Shaw, Jean Tague, Candy Schwartz.

Publications

Advances in Classification Research (Proceedings of the first ASIS SIG/CR Classification Research Workshop). *Eds.* Susan Humphrey, Barbara Kwasnick. Available from Learned Information, 143 Old Marlton Pike, Medford, NJ 08055.
Annual Review of Information Science and Technology. Available from Learned Information, 143 Old Marlton Pike, Medford, NJ 08055.
Bulletin of the American Society for Information Science. Available directly from ASIS.
Journal of the American Society for Information Science (formerly *American Documentation*). Available from John Wiley & Sons, 605 Third Ave., New York, NY 10016.
Modern Copyright Fundamentals. Ben Weil and Barbara Polansky. Available from Learned Information, 143 Old Marlton Pike, Medford, NJ 08055.
Proceedings of the ASIS Annual Meetings. Available from Learned Information, 143 Old Marlton Pike, Medford, NJ 08055.

Committee Chairpersons

Awards and Honors. Kay Denfeld.
Budget and Finance. N. Bernard Basch.
Conferences and Meetings. Joseph Canose.
Constitution and Bylaws. Jessica Milstead.
Education. Raymond Vondran.
Executive. Ann Prentice.
International Relations. Mary Ellen L. Jacob.
Inter-Society Cooperation. Samuel Beatty.
Membership. Marjorie M. K. Hlava.
Nominations. Tefko Saracovic.
Planning. Ann Prentice.
Professionalism. Lola Roseberry.
Public Affairs. John Clement.
Publications. Randolph Hock.
Research. Pat Molholt.
Standards. Nolan Pope.

American Theological Library Association

Executive Secretary, Susan E. Sponberg
820 Church St., Suite 300
Evanston, IL 60201

Object

"To bring its members into close working relationships with each other, to support theological and religious librarianship, to improve theological libraries, and to interpret the role of such libraries in theological education, developing and implementing standards of library service, promoting research and experimental projects, encouraging cooperative programs that make resources more available, publishing and disseminating literature and research tools and aids, cooperating with organizations having similar aims, and otherwise supporting and aiding theological education."

Founded 1947. Memb. (Inst.) 180; (Indiv.) 480. Dues (Inst.) $75 to $500, based on total library expenditure; (Indiv.) $15 to $100, based on salary scale. Year. Sept. 1–Aug. 31.

Membership

Persons engaged in professional library or bibliographical work in theological or religious fields and others who are interested in the work of theological librarianship.

Officers (July 1991–June 1992)

Pres. James Dunkly, Episcopal Divinity School, Weston School of Theology Libs., 99 Brattle St., Cambridge, MA 02138; *V.P.* Mary Bischoff, Jesuit/Krauss/McCormick Lib., 1100 E. 55 St., Chicago, IL 60615; *Secy.-Treas.* Robert A. Olsen, Jr., Brite Divinity School, Texas Christian Univ., Fort Worth, TX 76129.

Board of Directors

David Bundy, Myron Chace, Linda Corman, Robert Dvorak, Norman Kansfield, Seth Kasten, Russell Pollard, Richard D. Spoor, Norma S. Sutton, David Wartluft, Christine Wenderoth; *Exec. Dir.* Albert E. Hurd.

Publications

Index to Book Reviews in Religion.
Newsletter (q.; memb.; nonmemb. $10).
Proceedings (ann.; memb.; nonmemb. $20).
Religion Index One: Periodicals.
Religion Index Two: Multi-Author Works.
Research in Ministry: An Index to Doctor of Ministry Project Reports.

Committee Chairpersons and Other Officials

Annual Conference Committee. Sara Myers, Ira J. Taylor Lib., Iliff School of Theology, 2201 S. University Blvd., Denver, CO 80210.

Archivist. Boyd Reese, Office of History, Presbyterian Church (U.S.A.), 425 Lombard St., Philadelphia, PA 19147.

ATLA Representative to Committee Cataloging: Description and Access. Joyce L. Farris, Perkins Lib., Duke Univ., Durham, NC 27706.

ATLA Representative to the Council of National Library and Information Associations. Paul A. Byrnes, 69 Tiemann Pl., Apt. 44, New York, NY 10027.

Automation and Technology. Diane Choquette, Head, Public Services, Graduate Theological Union, 2400 Ridge Rd., Berkeley, CA 94709.

Bib-base User Group. William C. Miller, Nazarene Theological Seminary, 1700 E. Meyer Rd., Kansas City, MO 64131.

Chief Financial Officer. Patricia K. Adamek, ATLA, 820 Church St., Suite 300, Evanston, IL 60201.

Collection Evaluation and Development. M. Patrick Graham, Pitts Theological Lib., Emory Univ., Atlanta, GA 30322.

College and University Librarians. Marti Alt, General Humanities Bibliographer, Ohio State Univ. Libs., 1858 Neil Ave., Columbus, OH 43210-1286.

Newsletter. *Ed.* Donn Michael Farris, Divinity School Lib., Duke Univ., Durham, NC 27706.

Nominating. Seth Kasten, Union Theological Seminary, Burke Lib., 3041 Broadway, New York, NY 10027.

Oral History. Alice Kendrick, Evangelical Lutheran Church in America, 117 N. Brookside Ave., Freeport, NY 11520.

Proceedings. *Ed.* Betty A. O'Brien, United Theological Seminary, 1810 Harvard Blvd., Dayton, OH 45406.

Public Services. Judy Clarence, Reference Dept., California State Univ. Lib., Hayward, CA 94542.

Publication. Rev. George C. Papademetriou, Holy Cross Orthodox Seminary, 50 Goddard Ave., Brookline, MA 02146.

Rare Books and Special Collections. Roger L. Loyd, Bridwell Lib., Southern Methodist Univ., Dallas, TX 75275-0476.

Records Manager. Rev. Simeon Daly, O.S.B., Archabbey Lib., Saint Meinrad School of Theology, Saint Meinrad, IN 47577.

Relationship to NISO (Z39). Myron Chace, Lib. of Congress, Washington, DC 20540.

Statistician. Susan E. Sponberg, ATLA, 820 Church St., Suite 300, Evanston, IL 60201.

Technical Services. John Thompson, United Lib., 2121 Sheridan Rd., Evanston, IL 60201.

ARMA International
(Association of Records Managers and Administrators)

Executive Director, James P. Souders
4200 Somerset Dr., Suite 215, Prairie Village, KS 66208
913-341-3808

Object

"To promote a scientific interest in records and information management; to provide a forum for research and the exchange of ideas and knowledge; to foster professionalism; to develop and promulgate workable standards and practices; and to furnish a source of records and information management guidance through education and publication."

Membership

Membership application is available through ARMA Headquarters. Annual dues are $80 for international affiliation. Chapter dues vary from city to city. Membership categories are chapter member ($80 plus chapter dues), student member ($15), and unaffiliated members.

Officers (1991–1992)

Pres. Manker R. Harris, 8732 W. Berwyn, Apt. 1N, Chicago, IL 60656. Tel. 312-763-4455, Ext. 2665, FAX 312-714-8977; *Pres.-Elect.* Pat Dixon, Southland Corp., Box 711, Dallas, TX 75221. Tel. 214-828-5503, FAX 214-828-7223; *Immediate Past Pres. and Chpn. of the Board.* Wendy Shade, Iron Mountain Records Management, 1340 E. Sixth St., Suite 301, Los Angeles, CA 90021. Tel. 213-627-9006, FAX 213-627-9641; *Secy.-Treas.* James Allin Spokes, Records Management, Manitoba Hydro, Box 815, Winnipeg, MB R3C 2P4, Canada. Tel. 204-474-3295, FAX 204-475-9044; *Region V.P.s I.* Robert Nawrocki, GTE Contel Federal Systems, Box 10814, Chantilly, VA 22021-3808. Tel. 703-818-5126, FAX 703-818-5484; *II.* Debra K. Gearhart, State of Michigan, Dept. of Management and Budget, State Records Management Services, Box 30026, Lansing, MI 48909; *III.* Patricia Davis Sanders, McNair Law Firm Archives, Box 11390, Columbia, SC 29211; *IV.* Michael P. Flanagan, Union Pacific Railroad Co., 1416 Dodge St., Rm. 830, Omaha, NE 68179; *V.* Douglas P. Allen, Business Records Corp., 3103 Sasparilla Cove, Austin, TX 78748; *VI.* William E. Testerman, Hughes Aircraft Co., Box 45066, Bldg. C1/C103, Los Angeles, CA 90045-0066; *VII.* Gifford Salisbury, Box 59, Niagara Sq. Sta., Buffalo, NY 14201-0059; *VIII.* Richard Weinholdt, National Archives of Canada, 201 Weston St., Winnipeg, MB R3E 3H4, Canada; *IX.* Roy T. Radigan, Midtown Professional Records Center, 7208 Euclid Ave., Cleveland, OH 44103; *X.* Michael S. Cranston, File-Protek, Inc., Box 481, Portland, OR 97207; *XI.* Kenneth Hopkins,

ANACOMP, 4920 W. Cypress No. 107, Tampa, FL 33607; *XII.* Tyrone Butler, New York City Dept. of Records, 31 Chambers St., Rm. 305, New York, NY 10007.

Publication

Records Management Quarterly. Ed. Ira Penn, Box 4580, Silver Spring, MD 20914.

Committee Chairperson

Audit/Budget/Compensation. James Allin Spokes, Records Management, Manitoba Hydro, Box 815, Winnipeg, MB R3C 2P4, Canada.

Awards. David O. Stephens, Dataplex, Box 14975, Jackson, MS 39236.

Education Development. April Dmytrenko, Forms Technologies and Administration, Rockwell International Corp., 1701 Regency Dr., Seal Beach, CA 90740.

Industry Action. JoAnn Constantini, Fairfield Exec. Center, Ralph M. Parsons Co., 6120 S. Gilmore Rd., Fairfield, OH 45014.

Interorganizational Cooperative. Arthel Neff, Phillips Petroleum Co., 252A Adams Bldg., Bartlesville, OK 74004.

Legislative and Regulatory Affairs. Nancy Heaps, Computer Network Systems, Inc., 100 N. First St., Suite 103, Burbank, CA 91502.

Legislative and Regulatory Affairs – Canada (Subcommittee). Raphael A. Thierrin, Univ. of Calgary, 7 Beacham Rd. N.W., Calgary, AB T3K 2P8, Canada.

Legislative and Regulatory Affairs – New Zealand (Subcommittee). Alison Fraser, Acton Fraser Associates Ltd., Box 2907, Wellington, New Zealand.

Legislative and Regulatory Affairs – U.S. (Subcommittee). Richard P. Wilke, Chevron Corp., 575 Market St., San Francisco, CA 94105.

Long Range Planning. Manker R. Harris, 8732 W. Berwyn, Apt. 1N, Chicago, IL 60656.

Nominating. Wendy Shade, Iron Mountain Records Management, 1340 E. Sixth St., Suite 301, Los Angeles, CA 90021.

Professional Development. Mary Lou Hodge, Univ. of Pittsburgh, Services and Records, 3009 Cathedral of Learning, Pittsburgh, PA 15260.

1991 Conference Program. W. H. England, Record Systems, Inc., 11 Burwood Lane, San Antonio, TX 78216.

Public Relations, Marketing, and Membership. Linda Burns, c/o Cusack, 13 Foster Ct., Croton on Hudson, NY 10520.

Art Libraries Society of North America (ARLIS/NA)

Executive Director, Pamela J. Parry
3900 E. Timrod St., Tucson, AZ 85711
602-881-8479

Object

To foster excellence in art librarianship and visual resources curatorship for the advancement of the visual arts. Established 1972. Memb. 1,300. Dues (Inst.) $75; (Indiv.) $55; (Business Affiliate) $75; (Student/Retired/Unemployed) $35; (Sustaining) $175; (Sponsor) $500; (Overseas) $75. Year. Jan. 1–Dec. 31.

Membership

Open and encouraged for all those interested in visual librarianship, whether they be professional librarians, students, library assistants, art book publishers, art book dealers, art historians, archivists, architects, slide and photograph curators, or retired associates in these fields.

Officers (Feb. 1992–Jan. 1993)

Pres. B. J. Irvine; *V.P.* Deirdre Stam; *Secy.* Barbara Polowy; *Treas.* Edward Goodman; *Exec. Dir.* Pamela J. Parry; *Past Pres.* Merrill W. Smith.

Address correspondence to the executive director.

Executive Board

President, past president, president-elect, secretary, treasurer, and five regional representatives (Northeast, Midwest, South, West, and Canada).

Publications

ARLIS/NA Update (bi-mo.; memb.).
Art Documentation (q.; memb.).
Handbook and List of Members (ann.; memb.).
Occasional Papers (price varies).
Topical Papers (price varies).
Miscellaneous others (request current list from headquarters).

Committees

AAT Advisory.
Cataloging Advisory.
Conference.
Development.
International Relations.
Membership.
Gerd Muehsam Award.
Nominating.
Professional Development.
Publications.
Standards.
Travel Award.
George Wittenborn Award.

Chapters

Arizona; Central Plains; DC-Maryland-Virginia; Delaware Valley; Kentucky-Tennessee; Michigan; Midstates; Montreal-Ottawa-Quebec; New England; New Jersey; New York; Northern California; Northwest; Ohio; Southeast; Southern California; Texas; Twin Cities; Western New York.

Asian/Pacific American Librarians Association

President, Charlotte Chung-Sook Kim
Assistant Commissioner of Neighborhood Services
Chicago Public Library
400 S. State St., 10-S, Chicago, IL 60605
312-747-4212, FAX 312-747-4076

Object

"To provide a forum for discussing problems and concerns of Asian/Pacific American librarians; to provide a forum for the exchange of ideas by Asian/Pacific American librarians and other librarians; to support and encourage library services to the Asian/Pacific American communities; to recruit and support Asian/Pacific American librarians in the library/information science professions; to seek funding for scholarships in library/information science schools for Asian/Pacific Americans; and to provide a vehicle whereby Asian/Pacific American librarians can cooperate with other associations and organizations having similar or allied interests." Founded 1980; incorporated 1981; affiliated with ALA 1982. Dues (Inst.) $25; (Indiv.) $10; (Students/Unemployed Librarians) $5.

Membership

Open to all librarians and information specialists of Asian/Pacific descent working in U.S. libraries and information centers and other related organizations and to others who support the goals and purposes of APALA. Asian/Pacific Americans are defined as those who consider themselves Asian/Pacific Americans. They may be Americans of Asian/Pacific descent, Asian/Pacific people with the status of permanent residency, or Asian/Pacific people living in the United States.

Officers (June 1991–June 1992)

Pres. Charlotte Chung-Sook Kim, Chicago Public Lib., 400 S. State St., Chicago, IL 60605; *V.P./Pres.-Elect.* Marjorie H. Li, Rutgers Univ., College Ave., New Brunswick,

NJ 08904; *Secy.* Abdulfazal Kabir, Clark-Atlanta Univ., 223 James P. Brawley Dr. S.W., Atlanta, GA 30314; *Treas.* Yasuko Makino, C. V. Starr East Asian Lib., Columbia Univ., 300 Kent Hall, New York, NY 10027.

Advisory Committee

President, immediate past president, vice president/president-elect, secretary, treasurer, chairpersons of the regional chapters, and an elected representative of the standing committees.

Publications

Apala Newsletter. Eds. Jack T. Tsukamoto, Periodicals Libn., Ball State Univ., Muncie, IN 47306; Anna M. Wang, Systems Libn., Ohio State Univ. Libs., 124 Main Lib., 1858 Neil Ave. Mall, Columbus, OH 43210.

Committee Chairpersons

Awards. Elizabeth Hernandez Alaras, Foreign Language Lib., Chicago Public Lib.,

400 S. State St., Chicago, IL 60605.

Constitution and Bylaws. Eveline L. Yang, Head, ILL, Auraria Lib., Lawrence at 11 St., Denver, CO 80204.

Finance. Erlinda J. Regner, Libn., Chicago Public Lib., 400 S. State St., Chicago, IL 60605.

Local Arrangement. Yong Kyu Choo, Head, Korean Div., East Asiatic Lib., Univ. of California, Berkeley, CA 94720.

Membership. Sushila Shah, Catalog Libn., Macalester College Lib., 1600 Grand Ave., Saint Paul, MN 55105.

Nominations. Abdul J. Miah, Dir., Learning Resource Center, J. Sargent Reynolds Community College, 700 E. Jackson St., Richmond, VA 23261.

Program and Publicity. Heona Ahn, Head, Audio-Visual Dept., Chicago Public Lib., Sulzer Regional Lib., 4455 N. Lincoln Ave., Chicago, IL 60625.

Recruitment and Scholarship. Ganga Dakshinamurti, Coord., Bibliographic Database Management, Univ. of Manitoba, Winnipeg, Manitoba R3T 2N2, Canada.

Association for Federal Information Resources Management

Chairperson, Marvin Gordon
Grumman Data Systems
1000 Wilson Blvd., Suite 2800, Arlington, VA 22209
703-875-8514

Object

"Founded in 1979, AFFIRM is an organization of professionals associated to promote and advance the concept and practice of information resources management (IRM) in the government of the United States. AFFIRM carries out its goal through providing a forum for professionals in IRM to exchange ideas, exploring new techniques to improve the quality and use of federal information systems and resources, advocating effective application of IRM to all levels of the federal government, enhancing the professionalism of IRM personnel, and interacting with state and local government on IRM issues."

Membership

Regular membership is extended to professionals currently or formerly employed by the federal government in some capacity related to IRM. Persons who do not qualify for regular membership may join as associate members. The following component disciplines of IRM are represented: automatic data processing; library and technical information; paperwork management; privacy, freedom of information, and information security; records and statistical data collection; telecommunications; data administration; and other related areas. Dues (Regular) $25; (Assoc.) $35.

Officers (July 1991–June 1992)

Exec. Chpn. Marvin Gordon, Grumman Data Systems, 1000 Wilson Blvd., Suite 2800, Arlington, VA 22209. Tel. 703-875-8514; *Exec. V. Chpn.* Carol Naughton, Dir., Info. Resource Management, Overseas Private Investment Corp., 1015 M St. N.W., Washington, DC 20527. Tel. 202-457-7100; *Programs.* Marlene A. Palmer, Mobil Corp., Systems and Computer Services, 3225 Gallows Rd., Fairfax, VA 22037-0001. Tel. 703-846-5053; *Finance.* James P. Clancy, Software Solutions, 6106 Dory Landing, Burke, VA 22015. Tel. 703-671-0700; *Admin.* David P. Hale, Farm Credit Administration, 5566 First Statesman Lane, Alexandria, VA 22312. Tel. 703-883-4176.

Committee Chairpersons

Membership and Newsletter. Steve Whitney, 16 Crescent Place, Takoma Park, MD 20912. Tel. 301-270-4679.

Organizational Liaison. Ann Koestler, EDS, 1331 Pennsylvania Ave. N.W., Suite 1300, Washington, DC 20004. Tel. 202-637-6700.

Seminar. John C. Babcock, U.S. General Services Administration, 5621 Utah Ave. N.W., Washington, DC 20015. Tel. 202-501-3347.

Association for Information Management

Managing Director, David Kahn
6348 Munhall Ct., Box 374, McLean, VA 22101
703-790-0403

Object

To provide leadership in targeting and enhancing the abilities of all managers to ensure the efficient and effective delivery of information in order to further individual and organizational goals. The means to do this are through effective integration and management of technologies, content, and people. Established 1981. Memb. (Indiv.) 600.

Membership

Corporate planners, vice presidents of communication and marketing, administration managers, online users, data processing, telecommunications, librarianship, records management, office automation, and management information systems (MIS) personnel. Its primary focus is on the management of these information activities and on making the total information base supportive of management and the decision-making process. The Board of Directors is made up of leading information professionals in industry, academia, and government. Dues (Indiv.) private $100, public/academician $60; (Foreign) $135; (Student) $35.

Board of Directors

Chpn. Arlen R. Lessin, Chpn. and Pres., Lessin Technology Group; *V.Chpn.* Alan S. Lin-
den, Mgr., Dist. Marketing Operations, Wang Laboratories; *Treas.* Birtrun S. Kidwell, Jr., Dir., System Engineering, Computer Based Systems; Mark M. Adams, U.S. Navy; Gloria Aks, Libs. Supv., EBASCO Services; Thomas Dinenna, Dir., Technology Support Div., U.S. Census Bureau; Marvin Gordon, Pres., Vanguard Security Systems; James R. Guinaw, Deputy V.P., Grumman Data Systems Corp.; Juan Jover, Dir., Expense Management Services, American Express Travel Related Services; Scott I. Kostenbauder, Program Mgr., Technical Info., IBM Corp.; E. Norman Sims; Dick Sprague, Pres., Sprague Consulting; Margaret Telfer, Consultant, Key Indicators; Anthony E. Whyte, Pres., AMR International; Jean Young, Pres., Young & Assocs.; *Immediate Past Chpn.* Herbert R. Brinberg, Pres. and CEO, Parnassus Assocs. International; *Exec. Dir.* Susan Kahn.

Publications

AIM Network (mo.; memb.). Newsletter.

AIM 1990 Membership Profile Survey (memb. $20; nonmemb. $35).

Who's Who in Information Management (ann.; memb.; nonmemb. $60).

Association for Information and Image Management

Executive Director, Sue Wolk
1100 Wayne Ave., Silver Spring, MD 20910
301-587-8202, FAX 301-587-2711

Object

To promote and advance the development and use of systems, services, and technologies that store, retrieve, and manipulate images of documents to increase the effectiveness of public and private organizations.

Officers

Pres. Phillip R. Trapp, TRW Financial Systems, 2001 Center St., Berkeley, CA 94704;

V.P. Michael L. Thomas, MSTC, 3541 Chain Bridge Rd., Fairfax, VA 22030-2793; *Treas.* Beverlee Nunnari, Reliance Electric, 24800 Tungsten Rd., Cleveland, OH 44117.

Publications

fyi/im newsletter (24 per year; memb.). *Ed.* Katie Brophy.
INFORM (10 per year; memb.). *Ed.* Gregory E. Kaebnick.

Association for Library and Information Science Education

Executive Director, Sally Nicholson
4101 Lake Boone Trail, Suite 201, Raleigh, NC 27607-4916
919-787-5181, FAX 919-787-4916

Object

"To promote excellence in research, teaching, and service for library and information science education." Founded 1915. Memb. 680. Dues (Inst.) with ALA accredited programs $250; all others $150; (International Affiliate Inst.) $75; (Indiv.) $20 or $40. Year. Sept. -Aug.

Membership

Any library/information science school with a program accredited by the ALA Committee on Accreditation may become an institutional member. Any school that offers a graduate degree in librarianship or a cognate field but whose program is not accredited by the ALA Committee on Accreditation may become an institutional member at the lower rate. Any school outside the United States and Canada offering a program comparable to that of institutional membership may become an international affiliate institutional member.

Any faculty member, administrator, librarian, researcher, or other individual employed full time may become a personal member.

Any retired or part-time faculty member, student, or other individual employed less than full time may become a personal member at the lower rate.

Officers (Jan. 1992–Jan. 1993)

Pres. Adele M. Fasick, Dean, Faculty of Lib. and Info. Science, Univ. of Toronto, 140 Saint George St., Toronto, ON M5F 1A1; *V.P./ Pres.-Elect.* Timothy W. Sineath, College of Lib. and Info. Science, Univ. of Kentucky, Lexington, KY 40506; *Secy.-Treas.* Robert Grover, School of Lib. and Info. Management, Emporia State Univ., 1200 Commercial St., Emporia, KS 66801.

Directors

Fred W. Roper, College of Lib. and Info. Science, 113 Davis College, Univ. of South Carolina, Columbia, SC 29208; Darlene E. Weingand, School of Lib. and Info. Studies, Univ. of Wisconsin, Madison, WI 53706; Ronald R. Powell, School of Lib. and Informational Science, Univ. of Missouri, Columbia, MO 65211; Ruth A. Palmquist, Graduate

School of Lib. and Info. Science, Univ. of Tennessee, Knoxville, TN 37996.

Council of Deans and Directors

Chpn. Martha Hale.

Publications

ALISE Library and Information Science Education Statistical Report (ann.; $32; foreign $34).
Journal of Education for Library and Information Science (5 per year; $50; foreign $60).

Committee Chairpersons

Awards and Honors. Joan Durrance, School of Info. and Lib. Studies, Univ. of Michigan, Ann Arbor, MI 48109-1092.
Communications and Public Relations.
Conference.
Editorial Board.
Governmental Relations.
International.

Research. Daniel O'Connor, Rutgers School of Communications, Info. and Lib. Studies, New Brunswick, NJ 08903.

Representatives

ALA SCOLE. Ronald Powell, School of Lib. and Info. Science, Univ. of Missouri, Columbia, MO 65211.
ASIS. Timothy Sineatis, College of Lib. and Info. Science, Univ. of Kentucky, Lexington, KY 40506-0039.
IFLA. Adele M. Fasick; and Mohammed M. Aman (Section on Education and Training), School of Lib. and Info. Science, Univ. of Wisconsin, Milwaukee, WI 53201; Ismail Abdullahi (Section on Education and Training), Univ. of Southern Mississippi, School of Lib. Science, Hattiesburg, MS 39406; S. Michael Malinconico (Section on Information Technology), Univ. of Alabama, School of Lib. and Info. Studies, Tuscaloosa, AL 35487.
Medical Lib. Assn. Fred Roper.
Special Libs. Assn. Beth Paskoff, School of Lib. and Info. Science, Louisiana State Univ., Baton Rouge, LA 70803.

Association of Academic Health Sciences Library Directors

Administrative Assistant, Sandra Bailey Wilson
Houston Academy of Medicine–Texas Medical Center Library, Houston, TX 77030
713-790-7060

Object

"To promote, in cooperation with educational institutions, other educational associations, government agencies, and other non-profit organizations, the common interests of academic health sciences libraries located in the United States and elsewhere, through publications, research, and discussion of problems of mutual interest and concern, and to advance the efficient and effective operation of academic health sciences libraries for the benefit of faculty, students, administrators, and practitioners."

Membership

Regular membership is available to nonprofit educational institutions operating a school of health sciences that has full or provisional accreditation by the Association of American Medical Colleges. Regular members shall be represented by the chief administrative officer of the member institution's health sciences library.

Associate membership (and nonvoting representation) is available to organizations having an interest in the purposes and activities of the association.

Dues (Inst.) $300; (Assoc. Inst.) $150.

Officers (Nov. 1991–Nov. 1992)

Pres. Rachael K. Anderson, Health Sciences Center Lib., Univ. of Arizona, Tucson, AZ 85724; *Pres.-Elect.* Judith Messerle; *Secy.-Treas.* Lynn Kasner Morgan; *Past Pres.* Alison Bunting.

Board of Directors

Carol A. Burns, Michael Homan, Edward W. Tawyea.

Association of Christian Librarians

Executive Director, Wava Bueschlen
Box 4, Cedarville, OH 45314

Object

". . . to meet the needs of evangelical Christian librarians serving in institutions of higher learning. The Association shall promote high standards of professionalism in library work as well as projects that encourage membership participation in serving the academic library community." Founded 1956. Memb. (Indiv.) 301. Dues (Indiv.) $16–$38, based on salary scale. Year: Conference to Conference (2nd week in June).

Membership

A full member shall be a Christian librarian subscribing to the purposes of the corporation who is affiliated with an institution of higher learning. Associate members include those who are in agreement with the purposes of the corporation but who are not affiliated with institutions of higher learning or who are non-librarians.

Officers (June 1991–June 1992)

Pres. Nancy Olson, Lincoln Christian College, Lincoln, IL 62656; *V.P.* Bea Flinner, Southern Nazarene Univ., 4115 N. College, Bethany, OK 73008; *Secy.* Sharon Bull, Point Loma Nazarene College, San Diego, CA 92106; *Treas.* Stephen Brown, Cedarville College, Cedarville, OH 45314; *Public Relations Dir.* Woodvall Moore, Evangel College, Springfield, MO 65803; *Business Mgr.* Janice

Bosma, Cedarville College, Cedarville, OH 45314.

Board of Directors

Clem Guthro, Vihari Hivale, Clyde Root, Wendell Thompson, Ferne Weimer.

Publications

Christian Librarian (q.; memb.; nonmemb. $20).
Christian Periodical Index.

Committee Chairpersons

Archivist. Janice Bosma, Cedarville College, Cedarville, OH 45314.
Bible College Section. Lynn Anderson, Central Bible College, 1315 E. Wheatridge, Springfield, MO 65803.
Christian Librarian. *Ed.* Ronald Jordahl, Prairie Bible Institute, Three Hills, AB T0M 2A0, Canada.
Christian Periodical Index. Douglas Butler, Asbury College, 202 S. Walnut, Wilmore, KY 40390.
Commission for International Library Assistance. Ken Gill, BGC Lib., Wheaton College, Wheaton, IL 60187.
Liberal Arts Section. Clem Guthro, Point Loma Nazarene College, San Diego, CA 92107.
Program. Bea Flinner, Southern Nazarene Univ., 4115 N. College, Bethany, OK 73008.

Association of Jewish Libraries

c/o National Foundation for Jewish Culture
330 Seventh Ave., 21st fl., New York, NY 10001
212-629-0500

Object

"To promote the improvement of library services and professional standards in all Jewish libraries and collections of Judaica; to serve as a center of dissemination of Jewish library information and guidance; to encourage the establishment of Jewish libraries and collections of Judaica; to promote publication of literature which will be of assistance to Jewish librarianship; and to encourage people to enter the field of librarianship." Organized in 1965 from the merger of the Jewish Librarians Association and the Jewish Library Association. Memb. 890. Dues (Inst.) $25; (Student/Retired) $18. Year. July 1–June 30.

Officers (June 1991–June 1993)

Pres. Linda P. Lerman, Yale Univ., Sterling Memorial Lib., Box 1603A, Yale Sta., New Haven, CT 06520; *Past Pres.* Marcia Posner, Federation of Jewish Philanthropies Lib., 130 E. 59 St., New York, NY 10022; *V.P./Pres.-Elect.* Ralph R. Simon, Sindell Lib., Temple EmanuEl, 2200 S. Green Rd., Cleveland, OH 44121; *V.P. Memb.* Aviva Astrinsky, Anneberg Research Inst. Lib., 420 Walnut St., Philadelphia, PA 19106. Tel. 215-238-1290, Ext. 104; *Treas.* Toby G. Rossner, Bureau of Jewish Education of Rhode Island, 130 Sessions St., Providence, RI 02906; *Rec. Secy.* Esther Nussbaum, Ramaz Upper School Lib.,

60 E. 78 St., New York, NY 10021; *Corresponding Secy.* Tzivia Atik, Jewish Theological Seminary of America Lib., 3080 Broadway, New York, NY 10027. Tel. 212-678-8092; *Publns.* V.P. David J. Gilner, Hebrew Union College Lib., 3101 Clifton Ave., Cincinnati, OH 45220-2488.

Address correspondence to the Association.

Publications

AJL Newsletter (q.). *Eds.* Irene S. Levin-Wixman, Judaica Lib., Temple EmanuEl, 190 N. County Rd., Palm Beach, FL 33480; Hazel Karp, Hebrew Academy of Atlanta Lib., 5200 Northland Dr., Atlanta, GA 30342.

Judaica Librarianship (irreg.). *Eds.* Marcia Posner; and Bella Hass Weinberg, YIVO Lib., 1048 Fifth Ave., New York, NY 10028.

Miscellaneous others (request current list from David Gilner, AJL, Hebrew Union College Lib., 3101 Clifton Ave., Cincinnati, OH 45220-2488).

Division Presidents

Research and Special Library. Zachary Baker. Synagogue, School, and Center Libraries. Merrily Hart.

Association of Librarians in the History of the Health Sciences

President, Philip Teigen
National Library of Medicine, Bethesda, MD 20894
301-496-5405

Object

This Association is established exclusively for educational purposes to serve the professional interests of librarians, archivists, and

other specialists actively engaged in the librarianship of the history of the health sciences by promoting the exchange of information and by improving the standards of service.

Membership

Voting members shall be limited to persons who have professional responsibilities for library and archives collections and services in the history of the health sciences. Nonvoting membership shall be open to persons interested in the concerns of the Association.

Officers (May 1992–May 1993)

Pres. Edward T. Morman, Institute of History of Medicine, Johns Hopkins Univ., 1900 E. Monument St., Baltimore, MD 21205-2169. Tel. 301-955-9159; *Secy.-Treas.* Edwina Walls, Libn., Univ. of Arkansas for Medical Sciences, 4301 W. Markham, Little Rock, AR 72205; *Ed.* Judith Overmier, School of Lib. and Info. Studies, Univ. of Oklahoma, 410 W. Brooks, Rm. 123, Norman, OK 73019-0528.

Steering Committee

Inci Bowman, Moody Medical Lib., Galveston, TX 77550.

Committees

Nominating. Adele Lerner, 122 W. 74 St., Apt. 2B, New York, NY 10023.
Publications. Kathy Donahue, Louise Darling Biomedical Lib., UCLA, 10833 Le Conte Ave., Los Angeles, CA 90024.
Program. Nancy Zinn, Special Collections Libn., Univ. of California Lib., San Francisco, CA 94143-0840.

Publication

Watermark (q.; memb.; nonmemb. $15). *Ed.* Judith Overmier, School of Lib. and Info. Studies, Univ. of Oklahoma, 401 W. Brooks, Norman, OK 73019-0528.

Association of Research Libraries

Executive Director, Duane E. Webster
1527 New Hampshire Ave. N.W., Washington, DC 20036
202-232-2466

Object

To identify and influence forces affecting the future of research libraries in the process of scholarly communication; to promote equitable access to, and effective use of, recorded knowledge in support of teaching, research, scholarship, and community service. Established 1932 by the chief librarians of 43 research libraries. Memb. (Inst.) 119. Dues $10,400. Year. Jan.–Dec.

Membership

Membership is institutional.

Officers (Oct. 1991–Oct. 1992)

Pres. Arthur Curley, Boston Public Lib., Boston, MA 02117; *Pres.-Elect.* Susan K. Nutter, North Carolina State Univ. Libs., Raleigh, NC 27695-7111; *Past Pres.* Marilyn J. Sharrow, Univ. of California, Davis Libs., Davis, CA 95616.

Board of Directors

Harold Billings, Univ. of Texas Libs.; John Black, Univ. of Guelph Lib.; Jerry D. Campbell, Duke Univ. Libs.; Joan Chambers, Colorado State Univ. Lib.; Nancy Cline, Pennsylvania State Univ. Lib.; Arthur Curley, Boston Public Lib.; Sul Lee, Univ. of Oklahoma Lib.; Emily R. Mobley, Purdue Univ. Lib.; Susan K. Nutter, North Carolina State Univ. Libs.

Publications

ARL: A Bimonthly Newsletter of Research Libraries Issues and Actions (6 per year; $40).
ARL Annual Salary Survey (ann.; $60).
ARL Minutes (s. ann.; $60).
ARL Statistics (ann.; $60).
Cataloging Titles in Microform Sets. Report based on a study conducted for ARL in 1980 by Information Systems Consultants,

Inc., Richard W. Boss, principal investigator ($12).

The Changing System of Scholarly Communication. Report of the ARL Task Force on Scholarly Communication ($1).

Cumulated ARL University Library Statistics, 1962–1963 through 1978–1979. Compiled by Kendon Stubbs and David Buxton ($15).

Directory of Electronic Journals, Newsletters, and Academic Discussion Lists. Compiled by Michael Strangelove and Diane Kovacs (1991, rev. early 1992; $20).

The Gerould Statistics, 1907/08–1961/62. A compilation of data on ARL libraries, begun in 1908 by James Thayer Gerould and later continued as the "Princeton University Library Statistics." Compiled by Robert Molyneux ($25).

The Higher Education Act, Title II-C Program: Strengthening Research Library Resources — A Ten Year Profile and an Assessment of the Program's Effects upon the Nation's Scholarship. By Samuel Allen Streit ($20).

Linked Systems. Papers from the May 1988 ARL Membership meeting ($10).

Mass Deacidification Systems: Planning and Managerial Decision Making. By Karen Turko, Univ. of Toronto ($15).

Meeting the Preservation Challenge. Papers from the October 1987 ARL Membership meeting. Edited by Jan Merrill-Oldham ($28).

Microform Sets in U.S. and Canadian Libraries. Report of a Survey on the Bibliographic Control of Microform Sets contributed by the Association of Research Libraries Microform Project ($12).

Plan for a North American Program for Coordinated Retrospective Conversion. Report of a study conducted by the Association of Research Libraries, prepared by Jutta Reed-Scott ($15).

Preservation Program Models: A Study Project and Report. By Jan Merrill-Oldham, Carolyn Clark-Morrow, and Mark Roosa ($40).

Preservation Statistics. Statistics and analysis on personnel, expenditures, and categories of treatments (ann.; $60).

Preserving Knowledge: The Case for Alkaline Paper. Briefing packet and collection of articles, prepared in collaboration with ALA, Commission on Preservation and Access, and the National Humanities Alliance ($18).

Report of the ARL Serials Prices Project. A compilation of reports examining the serials prices problems ($60).

Research Library Statistics, 1907/08 through 1987/88. Machine-readable datafile on diskettes, with printed documentation. Compiled by Kendon Stubbs and Robert Molyneux ($150).

Technology and the Future of Scholarly Exchange. Papers from the May 1989 ARL Membership Meeting in Providence, RI ($30).

Technology and U.S. Government Information Policies: Catalysts for New Partnerships. Report of the ARL Task Force on Government Information in Electronic Formats ($5).

Committee Chairpersons

Access. Nancy Eaton, Iowa State Univ. Lib., Ames, IA 50011.

ARL Statistics. Kent Hendrickson, Univ. of Nebraska Lib., Lincoln, NE 68588-0410.

Information Policies. Merrily Taylor, Brown Univ. Lib., Providence, RI 02912.

Management of Research Library Resources. Joanne Euster, Rutgers Univ. Lib., New Brunswick, NJ 08903.

Nominations. Susan K. Nutter, North Carolina State Univ. Libs., Raleigh, NC 27695-7111.

Preservation of Research Library Materials. William Studer, Ohio State Univ. Lib., Columbus, OH 43210.

Research Collections. Charles Osburn, Univ. of Alabama Libs., Tuscaloosa, AL 35487-0266.

Scholarly Communications Committee. Paul Gherman, Virginia Polytechnic Institute and State Univ. Libs., Blacksburg, VA 24061.

Task Force Chairpersons

Minority Recruitment. Joseph Boiss, Univ. of California Lib., Santa Barbara, CA 93106.

Units

Coalition for Networked Information. Formed by ARL, CAUSE, and EDUCOM in March 1990 to explore the promise of high-performance computers and advanced networks for enriching scholarship and enhancing intellectual productivity.

Office of Management Services. Provides consulting, training, and publishing services on the management of human and material resources in libraries.

Office of Research and Development. To pursue the ARL research agenda through the identification and development of projects in support of the research library community's mission.

Office of Scientific and Academic Publishing. Established in 1990 to identify and influence the forces affecting the production, dissemination, and use of scholarly and scientific information.

ARL Membership in 1990

Nonuniversity Libraries

Boston Public Lib.; Canada Institute for Scientific and Technical Info.; Center for Research Libs.; Linda Hall Lib.; Lib. of Congress; National Agricultural Lib.; National Lib. of Canada; National Lib. of Medicine; New York Public Lib.; New York State Lib.; Newberry Lib.; Smithsonian Institution Libs.

University Libraries

Alabama; Alberta; Arizona; Arizona State; Boston; Brigham Young; British Columbia; Brown; California (Berkeley); California (Davis); California (Irvine); California (Los Angeles); California (Riverside); California (San Diego); California (Santa Barbara); Case Western Reserve; Chicago; Cincinnati; Colorado; Colorado State; Columbia; Connecticut; Cornell; Dartmouth; Delaware; Duke; Emory; Florida; Florida State; Georgetown; Georgia; Georgia Institute of Technology; Guelph; Harvard; Hawaii; Houston; Howard; Illinois (Chicago); Illinois (Urbana); Indiana; Iowa; Iowa State; Johns Hopkins; Kansas; Kent State; Kentucky; Laval; Louisiana State; McGill; McMaster; Manitoba; Maryland; Massachusetts; Massachusetts Institute of Technology; Miami; Michigan; Michigan State; Minnesota; Missouri; Nebraska; New Mexico; New York; North Carolina; North Carolina State; Northwestern; Notre Dame; Ohio State; Oklahoma; Oklahoma State; Oregon; Pennsylvania; Pennsylvania State; Pittsburgh; Princeton; Purdue; Queen's (Kingston, Canada); Rice; Rochester; Rutgers; Saskatchewan; South Carolina; Southern California; Southern Illinois; Stanford; SUNY (Albany); SUNY (Buffalo); SUNY (Stony Brook); Syracuse; Temple; Tennessee; Texas; Texas A & M; Toronto; Tulane; Utah; Vanderbilt; Virginia; Virginia Polytechnic; Washington; Washington State; Waterloo; Wayne State; Western Ontario; Wisconsin; Yale; York.

Association of Visual Science Librarians

Chairperson, Lynne Silvers, Librarian
New England College of Optometry, 420 Beacon St., Boston, MA 02115

Object

"To foster collective and individual acquisition and dissemination of visual science information, to improve services for all persons seeking such information, and to develop standards for libraries to which members are attached." Founded 1968. Memb. (U.S.) 55; (Foreign) 13.

Publications

Opening Day Book Collection – Visual Science.

PhD Theses in Physiological Optics (irreg.).
Standards for Visual Science Libraries.
Union List of Vision-Related Serials (irreg.).

Meetings

Annual meeting held in December in connection with the American Academy of Optometry; midyear mini-meeting with the Medical Library Association.

Beta Phi Mu

(International Library and Information Science Honor Society)
Executive Secretary, Blanche Woolls
School of Library and Information Science
University of Pittsburgh, Pittsburgh, PA 15260

Object

"To recognize high scholarship in the study of librarianship and to sponsor appropriate professional and scholarly projects." Founded at the University of Illinois in 1948. Memb. 23,000.

Membership

Open to graduates of library school programs accredited by the American Library Association who fulfill the following requirements: complete the course requirements leading to a fifth year or other advanced degree in librarianship with a scholastic average of 3.75 where A equals 4 points (this provision shall also apply to planned programs of advanced study beyond the fifth year that do not culminate in a degree but that require full-time study for one or more academic years); receive a letter of recommendation from their respective library schools attesting to their demonstrated fitness of successful professional careers. Former graduates of accredited library schools are also eligible on the same basis.

Officers

Pres. (1991–1993) Norman Horrocks, V.P., Editorial, Scarecrow Press, 52 Liberty St., Box 4167, Metuchen, NJ 08840; *V.P./Pres.-Elect (1991–1993)*. Elfreda A. Chatman, School of Lib. and Info. Science, Univ. of North Carolina, Chapel Hill, NC 27599-3360; *Past Pres.* Joseph J. Mika, Dir., Lib. Science Program, Wayne State Univ., 106 Kresge Lib., Detroit, MI 48202; *Treas. (1991–1994)*. Dennis K. Lambert, Head of Collection Management, Falvey Memorial Lib., Villanova Univ., Villanova, PA 19085-1684; *Exec. Secy.* Blanche Woolls, Chpn., Lib. Science Dept., School of Lib. and Info. Science, Univ. of Pittsburgh, Pittsburgh, PA 15260.

Directors

(1992) Beverly Joyce, Univ. of Oklahoma Libs., 401 W. Brooks, Norman, OK 73072; Mary Krutulis, School of Lib. and Info. Science, Indiana Univ., Lib. 011, Bloomington, IN 47405; (1993) Carl F. Orgren, School of Lib. and Info. Science, Univ. of Iowa, Iowa City, IA 52242; Sue Webreck Alman, School of Lib. and Info. Science, Univ. of Pittsburgh, Pittsburgh, PA 15260; *Dir.-at-Large.* Mary Biggs, Dir., Mercy College Libs., 555 Broadway, Dobbs Ferry, NY 10522.

Publications

Beta Phi Mu Monograph Series. Book-length scholarly works based on original research in subjects of interest to library and information professionals. Available from Greenwood Press, 88 Post Rd. W., Box 5007, Westport, CT 06881-9990.

Chapbook Series. Limited editions on topics of interest to information professionals. Call Beta Phi Mu for availability.

Newsletter Ed. Charles A. Seavey.

Chapters

Alpha. Univ. of Illinois, Grad. School of Lib. and Info. Science, Urbana, IL 61801; *Beta*. Univ. of Southern California, School of Lib. Science, University Park, Los Angeles, CA 90007; *Gamma*. Florida State Univ., School of Lib. Science, Tallahassee, FL 32306; *Delta* (Inactive). Loughborough College of Further Education, School of Libnshp., Loughborough, England; *Epsilon*. Univ. of North Carolina, School of Lib. Science, Chapel Hill, NC 27514; *Zeta*. Atlanta Univ., School of Lib. and Info. Studies, Atlanta, GA 30314; *Theta*. Pratt Institute, Grad. School of Lib. and Info. Science, Brooklyn, NY 11205; *Iota*. Catholic Univ. of America, School of Lib. and Info. Science, Washington, DC 20064; Univ. of Maryland, College of Lib. and Info. Services, College Park, MD 20742; *Kappa*.

Western Michigan Univ., School of Libnshp., Kalamazoo, MI 49008; *Lambda*. Univ. of Oklahoma, School of Lib. Science, Norman, OK 73019; *Mu*. Univ. of Michigan, School of Lib. Science, Ann Arbor, MI 48109; *Nu* (Inactive); *Xi*. Univ. of Hawaii, Grad. School of Lib. Studies, Honolulu, HI 96822; *Omicron*. Rutgers Univ., Grad. School of Lib. and Info. Studies, New Brunswick, NJ 08903; *Pi*. Univ. of Pittsburgh, School of Lib. and Info. Science, Pittsburgh, PA 15260; *Rho*. Kent State Univ., School of Lib. Science, Kent, OH 44242; *Sigma*. Drexel Univ., School of Lib. and Info. Science, Philadelphia, PA 19104; *Tau* (Inactive). State Univ. of New York at Geneseo, School of Lib. and Info. Science, Geneseo, NY 14454; *Upsilon*. Univ. of Kentucky, College of Lib. Science, Lexington, KY 40506; *Phi* (Inactive). Univ. of Denver, Grad. School of Libnshp. and Info. Management, Denver, CO 80208; *Chi*. Indiana Univ., School of Lib. and Info. Science, Bloomington, IN 47401; *Psi*. Univ. of Missouri at Columbia, School of Lib. and Info. Sciences, Columbia, MO 65211; *Omega* (Inactive). San Jose State Univ., Div. of Lib. Science, San Jose, CA 95192; *Beta Alpha*. Queens College, City College of New York, Grad. School of Lib. and Info. Studies, Flushing, NY 11367; *Beta Beta*. Simmons College, Grad. School of Lib. and Info. Science, Boston, MA 02115; *Beta Delta*. State Univ. of New York at Buffalo, School of Info. and Lib. Studies, Buffalo, NY 14260; *Beta Epsilon*. Emporia State Univ., School of Lib. Science, Emporia, KS 66801; *Beta Zeta*. Louisiana State Univ., Grad. School of Lib. Science, Baton Rouge, LA 70803; *Beta Eta*. Univ. of Texas at Austin, Grad. School of Lib. and Info. Science, Austin, TX 78712; *Beta Theta*. Brigham Young Univ., School of Lib. and Info. Science, Provo, UT 84602; *Beta Iota*. Univ. of Rhode Island, Grad. Lib. School, Kingston, RI 02881; *Beta Kappa*. Univ. of Alabama, Grad.

School of Lib. Service, University, AL 35486; *Beta Lambda*. North Texas State Univ., School of Lib. and Info. Science, Denton, TX 76203; Texas Woman's Univ., School of Lib. Science, Denton, TX 76204; *Beta Mu*. Long Island Univ., Palmer Grad. Lib. School, C. W. Post Center, Greenvale, NY 11548; *Beta Nu*. Saint John's Univ., Div. of Lib. and Info. Science, Jamaica, NY 11439; *Beta Xi*. North Carolina Central Univ., School of Lib. Science, Durham, NC 27707; *Beta Omicron*. Univ. of Tennessee at Knoxville, Grad. School of Lib. and Info. Science, Knoxville, TN 37916; *Beta Pi*. Univ. of Arizona, Grad. Lib. School, Tucson, AZ 85721; *Beta Rho*. Univ. of Wisconsin at Milwaukee, School of Lib. Science, Milwaukee, WI 53201; *Beta Sigma*. Clarion State College, School of Lib. Science, Clarion, PA 16214; *Beta Tau*. Wayne State Univ., Div. of Lib. Science, Detroit, MI 48202; *Beta Upsilon* (Inactive). Alabama A & M Univ., School of Lib. Media, Normal, AL 35762; *Beta Phi*. Univ. of South Florida, Grad. Dept. of Lib., Media, and Info. Studies, Tampa, FL 33620; *Beta Psi*. Univ. of Southern Mississippi, School of Lib. Service, Hattiesburg, MS 39406; *Beta Omega*. Univ. of South Carolina, College of Libnshp., Columbia, SC 29208; *Beta Beta Alpha*. Univ. of California, Los Angeles, Grad. School of Lib. and Info. Science, Los Angeles, CA 90024; *Beta Beta Gamma*. Rosary College, Grad. School of Lib. and Info. Science, River Forest, IL 60305; *Beta Beta Delta*. Univ. of Cologne, Germany; *Beta Beta Epsilon*. Univ. of Wisconsin at Madison, Lib. School, Madison, WI 53706; *Beta Beta Theta*. Univ. of Iowa, School of Lib. and Info. Science, Iowa City, IA 52242; *Beta Beta Zeta*. Univ. of North Carolina at Greensboro, Dept. of Lib. Science and Educational Technology, Greensboro, NC 27412; *Pi Lambda Sigma*. Syracuse Univ., School of Info. Studies, Syracuse, NY 13210.

Bibliographical Society of America

Executive Secretary, Marjory Zaik
Box 397, Grand Central Station, New York, NY 10163
212-995-9151

Object

"To promote bibliographical research and to issue bibliographical publications." Organized 1904. Memb. 1,300. Dues $30. Year. Jan.–Dec.

Officers (Jan. 1991–Jan. 1993)

Pres. Ruth Mortimer, Smith College, Box 775, Williamsburg, MA 01096; *V.P.* J. William Matheson; *Treas.* R. Dyke Benjamin, Lazard Freres and Co., One Rockefeller Plaza, New York, NY 10020; *Secy.* Marie E. Korey, 37 Coulson Ave., Toronto, ON M4V 1Y3, Canada.

Council

(1992) Sandra Alston; William P. Barlow, Jr.; Ralph W. Franklin; John Lancaster; (1993) Alexandra Mason; William S. Peterson; David L. Vander Meulen; James E. Walsh.

Publication

Papers (q.; memb.). *Ed.* William S. Peterson, Dept. of English, Univ. of Maryland, College Park, MD 20742.

Committee Chairpersons

Fellowship Program. Richard G. Landon, Thomas Fisher Lib., Univ. of Toronto, Toronto, ON M5S 1A5, Canada.
Publications. John Lancaster, Amherst College, Box 775, Williamsburg, MA 01096.

Canadian Association for Information Science
(Association Canadienne des Sciences de l'Information)

140 Saint George St., Toronto, ON M5S 1A1, Canada
416-978-8876

Object

Brings together individuals and organizations concerned with the production, manipulation, storage, retrieval, and dissemination of information with emphasis on the application of modern technologies in these areas. CAIS is dedicated to enhancing the activity of the information transfer process, utilizing the vehicles of research, development, application, and education, and serving as a forum for dialogue and exchange of ideas concerned with the theory and practice of all factors involved in the communication of information. Dues (Inst.) $150; (Regular) $65; (Student) $30.

Membership

Institutions and individuals interested in information science and involved in the gathering, organization, and dissemination of information (computer scientists, documentalists, information scientists, librarians, journalists, sociologists, psychologists, linguists, administrators, etc.) can become members of the Canadian Association for Information Science.

Officers (Jan. 1992–Dec. 1992)

Pres. Ernst J. Schuegraf, Box 55, Saint Francis Xavier Univ., Antigonish, NS B2G 1C0. Tel. 902-867-2269; *Past Pres.* Bryan Getchell, Bell Information Systems, 100 Dundas St., 3rd fl., London, ON N6A 4L6. Tel. 519-663-6865; *Treas.* Kent Weaver, Toronto Univ. Lib., 130 Saint George St., Toronto, ON M5S 1A5. Tel. 416-978-7292; *Publications Dir.* Charles Meadow, Faculty of Lib. and Info. Science, Toronto Univ., 140 Saint George St., Toronto, ON M5S 1A1. Tel. 416-978-4665; *Journal Ed.*

Joan Cherry, Faculty of Lib. and Info. Science, Toronto Univ., 140 Saint George St., Toronto, ON M5S 1A1. Tel. 416-978-4663; *Secy.* Mary Nash, Nash Information Services, 1975 Bel Air Dr., Ottawa, ON K2C 0X1.

Board of Directors

CAIS West Chapter. Jocelyn Godolphin.

Ottawa Chapter. Pat Johnston.
Toronto Chapter. Maggie Weaver.

Publications

Canadian Conference of Information Science: Proceedings (ann.).
Canadian Journal of Information Science (q.; $95; outside Canada $110).

Canadian Library Association

Executive Director, Karen Adams
200 Elgin St., Ottawa, ON K2P 1L5, Canada
613-232-9625, FAX 613-563-9895

Object

To provide leadership in the promotion, development, and support of library and information services in Canada for the benefit of Association members, the profession, and Canadian society. Offers library school scholarship and book awards; carries on international liaison with other library associations; makes representation to government and official commissions; offers professional development programs; and supports intellectual freedom. Founded in Hamilton in 1946, CLA is a nonprofit voluntary organization governed by an elected executive council. Memb. (Indiv.) 4,000; (Inst.) 1,000. Dues (Indiv.) $55 to $180, depending on salary; (Inst.) from $150 up, graduated on budget basis. Year. Anniversary date renewal.

Membership

Open to individuals, institutions, and groups interested in librarianship and in library and information services.

Officers (1991–1992)

Pres. Marnie Swanson, McPherson Lib., Univ. of Victoria, Box 180, Victoria, BC V8W 3H5. Tel. 604-721-8211; *1st V.P./Pres.-Elect.* Margaret Andrewes, R.R. 3, Beamsville, ON L0R 1B0. Tel. 416-563-4639; *Treas.* Richard Birkett, 322 Gloucester St., Oakville, ON L6J 3X1. Tel. 416-849-7267; *Past Pres.* Ernie Ingles, Rm. 502, Cameron Lib., Univ. of Alberta, Edmonton, AB T6G 2J8. Tel. 403-492-5569.

Executive Council

Table officers, divisional presidents, and councillors-at-large.

Publications

Canadian Library Journal (6 per year; Canada $45; U.S. $50; International $55. Prices in Canadian dollars.)
CM: Canadian Materials for Schools and Libraries (6 per year; $42).
Feliciter (10 issues; monthly newsletter).

Division Representatives

Canadian Association of College and University Libraries. Hazel Fry, 66 Woodmeadow Close S.W., Calgary, AB T2W 4L8.
Canadian Association of Public Libraries. Don Mills, Mississauga Lib. System, 301 Burnhamthorpe Rd. W., Mississauga, ON L5B 3Y3.
Canadian Association of Special Libraries and Information Services. Marilyn Rennick, Morisset Lib., Univ. of Ottawa, Ottawa, ON K1N 9A5.
Canadian Library Trustee Association. Agnes Richard, 5 Grandy Ave., Gander, NF A1V 1B3.
Canadian School Library Association. Gloria Hersak, Manitoba Education and Training, 1181 Portage Ave., Winnipeg, MB R3R 2P3.

Catholic Library Association

Executive Director, Anthony Prete
461 W. Lancaster Ave., Haverford, PA 19041
215-649-5250, FAX 215-896-1991

Object

The promotion and encouragement of Catholic literature and library work through cooperation, publications, education, and information. Founded 1921. Memb. 1,300. Dues $45–$500. Year. July–June.

Officers

Pres. Rev. Paul J. DeAntoniis, O. Praem., Archmere Academy, 3600 Philadelphia Pike, Claymont, DE 19703; *Pres.-Elect.* Paul J. Ostendorf, FSC, Saint Mary's College of Minnesota, 700 Terrace Heights, Winona, MN 55987; *Past Pres.* Emmett Corry, OSF, Div. of Lib. and Info. Science, Saint John's Univ., Jamaica, NY 11439.

Address correspondence to the executive director.

Executive Board

Officers; Joy Choppin, Georgetown Preparatory School, 10900 Rockville Pike, Rockville, MD 20852; Tina-Karen Forman, UCLA Research Lib., 405 Hilgard Ave., Los Angeles, CA 90024; Bonaventure Hayes, OFM, Christ the King Seminary, East Aurora, NY 14052-0607; Molly M. Lyons, Saint Patrick's Seminary, 325 Middlefield Ave., Menlo Park, CA 94025; Bert A. Thompson, Illinois Benedictine College, 5700 College Rd., Lisle, IL 60532; Barbara H. Weathers, Duchesne Academy, 10202 Memorial Dr., Houston, TX 77024.

Publications

Catholic Library World (6 per year plus *Handbook* and *Membership Directory*; memb.; nonmemb. $60).
Catholic Periodical and Literature Index (subscription). *Ed.* Dana Cernaianu.

Representatives

ALA RTSD Committee on Cataloging: Description and Access. Tina-Karen Forman, UCLA Research Lib., 405 Hilgard Ave., Los Angeles, CA 90024.
ALA Standing Committee on Library Education. Sister Lauretta McCusker, OP, Rosary College, Grad. School of Lib. and Info. Science, 7900 Division St., River Forest, IL 60305.
American Theological Library Association. Rev. Kenneth O'Malley, CP, Catholic Theological Union, 5401 S. Cornell St., Chicago, IL 60615.
Catholic Press Association. Michael W. Rechel, Catholic Lib. Assn., 461 W. Lancaster Ave., Haverford, PA 19041.
Council of National Library and Information Associations. Sister Marie Melton, RSM, Saint John's Univ. Libs., Grand Central & Utopia Pkwys., Jamaica, NY 11439.
Society of American Archivists. H. Warren Willis, U.S. Catholic Conference, 3211 Fourth St. N.E., Washington, DC 20017-1194.
Special Libraries Association. Mary L. Westermann, Palmer School of Lib. and Info. Science, C. W. Post Campus, Long Island Univ., Greenvale, NY 11548.

Section Chairpersons

Academic Libraries. Kathy Jastrab, Sacred Heart School of Theology, Box 429, Hales Corners, WI 53130-0429.
Archives. Rev. Gerald Garry, Divine Word College, Epworth, IA 52045.
Children's Libraries. Madeline Muller, Media Lib., Diocese of Youngstown, 225 Elm St., Youngstown, OH 44503.
High School Libraries. Maryanne Niehaus, York Catholic H.S. Lib., York, PA 17403.
Library Education. Gertrude Koh, Rosary College, Grad School of Lib. and Info. Science, 7900 Division St., River Forest, IL 60305.

Parish/Community Libraries. Mary Catherine Blooming, Saint Agatha School of Religion, 603 Bridge St., Ellwood City, PA 16117.

Round Table Chairpersons

Bibliographic Instruction. Sister Margaret Ruddy, OSF, Cardinal Stritch College Lib., 6801 N. Yates Rd., Milwaukee, WI 53217.
Cataloging and Classification. Tina-Karen Forman, UCLA Research Lib., 405 Hilgard Ave., Los Angeles, CA 90024.

Committee Chairpersons

Catholic Library World Editorial. Arnold Rzepecki, Sacred Heart Seminary College Lib., 2701 W. Chicago Blvd., Detroit, MI 48206.
Catholic Periodical and Literature Index. Sister Ellen Gaffney, RDC, Saint Joseph Seminary, Corrigan Memorial Lib., 201 Seminary Ave., Yonkers, NY 10704.
Constitution and Bylaws. Mary A. Grant, Saint John's Univ. Health Education Resource Center, Grand Central & Utopia Pkwys., Jamaica, NY 11439.
Elections. Carol Baker, Saint Gertrude School, 6551 Miami Ave., Cincinnati, OH 45243.
Finance. Rev. Paul J. DeAntoniis, O. Praem., Archmere Academy, 3600 Philadelphia Pike, Claymont, DE 19703.

Grant Development. Sister Jean R. Bostley, SSJ, Saint Joseph Central H.S., 22 Maplewood Ave., Pittsfield, MA 01201.
Membership Development. Carolyn W. Field, Catholic Lib. Assn., 461 W. Lancaster Ave., Haverford, PA 19041.
Nominations. Mary A. Grant, Saint John's Univ. Health Education Resource Center, Grand Central & Utopia Pkwys., Jamaica, NY 11439.
Public Relations. Sister Mary Elizabeth Gallagher, SSJ, College of Our Lady of the Elms, Alumnae Lib., 291 Springfield St., Chicopee, MA 01013.
Publications. Sister Marie Melton, RSM, Saint John's Univ. Libs., Grand Central & Utopia Pkwys., Jamaica, NY 11439.
Scholarship. Peggy Sullivan, 1508 Kennicott Ct., Sycamore, IL 60178.

Special Appointments

American Friends of the Vatican Library Board. Emmett Corry, OSF, Div. of Lib. and Info. Science, Saint John's Univ., Grand Central & Utopia Pkwys., Jamaica, NY 11439.
Convention Program Coordinator. Catholic Lib. Assn., 461 W. Lancaster Ave., Haverford, PA 19041.
Parliamentarian. Rev. Joseph P. Browne, CSC, Univ. of Portland Lib., 500 N. Willamette Blvd., Portland, OR 97203-5798.

Chief Officers of State Library Agencies

c/o The Council of State Governments
Iron Works Pike, Box 11910, Lexington, KY 40578-9989

Object

The object of COSLA is to provide "a means of cooperative action among its state and territorial members to strengthen the work of the respective state and territorial agencies. Its purpose is to provide a continuing mechanism for dealing with the problems faced by the heads of these agencies which are responsible for state and territorial library development."

Membership

The Chief Officers of State Library Agencies is an independent organization of the men and women who head the state and territorial agencies responsible for library development. Its membership consists solely of the top library officers of the 50 states, the District of Columbia, and one territory, variously designated as state librarian, director, commissioner, or executive secretary.

Officers (1990–1992)

Pres. Barratt Wilkins, State Libn., State Lib. of Florida, R. A. Gray Bldg., Tallahassee, FL 32399-0250; *V.P.* Nancy L. Zussy, State Libn., Washington State Lib., AJ-11, Olympia, WA 98504-0111; *Secy.* Rod Wagner, Dir., Nebraska Lib. Commission, 1420 P St., Lincoln, NE 68508; *Treas.* C. Ray Ewick, Dir., Indiana State Lib., 140 N. Senate Ave., Indianapolis, IN 46204.

Directors

Officers; *Immediate Past Pres.* Richard M. Cheski, State Libn., State Lib. of Ohio, 65 S. Front St., Columbus, OH 43266-0334; two elected members: Amy Owen, Dir., Utah State Lib., 2150 S. 300 W., Suite 16, Salt Lake City, UT 84115; J. Maurice Travillian, Asst. State Superintendent for Libs. and Dir., Maryland State Dept. of Educ., Div. of Lib. Development and Services, 200 W. Baltimore St., Baltimore, MD 21201.

Chinese-American Librarians Association

Executive Director, Eveline Yang
c/o Auraria Library, Lawrence at 11 St., Denver, CO 80204
303-556-2911

Object

"(1) To enhance communications among Chinese-American librarians as well as between Chinese-American librarians and other librarians; (2) to serve as a forum for discussion of mutual problems and professional concerns among Chinese-American librarians; (3) to promote Sino-American librarianship and library services; and (4) to provide a vehicle whereby Chinese-American librarians may cooperate with other associations and organizations having similar or allied interest."

Membership

Membership is open to everyone who is interested in the association's goals and activities. Memb. 450. Dues (Regular) $15; (Student/Nonsalaried) $7.50; (Inst.) $45; (Permanent) $200.

Officers (July 1991–June 1992)

Pres. Roy Chang; *V.P./Pres.-Elect.* Carl C. Chan; *Exec. Dir.* Eveline Yang; *Treas.* Peter Wang.

Publications

Journal of Library and Information Science (2 per year; memb.; nonmemb. $15).
Membership Directory (memb.).

Newsletter (3 per year; memb.; nonmemb. $10).

Committee Chairpersons

Award. Robert Chang.
Constitution and Bylaw. Betty Tsai.
Finance. Dora Chen.
Membership. Doris Tseng.
Nomination. Amy Seetoo.
Program Planning. Carl Chan.
Public Relations. Susana Liu.
Publications. Wilfred Fong.
Scholarship. Suzanne Lo.

Chapter Presidents

California. Susan Ma.
Greater Mid-Atlantic. Margaret Feng.
Midwest. Cynthia Hsieh.
Northeast. Karen Hsu.
Southwest. Cecilia Wang.

Journal Officers

Newsletter Eds. Ingrid Hsieh-Yee, 910 Primrose Rd., Apt. 203, Annapolis, MD 21403. Tel. 301-263-9335; May Chan Rathbone, Univ. of Washington Libs., FM-25, Seattle, WA 98195. Tel. 206-543-1760.

Church and Synagogue Library Association

Executive Director, Lorraine E. Burson
Box 19357, Portland, OR 97280-0357
503-244-6919

Object

"To act as a unifying core for the many existing church and synagogue libraries; to provide the opportunity for a mutual sharing of practices and problems; to inspire and encourage a sense of purpose and mission among church and synagogue librarians; to study and guide the development of church and synagogue librarianship toward recognition as a formal branch of the library profession." Founded 1967. Dues (Inst.) $100; (Affiliated) $50; (Church/Synagogue) $30; (Indiv.) $16. Year. July 1991–June 1992.

Officers (July 1991–June 1992)

Pres. E. Ruth Schneider, 1736 Juniper Dr., No. 199, Bowling Green, OH 43402; *1st V.P./ Pres.-Elect.* Joyce Allen, 3815 N. Bolton Ave., Indianapolis, IN 46226; *2nd V.P. Memb. and Public Relations.* Cheri Grout, 132 Foxwood Dr., Brownsburg, IN 46112; *Treas.* Lois S. Seyfrit, 15923 Yukon Lane, Derwood, MD 20855; *Past Pres.* Vera G. Hunter, 5511 First St. N.E., Washington, DC 20011; *Publications Ed.* Lorraine E. Burson, Box 19357, Portland, OR 97280-0357.

Executive Board

Officers; committee chairpersons.

Publications

Basic Book List for Church Libraries, 4th rev. ed. Bernard E. Deitrick (nonmemb. $5.95).
Church and Synagogue Libraries (bi-mo.; memb.; nonmemb. $18; Canada $21). *Ed.* Lorraine E. Burson.
Church and Synagogue Library Resources, 5th rev. *ed.* Dorothy Rodda (nonmemb. $5.95).
CSLA Guide No. 1. Setting Up a Library: How to Begin or Begin Again (nonmemb. $5.95).

CSLA Guide No. 2, 2nd rev. ed. *Promotion Planning All Year Round* (nonmemb. $5.95).
CSLA Guide No. 3, rev. ed. *Workshop Planning* (nonmemb. $8).
CSLA Guide No. 4, rev. ed. *Selecting Library Materials* (nonmemb. $4.75).
CSLA Guide No. 5. Cataloging Made Easy (nonmemb. $8.35).
CSLA Guide No. 6. Standards for Church and Synagogue Libraries (nonmemb. $5.95).
CSLA Guide No. 7. Classifying Church or Synagogue Library Materials (nonmemb. $5.95).
CSLA Guide No. 8. Subject Headings for Church or Synagogue Libraries (nonmemb. $8.35).
CSLA Guide No. 9. A Policy and Procedure Manual for Church and Synagogue Libraries (nonmemb. $4.75).
CSLA Guide No. 10. Archives in the Church or Synagogue Library (nonmemb. $5.95).
CSLA Guide No. 11. Planning Bulletin Boards for Church and Synagogue Libraries (nonmemb. $8.35).
CSLA Guide No. 12. Getting the Books Off the Shelves: Making the Most of Your Congregation's Library (nonmemb. $9).
CSLA Guide No. 13. The ABC's of Financing Church and Synagogue Libraries: Acquiring Funds, Budgeting, Cash Accounting (nomemb. $7.25).
CSLA Guide No. 14. Recruiting and Training Volunteers for Church and Synagogue Libraries (nonmemb. $7.25).
CSLA Guide No. 15. Providing Reference Service in Church and Synagogue Libraries (nonmemb. $8.35).
CSLA Guide No. 16. The Bible in Church and Synagogue Libraries (nonmemb. $7.25).
The Family Uses the Library. Leaflet (15 cents; nonmemb. $8.50/100).
Helping Children Through Books: Annotated Bibliography, 3rd rev. ed. (nonmemb. $7.25).
Know Your Neighbor's Faith: An Annotated Interfaith Bibliography (nonmemb. $4.75).

Religious Books for Children: An Annotated Bibliography, rev. ed. (nonmemb. $8.35).
The Teacher and the Library, a Partnership. Leaflet (15 cents; nonmemb. $8.50/100).

Committee Chairpersons

Awards. Lottie Kula.
Chapters. Maryann Dotts.

Continuing Education. Elsie Lehman.
Finance and Fund Raising. Emil Hirsch.
Library Services. Diane van Naerssen.
Nominations and Elections. Naomi Kauffman.
Personnel. Vera G. Hunter.
Publications. Arthur W. Swarthout.

Council of National Library and Information Associations

1700 18th St. N.W., Washington, DC 20009

Object

To provide a central agency for cooperation among library/information associations and other professional organizations of the United States and Canada in promoting matters of common interest.

Membership

Open to national library/information associations and organizations with related interests of the United States and Canada. American Assn. of Law Libs.; American Lib. Assn.; American Society of Indexers; American Theological Lib. Assn.; Art Libs. Society of North America; Assn. of Christian Libns.; Assn. of Jewish Libs.; Catholic Lib. Assn.; Chinese-American Libns. Assn.; Church and Synagogue Lib. Assn.; Council of Planning Libns.; Lib. Binding Institute; Lutheran Church Lib. Assn.; Medical Lib. Assn.; Music Lib. Assn.; National Libns. Assn.; Society of American Archivists; Special Libs. Assn.; Theatre Lib. Assn.

Officers (June 1991–June 1992)

Chpn. David Bender, Special Libs. Assn., 1700 18th St. N.W., Washington, DC 20009; *V.Chpn./Chpn.-Elect.* Kathleen Haefliger, 954 Galen Dr., State College, University Park, PA 16803; *Past Chpn.* D. Sherman Clarke, Amon Carter Museum, Box 2365, Fort Worth, TX 76113; *Secy./Treas.* Marie Melton, RSM, Saint John's Univ. Lib., Rm. 322, Grand Central and Utopia Pkwys., Jamaica, NY 11439.

Directors

Muriel Regan, Gossage Regan Associates, 25 W. 43 St., Suite 810–812, New York, NY 10036 (1991–1994); Madeline Taylor, George F. Smith Lib., Univ. of Medicine and Dentistry of New Jersey, 30 12th Ave., Newark, NJ 07103 (1989–1992); Susan Watkins, 29 Beach St., Wollaston, MA 02170 (1990–1993).

Council of Planning Librarians

Publications Office, 1313 E. 60 St., Chicago, IL 60637-2897
312-947-2163

Object

To provide a special interest group in the field of city and regional planning for libraries and librarians, faculty, professional planners, university, government, and private planning organizations; to provide an opportunity for exchange among those interested in problems of library organization and research and in the dissemination of information about city and regional planning; to sponsor programs of service to the planning profession and librarianship; to advise on library organization for new planning programs; and to aid and support administrators, faculty, and librarians in their efforts to educate the public and their appointed or elected representatives to the necessity for strong library programs in support of planning. Founded 1960. Memb. 242. Dues (Inst.) $45; (Indiv.) $25; (Student) $15. Year. July 1–June 30.

Membership

Open to any individual or institution that supports the purpose of the council, upon written application and payment of dues to the treasurer.

Officers (1991–1992)

Pres. M. Kay Mowery, Univ. of Georgia, Experiment Sta., Griffin, GA 30223-1797; *V.P./Pres.-Elect.* Thelma Helyar, Univ. of Kansas, Institute for Public Policy and Business Research, 607 Blake Hall, Lawrence, KS 66045-2960; *Secy.* Anna S. Sanchez, Tucson Planning Dept., Box 27210, Tucson, AZ 85726; *Treas.* Gretchen F. Beal, Knoxville–Know County Metropolitan Planning Commission, 400 Main Ave., Knoxville, TN 37902.

Publications

CPL Bibliographies (approx. 20 published per year) may be purchased on standing order or by individual issue. Catalog sent upon request. The following is only a partial list of publications:

No. 253. *An Annotated Bibliography and Index Covering CPL Bibliographies 1–253, January 1979–December 1989.* Patricia Coatsworth, Mary Ravenhall, and James Hecimovich ($20).

No. 254. *Automation in Local Government: A Partially Annotated Bibliography.* Elaine Gray ($16).

No. 255. *Planning in Rural and Small Town Communities: A Partially Annotated Bibliography.* Dennis A. Jenks ($16).

No. 256. *Government Information Sources for Architecture and Planning Research: Selected California, U.S., and International Documents.* Charles Eckman ($12).

No. 257. *Siting of Powerlines and Communication Towers: A Bibliography on the Po-*

tential Health Effects of Electric and Magnetic Fields. Lynne De Merritt ($16).

No. 258. *International Labor Migration: Bibliography.* Peter V. Schaefer ($16).

No. 259. *There Goes the Neighborhood . . . A Summary of Studies Addressing the Most Often Expressed Fears about the Effects of Group Homes in Neighborhoods in Which They Are Placed.* Community Residences Information Services Program ($16).

No. 260. *Venture Capital: A Select Bibliography for Professional Planners, Policy-Makers, and the Interested Lay Person.* Chris Thompson and Kristin Bayer ($16).

No. 261. *Groundwater: Overview of Issues, a Partially Annotated Bibliography.* Elaine Gray ($16).

No. 262. *Urban Planning in Latin America: Lessons from the 1980s.* Christine Cook ($16).

No. 263. *The Role of Service Industries in Rural Economic Development.* Amy Glasmeier and Gayle Borchard ($16).

No. 264. *Mediation and Negotiation for Planning, Land Use Management, and Environmental Protection: An Annotated Bibliography of Materials for the Period 1980–1989.* Richard G. RuBino and Harvey M. Jacobs ($20).

No. 265. *Wetlands: An Overview of the Issues.* Elaine Gray ($12).

No. 266. *Industry, the Environment, and Corporate Social Responsibility: A Selected and Annotated Bibliography.* Sonia Labatt ($16).

No. 267. *Airborne Radioactive Emissions from Nuclear Facilities: A Bibliography.* Frederick Frankena and Joann Koelln Frankena ($16).

No. 268. *Geographic Information Systems: A Partially Annotated Bibliography.* Michael A. Wilson ($16).

No. 269. *Survey Research.* Richard Langendorf ($16).

No. 270. *Fair Share Housing: A Partially Annotated Bibliography.* Judith Brownlow ($16).

No. 271. *Planning in Scandinavia: An Annotated Bibliography of English Language Materials Published 1980–1989.* Mary D. Ravenhall ($16).

No. 272. *Mail Surveys: A Comprehensive Bibliography 1974–1989.* Don A. Dillman and Roberta L. Sangster ($16).

No. 273. *Housing in Developing Countries: A Select Bibliography and Field Statement.* Ayse Pamuk ($16).

No. 274. *Where to Find Employment Advertisements for Planners: An Annotated Bib-* *liography of Journal Titles.* Deborah German and others. ($10).

No. 275. *Pedestrian and Street Life Bibliography.* David R. Hill and Leslie Ragan ($16).

Council on Library Resources

1785 Massachusetts Ave. N.W., Suite 313, Washington, DC 20036
202-483-7474, FAX 202-483-6410

Object

A private operating foundation, the Council seeks to assist in finding solutions to the problems of libraries, particularly academic and research libraries. In pursuit of this aim, the Council conducts its own projects, makes grants to and contracts with other organizations and individuals, and calls upon many others for advice and assistance with its work. The Council was established in 1956 by the Ford Foundation, and it now receives support from a number of private foundations and other sources. Current program emphases include research and analysis; improvement of library operations and management; and librarianship and professional education.

Membership

The Council's membership and board of directors is limited to 25.

Officers

Chpn. Maximilian Kempner; *V.Chpn.* Charles Churchwell; *Pres.* W. David Penniman; *Secy.-Treas.* Mary Agnes Thompson.

Address correspondence to headquarters.

Publications

Annual Report.
CLR Reports (newsletter).

Federal Library and Information Center Committee

Executive Director, Mary Berghaus Levering
Library of Congress, Washington, DC 20540
202-707-4800

Object

The Committee makes recommendations on federal library and information policies, programs, and procedures to federal agencies and to others concerned with libraries and information centers.

The Committee coordinates cooperative activities and services among federal libraries and information centers and serves as a forum to consider (1) issues and policies that affect federal libraries and information centers, (2) needs and priorities in providing information services to the government and to the nation at large, and (3) efficient and cost-effective use of federal library and information resources and services.

Furthermore, the Committee promotes (1) improved access to information, (2) continued development and use of the Federal Library and Information Network (FEDLINK), (3) research and development in the application of new technologies to federal libraries and information centers, (4) improvements in the management of federal libraries and information centers, and (5) relevant education opportunities. Founded 1965.

Membership

Libn. of Congress, Dir. of the National Agricultural Lib., Dir. of the National Lib. of Medicine, representatives from each of the other executive departments, and representatives from each of the following agencies: National Aeronautics and Space Admin., National Science Foundation, Smithsonian Institution, U.S. Supreme Court, U.S. Info. Agency, National Archives and Records Admin., Admin. Offices of the U.S. Courts, Defense Technical Info. Center, Government Printing Office, National Technical Info. Service, and Office of Scientific and Technical Info. (Dept. of Energy), Executive Office of the President, Department of the Army, Department of the Navy, Department of the Air Force, and chairperson of the FEDLINK Advisory Council. Fifteen additional voting member agencies shall be selected on a rotating basis by the voting members of FEDLINK and nine rotating members through selection by the permanent members of the Committee. These rotating members will serve three terms. One representative from each of the following agencies is invited as an observer to committee meetings: General Accounting Office, General Services Admin., Joint Committee on Printing, National Commission on Libs. and Info. Science, Office of Manage-

ment and Budget, Office of Personnel Management, and Library of Congress Financial Services Directorate.

Officers

Chpn. James H. Billington, Libn. of Congress; *Chpn. Designate.* Donald C. Curran, Assoc. Libn. for Constituent Services, Lib. of Congress; *Exec. Dir.* Mary Berghaus Levering, Federal Lib. and Info. Center Committee, Lib. of Congress, Washington, DC 20540.

Address correspondence to the executive director.

Publications

Annual FLICC Forum on Federal Information Policies (summary and papers).
Annual Report (Oct.).
FEDLINK Technical Notes (mo.).
FLICC Newsletter (q.).

Federal Publishers Committee

Chairperson, John Weiner
Energy Information Administration, EI-23, Mail Sta. 2H087,
1000 Independence Ave. S.W., Washington, DC 20585
202-586-6537, FAX 202-586-0114

Object

To foster and promote effective management of data development and dissemination in the federal government through exchange of information and to act as a focal point for federal agency publishing.

Membership

Membership is available to persons involved in publishing and dissemination in federal government departments, agencies, and corporations, as well as independent organizations concerned with federal government publishing and dissemination. Some key federal government organizations represented are

the Joint Committee on Printing, Government Printing Office, National Technical Info. Service, National Commission on Libs. and Info. Sciences, and the Lib. of Congress. Meetings are held monthly during business hours. Memb. 650.

Officers

Chpn. John Weiner; *Secy.* Marilyn Marbrook.

Committee Chairpersons

Programs. Sandra Smith.
Task Force Activity. June Malina.

Information Industry Association

Public Relations Director, Susan E. Goewey
555 New Jersey Ave. N.W., Suite 800, Washington, DC 20001
202-639-8262

Membership

For details on membership and dues, write to the association headquarters. Memb. More than 460.

Staff

Pres. David C. Fullarton; *Senior V.P. Government Relations.* Kenneth B. Allen; *V.P. Memb.* Judith Angerman; *V.P. and Counsel, Government Relations.* Steven J. Metalitz; *Dir. Program Planning and Development.* Michael Atkin; *Dir. Memb. Services.* Carol Madden; *Systems Mgr.* Rebecca L. Lake; *Meetings Mgr.* Melissa Tancredi; *Communications Dir.* Kevin A. Siegel; *Dir. Global Business Development.* Robert A. Vitro; *Dir. Public Relations.* Susan Goewey; *Dir. of Admin.* Monna Heuer.

Board of Directors

Chpn. Phyllis B. Steckler, Oryx Press; *Chpn.- Elect.* John F. Hockenberry, Washington Post Company; *Past Chpn.* Thomas Pace, Dow Jones & Co.; *Treas.* Hugh J. Yarrington, Bureau of National Affaris; *Secy.* Andrew Prozes, Southam Business Communications, Inc.; *V.Chpns.* Matilda Butler, Knowledge Access International; Lawrence L. Wills, IBM Corp.; Steven Graham, AT&T; Linda Laskowski, US West Communications; Peggy Miller, Prodigy Services; Joseph C. Rhyne, Mead Data Central; Peter F. Urbach, Reed Publishing (USA); William Whitenack, Dun & Bradstreet Credit Services; *Membs.* William P. Giglio, McGraw-Hill Inc.; Thomas J. McLeod, West Publishing Co.; Michael J.

Timbers, Information Handling Service; Thomas Haley, New York Stock Exchange; *Ex officio. Counsel.* Peter A. Marx, Marx Group.

Division Chairpersons

Database and Publishing. J. Parke Malcolm, Univ. Microfilms International.
Electronic Services. Mark Walsh, CUC On-line Services.
Financial Information Services. W. Leo McBlain, ADP Brokerage Info. Services.
Voice Information Services. Peter Brennan, Optima Direct.

Council Chairpersons

Global Business Development. Wayne G. Moran, Mortek Group.
Management and Technology. William Giglio, McGraw-Hill.
Public Policy and Government Relations. Michael Brewer, Dun & Bradstreet.

Publications

Artificial Intelligence: Reality or Fantasy?
Contracts in the Information Industry I (1989).
Contracts in the Information Industry II (1990).
European Multimedia Yearbook '92.
The Information Millennium: Alternative Futures (1986).
Information Sources (1992).
The Second Generation of CD-ROM (1990).
Strategic Information Systems (1988).
Valuing and Financing Information Companies (1989).

International Council of Library Association Executives

President, Bonnie Beth Mitchell, Exec. Dir., Ohio Lib. Assn.,
67 Jefferson Ave., Columbus, OH 43215
614-221-9057

Object

"To provide an opportunity for the exchange of information, experience, and opinion on a continuing basis through discussion, study and publication; to promote the arts and sciences of educational association management; and to develop and encourage high standards of professional conduct." Conducts workshops and institutes; offers specialized education.

Membership

Membership is available to chief paid executives engaged in the management of library associations. Founded 1975. Dues $25. Year. July 1–June 30.

Officers (July 1991–June 1992)

Pres. Bonnie Beth Mitchell, Exec. Dir., Ohio Lib. Assn., 67 Jefferson Ave., Columbus, OH 43215. Tel. 614-221-9057; *Secy./Treas.* Margaret S. Bauer, Exec. Dir., Pennsylvania Lib. Assn., 3107 N. Front St., Harrisburg, PA 17110. Tel. 717-233-3113; *Past Pres.* Mary Sue Ferrell, Exec. Dir., California Lib. Assn., 717 K St., Suite 300, Sacramento, CA 95814. Tel. 916-447-8541.

Meetings

Two meetings are held annually in conjunction with those of the American Library Association in January and June. Elections are held during the June meeting.

Lutheran Church Library Association

Executive Director, Leanna D. Kloempken
122 W. Franklin Ave., Minneapolis, MN 55404
612-870-3623

Object

"To promote the growth of church libraries by publishing a quarterly journal, *Lutheran Libraries*; furnishing booklists; assisting member libraries with technical problems; and providing meetings for mutual encouragement, assistance, and exchange of ideas among members." Founded 1958. Memb. 1,800. Dues $25, $37.50, $50, $75, $100, $500, $1,000. Year. Jan.–Jan.

Officers (Jan. 1991–Jan. 1993)

Pres. Elaine Hanson, 1928 Limetree Lane, Mountain View, CA 94040; *V.P.* Robert Kruger, 15180 County Rd. 40, Carver, MN 55315; *Secy.* Gloria Landborg, 1109 W. 37 St., Sioux Falls, SD 57105; *Treas.* Marilyn Anderson, 5328 51st Ave. N., Minneapolis, MN 55429.

Address correspondence to the executive director.

Directors

O. G. Beckstrand II, Lucille Christianson, Paul Dahlberg, Virgie Erickson, Ardis Jordahl, Vernita Kennen, Hazel Woodruff.

Publication

Lutheran Libraries (q.; memb.; nonmemb. $20). *Ed.* Ron Klug, 1115 S. Division St., Northfield, MN 55057.

Board Chairpersons

Advisory. Rev. Rolf Aaseng, 2450 Cavell Ave. S., Minneapolis, MN 55426.

Council of National Library and Information Associations. Wilma W. Jensen, 3620 Fairlawn Dr., Minnetonka, MN 55345.

Finance. Rev. Carl Manfred, 5227 Oaklawn Ave., Minneapolis, MN 55436.

Library Services Board. Betty LeDell, Grace Lutheran of Deephaven, 15800 Sunset Dr., Minnetonka, MN 55343.

Membership. Lorraine Setterlund, 1403 S.W. Second St., New Brighton, MN 55112.

Publications Board. Rod Olson, Augsburg Publishing House, 426 S. Fifth, Box 1209, Minneapolis, MN 55440.

Medical Library Association

Executive Director, Carla Funk
6 N. Michigan Ave., Suite 300, Chicago, IL 60602
312-419-9094

Object

The Medical Library Association was founded in 1898 and incorporated in 1934. MLA's major purposes are (1) to foster medical and allied scientific libraries, (2) to promote the educational and professional growth of health science librarians, and (3) to exchange medical literature among the members. Through its programs and publications, MLA encourages professional development of its membership, whose foremost concern is dissemination of health sciences information for those in research, education, and patient care.

Membership

MLA has 1,500 institutional members and 3,500 individual members. Institutional members are medical and allied scientific libraries. Institutional member dues are based on the number of subscriptions: (up to 199) $175; (200–299) $235; (300–599) $285; (600–999) $345; (1,000 +) $410. Individual MLA members are people who are (or were at the time membership was established) engaged in professional library or bibliographic work in medical and allied scientific libraries or people who are interested in medical or allied scientific libraries. Dues (Indiv.) $105; (Emeritus) $45; (Sustaining) $345.

Officers

Pres. Richard A. Lyders, Houston Academy of Medicine, Texas Medical Center Lib., 1133 M. D. Anderson Blvd., Houston, TX 77030; *Pres.-Elect.* Jacqueline D. Bastille, Treadwell Lib., Massachusetts General Hospital, Fruit St., Boston, MA 02114; *Past Pres.* Lucretia

W. McClure, Edward G. Miner Lib., Univ. of Rochester School of Medicine and Dentistry, 601 Elmwood Ave., Rochester, NY 14642.

Directors

(1989–1992) Carol G. Jenkins, Julia Sollenberger; (1990–1993) Jacqueline D. Doyle, Carolyn Anne Reid, Mary L. Ryan, Joan S. Zenan; (1991–1994) Karen Brewer, Frances A. Bischoff McNeely.

Publications

Bulletin of the Medical Library Association (q.; $130).

Current Catalog Proof Sheets (w. plus mo. index; $140).

Handbook of Medical Library Practice, vols. 1–3 ($80; nonmemb. $100).

Hospital Library Management ($56; nonmemb. $70).

Introduction to Reference Sources in the Health Sciences ($20.40; nonmemb. $27.20).

MEDLINE: A Basic Guide to Searching ($19.20; nonmemb. $25.60).

MLA Directory (ann.; $39.50; nonmemb. $43.75).

MLA News (10 per year; $46).

Miscellaneous others (request current list from association headquarters).

Standing Committee Chairpersons

Awards. Mary Ann Hoffman, Fordham Health Sciences Lib., Wright State Univ., School of Medicine, Box 927, Dayton, OH 45401-0927.

Books Panel. Daniel T. Richards, Dana Biomedical Lib., Dartmouth-Hitchcock Medical Center, Hanover, NH 03756.

Bulletin Consulting Editors Panel. Naomi C. Broering, Dahlgren Memorial Lib., Georgetown Univ., Medical Center, Pre-clinical Science Bldg., 3900 Reservoir Rd. N.W., Washington, DC 20007.

Bulletin Evaluation. Debra S. Ketchell, Health Sciences Lib. SB-55, Univ. of Washington, Seattle, WA 98195.

Bylaws. James A. Curtis, Health Sciences Lib., Univ. of North Carolina, CB 7585, Chapel Hill, NC 27599-7585.

Continuing Education. Gale A. Dutcher, National Lib. of Medicine, 8600 Rockville Pike, Bethesda, MD 20894.

Credentialing. M. Sandra Wood, George T. Harrell Lib., Milton S. Hershey Medical Center, Pennsylvania State Univ., Box 850, Hershey, PA 17033.

Exchange Advisory. Mary J. Jarvis, Medical Lib., Methodist Hospital, 3615 19th St., Lubbock, TX 79410.

Executive. Richard A. Lyders, Houston Academy of Medicine, Texas Medical Center Lib., 1133 M. D. Anderson Blvd., Houston, TX 77030.

Finance. Joan S. Zenan, Savitt Medical Lib., Univ. of Nevada, School of Medicine, c/o Rosalyn Casey, Reno, NV 89557-0046.

Governmental Relations. June Glaser, Basil G. Bibby Lib., Eastman Dental Center, 625 Elmwood Ave., Rochester, NY 14620.

Grants and Scholarship. Janet Minnerath, Medical Lib., Univ. of Oklahoma, College of Medicine, 2808 S. Sheridan, Tulsa, OK 74129.

Health Sciences Library Technicians. Van B. Afes, Louis Calder Memorial Lib., Univ. of Miami School of Medicine, Box 016950, Miami, FL 33101.

Hospital Libraries. Phyllis C. Gillikin, Northwest AHEC Lib. at Hickory, Catawba Memorial Hospital, 810 Fairgrove Church Rd., Hickory, NC 28602-9643.

Joseph Leiter NLM/MLA Lectureship. Lois Ann Colaianni, National Lib. of Medicine, 8600 Rockville Pike, Bethesda, MD 20894.

Membership. Gail A. Yokote, UCLA Biomedical Lib., Center for the Health Sciences, 10833 Le Conte Ave., Los Angeles, CA 90024-1798; Rosanne Labree, Mental Health Sciences Lib., McLean Hospital, 115 Mill St., Belmont, MA 02178.

National Program (1992). Pamela Jean Jajko, Lib. and Info. Center, El Camino Hospital, 2500 Grant Rd., Box 7025, Mountain View, CA 94039-7025.

National Program (1993). Rick B. Forsman, Denison Memorial Lib., Univ. of Colorado Health Science Center, 4200 E. Ninth Ave., Denver, CO 80262.

News Evaluation. Ellen R. Cooper, Solvay Pharmaceuticals Lib., 901 Sawyer Rd., Marietta, GA 30062.

Nominating. Jacqueline D. Bastille, Treadwell Lib., Massachusetts General Hospital, Fruit St., Boston, MA 02114.

Profession Recognition Review Panel. Julie Kuenzel Kwan, Science and Engineering Lib., Univ. of Southern California, University Park, Los Angeles, CA 90089-0481.

Publications. Connie Poole, Medical Lib., Southern Illinois Univ., School of Medicine, Box 19231, Springfield, IL 62794-9231.

Publishing and Information Industries Relations. Leonoor Ingraham-Swets, Lewis O. Cannell Lib., Clark College, 1800 E. McLoughlin Blvd., Vancouver, WA 98663.

Status and Economic Interests of Health Sciences Library Personnel. Dorothy A. Spencer, Kauffman Lib., California School of Professional Psychology, 1350 M St., Fresno, CA 93721.

Ad Hoc Committees

Committee to Establish Cunningham Endowment. Robert G. Cheshier, Cleveland Health Science Lib., 2119 Abington Rd., Cleveland, OH 44106-4914.

Joint MLA/AAHSLD Legislative Task Force. Carol G. Jenkins, Health Sciences Lib., Univ. of North Carolina at Chapel Hill, Box 7585, Chapel Hill, NC 27599-7585.

Second White House Conference on Library and Information Services (WHCLIS) Task Force. June Glaser, Basil G. Bibby Lib., Eastman Dental Center, 625 Elmwood Ave., Rochester, NY 14620.

Task Force on Knowledge and Skills. Fred W. Roper, College of Lib. and Info. Science,

Univ. of South Carolina, Columbia, SC 29208.

Representatives

American Association for the Advancement of Science, Section T: Information, Computing and Communication, Consortium of Affiliates for International Programs. Susan Crawford.
American Association of Colleges of Pharmacy, Inc., Librarians Section. Nancy F. Fuller.
American Library Association Coalition of Organizations for the Public Good. Maxine A. Hanke.
American Library Association, Committee on Cataloging, Description, and Access. Steven J. Squires.
American Library Association, Reference and Adult Services Division, Interlibrary Loan Committee. Susan T. Lyon.
American Medical Informatics Association. Mary M. Horres.
Association of Academic Health Sciences Library Directors. Logan Ludwig.
Canadian Health Libraries Association/Association des Bibliothèques de la Santé du Canada. Edean Berglund.
CNLIA Ad Hoc Committee on Copyright Law, Practice, and Implementation. Lucretia W. McClure; (*Alternate*) Raymond A. Palmer.

Continuing Library Education Network and Exchange. Reneta Webb.
Copyright Society. Lucretia W. McClure.
Council of National Library and Information Associations, Inc. Judie Malamud.
Documentation Abstracts, Inc., Board of Directors. Karen L. Brewer; (*Alternate*) Mark E. Funk.
European Association for Health Information and Libraries. Susan Crawford.
Friends of the National Library of Medicine, Board of Directors. Lucretia W. McClure, Nancy M. Lorenzi, Raymond A. Palmer.
Interagency Council on Library Resources for Nursing. Jacqueline L. Picciano; (*Alternate*) Dawn Bick.
International Federation of Library Associations and Institutions. Raymond A. Palmer.
National Information Standards Organization. Rick B. Forsman.
Network Advisory Committee to the Library of Congress. Erika Love; (*Alternate*) Peter Stangl.
North American Serials Interest Group. Barbara A. Carlson.
Patient Education in the Primary Care Setting (Annual Conference). Carolyn Ruby.
Symposium on Computer Applications in Medical Care. (No individual representative.)
White House Conference on Library and Information Services II. June Glaser.

Miniature Book Society, Inc.

President, Robert E. Massmann
478 Glen St., New Britain, CT 06051
203-223-5009

Object

Miniature books are those classified as three inches tall or less. The Miniature Book Society, Inc. is a nonprofit organization chartered in 1983 by the State of Ohio. Its purposes are to sustain an interest in all phases of miniature books; to provide a forum for the exchange of ideas; and to serve as a clearinghouse for information about miniature books. Memb.

475. Dues (U.S.) Single, $25; Couples/Corporate, $35; (Foreign) Single, $40; Couples/Corporate, $50. Year. Jan. 1–Dec. 31.

Officers

Pres. Robert E. Massman, 478 Glen St., New Britain, CT 06051; *V.P.* Eileen Beth Cummings, 405 W. Washington St., No. 22, San

Diego, CA 92103; *Secy.* Richard M. Childs, 5800 Windsor Dr., Fairway, KS 66205; *Treas.* Rev. Joseph L. Curran, Box 127, Sudbury, MA 01776.

Directors

Arthur A. Kier, 506 Buell Ave., Joliet, IL 60435; Ian Macdonald, 11 Low Rd., Castlehead, Paisley PA2 6AQ, Scotland; Doris

Selmer, 55 E. Arthur Ave., Arcadia, CA 91006; Mae Hightower-Vandamm, 2207 Highland Pl., Wilmington, DE 19805.

Publication

Miniature Book Society Newsletter (q.), *Ed.* Donn W. Sanford, 28350 Brandenburg Rd., Ingleside, IL 60041.

Music Library Association

Box 487, Canton, MA 02021
617-828-8450, FAX 617-828-8915

Object

"To promote the establishment, growth, and use of music libraries; to encourage the collection of music and musical literature in libraries; to further studies in musical bibliography; to increase efficiency in music library service and administration; and to promote the profession of music librarianship." Founded 1931. Memb. about 1,900. Dues (Inst.) $65; (Indiv.) $50; (Student) $25. Year. Sept. 1–Aug. 31.

Officers

Pres. Don L. Roberts, Music Lib., Northwestern Univ., Evanston, IL 60208-2300; *Past Pres.* Susan T. Sommer, N.Y. Public Lib., 111 Amsterdam Ave., New York, NY 10023; *Rec. Secy.* Nancy Bren Nuzzo, 68 Hillside Dr., Williamsville, NY 14221; *Treas.* Diane Parr Walker, 1437 Rugby Ave., Charlottesville, VA 22901-3848; *Exec. Secy.* A. Ralph Papakhian, Music Lib., Indiana Univ., Bloomington, IN 47405.

Members-at-Large

(1990–1992) Joseph M. Boonin, Jerona Music Corp.; Joan Swanekamp, Eastman School of Music, Univ. of Rochester; Ross Wood, Wellesley College; (1991–1993) James P. Cassaro, Cornell Univ.; Jane Gottlieb, Julliard School; Sherry L. Vellucci, Westminster Choir College.

Special Officers

Business Mgr. James S. P. Henderson, Box 487, Canton, MA 02021.
Convention Mgr. Christine Hoffman, N.Y. Public Lib., 111 Amsterdam Ave., New York, NY 10023.
Placement. Paula D. Matthews, Bates College, Ladd Lib., Lewiston, ME 04240.
Publicity. Richard E. Jones, 1904 Sandlewood Dr., Greencastle, IN 46135-9214.

Publications

MLA Index Series (irreg.; price varies).
MLA Newsletter (q.; memb.).
MLA Technical Reports (irreg.; price varies).
Music Cataloging Bulletin (mo.; $20).
Notes (q.; indiv. $45; inst. $60).

Committee Chairpersons

Administration. Carol Tatian, Brown Univ. Tel. 401-863-3999.
Awards and Publications. Harold Diamond, Lehman College; Walter Gerboth Award. Maria Calderisi, National Lib. of Canada. Tel. 613-996-7514.
Bibliographic Control. J. Bradford Young, Univ. of Pennsylvania. Tel. 215-898-6715.
Development. Geraldine Ostrove, Music Div., Lib. of Congress. Tel. 202-707-5503.
Education. Laura Dankner, Loyola Univ., New Orleans. Tel. 504-865-2367.
Finance. Gordon Theil, UCLA Music Lib. Tel. 213-825-4882.

Legislation. Mary Davidson, Sibley Music Lib., Rochester, NY. Tel. 716-274-1350.
Nominating. Richard Griscom, Univ. of Louisville. Tel. 502-588-5659.
Preservation. John Shepard, N.Y. Public Lib. Tel. 212-870-1654.
Public Libraries. Richard Schwegel, Chicago Public Lib. Tel. 312-269-2886.

Publications. Ruth Henderson, City Univ. of N.Y. Tel. 212-690-4174.
Reference and Public Service. Judy Tsou, Univ. of California, Berkeley. Tel. 415-643-6197.
Resource Sharing and Collection Development. John H. Roberts, Univ. of California, Berkeley. Tel. 415-642-2428.

National Association of Government Archives and Records Administrators

Executive Secretary, Bruce W. Dearstyne
New York State Archives
10A46 Cultural Education Center, Albany, NY 12230
518-473-8037

Object

Founded in 1984, the Association is successor to the National Association of State Archives and Records Administrators, which had been established in 1974. NAGARA is a growing nationwide association of local, state, and federal archivists and records administrators, and others interested in improved care and management of government records. NAGARA promotes public awareness of government records and archives management programs, encourages interchange of information among government archives and records management agencies, develops and implements professional standards of government records and archival administration, and encourages study and research into records management problems and issues. NAGARA is an adjunct member of the Council of State Governments.

Membership

State archival and records management agencies are NAGARA's sustaining members, but individual membership is open to local governments, federal agencies, and to any individual or organization interested in improved government records programs.

Officers

Pres. Ron Tryon, South Carolina Dept. of Archives and History; *V.P.* Edwin C. Bridges, Alabama Dept. of Archives and History; *Secy.* Brenda Banks, Georgia Dept. of Archives and History; *Treas.* James Moore, Western Washington Univ.

Publications

Clearinghouse (q.; memb.).
Government Records Issues (series).
Information Clearinghouse Needs of the Archival Profession (report).
Preservation Needs in State Archives (report).
Program Reporting Guidelines for Government Records Programs.

National Information Standards Organization

Executive Director, Patricia Harris
Box 1056, Bethesda, MD 20827
301-975-2814, FAX 301-869-8071

Object

To develop technical standards used in libraries, publishing, and information services. Experts from the information field volunteer to lend their expertise in the development and writing of NISO standards. The standards are approved by the consensus of NISO's voting membership, which consists of 65 voting members representing libraries, government, associations, and private businesses and organizations. NISO is supported by its membership and corporate grants. Formerly a committee of the American National Standards Institute (ANSI), NISO, formed in 1939, was incorporated in 1983 as a nonprofit educational organization. NISO is accredited by ANSI and serves as the U.S. Technical Advisory Group to ISO/TC 46.

Membership

Open to any organization, association, government agency, or company — national in scope — willing to participate in and having substantial concern for the development of NISO standards.

Officers

Chpn. James Rush, PALINET, Philadelphia, PA; *Past Chpn.* Paul Evan Peters, Coalition for Networked Information, Washington, DC; *V.Chpn./Chpn.-Elect.* Michael Mellinger, Data Research Associates, Saint Louis, MO; *Treas.* Heike Kordish, New York Public Lib., New York, NY; Lois Granick, American Psychological Assn., Arlington, VA; Bill Bartenbach, Engineering Information, New York, NY; Peter J. Paulson, OCLC–Forest Press, Albany, NY; Susan H. Vita, Lib. of Congress, Washington, DC; Shirley K. Baker, Washington Univ., Saint Louis, MO; Michael J. McGill, Ameritech Info. Systems, Dublin, OH; Lois Ann Colaianni, National Lib. of Medicine, Bethesda, MD; Connie Greaser, American Honda, Torrance, CA; Karen Runyan, Houghton Mifflin Co., Burlington, MA.

Publications

Information Standards Quarterly (q.; $40; foreign $50). *Ed.* Pat Ensor.
NISO Published Standards. List available from headquarters; order from Transaction Publishers, Order Dept., Rutgers Univ., New Brunswick, NJ 08903. Tel. 908-932-2280.

National Librarians Association

Secretary-Treasurer, Peter Dollard
Box 486, Alma, MI 48801

Object

"To promote librarianship, to develop and increase the usefulness of libraries, to cultivate the science of librarianship, to protect the interest of professionally qualified librarians, and to perform other functions necessary for the betterment of the profession of librarians, rather than as an association of libraries." Established 1975. Memb. 200. Dues $20/year;

$35/2 years; (Students, Retired, and Unemployed Libns.) $10. Floating membership year.

Membership

Any person interested in librarianship and libraries who holds a graduate degree in library science may become a member upon election by the executive board and payment of the annual dues. The executive board may authorize exceptions to the degree requirements for applicants who present evidence of outstanding contributions to the profession. Student membership is available to those graduate students enrolled full time at any ALA accredited library school.

Officers

Pres. Alvin Bailey, Denison (Texas) Public Library; *Secy.-Treas.* Peter Dollard.

Publication

National Librarian (q.; $15). *Ed.* Peter Dollard.

Society for Scholarly Publishing

10200 W. 44 Ave., Suite 304
Wheat Ridge, CO 80033
303-422-3914

Object

To draw together individuals involved in the process of scholarly publishing. This process requires successful interaction of the many functions performed within the scholarly community. SSP provides the leadership for such interaction by creating the opportunities for the exchange of information and opinions among scholars, editors, publishers, librarians, printers, booksellers, and all others engaged in scholarly publishing.

Membership

Open to all with an interest in scholarly publishing and information dissemination. There are four categories of membership: individual, $50; contributing, $250; sustaining (organizational), $500; and sponsoring, $1,500. Year. Jan. 1–Dec. 31.

Officers (July 1990–June 1992)

Pres. Judy C. Holoviak, American Geophysical Union, 2000 Florida Ave. N.W., Washington, DC 20009. Tel. 202-462-6900, Ext. 218, FAX 202-328-0566; *V.P.* Robert Shirrell, Univ. of Chicago Press, 5720 S. Woodlawn, Chicago, IL 60637. Tel. 312-702-8785, FAX 312-702-0694; *Secy.-Treas.* Michael Leonard, MIT Press, 55 Hayward St., Cambridge, MA 02142. Tel. 617-253-5250, FAX 617-258-6779.

Board of Directors

Officers; Arly Allen, Allen Press, Inc., 1041 New Hampshire, Lawrence, KS 66044. Tel. 913-843-1234, FAX 913-843-1244; Robert E. Baensch, Rizzoli International Publications, 300 Park Ave. S., New York, NY 10010. Tel. 212-387-3503, FAX 212-387-3535; Richard Dougherty, Mountainside Publications, Box 8330, Ann Arbor, MI 48109. Tel. 313-764-9376, FAX 313-764-2475; Karen Hunter, Elsevier Science Publications, 655 Sixth Ave., New York, NY 10010. Tel. 212-633-3787, FAX 212-633-3764; Edward Huth, 1124 Morris Ave., Bryn Mawr, PA 19010. Tel. 215-525-9494, FAX 215-525-7436; Christine Lamb, Little, Brown & Co., 34 Beacon St., Boston, MA 02108; Tel. 617-859-5645, FAX 617-859-0629; Robert H. Marks, Publications Div., American Chemical Society, 1155 16th St. N.W., Washington, DC 20036. Tel. 202-872-4556, FAX 202-872-6060; Herb Morton, 7106 Laverock Lane, Bethesda, MD 20817. Tel. 301-229-1718; Cynthia Smith, Aspen Publishers, 200 Orchard Ridge Dr., Gaithersburg, MD 20878. Tel. 301-417-7560, FAX 301-417-7550.

Committee Chairpersons

Annual Meeting. Patricia Scarry.
Budget and Finance. Chris Johnson.
Education. Barbara Meyers.
Executive. Judy Holoviak.
Membership. Sandra Whisler.
Nominations. Margaret Foti.
Planning. Robert Shirrell.
Publications. Mary Lane.

Meetings

An annual meeting is conducted in either May or June. The location changes each year.

Additionally, SSP conducts several seminars throughout the year.

Society of American Archivists

Executive Director, Anne P. Diffendal
600 S. Federal St., Suite 504, Chicago, IL 60605
312-922-0140

Object

"To promote sound principles of archival economy and to facilitate cooperation among archivists and archival agencies." Founded 1936. Memb. 4,600. Dues (Indiv.) $55–$155, graduated according to salary; (Assoc.) $55, domestic; (Student) $35, with a two-year maximum on membership; (Inst.) $200; (Sustaining) $400.

Officers (1991–1992)

Pres. Frank Burke, Univ. of Maryland; *V.P.* Anne Kenney, Cornell Univ.; *Treas.* William Maher, Univ. of Illinois at Champaign.

Council

Brenda Banks, Anne Van Camp, James Fogerty, Mary Janzen, Rand Jimerson, Waverly Lowell, James O'Toole, Robert Sink, William Wallach.

Staff

Exec. Dir. Anne P. Diffendal; *Memb. Asst.* Bernice E. Brack; *System Admin.* Jim Sauder; *Managing Ed.* Teresa Brinati; *Publns. Asst.* Troy Sturdivant; *Bookkeeper.* Ana Joyce; *Senior Archivist.* Jane Kenamore.

Publications

American Archivist (q.; $75; foreign $90). *Ed.* Richard Cox; *Managing Ed.* Teresa Brinati. Books for review and related correspondence should be addressed to the managing editor.
SAA Newsletter (6 per year; memb.). *Ed.* Teresa Brinati.

Special Libraries Association

Executive Director, David R. Bender
1700 18th St. N.W., Washington, DC 20009
202-234-4700, FAX 202-265-931

Object

"To provide an association of individuals and organizations having a professional, scientific, or technical interest in library and information science, especially as these are applied in the recording, retrieval, and dissemination of knowledge and information in areas such as the physical, biological, technical and social sciences, the humanities, and business; and to promote and improve the communication, dissemination, and use of such information and knowledge for the benefit of libraries or other educational organizations." Organized 1909. Memb. 13,000. Dues (Sustaining) $300; (Indiv.) $75; (Student) $15. Year. Jan.–Dec. or July–June.

Publications

Special Libraries (q.) and *SpeciaList* (mo.). Cannot be ordered separately ($60 for both; foreign $65). *Ed.* Maria Barry.

Officers (July 1991–June 1992)

Pres. Guy L. St. Clair, OPL Resources, 1701 16th St. N.W., Suite 644, Washington, DC 20009. Tel. 202-234-9824, FAX 202-234-9824; *Pres.-Elect.* Catherine D. Scott, Smithsonian Institution Libs., Central Reference and Loan Dept., NHB 27, Washington, DC 20560. Tel. 202-357-2139, FAX 202-786-2443; *Past Pres.* Ruth K. Seidman, Massachusetts Institute of Technology, Science and Engineering Libs., Rm. 10-500, Cambridge, MA 02139. Tel. 617-253-7741, FAX 617-258-5623; *Treas.* Richard E. Wallace, A. E. Staley Manufacturing Co., Technical Info. Center, 2200 Eldorado St., Decatur, IL 62525. Tel. 217-421-3283, FAX 217-421-2519; *Chapter Cabinet Chpn.* Marilyn Stark, U.S. Geological Survey Lib., MS 914, Box 25046, Denver Federal Center, Denver, CO 80225. Tel. 303-236-1004, FAX 303-236-0015; *Chapter Cabinet Chpn.-Elect.* Charlene M. Baldwin, Univ. of Arizona, Map Lib., Tucson, AZ 85721. Tel. 602-621-2610, FAX 602-621-9733; *Div. Cabinet Chpn.* Marjorie Hlava, Access Innovations, Box 40130, Albuquerque, NM 87196. Tel. 505-265-3591, FAX 505-256-1080; *Div. Cabinet Chpn.-Elect.* Marjorie A. Wilson, SRI International Lib., 333 Ravenswood Ave., Menlo Park, CA 94025. Tel. 415-859-5980, FAX 415-859-2936; *Secy.* L. Susan Hayes, Encore Computer Corp., MS 408, 6901 W. Sunrise Blvd., Fort Lauderdale, FL 33313. Tel. 305-797-5933, FAX 305-797-5940.

Directors

Officers; Mary E. Dickerson, Ontario Legislative Lib., Legislative Bldg., Queens Park, Toronto, ON M7A 1A2, Canada. Tel. 416-325-3940, FAX 416-325-3925; Elizabeth B. Eddison, Inmagic, 2067 Massachusetts Ave., Cambridge, MA 02140. Tel. 617-661-8124, FAX 617-661-6901; Beth Paskoff, Louisiana State Univ., School of Lib. and Info. Science, Baton Rouge, LA 70803. Tel. 504-388-1480, FAX 504-388-6400; Sylvia E. A. Piggott, Bank of Montreal, Business Info. Center, Box 6002, 129 Saint Jacques Place d'Armes, Montreal, PQ H2Y 3S8, Canada; Lois Webster, American Nuclear Society Lib., 555 N. Kensington Ave., La Grange Park, IL 60525. Tel. 708-352-6611, FAX 708-352-0499.

Committee Chairpersons

Affirmative Action. Nettie Seaberry, Reader's Digest, General Book Div., 260 Madison Ave., New York, NY 10016. Tel. 212-850-7043.

Association Office Operations. Guy St. Clair, OPL Resources, 1701 16th St. N.W., Suite 644, Washington, DC 20009. Tel. 202-234-9824.

Awards and Honors. Muriel B. Regan, Gossage Regan Associates, Inc., Suite 810-812, 25 W. 43 St., New York, NY 10036. Tel. 212-869-3348.

Bylaws. M. Kay Mowery, Univ. of Georgia, Georgia Experiment Sta. Lib., 1109 Experiment St., Griffin, GA 30223. Tel. 404-228-7238.

Cataloging. Stephanie D. Tolson, Saint Louis Community College, Instruction Resource Center, 5460 Highland Park Dr., Saint Louis, MO 63110. Tel. 314-652-5733.

Committee on Committees. Laura N. Gasaway, Univ. of North Carolina, Law Lib., CB 3385, Chapel Hill, NC 27599. Tel. 919-962-1049.

Conference Program Committee for 1992 (San Francisco). Barbara P. Semonche, Univ. of North Carolina, School of Journalism, Howell Hall CB 3365, Chapel Hill, NC 27599. Tel. 919-962-1204.

Conference Program Committee for 1993 (Cincinnati). Rebecca B. Vargha, National Humanities Center Libs., 7 Alexander Dr., Research Triangle Park, NC 27709. Tel. 919-549-0661.

Consultation Services. E. Louisa Worthington, Schering & Plough Lib., E25-131, Massachusetts Institute of Technology, 77 Massachusetts Ave., Cambridge, MA 02139. Tel. 617-253-6575.

Copyright Law Implementation. Sally Wiant, Washington and Lee Univ., Lewis Hall, Lexington, VA 24450.

Finance. Richard E. Wallace, A. E. Staley Manufacturing Co., Technology Info. Center, 2200 Eldorado St., Decatur, IL 62525. Tel. 217-423-4411.

Government Relations. Lynne K. McCay, Lib. of Congress, Congressional Research Service, Washington, DC 20540. Tel. 202-707-1415.

International Relations. Katherine M. Richards, 1505 Purdue Ave. No. 301, Los Angeles, CA 90025. Tel. 213-563-4868.

Meckler Award. Gloria J. Zamora, Sandia National Laboratories, Info. Research Organization 400, Albuquerque, NM 87185. Tel. 505-844-3909.

Networking. Hope Tillman, Dir. of Libs., Babson College, Horn Lib., Babson Park, MA 02157. Tel. 617-239-4259.

Professional Development. Judy MacFarlane, Peat Marwick Thorne Lib., 1155 Blvd. René Levesque W., Montreal, PQ H3B 2J9, Canada. Tel. 514-879-3428.

Public Relations. M. Hope Coffman, Charles S. Draper Lab Inc., 555 Technology Sq., Cambridge, MA 02139. Tel. 617-258-3555.

Publisher Relations. Pamela R. Palmer, Memphis State Univ., Memphis, TN 38152. Tel. 901-678-2208.

Research. Susan M. Hill, National Assn. of Broadcasters Lib., 1771 N St. N.W., Washington, DC 20036. Tel. 202-429-5488.

SLA Scholarship. Eleanor A. MacLean, McGill Univ., Blacker Wood Lib., 3459 McTavish St., Montreal, PQ H3A 1Y1, Canada. Tel. 514-398-4744.

Standards. Sharyn J. Ladner, Univ. of Miami, Richter Lib., Box 248214, Coral Gables, FL 33124. Tel. 305-284-4067.

Strategic Planning. L. Susan Hayes, Encore Computer Corp., MS 408, 6901 W. Sunrise Blvd., Fort Lauderdale, FL 33313. Tel. 305-797-5933.

Student Relations. Fred W. Roper, Univ. of South Carolina, College Lib. Info. Science, Columbia, SC 29208. Tel. 803-777-3858.

Tellers. James L. Olsen, Jr., 5905 Landon Lane, Bethesda, MD 20817. Tel. 301-229-5084.

H. W. Wilson Company Award. Lynda W. Moulton, Comstow Info. Service, Box 277, Harvard, MA 01451. Tel. 508-772-2001.

Theatre Library Association

Secretary-Treasurer, Richard M. Buck
New York Public Library for the Performing Arts
111 Amsterdam Ave., New York, NY 10023-7498

Object

"To further the interests of collecting, preserving, and using theatre, cinema, and performing arts materials in libraries, museums, and private collections." Founded 1937. Memb. 500. Dues (Indiv.) $20; (Inst.) $25. Year. Jan. 1–Dec. 31.

Officers (1991–1992)

Pres. James Poteat, New York Public Lib., 111 Amsterdam Ave., New York, NY 10023-7498; *V.P.* Bob Taylor, Asst. Curator, Billy Rose Theatre Collection, New York Public Lib. for the Performing Arts, 111 Amsterdam Ave., New York, NY 10023-7410; *Secy.-Treas.* Richard M. Buck, Asst. to the Exec. Dir., New York Public Lib. for the Performing Arts, 111 Amsterdam Ave., New York, NY 10023-7410; *Rec. Secy.* Maryann Chach, Archivist of the Shubert Archives, Lyceum Theatre, 149 W. 45 St., New York, NY 10036.

Executive Board

Susan Brady, Nena Couch, Rosemary Cullen, Geraldine Duclow, Steven Higgins, Catherine Johnson, Brigitte Kueppers, Louis A. Rachow, Richard Wall, Frederic W. Wilson, Walter Zvonchenko; *Ex officio.* Barbara Naomi Cohen-Stratyner, Alan J. Pally; *Honorary.* Paul Myers.

Publications

Broadside (q.; memb.). *Ed.* Alan J. Pally. *Performing Arts Resources* (ann.; memb.). *Ed.* Barbara Naomi Cohen-Stratyner.

Committee Chairpersons

Awards. Steven Vallillo.
Collection Resources. Walter Zvonchenko.
Long-Range Planning. To be appointed.
Membership. Geraldine Duclow.
Nominations. Richard Wall.
Program and Special Events. Richard M. Buck.
Publications. To be appointed.

State, Provincial, and Regional Library Associations

The associations in this section are organized under three headings: United States, Canada, and Regional associations. Both the United States and Canada are represented under Regional associations.

United States

Alabama

Memb. 1,450. Term of Office. Apr. 1991–Apr. 1992. Publication. *The Alabama Librarian* (9 per year). *Ed.* Kathy Vogel, 122 Plateau Rd., Montevallo 35115.

Pres. Geraldine Bell, 410 S. 13 St., Birmingham 35233; *Pres.-Elect.* Jane Keeton, 3020 Parkbrook Rd., Birmingham 35213; *Exec. Dir.* Barbara F. Black, 400 S. Union St., Suite 255, Montgomery 36104.

Address correspondence to the executive director.

Alaska

Memb. 475. Term of Office. Mar. 1992–Mar. 1993. Publication. *Sourdough* (q.).

Pres. Gaylin Fuller, Tuzzy Lib., Pouch 7337, Barrow 99723. Tel. 907-852-0246; *Secy.* Joyce Jenkins, Petersburg Public Lib., Box 549, Petersburg 99833. Tel. 907-772-3349; *Treas.* Karen Weiland, Valdez Consortium Lib., Box 609, Valdez 99686. Tel. 907-835-4632.

Address correspondence to the secretary.

Arizona

Memb. 1,230. Term of Office. Nov. 1991–Nov. 1992. Publication. *ASLA Newsletter* (mo.). *Ed.* Adrienne Sanden, 4515 N. 49 Place, Phoenix 85018. Tel. 602-840-9443.

Pres. Judy Register, Scottsdale Public Lib., 10101 N. 90 St., Scottsdale 85258. Tel. 602-391-6060; *Treas.* Marianna Hancin, Glendale Public Lib., 5959 W. Brown, Glendale 85302; *Exec. Secy.* Jim Johnson, 13832 N. 32 St. No. C1-7, Phoenix 85032.

Address correspondence to the president.

Arkansas

Memb. 800. Term of Office. Jan.–Dec. 1992. Publication. *Arkansas Libraries* (bi-mo.).

Pres. Margaret Crank, Arkansas Dept. of Educ., 4 Capitol Mall, Little Rock 72201. Tel. 501-682-4396; *Exec. Dir.* Sherry Walker, Arkansas Lib. Assn., 1100 N. University, Suite 109, Little Rock 72207. Tel. 501-661-1127.

Address correspondence to the executive director.

California

Memb. 2,300. Term of Office. Dec.–Nov. Publication. *California Libraries.*

Pres. Tobin deLeon Clarke, San Joaquin Delta College, Stockton; *V.P./Pres.-Elect.* Neel Parikh, San Francisco Public Lib.; *Past Pres.* Catherine E. Lucas, San Diego County Lib.; *Treas.* Linda Crowe, Peninsula Lib. System, Belmont; *ALA Chapter Councillor.* Betty J. Blackman, California State Univ., Dominguez Hills; *Exec. Dir.* Mary Sue Ferrell, California Lib. Assn., 717 K St., Suite 300, Sacramento 95814.

Address correspondence to the executive director.

Colorado

Memb. 863. Term of Office. Oct. 1991–Oct. 1992. Publication. *Colorado Libraries* (q.). *Ed.* Nancy Carter, Music Lib., Campus Box 184, Univ. of Colorado, Boulder 80309.

Pres. Judy Zelenski, Central Colorado Lib. System, 4350 Wadsworth, No. 340, Wheat Ridge 80033; *Pres.-Elect.* Rick Friddle, Pikes Peak Community College LRC, Colorado Springs 80906; *Treas.* Gail Dow, Denver Public Lib., 1330 Fox St., Denver 80204; *Assn. Office.* Box 489, Pinecliffe 80471. Tel. 303-940-9943.

Address correspondence to the association office.

Connecticut

Memb. 1,100. Term of Office. July 1991–June 1992. Publication. *Connecticut Libraries* (11 per year). *Ed.* David Kapp, 4 Llynwood Dr., Bolton 06040. Tel. 203-647-0697.

Pres. Marcia Trotta, Meriden Public Lib., 105 Miller St., Meriden 06450. Tel. 203-238-2344; *V.P./Pres.-Elect.* Peter Chase, Plainville Public Lib., 56 E. Main St., Plainville 06062. Tel. 203-793-0221; *Treas.* Sherry Hupp, Hamden Lib., 2901 Dixwell Ave., Hamden 06518. Tel. 203-288-6005; *Managing Dir.* M. Suzanne C. Berry; *Assn. Administrator.* Tessa Wilusz, Connecticut Lib. Assn., 638 Prospect Ave., Hartford 06105. Tel. 203-232-4825.

Address correspondence to the association administrator.

Delaware

Memb. 355. Term of Office. Apr. 1992–Apr. 1993. Publication. *DLA Bulletin* (3 per year).

Pres. Robert Wetherall, Dover Public Lib., 45 S. State St., Dover 19901. Tel. 302-736-7030; *Secy.* Jim McCloskey, Delaware State Hospital Medical Lib., 1901 N. Dupont Hwy., New Castle 19720. Tel. 302-421-6368; *Past Pres.* Elizabeth M. Simmons, Kirkwood Highway Lib., 6000 Kirkwood Hwy., Wilmington 19808. Tel. 302-995-7663.

Address correspondence to DLA, Box 1843, Wilmington 19899.

District of Columbia

Memb. 900. Term of Office. Sept. 1991–Aug. 1992. Publication. *INTERCOM* (mo.).

Pres. Susan Fifer Canby, National Geographic Society, 17 and M Sts. N.W., Washington 20036. Tel. 202-857-7787; *V.P./Pres.-Elect.* Hardy Franklin, D.C. Public Lib., 901 G St. N.W., Washington 20001. Tel. 202-727-1101; *Secy.* Edrue Ivory, Prince George's County Memorial Lib., 6200 Oxon Hill Rd., Oxon Hill, MD 20745; *Treas.* Sue Uebelacker, Prince George's County Memorial Lib., 2398 Iverson St., Hillcrest Heights, MD 20748.

Address correspondence to the president.

Florida

Memb. (Indiv.) 1,378; (In-state Inst.) 83. Term of Office. July 1991–June 1992.

Pres. Al Trezza, FSU School of Lib. and Info. Studies, 2205 Napoleon Bonaparte Dr., Tallahassee 32308. Tel. 904-644-8116; *V.P./Pres.-Elect.* Ann W. Williams, Alachua County Lib. Dist., 401 E. University Ave., Gainesville 32601; *Secy.* Betty A. Scott, State Lib. of Florida, R. A. Gray Bldg., Tallahassee 32399; *Treas.* Charles Parker, State Lib. of Florida, R. A. Gray Bldg., Tallahassee 32399; *Exec. Secy.* Marjorie Stealey, Florida Lib. Assn., 1133 W. Morse Blvd., Suite 201, Winter Park 32789. Tel. 407-647-8839.

Address correspondence to the executive secretary.

Georgia

Memb. 1,055. Term of Office. 1991–1993. Publication. *Georgia Librarian. Ed.* Joanne Lincoln, Atlanta Public Schools, 2930 Forrest Hill Dr., Atlanta 30315. Tel. 404-827-8725.

Pres. Sharon Self, Media Center, Hardaway H.S., Columbus 31995. Tel. 404-649-0748; *1st V.P./Pres.-Elect.* Donna Mancini, DeKalb County Public Lib., 1300 Commerce Dr., Decatur 30030. Tel. 404-371-3045; *2nd V.P.* Anita J. O'Neal, Anderson Park Elementary School, 2050 Tiger Flowers Dr. N.W., Atlanta 30314. Tel. 404-792-5914; *Secy.* Kristina Brockmeier, Clayton State College Lib., 5900 N. Lee St., Morrow 30260. Tel. 404-961-3520. *Treas.* Richard Leach, East Central Georgia Regional Lib., 902 Greene St., Augusta 30901. Tel. 404-821-2600.

Address correspondence to the president.

Hawaii

Memb. 450. Publications. *HLA Membership Directory* (ann.); *HLA Newsletter* (q.); *HLA Journal* (irreg.).

Pres. Anthony Oliver, 585-B Kawainui St., Kailua 96734. Tel. 808-586-2424; *Pres.-Elect./Conference Chpn.* Floriana Cofman, 1054 Green St., No. 302, Honolulu 96822. Tel. 808-395-2321.

Address correspondence to the association, Box 4441, Honolulu 96812-4441.

Idaho

Memb. 500. Term of Office. Oct. 1991–Oct. 1992. Publication. *The Idaho Librarian* (q.). *Ed.* Mary Bolin, Univ. of Idaho Lib., Moscow 83843. Tel. 208-885-7737.

Pres. Betty Holbrook, Pocatello Public Lib., Pocatello 83201. Tel. 208-232-1263; *Pres.-Elect.* Pat Stewart, Moscow Jr. High Lib., Moscow 83843. Tel. 208-882-3577; *Treas.* Camille Wood, Nampa Public Lib., Nampa 83651. Tel. 208-465-2264; *Secy.* Sandra Shropshire, Idaho State Univ. Lib., Pocatello 83209. Tel. 208-236-2671.

Address correspondence to the secretary.

Illinois

Memb. 4,100. Term of Office. July 1, 1991–June 30, 1992. Publication. *ILA Reporter* (10 per year).

Pres. Brent Crossland, R.R. 1, Box 46, Bowen 62316. Tel. 217-842-5216; *V.P.* Jo K. Potter, Alpha Park Public Lib., 3527 S. Airport Rd., Bartonville 61607. Tel. 309-697-3822; *Treas.* Lois Schultz, Suburban Lib. System, 125 Tower Dr., Burr Ridge 60521. Tel. 708-325-6640; *Exec. Dir.* Barbara Manchak Cunningham, Illinois Library Association, 33 W. Grand Ave., Suite 301, Chicago 60610. Tel. 312-644-1896, FAX 312-644-1899.

Address correspondence to the executive director.

Indiana

Memb. (Indiv.) 1,000; (Inst.) 200. Term of Office. May 1991–May 1992. Publications. *Focus on Indiana Libraries* (11 per year). *Ed.* Raquel M. Ravinet; *Indiana Libraries* (q.). *Ed.* Jackie Nytes, Indianapolis–Marion County Public Lib., Box 211, Indianapolis 46202. Tel. 317-269-1700.

Pres. Pat Steele, Indiana Univ., Bloomington 47401; *1st V.P.* Beverly Martin, Johnson County Public Lib., 401 S. State St., Franklin 46131; *Secy.* Jan Yeager, Monroe County Public Lib., Bloomington 47408; *Treas.* Sally Otte, 5251 N. Delaware, Indianapolis 46220.

Address correspondence to the Indiana Lib. Federation, 1500 N. Delaware St., Indianapolis 46202. Tel. 317-636-6613, FAX 317-634-9503.

Iowa

Memb. 1,813. Term of Office. Jan.–Dec. 1992. Publication. *The Catalyst* (bi-mo.). *Ed.* Naomi Stovall.

Pres. Julie Huiskamp, Cresco Public Lib., 320 N. Elm, Cresco 52136.

Address correspondence to Iowa Lib. Assn., 823 Insurance Exchange Bldg., Des Moines 50309. Tel. 515-243-2172.

Kansas

Memb. 1,000. Term of Office. July 1, 1991–June 30, 1992. Publications. *KLA Newsletter* (q.); *KLA Membership Directory* (ann.).

Pres. Joe McKenzie, Salina Public Lib., 301 W. Elm, Salina 67401. Tel. 913-825-4624; *Pres.-Elect.* Kent Oliver, Olathe Public Lib., 201 E. Park, Olathe 66061. Tel. 913-764-2259; *Exec. Secy.* Leroy Gattin, SCKLS, 901 N. Main, Hutchinson 67501. Tel. 316-663-2501; *Secy.* Gayle Willard, Kansas State Univ., Veterinary Medical Lib., Manhattan 66506; *Treas.* Marcella Ratzlaff, Hutchinson Public Lib., Hutchinson 67501.

Address correspondence to the president or executive secretary.

Kentucky

Memb. 1,900. Term of Office. Oct. 1991–Oct. 1992. Publication. *Kentucky Libraries* (q.).

Pres. Rose Gabbard, Box 313, Beattyville 41311; *Pres.-Elect.* Candace B. Wilson, Box 370, Russell Springs 42642; *Secy.* June Martin, Eastern Kentucky Univ., John Grant Crabbe Lib., Richmond 40475; *Exec. Secy.* John T. Underwood, 1501 Twilight Trail, Frankfort 40601. Tel. 502-223-5322.

Address correspondence to the association, 1501 Twilight Trail, Frankfort 40601.

Louisiana

Memb. (Indiv.) 1,710; (Inst.) 78. Term of Office. July 1991–June 1992. Publication. *LLA Bulletin* (q.).

Pres. Anna Perrault, 5609 Valley Forge, Baton Rouge 70808. Tel. 504-388-8538, FAX 504-388-6992; *1st V.P./Pres.-Elect.* Earl D. Hart, 2026 Robert St., New Orleans 70115. Tel. 504-286-6528; *Secy.* Norma H. Martin,

8335 Summa Ave., F-2, Baton Rouge 70809. Tel. 504-388-2217, FAX 504-388-6992; *Parliamentarian*. Virginia R. Smith, Box 517, Saint Francisville 70775; *Past Pres*. Elizabeth E. Bingham, 14215 Harwood Ave., Baton Rouge 70816.

Address correspondence to the LLA Office, Box 3058, Baton Rouge 70821.

Maine

Memb. 1,100. Term of Office. (Pres., V.P.) Spring 1992–Spring 1993. Publications. *Mainely Libraries* (4 per year); *Maine Memo* (mo.).

Pres. Barbara Rice, Bangor Public Lib., Bangor 04401; *Secy*. Charles Howell, Millinocket Memorial Lib., Millinocket 04462; *Treas*. Steve Podgajny, Curtis Memorial Lib., Pleasant St., Brunswick 04011.

Address correspondence to MLA, c/o Maine Municipal Assn., Local Government Center, 37 Community Dr., Augusta 04330. Tel. 207-623-8429.

Maryland

Memb. 1,300. Term of Office. July 1991–June 1992. Publication. *The Crab*.

Pres. Beth Babikow, Baltimore County Public Lib., 320 York Rd., Towson 21204. Tel. 410-887-6131; *1st V.P./Pres.-Elect*. John G. Ray III, Loyola/Notre Dame Lib., 200 Winston Ave., Baltimore 21212. Tel. 410-532-8788; *2nd V.P.* William G. Wilson, CLIS, Univ. of Maryland, College Park 20742; *Secy*. Susan Paznekas, Maryland State Department of Lib. Development Services, 200 W. Baltimore St., Baltimore 21201. Tel. 410-333-2122; *Treas*. Fran McClure; *Assn. Mgr*. Dinah Kappus, MLA Office, 400 Cathedral St., 3rd fl., Baltimore 21201. Tel. 410-727-7422.

Address correspondence to the association manager.

Massachusetts

Memb. (Indiv.) 950; (Inst.) 100. Term of Office. July 1991–June 1993. Publication. *Bay State Librarian* (10 per year).

Pres. Bonnie L. O'Brien, Shrewsbury Public Lib., 609 Main St., Shrewsbury 01545. Tel. 508-842-0081; *V.P.* Monica Grace, Framingham Public Lib., 49 Lexington St., Framingham 01701. Tel. 508-879-3570; *Secy*. Nancy R. Browne, Boston Public Lib., Box 286, Boston 02117-0286. Tel. 617-536-5400, Ext. 420; *Treas*. Brian Donoghue, Massachusetts Bd. of Lib. Commissioners, 648 Beacon St., Boston 02215. Tel. 617-267-9400; *Past Pres*. Anne O'Brien, Pollard Memorial Lib., 401 Merrimack St., Lowell 01852. Tel. 508-970-4120; *Exec. Secy*. Barry Blaisdell, Massachusetts Lib. Assn., Countryside Offices, 707 Turnpike St., North Andover 01845. Tel. 508-686-8543.

Address correspondence to the executive secretary.

Michigan

Memb. (Indiv.) 2,200; (Inst.) 300. Term of Office. June 1991–June 1992. Publication. *Michigan Librarian Newsletter* (10 per year).

Pres. Jean Houghton, Lib. Dir., Saginaw Valley State Univ., University Center 48710; *Treas*. Phyllis Jose, Dir., Oakland County Reference Lib., Pontiac 48341; *Exec. Dir*. Marianne Gessner, Michigan Lib. Assn., 1000 Long Blvd., Suite 1, Lansing 48911. Tel. 517-694-6615.

Address correspondence to the executive director.

Minnesota

Memb. 875. Term of Office. (Pres., V.P.) Jan. 1, 1992–Dec. 31, 1992; (Treas.) Jan. 1, 1992–Dec. 31, 1993; (Secy.) Jan. 1, 1991–Dec. 31, 1992. Publication. *MLA Newsletter* (10 per year).

Pres. Janet Kinney, Saint Catherine Lib., 2004 Randolph Ave., Saint Paul 55105; *ALA Chapter Councillor*. Janice Feye-Stukas, Lib. Development and Services, 440 Capitol Sq., 500 Cedar St., Saint Paul 55101; *Secy*. Carol P. Johnson, 1122 N. 30 Ave., Saint Cloud 56303; *Treas*. Heidi Hoks, Box 593, Thief River Falls 56701; *Admin. Secy*. JoAnne Kelty, Minnesota Lib. Assn., 1315 Lowry Ave. N., Minneapolis 55411-1398. Tel. 612-521-1735.

Address correspondence to the administrative secretary.

Mississippi

Memb. 1,100. Term of Office. Jan.–Dec. 1992. Publication. *Mississippi Libraries.*

Pres. Ken Chapman, 111 Hillcrest Dr., Brookhaven 39601; *V.P./Pres.-Elect.* Sherry Laughlin, 2023 Ridgeway Lane, Hattiesburg 39401; *Treas.* Sue Maisel, 544 Will-O-Wisp Way, Jackson 39204; *Exec. Secy.* Sharon L. Buchanan, MLA Office, Box 20448, Jackson 39289-1448. Tel. 601-352-3917.

Address correspondence to the executive secretary.

Missouri

Memb. 1,000. Term of Office. Sept. 1991–Oct. 1992. Publication. *MO INFO* (6 per year). *Ed.* Jean Ann McCartney.

Pres. Kurt Lamb, Mexico–Audrain County Lib., 305 W. Jackson, Mexico 65265. Tel. 314-581-4939; *V.P./Pres.-Elect.* Annie Linnemeyer, Dir., Springfield–Greene County Lib., MPO Box 760, Springfield 65801. Tel. 417-869-4621; *Secy.* Patricia Gass. Tel. 816-263-4426; *Chpn., Budget and Finance.* Valerie Darst; *Exec. Dir.* Jean Ann McCartney, Missouri Lib. Assn., 1015 E. Broadway, Suite 215, Columbia 65201. Tel. 314-449-4627.

Address correspondence to the executive director.

Montana

Memb. 600. Term of Office. July 1, 1991–June 30, 1992. Publication. *Library Focus, the Newsletter of the Montana Library Association* (4 per year). *Eds.* Gregg Sapp and Rick Dyson, Montana State Univ. Libs., Bozeman 59717.

Pres. Diane Van Gorden, Box 73, Baker 59313-0073; *V.P./Pres.-Elect.* Steve Cottrell, 918 S. Black, Bozeman 59715; *Past Pres.* Beverly Knapp, 1317 S. Black, Bozeman 59715; *Rec. Secy.* Coby Johnson, Mansfield Lib., Univ. of Montana, Missoula 59812.

Address correspondence to MLA, Box 954, Bozeman 59771-0954. Tel. 406-587-3346.

Nebraska

Memb. 1,000. Term of Office. Oct. 1991–Oct. 1992. Publication. *NLA Quarterly.*

Pres. Sharon McCaslin, Peru State College Lib., Peru 68421; *V.P./Pres.-Elect.* Sarah Watson, Omaha Public Lib., 2918 N. 60, Omaha 68104. Tel. 402-444-4846; *Secy.* Gale Kosalka, 5003 Sunset Dr., Ralston 68127; *Treas.* Kate Marek, S.E. Lib. System, c/o Union College Lib., Lincoln 68506. Tel. 402-486-2555; *Exec. Secy.* Fiona Turnbull, Bellevue College Lib., Galvin Rd. at Harvell Dr., Bellevue 68005. Tel. 402-293-2011.

Address correspondence to the executive secretary.

Nevada

Memb. 250. Term of Office. Jan. 1, 1992–Dec. 31, 1992. Publication. *Highroller* (4 per year).

Pres. Leon Wright, Sierra View Branch Lib., 4001 S. 827-Virginia, Reno 89509. Tel. 702-827-3232; *Exec. Secy.* Carol Madsen, Nevada State Library and Archives, Capitol Complex, Carson City 89710. Tel. 702-887-2620; *Treas.* Duncan McCoy, Boulder City Lib., 813 Arizona, Boulder City 89005. Tel. 702-293-1281; *Past Pres.* Danny Lee, State Farm Insurance, 2560 S. Maryland Pkwy., Suite 6, Las Vegas 89109. Tel. 702-737-7150.

Address correspondence to the executive secretary.

New Hampshire

Memb. 700. Term of Office. June 1992–May 1993. Publication. *NHLA Newsletter* (bi-mo.).

Pres. Catherine Redden, Leach Lib., 276 Mammoth Rd., Londonderry 03053. Tel. 603-432-1132; *V.P.* Margaret Marschner, Conway Public Lib., Box 2100, Conway 03818. Tel. 603-447-5552; *Secy.* Carl Heidenblad, Nesmith Lib., 3 N. Lowell Rd., Windham 03087. Tel. 603-432-7154; *Treas.* Charles LeBlanc, New Hampshire State Lib., 20 Park St., Concord 03301-6303.

Address correspondence to NHLA, Box 2332, Concord 03302-2332.

New Jersey

Memb. 1,700. Term of Office. May 1992–Apr. 1993. Publications. *New Jersey Libraries* (q.); *New Jersey Libraries Newsletter* (mo.).

Pres. Nancy Vernon, Madison Public Lib., 39 Keep St., Madison 07940; *Past Pres.* Abigail Studdiford, Middlesex County College Lib., Woodbridge Ave., Edison 08818; *V.P./Pres.-Elect.* Jane Crocker, Gloucester County College Lib., Tanyard Rd., Sewell 08080; *Treas.* Susan Persak, Chester Lib., 250 Route 24, Chester 07930; *Exec. Dir.* Patricia Tumulty, New Jersey Lib. Assn., 4 W. Lafayette St., Trenton 08607. Tel. 609-394-8032.

Address correspondence to the executive director, Box 1534, Trenton 08607.

New Mexico

Memb. 500. Term of Office. Apr. 1992–Apr. 1993. Publication. *New Mexico Library Association Newsletter.* Ed. Stefanie Wittenbach, 8227 Constitution N.E., Albuquerque 87110.

Pres. Drew Harrington, 4404 De La Cruz N.W., Albuquerque 87107. Tel. 505-828-3218; *1st V.P.* Alison Almquist; *Treas.* David Null, 9874 Menaul N.E., Apt. H-8, Albuquerque 87112; *ALA Councillor.* Ben Wakashige, 4552 Grandview, Silver City 88061.

Address correspondence to the association, 4 Mariposa Rd., Santa Fe 87505.

New York

Memb. 3,200. Term of Office. Nov. 1991–Oct. 1992. Publication. *NYLA Bulletin* (10 per year). *Ed.* Gail Sacco.

Pres. Janet M. Welch, Rochester Regional Lib. Council, 302 N. Goodman St./Village Gate, Rochester 14607; *V.P./Pres.-Elect.* Sheryl Egger, W. Irondequoit School Dist., 260 Cooper Rd., Rochester 14617; *Treas.* Carol Ann Desch, Worthman Lane, Rensselaer 12144; *Exec. Dir.* Susan Lehman Keitel, New York Library Assn., 252 Hudson Ave., Albany 12210. Tel. 518-432-6952; *Asst. to the Dir.* Carol A. Raphael; *Conference Coord.* Gail Ghazzawi.

Address correspondence to the executive director.

North Carolina

Memb. 2,500. Term of Office. Nov. 1991–Oct. 1993. Publication. *North Carolina Libraries* (q.). *Ed.* Frances Bradburn, Joyner Lib., East Carolina Univ., Greenville 27858.

Pres. Janet L. Freeman, Carlyle Campbell Lib., Meredith College, 3800 Hillsborough St., Raleigh 27607-5298. Tel. 919-829-8531; *V.P./Pres.-Elect.* Gwen Jackson, Southeast Technical Assistance Center, 2013 Lejeune Blvd., Jacksonville 28546. Tel. 919-577-8920; *Secy.* Waltrene M. Canada, F. D. Bluford Lib., N.C. A & T State Univ., Greensboro 27411. Tel. 919-334-7617; *Treas.* Wanda Brown Cason, Wake Forest Univ. Lib., Box 7777, Reynolda Sta., Winston-Salem 27109-7777. Tel. 919-759-5094.

Address correspondence to the secretary.

North Dakota

Memb. (Indiv.) 423; (Inst.) 32. Term of Office. Oct. 1991–Sept. 1992. Publication. *The Good Stuff* (q.). *Ed.* Michael Hurley, Chester Fritz Lib., UND School of Law, Rm. 161, Grand Forks 58202.

Pres. Marcella Schmaltz, Bismarck State College Lib., 1500 Edwards Ave., Bismarck 58501; *V.P./Pres.-Elect.* Jan Hendrickson, Hazen Public Lib., Box 471, Hazen 58545; *Secy.* Eileen Kopren, Dickinson State Univ., 291 Campus Ave., Dickinson 58601; *Treas.* Leeila Bina, Q&R Medcenter One Health Sciences Lib., 622 Ave. A East, Bismarck 58501.

Address correspondence to the secretary.

Ohio

Memb. 2,916. Term of Office. Nov. 2, 1991–Nov. 6, 1992. Publication. *Ohio Libraries* (6 per year).

Pres. Patricia Latshaw, Akron–Summit County Public Lib., 55 S. Main St., Akron 44326. Tel. 216-762-7621; *V.P./Pres.-Elect.* Alan C. Hall, Public Lib. of Steubenville–Jefferson County, 407 S. Fourth St., Steubenville 43952. Tel. 614-282-9782; *Secy.* Susan B. Hagloch, Tuscarawas County Public Lib., 121 Fair Ave. N.W., New Philadelphia 44663. Tel. 216-364-4474.

Address correspondence to OLA, 67 Jefferson Ave., Columbus 43215. Tel. 614-221-9057.

Oklahoma

Memb. (Indiv.) 1,050; (Inst.) 60. Term of Office. July 1991–June 1992. Publication. *Oklahoma Librarian* (bi-mo.).

Pres. Carol Casey, State Dept. of Educ., 2500 Lincoln Blvd., Oklahoma City 73105. Tel. 405-521-2956; *V.P./Pres.-Elect.* Edward R. Johnson, Oklahoma State Univ., Edmon Low Lib., Stillwater 74078. Tel. 405-744-6321; *Secy.* Debra Engel, Pioneer Lib. System, 225 N. Webster, Norman 73069. Tel. 405-321-1481; *Treas.* Joan Jester, Metropolitan Lib. System, 131 Dean A. McGee, Oklahoma City 73102. Tel. 405-235-0571; *Exec. Dir.* Kay Boies, 300 Hardy Dr., Edmond 73013. Tel. 405-348-0506.

Address correspondence to the executive director.

Oregon

Memb. (Indiv.) 975; (Inst.) 50. Term of Office. Sept. 1991–Aug. 1992. Publication. *Oregon Library News* (mo.). *Ed.* Walter Krafton-Minkel, 3425 N.E. 18 St., Portland 97212. Tel. 503-221-7725.

Pres. Maureen Sloan, Oregon Grad. Institute Lib., 19600 N.W. Von Neumann Dr., Beaverton 97006. Tel. 503-690-1060; *V.P./ Pres.-Elect.* Deborah Jacobs, Corvallis Public Lib., Corvallis 97339; *Secy.* Blythe Jorgensen, 24400 Siletz Hwy., Toledo 97391.

Address correspondence to the secretary.

Pennsylvania

Memb. 1,750. Term of Office. Oct. 1991–Oct. 1992. Publication. *PLA Bulletin* (8 per year).

Pres. Diane Ambrose, Beaver County Lib. System, 1260 N. Brodhead Rd., Monaca 15061. Tel. 412-728-3737; *Exec. Dir.* Margaret S. Bauer, CAE, Pennsylvania Lib. Assn., 3107 N. Front St., Harrisburg 17110. Tel. 717-233-3113.

Address correspondence to the association, 3107 N. Front St., Harrisburg 17110.

Rhode Island

Memb. (Indiv.) 451; (Inst.) 37. Term of Office. Nov. 1991–Nov. 1992. Publication. *Rhode Island Library Association Bulletin.* *Ed.* Judith A. Paster.

Pres. Judith A. Paster, Free-Lance Libn. Tel. 401-467-8898; *V.P./Pres.-Elect.* Janet A. Levesque, Cumberland Public Lib., 1464 Diamond Hill Rd., Cumberland 02864. Tel. 401-333-2552; *Secy.* Deborah Mongeau, Univ. of Rhode Island Lib., Kingston 02881-0803. Tel. 401-792-4610; *Treas.* Judith H. Bell, Jamestown Philomenian Lib., 26 North Rd., Jamestown 02835. Tel. 401-423-2665; *Past Pres.* John Fox Cory, Cranston Public Lib., 140 Sockanosett Cross Rd., Cranston 02920. Tel. 401-943-9080; *Memb.-at-Large.* Joan C. Prescott, Rogers Free Lib., Hope St., Bristol 02809. Tel. 401-253-6948; *NELA Councillor.* Eileen Socha, Weaver Memorial Lib., 41 Grove Ave., East Providence 02914. Tel. 401-434-2453; *ALA Councillor.* Carol S. Drought, Warwick Public Lib., 600 Sandy Lane, Warwick 02886. Tel. 401-739-5440.

Address correspondence to the secretary.

South Carolina

Memb. 800. Term of Office. Nov. 1991–Nov. 1992.

Pres. David Cohen, College of Charleston, 66 George St., Charleston 29424. Tel. 803-792-5530; *V.P./Pres.-Elect.* Claude Blakeley, 14 Crestline Rd., Greenville 29609. Tel. 803-233-6733.

Address correspondence to the president.

South Dakota

Memb. (Indiv.) 520; (Inst.) 62. Term of Office. Oct. 1991–Oct. 1992. Publication. *Bookmarks* (bi-mo.). *Ed.* Susan Richards, South Dakota State Univ., H. M. Briggs Lib., Brookings 57007.

Pres. Leon Raney, South Dakota State Univ., H. M. Briggs Lib., Box 2115, Brookings 57007-2115. Tel. 605-688-5557; *V.P./ Pres.-Elect.* Terri Davis, Deadwood Public Lib., Box 63, Deadwood 57732-0063; *Past Pres.* Mary Schwartz, Redfield H.S. Lib., Box 560, Redfield 57469-0560. Tel. 605-472-0560; *Secy.* Mary Caspers, South Dakota State Univ., H. M. Briggs Lib., Box 2115, Brookings 57007-2115. Tel. 605-688-5571; *Treas.* Lee Crary, Bison H.S., Box 242, Bison 57620-0242; *ALA Councillor.* Judy Johnson, Central H.S. Lib., 433 Mount Rushmore Rd. N., Rapid City 57701-2754. Tel. 605-394-4023; *MPLA Rep.* Mary Homan, Patrick Henry Jr. H.S. Lib., 2200 S. Fifth, Sioux Falls 57105-4099. Tel. 605-331-7639.

Address correspondence to the association, Box 673, Pierre 57501.

Tennessee

Memb. 1,057. Term of Office. July 1991–July 1992. Publication. *Tennessee Librarian* (q.).
Pres. Joseph Jones, Trustee, Forked Deer Regional Lib., Newbern 38059. Tel. 901-627-2807; *V.P./Pres.-Elect.* Patricia L. Watson, Dir., Knox County Public Lib., 500 W. Church Ave., Knoxville 37902. Tel. 615-544-5701; *Exec. Secy.* Betty Nance, Box 158417, Nashville 37215-8417. Tel. 615-297-8316.
Address correspondence to the executive secretary.

Texas

Memb. 5,311. Term of Office. Apr. 1991–Apr. 1992. Publications. *Texas Library Journal* (q.); *TLAcast* (9 per year).
Pres. Cynthia A. Gray, Palestine Public Lib., 1101 N. Cedar, Palestine 75801. Tel. 903-729-8087; *Exec. Dir.* Patricia H. Smith, TLA Office, 3355 Bee Cave Rd., Suite 603, Austin 78746-6763. Tel. 512-328-1518, FAX 512-328-8852.
Address correspondence to the executive director.

Utah

Memb. 600. Term of Office. May 1991–Apr. 1992. Publication. *UTAH Libraries News* (bi-mo.).
Pres. Carol Hansen, Stewart Lib., Weber State Univ., Ogden 84408-2901. Tel. 801-626-6071; *Rec. Secy.* Jane Smith, Utah State Lib. Commission. Tel. 801-466-5888 ext. 40; *Exec. Secy.* Donald H. Trottier.
Address correspondence to the association office, 2150 S. 300 W., Suite 16, Salt Lake City 84115.

Vermont

Memb. 450. Term of Office. May 1991–May 1992. Publication. *VLA News* (10 per year).
Pres. Linda McSweeney, Hartness Lib., Vermont Technical College, Randolph Center 05061. Tel. 802-728-3391; *V.P./Pres.-Elect.* Paula Baker, Rutland Free Lib., 10 Court St., Rutland 05701. Tel. 802-773-1860; *Secy.* Jean Fournier, Samuel Read Hall Lib., Lyndon State College, Lyndonville 05851. Tel. 802-626-9371; *Treas.* Daphne Bartholomew,

Poultney Public Lib., Main St., Poultney 05764. Tel. 802-287-5556; *ALA Councillor.* Sally Reed, Ilsley Lib., Main St., Middlebury 05753. Tel. 802-388-4095; *NELA Rep.* Anita Danigelis, Fletcher Free Lib., 235 College St., Burlington 05401. Tel. 802-863-3403.
Address correspondence to the president.

Virginia

Memb. 1,400. Term of Office. Jan. 1, 1992–Dec. 31, 1992. Publications. *Virginia Librarian* (q.). *Ed.* Patsy Hansel, Williamsburg Regional Lib., 515 Scotland Rd., Williamsburg 23185; *VLA Newsletter* (10 per year). *Ed.* Rebecca Laine, Longwood College Lib., Farmville 23173.
Pres. Steve Matthews, Foxcroft School, Currier Lib., Middleburg 22117; *V.P.* Liz Hamilton, Campbell County Public Lib., Box 310, Rustburg 24588; *2nd V.P.* Jim Gwin, Univ. of Richmond, Boatwright Lib., Richmond 23173; *Secy.* Linda Farynk, Old Dominion Univ. Lib., Norfolk 23529; *Exec. Dir.* Deborah M. Trocchi, VLA, 669 S. Washington St., Alexandria 22314. Tel. 703-519-7853, FAX 703-519-7732; *ALA Councillor.* Tom Hehman, Meherrin Lib., 133 W. Hicks St., Lawrenceville 23868.
Address correspondence to the executive director.

Washington

Memb. 1,125. Term of Office. Aug. 1, 1991–July 31, 1992. Publications. *Alki* (3 per year); *WLA Link* (5 per year).
Pres. Barbara Tolliver, King County Lib. System, 300 Eighth Ave. N., Seattle 98109. Tel. 206-684-6615.
Address correspondence to WLA, 1232 143rd Ave. S.E., Bellevue 98007. Tel. 206-747-6917.

West Virginia

Memb. (Indiv.) 676; (Inst.) 97. Term of Office. Dec. 1991–Nov. 1992. Publication. *West Virginia Libraries.* *Ed.* Yvonne Farley, Saint Albans Public Lib., Sixth Ave. & Fourth St., Saint Albans 25177.
Pres. Pamela Ford, James E. Morrow Lib., Marshall Univ., Huntington 25755. Tel. 304-696-2312; *V.P./Pres.-Elect.* Matt Onion, Ca-

bell County Public Lib., 455 Ninth St. Plaza, Huntington 25701. Tel. 304-523-9551; *2nd V.P.* J. D. Waggoner, West Virginia Lib. Commission, Cultural Center, Charleston 25305. Tel. 304-348-2531; *Secy.* Judy Duncan, Kanawha County Public Lib., 123 Capitol St., Charleston 25303. Tel. 304-343-4646; *Treas.* David Childers, West Virginia Lib. Commission, Cultural Center, Charleston 25305. Tel. 304-348-2041; *ALA Councillor.* Tom Brown, Box 901, Athens 24712. Tel. 304-327-4050.

Address correspondence to the president.

Wisconsin

Memb. 1,725. Term of Office. Jan.–Dec. 1992. Publication. *WLA Newsletter* (6 per year).

Pres. Kathy Pletcher, Cofrin Lib., UW-Green Bay, 2420 Nicolet Dr., Green Bay 54311-7001; *V.P./Pres.-Elect.* Mildred N. Larson, L. E. Philips Memorial Lib., 400 Eau Claire, Eau Claire 54701.

Address correspondence to the association, 4785 Hayes Rd., Madison 53704-7364. Tel. 608-242-2040, FAX 608-242-2050.

Wyoming

Memb. (Indiv.) 450; (Inst.) 21; (Subscribers) 24. Term of Office. Oct. 1991–Oct. 1992.

Pres. Dorothy Middleton, East High Libn., Cheyenne 82001. Tel. 307-635-2461 ext. 62; *V.P./Pres.-Elect.* Laurn Wilhelm, Univ. of Wyoming Libs., Box 3374, Laramie 82071. Tel. 307-766-2527; *Exec. Secy.* Laura Grott, Box 1387, Cheyenne 82001. Tel. 307-632-7622.

Address correspondence to the executive secretary.

Guam

Memb. 35. Publication. *Guam Library Association News* (mo. during school year).

Pres. Jeannetta Caplan, Univ. of Guam, UOG Sta., Mangilao 96923. Tel. 671-632-2507; *V.P. Programs.* Linda Schlekau, Upi Elementary, Yigo 96930. Tel. 671-653-5305; *V.P. Memb.* Chih Wang, Univ. of Guam, UOG Sta., Mangilao 96923; *Treas.* Jeanne Jewell, M. U. Lujan Elementary School, Yona 96914. Tel. 671-789-2442; *ALA Councillor.* Mark

Goniwiecha, R. F. K. Memorial Lib., Univ. of Guam, UOG Sta., Mangilao 96923. Tel. 671-734-5929; *Secy.* M. E. Odom, Agat Elementary, Agat 96928. Tel. 671-565-2238.

Address correspondence to Guam Lib. Assn., Box 22515 GMF, Barrigada 96921.

Puerto Rico

Memb. 250. Publications. *Boletín* (ann.); *Cuadernos Bibliotecológicos* (irreg.); *Informa* (mo.); *Cuadernos Bibliográficos* (irreg.).

Pres. Aura Jiménez de Panepinto.

Address correspondence to the Sociedad de Bibliotecarios de Puerto Rico, Apdo. 22989, UPR Sta., Rio Piedras 00931.

Virgin Islands

Saint Croix Lib. Assn. Memb. 48. Publications. *SCLA Newsletter* (q.); *Studies in Virgin Islands Librarianship* (irreg.)

Pres. Wallace Williams, Florence A. Williams Public Lib., 49-50 King St., Christiansted, Saint Croix 00820.

Address correspondence to the president.

Canada

Alberta

Memb. 700. Term of Office. May 1992–Apr. 1993. Publication. *Letter of the L.A.A.* (5 per year).

Pres. Pat Jobb, Peace Lib. System, 8301 110th St., Grand Prairie T8V 6T2; *Past Pres.* Nora Robinson, AVC Lib., 332 Sixth Ave. S.E., Calgary T2G 4S6; *Exec. Asst.* Christine Sheppard, 117 Superior Ave. S.W., Calgary T3C 2H8.

Address correspondence to the association, Box 64197, 5512 Fourth St. N.W., Calgary T2K 6J1. Tel. 403-228-0898, FAX 403-228-0929.

British Columbia

Memb. 848. Term of Office. Apr. 1991–May 1992. Publication. *BCLA Reporter. Ed.* Terry Dobroslavic.

Pres. Nancy Hannum. *V.P. Pres.-Elect.* Sylvia Crooks.

Address correspondence to BCLA, 110-6545 Bonsor Ave., Burnaby, V5H 1H3. Tel. 604-430-9633.

Manitoba

Memb. 300. Term of Office. Spring 1991–Spring 1992. Publication. *Newsline* (mo.).
Pres. Eric Marshall, Box 176, Winnipeg R3C 2G9. Tel. 204-943-4567.
Address correspondence to the president.

Ontario

Memb. Over 3,750. Term of Office. Nov. 1991–Nov. 1992. Publications. *Focus* (q.); *Inside OLA* (bi-mo.); *The Teaching Librarian* (q.).
Pres. Paula de Ronde, Toronto Public Lib. Tel. 416-393-7518; *V.P./Pres.-Elect.* Allison Craig, West Carleton Secondary School, Ottawa. Tel. 613-832-2773; *Past Pres.* Stan Skrzeszewski, Southern Ontario Lib. Service, London. Tel. 519-433-8411; *Treas.* Gordon Thomson, North York Public Lib. Tel. 416-395-5602.
Address correspondence to OLA, 100 Lombard St., Suite 303, Toronto M5C 1M3. Tel. 416-363-3388, FAX 416-941-9581.

Quebec

Memb. (Indiv.) 170; (Inst.) 42; (Commercial) 7. Term of Office. May 1991–May 1992. Publications. *ABQ/QLA Bulletin* (3 per year); *QASL Newsletter* (3 per year).
Pres. Susan Perles, John F. Kennedy H.S., 3030 Villeray, Montreal, H2A 1E7; *V.P./ Pres.-Elect.* Eva Raby, Jewish Public Lib., 5151 Cote Ste.-Catherine Rd., Montreal H3W 1M6; *Exec. Secy.* Marie Eberlin, Quebec Lib. Assn., Box 2216, Dorval H9S 5J4. Tel. 514-630-4875.
Address correspondence to the executive secretary.

Saskatchewan

Memb. 200. Term of Office. July 1991–June 1992. Publication. *Saskatchewan Library Association Forum* (5 per year).
Pres. Heather West, SLA Office, 208-1850 Cornwall St., Regina S4P 2K2. Tel. 306-780-9413; *Exec. Dir.* Judy A. Livingston, Box 3388, Regina S4P 3H1. Tel. 306-780-9413, FAX 306-347-7500.
Address correspondence to the executive director.

Regional

Atlantic Provinces: N.B., Nfld., N.S., P.E.I.

Memb. (Indiv.) 350; (Inst.) 40. Term of Office. May 1991–Apr. 1992. Publications. *APLA Bulletin* (bi-mo.); *Membership Directory and Handbook* (ann.).
Pres. Judy Head; *Past Pres.* Andrea John; *V.P. Nova Scotia.* Gwen Whitford; *V.P. Prince Edward Island.* Priscilla Ykelenstam; *V.P. New Brunswick.* Susan Collins; *V.P. Newfoundland.* Elinor Benjamin; *V.P./Pres.-Elect.* Suzanne Sexty. Tel. 709-737-7427; *V.P. Memb.* Leslye McVicar; *Secy.* Faye Hopkins. Tel. 902-562-3279; *Treas.* Peter Glenister; *APLA Bulletin Ed.* Bradd Burningham.
Address correspondence to Atlantic Provinces Lib. Assn., c/o School of Lib. and Info. Studies, Dalhousie Univ., Halifax, NS B3H 4H8.

Middle Atlantic: Del., D.C., Md., Va., W. Va.

Term of Office. June 1991–July 1992.
Pres. Kitty Hurrey, Southern Maryland Regional Lib., Box 459, Charlotte Hall, MD 20622. Tel. 301-934-9442; *V.P.* Ernest P. Kallay, Jr., Lib. Dir., Clarksburg Harrison Public Lib., 404 W. Pike St., Clarksburg, WV 26301. Tel. 304-624-4411; *Treas.* Darrell Lemke, 9207 Chanute Dr., Bethesda, MD 20814.
Address correspondence to the president.

Midwest: Ill., Ind., Minn., Ohio

Term of Office. Oct. 1991–Nov. 1994.
Pres. Patricia Llerandi, Schaumburg Township Lib., 32 W. Library Lane, Schaumburg, IL 60194. Tel. 708-885-3373 ext. 150; *Treas.* Bonnie Beth Mitchell, Ohio Lib. Assn., 40 S. Third St., Suite 230, Columbus, OH 43215. Tel. 614-221-9057; *Past Pres.* James L. Wells, Dir., Washington County Lib., 2150 Radio Dr., Woodbury, MN 55125. Tel. 612-731-8487.

Address correspondence to the president, Midwest Federation of Lib. Assns.

Mountain Plains: Ariz., Colo., Kans., Mont., Nebr., Nev., N. Dak., Okla., S. Dak., Utah, Wyo.

Memb. 920. Term of Office. One year. Publications. *MPLA Newsletter* (bi-mo.). *Ed. and Adv. Mgr.* Jim Dertien, Sioux Falls Public Lib., 201 N. Main Ave., Sioux Falls, SD 57102. Tel. 605-339-7115; *Membership Directory* (ann.).

Pres. Corky Walters, Wyoming State Lib., Supreme Court Bldg., Cheyenne, WY 82002. Tel. 307-777-7281; *Exec. Secy.* Joe Edelen, I. D. Weeks Lib., Univ. of South Dakota, Vermillion, SD 57069. Tel. 605-677-6082.

Address correspondence to the executive secretary.

New England: Conn., Maine, Mass., N.H., R.I., Vt.

Memb. (Indiv.) 1,200; (Inst.) 100. Term of Office. One year (Treas., Dirs. two years). Publication. *New England Libraries* (6 per year). *Ed.* Renee Olson, Reading Public Lib., 64 Middlesex Ave., Reading, MA 01867. Tel. 617-944-0840.

Pres. Patricia Holloway, Southeastern Connecticut Lib. Assn., Avery Point, Groton, CT 06340. Tel. 203-445-5577; *V.P./Pres.-Elect.* Nancy Vincent, Keene Public Lib., 60 Winter St., Keene, NH 03431. Tel. 603-352-0157; *Secy.* Sally Reed, Ilsley Public Lib., Main St., Middlebury, VT 05753. Tel. 802-388-4095; *Treas.* Mary Balmer, Babbidge Lib. U-5A, Univ. of Connecticut, Storrs, CT 06269-1005. Tel. 203-486-2219; *Dirs.* Penny Pillsbury, Brownell Lib., 6 Lincoln St., Essex Junction, VT 05452. Tel. 802-878-6954; Anne Parent, Central Massachusetts Regional Lib. System, Salem Square, Worcester, MA 01608. Tel. 508-799-1654; *Past Pres.* Betsy Wilkens, Capitol Region Lib. Council, 599 Matianuck Rd., Windsor, CT 06095. Tel. 203-549-0404.

Address correspondence to the executive secretary, NELA.

Southeastern: Ala., Fla., Ga., Ky., La., Miss., N.C., S.C., Tenn., Va., W. Va.

Memb. 2,000. Term of Office. Oct. 1990–Oct. 1992. Publication. *The Southeastern Librarian* (q.).

Pres. James E. Ward, Box 4146, David Lipscomb Univ., Nashville, TN 37040. Tel. 615-269-1000 ext. 2283; *V.P./Pres.-Elect.* Gail Lazenby, Cobb County Public Lib., Roswell, GA 30060; *Secy.* Linda H. Perkins, 9707 Holiday Dr., Louisville, KY 40272; *Treas.* Linda S. Gill, N101 Forest Oaks, 1002 E. Northfield Blvd., Murfreesboro, TN 37130; *Exec. Secy.* Claudia Medori, SELA, Box 987, Tucker, GA 30085. Tel. 404-939-5080.

Address correspondence to the executive secretary, SELA.

Pacific Northwest: Alaska, Idaho, Mont., Oreg., Wash., Alberta, B.C.

Memb. (Active) 725; (Subscribers) 160. Term of Office. Oct. 1991–Sept. 1992. Publication. *PNLA Quarterly. Ed.* Katherine G. Eaton, 1631 E. 24 Ave., Eugene, OR 97403. Tel. 503-344-2027.

Pres. Don Miller, Seattle Public Lib., Greenlake Branch, 7364 E. Greenlake Dr. N., Seattle, WA 98115. Tel. 206-684-7546; *1st V.P./Pres.-Elect.* June Pinnell-Stephens, Fairbanks North Star Borough Public Lib. and Regional Center, Noel Wien Lib., 1215 Cowles St., Fairbanks, AK 99701. Tel. 907-452-5177; *2nd V.P.* Bonnie Schuster, Univ. of Montana, 403 Evans, Missoula, MT 59801. Tel. 406-243-6800; *Secy.* Elaine C. Leppert, Caldwell Public Lib., 1010 Dearborn St., Caldwell, ID 83605. Tel. 208-459-3242.

Address correspondence to the president.

State Library Agencies

The state library administrative agencies in each of the states will have the latest information on their state plan for the use of federal funds under the Library Services and Construction Act. The directors and addresses of these state agencies are listed below.

Alabama

Alice G. Stephens, Interim Dir., Alabama Public Lib. Services, 6030 Monticello Dr., Montgomery 36130-2001. Tel. 205-277-7330. FAX 205-272-9419.

Alaska

Karen Crane, Dir., Div. of State Libs., Archives, and Museums, Dept. of Educ., Box G, Juneau 99811-0571. Tel. 907-465-2910. FAX 907-465-2665.

Arizona

Sharon Womack, Dir., Dept. of Libs., Archives, and Public Records, 1700 W. Washington, Suite 16, State Capitol, Phoenix 85007-2896. Tel. 602-542-4035. FAX 602-256-6372.

Arkansas

John A. (Pat) Murphey, Jr., State Libn., Arkansas State Lib., One Capitol Mall, Little Rock 72201-1081. Tel. 501-682-1526 or 2848. FAX 501-682-1529.

California

Gary E. Strong, State Libn., California State Lib., Box 942837, Sacramento 94237-0001. Tel. 916-654-0174. FAX 916-654-0064.

Colorado

Nancy M. Bolt, Asst. Commissioner, Colorado State Lib., 201 E. Colfax, Denver 80203. Tel. 303-866-6733. FAX 303-830-0793.

Connecticut

Richard Akeroyd, State Libn., Connecticut State Lib., 231 Capitol Ave., Hartford 06106. Tel. 203-566-4301. FAX 203-566-8940.

Delaware

Jeff Lewis, Asst. Secy., Dept. of State, Townsend Bldg., Box 1401, Dover 19903-1401. Tel. 302-739-4711. FAX 302-739-3811.

District of Columbia

Hardy R. Franklin, Dir., D.C. Public Lib., 901 G St. N.W., Washington 20001. Tel. 202-727-1101. FAX 202-727-1129.

Florida

Barratt Wilkins, State Libn., State Lib. of Florida, R. A. Gray Bldg., Tallahassee 32399-0250. Tel. 904-487-2651. FAX 904-488-2746.

Georgia

Joe Forsee, Dir., Div. of Public Lib. Services, 156 Trinity Ave. S.W., Atlanta 30303-3692. Tel. 404-656-2461. FAX 404-656-9447.

Hawaii

Bartholomew A. Kane, State Libn., Hawaii State Public Lib. System, 465 S. King St., Rm. B1, Honolulu 96813. Tel. 808-548-5597 or 96. FAX 808-548-5588.

Idaho

Charles A. Bolles, State Libn., Idaho State Lib., 325 W. State St., Boise 83702-6072. Tel. 208-334-5124. FAX 208-334-4016.

Illinois

Bridget L. Lamont, Dir., Illinois State Lib., 300 S. 2nd St., Springfield 62701-1796. Tel. 217-782-2994. FAX 217-782-4326.

Indiana

C. Ray Ewick, Dir., Indiana State Lib., 140 N. Senate Ave., Indianapolis 46204-2296. Tel. 317-232-3692. FAX 317-232-3728.

Iowa

Christie Brandau, Acting Dir., State Lib. of Iowa, Dept. of Cultural Affairs, E. 12 and Grand, Des Moines 50319. Tel. 515-281-4105. FAX 515-281-3384.

Kansas

Duane F. Johnson, State Libn., Kansas State Lib., 3rd fl., State Capitol, Topeka 66612-1593. Tel. 913-296-3296. FAX 913-296-6650.

Kentucky

James A. Nelson, State Libn./Commissioner, Kentucky Dept. for Libs. and Archives, 300 Coffee Tree Rd., Box 537, Frankfort 40602-0537. Tel. 502-875-7000. FAX 502-564-5773.

Louisiana

Thomas F. Jaques, State Libn., State Lib. of Louisiana, Box 131, Baton Rouge 70821-0131. Tel. 504-342-4923. FAX 504-342-7335.

Maine

J. Gary Nichols, State Libn., Maine State Lib., State House Sta. 64, Augusta 04333. Tel. 207-289-5620. FAX 207-622-0933.

Maryland

Maurice Travillian, Asst. State Superintendent for Libs., Div. of Lib. Development and Services, Maryland State Dept. of Educ., 200 W. Baltimore St., Baltimore 21201-2595. Tel. 301-333-2113. FAX 301-333-2507.

Massachusetts

Irene Levitt, Acting Dir., Massachusetts Bd. of Lib. Commissioners, 648 Beacon St., Boston 02215. Tel. 617-267-9400. FAX 617-421-9833.

Michigan

James W. Fry, State Libn., Lib. of Michigan, Box 30007, 717 Allegan St., Lansing 48909. Tel. 517-373-1580. FAX 517-373-5700.

Minnesota

William G. Asp, Dir., Office of Lib. Development and Services, Minnesota Dept. of Educ., 440 Capitol Square Bldg., 550 Cedar St., St. Paul 55101. Tel. 612-296-2821. FAX 612-296-3272.

Mississippi

David M. Woodburn, Dir., Mississippi Lib. Commission, 1221 Ellis Ave., Box 10700, Jackson 39209-0700. Tel. 601-359-1036. FAX 601-354-4181.

Missouri

Monteria Hightower, Assoc. Commissioner for Libs./State Libn., Missouri State Lib., Box 387, 2002 Missouri Blvd., Jefferson City 65102-0387. Tel. 314-751-2751. FAX 314-751-3612.

Montana

Richard T. Miller, State Libn., Montana State Lib., 1515 E. 6 Ave., Helena 59620. Tel. 406-444-3115. FAX 406-444-5612.

Nebraska

Rod Wagner, Dir., Nebraska Lib. Commission, 1420 P St., Lincoln 68505. Tel. 402-471-2045. FAX 402-471-2083.

Nevada

Joan Kerschner, State Libn., Nevada State Lib. and Archives, Capitol Complex, Carson City 89710. Tel. 702-687-5160. FAX 702-887-2630.

New Hampshire

Kendall Wiggin, State Libn., New Hampshire State Lib., 20 Park St., Concord 03301-6303. Tel. 603-271-2397. FAX 603-271-2005.

New Jersey

Donna Dziedzic, Acting Asst. Commissioner for Educ./State Libn., Div. of State Lib., Archives and History, 185 W. State St., Trenton 08625-0520. Tel. 609-292-6200. FAX 609-292-2746.

New Mexico

Karen J. Watkins, State Libn., New Mexico State Lib., 325 Don Gaspar St., Santa Fe 87503. Tel. 505-827-3804. FAX 505-827-3820.

New York

Joseph F. Shubert, State Libn./Asst. Commissioner for Libs., New York State Lib., Rm. 10C34, C.E.C., Empire State Plaza, Albany 12230. Tel. 518-474-5930. FAX 518-474-2718.

North Carolina

Howard F. McGinn, Dir./State Libn., Dept. of Cultural Resources, Div. of State Lib., 109 E. Jones St., Raleigh 27601-2807. Tel. 919-733-2570. FAX 919-733-8748.

North Dakota

Patricia L. Harris, State Libn., North Dakota State Lib., Liberty Memorial Bldg., 604 E. Blvd., Capitol Grounds, Bismarck 58505-0800. Tel. 701-224-2492. FAX 701-224-2040.

Ohio

Richard M. Cheski, Dir., State Lib. of Ohio, 65 S. Front St., Columbus 43266-0334. Tel. 614-644-7061. FAX 614-644-6845.

Oklahoma

Robert L. Clark, Jr., State Libn., Oklahoma Dept. of Libs., 200 N.E. 18 St., Oklahoma City 73105-3298. Tel. 405-521-2502. FAX 405-525-7804.

Oregon

Jim Scheppke, Acting State Libn., Oregon State Lib., Salem 97310-0640. Tel. 503-378-4367. FAX 503-588-7119.

Pennsylvania

Sara Parker, State Libn., State Lib. of Pennsylvania, Box 1601, Harrisburg 17105. Tel. 717-787-2646. FAX 717-783-2070.

Rhode Island

Barbara Weaver, State Libn., Rhode Island Dept. of State Lib. Services, 300 Richmond St., Providence 02903-4222. Tel. 401-277-2726. FAX 401-351-1311.

South Carolina

James B. Johnson, Jr., Dir., South Carolina State Lib., 1500 Senate St., Box 11469, Columbia 29211. Tel. 803-734-8666. FAX 803-734-8676.

South Dakota

Jane Kolbe, State Libn., South Dakota State Lib., 800 Governors Dr., Pierre 57501-2294. Tel. 605-773-3131. FAX 605-773-4950.

Tennessee

Edwin Gleaves, State Libn./Archivist, Tennessee State Lib. and Archives, 403 Seventh Ave. N., Nashville 37243-0312. Tel. 615-741-3158. FAX 615-741-6471.

Texas

William Gooch, Dir./State Libn., Texas State Lib., Box 12927, Capitol Sta., Austin 78711. Tel. 512-463-5460. FAX 512-463-5436.

Utah

Amy Owen, Dir., Utah State Lib., 2150 S. 300 W., Suite 16, Salt Lake City 84115. Tel. 801-466-5888. FAX 801-533-4657.

Vermont

Patricia E. Klinck, State Libn., State of Vermont, Dept. of Libs., c/o State Office Bldg. Post Office, Montpelier 05609-0601. Tel. 802-828-3265. FAX 802-828-2199.

Virginia

John C. Tyson, State Libn., Virginia State Lib. and Archives, 11 St. at Capitol Sq., Richmond 23219. Tel. 804-786-2332. FAX 804-786-5855.

Washington

Nancy Zussy, State Libn., Washington State Lib., AJ-11, Olympia 98504-0111. Tel. 206-753-2915. FAX 206-586-7575.

West Virginia

Frederick J. Glazer, Dir., West Virginia Lib. Commission, Science and Cultural Center, Charleston 25305. Tel. 304-348-2041. FAX 304-348-2044.

Wisconsin

Leslyn M. Shires, Asst. Superintendent, Div. of Lib. Services, Wisconsin Dept. of Public Instruction, 125 S. Webster St., Box 7841, Madison 53707-7841. Tel. 608-266-2205. FAX 608-267-3579.

Wyoming

Suzanne J. LeBarron, State Libn., Wyoming State Lib., Supreme Court Bldg., Cheyenne 82002. Tel. 307-777-7283. FAX 307-777-6289.

American Samoa

Emma C. Penn, Program Director, Office of Lib. Services, Box 1329, Pago Pago 96799. Tel. 011-684-633-1181 or 1182.

Guam

Frank R. San Agustin, Territorial Libn., Nieves M. Flores Memorial Lib., 254 Martyr St., Agana 96910. Tel. 671-677-6913. FAX 671-477-9777.

Northern Mariana Islands

William Matson, Federal Programs Coordinator, Dept. of Educ., Commonwealth of the Northern Mariana Islands, Saipan 96950. DC Contact: Luis A. Benavente. Tel. 202-673-5869.

Palau (Republic of)

Masa-Aki N. Emesiochl, Federal Grants Coordinator, Office of Lib. and Social Services, Bureau of Education, Box 189, Koror 96940. DC Contact: Tel. 202-624-7795.

Puerto Rico

Celeste Benitez, Secy., Dept. of Educ., Apartado 759, Box 11496, Hato Rey 00919. Tel. 809-751-5972. FAX 809-754-0843.

Virgin Islands

Jeannette Allis Bastian, Dir. and Territorial Libn., Div. of Libs., Archives and Museums, 23 Dronningens Gade, St. Thomas 00802. Tel. 809-774-4307. FAX 809-775-1887.

State School Library Media Associations

Alabama

Alabama Lib. Assn., Children's and School Libns. Div. Memb. 450. Term of Office. Apr. 1991–Apr. 1992. Publication. *The Alabama Librarian* (7 per year).

Chpn. Tywanna Burton, 607 Candle Lane, Birmingham 35214. Tel. 205-979-3030; *Exec. Dir.* Barbara Black, 400 S. Union St., No. 255, Montgomery 36104.

Address correspondence to the executive director.

Arizona

School Lib. Media Div., Arizona State Lib. Assn. Memb. 500. Term of Office. Nov. 1991–Oct. 1992. Publication. *ASLA Newsletter.*

Pres. Cathy Bonnell, Ironwood Elementary School, 14850 N. 39 Ave., Phoenix 85023. Tel. 602-866-5165; *Pres.-Elect.* Shirley Dresbach, Monte Vista School, 2702 E. Flower St., Phoenix 85016. Tel. 602-257-2800; *Secy.* Linda Renfro, Blue Ridge Elementary School, Box 885, Lakeside 85929. Tel. 602-368-6126.

Address correspondence to the president.

Arkansas

Arkansas Assn. of School Lib. Media Educators. Term of Office. Oct. 1991–Oct. 1992.

Chpn. Rachel Byrd, 202 Stonehenge, Hot Springs 71901. Tel. 501-262-1530; *V.Chpn.* Grace Donoho, 405 Indian Trail, Springdale 72764. Tel. 501-750-4930; *Secy.-Treas.* Vicki Smith, 401 W. 24, Apt. 108, Fayetteville 72701. Tel. 501-824-5947.

California

California Media and Lib. Educators Assn., 1499 Old Bayshore Hwy., Suite 142, Burlingame 94010. Tel. 415-692-2350. Job Hotline. Tel. 415-697-8832. Memb. 1,700. Term of Office. June 1991–May 1992. Publication. *CMLEA Journal.* Ed. Barbara Jeffus.

Pres. Penny Kastanis, 8081 Center Pkwy., Sacramento 95823; *Pres.-Elect.* Ellis Vance, 1111 Van Ness, Fresno 93721; *Secy.* Margaret Baker, 5333 N. Locan, Clovis 93612; *Treas.* Margery Findlay, Rio Linda U.S.D., 6450 20th St., Rio Linda 95673; *Business Office Secy.* Nancy D. Kohn, CMLEA, 1499 Old Bayshore Hwy., Suite 142, Burlingame 94010.

Address correspondence to the business office secretary.

Colorado

Colorado Educational Media Assn. Memb. 650. Term of Office. Feb. 1992–Feb. 1993.

Pres. Roberta Ponis, 6997 Robb St., Arvada 80004; *Secy.* Janet Fleharty, 1309 Wynkoop Dr., Colorado Springs 80909; *Exec. Secy.* Mary Anne Strasser, Box 22814, Wellshire Sta., Denver 80222. Tel. 303-756-6023.

Address correspondence to the executive secretary.

Connecticut

Connecticut Educational Media Assn. Term of Office. May 1991–May 1992. Publications. *CEMA Update Monthly;* CEMA videotape "The School Library Media Specialist—A Continuing Story," available in 1/2" ($35) or 3/4" Umatic ($40).

Pres. Mary Ann Pellerin, 228 Morningside Dr. E., Bristol 06010. Tel. 203-589-5031; *V.P.* Carolyn Marcato, 155 Catalpa Rd., Wilton 06897. Tel. 203-762-2547; *Secy.* June Bray, 143 Larrabee St., East Hartford 06108. Tel. 203-289-7205; *Treas.* Judy Whitcomb, 57 Idylwood Dr., Northford 06472. Tel. 203-484-9172; *Admin. Secy.* Anne Weimann, 25 Elmwood Ave., Trumbull 06611. Tel. 203-372-2260.

Address correspondence to the administrative secretary.

Delaware

Delaware School Lib. Media Assn., Div. of Delaware Lib. Assn. Memb. 100. Term of Office. Apr. 1992–Apr. 1993. Publications. *DSLMA Newsletter* (irreg.); column in *DLA Bulletin* (3 per year).

Pres. Judy Mims, Caesar Rodney H.S., 239 Old North Rd., Camden 19934. Tel. 302-697-2161.

District of Columbia

District of Columbia Assn. of School Libns. Memb. 93. Term of Office. Aug. 1991–July 1993. Publication. *Newsletter* (4 per year).

Pres. Beverly J. Wheeler, T. Roosevelt H.S., 4301 13th St. N.W., Washington 20011. Tel. 202-576-6131; *V.P.* Cheryl M. Haynes; *Rec. Secy.* Anita Drayton; *Treas.* Lydia Jenkins; *Financial Secy.* Margie Riley; *Corres. Secy.* Sharon Sorrels, Banneker H.S., 800 Euclid St. N.W., Washington 20001.

Address correspondence to the corresponding secretary.

Florida

Florida Assn. for Media in Education, Inc. Memb. 1,450. Term of Office. Oct. 1991–Oct. 1992. Publication. *Florida Media Quarterly. Ed.* Nell Brown, Box 306, Bunnell 32010. Tel. 904-445-6080.

Pres. Marion Cannon, 6732 Magnolia Pt. Circle, Orlando 32810. Tel. 407-298-0756; *Pres.-Elect.* Donna Heald, 1941 N.E. 51 St., No. 48, Fort Lauderdale 33308. Tel. 305-572-1336; *V.P.* Jan B. Buchanan, 206 Fairway Dr., Longwood 32779. Tel. 407-365-4670; *Secy.* Sue Orth, 541 Manor Rd., Maitland 32751. Tel. 407-363-4822; *Treas.* Sherie Bargar, 4377 Weeping Willow Circle, Casselberry 32707. Tel. 407-647-4432; *Assn. Exec.* Mary Margaret Rogers, Box 13119, Tallahassee 32317. Tel. 904-893-5396.

Address correspondence to the association executive.

Georgia

School Lib. Media Div., Georgia Lib. Assn. Term of Office. Oct. 1991–Oct. 1993.

Chpn. Gordon Baker, Eagle's Landing H.S., 301 Tunis Rd., McDonough 30253. Tel. 404-954-9515; *Pres.* Sharon Self, Hardaway H.S., Columbus 31995. Tel. 404-649-0748; *Secy.* Kristina C. Brockmeier, Clayton State College Lib., Morrow 30260. Tel. 404-289-7527.

Address correspondence to the Georgia Lib. Assn., Box 39, Young Harris 30582. Tel. 404-379-3526.

Hawaii

Hawaii Assn. of School Libns. Memb. 280. Term of Office. June 1991–May 1992.

Pres. Linda Kim. Tel. 808-623-1552.

Address correspondence to the association, Box 23019, Honolulu 96823.

Idaho

Educational Media Div. of the Idaho Lib. Assn. Memb. 125. Term of Office. Oct. 1990–Oct. 1992. Publication. Column in *The Idaho Librarian* (q.).

Chpn. Joanne Sutton, Moscow School Dist. No. 281, 410 E. Third St., Moscow 83843. Tel. 208-882-1120; *Chpn.-Elect.* Susan Van Orden, Hawthorn Jr. High, 1025 W. Eldredge St., Pocatello 83201. Tel. 208-237-1680; *Secy.* Marie Scharnhorst, Box 115, Genesee 83832.

Address correspondence to the chairperson.

Illinois

Illinois School Lib. Media Assn. Term of Office. July 1, 1991–June 30, 1992.

Pres. Caroline Campbell, R.R. 4, Box 26D, Pekin 61554. Tel. 309-699-4411; *Pres.-Elect.* Kathleen L. Shannon, 312 Osage, Park Forest 60466. Tel. 708-210-2984.

Address correspondence to the association, 609 W. Douglas, Fairfield 62837.

Indiana

Assn. for Indiana Media Educators. Memb. 950. Term of Office. (Pres.) May 1, 1991–Apr. 30, 1992. Publication. *Indiana Media Journal.*

Pres. Linda Mills, Washington Elementary, Greensburg 47240. Tel. 812-663-2881; *Pres.-Elect.* Judy Hays, Avon H.S., Indianapolis 46234. Tel. 317-272-2586; *Exec. Secy.* Lawrence Reck, School of Education, Indiana State Univ., Terre Haute 47809. Tel. 812-237-2926.

Address correspondence to the executive secretary.

Iowa

Iowa Educational Media Assn. Memb. 550. Term of Office. Apr. 1992–Mar. 1993. Publication. *Iowa Media Message* (6 per year). *Ed.* Eric Maehl, Arrowhead Area Education Agency, Box 1399, Fort Dodge 50501. *Pres.* Ilene Rewerts McLain, Davenport Schools, 1002 W. Kimberley, Davenport 52806; *Secy.* Cathy Lawyer; *Treas.* Loretta Moon, Iowa Falls H.S., Iowa Falls 50126; *Dirs.* (1992) Mary Ann Emerick, Jo Rae Peiffer, Laura Pratt; (1993) Roger Volker, Curtis Jensen, Rebecca Mounsdon; (1994) Kay Rewerts, Sharon Smaldino, Ron Enger.

Address correspondence to the president.

Kansas

Kansas Assn. of School Libns. Memb. 700. Term of Office. July 1991–June 1992. Publication. *KASL Newsletter* (s. ann.).

Pres. Sharon Dietz, Indian Valley Elementary School, 11600 Knox, Overland Park 66210. Tel. 913-345-7450; *V.P./Pres.-Elect* Judy Eller, Sedgwick Jr.-Sr. H.S., Sedgwick 67135. Tel. 316-772-5155; *Treas.* Margie Eaton, 363 N. Elizabeth, Wichita 67203. Tel. 316-263-4257; *Secy.* Shelia Blume, 227 Fifth St., Phillipsburg 67661; *Business Mgr.* Kay Mounkes, Westridge Middle School, 9300 Nieman, Shawnee Mission 66214. Tel. 913-888-5214.

Address correspondence to the business manager.

Kentucky

Kentucky School Media Assn. Memb. 628. Term of Office. Oct. 1991–Oct. 1992. Publication. *KSMA Newsletter.*

Pres. Neata Wiley, 701 Carter Lane, Bowling Green 42103. Tel. 502-781-3313; *V.P./Pres.-Elect.* Sally Livingston, 116 Heady Ave., Louisville 40207. Tel. 502-894-8554; *Secy.* Becky Stephens, 103 Cathy St., Elizabethtown 42701. Tel. 502-769-2252; *Treas.* Sandra Moran, Warren East H.S., 6867 Louisville Rd., Bowling Green 42101. Tel. 502-781-1277.

Address correspondence to the president.

Louisiana

Louisiana Assn. of School Libns., c/o Louisiana Lib. Assn., Box 3058, Baton Rouge 70821. Memb. 582. Term of Office. July 1, 1991–June 30, 1992.

Pres. Idella A. Washington, 2260 Hampton Dr., Harvey 70058; *1st V.P.* Molly Storey Bethea, 1011 Peyton, Benton 71006; *Secy.* Mary Read, 1025 Seventh St., Lake Charles 70601.

Address correspondence to the association.

Maine

Maine Educational Media Assn. Memb. 300. Term of Office. May 1991–May 1992. Publication. *Mainely Libraries* (with the Maine Lib. Assn.).

Pres. JeriAnn Holt, Erskine Academy, RFD 6, Box 547, Augusta 04330. Tel. 207-445-2962; *1st V.P.* Ellen Berrie, Harpswell Islands School, R.R. 2, Box 2066, Brunswick 04011; *2nd V.P.* David Anderson, Thornton Academy, 438 Main St., Saco 04072. Tel. 207-282-3361; *Secy.* Linda Gustafson, Belfast Area H.S., Belfast 04915; *Treas.* Mary Jean Cowing, Buker Jr. H.S., Armory St., Augusta 04330.

Address correspondence to the president.

Maryland

Maryland Educational Media Organization (MEMO). Term of Office. July 1, 1991–June 30, 1992. Publication. *MEMORANDOM.*

Pres. Anna Smink, 11228 Green Watch Way, Gaithersburg 20878; *Secy.* Gail Bailey, 5409 Sweet Air Rd., Baldwin 21013; *Treas.* Carol Schmidt, 5631 Knollwood Rd., Bethesda 20816.

Address correspondence to the association, Box 21127, Catonsville 21228.

Massachusetts

Massachusetts Assn. for Educational Media. Memb. 500. Term of Office. June 1, 1992–May 31, 1993. Publication. *Media Forum* (q.).

Pres. Barbara Selvitella, Foxboro H.S., 120 South St., Foxboro 02035; *Treas.* Gail Thomas, Medway High and Middle Schools, 45 Holliston St., Medway 02053; *Admin. Asst.* Nancy Johnson, 41 Waverly St., Brookline 02146-6833. Tel. 617-566-5645.

Address correspondence to the administrative assistant.

Michigan

Michigan Assn. for Media in Education (MAME). Term of Office. Jan. 1992–Dec. 1992.

Pres. Barbara Wallace, Wyandotte Public Schools, 540 Eureka Rd., Wayne 48192. Tel. 313-246-1048; *Pres.-Elect.* Mary Adrion, Kent Intermediate School Dist., 2930 Knapp N.E., Grand Rapids 49505; Tel. 616-364-1333; *Secy.* Terence Madden, Ann Arbor Public Schools, 2555 S. State St., Ann Arbor 48104. Tel. 313-994-2220; *Treas.* Jan Landsberg, South Redford Schools, 26255 Schoolcraft Rd., Redford 48239. Tel. 313-535-4000; *Past Pres.* Peggy Sanford, Saugatuck Public Schools, Box 186, Saugatuck 49453. Tel. 616-857-2133; *V.P. for Special Interest Groups.* Judy Evers, Hillsdale Community Schools, 30 S. Norwood Ave., Hillsdale 49242; *V.P. for Regions.* Susan Schwartz, REMC 13, 210 State St., Mason 48854. Tel. 517-676-1277; *Exec. Dir.* Burton H. Brooks.

Address correspondence to the executive director, MAME, 6810 S. Cedar St., Suite 8, Lansing 48911. Tel. 517-699-1717, 616-842-9195.

Minnesota

Minnesota Educational Media Organization. Memb. 840. Term of Office. (Pres.) June 1992–1993 (other offices 2 years in alternating years). Publications. *Minnesota Media*; *ImMEDEAte*; *MEMOrandum* (mo.).

Pres. Fran McDonald, Rte. 1, Box 173, Kasota 56050. Tel. 507-389-1965; *Past Pres.* Judy G. Bull, 908 S.E. 12 Ave., Forest Lake 50825. Tel. 612-770-4741; *Secy.* Maureen Guentzel, Box 641, Rush City 55069; *Treas.* Jan Sorell; *Admin. Secy.* Carolyn Fredell, 408 Quarry Lane, Stillwater 55082. Tel. 612-439-5795.

Address correspondence to the administrative secretary.

Mississippi

Mississippi Lib. Assn., School Section. Memb. 200. Term of Office. Jan.–Dec.

Chpn. Annette Wilson, Clinton H.S., 711 Lakeview Dr., Clinton 39056. Tel. 601-924-5656; *V.Chpn.* Josie Roberts, Purvis Elementary School, Purvis 39475; *Secy.* Janine Eaton, Provine H.S., Jackson 39208. Tel. 601-960-5393.

Missouri

Missouri Assn. of School Libns. Memb. 903. Term of Office. June 1991–May 1992.

Pres. Lynne Stype, Republic Middle School, 518 N. Hampton, Republic 65738. Tel. 417-732-1814; *Pres.-Elect.* Judy Mahoney, Fox Hill Elementary, 545 N.E. 106 St., Kansas City 64155. Tel. 816-734-2900.

Address correspondence to MASL, Box 22476, Kansas City 64113-2476. Tel. 816-361-9175.

Montana

Montana School Lib. Media Div., Montana Lib. Assn. Term of Office. June 1991–May 1992.

Pres. Peggy Kimmet, 240 Maverick Rd., Hardin 59034. Tel. 406-665-1464; *V.P./Pres.-Elect.* Margaret Kernan, 2045 Gold Rush, Helena 59601. Tel. 406-442-5437.

Address correspondence to the president.

Nebraska

Nebraska Educational Media. Assn. Memb. 350. Term of Office. July 1, 1991–June 30, 1992. Publication. *NEMA News* (4 per year). *Ed.* c/o Box 286, Henderson 68371.

Pres. Deborah Levitov, Park Elementary School, 714 F St., Lincoln 68508. Tel. 402-436-1159; *Pres.-Elect.* Ella Epp, Henderson Public Schools, 15 and Front St., Henderson 68371. Tel. 402-723-4434; *Past Pres.* Jon Wibbels, Educational Service Unit No. 10, Box 850, Kearney 68848. Tel. 308-237-5927; *Secy.* Barbara Hansen, Norfolk Jr. H.S., Fifth and Pasewalk, Norfolk 68701. Tel. 402-371-2241; *Treas.* Ken Hughes, North Platte Public Schools, 301 W. F St., North Platte 69101. Tel. 308-532-8304.

Address correspondence to the president.

Nevada

Nevada School and Children's Lib. Section, Nevada Lib. Assn. Memb. 100. Publication. *HighRoller. Ed.* David Robrock, James R. Dickinson Lib., Univ. of Nevada, 4505 S. Maryland Pkwy., Las Vegas 89154.

Pres. Ed Iverson, 495 S. Bailey, Fallon 89406.

New Hampshire

New Hampshire Educational Media Assn. Memb. 265. Term of Office. June 1991–June 1992. Publication. *Online* (5 per year).

Pres. Harvey Hayashi, Londonderry Jr. H.S., 313 Mammoth Rd., Londonderry 03053. Tel. 603-432-6925; *V.P.* Susan Ballard, Londonderry School Dist., 268 Mammoth Rd., Londonderry 03053. Tel. 603-432-6920; *V.P.-Elect.* Margaret Beale, Hollis Jr. H.S., Hollis 03049. Tel. 603-465-2223; *Treas.* Jeff Kent, Broken Ground School, Concord 03301. Tel. 603-225-0825; *Rec. Secy.* Joan Abbot, Bicentennial Elementary School, E. Dunstable Rd., Nashua 03062. Tel. 603-594-4382; *Corres. Secy.* Libby Robbie, Lebanon H.S., 195 Hanover St., Lebanon 03766. Tel. 603-448-2055.

Address correspondence to the president.

New Jersey

Educational Media Assn. of New Jersey (EMAnj). Memb. 1,000. Term of Office. June 1991–June 1992. Publications. *Signal Tab* (newsletter, mo.); *Emanations* (journal, 2 per year).

Pres. Madeline Ianni, 114 Walt Whitman Blvd., Cherry Hill 08003; *Pres.-Elect.* Marianne Ramirez, 17 Diamond Ct., Glen Rock 07452; *V.P.* Mary Jane Smith, 4 Wilbur Terr., Sayreville 08872; *Rec. Secy.* Emily Snitow, 890 Talcott Rd., Westfield 07090; *Corres. Secy.* Marcelyn Young, 415 Valentine St., Highland Park 08904; *Treas.* Marcia Wolfe, 22 Stacy Dr., Belle Mead 08502.

Address correspondence to the president.

New Mexico

New Mexico Lib. Assn., School Libs. Children and Young Adult Services Div. Memb. 240. Term of Office. Apr. 1992–Apr. 1993.

Chpn. Serena Douglas, Belen Jr. H.S., 400 S. Fourth St., Belen 87002. Tel. 505-864-2422.

Address correspondence to the chairperson.

New York

School Lib. Media Sec., New York Lib. Assn., 252 Hudson St., Albany 12210. Tel. 518-432-6952, 800-252-6952. Memb. 1,100. Term of Office. Oct. 1991–Oct. 1992. Publications. *SLMSgram* (q.); participates in *NYLA Bulletin* (mo. except July and Aug.).

Pres. Rocco Staino, Ulster BOCES SLS, 175 Rte. 32 N., New Paltz 12561. Tel. 914-255-1402; *V.P./Pres.-Elect.* Judy Gray, Nottingham H.S. Lib., 3100 E. Genesee St., Syracuse 13224. Tel. 315-425-6533; *Past Pres.* Beatrice Angus, Madison-Oneida SLS, 614 Sherrill Rd., Sherrill 13461. Tel. 315-363-0451; *V.P. Communications.* Glenda Rowe, Saranac Central School, Saranac 12981. Tel. 518-293-6602. *V.P. Conferences.* Carolyn Giambra, Williamsville North H.S., 1595 Hopkins Rd., Williamsville 14221. Tel. 716-626-8529; *Secy.* Jan Siebold, Parkdale Elementary School, East Aurora 14052. Tel. 716-652-2100; *Treas.* Joan DiSanto, Saint Lawrence Lewis SLS, Box 310, Norwood 13668; *Bur. of School Lib. Media Liaison.* Robert Barron, State Educ. Dept., Rm. 676, Education Bldg. Annex, Albany 12234. Tel. 518-474-2468; *Div. of Lib. Development Liaison.* Joseph Mattie, Rm. 10B41, Cultural Education Center, Empire State Plaza, Albany 12230. Tel. 518-474-4970.

Address correspondence to the president or secretary.

North Carolina

North Carolina Assn. of School Libns. Memb. 1,000. Term of Office. Oct. 1991–Oct. 1993.

Chpn. Nona Pryor, Rte. 1, Box 510, Randleman 27317. Tel. 919-431-4452; *Chpn.-Elect.* Augie Beasley, East Mecklenburg H.S., 6800 Monroe Rd., Charlotte 28212. Tel. 704-343-6430.

Address correspondence to the chairperson.

North Dakota

North Dakota Lib. Assn., School Media Sec. Memb. 70. Term of Office. Sept. 1991–Sept. 1992. Publication. *The Good Stuff.*

Pres. Melody Kuehn, Minot H.S., Minot 58701. Tel. 701-857-4641; *Pres.-Elect.* Jackie Basaraba, Williston H.S., Williston 58801.

Tel. 701-572-0967; *Secy.* Charlotte Hill, Bismarck Public Schools, Bismarck 58501. Tel. 701-221-3421.

Address correspondence to the president.

Ohio

Ohio Educational Lib. Media Assn. Memb. 1,300. Term of Office. Jan.–Dec. 1992. Publication. *Ohio Media Spectrum* (q.).

Pres. Anthony Marshalek, Northeast Ohio IMC, Warren 44485; *Pres.-Elect.* Janice Thomas, 3549 Malley St., Akron 44319; *Exec. Dir.* Ann W. Hanning, 67 Jefferson Ave., Columbus 43215. Tel. 614-221-9057.

Address correspondence to the executive director.

Oklahoma

Oklahoma Assn. of School Lib. Media Specialists. Memb. 326. Term of Office. July 1, 1991–June 30, 1992. Publication. *Information Powerline.*

Chpn. Jonette S. Ellis, Enid Public Schools, 500 S. Independence, Enid 73701. Tel. 405-249-3558; *Chpn.-Elect.* Jeannie Johnson, Choctaw Jr. H.S., Choctaw 73020. Tel. 405-390-2207; *Secy.* Christie Hefner, Eisenhower Elementary School, Norman 73070. Tel. 405-366-5879; *Treas.* Ginger Parker, Box 721978, Norman 73070. Tel. 405-321-6903.

Address correspondence to the chairperson.

Oregon

Oregon Educational Media Assn. Memb. 700. Term of Office. Oct. 1, 1991–Sept. 30, 1992. Publication. *INTERCHANGE.*

Pres. Ruth Herbert; *Past Pres.* Rod Hevland; *Pres.-Elect.* Cathi Rooth; *Exec. Secy.* Sherry Hevland, 16695 S.W. Rosa Rd., Beaverton 97007. Tel. 503-649-5764.

Address correspondence to the executive secretary.

Pennsylvania

Pennsylvania School Libns. Assn. Term of Office. July 1, 1992–June 30, 1994. Publication. *Learning and Media* (4 per year).

Pres. Sally Myers, 337 Roley St., Belle Vernon 15012; *Past Pres.* Janice S. Dysart, R.D. 1, Box 196, Orangeville 17859. Tel. 717-683-5004.

Address correspondence to the president.

Rhode Island

Rhode Island Educational Media Assn. Memb. 290. Term of Office. June 1, 1991–May 31, 1992. Publication. *RIEMA Newsletter* (5 per year). *Ed.* Susan Bryan, 26B Tamarac Dr., Greenville 02828. Tel. 401-949-4230.

Pres. Bette G. Dion, 8 Evelyn Dr., Bristol 02809. Tel. 401-253-9345; *Pres.-Elect.* Cheryl McCarthy, 154 Carriage Dr., Portsmouth 02871. Tel. 401-848-7689; *V.P.* Gretchen P. Bernier, 230 Cumberland Rd., Warwick 02886. Tel. 401-885-5323; *Secy.* Janice Carreau, RFD 1, Box 486, Mystic, CT 06355. Tel. 203-536-7066; *Treas.* Joseph Light, 34 George St., Westerly 02891. Tel. 401-596-3173; *Memb. Chair.* Michael Mello, 486 Water St., Portsmouth 02871. Tel. 401-683-4499.

Address correspondence to the association, Box 762, Portsmouth 02871.

South Carolina

South Carolina Assn. of School Libns. Memb. 1,050. Term of Office. June 1, 1991–May 31, 1992. Publication. *Media Center Messenger* (5 per year).

Pres. Laura Blanchard, 36 Fairway Lakes, Myrtle Beach. Tel. 803-448-4679; *Pres.-Elect.* Judy Roumillat, 4515 Paramount Rd., Charleston. Tel. 803-554-0562.

Address correspondence to the association, Box 2442, Columbia 29202.

South Dakota

South Dakota School Lib. Media Assn., Sec. of the South Dakota Lib. Assn. and South Dakota Education Assn. Term of Office. Oct. 1991–Oct. 1992.

Pres. Bonnie Harrison; *Pres.-Elect.* Mary Gillick; *Secy.-Treas.* Rosalie Aslesen, Spearfish H.S., Spearfish 57783. Tel. 605-642-2612.

Address correspondence to the secretary-treasurer.

Tennessee

Tennessee Education Assn., Tennessee Assn. of School Libns. Term of Office. May 1991–Nov. 1992.

Pres. Nell Booker, 921 Burchwood Ave., Nashville 37216; *V.P.* Margaret Martin, 3016 High Acres Dr., Kingsport 37663; *Secy.* Marilyn Kemp, 35 Sunnymeade, Jackson 38305; *Treas.* Jane Sparks, 5513 Lakeshore Dr., Knoxville 37920.

Address correspondence to the president.

Texas

Texas Assn. of School Libns. Memb. 2,595. Term of Office. Apr. 1991–Apr. 1992. Publication. *Media Matters* (3 per year).

Chpn. Nancy Blumel, 1901 Jamaica Lane, Sherman 75090. Tel. 214-892-9115; *V.Chpn.* Laura Edwards, Box 1292, Coppell 75019. Tel. 214-393-3030; *Secy.-Treas.* Donna Pohl, 3634 Oak Creek Dr., San Angelo 76904. Tel. 915-658-6571.

Address correspondence to an officer or to TASL, 3355 Bee Cave Rd., Suite 603, Austin 78746. Tel. 512-328-1518.

Utah

Utah Educational Lib. Media Assn. Memb. 400. Term of Office. Mar. 1992–Mar. 1993. Publication. *UELMA Newsletter* (5 per year).

Pres. Michael Hirschi, Roy H.S., 2150 W. 4800 S., Roy 84067. Tel. 801-774-4922; *V.P./ Pres.-Elect.* Ilona Pierce, Jordan Dist. Media Center, 9361 S. 300 E., Sandy 84070. Tel. 801-565-7410; *Secy.* Barbara Kerr, S. Cache Middle School, 29 N. 400 W., Hiram 84319. Tel. 801-245-4051; *Exec. Secy.* David Walton, Alpine School Dist. Media Center, 50 N. Center, American Fork 84003. Tel. 801-756-8470.

Address correspondence to the executive secretary.

Vermont

Vermont Educational Media Assn. Memb. 170. Term of Office. May 1991–May 1992. Publication. *VEMA News* (q.).

Pres. Martha Day, UVM Media Lib., Pomeroy Hall, Burlington 05405. Tel. 802-656-1949; *Pres.-Elect.* Melissa Malcolm, Mount Abraham Union H.S., Bristol 05443.

Tel. 802-453-2333; *Secy.* Karen Hennig, Craftsbury Academy, Craftsbury 05826. Tel. 802-586-2541; *Treas.* Pat Nelson, Berlin Elementary School, Montpelier 05602. Tel. 802-223-2796.

Address correspondence to the president.

Virginia

Virginia Educational Media Assn. Term of Office. Nov. 1991–Nov. 1992.

Pres. Anne Jordan, Norfolk Public Schools, 800 E. City Hall Ave., Norfolk 23510. Tel. 804-441-2600; *Pres.-Elect.* Jane James, Roanoke County Public Schools, 526 College Ave., Salem 24153. Tel. 703-985-3913; *Treas.* Eileen Godwin, 11300 Yorkshire Ct., Fredericksburg 22401. Tel. 703-720-2336; *Past Pres.* Betty Hutsler, Frederick County Public Schools, Box 3508, Winchester 22601. Tel. 703-662-3888, ext. 140.

Address correspondence to the president.

Washington

Washington Lib. Media Assn. Memb. 1,150. Term of Office. Oct. 1991–Oct. 1992. Publication. *The Medium* (3 per year). *Ed.* Sue Weiss, 23708 107th Place W., Edmonds 98020-5238. Tel. 206-546-2715.

Pres. Elaine Twogood, 2539 56th Ave. N.E., Tacoma 98422. Tel. 206-927-5298; *Pres.-Elect.* Kathy Lemmer, 7412 84th St. Ct. S.W., Tacoma 98498. Tel. 206-588-8122; *Past Pres.* Carol Mackey, 9508 N.W. Ninth, Vancouver 98665. Tel. 206-573-5533; *V.P.* Dee Whyte, 2615 David Ct. E., Tacoma 98424. Tel. 206-922-5623; *Secy.* Janet Brown, 5702 16th Ave. S.E., Apt. B, Lacey 98503. Tel. 206-459-8594; *Treas.* Barbara J. Baker, Box 1413, Bothell 98041. Tel. 206-489-6258.

Address correspondence to the president.

West Virginia

West Virginia Educational Media Assn. Memb. 150. Term of Office. Apr. 1992–Apr. 1993. Publication. *WVEMA Newsletter.*

Pres. Linda Freeman, RFD 2, Box 264, Elkins 26241. Tel. 304-636-8993; *Pres.-Elect.* Lynn Bennett, Rte. 1, Box 282, Salem 26426.

Address correspondence to the president.

Wisconsin

Wisconsin Educational Media Assn. Memb. 870. Term of Office. Mar. 1992–Apr. 1994. Publications. *Dispatch* (newsletter; 6 times per year); *Wisconsin Ideas in Media* (ann.).
Pres. Nels Aakre, N6176 Summerglow Tr., Onalaska 54650. Tel. 608-789-7737; *Past Pres.* Jim Klein, 530 W. Capitol Dr., Appleton 54911. Tel. 414-832-6133.
Address correspondence to the president.

Wyoming

Wyoming Lib. Assn., School Lib. Media Sec. Memb. 50. Term of Office. Oct. 1991–Oct. 1992.
Pres. Kelly Kraft, Sheridan H.S., 1056 Long Dr., Sheridan 82801. Tel. 307-672-2495, Ext. 234; *V.P./Pres.-Elect.* Barbara Wegner, Cody Jr. H.S., 920 Beck Ave., Cody 82414. Tel. 307-587-4273.
Address correspondence to the president.

Puerto Rico

Puerto Rico Assn. of School Libns. (ABESPRI). Memb. 498. Publications. *ABESPRINF* (4 per year); *BIBESCO* (every 2 years).
Pres. Juanín Núñez (1990-1992); *Pres.-Elect.* Shirley Kennerley (1992-1994).
Address correspondence to the Asociación de Bibliotecarios Escolares de Puerto Rico, Box 1559, Hato Rey, PR 00919-1559.

State Supervisors of School Library Media Services

Alabama

Jane Bandy Smith, Educational Specialist, Lib. Media Services, Gordon Persons Bldg., Rm. 3345, 50 N. Ripley St., Montgomery 36130-3901. Tel. 205-242-8082, FAX 205-242-0482.

Alaska

B. Jo Morse, Alaska State Lib., School Lib./Media Coord., 3600 Denali, Anchorage 99503. Tel. 907-261-2977.

Arizona

Irene Munger, State Dept. of Educ., 1535 W. Jefferson, Phoenix 85007. Tel. 602-542-3052.

Arkansas

Margaret Crank, Lib. Media Program Specialist, Arkansas Dept. of Educ., Arch Ford Bldg., 4 Capitol Mall, Rm. 405B, Little Rock 72201. Tel. 501-682-4396.

Colorado

Nancy M. Bolt, Asst. Commissioner, Colorado State Lib., 201 E. Colfax Ave., Denver 80203. Tel. 303-866-6900, FAX 303-830-0793.
Lynda Welborn, Senior Consultant, School Media, Colorado Dept. of Educ., 201 E. Colfax Ave., Denver 80203. Tel. 303-866-6730, FAX 303-830-0793.

Connecticut

Betty B. Goyette, Coord., Learning Resources and Technology Unit, and Instructional Television Lib. Media Consultant; Linda Naimi, Assoc. Consultant, Computers in Instruction; and Dorothy M. Headspeth, Info. Specialist, Learning Resources and Technology Unit, State Dept. of Educ., Box 2219, Hartford 06145. Tel. 203-566-2250.

District of Columbia

Marie Harris Aldridge, Supervising Dir., Lib. Services, Dist. of Columbia Public Schools, Wilkinson Annex, Pomeroy Rd. and Erie St. S.E., Washington 20020. Tel. 202-767-8643.

Florida

Sandra W. Ulm, Administrator, School Lib. Media Services, Florida Dept. of Educ., 344 Florida Education Center, 325 W. Gaines St., Tallahassee 32399. Tel. 904-488-8184.

Georgia

Nancy V. Paysinger, Dir., Media Programs, Div. of Curriculum and Instruction, Georgia Dept. of Educ., Twin Towers E., Suite 2054, Atlanta 30334. Tel. 404-656-2418.

Hawaii

Patsy Izumo, Dir., Special Instructional Programs and Services Branch, State Dept. of Educ., 641 18th Ave., Honolulu 96816. Tel. 808-732-5535.

Illinois

Marie Rose Sivak, Educational Consultant, Curriculum Improvement Sec.; Byron Bartlett, Instructional TV Specialist; and Mark Wancket, Educational Consultant, TV Unit, State Bd. of Educ., 100 N. First St., Springfield 62777. Tel. 217-782-2826 (Sivak), 217-782-9374 (Bartlett, Wancket).

Indiana

Jacqueline G. Morris, Learning Resources, Center for School Improvement and Performance, Indiana Dept. of Educ., 229 State House, Indianapolis 46204. Tel. 317-232-9125.

Iowa

Betty Jo Buckingham, Consultant, Educational Media, State Dept. of Educ., Grimes State Office Bldg., Des Moines 50319-0146. Tel. 515-281-3707.

Kansas

June Saine Level, Lib. Media Specialist, Educational Assistance Sec., Kansas State Dept. of Educ., 120 E. Tenth St., Topeka 66612. Tel. 913-296-3434.

Kentucky

Judy L. Cooper, Consultant for School Media Services, State Dept. of Educ., 1809 Capital Plaza Tower, 500 Mero St., Frankfort 40601. Tel. 502-564-7168.

Maine

Walter J. Taranko, Coord., Media Services, Maine State Lib., LMA Bldg., State House Sta. 64, Augusta 04333. Tel. 207-289-5620.

Maryland

Gail C. Bailey, Acting Chief, School Lib. Media Services and State Media Services Branch, Div. of Lib. Development and Services, State Dept. of Educ., 200 W. Baltimore St., Baltimore 21201. Tel. 301-333-2125.

Massachusetts

Candace Boyden, Dept. of Educ., 1385 Hancock St., Quincy 02169. Tel. 617-770-7512.

Michigan

Daniel W. Schultz, Asst. Superintendent, Educational Technology and Grants, Michigan Dept. of Educ., Box 30008, Lansing 48909. Tel. 517-373-6331.

Minnesota

Joan C. Wallin, Supv., Learning Resources and Strategies Unit, Minnesota Dept. of Educ., 660 Capitol Sq. Bldg., Saint Paul 55101. Tel. 612-296-1570.

Mississippi

Carol R. Furr, State Dept. of Educ., Educational Media Services, Box 771, Jackson 39205. Tel. 601-359-3778.

Missouri

Sandra Cullers, Supv., Missouri School Improvement Program, Dept. of Elementary and Secondary Education, Box 480, Jefferson City 65102. Tel. 314-751-3078.

Montana

Lorrie Monprode-Holt, Lib. Media Specialist, Office of Public Instruction, 1300 11th Ave., Helena 59601. Tel. 406-444-2979, FAX 406-444-3924.

Nebraska

Dan Mook, State Dept. of Educ., Liaison to School Lib. Media Programs, Box 94987, 301 Centennial Mall S., Lincoln 68509. Tel. 402-471-0535.

Nevada

Jody Gehrig, Lib. Media Consultant, State Dept. of Educ., Capitol Complex, 400 W. King St., Carson City 89710. Tel. 702-687-3136.

New Hampshire

Susan C. Snider, Curriculum Supv., Lib. Media Services, State Dept. of Educ., Div. of Instructional Services, 101 Pleasant St., Concord 03301. Tel. 603-271-2632.

New Jersey

Jean E. Harris, Consultant, State Dept. of Educ., State Lib., 185 W. State St., CN 520, Trenton 08625-0520. Tel. 609-292-6245.

New Mexico

Mary Jane Vinella, Lib./Media Consultant, Dept. of Educ., Education Bldg., Santa Fe 87501-2786. Tel. 505-827-6504.

New York

Robert E. Barron, Chief, Bur. of School Lib. Media Programs, State Educ. Dept., Rm. 676 EBA, Albany 12234. Tel. 518-474-2468.

North Carolina

Elsie L. Brumback, Dir. of Media and Technology, Dept. of Public Instruction, Raleigh 27603-1712. Tel. 919-733-3170.

North Dakota

Patricia Herbel, Dir., Elementary Education, Dept. of Public Instruction, State Capitol, 600 East Blvd., Bismarck 58505. Tel. 701-224-2295.

Ohio

Carl Carter, Lib./Media Consultant, Ohio Dept. of Educ., 65 S. Front St., Rm. 611, Columbus 43266-0308. Tel. 614-466-9272.

Oklahoma

Bettie Estes-Rickner, Dir.; Betty Riley, Carol Casey, David Titus, Coords., Library Media Sec., State Dept. of Educ., 2500 N. Lincoln Blvd., Oklahoma City 73105-4599. Tel. 405-521-2956.

Oregon

James W. Sanner, Specialist, Instructional Technology, Oregon Dept. of Educ., 700 Pringle Pkwy. S.E., Salem 97310. Tel. 503-378-8004.

Pennsylvania

Vacant, Div. of School Lib. Media Services, State Dept. of Educ., 333 Market St., Harrisburg 17126-0333. Tel. 717-787-6704.

Rhode Island

Edward T. Costa, Dir., School Support Services, Rhode Island Dept. of Elementary and Secondary Education, 22 Hayes St., Providence 02908. Tel. 401-277-2638.

South Carolina

To be appointed, Lib./Media Consultant, State Dept. of Educ., Rutledge Bldg., Rm. 801, Columbia 29201. Tel. 803-734-8378.

South Dakota

Donna Gilliland, School Lib./Media Coord., South Dakota State Lib., 800 Governors Dr., Pierre 57501-2294. Tel. 605-773-3131.

Tennessee

Betty Latture, Consultant, Lib./Media Services, Tennessee Dept. of Educ., Cordell Hull Bldg., 4th fl., North Wing, Nashville 37243-0379. Tel. 615-741-0874.

Texas

June Kahler, Dir., Lib. Media Program, Texas Education Agency, 1701 N. Congress, Austin 78701-1494. Tel. 512-463-9556.

Utah

Steven R. Mecham, Assoc. Superintendent, Instructional Services, State Office of Educ., 250 E. Fifth S., Salt Lake City 84111. Tel. 801-538-7515.

Vermont

Leda Schubert, School Lib./Media Consultant, Vermont Dept. of Educ., Montpelier 05620. Tel. 802-828-3111.

Virginia

Gloria K. Barber, Assoc., Lib./Media, Dept. of Educ., Box 6Q, 101 N. 14 St., Richmond 23219. Tel. 804-225-2539.

Washington

John C. Rutherford, Supv., Learning Resources Services, Office of State Superintendent of Public Instruction, Old Capitol Bldg., Box 47200, Olympia 98504. Tel. 206-753-6723.

West Virginia

Wanda Kirchner, Coord., Instructional Technology, West Virginia Dept. of Educ., Capitol Complex, Bldg. 6, Rm. B-346, Charleston 25305. Tel. 304-348-3538.

Wisconsin

Carolyn Winters Folke, Dir., Bur. for Instructional Media and Technology, State Dept. of Public Instruction, Box 7841, Madison 53707. Tel. 608-266-1965.

Wyoming

Nancy Leinius, Education Programs Specialist, Wyoming Dept. of Educ., Hathaway Bldg., Cheyenne 82002. Tel. 307-777-6226.

American Samoa

Eddie Manuma, Supv., Office of Lib. Services, Dept. of Educ., Box 1329, Pago Pago 96799. Tel. (011) 684-633-4474.

Marshall Islands

Tamar A. Jordan, Libn., National Archives, Box 629, Majuro, Marshall Islands 96960.

Northern Mariana Islands

Malinda S. Matson, Dir., Lib. Services, Northern Marianas College, Box 1250, Saipan, MP 96950.

Puerto Rico

Luz M. Estrada, Asst. Secy., Education Extension Area, Dept. of Educ., Box 759, Hato Rey 00919. Tel. 809-753-9211.

Virgin Islands

Fiolina B. Mills, State Dir., State Media Lib. Services, Virgin Islands Dept. of Educ., 44-46 Kongens Gade, St. Thomas 00801. Tel. 809-776-2573, 809-774-5339.

International Library Associations

Inter-American Association of Agricultural Librarians and Documentalists

c/o IICA-CIDIA, Apdo. 55-2200, Coronado, Costa Rica

Object

"To serve as liaison among the agricultural librarians and documentalists of the Americas and other parts of the world; to promote the exchange of information and experiences through technical publications and meetings; to promote the improvement of library services in the field of agriculture and related sciences; to encourage the improvement of the professional level of the librarians and documentalists in the field of agriculture in Latin America."

Officers

Pres. Piedad Montaño de Mayolo, CIAT, Colombia; *V.P.* Susana Sperry, EMBRAPA, Brazil; *Exec. Secy.* Ghislaine Poitevien, c/o IICA-CIDIA, Apdo. 55-2200, Coronado, Costa Rica.

Publications

AIBDA Actualidades (irreg.).
Boletín Especial (irreg.).
Boletín Informativo (3 per year).
Diccionario Histórico del Libro y de la Biblioteca (U.S. price: Memb. $15 plus postage; nonmemb. $20 plus postage).
Guía para Bibliotecas Agrícolas, by Olga Lendvay (U.S. price: Memb. $10 plus postage; nonmemb. $15 plus postage).
Páginas de Contenido: Ciencias de la Información (q.).
Revista AIBDA (2 per year; Memb. $10 plus postage; nonmemb. $25 for institutions and $20 for individuals plus postage).

International Association of Agricultural Librarians and Documentalists

c/o J. van der Burg, Acting Secretary-Treasurer,
PUDOC, Jan Kophuis, Box 4, 6700 AA Wageningen, The Netherlands

Object

"The Association shall, internationally and nationally, promote agricultural library science and documentation as well as the professional interest of agricultural librarians and documentalists." Founded 1955. Memb. 634. Dues (Inst.) $70; (Indiv.) $25.

Officers

Pres. J. H. Howard, National Agricultural Lib., Beltsville, MD 20705; *Sr. V.P.* Syed Salim Agha, Lib. Universiti Pertanian Malaysia, 43400 UPM, Serdang, Selangor, Malaysia; *Jr. V.P.* W. Laux, Biologische Bundesanstalt, Königin-Luise-Strasse 19, W-1000 Berlin 33, Germany; *Secy.-Treas.* J. van der Burg, PUDOC, Box 4, 6700 AA Wageningen, The Netherlands; *Ed.* A. P. Powell, Agriculture Lib., Agriculture Science Center-North, Lexington, KY 40546.

Executive Committee

C. Boast, USA; E. Herpay, Hungary; J. Kennedy-Olsen, USA; J. R. Metcalfe, UK; T. Niang, Senegal; N. W. Posnett, UK; V.

Pozdnyakov, former Soviet Union; J. M. Schippers, The Netherlands; J. C. Sison, Philippines; W. E. Umbima, Kenya; representatives of national associations of agricultural librarians and documentalists.

Publications

Quarterly Bulletin of the IAALD (memb.).
World Directory of Agricultural Information Resource Centres.

International Association of Law Libraries

c/o The University of Chicago, D'Angelo Law Library,
1121 E. 60 St., Chicago, IL 60637

Object

"To promote on a cooperative, non-profit, and fraternal basis the work of individuals, libraries, and other institutions and agencies concerned with the acquisition and bibliographic processing of legal materials collected on a multinational basis, and to facilitate the research and other uses of such materials on a worldwide basis." Founded 1959. Memb. Over 600 in 60 countries.

Officers (1989–1992)

Pres. Adolf Sprudzs, Univ. of Chicago, D'Angelo Law Lib., 1121 E. 60 St., Chicago, IL 60637; *1st V.P.* John Rodwell, Kensington, Australia; *2nd V.P.* Yoshiro Tsuno, Tokyo, Japan; *Secy.* Timothy Kearley, Baton Rouge, LA; *Treas.* Ivan Sipkov, Washington, DC.

Board Members (1989–1992)

Katalin Balázs-Veredy, Hungary; Marga Coing, Germany; David Combe, USA; Sng Yok Fong, Singapore; Igor I. Kavass, USA; Arno Liivak, USA; June Renie, Trinidad and Tobago; Joachim Schwietzke, Germany.

Services

1. The dissemination of professional information through the *International Journal of Legal Information*, through continuous contacts with formal and informal national groups of law librarians, and through work within other international organizations, such as IFLA.

2. Continuing education through one-week IALL Seminars in International Law Librarianship.

3. The preparation of special literature for law librarians, such as the *European Law Libraries Guide*, and of introductions to basic foreign legal literature.

4. Direct personal contacts and exchanges between IALL members.

Publications

The IALL Messenger (newsletter, irreg.).
International Journal of Legal Information (3 per year). *Ed.-in-Chief.* Ivan Sipkov, 4917 Butterworth Place N.W., Washington, DC 20016.

International Association of Metropolitan City Libraries

c/o Chr. Relly, Director, Pestalozzi-Bibliothek,
Zähringerstr. 17, CH-8001 Zurich, Switzerland

Object

INTAMEL is a platform for professional communication and information for libraries of cities with 400,000 or more inhabitants. INTAMEL has more than 100 members in approximately 40 countries.

Officers

Pres. M. P. K. Barnes, Dir. of Libs. and Art Galleries, Guildhall Lib., Aldermanbury, London EC2P 2EJ, England; *Secy.-Treas.* Chr. Relly, Dir., Pestalozzi-Bibliothek, Zähringerstr. 17, CH-8001 Zurich, Switzerland.

Publications

Annual International Statistics of City Libraries (INTAMEL).

INTAMEL Newsletter.
Various lecture papers.

International Association of Music Libraries, Archives and Documentation Centres (IAML)

c/o Veslemöy Heintz, Secretary-General
Svenskt musikhistoriskt arkiv, Box 16326, S-103 26 Stockholm, Sweden

Object

"To promote the activities of music libraries, archives, and documentation centers and to strengthen the cooperation among them; to promote the availability of all publications and documents relating to music and further their bibliographical control; to encourage the development of standards in all areas that concern the association; and to support the protection and preservation of musical documents of the past and the present." Memb. 1,800.

Board Members (1989–1992)

Pres. Catherine Massip, Dir., Département de la Musique, Bibliothèque Nationale, 58 rue Richelieu, F-75084 Paris Cedex 02, France; *Past Pres.* Maria Calderisi, National Lib. of Canada, 395 Wellington St., Ottawa, ON K1A 0N4, Canada; *V.P.* Lenore Coral, Music Library, Cornell Univ., Ithaca, NY 14853; Julius Húlek, Music Dept., National Lib. of the CR, Klementinum 190, 11001 Prague 1, Czechoslovakia; Knud Ketting, Aalborg symfoniorkester, Kjellerupsgade 14, DK-9000 Aalborg, Denmark; Wolfgang

Krueger, Fachhochschule für Bibliothekswesen, Wolframstr. 32, W-7000 Stuttgart 1, Germany; *Secy.-Gen.* Veslemöy Heintz, Svenskt musikhistoriskt arkiv, Box 16326, S-103 26 Stockholm, Sweden; *Treas.* Don L. Roberts, Music Lib., Northwestern Univ., Evanston, IL 60208.

Publication

Fontes Artis Musicae (4 per year; memb.). *Ed.* Brian Redfern, 27 Plantation Rd., Leighton Buzzard LU7 7HJ, England.

Professional Branches

Broadcasting and Orchestra Libraries. Helen Faulkner, 26 Vere Rd., Brighton, Sussex BN1 4NR, England.
Libraries in Music Teaching Institutions. Michèle Lancelin, Bibliothèque du Conservatoire National de Région, 22 rue de la Belle Feuille, F-92100 Boulogne, France.
Public Libraries. Maria Nyéki, 115 rue J. Bleuzen, F-92170 Vanves, France.
Research Libraries. Hugh Cobbe, Music Libn., British Lib., Great Russell St., London WC1B 3DG, England.

International Association of Orientalist Librarians

c/o Julia L. Y. Chan, Secretary-Treasurer
Assistant Librarian, University of Hong Kong Library,
Pokfulam Rd., Hong Kong

Object

"To promote better communication among Orientalist librarians and libraries, and others in related fields, throughout the world; to pro-

vide a forum for the discussion of problems of common interest; to improve international cooperation among institutions holding research resources for Oriental Studies." The term *Ori-*

ent here specifies the Middle East, East Asia, and the South and Southeast Asia regions.

Founded in 1967 at the 27th International Congress of Orientalists (ICO) in Ann Arbor, Michigan. Affiliated with the International Federation of Library Associations and Institutions (IFLA) and International Congress for Asian and North African Studies (formerly ICO).

Officers

Pres. Lai-bing Kan; *Secy.-Treas.* Julia L. Y. Chan; *Ed.* Michael J. Costin.

Publication

International Association of Orientalist Librarians Bulletin (s. ann.; memb.).

International Association of School Librarianship

c/o Jean Lowrie, Executive Secretary
Box 1486, Kalamazoo, MI 49005

Object

"To encourage the development of school libraries and library programs throughout all countries; to promote the professional preparation of school librarians; to bring about close collaboration among school libraries in all countries, including the loan and exchange of literature; to initiate and coordinate activities, conferences, and other projects in the field of school librarianship." Founded 1971. Memb. (Indiv.) 800; (Assn.) 41.

Officers and Executive Board

Pres. Lucille C. Thomas, USA; *V.P.* Sigrunklara Hannisdöttir, Iceland; *Treas.* Donald Adcock, USA; *Exec. Secy.* Jean Lowrie, USA; *Dirs.* Beatrice Anderson, Jamaica; Gerald Brown, Canada; David Elaturoti, Nigeria; Gloria Hall, Bolivia; Gunilla Janlert, Sweden; Takeshi Murofushi, Japan; Fay Nicholson, Australia; Melvin Rainey, Fiji; Felix Tawete, Swaziland.

Publications

Books and Borrowers.
Getting Started: A Bibliography of Ideas and Procedures (o.p.).
IASL Conference Proceedings (ann.).
IASL Monograph Series.
IASL Newsletter (q.).
Indicators of Quality for School Library Media Programs.
Persons to Contact for Visiting School Libraries/Media Centers, 6th ed.

U.S. Members

American Assn. of School Libs.; Assn. de Bibliotecarios Escolares de Puerto Rico; Educational Media Assn. of New Jersey; Hawaii School Lib. Assn.; Illinois Assn. for Media in Education; Louisiana Assn. of School Libns.; Maryland Educational Media Organization; Michigan Assn. for Media in Education; Oregon Educational Media Assn.; Virginia Educational Media Assn.; Washington Lib. Media Assn.

International Association of Sound Archives

c/o Sven Allerstrand, Director,
The National Archive of Recorded Sound and Moving Images (ALB),
Box 7371, S-103 91 Stockholm, Sweden

Object

The International Association of Sound Archives (IASA) is a nongovernmental UNESCO-affiliated organization. It was established in

1969 in Amsterdam to allow international cooperation among archives that preserve recorded sound documents. IASA interests lie in a wide variety of recorded sound, including music and cover problems common to the variety of collections with which the association deals: problems of acquisition, preservation, organization, documentation, copyright, accessibility, distribution, and the technical aspects of recording and playback. The association is actively involved in the preservation, organization, and use of sound recordings, techniques of recording, and methods of reproducing sound in all fields in which the audio medium is used; the exchange of recordings among archives and of related literature and information; and in all subjects relating to the professional work of sound archives and archivists.

Membership

Open to all categories of archives and other institutions that preserve sound recordings, and to organizations and individuals having a serious interest in the purposes or welfare of IASA. The association includes members representing national archives; archives of music, history, literature, drama, and folklife recordings; collections of oral history, natural history, bioacoustic, and medical sounds; recorded linguistic and dialect surveys; and radio and television sound archives.

Officers (1990–1993)

Pres. Gerald D. Gibson, 118 Monroe St., Apt. 410, Rockville, MD 20850; *V.P.s.* Gior-

gio Adamo, Discoteca di Stato, Via Caetani 32, I-00186 Rome, Italy; Hans Bosma, Gruttoweide 215, 6708 BG Wageningen, The Netherlands; Magdalena Csève, Hungarian Radio, Documentation Dept., Bródy Sandór u. 5-7, H-1800 Budapest, Hungary; *Past Pres.* Helen P. Harrison, Open Univ. Lib., Walton Hall, Milton Keynes MK7 6AA, England; *Ed.* Grace Koch, Australian Institute of Aboriginal and Torres Strait Islander Studies (AIATSIS), Box 553, Canberra, A.C.T. 2601, Australia; *Treas.* Marit Grimstad, Programarkivet, NRK, N-0340 Oslo 3, Norway; *Secy.-Gen.* Sven Allerstrand, ALB, Box 7371, S-103 91 Stockholm, Sweden.

Publications

An Archive Approach to Oral History, by David Lance (1978).
Directory of Members, 2nd edition, compiled by Grace Koch (1982; ISBN 0-946475-00-8; o.p.).
Phonographic Bulletin (journal; ISSN 2533-004X). Index issues 1–40, 1971–1984.
Selection in Sound Archives, edited by Helen Harrison (1984; ISBN 0-946475-02-4).
Sound Archives: A Guide to Their Establishment and Development, edited by David Lance (1983; ISBN 0-946475-01-6).

International Association of Technological University Libraries

c/o President, Gerard A. J. S. van Marle,
Twente University of Technology Library,
Box 217, 7500 AE Enschede, The Netherlands

Object

"To provide a forum where library directors can meet to exchange views on matters of current significance in the libraries of Universities of Science and Technology." Research projects identified as being of sufficient interest may be followed through by working parties or study groups.

Membership

Ordinary, official observer, sustaining, and nonvoting associate. Membership fee is 160

guilders per year (430 guilders for 3 years, 680 guilders for 5 years). Memb. 198 (in 41 countries).

Officers and Executives

Pres. Gerard A. J. S. van Marle, Twente Univ. of Technology Lib., Box 217, 7500 AE Enschede, The Netherlands; *Secy.* Michael Breaks, Libn., Heriot-Watt Univ., Riccarton, Edinburgh EH14 4AS, Scotland; *Treas.* Annette Winkel-Schwarz, National Technological Lib. of Denmark, Anker Engellundsvej 1,

DK-2800 Lyngby, Denmark; *1st V.P.* Nancy Fjällbrant, Sweden; *2nd V.P.* Anna Dömötor, Hungary; *Membs.* Tom Cochrane, Australia; Dietmar Brandes, Germany; *Immediate Past Pres.* Elin Törnudd, Finland; *North American Regional Group Chpn.* Jay K. Lucker, USA; *IATUL Proceedings Editorial Bd. Chpn.* Dennis Shaw, UK; *Ed.* Joan Hardy, Central Libs., Imperial College, London, England; *IATUL News Ed.* Nancy Fjällbrant, Sweden

Publications

IATUL News (irreg.).
IATUL Proceedings (ann.).

International Council on Archives

Executive Director, 60 rue des Francs-Bourgeois, F-75003 Paris, France

Object

"To establish, maintain, and strengthen relations among archivists of all lands, and among all professional and other agencies or institutions concerned with the custody, organization, or administration of archives, public or private, wherever located." Established 1948. Memb. 1,100 (representing 150 countries and territories). Dues (Indiv.) $50; (Inst.) $50; (Archives Assns.) $50 or $100; (Central Archives Directorates) $250 or $115 minimum, computed on the basis of GNP per capita.

Officers

Exec. Dir. Charles Kesckeméti.

Publications

Archivum (ann.; memb. or subscription to K. G. Saur Verlag, Ortlerstr. 8, Postfach 70 16 20, W-8000 Munich 70, Germany).
Guide to the Sources of the History of Nations (Latin American Series, 12 vols. pub.; African Series, 14 vols. pub.; Asian Series, 13 vols. pub.).
ICA Bulletin (s. ann.; memb., or $15).
Janus (s. ann.; memb.)
List of other publications available from the executive director.

International Federation for Information and Documentation (FID)

Box 90402, 2509 LK The Hague, The Netherland

Object

"To promote, through international cooperation, research in and development of information science, information management, and documentation, which includes inter alia the organization, storage, retrieval, repackaging, dissemination, value adding to information, and evaluation of information, however recorded, in the fields of science, technology, industry, social sciences, arts, and humanities."

Program

FID devotes much of its attention to corporate information; industrial, business, and finance information; information policy research; the application of information technology; information service management; the marketing of information systems and services; content analysis, for example, in the design of database systems; linking information and human resources; and the repackaging of information for specific user audiences. The following commissions, committees, and groups have been established to execute FID's program of activities: *Regional Commissions:* Commission for Western, Eastern and Southern Africa (FID/CAF), Commission for Asia and Oceania (FID/CAO), Commission for Latin America (FID/CLA), Commission for Northern Africa and the Near East (FID/NANE), Regional Organization for Europe

(FID/ROE) (currently being formed); *Committees:* Classification Research, Education and Training, Information for Industry, Information Policies and Programmes, Linguistics in Information and Documentation, Patents Information and Documentation, Research on the Theoretical Basis of Information, Social Sciences Documentation and Information, Universal Decimal Classification; *Special Interest Groups:* Advisory Services for Small and Medium-Sized Enterprises; Banking, Finance, and Insurance Information; Executive Information Systems; Roles, Careers, and Development of the Modern Information Professional; Marketing Systems and Services; Safety Control and Risk Management; Training for Information Resources Management; new groups to be formed on: environmental information, information technology, information for public administration.

Officers

Pres. Ritva T. Launo, ALKO Ltd., Box 350, SF-00101 Helsinki, Finland; *V.Ps.* Yuzuru Fujiwara, Institute of Electronics and Info. Science, Univ. of Tsukuba, Tsukuba-shi, Ibaraki, 305 Japan; P. V. Nesterov, VINITI, ul. Usievicha 201, Moscow 125219, Russia; Elmer V. Smith, Canada Institute for Scientific and Technical Info. (CISTI), National Research Council of Canada, Ottawa, ON K1A 0S2, Canada; *Treas.* Roger Bowes, Aslib, Information House, 20-24 Old St., London EC1V 9AP, England; *Councillors.* J. R. P. Alvarez-Ossorio, Madrid, Spain; Margarita Almada de Ascencio, Mexico D.F.,

Mexico; Barry L. Burton, Hong Kong; Tamás Földi, Budapest, Hungary; Forest W. Horton, Jr., Washington, D.C., USA; Karl Kalseth, Stabekk, Norway; Zh. Marinov, Sofia, Bulgaria; Antonio L. Carvalho de Miranda, Brasilia D.F., Brazil; R. Ogwang-Ameny, Kampala, Uganda; Anna M. Prat Trabal, Santiago, Chile; Neva Tudor Silovic, Zagreb, Yugoslavia; Karl A. Stroetmann, Cologne, Germany. *Belgian Memb.* L. Van Simaeys, Louvain-la-Neuve, Belgium; *Exec. Dir.* Ben G. Goedegebuure, The Hague, The Netherlands; *Pres. FID/CLA.* H. Arango Sales, Havana, Cuba; *Pres. FID/CAO.* I. Dickson, Clayton, Victoria, Australia; *Pres. FID/CAF.* M. H. Wali, Lagos, Nigeria.

Address all correspondence to the executive director, Box 90402, 2509 LK The Hague, The Netherlands.

Publications

FID Annual Report (ann.).
FID Directory (bienn.).
FID News Bulletin (mo.) with supplements *Document Delivery and Reproduction* (q.) and *Research Reviews in Documentation and Librarianship* (irreg.).
FID Publications List (irreg.).
International Forum on Information and Documentation (q.).
Newsletter on Education and Training Programmes for Information Personnel (q.).
Proceedings of congresses; Universal Decimal Classification editions; manuals; directories; bibliographies on information science, documentation, mechanization, linguistics, training, and classification.

International Federation of Film Archives (FIAF)

Secretariat, 190 rue Franz Merjay, B-1180 Brussels, Belgium
(32-2) 343-06-91, FAX (32-2) 343-76-22

Object

"To facilitate communication and cooperation between its members, and to promote the exchange of films and information; to maintain a code of archive practice calculated to satisfy all national film industries, and to encourage industries to assist in the work of the Federation's members; to advise its members on all matters of interest to them, especially the preservation and study of films; to give every possible assistance and encouragement to new film archives and to those interested in creating them." Founded in Paris, 1938. Affiliates: 93 (in 60 countries).

Officers

Pres. Robert Daudelin, Canada; *Secy.-Gen.* Eva Orbanz, Germany; *Treas.* Anna-Lena Wibom, Sweden; *V.P.s.* Christian Dimitriu, Switzerland; Maria-Rita Galvão, Brazil.
Address correspondence to B. van der Elst, executive secretary, c/o the Secretariat.

Executive Committee

Officers; Michelle Aubert, France; David Francis, USA; Clyde Jeavons, England; Manuel Martinez Carril, Uruguay; Vladimir Opela, Czechoslovakia; Guy-Claude Rochemont, France; Robert Rosen, USA; Henning Schou, Australia.

Publications

Annual Bibliography of FIAF Members' Publications.
Bibliography of National Filmographies.
Cinema 1900–1906, An Analytical Study.
Evaluating Computer Cataloguing Systems, by Roger Smither (a guide for film archivists).
FIAF Bulletin.
FIAF Cataloguing Rules for Film Archives.
Glossary of Filmographic Terms in English, French, German, Spanish, and Russian (a second version in 12 languages).
Handbook for Film Archives (available in English or French).
International Directory to Film & TV Documentation Sources.
International Index to Film Periodicals (cumulative volumes).
International Index to Film Television Periodicals (microfiche service).
International Index to Television Periodicals (cumulative volumes).
Physical Characteristics of Early Films as Aids to Identification by H. Brown.
The Preservation and Restoration of Colour and Sound in Films.
Proceedings of the FIAF Symposiums; 1977: *L'Influence du Cinéma Sovietique Muet sur le Cinéma Mondial/The Influence of Silent Soviet Cinema on World Cinema;* 1978: *Cinéma 1900–1906;* 1980: *Problems of Selection in Film Archives;* 1985: *The Slapstick.*
Study on the Usage of Computers for Film Cataloguing.

International Federation of Library Associations and Institutions (IFLA)

c/o The Royal Library, Box 95312, 2509 CH The Hague, The Netherlands

Object

"To promote international understanding, cooperation, discussion, research, and development in all fields of library activity, including bibliography, information services, and the education of library personnel, and to provide a body through which librarianship can be represented in matters of international interest." Founded 1927. Memb. (Lib. Assns.) 180; (Inst.) 903; (Aff.) 182; 124 countries.

Officers and Executive Board

Pres. Robert Wedgeworth, School of Lib. Service, Columbia Univ., New York, NY; *1st V.P.* Russell Bowden, Lib. Assn., London, England; *2nd V.P.* Natalya Igumnova, Lenin State Lib., Moscow, Russia; *Treas.* Marcelle Beaudiquez, C.C.B.T., Bibliothèque Nationale, Paris, France; *Exec. Bd.* Warren Horton, National Lib. of Australia, Canberra, Australia; Robert D. Stueart, GSLIS, Simmons College, Boston, MA; Eeva-Maija Tammekann, Lib. of Parliament, Helsinki, Finland; Marta Terry, Biblioteca Nacional, Havana, Cuba; *Ex officio memb.* David W. G. Clements, British Lib., London, England; *Secy. Gen.* Paul Nauta; *Coord. Professional Activities* Winston Roberts; *IFLA Office for Universal Bibliographic Control and International MARC Program Dir.* Kurt Nowak; *Program Off.* Marie-France Plassard, c/o Deutsche Bibliothek, Frankfurt/Main, Germany; *IFLA International Program for UAP Program Dir.* David Bradbury; *Program Off.* Graham Cornish, c/o British Lib. Document Supply Centre, Boston Spa, Wetherby, West

Yorkshire, England; *IFLA Office for Preservation and Conservation Program Dir.* Merrily Smith, c/o Lib. of Congress, Washington, DC; *IFLA Office for University Dataflow and Telecommunications Program Dir.* Leigh Swain; *Program Off.* Paula Tallim, c/o National Lib. of Canada, Ottawa, Canada; *IFLA Office for the Advancement of Librarianship in the Third World Program Dir.* Birgitta Bergdahl, c/o Uppsala Univ. Lib., Uppsala, Sweden; *IFLA Office for International Lending Dir.* David Bradbury; *Publications Committee Chpn.* Hope Clement, National Lib. of Canada, Ottawa, Canada; *Members.* Russell Bowden, Lib. Assn., London, England; Derek Law, Kings College Lib., London, England; Barry Wiebenga, Frederick Muller Academy, Amsterdam, The Netherlands.

Publications

IFLA Annual.
IFLA Directory (bienn.).
IFLA Journal (q.).

IFLA Professional Reports.
IFLA Publications Series.
International Cataloguing and Bibliographic Control (q.).
PAC Newsletter.
UAP Newsletter (s. ann.).
UDT Newsletter.

American Membership

American Assn. of Law Libs.; American Lib. Assn.; Art Libs. Society of North America; Assn. for Lib. and Info. Science Education; Assn. for Population Planning/Family Planning Libs.; Assn. of Research Libs.; International Assn. of Law Libs.; International Assn. of Orientalist Libns.; International Assn. of School Libns.; Medical Lib. Assn.; Special Libs. Assn. *Institutional Membs.* There are 143 libraries and related institutions that are institutional members or affiliates of IFLA in the United States (out of a total of 911), and 78 personal affiliates (out of a total of 154).

International Organization for Standardization (ISO)

ISO Central Secretariat
1 rue de Varembé, Case postale 56, CH-1211 Geneva 20, Switzerland

Object

"To promote the development of standardization and related activities in the world with a view to facilitating international exchange of goods and services, and to developing cooperation in the sphere of intellectual, scientific, technological, and economic activity."

Officers

Pres. R. Phillips, Canada; *V.P.* B. Vaucelle, France; *Secy.-Gen.* L. D. Eicher.

Technical Work

The technical work of ISO is carried out by over 172 technical committees. These include:

ISO/TC—Information and documentation (Secretariat, Deutsches Institut für Normung, Burggrafenstr. 6, Postfach 1107, W-1000 Berlin 30, Germany). Scope: Standardization of practices relating to libraries, documentation and information centers, indexing and abstracting services, archives, information science, and publishing.

ISO/TC 37—Terminology (principles and coordination) (Secretariat, Österreiches Normungsinstitut, Heinestr. 38, Postfach 130, A-1021 Vienna, Austria). Scope: Standardization of methods for creating, compiling, and coordinating terminologies.

ISO/IEC JTC 1 (Joint technical committee for information technology) (Secretariat, American National Standards Institute, 11 W. 42 St., 13th fl., New York, NY 10036). Scope: Standardization in the field of information technology.

Publications

Bulletin (mo.).
Catalogue (ann.).
Liaisons.
Member Bodies.
Memento (ann.).

Foreign Library Associations

The following list of regional and national foreign library associations is a selective one. A more complete list of foreign and international library associations can be found in *International Literary Market Place* (R. R. Bowker).

Regional

Africa

Standing Conference of African Lib. Schools, c/o School of Libns., Archivists & Documentalists, Université Cheikh Anta Diop de Dakar, B.P. 3252, Dakar, Senegal.

Standing Conference of African Univ. Libs., Eastern Area, c/o Univ. of Nairobi Lib., Box 30197, Nairobi, Kenya.

Standing Conference of African Univ. Libs., Western Area, c/o Jean Aboghe-Obyan, Bibliothèque Universitaire, Université Omar Bongo, Libreville, Gabon.

Standing Conference of Eastern, Central, and Southern African Libns., c/o Tanzania Lib. Assn., Box 2645, Dar-es-Salaam, Tanzania.

The Americas

Asociación de Bibliotecas Universitarias, de Investigación e Institucionales del Caribe-ACURIL (Assn. of Caribbean Univ., Research and Institutional Libs.), *Exec. Secy.* Oneida R. Ortiz, Apdo. Postal S, Estación de la Universidad, San Juan, Puerto Rico 00931, or Calle Humacao 39, Villa Avila, Guaynabo, Puerto Rico 00657.

Seminar on the Acquisition of Latin American Lib. Materials, SALALM Secretariat, *Exec. Secy.* Sharon Moynahan, General Lib., Univ. of New Mexico, Albuquerque, NM 87131-1466.

Asia

Congress of Southeast Asian Libns. (CONSAL), c/o Prochak Pumvises and Thara Kanakamani, National Library of Thailand, Samsen Rd., Bangkok 10300, Thailand.

The Commonwealth

Commonwealth Lib. Assn. (COMLA), c/o *Hon. Exec. Secy.* Norma Y. Amenu-Kpodo, Box 144, Mona, Kingston 7, Jamaica.

Standing Conference on Lib. Materials on Africa, c/o *Secy.* M. A. Cousins, Foreign and Commonwealth Office, Cornwall House, Stamford St., London SE1 9NS, England.

Europe

LIBER - Ligue des Bibliothèques Européenes de Recherche (Assn. of European Research Libs.), c/o H.-A. Koch, Staats- und Universitätsbibliothek, Postfach 330160, W-2800 Bremen 33, Germany.

Nordisk Videnskabeligt Bibliotekarforbund (Scandinavian Federation of Research Libns.), c/o Marta Honko, Libn., Abo Academy Lib., Domkyrkogatan 2-4, 20500 Abo, Finland.

Pacific Islands

Pacific Islands Association of Libraries and Archives, c/o *Exec. Secy.* Arlene Cohen, RFK Lib., Univ. of Guam, UOG Sta., Mangilao, Guam 96923. *Pres.* Dakio Syne.

National

Australia

Australian Lib. and Info. Assn., Box E441, Queen Victoria Terr., ACT 2600. *Exec. Dir.* Sue Kosse.

State Libs. Council of Australia, *Chpn.* D. H. Stephens, State Libn., State Lib. of Queensland, Cultural Centre, Southbank, South Brisbane, Queensland 4000.

Austria

Büchereiverband Österreichs (Assn. of Austrian Public Libs. and Libns.), *Chpn.* Franz Pscher; *Secy.* Heinz Buchmüller, Lange Gasse 37, A-1080 Vienna.

Österreichische Gesellschaft für Dokumentation und Information (Austrian Society for Documentation and Info.), *Exec. Secy.* Bruno Hofer, c/o Österreichisches Normungsinstitut, Heinestrasse 38, Postfach 130, A-1021 Vienna.
Vereinigung Österreichischer Bibliothekare (Assn. of Austrian Libns.), *Pres.* Magda Strebl, c/o Österreichische Nationalbibliothek, Josefsplatz 1, A-1015 Vienna; *Secy.* Marianne Jobst-Rieder.

Belgium

Archives et Bibliothèques de Belgique/Archief-en Bibliotheekwezen in België (Archives and Libs. of Belgium), *Exec. Secy.* T. Verschaffel, Bibliothèque Royale Albert I, 4 blvd. de l'Empereur, B-1000 Brussels.
Association Belge de Documentation/Belgische Vereniging voor Documentatie (Belgian Assn. for Documentation), blvd. L. Schmidt-laan 119, B.3, B-1040 Brussels. *Pres.* Paul Hubot.
Institut d'Enseignement Supérieur Social de la Communauté Française de Belgique, Sec. Bibliothécaires-Documentalistes-Gradués (State Institute of Higher Social Education, Libn., and Documentalist Sec.), rue de l'Abbaye 26, B-1050 Brussels. *Dir.* Roselyne Simon-Saint-Hubert.
Vereniging van Religieus-Wetenschappelijke Bibliothécarissen (Assn. of Theological Libns.), Minderbroederstr. 5, B-3800 Saint Truiden. *Exec. Secy.* K. Van de Casteele, Groenenborgerlaan 149, B-2020 Antwerp.
Vlaamse Vereniging voor Bibliotheek-, Archief-, en Documentatiewezen (Flemish Assn. of Libns., Archivists, and Documentalists), *Pres.* J. Cooymans; *Secy.* L. van den Bosch, Goudbloemstraat 10, B-2060 Antwerp.

Bolivia

Asociación Boliviana de Bibliotecarios (Bolivian Lib. Assn.), c/o Biblioteca y Archivo Nacional, Calle Bolivar, Sucre.

Brazil

Associação dos Arquivistas Brasileiros (Assn. of Brazilian Archivists), Praia de Botafogo 186, Sala B-217, CEP 22253 Rio de Janeiro. *Pres.* Jaime Antunes da Silva.
Federação Brasileira de Associações de Bibliotecários (Brazilian Federation of Libn. Assns.), c/o *Pres.* Mrian Salvadore Nascimento, Rua Avanhandava, 40-CJ. 110, Bela Vista, CEP 01306 Sao Paulo.

Bulgaria

Sâjuz na bibliotechnite i informatzionnite rabotnitzi (Union of Libns. and Info. Officers), 4 pl. Slaveikov, Rm. 501, Sofia 1000. *Pres.* Tatyana Yanakieva.

Canada

Bibliographical Society of Canada/La Société bibliographique du Canada, Box 575, Postal Sta. P, Toronto, ON M5S 2T1. *Secy.* Anne Dondertman.
Canadian Assn. for Info. Science/Association Canadienne de Science de l'Information, Univ. of Toronto, 140 Saint George St., Toronto, ON M5S 1A1. Tel. 416-978-8876, FAX 416-971-1399.
Canadian Council of Lib. Schools/Conseil Canadien des Ecoles de Bibliothéconomie, *Pres.* J. Andrew Large, Graduate School of Lib. and Info. Studies, McGill Univ., Montreal, PQ H3A 1Y1.
Canadian Lib. Assn., *Exec. Dir.* Karen Adams, 200 Elgin St., 6th fl., Ottawa, ON K2P 1L5. (For detailed information on the Canadian Lib. Assn. and its divisions, see "National Library and Information-Industry Associations, United States and Canada;" for information on the library associations of the provinces of Canada, see "State, Provincial, and Regional Library Associations.")

Chile

Colegio de Bibliotecarios de Chile A.G. (Chilean Lib. Assn.), *Pres.* María A. Calabacero Jiménez; *Secy.-Gen.* Mónica Núñez Navarrete, Box 3741, Santiago.

China (Taiwan)

Library Assn. of China, c/o National Central Lib., 20 Chung-shan S. Rd., Taipei. *Exec. Dir.* Teresa Wang Chang.

Colombia

Asociación Colombiana de Bibliotecarios-ASCOLBI (Colombian Assn. of Libns.), Apdo. Aéreo 30883, Bogotá, D.E.

Costa Rica

Asociación Costarricense de Bibliotecarios (Assn. of Costa Rican Libns.), Apdo. Postal 3308, San Jose.

Cyprus

Kypriakos Synthesmos Vivliothicarion (Lib. Assn. of Cyprus), c/o Pedagogical Academy, Box 1039, Nikosia. *Secy.* Paris G. Rossos.

Czechoslovakia

Spolok slovenských knihovníkov (Slovak Libns. Assn.), *Pres.* Štefan Kimlička, Kapitulská 3, 811 01 Bratislava.
Ústřední knihovnická rada ČR (Central Lib. Council of the Czech Republic), c/o Dept. of Libs., Ministry of Culture, Valdštejnské nám. 4, 118 11 Prague 1.

Denmark

Arkivforeningen (The Archives Society), *Exec. Secy.* Steen Ousager, Landsarkivet for Sjaelland, Box 661, Jagtvej 10, DK-2200 Copenhagen N.
Danmarks Biblioteksforening (Danish Lib. Assn.), *Pres.* Søren Møller, Trekronergade 15, DK-2500 Valby-Copenhagen.
Danmarks Forskningsbiblioteksforening (Danish Research Lib. Assn.), *Pres.* Niels Mark; *V.P.* Lars Bjørnshauge; *Secy.* Birte Preisler, Statsbiblioteket, Universitetsparken, DK-8000 Aarhus C.
Danmarks Skolebiblioteksforening (Assn. of Danish School Libs.), *Exec. Secy.* Niels Jacobsen, Norrebrogade 159, DK-2200 Copenhagen N.

Dominican Republic

Asociación Dominicana de Bibliotecarios (Dominican Lib. Assn.), c/o Biblioteca Nacional, Plaza de la Cultura, Santo Domingo. *Pres.* Prospero J. Mella Chavier.

El Salvador

Asociación de Bibliotecarios de El Salvador (El Salvador Lib. Assn.), c/o Biblioteca Nacional, 8A Avda. Norte y Calle Delgado, San Salvador.

Ethiopia

Ye Ethiopia Betemetshaft Serategnoch Mahber (Ethiopian Lib. Assn.), Box 30530, Addis Ababa.

Finland

Kirjastonhoitajat ja informaatikot/Bibliotekarier och informatiker r.y. (Assn. of Research and Univ. Libns.), *Exec. Secy.* Marketta Honkanen, Akavatalo, Rautatieläisenk 6, SF-00520 Helsinki.
Suomen Kirjastoseura/Finlands Biblioteksförening (Finnish Lib. Assn.), *Secy.-Gen.* Tuula Haavisto, Museokatu 18 A, SF-00100 Helsinki 10.
Tietopalveluseura/Samfundet för Informationstjänst i Finland (Finnish Society for Info. Services), Harakantie 2, SF-02600 Espoo. *Secy.* Gunilla Heikkinen.

France

Association des Archivistes Français (Assn. of French Archivists), *Pres.* Michel Maréchal; *Exec. Secys.* P. Arnauld and E. Gautier-Desuaux, 60 rue des Francs-Bourgeois, F-75141 Paris Cedex 03.
Association des Bibliothécaires Français (Assn. of French Libns.), *Pres.* Françoise Danset, 7 rue des Lions-Saint-Paul, F-75004 Paris.
Association des Bibliothèques Ecclésiastiques de France (Assn. of French Theological Libs.), *Secy.* Françoise Dupuy, 6 rue du Regard, F-75006 Paris.
Association Française des Documentalistes et des Bibliothécaires Spécialisés (Assn. of French Info. Scientists and Special Libns.), *Exec. Secy.* Eric Sutter, 12 rue Claude Tillier, F-75012 Paris.

Germany

Arbeitsgemeinschaft der Kunstbibliotheken (Working Group of Art Libs.), c/o *Chpn.* Eberhard Slenczka, Bibliothek des Germanischen Nationalmuseums Nürnberg, Postfach 9586, Kornmarkt 1, W-8500 Nuremberg 11.

Arbeitsgemeinschaft der Spezialbibliotheken (Assn. of Special Libs.), *Chpn.* Wolfrudolf Laux, Kekulé-Bibliothek, W-5090 Leverkusen-Bayerwerk.

Deutsche Gesellschaft für Dokumentation e.V. (German Society for Documentation), Hanauer Landstr. 126-128, W-6000 Frankfurt am Main 1. *Pres.* Arnoud de Kemp.

Deutscher Bibliotheksverband e.V. (German Lib. Assn.), *Secy.* Karin Pauleweit, Bundesallee 184/185, W-1000 Berlin 31.

Verband der Bibliotheken des Landes Nordrhein–Westfalen e.V. (Assn. of Libs. in the Federal State of North Rhine–Westphalia), *Chpn.* Bernhard Adams, Bibliotheksdirektor, Vorsitzender, Universitätsbibliothek Bochum, Universitäts str. 150, W-4630 Bochum.

Verein der Bibliothekare an Öffentlichen Bibliotheken e.V. (Assn. of Libns. at Public Libs.), *Chpn.* Birgit Dankert; *Secy.* Katharina Boulanger, Postfach 1324, W-7410 Reutlingen 1.

Verein der Diplom-Bibliothekare an wissenschaftlichen Bibliotheken (Assn. of Graduated Libns. at Academic Libs.), *Chpn.* Hans-J. Kuhlmeyer, c/o Niedersächsische Staats- und Universitätsbibliothek, Prinzenstr. 1, W-3400 Göttingen.

Verein deutscher Archivare (Assn. of German Archivists), *Chpn.* Hermann Rumschöttel, Generaldirektion der Staatlichen Archive Bayerns, Schönfeldstr. 5, Postfach 22 11 52, W-8000 Munich 22.

Verein Deutscher Bibliothekare e.V. (Assn. of German Libns.), *Pres.* Roswitha Poll; *Secy.* Peter te Boekhorst, Universitätsbibliothek Münster, Krummer Timpen 3-5, W-4400 Münster.

Ghana

Ghana Lib. Assn., *Exec. Secy.* D. B. Addo, Box 4105, Accra.

Great Britain

See United Kingdom.

Guatemala

Asociación Bibliotecológica de Guatemala (Lib. Assn. of Guatemala), c/o Dir., Biblioteca Nacional de Guatemala, 5A Avda. 7-26, Zona 1, Guatemala City.

Guyana

Guyana Lib. Assn., 76-77 Main St., Box 10240, Georgetown.

Hong Kong

Hong Kong Lib. Assn., *Pres.* Colin Storey, c/o Box 10095, G.P.O., Hong Kong.

Hungary

Magyar Könyvtárosok Egyesülete (Assn. of Hungarian Libns.), *Pres.* Tibor Horváth; *Secy.* István Papp, Szabó Ervin tér 1, H-1088 Budapest.

Tájékoztatási Tudományos Tanács (Info. Science Council), c/o Pál Gágyor, Kossuth tér 6-8, Budapest 1055.

Iceland

Bókavaroafélag Islands (Icelandic Lib. Assn.), *Pres.* Hildur G. Eythorsdottir, Box 1497, 121 Reykjavik.

India

Indian Assn. of Special Libs. and Info. Centres, *Gen. Secy.* S. M. Ganguly, P-291, CIT Scheme 6M, Kankurgachi, Calcutta 700054.

Indonesia

Ikatan Pustakawan Indonesia (Indonesian Lib. Assn.), *Pres.* Soekarman Kartosedono; *Secy.-Gen.* Hernandono, Jalan Medan Merdeka, Selatan 11, Jakarta 10012.

Iraq

Iraqi Lib. Assn., c/o National Lib., Dab-el-Muaddum, Baghdad.

Ireland

Cumann Leabharlann Na h-Eireann (Lib. Assn. of Ireland), *Pres.* Deirdre Ellis-King; *Hon. Secy.* Fionnuala Hanrahan, 53 Upper Mount St., Dublin 2.

Cumann Leabharlannaith Scoile (Irish Assn. of School Libns.), c/o *Exec. Secy.* Sister Mary Columban, Loreto Convent, Foxrock Co., Dublin.

Italy

Associazione Italiana Biblioteche (Italian Libs. Assn.), *Secy.* L. Bellingeri, C.P. 2461, I-00100 Rome A-D.

Associazione Nazionale Archivistica Italiana (National Assn. of Italian Archivists), *Secy.* Enrica Ormanni, Via Guido d'Arezzo 18, I-00198 Rome.

Jamaica

Jamaica Lib. Assn., *Secy.* Maureen Kerr-Campbell; Box 58, Kingston 5.

Japan

Information Science and Technology Assn., Japan (INFOSTA-NIPDOK), *Pres.* Yukio Nakamura; *Dir. and Secy.-Gen.* Yukio Ichikawa, Sasaki Bldg., 5-7 Koisikawa 2-chome, Bunkyo-ku, Tokyo 112.

Nihon Toshokan Kyôkai (Japan Lib. Assn.), *Secy.-Gen.* Hitoshi Kurihara, 1-10, Taishido 1-chome, Setagaya-ku, Tokyo 154.

Senmon Toshokan Kyôgikai (Japan Special Libs. Assn.), *Exec. Dir.* Naotake Ito, c/o National Diet Lib., 1-10-1 Nagata-cho, Chiyoda-ku, Tokyo 100.

Jordan

Jordan Lib. Assn., Box 6289, Amman.

Korea (Democratic People's Republic of)

Lib. Assn. of the Democratic People's Republic of Korea, *Secy.* Li Geug, Central Lib., Box 200, Central District, Pyongyang.

Korea (Republic of)

Hanguk Tosogwan Hyophoe (Korean Lib. Assn.), c/o Dept. of Lib. Science, Sung Kyun Kwan Univ., 53 Myonglyun-dong 3-ka, Chonguo-ku, Seoul 110-745.

Laos

Association des Bibliothécaires Laotiens (Laos Lib. Assn.), Direction de la Bibliothèque Nationale, Ministry of Education, Box 704, Vientiane.

Malaysia

Persatuan Perpustakaan Malaysia (Lib. Assn. of Malaysia), *Secy.* Raslin Abu Bakar, Box 12545, 50782 Kuala Lumpur.

Mauritania

Association Mauritanienne des Bibliothécaires, des Archivistes et des Documentalistes (Mauritanian Assn. of Libns., Archivists, and Documentalists), c/o *Pres.* Oumar Diouwara, Dir., National Lib., B.P. 20, Nouakchott.

Mexico

Asociación Mexicana de Bibliotecarios, A.C. (Mexican Assn. of Libns.), *Pres.* Estela Morales Campos, Apdo. 27-651, CP 06760, Mexico, D.F.

The Netherlands

Nederlandse Vereniging van Bibliothecarissen, Documentalisten en Literatuuronderzoekers (Dutch Lib. Assn.), c/o H. J. Krikke-Scholten, Nolweg 13 d, 4209 AW Schelluinen.

UKB—Samenwerkingsverband van de Universiteitsbibliotheken, de Koninklijke Bibliotheek en de Bibliotheek van de Koninklijke Nederlandse Akademie van Wetenschappen (Assn. of Univ. Libs., the Royal Lib., and the Lib. of the Netherlands Academy of Arts and Sciences), *Exec. Secy.* J. H. de Swart, c/o Bibliotheek Vrije Universiteit, De Boelelaan 1103, 1081 HV Amsterdam.

Koninklijke Vereniging van Archivarissen in Nederland (Royal Assn. of Archivists in the Netherlands), *Exec. Secy.* C. C. van der Woude, Postbus 11645, 2502 AP The Hague.

Vereniging voor het Theologisch Bibliothecariaat (Assn. of Theological Libns.), *Exec. Secy.* P. J. A. Nissen, Postbus 289, 6500 AG Nijmegen.

New Zealand

New Zealand Lib. Assn., *Gen. Secy.* Lydia Klimovitch, 20 Brandon St., Box 12-212, Wellington 1.

Nicaragua

Biblioteca Universitaria, Universidad Centroamericana, Apdo. 69, Managua. *Dir.* Conny Mendez R.

Nigeria

Nigerian Lib. Assn., *Pres.* J. O. Fasanya; *Treas.* U. I. Mbofung; *Secy.* L. I. Ehigiator, c/o The Library Polytechnic, Box 22, U.I. P.O., Ibadan.

Norway

Arkivarforeningen (Assn. of Archivists), *Secy.* Anne Hals, Postboks 10, Kringsjåa, N-0807 Oslo 8.
Norsk Bibliotekforening (Norwegian Lib. Assn.), *Secy.-Treas.* B. Aaker, Malerhaugveien 20, N-0661 Oslo.
Norsk Fagbibliotekforening (Norwegian Assn. of Special Libs.), *Chpn.* Else-Margrethe Bredland, Malerhaugveien 20, N-0661 Oslo.

Pakistan

Pakistan Lib. Assn. (FBC), c/o Pakistan Institute for Development Economy, Univ. Campus, Box 1091, Islamabad.
Society for the Promotion and Improvement of Libs., *Pres.* Hakim Mohammed Said, Al-Majeed, Hamdard Centre, Nazimabad, Karachi 18.

Paraguay

Asociación de Bibliotecarios Universitarios del Paraguay (Paraguayan Assn. of Univ. Libns.), c/o Escuela de Bibliotecnologia, Universidad Nacional de Asunción, Casilla de Correo, 1408 Asuncion.

Peru

Asociación Peruana de Archiveros (Assn. of Peruvian Archivists), Archivo General de la Nación, C. Manuel Cuadros s/n., Palacio de Justicia, Apdo. 3124, Lima 100.
Asociación Peruana de Bibliotecas, Bellavista 561, Miraflores, Apdo. 995, Lima 18.

Philippines

Assn. of Special Libs. of the Philippines, *Pres.* Lourdes Pereyra, College of Public Admin. Lib., Box 4118, Manila D-406.
Philippine Lib. Assn., Inc., *Pres.* Loreta L. Serina, The National Lib. Bldg., Rm. 301, T. M. Kalaw St., Ermita, Manila 2801.

Poland

Stowarzyszenie Bibliotekarzy Polskich (Polish Libns. Assn.), *Pres.* Stanislaw Czajka; *Gen. Secy.* Jozef Zajac, ul. Konopczyńskiego 5/7, 00-953 Warsaw.

Portugal

Associação Portuguesa de Bibliotecários, Arquivistas e Documentalistas (Portuguese Assn. of Libns., Archivists, and Documentalists) *Chpn.* João Gonçalves, Rua Ocidental ao Campo Grande 83, 1751 Lisbon.

Romania

Asociatia Bibliotecarilor din Romania (Romanian Libns. Assn.), *Pres.* G. Botez, Biblioteca Centrala de Stat, Strada Ion Ghica 4, 79708 Bucharest.

Senegal

Association Sénégalaise des Bibliothécaires, Archivistes et Documentalistes, c/o EBAD, B.P. 3252, Dakar. *Pres.* Mariétou Diongue Diop; *Secy. Gen.* Emmanuel Kabou.

Sierra Leone

Sierra Leone Lib. Assn., Box 326, Rokei St., Freetown.

Singapore

Lib. Assn. of Singapore, *Hon. Secy.* Glenda Gwee, Bukit Merah Central, Box 0693, Singapore 9115.

South Africa

African Lib. Assn. of South Africa, *Secy.-Treas.* A. N. Kambule, c/o Lib., Univ. of the North, Private Bag X5090, 07000 Pietersburg.

Spain

Instituto de Información y Documentación en Ciencia y Tecnologia, *Secy.* Milagros Villarreal de Benito, Joaquín Costa 22, 28002 Madrid.

Sri Lanka

Sri Lanka Lib. Assn., *Pres.* S. M. Kamaldeen; *Gen. Secy.* Nanda Fernando, Sri Lanka Institute of Development Administration, 28/10 Malalasekera Mawatha, Colombo 7.

Sweden

Svenska Arkivsamfundet (Swedish Archival Assn.), c/o Riksarkivet, Box 12541, S-102 29 Stockholm.

Svenska Bibliotekariesamfundet (Swedish Assn. of Univ. and Research Libs.), c/o *Secy.* Staffan Lööf, Högskolan i Borås, Bibliotekshögskolan, Box 874, S-501 15 Borås.

Sveriges Allmänna Biblioteksförening (Swedish Lib. Assn.), *Pres.* H. Larsen, Box 3127, S-103 62 Stockholm.

Sveriges Vetenskapliga Specialbiblioteks Förening (Assn. of Special Research Libs.), *Pres.* Anders Ryberg; *Secy.* Birgitta Fridén, c/o Utrikesdepartementets bibliotek, Box 16121, S-103 23 Stockholm.

Tekniska Litteratursällskapet (Swedish Society for Technical Documentation), *Secy.* Birgitta Levin, Box 5073, S-102 42 Stockholm 5.

Vetenskapliga Bibliotekens Tjänstemannaförening (Assn. of Research Lib. Employees), *Pres.* Anders Schmidt, Lund Univ. Lib., Box 3, S-221 00 Lund.

Switzerland

Schweizerische Vereinigung für Dokumentation/Association Suisse de Documentation (Swiss Assn. of Documentation), *Secy.-Treas.* W. Bruderer, BID GD PTT, CH-3030 Bern.

Vereinigung Schweizerischer Archivare (Assn. of Swiss Archivists), c/o Hans Ulrich Wipf, Fronwagplatz 24, CH-8200 Schaffhausen.

Vereinigung Schweizerischer Bibliothekare/Association des Bibliothécaires Suisses/Associazione dei Bibliotecari Svizzeri (Assn. of Swiss Libns.), *Exec. Secy.* W. Treichler, Hallwylstr. 15, CH-3003 Bern.

Tanzania

Tanzania Lib. Assn., Box 2645, Dar-es-Salaam.

Tunisia

Association Tunisienne des Documentalistes, Bibliothécaires et Archivistes (Tunisian Assn. of Documentalists, Libns., and Archivists), *Exec. Secy.* Mohamed Abdeljaoued, B.P. 380, 1015 Tunis.

Turkey

Türk Kütüphaneciler Derneği (Turkish Libns. Assn.), Elgün Sokaği 8/8, Yenisehir, Ankara.

Uganda

Uganda Lib. Assn., *Secy.* L. M. Ssengero, Box 5894, Kampala.

United Kingdom

ASLIB (The Assn. for Info. Management), *Chief Exec.* Roger Bowes, Information House, 20-24 Old St., London EC1V 9AP, England.

Assn. of British Theological and Philosophical Libs., *Hon. Secy.* Alan F. Jesson, Bible Society's Lib., c/o Univ. Lib., West Rd., Cambridge CB3 9DR, England.

Bibliographical Society, *Hon. Secy.* M. M. Foot, British Lib., Humanities and Social Sciences, Great Russell St., London WC1B 3DG, England.

British and Irish Assn. of Law Libns., *Hon. Secy.* H. C. Boucher, Info. Mgr., Pinsent & Co., Post and Mail House, 26 Colmore Circus, Birmingham B4 6BH, England.

The Lib. Assn., *Chief Exec.* George Cunningham, 7 Ridgmount St., London WC1E 7AE, England.

Private Libs. Assn., *Hon. Secy.* Frank Broomhead, 16 Brampton Grove, Kenton, Harrow, Middlesex HA3 8LG, England.

School Lib. Assn., *Exec. Secy.* Valerie Fea, Liden Lib., Barrington Close, Liden, Swindon, Wiltshire SN3 6HF, England.

Scottish Lib. Assn., a branch of the Lib. Assn., Motherwell Business Centre, Coursington Rd., Motherwell ML1 1PW, Scotland. *Exec. Secy.* Robert Craig.

Society of Archivists, c/o *Exec. Secy.*, Information House, 20-24 Old St., London EC1V 9AP, England.

Standing Conference of National and Univ. Libs., *Exec. Secy.* G. Pentelow, Secretariat and Registered Office, 102 Euston St., London NW1 2HA, England.

Welsh Lib. Assn., a branch of the Lib. Assn., *Hon. Secy.* Elspeth Mitcheson, Pencadlys Llyfrgell Gwynedd/Gwynedd Lib. Headquarters, Swyddfa'r Sir, County Offices, Caernarvon LL55 ISH, Wales.

Uruguay

Agrupación Bibliotecológica del Uruguay (Lib. Documentation, Numismatics and Archive Science Assn. of Uruguay), *Pres.* Luis Alberto Musso, Cerro Largo 1666, Montevideo.

Venezuela

Colegio de Bibliotecólogos y Archivólogos de Venezuela (Assn. of Venezuelan Libns. and Archivists), Apdo. 6283, Caracas 101.

Yugoslavia

Društvo Bibliotečkih Radnika Srbije (Society of Lib. Workers of Serbia), *Pres.* Dobrivoje Mladenović; *Secy.* Vera Crljić, Skerlićeva 1, YU-11000 Belgrade.

Društvo Bibliotekara Bosne i Hercegovine (Lib. Assn. of Bosnia and Herzegovina), *Exec. Secy.* Ćukac Neda, Obala V. Stepe 42, YU-71000 Sarajevo.

Hrvatsko Bibliotekarsko Društvo (Croatian Lib. Assn.), *Pres.* Srećko Jelušić; *Exec. Secy.* Tinka Katić, National and Univ. Lib., Marulićev trg 21, YU-41000 Zagreb.

Sojuz na Društvata na Bibliotékarite na Makedonija (Union of Libns. Assn. of Macedonia), Bul. "Goce Delčev" br. 6, Box 566, YU-91000 Skopje. *Secy.* Poliksena Matkovska.

Zveza Bibliotekarskih Društev Slovenije (Society of the Lib. Assns. of Slovenia), *Exec. Secy.* Silva Novljan, Turjaška 1, YU-61000 Ljubljana.

Zambia

Zambia Lib. Assn., Box 32839, Lusaka.

Zimbabwe

Zimbabwe Lib. Assn., Box 3133, Harare.

Directory of Book Trade and Related Organizations

Book Trade Associations, United States and Canada

For more extensive information on the associations listed in this section, see the annual editions of the *Literary Market Place* (R. R. Bowker).

Advertising Typographers Assn. of America, Inc., 161 Sergeantsville Locktown Rd., Stockton, NJ 08559. *Exec. Secy.* David Fort. Tel. 908-782-4055.

American Booksellers Assn., Inc., 560 White Plains Rd., Tarrytown, NY 10591. Tel. 914-631-7800. *Pres.* Joyce Meskis, Tattered Cover Book Store, Denver, Colo.; *V.P.* Chuck Robinson, Village Books, Bellingham, Wash.; *Secy.* Neal Coonerty, Bookshop Santa Cruz, Santa Cruz, Calif.; *Treas.* Avin Mark Domnitz, Harry W. Schwartz Bookshops, Milwaukee, Wis.; *Publications Dir.* Dan Cullen; *Conventions and Meetings Dir.* Eileen Dengler.

American Institute of Graphic Arts, 1059 Third Ave., New York, NY 10021. Tel. 212-752-0813. *Pres.* Anthony Russell; *Dir.* Caroline W. Hightower.

American Medical Publishers Assn. *Pres.* John Febiger Spahr, Jr., Lea & Febiger, 200 Chester Field Pkwy., Malvern, PA 19355-9725. Tel. 215-251-2230; *Pres.-Elect.* Daniel J. Doody, Mosby-Year Book, Inc., 200 N. LaSalle St., Chicago, IL 60601. Tel. 312-726-9733; *Secy.-Treas.* Mary K. Cowell, Raven Press, 1185 Ave. of the Americas, New York, NY 10036. Tel. 212-930-9500.

American Printing History Assn., Box 4922, Grand Central Sta., New York, NY 10163. *Pres.* Peter Van Wingen; *V.P. Programs.* Mary Phalen; *V.P. Publications.* Jerry Kelly; *V.P. Memb.* Martin Hutner; *Treas.* John Hench; *Ed., Printing History.* David Pankow; *Exec. Secy.* Stephen Crook.

American Society of Indexers, Inc., 1700 18th St. N.W., Washington, DC 20009. Tel. 202-328-7110. *Pres.* Diana Witt, Diana Witt Assocs., 201 Sheridan Ave. S., Minneapolis, MN 55405. Tel. 612-377-5394; *Rec. Secy.* Cecelia Wittmann, 1146 South Plaza, Springfield, MO 65804. Tel. 417-865-8731; *V.P.* Linda Fetters, Box 386, Port Aransas, TX 78373. Tel. 512-749-6634; *Treas.* Clifton Anderson, Box 4770, Charlottesville, VA 22905. Tel. 804-973-2889.

American Society of Journalists and Authors, 1501 Broadway, Suite 302, New York, NY 10036. Tel. 212-997-0947, FAX 212-768-7414. *Pres.* Florence Isaacs; *Exec. Dir.* Alexandra Cantor.

American Society of Magazine Photographers, 419 Park Ave. S., Suite 11407, New York, NY 10016. Tel. 212-889-9144. *Exec. Dir.* Richard Weisgrau; *Pres.* Vince Streano; *Admin. Dir.* Terri Guttilla.

American Society of Picture Professionals, Inc., c/o H. Armstrong Roberts, 4203 Locust St., Philadelphia, PA 19104. Tel. 215-383-6300. *National Pres.* John C. Weiser, Time-Life Books, 777 Duke St., Alexandria, VA 22314. Tel. 703-838-7423; *Memb. Chpn.* Mindy Klarman, Macmillan/McGraw-Hill School Div., 866 Third Ave., 4th fl., New York, NY 10022. Tel. 212-702-4705; *National Secy.* Mary Ann Platts, Box 92397, Milwaukee, WI 53202. Tel. 414-765-9442.

American Translators Assn., 1735 Jefferson Davis Hwy., Suite 903, Arlington, VA 22202. Tel. 703-892-1500. *Pres.* Leslie A. Willson; *Secy.* Nicholas Hartman; *Treas.* Mercedes Pellett; *Exec. Dir.* Ed Rugenstein.

Antiquarian Booksellers Assn. of America, 50 Rockefeller Plaza, New York, NY 10020. Tel. 212-757-9395, FAX 212-459-0307. *Pres.* Muir Dawson; *V.P.* Peter Howard; *Secy.* Jeffrey Marks; *Treas.* Robert Fleck; *Exec. Dir.* Liane Wood-Thomas. Address correspondence to the executive director.

Assn. of American Publishers, 220 E. 23 St., New York, NY 10010. Tel. 212-689-8920. *Pres.* Nicholas Veliotes; *Exec. V.P.* Thomas D. McKee; *Sr. V.P.* Donald A. Eklund; *Dirs.* Parker B. Ladd, Barbara J. Meredith; *Washington Office.* 1718 Connecticut Ave. N.W., Washington, DC 20009. Tel. 202-232-3335; *Dirs.* Judith Platt, Diane G. Rennert, Carol A. Risher; *Chpn.* Jerome S. Rubin, Times Mirror Co.; *V.Chpn.* Charles R. Ellis, John Wiley and Son; *Treas.* Barbara J. Morgan, Reader's Digest Assn.; *Secy.* Loren A. Korte, D. C. Heath & Co.

Assn. of American University Presses, 584 Broadway, Suite 410, New York, NY 10012. Tel. 212-941-6610. *Pres.* David Bartlett, Dir., Temple Univ. Press; *Exec. Dir.* Peter C. Grenquist. Address correspondence to the executive director or to Hollis A. Holmes, Asst. Exec. Dir.

Assn. of Authors' Representatives, Inc., 10 Astor Place, 3rd fl., New York, NY 10003. Tel. 212-353-3709. *Pres.* Georges Borchardt; *Exec. Secy.* Ginger Knowlton.

Assn. of Book Travelers, c/o *Pres.* Irving Harbus, Box 1795, New York, NY 10185. Tel. 212-206-7715; *Treas.* Paul Drougas. Address correspondence to the president.

Assn. of Canadian Publishers, 260 King St. E., Toronto, ON M5A 1K3, Canada. Tel. 416-361-1408, FAX 416-361-0643. *Dir.* Roy MacSkimming. Address correspondence to the director.

Assn. of Jewish Book Publishers, 838 Fifth Ave., New York, NY 10021. *Pres.* Rabbi Elliot L. Stevens. Address correspondence to the president.

Assn. of the Graphic Arts, 5 Penn Plaza, New York, NY 10001. Tel. 212-279-2100. *Pres.* William Dirzulaitis; *Dir. Memb.* Maureen Christensen; *Dir. Government Affairs.* Barry Ziman; *Dir. Ed.* Linda E. Nahum; *Office Mgr.* Susan Turturo.

Book Industry Study Group, Inc., 160 Fifth Ave., New York, NY 10010. Tel. 212-929-1393, FAX 212-989-7542. *Chpn.* Laura Conley; *V.Chpn.* James Buick; *Treas.* Seymour Turk; *Secy.* Robert W. Bell; *Managing Agent.* SKP Assocs. Address correspondence to William G. Raggio.

Book Manufacturers Institute, 111 Prospect St., Stamford, CT 06901. Tel. 203-324-9670. *Pres.* Jerry D. Butler, R. R. Donnelley & Sons; *Exec. V.P.* Douglas E. Horner. Address correspondence to the executive vice president.

Book Publicists of Southern California, 6464 Sunset Blvd., Suite 580, Hollywood, CA 90028. Tel. 213-461-3921, FAX 213-461-0917. *Pres.* Irwin Zucker; *V.P.* Sol Marshall; *Secy.* Joe Sorrentino; *Treas.* Nina Mills.

Book Week Headquarters, Children's Book Council, Inc., 568 Broadway, New York, NY 10012. Tel. 212-966-1990. *Pres.* John Donovan; *Publications/Marketing Dir.* Maria Juarez; *Chpn.* Dinah Stevenson, Clarion Books, 215 Park Ave. S., New York, NY 10003. Tel. 212-420-5800.

Bookbinders' Guild of New York, c/o *Secy.* Sheila Anderson, W. H. Freeman, 51 Madison Ave., New York, NY 10010. Tel. 212-576-9400; *Pres.* Janet McCarthy Grimm, Lindenmeyr Book Publishing Papers, 100 Park Ave., New York, NY 10011. Tel. 212-557-0262.

Bookbuilders of Boston, Inc., c/o *Pres.* Sharon Grant, Progressive Typographers, Inc., 26 Haven St., Dover, MA 02030. Tel. 508-785-0393; *1st V.P.* Nancy Fenton; *Treas.* Roland Ochsenbein.

Bookbuilders West, Box 883666, San Francisco, CA 94188. *Pres.* Roy A. Wallace, Maple-Vail Book Mfg. Group. Tel. 510-934-1440.

Canadian Book Publishers' Council, 250 Merton St., Suite 203, Toronto, ON M4S 1B1, Canada. Tel. 416-322-7011, FAX 416-322-6999. *Pres.* Bill Hushion, McClelland & Stewart; *1st V.P.* John Hirst, Times Mirror; *Treas.* Andrew Nopper, Distican; *Past*

Pres. George Bryson, Chpn., Addison-Wesley; *Exec. Dir.* Jacqueline Hushion; *Special Interest Groups.* The School Group, The College Group, The Trade Group.

Canadian Booksellers Assn., 301 Donlands Ave., Toronto, ON M4J 3R8, Canada. Tel. 416-467-7883. *Convention Mgr.* Lynda Joyet; *Exec. Dir.* Ingrid van Rotterdam.

Catholic Book Publishers Assn., c/o *Secy.* Charles Roth, Roth Advertising, Inc., 333 Glen Head Rd., Old Brookville, NY 11545. Tel. 516-671-9292; *Pres.* Dan Juday, U.S. Catholic Conference, 3211 Fourth St. N.E., Washington, DC 20017. Tel. 202-541-3090.

Chicago Book Clinic, 111 E. Wacker Dr., Suite 200, Chicago, IL 60601-4298. Tel. 312-946-1700. *Pres.* Danielle Greenwood; *Pres.-Elect.* Eugene Wheetley; *Secy.* Davis L. Scott; *Treas.* Kay Solt.

Chicago Publishers Assn., c/o *Pres.* Robert J. R. Follett, Follett Corp., 1000 W. Washington Blvd., Chicago, IL 60607. Tel. 312-666-4300.

Children's Book Council, Inc., 568 Broadway, New York, NY 10012. Tel. 212-966-1990. *Pres.* John Donovan; *Exec. V.P.* Paula Quint; *Chpn.* Jean Feiwel, Scholastic, Inc., 730 Broadway, New York, NY 10003. Tel. 212-505-3000.

Christian Booksellers Assn., Box 200, Colorado Springs, CO 80901. Tel. 719-576-7880. *Pres.* William R. Anderson.

Copyright Society of the U.S.A., Columbia Univ. Law School, 435 W. 116 St., New York, NY 10027. Tel. 212-854-7696, FAX 212-854-8472. *Pres.* Walter Josiah; *Admin. Asst.* Nadine Baker-Barrett.

Council on Interracial Books for Children, Inc., 1841 Broadway, New York, NY 10023. Tel. 212-757-5339.

Evangelical Christian Publishers Assn., 3225 S. Hardy Dr., Suite 101, Tempe, AZ 85282. Tel. 602-966-3998, FAX 602-966-1944. *Exec. Dir.* Doug Ross.

Graphic Artists Guild, 11 W. 20 St., 8th fl., New York, NY 10011. Tel. 212-463-7730. *Pres.* Frederick H. Carlson.

Guild of Book Workers, 201 E. Capitol St. S.E., Washington, DC 20003. Tel. 202-544-4600. *Pres.* Franklin Mowery.

International Assn. of Printing House Craftsmen, Inc., 7042 Brooklyn Blvd., Minneapolis, MN 55429-1370. Tel. 612-560-1620.

Pres. John Berthelsen; *Exec. Dir.* Kevin P. Keane.

International Copyright Information Center, c/o Assn. of American Publishers, 1718 Connecticut Ave. N.W., 7th fl., Washington, DC 20009-1148. Tel. 202-232-3335, FAX 202-745-0694. *Dir.* Carol A. Risher.

International Standard Book Numbering U.S. Agency, 121 Chanlon Rd., New Providence, NJ 07974. Tel. 908-665-6700, FAX 908-464-3553. *Dir.* Emery Koltay; *Officers.* Lynn DeVita, Diana Fumando, Bill McCahery, Don Riseborough, Albert Simmonds, Peter Simon.

Jewish Book Council, 15 E. 26 St., New York, NY 10010. Tel. 212-532-4949, FAX 212-481-4174. *Pres.* Leonard Gold; *Dir.* Paula Gribetz Gottlieb.

Library Binding Institute, 7401 Metro Blvd., Suite 325, Edina, MN 55439. *Exec. Dir.* Sally Grauer.

Magazine and Paperback Marketing Institute, 4000 Coolidge Ave., Baltimore, MD 21229. Tel. 301-525-3355. *Exec. V.P.* Don DeVito.

Metropolitan Lithographers Assn., 950 Third Ave., Suite 1500, New York, NY 10022. Tel. 212-838-8480. *Pres.* Carl Grossman; *Exec. Dir.* Jane B. Bernd.

Mid-America Publishers Assn., c/o *Exec. Dir.* Jerry Kromberg, Box 30242, Lincoln, NE 68503-0242. Tel. 402-466-9665.

Minnesota Book Publishers Roundtable. *Pres.* Pamela Johnson, Univ. of Minnesota Press, 2037 University Ave. S.E., Minneapolis, MN 55414; *V.P.* Chris Faatz, Graywolf Press, 2402 University Ave., Suite 203, St. Paul, MN 55114; *Secy.-Treas.* Brad Vogt, The Liturgical Press, Collegeville, MN 56321. Tel. 612-363-2538. Address correspondence to the secretary-treasurer.

National Assn. of College Stores, 500 E. Lorain St., Oberlin, OH 44074-1294. Tel. 216-775-7777, FAX 216-775-4769. *Exec. Dir.* Garis F. Distelhorst.

National Council of the Churches of Christ in the U.S.A., Dept. of Education, Communication, and Discipleship, Friendship Press, 475 Riverside Dr., New York, NY 10115-0050. Tel. 212-870-2048. *Assoc. Gen. Secy.* Rev. Martin Bailey.

New Mexico Book League, 8632 Horacio Place N.E., Albuquerque, NM 87111. Tel. 505-299-8940. *Exec. Dir.* Dwight A. Myers;

Pres. Saul Cohen; *V.P.* Mary Powell; *Treas.* C. Rittenhouse; *Ed.* Carol A. Myers.

New York Rights and Permissions Group, c/o *Chpn.* Jeanne A. Gough, Gale Research, Inc., 835 Penobscot Bldg., Detroit, MI 48226. Tel. 313-961-6813.

Northern California Booksellers Assn., 1339 61st St., Emeryville, CA 94608. Tel. 510-601-6922, FAX 510-601-8398. *Exec. Dir.* Melissa Mytinger.

Periodical and Book Assn. of America, Inc., 120 E. 34 St., New York, NY 10016. Tel. 212-689-4952, FAX 212-545-8328. *Pres.* Robert Woltersdorf; *V.P.s.* Michael McCarthy, James Miller; *Treas.* Keith Furman; *Secy.* Edward Handi; *Exec. Dir.* Michael Morse; *Legal Counsel.* Lee Feltman; *Advisers to the Pres.* Irwin Billman, Harold Clarke, Norman Jacobs.

Periodical Marketers of Canada, c/o *Pres.* John Marshall, H. H. Marshall Ltd., 3731 Mackintosh St., Box 9301, Sta. A, Halifax, NS B3K 5N5, Canada. Tel. 902-454-8381, FAX 902-455-3652; *V.P.* Alex Petraitis, Metro Toronto News Co., 120 Sinnott Rd., Scarborough, ON M1L 4N1, Canada. Tel. 416-752-8720; *Secy.-Treas.* Steve Shepherd, Ottawa Valley News Co. Ltd., Box 157, Arnprior, ON K7S 3H4, Canada. Tel. 613-623-3197. Address correspondence to PMC, Suite 503, 2 Berkeley St., Toronto, ON M5A 2W3, Canada. Tel. 416-363-4549, FAX 416-363-6691.

Philadelphia Book Clinic. *Secy.-Treas.* Thomas Colaiezzi, Lea & Febiger, 200 Chester Field Pkwy., Malvern, PA 19355-9725. Tel. 215-251-2230, FAX 215-251-2229.

Proofreaders Club of New York, c/o *Pres.* Allan Treshan, 38-15 149th St., Flushing, NY 11354.

Publishers Advertising and Marketing Assn., c/o *Secy.* Allison Gray, Baker & Taylor Books, Box 6920, 652 E. Main St., Bridgewater, NJ 08807; *Pres.* Catherine Tice, New York Review of Books, 250 W. 57 St., New York, NY 10107. Tel. 212-757-8070; *V.P.* Lee Wiggins, Macmillan, 866 Third Ave., New York, NY 10022. Tel. 212-702-6874; *Treas.* Judy Murphy Polvay, New Yorker, 29 W. 43 St., New York, NY 10036. Tel. 212-840-3800.

Publishers' Publicity Assn., c/o *Pres.* Helene Atwan, Farrar, Straus & Giroux, 19 Union Sq. W., New York, NY 10003. Tel. 212-206-5323; *V.P.* Jeffrey Seroy, Oxford Univ. Press, 200 Madison Ave., New York, NY 10016. Tel. 212-889-0191; *Secy.* Patricia Eisemann, Simon & Schuster, 1230 Ave. of the Americas, New York, NY 10020. Tel. 212-698-7641; *Treas.* Beth Davey, Little, Brown & Co., 205 Lexington Ave., New York, NY 10016. Tel. 212-683-0660.

Religion Publishing Group, c/o *Secy.* Charles Roth, Roth Advertising, Inc., 333 Glen Head Rd., Old Brookville, NY 11545. Tel. 516-671-9292; *Pres.* Michael Leach, Crossroad/Continuum Publishing Group, 370 Lexington Ave., New York, NY 10017. Tel. 212-532-3650.

Research and Engineering Council of the Graphic Arts Industry, Inc., Box 639, Chadds Ford, PA 19317. Tel. 215-388-7394. *Pres.* Judith A. Booth; *Exec. V.P./Secy.* Robert T. Peters; *Exec. V.P./Treas.* James K. Henderson; *Managing Dir.* Fred M. Rogers.

Society of Photographer and Artist Representatives, Inc., 1123 Broadway, Rm. 914, New York, NY 10010. Tel. 212-924-6023. *Pres.* Sam Bernstein; *1st V.P.* Susan Gomberg; *2nd V.P.* Gary Hurewitz; *Treas.* Alison Korman; *Secy.* Randy Cole.

Southern California Booksellers Assn., Box 92495, Pasadena, CA 91109. *Pres.* Gwen Feldman, Samuel French Bookshop, 7623 Sunset Blvd., Hollywood, CA 90046. Tel. 213-876-0570 (bookstore).

Technical Assn. of the Pulp and Paper Industry, Technology Park/Atlanta, Box 105113, Atlanta, GA 30348-5113. Tel. 404-446-1400. *Pres.* F. Keith Hall; *V.P.* Ronald B. Estridge; *Exec. Dir./Treas.* W. L. Cullison.

West Coast Book People Assn., 27 McNear Dr., San Rafael, CA 94901. *Secy.* Frank G. Goodall. Tel. 415-459-1227.

Women's National Book Assn., 160 Fifth Ave., New York, NY 10010. Tel. 212-675-7805. *Pres.* Patti Breitman, 12 Rally Ct., Fairfax, CA 94930. Tel. 415-459-1666; *V.P.* Carolyn T. Wilson, 1115 Grandview Dr., Nashville, TN 37204. Tel. 615-269-1000 ext. 2441; *Secy.* Margaret E. Auer, Dir. of Libs., Univ. of Detroit, Box 19900, Detroit, MI 48219-3599. Tel. 313-993-1090; *Treas.* Sylvia Cross, 19824 Septo St., Chatsworth, CA 91311. Tel. 818-886-8448; *Past Pres.* Marie Cantlon, 8 Whittier Place, No. 21-A,

Boston, MA 02114. Tel. 617-720-3992; *Chapter Pres.: Binghamton.* Melva L. Naylor, 6 Bennett Ave., Binghamton, NY 13905. Tel. 607-722-4085; *Boston.* Josephine Fang, 156 Common St., Belmont, MA 02178. Tel. 617-489-2391; *Detroit.* Barbara Wallace, 70 Poplar, Wyandotte, MI 48192. Tel. 313-246-8357; *Los Angeles.* Sue MacLaurin, 3554 Crownridge Dr., Sherman Oaks, CA 91403. Tel. 818-501-3925; *Nashville.* Donna Paz, Davis-Kidd Booksellers, 4007 Hillsboro Pike, Nashville, TN 37215. Tel. 615-385-2645; *New York.* Beth Lieberman, 2 Horatio St., No. 12F, New York, NY 10014. Tel. 212-889-2299; *San Francisco.* Linda T. Mead, 379 Burning Tree Ct., Half Moon Bay, CA 94019. Tel. 415-726-3969; *Washington, D.C.* Diane Ullius, 5621 Sixth St. S., Arlington, VA 22204. Tel. 703-931-8610;

National Committee Chairs.: Development. Sandra K. Paul, SKP Associates, 160 Fifth Ave., New York, NY 10010. Tel. 212-675-7804; *Corres. Memb.* Etta Wilson, 7003 Chadwick Dr., No. 256, Brentwood, TN 37027. Tel. 615-370-3148; *Pannell Awards.* Ann Heidbreder Eastman, Eastman Associates, 3588 S. Viadel Jilguero, Green Valley, AZ 85614. Tel. 602-625-2887; *UN/UGO Rep.* Sally Wecksler, Wecksler-Incomco, 170 West End Ave., New York, NY 10023. Tel. 212-787-2239; *WNBA Award.* Carolyn T. Wilson, David Lipscomb Univ. Lib., 1115 Grandview Dr., Nashville, TN 37204. Tel. 615-269-1000 ext. 2441; *Bookwoman Eds.* LaVonne Taylor-Pickell, 15831 Olden St., No. 71, Sylmar, CA 91342. Tel. 818-898-1391; and Sue MacLaurin (see LA chapter).

International and Foreign Book Trade Associations

For Canadian book trade associations, see the preceding section, "Book Trade Associations, United States and Canada." For a more extensive list of book trade organizations outside the United States and Canada, with more detailed information, consult *International Literary Market Place* (R. R. Bowker), which also provides extensive lists of major bookstores and publishers in each country.

International

International League of Antiquarian Booksellers, c/o *Pres.* Anton Gerits, Delilaan 5, 1217 HJ Hilversum, The Netherlands.
International Publishers Assn., 3 ave. de Miremont, CH-1206 Geneva, Switzerland. *Secy.-Gen.* J. Alexis Koutchoumow.

National

Argentina

Cámara Argentina de Publicaciones (Argentine Publications Assn.), Lavalle 437, piso 6, Of. D, 1047 Buenos Aires. *Pres.* Manuel Rodriguez.
Cámara Argentina del Libro (Argentine Book Assn.), Avda. Belgrano 1580, piso 6, 1093 Buenos Aires. *Pres.* Jaime Rodrigué.
Federación Argentina de Librerías, Papelerías y Actividades Afinés, Juan D. Perón 111

3o. piso, 3500 Resistencia. *Pres.* Jacobo M. Rozenblum.

Australia

Assn. of Australian Univ. Presses, c/o La Trobe Univ. Press, Bundoora, Vic. 3083. *Pres.* I. G. Patterson.
Australian Book Publishers Assn., 89 Jones St., Suite 60, Ultimo, N. S. W. 2007. *Dir.* Susan Blackwell.
Australian Booksellers Assn., Box 173, North Carlton, Vic. 3054. *Dir.* S. Girling-Butcher.

Austria

Hauptverband der graphischen Unternehmungen Österreichs (Austrian Master Printers Assn.), Grünangergasse 4, A-1010 Vienna. *Pres.* Richard Gerin; *Gen. Secy.* Hans Inmann.

Hauptverband des österreichischen Buchhandels (Austrian Publishers and Booksellers Assn.), Grünangergasse 4, A-1010 Vienna. *Gen. Secy.* Otto Mang.

Österreichischer Verlegerverband (Assn. of Austrian Publishers), Grünangergasse 4, A-1010 Vienna. *Gen. Secy.* Otto Mang.

Verband der Antiquare Österreichs (Austrian Antiquarian Booksellers Assn.), Grünangergasse 4, A-1010 Vienna. *Gen. Secy.* Otto Mang.

Belgium

Association des Editeurs Belges (Belgian Assn. of Publishers of French-Language Books), blvd. Lambermont 140, Bte 1, B-1030 Brussels. *Pres.* Didier Platteau; *Dir.* Bernard Gérard.

Chambre Professionnelle Belge de la Librairie Ancienne et Moderne/Belgische Beroepskamer van Antiquaren (Belgian Assn. of Antiquarian and Modern Booksellers), Secretariat, 53 blvd. Saint Michel, B-1040 Brussels.

Vereniging ter Bevordering van het Vlaamse Boekwezen (Assn. for the Promotion of Flemish Books), Frankrijklei 93, B-2000 Antwerp. *Pres.* I. de Vries. Member organizations: Algemene Vlaamse Boekverkopersbond; Uitgeversbond-Vereniging van Uitgevers van Nederlandstalige Boeken; Verenigde Boeken Importeurs (Book Importers).

Bolivia

Cámara Boliviana del Libro (Bolivian Booksellers Assn.), Box 682, Edif. Las Palmas, Avda. 20 de Octubre 2005, La Paz.

Brazil

Associação Brasileira de Livreiros Antiquarios (Brazilian Assn. of Antiquarian Booksellers), Rua Visconde de Caravelas 17, 22271 Rio de Janeiro. *Pres.* Patrick Levy.

Associação Brasileira do Livro (Brazilian Booksellers Assn.), Av. 13 de Maio 23, andar 16, 20031 Rio de Janeiro.

Câmara Brasileira do Livro (Brazilian Book Chamber), Av. Ipiranga, 1267-10 andar, 01039 Sao Paulo. *Pres.* Ary Kuflik Benclowicz.

Sindicato Nacional dos Editores de Livros (Brazilian Book Publishers Assn.), Av. Rio Branco 37, 15 andar, Salas 1503/06 e 1510/12, 20090 Rio de Janeiro. *Pres.* Regina Bilac Pinto; *Exec. Secy.* Antonio Laskos.

Bulgaria

Central Board of Press and Book Publishing (formerly Darzhavno Sdruzhenie "Bulgarska Kniga i Pechat"), 11 Slaveykov Pl., Sofia 1000.

Chile

Cámara Chilena del Libro, Avda. Libertador B. O'Higgins 1370, Of. 501, Santiago. *Pres.* Eduardo Castillo; *Exec. Secy.* Carlos Franz.

Colombia

Cámara Colombiana del Libro (Colombian Publishers Council), Carrera 17A, No. 37-27, Apdo. Aéreo 8998, Bogota. *Exec. Dir.* Miguel Laverde Espejo; *Chpn.* Jorge Valencia Jaramillo.

Czechoslovakia

Ministerstvo kultury České republiky, oddělení knižní kultury a tisku (Czech Ministry of Culture, Dept. for Publishing and Book Trade), Valdštejnské nám. 4, 118 11 Prague 1.

Denmark

Danske Antikvarboghandlerforening (Danish Antiquarian Booksellers Assn.), Box 2184, DK-1017 Copenhagen. *Pres.* Poul Jan Poulsen.

Danske Boghandlerforening (Danish Booksellers Assn.), Boghandlernes Hus, Siljangade 6, DK-2300 Copenhagen S.

Danske Forlaeggerforening (Danish Publishers Assn.), Købmagergade 11, DK-1150 Copenhagen K. *Dir.* Erik V. Krustrup.

Finland

Kirja-ja Paperikauppojen Liitto ry (Finnish Booksellers and Stationers Assn.), Eerikinkatu 15-17 D 43-44, 00100 Helsinki. *Secy.* Olli Eräkivi.

Suomen Kustannusyhdistys (The Finnish Book Publishers' Assn.), Merimiehenkatu 12 A6, SF-00150 Helsinki. *Secy.-Gen.* Veikko Sonninen.

France

Editions du Cercle de la Librairie (Circle of Professionals of the Book Trade), 35 rue Grégoire-de-Tours, F-75279 Paris Cedex 06. *Dir.* Jean-Marie Doublet.

Fédération Française des Syndicats de Libraires (French Booksellers Assn.), 43 rue Château Dun, F-75009 Paris. *Pres.* Bernard Bollenot.

France Edition—Office de promotion internationale, 35 rue Grégoire-de-Tours, F-75006 Paris. *Gen. Mgr.* Patrick C. Dubs; *Secy.-Gen.* Marc Franconie.

Syndicat National de la Librairie Ancienne et Moderne (SLAM), 4 rue Gît-le-Coeur, F-75006 Paris. *Pres.* Alain Nicolas.

Syndicat National de l'Edition (French Publishers Assn.), 35 rue Grégoire-de-Tours, F-75279 Paris Cedex 06. *Pres.* A. Gründ; *Dir.* Alain-Roland Kirsch.

Syndicat National des Importateurs et Exportateurs de Livres (National Assn. of Book Importers and Exporters), 107 blvd. Saint Germain, F-75006 Paris.

Germany

Börsenverein des Deutschen Buchhandels e.V. (Assn. of German Publishers and Booksellers), Gerichtsweg 26, Postfach 146, 0-7010 Leipzig.

Bundesverband der Deutschen Versandbuchhändler e.V. (National Federation of German Mail-Order Booksellers), An der Ringkirche 6, W-6200 Wiesbaden. *Dirs.* Stefan Rutkowsky, Kornelia Wahl.

Landesverband der Buchhändler und Verleger in Niedersachsen e.V. (Provincial Federation of Booksellers and Publishers in Lower Saxony), Arndtstr. 5, W-3000 Hanover 1. *Managing Dir.* Wolfgang Grimpe.

Verband Deutscher Antiquare e.V. (German Antiquarian Booksellers Assn.), Braubachstr. 34, W-6000 Frankfurt-am-Main 1. *Pres.* Christine Pressler; *V.P.* Edmund Brumme.

Verband Deutscher Bühnenverleger e.V. (Federation of German Theatrical Publishers and Drama Agencies), Bismarckstr. 107, W-1000 Berlin 12.

Ghana

Ghana Booksellers Assn., Box 10367, Accra. *Gen. Secy.* Fred J. Reimmer.

Great Britain

See United Kingdom

Greece

Syllogos Ekdoton Vivliopolon (Publishers and Booksellers Assn. of Athens), 54 Themistocleus St., GR-106 81 Athens. *Pres.* B. Giannikos; *Secy.* A. Sarafianou.

Hungary

Magyar Könyvkiadók és Könyvterjesztök Egyesülése (Hungarian Publishers and Booksellers Assn.), Vörösmarty tér 1, H-1051 Budapest. *Pres.* István Bart; *Secy.-Gen.* Péter Zentai.

Iceland

Félag Islenskra Bókaútgefenda (Publishers' Assn.), Sudurlandsbraut 4A, 108 Reykjavik.

India

Booksellers and Publishers Assn. of South India, No. 8, 2nd fl., Sun Plaza, G. N. Chetty Rd., Madras 600006, Tamil Nadu.

Delhi State Booksellers and Publishers Assn., c/o The Students' Stores, Box 1511, Delhi 110006. *Pres.* Devendra Sharma.

Federation of Indian Publishers, 18/1-C, Institutional Area (Near JNU), New Delhi 110067. *Pres.* D. N. Malhotra; *Hon. Gen. Secy.* Anand Bhushan; *Exec. Dir.* Narinder Nath.

Indonesia

Ikatan Penerbit Indonesia (IKAPI) (Assn. of Indonesian Book Publishers), Jalan Kalipasir 32, Jakarta 10330. *Pres.* Rozali Usman.

Ireland

CLE: The Irish Book Publishers' Assn., Book House Ireland, 65 Middle Abbey St., Dublin 1.

Israel

Book and Printing Center of the Israel Export Institute, Box 50084, 29 Hamered St., 68 125 Tel Aviv. *Dir.* Corine Knafo.
Book Publishers Assn. of Israel, Box 20123, 29 Carlebach St., Tel Aviv. *Chpn.* Racheli Edelman; *Managing Dir.* Arie Friedler; *International Promotion and Literary Rights Dept. Dir.* Lorna Soifer.

Italy

Associazione Italiana Editori (Italian Publishers Assn.), Via delle Erbe 2, I-20121 Milan. *Secy.* Pietro Pizzoni.
Associazione Librai Antiquari d'Italia (Antiquarian Booksellers Assn. of Italy), Via J. Nardi 6, I-50132 Florence. *Pres.* Pietro Chellini.
Associazione Librai Italiani (Italian Booksellers Assn.), Corso Venezia 49, I-20121 Milan.

Jamaica

Booksellers Assn. of Jamaica, c/o Sangster's Book Stores, Ltd., Box 366, 101 Water Lane, Kingston. *Managing Dir.* S. Kumaraswamy.

Japan

Japan Book Importers Assn., Chiyoda Kaikan 21-4, Nihonbashi 1-chome, Chuo-ku, Tokyo 103. *Secy.* Mitsuo Shibata.
Japan Book Publishers Assn., 6 Fukuromachi, Shinjuku-ku, Tokyo 162. *Pres.* Toshiyuki Hattori; *Exec. Dir.* Toshikazu Gomi; *Secy.* Masaaki Shigehisa.
Japan Federation of Commercial Cooperatives of Bookstores, 1-2 Surugadai, Kanda, Chiyoda-ku, Tokyo 101.

Textbook Publishers Assn. of Japan (Kyokasho Kyokai), 1-9-28 Sengoku Kotoku, Tokyo 135. *Secy.* Masae Kusaka.

Kenya

Kenya Publishers Assn., Box 73580, Nairobi. *Secy.* David Mwata.

Korea (Republic of)

Korean Publishers Assn., 105-2, Sagan-dong, Chongno-gu, Seoul 110-190. *Pres.* Byong-ill Kwon; *V.P.s.* Nak-Joon Kim; Choon-Ho Na; Ki-Ung Yi; *Secy.-Gen.* Doo-young Lee.

Luxembourg

Confédération du Commerce Luxembourgeois — Groupement Libraires-Papetiers (Confederation of Retailers — Group for Stationers and Booksellers), 23 Centre Allée-Scheffer, Luxembourg. *Pres.* Jean-Claude Diderich; *Secy.* Christiane Kuhn.

Malaysia

Malaysian Book Publishers Assn., No. 10, Jalan 217, 46050 Petaling Jaya, Selangor Darul Ehsan. *Hon. Secy.* Thomas Soh.

The Netherlands

Koninklijke Nederlandse Uitgeversbond (Royal Dutch Publishers Assn.), Keizersgracht 391, 1016 EJ Amsterdam. *Secy.* R. M. Vrij.
Koninklijke Vereeniging ter bevordering van de belangen des Boekhandels (Royal Dutch Book Trade Assn.), Frederiksplein 1, Box 15007, 1001 MA Amsterdam. *Secy.* M. van Vollenhoven-Nagel.
Nederlandsche Vereeniging van Antiquaren (Antiquarian Booksellers Assn. of the Netherlands), Box 664, 1000 AR Amsterdam. *Pres.* John A. Vloemans; *Secy.* A. Gerits.
Nederlandse Boekverkopersbond (Booksellers Assn. of the Netherlands), Box 90731, 2509 LS The Hague. *Pres.* J. van der Plas; *Exec. Secy.* A. C. Doeser.

New Zealand

Book Publishers Assn. of New Zealand, Inc., Box 386, Auckland 2. *Pres.* J. Seymour; *Dir.* Dean Reynolds.

Booksellers New Zealand (Inc.), Book House, 86 Boulcott St., Box 11-377, Wellington. *Chief Exec.* John Schiff.

Nigeria

Nigerian Publishers Assn., 14 Awosika Ave., Off Osuntokun St., Box 2541, Bodija, Ibadan. *Pres.* Chief (Mrs.) M. A. Adekanye; *Secy.* Mgbechinyere Ugwuzor.

Norway

Bok og Papiransattes Forening (Norwegian Book Trade Employees Assn.), Øvre Vollgate 15, N-0158 Oslo 1. *Mgr.* Astrid Fagerbakke.

Den norske Bokhandlerforening (Norwegian Booksellers Assn.), Øvre Vollgate 15, N-0158 Oslo 1. *Dir.* Olav Gjerdene.

Norsk Musikkforleggerforening (Norwegian Music Publishers Assn.), Box 822, Sentrum, N-0104 Oslo 1. *Chpn.* Arne Damsgaard.

Norske Forleggerforening (Norwegian Publishers Assn.), Øvre Vollgate 15, N-0158 Oslo 1. *Dir.* Paul M. Rothe.

Pakistan

Pakistan Publishers and Booksellers Assn., YMCA Bldg., Shahra-e-Quaide-Azam, Lahore.

Paraguay

Cámara Paraguaya del Libro (Paraguayan Publishers Assn.), Casilla de Correo 1705, Asunción.

Peru

Cámara Peruana del Libro (Peruvian Publishers Assn.), Jirón Washington 1206, Of. 507-508, Lima 100. *Pres.* Andrés Carbone O.

Philippines

Philippine Book Dealers Assn., c/o National Bookstore, Rizal Ave., Manila. *Pres.* Socorro Ramos.

Philippine Educational Publishers Assn., 927 Quezon Ave., Quezon City 3008, Metro Manila. *Pres.* Jesus Ernesto R. Sibal.

Poland

Polskie Towarzystwo Wydawców Książek (Polish Publishers Assn.), ul. Mazowiecka 2/4, 00-048 Warsaw. *Pres.* Andrzej Karpowicz.

Stowarzyszenie Ksiegarzy Polskich (Assn. of Polish Booksellers), ul. Mokotowska 4/6, 00-641 Warsaw. *Pres.* Tadeusz Hussak.

Portugal

Associação Portuguesa de Editores e Livreiros (Portuguese Assn. of Publishers and Booksellers), Av. dos Estados Unidos da América 97-6, Esq. 1700 Lisbon. *Pres.* Francisco Espadinha; *Gen. Secy.* Jorge de Sá Borges; *Service Mgr.* José Narciso Vieira.

Romania

Romlibri, Piata Presei Libere 1, R-79715 Bucharest. *Deputy Gen. Dir.* Victor Mircea.

Singapore

Singapore Book Publishers Assn., 865 Mountbatten Rd., No. 05-28, Katong Shopping Centre, Singapore 1543. *V.P.* N. T. S. Chopra.

South Africa

Associated Booksellers of Southern Africa, Box 23832, Claremont 7735. *Pres.* Mrs. M. Hargraves; *V.P.* F. Nel.

Book Trade Assn. of South Africa, Box 32844, Braamfontein 2107. *Pres.* P.W. van Heerden.

South African Publishers Assn., Box 5197, Cape Town 8000. *Chpn.* W. R. van der Vyver; *Secy.* P. G. van Rooyen.

Spain

Centro del Libro y de la Lectura (Center for the Book and Reading), Santiago Rusiñol 8, 28040 Madrid. *Dir.* Natividad Correo.

Federación de Gremios de Editores de España (Spanish Federation of Publishers Assns.), Juan Ramón Jiménez, 45-9°, Izda. 28036, Madrid. *Pres.* D. Juan Salvat; *Secy.-Gen.* Ana Moltó.

Gremi d'Editors de Catalunya (Assn. of Catalonian Publishers), Valencia 279, La Planta, Barcelona 08009. *Pres.* P. Vicens i Rahola.

Gremi de Llibreters de Barcelona i Catalunya (Assn. of Barcelona and Catalonia Booksellers), c. Mallorca 272-274, 08037 Barcelona.

Sri Lanka

Booksellers Assn. of Sri Lanka, Box 244, Colombo 2. *Secy.* W. L. Mendis.

Sri Lanka Assn. of Publishers, 112 S. Mahinda Mawatha, Colombo 10.

Sweden

Svenska Antikvariatföreningen, Box 22549, S-104 22 Stockholm. *Pres.* Sigbjörn Ryö.

Svenska Bokförläggareföreningen (Swedish Publishers Assn.), Sveavägen 52, S-111 34 Stockholm. *Managing Dir.* Walo von Greyerz.

Svenska Bokhandlareföreningen (Swedish Booksellers Assn.), Skeppargatan 27, S-114 52 Stockholm. *Managing Dir.* Thomas Rönström.

Svenska Tryckeriföreningen (Swedish Printing Industries Federation), Blasieholmsgatan 4A, S-111 48 Stockholm. *Managing Dir.* Per Galmark; *Dir.* H. Hedberg.

Switzerland

Schweizerischer Buchhändler-und Verleger-Verband (Swiss German-Language Booksellers and Publishers Assn.), Baumackerstr. 42, CH-8050 Zurich. *Managing Dir.* Egon Räz.

Società Editori della Svizzera Italiana (Publishers Assn. for the Italian-Speaking Part of Switzerland), Box 2600, Viale Portone 4, CH-6501 Bellinzona.

Société des Libraires et Editeurs de la Suisse Romande (Assn. of Swiss French-Language Booksellers and Publishers), 2 ave. Agassiz, CH-1001 Lausanne. *Secy.* Robert Junod.

Vereinigung der Buchantiquare und Kupferstichhändler in der Schweiz (Vebuku)/ Syndicat de la librairie ancienne et du commerce de l'estampe en Suisse (Slaces) (Assn. of Swiss Antiquarians and Print Dealers), c/o *Pres.* Alain Moirandat, Erasmushaus, Haus der Bücher AG, Bäumleingasse 18, CH-4051 Basel.

Thailand

Publishers and Booksellers Assn. of Thailand, 20 Rajprasong Trade Centre, Bangkok 10502.

United Kingdom

Assn. of Learned and Professional Society Publishers, 48 Kelsey Lane, Beckenham, Kent BR3 3NE, England. *Secy.* B. T. Donovan.

Book Trust, Book House, 45 E. Hill, London SW18 2QZ, England. *Chief Exec.* Keith McWilliams.

Booksellers Assn. of Great Britain and Ireland, Minster House, 272 Vauxhall Bridge Rd., London SW1V 1BA, England. *Dir.* Tim Godfray.

Educational Publishers Council, 19 Bedford Sq., London WC1B 3HJ, England. *Dir.* John R. M. Davies; *Mgr.* Sandra Robertson.

National Federation of Retail Newsagents, Yeoman House, Sekforde St., Clerkenwell Green, London EC1R 0HD, England. *Admin. Mgr.* Christine Cairns.

Publishers Assn., 19 Bedford Sq., London WC1B 3HJ, England. *Chief Exec.* Clive Bradley; *Pres.* Paul Scherer; International and Public Affairs: *Dir.* Ian Taylor; Educational Publishers Council: *Dir.* John Davies; Council of Academic and Professional Publishers: *Dir.* John Davies.

Uruguay

Cámara Uruguaya del Libro (Uruguayan Publishing Council), Juan D. Jackson 1118, CP 11200, Montevideo. *Pres.* Vicente

Porcelli; *Secy.* Mauricio Delgado; *Mgr.* Ana Cristina Rodríguez.

Yugoslavia

Assn. of Yugoslav Publishers and Booksellers, Kneza Milosa str. 25, Box 883, Belgrade. *Pres.* Ognjen Lakićević.

Zambia

Booksellers' and Publishers' Assn. of Zambia, Box 320199, Lusaka. *Chpn.* G. B. Mwangilwa.

Zimbabwe

Booksellers Assn. of Zimbabwe, Box 3916, 69 Jason Moyo Ave., Harare. *Chpn.* A. V. Masiye.

Calendar

The list below contains information on association meetings or promotional events that are, for the most part, national or international in scope. State and regional library association meetings are also included. To confirm the starting or ending date of a meeting, which may change after the *Bowker Annual* has gone to press, contact the association directly. Addresses of library and book trade associations are listed in Part 6 of this volume. For information on additional book trade and promotional events, see the *Exhibits Directory*, published annually by the Association of American Publishers; *Chase's Calendar of Annual Events*, published by the Apple Tree Press, Box 10112, Flint, MI 48501; *Literary Market Place* and *International Literary Market Place*, published by R. R. Bowker; and the "Calendar" section in each issue of *Publishers Weekly* and *Library Journal*.

1992

May

1	Council of National Library and Information Associations	New York, NY
1–3	New York Book Fair	New York, NY
3–7	International Reading Association	Orlando, FL
5–8	Florida Library Association	Miami, FL
6–8	New Jersey Library Association	Secaucus, NJ
7–8	Maryland Library Association	Solomons Island, MD
7–8	SOLINET	Atlanta, GA
7–10	Alberta Library Association	Jasper, AB, Canada
8–10	Council of Planning Librarians	Washington, DC
11–13	Booksellers Association of Great Britain and Ireland	Glasgow, Scotland
11–13	New Hampshire Library Association	Bedford, NH
13–15	Association of Research Libraries	Charleston, SC
14–17	Prague International Book Fair	Prague, Czechoslovakia
15–21	Medical Library Association	Washington, DC
17–19	Maine Library Association/ Maine Educational Media Association	Orono, ME
20–21	Vermont Library Association/ Vermont Educational Media Association	Fairlee, VT

May *(cont.)*

20–22	Canadian Association for Information Science	Ottawa, ON, Canada
20–25	National Educational Film and Video Festival	Oakland/San Francisco, CA
21–25	International Symposium on the Development of Theory and Practice of Library and Information Science	Wuhan, China
21–25	Warsaw International Book Fair	Warsaw, Poland
22–23	American Society of Indexers	San Antonio, TX
23–26	American Booksellers Association	Anaheim, CA
26–29	International Association for Social Science Information Service and Technology	Madison, WI
27–30	American Film and Video Association	Chicago, IL
*	American Merchant Marine Library Association	New York, NY
*	INFOBASE International Trade Show for Information Management	Frankfurt, Germany

June

4–5	Rhode Island Library Association	Newport, RI
6–11	Special Libraries Association	San Francisco, CA
9–10	Association for Information Management	Cincinnati, OH
9–12	Association of Christian Librarians	Hollister, MO
10–12	International Electronic Publishing Research Centre	Milan, Italy
11–14	Bucharest International Book Fair	Bucharest, Romania
11–14	Canadian Library Association	Winnipeg, MB, Canada
11–14	Graphic Artists Guild	Washington, DC
15–17	International Electronic Publishing Exhibition	Tokyo, Japan
15–17	National Educational Computing Conference	Dallas, TX
15–26	Georgia Archives Institute	Atlanta, GA
17–20	American Theological Library Association	Dallas, TX
21–24	Association of American University Presses	Chicago, IL
22–25	Association for Information and Image Management	Anaheim, CA
23–25	U.K. Antiquarian Booksellers Association	London, England
23–27	LIBER International Book Fair	Madrid, Spain

*To Be Determined

June *(cont.)*

25–28	Australian Book Publishers Association	Sydney, NSW, Australia
6/25–7/1	International Council of Library Association Executives	San Francisco, CA
6/25–7/1	Chinese-American Librarians Association	San Francisco, CA
6/25–7/2	American Library Association/ Association for Library Service to Children/Public Library Association	San Francisco, CA
6/27–7/2	Christian Booksellers Association	Dallas, TX
29	Theatre Library Association	San Francisco, CA

July

11–19	Manila International Book Fair	Manila, Philippines
12–14	Church and Synagogue Library Association	Lansing, MI
15–18	National Association of Government Archives and Records Administrators	Washington, DC
17–19	U.K. Society of Indexers	Chester, England
18–23	American Association of Law Libraries	San Francisco, CA
29–31	Library of Congress Center for the Book/ British Library Centre for the Book	London, England

August

1–4	International Association of Printing House Craftsmen	Des Moines, IA
12–15	Pacific Northwest Library Association	Seattle, WA
14–17	Hong Kong International Book Fair	Hong Kong
8/26–9/8	São Paulo International Book Show	São Paulo, Brazil
8/27–9/5	International Federation of Library Associations and Institutions	New Delhi, India

September

3–6	St. Petersburg International Book Fair	St. Petersburg, Russia
4–7	Miniature Book Society	San Diego, CA
7–12	International Board on Books for Young People	Berlin, Germany
13	Houston International Hispanic Book Fair	Houston, TX

*To Be Determined

September *(cont.)*

13–17	Library and Information Technology Association	Denver, CO
14–18	Society of American Archivists	Montreal, PQ, Canada
16–19	Kentucky School Media Association	Orvensboro, KY
16–20	Lutheran Church Library Association	Columbus, OH
17–18	Oklahoma Association of School Library Media Specialists	Oklahoma City, OK
18–29	U.K. School Library Association	Manchester, England
21–26	U.K. Society of Archivists	Belfast, Northern Ireland
24–26	North Dakota Library Association	Fargo, ND
25–27	California Trade Show/Northern California Booksellers Association	Oakland, CA
9/26–10/3	Banned Books Week	U.S.A.
9/27–10/2	Australian Library and Information Association	Albury/Wodonga, NSW, Australia
9/29–10/3	Mountain Plains Library Association/ Wyoming Library Association	Cheyenne, WY
9/30–10/3	Idaho Library Association	Boise, ID
9/30–10/5	Frankfurt Book Fair	Frankfurt, Germany
*	Mickler Networking Conference	Amsterdam, Netherlands
*	Singapore International Festival of Books	Singapore

October

1–3	Idaho Library Association	Boise, ID
3	American Printing History Association	Princeton, NJ
4–6	Arkansas Library Association	Little Rock, AR
4–6	New England Library Association	Sturbridge, MA
7–9	Iowa Library Association	Waterloo, IA
7–9	Kentucky Library Association	Saint Mitchell, KY
7–9	Minnesota Library Association	Brainerd, MN
7–10	South Dakota Library Association	Pierre, SD
8–10	Nevada Library Association	Las Vegas, NV
8–10	Oregon Educational Media Association	Portland, OR
8–10	Washington Library Media Association	Everett, WA
9–12	Colorado Library Association	Beaver Creek, CO
14–15	Vermont Educational Media Association	*
14–17	Florida Association for Media in Education	Tampa, FL
15–17	West Virginia Library Association	Parkersburg, WV
16	Utah Educational Library Media Association	Salt Lake City, UT
19–22	Association of Records Managers and Administrators	Detroit, MI

*To Be Determined

October *(cont.)*

21–23	Association of Research Libraries	Washington, DC
21–23	Nebraska Educational Media Association/Nebraska Library Association	Lincoln, NE
21–23	South Carolina Library Association	Columbia, SC
21–25	American Association of School Librarians	Baltimore, MD
22–28	Belgrade International Book Fair	Belgrade, Yugoslavia
23–26	Michigan Library Association	Traverse City, MI
25–28	Evangelical Christian Publishers Association	Sanibel Island, FL
25–29	American Society for Information Science	Pittsburgh, PA
27–30	Mississippi Library Association	Jackson, MS
28–30	Wisconsin Library Association	La Crosse, WI
28–31	Michigan Association for Media in Education	Lansing, MI
29–31	Illinois School Library Media Association	Lincolnshire, IL
10/29–11/3	Periodical Marketers of Canada	Toronto, ON, Canada
10/31–11/4	Tokyo Book Fair	Tokyo, Japan
10/31–11/14	Pennsylvania Library Association	Pittsburgh, PA
*	Chief Officers of State Library Agencies	Bar Harbor, ME
*	Children's Book Week	U.K.

November

1–4	Book Manufacturers Institute	Naples, FL
1–4	California Library Association	Long Beach, CA
3–5	Ohio Library Association/ Ohio Educational Library Media Association	*
4–6	Tennessee Association for School Librarians	Gatlinburg, TN
11–15	New York Library Association	Syracuse, NY
14–17	California Library Association	Long Beach, CA
14–19	Salon du Livre de Montréal	Montreal, PQ, Canada
15–18	Information Industry Association	San Francisco, CA
16–22	Children's Book Week	U.S.A.
20–22	Theatre Library Association	Cambridge, MA
11/28–12/6	Guadalajara International Book Fair	Guadalajara, Mexico
*	California Media and Library Education Association	Sacramento, CA

*To Be Determined

December

2	Bookbuilders West	San Francisco, CA
4	Council of National Library and Information Associations	New York, NY
6–8	Educational Media Association of New Jersey	New Brunswick, NJ
27–30	Modern Language Association	New York, NY

1993

January

19–22	Association for Library and Information Science Education	Denver, CO
22–28	American Library Association/ Public Library Association	Denver, CO
27–29	Special Libraries Association	Phoenix, AZ
1/28–2/3	Art Libraries Society	San Francisco, CA
*	South Carolina Association of School Librarians	Charleston, SC

February

3–6	Music Library Association	San Francisco, CA
9–11	International Book Publishing Conference and Services Expo	New York, NY
2/27–3/7	Mexico City International Book Fair	Mexico City, Mexico
2/28–3/5	U.K. Christian Booksellers Association	Bournemouth, England

March

5–7	Michigan Association for Media in Education	Cedar, MI
9–13	Texas Library Association	San Antonio, TX
11–14	Luxembourg Book Festival	Luxembourg
19–24	Paris Book Show	Paris, France
22–26	Louisiana Library Association	Shreveport, LA
3/30–4/3	Oklahoma Library Association	Oklahoma City, OK

April

5–8	Association for Information and Image Management	Chicago, IL
18–24	Jerusalem International Book Fair	Jerusalem, Israel
18–24	National Library Week	U.S.A.

*To Be Determined

April *(cont.)*

21–24	Washington Library Association	Tacoma, WA
4/22–5/3	Colombia International Book Fair	Bogota, Colombia
25–28	Evangelical Christian Publishers Association	Hilton Head, SC
26–30	International Reading Association	San Antonio, TX
4/27–5/1	Illinois Library Association	Springfield, IL
4/29–5/2	Alberta Library Association	Jasper, AB, Canada
4/30–5/3	Council of Planning Librarians	Chicago, IL
*	Chief Officers of State Library Agencies	Washington, DC
*	Montana Library Association	Kalispell, MT
*	Buenos Aires International Book Fair	Buenos Aires, Argentina

May

5–9	Salon International du Livre et de la Presse	Geneva, Switzerland
13	Bookbuilders West	San Francisco, CA
14–20	Medical Library Association	Chicago, IL
16–18	Maine Library Association/ Maine Educational Media Association	Orono, ME
19–20	Vermont Library Association	Fairlee, VT
20–22	American Society of Indexers	Washington, DC
*	Booksellers Association of Great Britain and Ireland	Brighton, England

June

5–10	Special Libraries Association	Cincinnati, OH
8–11	Association of Christian Librarians	Mishawaka, IN
10–15	Periodical Marketers of Canada	Halifax, NS, Canada
17–20	Canadian Library Association	Hamilton, ON, Canada
6/24–7/1	American Library Association/ Association for Library Service to Children/Public Library Association	New Orleans, LA
26–29	Association of American University Presses	Snowbird, UT
28	Theatre Library Association	New Orleans, LA

July

11–13	Church and Synagogue Library Association	Houston, TX
*	Chinese-American Librarians Association	New Orleans, LA

*To Be Determined

August

11–14	Montana Library Association/ Pacific Northwest Library Association	Kalispell, MT
22–28	International Federation of Library Associations and Institutions	Barcelona, Spain
22–30	International Federation for Modern Languages and Literature	Brazil
*	Edinburgh Book Festival	Edinburgh, Scotland
*	International Association of Printing House Craftsmen	Buffalo, NY
*	Zimbabwe International Book Fair	Harare, Zimbabwe

September

2–5	Society of American Archivists	New Orleans, LA
17–19	California Trade Show/ Northern California Booksellers Association	Oakland, CA
23–25	North Dakota Library Association	Williston, ND
26–29	Pennsylvania Library Association	Philadelphia, PA
9/30–10/2	Nevada Library Association	Elko, NV
9/30–10/4	Mountain Plains Library Association	Aspen, CO

October

6–8	Minnesota Library Association	Rochester, MN
6–9	Idaho Library Association	Moscow, ID
6–9	South Dakota Library Association	Brookings, SD
7–9	Washington Library Media Association	Spokane, WA
10–12	Arkansas Library Association	Hot Springs, AR
12–17	American Institute of Graphic Arts	Miami, FL
13–15	Iowa Library Association	Ames, IA
18–22	Association of Records Managers and Administrators	Seattle, WA
18–22	Michigan Library Association	Lansing, MI
19–22	North Carolina Library Association	Winston–Salem, NC
20–23	Michigan Association for Media in Education	Kalamazoo, MI
24–27	Evangelical Christian Publishers Association	Palm Springs, CA
27–29	Nebraska Library Association/ Nebraska Educational Media Association	Grand Island, NE
27–30	Florida Association for Media in Education	Tampa, FL
*	American Printing History Association	Providence, RI

*To Be Determined

October *(cont.)*

*	Children's Book Week	U.K.
*	Oregon Educational Media Association	Eugene, OR

November

4–6	Illinois School Library Media Association	Effingham, IL
13–16	Periodical Marketers of Canada	Montreal, PQ, Canada
14–17	Information Industry Association	Washington, DC
15–21	Children's Book Week	U.S.A.
19–21	Theatre Library Association	New Orleans, LA
19–23	California Library Association	San Francisco, CA
11/27–12/5	Guadalajara Book Fair	Guadalajara, Mexico
*	Chief Officers of State Library Agencies	Honolulu, HI

December

8–10	South Carolina Library Association	*
27–30	Modern Language Association	Toronto, ON, Canada

*To Be Determined

Authors and Contributors

Baker, John F.
Bales, Kathleen
Bixby, Pamela
Blixrud, Julia C.
Bloss, Marjorie E.
Boone, Mary
Brandhorst, Ted
Burns, Ann
Chute, Adrienne
Cooke, Eileen D.
Cunningham, George
DeCandido, GraceAnne A.
DeCandido, Keith R. A.
Ensor, Pat
Evans, Gwynneth
Farberman, Rhea
Fox, Bette-Lee
Fry, Ray M.
Gerhardt, Lillian N.
Grannis, Chandler B.
Grant, W. Vance
Haar, John
Halstead, Kent
Harer, John B.
Hausrath, Don
Henderson, Carol C.
Hill, Richard B.
Ink, Gary
Kepley, David R.
Koltay, Emery

Lesley, J. Ingrid
Levering, Mary Berghaus
Lottman, Herbert R.
Lynch, Mary Jo
McClung, James W.
MacEoin, Dorothy Aukofer
Mahony, Alan P.
Maryles, Daisy
Mehnert, Robert
Metalitz, Steven J.
Miles, Carol
Miller, Marilyn L.
Myers, Margaret
Norris, Brian
Platt, Judith
Quinn, Judy
Raggio, William G.
Reid, Charles E.
Roberts, Rachel
Rogers, Michael
Rosenberg, Laurence C.
Schick, Frank L.
Schuman, Patricia Glass
Segal, JoAn S.
Serepca, Mark S.
Shontz, Marilyn
Thompson, Mary Agnes
Tomer, Christinger
Zipkowitz, Fay

Acronyms

A

AAAS. American Association for Advancement of Science

AALL. American Association of Law Libraries

AAP. Association of American Publishers

AASL. American Association of School Librarians

ABA. American Booksellers Association

ABFFE. American Booksellers Foundation for Free Expression

ACRL. Association of College and Research Libraries

AFC. American Folklife Center

AFFIRM. Association for Federal Information Resources Management

AGRICOLA. AGRICultural OnLine Access

AIM. Association for Information Management

AJL. Association of Jewish Libraries

ALA. American Library Association

ALCTS. Association for Library Collections and Technical Services

ALISE. Association for Library and Information Science Education

ALSC. Association for Library Service for Children

ALTA. American Library Trustee Association

AMMLA. American Merchant Marine Library Association

ANSI. American National Standards Institute

APALA. Asian/Pacific American Librarians Association

ARL. Association of Research Libraries

ARLIS/NA. Art Libraries Society of North America

ARMA. Association of Records Managers and Administrators, *see* ARMA International

ASCLA. Association of Specialized and Cooperative Library Agencies

ASIS. American Society for Information Science

ATLA. American Theological Library Association

B

BAFTA. British Academy of Film and Television Arts

BCR. Bibliographical Center for Research

BISAC. Book Industry Study Group, Book Industry Systems Advisory Committee

BISG. Book Industry Study Group, Inc.

BOS. American Booksellers Association, Booksellers Order Service

C

CAIS. Canadian Association for Information Science

CARL. Colorado Alliance of Research Libraries

CD-ROM. Compact Disc Read-Only Memory

CLA. Canadian Library Association; Catholic Library Association

CLASS. Cooperative Library Authority for Systems and Services

CLR. Council on Library Resources

CNI. Coalition for Networked Information

CNLIA. Council of National Library and Information Associations

COSLA. Chief Officers of State Library Agencies

CPC. Association of American Publishers, Children's Publishing Committee

CPL. Council of Planning Librarians

CSLA. Church and Synagogue Library Association

E

EPA. Environmental Protection Agency

ERIC. Educational Resources Information Center

F

FBI. Federal Bureau of Investigation

FIAF. International Federation of Film Archives

FID. International Federation for Information and Documentation

FLICC. Federal Library and Information Center Committee

FOIA. Freedom of Information Act

FPC. Federal Publishers Committee

FSCS. Federal-State Cooperative System for Public Library Data

G

GPO. Government Printing Office

H

HEA. Higher Education Act

I

IAALD. International Association of Agricultural Librarians and Documentalists

IALL. International Association of Law Libraries

IAML. International Association of Music Libraries, Archives and Documentation Centres

IAOL. International Association of Orientalist Librarians

IASA. International Association of Sound Archives

IASL. International Association of School Librarianship

IATUL. International Association of Technological University Libraries

IFLA. International Federation of Library Associations and Institutions

IIA. Information Industry Association

INTAMEL. International Association of Metropolitan City Libraries

IRIS. National Science Foundation, Division of Information, Robotics, and Intelligent Systems

ISBN. International Standard Book Number

ISO. International Organization for Standardization

ISQ. National Information Standards Organization, *Information Standards Quarterly*

ISSN. International Standard Serial Number

L

LAMA. Library Administration and Management Association

LARS. FEDLINK, Library Automation Resource Service

LC. Library of Congress

LIBER. Ligue des Bibliotheques Europeennes de Recherche

LITA. Library and Information Technology Association

LSCA. Library Services and Construction Act

M

MLA. Medical Library Association; Music Library Association

MLNC. Missouri Library Network Corporation

MURLs. Major Urban Resource Libraries

N

NAC. Network Advisory Committee

NAGARA. National Association of Government Archives and Records Administrators

NAL. National Agricultural Library

NARA. National Archives and Records Administration

NATDP. National Agricultural Library, National Agricultural Text Digitizing Project

NCES. National Center for Education Statistics

NCLIS. National Commission on Libraries and Information Science

NEH. National Endowment for the Humanities

NISO. National Information Standards Organization

NLA. National Librarians Association

NLM. National Library of Medicine

NREN. National Research and Education Network

NSF. National Science Foundation

NTIS. National Technical Information Service

O

OCLC. Online Computer Library Center

OGE. United States, Government Ethics, Office of

OIF. American Library Association, Intellectual Freedom, Office for

OMB. United States, Management and Budget, Office of

OPM. United States, Personnel Management, Office of

OSAP. Association of Research Libraries, Scientific and Academic Publishing, Office of

P

PLA. Public Library Association

PRA. Paperwork Reduction Act

PW. Publishers Weekly

R

RASD. American Library Association, Reference and Adult Services Division

RBOCs. Regional Bell Operating Companies

RLG. Research Libraries Group

RLIN. Research Libraries Information Network

RTSD. American Library Association, Resources and Technical Services Division. *See new name* Association for Library Collections and Technical Services

S

SAA. Society of American Archivists

SISAC. Book Industry Study Group, Serials Industry Systems Advisory Committee

SLA. Special Libraries Association

SLJ. School Library Journal

SSP. Society for Scholarly Publishing

STM. Scientific, Technical and Medical Publishers

T

TLA. Theatre Library Association

U

USIA. United States Information Agency

USIS. United States Information Service

USPS. United States Postal Service

V

VLIST. Virginia Library and Information Services Task Force

W

WHCLIS. White House Conference on Library and Information Services

WILS. Wisconsin Interlibrary Services

WLN. Western Library Network

Y

YALSA. American Library Association, Young Adult Library Services Association

Index of Organizations

Subject Index

Please note that many cross-references refer to organizations found in the Index of Organizations.

A

Abortion services, *Rust v. Sullivan* ruling, 41, 167, 174–175, 230

Academic books, prices and price indexes
books and periodicals, FYs 1976–1990, 416 (table)
British averages, 1989–1991, 496–497 (table)
German averages, 1989–1991, 498–499 (table)
North American, 1988–89 to 1990–91, 486–487 (table)
U.S. college books, averages, 1989–1991, 488–489 (table)
See also Association of American Publishers, Professional and Scholarly Publishing Division; Society for Scholarly Publishing

Academic libraries, *see* College and research libraries; National Center for Education Statistics, academic library survey

Acquisitions
expenditures
academic libraries, 406–407 (table)
government libraries, 410–411 (table)
public libraries, 404–405 (table)
special libraries, 408–409 (table)
Library of Congress trends, 141
LSCA Foreign Language Materials Acquisitions Program, 29–31, 290–291
funding, FY 1991, 291 (table)
school library price indexes, FYs 1976–1990, 418–420 (table)
Z39 standards, 207
See also Association of Research Libraries, collections services program *and* specific types of libraries, i.e., Public libraries

Adults, services for, *see* American Library Association, Reference and Adult

Services Division; Literacy programs; Senior citizens, library services for

Affirmative action; AAP activities, 188

African Americans, 148, 168

Agencies, library, *see* Library associations and agencies

Agents, literary, 23

Agricultural libraries, *see* Inter-American Association of Agricultural Librarians and Documentalists; International Association of Agricultural Librarians and Documentalists; National Agricultural Library

Alabama
Eastern European languages, collection development in, 30
LJ report, 5

Alaska
LJ report, 5

American history, role of library
LC's American Memory program, 137

Arab Americans, 42

Archives
acquisition expenditures
academic library, 406–407 (table)
government library, 410–411 (table)
public library, 404–405 (table)
special library, 408–409 (table)
See also International Council on Archives; International Federation of Film Archives; National Archives and Records Administration; National Association of Government Archives and Records Administrators; Society of American Archivists

Arizona
LJ report, 5
Mexican Americans, library services for, 30
Spanish Americans, library services for, 29–30

H.W. Wilson Foundation grant, 176
See also American Library Association,
 special projects; College Library
 Technology and Cooperation Grants
 Program; Higher Education Act;
 National Endowment for the Humanities; Scholarships and fellowships
Great Britain
 BAFTA and Library of Congress activities,
 135–136
 prices and price indexes, 494
 academic books, averages 1989–1991,
 496– 497 (table)

H

Handicapped, library services for the; LSCA
 funding, 307–308, 309 (table), 310
Hardcover books
 American book title production,
 1989–1991, 503 (table)
 bestsellers, 557–560
 fiction, 557–558
 nonfiction, 559–560
 prices and price indexes
 average per–volume prices, 1989–1991,
 506(tables)
 averages, 1988–1991, 485 (table)
 books and periodicals, FYs 1976–1990,
 416 (table)
 school library acquisitions, FYs 1976–
 1990, 418–420 (table)
 three cloth categories; *PW* announcement
 Fall ads, 508 (table)
 translations into English, 505 (table)
Hawaiian natives, library services under
 LSCA Title IV, 284–286
 basic grant awards, FY 1991, 287 (table)
Health sciences libraries, *see* Association of
 Academic Health Sciences Library
 Directors; Association of Librarians
 in the History of the Health Sciences;
 Medical Library Association; National Library of Medicine
Higher Education Act (HEA), 258–284
 appropriations for federal library and
 related programs, FY 1992, 215 (table)
 reauthorization, 213, 221
 Title II–A, *see* College Library Resources
 Program
 Title II–B funding history
 See also Library Career Training Pro-
 gram; Library Education Fellowship/

Trainee Program; Library Research
 and Demonstration Program
 Title II–C, *see* Strengthening Research
 Library Resources Program
 Title II–D, *see* College Library Technology
 and Cooperation Grants Program
Hill, Anita, 15
Homeless, library services for, 33–34
 Kreimer v. Morristown, 42
Housebound people, library services for, 34

I

Idaho
 LJ report, 7
Illinois
 Asian Americans, library services for, 29
 homeless, library services for, 33–34
 ILLINET/OCLC, 58
 LJ report, 7
 library usage, 34, 35
 Spanish–speaking Americans, library
 services for, 31
Immigrants, library services for
 Asian Americans, 28–29, 30
 Eastern Europeans, 30
 Mexican Americans, 30
 New Americans Project, 31
 Spanish Americans, 29–30, 31
Improvement of Information Access Act, 220
Indian tribes, library services to, *see* Native
 Americans, library services to
Indiana
 LJ report, 7
Information
 access to
 Improvement of Information Access
 Act, 220
 See also Federal Bureau of Investigation,
 Library Awareness Program; United
 States, information, access to
 technology, *see* Information technology
 See also ARMA International; Association
 for Information and Image Manage-
 ment; Association for Information
 Management; Education for librarians
 and librarianship; Federal Bureau of
 Investigation, Library Awareness
 Program; Information industry;
 Information Industry Association;
 Information science
Information industry
 associations, U.S. and Canadian, 603–668
 employment, *see* Placement